West's Law School
Advisory Board

CASES AND MATERIALS ON
MODERN PROPERTY LAW

Fourth Edition

By

Jon W. Bruce
Professor of Law, Vanderbilt University

James W. Ely, Jr.
Professor of Law and History, Vanderbilt University

AMERICAN CASEBOOK SERIES®

**WEST
GROUP**

ST. PAUL, MINN., 1999

*TEXT IS PRINTED ON 10% POST
CONSUMER RECYCLED PAPER*

To

Barbara, Kelly, and Tyler

———

Mickey

*

Preface

Property law is deeply rooted in history and tradition. It is, therefore, the dilemma of the property law teacher to strike a proper balance between emerging developments and traditional doctrine. To meet this challenge, these materials undertake to present the basic principles of property law in a somewhat different manner. We have created a series of hypothetical situations to serve as the backdrop for the presentation of both old and new property issues. This format is designed to provide a realistic contemporary context for the study of property law and to demonstrate that legal problems are invariably multifaceted. Further, we have placed landlord-tenant material at the beginning of the book to introduce fundamental property concepts in a relatively familiar setting, to illustrate how the common law evolves as general socio-economic conditions change, and to highlight the underlying tension between the legislative and judicial branches of government.

Our effort to treat a sometimes difficult subject in cogent and meaningful ways has been made easier by the fact that property is one of the most interesting areas of modern legal study. Indeed, the notion that property law is static has never been true. New ways of addressing societal concerns about property are constantly emerging. For example, controversial property innovations such as condominium conversion, seller disclosure requirements, and development exactions are integral parts of the legal fabric of real estate ownership. This book is designed to give the next generation of property lawyers an appreciation of the interrelationship between these contemporary developments and traditional doctrine. Thus, they will be prepared to deal with both commonplace legal problems and novel issues that will arise as the concept of property continues to change.

We believe that this goal is best accomplished by teaching straight through the book. The materials, however, are not so tightly tied together that a creative teacher cannot re-arrange their order.

One additional note: we believe that a first-year casebook should be a teaching tool, not an exhaustive treatment of every nuance of property law. We, therefore, have avoided lengthy notes and have omitted identification of counsel, footnotes, citations of authority, captions, and dissenting and concurring opinions from cases and readings without indication. We have also renumbered footnotes on occasion. Omitted textual material, of course, is indicated by ellipsis.

We wish to thank the following research assistants for their diligent and invaluable efforts: Henry J. Heyming, Geoffrey R. Schiveley, and Ross G. Shank for their work on this edition, and Raymond T. Abbott, Catherine A. Alder, Fred W. Bopp III, Fred S. Finkelstein, P. Perry Finney,

Amy K. Luigs, Sandeep Narang, Mark E. Pfeifer, Gregory D. Smith, and Amy E. Stutz for their work on earlier editions. We also thank the students in first-year property classes at Vanderbilt who have used prior versions of these materials. Their comments, questions, and encouragement contributed greatly to the final product. Further, we acknowledge the fine support services secretary Nan Paden provided for this edition.

In conclusion, we wish to express our continuing gratitude to our colleague C. Dent Bostick who served as co-author of the first two editions of this book. He has now attained emeritus status and did not participate in the preparation of the last two editions. His discerning comments and lively presence were missed.

JON W. BRUCE
JAMES W. ELY, JR.

Vanderbilt University
February, 1999

Acknowledgments

We gratefully acknowledge receiving reprint permissions for the following materials:

ABA Report, *Residential Real Estate Transactions: The Lawyer's Proper Role-Services-Compensation*, 14 Real Prop., Prob. & Tr. J. 581 (1979). Copyright © 1979, American Bar Association. Reprinted by permission of the Real Property, Probate and Trust Journal.

1 America Law of Property § 3.52 (1952). Copyright © 1952, Little, Brown and Company. Reprinted by permission of Little, Brown and Company.

Bostick, *Loosening the Grip of the Dead Hand: Shall We Abolish Legal Future Interests in Land*, 32 Vand.L.Rev. 1061, 1079-1080 (1979). Copyright © 1979, Vanderbilt University School of Law. Reprinted by permission of the Vanderbilt Law Review.

Browder, *The Taming of a Duty—The Tort Liability of Landlords*, 81 Mich.L.Rev. 99, 150 (1982). Copyright © 1982, Michigan Law Review Association. Reprinted by permission of the Michigan Law Review and the author.

FNMA/FHLMC Uniform Instruments–Multistate Fixed Rate Note (Form 3200 12/83) and Mortgage–Indiana-Single Family (Form 3015 9/90). Reprinted by permission of the Federal National Mortgage Association and the Federal Home Loan Mortgage Corporation.

B. Goldsmith, Little Gloria . . . Happy at Last 149 (Dell ed. 1980). Copyright © 1980, Barbara Goldsmith. Reprinted by permission of Alfred A. Knopf, Inc.

D. Hagman, Urban Planning and Land Development Control Law 289 (1971). Copyright © 1971, West Publishing Co. Reprinted with permission of the West Group.

J. Juergensmeyer & T. Roberts, Land Use Planning and Control Law § 4.16 (1998). Copyright © 1998, West Group. Reprinted with permission of the West Group.

Lease of apartment—Unfurnished, 11 Am.Jur. Legal Forms § 161.38 (2d ed.rev.1998). Copyright © 1998, West Group. Reprinted with permission of the West Group.

Mursten, *Florida's Regulatory Response to Condominium Conversion: The Roth Act*, 34 Miami L.Rev. 1077, 1082 (1980). Copyright © 1980, University of Miami Law Review. Reprinted by permission of the University of Miami Law Review.

G. Nelson & D. Whitman, Real Estate Finance Law §§ 1.1–1.5 (3d ed. 1994). Copyright © 1994, West Publishing Co. Reprinted with permission of the West Group.

Note, *Covenants Running with the Land: Viable Doctrine or Common Law Relic?*, 7 Hofstra L.Rev, 139, 174 (1978). Copyright © 1978, Hofstra Law Review Association. Reprinted by permission of the Hofstra Law Review Association and the author, Margot L. Rau.

Policy of Title Insurance (American Land Title Association Owner's Policy–Revised 10/17/92). Reprinted by permission of The American Land Title Association.

2 Powell on Real Property § 16.02[1] (1998). © 1998, Matthew Bender & Co., Inc. Reprinted by permission of Matthew Bender & Co., Inc.

Restatement (Second) of Property § 14.1 statutory note 1 (1977). Copyright © 1977 by The American Law Institute. Reprinted with the permission of The American Law Institute.

Uniform Listing Contract–Improved Residential–Class 1. Reprinted by permission of the Chattanooga Board of Realtors, Inc.

Uniform Marketable Title Act selected sections and comments (1990). This Act has been reprinted by permission of the National Conference of Commissioners on Uniform State Laws, and copies of the Act may be ordered from them at a nominal cost at 676 North St. Clair Street, Suite 1700, Chicago, Illinois 60611, (312) 915-0195.

Van Buren, *Dear Abby, Gold Found in Library*. Taken from the DEAR ABBY column by Abigail Van Buren. © UNIVERSAL PRESS SYNDICATE. Reprinted with permission. All rights reserved.

Warranty Deed, Copyright © 1986, 1990, 1991 by Indianapolis Bar Association (Rev. 10/91). Reprinted by permission of the Indianapolis Bar Association.

We also wish to thank the following individuals for providing us with background information about various cases or other assistance:

Mr. John Earle Chason, Attorney-at-Law, Bay Minette, Alabama.

Mr. Martin M. Green, Attorney-at-Law, St. Louis, Missouri.

Mr. Steven Miller, Curator, Museum of the City of New York, New York, New York.

Mr. Gary T Roberson, Manager, Marengo Cave Park, Marengo, Indiana.

Mr. Joe K. Telford, Attorney-at-Law, Gainesville, Georgia.

Summary of Contents

Table of Contents

Table of Cases

The principal cases are in bold type. Cases cited or discussed in the text are roman type. References are to pages. Cases cited in principal cases and within other quoted materials are not included.

CASES AND MATERIALS ON
MODERN PROPERTY LAW

Fourth Edition

*

Introduction

A CONTEMPORARY CONTEXT FOR THE STUDY OF PROPERTY LAW

The American Dream of home ownership is one of the more conspicuous characteristics of our society. This phenomenon is inextricably entwined with such property innovations as the conversion of rental apartments to condominiums, the disclosure requirements placed on real estate sellers, and the imposition of various exactions on developers. We have decided to use these and other recent developments in the property field as catalysts for your study of property law. We take this approach for several reasons. First, such topics illustrate the modern significance of traditional property law doctrine. Second, they combine broad socio-economic issues such as the continuing need for affordable housing with narrower but nonetheless significant matters such as the legal pitfalls in purchasing a home. Finally, sophisticated issues of this type challenge you at the outset of your legal studies to strive to perceive the interrelationship among a variety of legal principles, an ability necessary for the successful practice of law.

Some current property issues, including those noted above, are presented to you in the form of a series of hypothetical situations. These hypothetical situations are utilized as the starting point for analysis of many areas of property law. This format is designed to bring reality to the classroom. In life, legal problems are human problems. They arise because individuals disagree, misunderstand, forget, or otherwise act like human beings. The hypothetical situations serve as constant reminders that legal problems do not exist in a vacuum.

Chapter 1

LANDLORD–TENANT

Hypothetical Situation—Number 1

Ralph and Mary Lloyd are life-long residents of Centerville, a community of approximately 50,000 citizens located twenty miles from one of our nation's largest cities. The Lloyds are both sixty years old.

Five years ago, the Lloyds sold their house and rented the two-bedroom apartment they now occupy. Their apartment is located on the fifth floor of a six-story apartment building known as Harmony House. The building is owned by Daze Corporation. Centerville is growing rapidly, and Harmony House is in a convenient location, so there is a long waiting list for apartments.

The Lloyds recently heard a rumor that Daze Corporation has decided to convert Harmony House to a condominium. Although Daze Corporation has made no formal announcement as to its plan for Harmony House, the tenants are alarmed.

Shortly after the condominium conversion rumor circulated among the residents of Harmony House, the Lloyds' air conditioning unit broke down. Although Mary Lloyd made numerous calls to the rental manager at Daze Corporation, no one came to repair the unit. Other tenants in Harmony House had the same experience when they reported maintenance problems. This was unusual; previously Daze Corporation responded promptly to requests for repair work.

The tenants are concerned about one unrepaired item in particular. The lock on the side-door to Harmony House malfunctions. Often the door remains unlocked overnight. The Lloyds and other tenants are worried about criminals gaining access to the building through this unlocked door.

The residents of Harmony House decided to hold a general meeting to discuss the maintenance issue and the rumor about condominium conversion. Danielle Daze, president of Daze Corporation, declined an invitation to attend and did not send anyone to represent her.

At the tenants' meeting, it became apparent that tenants have different lease arrangements. Some tenants have long-term leases, others occupy their units on a month-to-month basis.

The meeting served as a forum for Jan Swanson, a long-time tenant of Harmony House, to advocate a four-prong approach for dealing with Daze Corporation. Her proposal called for the tenants to: (1) withhold rent until repairs were made, (2) report needed repairs to the Centerville Housing Code Inspector, (3) notify Daze Corporation that it will be held responsible for any criminal activity on the premises, and (4) refuse to vacate their apartments at the end of their current leases. This proposal generated a great deal of discussion, but the meeting was adjourned without any agreement among the tenants.

In the mail the next day, the Lloyds received notice from Daze Corporation that Harmony House is to be converted to a condominium. They were given the option of purchasing their unit or moving out at the end of their lease term. They are disturbed about recent developments and unsure about their rights under their current lease. They seek your advice.

Note

The condominium concept is discussed on pages 316–318. The move to convert apartment buildings to condominiums is a relatively recent development which has engendered considerable controversy. State and municipal laws have been adopted in some jurisdictions to regulate the conversion process. The conversion phenomenon is discussed on pages 318–319. You are not expected to become an expert on condominium conversion, but we will examine basic substantive areas of property law, such as landlord-tenant and concurrent ownership, that bear directly on the subject.

A. INTRODUCTION

In order to appreciate the rights and obligations of the Lloyds under their lease with Daze Corporation, it is necessary to examine the fundamentals of landlord-tenant law. The landlord-tenant relationship originated in medieval England where leases were utilized by lenders to secure loans and to avoid the Church's prohibition on charging interest. In those days, a lender often took possession of a borrower's property long enough to recover the loan principal, plus a handsome profit, from income produced by the land. The use of the lease for this purpose disappeared as other land security devices, such as the mortgage, were developed. *See* T. Plucknett, A Concise History of the Common Law 572, 574 (5th ed. 1956). The general lease concept, however, flourished. Landowners adopted it for their own purposes, using the lease as a means by which they could have someone cultivate the land and pay rent from the harvest. The practice of absentee ownership spread over the years to different types of real estate. Today leases cover factories, apartments, office buildings, stores, and houses. *See* 7 W. Holdsworth, A History of English Law 239 (1926).

1. IS A LEASE A CONVEYANCE OR A CONTRACT?

The early law did not recognize a lease as giving the tenant any interest in the leased property. This proved to be a poor arrangement principally because the tenant's possession was not adequately protected. Hence, procedures soon evolved to protect the tenant from physical interference by the landlord and third parties. Eventually, the landlord-tenant relationship became one in which the landlord was viewed as conveying a limited possessory interest in land to the tenant while at the same time retaining an ownership interest, known as a reversion. *See* 3 W. Holdsworth, A History of English Law 213–217 (1923).

Traditional landlord-tenant legal principles were developed on the basis of this conveyance theory and consequently were considered a part of property law. But, as buildings began to be leased with the land, the parties made specific agreements about such things as utilities, maintenance, and liability for injuries. As a result, modern landlord-tenant law includes many contractual principles which are used to interpret lease covenants. These contractual principles often collide with traditional property law. *See* Hicks, *The Contractual Nature of Real Property Leases*, 24 Baylor L.Rev. 443 (1972); Chase & Taylor, *Landlord and Tenant: A Study in Property and Contract*, 30 Vill.L.Rev. 571 (1985).

The current situation is well summarized in 2 Powell on Real Property § 16.02[1] (1998):*

> * * * [T]he background of the lease as a conveyance, built solidly by 1500, has a tremendous foreground, evolved largely since 1800, which is essentially contractual. The modern common law of landlord and tenant is a synthesis of these two historical perspectives on the lease transaction. Sometimes the background peeks through and controls; more often in modern law, the contractual foreground controls. The lawyer's task is to understand the differences that can result on specific issues from application of either property or contract principles, and to determine which of the two perspectives will control (or should be advocated) in any specific case.

> * * *

> * * * Thus, at present, the law of leases reflects its historical development: it remains a blend of property concepts and contractual doctrines developed for the service of a wide variety of objectives—agrarian, urban and financial. The "contractualization" of the lease is a useful and necessary development to the extent that it removes outmoded rules of landlord-tenant law. Contract rules, however, are not always the panacea for lease problems that they

may initially seem to be, nor are property rules always regressive in lease cases.

The advisability of the trend to supplant the conveyance theory with a contractual approach has been sharply questioned by one scholar who contends that the application of traditional contract principles to leases may prove an obstacle to reform of landlord-tenant law. Humbach, *The Common–Law Conception of Leasing: Mitigation, Habitability, and Dependence of Covenants*, 60 Wash.U.L.Q. 1213 (1983). *See also* Kelley, *Any Reports of the Death of the Property Law Paradigm for Leases Have Been Greatly Exaggerated*, 41 Wayne L. Rev. 1563 (1995).

2. STATUTORY MODIFICATION OF COMMON LAW: UNIFORM RESIDENTIAL LANDLORD AND TENANT ACT

An understanding of the concept of common law is crucial to a mastery of property. Common law is customary law. It derives its authority from usage, and from court rulings recognizing such usage. As applied in the royal courts of medieval England, the common law became a body of rules whose content was judicially fashioned. Yet common law also suggests a manner of reasoning in which courts use past experience and consideration of social policy as a means of analyzing new problems. *See* S. Milsom, Historical Foundations of the Common Law (2d ed. 1981); R. Pound, The Spirit of the Common Law (1921); Jones, *Our Uncommon Common Law*, 42 Tenn.L.Rev. 443 (1975).

Through a complex and much debated process, the colonists adopted the English common law as the basis of their jurisprudence. *See* J. Smith & T. Barnes, The English Legal System: Carryover to the Colonies (1975). Despite the upheaval caused by the American Revolution, the states continued to rely on common law. *See* Ely, *Law in a Republican Society: Continuity and Change in the Legal System of Postrevolutionary America*, in Perspectives on Revolution and Evolution 46 (R. Preston ed. 1979).

Today, except for Louisiana with its French–Spanish heritage, American states are common law jurisdictions. Of course, state courts interpret the common law differently and there are often striking variations from jurisdiction to jurisdiction. Moreover, state legislatures may change the common law by enacting statutes.

Although it is not educationally profitable to examine the statutes of each state, it is important for you to gain an appreciation of the effect of statutory developments on the common law. *See* Glendon, *The Transformation of American Landlord–Tenant Law*, 23 B.C.L. Rev. 503 (1982). We have selected the Uniform Residential Landlord and Tenant Act as a means of providing this perspective. You will be asked to consider the Act at various points throughout this chapter. The Act was prepared in the early 1970's by the National Conference of Commissioners on Uniform State Laws and recommended to the individual states for adoption. Approximately one-third of the states have adopted the Uniform Residential Landlord and Tenant Act in whole or substantial part. *See* 7B Uniform Laws Annotated 107 (Supp.1998). Note, however, that the Act covers only residential leases; it does not apply to commercial transactions.

3. SAMPLE LEASE

Following is the form lease that Daze Corporation used with some of the tenants in Harmony House. Read it for general understanding at this point. As we proceed through the materials in this chapter, you will be referred to specific sections of the lease and asked about their adequacy.

LEASE AGREEMENT*

By this agreement, made and entered into on _____ [date], between _____, referred to as "lessor," and _____, referred to as "lessee," lessor demises and lets to lessee, and lessee hires and takes as tenant of lessor, apartment no. _____ of the building _____ [known as _____], situated at _____ [address], _____ [city], _____ County, _____ [state], to be used and occupied by lessee as a residence and for no other use or purpose whatever, for a term of _____ years beginning on _____ [date], and ending on _____ [date], at a rental of $_____ per month, payable monthly, in advance, during the entire term of this lease, to lessor at _____ [address], _____ [city], _____ County, _____ [state], or to any other person or agent and at any other time or place that lessor may designate.

It is further mutually agreed between the parties as follows:

SECTION ONE
SECURITY DEPOSIT

On the execution of this lease, lessee deposits with lessor $_____, receipt of which is acknowledged by lessor, as security for the faithful performance by lessee of the terms of this lease agreement, to be returned to lessee, without interest, on the full and faithful performance by lessee of the provisions of this lease agreement.

SECTION TWO
NUMBER OF OCCUPANTS

Lessee agrees that the leased apartment shall be occupied by no more than _____ [number] persons, consisting of _____ [number] adults and _____ [number] children under the age of _____ years without the prior, express, and written consent of lessor.

SECTION THREE
ASSIGNMENT AND SUBLETTING

Without the prior, express, and written consent of lessor, lessee shall not assign this lease, or sublet the premises or any part of the premises. A consent by lessor to one assignment or subletting shall not be deemed to be a consent to any subsequent assignment or subletting.

---

* Found at 11 Am.Jur.Legal Forms § 161:38, Lease of apartment—Unfur- nished (2d ed. 1998 rev.). Reprinted with permission of the West Group.

SECTION FOUR
SHOWING APARTMENT FOR RENTAL

Lessee grants permission to lessor to show the apartment to new rental applicants at reasonable hours of the day, within _____ days of the expiration of the term of this lease.

SECTION FIVE
ENTRY FOR INSPECTION, REPAIRS, AND ALTERATIONS

Lessor shall have the right to enter the leased premises for inspection at all reasonable hours and whenever necessary to make repairs and alterations of the apartment or the apartment building, or to clean the apartment.

SECTION SIX
UTILITIES

Electricity, gas, telephone service, and other utilities are not furnished as a part of this lease unless otherwise indicated in this lease agreement. These expenses are the responsibility of and shall be obtained at the expense of lessee. Charges for _____ *[water and garbage service or as the case may be]* furnished to the apartment are included as a part of this lease and shall be borne by lessor.

SECTION SEVEN
REPAIRS, REDECORATION, OR ALTERATIONS

Lessor shall be responsible for repairs to the interior and exterior of the building, provided, however, repairs required through damage caused by lessee shall be charged to lessee as additional rent. It is agreed that lessee will not make or permit to be made any alterations, additions, improvements, or changes in the leased apartment without in each case first obtaining the written consent of lessor. A consent to a particular alteration, addition, improvement, or change shall not be deemed a consent to or a waiver of restrictions against alterations, additions, improvements, or changes for the future. All alterations, changes, and improvements built, constructed, or placed in the leased apartment by lessee, with the exception of fixtures removable without damage to the apartment and movable personal property, shall, unless otherwise provided by written agreement between lessor and lessee, be the property of lessor and remain in the leased apartment at the expiration or earlier termination of this lease.

SECTION EIGHT
ANIMALS

Lessee shall keep no domestic or other animals in or about the apartment or on the apartment house premises without the prior, express, and written consent of lessor.

SECTION NINE
WASTE, NUISANCE, OR UNLAWFUL USE

Lessee agrees that _____ *[he or she]* will not commit waste on the premises, or maintain or permit to be maintained a nuisance on the premises, or use or permit the premises to be used in an unlawful manner.

SECTION TEN
WAIVERS

A waiver by lessor of a breach of any covenant or duty of lessee under this lease is not a waiver of a breach of any other covenant or duty of lessee, or of any subsequent breach of the same covenant or duty.

SECTION ELEVEN
LESSEE'S HOLDING OVER

The parties agree that any holding over by lessee under this lease, without lessor's written consent, shall be a tenancy at will which may be terminated by lessor on _____ days' notice in writing.

SECTION TWELVE
PARKING SPACE

Lessee is granted a license to use parking space No. _____ in the apartment building for the purpose of parking one motor vehicle during the term of this lease.

SECTION THIRTEEN
OPTION TO RENEW

Lessee is hereby granted the option of renewing this lease for an additional term of _____ *[number]* _____ *[months or years]* on the same terms and conditions as contained in this lease agreement and at the _____ *[monthly or annual]* rent of $_____. If lessee elects to exercise this option, _____ *[he or she]* must give at least _____ days' written notice to lessor prior to the termination of this lease.

SECTION FOURTEEN
REDELIVERY OF PREMISES

At the end of the term of this lease, lessee shall quit and deliver up the premises to lessor in as good condition as they are now, ordinary wear, decay, and damage by the elements excepted.

SECTION FIFTEEN
DEFAULT

If lessee defaults in the payment of rent or any part of the rent at the times specified above, or if lessee defaults in the performance of or compliance with any other term or condition of this lease agreement _____ *[or of the regulations attached to and made a part of this lease agreement, which regulations shall be subject to occasional amendment or addition by lessor],* the lease, at the option of lessor, shall terminate and be forfeited, and lessor may reenter the premises and retake possession and recover damages, including costs and attorney fees. Lessee shall be given _____ *[written]* notice of any default or breach. Termination and forfeiture of the lease shall not result if, within _____ days of receipt of such notice, lessee has corrected the default or breach or has taken action reasonably likely to effect correction within a reasonable time.

SECTION SIXTEEN
DESTRUCTION OF PREMISES AND EMINENT DOMAIN

In the event the leased premises are destroyed or rendered untenantable by fire, storm, or earthquake, or other casualty not caused by the negligence of lessee, or if the leased premises are taken by eminent domain, this lease shall be at an end from such time except for the purpose of enforcing rights that may have then accrued under this lease agreement. The rental shall then be accounted for between lessor and lessee up to the time of such injury or destruction or taking of the premises, lessee paying up to such date and lessor refunding the rent collected beyond such date. Should a part only of the leased premises be destroyed or rendered untenantable by fire, storm, earthquake, or other casualty not caused by the negligence of lessee, the rental shall abate in the proportion that the injured part bears to the whole leased premises. The part so injured shall be restored by lessor as speedily as practicable, after which the full rent shall recommence and the lease continue according to its terms. Any condemnation award concerning the leased premises shall belong exclusively to lessor.

SECTION SEVENTEEN
DELAY IN OR IMPOSSIBILITY OF DELIVERY OF POSSESSION

In the event possession cannot be delivered to lessee on commencement of the lease term, through no fault of lessor or lessor's agents, there shall be no liability on lessor or lessor's agents, but the rental provided in this lease agreement shall abate until possession is given. Lessor or lessor's agents shall have _____ days in which to give possession, and if possession is tendered within that time, lessee agrees to accept the leased premises and pay the rental provided in this lease agreement. In the event possession cannot be delivered within that time, through no fault of lessor or lessor's agents, then this lease and all rights under this lease agreement shall be at an end.

SECTION EIGHTEEN
BINDING EFFECT

The covenants and conditions contained in this lease agreement shall apply to and bind the heirs, legal representatives, and assigns of the parties to this lease agreement, and all covenants are to be construed as conditions of this lease.

SECTION NINETEEN
GOVERNING LAW

It is agreed that this lease agreement shall be governed by, construed, and enforced in accordance with the laws of _____ *[state]*.

SECTION TWENTY
ATTORNEY FEES

In the event that any action is filed in relation to this lease agreement, the unsuccessful party in the action shall pay to the successful party, in addition to all the sums that either party may be called on to pay, a reasonable sum for the successful party's attorney fees.

SECTION TWENTY–ONE
TIME OF THE ESSENCE

It is specifically declared and agreed that time is of the essence of this lease agreement.

SECTION TWENTY–TWO
PARAGRAPH HEADINGS

The titles to the paragraphs of this lease agreement are solely for the convenience of the parties and shall not be used to explain, modify, simplify, or aid in the interpretation of the provisions of this lease agreement.

In witness whereof, each party to this lease agreement has caused it to be executed at _____ *[place of execution]* on the date indicated below.

[Signatures and date(s) of signing]

[Acknowledgments]

B. LEASES—CREATION AND CLASSIFICATION

1. CREATION—STATUTE OF FRAUDS

The landlord-tenant relationship is created by an express or implied agreement between the parties. The English Statute of Frauds (1677) required written evidence for certain lease agreements, contracts, and conveyances. Oral leases exceeding three years in duration had "the force and effect of leases or estates at will only." Enacted at a time when parol transactions were common, the measure was designed to make contractual and property dealings more secure by eliminating fraudulent practices. *See* 6 W. Holdsworth, A History of English Law 379–393 (1924). The Statute of Frauds has been adopted in some form by every state. Most modern statutes limit the maximum length of oral leases to one year. The application of the Statute of Frauds to real estate contracts and deeds will be considered in Chapter 4.

Problems and Questions

1. What is the effect of a lease that violates the Statute of Frauds? L orally rented T a store for a five-year term for a total rent of $60,000, payable in monthly installments of $1,000. T took possession and paid rent for six months. Is the lease void and T a trespasser? In formulating your response consider the discussion of tenancy at will on page 14.

2. In addition to the requirement that certain leases be in writing, the English Statute of Frauds and many American versions of that statute contain a separate provision that requires a writing for agreements not to be performed within one year from the date of "the making thereof." On May 18, L orally rented T a house for a one year term beginning July 1 and ending on June 30 the next year. Is the agreement in violation of the Statute of Frauds? The courts are split on the question. *See* Bell v. Vaughn, 46 Ariz. 515, 53 P.2d 61 (1935); Annot., *Parol Lease for Term of Years to Commence in Future as Within Statute of Frauds,* 111 A.L.R. 1465 (1937).

GEE v. NIEBERG

Missouri Court of Appeals, St. Louis District, 1973.
501 S.W.2d 542.

McMILLIAN, JUDGE.

This is an appeal by defendant Marvin C. Nieberg from a judgment of $315.00, plus interest, for a total of $337.05 entered by the Circuit Court of St. Louis County in favor of plaintiffs Sidney Gee and Margaret Gee. The controversy arose out of a landlord-tenant dispute and is concerned with the sufficiency of an oral agreement to terminate a written lease. We affirm the judgment of the Circuit Court.

Plaintiffs and defendant on July 18, 1969, entered into a written one-year lease. Occupancy was to commence on August 1, 1969. Monthly rental payments were $315.00 and plaintiffs paid to defendant one month's rent as a security deposit which was to be returned by defendant at the expiration of the lease, provided plaintiffs had discharged all the lease covenants required of them.

On [June] 28, 1970,[1] after having paid eleven months' rent in addition to the security deposit, plaintiffs moved. In support of their claim for the return of the security deposit, plaintiffs, by leave of the court, amended their petition to allege that the twelfth month of the lease had been mutually terminated by an oral agreement. Defendant denied any agreement to terminate the lease, and claimed the $315.00 security deposit for the last month's rent.

* * *

The unruly behavior of the Gee's four children provided the source of the dissension between these litigants, particularly at the swimming pool within the complex. Defendant-landlord testified as to his grave concern for the safety of the Gee children as well as that of others using the facility. Furthermore, he complained about the condition of the lawn adjacent to the Gee's apartment which the Gee children continued to trample with their bicycles although he had concrete sidewalks constructed.

Plaintiff Margaret Gee testified that after a conversation between her and defendant, wherein they agreed that "things had gone too far," defendant, when asked about the Gee's lease, said, "You find a place to live and I will release you." Immediately thereafter, Mrs. Gee went out, looked for, found another place, and moved. We find this sufficient consideration to support defendant's verbal promise.

Inasmuch as the one-year lease agreement between the parties was entered into on July 18, 1969, and was to begin August 1, 1969, it is obvious that the agreement itself extended for a period longer than one year. Pursuant to our statutes such an agreement, in order to be taken out of the ambit of the statute of frauds provision, must extend for one year or less. Consequently, the written lease was required by § 432.010, RSMo 1969, V.A.M.S., to be in writing for an action to be brought thereon. And as contended by defendant, we agree that the general rule, where the original contract is required by the statute of frauds to be in writing, is that it may not be modified or varied by a subsequent oral agreement.

The question here is whether the two parties attempted to modify the existing lease or whether the subsequent oral agreement was an abrogation of a written contract within the statute of frauds. While an oral modification of a contract coming within the statute of frauds is ordinarily regarded as invalidated by the statute, the trend of modern

---

1. Mr. Martin M. Green of St. Louis, attorney for the tenant, advised the authors that the July 28 date stated in the court's opinion is incorrect and that his client actually vacated the premises on June 28, 1970. We wish to thank Mr. Green for resolving this factual irregularity and for providing us with additional background information about the case. [Editors' Note.]

authority seems toward the view that an oral re[s]cission of an executory contract is valid notwithstanding the contract rescinded was one required by the statute of frauds to be in writing. Moreover, it is generally held that an oral agreement for the surrender of a written lease required by the statute of frauds to be in writing is within the statute, unless the unexpired term of the lease is less than that required by the statute to be in writing.

* * * Here, the purpose of the oral agreement was not to add to or change the nature of the parties' obligations under the old lease, but rather to bring it to an end so as to release the parties and abrogate the old lease entirely. Therefore, since the lease agreement was executory and the unexpired term was less than that required by the statute of frauds to be in writing, we hold that the lease was terminated by the subsequent executory oral agreement.

Accordingly, judgment affirmed.

Notes, Problems, and Questions

1. Would the court in *Gee* have reached a different conclusion if the lease had involved commercial property? *See* Johnson v. Ashkouti, 193 Ga.App. 810, 389 S.E.2d 27 (1989) (oral release ineffective because three-year commercial lease at issue was required to be in writing under Statute of Frauds).

2. Only $315.00 was involved in this controversy. Considering the high cost of litigation, why do you suppose the landlord appealed the decision of the trial court? Is there a better way to handle such disputes? *See* Kurtzberg & Henikoff, *Freeing the Parties From the Law: Designing an Interest and Rights Focused Model of Landlord/Tenant Mediation*, 1997, No. 1, *J.Disp.Resol.* 53; Comment, *Arbitration of Landlord–Tenant Disputes*, 27 Am.U.L.Rev. 407 (1978); *see also* Riskin, *Mediation and Lawyers*, 43 Ohio St.L.J. 29 (1982).

3. *Gee* is the first of numerous decisions you will analyze. The use of actual cases as a basis for study is pedagogically sound, but overemphasizes the litigation aspect of law practice. Throughout your studies, keep in mind that most lawyers are primarily counselors, negotiators, and drafters. *See* Bruce, *A Critique of the Litigation Emphasis of Legal Education*, 12 Stetson L.Rev. 593 (1983).

2. CLASSIFICATION BY DURATION

In our hypothetical situation, the tenants at Harmony House occupied their apartments under different lease arrangements. This matter requires further examination. Leases are usually classified by duration into four general categories.

a. Tenancy for a Fixed Term (Estate for Years)

A lease for any set period, be it six days, six weeks, six months, or six years, is a tenancy for a fixed term. Such a lease has been traditionally called an estate for years, but the label "tenancy for a fixed term" is similar to the terminology used in the Restatement (Second) of Property and conveys a more accurate image of the nature of the lease. *See* Restatement (Second) of Property, Landlord and Tenant § 1.4 (1977).

There is no common law limitation on the duration of a tenancy for a fixed term. Statutes in some states, however, set a maximum length for leases, *e.g.*, ninety-nine years, or convert long-term leases into absolute ownership interests. *See id.* at reporter's note & statutory note 3. *See also* the *Lonergan* case on page 123.

A tenancy for a fixed term terminates automatically at the end of the term. Absent agreement to the contrary, the landlord need not give advance notice to the tenant that the period stated in the lease is about to expire.

b. *Periodic Tenancy*

A lease giving the tenant possession of the leased property for successive identical periods of time is a periodic tenancy. The period may be a week, month, year, or other specified length of time, but a month-to-month tenancy is most common. Such an arrangement may be created by express agreement between the parties or imposed by operation of law where the parties fail to fix a lease term and rent is paid periodically.

The periodic tenancy is of potentially indefinite duration because it is automatically renewed for successive periods unless one of the parties gives proper notice to terminate. The type of notice required to terminate a periodic tenancy has been the subject of a great deal of controversy. The common law rules on notice to terminate are: (1) six months' notice for a year-to-year tenancy; (2) notice equal to the length of the period where the period is less than a year (e.g. one month's notice for a month-to-month tenancy); (3) the date for termination must be at the end of a period. The first two rules have been codified in many states, often with modification. The third common law rule survives intact in most jurisdictions. *See* 1 American Law of Property §§ 3.23, 3.90 (1952); Restatement (Second) of Property, Landlord and Tenant § 1.5 (1977).

Notes and Questions

1.   The Uniform Residential Landlord and Tenant Act § 4.301(a) & (b) (1974) expands the notice required to terminate a week-to-week residential tenancy to ten days and the notice to terminate a month-to-month residential tenancy to sixty days.

2.   Notice to terminate a periodic tenancy may be oral unless required to be in writing by the lease or by statute. Statutes in several states require only the landlord to give written notice. *See* Restatement (Second) of Property, Landlord and Tenant § 1.5 comment f, statutory note 2c, & reporter's note (1977).

3.   Is notice given during the middle of a period effective? If so, when? *See* S.D.G. v. Inventory Control Co., 178 N.J.Super. 411, 429 A.2d 394 (1981).

c. Tenancy at Will

A lease that may be terminated at the election of either party is a tenancy at will. At common law no advance notice was necessary. In many states, however, statutes provide for notice to terminate. Further, if rent is paid periodically, the arrangement generally is treated by the courts as a periodic tenancy and appropriate notice to terminate is required.

Although a tenancy at will may be created by express agreement, often it arises because the particular arrangement in question is neither a tenancy for a fixed term nor a periodic tenancy. For example, a tenancy at will is created when a property owner permits a friend or relative to occupy the property rent-free for an indefinite period of time, or when a tenant takes possession of property under an invalid lease. *See* 1 American Law of Property §§ 3.25, 3.27–3.31 (1952); Restatement (Second) of Property, Landlord and Tenant § 1.6 & reporter's note (1977).

Problems

1. T occupied L's house as a tenant at will. L died. How long may T remain in the house?

2. T and L agreed that T could occupy L's house as long as T wished. May L ever terminate the lease? If the lease were to run only as long as L wished, could T ever terminate it?

d. Tenancy at Sufferance (Holdover Tenant)

A tenant at sufferance, often called a holdover tenant, is one who remains on leased property after termination of the lease. Absent lease provision to the contrary, the landlord has the option to treat a tenant at sufferance as either a trespasser or a new tenant. *See* 1 American Law of Property § 3.32 (1952). The landlord's remedies in such a situation are explored later in this chapter. *See* pages 117–127.

Note

You will encounter this system of lease classification (tenancy for a fixed term, periodic tenancy, tenancy at will, and tenancy at sufferance) again in Chapter 3 where the full spectrum of interests in land is presented.

C. TENANT'S RIGHT TO POSSESSION AND QUIET ENJOYMENT

We have seen that early leases usually covered land which the tenant farmed to earn sufficient money to pay the rent. The system worked only if the tenant was able to take and hold physical possession of the property free from interference by the landlord. This section deals with the development of the law protecting the tenant in this regard.

1. POSSESSION AT THE COMMENCEMENT OF THE LEASE

Possession at commencement of the lease is important to lessees of both improved and unimproved property. For example, in our hypothetical situation, many of the tenants of Harmony House plan to move rather than purchase a condominium unit in the converted Harmony House. The Lloyds are among those who plan to rent elsewhere if they must leave Harmony House. They want to take possession of a new apartment at a convenient time. What if they sign a lease for an apartment in another building and then discover that the apartment is not available at the commencement date of the lease?

HANNAN v. DUSCH

Supreme Court of Appeals of Virginia, 1930.
154 Va. 356, 153 S.E. 824.

PRENTIS, C.J.

The declaration filed by the plaintiff, Hannan, against the defendant, Dusch, alleges that Dusch had on August 31, 1927, leased to the plaintiff certain real estate in the city of Norfolk, Va., therein described, for fifteen years, the term to begin January 1, 1928, at a specified rental; that it thereupon became and was the duty of the defendant to see to it that the premises leased by the defendant to the plaintiff should be open for entry by him on January 1, 1928, the beginning of the term, and to put said petitioner in possession of the premises on that date; that the petitioner was willing and ready to enter upon and take possession of the leased property, and so informed the defendant; yet the defendant failed and refused to put the plaintiff in possession or to keep the property open for him at that time or on any subsequent date; and that the defendant suffered to remain on said property a certain tenant or tenants who occupied a portion or portions thereof, and refused to take legal or other action to oust said tenant or tenants or to compel their removal from the property so occupied. Plaintiff alleged damages which he had suffered by reason of this alleged breach of the contract and deed, and sought to recover such damages in the action. There is no express covenant as to the delivery of the premises nor for the quiet possession of the premises by the lessee.

The defendant demurred to the declaration on several grounds, one of which was "that under the lease set out in said declaration the right of possession was vested in said plaintiff and there was no duty as upon the defendant, as alleged in said declaration, to see that the premises were open for entry by said plaintiff."

The single question of law therefore presented in this case is whether a landlord, who without any express covenant as to delivery or possession leases property to a tenant, is required under the law to oust trespassers and wrongdoers so as to have it open for entry by the tenant at the beginning of the term; that is, whether without an express covenant there is nevertheless an implied covenant to deliver possession.

For an intelligent apprehension of the precise question it may be well to observe that some questions somewhat similar are not involved.

It seems to be perfectly well settled that there is an implied covenant in such cases on the part of the landlord to assure to the tenant the legal right of possession; that is, that at the beginning of the term there shall be no legal obstacle to the tenant's right of possession. This is not the question presented. Nor need we discuss in this case the rights of the parties in case a tenant rightfully in possession under the title of his landlord is thereafter disturbed by some wrongdoer. In such case the tenant must protect himself from trespassers, and there is no obligation on the landlord to assure his quiet enjoyment of his term as against wrongdoers or intruders.

Of course, the landlord assures to the tenant quiet possession as against all who rightfully claim through or under the landlord.

The discussion then is limited to the precise legal duty of the landlord in the absence of an express covenant, in case a former tenant, who wrongfully holds over, illegally refuses to surrender possession to the new tenant. This is a question about which there is a hopeless conflict of the authorities. It is generally claimed that the weight of the authority favors the particular view contended for. There are, however, no scales upon which we can weigh the authorities. In numbers and respectability they may be quite equally balanced.

It is then a question about which no one should be dogmatic, but all should seek for that rule which is supported by the better reason.

That great annotator, Hon. A.C. Freeman, has collected the authorities as they were at the time he wrote, in 1909, in a note to Sloan v. Hart (150 N.C. 269, 63 S.E. 1037, 21 L.R.A. (N.S.) 239), 134 Am.St.Rep. 916. We shall quote from and paraphrase that note freely because it is the most succinct and the most comprehensive discussion of the question with which we are familiar.

It is conceded by all that the two rules, one called the English rule, which implies a covenant requiring the lessor to put the lessee in possession, and that called the American rule, which recognizes the lessee's legal right to possession, but implies no such duty upon the lessor as against wrongdoers, are irreconcilable.

The English rule is that, in the absence of stipulations to the contrary, there is in every lease an implied covenant on the part of the landlord that the premises shall be open to entry by the tenant at the time fixed by the lease for the beginning of his term. * * *

* * *

It must be borne in mind, however, that the courts which hold that there is such an implied covenant do not extend the period beyond the day when the lessee's term begins. If after that day a stranger trespasses upon the property and wrongfully obtains or withholds possession of it from the lessee, his remedy is against the stranger and not against the lessor.

It is not necessary for either party to involve himself in uncertainty, for by appropriate covenants each may protect himself against any doubt either as against a tenant then in possession who may wrongfully hold over by refusing to deliver the possession at the expiration of his own term, or against any other trespasser.

In Rhodes v. Purvis, 74 Ark. 227, 85 S.W. 235, 236, the lessor agreed that the terms should commence "from the date of the occupancy, which the contract provided should commence as soon as vacated by the present occupants." He was not able to eject them as soon as contemplated, and it was held that this provision exempted him from any liability to the new tenant for failure to deliver possession prior to such vacation by the tenants in possession.

As has been stated, the lessee may also protect himself by having his lessor expressly covenant to put him in possession at a specified time, in which case, of course, the lessor is liable for breach of his express covenant where a trespasser goes into possession or wrongfully holds possession, and thereby wrongfully prevents the lessee from obtaining possession.

* * *

[A] case which supports the English rule is Herpolsheimer v. Christopher, 76 Neb. 352, 107 N.W. 382, 111 N.W. 359, 360, 9 L.R.A. (N.S.) 1127, 14 Ann.Cas. 399, note. In that case the court gave these as its reasons for following the English rule: "We deem it unnecessary to enter into an extended discussion, since the reasons pro and con are fully given in the opinions of the several courts cited. We think, however, that the English rule is most in consonance with good conscience, sound principle, and fair dealing. Can it be supposed that the plaintiff in this case would have entered into the lease if he had known at the time that he could not obtain possession on the 1st of March, but that he would be compelled to begin a lawsuit, await the law's delays, and follow the case through its devious turnings to an end before he could hope to obtain possession of the land he had leased? Most assuredly not. It is unreasonable to suppose that a man would knowingly contract for a lawsuit, or take the chance of one. Whether or not a tenant in possession intends to hold over or assert a right to a future term may nearly always be known to the landlord, and is certainly much more apt to be within his knowledge than within that of the prospective tenant. Moreover, since in an action to recover possession against a tenant holding over the lessee would be compelled largely to rely upon the lessor's testimony in regard to the facts of the claim to hold over by the wrongdoer, it is more reasonable and proper to place the burden upon the person within whose knowledge the facts are most apt to lie. We are convinced, therefore, that the better reason lies with the courts following the English doctrine, and we therefore adopt it, and hold that ordinarily the lessor impliedly covenants with the lessee that the premises leased shall be open to entry by him at the time fixed in the lease as the beginning of the term."

In commenting on this line of cases, Mr. Freeman says this: "The above rule practically prohibits the landlord from leasing the premises while in the possession of a tenant whose term is about to expire, because notwithstanding the assurance on the part of the tenant that he will vacate on the expiration of his term, he may change his mind and wrongfully hold over. It is true that the landlord may provide for such a contingency by suitable provisions in the lease to the prospective tenant, but it is equally true that the prospective tenant has the privilege of insisting that his prospective landlord expressly agree to put him in possession of the premises if he imagines there may be a chance for a lawsuit by the tenant in possession holding over. It seems to us that to raise by implication a covenant on the part of the landlord to put the tenant into possession is to make a contract for the parties in regard to a matter which is equally within the knowledge of both the landlord and tenant."

So let us not lose sight of the fact that under the English rule a covenant which might have been, but was not, made is nevertheless implied by the court, though it is manifest that each of the parties might have provided for that and for every other possible contingency relating to possession by having express covenants which would unquestionably have protected both.

Referring then to the American rule: Under that rule, in such cases, "the landlord is not bound to put the tenant into actual possession, but is bound only to put him into legal possession, so that no obstacle in the form of a superior right of possession will be interposed to prevent the tenant from obtaining actual possession of the demised premises. If the landlord gives the tenant a right of possession he has done all that he is required to do by the terms of an ordinary lease, and the tenant assumes the burden of enforcing such right of possession as against all persons wrongfully in possession, whether they be trespassers or former tenants wrongfully holding over." This quoted language is Mr. Freeman's, and he cites * * * cases in support thereof * * *.

So that, under the American rule, where the new tenant fails to obtain possession of the premises only because a former tenant wrongfully holds over, his remedy is against such wrongdoer and not against the landlord, this because the landlord has not covenanted against the wrongful acts of another and should not be held responsible for such a tort, unless he has expressly so contracted. This accords with the general rule as to other wrongdoers, whereas the English rule appears to create a specific exception against lessors. It does not occur to us now that there is any other instance in which one clearly without fault is held responsible for the independent tort of another in which he has neither participated nor concurred, and whose misdoings he cannot control.

* * *

There are some underlying fundamental considerations. Any written lease, for a specific term, signed by the lessor, and delivered, is like a deed signed, sealed, and delivered by the grantor. This lease for fifteen years is and is required to be by deed. It is a conveyance. During the term the tenant is substantially the owner of the property, having the right of possession, dominion, and control over it. Certainly, as a general rule, the lessee must protect himself against trespassers or other wrongdoers who disturb his possession. It is conceded by those who favor the English rule that, should the possession of the tenant be wrongfully disturbed the second day of the term, or after he has once taken possession, then there is no implied covenant on the part of his landlord to protect him from the torts of others. The English rule seems to have been applied only where the possession is disturbed on the first day, or, perhaps more fairly expressed, where the tenant is prevented from taking possession on the first day of his term; but what is the substantial difference between invading the lessee's right of possession on the first or a later day? To apply the English rule you must imply a covenant on the part of the landlord to protect the tenant from the tort of another, though he has entered into no such covenant. This seems to be a unique exception, an exception which stands alone in implying a contract of insurance on the part of the lessor to save his tenant from all the consequences of the flagrant wrong of another person. Such an obligation is so unusual and the prevention of such a tort so impossible as to make it certain, we think, that it should always rest upon an express contract.

* * *

We are confirmed in our view by the Virginia statute, providing a summary remedy for unlawful entry or detainer, Code, § 5445 et seq. The adequate, simple, and summary remedy for the correction of such a wrong provided by that statute was clearly available to this plaintiff. It specifically provides that it shall lie for one entitled to possession in any case in which a "tenant shall detain the possession of land after his right has expired, without the consent of him who is entitled to the possession." Section 5445.

* * *

The plaintiff alleges in his declaration as one of the grounds for his action that the defendant suffered the wrongdoer to remain in possession, but the allegations show that [it was he] who declined to assert his remedy against the wrongdoer, and so he it was who permitted the wrongdoer to retain the possession. Just why he valued his legal right to the possession so lightly as not to assert it in the effective way open to him does not appear. Whatever ethical duty in good conscience may possibly have rested upon the defendant, the duty to oust the wrongdoer by the summary remedy provided by the unlawful detainer statute clearly rested upon the plaintiff. The law helps those who help themselves, generally aids the vigilant, but rarely the sleeping, and never the acquiescent.

[Judgment for defendant-landlord is] [a]ffirmed.

Notes and Questions

1. The English rule has gained support since the *Hannan* decision. *See* Weisenberger, *The Landlord's Duty to Deliver Possession: The Overlooked Reform,* 46 U.Cin.L.Rev. 937 (1978); *see also* Uniform Residential Landlord and Tenant Act §§ 2.103, 4.102 (1974).

2. What are the tenant's rights against the landlord when the landlord breaches its duty under either rule? *See* 1 American Law of Property § 3.37 (1952). *See also* Uniform Residential Landlord and Tenant Act § 4.102 (1974) for one legislative approach to the problem.

3. The *Hannan* decision notes that the parties may make a specific agreement about possession. Does section seventeen of the sample lease on page 9 adequately protect the interests of both parties?

2. QUIET ENJOYMENT DURING THE LEASE TERM

A covenant of quiet enjoyment is implied in leases in virtually all states and is expressly included in many written leases. The covenant is breached when the tenant is evicted by the landlord, by someone acting under the landlord's authority, or by someone asserting paramount title. *See* 1 American Law of Property §§ 3.47–3.50 (1952). Eviction by paramount title occurs, for example, when the landlord does not own the leased property and the true owner demands possession, or when a prior mortgage on the property is foreclosed. *See id.* at § 3.48; *see also* Restatement (Second) of Property, Landlord and Tenant § 4.1 (1977).

a. Actual Eviction

CAMATRON SEWING MACHINE, INC.
v. F.M. RING ASSOCIATES, INC.

Supreme Court of New York, Appellate Division, First Department, 1992.
179 A.D.2d 165, 582 N.Y.S.2d 396.

SULLIVAN, JUSTICE.

Plaintiff seeks a judicial declaration of the rights of the parties with respect to a planned alteration by the landlord under a lease entered into on July 18, 1984 between plaintiff and R.C.M. Maintenance Co., Inc., pursuant to which plaintiff, for a period of ten years commencing September 1, 1984 and ending August 31, 1994, rented the "store, basement space * * * and the entire seventh (7th) floor" at 142–146 West 24th Street in Manhattan. * * * Six weeks after entering into the lease, on August 29, 1984, R.C.M. assigned all of its rights under the lease to the defendants Ring.

Throughout the entire period of its tenancy, plaintiff has used the seventh floor as a warehouse, the basement area for manufacturing and the "store", which constitutes the entire rentable portion of the building's ground floor, both for manufacturing (back area) and to house its administrative and executive offices (front area). According to plaintiff, of all the demised space spread over three floors of the building, the "store" is the most vital to its operation since its day-to-day business operations are conducted from that space.

In August 1988, defendant Frank Ring informed plaintiff that defendants were planning a renovation of the lobby. Mr. Ring subsequently advised plaintiff that defendants intended to knock down the lobby wall adjacent to plaintiff's administrative office and move it inward three feet. This particular renovation, intended to ameliorate the lobby's awkward configuration, would eliminate 46.5 square feet from the store area, approximately 25% of plaintiff's administrative office.

Plaintiff objected to the proposed renovation on the ground that it would adversely affect its business operations by eliminating vital space. Since the renovation would, plaintiff argued, deprive it of possession of a portion of the leased space, it thus constituted a partial actual eviction. Defendants ignored plaintiff's protests, claiming that Article 13 of the lease authorized the contemplated diminution of plaintiff's leased area. Article 13, upon which defendants rely, provides, in pertinent part:

> Owner shall have the right at any time, without the same constituting an eviction and without incurring liability to Tenant therefor to change the arrangement and/or location of public entrances, passageways, doors, doorways, corridors, elevators, stairs, toilets, or other public parts of the building and to change the name, number or designation by which the building may be known.

After joinder of issue in the within lawsuit, plaintiff moved for summary judgment and injunctive relief prohibiting defendants from making any renovations or alterations which would deprive it of its leased area. Defendants cross-moved for summary judgment on the ground that Article 13 of the lease entitled them to make the renovations, which were *de minimis,* and for counsel fees. Defendants argued that the 46.5 square feet loss would constitute less than 1% of the total demised space, that is, store area, basement and seventh floor. The [trial] court denied summary judgment to plaintiff and granted defendants' cross-motion for summary judgment dismissing the complaint, holding that the lease authorized the renovations. Plaintiff appeals, while defendants cross-appeal from the denial of their request for legal fees. We modify to reverse the denial of summary judgment to plaintiff and the grant of same to defendants, to declare in plaintiff's favor and permanently enjoin defendants from proceeding with their proposed renovation to the extent it diminishes plaintiff's leasehold interest.

While Article 13 of the lease, cited by defendants as authorization for the contemplated taking and relied upon by the [trial] court in dismissing the complaint, permits changes in the location of, *inter alia,* the public entrances, passageways, doorways and corridors and "other public parts of the building", "without the same constituting an eviction", that reservation is limited to the building's public areas and does not, explicitly or implicitly, authorize the landlord to take a portion of the demised area. Absent such a reservation to the landlord, the tenant has the sole and exclusive right to undisturbed possession during the term of the lease and the landlord has no right to take possession of a part of the demised premises to the exclusion of the tenant. Since plaintiff has the exclusive right to occupy the 46.5 square feet area which will be taken as a result of defendants' relocation of a lobby wall, its loss of the use of that area constitutes an actual eviction, albeit partial, on the part of defendants. Moreover, contrary to defendants' argument, the contemplated taking is not *de minimis;* it constitutes 25% of the 201.5 square foot store space used for its administrative office. In 81 Franklin Co. v. Ginaccini, 160 A.D.2d 558, 554 N.Y.S.2d 207, the landlord's construction of an elevator shaft through the tenant's art gallery constituted, *inter alia,* a 1% diminution of the total demised space and was held to constitute a partial actual eviction entitling the tenant to a rent abatement.

The [trial] court's reliance on Bijan Designer For Men, Inc. v. St. Regis Sheraton Corp., 142 Misc.2d 175, 536 N.Y.S.2d 951, *affd,* 150 A.D.2d 244, 543 N.Y.S.2d 296, is misplaced. There, the tenant leased premises consisting of two-story retail space in the St. Regis Hotel. The store had an entrance on Fifth Avenue as well as entrances from the hotel's lobby and mezzanine. The court found that there was no actual eviction as a result of extensive renovation work which restricted customers' entry from the lobby and mezzanine, since the tenant had agreed that the landlord had the right to make repairs or alterations "either to the Hotel or the demised premises" and would not be liable for loss or interruption of the tenant's business as a result of the repairs or alterations. (142 Misc.2d at 178, 536 N.Y.S.2d 951.) Similarly, in Two Rector Street Corp. v. Bein, 226 App.Div. 73, 234 N.Y.S. 409, and Ernst v. Straus, 114 App.Div. 19, 99 N.Y.S. 597, cited by defendants, the landlord's entry was a temporary one and was for the purpose of making repairs and alterations pursuant to a provision in the lease giving the landlord permission to enter for such a purpose. In none of these cases did the landlord seek, as it does here, to deprive the tenant permanently of a portion of the leased space without any contractual right to do so.

Nor does the authorization given to the landlord to enter the demised premises to make necessary and "reasonably desirable" repairs or improvements constitute authorization of alterations which would take from the tenant a portion of its premises. Neither Article 13 nor any other provision of the lease authorizes a rearrangement of demised space or gives the landlord the right to make a renovation which would result in a diminution in the size of the demised premises.

* * *

All concur.

Notes and Questions

1. Assume the landlord moved the lobby wall late one night without the tenant's knowledge. Must the tenant continue to pay rent? Consider the

following analysis from Smith v. McEnany, 170 Mass. 26, 27–28, 48 N.E. 781, 781–782 (1897):

> * * * It is settled in this state, in accordance with the law of England, that a wrongful eviction of the tenant by the landlord from a part of the premises suspends the rent under the lease. The main reason which is given for the decisions is that the enjoyment of the whole consideration is the foundation of the debt and the condition of the covenant, and that the obligation to pay cannot be apportioned. It is also said that the landlord shall not apportion his own wrong, following an expression in some of the older English books. But this does not so much explain the rule as suggest the limitation that there may be an apportionment when the eviction is by title paramount or when the lessor's entry is rightful. It leaves open the question why the landlord may not show that his wrong extended only to a part of the premises. No doubt the question equally may be asked why the lease is construed to exclude apportionment, and it may be that this is partly due to the traditional doctrine that the rent issues out of the land, and that the whole rent is charged on every part of the land. But the same view naturally would be taken if the question arose now for the first time. The land is hired as one whole. If by his own fault the landlord withdraws a part of it he cannot recover either on the lease or outside of it for the occupation of the residue.

* * *

> * * * [A partial actual] eviction like the present does not necessarily end the lease, or other obligations of the tenant under it, such as the covenant to repair.

This view is still followed in many states. *See, e.g.*, 487 Elmwood, Inc. v. Hassett, 107 A.D.2d 285, 486 N.Y.S.2d 113 (1985). Nevertheless, certain jurisdictions apportion the rent when there is a partial actual eviction. Which is the better approach? *See* Restatement (Second) of Property, Landlord and Tenant § 6.1 reporter's note 6 (1977).

2.   The *Camatron Sewing Machine* case involved partial actual eviction. When the landlord wrongfully evicts the tenant from the entire premises, the tenant need not pay rent while ousted. The tenant may seek to regain possession or may terminate the lease and recover damages. "[T]he measure of damages is the difference between the rental value of the premises for the remainder of the term and the rent reserved in the lease, with such special damages as may have been within the contemplation of the parties." 1 American Law of Property § 3.52 (1952).

3.   Does a landlord breach the covenant of quiet enjoyment by making an opening in one of the apartment's windows and peeking into the apartment? *See* Kobouroff v. Blake, 16 Misc.2d 202, 183 N.Y.S.2d 934 (City of N.Y. Mun. Ct. 1959). *See generally* Stevens, *Intrusion Into Solitude and the Tenant's Right to Privacy*, 16 Real Estate L.J. 324 (1988).

b. *Constructive Eviction*

As indicated in the preceding section, the tenant does not have to pay rent if the landlord interferes with the tenant's possession (quiet enjoyment) of the premises. The early cases required an actual eviction to relieve the tenant of the obligation to pay rent. Eventually the courts recognized that the value of the tenant's possession might be effectively destroyed by the landlord's wrongful conduct that falls short of physical interference. Thus, today the covenant of quiet enjoyment may be breached by "constructive" as well as actual eviction. *See* 1 American Law of Property §§ 3.50–3.51 (1952).

In order for constructive eviction to occur, the landlord must breach some duty to the tenant. It is necessary that the duty be found outside the covenant of quiet enjoyment which imposes no specific obligation on the landlord, requiring only that the landlord not interfere with the tenant's possession. In some of the more recent cases on constructive eviction, however, the courts are quite vague about the legal duty the landlord is supposed to have violated, particularly where the "violation" is an act of omission. *See* Rapacz, *Origin and Evolution of Constructive Eviction in the United States,* 1 DePaul L.Rev. 69, 72–74, 79–84 (1951).

Once it is determined that the landlord has breached a duty, for example, failed to make repairs as required by the lease, the tenant may be able to claim constructive eviction. But is the doctrine of constructive eviction necessary? Cannot the tenant simply withhold rent until the landlord makes the repair or have the repair made and deduct the cost from the rent? Not under the common law of property where lease covenants are considered independent undertakings. Hence, if the landlord breaches a lease covenant such as a promise to make repairs, traditional property law permits the tenant to recover damages, but requires the tenant to continue to pay rent.[1] *See* 1 Friedman on Leases § 1.1 (4th ed. 1997).

The common law treatment of lease covenants as independent obligations developed because, from a property law perspective, the landlord fulfills the landlord's obligation by conveying a leasehold estate to the tenant. However, as discussed earlier in this chapter, the modern lease is much different from the type of lease employed at the time the common law developed. Today the typical lease deals primarily with shelter and services rather than undeveloped agricultural land and contains numerous covenants regarding these matters. Consequently,

---

1. Similarly, if the tenant failed to pay rent, early property law permitted the landlord to recover damages, but prevented the landlord from retaking possession. Landlords, however, soon routinely inserted forfeiture provisions in leases making the tenant's right to possession dependent upon paying rent and complying with other lease covenants. *See* section fifteen of the sample lease on page 8. Moreover, legislatures and courts in this country have changed the early common law and now generally permit the landlord to recover possession of the leased property when the tenant fails to pay rent. *See* Humbach, *The Common–Law Conception of Leasing: Mitigation, Habitability, and Dependence of Covenants,* 60 Wash.U.L.Q. 1213, 1229–1231 (1983).

there is a strong trend to apply contract law to leases, including the contractual principle that covenants are mutually dependent. But, before we examine this trend, let us see how courts have utilized the doctrine of constructive eviction to relieve the tenant of the burden imposed by the common law property rule that lease covenants are independent obligations. In this respect, the doctrine serves as a half-way step toward the application of contract principles to lease agreements. *See id.*

AUTOMOBILE SUPPLY CO. v. SCENE–IN–ACTION CORP.

Supreme Court of Illinois, 1930.
340 Ill. 196, 172 N.E. 35.

DUNN, C. J.

The Automobile Supply Company recovered a judgment by confession against the Scene-in-Action Corporation on a lease for $1,750 rent for the last five months of the term ending September 30, 1928, and $20 attorney's fees. The defendant made a motion to vacate the judgment, which was denied, and on appeal the Appellate Court affirmed the judgment. The record has been certified to us as a return to a writ of certiorari allowed on the petition of the defendant.

The defense alleged in the motion to vacate was a constructive eviction of the lessee by the breach of the landlord's covenant to furnish steam heat during ordinary business hours of the heating season, the premises having been rented by the defendant for office purposes and for the manufacture, sale, and shipping of electrical advertising display signs. The affidavit filed by the defendant in support of its motion to vacate showed that the office was rented for the use of the officers of the defendant, its clerks, stenographers, bookkeepers, and other employees, and the rest of the premises for the manufacture, sale, and shipping of electrical display advertising signs by artists, workmen, designers, mechanics, clerks, and other employees of the defendant; that it was necessary for the proper conduct of the business that not only the office but the workrooms should be kept at a comfortable temperature, otherwise the officers, clerks, stenographers, artists, designers, and workmen could not do a reasonable amount of work, or work of proper kind or accuracy; that the kind of work, the materials used, and the class of workmen and artists employed all required that the premises be kept at a reasonably comfortable degree of heat, all of which was well known to the plaintiff and its officers and agents at and before the execution and delivery of the lease; that the plaintiff did not furnish heat reasonably adequate to make the premises tenantable for office purposes or for the manufacture, sale, and shipment of electrical advertising display signs, but, on the contrary, in November, 1927, during cold days, the premises were without heat from two to five hours on several days; that during December, 1927, there were eight cold days when the premises were without heat from two to five hours each day; that one day for six hours the premises were without heat and were cold, uncomfortable, and untenantable for the purpose of which they were rented; that complaint was frequently made during this period to the plaintiff and its agents but without effect; that the plaintiff was indifferent, and though often requested did not attempt to remedy the matter or give adequate heat for the purpose for which the premises were rented; that on February 20, 1928, at the opening of the usual business hours, the temperature in the premises was below 50° owing to the negligence of the plaintiff in failing to heat them and the defendant was unable to do business until after 10 o'clock on that day, and the defendant gave notice to the plaintiff that, owing to the failure to comply with the terms of the lease, it would be terminated and canceled on April 30, 1928, and that the defendant would vacate the premises on that date; that no attempt was made by the plaintiff to better such conditions and on many days during February and March the temperature was below 50° Fahrenheit; that on April 9, 1928, it was below 50° upon the arrival of the employees, and remained so until after 11:30 owing to the negligence of the plaintiff and its employees; that during the months of November, December, February, March, and April, the defendant had from thirty to thirty-five employees on said premises who for a considerable time and parts of many days were unable to work because of the frigid temperature, and it was impossible to make the artistic designs, plates, pictures, photographs, and displays necessary in and about the manufacture of its signs unless the temperature was about 55° Fahrenheit; that a number of the employees of the defendant were rendered sick and unable to carry on their work by reason of colds caused by the lack of proper heat in the premises, and were obliged to go home and abandon their work, for days at a time, to the great loss and damage of the defendant, and at other times said employees labored under great handicaps and were unable to produce the amount and character of work which they ordinarily produced when the rooms were comfortably warm, thereby again causing great loss and damage to the defendant and the output of work was much less than it would have been if the premises had been kept adequately heated; that by reason of the premises, and especially the failure on the part of the plaintiff to furnish adequate heat, the defendant was deprived of the beneficial use and enjoyment of the premises leased, was unable to carry on its business, and was obliged to, and did, vacate and abandon the premises, and on April 30, 1928, surrendered them to the plaintiff and delivered the keys to its agent, who accepted them, and since that date and during the period for which the judgment for rent was confessed the defendant did not occupy the premises or any portion of them and has not been, and is not, a tenant of the plaintiff.

The eviction of a tenant from the possession or enjoyment of the demised premises, or any part thereof, by the landlord releases the tenant from the further payment of rent. Rent is the return made to the lessor by the lessee for his use of the land, and the landlord's claim for rent therefore depends upon the tenant's enjoyment of the land for the term of his contract. It follows that if the tenant is deprived of the premises by any agency of the landlord the obligation to pay rent ceases, because such obligation has force only from the consideration of the enjoyment of the premises. The eviction which will discharge the liability of the tenant to pay rent is not necessarily an actual physical expulsion from the premises or some part of them, but any act of the landlord which renders the lease unavailing to the tenant or deprives him of the beneficial enjoyment of the premises constitutes a constructive eviction of the tenant, which exonerates him from the terms and conditions of the lease and he may abandon it.

Not every act of a landlord in violation of his covenants or of the tenant's enjoyment of the premises under the lease will amount to a constructive eviction. Some acts of interference may be mere acts of trespass to which the term "eviction" is not applicable. To constitute an eviction there must be something of a grave and permanent character done by the landlord clearly indicating the intention of the landlord to deprive the tenant of the longer beneficial enjoyment of the premises in accordance with the terms of the lease. The failure of a landlord to furnish heat for the demised premises in accordance with the terms of his covenant in the lease justifies the tenant in removing from the premises, and if he does so he is discharged from the payment of rent thereafter. These facts constitute a constructive eviction. There can be no constructive eviction, however, without the vacating of the premises. Where a tenant fails to surrender possession after the landlord's commission of acts justifying the abandonment of the premises, the liability for rent will continue so long as possession of the premises is continued. Whether the acts of the landlord amount to a constructive eviction is ordinarily a question of fact for the decision of a jury, depending upon the circumstances of the particular case.

The affidavit in support of the motion to vacate the judgment did not show a defense to the claim for rent under the principles stated. Conceding, without deciding, that the affidavit stated with sufficient definiteness and particularity conditions in regard to the furnishing of heat which would have justified the vacating of the premises in December, on February 20, and on April 9, yet the defendant did not vacate them. It complained frequently in November and December. Its complaints were not heeded, and by its continued occupation of the premises it waived its right to terminate the lease for those breaches of the landlord's duty. The waiver, however, did not waive subsequent breaches, and when new breaches occurred in February, the plaintiff in error, in addition to its complaints, notified the defendant in error, not that it elected to determine the lease and vacate the property for the defendant in error's failure to furnish heat in accordance with its covenant, but that for the failure of the defendant in error to comply with the terms of the lease it would be terminated and canceled on April 30, more than two months after the giving of the notice, and that the plaintiff in error would vacate the premises on that date. It further appears that in February and March the temperature was below 50♦ Fahrenheit on many days, the number not stated nor for what length of time the low temperature continued on any day, but on April 9, the temperature was below 50♦ upon the arrival of the employees and so continued until 11:30 o'clock.

Where a landlord is guilty of such a breach of his duty to his tenant under the terms of the lease that the tenant would be justified in vacating the premises, he is not obliged to vacate immediately, but is entitled to a reasonable time in which to do so. What is such reasonable time is usually a question of fact, though under the circumstances of a particular case it may become a question of law. If the plaintiff in error on account of the failure of the defendant in error to furnish heat in December, as it had agreed, would then have been entitled to vacate the premises, it does not appear that it did so within a reasonable time, and it must therefore be regarded as having waived the defendant in error's breach of its covenant. Neither does it appear that the plaintiff in error vacated the premises within a reasonable time after February 20. If it had a right on that date to vacate the premises within a reasonable time for the previous breach of the defendant in error, it did not have the right to declare a termination of the lease to take effect two months later. And the same thing is true of the breach of April 9. The affidavit shows no cause of complaint subsequent to April 9. The burden of showing a vacation of the premises on account of the landlord's breach of his duty to the tenant under the lease within a reasonable time after such breach is upon the tenant. The affidavit sets out that by reason of the plaintiff's failure to furnish adequate heat the defendant was deprived of the beneficial use and enjoyment of the premises and was obliged to, and did, vacate and abandon them, and on April 30, 1928, surrendered them to the plaintiff and delivered the keys to its agent. The plaintiff in error no doubt stated the defense as strongly as the evidence would show it and the affidavit must be taken most strongly against it. It alleges that the defendant surrendered the premises to the plaintiff on April 30, and we cannot presume that it did so on any earlier day. The leased premises were the sixth floor of a building, and we cannot take judicial notice that three weeks was a reasonable time to vacate the premises after the last failure mentioned to furnish heat on April 9. The question was one of fact for the jury, and, in the absence of an allegation of fact tending to show the reasonableness of the time, there was no question to submit to the jury on behalf of the defendant, who had the burden of proof.

* * *

The judgment of the Appellate Court is affirmed.

Judgment affirmed.

Questions

1. What result in *Scene-In–Action Corp.* if the lease had not contained a provision requiring the landlord to supply heat? *See* Brendle's Stores, Inc. v. OTR, 978 F.2d 150 (4th Cir.1992) (tenant failed to establish constructive eviction because landlord had no duty to repair wall).

2. Recall that in our hypothetical situation, the Lloyds' broken air conditioning unit was not promptly repaired. Does this constitute constructive eviction?

3. How useful is the doctrine of constructive eviction to most tenants?

NET REALTY HOLDING TRUST v. NELSON

Superior Court of Connecticut, 1976.
33 Conn.Supp. 22, 358 A.2d 365.

GRILLO, JUDGE.

This action relates to a claim by the defendant lessees that they, having moved from the demised premises during the term of the lease and without paying the rental charges, are insulated from liability for that nonpayment since, by virtue of a violation by the plaintiff landlord of the orthodox "peace and quiet enjoyment" covenant in their lease, their right to the benefits of that provision has been denied them. Legalistically speaking, the plaintiff asserts an unjustified abandonment of the leased premises by the defendants, while the defendants contend they have been constructively evicted because of the plaintiff's breach of the covenant. Pragmatically speaking, the defendants maintain that the intrusion and continued presence of trespassers on the leased premises (part of a large shopping center owned by the plaintiff) and on the adjoining areas discouraged attendance at their establishment, forcing them to "close shop."

The premises in question were leased to the defendants, who operated a miniature golf course thereon, for a period of two years from January 15, 1975. The defendants left the premises about the middle of February, 1975. Window panels, adjacent to the corridors, would allow passersby and the curious to view the golf course. Groups of people would come on the premises even though they did not play. The golf course is one of many businesses and recreational facilities in the enclosed shopping center in the Meriden Mall. The course and shopping center attracted many young people, some of whom loitered boisterously on the premises. When that number exceeded, in the opinion of the defendants, a reasonable number, the security guard was called who would disperse the trespassers. Those persons, however, would eventually return. An altercation in the nature of an assault on the defendants' employee and a theft of the cash box of the defendants occurred because of those intruders. Ultimately, frustrated by incidents of the type outlined above, the ability of the defendants to carry on their business in an orderly fashion was jeopardized, business declined, and they ultimately abandoned the premises. Succinctly stated, the position of the defendants would seem to indicate that the plaintiff landlord should have taken action to preclude the detrimental activity heretofore set forth, that it was negligent in not so doing, and that that constituted a violation of their right to quiet enjoyment of the premises, justifying their canceling the lease.

The covenant of quiet enjoyment is that the grantee shall have legal quiet and peaceful * * * [possession] and is broken only by an entry on and an expulsion from the land or from actual disturbance of possession by virtue of some paramount title or right. A constructive eviction is said to arise when a landlord, while not actually depriving a tenant of possession, has done or suffered some act by which the premises are rendered untenantable. The defendants did not have the right to quit possession unless some act of the plaintiff rendered the premises uninhabitable, resulting in a constructive eviction. A disturbance or entry by a mere intruder is not sufficient to constitute a breach of a covenant of quiet enjoyment. The obligation of the landlord to protect his tenant relative to the tenant's right to quiet and peaceful possession and enjoyment extends only to evictions and disturbances caused by himself or by someone with a paramount title. Thus a hindrance of that enjoyment by a mere intruder is no ground of action for breach of covenant for quiet enjoyment.

The evidence in this case is clear that any interference with the defendants' tenancy was not done with the plaintiff's knowledge, permission or direction. Any relationship between the plaintiff and the acts of interference complained of was too attenuated for it to be held responsible for the disturbance of the defendants' tenancy. See Dietz v. Miles Holding Corporation, 277 A.2d 108 (D.C.App.) (congregating by "hippie people" on leased premises). Certainly if a covenant for quiet enjoyment is not broken by one who asserts an inferior right, it can hardly be validly maintained that the illegal activity of trespassers, assaulters and thieves that wreck a business is to be equated with a breach of that covenant by an innocent landlord.

Even assuming, arguendo, that it was incumbent on the plaintiff to assure the defendants' right to quiet enjoyment by positive steps, although the lease did not so provide, the plaintiff arranged for continuous patrolling of the mall by security guards. The merchants association of the mall also employed guards. Furthermore, the plaintiff consulted with the Meriden police department whose personnel admittedly also patrolled the mall. Even if we are to assume that acts of ordinary negligence on the part of a landlord, growing out of his contractual duties as a covenanter, amount to a constructive eviction, there is no evidence in the record to support a finding that this plaintiff was guilty of any negligence.

In construing one's obligations under a contract the surrounding circumstances should be considered. The defendants could reasonably expect that a shopping center encompassing many multifaceted recreation and business stores would attract thousands of persons including some undesirable trespassers when it entered into the lease. To have expected the quietude and decorum of a cloistered convent in a hustling, bustling business mall would have been completely unrealistic, as it would have been to suppose that the plaintiff could deter all the unpleasant incidents narrated above. The plaintiff took adequate preventive measures to minimize loitering, damage or injury to the defendants and their business.

The parties agreed that even though the plaintiff mitigated damages by rerental of the premises, the loss of rental during the vacancy amounted to $10,803.92.

Judgment may enter for the plaintiff to recover of the defendants the sum of $10,803.92, and attorney's fees of $1200.

Judgment may enter for the plaintiff on the counterclaim of the defendants.

Problem

Suppose protesters repeatedly blocked access to an office rented by a doctor who performs abortions. The landlord did not order the protesters to leave the building nor did the landlord provide security on Saturdays as required by the lease. Can the doctor vacate the premises and successfully claim constructive eviction? *See* Fidelity Mutual Life Insurance Company v. Robert P. Kaminsky, 768 S.W.2d 818 (Tex.App.1989).

BLACKETT v. OLANOFF

Supreme Judicial Court of Massachusetts, 1977.
371 Mass. 714, 358 N.E.2d 817.

WILKINS, JUSTICE.

The defendant in each of these consolidated actions for rent successfully raised constructive eviction as a defense against the landlords' claim. The judge found that the tenants were "very substantially deprived" of quiet enjoyment of their leased premises "*for a substantial time*" (emphasis original). He ruled that the tenants' implied warranty of quiet enjoyment was violated by late evening and early morning music and disturbances coming from nearby premises which the landlords leased to others for use as a bar or cocktail lounge (lounge). The judge further found that, although the landlords did not intend to create the conditions, the landlords "had it within their control to correct the conditions which * * * amounted to a constructive eviction of each [tenant]." He also found that the landlords promised each tenant to correct the situation, that the landlords made some attempt to remedy the problem, but they were unsuccessful, and that each tenant vacated his apartment within a reasonable time. Judgment was entered for each tenant; the landlords appealed; and we transferred the appeals here. We affirm the judgments.

The landlords argue that they did not violate the tenants' implied covenant of quiet enjoyment because they are not chargeable with the noise from the lounge. The landlords do not challenge the judge's conclusion that the noise emanating from the lounge was sufficient to constitute a constructive eviction, if that noise could be attributed to the landlords.[1] Nor do the landlords seriously argue that a constructive eviction could not be found as matter of law because the lounge was not on the same premises as the tenants' apartments. The landlords' principal contention, based on the denial of certain requests for rulings, is that they are not responsible for the conduct of the proprietors, employees, and patrons of the lounge.

Our opinions concerning a constructive eviction by an alleged breach of an implied covenant of quiet enjoyment sometimes have stated that the landlord must perform some act with the intent of depriving the tenant of the enjoyment and occupation of the whole or part of the leased premises. There are occasions, however, where a landlord has not intended to violate a tenant's rights, but there was nevertheless a breach of the landlord's covenant of quiet enjoyment which flowed as the natural and probable consequence of what the landlord did, what he failed to do, or what he permitted to be done. Charles E. Burt, Inc. v. Seven Grand Corp., 340 Mass. 124, 127, 163 N.E.2d 4 (1959) (failure to supply light, heat, power, and elevator services). Westland Housing Corp. v. Scott, 312 Mass. 375, 381, 44 N.E.2d 959 (1942) (intrusions of smoke and soot over a substantial period of time due to a defective boiler). Shindler v. Milden, 282 Mass. 32, 33–34, 184 N.E. 673 (1933) (failure to install necessary heating system, as agreed). Case v. Minot, 158 Mass. 577, 587, 33 N.E. 700 (1893) (landlord authorizing another lessee to obstruct the tenant's light and air, necessary for the beneficial enjoyment of the demised premises). Skally v. Shute, 132 Mass. 367, 370–371 (1882) (undermining of a leased building rendering it unfit for occupancy). Although some of our opinions have spoken of particular action or inaction by a landlord as showing a presumed intention to evict, the landlord's conduct, and not his intentions, is controlling.

The judge was warranted in ruling that the landlords had it within their control to correct the condition which caused the tenants to vacate their apartments. The landlords introduced a commercial activity into an area where they leased premises for residential purposes. The lease for the lounge expressly provided that entertainment in the lounge had to be conducted so that it could not be heard outside the building and would not disturb the residents of the leased apartments. The potential threat to the occupants of the nearby apartments was apparent in the circumstances. The landlords complained to the tenants of the lounge after receiving numerous objections from residential tenants. From time to time, the pervading noise would abate in response to the landlord's complaints. We conclude that, as [a] matter of law, the landlords had a right to control the objectionable noise coming from the lounge and that

---

1. There was evidence that the lounge had amplified music (electric musical instruments and singing, at various times) which started at 9:30 P.M. and continued until 1:30 A.M. or 2 A.M., generally on Tuesdays through Sundays. The music could be heard through the granite walls of the residential tenants' building, and was described variously as unbelievably loud, incessant, raucous, and penetrating. The noise interfered with conversation and prevented sleep. There was also evidence of noise from patrons' yelling and fighting.

the judge was warranted in finding as a fact that the landlords could control the objectionable conditions.

This situation is different from the usual annoyance of one residential tenant by another, where traditionally the landlord has not been chargeable with the annoyance. See Katz v. Duffy, 261 Mass. 149, 158 N.E. 264 (1927) (illegal sale of alcoholic beverages); DeWitt v. Pierson, 112 Mass. 8 (1873) (prostitution).[2] Here we have a case more like Case v. Minot, 158 Mass. 577, 33 N.E. 700 (1893), where the landlord entered into a lease with one tenant which the landlord knew permitted that tenant to engage in activity which would interfere with the rights of another tenant. There, to be sure, the clash of tenants' rights was inevitable, if each pressed those rights. Here, although the clash of tenants' interests was only a known potentiality initially, experience demonstrated that a decibel level for the entertainment at the lounge, acoustically acceptable to its patrons and hence commercially desirable to its proprietors, was intolerable for the residential tenants.

Because the disturbing condition was the natural and probable consequence of the landlords' permitting the lounge to operate where it did and because the landlords could control the actions at the lounge, they should not be entitled to collect rent for residential premises which were not reasonably habitable. Tenants such as these should not be left only with a claim against the proprietors of the noisome lounge. To the extent that our opinions suggest a distinction between nonfeasance by the landlord, which has been said to create no liability, and malfeasance by the landlord, we decline to perpetuate that distinction where the landlord creates a situation and has the right to control the objectionable conditions.

Judgments affirmed.

Question

Although the landlord generally has no responsibility for the actions of tenants, the landlord may attempt to remove a tenant because that tenant is

---

2. The general, but not universal, rule in this country is that a landlord is not chargeable because one tenant is causing annoyance to another (A.H. Woods Theatre v. North American Union, 246 Ill.App. 521, 526–527, [1927] [music from one commercial tenant annoying another commercial tenant's employees]), even where the annoying conduct would be a breach of the landlord's covenant of quiet enjoyment if the landlord were the miscreant. See Paterson v. Bridges, 16 Ala.App. 54, 55, 75 So. 260 (1917); Thompson v. Harris, 9 Ariz. App. 341, 345, 452 P.2d 122 (1969), and cases cited; 1 American Law of Property § 3.53 (A.J. Casner ed. 1952); Annot., 38 A.L.R. 250 (1925). Contra Kesner v. Consumers Co., 255 Ill.App. 216, 228–229 (1929) (storage of flammables constituting a nuisance); Bruckner v. Helfaer, 197 Wis. 582, 585, 222 N.W. 790 (1929) (residential tenant not liable for rent where landlord, with ample notice, does not control another tenant's conduct).

The rule in New York appears to be that the landlord may not recover rent if he has had ample notice of the existence of conduct of one tenant which deprives another tenant of the beneficial enjoyment of his premises and the landlord does little or nothing to abate the nuisance.

A tenant with sufficient bargaining power may be able to obtain an agreement from the landlord to insert and to enforce regulatory restrictions in the leases of other, potentially offending, tenants. See E. Schwartz, Lease Drafting in Massachusetts § 6.33 (1961).

disturbing other occupants of the building. *See* Humbach, *Landlord Control of Tenant Behavior: An Instance of Private Environmental Legislation*, 45 Fordham L.Rev. 223 (1976). The landlord may thereby avoid the constructive eviction issue presented in *Blackett*. What standard should the court use to determine whether the offending tenant can be removed?

LOUISIANA LEASING CO. v. SOKOLOW

Civil Court of the City of New York, 1966.
48 Misc.2d 1014, 266 N.Y.S.2d 447.

DANIEL E. FITZPATRICK, JUSTICE.

This is a proceeding to remove the respondents from the premises of the petitioner upon the ground that they are objectionable tenants. The applicable clauses in the lease between the parties contain the following:

> "15. No Tenant shall make or permit any disturbing noises in the building by himself, his family, servants, employees, agents, visitors and licensees, nor do or permit anything by such persons that will interfere with the rights, comforts or convenience of other tenants."

Paragraph 9 of said lease states in part as follows:

> "9. Tenant and Tenant's family, servants, employees, agents, visitors, and licensees shall observe faithfully and comply strictly with the Rules and Regulations set forth on the back of this lease, * * *. Tenant agrees that any violation of any of said Rules and Regulations by Tenant or by a member of Tenant's family, or by servants, or employees, or agents, or visitors, or licensees, shall be deemed a substantial violation by Tenant of this lease and of the Tenancy."

The landlord alleges that the noise from respondents' apartment is destroying the peace and quiet of the new tenants immediately underneath them. The claim is and the proof attempted to establish that the noise is of such a character as to constitute a violation of the provisions of the lease set out above. The respondents have been in possession over two and one-half years and their lease runs until December 31, 1966. It is significant that the respondents over that period gave no evidence of being objectionable until the new tenants, the Levins, moved in last October. From the court's opportunity to observe them, both the respondents and the tenants below seem to be people who under other circumstances would be congenial and happy neighbors. It is unfortunate that they have had to come to court to face each other in an eye-ball to eye-ball confrontation.

The respondents are a young couple with two small children, ages 4 and 2. It was admitted by them that the children do run and play in their apartment, but they say that they keep shoes off their feet when at home. The father says that he does walk back and forth at various times when at home, particularly to the refrigerator during the TV commercials and, also, to other areas of the apartment as necessity requires, but denies that he does this excessively or in a loud or heavy manner. They maintain that whatever noises emanate from their apartment are the normal noises of everyday living.

The tenants below, the Levins, are a middle-age couple who go to business each day. They are like many others of our fellow citizens, who daily go forth to brave the vicissitudes of the mainstream of city life. At the end of the toilsome day, like tired fish, they are only too happy to seek out these quiet backwaters of the metropolis to recuperate for the next day's bout with the task of earning a living. They have raised their own child and are past the time when the patter of little feet overhead is a welcome sound. They say they love their new apartment and that it is just what they have been looking for and would hate to have to give it up because of the noise from above. Mrs. Levin is associated with the publisher of a teen-age magazine and realizes that she is in a bind between her desire for present comfort and the possible loss of two future subscribers. She consequently hastens to add that she loves children and has no objection to the Sokolows because of them, that it is solely the noise of which she complains. So we have the issue.

The landlord's brief states that in its "view, the conduct that is even more objectionable than the noise, is the uncooperative attitude of the Tenants". This observation is probably prompted by testimony to the effect that Mr. Sokolow, one of the upstairs tenants, is reported to have said "This is my home, and no one can tell me what to do in my own home". This is a prevalent notion that stems from the ancient axiom that a man's home is his castle.

The difficulty of the situation here is that Mr. Sokolow's castle is directly above the castle of Mr. Levin. That a man's home is his castle is an old Anglo-legal maxim hoary with time and the sanction of frequent repetition. It expressed an age when castles were remote, separated by broad moors, and when an intruder had to force moat and wall to make his presence felt within. The tranquillity of the King's Peace, the seclusion of a clandestine romance and the opportunity, like Hamlet, to deliver a soliloquy from the ramparts without fear of neighborly repercussions were real. Times however change, and all change is not necessarily progress as some sage has perceptively reminded us. For in an era of modernity and concentrated urban living, when high-rise apartment houses have piled castle upon castle for some twenty or more stories in the air, it is extremely difficult to equate these modern counterparts with their drawbridged and turreted ancestors. The builders of today's cubicular confusion have tried to compensate for the functional construction by providing lobbies in Brooklyn Renaissance that rival in decor the throne room at Knossos. They have also provided built-in air-conditioning, closed circuit television, playrooms and laundromats. There are tropical balconies to cool the fevered brow in the short, hot northern summer; which the other nine months serve as convenient places to store the floor mop and scrub pail. On the debit side they also contain miles of utility and sanitary piping which convey sound throughout the building with all the gusto of the mammoth organ in the Mormon Tabernacle at Salt Lake City. Also, the prefabricated or frugally plastered walls have their molecules so critically near the separation level that they oppose almost no barrier at all to alien sounds from neighboring apartments. This often forces one into an embarrassingly auditory intimacy with the surrounding tenants. Such are the hazards of modern apartment house living. One of my brother justices, the Honorable Harold J. Crawford, has opined that in this day in our large cities it is fruitless to expect the solitude of the sylvan glen. In this we concur. Particularly so, when we consider that all of us are daily assaulted by the "roaring traffic's boom", the early-morning carillon of the garbage cans and the determined whine of homing super-sonic jets. Further, children and noise have been inseparable from a time whence the mind of man runneth not to the contrary. This Court, therefore, is not disposed to attempt anything so schizophrenic at this late date.

Weighing the equities in this difficult controversy, the court finds that the Sokolows were there first, with a record as good tenants. The Levins underneath seem to be good tenants also. This was attested to by the superintendent who was called upon to testify. He made the understatement of the year when he said, "I kept out of the middle of this fight. It's near Christmas and this is no time for me to fight with tenants"—a piece of homely pragmatism which would have gladdened the heart of William James.

In his own crude way the superintendent may have suggested the solution to this proceeding. This is a time for peace on earth to men of good will. As the court noted above, they are all nice people and a little mutual forbearance and understanding of each other's problems should resolve the issues to everyone's satisfaction.

The evidence on the main question shows that in October the respondents Sokolow were already in a fixed relationship to the landlord. The Levins, on the other hand, were not their position was a mobile one. They had the opportunity to ascertain what was above them in the event they decided to move in below. They elected to move in and afterwards attempted to correct the condition complained of. Since upon the evidence the overhead noise has been shown to be neither excessive nor deliberate, the court is not constrained to flex its muscles and evict the respondents. Upon the entire case the respondents are entitled to a final order dismissing the petition.

Question

Is there any remedy short of eviction available to a landlord against a disruptive tenant? What remedies are available to a tenant who is disturbed by another tenant? For example, what if a normally quiet tenant of Harmony House holds a noisy party one Saturday night?

D. CONDITION AND MAINTENANCE OF THE LEASED PREMISES

The tenants at Harmony House are disturbed by the failure of the rental manager to make necessary repairs. The Lloyds are particularly concerned about their malfunctioning air conditioning unit. In order to give sound advice in these matters, you must become acquainted with the parties' legal obligations to maintain the leased premises.

1. TRADITIONAL APPROACH

a. Landlord's Duty—Caveat Emptor

Although the common law protects the tenant's possession of the leased property, possession may be of little value if the premises are in disrepair. Hence, the separate question of maintenance arises. The traditional view is that the doctrine of caveat emptor applies. The tenant takes the premises "as is," and the landlord has no duty to repair. This approach originated at a time when the economy was primarily agrarian and raw land was the principal object of the lease. Any buildings on the property were incidental and the tenant, generally an experienced workman, could inspect existing structures and make necessary repairs. Although circumstances have changed dramatically, the caveat emptor doctrine lives on. *See* 2 Powell on Real Property § 16B.04 (1998).

Even the common law, however, recognizes exceptions to the caveat emptor rule for short-term leases of furnished dwellings, leases of buildings under construction, and cases where the landlord fraudulently misrepresents or conceals the condition of the property. The landlord is also required to maintain common areas. *See* 1 American Law of Property §§ 3.45, 3.78 (1952); Restatement (Second) of Property, Landlord and Tenant § 5.1 reporter's note 2 (1977).

Question

Why does the common law recognize the stated exceptions to the caveat emptor rule?

b. Tenant's Duty—Waste

SUYDAM v. JACKSON

Commission of Appeals of New York, 1873.
54 N.Y. 450.

Appeal from judgment of the General Term of the Court of Common Pleas for the city and county of New York, affirming a judgment in favor of plaintiff [landlord] * * *.

This action was brought to recover a quarter's rent alleged to be due under a lease of certain premises situate in the city of New York.

On the 30th of March, 1866, the plaintiff leased to the defendant the store known as No. 48 Front street, in the city of New York, for the term of three years from the 1st day of May, 1866, at the yearly rental of $2,600, payable quarterly. The lease contained no covenant to repair on the part of the landlord, but that the * * * water and gas-pipes were to be kept in repair by the lessee. The demised premises consisted of a store five stories high, the main floor being about seventy feet long; in the rear of the first floor there was an extension, about eight or nine feet in width, and extending no higher than the first story; the roof of the extension was of glass; it was occupied as an office. On the 1st day of May, 1868, the defendant left, at the plaintiffs' office, a notice that the premises were untenantable and unfit for occupancy, and that he surrendered possession of the same. The alleged untenantableness specified was that the roof, etc., had become "so injured, corroded and worn out by the action of the elements and by age, as to leak" in such a manner that the same were unfit for occupancy. In support of these allegations, the defendant's witnesses testified that after the tenants had been in possession nearly a year, the glass roof over the extension, in the rear of the first floor, began to leak in the beginning of 1867, when the snow broke up, about March of that year; that it began to leak a little at first, and afterward, during the ensuing summer and winter it leaked some, and leaked badly when it rained, rendering the office damp and admitting the water. That the glass roof of the extension was dilapidated and was decayed at the joining of the glass and the frame, and the crossing of the extension, where the leakage took place. Neither the defendant nor his sub-tenants repaired the glass roof when it began to leak from said decay, nor made any repairs. No proof was given as to any injury or damage to the premises during the term, except such as arose from natural decay, and no leakage, except that above noticed from the roof, over the extension in the rear.

At the conclusion of his evidence the court directed a verdict for the plaintiff * * *.

Earl, C. The sole defense to this action is based upon the statute (Laws of 1860, chap. 345) which provides "that the lessees or occupants of any building, which shall, without any fault or neglect on their part, be destroyed or be so injured by the elements or any other cause as to be untenantable and unfit for occupancy, shall not be liable or bound to pay rent to the lessors or owners thereof, after such destruction or injury, unless otherwise expressly provided by written agreement or covenant; and the lessees or occupants may thereupon quit and surrender possession of the leasehold premises, and of the land so leased or occupied."

The roof of the small extension, in the rear of the main building, became gradually out of repair so as to leak badly, and the sole question for us to determine is, whether the demised premises were thus "injured" within the meaning of the statute. The leaking was not caused by any sudden, unusual, or fortuitous circumstance, but seems to have been caused by gradual wear and decay. The courts below held that the case was not within the statute, and that the lessee remained liable for the rent.

To be able properly to understand this statute, it is well to see what the common law was before it was enacted, and to ascertain, if we can, the mischief it was intended to remedy. At common law the lessor was, without express covenant to that effect, under no obligation to repair, and if the demised premises became, during the term, wholly untenantable by destruction thereof by fire, flood, tempest or otherwise, the lessee still remained liable for the rent unless exempted from such liability by some express covenant in his lease. But the lessee was under an implied covenant, from his relation to his landlord, to make what are called "tenantable repairs." Comyn, in his work on Landlord and Tenant, at page 188, states the implied covenant or obligation of a lessee growing out of the relation of landlord and tenant to be, "to treat the premises demised in such manner that no injury be done to the inheritance, but that the estate may revert to the lessor undeteriorated by the willful or negligent conduct of the lessee. He is bound, therefore, to keep the soil in a proper state of cultivation, to preserve the timber and to support and repair the buildings. These duties fall upon him without any express covenant on his part, and a breach of them will, in general, render him liable to be punished for waste." The lessee was not bound to make substantial, lasting or general repairs, but only such ordinary repairs as were necessary to prevent waste and decay of the premises. If a window in a dwelling should blow in, the tenant could not permit it to remain out and the storms to beat in and greatly injure the premises without liability for permissive waste; and if a shingle or board on the roof should blow off or become out of repair, the tenant could not permit the water, in time of rain, to flood the premises, and thus injure them, without a similar liability. He being present, a slight effort and expense on his part could save a great loss; and hence the law justly casts the burden upon him. I am not aware that it was ever claimed that it was unjust that he should bear this burden, or that any complaint was ever made of the rule of law which cast it upon him. It cannot, therefore, be presumed that the statute of 1860 was passed to shift this burden from the lessee to the lessor.

But it was considered a hard rule that the tenant who had from ignorance or inadvertence failed to protect himself by covenants in his lease, should be obliged to pay rent in cases where, from fire, flood or other fortuitous causes, the premises were destroyed or so injured as to be untenantable, and I am of opinion that it was to change this rule and cast the misfortune upon the owner of the demised premises that the law was enacted. The statute provides for two alternatives when the premises are "destroyed" or "injured." The first alternative, evidently, has reference to a sudden and total destruction by the elements, acting with unusual power, or by human agency. The latter has reference to a case of injury to the premises, short of a total destruction, occasioned in the same way. If the legislature had intended to provide that the tenant should cease to be liable for rent when the premises from any cause became so damaged or out of repair as to be untenantable, it would have been easy to have expressed the intent in apt and proper language. The terms "destroyed" and "injured" do not, to my mind, convey the idea of gradual deterioration from the ordinary action of the elements in producing decay, common to all human structures.

I am, therefore, of the opinion that the courts below did not err in the construction which they gave to this statute * * *.

* * *

Reynolds, C. When the legislature attempts, by positive enactment, to remedy an evil that has apparently grown up with the common law, it may be fairly assumed that the evil to be cured is fully appreciated, and that by apt words the remedy is provided for, as it is, and should be, understood by the law-making power.

* * *

In construing a statute which operates to change a principle of the common law, we are to be guided by rules of construction that have been long approved, and the most prominent of which, on the subject of statutes altering the common law, is that adopted by Chief Justice Trevor in the case of Arthur v. Bohenham in the reign of Queen Anne (11 Modern, 149, 161), which, in some form, has been repeated in the most reliable digests, and supported by many prior and subsequent adjudications in the courts. He said that "the general rule in the exposition of all acts of parliament is that, in all doubtful matters, and where the expression is in general terms, they are to receive such a construction as may be agreeable to the common law in cases of that nature, for statutes are not presumed to make any alteration in the common law, further or otherwise than the statute does expressly declare; therefore, in all general matters the law does not presume the act did intend to make any alteration, for if the parliament had had that design they would have expressed it in the act." Applying this rule to the present case, it seems to me entirely clear that the statute of 1860 does not change or impair the obligation of a tenant to make ordinary repairs, unless he is relieved from that duty by some provision in his lease.

All concur.

Judgment affirmed.

Notes and Questions

1. What is the tenant's common law obligation regarding repair if the leased premises are destroyed by an earthquake? What about the tenant's common law obligation to pay rent in such a situation? How does the New York statute cited in *Suydam* alter the common law on rent payment? *See also* Uniform Residential Landlord and Tenant Act § 4.106 (1974).

2. The problem of destruction of the leased premises is often the subject of lease provision. Does section sixteen of the sample lease on page 8 adequately protect the tenant?

3. The *Suydam* case involved permissive waste. The *Sparkman* case which follows deals with a more common type of waste—voluntary waste.

SPARKMAN v. HARDY

Supreme Court of Mississippi, 1955.
223 Miss. 452, 78 So.2d 584.

Lee, Justice.

This cause originated by the bill of complaint of Mrs. Edd Metts Hardy [tenant] to compel the acceptance by Mrs. L.B. Sparkman [landlord] of monthly advance rent in the sum of $120 for the first floor and the rear four rooms on the second floor * * * of the Sparkman building in the City of Cleveland, Mississippi. The complainant alleged that she is the assignee of an original lease from Mrs. Sparkman to Marion J. Hardy, dated March 29, 1945, which was to run for a period of ten years, with the right of renewal, under certain conditions, for an additional fifteen years. It was charged that Mrs. Sparkman refused to accept the January 1952 rent; and such amount, together with the amount to accrue until the disposition of the cause, was paid into the registry of the court. * * *

The answer of Mrs. Sparkman admitted the receipt of rent from December 1945 to December 1951; that she refused acceptance of the January 1952 rent because complainant and her husband, Marion J. Hardy, made material changes and alterations in the building without her permission; and that they declined to restore the building to its former state, after she protested. She made her answer also a cross bill, in which it was charged * * * that a partition was placed in the building * * * leaving the store proper only 20 feet instead of 30 feet wide; that a part of the glass front, installed at great expense, was removed; that the acts of the Hardys converted the building into a different kind of structure, with consequent damage to its value; that such material changes constituted waste; and that the restoration of the building to its previous state will be expensive. She therefore prayed for the cancellation of the lease and the assignment, and for recovery of damages on account of the changes.

The answer of the cross defendant, Mrs. Hardy, admitted that certain changes were made, but denied that they were material ones. * * *

The court, at the conclusion of the hearing, validated the assignment to, and the title of, Mrs. Hardy in the lease, denied damages to Mrs. Sparkman on account of the changes, and directed the payment of rent * * * to Mrs. Sparkman. * * * From the final judgment, Mrs. Sparkman appealed.

When the lease was originally executed, Marion J. Hardy purposed to use the space for an electrical appliance shop, though there was no provision in the contract, which, in any case, limited the use. Neither was there a prohibition against its assignment or changes in the rental property. The changes, which are complained about, were made in August and September 1950. The partition cut the building into two parts for approximately 65 feet, with ten feet on the south side, which was converted into offices, and 20 feet on the north side, which was sublet for a jewelry shop. There was also a change in the front entrance. Mrs. Sparkman knew nothing about these changes until after they were made. She did not authorize them. She protested when she ascertained that they had been made, and demanded that the building be restored to its former condition. Her witnesses testified that it would cost a minimum of $840.90 and perhaps $1,000, or slightly more, to put the building in its former condition.

The evidence for the Hardys was to the effect that the changes were temporary in nature; that the building could be restored to its previous condition at small cost; that instead of damage to the building, the changes in fact increased its value. * * *

The case turns on whether or not the changes were material, and therefore amounted to waste.

In Moss Point Lumber Co. v. Harrison County, 89 Miss. 448, 42 So. 290, 300, 873, this Court said that: "Waste is defined to be any substantial injury done to the inheritance, by one having a limited estate, during the continuance of his estate." It was also there said that: " * * * it is a universal rule in this country that, unless exempted by the terms of the lease from responsibility for waste, a tenant is responsible for voluntary waste, whenever committed."

Undoubtedly material changes in a building, even though they may enhance the value, amount to waste. A good statement of the rule is given in Section 1615, Vol. 4, Thompson on Real Property, p. 118, as follows: "A tenant, whether rightfully in possession or not, cannot, without the consent of the landlord, make material changes or alterations in a building to suit his taste or convenience, and, if he does, it is waste. The law is undoubtedly so settled. Any material change in the nature or character of the buildings made by the tenant is waste, although the value of the property should be enhanced by the alteration."

In the absence of a provision to the contrary, the tenant had the right to make such temporary changes as were consistent and proper for the utilization of the leased premises. The changes did not affect the four walls, the foundation, or the roof. The reasonable value of the building was not shown; however, it appeared that it was insured for $15,000, and this affords a gauge by which it may be reasonably concluded that the building was worth at least that amount, and perhaps more. The parties to a ten-year lease, with a potential of fifteen additional years by renewal, in the absence of a prohibition to the contrary, must have contemplated that changes or rearrangements of the leased space could and would be made. All of the evidence showed that the former status can be restored at a cost ranging from several hundred to one thousand dollars a small per cent of the actual value of the building. Drawings and photographs were introduced in evidence. Besides the court, on the motion of the appellant, "made a minute inspection of all parts" of the building. Under the evidence in this case, the learned chancellor was fully warranted in finding that the changes are temporary and are not so material as to amount to waste.

It follows therefore that the decree appealed from must be, and is, affirmed.

Affirmed.

Notes and Questions

1. As to whether alteration of the leased premises constitutes waste, consider the following analysis in Crewe Corp. v. Feiler, 28 N.J. 316, 324, 146 A.2d 458, 462 (1958):

> The classic view is that a tenant may not make material changes or alterations in a building to suit his taste or convenience and that any material change in the nature or character of the buildings is waste, even though the value of the property be enhanced thereby.

> Undoubtedly, the concept of waste is far from rigid in its practical application. Conduct once permissible in an agrarian economy would today be proscribed, and acts then deemed wrongful would today be warranted. There are many variables. It is reasonable to assume that the parties to a 99–year lease contemplate the possibility of obsolescence, physical or economic, and hence intend a substantial right in the lessee to change the property in the interest of a fruitful enjoyment. In such situations, the reversionary interests are concerned more with the rental yield than with the character of the buildings. On the other hand, in short-term lettings, the landlord is interested not only in the rental income but as well in the basic integrity of the structures which will shortly return to his possession. There the lessee's right to alter or improve must be more sharply contained. No easy formula can be prescribed. The law seeks a reasonable result, consonant with the probable intent of the parties, which will permit beneficial enjoyment without injury to the landlord's estate. The answer must depend upon the nature and extent of the change in relation to the total facts.

How can the landlord protect against unwanted changes? *See* section seven of the sample lease on page 7.

2. The Uniform Residential Landlord and Tenant Act § 3.101 (1974) specifies the tenant's duties regarding maintenance of the leased premises. This section is, in a sense, a modern statement of the doctrine of waste.

3. In Three and One Company v. Geilfuss, 178 Wis.2d 400, 504 N.W.2d 393 (App.1993), tenants allowed their pets (a dog, a cat, and a rabbit) to use the rental unit "as a litter box," and consequently "carpeting throughout the premises was found to be permeated with cat urine and littered with animal feces." Are the tenants liable for permissive or voluntary waste?

4. In Kennedy v. Kidd, 557 P.2d 467 (Okla.App.1976), a month-to-month tenant died in the tenant's rented apartment. The following week the tenant's "partially decomposed body" was discovered. The landlord refurbished the leased premises to rid it of "putrid odors associated with the

decedent's body." Should the landlord be able to recover rent and the cost of rehabilitating the apartment from the tenant's estate?

5.   The parties may alter the common law of waste by agreement. For example, the landlord may expressly permit the tenant to cut all the timber on the leased premises or remove valuable minerals from the property. Does section nine of the sample lease on page 7 adequately cover this topic?

6.   The law of waste applies whenever someone other than the possessor has an interest in the property. Thus, questions of waste frequently arise outside the landlord-tenant area. Other situations in which waste may become an issue are discussed in Chapter 3.

2.   IMPLIED WARRANTY OF HABITABILITY

Although the common law caveat emptor rule discussed in the preceding section still generally applies to commercial leases, virtually all states have rejected its application to leases of residential property. In these jurisdictions, a warranty of habitability is implied in residential leases. *See* Cunningham, *The New Implied and Statutory Warranties of Habitability in Residential Leases: From Contract to Status,* 16 Urb. L.Ann. 3 (1979).

WADE v. JOBE

Supreme Court of Utah, 1991.
818 P.2d 1006.

DURHAM, JUSTICE:

In June 1988, defendant Lynda Jobe (the tenant) rented a house in Ogden, Utah, from plaintiff Clyde Wade (the landlord). Jobe had three young children. Shortly after she took occupancy, the tenant discovered numerous defects in the dwelling, and within a few days, she had no hot water. Investigation revealed that the flame of the water heater had been extinguished by accumulated sewage and water in the basement which also produced a foul odor throughout the house. The tenant notified the landlord, who came to the premises a number of times, each time pumping the sewage and water from the basement onto the sidewalk and relighting the water heater. These and other problems persisted from July through October 1988.

In November 1988, the tenant notified the landlord that she would withhold rent until the sewage problem was solved permanently. The situation did not improve, and an inspection by the Ogden City Inspection Division (the division) in December 1988 revealed that the premises were unsafe for human occupancy due to the lack of a sewer connection and other problems. Within a few weeks, the division made another inspection, finding numerous code violations which were a substantial hazard to the health and safety of the occupants. The division issued a notice that the property would be condemned if the violations were not remedied.

After the tenant moved out of the house, the landlord brought suit in the second circuit court to recover the unpaid rent.

* * *

At trial, the landlord was awarded judgment of unpaid rent of $770, the full rent due under the parties' original agreement.

This appeal followed

I.   WARRANTY OF HABITABILITY

At common law, the leasing of real property was viewed primarily as a conveyance of land for a term, and the law of property was applied to landlord/tenant transactions. At a time when the typical lease was for agricultural purposes, it was assumed that the land, rather than any improvements, was the most important part of the leasehold. *See generally* Javins v. First Nat'l Realty Corp., 428 F.2d 1071, 1077 (D.C.Cir.), cert. denied, 400 U.S. 925 (1970). Under the rule of caveat emptor, a tenant had a duty to inspect the premises to determine their safety and suitability for the purposes for which they were leased before entering a lease. Moreover, absent deceit or fraud on the part of the landlord or an express warranty to the contrary, the landlord had no duty to make repairs during the course of the tenancy. Under the law of waste, it was the tenant's implied duty to make most repairs.

Unlike tenants in feudal England, most modern tenants bargain for the use of structures on the land rather than the land itself. Modern tenants generally lack the necessary skills or means to inspect the property effectively or to make repairs. Moreover, the rule of caveat emptor assumes an equal bargaining position between landlord and tenant. Modern tenants, like consumers of goods, however, frequently have no choice but to rely on the landlord to provide a habitable dwelling. Where they exist, housing shortages, standardized leases, and racial and class discrimination place today's tenants, as consumers of housing, in a poor position to bargain effectively for express warranties and covenants requiring landlords to lease and maintain safe and sanitary housing. Javins, 428 F.2d at 1079; Green v. Superior Court, 10 Cal.3d 616, 111 Cal.Rptr. 704, 709, 517 P.2d 1168, 1173 (1974).

In consumer law, implied warranties are designed to protect ordinary consumers who do not have the knowledge, capacity, or opportunity to ensure that goods which they are buying are in safe condition. See Henningsen v. Bloomfield Motors, Inc., 32 N.J. 358, 161 A.2d 69, 78 (1960); Utah Code Ann. §§ 70A–2–314 to–316 (implied warranties contained in Uniform Commercial Code). The implied warranty of habitability has been adopted in other jurisdictions to protect the tenant as the party in the less advantageous bargaining position.

The concept of a warranty of habitability is in harmony with the widespread enactment of housing and building codes which reflect a legislative desire to ensure decent housing. It is based on the theory that the residential landlord warrants that the leased premises are habitable at the outset of the lease term and will remain so during the course of the tenancy. The warranty applies to written and oral leases, and to single-family as well as to multiple-unit dwellings. The warranty of habitability has been adopted, either legislatively or judicially, in over forty states and the District of Columbia.

In recent years, this court has conformed the common law in this state to contemporary conditions by rejecting the strict application of traditional property law to residential leases, recognizing that it is often more appropriate to apply contract law. Similarly, we have expanded landlord liability in tort. See Stephenson v. Warner, 581 P.2d 567 (Utah 1978) (landlord must use ordinary care to ensure leased premises are reasonably safe). Consistent with prevailing trends in consumer law, products liability law, and the law of torts, we reject the rule of caveat emptor and recognize the common law implied warranty of habitability in residential[1] leases.

The determination of whether a dwelling is habitable depends on the individual facts of each case. To guide the trial court in determining whether there is a breach of the warranty of habitability, we describe some general standards that the landlord is required to satisfy. We note initially that the warranty of habitability does not require the landlord to maintain the premises in perfect condition at all times, nor does it preclude minor housing code violations or other defects. Moreover, the landlord will not be liable for defects caused by the tenant. Further, the landlord must have a reasonable time to repair material defects before a breach can be established.

As a general rule, the warranty of habitability requires that the landlord maintain "bare living requirements," see Academy Spires, Inc. v. Brown, 111 N.J.Super. 477, 268 A.2d 556, 559 (1970), and that the premises are fit for human occupation. See Mease v. Fox, 200 N.W.2d 791 (Iowa 1972); Hilder v. St. Peter, 144 Vt. 150, 478 A.2d 202, 208 (1984). Failure to supply heat or hot water, for example, breaches the warranty. A breach is not shown, however, by evidence of minor deficiencies such as the malfunction of venetian blinds, minor water leaks or wall cracks, or a need for paint.

Substantial compliance with building and housing code standards will generally serve as evidence of the fulfillment of a landlord's duty to provide habitable premises. Evidence of violations involving health or safety, by contrast, will often sustain a tenant's claim for relief. At the same time, just because the housing code provides a basis for implication of the warranty, a code violation is not necessary to establish a breach so long as the claimed defect has an impact on the health or safety of the tenant.

In the instant case, in support of her claim that the premises were not in habitable condition, the tenant presented two city housing inspection reports detailing numerous code violations which were, in the words of the trial judge, "a substantial hazard to the health and safety of the

---

1. We do not decide whether the warranty is implied in commercial leases.

occupants." Those violations included the presence of raw sewage on the sidewalks and stagnant water in the basement, creating a foul odor. At trial, the tenant testified that she had repeatedly informed the landlord of the problem with the sewer connection and the resulting lack of hot water, but the landlord never did any more than temporarily alleviate the problem. The landlord did not controvert the evidence of substantial problems. At trial, the court granted judgment for the landlord, concluding that Utah law did not recognize an implied warranty of habitability for residential rental premises. As discussed above, we have now recognized the warranty. We therefore remand this case to the trial court to determine whether the landlord has breached the implied warranty of habitability as defined in this opinion. If the trial court finds a breach of the warranty of habitability, it must then determine damages.

A. Remedies

Under traditional property law, a lessee's covenant to pay rent was viewed as independent of any covenants on the part of the landlord. Even when a lessor expressly covenanted to make repairs, the lessor's breach did not justify the lessee's withholding rent. Under the prevailing contemporary view of the residential lease as a contractual transaction, however, the tenant's obligation to pay rent is conditioned upon the landlord's fulfilling his part of the bargain. The payment of rent by the tenant and the landlord's duty to provide habitable premises are, as a result, dependent covenants.

Once the landlord has breached his duty to provide habitable conditions, there are at least two ways the tenant can treat the duty to pay rent. The tenant may continue to pay rent to the landlord or withhold the rent.[2] If the tenant continues to pay full rent to the landlord during the period of uninhabitability, the tenant can bring an affirmative action to establish the breach and receive a reimbursement for excess rents paid. Rent withholding, on the other hand, deprives the landlord of the rent due during the default, thereby motivating the landlord to repair the premises.[3]

* * *

B. Damages

In general, courts have applied contract remedies when a breach of the warranty of habitability has been shown. One available remedy, therefore, is damages. Special damages may be recovered when, as a foreseeable result of the landlord's breach, the tenant suffers personal

2. In addition, some jurisdictions recognize rent application, also known as "repair and deduct," allowing the tenant to use the rent money to repair the premises. Because this remedy has not been relied on or sought in the instant case, we do not at this time make a ruling on its availability in Utah.

3. The majority of jurisdictions that permit rent withholding allow the tenant to retain the funds subject to the discretionary power of the court to order the deposit of the rent into escrow. Like the court in Javins, we think this type of escrow account would provide a useful protective procedure in the right circumstances.

injury, property damage, relocation expenses, or other similar injuries. See Mease v. Fox, 200 N.W.2d at 797; Restatement (Second) of Property, Landlord & Tenant § 10.2 (1977). General damages recoverable in the form of rent abatement or reimbursement to the tenant are more difficult to calculate.

Several different measures for determining the amount of rent abatement to which a tenant is entitled have been used by the courts. The first of these is the fair rental value of the premises as warranted less their fair rental value in the unrepaired condition. Under this approach, the contract rent may be considered as evidence of the value of the premises as warranted. Another measure is the contract rent less the fair rental value of the premises in the unrepaired condition. Methodological difficulties inherent in both of these measures, combined with the practical difficulties of producing evidence on fair market value,[4] however, limit the efficacy of those measures for dealing with residential leases. For this reason, a number of courts have adopted what is called the "percentage diminution" (or percentage reduction in use) approach which places more discretion with the trier of fact.

Under the percentage diminution approach, the tenant's recovery reflects the percentage by which the tenant's use and enjoyment of the premises has been reduced by the uninhabitable conditions. *See generally* Annotation, *Measure of Damages for Landlord's Breach of Implied Warranty of Habitability,* 1 A.L.R.4th 1182 (1980). In applying this approach, the trial court must carefully review the materiality of the particular defects and the length of time such defects have existed. It is true that the percentage diminution approach requires the trier of fact to exercise broad discretion and some subjective judgment to determine the degree to which the defective conditions have diminished the habitability of the premises. It should be noted, however, that despite their theoretical appeal, the other approaches are not objectively precise either. Furthermore, they involve the use of an expert witness's subjective opinion of the "worth" of habitable and uninhabitable premises.

As the foregoing discussion demonstrates, the determination of appropriate damages in cases of a breach of the warranty of habitability will often be a difficult task. None of the approaches described above is inherently illegitimate, but we think that the percentage diminution approach has a practical advantage in that it will generally obviate the need for expert testimony and reduce the cost and complexity of enforcing the warranty of habitability. We acknowledge the limitation of the method but conclude that it is as sound in its result as any other and more workable in practice. We will have to depend on development of the rule in specific cases to determine whether it will be universally applicable.

* * *

4. Under either approach, at least one market value is almost certain to require expert testimony. The production of such testimony will increase the cost, in time and money, of the typical case.

Conclusion

* * * [The trial court's] determination regarding the implied warranty of habitability * * * is reversed. We remand this case to the trial court to determine whether the landlord breached the implied warranty of habitability as defined in this opinion. If the trial court determines that he was not in breach, the landlord will be entitled to payment for all the past due rent. If the trial court determines that his breach of the warranty of habitability totally excused the tenant's rent obligation (i.e., rendered the premises virtually uninhabitable), the landlord's action to recover rent due will fail. If the trial court determines that the landlord's breach partially excused the tenant's rent obligation, the tenant will be entitled to a percentage rent abatement for the period during which the house was uninhabitable.

Notes and Questions

1. In addition to judicial activity in this area, numerous state legislatures have adopted statutes imposing a warranty of habitability in leases of residential property. *See, e.g.*, Uniform Residential Landlord and Tenant Act § 2.104 (1974); *see also*, Note, *The Unwarranted Implication of a Warranty of Fitness in Commercial Leases, An Alternative Approach*, 41 Vand.L.Rev. 1057, 1065–1066 (1988).

2. What is the economic effect of an implied warranty of habitability? Will it cause landlords to raise rents to cover the costs of repair and to abandon certain rental property as unprofitable? *See* Cunningham, *The New Implied and Statutory Warranties of Habitability on Residential Leases: From Contract to Status,* 16 Urb.L.Ann. 3, 138–153 (1979).

3. Should the tenant be allowed to waive the implied warranty of habitability? Although most courts will not permit waiver, a few do. *See id.* at 95–97; P.H. Investment v. Oliver, 818 P.2d 1018 (Utah 1991) (allowing express waiver of specifically listed defects); Bell, *The Mississippi Landlord–Tenant Act of 1991,* 61 Miss.L.J. 527, 542–545 (1991). Which is the better approach? The question of waiver may also be addressed by statute. *See* Uniform Residential Landlord and Tenant Act § 1.403(a)(1) (1974) which prohibits waiver of tenants' rights under the Act and compare it with § 2.104(c) & (d).

DAVIDOW v. INWOOD NORTH PROFESSIONAL GROUP—PHASE I

Supreme Court of Texas, 1988.
747 S.W.2d 373.

Spears, Justice.

* * *

Dr. Davidow entered into a five-year lease agreement with Inwood for medical office space. The lease required Dr. Davidow to pay Inwood $793.26 per month as rent. The lease also required Inwood to provide air conditioning, electricity, hot water, janitor and maintenance services, light fixtures, and security services. Shortly after moving into the office space, Dr. Davidow began experiencing problems with the building. The air conditioning did not work properly, often causing temperatures inside the office to rise above eighty-five degrees. The roof leaked whenever it rained, resulting in stained tiles and rotting, mildewed carpet. Patients were directed away from certain areas during rain so that they would not be dripped upon in the waiting room. Pests and rodents often infested the office. The hallways remained dark because hallway lights were unreplaced for months. Cleaning and maintenance were not provided. The parking lot was constantly filled with trash. Hot water was not provided, and on one occasion Dr. Davidow went without electricity for several days because Inwood failed to pay the electric bill. Several burglaries and various acts of vandalism occurred. Dr. Davidow finally moved out of the premises and discontinued rent payments approximately fourteen months before the lease expired.

Inwood sued Dr. Davidow for the unpaid rent and costs of restoration. Dr. Davidow answered by general denial and the affirmative defenses of material breach of the lease agreement, a void lease, and breach of an implied warranty that the premises were suitable for use as a medical office. The jury found that Inwood materially breached the lease, that Inwood warranted to Dr. Davidow that the lease space was suitable for a medical office, and that the lease space was not suitable for a medical office. * * * The trial court then rendered judgment that Inwood take nothing and that Dr. Davidow recover $9,300 in damages.

With one justice dissenting, the court of appeals reversed the trial court judgment and rendered judgment in favor of Inwood for unpaid rent. The court of appeals held that because Inwood's covenant to maintain and repair the premises was independent of Dr. Davidow's covenant to pay rent, Inwood's breach of its covenant did not justify Dr. Davidow's refusal to pay rent. The court of appeals also held that the implied warranty of habitability does not extend to commercial leaseholds and that Dr. Davidow's pleadings did not support an award of affirmative relief.

Inwood contends that the defense of material breach of the covenant to repair is insufficient as a matter of law to defeat a landlord's claim for unpaid rent. In Texas, the courts have held that the landlord's covenant to repair the premises and the tenant's covenant to pay rent are independent covenants. Thus, a tenant is still under a duty to pay rent even though his landlord has breached his covenant to make repairs.

This theory of independent covenants in leases was established in early property law prior to the development of the concept of mutually dependent covenants in contract law. At common law, the lease was traditionally regarded as a conveyance of an interest in land, subject to the doctrine of *caveat emptor*. The landlord was required only to deliver the right of possession to the tenant; the tenant, in return, was required to pay rent to the landlord. Once the landlord delivered the right of possession, his part of the agreement was completed. The tenant's duty to pay rent continued as long as he retained possession, even if the buildings on the leasehold were destroyed or became uninhabitable. The landlord's breach of a lease covenant did not relieve the tenant of his duty to pay rent for the remainder of the term because the tenant still retained everything he was entitled to under the lease, the right of possession. All lease covenants were therefore considered independent.

In the past, this court has attempted to provide a more equitable and contemporary solution to landlord-tenant problems by easing the burden placed on tenants as a result of the independence of lease covenants and the doctrine of *caveat emptor. See, e.g.,* Kamarath v. Bennett, 568 S.W.2d 658 (Tex.1978); Humber v. Morton, 426 S.W.2d 554 (Tex.1968). In *Kamarath v. Bennett,* we reexamined the realities of the landlord-tenant relationship in a modern context and concluded that the agrarian common-law concept is no longer indicative of the contemporary relationship between the tenant and landlord. The land is of minimal importance to the modern tenant; rather, the primary subject of most leases is the structure located on the land and the services which are to be provided to the tenant. The modern residential tenant seeks to lease a dwelling suitable for living purposes. The landlord usually has knowledge of any defects in the premises that may render it uninhabitable. In addition, the landlord, as permanent owner of the premises, should rightfully bear the cost of any necessary repairs. In most instances the landlord is in a much better bargaining position than the tenant. Accordingly, we held in *Kamarath* that the landlord impliedly warrants that the premises are habitable and fit for living. We further implicitly recognized that the residential tenant's obligation to pay rent is dependent upon the landlord's performance under his warranty of habitability.

When a commercial tenant such as Dr. Davidow leases office space, many of the same considerations are involved. A significant number of commentators have recognized the similarities between residential and commercial tenants and concluded that residential warranties should be expanded to cover commercial property. *See, e.g.,* Chused, *Contemporary Dilemmas of the Javins Defense: A Note on the Need for Procedural Reform in Landlord, Tenant Law,* 67 Geo.L.J. 1385, 1389 (1979); Greenfield & Margolies, *An Implied Warranty of Fitness in Nonresidential Leases,* 45 Albany L.Rev. 855 (1981); Levinson & Silver, *Do Commercial Property Tenants Possess Warranties of Habitability?,* 14 Real Estate L.J. 59 (1985); Note, *Landlord-Tenant, Should a Warranty of Fitness be Implied in Commercial Leases?,* 13 Rutgers L.J. 91 (1981); *see also* Restatement (Second) of Property § 5.1 reporter's note at 176 (1977).

It cannot be assumed that a commercial tenant is more knowledgeable about the quality of the structure than a residential tenant. A businessman cannot be expected to possess the expertise necessary to adequately inspect and repair the premises, and many commercial tenants lack the financial resources to hire inspectors and repairmen to assure the suitability of the premises. Additionally, because commercial tenants often enter into short-term leases, the tenants have limited economic incentive to make any extensive repairs to their premises.

Consequently, commercial tenants generally rely on their landlords' greater abilities to inspect and repair the premises.

* * *

There is no valid reason to imply a warranty of habitability in residential leases and not in commercial leases. Although minor distinctions can be drawn between residential and commercial tenants, those differences do not justify limiting the warranty to residential leaseholds. Therefore, we hold there is an implied warranty of suitability by the landlord in a commercial lease that the premises are suitable for their intended commercial purpose. This warranty means that at the inception of the lease there are no latent defects in the facilities that are vital to the use of the premises for their intended commercial purpose and that these essential facilities will remain in a suitable condition. If, however, the parties to a lease expressly agree that the tenant will repair certain defects, then the provisions of the lease will control.

We recognized in *Kamarath* that the primary objective underlying a residential leasing arrangement is "to furnish [the tenant] with quarters suitable for living purposes." *Kamarath,* 568 S.W.2d at 661. The same objective is present in a commercial setting. A commercial tenant desires to lease premises suitable for their intended commercial use. A commercial landlord impliedly represents that the premises are in fact suitable for that use and will remain in a suitable condition. The tenant's obligation to pay rent and the landlord's implied warranty of suitability are therefore mutually dependent.

The existence of a breach of the implied warranty of suitability in commercial leases is usually a fact question to be determined from the particular circumstances of each case. Among the factors to be considered when determining whether there has been a breach of this warranty are: the nature of the defect; its effect on the tenant's use of the premises; the length of time the defect persisted; the age of the structure; the amount of the rent; the area in which the premises are located; whether the tenant waived the defects; and whether the defect resulted from any unusual or abnormal use by the tenant. *Kamarath,* 568 S.W.2d at 661.

The jury found that Inwood leased the space to Dr. Davidow for use as a medical office and that Inwood knew of the intended use. The evidence and jury findings further indicate that Dr. Davidow was unable to use the space for the intended purpose because acts and omissions by Inwood rendered the space unsuitable for use as a medical office. The jury findings establish that Inwood breached the implied warranty of suitability. Dr. Davidow was therefore justified in abandoning the premises and discontinuing his rent payments.

Dr. Davidow further contends that the court of appeals erred in reversing the trial court's award of damages for Inwood's breach of the lease agreement. Specifically, Dr. Davidow claims that his pleadings gave sufficient notice of an affirmative cause of action for Inwood's breach of the lease. * * * We agree with the court of appeals that the pleading is insufficient to support the award by the trial court of affirmative relief for Dr. Davidow. Because Dr. Davidow failed to plead a basis for affirmative relief, we hold that the trial court erred in awarding him damages based on Inwood's alleged material breach of the lease agreement.

For the reasons stated, the part of the court of appeals judgment awarding Inwood damages for unpaid rent and attorney's fees is reversed and judgment is here rendered that Inwood take nothing. The part of the court of appeals judgment that Dr. Davidow recover nothing on his material breach claim is affirmed.

Notes and Questions

1. *Davidow* is the most aggressive and far-reaching opinion on this subject to date. Virtually all other courts have declined to imply a warranty of fitness in commercial leases. *See* Note, *The Unwarranted Implication of a Warranty of Fitness in Commercial Leases, An Alternative Approach,* 41 Vand.L.Rev. 1057 (1988); Note, *Modernizing Commercial Lease Law: The Case for an Implied Warranty of Fitness,* 19 Suffolk U.L.Rev. 929, 946–948 (1985). *See generally* Note, *An Economic Analysis of Implied Warranties of Fitness in Commercial Leases,* 94 Colum.L.Rev. 658 (1994) (contending that warranty of general fitness should be implied in commercial leases unless parties agree otherwise and that warranty of particular fitness should be implied in commercial leases in certain circumstances).

2. Courts may treat express covenants in commercial leases as mutually dependent without recognizing an implied warranty of fitness in such leases. *See* Richard Barton Enterprises, Inc. v. Tsern, 928 P.2d 368 (Utah 1996) (holding that tenant's covenant to pay rent under commercial lease was dependent on landlord's compliance with essential covenants, and that breach by landlord of covenant to make certain repairs warranted rent abatement). *See also* Note, *The Unwarranted Implication of a Warranty of Fitness in Commercial Leases—An Alternative Approach,* 41 Vand.L.Rev. 1057 (1988) (arguing against implying warranty of fitness or suitability in commercial landlord-tenant arrangements, but in favor of treating covenants expressed in commercial leases as mutually dependent).

3. Are not commercial tenants and residential tenants in fact in significantly different positions?

4. Is the nature of the commercial tenant's business significant?

3. EXPRESS COVENANT TO REPAIR

The landlord and tenant frequently agree in the lease about their respective obligations to repair. The effect of such an agreement in residential leases, of course, may be limited in states where a nonwaivable warranty of habitability is implied.

a. *Covenant by Landlord*

Sections five, seven, and sixteen of the sample lease on pages 7–8, place the obligation to repair on the landlord. The next case involves interpretation of similar lease covenants.

MORRIS v. DURHAM

Court of Appeals of Kentucky, 1969.
443 S.W.2d 642.

STEINFELD, JUDGE.

Chester G. Luxon and his wife Lillian, on January 14, 1964, leased to Dallas C. Morris for a period of ten years a portion of a building on Main Street in Richmond, Kentucky. Chester died in 1966 and the ownership passed to his widow Lillian, his son William E. Luxon, and his daughter Ann L. Durham. The entire building, of which the leased premises were a part, was destroyed by fire on the 8th day of February, 1968. Morris was a tenant on that date. Two days later Morris was given written notice that the lease was cancelled because of the destructive fire but he protested, claiming that the lease obligated the owners to rebuild. They refused to do so.

To settle the controversy the owners sued for a reformation of the lease, for a declaration that the lease was terminated and for damages " * * * in loss of rental caused by * * * wrongful claims and actions * * * "made and committed by Morris. He counterclaimed demanding that the court declare that it was the duty of the owners to rebuild within a reasonable time. The court held that the owners had the option to rebuild but were not required to do so, but if they rebuilt " * * * within a reasonable time" a " * * * building in substantially the same form it was in previous to the fire * * * said Lease will resume its binding effect upon the parties * * * from the date the rebuilt premises are ready for occupancy * * *." No damages were awarded and no reformation ordered. Tenant Morris appeals. We affirm.

Appellant makes only two arguments before us. He contends that "The language of the lease requires that appellees rebuild the premises" and that " * * * having elected to rebuild (they) cannot avoid the lease."

The lease contained two sections on which appellant relies, to wit:

"In the event said premises or any part thereof be destroyed or damaged by fire or other casualty so that the same shall thereby be rendered unfit for habitation or for the purposes herein designed, the rental herein above stipulated to be paid, or a just and proportionate part thereof, shall be suspended or abated until the premises shall have been by the Lessors rebuilt or repaired and put in proper condition for use and habitation, and the rental shall thereupon recommence immediately after the said rebuilding or repairing shall have been completed.

"The Lessor agrees to protect the building, together with the display window glass, [with] sufficient insurance policies, and in case of damage to the building by fire or by breakage of the windows or by any cause whatsoever, to make the necessary repairs at the earliest possible time, in order that the Lessee may not be inconvenienced longer than absolutely necessary. In case the Lessee is deprived of the use and occupancy of said building on account of damage by fire or flood, or any other cause beyond the control of the Lessee, then the Lessee shall not be required to pay to the Lessor the stipulated rental charges during that period."

He contends that this language indicated a clear intention " * * * that the leased premises would have to be rebuilt in the event of their destruction."

A lessor is not required to rebuild on substantial destruction by fire unless he is obligated to do so by the terms of the lease. In Davis v. Parker et al., 200 Ky. 847, 255 S.W. 836 (1923), we held the lessor did not have to rebuild a fire-destroyed building, the lease not imposing that obligation on him, although it contained the language requiring him to " * * * replace the buildings in the same condition as they now are * * *."

The first quoted section of the lease is similar to a provision in the lease discussed in Columbia Amusement Co. v. Hughes, Ky., 375 S.W.2d 813, in which we held it did not create an obligation to rebuild after fire destroyed the leased premises. Neither paragraph expressed an agreement to rebuild after complete destruction. We find no error in the chancellor's declaration that the owners were not required to rebuild.

On April 3, 1968 the attorney for the owners wrote Morris' attorney that his clients were willing to construct a new building in which Morris could become a tenant if he agreed to the proposed conditions. He did not accept. We do not interpret that letter as an election to rebuild. The judgment made proper provision for Morris in the event rebuilding occurs " * * * in substantially the same form as previously."

The judgment is affirmed.

All concur.

Problems and Questions

1. Why was the court hesitant to find an obligation to rebuild even though the landlord had already indicated a willingness to do so?

2. Assume a commercial lease is silent regarding repairs except for a provision that "Lessor, its successor or assigns, may at all reasonable times enter to view and make such repairs to the premises as may be necessary." Must the landlord make repairs? See Givens v. Union Investment Corp., 116 R.I. 539, 359 A.2d 40 (1976); see also 2 Powell on Real Property § 16B.04[4][a] (1998).

b. Covenant by Tenant

In the commercial area, the tenant often covenants to keep the leased property in repair.

BROWN v. GREEN

Supreme Court of California, 1994.
8 Cal.4th 812, 35 Cal.Rptr.2d 598, 884 P.2d 55.

ARABIAN, JUSTICE.

We granted review to consider the effect of the developing public awareness of environmentally hazardous building materials, and the often substantial cost of their abatement, on traditional rules allocating, as between lessor and lessee, the duty to make repairs and alterations to the leasehold required to comply with laws affecting commercial property. We conclude that settled and well-understood legal rules for determining which party has assumed the burdens of compliance and repair continue to yield fair and reasonable results when applied to leases of nonresidential property presenting abatement of hazardous materials issues.

Disputes between landlords and tenants of commercial property over responsibility for hazardous materials abatement are not, in other words, unique or so extraordinary in nature as to require special rules governing their resolution. In most cases, however, they *do* require a court presented with such a controversy not only to construe the relevant lease terms—terms that presumptively reflect the parties' intent—but to assess the result yielded by that analysis in light of established, judicially developed criteria designed to confirm the text-based conclusion that the parties agreed that the lessee would assume certain (often substantial) risks. Here, given a narrowly drawn compliance with laws clause, the absence of a lease provision expressly allocating responsibility for the abatement of environmentally hazardous materials, and a resultant ambiguity as to how the parties intended to allocate responsibility for compliance with government—ordered alterations unrelated to the lessees' use, we apply these established factors and conclude that the parties agreed the lessee would assume the burden of removing asbestos-laden materials from the building as required by a government abatement order.

We underline the context-dependent nature of both the inquiry and the result in cases such as this. We deal in this case with the long-term lease of an entire warehouse-like building by sophisticated business partners who had substantial experience in leasing commercial property: lessees who were on written notice of at least the *potential* for asbestos contamination prior to executing the lease, who inspected the building and elected not to investigate the possible presence of hazardous materials before negotiating and signing an agreement that by its terms shifted the major risks of property ownership to the lessee, negated any repair obligations on the part of the lessor, and omitted any representations respecting the condition of the property. In addition, the cost of complying with the mandated work, although substantial in absolute numbers, is less than 5 percent of the total rent payable over the life of the lease.

Under these circumstances, we have no difficulty in concluding that the Court of Appeal was correct in deciding that the lessees agreed to accept responsibility for the government-ordered abatement of asbestos-containing materials. As we explain, however, such determinations are usually closely tied, not only to the terms of the lease itself, but to the context in which it is made, assessed in light of a handful of factors designed to elucidate the probable intent of the parties. Contrary to the result we reach in this case, even though a lease may by its terms require the lessee to be responsible for all repairs and alterations, without limitation, the legal and practical scope of that duty may well be less, especially where a short-term commercial lease is at issue and the cost of compliance is more than a small fraction of the aggregate rent reserved over the life of the lease. Similarly, where questions regarding the duty to abate arise in a case presenting unforeseeable or hidden defects or conditions, the result may well be the opposite of the one we reach in this case.

Together, our opinions in this case and in *Hadian v. Schwartz* (1994) 8 Cal.4th 836, 35 Cal.Rptr.2d 589, 884 P.2d 46, also filed today, illustrate the relationship between the literal text of a nonresidential lease and the result yielded by applying these interpretive factors. In *Hadian*, we construe a preprinted, *short*-term lease with terms virtually identical to the one at issue in this case and conclude that, contrary to the purport of language placing an unqualified responsibility on the lessee for all building alterations and repairs, the conclusion arising from the literal text of the lease is negated by a consideration of the circumstances surrounding its execution. We reason in that case that, despite the unqualified language of the lease, the lessor rather than the lessee is responsible for a municipally ordered seismic upgrade of the leased building, at a cost that is almost one-half of the total rent payable over the life of the original lease and option combined.

Thus, although broadly applicable criteria for determining the repair and compliance with laws obligations of the parties to a nonresidential lease can be articulated, it does not follow that the outcome in a particular case can be easily forecast on the basis of the text of the lease alone. Each agreement must be evaluated in light of its individual terms under generally applicable contextual criteria and the principle of reasonable construction.

I

In 1984, Willet H. Brown purchased a 45,000–square foot building at 8921 Venice Boulevard in Los Angeles which he immediately leased to Hillcrest Motor Company, a West Los Angeles Cadillac dealership of which Brown was president and chief executive officer, for use in preparing automobiles for delivery to buyers. After he withdrew from the new car business in late 1985, Brown began looking for a potential lessee for the Venice Boulevard property; he enlisted a real property brokerage firm, Coldwell Banker, to find a tenant and broker the lease transaction. In April of 1986, Joseph Green, a partner in a retail furniture business with between 10 and 20 outlets in the Los Angeles area, all of which operated out of leased premises and grossed cumulative annual revenues of between $10 and $20 million, saw a listing for the property and made inquiries. The Green partnership later retained its own broker to facilitate lease negotiations with Brown's broker.

On May 8, 1987, following a discussion of terms between the two brokers and Green, Green and another partner signed on behalf of the partnership a two-page, preprinted document entitled "Proposal to Lease Industrial Space," given them by a Coldwell Banker agent, for Brown's consideration. At the foot of the second page of the proposal, just below Joseph Green's signature, appeared the following boxed text, in what appears to be 10–point type:

> "CONSULT YOUR ADVISORS—This document has been prepared for approval by your attorney. No representations or recommendation is made by Coldwell Banker as to the legal sufficiency or tax consequences of this document or the transaction to which it relates. These are questions for your attorney. [¶] In any real estate transaction, it is recommended that you consult with a professional, such as a civil engineer, industrial hygienist or other person, with experience in evaluating the condition of the property, including the possible presence of asbestos, hazardous materials and underground storage tanks."

At his deposition, Green testified that he had inspected the building by walking through it, had understood the boxed text, and had made a "deliberate" decision not to retain a professional to inspect the property for environmental hazards; the trial court made a finding of fact to that effect in its judgment. After additional negotiations between Brown, his son Michael (a vice-president of Hillcrest designated by Brown to oversee the lease transaction), and their broker and lawyer, and the Green partnership and their broker and lawyer, the parties reached agreement on June 25, 1987, and signed a written lease agreement. That document, a preprinted, six-page form published by the American Industrial Real Estate Association, was modified by the parties by several strikethroughs and interlineations and a three-page, typewritten "Addendum to Standard Industrial Lease—Net" attached to the modified form lease agreement; each page of the lease bore the initials of the signatories.

As modified and signed by the parties, the lease provided for a term of 15 years at a monthly rent of $28,500; the lessees agreed to pay the annual property taxes and to obtain and pay the premiums for liability (but not casualty) insurance on the building. A handful of other lease provisions are material in resolving the question presented in this suit. Paragraph 6.2(b), entitled "Compliance with Law," provided that "*Les-*

see shall, at Lessee's expense, comply promptly with all applicable statutes, ordinances, rules, regulations, orders, covenants and restrictions of record, and requirements in effect during the term or any part of the term hereof, regulating the use by the Lessee of the premises...." (Italics added.) In addition, paragraph 7.1 of the lease, "Maintenance, Repairs and Alterations," provided that "*Lessee* shall keep in good order, condition and repair the Premises and every part thereof, *structural* and non-structural (whether or not ... the need for such repairs occurs as a result of Lessee's use, any prior use, the elements or the age of such portion of the Premises) including, without limiting the generality of the foregoing, all plumbing, heating, air-conditioning." (Italics added.) Paragraph 7.4 of the lease purported to limit the Lessor's obligations by providing that "Except for the obligations of Lessor under paragraph 9 [specifying the obligations of the parties in the event the building was destroyed], it is intended by the parties hereto that *Lessor* have *no obligation in any manner whatsoever*, to *repair and maintain* the Premises nor the building located thereon nor the equipment therein, whether structural or nonstructural, all of which obligations are intended to be that of the *Lessee* under Paragraph 7.1 hereof...." (Italics added.)

In addition, subparagraphs 6.2(a) and 6.3(a) of the form lease agreement, by which the lessor warranted compliance with applicable laws and the condition of the property on the date the lessee took occupancy, were crossed out by the parties. Last, the lease set forth provisions requiring the lessee to indemnify and hold harmless the lessor against any claim arising from the use of the property during the term of the lease. According to the evidence, apart from the import of the notice appearing at the foot of the lease proposal, at the time the lease was executed, neither party had actual knowledge or reason to believe that the building contained asbestos, and the parties discussed neither that possibility nor, if discovered, which of them would bear the responsibility for its abatement; the trial court made an express finding of fact to that effect.

Less than two years after taking possession of the property and opening a retail furniture store, the Green partnership suffered business reverses at the Venice Boulevard location. In March of 1989, the partners held a liquidation sale and sublet the entire building to Green's son Ricky and his business partner, who continued to operate a retail furniture store under a new name. In the fall of that year, in the course of a routine inspection of the building, the county Department of Health Services (Department) found that debris containing friable asbestos had flaked onto the floor and furniture in the store's showroom. Ambient air samples of the interior of the building showroom were positive for the presence of airborne asbestos fibers at levels deemed harmful to humans. Soon after the inspection, the Department served the subtenants with a notice of asbestos contamination, advising them of its hazardous nature, and directing that it be abated; a copy of the Department's notice was mailed subsequently to Brown.

* * *

Amid charges and countercharges by the parties to the lease over who was responsible for arranging for and financing the cost of removing the asbestos laden material, the subtenants converted the retail furniture operation by moving the sales and showroom into what had been the warehouse portion of the building, and sealing off the area subject to the flaking debris. Ricky Green also sublet a small portion of the newly converted warehouse area. Although Ricky Green and his partner, as subtenants, paid rent on the property directly to Brown from April of 1989 to May of 1990, thereafter neither the Green partnership nor the subtenants paid any rent for the use of the building, which Ricky Green and his partner continued to occupy; as of the date of trial, the county had not pursued abatement proceedings against the site and no asbestos cleanup work had been undertaken.

Having failed to settle his differences with the lessees over responsibility for the asbestos cleanup, Brown filed this action against Green and his partners in November of 1990. The complaint sought as damages accrued rent (totaling $504,278.37, including property taxes, on the date judgment was entered) and the cost of the environmental cleanup, estimated by plaintiff's experts at $251,856, together with attorney fees as provided in the lease agreement. By agreement of the parties, the matter was tried before a superior court judge on a record consisting of stipulated facts, excerpts of deposition testimony, and documentary exhibits. After reviewing the record and hearing oral argument, the trial judge made findings of fact and filed a memorandum decision. Relying principally on our opinion in *Glenn R. Sewell Sheet Metal, Inc. v. Loverde* (1969) 70 Cal.2d 666, 75 Cal.Rptr. 889, 451 P.2d 721 (*Sewell*), the trial court concluded that the language of the relevant lease provisions allocated responsibility for asbestos removal and cleanup to the lessees; the court rejected the claim of the Green partners that because the lease did not expressly refer to the risk of asbestos or other environmental hazards, the parties had made no agreement with respect to that subject. The Court of Appeal affirmed the judgment of the trial court, concluding that our decision in *Sewell* was dispositive. We then granted the lessees' petition for review of the Court of Appeal judgment. We affirm.

II

A

We begin with an account of our reasoning in *Sewell, supra,* 70 Cal.2d 666, 75 Cal.Rptr. 889, 451 P.2d 721. In 1953, the Loverdes entered into a multi-year lease (with an option to renew) of property for use as an automobile repair shop. With the consent of the lessor, the Loverdes converted the property into a trailer park, using an on-site septic system to dispose of waste. Sometime later, Sewell sublet the entire property for the remaining three years of the option, intending to continue operating the trailer park. During the term of Sewell's sublease, county officials determined that the septic system was in danger of failing; they ordered Sewell to connect to a nearby public sewer or to cease using the property as a trailer park. After investigating the cost of complying with the county's order and finding it beyond his means, Sewell evicted his tenants, closed the park, and abandoned the property.

Sewell later sought declaratory relief to the effect that the Loverdes, rather than he, were responsible for payment of the accrued rent. The Loverdes cross-complained for the back rent and Sewell defended on the ground that the duty of complying with the county's order to connect to the public sewer fell on them. In an opinion for a unanimous court, Chief Justice Traynor held that under the terms of the lease and sublease, Sewell had the duty of complying with the county's order to cease using the septic system and connect to the public sewer and was thus liable for payment of the back rent. We reasoned that although neither party to a commercial lease owes a duty to *repair* leased property in the absence of an agreement allocating that responsibility, "[a] different conclusion must be reached ... when preventative or reparative actions are required by laws and orders governing the premises and their uses. In such a case public policy requires that someone at all times be obliged to comply with such laws and orders, and parties to a lease will not be permitted to create a hiatus in their respective duties of compliance.... Since the property owner is initially under the duty to comply with all laws and orders, he, as lessor, remains subject to that duty unless it is assumed by the lessee." (*Sewell, supra.*)

Our opinion noted that there are two principal ways in which a lessee can assume the duty of compliance with laws or government orders requiring the repair or alteration of commercial property. The first is by "voluntarily put[ting] the premises to uses different from those to which they were put before the creation of his tenancy, and thereby caus[ing] the premises to fall within the scope of existing laws not previously applicable to the premises...." (*Sewell, supra.*) Without such a rule, we noted, a lessee would "have the lessor at his mercy." (*Id.*) A lessee's responsibility for complying with laws may also be the subject of negotiations between the parties to the lease, and may be transferred from the lessor as an obligation undertaken by the lessee by agreement. Even in such cases, however, there is an implied limitation on the scope of the lessee's burden. "[T]he general rule is that a lessee's *unqualified* covenant to comply with applicable laws, *standing alone*, does not constitute an assumption of the duty to comply with those laws that require curative actions of a '*substantial*' nature." (*Id.*, italics added).

* * *

B

To both the trial court and the Court of Appeal, the lease terms at issue here and those parsed in *Sewell* were sufficiently alike to make our analysis in Sewell dispositive. Relying wholly on similarities in the texts of the two leases, and without discussing either the scope of the compliance with laws clause or the nature of the lessees' use, the Court of Appeal concluded that "[u]nder *Sewell*, the lease before us can only be read to transfer to the tenant the duty to abate the asbestos." Although we agree that the duty of compliance was transferred from the building owner to the lessees, we reach that result by a route different from the logic of the lease terms themselves that the Court of Appeal purported to deduce from our opinion in *Sewell*.

It is true that the compliance with laws clauses in both cases are, in substance, identical—both require the lessee to comply with laws, orders, etc., regulating the lessee's use of the property. The distinguishing feature of this case, however, is that, unlike *Sewell*, here it was not the lessee's particular use of the property that led to the government's compliance order. In *Sewell*, on the other hand, we relied on the fact that it was the lessee's use of the property as a trailer park that led to the county's demand that he modify the existing waste disposal system. * * *

Unlike the situation in *Sewell*, the lease at issue here does not contemplate a use of the property by the lessee of the sort likely to trigger a municipally ordered hazardous materials cleanup. It is clear from the record that the substantial cause of the flaking of the asbestos laden material was activity within the building that would have been typical of virtually any occupant, including the predecessor dealer preparation work undertaken by Hillcrest Motors. * * * Because the lessee's particular use of the property here is *not* one that triggered the county's abatement order, unlike the use at issue in *Sewell*, it lies outside the literal text of the compliance with laws clause of the lease.

* * *

Because the lessees' use of the property in this case lies outside the literal scope of the compliance with laws clause, it is unclear from that provision, standing alone, how the parties intended to allocate the risk of compliance with respect to government orders arising from property conditions unrelated to a particular use by the lessee. In the face of that ambiguity, we may properly consider other relevant provisions of the lease as well as the factors employed by the courts to determine the intent of the parties to a nonresidential lease, factors that, in the words of our opinion in *Sewell*, "offer insight into the probable intent of the parties" "despite the use of unqualified language" in the lease.

III

A

Although the Green partnership neither agreed expressly to comply with laws *not* regulating their use of the property, nor used the building in particular ways that triggered the county's asbestos abatement order, it *did* agree to a duty of repair that is, on its face, virtually global in scope. In combination with other features of the lease, the extent of that obligation strongly suggests that the parties intended to transfer to the lessees substantially *all* of the responsibilities of property ownership, including the duty to comply with the county-ordered asbestos cleanup.

Lessees urge us to adopt the contrary view with respect to the duty to comply with *government-mandated* alterations. They argue that, because the compliance clause of the lease only obligates them to comply with laws affecting their particular use of the property, and because the county's order mandating the replacement of the asbestos-containing material applies to *any* occupant of the building, the abatement order is outside the scope of paragraph 6.2 of the agreement and that is the end of the matter.

Although as noted, we agree that the text of the compliance clause of the lease literally applies only to governmental laws, orders, et cetera, regulating the *uses* made of the property by the lessee, that conclusion alone is not dispositive. Several circumstances surrounding the transaction persuade us that the parties intended that the Green partnership accept responsibility for government-mandated work on the building *unrelated* to the particular use made of it by the lessees.

An interpretation of the lease which places the burden of complying with the abatement order on the lessor would, we think, lead to a strained and unrealistic result, given the unqualified duty of repair imposed by the lease on the lessees and the absence of any significant obligations on the part of the lessor. Moreover, viewed through the prism of the economics of the transaction, we think the case for concluding that the lessees assumed a virtually unqualified burden of compliance with government-ordered alterations, maintenance and repair of the property is stronger here than in *Sewell* itself. Financial considerations implicit in the text of the lease agreement make it clear that Brown negotiated a "net" lease, an arrangement that is not uncommon in long-term commercial leases, especially of entire buildings. As one commentator on the characteristics of such leases has explained, "A net lease presumes the landlord will receive a fixed rent, without deduction for repairs, taxes, insurance, or any other charges, other than landlords' income taxes. Accordingly, the repair clause requires the tenant to make all repairs, inside and out, structural and otherwise, as well as all necessary replacements of the improvements on the premises (and to comply with all legal requirements affecting these improvements during the term). A lease is not 'net,' as this term is used in long-term leases, if the tenant's repair obligations are less than these." (1 Friedman on Leases (3d ed. 1990) Repairs, § 10.8.) The economic exchange supporting such "net" leases has been succinctly described as one under which "the landlord foregoes the speculative advantages of ownership in return for the agreed net rental. The tenant, in turn, gambles on the continued value of the location and the improvement[s].... and assumes all risks in connection therewith." (Van Doren, *Some Suggestions for the Drafting of Long Term Net and Percentage Leases*, (1951) 51 Colum.L.Rev. 186.)

The fact that the form lease used by the parties here bears the word "net" at the foot of each page and that the heading of the addendum negotiated by the parties and annexed to the lease used the word "net," while probative of the parties' intent, is not alone decisive. What is persuasive is a consideration of the provisions of the lease agreement as a whole, including its comparatively long 15–year term, the lessees' agreement to pay property taxes, to assume the risk of third party liability and to insure against that risk, the unqualified nature of the repair clause, the lessor's "negative" covenants with respect to any obligation to maintain or repair the property, and the elimination of any warranties on the part of the lessor.

It is, in short, reasonably clear *from the four corners of the agreement* itself that the parties intended to transfer from the lessor to the tenants the major burdens of ownership of real property over the life of the lease. * * *

B

Lessees and supporting amicus curiae press us to adopt a rule that the obligation to remove environmentally hazardous materials always falls on the lessor of commercial property *unless* the responsibility for their removal is *explicitly* allocated to the lessee by the text of the lease agreement. * * * We are not persuaded of the wisdom of adopting a bright line rule of the kind sought by lessees. Apart from the relative novelty of environmental cleanup demands, there is little to distinguish requiring a lessee to abate asbestos laden building materials and to replace, say, the entire roof of a large warehouse-like building of the sort involved in this case. We agree, however, that, given the differences between the use at issue here and the one in *Sewell*, it is appropriate to apply the factors enumerated in *Sewell* as "offer[ing] insight into the probable intent of the parties...."

Whether the parties actually intended the allocation of responsibilities suggested by the use of unqualified language in a lease is an inquiry better approached through the application of a handful of relevant factors than by a "four corners" analysis of the text that focuses exclusively on the interlocking provisions of the agreement itself and their legal consequences. Such an inquiry seems all the more appropriate in cases such a this one, involving the use of a so-called "form" lease, where the logic of preprinted terms may favor the interests of one party over that of the other and, even where interlineated by the parties, produce an unreasonable result. * * *

More significantly, in seeking the intent of the parties, courts can seldom safely rely solely on the text of the lease. * * *

We recognized explicitly in *Sewell* that in assessing the terms and the circumstances surrounding a nonresidential lease transaction, courts usually apply a handful of factors as "clues" or indicators as to whether the parties agreed that the lessee "assumed certain risks, despite the use of unqualified language." That proposition has long been bedrock law.

We examine the six factors as they apply to the record in this case.

(1) *The relationship of the cost of the curative action to the rent reserved.* Not surprisingly, lessees seize on the absolute cost of the asbestos disposal operation—set at $251,856 in the judgment entered by

the trial court—as confirming that the costs at issue here qualify as "substantial." The inquiry, however, is not quite so straightforward. Lessor points out that the roughly quarter million dollars estimated as necessary to finance asbestos-related disposal is less than 5 percent of the total rent reserved over the 15–year life of the lease, an expression of the value of the repair that throws a different light on the relative financial magnitude (and hardship) of the undertaking.

* * *

The relationship between the cost of compliance and the aggregate rent payable over the life of the lease is thus a significant factor in divining the probable intent of the parties and determining which of them agreed to bear the burden of compliance. In many—perhaps most—cases, it is likely that the cost of the mandated work, expressed as a percentage of the aggregate rent over the life of the lease, will tip in favor of the lessee. It is, after all, highly unlikely that a lessee would intend or expect to assume a repair/compliance burden that is, say, equal to or even a substantial fraction of the total rent over the life of the lease. The analysis is different, however, where, as in this case, the hazardous condition is discovered relatively early in a long-term lease, the total rent reserved over the life of the lease is a very high multiple (here, 20 times) of the cost of disposal, and the provisions of the lease agreement otherwise suggest that the parties intended that the lessees assume the major burdens of ownership.

(2) *The term for which the lease was made.* There is little question under this rubric that a lease for a term of 15 years is a comparatively lengthy one. * * *

The length of the lease term has significance for the determination of responsibility for government-ordered alterations for the reasons mentioned in the analysis of factor (1), above. Where the term of the lease is short, it is highly unlikely that the lessee would have expected to assume responsibility for the cost of alterations that are, in effect, capital improvements to the property that will benefit primarily the owner. Conversely, where the lease term is a comparatively long one, the lessee has more time in which to amortize the cost of the alterations and stands more in the shoes of the building owner.

(3) *The relationship of the benefit to the lessee to that of the reversioner.* No evidence was introduced at trial bearing on the projected useful life of the building. It is thus impossible to say on the basis of the record to what extent disposal of the asbestos laden material would benefit the lessor. Lessees argue that the benefits would be substantial, noting that, at the end of their term, the lessor would be in a position to market an "asbestos free" building, thus gaining a commercial advantage. Although that scenario seems a plausible one, it is also true that given the long-term nature of this 15–year lease and the fact that the hazardous material was discovered in only the third year of the term, the cleanup would be of substantial benefit to the lessees themselves. On

balance, then, given this record, the benefit of the mandated work will inure to *both* parties.

(4) *Whether the curative action is structural or nonstructural in nature.* Lessees point out that the removal and disposition of asbestos-containing fireproofing material is costly and expensive, requiring special equipment for containment of the material, warning signs, area evacuation and "moon-suited" workers. Moreover, because the removal here requires that the fireproofing material adhering to the building's structural beams be stripped, the work is literally "structural." That is true, of course, and under ordinary principles of construction might place the burden of cleanup on the lessor.

In the context of this case, however, the argument overlooks the fact that the lease agreement shifts, explicitly and systematically, responsibility for *all* repairs—expressly including "structural" repairs—to the tenants both by an affirmative provision (Par. 7.1) and by expressly absolving the lessor of any responsibility for repairs, whether or not "structural" (Par. 9), and that it does so in an overall context supporting the conclusion that the parties intended the lessees to assume the burdens of compliance and repair. The language of the lease is thus sufficiently definite and clear to negate the argument that "structural" alterations are not within the lessees' obligations.

(5) *The degree to which the lessee's enjoyment of the premises will be interfered with while the curative action is being undertaken.* Our review of the case law suggests that if the lessee's use of the premises is substantially interfered with by the work required to comply with a given law or government order, that fact supports an inference that the lessor accepted the burden of compliance. That supposition is consistent, we think, with the notion that the greater the magnitude (and the likely disruptive effect) of the compliance effort, the more likely it is to qualify as "substantial" and thus as part of the lessor's duty. Here, although the factual record is scanty on the point, it appears that the lessees were able to "work around" the flaking debris through the expediency of moving the retail sales operation into the former storage area and storing inventory in the area subject to delamination. The record is devoid of evidence as to whether this arrangement could be continued throughout the course of the actual abatement work, however. On balance, the most that can be concluded in light of the evidence is that the degree of interference is not so great as to weigh heavily in favor of a finding that the lessor accepted the compliance responsibility.

(6) *The likelihood that the parties contemplated the application of the particular law or order involved.* In light of the finding of the trial court and the evidence supporting it, we can only conclude that although neither party was *aware of* or had reason to believe hazardous materials were present within the building at the time the lease agreement was negotiated and signed, both had notice of the *possibility* that such a condition *might* exist, at least in the abstract. We think this fact is especially telling in a context in which lessees with substantial experi-

ence in retail leasing conceded that they had read and understood the notice at the foot of the lease proposal and elected not to pursue an investigation of that contingency. Although this factor is not dispositive of the question of responsibility for complying with the county-ordered abatement work, it is of considerable weight in leading us to conclude that the parties intended that the lessees would assume the burden of compliance with the abatement order. (We note, of course, the obvious fact that a finding of no abatement liability on the part of the lessee is likely where the condition at issue was unforeseeable or would not have been disclosed by a reasonable inspection of the site.)

C

An evaluation of the lease terms in light of factors substantially similar to those proposed by the lessees themselves leads us to conclude that the Court of Appeal was correct in ruling that the lessees assumed responsibility for removing the asbestos laden material from the building. That conclusion, we point out, does not necessarily follow in the typical *short-term* commercial lease. As several commentators have noted—and as our opinion in *Hadian v. Schwartz*, also filed today, confirms—application of the factors identified above will in many, perhaps even most, cases place the burden of compliance on the property owner, both because the cleanup substantially enhances the lessor's reversionary rather than the lessee's possessory interest, and because the cost of compliance may be a substantial percentage of the entire rent reserved over the life of the term. That conclusion, however, remains a mixed question of fact and law arising out of the provisions of *a particular agreement and its terms* and the context in which it arises, considered in light of established common law factors and the principle of reasonable construction, rather than one dependent on a bright line, a priori allocation of risk.

CONCLUSION

The judgment of the Court of Appeal is affirmed.

Question

A commercial tenant under a five-year lease was required by express provision to "maintain the building situated on the lease premises." Does this covenant obligate the tenant to pay the cost of replacing a leaking roof? *See* Mach v. Accettola, 112 Ohio App.3d 282, 678 N.E.2d 617 (1996).

AMOCO OIL COMPANY v. JONES

Court of Appeals of Minnesota, 1991.
467 N.W.2d 357.

OPINION

EDWARD D. MULALLY, JUDGE.

Amoco Oil Company challenges a directed verdict for respondent Llewellan K. Jones, claiming material fact issues exist regarding Jones' obligation to rebuild or restore leased property under a general repair and delivery covenant. We affirm.

FACTS

Respondent Jones operated a gas station which he had leased from appellant Amoco Oil Company (Amoco) since 1968. In general, Amoco agents provided a standard lease form for Jones' signature. Jones testified minimal negotiation was involved, "they presented the lease and you signed it or not." The parties entered the lease in question on October 26, 1984. The lease terms prohibited Jones from committing waste to the property, and further required that:

> (b) Lessee shall keep the Premises, together with the adjoining sidewalks and entrance driveways, in good repair, appearance, and order; and, at the expiration of this lease, or upon sooner termination thereof, Lessee shall surrender the Premises to Lessor in substantially as good condition as when received, ordinary wear and tear excepted.

> (c) Lessee shall perform necessary upkeep and maintenance to the Premises, and in so doing shall follow reasonable guides outlining proper care which Lessor may from time to time provide to Lessee. Lessee shall keep the Premises, including adjoining areas, alleys, and sidewalks, in clean, safe, and healthful condition.

The lease did not indicate which party was responsible for obtaining fire insurance. However, under the lease Amoco could terminate or choose not to renew the lease upon the occurrence of a variety of events, including:

> (j) Destruction of all or a substantial part of the Premises, it being understood that if the Premises are rendered untenantable, rent shall abate as of the date the Premises are rendered untenantable. In the event the Premises shall be subsequently rebuilt or replaced by Lessor and operated under a lessee franchise relationship, Lessor shall grant to Lessee a thirty (30) day right of first refusal of the new franchise * * *.

Fire broke out in the early morning of December 24, 1985, causing substantial damage and destruction to the station. Parts of the building suffered heavy smoke damage only, while other parts were nearly gutted. Neither party was negligent or otherwise at fault in causing the fire.

After the fire, Amoco terminated the lease because of "destruction of all or a substantial part" of the property. In its letter to Jones, Amoco stated "[t]he premises now cannot be used for a gasoline service station or anything else because of the level of damage to the structure and utility services." Amoco also stated that an Amoco representative would contact Jones "to discuss whether or not you would be willing to work with Amoco and contribute to rebuilding the premises." Amoco contacted a general contractor to inspect the property and submit an estimate for the cost of repairing or rebuilding the station. After receiving the estimate, Amoco leveled the remaining structure. Amoco then sued

Jones for breach of the lease, alleging Jones failed to return the station to Amoco in as good condition as when he received it.

At the jury trial Amoco's expert witness, Thomas Shamp, a general contractor, testified the reasonable cost of repairing the station was $118,850. Shamp testified parts of the station needed to be gutted, that he would take off "the skin" and reuse the shell of the building. Shamp also testified the roof needed to be completely replaced, as did some wall partitions, door jambs, and bathroom fixtures. Shamp stated other parts of the building (porcelain panels, floor tiles) could be cleaned and reused, although he did not know how effective the cleaning would be.

At the close of Amoco's evidence, the trial court directed a verdict in Jones' favor. The trial court found the lease terms did not contain a covenant to restore the property to its original state in the event of such severe destruction or damage, that Jones did not breach the lease, and entered judgment in favor of Jones. Amoco appeals.

ISSUE

Does a general repair and delivery covenant obligate a lessee to rebuild property destroyed or substantially damaged by fire, where the lessee is not at fault?

ANALYSIS

* * *

Common Law Rule

At common law, a lessee's covenant to repair property included an obligation to rebuild structures destroyed during the lease term, regardless of the lessee's fault in causing the destruction. *See* Lewis v. Real Estate Corp., 6 Ill.App.2d 240, 244, 127 N.E.2d 272, 275 (Ill.App.Ct. 1955). A lessee's covenant to return the leased property in the same condition as it was at the time of the letting, often combined with a covenant to repair, also imposed an obligation to rebuild, unless the lessee limited the covenant. Wattles v. South Omaha Ice & Coal Co., 50 Neb. 251, 256–58, 69 N.W. 785, 786 (1897). This rule arose because, at common law, the landlord conveyed an interest in the land to the tenant, who became the "owner" for the lease term. 1 M. Friedman, Friedman on Leases § 9.1 at 305–6 (1974).

> The common law rule may not have been inappropriate at the time
> * * *—an agricultural lease in which the improvements were mere-
> ly incidental. Damage to the house, or its destruction, might make
> life inconvenient but the land was still tillable.

Id. at 313. Thus, when the tenant covenanted to repair the property and return it in the same condition as when the lease was executed, the covenant included an obligation to rebuild regardless of the cause of the destruction.

Modern Trend

Jurisdictions are split regarding whether a general repair and delivery covenant requires a tenant to rebuild where the tenant is not at fault. *Compare Lewis,* 6 Ill.App.2d at 244, 127 N.E.2d at 275 (applying common law rule) *with Wattles,* 50 Neb. at 262, 69 N.W. at 788 (holding general repair and delivery covenant does not include covenant to rebuild). Some states have modified the rule by statute. *See, e.g.,* W.Va.Code § 36–4–13 (1988). Courts that have refused to apply the common law rule have done so on the ground that one cannot repair that which does not exist. *See, e.g.,* Realty & Rebuilding Co. v. Rea, 184 Cal. 565, 576, 194 P. 1024, 1029 (1920) ("To repair means to mend an old thing, not to make a new thing; to restore to a sound state something which has become partially diliapidated (sic), not to create something which has no existence.")

> This distinction between "repair" and "restore" rescued some tenants who had naively agreed to repair, with no suspicion of what the common law attributed to this covenant. However, a repair is a partial restoration and these terms do not necessarily present a clear contrast. Their difference may be of degree rather than of nature.

Friedman, § 9.1 at 307. Rather than rely on "magic words" to create a covenant to rebuild, courts look to the intent of the parties at the time of the lease execution and the plain meaning of the language used. Washington Hydroculture, Inc. v. Payne, 96 Wash.2d 322, 328, 635 P.2d 138, 141 (1981).

While Minnesota case law establishes a lessee's duty to repair leased property damaged through the lessee's negligence, these cases do not mandate application of the common law rule. Amoco contends a fact question exists regarding Jones' liability because the station suffered substantial damage which could be repaired without rebuilding the entire station. Under the common law rule this argument may have merit; however, we believe the common law rule is arbitrary and outdated. Application of the "magic" language places an unforeseen burden on the lessee, a burden which is most often outside both parties' contemplation. A lease is a contract which should be construed according to ordinary rules of interpretation. We believe the better approach is to interpret the lease according to its plain language to ascertain the parties' intent.

Because we reject the automatic application of the common law rule, Amoco's distinction between destroy and damage is irrelevant. Shamp's testimony does not bear on the parties' intent. Amoco drafted the lease, thus the lease is construed against Amoco. Amoco did not present any evidence to suggest the parties intended Jones to assume the risk of loss by fire. Rather, the plain language of the lease speaks of Jones' responsibility for "necessary upkeep and repairs," including maintenance of sidewalks and driveways. We agree with the trial court's conclusion that Amoco did not carry its burden to show the parties intended Jones to rebuild the property in the event of substantial damage or destruction.

DECISION

The trial court did not err in directing a verdict for Jones where the evidence was insufficient to present a fact question regarding the parties' intent.

Affirmed.

Question

What is the legal effect of section fourteen of the sample lease on page 8, which places a duty on the tenant to redeliver the premises "in as good condition as they are now, ordinary wear, decay, and damage by the elements excepted," in light of sections five, seven, and sixteen which place the duty to repair on the landlord?

E. LIABILITY FOR PERSONAL INJURY AND PROPERTY DAMAGE

The obligation to repair bears directly on the issue of tort liability for personal injury and property damage. For example, who is liable if someone is injured at Harmony House as a result of the rental manager's failure to make repairs?

1. TENANT'S LIABILITY TO THIRD PARTIES

HOWE v. KROGER CO.

Court of Civil Appeals of Texas, 1980.
598 S.W.2d 929.

ROBERTSON, JUSTICE.

Appellants Delores Gail Howe and Dennis Wayne Howe brought this action to recover for injuries Mrs. Howe sustained from a fall that occurred after she slipped on accumulated ice and snow on the sidewalk outside one of appellee's stores. Appellants alleged that appellee breached its duties to keep its premises in reasonably safe condition and to warn business invitees of dangerous conditions existing on its premises. The trial court entered summary judgment for appellee. We affirm.

On this appeal appellants argue that the summary judgment was erroneously granted because a genuine issue of fact exists concerning whether appellee breached the duties it had. * * * [B]oth sides agree that the real issue is whether the appellee had any duty to Mrs. Howe. Appellants rely on the general rule of premises liability that the occupier of premises is required to exercise ordinary care to keep his premises in a reasonably safe condition so that his invitees will not be injured, or to warn his invitees of any dangerous conditions. * * *

* * * Appellee first points out that the phrase "occupier of premises," as interpreted by Texas courts, means the party *in control* of premises. O'Connor v. Andrews, 81 Tex. 28, 33, 16 S.W. 628, 629 (1891). In *O'Connor* the court acknowledged the general rule that when an

entire building is leased to one tenant, the tenant is liable for injuries caused by dangerous conditions subsequently occurring thereon, absent lease provisions to the contrary.

When, however, a building consisting of a number of different apartments is divided among several tenants, each one of whom takes a distinct portion, and none of them rent the entire building, the rule must then be applied so as to make each tenant responsible only for so much as his lease includes, leaving the landlord liable for every part of the building not included in the actual holding of any one tenant.

* * * [Thus,] the general rule * * * [is] that liability follows control.

In Parker [v. Highland Park, 565 S.W.2d 512 (Tex.1978)] the Texas Supreme Court quoted section 360 of the Restatement (Second) of Torts, which holds a lessor liable to lessees and their guests for injuries caused by dangerous conditions on portions of the leased premises over which the lessor retains control. The court then examined several comments to this section, including comment *a*, which states that the lessee's knowledge of the dangerous condition will not relieve the lessor of liability to a guest of the lessee. The court quoted that comment as follows: "[The lessee's] knowledge may subject him to liability even to his own licensees, if he fails to warn them of the danger. *It will not, however, relieve the lessor of liability for his negligence in permitting the entrance to become dangerous.*" Appellants point to the first quoted sentence as indicating the supreme court's recognition of the extension of the general rule. Read in context, however, it is clear that the court was focusing on the second quoted sentence and that the first was mere surplusage in reaching the conclusion. We conclude that the first quoted sentence has not been adopted as law in Texas, but rather, that it is contrary to the existing law in Texas. That existing law, as exemplified by the cases cited above, is that an occupier of premises owes to his invitees a duty of ordinary care, which encompasses the duties to maintain those premises in reasonably safe condition and to warn of dangerous conditions on the premises. This duty, however, extends only to the limits of those premises and not beyond. We conclude that an occupier of premises has no greater duty than does the public generally regarding conditions existing outside his premises and not caused by the occupier. The question we must determine then is whether the sidewalk on which Mrs. Howe was injured was part of the premises which appellee occupied.

The lease signed by Kroger as lessee reads in pertinent part as follows: "All that portion of the tract of land not covered by buildings is to be Common Area for the joint use of all tenants, customers, invitees, and employees * * *. Landlord agrees, at its own expense, to maintain all Common Area in good repair, to keep such area clean, to remove snow and ice therefrom, to keep such area lighted during hours of darkness * * *." Since the sidewalk was "not covered by buildings," it was part of the "Common Area" over which Kroger had no control, and thus no responsibility to repair or warn. Both case law and the lease agreement, therefore, establish that appellee had no liability regarding injuries occurring on the sidewalk because no duty existed relative to areas outside the leased premises.

Accordingly, we hold that under the lease agreement entered into by appellee, it did not have control over areas outside the leased premises and thus, had no duty to maintain such areas in a reasonably safe condition for its business invitees or to warn them of dangerous conditions on such areas. Since no duty existed in this respect, appellants' point of error, contending that a fact issue existed concerning whether these duties were breached, is overruled.

* * *

Affirmed.

2. LANDLORD'S LIABILITY TO TENANT AND THIRD PARTIES

The common law rule is that the landlord is not liable for physical injury or property damage resulting from a dangerous condition on the leased premises. The caveat emptor concept supports this rule as to dangerous conditions existing at the commencement of the lease. The notion that the landlord has relinquished all possession and control of the leased premises to the tenant supports the rule as to dangerous conditions that arise during the lease term. *See* Restatement (Second) of Property, Landlord and Tenant Ch. 17 reporter's note to introductory note (1977).

The traditional immunity of the landlord is severely limited today by numerous exceptions. Indeed, the modern landlord is frequently under an express or implied duty to make repairs and may be liable in tort for failure to do so. *See* Browder, *The Taming of a Duty, The Tort Liability of Landlords*, 81 Mich.L.Rev. 99 (1982).

ROLLO v. CITY OF KANSAS CITY, KANSAS

United States District Court, D. Kansas, 1994.
857 F.Supp. 1441.

VAN BEBBER, DISTRICT JUDGE.

This is a negligence action arising out of injuries suffered by plaintiff Gerald Rollo when he fell down an elevator shaft at the warehouse space leased by Friendly Frank's from the City of Kansas City, Kansas. Plaintiff was inspecting the plumbing at the premises in preparation for submitting a bid to put in a shower for Friendly Frank's. In the Pretrial Order, plaintiff claims that his accident was proximately caused by the negligence of Friendly Frank's and the lessor of the space, the City of Kansas City, Kansas. Plaintiff also alleges what appears to be a claim predicated on a negligence per se theory based on the city's failure to comply with the Uniform Building Code's requirements regarding the inspection and repair of elevators.

This case is now before the court on Defendant Kansas City's Motion for Summary Judgment. The defendant city argues that it is entitled to summary judgment as a matter of law on the negligence claim because it owed no duty to the plaintiff on which a claim for negligence could be premised. The city also argues that as a matter of law it cannot be liable to the plaintiff under a theory of negligence *per se*. Both plaintiff and separate defendant Friendly Frank's have responded and oppose the motion. For the reasons stated in this memorandum and order, the motion is denied.

* * *

II. FACTUAL BACKGROUND

* * *

Friendly Frank's and the City of Kansas City, Kansas, entered into a warehouse lease agreement dated March 1, 1992, for the premises located at Public Levee Building 220D. The space was leased to Friendly Frank's for the purpose of wholesale distribution of comics, books, and cards. Friendly Frank's occupied Building 220D from the time it took possession in late February or early March, 1992, and continuously thereafter, including the day when plaintiff was injured.

The lease agreement provides that the city shall maintain the elevator in good working order, and that the city has the right to enter the leased premises to make inspections, and may halt operation of the elevator when necessary to make repairs or inspections. It also provides that Friendly Frank's is to promptly notify the city of any repairs needed to the elevator. At the time the premises were turned over to Friendly Frank's, the city made no inspection of the elevator.

On April 28, 1992, plaintiff Rollo had an appointment with Friendly Frank's manager, Debbie Christiansen, to inspect the premises for the purpose of bidding on the job of installing a shower into the leased space. Plaintiff was aware of the elevator's existence when he visited Friendly Frank's on April 28, 1992. On April 30, 1992, plaintiff Rollo returned to Friendly Frank's to further inspect the plumbing in preparation for his bid. While looking at the ceiling to inspect distance, plaintiff took a step backwards and fell into the elevator shaft. He fell one floor down and landed on top of the elevator which was being operated by Debbie Christiansen. He suffered a fracture of his right femur.

At the time of plaintiff's fall, Debbie Christiansen was operating the elevator without its safety gate in its proper upright position. The elevator is equipped with an "interlock device" which is intended to prevent operation of the elevator when the safety gate is not in the upright position in front of the entry to the elevator and the elevator shaft. The elevator was not working properly at the time of plaintiff's fall in that it could be used without the safety gate in an upright position.

* * *

None of the Friendly Frank's employees notified the city of any need for repair to the elevator, and it is controverted whether any Friendly Frank's employees or the city knew the elevator was not working as it was intended to work.

III. LANDLORD'S DUTY OF CARE

In its motion for summary judgment, the city argues that plaintiff's negligence claim against it must fail because under Kansas law and the uncontroverted facts of this case, the city owed no duty to plaintiff upon which a negligence claim can be based. Plaintiff contends that the city, as owner and landlord of the commercial building where he was injured, owed him a duty to keep the elevator in a reasonably safe condition.

Under Kansas law, in order to submit a triable negligence claim, plaintiff must establish that: (1) the city owed a duty to him, (2) a breach of that duty occurred, (3) plaintiff sustained damage, and (4) the damage was caused by the breach of duty. In the present case, plaintiff contends that the city's duty arises from its responsibility as landlord of the leased premises.

The general rule in Kansas is that * * * no liability rests upon a landlord, either to a tenant or to others entering the property, for defective conditions existing at the time of the lease. *Borders v. Roseberry*, 216 Kan. 486, 488, 532 P.2d 1366 (1975). The lessee, as the person in possession of the property, has the burden of maintaining the premises in a reasonably safe condition to protect persons who come upon the property. *Burch v. University of Kansas*, 243 Kan. 238, 241–42, 756 P.2d 431 (1988). Kansas courts have held that the landlord's duty of care owed to a tenant's guest is not controlled by licensee-invitee distinctions, but by the common-law rule that the landlord owes no duty to guests except in certain specific situations. There are six recognized exceptions to the no-duty rule. *Borders* 216 Kan. at 488, 532 P.2d 1366. Those exceptions include: (1) undisclosed dangerous conditions known to lessor and unknown to the lessee; (2) conditions dangerous to persons outside of the premises; (3) premises leased for admission of the public; (4) parts of land retained in lessor's control which lessee is entitled to use; (5) where lessor contracts to repair; and (6) negligence by lessor in making repairs.

In the present case, plaintiff argues that the city's liability flows from exceptions (3), (4), and (5).[1] The court will address each of these three exceptions in turn.

Premises Leased for Admission of the Public

Kansas recognizes the exception to the no-duty rule for landlords in cases where land is leased for a purpose which involves the admission of

---

1. In its memorandum in opposition to the motion for summary judgment, defendant Friendly Frank's also argues that the city is liable based on exception (1), for conditions known to the lessor and unknown to the lessee. In light of the court's conclusions regarding the other exceptions as set forth in this memorandum and order and because Friendly Frank's is not a plaintiff in this action, the court does not address this issue.

the public. *Id.* at 490, 532 P.2d 1366. Section 359 of the Restatement (Second) of Torts sets out the exception as follows:

Section 359. Land Leased for Purpose Involving Admission of Public

A lessor who leases land for a purpose which involved the admission of the public is subject to liability for physical harm caused to persons who enter the land for that purpose by a condition of the land existing when the lessee takes possession, if the lessor

(a) knows or by the exercise of reasonable care could discover that the condition involves an unreasonable risk of harm to such persons, and

(b) has reason to expect that the lessee will admit them before the land is put in safe condition for their reception, and

(c) fails to exercise reasonable care to discover or to remedy the condition, or otherwise to protect such persons against it.

Restatement (Second) of Torts § 359 comment (e) indicates that a landlord is subject to liability under this exception only for those persons admitted by the lessee for the purpose for which the land is held open. * * *

In light of comment (e)'s restriction on the landlord's liability under the public admission exception set out in section 359, the court concludes that in the present case the city would have no liability under this exception for the injuries suffered by plaintiff Rollo. Plaintiff was not a comic book distributor or retailer on the premises of Friendly Frank's to view inventory; he was a plumber who came on the premises in order to prepare an estimate for plumbing work. * * *

* * *

Where Lessor Contracts to Repair

Section 357 of the Restatement 2d of Torts confers liability on a landlord who has contracted to make a repair on leased property but has failed to exercise reasonable care in performing the contractual duty. Like section 359, this restatement section has also been adopted as Kansas law. Section 357 reads as follows:

Section 357. Where Lessor Contracts to Repair.

A lessor of land is subject to liability for physical harm caused to his lessee and others upon the land with the consent of the lessee or his sublessee by a condition of disrepair existing before or arising after the lessee has taken possession, if

(a) the lessor, as such, has contracted by a covenant in the lease or otherwise to keep the land in repair, and

(b) the disrepair creates an unreasonable risk to persons upon the land which the performance of the lessors agreement would have prevented, and

(c) the lessor fails to exercise reasonable care to perform his contract.

The terms of the lease define the extent of the duty imposed. Restatement (Second) of Torts § 357 cmt. (d).

In *Vieyra v. Engineering Investment Co.*, 205 Kan. 775, 778, 473 P.2d 44 (1970), the Kansas Supreme Court applied the section 357 exception to a case involving an injury caused by a malfunctioning elevator and held that unless a covenant in the lease required the lessor to inspect the premises, the landlord was not liable for any harm caused by the disrepair until the lessee gives the lessor notice of the need for repairs. In *Vieyra*, the terms of the lease obligated the lessor to make necessary repairs, not caused by the tenant's neglect, to the plumbing, lighting, dock facilities, and elevator in the leased premises. Additionally, the tenant in *Vieyra* made regular inspections of the elevator and reported needed repairs to the lessor.

The present case offers a scenario somewhat different from that of the *Vieyra* case. The terms of the lease involved here are different from those in *Vieyra*, and read as follows:

11. Elevator. In those premises leased to Lessee which are serviced by an elevator, Lessor shall maintain said elevator in good working order. Lessor shall have the right to enter upon the leased premises to make inspections, repairs, alterations, replacements, or improvements to the elevator and Lessee shall allow any city or other governmental inspector to make inspections as provided by law. Lessor reserves the right to stop service of the elevator, when necessary, by reason of accident, or emergency, or for repairs, alterations, replacements or improvements, which in the judgment of Lessor are desirable or necessary to be made, until said repairs, alterations, replacements or improvements shall have been completed. Lessor shall have no responsibility or liability for failure of operation of the elevator during said period or when prevented from so doing by laws, orders, or regulations of any federal, state, county or municipal authority or by strikes, accidents, or by any other causes whatever beyond Lessor's control.

Lessee covenants that Lessee and all of Lessee's employees, invitees and agents shall operate the elevator in a safe and careful manner complying with all weight limit and other operating instructions. Lessee shall be responsible for any and all damages caused to said elevator or the premises by the intentional abuse or operations of said elevator in violation of the weight limit or any other operational instruction.

Lessee covenants that Lessee will give Lessor prompt notice of any malfunctions, failures or needed repairs or maintenance of the elevator.

Defendant argues that under *Vieyra*, the city faces no liability for plaintiff's injuries because it had not been notified of any defect in the elevator and it was under no duty to inspect the elevator to discover defects. Plaintiff and Friendly Frank's argue that *Vieyra* is distinguishable from the present case and that the terms of the lease obligated the city to inspect as well as repair the elevator. Moreover, Friendly Frank's notes that it had just taken possession of the premises a few weeks before plaintiff's injury, and that the Friendly Frank's employees had no way of knowing that the elevator was not in proper working order.

The court concludes that the facts of the present case are distinguishable from *Vieyra* and the city may have liability for plaintiff's injury based upon its covenant to repair the elevator. Instrumental to this conclusion are the provisions in the lease which not only obligate the city to maintain the elevator in good working order, but also confer upon the city a right of entry to inspect or repair the elevator and a right to stop operation of the elevator when the city deems it necessary. The lease agreement in the *Vieyra* case included no such provisions.

Based upon these lease terms, the landlord's contractual obligation for maintenance of the elevator goes beyond the obligation to repair set out in the *Vieyra* contract. Although there is no direct contractual obligation under which the city must periodically inspect the elevator, the court concludes that the contract is at best ambiguous on the issue of inspections. Therefore, the lease agreement must be construed against its drafter, the city. In light of the city's right of entry for purposes of inspection and its right to stop operation of the elevator, the court does not construe the lease provision requiring the tenant to notify the city of any needed repair to be the exclusive mechanism which triggers the city's duty to maintain the elevator. It will be a question for the trier of fact to determine whether the city is liable for plaintiff's injury under Restatement (Second) § 357 or whether the city exercised reasonable care to keep the elevator in safe condition.

As an additional matter, the court notes that plaintiff contends that a genuine issue of material fact exists concerning the city's knowledge of the defective condition of the elevator. Plaintiff argues that the elevator in the premises leased to Friendly Frank's had in the past suffered malfunctions and that the city had a long history of problems with the elevators in the public levee buildings and that the city therefore had actual notice that the elevator was in need of repair. If plaintiff can prove that the city had actual knowledge of a problem with the elevator's safety mechanism, the city would have been contractually obligated to repair it. The city denies any knowledge of the elevator's defective condition. This genuine issue of material fact creates an alternative ground from denial of the city's motion for summary judgment on the issue of liability for conditions that a landlord contracts to repair.

Parts of Land Retained in Lessor's Control
which Lessee is Entitled to Use

Closely tied to the issue of the applicability of Restatement (Second) of Torts § 357 in the present case is the issue of whether the exception set out in Restatement (Second) of Torts § 360 applies. Section 360, which is often called the "common areas" exception, places upon a lessor "an affirmative obligation and duty to exercise reasonable care to inspect and make reasonably safe those parts of the premises retained in the lessor's control which the lessee and others lawfully upon the land with the consent of the lessee are entitled to use." *Burch*, 243 Kan. at 242, 756 P.2d 431 (quoting Restatement (Second) of Torts §§ 360 and 361).

Kansas courts have long recognized the duty of a lessor to keep common areas safe for tenants. The common areas exception has been applied to stairways, hallways, and other portions of a lessor's property over which multiple tenants have rights of passage. The Kansas Pattern Jury Instruction applicable to a landlord's duty for "reserved parts" is written in terms of areas reserved for the common use of different tenants. There are no Kansas cases extending the "common areas" exception to areas within a tenant's premises over which the landlord has retained control.

Because there are no Kansas cases extending the exception in section 360 to areas within a tenant's leased premise[s] over which the lessor retains control, and because the language of section 360 itself is set out in terms of areas "appurtenant to the part leased" to the tenant, the court concludes that there is no basis for liability on the part of the city under this exception.

IV. NEGLIGENCE PER SE LIABILITY

In the second part of its motion for summary judgment, the city argues that plaintiff should not be able to recover against it on a theory of negligence *per se*. This issue was briefed extensively by the parties. Although the complaint does not include a claim termed "negligence *per se*" against the city, the pretrial order includes among plaintiff's factual contentions and legal theories a claim based on the city's failure to comply with ordinances concerning the inspection and maintenance of elevators. Therefore, the court will address the negligence per se issue.

Negligence *per se* is a term of art which refers to a violation of a specific requirement of a law or ordinance. * * *

* * *

* * * [T]his court concludes that liability may be predicated on a negligence *per se* theory in the present case. Whether or not plaintiff's injuries were proximately caused by any non-compliance with the building code provisions concerning elevators will be a question of fact for trial. The city's motion for summary judgment on this issue is denied.

IT IS, THEREFORE, BY THE COURT ORDERED that Defendant Kansas City's Motion for Summary Judgment is denied.

* * *

NEWTON v. MAGILL

Supreme Court of Alaska, 1994.
872 P.2d 1213.

MATTHEWS, JUSTICE.

This is a slip and fall case brought by a tenant against her landlord. The superior court granted summary judgment in favor of the landlord based on the traditional common law rule that a landlord is generally not liable for dangerous conditions in leased premises. We hold that this rule no longer applies in view of the legislature's enactment of the Uniform Residential Landlord and Tenant Act, and therefore reverse.

I. FACTS AND PROCEEDINGS

In the summer of 1988, Darline Newton moved from Idaho to Petersburg to join her husband, Stan, who had moved to Alaska a few months earlier. In Petersburg, Stan Newton had leased a house in a trailer park owned by Enid and Fred Magill.

The front door of the house opened onto a wooden walkway about six feet long and five feet wide. This walkway served the Newtons' house. It was partly covered by an overhanging roof, had no hand railing, and no "anti-slip" material on its surface.

On November 20, 1988, Darline Newton slipped and fell on the walkway, breaking her ankle. The Newtons filed suit against the Magills claiming that the walkway had been slippery and hazardous for a considerable period of time prior to the accident, that the Magills had a duty to remedy its condition, and that they negligently failed to do so.

The Magills moved for summary judgment on the ground that the tenants were responsible for "any slippery conditions resulting from rain" under both the common law and the Uniform Residential Landlord and Tenant Act (URLTA) as adopted in Alaska, AS 34.03.010–380. The Magills argued, further, that they could not be liable under a latent defect theory because the walkway was not defective; further, even assuming that it had a tendency to become dangerously slippery when wet, this hazard should have been obvious to the tenants. The superior court granted the motion. The court ruled:

> Plaintiff's ... claim is barred by Alaska's interpretation of the Uniform Residential Landlord [and] Tenant Act; AS 34.03.010–380. In *Coburn v. Burton*, 790 P.2d 1355, 1357 (Alaska 1990), the Supreme Court held that the landlord had the duty to keep common areas in a safe and clean condition, while at the same time, the tenant had a correlative duty to keep areas occupied and used solely by the tenant in a clean and safe condition. Here, the injury did not occur in a common area. The plaintiff states that she slipped and fell on the entryway, which was for the sole use of the plaintiff to enter the single-family residence. Pursuant to *Coburn*, the plaintiff had

the duty to keep the entry-way in a clean and safe condition. The defendant could not have breached the plaintiff's duty.

Additionally, there is no evidence that the entryway was latently defective. The plaintiff even admits that no complaints were made to the defendant about the entryway.

The Newtons moved to reconsider. The court denied the motion in a written order which stated, after noting that the accident occurred in an area which the Newtons had a duty to maintain:

Nevertheless, the Newtons argue that other circumstances involved here should require the burden to remain with the Magills. They argue that the entryway had latent or design defects. The fact that the entryway did not have a handrail, a gutter on the roof, or anti-slip material on the boards are not latent defects. These conditions existed in plain view and the Newtons knew these conditions existed. This is not a case involving a guest unfamiliar with the house or entryway. Mrs. Newton lived in the house for nearly five months before the fall. The Newtons used the entryway daily and it rained on numerous days before [the accident].

Even if the lack of a gutter and a handrail could be considered design defects, given the width of the entryway and its outside location, it is difficult to see, and the Newtons have offered no evidence to suggest, how these fixtures would have played any role in preventing the accident. Furthermore, the parties have not argued that the handrail or the rain gutters are required by any building code, ordinance or statute.

The anti-slip material is not a design problem, but is a maintenance problem. As noted above, the duty to maintain the entryway rests with the Newtons.

From this order the Newtons have appealed.

* * *

III. Discussion

The Newtons describe Petersburg as a city where "constant drizzle" is "prevalent" except in the summer "when the rainfall is broken by periods of sun." They contend that the wet climate fosters the growth of a plant organism on exposed wooden boards, causing them to become dangerously slippery when wet. To guard against this tendency, the Newtons contend that permanent installation of some sort of anti-slip device is necessary. They argue that the general community standard in Petersburg is to install such devices.

Under the traditional common law rule governing the liability of a landlord, failure by the Magills to meet the community standard, assuming it exists, would be irrelevant. The traditional rule is that real property lessors are not liable to their tenants for injuries caused by dangerous conditions on the property. *City of Fairbanks v. Schaible*, 375 P.2d 201, 205 (Alaska 1962); Restatement (Second) of Torts §§ 335, 356

(1965). There are exceptions to this rule of non-liability. If the dangerous condition is not reasonably apparent or disclosed, if it exists on a part of the premises which remains subject to the landlord's control, if the landlord has undertaken to repair the condition, or if the property is leased for a purpose which involves admission of the public, the landlord is subject to liability for negligence. None of these exceptions applies to this case.

The general rule of landlord immunity follows from the conception of a lease as a conveyance of an estate in land under which the lessee becomes, in effect, the owner for the term of the lease. As such, the lease was subject to the principle of *caveat emptor*. The tenant had to "inspect the land for himself and take it as he finds it, for better or for worse." William L. Prosser, *Law of Torts* § 63 at 400 (4th ed. 1971).

The courts of a number of jurisdictions have begun to discard this common law rule, however, in favor of the principle that landlords are liable for injuries caused by their failure to exercise reasonable care to discover or remedy dangerous conditions. These courts have relied in part on statutory or common law warranties of habitability and in part on a belief that the rule of landlord immunity is inconsistent with modern needs and conditions.

The decision which began the trend imposing a general duty of care upon landlords was *Sargent v. Ross*, 113 N.H. 388, 308 A.2d 528 (N.H.1973). *Sargent* involved the death of a tenant's four-year-old daughter in a fall from an outdoor stairway attached to an apartment house. The tenant brought a wrongful-death action against the landlord, alleging negligence in the construction and maintenance of the stairway. Evidence indicated that the stairs were dangerously steep and the railing was insufficient to prevent the child from falling over the side. The jury returned a verdict for plaintiff.

In affirming, the New Hampshire Supreme Court indicated that it might have analyzed the case as falling within an exception to the common law rule of landlord immunity, but declined to do so. Although the stairway was not a common passageway, the court might have strained to find that the landlord still retained some control over it; the court might also have found a hidden defect, at least as to the infant decedent; or the court might have found that the landlord had been negligent in making repairs to the stairway. Instead, the court stated: "We think that now is the time for the landlord's limited tort immunity to be relegated to the history books where it more properly belongs." The court held that "landlords as other persons must exercise reasonable care not to subject others to an unreasonable risk of harm," and, more fully, "[a] landlord must act as a reasonable person under all of the circumstances including the likelihood of injury to others, the probable seriousness of such injuries, and the burden of reducing or avoiding the risk." The court noted that this was a natural extension of a prior holding which had recognized an implied warranty of habitability in the landlord-tenant relationship.

* * *

With the 1974 adoption in Alaska of the URLTA, the theoretical foundation of the traditional rule of *caveat emptor* has been undermined in this state as well. Landlords subject to the act have a continuing duty to "make all repairs and do whatever is necessary to put and keep the premises in a fit and habitable condition." AS 34.03.100(a)(1). This means that landlords retain responsibility for dangerous conditions on leased property.

The duty of a tenant is to "keep that part of the premises occupied and used by the tenant as clean and safe as the condition of the premises permit[s]." AS 34.03.120(1). This obligation exists as part of the same statute which defines the landlord's obligation to "make all repairs and do whatever is necessary to put and keep the premises in a fit and habitable condition." AS 34.03.100(a)(1). It follows that the legislature intended these obligations to be reconcilable. Reconciliation can be accomplished by interpreting the tenant's duty to pertain to activities such as cleaning, ice and snow removal, and other light maintenance activities pertaining to the safety of the premises which do not involve an alteration of the premises, whereas the landlord's duty relates to the physical state of the premises. This distinction is suggested by the phrase "as the condition of the premises permit[s]" in section 120(1). In context this must refer to the inherent physical qualities of the premises.

Our case law has also reflected the trend toward a more general duty of care for landlords. In *Webb v. City & Borough of Sitka*, 561 P.2d 731 (Alaska 1977), we rejected the prevailing common law view that a landlord's duty was controlled by the rigid classification of the person seeking compensation as a trespasser, licensee or invitee. Instead, we adopted a rule based on general tort law that an owner "must act as a reasonable person in maintaining his property in a reasonably safe condition in view of all the circumstances, including the likelihood of injury to others, the seriousness of the injury, and the burden on the respective parties of avoiding the risk." *Id.* at 733.

We now further expand the landlord's duty of care in aligning Alaska with the jurisdictions following *Sargent*, and thus reject the traditional rule of landlord immunity reflected in *Schaible*. We do this because it would be inconsistent with a landlord's continuing duty to repair premises imposed under the URLTA to exempt from tort liability a landlord who fails in this duty. The legislature by adopting the URLTA has accepted the policy reasons on which the warranty of habitability is based. These are the need for safe and adequate housing, recognition of the inability of many tenants to make repairs, and of their financial disincentives for doing so, since the value of permanent repairs will not be fully realized by a short-term occupant. The traditional rule of landlord tort immunity cannot be squared with these policies.

* * *

Our rejection of the general rule of landlord immunity does not make landlords liable as insurers. Their duty is to use reasonable care to discover and remedy conditions which present an unreasonable risk of harm under the circumstances. Nor does our ruling mean that questions as to whether a dangerous condition existed in an area occupied solely by the tenant or in a common area, or whether the condition was apparent or hidden, are irrelevant. These are circumstances which must be accounted for in customary negligence analysis. They may pertain to the reasonableness of the landlord's or the tenant's conduct and to the foreseeability and magnitude of the risk. In particular, a landlord ordinarily gives up the right to enter premises under the exclusive control of the tenant without the tenant's permission. The landlord's ability to inspect or repair tenant areas is therefore limited. In such cases "a landlord should not be liable in negligence unless he knew or reasonably should have known of the defect and had a reasonable opportunity to repair it." *Young v. Garwacki*, 380 Mass. 162, 402 N.E.2d 1045, 1050 (1980).

The trial court observed in this case that slipperiness can be regarded as a hazard which comes within the tenant's maintenance duties rather than the duties of the landlord to keep the premises safe. A tenant can throw sand onto wet and slippery boards. On the other hand, this method has limitations, especially in an area of near constant rainfall. A jury could find that a landlord in such an area should take any one of a number of steps relating to the physical condition of the premises which would prevent a board walkway from becoming dangerously slippery when wet.

IV. Conclusion

In our view genuine issues of material fact exist as to whether the appellees breached their duty to Darline Newton to exercise reasonable care in light of all the circumstances with respect to the condition of the walkway. Determination of whether that duty was breached should be left for the trier of fact. We therefore REVERSE the trial court's grant of summary judgment in favor of the Magills and REMAND this case for further proceedings.

Question

Other courts also have found that tort liability flows from the breach of an implied warranty of habitability. Is this a wise approach? *See* Johnson v. Scandia Associates, Inc., 641 N.E.2d 51 (Ind.App.1994) (concluding that "professional" landlord may be liable for personal injuries stemming from breach of judicially recognized implied warrant of habitability); 2 Powell on Real Property § 16B.08[2][e](1998).

FELD v. MERRIAM

Supreme Court of Pennsylvania, 1984.
506 Pa. 383, 485 A.2d 742.

McDermott, Justice.

Peggy and Samuel Feld were tenants in the large Cedarbrook Apartment complex, consisting of 150 acres and 1,000 apartments housed in three high rise buildings. For an extra rental fee the apartments are serviced by parking garages adjacent to the apartment buildings. On the evening of June 27, 1975, about 9:00 P.M., the Felds, returning from a social engagement, drove as usual to their allotted space in the parking garage. Then began the events that brings before us the question of a landlord's liability for the criminal acts of unknown third persons. We are not unaware of the social, economic and philosophic dimensions of the questions posed.

While the Felds were parking their car, they were set upon by three armed felons. At gun point, accompanied by two of the felons, they were forced to the back seat of their car. Followed by the third felon in an "old, blue broken down car," they were driven past the guard on duty at the gate, out into the night, to the ferine disposal of three criminals. To clear the car for their main criminal purpose, the felons started to force Mr. Feld into the trunk of the car. Mrs. Feld pled her husband's illness and to save him, offered herself for her husband's life. Thereupon the felons released Mr. Feld on a deserted street corner and drove Mrs. Feld to the lonely precincts of a country club. There is no need to recite the horrors that brave and loving woman suffered. Suffice it to say they extorted a terrible penalty from her defenseless innocence.

The Felds brought suit against the appellees, owners of the complex, alleging a duty of protection owed by the landlord, the breach of the duty, and injuries resulting therefrom. Named as defendants were John Merriam, Thomas Wynne, Inc., the Cedarbrook Joint Venture, and Globe Security Systems, Inc. Following an eight-day trial, the jury returned a plaintiff's verdict and a judgment totaling six million dollars against Merriam, Thomas Wynne, Inc., and the Cedarbrook Joint Venture. The jury absolved Globe Security of any liability. Common Pleas, per the Honorable Jacob Kalish, denied motions for a new trial, judgment N.O.V. and remittitur.

On appeal the Superior Court affirmed the lower court, with the exception that the award of punitive damages to Samuel Feld was reduced by one half. Both Cedarbrook and Mr. Feld filed petitions for allowance of appeal, which were granted. We now reverse.

I

The threshold question is whether a landlord has any duty to protect tenants from the foreseeable criminal acts of third persons, and if so, under what circumstances. Well settled law holds landlords to a duty to protect tenants from injury rising out of their negligent failure to maintain their premises in a safe condition. That rule of law is addressed to their failure of reasonable care, a failure of care caused by their own negligence, a condition, the cause of which was either known or knowable by reasonable precaution. The criminal acts of a third person belong to a different category and can bear no analogy to the unfixed radiator, unlighted steps, falling ceiling, or the other myriad possibilities of one's personal negligence. To render one liable for the deliberate criminal acts of unknown third persons can only be a judicial rule for given limited circumstances.

The closest analogy is the duty of owners of land who hold their property open to the public for business purposes. They are subject to liability for the accidental, negligent or intentionally harmful acts of third persons, as are common carriers, innkeepers and other owners of places of public resort. * * * The reason is clear; places to which the general public are invited might indeed anticipate, either from common experience or known fact, that places of general public resort are also places where what men can do, they might. One who invites all may reasonably expect that all might not behave, and bears responsibility for injury that follows the absence of reasonable precaution against that common expectation. The common areas of an apartment complex are not open to the public, nor are the general public expected or invited to gather there for other purposes than to visit tenants.

Tenants in a huge apartment complex, or a tenant on the second floor of a house converted to an apartment, do not live where the world is invited to come. Absent agreement, the landlord cannot be expected to protect them against the wiles of felonry any more than the society can always protect them upon the common streets and highways leading to their residence or indeed in their home itself.

An apartment building is not a place of public resort where one who profits from the very public it invites must bear what losses that public may create. It is of its nature private and only for those specifically invited. The criminal can be expected anywhere, any time, and has been a risk of life for a long time. He can be expected in the village, monastery and the castle keep.

In the present case the Superior Court departed from the traditional rule that a person cannot be liable for the criminal acts of third parties when it held "that in all areas of the leasehold, particularly in the area under his control, the landlord is under a duty to provide adequate security to protect his tenants from the foreseeable criminal actions of third persons." Feld v. Merriam, et al., 314 Pa.Super. 414, 427, 461 A.2d 225, 231 (1983).

The Superior Court viewed the imposition of this new duty as merely an extension of the landlord's existing duty to maintain the common areas to be free from the risk of harm caused by physical defects. However, in so holding that court failed to recognize the crucial distinction between the risk of injury from a physical defect in the property, and the risk from the criminal act of a third person. In the former situation the landlord has effectively perpetuated the risk of injury by refusing to correct a known and verifiable defect. On the other hand, the risk of injury from the criminal acts of third persons arises not from the conduct of the landlord but from the conduct of an unpredictable independent agent. To impose a general duty in the latter case would effectively require landlords to be insurers of their tenants safety: a burden which could never be completely met given the unfortunate realities of modern society.

Our analysis however does not stop here, for although there is a general rule against holding a person liable for the criminal conduct of another absent a preexisting duty, there is also an exception to that rule, i.e., where a party assumes a duty, whether gratuitously or for consideration, and so negligently performs that duty that another suffers damage.

This exception has been capsulized in Section 323 of the Restatement (Second) of Torts, which provides:

> § 323.   Negligent Performance of Undertaking to Render Services
>
> One who undertakes, gratuitously or for consideration, to render services to another which he should recognize as necessary for the protection of the other's person or things, is subject to liability to the other for physical harm resulting from his failure to exercise reasonable care to perform his undertaking, if
>
> (a) his failure to exercise such care increases the risk of such harm, or
>
> (b) the harm is suffered because of the other's reliance upon the undertaking.

Previously we adopted this section as an accurate statement of the law in this Commonwealth.

Expounding on the proper application of Section 323 the drafters indicated that

> [T]his Section applies to any undertaking to render services to another which the defendant should recognize as necessary for the protection of the other's person or things. It applies whether the harm to other or his things results from the defendant's negligent conduct in the manner of his performance of the undertaking, or from his failure to exercise reasonable care to complete it or to protect the other when he discontinues it.

Comment (a) § 323 Restatement (Second) of Torts. These comments are particularly relevant in a situation such as the present where a landlord undertakes to secure the areas within his control and possibly fosters a reliance by his tenants on his efforts.

Absent therefore an agreement wherein the landlord offers or voluntarily proffers a program, we find no general duty of a landlord to protect tenants against criminal intrusion. However, a landlord may, as indicated, incur a duty voluntarily or by specific agreement if to attract or keep tenants he provides a program of security. A program of security is not the usual and normal precautions that a reasonable home owner would employ to protect his property. It is, as in the case before us, an extra precaution, such as personnel specifically charged to patrol and protect the premises. Personnel charged with such protection may be expected to perform their duties with the usual reasonable care required under standard tort law for ordinary negligence. When a landlord by agreement or voluntarily offers a program to protect the premises, he must perform the task in a reasonable manner and where a harm follows a reasonable expectation of that harm, he is liable. The duty is one of reasonable care under the circumstances. It is not the duty of an insurer and a landlord is not liable unless his failure is the proximate cause of the harm.

A tenant may rely upon a program of protection only within the reasonable expectations of the program. He cannot expect that a landlord will defeat all the designs of felonry. He can expect, however, that the program will be reasonably pursued and not fail due to its negligent exercise. If a landlord offers protection during certain periods of the day or night a tenant can only expect reasonable protection during the periods offered. If, however, during the periods offered, the protection fails by a lack of reasonable care, and that lack is the proximate cause of the injury, the landlord can be held liable. A tenant may not expect more than is offered. If, for instance, one guard is offered, he cannot expect the same quality and type of protection that two guards would have provided, nor may he expect the benefits that a different program might have provided. He can only expect the benefits reasonably expected of the program as offered and that that program will be conducted with reasonable care.

In the present case the trial judge, when instructing the jury, was placed in the unenviable position of predicting how we would resolve this difficult question. Although we commend him on his endeavor, we are constrained to reverse the verdict, since the jury instructions which were given imposed upon the landlord a duty greater than that which we today hold to have existed.

* * *

ZAPPALA, JUSTICE, concurring.

* * *

Where, as here, the conduct of the parties is regulated neither by statute, ordinance, or regulation, nor by the lease-contract itself, the courts have struggled with the issue of whether liability may be imposed upon a landlord for criminal acts. The conflicting resolutions of this issue result from the courts' attempts to respond to what is essentially a social problem, rather than a landlord-tenant problem. The risk of harm from criminal conduct is not peculiar to the landlord-tenant relationship. It is a risk that one encounters in society at large. Any attempt by a landlord to insulate tenants from this risk must necessarily fail. Therefore, the mere fact that a tenant may be exposed to that risk cannot be the basis for imposing liability.

As has been ably detailed in the Opinion of the Court, although the creation of the landlord-tenant relationship in and of itself does not impose a duty on the landlord to provide security services to a tenant, where a landlord voluntarily undertakes to provide protection from criminal acts he has a duty to do so reasonably. Liability is to be imposed only where the measures taken by the landlord either are unreasonable to reduce the risk of harm or have the effect of increasing the risk of harm; or where the landlord fails to maintain the measures which have been adopted in their normal operable condition.

* * *

Notes and Questions

1.   Does *Feld* adopt an unduly narrow scope for a landlord's liability concerning criminal acts against tenants? *See* Comment, *Landlord Liability for Criminal Acts Perpetrated Against Tenants: The Pennsylvania Approach,* 91 Dick.L.Rev. 779 (1987). For additional decisions holding that landlords have no general duty to protect their tenants from criminal acts of third parties, see Bartley v. Sweetser, 319 Ark. 117, 890 S.W.2d 250 (1994); C.S. v. Sophir, 220 Neb. 51, 368 N.W.2d 444 (1985) (observing that "landlords are not insurers that a tenant will be protected at all times"); Walls v. Oxford Management Company, Inc., 137 N.H. 653, 633 A.2d 103 (1993) (noting exceptions for "known defective condition on a premises that enhances the risk of crime" and for failure to use reasonable care in providing security required by contract or voluntarily undertaken); Cramer v. Balcor Property Management, Inc., 312 S.C. 440, 441 S.E.2d 317 (1994). There is also authority that a landlord does not have a duty to safeguard a tenant against the criminal acts of another tenant, Miller v. Whitworth, 193 W.Va. 262, 455 S.E.2d 821 (1995), nor a duty to protect a social guest of a tenant from criminal activity by third parties, Jack v. Fritts, 193 W.Va. 494, 457 S.E.2d 431 (1995). A number of courts have likewise determined that a landlord has no duty to protect tenants from crime on off-site premises not under the landlord's control. *See* Kuzmicz v. Ivy Hill Park Apartments, Inc., 147 N.J. 510, 688 A.2d 1018 (1997).

2.   In Trentacost v. Brussel, 82 N.J. 214, 228, 412 A.2d 436, 443 (1980) the Supreme Court of New Jersey declared:

> We now conclude * * * that the landlord's implied warranty of habitability obliges him to furnish reasonable safeguards to protect tenants from foreseeable criminal activity on the premises. * * * Since the landlord's implied undertaking to provide adequate security exists independently of his knowledge of any risks, there is no need to prove notice of such a defective and unsafe condition to establish the landlord's contractual duty. It is enough that defendant did not take measures which were in fact reasonable for maintaining a habitable residence.

One authority has observed: "The *Brussel* decision seems to hold landlords strictly accountable for every crime committed on their property, without regard to the reasonableness of their precautions or their knowledge of any risk." Browder, *The Taming of a Duty, The Tort Liability of Landlords,* 81 Mich.L.Rev. 99, 150 (1982). Do you agree with this assessment? Is such a standard of liability appropriate?

In the *Walls* case noted in the immediately preceding note, the Supreme Court of New Hampshire specifically rejected the notion that an implied warranty of habitability imposes a duty on landlords to protect their tenants from criminal acts of third parties. Is this a better approach?

3. In Kline v. 1500 Massachusetts Avenue Apartment Corp., 439 F.2d 477 (D.C.Cir.1970) the court imposed a duty on landlords to keep the premises reasonably free from foreseeable crime. This result was predicated upon the landlord having notice of crime in the common areas. *See also* Pamela W. v. Millsom, 25 Cal.App.4th 950, 30 Cal.Rptr.2d 690 (1994) (concluding neither landlords of rental condominium unit nor condominium owners association had duty to provide security against attack by "stalker" where they had no notice that specific crimes of similar nature had been committed on property). Some courts, however, have taken the position that criminal activity may be foreseeable even though no prior criminal acts have been committed on the premises. *See, e.g.,* Sharp v. W.H. Moore, 118 Idaho 297, 796 P.2d 506 (1990); Shea v. Preservation Chicago, Inc., 206 Ill.App.3d 657, 151 Ill.Dec. 749, 565 N.E.2d 20 (1990). Which is the better approach to foreseeability? *See generally* Note, *Landlord Liability for Crimes Committed by Third Parties Against Tenants on the Premises,* 38 Vand.L.Rev. 431 (1985).

4. Recall that the lock on the side-door to Harmony House has been malfunctioning. Suppose a third party gained access to the building through the unlocked door and assaulted the Lloyds in the hallway outside their apartment. Can they successfully pursue a claim against Harmony House?

3. VALIDITY OF EXCULPATORY CLAUSES

It is common for leases to contain a provision absolving the landlord from liability for personal injury and property damage that occurs on the leased premises or in common areas. The following case considers the validity of these exculpatory clauses.

CRAWFORD v. BUCKNER

Supreme Court of Tennessee, 1992.
839 S.W.2d 754.

Opinion

Anderson, Justice.

The determinative issue raised in this appeal is whether an exculpatory clause in a residential lease bars recovery against the landlord for negligence which causes the tenant injury. The trial court granted the landlords' motion for summary judgment, holding that the tenant's tort action was barred by the exculpatory clause. The Court of Appeals affirmed. Because we conclude that the exculpatory clause is void as against public policy, we reverse the Court of Appeals and remand.

FACTUAL BACKGROUND

On December 16, 1988, the plaintiff, Linda Crawford, rented an apartment from the defendants, Tobe McKenzie and McKenzie Development Corporation. As a condition of rental, Crawford was required to sign the defendants' standard form lease, which contained an exculpatory clause providing that:

> [t]enant agrees that the landlord, his agents and servants shall not be liable to tenant or any person claiming through tenant, for any injury to the person or loss of or damage to property for any cause. Tenant shall hold and save landlord harmless for any and all claims, suits, or judgments for any such damages or injuries however occurring.

On February 21, 1989, two months after Crawford rented her apartment, a fire started in the apartment of Debra and Larry Buckner, who lived in the apartment below the plaintiff. The fire quickly spread to the plaintiff's apartment, blocking her exit through the front, and only, door. To escape the fire, Crawford jumped from a window in her second story apartment. When she landed, the plaintiff suffered numerous injuries, partly due to the debris on the ground behind her apartment building.

Crawford later filed a tort action in Bradley County naming the Buckners, Tobe McKenzie, and McKenzie Development Corporation as defendants. The complaint alleged that the landlords were negligent in failing to maintain the fire alarm, the premises behind her apartment, and in continuing to allow the Buckners to reside at the apartment complex after numerous altercations and complaints. * * *

The landlord defendants answered that the plaintiff's action was barred by the exculpatory clause of the lease and filed a motion for summary judgment.

At the hearing on the landlords' motion for summary judgment, the trial court concluded the exculpatory clause in the lease was enforceable. * * * The Court of Appeals affirmed.

EXCULPATORY LEASE PROVISIONS

An exculpatory clause in the context of a landlord-tenant relationship refers to a clause which deprives the tenant of the right to recover damages for harm caused by the landlord's negligence by releasing the landlord from liability for future acts of negligence.

The rationale underlying the argument for enforceability of such clauses has often been based upon the doctrine of freedom of contract. Courts employing that reasoning have said:

> that the public policy in apparent conflict with the freedom of contract argument in real-estate lease exculpatory clause cases, namely, that a landlord should be liable for the negligent breach of a

duty which is owed to his tenant, is subservient to the doctrine that a person has the right to freely contract about his affairs. Some cases, especially the older ones, have reasoned that the relationship of landlord and tenant is in no event a matter of public interest, but is purely a private affair, so that such clauses cannot be held void on purely public policy grounds.

John D. Perovich, Annotation, *Validity of Exculpatory Clause in Lease Exempting Lessor From Liability,* 49 A.L.R.3d 321, 325 (1973).

However, because of the burden-shifting effect of such clauses which grant immunity from the law, it is not surprising that their validity has been challenged and that courts have reached different conclusions as to their enforceability.

As early as 1938 Williston recognized that while such exculpatory clauses were recognized as "legal", many courts had shown a reluctance to enforce them. Even then, courts were disposed to interpret them strictly so they would not be effective to discharge liability for the consequences of negligence in making or failing to make repairs. 6 Williston, *A Treatise on the Law of Contracts* § 1751C p. 4968 (Rev. ed. 1938).

McCutcheon v. United Homes Corp., 79 Wash.2d 443, 486 P.2d 1093, 1095 (1971).

For example, courts have held that such clauses may be void as against public policy where the landlord had greater bargaining power so that the tenant must accept the lease as written, or where the tenant was unaware of or did not fully understand the clause's effect, or where the clause was overly broad or was unconscionable. *See* Annotation, *Validity of Exculpatory Clause,* 49 A.L.R.3d at 325–26.

The defendant contends that freedom to contract in the residential lease setting is the majority rule in the United States, and that holding exculpatory provisions in residential leases invalid on public policy grounds would require this court to adopt the minority rule. Our research of the cases in this area, however, demonstrates that there is no true majority rule. We find, as the Washington Supreme Court found, that there is no majority rule, "only numerous conflicting decisions, decisions concerned with contracts of indemnity, cases relating to property damage under business leases, and a disposition of the courts to emasculate such exculpatory clauses by means of strict construction." McCutcheon v. United Homes Corp., *supra,* 486 P.2d at 1096.

Tennessee courts have long recognized that, subject to certain exceptions, parties may contract that one shall not be liable for his negligence to another. One exception, for example, is that a common carrier cannot by contract exempt itself from liability for a breach of duty imposed on it for the benefit of the public.

Although the earlier cases recognized that there were exceptions to the rule made for the benefit of the public, no case considered the public interest issue until this Court's decision in Olson v. Molzen, 558 S.W.2d

429 (Tenn.1977). We held in *Olson* that if an exculpatory provision [a]ffects the public interest, it is void as against public policy, despite the general rule that parties may contract that one shall not be liable for his negligence to another. We said that an exculpatory contract signed by a patient as a condition of receiving medical treatment is invalid as contrary to public policy and may not be pleaded as a bar to the patient's suit for negligence.

* * *

The plaintiff here contends that the exculpatory provision in her lease falls squarely within the criteria set forth in *Olson*. As a result, the plaintiff argues that we should * * * hold that the exculpatory provision in her lease is void as against public policy. In order to determine whether an exculpatory provision affects the public interest, we adopted the following criteria in *Olson* from Tunkl v. Regents of University of California, 60 Cal.2d 92, 383 P.2d 441, 32 Cal.Rptr. 33 (1963):

[a.] It concerns a business of a type generally thought suitable for public regulation.

[b.] The party seeking exculpation is engaged in performing a service of great importance to the public, which is often a matter of practical necessity for some members of the public.

[c.] The party holds himself out as willing to perform this service for any member of the public who seeks it, or at least for any member coming within certain established standards.

[d.] As a result of the essential nature of the service, in the economic setting of the transaction, the party invoking exculpation possesses a decisive advantage of bargaining strength against any member of the public who seeks his services.

[e.] In exercising a superior bargaining power the party confronts the public with a standardized adhesion contract of exculpation, and makes no provision whereby a purchaser may pay additional reasonable fees and obtain protection against negligence.

[f.] Finally, as a result of the transaction, the person or property of the purchaser is placed under the control of the seller, subject to the risk of carelessness by the seller or his agents.

Olson, 558 S.W.2d at 431. In adopting these factors, we stated that "[i]t is not necessary that all be present in any given transaction, but generally a transaction that has some of these characteristics would be offensive." *Id.*

Applying the *Olson* criteria to the facts of this case, first, we conclude a residential lease concerns a business of a type that is generally thought suitable for public regulation. Our conclusion is bolstered by the fact that the legislature of this state has seen fit to regulate this area, and that other states, such as Illinois, Maryland, Massachusetts, and New York, have enacted legislation regulating the residential landlord-tenant relationship. *See* John D. Perovich, Annotation, *Validity of Exculpatory Clause in Lease Exempting Lessor From Liability,* 49 A.L.R.3d 321 (1973).

Second, it is clear we no longer live in an agrarian society where land, not housing, was the important part of a rental agreement. Nor do we live in an era of the occasional rental of rooms in a private home or over the corner grocery. Residential landlords offer shelter, a basic necessity of life, to more than a million inhabitants of this state. In 1990 in Tennessee, 32 percent of the total occupied housing units in the state were rental units. Accordingly, it is self-evident that a residential landlord is engaged in performing a service of great importance to the public, which is often a matter of practical necessity for some members of the public. In addition, a residential landlord holds itself out as willing to perform a service for any member of the public who seeks it. Therefore, we conclude that the residential landlord-tenant relationship falls within the second and third public interest criteria.

With respect to the fourth public interest criterion, as a result of the essential nature of the service and the economic setting of the transaction, a residential landlord has a decisive advantage in bargaining strength against any member of the public who seeks its services. A potential tenant is usually confronted with a "take it or leave it" form contract, which the tenant is powerless to alter. The tenant's only alternative is to reject the entire transaction.

Moreover, due to its superior bargaining position, a residential landlord confronts the public with a standardized adhesion contract of exculpation, which contains no provision whereby a tenant can pay additional reasonable fees to obtain protection from the landlord's negligence. The lease in this case is a good example. In her affidavit in opposition to the defendants' motion for summary judgment, Crawford testified that she was given the defendants' standard lease form to sign, and was never offered the opportunity to pay additional reasonable fees to obtain protection from the landlords' negligence. We determine that the residential landlord-tenant relationship falls within the fifth *Olson* criterion.

Finally, we conclude that by definition a residential lease places the person and the property of the tenant under the control of the landlord, subject to the risk of carelessness by the landlord and his agents. * * * Therefore, it follows that the landlord-tenant relationship falls within the final public interest criterion set forth in *Olson.*

Accordingly, we find that the residential landlord-tenant relationship here satisfies all six of the public interest criteria adopted in *Olson.* * * *

However, the defendants insist that a residential lease between a landlord and a tenant is a purely private affair, and not a matter of public interest. We disagree. We rejected this same argument in *Olson* and find persuasive the reasoning of the Washington Supreme Court, which, in response to the very same argument, stated:

[W]e are not faced merely with the theoretical duty of construing a provision in an isolated contract specifically bargained for by *one landlord and one tenant* as a purely private affair. Considered realistically, we are asked to construe an exculpatory clause, the generalized use of which may have an impact upon thousands of potential tenants.

McCutcheon v. United Homes Corp., 79 Wash.2d 443, 449–50, 486 P.2d 1093, 1097 (1971) (emphasis in original).

Based on the foregoing, we conclude that the exculpatory clause in the residential lease in this case is contrary to public policy. In reaching this conclusion, we join a growing number of states. * * * [T]he legislature of this state has enacted the Uniform Residential Landlord and Tenant Act, albeit in only a few counties, which prohibits exculpatory provisions in residential leases. In addition, at least four states have limited by statute the freedom of contract concept as applied to exculpatory provisions in residential leases. *See* Ill.Ann.Stat. ch. 80, para. 91 (Smith–Hurd 1987); N.Y. General Obligations Law § 5–321 (McKinney 1989); Md.Real Property Code Ann. § 8–105 (1988); and Mass.Gen.Laws Ann. ch. 186, § 15 (West 1991). Moreover, at least eleven states and the District of Columbia by judicial decision have declared exculpatory lease clauses void as against public policy under the facts developed in those cases. *See* Lloyd v. Service Corp. of Alabama, 453 So.2d 735 (Ala.1984); Henrioulle v. Marin Ventures, Inc., 20 Cal.3d 512, 573 P.2d 465, 143 Cal.Rptr. 247 (1978) (en banc); Tenants Council of Tiber Island–Carrollsburg Square v. DeFranceaux, 305 F.Supp. 560 (D.D.C.1969); Old Town Development Co. v. Langford, 349 N.E.2d 744 (Ind.App.1976); Feldman v. Stein Building & Lumber, 6 Mich.App. 180, 148 N.W.2d 544 (1967); Cappaert v. Junker, 413 So.2d 378 (Miss.1982); Papakalos v. Shaka, 91 N.H. 265, 18 A.2d 377 (1941); Kuzmiak v. Brookchester, Inc., 33 N.J.Super. 575, 111 A.2d 425 (1955); Galligan v. Arovitch, 421 Pa. 301, 219 A.2d 463 (1966); Crowell v. Housing Authority of the City of Dallas, 495 S.W.2d 887 (Tex.1973); McCutcheon v. United Homes Corp., *supra,* 79 Wash.2d 443, 486 P.2d 1093 (1971); College Mobile Home Park & Sales, Inc. v. Hoffmann, 72 Wis.2d 514, 241 N.W.2d 174 (1976).

Finally, the defendants argue that declaring public policy in Tennessee is the province of the legislature. Since the legislature has specifically chosen to limit application of the Uniform Residential Landlord and Tenant Act, and its section prohibiting exculpatory provisions in residential leases, to the most populous counties, the defendants contend that the public policy in those counties not covered by the Act still favors freedom of contract. We disagree.

"The public policy of Tennessee 'is to be found in its constitution, statutes, judicial decisions and applicable rules of common law.[' "] Smith v. Gore, 728 S.W.2d 738, 747 (Tenn.1987) (quoting State ex rel. Swann v. Pack, 527 S.W.2d 99, 112 n. 17 (Tenn.1975), cert. denied, 424 U.S. 954 (1976)). Primarily, it is for the legislature to determine the public policy of the state, and only in the absence of any declaration in the Constitution and statutes may public policy be determined from judicial decisions. However, where there is no declaration in the Constitution or the statutes, and the area is governed by common law doctrines, it is the province of the courts to consider the public policy of the state as reflected in old, court-made rules.

The rule that, subject to certain exceptions, parties are free to contract that one shall not be liable to the other for his negligence, * * * is a judicial declaration of public policy. *See* Chazen v. Trailmobile Inc., 215 Tenn. 87, 384 S.W.2d 1 (1964). In addition, the exception to the freedom of contract rule for exculpatory clauses affecting the public interest is also a judicial declaration of public policy.

We conclude that in the residential landlord-tenant relationship, the public policy against exculpatory clauses affecting the public interest should control lease provisions limiting a landlord's liability to its tenants. Our conclusion is not changed by the fact that in 1975 the legislature limited the coverage of the Uniform Residential Landlord and Tenant Act to counties having a population of more than 200,000 according to the 1970 Census, or any subsequent federal census. On the contrary, we note that the Act's language permits any county in the state to grow into the population classification and that the legislature, effective July 1, 1992, reduced the population classification to counties having a population of more than 68,000.

We observe that the Act broadly regulates the landlord-tenant relationship, covers much more than just exculpatory lease provisions, and declares public policy for counties which now fit in the population class and for those who "grow into it." Accordingly, we determine that the Act declares no public policy in the area of exculpatory clauses for the least populous counties of the state. Therefore, we conclude the limited application of the Act is not a declaration by the legislature that the public policy of Tennessee favors freedom of contract for residential leases in the counties not covered by the Act.

Accordingly, we hold that under the facts here, the lease clause limiting the residential landlord's liability for negligence to its tenants is void as against public policy. * * *

The Court of Appeals' judgment is reversed, and the cause is remanded to the trial court for proceedings consistent with this Opinion. The costs of this appeal are taxed to the defendants, Tobe McKenzie and McKenzie Development Corporation.

Questions

1. Suppose a landlord and tenant included an exculpatory clause in a residential lease in exchange for reduced rent. Is the clause enforceable in this jurisdiction or elsewhere? *Compare* Stanley v. Creighton Co., 911 P.2d 705 (Colo.App.1996) (invoking public policy in striking down exculpatory clause in residential lease and distinguishing between residential leases and commercial leases) *with* Warren v. Paragon Technologies Group, Inc., 950 S.W.2d 844, 845 (Mo.1997) (stating in reference to exculpatory clause in

residential lease: "Releases of future negligence are not void as against public policy, though they are disfavored and strictly construed.").

2. Are exculpatory clauses in commercial leases enforceable?

F. ASSIGNMENT AND SUBLEASE

The Lloyds are thinking about moving from Harmony House before their lease ends if they can locate adequate housing elsewhere. They contacted you and asked whether they will encounter any problems if they "sublet" their apartment. This section is designed to provide you with the foundation upon which to base your advice to them.

DAYENIAN v. AMERICAN NATIONAL BANK AND TRUST COMPANY OF CHICAGO

Appellate Court of Illinois, First District, 1980.
91 Ill.App.3d 622, 47 Ill.Dec. 83, 414 N.E.2d 1199.

GOLDBERG, PRESIDING JUSTICE:

Ursula Dayenian (plaintiff) brought this action for specific performance against 900/910 Lake Shore Drive Development Company and American National Bank and Trust Company of Chicago, as Trustee under Trust No. 46033, (defendants), to compel the conveyance of a condominium unit to plaintiff. The trial court granted summary judgment for defendants. Plaintiff appeals.

The following facts appear from the motion for summary judgment and attached affidavits. On July 14, 1978, plaintiff entered into a lease with Monticello Realty Corporation, agents for the lessor, to rent a unit in an apartment building from October 1, 1978, to September 30, 1980. On October 26, 1978, plaintiff signed a portion of the printed lease headed "ASSIGNMENT" which states:

"For value received, the undersigned Lessee hereby assigns all the Lessee's right, title and interest in and to the within lease from and after December 1, 1978 unto W. Carlton Lambert * * *. It is expressly agreed this assignment shall not release or relieve the undersigned, as Original Lessee, from any liability under the covenants of the lease * * *."

On November 8, 1978, in a portion of the lease headed "ACCEPTANCE OF ASSIGNMENT," W. Carlton Lambert, described as "the undersigned Assignee," assumed:

"the obligations of said lease imposed on the Lessee and promises to make all payments and to keep and perform all conditions and covenants of the lease by the Lessee to be kept and performed commencing December 1, 1978 * * *."

Also on November 8, 1978, Monticello Realty Corporation executed a portion of the lease headed "CONSENT TO ASSIGNMENT" whereby it:

"consent[ed] to the above Assignment upon the express condition that Original Lessee shall remain liable for the prompt payment of the Rent and the keeping and performance of all conditions and covenants of the lease by the lessee to be kept and performed."

On March 13, 1979, the defendant 900/910 Lake Shore Drive Development Company mailed to W. Carlton Lambert a notice of intent to convert the apartment building into a condominium. This was apparently done to comply with Ill.Rev.Stat.1979, ch. 30, par. 330(a) and Chicago Municipal Code 100.2–6C (1979) which in essence provide that any "tenant" who was a "tenant" on the date the notice of intent was given shall have the right of first refusal to purchase the apartment if he so responds within the time allowed. W. Carlton Lambert never manifested an intent to purchase the unit and never responded within the time permitted. On May 31, 1979, the developer entered into a contract to sell the unit to another party.

Plaintiff contends she should have been given the right of first refusal to purchase the unit because she was the tenant of the apartment at the time the notice to convert was sent on March 13, 1979. She claims the transfer to W. Carlton Lambert should be construed as a sublease.

The dispositive issue, therefore, is whether the transaction of December 1, 1978, constituted a sublease or an assignment. Whether the transaction is actually a sublease or an assignment is a question of law.

"The prime consideration in construing an instrument is to ascertain and effectuate the intention of the parties at the time of execution." (*Chemical Petroleum Exchange, Inc.*, 81 Ill.App.3d 1005, 1009, 37 Ill.Dec. 110, 401 N.E.2d 1203.) Generally, an assignment of a lease occurs "where the lessee transfers the entire unexpired remainder of the term created by his lease." (*Urban Investment and Development Co.*, 25 Ill.App.3d 546, 551, 323 N.E.2d 588.) In other words, in an assignment one transfers his whole estate "without reserving a reversionary interest to himself [and] a privity of estate is immediately created between his transferee and the original lessor * * *." (*Danaj v. Anest* (1979), 77 Ill.App.3d 533, 534, 33 Ill.Dec. 19, 396 N.E.2d 95; *Urban Investment and Development Co.*, 25 Ill.App.3d 546, 551, 323 N.E.2d 588). But if the transferor retains or reserves any reversionary interest, "the privity of estate between the transferee and the original lessor is not established and there is no assignment." *Danaj*, 77 Ill.App.3d 533, 534, 33 Ill.Dec. 19, 396 N.E.2d 95; *Urban Investment and Development Co.*, 25 Ill.App.3d 546, 551, 323 N.E.2d 588.

The plaintiff in the instant case transferred the entire remainder of her estate and did not retain any reversionary interest. The document stated she conveyed "all the Lessee's right, title and interest in and to the within lease from and after December 1, 1978 * * *." Upon this transfer, a privity of estate was immediately created between W. Carlton Lambert and the Monticello Realty Corporation, agents for the original lessor. This left plaintiff with no interest in the estate. Plaintiff remained only a surety to guarantee performance of the lease by the assignee, Lambert. We conclude an assignment was created here. "[A] lessee for a term of years who assigns his lease parts with all his rights thereunder." *(Bevelheimer v. Gierach* (1975), 33 Ill.App.3d 988, 992, 339 N.E.2d 299.) Accordingly, plaintiff was not a tenant at the time notice to convert was given and plaintiff had no right of first refusal.

Plaintiff contends use of the term "sublease" by the parties in correspondence and office memoranda was evidence of an intent that plaintiff should retain a reversionary interest. Plaintiff depends upon a letter dated October 18, 1978, sent to plaintiff by management referring to the lease assignment as a "sublease form" ; an office memorandum dated October 26, 1978, making the same reference; a letter dated November 8, 1978, to plaintiff's assignee from management using the word "subleasing"; and a management office memo dated November 8, 1978, using the word "sublet."

We reject this argument. "[T]he legal effect to be given an instrument is not to be determined by the label it bears or the technical terms it contains * * *." *(Chemical Petroleum Exchange, Inc.,* 81 Ill.App.3d 1005, 1009, 37 Ill.Dec. 110, 401 N.E.2d 1203; *Urban Investment Development Co.,* 25 Ill.App.3d 546, 551, 323 N.E.2d 588.) As above shown, the document executed by plaintiff was simply and only an assignment. The language used by the parties in referring to the clear and unambiguous assignment of the lease is neither competent nor proper to attempt to vary its legal effect or determine its meaning.

For these reasons we find no genuine issue as to any material fact is presented by this record. The judgment appealed from is affirmed.

* * *

ROWE v. GREAT ATLANTIC & PACIFIC TEA CO., INC.

Court of Appeals of New York, 1978.
46 N.Y.2d 62, 412 N.Y.S.2d 827, 385 N.E.2d 566.

OPINION OF THE COURT

GABRIELLI, JUDGE.

We are called upon to determine whether a certain real property lease agreement contains an implied covenant limiting the lessee's power to assign the lease. The property subject to the lease is located in Sag Harbor, New York. In 1964, petitioner, Robert Rowe, an experienced attorney and businessman and the owner of the land involved herein, leased the property to respondent Great Atlantic & Pacific Tea Co. (A & P) for use as a "general merchandise business". The agreement required Rowe to erect a building on the property, and provided for a yearly rental of $14,000 for a 10–year term. It also granted A & P options to renew for two additional seven-year periods, at a slightly lower rental. The lease contained no restrictions on assignment of the lease by A & P.

Rowe constructed the building as agreed, and A & P took possession and utilized the premises for a supermarket.

Some years later, both parties sought to renegotiate the agreement. Rowe desired a higher rental because of increases in taxes and other expenses, while A & P wished to have the building enlarged. Following protracted negotiations, a new lease was executed in 1971, in which it was provided that Rowe would expand the building by an additional 6,313 square feet, and that the base rental would be increased to $34,420 per year. This figure was reached by estimating the cost to Rowe of the improvements to the building and then computing a rate of return agreed to by the parties and adding that to the old rental. The new lease was for a period of 15 years, and provided A & P with the option to renew for three additional seven-year periods at the same rental. In addition to the base rental, the new lease provided that Rowe was to receive 1 1/2% of the store's annual gross receipts in excess of $2,294,666 and less than $5,000,000. In other words, unless gross receipts reached the $2,294,666 mark, the percentage clause would be inoperable. There was no warranty, stipulation or promise by A & P that sales would climb to the minimum necessary to trigger the percentage clause. The lease contained no restriction on the lessee's right to assign the lease. Nor did it make any reference to assignability other than providing that the lease would bind the heirs and assigns of the parties.

Unfortunately for all concerned, the new store did not fare as well as had been hoped. Indeed, A & P entered into a period of retrenchment in which it decided to close several of its less profitable stores, and the Sag Harbor store was one of those selected. Following months of discussion with Rowe and others, and over Rowe's objections, A & P in 1975 shut down its operation in Sag Harbor and assigned the lease of the premises to respondent Southland Corp., which operates a chain of supermarkets under the name Gristede Brothers. Rowe then commenced this proceeding seeking to recover possession of the premises as well as money damages. His claim is premised on the theory that A & P breached an implied covenant against assignment without consent of the lessor.

Following a nonjury trial, Supreme Court dismissed the petition on the merits, concluding that in the absence of bad faith, which was not shown, A & P had the unqualified right to assign the lease since there existed no provision limiting that right.

* * *

Petitioner appealed and the Appellate Division reversed.

* * *

A lease agreement, like any other contract, essentially involves a bargained-for exchange between the parties. Absent some violation of law or transgression of a strong public policy, the parties to a contract are basically free to make whatever agreement they wish, no matter how unwise it might appear to a third party. It is, of course, far too late in the day to seriously suggest that the law has not made substantial inroads into such freedom of private contracts. There exists an unavoidable tension between the concept of freedom to contract, which has long been basic to our socioeconomic system, and the equally fundamental belief that an enlightened society must to some extent protect its members from the potentially harsh effects of an unchecked free market system. Thus, rightly or wrongly, society has chosen to intervene in various ways in the dealings between private parties. This intervention is perhaps best exemplified by statutes mandating the express or implicit inclusion of certain substantive or procedural provisions in various types of contracts. It is also illustrated by judicial decisions to the effect that there exists in every contract certain implied-by-law covenants, such as the promise to act with good faith in the course of performance. In a similar vein, the law has developed the concept of unconscionability so as to prevent the unjust enforcement of onerous contractual terms which one party is able to impose under the other because of a significant disparity in bargaining power. Despite all this, there yet remains substantial room for bargaining by the parties.

Contrary to petitioner's contentions, this appeal does not implicate any of the methods utilized by society to police both the substance of contracts and the process of contracting. There has been no violation of law or of public policy, nor does it appear that A & P acted in bad faith. Moreover, the status of the parties to this contract is not such that the doctrine of unconscionability would normally be applicable even if there were any indications that the contract was unusually one-sided. Finally, we are not here confronted with a situation in which a party seeks to apply a covenant which must be implied by law in a particular contract. Rather, it is petitioner's claim that the parties in fact impliedly did agree that A & P could not assign the lease without Rowe's permission, and simply neglected, for one reason or another, to verbalize that understanding and to incorporate it into their written contract.

That a particular provision has not been expressly stated in a contract does not necessarily mean that no such covenant exists. * * * "[T]he undertaking of each promisor in a contract must include any promises which a reasonable person in the position of the promisee would be justified in understanding were included" (5 Williston, Contracts [rev.ed., 1937], § 1293, p. 3682).

Nonetheless, a party who asserts the existence of an implied-in-fact covenant bears a heavy burden, for it is not the function of the courts to remake the contract agreed to by the parties, but rather to enforce it as it exists. Thus, a party making such a claim must prove not merely that it would have been better or more sensible to include such a covenant, but rather that the particular unexpressed promise sought to be enforced is in fact implicit in the agreement viewed as a whole. This is especially so where, as here, the implied covenant sought to be recognized and enforced is of a type not favored by the courts.

It has long been the law that covenants seeking to limit the right to assign a lease are "restraints which courts do not favor. They are construed with the utmost jealousy, and very easy modes have always been countenanced for defeating them" (Riggs v. Pursell, 66 N.Y. 193, 201). This is so because they are restraints on the free alienation of land, and as such they tend to prevent full utilization of the land, which is contrary to the best interests of society. Since such covenants are to be construed strictly even if expressly stated, it follows that a court should not recognize the existence of an implied limitation upon assignment unless the situation is such that the failure to do so would be to deprive a party of the benefit of his bargain.

In the case presently before us petitioner Rowe has failed to prove the existence of an implied covenant limiting the lessee's right to assign the lease. Such a covenant is to be recognized only if it is clear that a reasonable landlord would not have entered into the lease without such an understanding, for it is only in such a situation that it can be said with the requisite certainty that to refuse to recognize such a covenant would be to deprive the landlord of the fruits of his bargain. This is not such a case.

An implied covenant limiting the right to assign will often be found in those situations in which it is evident that the landlord entered into the lease in reliance upon some special skill or ability of the lessee which will have a material effect upon the fulfillment of the landlord's reasonable contractual expectations. In the typical lease in which the landlord is assured of a set monthly rent, and has not placed any unusual restrictions upon the use of the premises, there is no occasion to find an implied covenant precluding or limiting assignment. This is so because the only reasonable expectation of the landlord is that the rent will be paid and the premises not abused, and thus the identity of the tenant is not material to the landlord's expectations under the lease. If, however, the expectations of the landlord are substantially dependent upon some special skill or trait of the lessee, the lack of which might endanger the lessor's legitimate contractual expectations, then it may be appropriate to find the existence of an implied covenant limiting the right to assign, for in such circumstances no reasonable person would enter into the contract without assurance that the tenant could not be replaced by an assignee lacking the requisite skills or character traits. Even in such a case, however, the implied restrictions must of course be limited to the extent possible without destroying the landlord's legitimate interests.

The type of situation in which a court may properly find that there exists a covenant limiting the right to assign is illustrated by the factual pattern which confronted the court in Nassau Hotel Co. v. Barnett & Barse Corp., 212 N.Y. 568, 106 N.E. 1036, affg. on opn. at 162 App.Div. 381, 147 N.Y.S. 283. There, the owner of a hotel had leased the hotel and all its appurtenances to two men, one of whom was an experienced hotel manager. The lease granted them " 'the exclusive possession, control and management' "of the hotel, and they not only became responsible " 'for the operation * * * and maintenance' "of the hotel, but also promised that they would operate it " 'at all times in a first-class, business-like manner' "(162 App.Div. at p. 382, 147 N.Y.S. at p. 284). In lieu of any set rental, the owner was to receive 19% of the gross receipts of the hotel. Subsequently, the lessees assigned the lease to a corporation and the landlord sued to recover the premises. The courts concluded that the lease could not be assigned without the owner's consent, even though the lease did not contain a provision limiting the lessees' power to assign, because the entire agreement indicated conclusively that a fundamental premise of the agreement was that the two original lessees would operate the hotel. This was so in part because the landlord had agreed to accept a percentage of the receipts in place of rent, and thus his legitimate expectations were completely dependent on the ability and honesty of the two individual lessees. To deprive him of the right to depend on the fact that the hotel was being operated by the individuals with whom he had contracted would have been to deprive him of a substantial element of his reasonable and legitimate contractual expectations.

Although the existence of the percentage clause was a significant factor in that decision, it alone was not dispositive. Rather, the court properly considered the entire agreement, with its emphasis on the operation of the hotel and the implicit dependence of the landlord upon the identity of the operators of the hotel. Thus, while a percentage clause in a lease is some sign of an implied agreement to limit the lessee's power to assign the lease, its significance will vary with the other terms of the lease, the surrounding circumstances, the nature of the business conducted upon the premises, and the identities and expectations of the parties.

Although the lease we are called upon to interpret today does contain a percentage clause, it is a far cry from that involved in *Nassau Hotel*. There, the percentage of gross receipts to be received by the landlord was the only value the landlord was to receive from the agreement, for there was no set rental. Here, in contradistinction, the landlord is provided with an annual rental of some $34,420 in addition to whatever amount he might receive pursuant to the percentage clause. We would also emphasize that the percentage clause does not result in any additional income to the landlord until and unless the store first attains sales of over $2,294,666 in a particular year. Of some interest is the fact that this figure is considerably higher than the previous record gross sales at the Sag Harbor store at the time the lease was entered into. It is thus evident that the percentage clause, although doubtless of considerable interest to the landlord as a hedge against inflation and as a means of sharing in the hoped for success of the store, was not a material part of the lessor's fundamental expectations under the lease. Hence, it cannot be said that the lease was entered into in sole reliance upon the skill, expertise, and reputation of A & P, and thus there is no reason to find an implied covenant limiting the lessee's right to assign the lease.

This conclusion is buttressed by consideration of the circumstances surrounding and preceding the making of the new lease in 1971. It should not be forgotten that at that time the landlord was bound by a long-term lease which provided substantially less rent per square foot of store space than does the current lease, taking into account the expansion in size of the store. Indeed, examination of the two leases indicates that even absent the percentage clause, the new lease was an improvement over the old from the landlord's point of view. Moreover, comparison with other supermarket leases indicates that the base rental in the new lease is not out of line with the rentals reserved in other leases. Thus we cannot agree with the Appellate Division that it is "not substantial".

Of additional interest is the identity of the parties to this agreement. Petitioner is an experienced attorney and businessman knowledgeable in real estate transactions. A & P is, of course, a national firm presumably represented by capable agents. The negotiations which resulted in the new lease were long and exhaustive, dealing with a variety of topics, and the lease itself is obviously the result of a process of give and take. Although A & P might well have agreed to include a provision limiting its right to assign the lease had petitioner insisted upon such a clause, we may safely assume that petitioner would have had to pay a price for that concession. In these circumstances, the courts should be extremely reluctant to interpret an agreement as impliedly stating something which the parties have neglected to specifically include. As we have previously declared in a similar context, "such lack of foresight does not create rights or obligations" (Mutual Life Ins. Co. of N.Y. v. Tailored Woman, 309 N.Y. 248, 253, 128 N.E.2d 401, 403).

Finally, although not necessary to our disposition of this appeal, we would note that even were the circumstances such as to support the conclusion that the lease contains a provision limiting the lessee's right to assign the lease, that finding alone would not justify judgment in favor of petitioner. It would then be necessary to further consider whether that implied restriction would in fact be violated by assignment of the lease to another supermarket chain in light of all the facts and circumstances.

Accordingly, the order appealed from should be reversed, with costs, and the judgment of Supreme Court, Suffolk County, reinstated.

Question

When a commercial lease contains a percentage rental clause, should courts imply a covenant that the tenant will remain in business on the leased premises? *Compare* Nalle v. Taco Bell Corp., 914 S.W.2d 685 (Tex. App.1996) (affirming refusal to imply covenant requiring tenant to keep restaurant open even though lease contained percentage rental clause over and above base rent) *with* East Broadway Corp. v. Taco Bell Corp., 542 N.W.2d 816 (Iowa 1996) (determining lease contained implied covenant that tenant continue to conduct business on premises because agreement included significant percentage rental provision in addition to base rent). *See also* Pequot Spring Water Company v. Brunelle, 243 Conn. 928, 46 Conn.App. 187, 698 A.2d 920 (1997); Casa D'Angelo, Inc. v. A & R Realty Company, 553 N.E.2d 515 (Ind.App.1990); Worcester–Tatnuck Square CVS, Inc. v. Kaplan,

33 Mass.App.Ct. 499, 601 N.E.2d 485 (1992); Aneluca Associates v. Lombardi, 620 A.2d 88 (R.I.1993).

JULIAN v. CHRISTOPHER

Court of Appeals of Maryland, 1990.
320 Md. 1, 575 A.2d 735.

CHASANOW, JUDGE.

In 1961, this Court decided the case of Jacobs v. Klawans, 225 Md. 147, 169 A.2d 677 (1961) and held that when a lease contained a "silent consent" clause prohibiting a tenant from subletting or assigning without the consent of the landlord, landlords had a right to withhold their consent to a subletting or assignment even though the withholding of consent was arbitrary and unreasonable.

* * * We now have before us the issue of whether the common law rule applied in *Klawans* should be changed.

In the instant case, the tenants, Douglas Julian and William J. Gilleland, III, purchased a tavern and restaurant business, as well as rented the business premises from landlord, Guy D. Christopher. The lease stated in clause ten that the premises, consisting of both the tavern and an upstairs apartment, could not be assigned or sublet "without the prior written consent of the landlord." Sometime after taking occupancy, the tenants requested the landlord's written permission to sublease the upstairs apartment. The landlord made no inquiry about the proposed sublessee, but wrote to the tenants that he would not agree to a sublease unless the tenants paid additional rent in the amount of $150.00 per month. When the tenants permitted the sublessee to move in, the landlord filed an action in the District Court of Maryland in Baltimore City requesting repossession of the building because the tenants had sublet the premises without his permission.

At the district court trial, the tenants testified that they specifically inquired about clause ten, and were told by the landlord that the clause was merely included to prevent them from subletting or assigning to "someone who would tear the apartment up." The district court judge refused to consider this testimony. He stated in his oral opinion that he would "remain within the four corners of the lease, and construe the document strictly," at least as it pertained to clause ten. Both the District Court and, on appeal, the Circuit Court for Baltimore City found in favor of the landlord. The circuit judge noted: "If you don't have the words that consent will not be unreasonably withheld, then the landlord can withhold his consent for a good reason, a bad reason, or no reason at all in the context of a commercial lease, which is what we're dealing with." We granted certiorari to determine whether the *Klawans* holding should be modified in light of the changes that have occurred since that decision.

While we are concerned with the need for stability in the interpretation of leases, we recognize that since the *Klawans* case was decided in

1961, the foundations for that holding have been substantially eroded. The *Klawans* opinion cited *Restatement of Property* § 410 as authority for its holding. The current *Restatement (Second) of Property* § 15.2 rejects the *Klawans* doctrine and now takes the position that:

> A restraint on alienation without the consent of the landlord of the tenant's interest in the leased property is valid, but the landlord's consent to an alienation by the tenant cannot be withheld unreasonably, unless a freely negotiated provision in the lease gives the landlord an absolute right to withhold consent.

Another authority cited in *Klawans* in support of its holding was 2 R. Powell, *Powell on Real Property*. The most recent edition of that text now states:

> Thus, if a lease clause prohibited the tenant from transferring his or her interest without the landlord's consent, the landlord could withhold consent arbitrarily. This result was allowed because it was believed that the objectives served by allowing the restraints outweighed the social evils implicit in them, inasmuch as the restraints gave the landlord control over choosing the person who was to be entrusted with the landlord's property and was obligated to perform the lease covenants.

> It is doubtful that this reasoning retains full validity today. Relationships between landlord and tenant have become more impersonal and housing space (and in many areas, commercial space as well) has become scarce. These changes have had an impact on courts and legislatures in varying degrees. Modern courts almost universally adopt the view that restrictions on the tenant's right to transfer are to be strictly construed.

2 R. Powell, *Powell on Real Property* § 248[1] (1988).

Finally, in support of its decision in *Klawans,* this Court noted that, "although it, apparently, has not been passed upon in a great number of jurisdictions, the decisions of the courts that have determined the question are in very substantial accord." *Klawans,* 225 Md. at 151, 169 A.2d at 679. This is no longer true. Since *Klawans,* the trend has been in the opposite direction. ["The modern trend is to impose a standard of reasonableness on the landlord in withholding consent to a sublease unless the lease expressly states otherwise."] *Campbell v. Westdahl,* 148 Ariz. 432, 715 P.2d 288, 292 (Ariz.Ct.App.1985).

* * *

Traditional property rules favor the free and unrestricted right to alienate interests in property. Therefore, absent some specific restriction in the lease, a lessee has the right to freely alienate the leasehold interest by assignment or sublease without obtaining the permission of the lessor.[1]

---

1. The common law right may have some limitations. For example, a lessee may not sublet or assign the premises to be used in a manner which is injurious to the property or inconsistent with the terms of the original lease.

Contractual restrictions on the alienability of leasehold interests are permitted. Consequently, landlords often insert clauses that restrict the lessee's common law right to freely assign or sublease. Probably the most often used clause is a "silent consent" clause similar to the provision in the instant case, which provides that the premises may not be assigned or sublet without the written consent of the lessor.

In a "silent consent" clause requiring a landlord's consent to assign or sublease, there is no standard governing the landlord's decision. Courts must insert a standard. The choice is usually between 1) requiring the landlord to act reasonably when withholding consent, or 2) permitting the landlord to act arbitrarily and capriciously in withholding consent.

Public policy requires that when a lease gives the landlord the right to withhold consent to a sublease or assignment, the landlord should act reasonably, and the courts ought not to imply a right to act arbitrarily or capriciously. If a landlord is allowed to arbitrarily refuse consent to an assignment or sublease, for what in effect is no reason at all, that would virtually nullify any right to assign or sublease.

Because most people act reasonably most of the time, tenants might expect that a landlord's consent to a sublease or assignment would be governed by standards of reasonableness. Most tenants probably would not understand that a clause stating "this lease may not be assigned or sublet without the landlord's written consent" means the same as a clause stating "the tenant shall have no right to assign or sublease." Some landlords may have chosen the former wording rather than the latter because it vaguely implies, but does not grant to the tenant, the right to assign or sublet.

There are two public policy reasons why the law enunciated in *Klawans* should now be changed. The first is the public policy against restraints on alienation. The second is the public policy which implies a covenant of good faith and fair dealing in every contract.

Because there is a public policy against restraints on alienation, if a lease is silent on the subject, a tenant may freely sublease or assign. Restraints on alienation are permitted in leases, but are looked upon with disfavor and are strictly construed. If a clause in a lease is susceptible of two interpretations, public policy favors the interpretation least restrictive of the right to alienate freely. Interpreting a "silent consent" clause so that it only prohibits subleases or assignments when a landlord's refusal to consent is reasonable, would be the interpretation imposing the least restraint on alienation and most in accord with public policy.

Since the *Klawans* decision, this Court has recognized that in a lease, as well as in other contracts, "there exists an implied covenant that each of the parties thereto will act in good faith and deal fairly with the others." Food Fair v. Blumberg, 234 Md. 521, 534, 200 A.2d 166, 174

(1964). When the lease gives the landlord the right to exercise discretion, the discretion should be exercised in good faith, and in accordance with fair dealing; if the lease does not spell out any standard for withholding consent, then the implied covenant of good faith and fair dealing should imply a reasonableness standard.

We are cognizant of the value of the doctrine of *stare decisis,* and of the need for stability and certainty in the law. However, as we noted in Harrison v. Mont. Co. Bd. of Educ., 295 Md. 442, 459, 456 A.2d 894, 903 (1983), a common law rule may be modified "where we find, in light of changed conditions or increased knowledge, that the rule has become unsound in the circumstances of modern life, a vestige of the past, no longer suitable to our people." The *Klawans* common law interpretation of the "silent consent" clause represents such a "vestige of the past," and should now be changed.

REASONABLENESS OF WITHHELD CONSENT

In the instant case, we need not expound at length on what constitutes a reasonable refusal to consent to an assignment or sublease. We should, however, point out that obvious examples of reasonable objections could include the financial irresponsibility or instability of the transferee, or the unsuitability or incompatibility of the intended use of the property by the transferee. We also need not expound at length on what would constitute an unreasonable refusal to consent to an assignment or sublease. If the reasons for withholding consent have nothing to do with the intended transferee or the transferee's use of the property, the motivation may be suspect. Where, as alleged in this case, the refusal to consent was solely for the purpose of securing a rent increase, such refusal would be unreasonable unless the new subtenant would necessitate additional expenditures by, or increased economic risk to, the landlord.

PROSPECTIVE EFFECT

The tenants ask us to retroactively overrule *Klawans,* and hold that in all leases with "silent consent" clauses, no matter when executed, consent to assign or sublease may not be unreasonably withheld by a landlord. We decline to do so. In the absence of evidence to the contrary, we should assume that parties executing leases when *Klawans* governed the interpretation of "silent consent" clauses were aware of *Klawans* and the implications drawn from the words they used. We should not, and do not, rewrite these contracts.

* * *

For leases with "silent consent" clauses which were entered into before the mandate in this case, *Klawans* is applicable, and we assume the parties were aware of the court decisions interpreting a "silent consent" clause as giving the landlord an unrestricted right to withhold consent.

For leases entered into after the mandate in this case, if the lease contains a "silent consent" clause providing that the tenant must obtain the landlord's consent in order to assign or sublease, such consent may not be unreasonably withheld. If the parties intend to preclude any transfer by assignment or sublease, they may do so by a freely negotiated provision in the lease. If the parties intend to limit the right to assign or sublease by giving the landlord the arbitrary right to refuse to consent, they may do so by a freely negotiated provision of the lease clearly spelling out this intent. For example, the clause might provide, "consent may be withheld in the sole and absolute subjective discretion of the lessor."

* * *

The tenants in the instant case should get the benefit of the interpretation of the "silent consent" clause that they so persuasively argued for, unless this interpretation would be unfair to the landlord. We note that the tenants testified they were told that the clause was only to prevent subleasing to "someone who would tear the apartment up." Therefore, we will reverse the judgment of the Circuit Court with instructions to vacate the judgment of the District Court and remand for a new trial. At that trial, the landlord will have the burden of establishing that it would be unfair to interpret the "silent consent" clause in accordance with our decision that a landlord must act reasonably in withholding consent. He may establish that it would be unfair to do so by establishing that when executing the lease he was aware of and relied on the *Klawans* interpretation of the "silent consent" clause. We recognize that we may be giving the tenants a benefit that other tenants with leases entered into before our mandate will not receive. * * *

Notes, Problems, and Questions

1. In the absence of a lease provision limiting assignment and sublease, what are the tenant's rights regarding transfer of the leasehold?

2. Notwithstanding the trend of decisions noted in *Julian,* a number of courts continue to follow the traditional view that, absent a lease provision, a landlord is under no obligation to act reasonably in withholding consent to a proposed assignment or sublease pursuant to a consent to transfer clause. *See, e.g.,* First Federal Savings Bank of Indiana v. Key Markets, Inc., 559 N.E.2d 600 (Ind.1990); 21 Merchants Row Corporation v. Merchants Row, Inc., 412 Mass. 204, 587 N.E.2d 788 (1992). Does this represent a better approach?

3. What constitutes a reasonable objection to an assignment or sublease under a consent to transfer clause? *See* Worcester–Tatnuck Square CVS, Inc. v. Kaplan, 33 Mass.App.Ct. 499, 601 N.E.2d 485 (1992).

4. In Kendall v. Ernest Pestana, Inc., 40 Cal.3d 488, 220 Cal.Rptr. 818, 709 P.2d 837 (1985) the court held that a commercial landlord may withhold consent to an assignment or sublease under a consent to transfer clause only when the landlord has a commercially reasonable objection. However, a landlord in California can enforce without reason a recapture clause in a

lease giving it the right to terminate the leasehold upon the tenant's request to assign or sublease. *See* Carma Developers (California), Inc. v. Marathon Development California, Inc., 2 Cal.4th 342, 6 Cal.Rptr.2d 467, 826 P.2d 710 (1992). Does the *Carma Developers* decision undermine the requirement that consent to a proposed transfer cannot be unreasonably withheld?

5. The common law Rule in Dumpor's Case provides that a clause in a lease not to assign without the landlord's consent cannot be divided. Consequently, the landlord's consent to one assignment ends the restriction thereby making the lease freely assignable. The Rule lives on in many jurisdictions. What policy promotes its continued existence? A landlord may easily circumvent the Rule by providing that consent to a particular assignment is not a waiver of the right to consent to subsequent assignments. *See* 1 American Law of Property § 3.58 (1952); Restatement (Second) of Property, Landlord & Tenant § 16.1 reporter's note 7 (1977). *See also* section three of the sample lease on page 6.

6. The question of waiver may arise in other contexts. It has been held that, because consent to transfer clauses are strictly construed, the lessor's acceptance of rent from a sublessee or an assignee constitutes a waiver of such a restriction. *See* Taylor Oil Co. v. Contemporary Industries Corp., 305 N.W.2d 854 (S.D.1981).

FIRST AMERICAN NATIONAL BANK OF NASHVILLE v. CHICKEN SYSTEM OF AMERICA, INC.

Court of Appeals of Tennessee, Middle Section, 1980.
616 S.W.2d 156.

LEWIS, JUDGE.

This case arose out of a lease entered into on May 28, 1968, between plaintiff First American National Bank, Trustee, (First American) and defendant Chicken System of America, Inc., (Chicken System). The lease contained a provision which expressly prohibited any assignment or subletting without the written consent of First American. The lease was for a term of 180 months from May 28, 1968, at a rental of $1049.08 per month, and in addition Chicken System was required to pay premiums on all insurance and to pay all real estate taxes. Chicken System entered and took possession of the premises under the lease and paid all obligations to and including the month of April, 1969. On April 30, 1969, the President of defendant Performance Systems, Inc., (PSI) wrote to C.H. Wright of Wriking Foods/Beverage Systems, Inc., the parent company of Chicken System. We set out the pertinent parts of that letter:

> This will confirm our mutual agreement for the purchase by us at March 30, 1969, of the Minnie Pearl's Chicken retail outlets owned by your subsidiaries at Murfreesboro Road and Nolensville Road, Nashville, Tennessee, for the sum of $137,329, plus $24,-895.00. We will assume the contract payable to the Third National Bank, Nashville, Tennessee, for the Nolensville Road Store, together with the rent deposit note to us on Murfreesboro Road per schedule

attached. At the time of closing you will discharge your equipment note to Nashco Equipment and Supply Company in the amount of $24,895.00. For the price mentioned above and the assumption of these liabilities, we will acquire from you all inventories, store equipment, rent deposits and your franchise to operate these outlets.

You understand and agree that other liabilities relating to the operation of these stores incurred by you are for your account, except that the real estate and sign leases are our responsibility after April 30, 1969.

On May 5, 1969, First American was advised by Gale Smith & Company of insurance cancellations on the leased property and was informed of Gale Smith's understanding that the business had been purchased by PSI. Prior to that time First American had no knowledge of any agreement or possible agreement between Chicken System and PSI.

On May 8, 1969, First American's counsel wrote PSI in regard to the insurance coverage and also informed PSI that the premises could only be subleased with the written consent of First American. On June 6, 1969, First American's Counsel wrote to all concerned parties. Pertinent portions of that letter are as follows:

Under Section 24 of the lease agreement there may be no assignment or subletting without the written consent of the lessor. I wish to make it plain that as of this time no such consent has been given, nor will any such consent be given unless there is a formal request in writing, requesting same. Upon our receipt of such a written request, we will submit the proposal to those three individuals who have guaranteed performance of the lease by Chicken System of America, Inc., and if they have no objection to the assignment or sub-letting and will continue bound on their guaranty agreement, the Bank will probably have no objection to consenting to a sub-lease or assignment.

The guarantors did not at any time agree to remain bound on their guaranty agreement if the premises were sublet or assigned to PSI. The guarantors were originally defendants in this suit, but prior to trial a nonsuit as to them was taken by First American. There were several letters written by plaintiff's counsel and PSI's counsel regarding subletting or assignment, but at no time did First American ever consent to an assignment of the lease from Chicken System to PSI.

PSI entered the premises and took possession and from May 1, 1969, through October, 1970, paid rent to First American. On November 1, 1970, PSI defaulted in payment of the rent and vacated the premises. Thereafter, First American filed suit in the Chancery Court for Davidson County against Chicken System and PSI and sought rent, insurance, taxes, and maintenance under the terms of the lease agreement due and owing until September 1, 1972. PSI's primary defense was that First American had withheld consent, that absent consent by First American the "assignment" from Chicken System to PSI was invalid and PSI was merely a tenant at suffera[nce], and that when PSI vacated the premises in November, 1970, its obligations and rights under the lease were suspended. The Chancellor held that the lack of consent could be waived by First American and could not be raised by PSI as a defense, that PSI's surrender of the premises in November, 1970, did not terminate privity of estate between it and First American, and that PSI was liable to First American for obligations of the lease running with the land, including the obligation to pay rent. PSI appealed, and the Supreme Court affirmed the Chancellor. First American National Bank v. Chicken System of America, Inc., 510 S.W.2d 906 (Tenn.1974). The Court stated: "[T]here is privity of estate between an original lessor and a subsequent assignee that makes the assignee fully responsible to the lessor for the lease provisions." *Id.* at 908. The Court remanded to the Chancery Court for the purpose of ascertaining damages. The damages were stipulated, but the Chancellor allowed interest on the recovery. PSI again appealed to the Supreme Court which again affirmed the Chancellor. Performance Systems, Inc. v. First American National Bank, 554 S.W.2d 616 (Tenn. 1977).

Following PSI's default in the payment of rent in November, 1970, First American, along with PSI, made efforts to find another tenant for the premises and received some ten proposals. PSI wrote First American and granted approval for First American to enter the premises in the interest of subleasing the land and permanent improvements. On June 1, 1971, PSI wrote First American again and stated: "It is important that we place a tenant in the property at the earliest possible time." First American, without consulting PSI or requesting PSI's consent, entered into a lease with Rodney E. and Melanie Fortner, d/b/a Sir Pizza of Madison, for a term of 60 months beginning the first day of September, 1972, at a rental of $600 per month. The Sir Pizza lease was renewed effective September 1, 1977, for a rental of $1000 per month.

First American has brought this suit for the deficiency in the rent and other obligations occurring after September 1, 1972, the date of the Sir Pizza lease. This case was presented to the Trial Court on stipulated facts, and the Chancellor found that First American was entitled to recover $47,384.27 from PSI. PSI has appealed. While both PSI and First American have set forth issues, we are of the opinion that answering only the following question is necessary to resolve this case. Is PSI liable to First American under either privity of estate or privity of contract?

PRIVITY OF ESTATE

Three legal factors arise to create a liability running from the assignee of a leasehold to the lessor (a) privity of estate (b) covenants in the lease running with the land and (c) actual assumption of the covenants of the lease by the assignee. An assignee of a lease is bound by privity of estate to perform the express covenants which run with the land, but, in the absence of express agreement on his part, he is liable only on such covenants as run with the land and only during such time as he holds the term. (Footnote omitted.)

3A Thompson on Real Property § 1216 (1959).

> An assignee, unless he has personally assumed the obligation of the lease, may absolve himself from further liability by an act which terminates his privity of estate. [The lessee's assignee] has the benefit and the burden of all covenants running with the land as long as he holds the estate. Liability of the assignee to the lessor, being based solely on privity of estate, does not continue after he transfers his interest to another. The assignee may thus put an end to his liability by making a further assignment, and this * * * although the second assignee is financially irresponsible. (Footnotes omitted.)

1 American Law of Property (A. Casner ed. 1952) § 3.61.

In accord with this rule is McLean v. Caldwell, 107 Tenn. 138, 64 S.W. 16 (1901), in which the Court stated:

> As a general rule, the assignee of a lease is only liable for rents while in possession, *provided he reassigns the lease to the lessor or any other person;* and it does not matter that such assignment is made to a beggar, a minor, a married woman, a prisoner, or an insolvent, or to one hired to take the assignment, or made expressly to rid himself of liability. * * * (Emphasis added.)

> The reason is that such reassignment and surrender of possession terminate the privity of estate existing between him and the landlord. (Citations omitted.)

Id. at 140–41, 64 S.W. at 16–17.

A.D. Juilliard & Co. v. American Wollen Co., 69 R.I. 215, 32 A.2d 800 (1943), is closely akin in facts to the case at bar. There the landlord leased premises to a lessee which, in turn, assigned the lease to the defendant. Thereafter, the defendant reassigned to a third party. The defendant assignee there, as here, had not expressly assumed the lease. The lessor there, as First American here, contended "that the assignee of a lease of real property * * * is liable for the payment of the stipulated rent for the entire unexpired term, notwithstanding that the assignee did not agree to assume such obligation and assigned the lease before the expiration of the term." *Id.* at 216, 32 A.2d at 801. The Court, in *Juilliard,* stated:

> This contention is contrary to the overwhelming weight of authority both in England and this country * * *. [T]he courts in this country have consistently held that, in the absence of the assumption by the assignee of the obligations of the lease, the liability of such assignee to the lessor rests in privity of estate which is terminated by a new assignment of the lease made by the assignee.

Id. With this rule, First American says it "has no quarrel." It insists, however, that the rule has no relevance to the case at bar since there was not a reassignment by PSI but a reletting of the premises by First American for the benefit of PSI. This contention is a distinction without difference. While mere abandonment by PSI without reassignment of the lease would not have terminated privity of estate, McLean v. Caldwell, 107 Tenn. 138, 141, 64 S.W. 16, 17 (1901), there was a reletting of the premises on September 1, 1972, by First American. When First American relet the premises to Sir Pizza, PSI's possessory rights to the premises terminated just as if PSI had reassigned the lease. Privity of estate terminated, and PSI had no further leasehold interest in the premises.

First American's contention that PSI is charged with knowledge of the covenants of the lease is correct only so long as the basis of liability exists, *i.e.*, during privity of estate. When privity of estate ended between First American and PSI, PSI was no longer charged with knowledge of the covenants of the lease. An assignee who has not assumed the lease "stands in the shoes" of the original lessee only for covenants that run with the land and then only during privity of estate. If this were not so, then the "dumping" of an unfavorable lease would not be possible. Tennessee clearly recognizes that an assignee who has not assumed the lease may "dump it."

PRIVITY OF CONTRACT

First American contends that the following stipulated facts "demonstrate that PSI assumed the obligations of the Chicken System lease thereby placing it in privity of contract with First American":

    1. An agreement was entered into between Chicken System of America, Inc. and Performance Systems, Inc., which is reflected in a letter dated April 30, 1969, from Edward G. Nelson, President of Performance Systems, Inc., to C.H. Wright of Wriking Food/Beverage Systems, Inc., the parent company of Chicken System of America, Inc.

    2. The letter, as it related to PSI's purchase of the Nolensville Road store, provided in relevant part that "You understand and agree that other liabilities relating to the operation of these stores incurred by you are for your account, except that the real estate and sign leases are our responsibility [PSI] after April 30, 1969.

    3. After April 30, 1969, neither Chicken System of America, nor its parent corporation paid any rent on the property. Rent on the property was paid by PSI from May 1, 1969 through October, 1970, and PSI was in possession of the premises during that time.

First American cites Sander v. Piggly Wiggly Stores, Inc., 20 Tenn. App. 107, 95 S.W.2d 1266 (1936), and says that the facts there "strikingly resemble" the facts in the case at bar. We disagree.

* * *

In *Sander* the assignee acknowledged that it had assumed the lease contract, and the Court found that the assignee had agreed to perform the covenants of the lease. In the case at bar, we find no such acknowledgement.

In Hart v. Socony–Vacuum Oil Co., 291 N.Y. 13, 50 N.E.2d 285 (1943), several years after an oral assignment of the lease the assignee signed a modification agreement in regard to the insurance requirements of the lease. The modification agreement contained the following provision: "It is further mutually understood and agreed that except as herein expressly modified, all other provisions and covenants contained in said lease shall remain in full force and effect." *Id.* at 15, 50 N.E.2d at 286. In rejecting the lessor's argument that this agreement was a personal assumption of the covenants of the lease on the part of the assignee, the Court stated:

> There is strong authority which says that to hold liable an assignee under a lease, after he has given up the lease and vacated the premises, there must be produced an express promise by him to perform the covenants of the lease. * * * [S]uch an express covenant is never assumed to have been made it must always be proven. * * * It is not every reference to, or mention of, the covenants of a lease, by an assignee, that amounts to an assumption by him. Even where he covenants that his assignment is to be "subject" to the terms of the lease, that language, without more definite words of promise, does not make him liable as by privity of contract. (Citations omitted.)

Id. at 15–18, 50 N.E.2d at 286–87.

* * *

※Before there is privity of contract between the assignee and the lessor, there must be an actual assumption of the lease. In the case at bar there was not an actual assumption, only a mere acceptance of an assignment. ※

* * *

"The mere acceptance of an assignment is not an assumption. Every assignment requires acceptance, * * * yet 'an assignee * * * who does not assume the performance of the covenants of the lease holds the lease merely under a privity of estate * * * .'" Packard–Bamberger & Co. v. Maloof, 89 N.J.Super. 128, 214 A.2d 45, 46–47 (1965) (quoting annot. 148 A.L.R. 196 (1944)).

While no contention is made that there was a written contract between PSI and First American, First American argues, nevertheless, that certain statements made by PSI to other parties after the assignment by Chicken System to PSI created privity of contract between First American and PSI. First American cites Crow v. Kaupp, 50 S.W.2d 995 (Mo.1932), in support of this contention. *Crow* is readily distinguishable from the case at bar. In *Crow* the assignee assumed the lease by written assignment which provided, in pertinent part: "'[T]he second parties * * * hereby further bind and obligate themselves, their heirs and assigns, to assume the payment of all rent * * * to the said * * * owner * * * it being understood that the second parties hereto assume the above mentioned contract, together with all liabilities and obligations created thereby. * * * ' ''*Id.* at 996–97. The assignee, in *Crow,* made a complete and detailed assumption of the lease. In the case at bar, the assignment to PSI by Chicken System was oral, and PSI made no promise at any time to be bound to First American.

We are of the opinion that privity of estate between First American and PSI terminated upon PSI's abandonment of the premises and the reletting of the premises to Sir Pizza by First American. We further hold that there was no privity of contract between PSI and First American.

* * *

The judgment of the Chancellor as to Performance Systems, Inc. is reversed and dismissed with costs to First American. The case is remanded to the Chancery Court for collection of costs and any other necessary proceedings.

* * *

Notes and Questions

1. As the *Chicken System* case indicates, the tenant's assignee is in privity of estate with the landlord and thus, is liable for rent. The assignee is also burdened or benefited by all other lease covenants that run with the land. A covenant runs with the land if it touches and concerns the land (is not merely personal in nature) and is intended by the original parties to bind or benefit successors. The wording of the lease usually clearly indicates this intention. The tenant's assignee, therefore, must make repairs if the tenant covenanted to do so. Similarly, the assignee may require the landlord to make repairs if the landlord covenanted with the tenant to do so. These principles apply with equal force to the landlord's successors. *See* 2 American Law of Property §§ 9.1–9.7 (1952); Restatement (Second) of Property, Landlord and Tenant §§ 16.1 & 16.2 (1977).

You will encounter the concept of covenants running with the land ("real covenants") in more detail in the subsection of Chapter 3 dealing with covenants in deeds. *See* pages 392–448. At this point, it is sufficient for you to be aware of the general distinction between personal covenants that bind only the parties to them and covenants running with the land which bind successors to the original parties even if the successors do not expressly assume the obligation contained in the covenant.

2. What was the liability of the original tenant, Chicken System, for unpaid rent? Consider the following statement from Insley v. Myers, 192 Md. 292, 298, 64 A.2d 126, 128 (1949):

> The general law is that *expressed* stipulations in a lease continue to be binding on the lessee, in spite of an assignment and its recognition by the landlord, one of those expressed stipulations being the covenant to pay rent. * * * When the lessee parts with the estate, with the consent of the lessor, he thereby destroys the privity, and there is no further obligation on his part to pay rent, unless he is bound by a covenant, but if he has expressly covenanted to pay, he is held in privity of contract, which lasts until the contract is discharged. Under such circumstances, the lessor has the right to proceed against the original lessee, and also

the assignee, although, of course, he can obtain but one satisfaction of his debt.

A tenant who has assigned remains liable to the landlord as a surety. What does this mean?

3. What is the legal relationship among the landlord, the tenant, and a subtenant after the execution of a valid sublease? *See* 1 American Law of Property § 3.62 (1952).

4. Suppose the landlord assigns the reversion to X. What is the legal relationship between the tenant and X?

G. TERMINATION OF THE LANDLORD–TENANT RELATIONSHIP

Recall that in our hypothetical situation, one tenant proposed that Harmony House tenants refuse to vacate their apartments at the end of their current leases. This proposal raises the general question of how the landlord-tenant relationship may be terminated. Reconsider at this point the material on pages 12–14 which classifies leases by duration and discusses the notice required to terminate each type of lease.[1] Also review footnote 1 on page 24 which discusses the landlord's right to retake possession of the leased property upon the tenant's failure to pay rent or observe other lease terms.

Problem

L rented an apartment to T. The lease provided that only T and members of her "immediate family" could occupy the apartment. T permitted her boyfriend to move into the apartment. Can L evict T? *See* Hudson View Properties v. Weiss, 59 N.Y.2d 733, 463 N.Y.S.2d 428, 450 N.E.2d 234 (1983).

1. HOLDOVER TENANT

This subsection deals with the problem of the holdover tenant (tenant at sufferance)—one who remains on the premises after the lease ends. *See* page 14.

CLAIRTON CORPORATION v. GEO–CON, INC.

Superior Court of Pennsylvania, 1993.

431 Pa.Super. 34, 635 A.2d 1058.

CIRILLO, JUDGE.

1. Assume that our hypothetical situation arises in a jurisdiction which does not regulate condominium conversion. Thus, the standard notice-to-terminate requirements apply to the Harmony House conversion situation. Some state and local governments, however, have enacted legislation that requires additional notice to tenants in a building to be converted to a condominium. *See* discussion of condominium conversion on pages 31–319.

This is an appeal from an order entered in the Court of Common Pleas of Allegheny County denying appellant Clairton Corporation's (Lessor) motion for post-trial relief. We affirm.

Lessor and appellee Geo–Con, Inc. (Tenant) were parties to a commercial lease for a business premises located in Monroeville, Pennsylvania. The lease was for a term of two years. At the expiration of the two-year term, which was September 15, 1990, Tenant, with the consent of Lessor, remained on the premises for approximately seven months. During that time, Tenant continued to pay the same monthly installment rate as provided for in the two-year lease. The lease, which had been signed by the parties on August 10, 1988, provides in pertinent part:

> TO HAVE AND TO HOLD THE said premises for a full term of two years, commencing on September 15, 1988.

> * * *

> The Tenant shall pay as rental hereunder the sum of One Hundred Seventy Three Thousand Eight Hundred Seventy–Seven and 36/xx Dollars in 24 equal monthly installments, without demand, of Seven Thousand Two Hundred Forty Four and 89/xx, beginning on the commencement of the term and on the first day of each calendar month thereafter.

> * * *

The lease did not include a "hold-over" provision and, at the end of the two-year term, the parties had made no definite new arrangements. Tenant eventually vacated the premises in April, 1991.

Lessor filed a complaint seeking to recover rent for the remainder of the one year hold-over term from early April, 1991 through September 14, 1991. Tenant claimed that it did not hold over; it was engaged in negotiations for a new lease for additional rental space with Lessor and, thus, became a month-to-month tenant. A non-jury trial ensued, whereupon a verdict was entered in favor of Lessor in the amount of $1,466.50.[1] Lessor, believing the verdict to be inadequate, filed post-trial motions which were argued and denied. This timely appeal followed. Lessor raises the following issue for our review:

---

1. At trial, the Lessor had claimed the following items of damage: (1) unpaid rent for the remainder of the one-year holdover term ending September 14, 1991, being a total of $39,846.90; plus, (2) late charges as required by the lease in the amount of $4,081.44; plus, (3) a partial underpayment of rent during one month of the original term of the lease in the amount of $967.50; minus, (4) a credit for a security deposit in the amount of $950.00.

The trial judge awarded damages as follows: (1) instead of unpaid rent for the remainder of the one-year hold-over term, only per diem rental from March 31, 1991 through April 6, 1991 (the date Tenant vacated the property), which totaled $1,449.00; plus, (2) nothing for late charges; plus, (3) the partial underpayment of rent during one month of the original term of the lease in the amount of $967.50; minus, (4) a credit for a security deposit in the amount of $950.00. Accordingly, the total damage award amounted to $1,466.50.

Where a tenant for a term of years holds over after the expiration of the original term with the consent of the lessor, and where no definite new arrangement has been made between the lessor and the tenant, is the hold-over tenancy for a term of one year?

In support of its claim, Lessor cites principles established at common law. Specifically, when a lease for a term of years expires, and the lessee remains in possession, the landlord may, at his option, treat the lessee as a hold-over tenant; such law implies that the possession of the hold-over is subject to the same terms, conditions, and covenants as the old lease. Lessor relies primarily on *Routman v. Bohm*, 194 Pa.Super. 413, 168 A.2d 612 (1961), where it was specifically held that the tenants, who had held over after an expiration of a three-year lease and continued to pay the same monthly rent, became tenants from year to year. The court in *Routman* set forth the following rule of law:

> [W]here following the expiration of a tenancy for a term of one or more years, the tenant with the consent of the landlord holds over, prima facie, *in the absence of evidence showing a contrary intent*, the normal inference from the conduct of the parties is that they thus exhibited an intent to convert the tenancy into one from year to year.

(emphasis added).

In further support of its position, Lessor relies upon *Harvey v. Gunzberg*, 148 Pa. 294, 23 A. 1005 (1892), one of the cases cited by this court in *Routman*. In *Harvey*, the Pennsylvania Supreme Court proclaimed that where a tenant holds over after the expiration of his term, and no different arrangement has been made between the landlord and tenant, a tenancy for another year is created.

In its evaluation of the foregoing precedent, the trial court in this case found "evidence showing a contrary intent," *Routman, supra* regarding the term of Tenant's "hold-over." There is no question that Tenant continued to pay, and the Lessor continued to accept, the monthly rental rate set forth in the expired lease. The record also reflects that, from approximately August, 1990 (one month before the termination of the two-year lease), through April, 1991 (when Tenant vacated the premises), the Lessor and Tenant were involved in negotiations for a new lease. The negotiations mostly centered around the fact that Tenant desired an increased amount of rental space.[2] At no time during their negotiations was there discussion of whether Tenant was occupying the space on a hold-over basis for a year or on a hold-over basis from month to month.[3] Thus, in light of the fact that there was an

---

2. At the time that the lease was in effect Tenant occupied 7,000 square feet of Lessor's rental space; Tenant wanted the new lease to provide an additional 3,000 square feet of space. The record reflects that Lessor was slow in responding to Tenant's requests for this new agreement.

3. On cross-examination, Joseph Jonnet, President of the Lessor corporation, testified as follows:

Q. So is it correct to say that you and Steve [Mr. Jonnet's nephew] decided that you would just simply treat it as a one-year election on your part, the landlord's

attempt to have a new lease drafted, the trial court refused to hold that Tenants had agreed to another yearly lease, finding, *inter alia*, that the parties' intent was contrary to the creation of a hold-over tenancy. We agree.

In addition to citing *Routman* and distinguishing it from the instant case, the trial court pointed to no other law in support of its conclusion. Indeed, our research on this specific issue reveals a scarcity of authority. We are convinced, however, that a hold-over for a term of one year was *not* created under the instant set of circumstances.

"[I]t is established law that mere continuance in possession and payment of rent does not *of itself* constitute a renewal of the lease with all its provisions." *Young Men's Christian Association v. Harbeson*, 407 Pa. 489, 492, 180 A.2d 916, 918 (1962) (emphasis added). In *Harbeson*, the lessee sought specific performance of an option to purchase certain property, as specified in a lease agreement between the lessee and lessor. The Pennsylvania Supreme Court specifically held that the lease agreement, including the option clause, was *not* renewed for a second five-year term when the lessee continued in possession of the property after the end of the first term. Rather, the Court looked to the specific facts of the case and came to the conclusion that there was a mutually agreed upon modification of the original lease agreement, the modification being the elimination of the option to purchase. Significantly, the Court took into account the fact that the lessor informed the lessee that he would no longer sell at the option price and that such price was to be renegotiated. Thus, when the lessee continued possession at the termination of the lease, his acceptance of the modification was implied.

We decline to follow Lessor's strict interpretation of the rule set forth in *Routman* and *Harvey* and, in light of the facts at hand, will instead adopt a more flexible approach. Like the court in *Harbeson*, we are of the opinion that Tenant's possession of the premises after the termination of the lease, in and of itself, does not automatically bind them to a renewal of their original lease agreement. When we consider the surrounding circumstances, specifically the failed renegotiation of the lease, we refuse to hold Tenant liable for another entire year's rent. *See Severance v. Heyl & Patterson, Inc.*, 308 Pa. 101, 108, 162 A. 171, 173 (1932) ("[t]he fact that money was paid as rent does not establish any particular term or holding and if the beginning of the tenancy or its length is in question, these facts must be shown by other evidence"); *Peterson v. Schultz*, 162 Pa.Super. 469, 58 A.2d 360 (1948) (fact that tenant has paid rent after expiration of term and the landlord has accepted it is not an affirmance of the lease for a new year but merely evidence of affirmance which may be rebutted by proof that such was not the intention of the parties). Lessor's acceptance of Tenant's rent, combined with Lessor's involvement in negotiations for a new lease to

part, and didn't feel an obligation to tell them anything; is that right?

  A. Well, I felt they knew it.

Q. And how—

A. It's the law.

include more rental space for Tenant, clearly implies that Lessor knew that the terms and conditions of the old lease would not have been acceptable to Tenant. It can be deduced, therefore, that under these circumstances, the creation of a month to month lease was more appropriate.

In further support of our conclusion, we are persuaded by the following language set forth in *Southern Ry. Co. v. Peple*, 228 F. 853 (4th Cir.Va.1915):

> Continuance in possession by a tenant, with the payment of rent, will usually be regarded as renewal of the lease; the acceptance of the rent by the lessor being considered a waiver of any right to notice of intention to renew. *But this rule does not apply where the possession is retained and the rent paid pending negotiations with respect to the renewal of the lease.*

(emphasis added); *see also* 45 A.L.R.2d 841, § 6.[4] *Peple* involved a proceeding in which a lessor alleged that a right to renew a lease had not been exercised. The court held that the lessor had waived the notice requirement in the lease asking for ninety days' notice for exercise of the option to renew. In reaching this conclusion, the court looked to the following factors: the lessor knew that expense and labor had been incurred and plans had been laid out for the future in reliance on renewal of the lease; the lessor had allowed the lessee to remain in possession and pay rent and taxes after the end of the initial term, pending negotiations for a possible new lease; the lessor had delayed for approximately five weeks after receiving a sixty day notice from the lessee; and the lessor had responded to such notice that lessor would renew the lease on receiving a more formal letter from the lessee.

We find it significant that, in finding for the lessee, the court in *Peple* looked to the fact that the lessor had allowed the lessee to remain in possession of the property after the lease had ended, that negotiations for a new lease were pending, and that the lessor had delayed in responding to the notice received from the lessee. The court focused on the conduct of the lessor in determining that the lessor had accepted the lessee's notice to renew. Although the instant case does not involve an option to renew, *Peple* lends analogous support for our decision to uphold the implication of a month to month lease. In reaching this decision, we, too, look to Lessor's conduct involving negotiations for a new lease, along with the delay incurred in doing so. When these factors

---

4. Landlord's consent to extension or renewal of lease as shown by acceptance of rent from tenant holding over:

§ 6. Circumstances rendering rule inapplicable; receipt of rent during negotiations for new lease.

Where a tenant remains in possession of realty after the expiration of his term, and during a period in which he and the landlord are negotiating for a new lease, and the landlord accepts rent for this period, it is uniformly held that such acceptance is not a manifestation of the landlord's consent to an extension or renewal of the lease.

45 A.L.R.2d 841, § 6.

are considered, it is clear that the parties' intent was not to enter into the same lease as was originally executed.

Our refusal to focus solely on the fact that Tenant has remained in possession of the property after the expiration of the lease is not in conflict with the rules set forth in *Routman* and *Harvey*; rather, it is consistent with them. In fact, the reasoning employed here can be considered an example of *Routman's* "contrary intent" exception to the general rule regarding holdovers. Thus, because the parties' conduct evidenced an intent to enter into a new agreement, even though a new lease never actually came to fruition, such conduct was sufficient to invoke an exception to the common law rule making Tenant liable for another year's rent. In the interest of fairness, we will not disturb the trial court's conclusion, and hold that Tenant's occupation of the premises after the original lease had expired became a month to month tenancy.

Order affirmed.

Notes and Questions

1. In A.H. Fetting Manufacturing Jewelry Co. v. Waltz, 160 Md. 50, 152 A. 434 (1930) negotiations for a new lease failed, but the tenant remained in possession of the premises for a month following expiration of the five-year lease. The court ruled that the landlord, at its election, could treat the holdover tenant as a tenant from year-to-year under the terms of the original lease. What rationale supports such a result? Is the decision consistent with the decision in *Clairton Corporation*?

2. May the landlord hold the tenant liable for another term if the tenant is prevented from moving because the tenant or a member of the tenant's family is critically ill? *See* 1 American Law of Property § 3.34 (1952).

3. When a landlord treats a holdover tenant as a tenant rather than a trespasser, a question arises about the duration of the tenancy. To resolve this issue, the courts look to the length of the original lease and the manner in which rent was reserved. *See* 1 American Law of Property § 3.35 (1952). In some states, statutes cover the subject. *See* N.J.Stat.Ann. § 46:8–10 (West 1989) (holdover tenant shall be treated as tenant from month-to-month); Nev.Rev.Stat.Ann. § 118A.470 (Michie 1993) (tenant holding over regarded as tenant from month-to-month); Wis.Stat.Ann. § 704.25 (West 1981 & Supp. 1997) (landlord may treat nonresidential holdover tenant as a year-to-year tenant, but may consider residential holdover tenant as month-to-month tenant).

4. What remedy is available if the landlord does not wish the holdover tenant to remain on the leased premises?

5. How does section eleven of the sample lease on page 8 affect the landlord's rights against a holdover tenant?

LONERGAN v. CONNECTICUT FOOD STORE, INC.

Supreme Court of Connecticut, 1975.
168 Conn. 122, 357 A.2d 910.

LONGO, ASSOCIATE JUSTICE.

The plaintiff, Evelyn P. Lonergan, is the owner of a building, located at 1166 Main Street in Willimantic, consisting of two separate units rented as retail stores. In April, 1962, her husband began negotiating with the defendant's district representative for the leasing of the store that was vacant. Her husband, now deceased, informed her of the negotiations, and she authorized him to enter into a lease on her behalf for a reasonable period of time of approximately five years.

The written lease was prepared by the defendant. The lease which has been made a part of the record, was for a term of five years beginning May 1, 1962. Paragraph 14 of the lease, however, contained the following provision for renewal: "Upon the expiration of the term of this Lease, the same, including this clause, shall automatically be extended for a period of one year and thence from year to year, unless the Lessee shall give notice to the Lessor of termination at least sixty (60) days before the end of the original term or any extension thereof."

The plaintiff, claiming that the lease did not create a right to perpetual renewal in the lessee, on numerous occasions demanded that the defendant vacate the premises upon the termination of the five-year term on April 30, 1967. Nonetheless, the defendant occupied the premises from the date of the lease and indicated no willingness to vacate voluntarily.

The action in four counts was instituted by the plaintiff on December 3, 1969, claiming possession of the premises, damages and cancellation of the lease. The case was referred to Hon. Joseph E. Klau, state referee, who, upon a hearing, found the issues for the plaintiff on all counts and granted all of the relief sought including $9485 in damages. The defendant has appealed from the judgment.

I

The defendant has assigned error in the conclusion of the referee, hereinafter referred to as the court, that the language of the lease could not be interpreted as creating a right in the lessee to renew the lease perpetually.

* * *

Although this is the first occasion this court has had to rule on the issue, it is well settled in most other jurisdictions that, absent statutory provision to the contrary, the right to perpetual renewal of a lease is not forbidden by the law, either upon the ground that it creates a perpetuity or a restraint on alienation or upon any other ground, and such provisions, when properly entered into, will be enforced.

We acknowledge the clear weight of authority as stating the correct view of the law on this issue.

Courts do not favor perpetual leases, however; thus a provision in a lease will not be construed as conferring a right to a perpetual renewal "unless the language is so plain as to admit of no doubt of the purpose to provide for perpetual renewal." Thaw v. Gaffney, 75 W.Va. 229, 232, 83 S.E. 983, 985; see also McLean v. United States, 316 F.Supp. 827, 832–34 (E.D.Va.). Furthermore, "[a] perpetuity will not be regarded as created from an ordinary covenant to renew." *McLean v. United States, supra* 829. Rather, "[t]here must be some peculiar and plain language before it will be assumed that the parties intended to create it." Winslow v. Baltimore & O.R. Co., 188 U.S. 646, 655.

In this connection, we have stated that in determining the intention of the parties to a lease, "[t]he controlling factor is the intent expressed in the lease, not the intent which the parties may have had or which the court believes they ought to have had." Ingalls v. Roger Smith Hotels Corporation, 143 Conn. 1, 6, 118 A.2d 463, 465. Rather, "the lease must be construed as a whole and in such a manner as to give effect to every provision, if reasonably possible." *Ingalls v. Roger Smith Hotels Corporation, supra.*

The language in paragraph 14 of the instant lease, insofar as it purports to create in the lessee the right of perpetual renewal, is far from clear. It states that, upon the expiration of the original five-year term, the lease, "including this clause, *shall automatically be extended* for a period of one year and *thence from year to year, unless the Lessee shall give notice* to the Lessor of termination at least sixty (60) days before the end of the original term or any extension thereof." (Emphasis added.) Nowhere in the provision appear any of the words customarily used to create a perpetual lease, such as "forever," "for all time," and "in perpetuity," words whose presence or absence in a lease is of considerable significance to a court in deciding whether a right of perpetual renewal was intended by the parties. It is true that the words in paragraph 14 emphasized above presume to characterize the successive renewals of the lease as self-executing (i.e., "automatic"). But such language is construed as creating a perpetual lease only when the renewal period to which it refers is for a specific term, usually as long as that provided in the original lease. In the instant lease, these words are used in combination with language describing the renewal period as one "from year to year." Where words of perpetuity are absent from the lease, courts generally do not construe a clause which establishes a renewal period as one merely "from year to year" as expressing an intention of the parties to create a perpetual lease.

Moreover, neither paragraph 14, nor any other clause in the lease, provides for escalation of rent beyond the $175 per month agreed upon by the parties in paragraph 3. Of course, failure to include an escalation clause is not fatal; perpetual renewal upon the same terms as the original lease is an enforceable option. But an agreement to that effect is of such critical importance to parties creating a perpetual lease that it is generally stipulated in the same provision as that which creates the right in the lessee to perpetual renewal. In the present lease, the lessor agreed, in paragraph 8, to repair the demised buildings and to repair and restore them in the event of partial or total destruction; in paragraph 12 the lessor agreed to pay all taxes, charges and assessments, including charges relating to the use of water. The absence of an escalation clause to provide a source of revenue from which the lessor might meet her continuing obligations under these two paragraphs strongly suggests that the creation of a right to perpetual renewal was not the intention expressed by the parties in paragraph 14.

A review of the lease in its entirety establishes that there are sufficient facts to support the court's conclusion that the instrument does not create a right in the lessee to renew the lease perpetually. However, while the language of paragraph 14 did not clearly and unambiguously express an intention to create a perpetual lease, it specifically provides that the lease should be extended upon the expiration of the five-year term "for a period of one year and thence from year to year." In some cases, where the clause in question provides for renewal or extension only "from year to year," courts have concluded that the lessee does not thereby have a right to even one renewal but rather that what results is a tenancy from year to year terminable by either party upon proper notice. Such an approach is inappropriate here, since paragraph 14 is precise in providing not simply that the lease should be extended "from year to year" but that it should be extended for the definite period of one year upon the expiration of the original five-year term of the lease. We have stated that "[w]hen the plain meaning and intent of the language is clear, a clause in a written lease cannot be enlarged by construction. There is no room for construction where the terms of a writing are plain and unambiguous, and it is to be given effect according to its language." Collins v. Sears, Roebuck and Co., 164 Conn. 369, 373–74, 321 A.2d 444, 448. Moreover, the general rule is that where doubt exists as to the intention of the parties to create a right to perpetual renewal, the provision in the lease purporting to create this right is viewed as establishing the length of the renewal period, the right to one such renewal, and thereafter, at most, a periodic tenancy terminable by either party upon giving proper notice.

We conclude that the language in paragraph 14 confers upon the lessee the right to one renewal for a period of one year beyond the term of the original lease, and establishes thereafter the possibility of a periodic tenancy terminable by either party. Thus, although there is ample evidence to support the court's conclusion that the language of paragraph 14 does not create a right to renew the lease perpetually, it does not follow therefrom as the court also concluded, that upon the expiration of the original term the lessee became a "tenant at sufferance," i.e., one who came into possession of land rightfully but continues in possession wrongfully after his right thereto has terminated. Nor does it follow, as the court also concluded, that the defendant's right to possession ceased and the plaintiff was entitled to immediate possession on May 1, 1967, instead of May 1, 1968. To that extent the court erred in that these conclusions were inconsistent with the facts found, and involved the application of an erroneous rule of law material to the case.

The court's error in this respect, however, is of no significance in this case. Under the terms of the lease, the defendant's right to possession of the premises, as we have indicated, terminated on April 30, 1968, with the expiration of the one-year renewal period. At trial the plaintiff acknowledged the defendant's right to possession during this one-year renewal period and declined to make any claim for damages suffered during that period. The plaintiff, however, has consistently manifested an intention not to treat the defendant as entitled to possession for any length of time beyond the expiration of the initial renewal period; although the defendant continued to offer rental payments, the court found that on numerous occasions after the expiration of the lease the plaintiff demanded that the defendant vacate the leased premises, and it found that the plaintiff never intended the lease to be renewed perpetually by the defendant. Accordingly, after April 30, 1968, the defendant, in refusing to vacate upon the plaintiff's demand, continued in possession wrongfully and became a tenant at sufferance.[1] The court correctly concluded that the plaintiff was entitled to damages for unlawful retention of the property by the defendant after May 1, 1968, these damages consisting of the fair rental value of the property for the period during which the defendant remained in unlawful possession. Implicit in this conclusion is the further conclusion that the plaintiff on May 1, 1968, also became entitled to immediate possession of the premises. The court, indeed, adopted this conclusion in its judgment, wherein it stated that "the plaintiff is entitled to immediate possession of the premises and for damages for unlawful * * * [retention] *since May 1, 1968.*" (Emphasis added.) This court will not remand a case to correct an erroneous conclusion where the judgment is properly supported by valid grounds.

II

The defendant next assigns error in the court's evaluation of the damages due the plaintiff as an amount totaling $9485. This sum represented the difference between what the court concluded to be the fair market rental of the property and the amount actually received by the plaintiff, the period of computation extending from May 1, 1968, a year after the original five-year term of the lease expired, through June 15, 1973, the date on which judgment was rendered.

The obligation of the defendant, as a tenant at sufferance, with respect to damages was to pay the reasonable rental value of the property which it occupied without the plaintiff's consent. Essentially, the defendant has challenged the court's assessment of the fair rental

---

1. The presumption that a periodic tenancy has resulted can be overcome by a finding of a contrary intention on the part of the lessor alone. Continued demand and acceptance of rent by the lessor need not negate an intention by the lessor, otherwise clearly expressed, not to allow the lessee to hold over upon the expiration of a term stipulated in the lease.

value of the subject premises during the period in question. No attack, however, has been made upon the subordinate facts found by the court which establish, inter alia, the fair market rental for premises similar to the subject premises during the period in question and the prevailing rate for comparable rental property during the same period. Rather, in urging upon us this assignment of error, the defendant asks us to consider certain facts which the defendant has never requested be added to the finding, and other facts which it has requested be added to the finding, but which the plaintiff has disputed. This court is without power to add to the finding facts which are not undisputed. Left undisturbed, the facts in the finding as such fully support the court's conclusion as to the fair rental of the subject premises during the period, so that we cannot say that the court erred in fixing damages at $9485.

* * *

[In Part III of the opinion, the court found that the lower court had erroneously cancelled the lease. Thus, the court required that the judgment be modified to correspond with this finding.]

There is error in part, the judgment is set aside and the case is remanded with direction to render judgment as on file except as corrected to accord with Part III of this opinion.

Notes and Questions

1. For a decision reaching a similar result to that in *Lonergan,* see Schroeder v. Johnson, 696 So.2d 498 (Fla.App.1997) (successive renewal clause interpreted in light of judicial hostility to perpetual leases).

2. Is section thirteen of the sample lease on page 8 an adequate renewal provision?

3. The landlord in *Lonergan* was eventually able to recover possession of the leased premises. Often the landlord is anxious to evict a holdover tenant. The following subsection concerns the eviction process.

2. SUMMARY EVICTION

There exists in every state a summary, efficient and economical method for the recovery of possession of leased property from a tenant who has improperly held over after the termination of his lease. Local practice varies greatly, and any landlord or incoming tenant who desires to use the remedy must make an investigation into the particular requirements of the governing statute. It should be noted that in some jurisdictions, particularly in larger cities, a separate housing court has concurrent jurisdiction, with the court of general jurisdiction, over matters dealing with housing, including summary proceedings for possession of property.

Restatement (Second) of Property, Landlord and Tenant § 14.1 statutory note 1 (1977).

As noted above, states have generally enacted wrongful detainer statutes providing for expedited eviction procedures when a tenant has failed to pay rent or violated some other lease provision. In Lindsey v. Normet, 405 U.S. 56 (1972), the Supreme Court upheld, against due process and equal protection challenges, the constitutionality of provisions in a wrongful detainer statute which mandated an early trial and limited triable issues to the tenant's default. The Court stressed the importance of a rapid and peaceful settlement of landlord-tenant disputes. Rejecting the contention that there was a constitutional right to housing, the Court ruled:

> We do not denigrate the importance of decent, safe, and sanitary housing. But the Constitution does not provide judicial remedies for every social and economic ill. We are unable to perceive in that document any constitutional guarantee of access to dwellings of a particular quality, or any recognition of the right of a tenant to occupy the real payment of rent or otherwise contrary to the terms of the relevant agreement. Absent constitutional mandate, the assurance of adequate housing and the definition of landlord-tenant relationships are legislative, not judicial, functions. Nor should we forget that the Constitution expressly protects against confiscation of private property or the income therefrom.

Id. at 74.

BASS v. BOETEL & CO.

Supreme Court of Nebraska, 1974.
191 Neb. 733, 217 N.W.2d 804.

Spencer, Justice.

Plaintiffs, dispossessed tenants of business premises at Rockbrook Center in Omaha, Nebraska, sued their landlord and the latter's agent to recover damages. Admitting default in payment of rents, they alleged that defendants, by the use of self-help, removed and detained certain personal property belonging to plaintiffs. A jury returned a verdict of $12,000 for plaintiffs, and defendants appeal. We reverse.

On September 24, 1968, plaintiffs entered into a written lease of the premises with defendants' predecessor in interest. Rent was payable monthly at the rate of $400 for a period of 3 years. On April 20, 1971, the Rockbrook Center area was acquired by defendants. The transaction included an assignment of one-third of the April rent.

Carl Bass, one of the plaintiffs, operated a billiard parlor on the premises. His business was seasonal, greater in the winter than in the summer. In 1970, he was unable to pay rent to defendants' predecessor for a period of 3 months, but was permitted to make up the payments during the following 3 months. At the time of the transfer of the premises to defendants, Bass had not paid the April rent. He paid no rent to defendants. As of June 1, 1971, he was indebted to them for the rent from April 21, 1971. This is the subject of a counterclaim. Defendants were awarded a judgment of $600 against the plaintiffs. No cross-appeal was taken so this judgment is not in controversy.

When Bass attempted to open for business on June 1, 1971, he found defendants had changed the outside locks on the billiard parlor. He went to their office to discuss the matter but was refused a key. He subsequently hired a locksmith, had the locks changed, and went in to resume business. When the locksmith opened the door, the alarm went off and the security patrol showed up and asked for his identification. Shortly thereafter representatives of defendants appeared and told Bass he could no longer occupy the premises. He stayed in the premises a short while and then sought legal advice. When he left he removed his books, money from the cash register, some standing ashtrays, and a case for pool cues from the premises. When he returned to the premises the locks had again been changed, and he could not reenter. Subsequently he learned that the remainder of his equipment, with the exception of the carpeting, had been removed from the premises.

Bass was never given a written notice to quit as required by statute, nor served with legal process. Defendants removed the personal property claimed by Bass from the billiard parlor. They subsequently gave his attorney an inventory list. The property was placed in defendants' warehouse for storage pending the outcome of this litigation. The premises were relet to another tenant.

* * *

Defendants assert they possessed the right to use self-help as a matter of law; the evidence was insufficient to sustain a finding on the facts or amount of damages; erroneous exclusion of the issue of abandonment; and instructional error relating to damages.

The lease asserted ownership of the landlord, defendants' predecessor, in the tenant's fixtures, except movable office fixtures and trade fixtures. In the event of default in payment of rent, the lease provided as follows: "* * * the Lessor may * * * without demand * * * or notice * * * at once declare this lease terminated, and the Lessor may reenter said premises without any formal notice or demand and hold and enjoy the same thenceforth as if these presents had not been made, * * *."

The lease also provided: "If the Lessee shall not promptly remove all his property * * * whenever the Lessor shall become entitled to * * * possession * * * as herein agreed, the Lessor may, without notice, remove the same * * * in any manner * * *, or if the Lessee shall at any time vacate or abandon said premises, and leave any * * * chattels * * * for a period of ten days after such vacation or abando[n]ment, or after the termination of this lease in any manner * * * then the Lessor shall have the right to sell * * * said * * * chattels * * * without * * * notice to the Lessee, or any notice of sale, all notices required by statute or otherwise being hereby expressly waived, * * *. * * * all * * * chattels, fixtures and other personal property belonging to * * * Lessee, which are, or may be put into the said leased premises during said term, whether exempt or not from sale under execution or attachment * * *, shall at all times be bound with a first lien in favor of * * * Lessor, and shall be chargeable for all rent * * * which * * * lien may be enforced in like manner as a chattel mortgage, or in any other manner afforded by law.''

The lease also provided that personal property was at the risk of plaintiffs only that '' * * * the Lessor shall not be * * * liable for any damage * * * caused in any * * * manner whatsoever.''

Plaintiffs' second amended petition pleaded two causes of action. The first alleged breach of quiet enjoyment and loss of financial and business standing as well as public ridicule and ignominy as a result of being locked out of the business premises. The second cause of action alleged the wrongful taking and detention of plaintiffs' personal property.

Defendants argue that wrongful eviction and abandonment were issues of law and that by the terms of the lease they were given the right to take possession of the premises and the personal property. The law on forcible entry and detainer has long been otherwise.

In Myers v. Koenig (1877), 5 Neb. 419, this court stated: ''One great object of the forcible entry act is to prevent even rightful owners from taking the law into their own hands and attempting to recover by violence, what remedial powers of a court would give them in a peaceful mode.''

In Watkins v. Dodson (1955), 159 Neb. 745, 68 N.W.2d 508, after quoting the above language, this court said: ''It was the purpose of the statute relating to forcible entry and detainer to prevent parties to a litigable controversy like the present from taking the law into their own hands. The issue was not ownership or title, but 'lawful and peaceable entry,' * * * .''

To accept defendants' argument would scuttle our forcible entry and detainer statute. Self-help, relating to the repossession of real estate, has long been contrary to the public policy of Nebraska and is not to be condoned. The lockout herein was unlawful. The right of a landlord legally entitled to possession to dispossess a tenant without legal process is the subject of an annotation in 6 A.L.R.3d 177. At page 186, we find the following statement: ''An increasing number of jurisdictions uphold what seems to be the modern doctrine that a landlord otherwise entitled to possession must, on the refusal of the tenant to surrender the leased premises resort to the remedy given by law to secure it; otherwise he would be liable in damages for using force or deception to regain possession.''

Plaintiffs were in lawful possession of the premises even though they had failed to make rental payments as specified by the lease. The fact that they were in default gave defendants the right to declare a forfeiture and to recover the leased premises by legal means. Instead, they resorted to self-help and are liable for the consequences.

* * *

The only issue submitted to the jury was the wrongful taking and detention of plaintiffs' personal property as the result of their being unlawfully and forcibly dispossessed of the leased premises. Defendants' unlawful seizure of the property of plaintiffs could not be justified on the ground that rent was due and owing, as defendants might have proceeded legally to enforce whatever legal or equitable claims they might have had. Instead, defendants saw fit to wrongfully and unlawfully seize and detain plaintiffs' property. The trial court properly instructed the jury that a person having a lien upon the property of another must enforce that lien by proper legal action rather than by force.

No specific damage instruction was submitted by the court. The jury was merely advised to determine the nature, extent, and amount of the damages sustained by plaintiffs as a result of the forcible taking and detention of their personal property by defendants.

* * *

* * * It is always the duty of the court to instruct the jury as to the proper basis upon which damages are to be estimated. The jury should be fully and fairly informed as to the various items or elements of damage which it should take into consideration in arriving at its verdict. Otherwise, the jury may be confused and misled.

* * *

For the reasons given, the judgment is reversed and the cause remanded to the District Court for a new trial in conformity with this opinion.

Reversed and remanded.

BOSLAUGH, JUSTICE (concurring).

With respect to the matter of self-help relating to the repossession of real estate, the following statement from the opinion of Mr. Justice Marshall in Pernell v. Southall Realty, 416 U.S. 363 seems appropriate: "Some delay, of course, is inherent in any fair-minded system of justice. A landlord-tenant dispute, like any other lawsuit, cannot be resolved with due process of law unless both parties have had a fair opportunity to present their cases. Our courts were never intended to serve as rubber stamps for landlords seeking to evict their tenants, but rather to see that justice be done before a man is evicted from his home."

NEWTON, JUSTICE (dissenting).

I respectfully dissent. Under existing Nebraska law, a landlord cannot evict a tenant by force or artifice even though the landlord is entitled to possession. See, Anderson v. Carlson, 86 Neb. 126, 125 N.W. 157; Miller v. Maust, 128 Neb. 453, 259 N.W. 181; Barnes v. Davitt, 160 Neb. 595, 71 N.W.2d 107. These are all cases in forcible entry and detainer where the only issue was the right of possession. In such cases damages were not an issue. Furthermore, in none of these cases was a lease involved which contained a provision for reentry on breach. These cases represent an exercise in futility. In each instance the tenant, who wrongfully held possession in the first place, was returned to possession. This simply meant that the landlord would have to bring a second action in forcible entry and detainer to obtain possession from a defaulting tenant or trespasser. I believe it inadvisable to extend or rule to cases where the lease contract authorizes reentry on breach or termination of the lease. I favor following the weight of authority as outlined in Annotation, 6 A.L.R.3d 194.

The right of a landlord to reenter for default in payment of rent or a wrongful holding over should be permitted where the lease provides for reentry and it can be accomplished without violence. This is similar to the right of a conditional sale vendor to take possession of the security on default by peaceful means. See § 9–503, U.C.C.

How can a rule such as is advocated in the majority opinion be justified? It is said that it prevents violence and therefore is required by public policy. This is untrue as the rule I have proposed, like that dealing with the repossession of a conditional sales contract security interest, authorizes only peaceful repossession. Contractual rights should not be nullified without good reason.

On the question of whether a party not entitled to possession of realty who is ejected by force or artifice may recover damages, there is a split in the authorities. There is not a single Nebraska case permitting such recovery. The decisions seem to indicate approval of Ish v. Marsh, 1 Neb. (Unoff.) 864, 96 N.W. 58, which approved an instruction that one not entitled to possession cannot recover damages when forcibly ejected except in the event due care was not used in removing his property.

* * *

In the absence of a willful destruction of the evicted party's property or a physical assault, I would deny recovery. This is particularly true in cases where the lease provides that the landlord shall have a lien on the tenant's property on the demised premises to secure accrued rentals. In 49 Am.Jur.2d, Landlord and Tenants, § 677, p. 642, it is stated: "It is competent for the parties to a lease to stipulate that the landlord shall have a lien on the crops or the personal property of the tenant which may be brought upon the leased premises, which, even if invalid at common law, will be given effect in equity."

Notes and Questions

1.   The self-help issue addressed in *Bass* has been considered by other courts. *Compare* Rucker v. Wynn, 212 Ga.App. 69, 71, 441 S.E.2d 417, 420 (1994) ("'[W]here under the terms of a commercial lease a landlord has the right to reenter and take possession of the premises without recourse to legal proceedings, he may do so and effect a self-help eviction if this can be accomplished without a breach of the peace.") *with* Whalen v. Taylor, 278 Mont. 293, 925 P.2d 462 (1996) (landlord's self-help action in changing locks to apartment of tenant who failed to pay rent constituted violation of state statute governing eviction procedures). Several states still permit some form of self-help, but no jurisdiction retains the common law rule permitting the

landlord to use all necessary force. *See* Restatement (Second) of Property, Landlord and Tenant § 14.1 statutory note 7 (1977); Bell, *The Mississippi Landlord–Tenant Act of 1991,* 61 Miss. L.J. 527, 560–562 (1991). *See also* Restatement (Second) of Property, Landlord and Tenant § 14.2 for a discussion of the relationship between self-help and summary eviction procedures and § 14.3 for limits on self-help where it is an available remedy.

2. The lease in *Bass* provided that the landlord had a lien on the tenant's property on the leased premises and could remove and sell the property without notice. Such clauses have received a mixed reception from modern courts and legislatures.

At common law, even without such a lease clause, the landlord could enter the leased premises and seize the tenant's personal property as security for overdue rent. This common law right was called distress or distraint. Later an English statute gave the landlord the power to sell the seized goods and to apply the proceeds to the rent. *See* 2 American Law of Property § 9.47 (1952).

Distress for rent has been abolished by statute in some states. *See, e.g.,* Uniform Residential Landlord and Tenant Act § 4.205(b)(1974). Statutes in other jurisdictions recognize the remedy, but require enforcement by a public official. *See* 1 American Law of Property § 3.72 (1952). Statutes of this type which permit seizure of the tenant's goods without notice and a hearing, however, have been held unconstitutional as a denial of due process by some courts. *See* Restatement (Second) of Property, Landlord and Tenant § 12.1 reporter's note 12 & statutory note 5 (1977).

3. Under Uniform Residential Landlord and Tenant Act § 4.105(a) (1974), the tenant may file a defense or counterclaim in a summary eviction proceeding. *See also* P.H. Investment v. Oliver, 818 P.2d 1018 (Utah 1991) (permitting tenant to assert breach of warranty of habitability as defense in summary eviction action). Does this development undermine the objective of a speedy determination of eviction disputes?

3. RETALIATORY EVICTION

Recall that at the Harmony House tenants meeting, one tenant urged all tenants to report needed repairs to the Centerville Housing Code Inspector. The Lloyds are concerned that the Daze Corporation may try to evict them if they contact the Housing Code Inspector about their broken air conditioner.

EDWARDS v. HABIB

United States Court of Appeals, District of Columbia Circuit, 1968.
130 U.S.App.D.C. 126, 397 F.2d 687, certiorari denied 393 U.S. 1016 (1969).

J. SKELLY WRIGHT, CIRCUIT JUDGE:

In March 1965 the appellant, Mrs. Yvonne Edwards, rented housing property from the appellee, Nathan Habib, on a month-to-month basis. Shortly thereafter she complained to the Department of Licenses and Inspections of sanitary code violations which her landlord had failed to remedy. In the course of the ensuing inspection, more than 40 such violations were discovered which the Department ordered the landlord to correct. Habib then gave Mrs. Edwards a 30–day statutory notice to vacate and obtained a default judgment for possession of the premises. Mrs. Edwards promptly moved to reopen this judgment, alleging excusable neglect for the default and also alleging as a defense that the notice to quit was given in retaliation for her complaints to the housing authorities. Judge Greene, sitting on motions in the Court of General Sessions, set aside the default judgment and, in a very thoughtful opinion, concluded that a retaliatory motive, if proved, would constitute a defense to the action for possession. At the trial itself, however, a different judge apparently deemed evidence of retaliatory motive irrelevant and directed a verdict for the landlord.

Mrs. Edwards then appealed to this court for a stay pending her appeal to the District of Columbia Court of Appeals, and on December 3, 1965, we granted the stay, provided only that Mrs. Edwards continue to pay her rent. Edwards v. Habib, 125 U.S.App.D.C. 49, 366 F.2d 628 (1965). She then appealed to the DCCA, which affirmed the judgment of the trial court. 227 A.2d 388 (1967). In reaching its decision the DCCA relied on a series of its earlier decisions holding that a private landlord was not required, under the District of Columbia Code, to give a reason for evicting a month-to-month tenant and was free to do so for any reason or for no reason at all. The court acknowledged that the landlord's right to terminate a tenancy is not absolute, but felt that any limitation on his prerogative had to be based on specific statutes or very special circumstances. Here, the court concluded, the tenant's right to report violations of law and to petition for redress of grievances was not protected by specific legislation and that any change in the relative rights of tenants and landlords should be undertaken by the legislature, not the courts. We granted appellant leave to appeal that decision to this court. We hold that the promulgation of the housing code by the District of Columbia Commissioners at the direction of Congress impliedly effected just such a change in the relative rights of landlords and tenants and that proof of a retaliatory motive does constitute a defense to an action of eviction. Accordingly, we reverse the decision of the DCCA with directions that it remand to the Court of General Sessions for a new trial where Mrs. Edwards will be permitted to try to prove to a jury that her landlord who seeks to evict her harbors a retaliatory intent.

Appellant has launched a constitutional challenge to the judicial implementation of 45 D.C.Code §§ 902 and 910 in aid of a landlord who is evicting because his tenant has reported housing code violations on the premises. * * *

* * *

Appellant argues first that to evict her because she has reported violations of the law to the housing authorities would abridge her First

Amendment rights to report violations of law and to petition the government for redress of grievances. * * *

* * *

But we need not decide whether judicial recognition of this constitutional defense is constitutionally compelled. We need not, in other words, decide whether 45 D.C.Code § 910 could validly compel the court to assist the plaintiff in penalizing the defendant for exercising her constitutional right to inform the government of violations of the law; for we are confident that Congress did not intend it to entail such a result.

45 D.C.Code § 910, in pertinent part, provides:

"Whenever * * * any tenancy shall be terminated by notice as aforesaid [45 D.C.Code § 902], and the tenant shall fail or refuse to surrender possession of the leased premises, * * * the landlord may bring an action to recover possession before the District of Columbia Court of General Sessions, as provided in sections 11–701 to 11–749."

And 16 D.C.Code § 1501, in pertinent part, provides:

"When a person detains possession of real property * * * after his right to possession has ceased, the District of Columbia Court of General Sessions * * * may issue a summons to the party complained of to appear and show cause why judgment should not be given against him for restitution of possession."

These provisions are simply procedural. They neither say nor imply anything about whether evidence of retaliation or other improper motive should be unavailable as a defense to a possessory action brought under them. It is true that in making his affirmative case for possession the landlord need only show that his tenant has been given the 30–day statutory notice, and he need not assign any reason for evicting a tenant who does not occupy the premises under a lease. But while the landlord may evict for any legal reason or for no reason at all, he is not, we hold, free to evict in retaliation for his tenant's report of housing code violations to the authorities. As a matter of statutory construction and for reasons of public policy, such an eviction cannot be permitted.

The housing and sanitary codes, especially in light of Congress' explicit direction for their enactment, indicate a strong and pervasive congressional concern to secure for the city's slum dwellers decent, or at least safe and sanitary, places to live. Effective implementation and enforcement of the codes obviously depend in part on private initiative in the reporting of violations. Though there is no official procedure for the filing of such complaints, the bureaucratic structure of the Department of Licenses and Inspections establishes such a procedure, and for fiscal year 1966 nearly a third of the cases handled by the Department arose from private complaints. To permit retaliatory evictions, then, would clearly frustrate the effectiveness of the housing code as a means of upgrading the quality of housing in Washington.

As judges, "we cannot shut our eyes to matters of public notoriety and general cognizance. When we take our seats on the bench we are not struck with blindness, and forbidden to know as judges what we see as men." Ho Ah Kow v. Nunan, C.C.D.Cal., 12 Fed.Cas. 252, 255 (No. 6546) (1879). In trying to effect the will of Congress and as a court of equity we have the responsibility to consider the social context in which our decisions will have operational effect. In light of the appalling condition and shortage of housing in Washington, the expense of moving, the inequality of bargaining power between tenant and landlord, and the social and economic importance of assuring at least minimum standards in housing conditions, we do not hesitate to declare that retaliatory eviction cannot be tolerated. There can be no doubt that the slum dweller, even though his home be marred by housing code violations, will pause long before he complains of them if he fears eviction as a consequence. Hence an eviction under the circumstances of this case would not only punish appellant for making a complaint which she had a constitutional right to make, a result which we would not impute to the will of Congress simply on the basis of an essentially procedural enactment, but also would stand as a warning to others that they dare not be so bold, a result which, from the authorization of the housing code, we think Congress affirmatively sought to avoid.

The notion that the effectiveness of remedial legislation will be inhibited if those reporting violations of it can legally be intimidated is so fundamental that a presumption against the legality of such intimidation can be inferred as inherent in the legislation even if it is not expressed in the statute itself. Such an inference was recently drawn by the Supreme Court from the federal labor statutes to strike down under the supremacy clause a Florida statute denying unemployment insurance to workers discharged in retaliation for filing complaints of federally defined unfair labor practices. While we are not confronted with a possible conflict between federal policy and state law, we do have the task of reconciling and harmonizing two federal statutes so as to best effectuate the purposes of each. The proper balance can only be struck by interpreting 45 D.C.Code §§ 902 and 910 as inapplicable where the court's aid is invoked to effect an eviction in retaliation for reporting housing code violations.

This is not, of course, to say that even if the tenant can prove a retaliatory purpose she is entitled to remain in possession in perpetuity. If this illegal purpose is dissipated, the landlord can, in the absence of legislation or a binding contract, evict his tenants or raise their rents for economic or other legitimate reasons, or even for no reason at all. The question of permissible or impermissible purpose is one of fact for the court or jury, and while such a determination is not easy, it is not significantly different from problems with which the courts must deal in a host of other contexts, such as when they must decide whether the employer who discharges a worker has committed an unfair labor practice because he has done so on account of the employee's union activities. As Judge Greene said, "There is no reason why similar factual judgments cannot be made by courts and juries in the context of economic retaliation [against tenants by landlords] for providing information to the government.''

Reversed and remanded.

Notes, Problems, and Questions

1. Today the defense of retaliatory eviction is recognized in a majority of states by either court decision or statute. *See* Restatement (Second) of Property, Landlord and Tenant § 14.8 statutory note & § 14.9 reporter's note 1 (1977). *See, e.g.*, Wright v. Brady, 126 Idaho 671, 889 P.2d 105 (App.1995); Building Monitoring Systems, Inc. v. Paxton, 905 P.2d 1215 (Utah 1995). Moreover, the concept has been expanded in many states to a defense of retaliatory action. In these jurisdictions, a landlord is prohibited from retaliating against a tenant by raising rent or decreasing services. *See* Restatement (Second) of Property, Landlord and Tenant § 14.8 & statutory note (1977). *See, e.g.*, Uniform Residential Landlord and Tenant Act § 5.101(a) (1974).

2. Under the Uniform Residential Landlord and Tenant Act § 5.101(a) (1974) the tenant is protected from retaliation for reporting housing code violations, complaining to the landlord, or joining a tenant's union. Should other tenant activity be protected?

3. Should the defense of retaliatory eviction be recognized where the tenant complains to public authorities, but the landlord is not in violation of the housing code? *See* Dickhut v. Norton, 45 Wis.2d 389, 173 N.W.2d 297 (1970); Wilkins v. Tebbetts, 216 So.2d 477 (Fla.App.1968), *cert. dismissed* 222 So.2d 753 (Fla.1969).

4. How can a tenant prove the landlord's retaliatory purpose? *See* Uniform Residential Landlord and Tenant Act § 5.101(b) (1974) which imposes a rebuttable presumption that eases the tenant's burden of proof.

5. Once a tenant has established the defense of retaliatory eviction, how can the landlord show that the illegal purpose no longer exists? *See* Robinson v. Diamond Housing Corp., 463 F.2d 853 (D.C.Cir.1972).

6. Is the tenant limited to asserting retaliatory action as a defense or may the tenant recover damages from the landlord in an independent cause of action? *Compare* Sims v. Century Kiest Apartments, 567 S.W.2d 526 (Tex.Civ.App.1978) *and* Murphy v. Smallridge, 196 W.Va. 35, 468 S.E.2d 167 (1996) *with* Weisman v. Middleton, 390 A.2d 996 (D.C.App.1978). In this regard consider §§ 4.107 and 5.101 of the Uniform Residential Landlord and Tenant Act (1974).

7. Should the defense of retaliatory eviction be accepted in a commercial context? *Compare* William C. Cornitius, Inc. v. Wheeler, 276 Or. 747, 556 P.2d 666 (1976) *with* Windward Partners v. Delos Santos, 59 Hawaii 104, 577 P.2d 326 (1978). *See also* Restatement (Second) Property, Landlord and Tenant § 14.8 reporter's note 1 (1977).

8. In 1974, New Jersey effectuated a basic change in landlord-tenant law with the adoption of the Anti–Eviction Act. N.J.Stat.Ann. § 2A:18–61.1 (1987 & Supp.1998). The statute provides that no landlord of a residential property "may evict or fail to renew any lease of any premises * * * except

for good cause * * * "The enumerated grounds for good cause include failure to pay rent, disorderly or destructive behavior, violation of lease covenants or "reasonable rules and regulations of the landlord," or non-payment of reasonable rent increases. The landlord may withdraw the property from the housing market, but a three-year notice is required for condominium conversion. Note, *New Jersey's Anti–Eviction Act,* 11 Seton Hall L.Rev. 311 (1980). What effect will this statute have on the housing market in New Jersey? Does the statute represent a sound approach? *See* Les Gertrude Associates v. Walko, 262 N.J.Super. 544, 621 A.2d 522 (1993) (finding tenant's stealing money from coin-operated washing machine owned by landlord did not constitute good cause for eviction under statute). *See generally* Bell, *Providing Security of Tenure for Residential Tenants: Good Faith as a Limitation on the Landlord's Right to Terminate,* 19 Ga.L.Rev. 483 (1985); Salzberg & Zibelman, *Good Cause Eviction,* 21 Willamette L.Rev. 61 (1985).

4. ILLEGAL ACTIVITY BY TENANT

PHILLIPS NEIGHBORHOOD HOUSING TRUST v. BROWN

Court of Appeals of Minnesota, 1997.
564 N.W.2d 573.

HAROLD W. SCHULTZ, JUDGE.

After appellant's 20-year-old son, a co-tenant of her apartment, was found to have illegal drugs on the premises in violation of the lease, respondent landlord brought this unlawful detainer action to recover possession of the apartment. The housing referee found for the landlord. Appellant sought judicial review of the referee's decision, and the district court affirmed. Because the lease clearly gives respondent the right to cancel the lease and bring an unlawful detainer action against a tenant who engages in illegal activity on the premises, we affirm.

FACTS

Respondent Phillips Neighborhood Housing Trust, c/o Perennial Properties, Inc. (PNHT), owns and operates rental property in Minneapolis. PNHT residents receive federal assistance with their rent payments. Appellant Mary Brown and her son, Anthony Brown, 20, applied for and received PNHT occupancy.

PNHT management went over the lease regulations with Mary and Anthony Brown, who indicated that they understood the lease. Anthony Brown was required to sign the lease because he was an adult. He, Mary Brown, and her two minor daughters were listed as persons who live in the apartment. Mary Brown testified that she intended to have Anthony Brown live with her in the apartment so she could maintain more control over him.

Less than a week after the Browns moved in, police were called to the apartment because Anthony Brown was threatening violence. The police found crack cocaine in the apartment. It is undisputed that the cocaine was the property of Anthony Brown and that neither Mary Brown nor her daughters knew of its presence. Pursuant to PNHT's policy of terminating leases when illegal drugs are found in an apartment and to its lease providing for cancellation in case of illegal activity, it terminated the Browns' lease as of June 30, 1996, and brought an unlawful detainer action.

ISSUE

When a lease provides that a landlord may cancel the lease and bring an unlawful detainer action against a tenant who engages in illegal activity, and one of two co-tenants engages in illegal activity, may the landlord bring an unlawful detainer action to recover possession of the premises?

ANALYSIS

Standard of Review

Unlawful detainer is a civil proceeding, and the only issue for determination is whether the facts alleged in the complaint are true. Our standard of review is whether the trial court's findings of fact are clearly erroneous.

Minneapolis Community Dev. Agency v. Smallwood, 379 N.W.2d 554, 555 (Minn.App.1985).

The lease agreement signed by Mary and Anthony Brown provided that:

> RESIDENT Promises * * * not to act in a loud, * * * unlawful or dangerous manner * * * or to allow his/her family or guests to do so * * * [and] to refrain from such illegal activity or other activities on or away from the premises which impairs or down grades the physical or social environment * * * [and that v]iolation of any of the provisions of this section * * * is a material violation of this lease and at its option MANAGEMENT may cancel this lease and bring unlawful detainer proceedings to evict RESIDENT.

It is undisputed that Anthony Brown, a resident in terms of the lease, had illegal drugs on the premises. Pursuant to the lease, PNHT then had the option to cancel the lease and bring unlawful detainer proceedings. It exercised that option.

Appellant argues first that the lease should not have been cancelled, but rewritten, eliminating Anthony Brown as a lessee and resident. However, PNHT was entitled to have its lease enforced, not rewritten. *See id.* at 556 ("[A] landlord's right of action for unlawful detainer is complete upon a tenant's violation of a lease condition."); *Minneapolis Pub. Hous. Auth. v. Greene*, 463 N.W.2d 558 (Minn.App.1990) (upholding eviction upon lease termination of all tenants where a controlled substance was found on the premises and the son of one tenant was arrested for possession).

Appellant also argues that she did not violate the lease and that she had no control over Anthony, who did violate it. However, the lease provides that if the prohibition against drugs is violated, PNHT has the option of voiding the lease. Appellant's right to the apartment derives only from the lease. "It is well established that a tenant under various public housing programs possesses no absolute right to public housing and may be evicted for lease violations or other good cause." *Smallwood*, 379 N.W.2d at 556. Under the terms of the lease appellant signed and said she understood, PNHT is entitled to cancel the lease and pursue an unlawful detainer against appellant.

We are aware that eviction is a harsh remedy that will not be enforced when the party seeking eviction has another adequate remedy. *See 1985 Robert St. Assoc. v. Menard, Inc.*, 403 N.W.2d 900, 902 (Minn.App.1987). However, PNHT has an obligation to provide a safe environment for its tenants, and there is a strong public policy interest in eliminating drugs from subsidized housing. Evicting those who violate the lease by having controlled substances in their apartments is PNHT's most effective, if not its only effective, means of eliminating drugs and providing a safe environment. "[T]he Housing Authority is not required to permit lessees to remain in its project if they are dangerous, destructive, or harmful to others." *Smallwood*, 379 N.W.2d at 557.

Because the lease so clearly provides that PNHT may cancel the lease and recover possession of the premises when a resident engages in illegal activity, we need not address whether Minn.Stat. § 504.181 (1996) also provides that right.

Decision

Pursuant to the terms of their lease agreement, PNHT had the right to bring an unlawful detainer action to recover an apartment when a resident of that apartment violated the lease prohibition of illegal activity.

Affirmed.

Notes and Questions

1. *Phillips Neighborhood Housing Trust* raises the question of what the landlord may do when the tenant uses the premises for illegal purposes. At common law the landlord could recover damages and obtain injunctive relief against the tenant's illegal use of the premises. Today, statutes in several states also give the landlord the option of terminating the lease if the tenant engages in certain specified illegal activity on the leased premises. The landlord, of course, could reserve a similar right in the lease itself. *See* Restatement (Second) of Property, Landlord and Tenant § 12.5, reporter's note & statutory note (1977). *See also* section nine of the sample lease on page 7.

2. Illegal drug transactions by tenants pose an acute dilemma for landlords. Congress has provided for civil forfeiture of real property used in connection with violations of federal drug control laws. Apartment buildings are subject to forfeiture when tenants have committed drug-related offenses.

See Glesner, *Landlords as Cops: Tort, Nuisance & Forfeiture Standards Imposing Liability on Landlords For Crime on the Premises,* 42 Case W.Res.L.Rev. 679, 740–756 (1992); Note, *Real Property Forfeiture Under Federal Drug Laws: Does the Punishment Outweigh the Crime?,* 20 Hastings Const.L.Q. 247, 263–264 (1992). What steps should landlords take in the event that tenants engage in illegal drug activities?

3.   Ordinances in some localities have imposed on landlords the responsibility for regulating the activity of tenants and preventing illegal conduct. *See* Bloomsburg Landlords Association, Inc. v. Town of Bloomsburg, 912 F.Supp. 790 (M.D.Pa.1995) (upholding constitutionality of ordinance requiring landlords to curtail disruptive behavior by tenants); Zeman v. City of Minneapolis, 552 N.W.2d 548 (Minn.1996) (sustaining constitutionality of ordinance authorizing revocation of city rental license where landlord failed to take appropriate action to curtail tenants' disorderly behavior). Do such ordinances in effect mandate that landlords perform police functions? *See generally* Kanner, *California Makes Landlords Do the Police's Job,* Wall Street Journal, Jan. 27, 1993, at A17.

5.   ABANDONMENT AND SURRENDER

MESILLA VALLEY MALL COMPANY v. CROWN INDUSTRIES

Supreme Court of New Mexico, 1991.
111 N.M. 663, 808 P.2d 633.

OPINION

RANSOM, JUSTICE.

This appeal is from a decision of the trial court that the lessor had accepted the lessee's surrender of a leasehold, relieving the lessee of any further obligation under the lease. There being substantial evidence to support the factual findings of the trial court, and having no disagreement on the applicable principles of law, we affirm.

The essential facts of this case are few and uncontested. Crown Industries, doing business as Lemon Tree, Inc., occupied retail premises at the Mesilla Valley Mall in Las Cruces under a long-term lease with the Mesilla Valley Mall Company. Lemon Tree had attempted to renegotiate the terms of the lease, but the Mall Company refused to make adjustments. Lemon Tree advised the Mall Company that it simply would vacate the premises, and it did so on January 20, 1989. Rent was paid only to February 1, and the unpaid rent under the unexpired portion of the lease totaled $35,056.58.

The Mall Company repossessed the premises and, beginning on February 1, 1989, allowed the Las Cruces Museum of Natural History to occupy the space rent free in the interest of promoting good community relations. The Museum remodeled the premises for its own use and has occupied the premises continuously since it first took possession. The Mall Company describes the Museum as a tenant at sufferance. In the past, the Museum has occupied several locations in the Mall. The

Museum occupied these locations, and the space at issue in this case, with the understanding that it would immediately vacate the premises at the request of the Mall Company should another rent-paying tenant become available.

In April 1989 the Mall Company brought suit to collect all amounts due under the lease. At trial Lemon Tree raised the affirmative defense of surrender and acceptance. The trial court determined that after the lessee had abandoned the property the Museum's rent-free tenancy was for the benefit of the lessor and not the lessee, and that this use was inconsistent with the rights of the lessee. Specifically, the court found "nothing in the lease agreement allowed the Mall to re-enter the property for any other purpose [than to relet for the benefit of the tenant], and, in particular to re-lease the property for no rent and for its own benefit." The court concluded that under the doctrine of surrender and acceptance the lease agreement terminated on February 1, 1989.

In the absence of legal justification, a tenant who abandons occupancy before the expiration of a lease remains liable for rent for the remainder of the term; and, under traditional common-law property rules, the landlord is under no obligation to relet the premises to mitigate the tenant's liability under the lease. 2 R. Powell, *The Law of Real Property* & 249[1] (1991); *Restatement (Second) of Property, Landlord & Tenant* § 12.1(3) (1977). The landlord, however, may elect to retake possession on behalf of the tenant and to relet the premises for the tenant's account. Noce v. Stemen, 77 N.M. 71, 419 P.2d 450 (1966); Heighes v. Porterfield, 28 N.M. 445, 214 P. 323 (1923). Or, the landlord may choose to accept what is in effect the tenant's offer to surrender the leasehold, thereby terminating the lease and leaving the tenant liable only for rent that accrued before the acceptance. *Id.; Restatement (Second) of Property, Landlord & Tenant* § 12.1(3)(a) (1977).

A surrender and acceptance of the lease may arise either from the express agreement of the parties or by operation of law. Here, there is no contention that there was a surrender and acceptance by express agreement of the parties. A surrender by operation of law only can occur when the conduct of the landlord is inconsistent with the continuing rights of the tenant under the lease. Thus, where the landlord has reappropriated the property for his own use and benefit and not for the benefit of the original tenant as well, surrender and the acceptance results by operation of law. Cancellation of the lease occurs under principles of estoppel, because it would be inequitable for either landlord or tenant to assert the continued existence of the lease.

In this case Lemon Tree claims the Mall Company relet the premises solely for its own benefit. The Mall Company admits the presence of the Museum attracts large numbers of potential customers to the Mall and so benefits the Mall Company and its tenants, but the Mall Company claims its actions were permissible under the lease and the lease is controlling. In this case it is true that the lease provides the lessor may relet the premises without terminating the lease. When a clause in a lease permits the landlord to relet the premises, the clause creates a presumption that the re-entry and reletting of the premises was not the acceptance of a surrender or a termination of the lease. However, the reletting still must be for the benefit of the original tenant as well as for the justifiable ends of the landlord. If not, the landlord's actions would be inconsistent with a continued landlord-tenant relationship to which the landlord seeks to hold the tenant. We are in substantial agreement on this point with the discussion of Milton R. Friedman in his respected treatise on leases.

> Any reletting under a survival clause must be for the tenant's benefit in order to preserve the landlord's rights under the clause. A tenant is released, despite a survival clause, if the landlord resumes possession for his own use. A tenant is also released when a landlord relets to a third person rent-free, a result fair enough in view of the lack of benefit to the original tenant. Reletting with a rent concession does not release the original tenant but abates his liability for the period covered by the concession.

2 M. Friedman, *Friedman on Leases* § 16.302, at 1001 (3d ed. 1990).

The lease provisions in this case regarding reletting are consistent with these principles; that is, the lease itself suggests that any reletting will benefit the original tenant. The lease states that if the landlord elects to relet in the event of abandonment of the leased premises, then *rentals received* by the landlord shall be applied against the debts of the tenant who shall remain liable for any deficiency, and any residue shall be held by the landlord and applied in payment of future rent as it becomes due. The lease clearly anticipates *some* payment of rent and in no way suggests that the Mall Company can simply donate the occupancy of the premises to a third party or use the property for any purpose whatsoever.

We believe there was substantial evidence to support the court's finding that the re-entry was for the lessor's own benefit and not for the benefit of the tenant. Consequently, that finding is binding upon us even though there was strong evidence to support a finding to the contrary.[1] The court's conclusion necessarily follows: The Mall Company accepted the surrender of the lease and the lease was terminated by operation of law on February 1, 1989. For these reasons we affirm the judgment of the trial court.

We remand for the trial court to hear and decide the issue of attorney fees to which Lemon Tree may be entitled on appeal under the

---

1. The Mall Company made efforts to release the premises by advertising the space at national trade shows, and by showing the premises to persons or businesses interested in leasing premises in the mall. The Museum understood that it would be required to move on as little as one day's notice if a paying tenant were found for the space. The leasing agent testified the Museum's occupancy in no way affected his abili-ty to relet the premises. The lease provided that reentry by the Mall Company "shall [not] be construed as an election to terminate this lease nor shall it cause a forfeiture of rents or other charges remaining to be paid during the balance of the term hereof, unless a written notice of such intention be given." No written notice was given Lemon Tree.

provision of the lease agreement that the party prevailing in any action brought thereunder shall be entitled to recover its attorney fees.

It Is So Ordered.

Notes and Questions

1. When the landlord chooses to allow the abandoned premises to lie vacant and to seek rent from the tenant, the common law allows the landlord to recover rent only as it falls due, not future rent. *See* tenBraak v. Waffle Shops, Inc., 542 F.2d 919 (4th Cir.1976). However, the parties generally may alter this principle by including in the lease an acceleration clause authorizing the landlord to recover rent for the entire term upon the tenant's breach. *See, e.g.,* Coast Federal Savings and Loan Association v. DeLoach, 362 So.2d 982 (Fla.App.1978), *reasserting jurisdiction after remand* 376 So.2d 1190 (Fla.App.1979). If the landlord enforces a rent acceleration clause, the landlord cannot also recover possession for the landlord's own purposes before the end of the lease term. *See* Quintero–Chadid Corp. v. Gersten, 582 So.2d 685 (Fla.App.1991). For discussion of rent acceleration clauses, see 1 Friedman on Leases § 5.3 (4th ed. 1997).

2. Although the court in *Mesilla Valley Mall* indicated that the landlord could relet without terminating the lease, a split of authority exists on that question. In a handful of states, the lease terminates automatically upon reletting. *See* McGrath v. Shalett, 114 Conn. 622, 159 A. 633 (1932); 2 Friedman on Leases § 16.302 (4th ed. 1997).

AUSTIN HILL COUNTRY REALTY, INC. v. PALISADES PLAZA, INC.

Supreme Court of Texas, 1997.
948 S.W.2d 293.

SPECTOR, JUSTICE, delivered the opinion for a unanimous Court.

* * *

The issue in this case is whether a landlord has a duty to make reasonable efforts to mitigate damages when a tenant defaults on a lease. The court of appeals held that no such duty exists at common law. We hold today that a landlord has a duty to make reasonable efforts to mitigate damages. Accordingly, we reverse the judgment of the court of appeals and remand for a new trial.

I.

Palisades Plaza, Inc., owned and operated an office complex consisting of four office buildings in Austin. Barbara Hill, Annette Smith, and David Jones sold real estate in Austin as a Re/Max real estate brokerage franchise operating through Austin Hill Country Realty, Inc. On September 15, 1992, the Palisades and Hill Country executed a five-year commercial office lease for a suite in the Palisades' office complex. An addendum executed in connection with the lease set the monthly base rent at $3,128 for the first year, $3,519 for the second and third years, and $3,910 for the fourth and fifth years. The parties also signed an improvements agreement that called for the Palisades to convert the shell office space into working offices for Hill Country. The lease was to begin on the "commencement date," which was defined in the lease and the improvements agreement as either (1) the date that Hill Country occupied the suite, or (2) the date that the Palisades substantially completed the improvements or would have done so but for "tenant delay." All parties anticipated that the lease would begin on November 15, 1992.

By the middle of October 1992, the Palisades had nearly completed the improvements. Construction came to a halt on October 21, 1992, when the Palisades received conflicting instructions about the completion of the suite from Hill on one hand and Smith and Jones on the other. By two letters, the Palisades informed Hill Country, Hill, Smith, and Jones that it had received conflicting directives and would not continue with the construction until Hill, Smith, and Jones collectively designated a single representative empowered to make decisions for the trio. Hill, Smith, and Jones did not reply to these letters.

In a letter dated November 19, 1992, the Palisades informed Hill Country, Hill, Smith, and Jones that their failure to designate a representative was an anticipatory breach of contract. The parties tried unsuccessfully to resolve their differences in a meeting. The Palisades then sued Hill Country, Hill, Smith, and Jones (collectively, "Hill Country") for anticipatory breach of the lease.

At trial, Hill Country attempted to prove that the Palisades failed to mitigate the damages resulting from Hill Country's alleged breach. In particular, Hill Country introduced evidence that the Palisades rejected an offer from Smith and Jones to lease the premises without Hill, as well as an offer from Hill and another person to lease the premises without Smith and Jones. Hill Country also tried to prove that, while the Palisades advertised for tenants continuously in a local newspaper, it did not advertise in the commercial-property publication "The Flick Report" as it had in the past. Hill Country requested an instruction asking the jury to reduce the Palisades' damage award by "any amount that you find the [Palisades] could have avoided by the exercise of reasonable care." The trial judge rejected this instruction, stating, "Last time I checked the law, it was that a landlord doesn't have any obligation to try to fill the space." The jury returned a verdict for the Palisades for $29,716 in damages and $16,500 in attorney's fees. The court of appeals affirmed that judgment.

II.

In its only point of error, Hill Country asks this Court to recognize a landlord's duty to make reasonable efforts to mitigate damages when a tenant breaches a lease. * * *

* * *

The traditional common law rule regarding mitigation dictates that landlords have no duty to mitigate damages. See Dawn R. Barker, Note, *Commercial Landlords' Duty upon Tenants' Abandonment—To Mitigate?*, 20 J. Corp. L. 627, 629 (1995). This rule stems from the historical concept that the tenant is owner of the property during the lease term; as long as the tenant has a right to poss[ess] the land, the tenant is liable for rent. See *Reid v. Mutual of Omaha Ins. Co.*, 776 P.2d 896, 902, 905 (Utah 1989). Under this rule, a landlord is not obligated to undertake any action following a tenant's abandonment of the premises but may recover rents periodically for the remainder of the term.

* * *

Texas courts have consistently followed this no-mitigation rule in cases involving a landlord's suit for past due rent.

Some Texas courts have, however, required a landlord to mitigate damages when the landlord seeks a remedy that is contractual in nature, such as anticipatory breach of contract, rather than a real property cause of action. * * *

Other Texas courts have required a landlord to mitigate damages when the landlord reenters or resumes control of the premises. Thus, a landlord currently may be subject to a mitigation requirement depending upon the landlord's actions following breach and the type of lawsuit the landlord pursues.

III.

In discerning the policy implications of a rule requiring landlords to mitigate damages, we are informed by the rules of other jurisdictions. Forty-two states and the District of Columbia have recognized that a landlord has a duty to mitigate damages in at least some situations: when there is a breach of a residential lease, a commercial lease, or both.

Only six states have explicitly held that a landlord has no duty to mitigate in any situation. In South Dakota, the law is unclear.

Those jurisdictions recognizing a duty to mitigate have emphasized the change in the nature of landlord-tenant law since its inception in medieval times. At English common law, the tenant had only contractual rights against the landlord and therefore could not assert common-law real property causes of action to protect the leasehold. Over time, the courts recognized a tenant's right to bring real property causes of action, and tenants were considered to possess an estate in land. The landlord had to give the tenant possession of the land, and the tenant was required to pay rent in return. As covenants in leases have become more complex and the structures on the land have become more important to the parties than the land itself, courts have begun to recognize that a lease possesses elements of both a contract and a conveyance. *See, e.g., Schneiker v. Gordon*, 732 P.2d 603, 607–09 (Colo.1987); *Reid v. Mutual of Omaha Ins. Co.*, 776 P.2d 896, 902, 904 (Utah 1989). Under contract principles, the lease is not a complete conveyance to the tenant for a specified term such that the landlord's duties are fulfilled upon deliverance of the property to the tenant. Rather, a promise to pay in a lease is essentially the same as a promise to pay in any other contract, and a breach of that promise does not necessarily end the landlord's ongoing duties. *Wright v. Baumann*, 239 Or. 410, 398 P.2d 119, 121 (1965). Because of the contractual elements of the modern lease agreement, these courts have imposed upon the landlord the contractual duty to mitigate damages upon the tenant's breach.

Public policy offers further justification for the duty to mitigate. First, requiring mitigation in the landlord-tenant context discourages economic waste and encourages productive use of the property. As the Colorado Supreme Court has written:

> Under traditional property law principles a landlord could allow the property to remain unoccupied while still holding the abandoning tenant liable for rent. This encourages both economic and physical waste. In no other context of which we are aware is an injured party permitted to sit idly by and suffer avoidable economic loss and thereafter to visit the full adverse economic consequences upon the party whose breach initiated the chain of events causing the loss.

Schneiker, 732 P.2d at 610. A mitigation requirement thus returns the property to productive use rather than allowing it to remain idle. Public policy requires that the law "discourage even persons against whom wrongs have been committed from passively suffering economic loss which could be averted by reasonable efforts." *Wright*, 398 P.2d at 121 (quoting C. McCormick, Handbook on the Law of Damages, § 33 (1935)).

Second, a mitigation rule helps prevent destruction of or damage to the leased property. If the landlord is encouraged to let the property remain unoccupied, "the possibility of physical damage to the property through accident or vandalism is increased." *Schneiker*, 732 P.2d at 610.

Third, the mitigation rule is consistent with the trend disfavoring contract penalties. Courts have held that a liquidated damages clause in a contract must represent a reasonable estimate of anticipated damages upon breach. "Similarly, allowing a landlord to leave property idle when it could be profitably leased and forc[ing] an absent tenant to pay rent for that idled property permits the landlord to recover more damages than it may reasonably require to be compensated for the tenant's breach. This is analogous to imposing a disfavored penalty upon the tenant." *Reid*, 776 P.2d at 905–06.

Finally, the traditional justifications for the common law rule have proven unsound in practice. Proponents of the no-mitigation rule suggest that the landlord-tenant relationship is personal in nature, and that the landlord therefore should not be forced to lease to an unwanted tenant. Modern lease arrangements, however, are rarely personal in nature and are usually business arrangements between strangers. Further, the landlord's duty to make reasonable efforts to mitigate does not require that the landlord accept replacement tenants who are financial risks or whose business was precluded by the original lease.

The overwhelming trend among jurisdictions in the United States has thus been toward requiring a landlord to mitigate damages when a tenant abandons the property in breach of the lease agreement. Those courts adopting a mitigation requirement have emphasized the contractual elements of a lease agreement, the public policy favoring productive use of property, and the practicalities of the modern landlord-tenant arrangement as supporting such a duty.

IV.

We are persuaded by the reasoning of those courts that recognize that landlords must mitigate damages upon a tenant's abandonment and failure to pay rent. This Court has recognized the dual nature of a lease as both a conveyance and a contract. Under a contract view, a landlord should be treated no differently than any other aggrieved party to a contract. Further, the public policy of the state of Texas calls for productive use of property as opposed to avoidable economic waste. As Professor McCormick wrote over seventy years ago, the law

> which permits the landlord to stand idly by the vacant, abandoned premises and treat them as the property of the tenant and recover full rent, [should] yield to the more realistic notions of social advantage which in other fields of the law have forbidden a recovery for damages which the plaintiff by reasonable efforts could have avoided.

Charles McCormick, *The Rights of the Landlord Upon Abandonment of the Premises by the Tenant*, 23 Mich.L.Rev. 211, 221–22 (1925). Finally, we have recognized that contract penalties are disfavored in Texas. *Stewart v. Basey*, 150 Tex. 666, 245 S.W.2d 484, 486 (1952) (landlord should not receive more or less than actual damages upon tenant's breach). A landlord should not be allowed to collect rent from an abandoning tenant when the landlord can, by reasonable efforts, relet the premises and avoid incurring some damages. We therefore recognize that a landlord has a duty to make reasonable efforts to mitigate damages when the tenant breaches the lease and abandons the property, unless the commercial landlord and tenant contract otherwise.

V.

To ensure the uniform application of this duty by the courts of this state, and to guide future landlords and tenants in conforming their conduct to the law, we now consider several practical considerations that will undoubtedly arise. We first consider the level of conduct by a landlord that will satisfy the duty to mitigate. The landlord's mitigation duty has been variously stated in other jurisdictions. *See, e.g., Reid*, 776 P.2d at 906 ("objective commercial reasonableness"); *Schneiker*, 732 P.2d at 611 ("reasonable efforts"); Cal. Civ.Code § 1951.2(c)(2) ("reasonably and in a good-faith effort"). Likewise, the courts of this state have developed differing language regarding a party's duty to mitigate in other contexts. We hold that the landlord's duty to mitigate requires the landlord to use objectively reasonable efforts to fill the premises when the tenant vacates in breach of the lease.

We stress that this is not an absolute duty. The landlord is not required to simply fill the premises with any willing tenant; the replacement tenant must be suitable under the circumstances. Nor does the landlord's failure to mitigate give rise to a cause of action by the tenant. Rather, the landlord's failure to use reasonable efforts to mitigate damages bars the landlord's recovery against the breaching tenant only to the extent that damages reasonably could have been avoided. Similarly, the amount of damages that the landlord actually avoided by releasing the premises will reduce the landlord's recovery.

Further, we believe that the tenant properly bears the burden of proof to demonstrate that the landlord has mitigated or failed to mitigate damages and the amount by which the landlord reduced or could have reduced its damages. The traditional rule in other contexts is that the breaching party must show that the nonbreaching party could have reduced its damages. In the landlord-tenant context, although there is some split of authority, many other jurisdictions have placed the burden of proving mitigation or failure to mitigate upon the breaching tenant.

* * *

The final issue to resolve regarding the duty to mitigate is to which types of actions by the landlord the duty will apply. Traditionally, Texas courts have regarded the landlord as having four causes of action against a tenant for breach of the lease and abandonment. First, the landlord can maintain the lease, suing for rent as it becomes due. Second, the landlord can treat the breach as an anticipatory repudiation, repossess, and sue for the present value of future rentals reduced by the reasonable cash market value of the property for the remainder of the lease term. Third, the landlord can treat the breach as anticipatory, repossess, release the property, and sue the tenant for the difference between the contractual rent and the amount received from the new tenant. Fourth, the landlord can declare the lease forfeited (if the lease so provides) and relieve the tenant of liability for future rent.

The landlord must have a duty to mitigate when suing for anticipatory repudiation. Because the cause of action is contractual in nature, the contractual duty to mitigate should apply. The landlord's option to maintain the lease and sue for rent as it becomes due, however, is more troubling. To require the landlord to mitigate in that instance would force the landlord to reenter the premises and thereby risk terminating the lease or accepting the tenant's surrender. We thus hold that, when exercising the option to maintain the lease in effect and sue for rent as it becomes due following the tenant's breach and abandonment, the landlord has a duty to mitigate only if (1) the landlord actually reenters, or (2) the lease allows the landlord to reenter the premises without accepting surrender, forfeiting the lease, or being construed as evicting the tenant. A suit for anticipatory repudiation, an actual reentry, or a contractual right of reentry subject to the above conditions will therefore give rise to the landlord's duty to mitigate damages upon the tenant's breach and abandonment.

VI.

In their first amended answer, Hill Country and Barbara Hill specifically contended that the Palisades failed to mitigate its damages. Because the court of appeals upheld the trial court's refusal to submit their mitigation instruction, we reverse the judgment of the court of appeals and remand for a new trial.

Note

Uniform Residential Landlord and Tenant Act § 4.203(c) (1974) incorporates the mitigation of damages concept.

6. RETENTION OF SECURITY DEPOSIT

Leases typically contain a provision requiring the tenant to make a security deposit. *See* section one of the sample lease on page 6. When the tenant abandons the premises, the landlord usually retains the tenant's security deposit. Although such action may be appropriate in the case of abandonment, landlords sometimes keep security deposits under questionable circumstances. *See* 1 American Law of Property § 3.73 (1952). Consequently, statutes have been enacted in several states limiting the amount of the deposit, requiring that it be refunded within a certain time, and specifying that any deductions be itemized. Some state statutes also require the landlord to pay interest on certain deposits. *See* Restatement (Second) Property, Landlord and Tenant § 12.1 statutory note 6 (1977); Uniform Residential Landlord and Tenant Act § 2.101 & comment (1974).

BRUCE v. ATTAWAY

Supreme Court of New Mexico, 1996.
121 N.M. 755, 918 P.2d 341.

FROST, CHIEF JUSTICE.

Plaintiff–Appellant Elmer Bruce appeals from a judgment of $125.00 in favor of Defendant–Appellee Vaughn Attaway. Bruce contends that Attaway improperly retained his $150.00 security deposit in violation of the Uniform Owner–Resident Relations Act, NMSA 1978, §§ 47–8–1 to 51 (Repl.Pamp.1995) (the Act). We affirm.

I. FACTS

On September 27, 1993, Bruce entered into an agreement to rent an apartment from Attaway. Before moving in, Bruce paid Attaway one month's rent, totalling $275.00, for the month of October. Bruce also paid a security deposit of $150.00. On October 17, 1993, Bruce vacated the premises without providing thirty-days' notice to Attaway, as required by the Act, § 47–8–37. Attaway retained Bruce's $150.00 security deposit. Attaway did not send Bruce an itemization of deductions from the security deposit. Attaway does not claim on appeal that Bruce damaged the premises or that Attaway retained the security deposit to pay for repairs necessitated by Bruce's occupancy.

Bruce sued Attaway in magistrate court for return of the security deposit. The magistrate court dismissed Bruce's claim. Bruce appealed the dismissal to the district court. After a trial de novo, the district court found in favor of Attaway. The court found that Bruce did not provide thirty-days' notice before moving out and concluded that Bruce owed Attaway $275.00 for November rent. The court offset the $150.00 security deposit and awarded Attaway $125.00, the remainder of the November rent amount.

II. DISCUSSION

In this case we are once again asked to interpret Section 47–8–18 of the Act. The pertinent parts of this section provide:

> C. Upon termination of the residency, property or money held by the owner as deposits may be applied by the owner to the payment of rent and the amount of damages which the owner has suffered by reason of the resident's noncompliance with the rental agreement or Section 47–8–22 NMSA 1978. No deposit shall be retained to cover normal wear and tear. In the event actual cause exists for retaining any portion of the deposit, the owner shall provide the resident with an itemized written list of the deductions from the deposit and the balance of the deposit, if any, within thirty days of the date of termination of the rental agreement or resident departure, whichever is later. The owner is deemed to have complied with this section by mailing the statement and any payment required to the last known address of the resident. Nothing in this section shall preclude the owner from retaining portions of the deposit for nonpayment of rent or utilities, repair work or other legitimate damages.

> If the owner fails to provide the resident with a written statement of deductions from the deposit and the balance shown by the statement to be due, within thirty days of the termination of the tenancy, the owner:

>> (1) shall forfeit the right to withhold any portion of the deposit;

>> (2) shall forfeit the right to assert any counterclaim in any action brought to recover that deposit;

>> (3) shall be liable to the resident for court costs and reasonable attorneys' fees; and

>> (4) shall forfeit the right to assert an independent action against the resident for damages to the rental property.

Section 47–8–18.

Bruce argues that Attaway forfeited his right to retain the security deposit by failing to send him a written itemization of damages as required by Section 47–8–18(D). For support, Bruce relies on *Garcia v. Thong*, 119 N.M. 704, 895 P.2d 226 (1995), a case in which we recently addressed the proper interpretation of Section 47–8–18.

Garcia involved a landlord who retained a tenant's security deposit to pay for alleged damages to the property, without providing written itemization of deductions from the deposit. We held that, under Section 47–8–18, if a landlord does not provide the former tenant with an itemized listing of damages to the property within thirty days of vacancy, the landlord forfeits any "right to withhold any portion of the deposit or to file suit for the alleged damages" to the property.

However, this case presents a slightly different question than that in *Garcia*. Here we are not confronted with a landlord retaining some or all of a security deposit to pay for alleged property damage. Instead, Attaway applied the security deposit to a rent payment owed by Bruce when Bruce failed to give proper notice before terminating the rental agreement.

Section 47–8–37(B) of the Act governs termination of a monthly rental agreement. This Section provides, "The owner or the resident may terminate a month-to-month residency by a written notice given to the other at least thirty days prior to the periodic rental date specified in the notice." Bruce concedes that he did not provide notice of his intended termination thirty days prior to October 31, 1993. Accordingly, Bruce was still responsible for paying rent for the month of November in the amount of $275.00. See *T.W.I.W., Inc. v. Rhudy*, 96 N.M. 354, 358, 630 P.2d 753, 757 (1981) (holding that termination notice set for period shorter than thirty days only took effect at the end of rental period following thirty-day interval).

Attaway contends that because Bruce did not pay rent for November, Attaway was entitled to apply the security deposit to Bruce's deficient rent payment without sending a written itemization. We agree. As we explained in *Garcia*, the purpose of Section 47–8–18 is to prevent the unexplained retention of security deposits to pay for alleged damages to the property. One problem addressed by this notice and accounting requirement is the fact that after the tenant vacates the property, the landlord has sole control over the premises. If the landlord were allowed to retain the security deposit without providing an itemized accounting of damages to the tenant within thirty days, the landlord would then be in the advantageous position of having the opportunity to make unnecessary repairs or excessive improvements at the tenant's expense. In the process, the landlord could end up removing any evidence of the alleged damage, thereby denying the tenant any effective means of challenging the landlord's assertions of property damage or contesting the reasonableness of the amount withheld. It is for this reason we held in *Garcia* that failure to comply with Section 47–8–18(C) results in forfeiture of any "right to withhold any portion of the deposit or to file suit *for the alleged damages*" to the property. (emphasis added).

These same considerations do not exist when the landlord applies the security deposit to a deficient rent payment. See § 47–8–18(C) (allowing owner to apply deposit to rent payment). Under such circumstances, the amount in controversy is fixed and certain, and neither party is at an unfair advantage in proving whether the rent payment is deficient. Section 47–8–18, therefore, would not mandate an itemized accounting of a deposit applied to a deficient rent payment when the amount of the payment is not at issue.

* * *

III. CONCLUSION

For the foregoing reasons, we affirm the judgment of the trial court.

* * *

Problem

After the expiration of an apartment lease, the landlord withheld part of the tenant's security deposit by mistake, refunding the amount mistakenly withheld after the expiration of the thirty-day statutory period for returning deposits. Is the landlord liable under a provision in the statute permitting tenants to recover damages from landlords who "wrongfully" withhold security deposits? *See* Battis v. Hofmann, 832 S.W.2d 937 (Mo.App.1992).

7. COMMERCIAL FRUSTRATION

SMITH v. ROBERTS

Appellate Court of Illinois, Fourth District, 1977.
54 Ill.App.3d 910, 12 Ill.Dec. 648, 370 N.E.2d 271.

MILLS, JUSTICE.

We have here a lease.

And with it we have the doctrine of commercial frustration.

The trial judge held that the doctrine applied and that the lease was terminated thereby.

He was right. We affirm.

The Smiths and Roberts Brothers entered into a lease agreement for the rental of the first floor and basement of property located in Springfield at 111–113 North Sixth Street. Roberts Brothers was already operating a men's clothing store next to the leased premises and intended to make an opening through their east wall and Smiths' west wall in order to establish a department which would be called the Gas Light Room. Thereafter, the main store building of Roberts Brothers was completely destroyed by fire. Questions concerning the rights and liabilities of the parties under the lease were raised as a result of that conflagration and those questions then ripened into litigation.

After Roberts Brothers failed to reoccupy the leased premises—which suffered only smoke damage, the Smiths filed suit for breach of the lease. * * * The trial court found that the lease had been terminated because the destruction of Roberts Brothers' main store excused performance on its part. * * *

We concur with the trial judge and affirm.

In their complaint, the Smiths alleged that the clothing store had violated its obligations under the lease and that the leased premises had been restored and repaired according to provisions of the lease. Roberts Brothers' defense to the complaint was two-fold: (1) the lease had been terminated because of the "doctrine of commercial frustration"; and (2) the lease had been terminated because of the "doctrine of constructive eviction". We need only consider the first defense since it is dispositive of the question.

At issue is the doctrine of *commercial frustration:*

"The doctrine of frustration is an extension of this exception to cases where the cessation or nonexistence of some particular condition or state of things has rendered performance impossible and the object of the contract frustrated. It rests on the view that where from the nature of the contract and the surrounding circumstances the parties when entering into the contract must have known that it could not be performed unless some particular condition or state of things would continue to exist, the parties must be deemed, when entering into the contract, to have made their bargain on the footing that such particular condition or state of things would continue to exist, and the contract therefore must be construed as subject to an implied condition that the parties shall be excused in case performance becomes impossible from such condition or state of things ceasing to exist." Leonard v. Autocar Sales & Service Co. (1945) 392 Ill. 182, 187–188, 64 N.E.2d 477, 479–480, cert. denied, 327 U.S. 804.

The doctrine of commercial frustration is not to be applied liberally. However, the defense of commercial frustration is a viable doctrine in Illinois and will be applied when the defendant has satisfied two rigorous tests: (1) the frustrating event was not reasonably foreseeable; and (2) the value of counterperformance by the less[or] had been totally or nearly totally destroyed by the frustrating cause.

The factual circumstances here satisfy these stringent tests. First, although it might be foreseeable that the main Roberts Brothers' store would be destroyed and the leased premises would remain intact, it is a remote contingency to provide for in a lease. The parties were, in fact, diligent enough to put a catastrophe clause in the lease concerning destruction of the *leased* premises. We find that their failure to include such a clause as to Roberts Brothers' main store was not due to a lack of diligence since such a contingency was not reasonably foreseeable.

The second horn of the two-prong test is also satisfied the value of the Smith counterperformance was totally or nearly totally destroyed. Although it would be physically possible to operate the leased premises as a separate entity, testimony revealed that operations would have to be changed drastically in order to make the premises self-sufficient. Furthermore, the record clearly demonstrates that the leased premises were never intended to be autonomous. Therefore, the trial court's finding that the existence of the main store was an implied condition of the contract between the parties and that its destruction frustrated the lease is an accurate interpretation of the lease. The court's finding results in the fairest disposition of the parties' respective interests.

* * *

Affirmed.

Notes and Questions

1. In contrast to *Smith*, other courts have been reluctant to terminate leases under the doctrine of commercial frustration. *See* Butler Manufacturing Company, Inc. v. Americold Corporation, 850 F.Supp. 952 (D.Kan.1994) (concluding that fire at warehouse facility was foreseeable, and observing that "Kansas courts have been extremely strict in determining whether a supervening event was reasonably foreseeable and controllable by the parties"); Lloyd v. Murphy, 25 Cal.2d 48, 153 P.2d 47 (1944) (finding that automobile dealer was not entitled to terminate lease because United States involvement in World War II and consequent restrictions on sale of cars was deemed foreseeable). What policy objective is served by these decisions?

2. Is a tenant's right to assign or sublease the premises relevant in determining whether the value of the lease has been destroyed?

H. GOVERNMENTAL INVOLVEMENT IN THE RENTAL HOUSING MARKET

1. RENT CONTROL

Regulation of maximum rents and rental practices has long been a source of controversy. Concerned about an inadequate supply of rental housing and high rent charges, some localities have enacted rent control ordinances. Such laws in effect treat privately-owned rental property as a regulated public utility. Landlords often assert that these ordinances constitute an unconstitutional taking of their property without compensation in violation of the Fifth Amendment. *See, e.g.,* Pennell v. City of San Jose, 485 U.S. 1 (1988). *See generally* J. Ely, *The Guardian of Every Other Right: A Constitutional History of Property Rights* 114–115 (2d ed. 1998) (discussing origins of rent control).

152 VALPARAISO ASSOCIATES v. CITY OF COTATI

California Court of Appeal, First District, 1997.
56 Cal.App.4th 378, 65 Cal.Rptr.2d 551.

PETERSON, PRESIDING JUSTICE.

Appellants 152 Valparaiso Associates, 402 Grand Avenue Associates, and 378 Belmont Associates contend the trial court wrongly sustained a demurrer and dismissed this lawsuit, which alleges that the rent control system of respondents the City of Cotati and the Cotati Rent Appeals Board has accomplished a taking of appellants' property without just compensation, in violation of the Fifth and Fourteenth Amendments to the United States Constitution and article I, section 19 of the California Constitution. We agree and, therefore, vacate the judgment of dismissal.

I. FACTS AND PROCEDURAL HISTORY

Appellants are the owners of residential rental property in Cotati. Their property is subject to respondents' rent control ordinance and regulations.

The stated purpose of respondents' rent control laws includes the preservation of an affordable stock of residential rental units in the city for low income renters, renters who are aged or on fixed incomes, and students.

However, according to the allegations of the first amended complaint and the United States Census Bureau figures referred to therein, respondents' rent control laws have not advanced those goals. The complaint supported by the census data referenced and incorporated therein alleges: (1) The city has suffered a loss of its housing stock of rental apartments, even though every comparable city in Northern California without rent control has experienced an increase in its rental housing supply; (2) the number of low income renters has "dropped dramatically" in the city, even though in cities without rent control, the number of such low income renters has increased; (3) the "reduced availability of affordable housing caused by the Rent Ordinance" has caused the number of college students living in the city to decline. Appellants contend that respondents' rent control laws, to which appellants' property is subject, have, thus, "failed to substantially advance" the stated objectives of the rent control laws, since the results those laws have produced are simply the "gentrification" of Cotati.

Appellants, who are subject to those rent control laws, made certain capital improvements to their rental property. They sought a rent increase sufficient to give them a fair return on their investment in those capital improvements. The rent board refused to grant any such increase. As a result, appellants' allege the rate of return on their investments will be zero, resulting in an unconstitutional taking of their investment property.

In sum, appellants allege that respondents' rent control ordinances effected an unconstitutional taking of appellants' property, because they failed to substantially advance their stated public goals and denied appellants a fair return on their investment.

The trial court sustained without leave to amend a demurrer to appellants' first amended complaint encompassing such allegations. Appellants filed a timely appeal from a resulting judgment dismissing that complaint.

II. Discussion

The trial court erred in sustaining the demurrer to the first amended complaint. Appellants have alleged facts which, if true, would tend to establish that respondents' rent control laws have effected a taking of appellants' property, in violation of the federal and California Constitutions. We vacate the dismissal and remand with instructions to overrule the demurrer.

A. Background of Rent Control Decisions

This court (Division Five) has had many occasions to review the tortured history of rent control in California, most recently in *City of Berkeley v. City of Berkeley Rent Stabilization Bd.* (1994) 27 Cal.App.4th 951, 958–961, 33 Cal.Rptr.2d 317 (*Berkeley Rent*). We summarize that history very briefly here, in order to provide necessary legal background.

Our Supreme Court first overturned a rent control law as unconstitutional in *Birkenfeld v. City of Berkeley* (1976) 17 Cal.3d 129, 169, 130 Cal.Rptr. 465, 550 P.2d 1001 (*Birkenfeld*). The *Birkenfeld* court held that the Berkeley rent control law before it "drastically and unnecessarily restricts the rent control board's power to adjust rents, thereby making inevitable the arbitrary imposition of unreasonably low rent ceilings. It is clear that if the base rent for all controlled units were to remain as the maximum rent for an indefinite period many or most rent ceilings would be or become confiscatory."

In light of *Birkenfeld*, the Berkeley rent laws were amended to provide for periodic upward adjustments of rent levels, in order to prevent the gradual confiscation of property. Our Supreme Court subsequently upheld those amended laws against a facial challenge in *Fisher v. City of Berkeley* (1984) 37 Cal.3d 644, 679–684, 209 Cal.Rptr. 682, 693 P.2d 261 (*Fisher*). The *Fisher* court specifically noted that under the revised ordinance, the rent board had the power to adjust rents upward in order to allow landlords a reasonable return on their investment. The *Fisher* court also cautioned, however: "We must stress ... the limited scope of our inquiry in facial challenges. ... As we made clear in *Birkenfeld*, whether rental regulations are fair or confiscatory depends ultimately on the result reached."

Berkeley was not the only city to enact rent control laws, and our Supreme Court was not the only court which was required to deal with these issues. This court (Division Five) first dealt with the Cotati rent control laws in *Cotati Alliance for Better Housing v. City of Cotati* (1983) 148 Cal.App.3d 280, 195 Cal.Rptr. 825 (*Cotati I*). In *Cotati I*, we held such a rent control ordinance is not facially unconstitutional if it provides landlords " 'a fair and reasonable return on their investment.' " Of course, the corollary to that holding is that a rent control ordinance which fails to actually provide a fair and reasonable rate of return in practice is unconstitutional, because it has taken private property without proper compensation. As we noted in *Cotati I*, the failure of a rent control law to provide a fair return on investment "might well violate prohibitions against the taking of private property for public use without just compensation contained in the ... United States Constitution and article I, section 19, of the California Constitution."

* * *

* * * [I]n *Berkeley Rent* * * * we concluded: "The judicial response to over two decades of ... rent control controversies has consistently established these principles: Rent control schemes are unconstitutional if they deprive a landlord of a fair return on his investment; that condition [requiring a fair rate of return] if not present in an ordinance will be implied therein; and whether rental regulations are fair or (unconstitutionally) confiscatory is determined by the result they produce." Under *Berkeley Rent*, therefore, it is the *result produced*, not merely the result intended, which must be examined in determining whether a rent control ordinance has unconstitutionally taken private property without just compensation.

B. Application of Precedent and Constitutional Principles to the Case at Bench

The constitutional focus on the results produced by rent control laws is critical in this case. Appellants' first amended complaint alleged certain results were produced by respondents' rent control laws; and for purposes of ruling on this appeal from a judgment of dismissal following the sustaining of a demurrer without leave to amend, we are required to treat those results as legally established. * * *

We are, therefore, required to assume, for purposes of ruling on this appeal, that the results produced by rent control in Cotati were as follows. Contrary to the stated purposes of respondents' rent control program, the results it produced were that poor people, the aged, students, and those on fixed incomes were gradually driven out of Cotati; and the stock of affordable rental apartments was not preserved, but instead was significantly depleted. In addition, appellants allege and we are required to assume that the rent board, contrary to the requirements of providing a fair rate of return, has decided appellants' rate of return on their capital improvements to their property should be zero. Under those posited factual circumstances, we are asked to determine whether it is an unconstitutional taking for the rent board to deny any rate of return on such investment to property owners, resulting in poor people and others who need rental housing being driven from the city. We conclude appellants have stated a claim for an unconstitutional taking of their property under the posited facts.

As the federal and California Supreme Courts have repeatedly observed, "The application of a general ... law to particular property effects a taking if the ordinance does not substantially advance legitimate state interests, *or* denies an owner economically viable use of his land." (*Agins v. Tiburon* (1980) 447 U.S. 255, 260; accord, *Ehrlich v. City of Culver City* (1996) 12 Cal.4th 854, 870, 50 Cal.Rptr.2d 242, 911 P.2d 429.) In the present case, appellants have alleged a state of facts which satisfies both prongs of this *Agins* test, by contending and offering to prove that respondents' rent control laws have not substantially advanced legitimate state interests and have denied appellants any rate of return on their investments in capital improvements to their property. Under the more recent federal Supreme Court cases, general land use regulations will be held to have effected a regulatory taking if the results produced by the regulatory scheme do not advance a legitimate state interest. (See *Nollan v. California Coastal Comm'n* (1987) 483 U.S. 825, 834); *Dolan v. City of Tigard* (1994) 512 U.S. 374, 385.) Under the so-called *Nollan/Dolan* test, which also stems from the language of *Agins*, a property owner may challenge a regulatory taking if it does not advance a legitimate state interest, even if the taking does not deprive the property owner of *all* economically viable use of the property.

* * *

In the context of the present case, there are also compelling constitutional reasons underlying our analysis. As the federal Supreme Court reemphasized most recently in *Dolan*: "One of the principal purposes of the Takings Clause is 'to bar Government from forcing some people alone to bear public burdens which, in all fairness and justice, should be borne by the public as a whole.'" (512 U.S. at p. 384, quoting from *Armstrong v. United States* (1960) 364 U.S. 40, 49). If housing the poor and other vulnerable groups is a legitimate public burden—and we do not doubt that it is—then " 'in all fairness and justice' "and under the federal and California Constitutions, appellants contend this burden must be borne by the public as a whole, not just owners of rental property. It is not only unconstitutional, it is also—appellants suggest—futile and self-defeating to attempt to finance relief for the poor by regulatory exactions on local owners of private rental property. Such exactions might be justified as attempts to support a legitimate state interest, but they could still constitute takings. In addition, if the true purpose of rent control is indeed providing housing to the poor, then an examination of the actual results produced by such policies might be relevant to show they do not in fact substantially advance this interest. If that were shown, then this might suggest such rent control policies actually serve other purposes, at the expense of property owners, who are not so numerous as tenants. The danger that private property will be taken for an alleged public use by a local electoral majority is ever present in a rent control scheme; and we must examine the results produced, not simply the noble intentions, of such programs to determine their true constitutional effect.

We must for these reasons also reject respondents' argument that their demurrer was properly sustained because appellants' allegations— that rent control in Cotati has not served any legitimate state interest— are simply allegations and are only supported by the most recent United States Census Bureau data. Respondents seem to contend that the most recent census data is not current enough to support such allegations, and that a demurrer may be sustained unless appellants present some more recent, incontrovertible proof in the pleadings. There are numerous problems with this argument. First, for purposes of a demurrer, the courts must accept all properly pleaded allegations as true. We are not concerned at this stage with the means by which appellants might prove their allegations. Second, respondents' argument that the most recent U.S. census data, issued to the public 17 months before the filing of this lawsuit and within a few months of the rent board action challenged here, lacks evidentiary significance because another decennial census will be conducted in the year 2000, ignores pertinent state and federal authority. The most recent U.S. decennial census data is favored by an evidentiary presumption, which requires "clear and convincing" evidence to rebut it.

California courts also routinely rely on the data from the most recent federal decennial census, even though it may necessarily be somewhat out of date, because it is still the best available source of such information.

We further observe that respondents are free if they wish, in later trial court proceedings, to attempt to introduce contrary evidence of subsequent census data, if it exists, allegedly showing, inter alia, that despite the documented exodus from Cotati by the poor and other groups reflected in the most recent federal decennial census, poor people have in fact more recently flocked to Cotati to live in an increasing inventory of rental apartments; that respondents' rent control laws are applied so as to lure private investors and builders; or that the latter will receive a reasonable rate of return on their investment.

We need only hold here that respondents were proscribed from barring appellants' allegations and proof by filing a demurrer, based on allegations such contrary evidence was or would be supported by more recent population data.

* * *

The time has arrived to litigate the truth or falsity of appellants' contentions that Cotati's application of its rent control program has unconstitutionally confiscated landlords' property. Confiscation may or may not have occurred in this case; and respondents' rent control ordinance may or may not have substantially advanced some legitimate state interest, while avoiding the unlawful taking of landlords' property. Those issues remain to be determined under the allegations of appellants' pleading, combining a first amended complaint for inverse condemnation and a petition for writ of administrative mandate; and we remand this matter to the trial court for that purpose.

III. DISPOSITION

The judgment of dismissal is vacated. The matter is remanded to the trial court with instructions to overrule the demurrer.

Notes and Questions

1.   The Supreme Court of California subsequently limited the potential reach of *152 Valparaiso Associates*. In Santa Monica Beach, Ltd. v. Superior Court of Los Angeles County, 81 Cal.Rptr.2d 93, 968 P.2d 993 (1999), a sharply divided court denied a landlord the opportunity to present evidence that a rent control scheme failed to advance a legitimate state interest and therefore constituted a taking of property. Stressing deference to legislative authority over economic matters, the majority rejected a facial-like challenge to a local rent control ordinance and brushed aside the argument that the law did not promote its stated goal.

2.   At issue in Richardson v. City and County of Honolulu, 124 F.3d 1150 (9th Cir.1997), *cert. denied*, 119 S.Ct. 168 and 119 S.Ct. 275 (1998), was a rent control ordinance which allowed owners to sell condominium units at a premium because the lease of the ground was fixed at a rate below market value. The court concluded that the ordinance did not further the public interest of creating affordable housing, and thus effected a regulatory taking of property in violation of the Fifth Amendment.

3.   Although rent control ordinances usually have been sustained against constitutional challenge, federal and state courts have ruled that under the Constitution landlords are entitled to a reasonable rate of return on their investment. Rent control provisions which do not provide for a reasonable return have been invalidated as confiscatory in nature. *See, e.g.,* Westwinds Mobile Home Park v. Mobilehome Rental Review Board, 30 Cal.App.4th 84, 35 Cal.Rptr.2d 315 (1994); Cromwell Associates v. Mayor and Council of Newark, 211 N.J.Super. 462, 511 A.2d 1273 (1985).

4.   Some rent control ordinances also limit the right of landlords to demolish rental property or to convert the premises to other uses. Do such restrictions amount to a taking of property? *See* Seawall Associates v. City of New York, 74 N.Y.2d 92, 544 N.Y.S.2d 542, 542 N.E.2d 1059 (1989), *cert. denied* 493 U.S. 976 (1989) (ordinance placing moratorium on demolition or conversion of single-room occupancy hotels and requiring owners to lease them at controlled rents found to be an unconstitutional taking of owners' property). A California statute recognizes the ability of landlords to withdraw property from the rental market. Cal.Govt.Code §§ 7060–7060.7 (West Supp.1993).

5.   Mobile home rent control ordinances have been a source of litigation. In Yee v. City of Escondido, 503 U.S. 519 (1992), the Supreme Court sustained a California law that severely restricted the right of mobile park owners to evict tenants. Does the rental of mobile home pads present unusual problems?

6.   A number of state legislatures have adopted statutes forbidding municipalities from enacting rent control ordinances. *See, e.g.,* Colo.Rev.Stat. § 38–12–301 (1997) (residential rental property); Ga.Code Ann. § 44–7–19 (1991) (residential rental property); 50 Ill.Comp.Stat.Ann. 825/1–825/99 (West Supp. 1998); Mass.Gen.Laws.Ann. ch.40P, §§ 1–5 (West Supp.1998);

N.C.Gen.Stat. § 42–14.1 (1994) (residential or commercial rental property). *See also* N.J.Stat.Ann. §§ 2A:42–84.1 to 2A:42–84.6 (West 1987 & Supp. 1998) (exempting certain new multiple dwellings from rent control ordinances). What is the practical effect of such statutes?

Lawmakers in several states have taken steps to weaken rent control. A California statute authorizes landlords to increase rent for new tenants notwithstanding local ordinances. Cal.Civ.Code §§ 1954.52–1954.53 (West Supp.1998). Similarly, the New York legislature enacted the Rent Regulation Reform Act of 1997, 1997 Sess. Law News of N.Y. ch. 116 (S. 5553, A. 8346) (McKinney's), which made a number of significant modifications in the rent control scheme for New York City. Foremost among these were expanded decontrol for high rental apartments, larger rent increases upon vacancy, and procedural changes to facilitate eviction of non-paying tenants. *See* Caras & Levine, *New York's Rent Regulation Reform Act of 1997*, 13 No.3 Real Est.Fin.J. 42 (1998).

7. Rent control statutes often produce anomalous windfall situations for particular individuals. Tenants may be reluctant to relinquish rent-controlled units and may permit friends to make covert use of their apartments. This practice figured prominently in Tom Wolfe's popular novel, *The Bonfire of the Vanities* (1987).

8. The debate over the constitutionality and desirability of rent control continues unabated. *See, e.g.,* Epstein, *Rent Control and the Theory of Efficient Regulation*, 54 Brook.L.Rev. 741 (1988); Radford, *Why Rent Control Is a Regulatory Taking*, 6 Fordham Envtl.L.J. 755 (1995); Note, *The Constitutionality of Rent Control Restrictions on Property Owners' Dominion Interests*, 100 Harv.L.Rev. 1067 (1987).

2. WHEN THE GOVERNMENT IS LANDLORD

The landlord in our hypothetical situation is a private corporation. Thus, our discussion of the landlord-tenant relationship has proceeded on the basis that the government was not involved in the lease arrangement. The rules governing the landlord-tenant relationship, however, are altered considerably when public housing or publicly subsidized housing is at issue. *See* Joy v. Daniels, 479 F.2d 1236 (4th Cir.1973).

Judicial decisions and administrative regulations which govern eviction from public housing or publicly subsidized housing have become extremely complex. Department of Housing and Urban Development (HUD) regulations provide that a landlord must show good cause to evict a tenant from certain public housing (24 C.F.R. § 966.4(*l*)(2) (1997)) and certain publicly subsidized housing (24 C.F.R. § 247.3(a) (1997)). Difficult questions remain. (1) What constitutes good cause? The regulations cited above provide general guidance, but not definite answers. *See* The National Housing Law Project, HUD Housing Programs, Tenant's Rights §§ 14.2.2, 14.3.3 (1994 & Supp. 1996) for a discussion of good cause. *See also Phillips Neighborhood Housing Trust* on page 138. (2) What procedures must be employed to make a good cause determination? *Compare* Owens v. Housing Authority of Stamford, 394 F.Supp. 1267

(D.Conn.1975) (holding that state summary eviction procedures did not meet due process requirements and that public housing tenant was entitled to separate administrative hearing prior to institution of eviction proceedings) *with* Jeffries v. Georgia Residential Finance Authority, 503 F.Supp. 610 (N.D.Ga.1980) (separate administrative hearing unnecessary because state court proceeding met due process requirements). HUD has set forth procedural requirements for certain public housing projects (24 C.F.R. §§ 966.50 *et seq.* (1997)), and one court has held that HUD regulations can require that a tenant be given the opportunity for a separate administrative hearing even if state eviction procedures meet due process standards. King v. Housing Authority of City of Huntsville, 670 F.2d 952 (11th Cir.1982). *See* The National Housing Law Project, HUD Housing Programs, Tenant's Rights §§ 14.2.3, 14.3.4 (1994 & Supp.1996) for further discussion of procedural requirements.

Maintenance of public housing is another critical issue. HUD regulations require that a warranty of habitability be included in certain public housing leases (24 C.F.R. § 966.4(e) (1997)) and provide for an abatement of the rent if the owner is given notice and does not make repairs within a reasonable time (24 C.F.R. § 966.4(h)(4) (1997)). Moreover, several courts have ruled that an implied warranty of habitability is applicable to public housing. Hence, these courts have allowed tenants to withhold or recover rent where their apartments are below standard. *See* Allen v. Housing Authority of the County of Chester, 683 F.2d 75 (3d Cir.1982); Conille v. Secretary of Housing and Urban Development, 840 F.2d 105 (1st Cir.1988); Note, *The Incorporation of the Implied Warranty of Habitability in Public Housing Programs,* 38 Wash.U.J.Urb. & Contemp.L. 205, 216–226 (1990).

Chapter 2

PERSONAL PROPERTY

Hypothetical Situation—Number 2

The Lloyds do not wish to purchase the condominium unit to which their apartment is being converted. Instead, they have rented a one-bedroom apartment in another area of the city. Because their new apartment is considerably smaller than their current one, they have decided to store some furniture and to give china and a set of silver candlesticks to their daughter. They mentioned that they will contact you if they experience any legal problems in carrying out their plans.

A. INTRODUCTION: REALTY v. PERSONALTY

The common law drew a distinction between real property (rights in land) and personal property (rights in chattels). These terms were originally the result of different forms of actions. Real actions were those in which the prevailing plaintiff recovered the actual object of the lawsuit. Given the unique importance of land in the feudal system, real actions were primarily employed in litigation concerning land. In *actiones in personam,* on the other hand, the successful plaintiff recovered only damages for wrongs to the plaintiff's property.

Personal property is divided into two categories. Tangible personal property consists of physical objects such as animals, furniture, jewelry, and vehicles. Intangible personal property, including bank accounts, stock, and debts, is really a claim against third parties. Intangible personalty is central to modern commercial life. Yet such property is not subject to physical possession and consequently poses special problems.

This chapter is designed to give you a broad introduction to the acquisition, protection, and transfer of personal property. In your study of this topic, you may wish to consult R. Brown, The Law of Personal Property (3d ed. 1975).

B. WILD ANIMALS

In order to properly advise the Lloyds about the storage and gift of personal property, it is important that you appreciate the significance of possession. *See generally* Rose, *Possession as the Origin of Property*, 52 U.Chi.L.Rev. 73 (1985). The complex concept of possession is profitably introduced by examining the law governing the acquisition of title to wild animals.

PIERSON v. POST

Supreme Court of New York, 1805.
3 Caines 175, 2 Am.Dec. 264.

This was an action of trespass on the case commenced in a justice's court, by the present defendant [*Post*] against the now plaintiff [*Pierson*].

The declaration stated that *Post*, being in possession of certain dogs and hounds under his command, did, "upon a certain wild and uninhabited, unpossessed and waste land, called the beach, find and start one of those noxious beasts called a fox," and whilst there hunting, chasing and pursuing the same with his dogs and hounds, and when in view thereof, *Pierson*, well knowing the fox was so hunted and pursued, did, in the sight of *Post*, to prevent his catching the same, kill and carry it off. A verdict having been rendered for the plaintiff below [*Post*], the defendant there [*Pierson*] sued out a *certiorari*, and now assigned for error, that the declaration and the matters therein contained were not sufficient in law to maintain an action.

* * *

TOMPKINS, J. delivered the opinion of the court. This cause comes before us on a return to a *certiorari* directed to one of the justices of *Queens* county.

The question submitted by the counsel in this cause for our determination is, whether *Lodowick Post,* by the pursuit with his hounds in the manner alleged in his declaration, acquired such a right to, or property in, the fox, as will sustain an action against *Pierson* for killing and taking him away?

* * *

It is admitted that a fox is an animal *ferae naturae,* and that property in such animals is acquired by occupancy only. These admissions narrow the discussion to the simple question of what acts amount to occupancy, applied to acquiring right to wild animals?

If we have recourse to the ancient writers upon general principles of law, the judgment below is obviously erroneous. *Justinian's Institutes,* lib. 2. tit. 1. s. 13, and *Fleta,* lib. 3. e. 2. p. 175. adopt the principle, that pursuit alone vests no property or right in the huntsman; and that even pursuit, accompanied with wounding, is equally ineffectual for that purpose, unless the animal be actually taken. The same principle is recognized by *Bracton,* lib. 2. c. 1. p. 8.

Puffendorf, lib. 4. c. 6. s. 2. and 10. defines occupancy of beasts *ferae naturae,* to be the actual corporal possession of them, and *Bynkershoek* is cited as coinciding in this definition. It is indeed with hesitation that *Puffendorf* affirms that a wild beast mortally wounded, or greatly maimed, cannot be fairly intercepted by another, whilst the pursuit of the person inflicting the wound continues. The foregoing authorities are decisive to show that mere pursuit gave *Post* no legal right to the fox, but that he became the property of *Pierson,* who intercepted and killed him.

It therefore only remains to inquire whether there are any contrary principles, or authorities, to be found in other books, which ought to induce a different decision. Most of the cases which have occurred in *England,* relating to property in wild animals, have either been discussed and decided upon the principles of their positive statute regulations, or have arisen between the huntsman and the owner of the land upon which beasts *ferae naturae* have been apprehended; the former claiming them by title of occupancy, and the latter *ratione soli.* Little satisfactory aid can, therefore, be derived from the English reporters.

Barbeyrac, in his notes on *Puffendorf,* does not accede to the definition of occupancy by the latter, but, on the contrary, affirms, that actual bodily seizure is not, in all cases, necessary to constitute possession of wild animals. He does not, however, *describe* the acts which, according to his ideas, will amount to an appropriation of such animals to private use, so as to exclude the claims of all other persons, by title of occupancy, to the same animals; and he is far from averring that pursuit alone is sufficient for that purpose. To a certain extent, and as far as *Barbeyrac* appears to me to go, his objections to *Puffendorf's* definition of occupancy are reasonable and correct. That is to say, that actual bodily seizure is not indispensable to acquire right to, or possession of, wild beasts; but that, on the contrary, the mortal wounding of such beasts, by one not abandoning his pursuit, may, with the utmost propriety, be deemed possession of him; since, thereby, the pursuer manifests an unequivocal intention of appropriating the animal to his individual use, has deprived him of his natural liberty, and brought him within his certain control. So also, encompassing and securing such animals with nets and toils, or otherwise intercepting them in such a manner as to deprive them of their natural liberty, and render escape impossible, may justly be deemed to give possession of them to those persons who, by their industry and labour, have used such means of apprehending them.

* * *

The case now under consideration is one of mere pursuit, and presents no circumstances or acts which can bring it within the definition of occupancy by *Puffendorf,* * * * or the ideas of *Burbeyrac* upon that subject.

* * *

We are * * * inclined to confine possession or occupancy of beasts *ferae naturae,* within the limits prescribed by the learned authors above cited, for the sake of certainty, and preserving peace and order in society. If the first seeing, starting, or pursuing such animals, without having so wounded, circumvented or ensnared them, so as to deprive them of their natural liberty, and subject them to the control of their pursuer, should afford the basis of actions against others for intercepting and killing them, it would prove a fertile source of quarrels and litigation.

However uncourteous or unkind the conduct of *Pierson* towards *Post,* in this instance, may have been, yet his act was productive of no injury or damage for which a legal remedy can be applied. We are of opinion the judgment below was erroneous, and ought to be reversed.

LIVINGSTON, J. [Dissenting].

* * *

This is a knotty point, and should have been submitted to the arbitration of sportsmen, without poring over *Justinian, Fleta, Bracton, Puffendorf, Locke, Barbeyrac,* or *Blackstone,* all of whom have been cited; they would have had no difficulty in coming to a prompt and correct conclusion.

* * *

But the parties have referred the question to our judgment, and we must dispose of it as well as we can, from the partial lights we possess, leaving to a higher tribunal, the correction of any mistake which we may be so unfortunate as to make. By the pleadings it is admitted that a fox is a "wild and noxious beast."

* * *

His depredations on farmers and on barn yards, have not been forgotten; and to put him to death wherever found, is allowed to be meritorious, and of public benefit. Hence it follows, that our decision should have in view the greatest possible encouragement to the destruction of an animal, so cunning and ruthless in his career. But who would keep a pack of hounds; or what gentleman, at the sound of the horn, and at peep of day, would mount his steed, and for hours together * * * pursue the windings of this wily quadruped, if, just as night came on, and his stratagems and strength were nearly exhausted, a saucy intruder, who had not shared in the honours or labours of the chase, were permitted to come in at the death, and bear away in triumph the object of pursuit? Whatever *Justinian* may have thought of the matter, it must be recollected that his code was compiled many hundred years ago, and it would be very hard indeed, at the distance of so many centuries, not to have a right to establish a rule for ourselves. In his day, we read of no order of men who made it a business, in the language of the declaration in this cause, "with hounds and dogs to find, start, pursue, hunt, and chase," these animals, and that, too, without any other motive than the preservation of *Roman* poultry; if this diversion had been then in fashion, the lawyers who composed his institutes, would have taken care not to pass it by, without suitable encouragement. If any thing, therefore, in the digests or pandects shall appear to militate against the defendant in error, who, on this occasion, was the foxhunter, we have only to say * * * if men themselves change with the times, why should not laws also undergo an alteration?

It may be expected, however, by the learned counsel, that more particular notice be taken of their authorities. I have examined them all, and feel great difficulty in determining, whether to acquire dominion over a thing, before in common, it be sufficient that we barely see it, or know where it is, or wish for it, or make a declaration of our will respecting it; or whether, in the case of wild beasts, setting a trap, or lying in wait, or starting, or pursuing, be enough; or if an actual wounding, or killing, or bodily tact and occupation be necessary. Writers on general law, who have favoured us with their speculations on these points, differ on them all; but, great as is the diversity of sentiment among them, some conclusion must be adopted on the question immediately before us. After mature deliberation, I embrace that of *Barbeyrac,* as the most rational, and least liable to objection.

* * *

He ordained, that if a beast be followed with *large dogs and hounds,* he shall belong to the hunter, not to the chance occupant; and in like manner, if he be killed or wounded with a lance or sword; but if chased with *beagles only,* then he passed to the captor, not to the first pursuer. If slain with a dart, a sling, or a bow, he fell to the hunter, if still in chase, and not to him who might afterwards find and seize him.

Now, as we are without any municipal regulations of our own, and the pursuit here * * * being with dogs and hounds of *imperial stature,* we are at liberty to adopt one of the provisions just cited: * * * that property in animals *ferae naturae* may be acquired without bodily touch or manucaption, provided the pursuer be within reach, or have a *reasonable* prospect (which certainly existed here) of taking, what he has *thus* discovered an intention of converting to his own use.

When we reflect also that the interest of our husbandmen, the most useful of men in any community, will be advanced by the destruction of a beast so pernicious and incorrigible, we cannot greatly err, in saying, that a pursuit like the present, through waste and unoccupied lands, and which must inevitably and speedily have terminated in corporal possession, or bodily *seisin,* confers such a right to the object of it, as to make any one a wrongdoer, who shall interfere and shoulder the spoil. The *justice's* judgment ought, therefore, in my opinion, to be affirmed.

Judgment of reversal.

Notes and Questions

1. Note that both the majority and the dissent make judgments about social policy. Which is more persuasive? Is this an appropriate function for courts in a democratic society? *See generally* M. Horwitz, The Transformation of American Law, 1780–1860 (1977).

2. In Chapter 89 of the literary classic *Moby Dick* (1851), Herman Melville discusses the significance of possession in the context of capturing wild animals. He first notes that in the whaling industry there is an unwritten code: "I. A Fast–Fish belongs to the party fast to it. II. A Loose–Fish is fair game for anyone who can soonest catch it." Next, Melville points out that the code has been difficult to apply. In this regard, he analyzes an English case in which it was held that one who takes a Loose–Fish has the right to keep any harpoons and loose line attached to it. Melville then contends that the concept of possession often is "the whole of the law." He compares life's Fast–Fish such as rent or interest on a loan with its Loose–Fish such as thoughts and religious beliefs, and concludes by asking: "And what are you, reader, but a Loose–Fish and a Fast–Fish, too?"

STATE v. BARTEE

Court of Appeals of Texas, San Antonio 1994.
894 S.W.2d 34.

ONION, JUSTICE.

These appeals are taken by the State from pretrial orders setting aside indictments * * *. These orders were on motions to set aside the indictments which attacked the facial validity of the indictments.

These appeals present rather novel and interesting legal questions and are possibly a case of first impression as to whether a white-tailed deer can be the subject of the theft and criminal mischief statutes, and whether the State of Texas may be alleged as an owner in such situations. * * *

* * *

In order to be the subject of larceny the thing or property taken must be capable of individual ownership. Theft and larceny are substantially the same offense.

The criminal mischief statute in effect at the time of the alleged offense provided in pertinent part:

(a) A person commits an offense if, without the effective consent of the owner:

(1) he intentionally or knowingly damages or destroys the tangible property of the owner....

"Property" subject to criminal mischief had the same definition as "property" under the applicable theft statute at the time of the alleged offense.

We find nothing in the Penal Code itself to exclude white-tailed deer and deer antlers from being the subject of the theft or criminal mischief statutes. We must examine other statutes, caselaw and authorities in pursuit of an answer to the questions presented.

We begin by flipping through the pages of time. History reveals a long recognition of common ownership in game and wild animals and its developing subjectivity to governmental authority. At one point the law of ancient Athens forbade the killing of game. Roman law recognized common ownership, but imposed its regulations on the taking of wild animals. There is a history of varying controls exercised by the lawgiving power over the right of a citizen to acquire a qualified ownership in animals *ferae naturae* evidenced by the Salic law, exemplified by the legislation of Charlemagne, and later by the Napoleonic Code which permitted police regulations to direct the manner in which common ownership was to be enjoyed.

The common law of England also based property in game upon the principle of common ownership, and therefore treated it as subject to governmental authority. In *State v. Ward*, 328 Mo. 658, 40 S.W.2d 1074, 1077 (1931) the Supreme Court of Missouri wrote:

> At a very remote time the right and power of the sovereign authority to regulate and control the taking of wild animals were asserted and recognized. Originally, the title seems to have been regarded as vested in the sovereign as a personal prerogative; but, on the granting of Magna Charta and the Charter of the Forest by Henry III in 1225, the rights of the sovereign in unreclaimed wild animals were limited, and the rule of the Roman Law restricting the sovereign power to controlling and regulating the taking of such animals became the common law of England. The rule of the Civil Law recognizing the qualified title of the sovereign in wild animals, having been adopted by England, became the common law of the United States, and here the rule is that the general ownership of wild animals, as far as they are capable of ownership, is in the state, not as a proprietor, but in its collective sovereign capacity as the representative and for the benefit of all its citizens in common.

The attribute of government to control the taking of animals *ferae naturae* (wild animals) which was recognized and enforced by the common law of England was vested in the American colonial governments where not denied by their characters or in conflict with grants of the royal prerogative. The power which the colonies possessed passed to the states with separation from the mother country, and remains in the states until the present time in so far as its exercise is not incompatible with rights which were conveyed to the federal government by the United States Constitution.

In Texas, it has been said that the common law provides that animals *ferae naturae* belong to the state and no individual property rights exist as long as the animal remains wild, unconfined, and undomesticated. Unqualified property rights in wild animals can arise when they are legally removed from their natural liberty and made the subjects of man's dominion. This qualified right is lost, however, if the animal regains its natural liberty.

This same theme is well expressed in 3A C.J.S. *Animals* § 8 at 478–79 (1973), where, in addition, it is stated:

> Whether one has secured a property right to an animal *ferae naturae* will be determined by whether the animal has been reduced to possession, and not by its habits.

> If the person who reduces an animal from the wild state does so in compliance with the law, he gains ownership of it; otherwise, its ownership remains in the state. A wrongful reducing to possession of creature *ferae naturae* cannot form the basis of ownership.

In *Runnels v. State*, 152 Tex.Crim. 268, 213 S.W.2d 545, 547 (1948), the Court of Criminal Appeals discussed when wild animals became subject to theft. The Court wrote:

> Wild animals are not subject to theft until they become the property of an owner. This they do immediately upon being reduced to possession. *Jones v. State*, 119 Tex.Cr.R. 126, 45 S.W.2d 612 [(1931)]. This seems to be the settled law in all jurisdictions. Mr. X captures a wildcat. It is a wildcat still, but it immediately becomes his property. The fisherman becomes the owner of his catch as soon as he secures possession. It is wild game still, but is the subject of theft.

The reason behind the principle expressed in *Runnels* is that the gist of the offense of theft consists in the misappropriation of another person's property. Jones recognized that when wild animals, including deer, become property it was such property that would pass to the executors and administrators of a deceased person's estate. Thus, it is legally possible for an individual to have qualified property rights in a wild animal, particularly a deer.

Most states of this nation have enacted laws for the protection and preservation of game. It has been said that statutes placing ownership and control of wild animals in the state are but an expression of both the civil and the common law on the subject. The power to so legislate is not normally questioned. The Texas legislature may make laws for the protection of public rights in wild game including the right to regulate the method of hunting.

Section 1.011(a) of the Texas Parks and Wildlife Code provides "(a) All wild animals, fur-bearing animals, wild birds, and wild fowl inside the borders of this state are *the property of the people of this state*." Tex. Parks & Wildlife Code Ann. § 1.011(a) (Vernon 1991)(Emphasis added). The emphasized phrase or the phrase "property of the public" are found in all the statutory forerunners of section 1.011 as far back as 1907. With regard to the ownership of wild animals, we do not find that the various statutes enacted over the years have departed from the common law. The statutory phrase "property of the people of this state" does not appear to have been interpreted by our courts. Despite its use in various statutes over the years, our courts have consistently referred to the ownership of wild animals as being in "the state" or belonging to "the state."

* * *

While the legislature has declared that all wild animals are property of the people of this state, these elected representatives of the people, in order to protect the common ownership and to properly regulate and protect wild animals and game, have entrusted a state agency with the power and responsibility to do so under statutes enacted, and by regulations adopted, as provided by law. The power of the state agency is to be exercised like all other powers of government as a trust for the benefit of the people and not as a prerogative for the advantage of the government or for the benefit of private individuals. The very purpose of the wildlife conservation act "is to provide a comprehensive method for the conservation of an ample supply of wildlife resources on a statewide basis to insure reasonable and equitable enjoyment of the privileges of ownership and pursuit of wildlife resources." Tex.Parks & Wildlife Code Ann. § 61.002 (Vernon 1991). The law is made flexible to enable the Parks and Wildlife Commission to deal effectively with changing conditions. The State, through its agency, represents the common ownership of wild animals. The people have the right to change this arrangement if they so desire. The State, as trustee, has the power to regulate the taking and acquisition of property in wild animals by individuals by imposing such restrictions and conditions as the legislature may see fit. Wholly apart from its authority to protect the common ownership of wild animals, the right of the State to preserve wild animals cannot be disputed due to the undoubted existence of a police power to that end.

In the Parks and Wildlife Code the legislature has provided for scientific breeders of white-tailed deer. The Parks and Wildlife Department is authorized to issue permits to qualified persons to possess white-tailed deer for propagation, management, and scientific purposes. Among the privileges of the permit is the right of the scientific breeder to engage in the business of breeding white-tailed deer, and for that purpose to hold in possession and in captivity white-tailed deer for propagation or sale. The implication is that the proceeds of any sale may be retained by the scientific breeder. Permits may also be granted to individuals by the department for the trapping, transportation and transplanting of "wild white-tailed deer" from areas overpopulated by such deer to other areas of the state, all without cost to the State government. There may be other examples, but clearly while acting under permits from the State, the scientific breeder and the transporter would legally have qualified rights of ownership or possession of the white-tailed deer. As we have already seen, wild animals legally reduced to possession may be the subject of theft. Likewise, the white-tailed deer in the legal possession of a scientific breeder or transporter with the consent of the State may be the subject of theft, and for that matter, criminal mischief as well. It must be recognized then that the prosecution may bring theft and criminal mischief charges concerning white-tailed deer but only in limited and very circumscribed situations. A white-tailed deer in its natural state of liberty cannot be the subject of the theft and criminal mischief statutes. This is undoubtedly one of the reasons why we have been unable to find a single reported case in Texas involving the theft of deer from the State. The prosecutor in charging theft or criminal mischief involving a white-tailed deer must be extremely careful in choosing the proper allegations in the State's pleadings, but also keenly aware of the facts which will support those allegations. Otherwise, the prosecutor may be up the creek without the proverbial paddle.

* * *

SUMMARY

White-tailed deer in their natural state of liberty are not the proper subject of the criminal offenses of theft and criminal mischief. In limited and circumscribed situations, however, qualified property rights may be legally acquired in white-tailed deer and these deer may be the subject of theft and criminal mischief. White-tailed deer antlers legally acquired may also be the subject of theft. The State of Texas may be alleged as "owner" of property in theft and criminal mischief cases. An indictment returned by a legally constituted grand jury and valid on its face is sufficient to mandate a trial of the charge on its merits.

* * *

The orders setting aside the indictments are reversed and the causes are remanded to the trial court.

RICKHOFF, JUSTICE concurring.

* * *

I agree with the majority "that white-tailed deer in their natural state of liberty cannot be the subject of theft." As the majority observes, animals are either wild (ferae naturae) or domestic (domitae naturae). No one, not even the state, "owns" wild animals, at least in the proprietary sense, when they are in their natural habitat.

I also agree that we cannot assume, as the trial judge apparently did in this case, that "[t]he white-tailed deer named in the indictment is a 'wild animal,'" or as the majority says, that the deer was "in its natural state of liberty."

The majority observes that white-tailed deer in the possession of a scientific breeder or transporter may be the subject of theft or criminal mischief, or that "[t]here may be other examples" that allow such qualified rights of ownership or possession of white-tailed deer. If this is so, then I believe there are many white-tailed deer that are privately owned in Texas that could be the subject of a theft or criminal mischief indictment and in the future there will be many thousands.

If the majority is merely holding that it is possible for a white-tailed deer to become personal property and that, accordingly, it will be difficult for the State to prove the deer in this case was owned by the State, then I agree. Here, the State was alleged in very general terms to be the owner of a particular deer. As the majority correctly notes, this may be sufficient for purposes of an indictment, but how is it going to prove this deer was reduced to possession by the State? * * *

* * *

Notes and Problems

1.   The Charleston Courier, June 5, 1827, at 2, reported on a New York case:

> Stealing a Duck—A person was convicted at the last term of the criminal court of stealing a duck. On the prisoner's being brought to the bar to receive his sentence, the Recorder stated, that he thought the indictment defective, as it did not charge it to be a dead duck; for it might have been a wild duck (ferae naturae) the taking of which would not be a crime.

2.   Actions by the federal and state governments to relocate wild animals to their native ranges have generated a lively debate. *See* Moerman v. State, 17 Cal.App.4th 452, 21 Cal.Rptr.2d 329 (1993) (holding that state does not own or control wild animals, and that damage caused by wildlife does not constitute a taking of property for which compensation is constitutionally required).

3.   How long does the ownership of a captured wild animal continue? William Blackstone declared: "[Animals *ferae naturae*] are no longer the property of a man, than while they continue in his keeping or actual possession: but, if at any time they regain their natural liberty, his property instantly ceases; unless they have *animum revertendi,* which is only to be known by their usual custom of returning." 2 Blackstone, Commentaries on the Laws of England 392 (1766).

4.   O operates a game farm, and holds an American Elk on O's land. The elk escapes. Subsequently H shoots and kills the elk on land not belonging to O. O brings an action to recover the value of the elk from H. You represent H. What argument will you make? *See* Wiley v. Baker, 597 S.W.2d 3 (Tex.Civ.App.1980).

5.   Do not be deceived by the cases on wild animals. They pose difficult analytical problems and raise important social questions. Despite the current interest in wildlife protection, there has been little scholarly investigation of the laws governing wild animals. Yet societal measures to regulate the killing of wildlife present issues of environmental preservation, property rights, gun control, class and ethnic divisions, federal-state relations, and law enforcement. *See* T. Lund, American Wildlife Law (1980).

C. FOUND PROPERTY

BENJAMIN v. LINDNER AVIATION, INC.

Supreme Court of Iowa, 1995.
534 N.W.2d 400.

TERNUS JUSTICE.

Appellant, Heath Benjamin, found over $18,000 in currency inside the wing of an airplane. At the time of this discovery, appellee, State Central Bank, owned the plane and it was being serviced by appellee, Lindner Aviation, Inc. All three parties claimed the money as against the true owner. After a bench trial, the district court held that the currency was mislaid property and belonged to the owner of the plane. The court awarded a finder's fee to Benjamin. Benjamin appealed and Lindner Aviation and State Central Bank cross-appealed. We reverse on the bank's cross-appeal and otherwise affirm the judgment of the district court.

I. BACKGROUND FACTS AND PROCEEDINGS.

In April of 1992, State Central Bank became the owner of an airplane when the bank repossessed it from its prior owner who had defaulted on a loan. In August of that year, the bank took the plane to Lindner Aviation for a routine annual inspection. Benjamin worked for Lindner Aviation and did the inspection.

As part of the inspection, Benjamin removed panels from the underside of the wings. Although these panels were to be removed annually as part of the routine inspection, a couple of the screws holding the panel on the left wing were so rusty that Benjamin had to use a drill to remove them. Benjamin testified that the panel probably had not been removed for several years.

Inside the left wing Benjamin discovered two packets approximately four inches high and wrapped in aluminum foil. He removed the packets from the wing and took off the foil wrapping. Inside the foil was paper currency, tied in string and wrapped in handkerchiefs. The currency was predominately twenty-dollar bills with mint dates before the 1960s, primarily in the 1950s. The money smelled musty.

Benjamin took one packet to his jeep and then reported what he had found to his supervisor, offering to divide the money with him. However, the supervisor reported the discovery to the owner of Lindner Aviation, William Engle. Engle insisted that they contact the authorities and he called the Department of Criminal Investigation. The money was eventually turned over to the Keokuk police department.

Two days later, Benjamin filed an affidavit with the county auditor claiming that he was the finder of the currency under the provisions of

Iowa Code chapter 644 (1991).[1] Lindner Aviation and the bank also filed claims to the money. The notices required by chapter 644 were published and posted. *See* Iowa Code § 644.8 (1991). No one came forward within twelve months claiming to be the true owner of the money. *See id.* § 644.11 (if true owner does not claim property within twelve months, the right to the property vests in the finder).

Benjamin filed this declaratory judgment action against Lindner Aviation and the bank to establish his right to the property. The parties tried the case to the court. The district court held that chapter 644 applies only to "lost" property and the money here was mislaid property. The court awarded the money to the bank, holding that it was entitled to possession of the money to the exclusion of all but the true owner. The court also held that Benjamin was a "finder" within the meaning of chapter 644 and awarded him a ten percent finder's fee. See id. § 644.13 (a finder of lost property is entitled to ten percent of the value of the lost property as a reward).

Benjamin appealed. He claims that chapter 644 governs the disposition of all found property and any common law distinctions between various types of found property are no longer valid. He asserts alternatively that even under the common law classes of found property, he is entitled to the money he discovered. He claims that the trial court should have found that the property was treasure trove or was lost or abandoned rather than mislaid, thereby entitling the finder to the property.

The bank and Lindner Aviation cross-appealed. Lindner Aviation claims that if the money is mislaid property, it is entitled to the money as the owner of the premises on which the money was found, the hangar where the plane was parked. It argues in the alternative that it is the finder, not Benjamin, because Benjamin discovered the money during his work for Lindner Aviation. The bank asserts in its cross-appeal that it owns the premises where the money was found—the airplane—and that no one is entitled to a finder's fee because chapter 644 does not apply to mislaid property.

II. STANDARD OF REVIEW.

* * *

Whether the money found by Benjamin was treasure trove or was mislaid, abandoned or lost property is a fact question. 1 Am.Jur.2d *Abandoned, Lost, and Unclaimed Property* § 41, at 49 (2d ed. 1994) (hereinafter "1 Am.Jur.2d *Abandoned Property*"). Therefore, the trial court's finding that the money was mislaid is binding on us if supported by substantial evidence.

---

1. Chapter 644 was renumbered by the editors of the 1995 Iowa Code and is now found in chapter 556F.

III. Does Chapter 644 Supersede the Common Law Classifications of Found Property?

Benjamin argues that chapter 644 governs the rights of finders of property and abrogates the common law distinctions between types of found property. As he points out, lost property statutes are intended "to encourage and facilitate the return of property to the true owner, and then to reward a finder for his honesty if the property remains unclaimed." *Paset v. Old Orchard Bank & Trust Co.*, 62 Ill.App.3d 534, 19 Ill.Dec. 389, 393, 378 N.E.2d 1264, 1268 (1978) (interpreting a statute similar to chapter 644). These goals, Benjamin argues, can best be achieved by applying such statutes to all types of found property.

* * *

Although a few courts have adopted an expansive view of lost property statutes, we think Iowa law is to the contrary. In 1937, we quoted and affirmed a trial court ruling that "the old law of treasure trove is not merged in the statutory law of chapter 515, 1935 Code of Iowa." *Zornes v. Bowen*, 223 Iowa 1141, 1145, 274 N.W. 877, 879 (1937). Chapter 515 of the 1935 Iowa Code was eventually renumbered as chapter 644. The relevant sections of chapter 644 are unchanged since our 1937 decision. As recently as 1991, we stated that "[t]he rights of finders of property vary according to the characterization of the property found." *Ritz v. Selma United Methodist Church*, 467 N.W.2d 266, 268 (Iowa 1991). We went on to define and apply the common law classifications of found property in deciding the rights of the parties. As our prior cases show, we have continued to use the common law distinctions between classes of found property despite the legislature's enactment of chapter 644 and its predecessors.

The legislature has had many opportunities since our decision in *Zornes* to amend the statute so that it clearly applies to all types of found property. However, it has not done so. When the legislature leaves a statute unchanged after the supreme court has interpreted it, we presume the legislature has acquiesced in our interpretation. Therefore, we presume here that the legislature approves of our application of chapter 644 to lost property only. Consequently, we hold that chapter 644 does not abrogate the common law classifications of found property. We note this position is consistent with that taken by most jurisdictions. *See, e.g., Bishop v. Ellsworth*, 91 Ill.App.2d 386, 234 N.E.2d 49, 51 (1968) (holding lost property statute does not apply to abandoned or mislaid property); *Foster v. Fidelity Safe Deposit Co.*, 264 Mo. 89, 174 S.W. 376, 379 (1915) (refusing to apply lost property statute to property that would not be considered lost under the common law); *Sovern v. Yoran*, 16 Or. 269, 20 P. 100, 105 (1888) (same); *Zech v. Accola*, 253 Wis. 80, 33 N.W.2d 232, 235 (1948) (concluding that if legislature had intended to include treasure trove within lost property statute, it would have specifically mentioned treasure trove).

In summary, chapter 644 applies only if the property discovered can be categorized as "lost" property as that term is defined under the common law. Thus, the trial court correctly looked to the common law classifications of found property to decide who had the right to the money discovered here.

IV. Classification of Found Property.

Under the common law, there are four categories of found property: (1) abandoned property, (2) lost property, (3) mislaid property, and (4) treasure trove. *Ritz*, 467 N.W.2d at 269. The rights of a finder of property depend on how the found property is classified.

A. *Abandoned property*. Property is abandoned when the owner no longer wants to possess it. Abandonment is shown by proof that the owner intends to abandon the property and has voluntarily relinquished all right, title and interest in the property. Abandoned property belongs to the finder of the property against all others, including the former owner.

B. *Lost property*. "Property is lost when the owner unintentionally and involuntarily parts with its possession and does not know where it is." *Id.* (citing *Eldridge v. Herman,* 291 N.W.2d 319, 323 (Iowa 1980)). Stolen property found by someone who did not participate in the theft is lost property. Under chapter 644, lost property becomes the property of the finder once the statutory procedures are followed and the owner makes no claim within twelve months.

C. *Mislaid property*. Mislaid property is voluntarily put in a certain place by the owner who then overlooks or forgets where the property is. It differs from lost property in that the owner voluntarily and intentionally places mislaid property in the location where it is eventually found by another. In contrast, property is not considered lost unless the owner parts with it involuntarily. [S]ee *Hill v. Schrunk,* 207 Or. 71, 292 P.2d 141, 143 (1956) (carefully concealed currency was mislaid property, not lost property).

The finder of mislaid property acquires no rights to the property. The right of possession of mislaid property belongs to the owner of the premises upon which the property is found, as against all persons other than the true owner.

D. *Treasure trove*. Treasure trove consists of coins or currency concealed by the owner. It includes an element of antiquity. To be classified as treasure trove, the property must have been hidden or concealed for such a length of time that the owner is probably dead or undiscoverable. Treasure trove belongs to the finder as against all but the true owner.

V. Is There Substantial Evidence to Support the Trial Court's Finding That the Money Found by Benjamin Was Mislaid?

We think there was substantial evidence to find that the currency discovered by Benjamin was mislaid property. In the *Eldridge* case, we examined the location where the money was found as a factor in determining whether the money was lost property. [A]ccord 1 Am.Jur.2d

Abandoned Property § 6, at 11–12 ("The place where money or property claimed as lost is found is an important factor in the determination of the question of whether it was lost or only mislaid."). Similarly, in *Ritz*, we considered the manner in which the money had been secreted in deciding that it had not been abandoned.

The place where Benjamin found the money and the manner in which it was hidden are also important here. The bills were carefully tied and wrapped and then concealed in a location that was accessible only by removing screws and a panel. These circumstances support an inference that the money was placed there intentionally. This inference supports the conclusion that the money was mislaid. *Jackson v. Steinberg*, 186 Or. 129, 200 P.2d 376, 378 (1948) (fact that $800 in currency was found concealed beneath the paper lining of a dresser indicates that money was intentionally concealed with intention of reclaiming it; therefore, property was mislaid, not lost); *Schley v. Couch*, 155 Tex. 195, 284 S.W.2d 333, 336 (1955) (holding that money found buried under garage floor was mislaid property as a matter of law because circumstances showed that money was placed there deliberately and court presumed that owner had either forgotten where he hid the money or had died before retrieving it).

The same facts that support the trial court's conclusion that the money was mislaid prevent us from ruling as a matter of law that the property was lost. Property is not considered lost unless considering the place where and the conditions under which the property is found, there is an inference that the property was left there unintentionally. [S]ee *Sovern*, 20 P. at 105 (holding that coins found in a jar under a wooden floor of a barn were not lost property because the circumstances showed that the money was hidden there intentionally); *see Farrare v. City of Pasco*, 68 Wash.App. 459, 843 P.2d 1082, 1084 (1992) (where currency was deliberately concealed, it cannot be characterized as lost property). Contrary to Benjamin's position the circumstances here do not support a conclusion that the money was placed in the wing of the airplane unintentionally. Additionally, as the trial court concluded, there was no evidence suggesting that the money was placed in the wing by someone other than the owner of the money and that its location was unknown to the owner. For these reasons, we reject Benjamin's argument that the trial court was obligated to find that the currency Benjamin discovered was lost property.

We also reject Benjamin's assertion that as a matter of law this money was abandoned property. Both logic and common sense suggest that it is unlikely someone would voluntarily part with over $18,000 with the intention of terminating his ownership. The location where this money was found is much more consistent with the conclusion that the owner of the property was placing the money there for safekeeping. *See Ritz*, 467 N.W.2d at 269 (property not abandoned where money was buried in jars and tin cans, indicating a desire by the owner to preserve it); *Jackson*, 200 P.2d at 378 (because currency was concealed intentionally and deliberately, the bills could not be regarded as abandoned property); 1 Am.Jur.2d *Abandoned Property* § 13, at 17 (where property is concealed in such a way that the concealment appears intentional and deliberate, there can be no abandonment). We will not presume that an owner has abandoned his property when his conduct is consistent with a continued claim to the property. Therefore, we cannot rule that the district court erred in failing to find that the currency discovered by Benjamin was abandoned property.

Finally, we also conclude that the trial court was not obligated to decide that this money was treasure trove. Based on the dates of the currency, the money was no older than thirty-five years. The mint dates, the musty odor and the rusty condition of a few of the panel screws indicate that the money may have been hidden for some time. However, there was no evidence of the age of the airplane or the date of its last inspection. These facts may have shown that the money was concealed for a much shorter period of time.

Moreover, it is also significant that the airplane had a well-documented ownership history. The record reveals that there were only two owners of the plane prior to the bank. One was the person from whom the bank repossessed the plane; the other was the original purchaser of the plane when it was manufactured. Nevertheless, there is no indication that Benjamin or any other party attempted to locate and notify the prior owners of the plane, which could very possibly have led to the identification of the true owner of the money. Under these circumstances, we cannot say as a matter of law that the money meets the antiquity requirement or that it is probable that the owner of the money is not discoverable.

We think the district court had substantial evidence to support its finding that the money found by Benjamin was mislaid. The circumstances of its concealment and the location where it was found support inferences that the owner intentionally placed the money there and intended to retain ownership. We are bound by this factual finding.

VI. Is the Airplane Or the Hangar the "Premises" Where the Money Was Discovered?

Because the money discovered by Benjamin was properly found to be mislaid property, it belongs to the owner of the premises where it was found. Mislaid property is entrusted to the owner of the premises where it is found rather than the finder of the property because it is assumed that the true owner may eventually recall where he has placed his property and return there to reclaim it.

We think that the premises where the money was found is the airplane, not Lindner Aviation's hangar where the airplane happened to be parked when the money was discovered. The policy behind giving ownership of mislaid property to the owner of the premises where the property was mislaid supports this conclusion. If the true owner of the money attempts to locate it, he would initially look for the plane; it is unlikely he would begin his search by contacting businesses where the airplane might have been inspected. Therefore, we affirm the trial court's judgment that the bank, as the owner of the plane, has the right to possession of the property as against all but the true owner.

VII.   Is Benjamin Entitled to a Finder's Fee?

Benjamin claims that if he is not entitled to the money, he should be paid a ten percent finder's fee under section 644.13. The problem with this claim is that only the finder of *"lost* goods, money, bank notes, and other things" is rewarded with a finder's fee under chapter 644. Iowa Code § 644.13 (1991). Because the property found by Benjamin was mislaid property, not lost property, section 644.13 does not apply here. The trial court erred in awarding Benjamin a finder's fee.

VIII.   Summary.

We conclude that the district court's finding that the money discovered by Benjamin was mislaid property is supported by substantial evidence. Therefore, we affirm the district court's judgment that the bank has the right to the money as against all but the true owner. This decision makes it unnecessary to decide whether Benjamin or Lindner Aviation was the finder of the property. We reverse the court's decision awarding a finder's fee to Benjamin.

AFFIRMED IN PART; REVERSED IN PART.

Snell, Justice (dissenting).

I respectfully dissent.

The life of the law is logic, it has been said. *See Davis v. Aiken*, 111 Ga.App. 505, 142 S.E.2d 112, 119 (1965) (quoting Sir Edward Coke). If so, it should be applied here.

* * *

After considering the four categories of found money, the majority decides that Benjamin found mislaid money. The result is that the bank gets all the money; Benjamin, the finder, gets nothing. Apart from the obvious unfairness in result, I believe this conclusion fails to come from logical analysis.

Mislaid property is property voluntarily put in a certain place by the owner who then overlooks or forgets where the property is. *Ritz v. Selma United Methodist Church*, 467 N.W.2d 266, 268 (Iowa 1991). The property here consisted of two packets of paper currency totalling $18,910, three to four inches high, wrapped in aluminum foil. Inside the foil, the paper currency, predominantly twenty dollar bills, was tied with string and wrapped in handkerchiefs. Most of the mint dates were in the 1950s with one dated 1934. These packets were found in the left wing of the Mooney airplane after Benjamin removed a panel held in by rusty screws.

These facts satisfy the requirement that the property was voluntarily put in a certain place by the owner. But the second test for determining that property is mislaid is that the owner "overlooks or forgets where the property is." *See Ritz*, 467 N.W.2d at 269. I do not believe that the facts, logic, or common sense lead to a finding that this requirement is met. It is not likely or reasonable to suppose that a person would secrete $18,000 in an airplane wing and then forget where it was.

Cases cited by the majority contrasting "mislaid" property and "lost" property are appropriate for a comparison of these principles but do not foreclose other considerations. After finding the money, Benjamin proceeded to give written notice of finding the property as prescribed in Iowa Code chapter 644 (1993), "Lost Property." As set out in section 556F.8, notices were posted on the courthouse door and in three other public places in the county. In addition, notice was published once each week for three consecutive weeks in a newspaper of general circulation in the county. Also, affidavits of publication were filed with the county auditor who then had them published as part of the board of supervisors' proceedings. Iowa Code § 556F.9. After twelve months, if no person appears to claim and prove ownership of the property, the right to the property rests irrevocably in the finder. Iowa Code § 556F.11.

The purpose of this type of legal notice is to give people the opportunity to assert a claim if they have one. If no claim is made, the law presumes there is none or for whatever reason it is not asserted. Thus, a failure to make a claim after legal notice is given is a bar to a claim made thereafter.

Benjamin followed the law in giving legal notice of finding property. None of the parties dispute this. The suggestion that Benjamin should have initiated a further search for the true owner is not a requirement of the law, is therefore irrelevant, and in no way diminishes Benjamin's rights as finder.

The scenario unfolded in this case convinces me that the money found in the airplane wing was abandoned. Property is abandoned when the owner no longer wants to possess it. The money had been there for years, possibly thirty. No owner had claimed it in that time. No claim was made by the owner after legally prescribed notice was given that it had been found. Thereafter, logic and the law support a finding that the owner has voluntarily relinquished all right, title, and interest in the property. Whether the money was abandoned due to its connection to illegal drug trafficking or is otherwise contraband property is a matter for speculation. In any event, abandonment by the true owner has legally occurred and been established.

I would hold that Benjamin is legally entitled to the entire amount of money that he found in the airplane wing as the owner of abandoned property.

Notes, Problems, and Questions

1.   **GOLD FOUND IN LIBRARY***

By Abigail Van Buren

DEAR ABBY: I live in Salisbury, Mass., and I use the Newbury public library quite often.

---

* Taken from the DEAR ABBY column by Abigail Van Buren. © UNIVERSAL PRESS SYNDICATE. Reprinted with permission. All rights reserved.

I recently checked out an old book and brought it home to read. When I started to read it, I got the shock of my life. There, in the second chapter, was an old $5,000 bill! It's good. I have already checked it out.

What do I do? Keep it, or take it back to the library and find out if someone has reported it lost or misplaced?

I really want to do the right thing. Of course I would like to keep it, but not if it belongs to somebody else.

Please advise me.

                                    FINDERS KEEPERS

DEAR FINDERS: Take the $5,000 bill back to the library and ask them to try to find the owner. If they are unable to locate him (or her), the money is yours. (And check with a lawyer before you do anything.)

Comment on Dear Abby's advice.

2. Should found property be divided between the finder and the owner of the land upon which it was found? *See* Helmholz, *Equitable Division and the Law of Finders,* 52 Fordham L.Rev. 313 (1983).

3. Under English common law, treasure trove was a special category of lost property which belonged to the crown. As indicated in *Benjamin,* however, it has been generally held in the United States that treasure trove goes to the finder. *See* R. Brown, The Law of Personal Property § 3.3 (3d ed. 1975). A limited number of jurisdictions have rejected the doctrine of treasure trove as incompatible with modern society, and have held that hidden property belongs to the owner of the locus in quo. *See, e.g., Morgan v. Wiser,* 711 S.W.2d 220 (Tenn.App.1985) (declaring that treasure trove rule encourages trespass); *see also* Comment, *Property Owners' Constructive Possession of Treasure Trove: Rethinking the Finders Keepers Rule,* 38 U.C.L.A. L.Rev. 1659 (1991) (arguing for abolition of treasure trove).

4. Under certain circumstances, title to personal property may be acquired by adverse possession. *See* Note 6 on page 584.

FAVORITE v. MILLER

Supreme Court of Connecticut, 1978.
176 Conn. 310, 407 A.2d 974.

BOGDANSKI, ASSOCIATE JUSTICE.

On July 9, 1776, a band of patriots, hearing news of the Declaration of Independence, toppled the equestrian statue of King George III, which was located in Bowling Green Park in lower Manhattan, New York. The statue, of gilded lead, was then hacked apart and the pieces ferried over

Long Island Sound and loaded onto wagons at Norwalk, Connecticut, to be hauled some fifty miles northward to Oliver Wolcott's bullet-molding foundry in Litchfield, there to be cast into bullets. On the journey to Litchfield, the wagoners halted at Wilton, Connecticut, and while the patriots were imbibing, the loyalists managed to steal back pieces of the statue. The wagonload of the pieces lifted by the Tories was scattered about in the area of the Davis Swamp in Wilton and fragments of the statue have continued to turn up in that area since that time.

Although the above events have been dramatized in the intervening years, the unquestioned historical facts are: (1) the destruction of the statue; (2) cartage of the pieces to the Wolcott Foundry; (3) the pause at Wilton where part of the load was scattered over the Wilton area by loyalists; and (4) repeated discoveries of fragments over the last century.

In 1972, the defendant, Louis Miller, determined that a part of the statue might be located within property owned by the plaintiffs. On October 16 he entered the area of the Davis Swamp owned by the plaintiffs although he knew it to be private property. With the aid of a metal detector, he discovered a statuary fragment fifteen inches square and weighing twenty pounds which was embedded ten inches below the soil. He dug up this fragment and removed it from the plaintiffs' property. The plaintiffs did not learn that a piece of the statue of King George III had been found on their property until they read about it in the newspaper, long after it had been removed.

In due course, the piece of the statue made its way back to New York City, where the defendant agreed to sell it to the Museum of the City of New York for $5500. The museum continues to hold it pending resolution of this controversy.

In March of 1973, the plaintiffs instituted this action to have the fragment returned to them and the case was submitted to the court on a stipulation of facts. The trial court found the issues for the plaintiffs, from which judgment the defendant appealed to this court. The sole issue presented on appeal is whether the claim of the defendant, as finder, is superior to that of the plaintiffs, as owners of the land upon which the historic fragment was discovered.

Traditionally, when questions have arisen concerning the rights of the finder as against the person upon whose land the property was found, the resolution has turned upon the characterization given the property. Typically, if the property was found to be "lost" or "abandoned," the finder would prevail, whereas if the property was characterized as "mislaid," the owner or occupier of the land would prevail.

Lost property has traditionally been defined as involving an involuntary parting, i.e., where there is no intent on the part of the loser to part with the ownership of the property. Abandonment, in turn, has been defined as the voluntary relinquishment of ownership of property without reference to any particular person or purpose; i.e., a "throwing away" of the property concerned; while mislaid property is defined as that which is intentionally placed by the owner where he can obtain custody of it, but afterwards forgotten.

It should be noted that the classification of property as "lost," "abandoned," or "mislaid" requires that a court determine the intent or mental state of the unknown party who at some time in the past parted with the ownership or control of the property.

The trial court in this case applied the traditional approach and ruled in favor of the landowners on the ground that the piece of the statue found by Miller was "mislaid." The factual basis for that conclusion is set out in the finding, where the court found that "the loyalists did not wish to have the pieces [in their possession] during the turmoil surrounding the Revolutionary War and hid them in a place where they could resort to them [after the war], but forgot where they put them."

The defendant contends that the finding was made without evidence and that the court's conclusion "is legally impossible now after 200 years with no living claimants to the fragment and the secret of its burial having died with them." While we cannot agree that the court's conclusion was legally impossible, we do agree that any conclusion as to the mental state of persons engaged in events which occurred over two hundred years ago would be of a conjectural nature and as such does not furnish an adequate basis for determining rights of twentieth century claimants.

The defendant argues further that his rights in the statue are superior to those of anyone except the true owner (i.e., the British government). He presses this claim on the ground that the law has traditionally favored the finder as against all but the true owner, and that because his efforts brought the statue to light, he should be allowed to reap the benefits of his discovery. In his brief, he asserts: "As with archeologists forever probing and unearthing the past, to guide man for the betterment of those to follow, explorers like Miller deserve encouragement, and reward, in their selfless pursuit of the hidden, the unknown."

There are, however, some difficulties with the defendant's position. The first concerns the defendant's characterization of himself as a selfless seeker after knowledge. The facts in the record do not support such a conclusion. The defendant admitted that he was in the business of selling metal detectors and that he has used his success in finding the statue as advertising to boost his sales of such metal detectors, and that the advertising has been financially rewarding. Further, there is the fact that he signed a contract with the City Museum of New York for the sale of the statuary piece and that he stands to profit thereby.

Moreover, even if we assume his motive to be that of historical research alone, that fact will not justify his entering upon the property of another without permission. It is unquestioned that in today's world even archeologists must obtain permission from owners of property and the government of the country involved before they can conduct their explorations. Similarly, mountaineers must apply for permits, sometimes years in advance of their proposed expeditions. On a more familiar level, backpackers and hikers must often obtain permits before being allowed access to certain of our national parks and forests, even though that land is public and not private. Similarly, hunters and fishermen wishing to enter upon private property must first obtain the permission of the owner before they embark upon their respective pursuits.

Although few cases are to be found in this area of the law, one line of cases which have dealt with this issue has held that except where the trespass is trivial or merely technical, the fact that the finder is trespassing is sufficient to deprive him of his normal preference over the owner of the place where the property was found. The basis for the rule is that a wrongdoer should not be allowed to profit by his wrongdoing. Another line of cases holds that property, other than treasure trove, which is found embedded in the earth is the property of the owner of the locus in quo. Allred v. Biegel, 240 Mo.App. 818, 219 S.W.2d 665 (1949) (prehistoric Indian canoe); Elwes v. Brigg Gas Co., 33 Ch. 562 (1886) (prehistoric boat). The presumption in such cases is that possession of the article found is in the owner of the land and that the finder acquires no rights to the article found.

The defendant, by his own admission, knew that he was trespassing when he entered upon the property of the plaintiffs. He admitted that he was told by Gertrude Merwyn, the librarian of the Wilton Historical Society, *before* he went into the Davis Swamp area, that the land was privately owned and that Mrs. Merwyn recommended that he call the owners, whom she named, and obtain permission before he began his explorations. He also admitted that when he later told Mrs. Merwyn about his discovery, she again suggested that he contact the owners of the property, but that he failed to do so.

In the stipulation of facts submitted to the court, the defendant admitted entering the Davis Swamp property "with the belief that part of the 'King George Statue' * * * might be located within said property and with the intention of removing [the] same if located." The defendant has also admitted that the piece of the statue which he found was embedded in the ground ten inches below the surface and that it was necessary for him to excavate in order to take possession of his find.

In light of those undisputed facts the defendant's trespass was neither technical nor trivial. We conclude that the fact that the property found was embedded in the earth and the fact that the defendant was a trespasser are sufficient to defeat any claim to the property which the defendant might otherwise have had as a finder.

There is no error.

Notes

1. Mr. Steven Miller, Curator, Museum of the City of New York, has advised the authors that the contested statuary fragment was ultimately purchased by the Museum and placed on display.

2. The discovery of abandoned sunken vessels in territorial waters has raised questions as to the rights of a finder. There has been confusion over the ownership and management of these shipwrecks. As a result, considerable litigation arose between finders and states which asserted title to sunken vessels based on the doctrine of sovereignty. To resolve this matter Congress enacted the Abandoned Shipwreck Act of 1987. Under this measure the United States asserts its title to abandoned shipwrecks and transfers such title to the state in whose submerged land the shipwreck is located. The Act specifically provides that the law of salvage and finders shall not apply to such sunken vessels. 43 U.S.C.A. §§ 2101–2106 (West Supp. 1998). *See generally* McLaughlin, *Roots, Relics and Recovery: What Went Wrong With the Abandoned Shipwreck Act of 1987*, 19 Colum.-VLA J.L. & Arts 149 (1995); Note, *Abandoned Shipwreck Act of 1987: Navigating Turbulent Constitutional Waters*, 10 Bridgeport L.Rev. 361 (1990).

D. BAILMENTS

Bailment has been broadly defined as "the rightful possession of goods by one who is not the owner." 9 S. Williston, A Treatise on the Law of Contracts § 1030 (3d ed. 1967). Some courts, however, utilize a more restrictive definition of bailment as a delivery of property pursuant to a contract. *See, e.g.,* B.A. Ballou and Company, Inc. v. Citytrust, 218 Conn. 749, 591 A.2d 126 (1991). The existence of differing definitions may explain some of the doctrinal confusion that has plagued the law of bailments, but it does not tell us anything about the rights and duties of a bailor and bailee. *See* R. Brown, The Law of Personal Property § 10.1 (3d ed.1975). Such matters are explored in this section.

Bailments are at the heart of many commercial arrangements. Indeed, certain commercial bailments are covered extensively by Article 7 of the Uniform Commercial Code. Banks, common carriers, pawnbrokers, and warehouses make a business of being bailees. You are a bailee when you rent an automobile or piece of equipment. Gratuitous bailments are also common, as when you borrow a book from a friend.

In our hypothetical situation, the warehouseman that accepts the Lloyds' furniture for storage is a bailee. What are the warehouseman's rights and obligations?

ALLEN v. HYATT REGENCY—NASHVILLE HOTEL

Supreme Court of Tennessee, 1984.
668 S.W.2d 286.

HARBISON, JUSTICE.

In this case the Court is asked to consider the nature and extent of the liability of the operator of a commercial parking garage for theft of a vehicle during the absence of the owner. Both courts below, on the basis of prior decisions from this state, held that a bailment was created when the owner parked and locked his vehicle in a modern, indoor, multi-story garage operated by appellant in conjunction with a large hotel in downtown Nashville. We affirm.

There is almost no dispute as to the relevant facts. Appellant is the owner and operator of a modern high-rise hotel in Nashville fronting on the south side of Union Street. Immediately to the rear, or south, of the main hotel building there is a multi-story parking garage with a single entrance and a single exit to the west, on Seventh Avenue, North. As one enters the parking garage at the street level, there is a large sign reading "Welcome to Hyatt Regency–Nashville." There is another Hyatt Regency sign inside the garage at street level, together with a sign marked "Parking." The garage is available for parking by members of the general public as well as guests of the hotel, and the public are invited to utilize it.

On the morning of February 12, 1981, appellee's husband, Edwin Allen, accompanied by two passengers, drove appellee's new 1981 automobile into the parking garage. Neither Mr. Allen nor his passengers intended to register at the hotel as a guest. Mr. Allen had parked in this particular garage on several occasions, however, testifying that he felt that the vehicle would be safer in an attended garage than in an unattended outside lot on the street. The single entrance was controlled by a ticket machine. The single exit was controlled by an attendant in a booth just opposite to the entrance and in full view thereof. Appellee's husband entered the garage at the street level and took a ticket which was automatically dispensed by the machine. The machine activated a barrier gate which rose and permitted Mr. Allen to enter the garage. He drove to the fourth floor level, parked the vehicle, locked it, retained the ignition key, descended by elevator to the street level and left the garage. When he returned several hours later, the car was gone, and it has never been recovered. Mr. Allen reported the theft to the attendant at the exit booth, who stated, "Well, it didn't come out here." The attendant did not testify at the trial.

Mr. Allen then reported the theft to security personnel employed by appellant, and subsequently reported the loss to the police. Appellant regularly employed a number of security guards, who were dressed in a distinctive uniform, two of whom were on duty most of the time. These guards patrolled the hotel grounds and building as well as the garage and were instructed to make rounds through the garage, although not necessarily at specified intervals. One of the security guards told appellee's husband that earlier in the day he had received the following report:

"He said, 'It's a funny thing here. On my report here a lady called me somewhere around nine-thirty or after and said that there was someone messing with a car.'"

The guard told Mr. Allen that he closed his office and went up into the garage to investigate, but reported that he did not find anything unusual or out of the ordinary.

Customers such as Mr. Allen, upon entering the garage, received a ticket from the dispensing machine. On one side of this ticket are instructions to overnight guests to present the ticket to the front desk of the hotel. The other side contains instructions to the parker to keep the ticket and that the ticket must be presented to the cashier upon leaving the parking area. The ticket states that charges are made for the use of parking space only and that appellant assumes no responsibility for loss through fire, theft, collision or otherwise to the car or its contents. The ticket states that cars are parked at the risk of the owner, and parkers are instructed to lock their vehicles.[1] The record indicates that these tickets are given solely for the purpose of measuring the time during which a vehicle is parked in order that the attendant may collect the proper charge, and that they are not given for the purpose of identifying particular vehicles.

The question of the legal relationship between the operator of a vehicle which is being parked and the operator of parking establishments has been the subject of frequent litigation in this state and elsewhere. The authorities are in conflict, and the results of the cases are varied.

It is legally and theoretically possible, of course, for various legal relationships to be created by the parties, ranging from the traditional concepts of lessor-lessee, licensor-licensee, bailor-bailee, to that described in some jurisdictions as a "deposit." Several courts have found difficulty with the traditional criteria of bailment in analyzing park-and-lock cases. One of the leading cases is *McGlynn v. Parking Authority of City of Newark*, 86 N.J. 551, 432 A.2d 99 (1981). There the Supreme Court of New Jersey reviewed numerous decisions from within its own state and from other jurisdictions, and it concluded that it was more "useful and straightforward" to consider the possession and control elements in defining the duty of care of a garage operator to its customers than to consider them in the context of bailment. That Court concluded that the "realities" of the relationship between the parties gave rise to a duty of reasonable care on the part of operators of parking garages and parking lots. It further found that a garage owner is usually better situated to protect a parked car and to distribute the cost of protection through parking fees. It also emphasized that owners usually expect to receive their vehicles back in the same condition in which they left them and that the imposition of a duty to protect parked vehicles and their contents was consistent with that expectation. The Court went further and stated that since the owner is ordinarily absent when theft or damage occurs, the obligation to come forward with affirmative evidence of negligence could impose a difficult, if not insurmountable, burden upon him. After considering various policy considerations, which it acknowledged be the same as those recognized by courts holding that a bailment is created, the New Jersey Court indulged or authorized a

---

1. It is not insisted that the language of the ticket is sufficient to exonerate appellant, since the customer is not shown to have read it or to have had it called to his attention. *See Savoy Hotel Corp. v. Sparks*, 57 Tenn.App. 537, 421 S.W.2d 98 (1967).

presumption of negligence from proof of damage to a car parked in an enclosed garage. 432 A.2d at 105.[2]

Although the New Jersey Court concluded that a more flexible and comprehensive approach could be achieved outside of traditional property concepts, Tennessee courts generally have analyzed cases such as this in terms of sufficiency of the evidence to create a bailment for hire by implication. We believe that this continues to be the majority view and the most satisfactory and realistic approach to the problem, unless the parties clearly by their conduct or by express contract create some other relationship.

The subject has been discussed in numerous previous decisions in this state. One of the leading cases is *Dispeker v. New Southern Hotel Co.*, 213 Tenn. 378, 373 S.W.2d 904 (1963). In that case the guest at a hotel delivered his vehicle to a bellboy who took possession of it and parked it in a lot adjoining the hotel building. The owner kept the keys, but the car apparently was capable of being started without the ignition key. The owner apparently had told the attendant how to so operate it. Later the employee took the vehicle for his own purposes and damaged it. Under these circumstances the Court held that a bailment for hire had been created and that upon proof of misdelivery of the vehicle the bailee was liable to the customer.

In the subsequent case of *Scruggs v. Dennis*, 222 Tenn. 714, 440 S.W.2d 20 (1969), upon facts practically identical to those of the instant case, the Court again held that an implied bailment contract had been created between a customer who parked and locked his vehicle in a garage. Upon entry he received a ticket dispensed by a machine, drove his automobile to the underground third level of the garage and parked. He retained his ignition key, but when he returned to retrieve the automobile in the afternoon it had disappeared. It was recovered more than two weeks later and returned to the owner in a damaged condition.

In that case the operator of the garage had several attendants on duty, but the attendants did not ordinarily operate the parked vehicles, as in the instant case.

Although the Court recognized that there were some factual differences between the *Scruggs* case and that of *Dispeker v. New Southern Hotel Co., supra*, it concluded that a bailment had been created when the owner parked his vehicle for custody and safe keeping in the parking garage, where there was limited access and where the patron had to present a ticket to an attendant upon leaving the premises.

* * *

On the contrary, in the case of *Rhodes v. Pioneer Parking Lot, Inc.*, 501 S.W.2d 569 (Tenn.1973), a bailment was found not to exist when the owner left his vehicle in an open parking lot which was wholly unattend-

---

2. Other courts, declining to find a bailment, have onerated the customer with proving negligence. *E.g., Central Parking System v. Miller*, 586 S.W.2d 262 (Ky.1979).

ed and where he simply inserted coins into a meter, received a ticket, then parked the vehicle himself and locked it.

* * *

In the instant case, appellee's vehicle was not driven into an unattended or open parking area. Rather it was driven into an enclosed, indoor, attended commercial garage which not only had an attendant controlling the exit but regular security personnel to patrol the premises for safety.

Under these facts we are of the opinion that the courts below correctly concluded that a bailment for hire had been created, and that upon proof of nondelivery appellee was entitled to the statutory presumption of negligence provided in T.C.A. § 24–5–111.

We recognize that there is always a question as to whether there has been sufficient delivery of possession and control to create a bailment when the owner locks a vehicle and keeps the keys. Nevertheless, the realities of the situation are that the operator of the garage is, in circumstances like those shown in this record, expected to provide attendants and protection. In practicality the operator does assume control and custody of the vehicles parked, limiting access thereto and requiring the presentation of a ticket upon exit. As stated previously, the attendant employed by appellant did not testify, but he told appellee's husband that the vehicle did not come out of the garage through the exit which he controlled. This testimony was not amplified, but the attendant obviously must have been in error or else must have been inattentive or away from his station. The record clearly shows that there was no other exit from which the vehicle could have been driven.

Appellant made no effort to rebut the presumption created by statute in this state (which is similar to presumptions indulged by courts in some other jurisdictions not having such statutes). While the plaintiff did not prove positive acts of negligence on the part of appellant, the record does show that some improper activity or tampering with vehicles had been called to the attention of security personnel earlier in the day of the theft in question, and that appellee's new vehicle had been removed from the garage by some person or persons unknown, either driving past an inattentive attendant or one who had absented himself from his post, there being simply no other way in which the vehicle could have been driven out of the garage.

Under the facts and circumstances of this case, we are not inclined to depart from prior decisions or to place the risk of loss upon the consuming public as against the operators of commercial parking establishments such as that conducted by appellant. We recognize that park-and-lock situations arise under many and varied factual circumstances. It is difficult to lay down one rule of law which will apply to all cases. The expectations of the parties and their conduct can cause differing legal relationships to arise, with consequent different legal results. We do not find the facts of the present case, however, to be at variance with the legal requirements of the traditional concept of a bailment for hire. In our opinion it amounted to more than a mere license or hiring of a space to park a vehicle, unaccompanied by any expectation of protection or other obligation upon the operator of the establishment.

The judgment of the courts below is affirmed at the cost of appellant. The cause will be remanded to the trial court for any further proceedings which may be necessary.

DROWOTA, JUSTICE, dissenting.

In this case we are asked to consider the nature and extent of liability of the operator of a commercial "park and lock" parking garage. In making this determination, we must look to the legal relationship between the operator of the vehicle and the operator of the parking facility. The majority opinion holds that a bailment contract has been created, and upon proof of non-delivery Plaintiff is entitled to the statutory presumption of negligence provided in T.C.A. § 24–5–111. I disagree, for I find no bailment existed and therefore the Plaintiff does not receive the benefit of the presumption. Consequently, the Plaintiff had the duty to prove affirmatively the negligence of the operator of the parking facility and this Plaintiff failed to do.

* * *

From its earliest origins, the most distinguishing factor identifying a bailment has been delivery. Our earliest decisions also recognize acceptance as a necessary factor, requiring that possession and control of the property pass from bailor to bailee, to the exclusion of control by others. The test thus becomes whether the operator of the vehicle has made such a delivery to the operator of the parking facility as to amount to a relinquishment of his exclusive possession, control, and dominion over the vehicle so that the latter can exclude it from the possession of all others. If so, a bailment has been created.

* * *

The difficulty in these types of cases seems to arise when the traditional elements of bailment are missing and courts must determine whether there is an implied bailment created by implication from the surrounding circumstances and the conduct of the parties.

* * *

The majority opinion "recognize[s] that there is always a question as to whether there has been sufficient delivery of possession and control to create a bailment when the owner locks a vehicle and keeps the keys." The majority finds that "in practicality the operator does assume control and custody of the vehicles parked, limiting access thereto and requiring the presentation of a ticket upon exit." The majority opinion, as did the *Scruggs* court, finds custody and control implied because of the limited access and because "the presentation of a ticket upon exit" is required. I cannot agree with this analysis as creating a bailment situation. I do not believe that based upon the fact that a ticket was required to be presented upon leaving, that this factor created a proper basis upon which to find a bailment relationship. The ticket did not identify the vehicle or the operator of the vehicle, as do most bailment receipts. The cashier was not performing the traditional bailee role or identifying and returning a particular article, but instead was merely computing the amount owed and accepting payment due for use of a parking space. I do not believe the Defendant exercised such possession and control over Plaintiff's automobile as is necessary in an implied bailment.

* * * The full transfer of possession and control, necessary to constitute delivery, should not be found to exist simply by the presentation of a ticket upon exit. In the case at bar, I find no such delivery and relinquishment of exclusive possession and control as to create a bailment. Plaintiff parked his car, locked it and retained the key. Certainly Defendant cannot be said to have sole custody of Plaintiff's vehicle, for Defendant could not move it, did not know to whom it belonged, and did not know when it would be reclaimed or by whom. Anyone who manually obtained a ticket from the dispenser could drive out with any vehicle he was capable of operating. Also, a cashier was not always on duty. When on duty, so long as the parking fee was paid—by what means could the Defendant reasonably exercise control? The necessary delivery and relinquishment of control by the Plaintiff, the very basis upon which the bailment theory was developed, is missing.

We should realize that the circumstances upon which the principles of bailment law were established and developed are not always applicable to the operation of the modern day automated parking facility. The element of delivery, of sole custody and control are lacking in this case.

Problems and Questions

1. What are the elements of a bailment? Did the plaintiff deliver the automobile to the defendant? For a case which adopts the reasoning of the dissenting opinion in *Allen,* see Central Parking System v. Miller, 586 S.W.2d 262 (Ky.1979).

2. Assume that the plaintiff parked the automobile in an unattended park and lock lot. Same result as in *Allen*? *See* Colwell v. Metropolitan Airports Commission, Inc., 386 N.W.2d 246 (Minn.App.1986).

3. A's airplane was damaged by a motor vehicle while it was parked at B's airport facility pursuant to a storage contract. The airplane which could be started without a key was parked in a designated space and held with tie-down ropes provided by B. B contends that there was no bailment. Do you agree? *See* Aerowake Aviation, Inc. v. Winter, 423 So.2d 165 (Ala.1982).

4. What is the significance of finding that a bailment exists? *See* Helmholz, *Bailment Theories and the Liability of Bailees: The Elusive Uniform Standard of Reasonable Care,* 41 Kan.L.Rev. 97 (1992).

BUENA VISTA LOAN & SAVINGS
BANK v. BICKERSTAFF

Court of Appeals of Georgia, 1970.
121 Ga.App. 470, 174 S.E.2d 219.

This action is based on the alleged mysterious disappearance of $9,400 in cash from a safe deposit box which the plaintiff customer had rented from the defendant bank. The bank appeals from the denial of a summary judgment.

* * *

JORDAN, PRESIDING JUDGE.

The plaintiff bases his claim primarily on the breach of a bailor-bailee relationship with the bank in respect to the alleged missing contents of the box, or, in the alternative, if the relationship is not that of a bailor-bailee, at least a duty on the part of the bank to exercise ordinary care to safeguard the contents of the box, contending that the evidence of negligence in this respect is sufficient to create a jury question.

The defendant relies on the decision in Tow v. Evans, 194 Ga. 160, 20 S.E.2d 922 defining the relationship between the bank and a customer to whom it leases a safe deposit box in its vault as that of lessor and lessee, * * * and, viewing this relationship as merely one of landlord and tenant, contends that the bank incurs no liability by reason of the mysterious disappearance of the money. The bank argues further that even if the defendant was under a duty in some manner to protect the contents of the box, the evidence fails to disclose any breach that could be regarded as the proximate cause of the loss.

We do not regard the mere labeling of the relationship in Tow v. Evans, supra, as that of lessor and lessee * * * as a holding which is dispositive of the relationship between the bank and a boxholder in respect to safeguarding the contents of the box and liability of the bank to the customer for a mysterious disappearance of the contents. Except to determine that the relationship of lessor and lessee was such as to preclude the use of statutory garnishment, the court in that case made no attempt to define the duties of the lessor towards its lessee in respect to the lease of a safe deposit box. Both lease and bailment are indicative of a contractual relationship, and the terms are not necessarily mutually exclusive. A lease may refer to a contract involving realty or personalty, or both, whereas a bailment involves the custody of personalty.

Whatever the label attached to the contract here involved, the facts demand a determination that the bank was involved in an undertaking for a consideration to safeguard the personal property of another in respect to whatever was placed in the safe deposit box, without acquiring any knowledge of the contents of the box, and that it exercised complete dominion at all times over this box, regardless of its contents, except when the customer requested access thereto.

* * *

The parties do not cite, and research fails to disclose any Georgia decision directly in point. The early case of Merchants' National Bank of Savannah v. Guilmartin, 88 Ga. 797, 15 S.E. 831 recognizes a special deposit of securities for the accommodation of the customer, for which he received a receipt, as creating a gratuitous bailment, obligating the bank to exercise slight diligence, which could be met, in respect to a loss caused by the felonious appropriation by a cashier, "when it does its full duty in selecting a proper person, and in not disregarding indications of dishonesty which ought to arouse suspicion and investigation." When the same case was before the court again, 93 Ga. 503, at p. 506, 21 S.E. 55 the court stated that nothing less than actual proof of the standard of diligence imposed on the bank would satisfy the requirement of the law. To the same effect, see Merchants' National Bank of Savannah v. Carhart, 95 Ga. 394, 22 S.E. 628.

Summarized, these cases impose upon the bank, once the fact of loss * * * is shown, the duty of affirmatively showing the exercise of the required degree of care, and this is in accord with the law of bailment as it now exists in this State.

* * *

We view the relationship here created, as between the customer and the bank, as one of bailor and bailee, making the bank a depositary for hire under a duty to exercise ordinary care, the proof of which is cast upon the bank after proof of the fact of loss by the customer[.] Code § 12–104.[1] This burden on the bailee is regarded as a presumption of negligence, i.e., a rebuttable inference, thus placing on the bailee the affirmative duty of producing evidence of its diligence. Where some evidence of this nature is adduced in the trial of a case, whether the bailee has overcome the rebuttable inference would ordinarily be a matter for jury determination. But this is a duty imposed by the law of bailment on the bank which it must meet to preserve an issue for jury determination and the bank, as the movant for summary judgment, in order to prevail, has the greater burden of showing the absence of any genuine issue of fact as to a material matter and that as a matter of law it is entitled to judgment. In short, in the posture of the present case, it must appear from the consideration of the pleadings and evidence that as a matter of law the bank did all that was required of it, in the exercise of ordinary care under the circumstances, to protect the contents of the safe deposit box. What constitutes the exercise of ordinary care, or the lack of it, is ordinarily a jury question, and the evidence here, which discloses, among other things, practices which fall below acceptable

---

1. Ga. Code Ann. § 44–12–44 (1982) (previously § 12–104) provides: "In all cases of bailment, after proof of loss by the bailor, the burden of proof is on the bailee to show proper diligence." [Editors' note.]

standards in the industry, does not eliminate, as a permissible jury determination, that the failure to meet acceptable standards in the industry is a failure to exercise ordinary care which constitutes the proximate cause of the mysterious disappearance.

In view of the foregoing the trial court properly refused to grant a summary judgment for the bank.

Judgment affirmed.

Problems and Questions

1. Why should a bailee have the burden of proving that a loss did not result from its negligence?

2. When X rented a safe deposit box from Friendly Bank, X signed a contract which provided in part:

> It is expressly understood * * * that in making this lease the Bank does not assume the relation and duty of bailee and shall not be liable for loss or damage to, the contents of said box, caused by burglary, fire or any cause whatsoever, but that the entire risk of such loss or damage is assumed by the lessee.

An unauthorized person gained access to X's safe deposit box, with the resulting loss of $250,000 in bearer bonds. X brings suit against Friendly Bank. The Bank raises the contract as a defense. What result? *See* Farmers Bank of Greenwood v. Perry, 301 Ark. 547, 787 S.W.2d 645 (1990); Sniffen v. Century National Bank of Broward, 375 So.2d 892 (Fla.App.1979).

3. One may come into control of a particular item contrary to expectation or desire. What are the responsibilities of such constructive bailees?

SHAMROCK HILTON HOTEL v. CARANAS

Texas Court of Civil Appeals, 1972.
488 S.W.2d 151.

BARRON, JUSTICE.

This is an appeal in an alleged bailment case from a judgment non obstante veredicto in favor of plaintiffs below.

Plaintiffs, husband and wife, were lodging as paying guests at the Shamrock Hilton Hotel in Houston on the evening of September 4, 1966, when they took their dinner in the hotel restaurant. After completing the meal, Mr. and Mrs. Caranas, plaintiffs, departed the dining area leaving her purse behind. The purse was found by the hotel bus boy who, pursuant to the instructions of the hotel, dutifully delivered the forgotten item to the restaurant cashier, a Mrs. Luster. The testimony indicates that some short time thereafter the cashier gave the purse to a man other than Mr. Caranas who came to claim it. There is no testimony on the question of whether identification was sought by the cashier. The purse allegedly contained $5.00 in cash, some credit cards, and ten pieces of jewelry said to be worth $13,062. The misplacement of the purse was realized the following morning, at which time plaintiffs notified the hotel authorities of the loss.

Plaintiffs filed suit alleging negligent delivery of the purse to an unknown person and seeking a recovery for the value of the purse and its contents.

The trial was to a jury which found that the cashier was negligent in delivering the purse to someone other than plaintiffs, and that this negligence was a proximate cause of the loss of the purse. The jury further found that plaintiffs were negligent in leaving the purse containing the jewelry in the hotel dining room, and that this negligence was a proximate cause of the loss.

A motion for judgment n.o.v. and to disregard findings with respect to the findings that plaintiffs' negligence was a proximate cause of the loss of the purse and its contents was granted, and judgment was entered by the trial court for plaintiffs in the amount of $11,252.00 plus interest and costs. Shamrock Hilton Hotel and Hilton Hotels Corporation have perfected this appeal.

We find after a full review of the record that there is sufficient evidence to warrant the submission of appellees' issues complained of and to support the jury findings on the special issues to the effect that the misdelivery was negligence and a proximate cause of the loss to appellees.

* * *

Contrary to appellants' contention, we find that there was indeed a constructive bailment of the purse. The delivery and acceptance were evidenced in the acts of Mrs. Caranas' unintentionally leaving her purse behind in the hotel restaurant and the bus boy, a hotel employee, picking it up and taking it to the cashier who accepted the purse as a lost or misplaced item. The delivery need not be a knowingly intended act on the part of Mrs. Caranas if it is apparent that were she, the quasi or constructive bailor, aware of the circumstances (here the chattel's being misplaced) she would have desired the person finding the article to have kept it safely for its subsequent return to her.

As stated above, the evidence conclusively showed facts from which there was established a bailment with the Caranases as bailors and the hotel as bailee. The evidence also showed that the hotel, as bailee, had received Mrs. Caranas' purse and had not returned it on demand. Such evidence raised a presumption that the hotel had failed to exercise ordinary care in protecting the appellees' property. When the hotel failed to come forward with any evidence to the effect that it had exercised ordinary care, that the property had been stolen, or that the property had been lost, damaged or destroyed by fire or by an act of God, the appellees' proof ripened into proof by which the hotel's primary liability was established as a matter of law.

* * *

Further, this bailment was one for the mutual benefit of both parties. Appellees were paying guests in the hotel and in its dining room. Appellant hotel's practice of keeping patrons' lost personal items until they could be returned to their rightful owners, as reflected in the testimony, is certainly evidence of its being incidental to its business, as we would think it would be for almost any commercial enterprise which caters to the general public. Though no direct charge is made for this service there is indirect benefit to be had in the continued patronage of the hotel by customers who have lost chattels and who have been able to claim them from the management.

Having found this to have been a bailment for the mutual benefit of the parties, we hold that the appellants owed the appellees the duty of reasonable care in the return of the purse and jewelry, and the hotel is therefore liable for its ordinary negligence.

Appellants urge that if a bailment is found it existed only as to "the purse and the usual petty cash or credit cards found therein" and not to the jewelry of which the hotel had no actual notice. This exact question so far as we can determine has never been squarely put before the Texas Courts, but as appellants concede, the general rule in other jurisdictions is that a bailee is liable not only for lost property of which he has actual knowledge but also the property he could reasonably expect to find contained within the bailed property.

We believe appellants' contention raises the question of whether or not it was foreseeable that such jewelry might be found in a woman's purse in a restaurant of a hotel such as the Shamrock Hilton under these circumstances.

Although the burden may rest with the appellees to prove that the jewelry was a part of the total bailment and the issue of whether it was reasonably foreseeable that such jewelry might be contained within the lost purse ordinarily should have been submitted by appellees, it remains for the hotel to object to the omission of the issue if it wishes to avoid the possibility of deemed findings by the Court. We cannot say as a matter of law that there is no evidence upon which a jury could reasonably find that it was foreseeable that such jewelry might be found in a purse under such circumstances as here presented. It is known that people who are guests in hotels such as the Shamrock Hilton, a well-known Houston hotel, not infrequently bring such expensive jewelry with them, and it does not impress us as unreasonable under the circumstances that one person might have her jewelry in her purse either awaiting a present occasion to wear it or following reclaiming it from the hotel safe in anticipation of leaving the hotel.

We find that the question of whether it is reasonably foreseeable that a woman, under the circumstances of this case, might keep jewelry in a purse which is determinative of whether there was a bailment of jewelry and whether the negligence in losing the purse was a proximate cause of losing the jewelry, is an omitted issue in the grounds of recovery to which the submitted issues are reasonably or necessarily referable.

Appellants were on notice that recovery was sought primarily for the value of the jewelry and that the only ground for recovery was the hotel's negligence with respect to the bailment, purse and contents. This is reflected in appellants' second amended original answer where they allege that there was no bailment as to the jewelry within the purse.

The record reflects no timely objection to the issues submitted or to the omitting of a special issue, and therefore * * * we deem it to be found that one might reasonably expect to find valuable jewelry within a purse under the circumstances of this case in support of the judgment below. It follows that the findings of negligence and proximate cause of the loss of the purse apply to the jewelry as well, which is deemed to be a part of the bailment. There was no error in the judgment insofar as it was complained that there was no bailment of the jewelry and that there was no connection between the findings of negligence and proximate cause as regards the purse and the jewelry.

Appellant's final point of error complains of the trial court's granting of appellees' motion for judgment notwithstanding the verdict and disregarding the jury's findings on special issues that appellees' leaving the purse was negligence and a proximate cause of the loss of the jewelry. In support of this contention appellants cite Southwestern Hotel Co. v. Rogers, 183 S.W.2d 751 (Tex.Civ.App.El Paso 1944), aff'd 143 Tex. 343, 184 S.W.2d 835 (1945) and Driskill Hotel Co. v. Anderson, 19 S.W.2d 216 (Tex.Civ.App.Austin 1929, no writ), for the proposition that contributory negligence of a guest of a hotel is an absolute defense to a claim for jewelry or money lost in the hotel. Both cases, however, are distinguishable on the facts in that here the loss occurred *after* appellees had relinquished possession of the purse and its contents, and the hotel alone had assumed responsibility for the items.

* * *

The bus boy and cashier assumed possession and control of the purse per instructions of the hotel with respect to articles misplaced or lost by customers. * * * [O]nce the bailee assumed possession he alone had the duty to safeguard the bailed article. We find therefore under these facts that the negligence of Mrs. Caranas was not a cause " * * * which in a natural and continuous sequence produces an event * * * "of this nature.

* * *

The judgment of the trial court is affirmed.

SAM D. JOHNSON (dissenting).

If, as found by the majority, the evidence conclusively showed facts from which there was established a bailment, it is well to examine the relationship of the parties. Mrs. Caranas is characterized as a quasi or constructive bailor. The bailment is characterized as a mutual benefit and as a constructive bailment. If a bailment was created it was certainly unintentional. Mrs. Caranas had no intention of creating a bailment.

The hotel had no such intention. Neither, in fact, for a considerable period of time knew of its existence.

This, for two reasons forming the basis of this dissent, is at least true of the jewelry allegedly contained in the purse. First, it seems to be conceded that the hotel had no actual notice of the existence of the jewelry in the purse and there is no authority in this state for the proposition that a bailee is liable for property he could reasonably expect to find contained in the bailed property. Secondly, even if the foregoing were true it does not occur to this writer that it is reasonable to expect a purse, inadvertently left under a chair in a hotel's restaurant and not even missed by the owner until the next day, might contain ten pieces of jewelry valued at $13,062.00.

This dissent is therefore most respectfully submitted.

Notes and Questions

1. The bailee is under a contractual duty to redeliver the subject of the bailment to the bailor upon demand. Hence, under common law a bailee is strictly liable in the event of misdelivery to a third party. *See* R. Brown, The Law of Personal Property § 11.7 (3d ed. 1975). The Shamrock Hilton Hotel had clearly misdelivered plaintiff's property. Why is liability predicated on a showing of negligence?

2. The uncertainty of common law standards proved too great for many commercial dealings. As a consequence, statutes and standard form contracts have narrowed the scope of common law bailments. Analyze the following case. Has the Uniform Commercial Code changed the governing law?

SINGER COMPANY v. STOTT & DAVIS MOTOR EXPRESS, INC. and STODA CORPORATION

Supreme Court of New York, Appellate Division, Fourth Department, 1981.
79 A.D.2d 227, 436 N.Y.S.2d 508.

[Plaintiffs Singer Company and Sterling Millwork stored goods in a warehouse leased and operated by defendant Stoda Corporation in Auburn, New York. In 1974 a fire broke out in the warehouse, totally destroying plaintiffs' property. Plaintiffs alleged that the loss of their property was caused by Stoda's negligence. At trial the plaintiffs presented evidence showing that the defendant had taken inadequate fire precautions. The trial court dismissed plaintiffs' complaint for failure to establish a prima facie case.]

MOULE, JUSTICE.

Plaintiffs first contend that they established prima facie cases of negligence against defendant Stoda. * * *

They, therefore, maintain that the trial court erred in dismissing the complaints against these defendants.

In reviewing the dismissal of a plaintiff's complaint, the evidence must be examined in the light most favorable to plaintiff. Facts alleged by plaintiff and inferences which may be reasonably drawn from them must be accepted as true. The case should be submitted to the jury only where there is a rational process by which it could find for the plaintiff.

If plaintiff is to recover for bailee negligence, he must establish that a bailment relationship existed with respect to the destroyed goods, and that the bailee failed to exercise the required standard of care in storing the goods. The statutorily defined standard of care provides:

> (1) A warehouseman is liable for damages for loss of or injury to the goods caused by his failure to exercise such care in regard to them as a reasonably careful man would exercise under like circumstances but unless otherwise agreed he is not liable for damages which could not have been avoided by the exercise of such care.

(Uniform Commercial Code, § 7–204). This statute does not alter the common law, but codifies it.

Once plaintiff establishes delivery of the goods and the failure of the bailee to return them on demand, a prima facie case of negligence is made and the burden of coming forward with evidence tending to show due care shifts to the bailee. However, the burden of persuasion never shifts from the plaintiff to the bailee, and the bailee can rebut the prima facie case if it shows either how the loss occurred and that this was in no way attributable to its negligence, or that the requisite care was exercised in all respects to the bailed goods so that, regardless of how the accident transpired, it could not have been caused by any negligence on the bailee's part. If the goods have been destroyed by fire, the plaintiff has the burden to show that the loss resulted from the bailee's negligence.

The evidence presented at trial established a bailment relationship between plaintiffs and Stoda, delivery of the goods to Stoda and its failure to return them upon demand. This proof established plaintiffs' prima facie case of negligence and shifted the burden to the bailee of coming forward with evidence tending to show due care. Plaintiffs also went forward with proof of negligence on the part of Stoda, the evidence showing that the sprinkler system was inoperable; that Stoda was aware of this condition; that no watchmen were present; and that the fire alarm system could not be automatically activated. Expert testimony established that a properly operating sprinkler system could control the spread of the fire, and that an automatic alarm system would have been helpful given the close proximity of the fire department.

Under these circumstances, the issue of bailee negligence should have been submitted to the jury. Stoda did not successfully rebut plaintiffs' prima facie case of negligence by merely showing the fact that the goods were destroyed by fire, especially where plaintiffs went forward with proof of negligence. Plaintiffs produced sufficient evidence to establish a rational basis by which the jury could have found in their favor. Whether due caution requires a bailee to furnish the means for extinguishing fire, or provide an all-night watchman, has been held to be a question for the jury. Consequently, this cause of action by Singer and Sterling against Stoda should not have been dismissed.

Notes and Problems

1. For a case involving a fact pattern similar to that found in *Singer*, see Fleetguard, Inc. v. Dixie Box and Crating Co., 314 S.C. 471, 445 S.E.2d 459 (App.1994). In *Fleetguard*, the bailee was unable to rebut the presumption of negligence and thus, was found liable when filter paper stored by the bailor in the bailee's warehouse was damaged by smoke and water during a fire at the warehouse.

2. Suppose there had been no fire in *Singer*, but that Stoda had delivered the plaintiff's goods to a third party who possessed the proper documents. What result at common law? Does the following U.C.C. section change this result?

§ 7–404. No Liability for Good Faith Delivery Pursuant to Receipt or Bill

A bailee who in good faith including observance of reasonable commercial standards has received goods and delivered or otherwise disposed of them according to the terms of the document of title or pursuant to this Article is not liable therefor. This rule applies even though the person from whom he received the goods had no authority to procure the document or to dispose of the goods and even though the person to whom he delivered the goods had no authority to receive them.

CARR v. HOOSIER PHOTO SUPPLIES, INC.

Supreme Court of Indiana, 1982.
441 N.E.2d 450.

GIVAN, CHIEF JUSTICE.

Litigation in this cause began with the filing of a complaint in Marion Municipal Court by John R. Carr, Jr. (hereinafter "Carr"), seeking damages in the amount of $10,000 from defendants Hoosier Photo Supplies, Inc. (hereinafter "Hoosier") and Eastman Kodak Company (hereinafter "Kodak").

Carr was the beneficiary of a judgment in the amount of $1,013.60. Both sides appealed.

The Court of Appeals affirmed the trial court in its entirety.

Kodak and Hoosier now petition to transfer this cause to this Court. We hereby grant that petition and vacate the opinion of the Court of Appeals. For reasons we shall set out below, we remand the cause to the trial court with instructions to enter a judgment in favor of Carr in the amount of $13.60 plus interest. Each party is to bear its own costs.

The facts were established by stipulation agreement between the parties and thus are not in dispute. In the late spring or early summer of 1970, Carr purchased some Kodak film from a retailer not a party to this action, including four rolls of Kodak Ektachrome–X 135 slide film that are the subject matter of this dispute. During the month of August, 1970, Carr and his family vacationed in Europe. Using his own camera Carr took a great many photographs of the sites they saw, using among others the four rolls of film referred to earlier. Upon their return to the United States, Carr took a total of eighteen [18] rolls of exposed film to Hoosier to be developed. Only fourteen [14] of the rolls were returned to Carr after processing. All efforts to find the missing rolls or the pictures developed from them were unsuccessful. Litigation commenced when the parties were unable to negotiate a settlement.

The film Carr purchased, manufactured by Kodak, is distributed in boxes on which there is printed the following legend:

"Read This Notice"

"This film will be replaced if defective in manufacture, labeling, or packaging, or if damaged or lost by us or any subsidiary company even though by negligence or other fault. Except for such replacement, the sale, processing, or other handling of this film for any purpose is without other warranty of liability."

In the stipulation of facts it was agreed though Carr never read this notice on the packages of film he bought, he knew there was printed on such packages "a limitation of liability similar or identical to the Eastman Kodak limitation of liability." The source of Carr's knowledge was agreed to be his years of experience as an attorney and as an amateur photographer.

When Carr took all eighteen [18] rolls of exposed film to Hoosier for processing, he was given a receipt for each roll. Each receipt contained the following language printed on the back side:

"Although film price does not include processing by Kodak, the return of any film or print to us for processing or any other purpose, will constitute an agreement by you that if any such film or print is damaged or lost by us or any subsidiary company, even though by negligence or other fault, it will be replaced with an equivalent amount of Kodak film and processing and, except for such replacement, the handling of such film or prints by us for any purpose is without other warranty or liability."

Again, it was agreed though Carr did not read this notice he was aware Hoosier "[gave] to their customers at the time of accepting film for processing, receipts on which there are printed limitations of liability similar or identical to the limitation of liability printed on each receipt received by Carr from Hoosier Photo."

It was stipulated upon receipt of the eighteen [18] rolls of exposed film only fourteen [14] were returned to Hoosier by Kodak after processing. Finally, it was stipulated the four rolls of film were lost by either Hoosier or Kodak.

Kodak and Hoosier petition to transfer this cause to this Court. They allege the Court of Appeals erred when it decided two new questions of law. These errors are alleged to be: (1) that Hoosier's limitation of liability as a bailee for its own negligence, as reflected on the receipts given to Carr, was ineffective; and (2) that Kodak's limitation for its own negligence, as reflected on the boxes of film sold to Carr, was ineffective.

* * *

At the time Carr purchased the film in question the sale contract was completed. The box in which the film was packaged contained an offer by Kodak to enter into a bailment contract to process the film. This offer of bailment was accepted by Carr when he turned the film over to Hoosier and Kodak for processing.

We thus find the breach of contract occurring in the case at bar was a breach of a contract for bailment between the parties. In 8 Am.Jur.2d Bailments § 34 (1980), it is stated:

"Where property in an unmanufactured state is delivered by one person to another, on an agreement that it shall be manufactured or *converted in form,* or there is a delivery of chattels under an agreement that the party receiving them shall improve them by his labor or skill, whether the transaction is a sale or a bailment depends generally on *whether the product of the identical articles delivered is to be returned to the original owner, though in a new form. If it is to be so returned, it is a bailment* * * * . The intention of the parties is the controlling factor * * * ." (Emphasis added.) *Id.* at 769–70.

That either Kodak or Hoosier breached the bailment contract, by negligently losing the four rolls of film, was established in the stipulated agreement of facts. Therefore, the next issue raised is whether either or both, Hoosier or Kodak, may limit their liability as reflected on the film packages and receipts.

* * *

At the time Carr purchased the film, the box contained an offer by Kodak to process the film under the stated conditions. At that time no contract existed between Carr and Kodak. When Carr submitted the film for processing, he in effect accepted the terms and conditions of Kodak's offer.

We view the receipt issued by Hoosier as a reiteration of the offer by Kodak and a memorialization of the acceptance of the contract by the person submitting the film for processing. Hoosier was acting as the agent for Kodak in this regard.

The parties in this case cite us to two Indiana cases on the subject of the validity of contract terms purporting to limit one party's liability to another in the event of the former's breach of the contract by a negligent act.

In General Grain, Inc. v. International Harvester, (1968) 142 Ind. App. 12, 232 N.E.2d 616, the Court of Appeals held the exculpatory clause of a bailment contract between a garage owner and a customer was invalid. Likewise, in Weaver v. American Oil Co., (1971) 257 Ind. 458, 276 N.E.2d 144, this Court held a similar exculpatory clause of a lease was invalid and could not be enforced against Weaver.

However, a close reading of these cases shows neither may be read so broadly as to stand for the proposition all limitation of liability clauses in contracts are void as a matter of law. In *General Grain, supra,* the Court of Appeals acknowledged though the parties are free to negotiate and include terms in a contract as they see fit, some kinds of terms, including terms limiting one's liability for breach of the contract, may be voided as being contrary to public policy. The Court of Appeals observed a professional bailee is not permitted to enforce a limitation of his liability due to his negligence in losing or damaging bailed goods merely by posting a notice of such limitation or printing it on a receipt or claim check. The Court then continued:

"A notice or statement of terms, such as the one here in issue, is at most only a proposal. It does not bind a bailor delivering property to a bailee *unless the former assents to the terms proposed.* In this case there was no assent.

* * *

"The rule gains in force where (as the trial court found) the appellant did not have any knowledge of the disclaimer of liability." (Emphasis added.) *General Grain, supra,* 142 Ind.App. at 17, 232 N.E.2d at 619.

It must be pointed out in the *General Grain* case the trial court found the bailor whose remedy was limited by the exculpatory clause was not aware of the exculpatory language in the bailment contract.

In *Weaver, supra,* this Court held an exculpatory clause in a lease limiting American Oil's liability to Weaver, the lessee, for damages caused by American Oil's negligent acts was unconscionable and hence void. We pointed out in that case the facts showed Weaver had only a year and a half of high school education, that he "was not one who should be expected to know the law or understand the meaning of technical terms," and "the evidence showed Weaver had never read the lease prior to signing and that the clauses in the lease were never explained to him in a manner from which he could grasp their legal significance." *Weaver, supra,* 257 Ind. at 460–61, 276 N.E.2d at 146.

We summarized our view in *Weaver, supra,* in the following language:

"When a party can show that the contract, which is sought to be enforced, was in fact an unconscionable one, *due to a prodigious amount of bargaining power on behalf of the stronger party* [emphasis added], which is used to the stronger party's advantage and unknown to the lesser party, causing a great hardship and risk on the lesser party, the contract provision, or the contract as a whole, if the provision is not separable, should not be enforceable on the grounds that the provision is contrary to public policy. The party seeking to enforce such a contract has the burden of showing that the provision was explained to the other party and *came to his knowledge* and there was in fact *a real and voluntary meeting of the minds and not merely an objective meeting* [emphasis in original]." *Id.* at 464, 276 N.E.2d at 148.

The language quoted above, and the facts of the *Weaver* case, show a prerequisite to finding a limitation of liability clause in a contract unconscionable and therefore void is a showing of disparity in bargaining power in favor of the party whose liability is thus limited. The Court of Appeals in the *General Grain* case did not make this as clear as it might have in the opinion. However, that case was decided before *Weaver, supra.*

In the case at bar the stipulated facts foreclose a finding of disparate bargaining power between the parties or lack of knowledge or under-standing of the liability clause by Carr. The facts show Carr is an experienced attorney who practices in the field of business law. He is hardly in a position comparable to that of the plaintiff in *Weaver, supra.* Moreover, it was stipulated he was aware of the limitation of liability on both the film packages and the receipts. We believe these crucial facts belie a finding of disparate bargaining power working to Carr's disadvantage.

Contrary to Carr's assertions, he was not in a "take it or leave it position" in that he had no choice but to accept the limitation of liability terms of the contract. As cross-appellants Hoosier and Kodak correctly point out, Carr and other photographers like him do have some choice in the matter of film processing. They can, for one, undertake to develop their film themselves. They can also go to independent film laboratories not a part of the Kodak Company. We do not see the availability of processing as limited to Kodak.

Nor can we agree with Carr's contention, focusing on the language in both the *General Grain* and *Weaver* cases on the necessity of assent to such a term. Carr contends "knowledge" or "notice" do not constitute "assent." However, where, as here, a knowledgeable party, aware that such terms are part of the proposed contract, enters into the contract without indicating any non-acquiescence to those terms, we must assume he has assented to those terms.

* * *

In the case at bar, Carr's act of bringing the film to Hoosier and Kodak for processing, coupled with the awareness and understanding of the effect of the limitation of liability clause in the contracts, constitutes a manifestation of assent to those terms.

We hold the limitation of liability clauses operating in favor of Hoosier and Kodak were assented to by Carr; they were not unconscionable or void. Carr is, therefore, bound by such terms and is limited in his remedy to recovery of the cost of four boxes of unexposed Kodak Ektachrome–X 135 slide film.

The Court of Appeals' opinion in this case is hereby vacated. The cause is remanded to the trial court with instructions to enter a judgment in favor of appellant, John R. Carr, Jr., in the amount of $13.60, plus interest. Each party is to bear its own costs.

DeBruler, Justice, dissenting.

According to the agreed facts, we are confronted with two limitation of liability statements. One appears in print on the side of a small box containing a roll of Kodak film and the other appears on the reverse side of a receipt and claim check measuring one inch by two inches. Each purports to limit liability for damage or loss of film during processing due to "negligence or other fault."

* * *

As a general rule the law does not permit professional bailees to escape or diminish liability for their own negligence by posting signs or handing out receipts. The statements on the film box and claim check used by Kodak and Hoosier Photo are in all respects like the printed forms of similar import which commonly appear on packages, signs, chits, tickets, tokens and receipts with which we are all bombarded daily. No one does, or can reasonably be expected, to take the time to carefully read the front, back, and sides of such things. We all know their gist anyway.

The distinguished trial judge below characterizes these statements before us as "mere notices" and concludes that plaintiff below did not "assent" to them so as to render them a binding part of the bailment contract. Implicit here is the recognition of the exception to the general rule regarding such notices, namely, that they may attain the dignity of a special contract limiting liability where the bailor overtly assents to their terms. To assent to provisions of this sort requires more than simply placing the goods into the hands of the bailee and taking back a receipt or claim check. Such acts are as probative of ignorance as they are of knowledge. However, according to the agreed statement of facts, plaintiff Carr "knew" by past experience that the claim checks carried the limitation of liability statements, but he did not read them and was unaware of the specific language in them. There is nothing in this agreed statement that Carr recalled this knowledge to present consciousness at the time of these transactions. Obviously we all know many things which we do not recall or remember at any given time. The assent required by law is more than this; it is, I believe to perform an act of understanding. There is no evidence of that here.

The evidence presented tending to support the award of damages included an actual uncontroverted amount of $13.60 thereby precluding mere nominal damages. There was further evidence that 150 exposures were lost. The actual award of $1,014.60 amounted to between $6.00 and $7.00 per picture. Carr provided evidence that the pictures were of exceptional value to him, having been taken in a once-in-a-lifetime European trip costing $6000, including visits arranged there beforehand with relatives. The award was fair and just compensation for the loss of value to the owner and does not include sentimental or fanciful value.

The trial court judgment should be affirmed.

Note

For a thorough examination of exculpatory clauses in commercial bailments, see Note, *Bailor Beware: Limitations and Exclusions of Liability in Commercial Bailments,* 41 Vand.L.Rev. 129 (1988).

E. GIFTS

A gift is a voluntary transfer of property to another without consideration. Such donative transactions are very common and take many forms. The subject matter of the gift may pose special problems. It is easier to make a gift of a tangible chattel than stock or money in a bank account.

Property also may be transferred gratuitously at death by will or by intestate succession. It is important to distinguish transfer by will and intestate succession from gifts made prior to death.

Gifts may be either inter vivos or causa mortis. Both types of gifts require a showing of donative intent, delivery, and acceptance. An inter vivos gift takes effect presently and irrevocably. A gift causa mortis, one made in apprehension of death from an existing peril or illness, also takes effect presently. Gifts causa mortis, however, are revocable under certain circumstances. Indeed, this is the principal difference between the two types of gifts. Causa mortis gifts are revocable (a) by express revocation of the donor; (b) by the donor's recovery from the peril or illness; or (c) by death of the donee before the donor.

As you will recall, the Lloyds desire to give china and a set of silver candlesticks to their daughter. What problems are they likely to encounter?

IRVIN v. JONES

Supreme Court of Arkansas, 1992.
310 Ark. 114, 832 S.W.2d 827.

CORBIN, JUSTICE.

Appellants, Kenny Irvin, Doug Irvin, and Mike Irvin, are brothers. Their mother was once married to the nephew of appellee, Bernice Jones. While their mother was married to appellee's nephew, appellee bought seventeen $10,000 certificates of deposit payable to herself or each of her grandnieces and grandnephews respectively, as joint tenants with right of survivorship. Three of these seventeen certificates of deposit were made payable to appellee or each of the three appellants respectively, and are the subject of this appeal. The three certificates in question stated on their faces that they were "not negotiable—not transferrable—not subject to check" and that they were to be paid on return of the certificate properly endorsed. Appellee purchased the certificates solely with her money on March 12, 1985; the certificates were to mature in 48 months. Appellee cashed the three certificates in question on March 14, 1989, collecting $14,894.03 principal and interest for each certificate. Meanwhile, appellants' mother and appellee's nephew had divorced.

Appellants filed suit against appellee for conversion of the proceeds claiming the certificates were gifts *inter vivos*. Appellee filed a motion for summary judgment contending she only intended for appellants to have the certificates on her death, if she had not already cashed them and that she had never delivered possession of the certificates to appellants. The trial court stated that appellants admitted appellee never delivered the certificates to them and entered an order granting summary judgment because there were no genuine issues of material fact and appellee was entitled to judgment as a matter of law. The order was correct and we affirm it.

In addition to the hearing on the motion for summary judgment, the trial judge had before him affidavits, depositions, responses to interrogatories, and requests for production of documents. There were arguably disputed facts regarding whether or not appellee had the requisite intent to make an irrevocable gift *inter vivos*. However, neither appellee nor any of appellants dispute that appellee retained sole possession of the certificates at all times and that she never delivered them to appellants.

Our law determining a valid gift *inter vivos* is well established. The donor must have an irrevocable intent to make the gift and must deliver the gift to the donee.

* * *

* * * [I]n Wright v. Union Nat'l Bank, 307 Ark. 301, 304, 819 S.W.2d 698, 700–01 (1991), we stated [the] requirements as follows:

> Our law is clear that in order for an inter vivos gift to transpire it must be proven by clear and convincing evidence that (1) the donor was of sound mind; (2) an actual delivery of the property took place; (3) the donor clearly intended to make an immediate, present, and final gift; (4) the donor unconditionally released all future dominion and control over the property; and (5) the donee accepted the gift.

Over the years, we have focused on the requirement of delivery. In Baugh v. Howze, 211 Ark. 222, 226, 199 S.W.2d 940, 942 (1947), we quoted from Ragan v. Hill, 72 Ark. 307, 80 S.W. 150 (1904) and stated that:

> "In all gifts a delivery of the thing given is essential to their validity; for although every other step be taken that is essential to the validity of a gift, if there is no delivery, the gift must fail. Intention cannot supply it; words cannot supply it; actions cannot supply it; it

is an indispensable requisite, without which the gift fails, regardless of the consequences * * *."

Appellants do not dispute the foregoing recitation of the law of gifts *inter vivos*. They argue, however, that in this particular case, the foregoing requirements can be met in a less stringent manner. They seem to rely on the language in *Williams,* 66 Ark. 299, 50 S.W. 513, that there need only be "such delivery as the nature of the property will admit." As we have consistently applied the foregoing requirements to *inter vivos* gifts of certificates of deposit, we are not persuaded by appellants' argument. * * *

There can be no doubt that a certificate of deposit may be the subject of a gift *inter vivos*. We have stated that a promissory note, or any chose in action or other evidence of debt, may be the subject of a gift *inter vivos* and that a certificate of deposit falls into this category. Likewise, there can be no doubt that the requirements of intent and delivery apply to an *inter vivos* gift of a certificate of deposit. We have also stated that in order to constitute a valid gift of a certificate of deposit, there must be an intent by the donor that title pass immediately, and a delivery of the certificate.

In Hudson v. Bradley, 176 Ark. 853, 4 S.W.2d 534 (1928), we applied the law of gifts *inter vivos* to a case with facts very similar to the present case. In *Hudson,* a father bought certificates of deposit payable to himself or his son. As in the present case, the certificates in *Hudson* were purchased solely with the purchaser's money and were not subject to check. The *Hudson* case held there was not a valid gift *inter vivos* because the father retained possession of the certificates and never delivered them to his son.

In the present case, appellee stated in her affidavit that she kept physical possession of the certificates in her safe deposit box at all times. Appellants admit that they never had possession of the certificates. Thus, appellants offered no proof of the element of delivery, which the foregoing case law, especially *Hudson,* establishes is an essential element of the claim of a valid gift *inter vivos*.

* * *

As there was no proof that appellee delivered the certificates to appellants or to their agent, there is no proof of delivery, an essential element of appellants' claim. Therefore, * * * there is no remaining genuine issue of material fact, and appellee was entitled to judgment as a matter of law. The trial court committed no error in granting summary judgment.

Affirmed.

Notes, Problems, and Questions

1. Why do courts require delivery as an essential element of a gift? Delivery serves both a protective and an evidentiary function. It makes clear to the donor the significance of the transaction and furnishes objective

evidence of the donor's intent. *See* Mechem, *The Requirement of Delivery in Gifts of Chattels and of Choses in Action Evidenced by Commercial Instruments*, 21 Ill.L.Rev. 341 (1926); Rohan, *The Continuing Question of Delivery in the Law of Gifts*, 38 Ind.L.Rev. 1 (1962).

2.   A person can make a gift of personal property by delivery of the subject of the gift to a third party to hold for the intended donee. The third party holds the gift as the agent or trustee of the donee. *See* Innes v. Potter, 130 Minn. 320, 153 N.W. 604 (1915); R. Brown, The Law of Personal Property § 7.4 (3d ed. 1975). When the subject matter of the gift is already in the possession of a bailee of the donor, can the donor make a valid delivery by simply instructing the bailee to hold the property for the donee? *See* Payne v. Tobacco Trading Corp., 179 Va. 156, 18 S.E.2d 281 (1942).

3.   Suppose that O, wishing to make donations of stock to family members, directs a transfer of the stock on the books of the corporation. After the new certificates were issued but before they were physically delivered to the intended donees, O died. Can O's executor successfully claim that there was no delivery of the stock? *See* Owens v. Sun Oil Company, 482 F.2d 564 (10th Cir.1973.)

GRUEN v. GRUEN

Court of Appeals of New York, 1986.
68 N.Y.2d 48, 505 N.Y.S.2d 849, 496 N.E.2d 869.

SIMONS, JUDGE.

Plaintiff commenced this action seeking a declaration that he is the rightful owner of a painting which he alleges his father, now deceased, gave to him. He concedes that he has never had possession of the painting but asserts that his father made a valid gift of the title in 1963 reserving a life estate for himself. His father retained possession of the painting until he died in 1980. Defendant, plaintiff's stepmother, has the painting now and has refused plaintiff's requests that she turn it over to him. She contends that the purported gift was testamentary in nature and invalid insofar as the formalities of a will were not met or, alternatively, that a donor may not make a valid inter vivos gift of a chattel and retain a life estate with a complete right of possession. Following a seven-day nonjury trial, Special Term found that plaintiff had failed to establish any of the elements of an inter vivos gift and that in any event an attempt by a donor to retain a present possessory life estate in a chattel invalidated a purported gift of it. The Appellate Division held that a valid gift may be made reserving a life estate and, finding the elements of a gift established in this case, it reversed and remitted the matter for a determination of value (104 A.D.2d 171, 488 N.Y.S.2d 401). That determination has now been made and defendant appeals directly to this court, pursuant to CPLR 5601(d), from the subsequent final judgment entered in Supreme Court awarding plaintiff $2,500,000 in damages representing the value of the painting, plus interest. We now affirm.

The subject of the dispute is a work entitled "Schloss Kammer am Attersee II" painted by a noted Austrian modernist, Gustav Klimt. It was purchased by plaintiff's father, Victor Gruen, in 1959 for $8,000. On April 1, 1963 the elder Gruen, a successful architect with offices and residences in both New York City and Los Angeles during most of the time involved in this action, wrote a letter to plaintiff, then an undergraduate student at Harvard, stating that he was giving him the Klimt painting for his birthday but that he wished to retain the possession of it for his lifetime. This letter is not in evidence, apparently because plaintiff destroyed it on instructions from his father. Two other letters were received, however, one dated May 22, 1963 and the other April 1, 1963. Both had been dictated by Victor Gruen and sent together to plaintiff on or about May 22, 1963. The letter dated May 22, 1963 reads as follows:

"Dear Michael:

"I wrote you at the time of your birthday about the gift of the painting by Klimt.

"Now my lawyer tells me that because of the existing tax laws, it was wrong to mention in that letter that I want to use the painting as long as I live. Though I still want to use it, this should not appear in the letter. I am enclosing, therefore, a new letter and I ask you to send the old one back to me so that it can be destroyed.

"I know this is all very silly, but the lawyer and our accountant insist that they must have in their possession copies of a letter which will serve the purpose of making it possible for you, once I die, to get this picture without having to pay inheritance taxes on it.

"Love,

"s/Victor".

Enclosed with this letter was a substitute gift letter, dated April 1, 1963, which stated:

"Dear Michael:

"The 21st birthday, being an important event in life, should be celebrated accordingly. I therefore wish to give you as a present the oil painting by Gustav Klimt of Schloss Kammer which now hangs in the New York living room. You know that Lazette and I bought it some 5 or 6 years ago, and you always told us how much you liked it.

"Happy birthday again.

"Love,

"s/Victor".

Plaintiff never took possession of the painting nor did he seek to do so. Except for a brief period between 1964 and 1965 when it was on loan to art exhibits and when restoration work was performed on it, the painting remained in his father's possession, moving with him from New York City to Beverly Hills and finally to Vienna, Austria, where Victor

Gruen died on February 14, 1980. Following Victor's death plaintiff requested possession of the Klimt painting and when defendant refused, he commenced this action.

The issues framed for appeal are whether a valid inter vivos gift of a chattel may be made where the donor has reserved a life estate in the chattel and the donee never has had physical possession of it before the donor's death and, if it may, which factual findings on the elements of a valid inter vivos gift more nearly comport with the weight of the evidence in this case, those of Special Term or those of the Appellate Division. The latter issue requires application of two general rules. First, to make a valid inter vivos gift there must exist the intent on the part of the donor to make a present transfer; delivery of the gift, either actual or constructive to the donee; and acceptance by the donee. Second, the proponent of a gift has the burden of proving each of these elements by clear and convincing evidence.

DONATIVE INTENT

There is an important distinction between the intent with which an inter vivos gift is made and the intent to make a gift by will. An inter vivos gift requires that the donor intend to make an irrevocable present transfer of ownership; if the intention is to make a testamentary disposition effective only after death, the gift is invalid unless made by will.

Defendant contends that the trial court was correct in finding that Victor did not intend to transfer any present interest in the painting to plaintiff in 1963 but only expressed an intention that plaintiff was to get the painting upon his death. The evidence is all but conclusive, however, that Victor intended to transfer ownership of the painting to plaintiff in 1963 but to retain a life estate in it and that he did, therefore, effectively transfer a remainder interest in the painting to plaintiff at that time. Although the original letter was not in evidence, testimony of its contents was received along with the substitute gift letter and its covering letter dated May 22, 1963. The three letters should be considered together as a single instrument and when they are they unambiguously establish that Victor Gruen intended to make a present gift of title to the painting at that time. But there was other evidence for after 1963 Victor made several statements orally and in writing indicating that he had previously given plaintiff the painting and that plaintiff owned it. Victor Gruen retained possession of the property, insured it, allowed others to exhibit it and made necessary repairs to it but those acts are not inconsistent with his retention of a life estate. Furthermore, whatever probative value could be attached to his statement that he had bequeathed the painting to his heirs, made 16 years later when he prepared an export license application so that he could take the painting out of Austria, is negated by the overwhelming evidence that he intended a present transfer of title in 1963. Victor's failure to file a gift tax return on the transaction was partially explained by allegedly erroneous legal advice he received, and while that omission sometimes may indicate that the donor had no intention of making a present gift, it does not necessarily do so and it is not dispositive in this case.

Defendant contends that even if a present gift was intended, Victor's reservation of a lifetime interest in the painting defeated it. She relies on a statement from Young v. Young, 80 N.Y. 422 that " '[a]ny gift of chattels which expressly reserves the use of the property to the donor for a certain period, or * * * as long as the donor shall live, is ineffectual' "(id., at p. 436, quoting 2 Schouler, Personal Property, at 118). The statement was dictum, however, and the holding of the court was limited to a determination that an attempted gift of bonds in which the donor reserved the interest for life failed because there had been no delivery of the gift, either actual or constructive (see, id., at p. 434; see also, Speelman v. Pascal, 10 N.Y.2d 313, 319–320, 222 N.Y.S.2d 324, 178 N.E.2d 723). The court expressly left undecided the question "whether a remainder in a chattel may be created and given by a donor by carving out a life estate for himself and transferring the remainder" Young v. Young at p. 440. We answered part of that question in Matter of Brandreth, 169 N.Y. 437, 441–442, 62 N.E. 563 when we held that "[in] this state a life estate and remainder can be created in a chattel or a fund the same as in real property". The case did not require us to decide whether there could be a valid gift of the remainder.

Defendant recognizes that a valid inter vivos gift of a remainder interest can be made not only of real property but also of such intangibles as stocks and bonds. Indeed, several of the cases she cites so hold. That being so, it is difficult to perceive any legal basis for the distinction she urges which would permit gifts of remainder interests in those properties but not of remainder interests in chattels such as the Klimt painting here. The only reason suggested is that the gift of a chattel must include a present right to possession. The application of Brandreth to permit a gift of the remainder in this case, however, is consistent with the distinction, well recognized in the law of gifts as well as in real property law, between ownership and possession or enjoyment. Insofar as some of our cases purport to require that the donor intend to transfer both title and possession immediately to have a valid inter vivos gift, they state the rule too broadly and confuse the effectiveness of a gift with the transfer of the possession of the subject of that gift. The correct test is " 'whether the maker intended the [gift] to have *no effect* until after the maker's death, or whether he intended it to transfer *some present interest*' " McCarthy v. Pieret, 281 N.Y. 407, 409, 24 N.E.2d 102 [emphasis added]. As long as the evidence establishes an intent to make a present and irrevocable transfer of title or the right of ownership, there is a present transfer of some interest and the gift is effective immediately. Thus, in *Speelman v. Pascal*, we held valid a gift of a percentage of the future royalties to the play "My Fair Lady" before the play even existed. There, as in this case, the donee received title or the right of ownership to some property immediately upon the making of the gift but possession or enjoyment of the subject of the gift was postponed to some future time.

Defendant suggests that allowing a donor to make a present gift of a remainder with the reservation of a life estate will lead courts to effectuate otherwise invalid testamentary dispositions of property. The two have entirely different characteristics, however, which make them distinguishable. Once the gift is made it is irrevocable and the donor is limited to the rights of a life tenant not an owner. Moreover, with the gift of a remainder title vests immediately in the donee and any possession is postponed until the donor's death whereas under a will neither title nor possession vests immediately. Finally, the postponement of enjoyment of the gift is produced by the express terms of the gift not by the nature of the instrument as it is with a will.

DELIVERY

In order to have a valid inter vivos gift, there must be a delivery of the gift, either by a physical delivery of the subject of the gift or a constructive or symbolic delivery such as by an instrument of gift, sufficient to divest the donor of dominion and control over the property. As the statement of the rule suggests, the requirement of delivery is not rigid or inflexible, but is to be applied in light of its purpose to avoid mistakes by donors and fraudulent claims by donees. Accordingly, what is sufficient to constitute delivery "must be tailored to suit the circumstances of the case" (Matter of Szabo, 10 N.Y.2d at p. 98, 217 N.Y.S.2d 593, 176 N.E.2d 395). The rule requires that " '[t]he delivery necessary to consummate a gift must be as perfect as the nature of the property and the circumstances and surroundings of the parties will reasonably permit' "(*id.*).

Defendant contends that when a tangible piece of personal property such as a painting is the subject of a gift, physical delivery of the painting itself is the best form of delivery and should be required. Here, of course, we have only delivery of Victor Gruen's letters which serve as instruments of gift. Defendant's statement of the rule as applied may be generally true, but it ignores the fact that what Victor Gruen gave plaintiff was not all rights to the Klimt painting, but only title to it with no right of possession until his death. Under these circumstances, it would be illogical for the law to require the donor to part with possession of the painting when that is exactly what he intends to retain.

Nor is there any reason to require a donor making a gift of a remainder interest in a chattel to physically deliver the chattel into the donee's hands only to have the donee redeliver it to the donor. As the facts of this case demonstrate, such a requirement could impose practical burdens on the parties to the gift while serving the delivery requirement poorly. Thus, in order to accomplish this type of delivery the parties would have been required to travel to New York for the symbolic transfer and redelivery of the Klimt painting which was hanging on the wall of Victor Gruen's Manhattan apartment. Defendant suggests that such a requirement would be stronger evidence of a completed gift, but in the absence of witnesses to the event or any written confirmation of the gift it would provide less protection against fraudulent claims than have the written instruments of gift delivered in this case.

ACCEPTANCE

Acceptance by the donee is essential to the validity of an inter vivos gift, but when a gift is of value to the donee, as it is here, the law will presume an acceptance on his part. Plaintiff did not rely on this presumption alone but also presented clear and convincing proof of his acceptance of a remainder interest in the Klimt painting by evidence that he had made several contemporaneous statements acknowledging the gift to his friends and associates, even showing some of them his father's gift letter, and that he had retained both letters for over 17 years to verify the gift after his father died. Defendant relied exclusively on affidavits filed by plaintiff in a matrimonial action with his former wife, in which plaintiff failed to list his interest in the painting as an asset. These affidavits were made over 10 years after acceptance was complete and they do not even approach the evidence in Matter of Kelly (285 N.Y. 139, 148–149, 33 N.E.2d 62 [dissenting in part opn.]) where the donee, immediately upon delivery of a diamond ring, rejected it as "too flashy". We agree with the Appellate Division that interpretation of the affidavit was too speculative to support a finding of rejection and overcome the substantial showing of acceptance by plaintiff.

Accordingly, the judgment appealed from and the order of the Appellate Division brought up for review should be affirmed, with costs.

IN RE ESTATE OF GLADOWSKI

Supreme Court of Pennsylvania, 1979.
483 Pa. 258, 396 A.2d 631.

EAGEN, CHIEF JUSTICE.

This appeal challenges a final decree of the Court of Common Pleas of Allegheny County, Orphans' Court Division, which ruled in part that the proceeds of a savings bank account in the joint names of Joseph Gladowski, deceased, and his daughter, Ann Mazuran, are not an asset of the decedent's estate, but rather the property of Ann Mazuran. The appellants are three of the decedent's seven surviving children.

Joseph Gladowski died testate on September 30, 1976, at the age of eighty-five. He had come to the United States from Poland at the age of twelve and worked as a coal miner for forty years. A widower since 1936, Gladowski retired due to disability in 1951 at the age of sixty. Subsequently, he suffered from numerous serious physical ailments. His daughter, Ann Mazuran, lived with him and cared for him during his many illnesses.

The decedent was a party to four transactions which have a bearing on this case. On September 21, 1963, he executed a deed conveying title to his residence to himself, Joseph Gladowski, and Ann Mazuran as joint tenants with right of survivorship. On that same day, decedent executed a will naming Ann Mazuran executrix and authorizing her to sell all of his real estate and, after paying his debts and funeral expenses, to divide and distribute the residue of the estate in equal shares to his seven-named children.

On March 4, 1966, decedent opened a joint savings account in the names of Joseph Gladowski or Mrs. Ann Mazuran as joint tenants with right of survivorship. On June 26, 1975, decedent executed a second will naming Ann Mazuran executrix, devising his residence specifically to Ann Mazuran, and bequeathing the residue of his estate in equal shares to his seven-named children. The terms of this will are substantially the same as the earlier will except for the disposition of decedent's residence.

At the time of his death, decedent had the following: (1) the savings account held jointly with Ann Mazuran containing a balance of $16,-226.66 (The account was originally opened with a deposit of $217.40; all of the deposits consisted of decedent's money; on June 30, 1975, the account had a balance of $34,848.40; and, withdrawals did not begin until January 20, 1975, and were all signed by Ann Mazuran); (2) the residence held in joint tenancy with Ann Mazuran; (3) miner's death benefits in the amount of $2,000.00; and, (4) four life insurance policies designating Ann Mazuran as beneficiary and amounting to $1,682.91.

The Orphans' Court ruled Ann Mazuran was entitled to decedent's residence as the survivor of the joint tenancy, to the proceeds of the insurance policies as the designated beneficiary, and to the miner's benefits by virtue of her right as a member of decedent's household to the family exemption of $2,000.00. Appellants do not now contest these rulings. They challenge only the court's additional ruling denying their petition seeking to compel Ann Mazuran to pay over to decedent's estate proceeds of the joint bank account remaining at decedent's death and to account to the estate for funds which she withdrew from the joint account before his death. Appellants' petition was dismissed on the basis of the court's conclusion that the decedent had made a valid gift of the proceeds of the bank account to his daughter Ann during his lifetime.

Donative intent is one of the essential elements of a completed inter vivos gift. Under Pennsylvania law, the creation of a joint interest in a bank account with rights of survivorship, evidenced by the signatures of both parties, is *prima facie* evidence of the intent of the party funding the account to make an inter vivos gift to the other joint tenant.[1]

* * *

It is undisputed that both Joseph Gladowski and Ann Mazuran signed the contract with the bank, which read in part as follows:

---

1. Compare 20 Pa.C.S. § 6304(a) (Supp. 1978–79), applicable to accounts created after September 1, 1976, which provides, in part, that "[a]ny sum remaining on deposit at the death of a party to a joint account belongs to the surviving party or parties as against the estate of the decedent unless there is clear and convincing evidence of a different intent at the time the account is created."

"All deposits now or hereafter made in this account shall be held and owned by us as joint tenants with right of survivorship and not as tenants in common * * * and shall be withdrawable by appropriate order signed by either of us * * * . Upon the death of either of us, the surviving tenant shall be the sole owner of said account and the balance thereof."

This was sufficient to raise a presumption that, at the time the account was opened, Joseph Gladowski intended to make a gift of the proceeds to his daughter Ann. However, such a presumption may be overcome where there is clear, precise and convincing evidence to the contrary. We conclude this is such a case.

Ann Mazuran, who seeks the funds by virtue of the claimed gift inter vivos, admitted, during her testimony in the trial court, that the bank signature card did not reflect the entire agreement between her father and herself at the time the account was opened in 1966. She admitted her father wanted her name on the account as a matter of convenience so she could transact business on his behalf when he was physically unable to do so. She also stated that, when the account was opened in 1966, her father intended that, at the time of his death, the money in the account was to be equally divided among his children. But she further said that her father changed his mind "before 1970," after he became ill, and after the other children failed to visit or help in caring for him, and that her father then told her "he wanted me to have everything."

While the record is none too clear, the trial court apparently concluded a valid gift inter vivos was effected at the time the account was opened. This was error since it is clear from Ann Mazuran's own testimony that the donative intent essential to a completed gift inter vivos was not present in 1966 when the account was opened. Hence, the crucial issue is whether or not Ann Mazuran's testimony that "before 1970" her father changed his mind and then declared "he wanted me to have everything" is sufficient in law to establish a valid gift inter vivos of the account. Under the circumstances, we rule it is not.

The burden of proving the alleged gift was upon the claimant by clear, precise and convincing evidence. Titusville Trust Company v. Johnson, 375 Pa. 493, 100 A.2d 93 (1953). Contravening and speaking against the claimant's bare statement that, "before 1970," the father said "he wanted me to have everything" is the fact that, on June 26, 1975, the decedent executed a will bequeathing the residue of his estate in equal shares to his seven children. Other than the residence, the only assets decedent had at the time he executed the will and at his death were the joint savings account in his name and Ann's, the miner's death benefits amounting to $2,000.00 to which Ann was entitled by virtue of the family exemption, and the life insurance policies designating Ann as the beneficiary.

Additionally, the testimony of the scrivener of the second will tends to deny that a gift inter vivos of the bank account had previously been completed.

Attorney Dennis G. Nader, who prepared the will, testified that, although he knew the house would go to Ann Mazuran by operation of law and explained the concept of joint ownership to decedent, he nevertheless provided in the will for a bequest of the house to Ann. He further testified that the existence of a bank account in joint names with the right of survivorship was not brought to his attention and that he understood the residue of the estate was composed of cash. As to the amount of cash to be included in decedent's residuary estate for the purpose of determining federal estate tax liability, Attorney Nader testified as follows:

"A. The only ascertainment I made, I asked questions of both Mrs. Mazuran and Mr. Gladowski, as to what amount of cash was involved. The way I phrased it was 'was it over $5,000?' And then I went to over $25,000 and was it over $60,000. And the indication was that at least it was below $60,000. And that is the figure to the best of my recollection."

In addition, Attorney Nader testified:

"A. I drew up the will, and I explained to Mr. Gladowski that the house would go to his daughter. And I showed him the will and explained that everything else he had would be divided among the rest of his children. I didn't make reference to any specific bank account or any specific amount of cash."

If decedent had already effected an inter vivos gift of the joint savings account, there would have been no assets to form his residuary estate and the will provision would have been meaningless. On the basis of decedent's responses to questioning from Attorney Nader, we can infer that, on June 26, 1975, decedent had in excess of $25,000.00 which he wished divided among his children. Thus, he must have referred to the joint savings account as that to be divided among his children since this represented his sole cash asset.

We, therefore, conclude that the trial court erred in refusing to direct Ann Mazuran to account for the funds involved since the evidence was not clear, precise and convincing that a completed gift inter vivos thereof ensued.

Decree vacated and the record is remanded for further proceedings consistent with this opinion.

Costs on the estate.

Notes and Questions

1. Assume that the decedent intended a gift to Mrs. Mazuran. How might the decedent have more clearly manifested his desire that the proceeds of the account should pass to her?

2. Claimed gifts arising from joint bank accounts have been a frequent source of litigation. Many states have adopted statutes which establish a rebuttable presumption that the depositor of the funds intended a gift to the survivor of the proceeds remaining after the depositor's death. Courts often grapple with the nature of evidence sufficient to rebut such a statutory presumption. *See, e.g., In re* Estate of Combee, 601 So.2d 1165 (Fla.1992); Daniell v. Clein, 206 Ga.App. 377, 425 S.E.2d 344 (1992); Webb v. Williams, 188 W.Va. 7, 422 S.E.2d 484 (1992).

BRAUN v. BROWN

Supreme Court of California, 1939.
14 Cal.2d 346, 94 P.2d 348.

PULLEN, JUSTICE, *pro tem.*

* * *

The action was brought against the administrator of the estate of Julius H. Schmidt, deceased, to establish a gift *causa mortis* by deceased to plaintiff of certain personal property, and to quiet title thereto. This personal property, consisting of stocks, bonds, promissory notes, a diamond ring and bank deposit books during his lifetime belonged to Schmidt, and was kept in a safe deposit box in a bank in the city of Los Angeles. After the death of Schmidt, plaintiff attempted to take over the box and its contents, but upon refusal of the bank to surrender possession to her, she turned the key to the box over to defendant, who had previously obtained letters of administration in the estate of Schmidt, and upon the refusal of the administrator to recognize her claim to the property brought this action to secure the same or its value.

The underlying facts as revealed by the record briefly are that some time in 1922 Schmidt met Teresa A. Braun, the plaintiff, at a church bazaar in Chicago. He was then a man about 52 years of age and unmarried. In 1924 plaintiff, then a young woman, came to California with her parents, who established their home in Los Angeles. The following year Schmidt, who had retired from business, also came to Los Angeles, and from that time until his last illness spent several hours almost every day in the company of plaintiff, either in her home or accompanying her to and from her place of employment or escorting her to church and places of entertainment. During that time she received from him notes and Easter cards addressed to her in terms of friendship and endearment, and on more than one occasion he proposed marriage, which proposals were neither accepted nor encouraged by plaintiff. In 1925 he attempted to make her a gift of a diamond engagement ring, which she refused, and in 1926 he purchased and offered her an automobile, which she also refused to accept. The relationship between the two, however, continued very friendly and apparently did not abate.

On January 6, 1937, Schmidt complained to the sexton of his church that he did not feel well, and later in the day he suffered a slight paralytic stroke. The next day he was confined to his room and a doctor was called to attend him. A few days later Mr. Assmann, a brother-in-law, came over from Long Beach, where he was spending the winter, and remained with him almost continuously until Schmidt was taken to a hospital on January 26th, where he remained until his death on February 11, 1937.

After Schmidt was confined to his room by reason of illness, Miss Braun called upon him almost daily. On January 21st she called as usual. After some conversation about what had occurred that day at her place of employment Schmidt asked his brother-in-law, who was present, to bring to him his purse. He thereupon took from this purse a safe deposit key which he handed to plaintiff, saying, "Teresa, every thing in the box belongs to you," and, turning to Assmann, said, "Bernard, you hear, I want Teresa to have every thing in the box." He also told her that there was more than enough money in the box for her to live on and that she would not have to work any more. A day or so later Schmidt gave plaintiff a check for $175, drawn from funds other than those in the safe deposit box, and gave it to plaintiff in order that she might pay his hotel and hospital bills. Plaintiff then took the key and kept it among her effects at her home until after the death of Schmidt, when, as stated above, she gave it to the administrator and, upon his refusal to redeliver the key, this action was commenced.

The trial court confirmed the gift to plaintiff and ordered that the property be delivered to her or, in the alternative, the value thereof. It is from that judgment that this appeal is taken.

* * * [T]he basic question in controversy * * * is, did Schmidt on the 21st day of January, 1937, entertain and express the specific intention then and there to give to plaintiff the property in the safe deposit box; and did he then and there effectuate that intention by the delivery of that property to her, divesting himself of dominion thereover, and was he actuated therein by the thought of death, and did plaintiff accept the same?

* * *

The evidence fairly establishes that the gift was made by Schmidt during his last illness, and there can be little doubt from the evidence that the circumstances surrounding such illness impressed him with the expectation of death, and, by the delivery of the key and his statement to plaintiff he intended to set over to plaintiff all his interest in the property.

At the time of the making of the gift Schmidt was ill in bed in his hotel room; he had suffered a stroke and had told certain friends that he was not feeling well. He was arranging to go to a hospital and had made provision for plaintiff to pay his hotel and hospital bills. His brother-in-law, realizing the seriousness of his condition, had left his place of abode in Long Beach and had a cot moved into the room of Schmidt, so he could be near him all night; he was at times delirious; a doctor had examined him and advised hospital care. He was then about 67 years of age and had never theretofore been sick. He left the hotel January 26th and died 15 days later. Such circumstances could not but have caused even the most optimistic of men to contemplate to some degree at least the fact of death. Realizing, however, that under such circumstances any reference to or discussion of death is universally avoided by the patient, his friends and the doctor, section 1150 of the Civil Code declares that a gift made during the last illness or under circumstances which would naturally impress one with an expectation of speedy death is presumed to be a gift in view of death. This presumption is evidence and is sufficient to establish the fact unless rebutted.

But the fear of impending death is not a sole essential element of a gift *causa mortis*. The code predicates such a gift on either contemplation of death or peril of death; and as pointed out in Donovan v. Hibernia Sav. & Loan Soc., 90 Cal.App. 489 [265 Pac. 995], while one may make general statements to the effect that he is feeling fine, yet his condition may be known to him to be critical. One may realize himself to be in peril of death and yet not expect to die. He may still believe his chances to live are greater than his chances to die, yet prudently take steps to adjust his affairs in case of death.

* * *

Both the circumstantial evidence and the presumption raised by the provisions of the code are sufficient to support the finding that the gift by Schmidt to respondent was made by him in contemplation of death and was a gift *causa mortis*.

It is next urged by appellant that there is no substantial evidence in the record to support the finding that Schmidt had the specific intent then and there to give to plaintiff the contents of the safe deposit box, or did anything to effectuate delivery, or that plaintiff accepted the same.

As to the intent, we find that when Schmidt handed the key to plaintiff he said, "Every thing in the box belongs to you," and also said to plaintiff that she wouldn't have to work any more, there would be enough money there for her to live on, and, calling upon his brother-in-law as a witness, said, "Bernard, you hear, I want Teresa to have every thing in the box." Here are words of present donation, accompanied by the delivery into her hands of the means of access to the property in the presence of a witness particularly enjoined to act as such.

The mother of plaintiff * * * testified as to a conversation with Schmidt some five or six days after the delivery of the key, wherein Schmidt, according to her, said, "Yes, every thing what I have in the box belongs to Teresa; I told her that all the time," and also testified that at that time Schmidt "asked Bernard to make a paper out for that he want to sign it that every thing belongs to Teresa[.]" * * *

Appellant, analyzing this testimony, claims to find no express or direct words of gift or giving, nor any clear expression of intent that what had theretofore been the property of Schmidt then and there passed from him into the sole ownership of plaintiff. * * * [However,]

[a]ll that is required is that appropriate words of gift be used, and such words are here found. * * * "[Intention] is a question of fact to be determined like other questions of fact upon all the evidence in the case—the situation of the parties, their relationship, the circumstances surrounding the transaction, the apparent purpose in making the gift, the words spoken at the time, and the like. If the words accompanying the delivery of the thing can be said to be expressive of a gift and, in the light of the circumstances, consistent with the intention to give, the execution of a gift is established." [Mellor v. Bank of Willows, 173 Cal. 454, 160 P. 567]

Appellant stresses the fact that on more than one occasion after saying to plaintiff, "Every thing in the box belongs to you," he repeated to others, among them the mother, "Every thing what I have in the box belongs to Teresa," as indicating some future contingency. With this we cannot agree. Schmidt knew that he had not actually handed to plaintiff the physical possession of the contents of the box. He knew that at some future time she would actually possess herself of them. It was, therefore, of that future event and not the gift itself upon which his mind dwelt. So, also, the desire of Schmidt to sign a paper of some kind to confirm the fact that he had made a gift to respondent in no way affects the validity of the gift. * * *

Assuming, as appellant does, that the language used by Schmidt was ambiguous, and that some extrinsic evidence was necessary to clarify his intention, such is found in the relationship of plaintiff and the deceased; the proposals of marriage, the declaration of affection by donor, statements that he intended to give her his property and that she would not have to work, the absence of an immediate family or close relatives of Schmidt who might otherwise be natural objects of his bounty, his illness, all have force in explaining the acts of the donor, even if his words could be considered ambiguous. * * *

Appellant contends that plaintiff has failed to establish delivery. We are here dealing with personal property locked in a deposit box. The box was not capable of manual delivery, therefore, the well-recognized rule that a valid gift may be made under such circumstances by the transfer of the key thereto is applicable. Nor can any rule or regulation of the depository affect the validity of the gift to plaintiff. The court found that the sole means of access to the deposit box was one key which was in the possession of Schmidt; that during his last illness he handed over to plaintiff this key and at the time stated to her that he was thereby making a gift to her of all the contents of the box. With the evidence in the record supporting the finding, there can be no question as to the divestiture of dominion. Appellant makes some point of a second key. This key, however, was locked in the box and was accessible to the one alone who had control of the Schmidt key. This second key may, therefore, be dismissed from consideration.

Lastly, appellant claims that because plaintiff did not exercise her authority by using the key and taking possession of the property before the death of Schmidt the gift never became effective and failed for lack of acceptance. In Wilson v. Crocker First Nat. Bank, 12 Cal.App. (2d) 627 [55 Pac. (2d) 1208], it was contended but unsuccessfully that because a donee had not assumed dominion and withdrawn money from the bank prior to the death of the donor the gift was incomplete. In Paddock v. Fonner, 84 Cal.App. 652 [258 Pac. 423], although the gift failed because of lack of donative intent, the court held that the acceptance was sufficient if the donee received the bank book and order and took into his possession the means of obtaining the funds on deposit; and that he later offered to turn over to the administratrix of the estate the bank book for the purpose of adjudication of a dispute did not affect the validity of the gift as far as acceptance was concerned. To the same effect was the holding in Estate of Elliott, 312 Pa. 493 [167 Atl. 289, 90 A.L.R. 360], where the donee turned over the keys of the deposit box to the administratrix prior to suit.

* * * The judgment should be affirmed and it is so ordered.

Notes, Problems, and Questions

1. Suppose Schmidt retained the second key to the safe deposit box. Same result?

2. In the principal case Schmidt was on his deathbed when he handed over the key. Suppose that he was in good health at the time of the transaction. Would delivery of a key constitute a gift of the contents of the box?

3. What if Schmidt had recovered and had requested Braun to return the key, but she refused claiming that the contents of the box belonged to her?

4. O, believing that death was near, wrote a check for $10,000 payable to X and handed the check to X as a gift. O died. Shortly thereafter, X cashed the check. Z, administrator of O's estate, has demanded that X transfer the $10,000 to O's estate. Must X do so? *Compare* Woo v. Smart, 247 Va. 365, 442 S.E.2d 690 (1994) *with* Estate of Smith v. Sandt, 694 A.2d 1099 (Pa.Super.1997).

5. There is obvious tension between gifts causa mortis and the policy behind the Statute of Wills. The Statute requires that wills be written and signed by the testator in the presence of witnesses. These formalities protect the testator against fraud or undue influence, and help preclude a casual disposition of property. Since a testamentary bequest does not take effect until the testator's death, a testator near death could undercut the terms of the will by making gifts causa mortis. This has caused many courts to look with disfavor on causa mortis transactions and insist upon convincing evidence to uphold them.

6. O was seriously injured in an automobile accident. Acutely depressed, O wrote a note in which O "bequested" all of O's possessions to O's friend X, including "the check for $17,400." O then committed suicide. The police found the check endorsed in blank. As between X and O's administrator, who is entitled to the $17,400? *See* Scherer v. Hyland, 75 N.J. 127, 380

A.2d 698 (1977). *See also* Estate of Smith v. Sandt, 694 A.2d 1099 (Pa.Super.1997).

7. O, in apprehension of death, delivered to X a valuable vase with the intention that X keep it if O died. One week later O executed a will in which O specifically bequeathed the vase to Y. O died. Who owns the vase?

HEIMAN v. PARRISH

Supreme Court of Kansas, 1997.
262 Kan. 926, 942 P.2d 631.

McFARLAND, CHIEF JUSTICE:

The issue before us concerns the ownership of an engagement ring after the engagement was terminated.

The case was called for jury trial. After a brief in-chambers conference (no record of which is before us), the court orally decided the issue in open court. What transpired is concisely journalized as follows:

"The parties stipulate to the following facts:

"1. The issue to be determined is the ownership of an engagement ring.

"2. The plaintiff purchased the engagement ring.

"3. The ring was given to defendant as an engagement ring in contemplation of marriage between the parties.

"4. The plaintiff is the party who ended the relationship.

"5. Neither party stipulates to whose fault caused the relationship to terminate.

"Based upon the stipulated facts, the pleadings in the Court file, arguments of counsel and the supporting briefs, the Court finds as a matter of law that since the engagement ring was given in contemplation of marriage, the marriage itself is a condition precedent to the ultimate ownership of the ring. Since the parties did not perform the condition of marriage, the purchaser is entitled to the return of the ring. The Court further finds that the issue of who ended the relationship is not determinative of the ownership of the ring.

. . . .

"IT IS, THEREFORE ORDERED, ADJUDGED AND DECREED that the plaintiff is entitled to the return of the engagement ring and costs are assessed to the defendant."

Defendant appeals therefrom. Additional uncontroverted facts are that the ring was purchased in August 1994 for $9,033. Plaintiff terminated the engagement in October 1995. Defendant refused to return the ring, and this action was filed April 3, 1996. For the sake of simplicity, plaintiff will henceforth be referred as Jerod and defendant will be referred to as Heather.

* * *

The issues may be summarized as follows. Was the engagement ring a conditional gift given in contemplation of marriage? If this question is answered affirmatively, then, upon termination of the engagement, should ownership of the ring be determined on a fault or no-fault basis? These are issues of first impression in Kansas.

CONDITIONAL GIFT

Heather argues that the gift of an engagement ring should be gauged by the same standards as for any other inter vivos gift, and that, once delivery and acceptance have occurred, the gift is irrevocable. She contends Kansas does not recognize conditional gifts.

Jerod argues that an engagement ring is inherently a conditional gift, as it is given in contemplation of marriage. If the wedding does not occur, the ring should be returned to its donor.

To establish a gift inter vivos there must be (a) an intention to make a gift; (b) a delivery by the donor to the donee; and (c) an acceptance by the donee. The gift must be absolute and irrevocable. The elements of intent, delivery, and acceptance are usually questions of fact to be determined by the jury.

* * *

While there is a paucity of Kansas law on gifts in contemplation of marriage in general, and engagement rings in particular, courts in many other states have wrestled with the issues arising therefrom. Most courts recognize that engagement rings occupy a rather unique niche in our society.

* * *

By tradition and the mores of our society, an engagement ring is the symbol of the parties' mutual promises to marry. It is unlike any other gift given or exchanged by lovers. The single sentence "She returned his ring" illustrates this. These four words, standing alone, paint the picture of mutual promises to wed, a ring being given and received to symbolize these promises, and the intended bride reneging on her promise and so advising the would-be groom by returning the ring. No like picture is engendered by the phrase "She returned his bracelet." Nothing about the relationship of the parties or the circumstances surrounding the exchange can be implied from these four words.

An extensive discussion of the topic can be found in Annot., Rights in Respect of Engagement and Courtship Presents When Marriage Does Not Ensue, 46 A.L.R.3d 578.

In the absence of a contrary expression of intent, it is logical that engagement rings should be considered, by their very nature, conditional gifts given in contemplation of marriage. Once it is established the ring is an engagement ring, it is a conditional gift.

Other courts have reached a similar conclusion. *See Simonian v. Donoian*, 96 Cal.App.2d 259, 215 P.2d 119 (1950); *White v. Finch*, 3

Conn.Cir.Ct. 138, 209 A.2d 199 (1964); *Gill v. Shively*, 320 So.2d 415 (Fla.App. 4 Dist.1975); *Vann v. Vehrs*, 260 Ill.App.3d 648, 198 Ill.Dec. 640, 633 N.E.2d 102 (1994); *Harris v. Davis*, 139 Ill.App.3d 1046, 94 Ill.Dec. 327, 487 N.E.2d 1204 (1986); *Fierro v. Hoel*, 465 N.W.2d 669 (Iowa App.1990); *Aronow v. Silver*, 223 N.J.Super. 344, 538 A.2d 851 (1987); *Mate v. Abrahams*, 62 A.2d 754 (N.J.County Ct.1948); *Vigil v. Haber*, 119 N.M. 9, 888 P.2d 455 (1994); *Wion v. Henderson*, 24 Ohio App.3d 207, 494 N.E.2d 133 (1985); *Lyle v. Durham*, 16 Ohio App.3d 1, 473 N.E.2d 1216 (1984); *Spinnell v. Quigley*, 56 Wash.App. 799, 785 P.2d 1149 (1990); *Brown v. Thomas*, 127 Wis.2d 318, 379 N.W.2d 868.

Other types of property may be shown to be conditional gifts given in contemplation of marriage, but such a classification would require specific evidence of such intent as opposed to just showing the ring was an engagement ring given in contemplation of marriage. As was stated in *Fierro v. Hoel*, 465 N.W.2d at 671, of an engagement ring: "[T]here is no need to establish an express condition that marriage will ensue. A party meets the burden of establishing the conditional nature of the gift by proving by a preponderance of evidence that the gift was given in contemplation of marriage."

In the action herein, the parties stipulated that the object in dispute is an engagement ring given in contemplation of marriage. We conclude the district court correctly held that it was a conditional gift.

Fault or No Fault

We turn now to who is entitled to the ring under the facts herein. There is a split of authority on this issue. Should ownership be determined on the basis of fault? Or should a no-fault rule be applied and the ring returned to its donor after the engagement is broken, regardless of fault?

The annotation at 46 A.L.R.3d 578, previously cited, extensively summarizes the cases arising in this area and the rationales used to resolve them.

Generally, with regard to who is entitled to the engagement ring once the engagement has been broken, courts have taken two divergent paths. One rule states that when an engagement has been unjustifiably broken by the donor, the donor shall not recover the ring. However, if the engagement is broken by mutual agreement or, unjustifiably by the donee, the ring should be returned to the donor. This is the fault-based line of cases. The other rule, the so-called "modern trend," holds that as an engagement ring is an inherently conditional gift, once the engagement has been broken the ring should be returned to the donor. Thus, the question of who broke the engagement and why, or who was "at fault," is irrelevant. This is the no-fault line of cases.

Heather argues that we should adopt the fault-based rule and award the ring to her, as Jerod ended the engagement. Jerod, for obvious reasons, urges us to affirm the district court's adoption of the no-fault rule and award the ring to him.

Heather relies in part upon *Simonian v. Donoian*, 96 Cal.App.2d 259, 215 P.2d 119. The *Simonian* case is not persuasive as it turned on a California statute setting forth the parties' rights in gifts given in contemplation of marriage.

Justification for the fault-based rule was picturesquely stated in *Pavlicic v. Vogtsberger*, 390 Pa. 502, 507, 136 A.2d 127 (1957), as follows:

"A gift given by a man to a woman on condition that she embark on the sea of matrimony with him is no different from a gift based on the condition that the donee sail on any other sea. If, after receiving the provisional gift, the donee refuses to leave the harbor,—if the anchor of contractual performance sticks in the sands of irresolution and procrastination—the gift must be restored to the donor."

Presumably, if the donor of the ring was the party refusing to leave the pier, the Pennsylvania court would rule the donee was entitled to the ring.

Mate v. Abrahams, 62 A.2d at 754–55, applied the fault-based rule, stating:

"On principle, an engagement ring is given, not alone as a symbol of the status of the two persons as engaged, the one to the other, but as a symbol or token of their pledge and agreement to marry. As such pledge or gift, the condition is implied that if both parties abandon the projected marriage, the sole cause of the gift, it should be returned. Similarly, if the woman, who has received the ring in token of her promise, unjustifiably breaks her promise, it should be returned.

"When the converse situation occurs, and the giver of the ring, betokening his promise, violates his word, it would seem that a similar result should follow, i.e., he should lose, not gain, rights to the ring. In addition, had he not broken his promise, the marriage would follow, and the ring would become the wife's absolutely. The man could not then recover the ring. The only difference between that situation, and the facts at bar, is that the man has broken his promise. How, on principle, can the courts aid him, under such circumstances, to regain a ring which he could not regain, had he kept his promise? 'No man should take advantage of his own wrong.' Of course, were the breaking of the engagement to be justifiable, there would be no violation of the agreement legally, and a different result might follow."

Heather also cites *Spinnell v. Quigley*, 56 Wash.App. 799, 785 P.2d 1149 as supporting her argument. *Spinnell* considered the same question as is before us. Relying on 46 A.L.R.3d 578, discussed above, the *Spinnell* court used a contract theory in deciding the case. The court found that an engagement ring is a symbol of an agreement to marry. If that agreement is not performed, then the parties should be restored to their former positions and the ring should be returned. However, if the agreement is not performed because of a breach by the donor, the donor should not benefit from that breach by regaining the ring. In such a case, the ring should be retained by the donee. * * *

We turn now to the no-fault line of cases. In *Vigil v. Haber*, 119 N.M. at 10–11, 888 P.2d 455, the court held that the engagement ring was a conditional gift dependent upon the parties' future marriage, that the question of fault in the breaking of the engagement was irrelevant, and that, therefore, once the engagement had been terminated, the ring should be returned to the donor. The *Vigil* court discussed *Spinnell* in reaching this result and declined to follow its rule. The court noted that, although the practice of determining possession of the engagement ring based upon fault is the majority rule, it preferred the modern trend toward no-fault. Likening a broken engagement to a broken marriage, the court noted that no-fault divorce is the modern approach to a broken marriage. Thus, the court believed, a no-fault approach to a broken engagement was equally appropriate. Following the lead of Iowa, New Jersey, New York, and Wisconsin, the court held that when the condition precedent of marriage fails, an engagement gift must be returned.

The same result was reached in *Aronow v. Silver*, 223 N.J.Super. 344, 538 A.2d 851. Although "[t]he majority rule in this country concerning the disposition of engagement rings is a fault rule: the party who unjustifiably breaks the engagement loses the ring," the *Aronow* court believed the majority rule to be "sexist and archaic," giving the following explanation:

> "The history is traced in 24 A.L.R.2d at 582–586 [superseded by 46 A.L.R.3d 578]. In ancient Rome the rule was fault. When the woman broke the engagement, however, she was required not only to return the ring, but also its value, as a penalty. No penalty attached when the breach was the man's. In England, women were oppressed by the rigidly stratified social order of the day. They worked as servants or, if not of the servant class, were dependent on their relatives. The fact that men were in short supply, marriage above one's station rare and travel difficult abbreviated betrothal prospects for women. Marriages were arranged. Women's lifetime choices were limited to a marriage or a nunnery. Spinsterhood was a centuries-long personal tragedy. Men, because it was a man's world, were much more likely than women to break engagements. When one did, he left behind a woman of tainted reputation and ruined prospects. The law, in a de minimis gesture, gave her the engagement ring, as a consolation prize. When the man was jilted, a seldom thing, justice required the ring's return to him. Thus, the rule of life was the rule of law—both saw women as inferiors.

> . . . .

> "The majority rule, even without its constitutional infirmity, will not stand elementary scrutiny. Its foundation is fault, and fault, in an engagement setting, cannot be ascertained.

> "What fact justifies the breaking of an engagement? The absence of a sense of humor? Differing musical tastes? Differing

political views? The painfully-learned fact is that marriages are made on earth, not in heaven. They must be approached with intelligent care and should not happen without a decent assurance of success. When either party lacks that assurance, for whatever reason, the engagement should be broken. No justification is needed. Either party may act. Fault, impossible to fix, does not count."

In *Fierro v. Hoel*, 465 N.W.2d at 671–72, rejecting "an older majority line of cases" which follow the general principle that the donor of the engagement ring can recover the gift only if the engagement is dissolved by agreement or if the engagement is unjustifiably broken by the donee, the court held that "[i]f the wedding is called off, for whatever reason, the gift is not capable of becoming a completed gift and must be returned to the donor."

In *Brown v. Thomas*, 127 Wis.2d at 328, 379 N.W.2d 868, acknowledging that "most jurisdictions allow recovery of conditional engagement gifts only if the party seeking recovery has not unjustifiably broken off the engagement," the court declined to join them. The court believed that the answer to the question of, Who's at fault, often becomes "lost in the murky depths of contradictory, acrimonious, and largely irrelevant testimony by disappointed couples, their relatives and friends." Applying the same public policy it found embodied within Wisconsin's no-fault divorce law, the court held that the only relevant inquiry in conditional engagement gift cases is whether the condition under which the gift was made has failed. [S]ee also Lyle v. Durham, 16 Ohio App.3d 1, 473 N.E.2d 1216, (adopting no-fault rule in the absence of an agreement between the parties to the contrary).

After careful consideration, we conclude the no-fault line of cases is persuasive.

What is fault or the unjustifiable calling off of an engagement? By way of illustration, should courts be asked to determine which of the following grounds for breaking an engagement is fault or justified? (1) The parties have nothing in common; (2) one party cannot stand prospective in-laws; (3) a minor child of one of the parties is hostile to and will not accept the other party; (4) an adult child of one of the parties will not accept the other party; (5) the parties' pets do not get along; (6) a party was too hasty in proposing or accepting the proposal; (7) the engagement was a rebound situation which is now regretted; (8) one party has untidy habits that irritate the other; or (9) the parties[ ] have religious differences. The list could be endless.

* * *

The engagement period is one where each party should be free to reexamine his or her commitment to the other and be sure he or she desires the commitment of marriage to the other. If the promise to wed were rashly or improvidently made, public policy would be better served if the engagement promise to wed would be broken rather than the marriage vows.

The ring which was given on the promise of a future marriage and is the symbol of the parties' commitment to each other and their life together is, after the engagement is broken, a symbol of failed promises and hopes, hardly a treasured keepsake for its formerly betrothed wearer. Broken engagements engender hurt pride, anger, and wounded egos. They do not ordinarily present the major questions of changes in lifestyles, standards of living, etc., that broken marriages involve. Yet the legislature has applied the no-fault principle to divorces on the grounds of public policy. It is difficult to see how the public policies involving divorce and the division of marital property are best served by no-fault principles, but broken engagements should require a fault-based determination as to ownership of the engagement ring. Litigating fault for a broken engagement would do little but intensify the hurt feelings and delay the parties[ ] being able to get on with their lives.

We conclude that fault is ordinarily not relevant to the question of who should have ownership and possession of an engagement ring after the engagement is broken. Ordinarily, the ring should be returned to the donor, regardless of fault. As in the *Sommers* case, we recognize there may be "extremely gross and rare situations" where fault might be appropriately considered. No such rare situation has been suggested to be involved herein.

The district court did not err in awarding the ring to Jerod after concluding fault was irrelevant.

The judgment is affirmed.

CHRISTEL E. MARQUARDT, JUDGE, dissenting:

I respectfully dissent from the majority's holding.

The courts throughout our country seem to have difficulty in deciding which legal theory applies to ownership of an engagement ring when the engagement is broken. Is the engagement ring a gift or is it used as consideration for the promise to be engaged? If it is a gift, why is it not a completed gift? If it is a conditional gift, what makes it conditional? May a court infer a condition on a gift that was intended to be given and was delivered and accepted? If the ring is consideration for a contract, why not apply breach of contract rules?

"[W]here a transfer of property is made without consideration, the inference is that a gift was intended, not that the grantee was to hold the property for the benefit of the grantor." *Hansen v. Walker*, 175 Kan. 121, 123, 259 P.2d 242 (1953). Where there is an intent to make a gift, the gift is complete when it has been delivered and accepted. In applying gift law, Heather's position that the ring is a valid inter vivos gift is supported in that the engagement took place. As far as we know from the limited record, the gift was complete; all the conditions were met. Jerod, without fraud or coercion, intended to make the gift, and the ring was delivered by him and accepted by Heather.

* * *

Jerod makes no assertion that he told Heather that if the marriage did not take place, she would have to return the ring. The majority asserts that the condition was inferred and, as such, it was a revocable gift, stating: "In the absence of a contrary expression of intent, it is logical that engagement rings should be considered, by their very nature, conditional gifts given in contemplation of marriage." Those jurisdictions that rely on the analysis that an engagement ring is a conditional gift ignore general gift law, which holds that a gift is complete if there is intent, delivery, and acceptance.

We get into legal contortions when we adopt the majority's view that "an engagement ring is the symbol of the parties' mutual promises to marry." This statement indicates that the majority views the giving of an engagement ring as consideration for a contract. It is difficult to reconcile contract principles with this statement. If the parties have exchanged mutual promises, the consideration for the woman's promise to marry is the man's promise to marry. Under this analysis, the ring is transferred without consideration and is a gift. The majority then disregards the "mutual promise" statement and finds that an engagement ring is a conditional gift in contemplation of marriage.

A conditional gift is one that is conditioned or qualified, and the title does not vest in the donee. The majority states: "The engagement period is one where each party should be free to reexamine his or her commitment." Although that may not be the way some people view the engagement period, it has no bearing on the ownership of an engagement ring when an engagement is broken. The majority seems to intertwine the commitment to be engaged with the commitment to be married. The law does not ordinarily become involved with engagements; however, public policy mandates that the law be involved in the breakup of marriages. The commitment to be engaged is given at the time of the engagement, while the commitment to be married is given at the wedding ceremony.

The parties stipulated that the ring was given in contemplation of marriage. This stipulation does not lead to the conclusion that the ring was a conditional gift. Using the majority's analysis, the words "contemplation of marriage" are considered synonymous with "conditioned upon the marriage taking place." I disagree with this legal conclusion as there was no evidence to support such an interpretation here. This case was disposed of by the district court on the stipulated fact that the ring was given in contemplation of marriage. The district court did not consider the issue of intent. If intent was an issue, then the district court should not have disposed of the case on stipulated facts, and a trial should have been held to determine the factual issue of intent.

Applying the "no fault" concept to the ring does not take into account the many expenditures made by the woman in contemplation of marriage. What is the woman to do when she buys a costly dress that cannot be returned? In addition, a bride-to-be may make deposits on a place for the ceremony, a caterer, a reception hall, and entertainment;

buy items to be used jointly after the marriage; move from one city to another; etc.—all of which are costly and for the most part, nonrefundable. This court's ruling implies that these expenditures are irrelevant. Although Jerod is made whole, there is no attempt to put Heather back to her preengagement position, despite the fact that he breached the engagement agreement.

* * *

Most of the other jurisdictions cited by the majority that have dealt with rings and broken engagements hold that if the engagement is unjustifiably broken by the donor, the donor is not entitled to the return of the ring or other gifts. *See, e.g., Spinnell v. Quigley*, 56 Wash.App. 799, 785 P.2d 1149 (1990). This interpretation incorporates fault grounds while supporting a breach of contract concept.

Why should Jerod be rewarded for having broken the engagement contract? Returning the ring to Jerod rewards him for breaking the engagement. A party who breaches a contract is not usually rewarded for the breach. An engagement ring should not be given special treatment.

In the event of a broken engagement, the engagement ring should be considered a completed inter vivos gift. Regardless, Heather is entitled to keep the engagement ring whether this case is analyzed on the principles of gift law, contract law, or equity.

Notes and Problems

1. For another engagement ring case reaching a similar conclusion, see *Lindh v. Surman*, 702 A.2d 560 (Pa.Super.1997).

2. Some states have enacted statutes that bear on this question. For example, Cal.Civ.Code Ann. § 1590 (West 1982) provides:

> Where either party to a contemplated marriage in this State makes a gift of money or property to the other on the basis or assumption that the marriage will take place, in the event that the donee refuses to enter into the marriage as contemplated or that it is given up by mutual consent, the donor may recover such gift or such part of its value as may, under all the circumstances of the case, be found by a court or jury to be just.

3. Suppose third persons send wedding presents to one or both of the engaged couple. Can the donors recover these presents when the engagement is broken?

F. FIXTURES

A fixture is an item of personal property attached to land in such a way that it becomes part of the realty, but retains its identity. Controversy as to whether an item is a fixture may arise in situations where one party is entitled to the land and another party is entitled to personal property on the land. Thus, disagreement on the fixture issue occurs in cases involving executor and heir, seller and purchaser, mortgagor and mortgagee, landlord and tenant, and life tenant and remainderman. *See* 8 Powell on Real Property ¶ 651 (1998).

EVERITT v. HIGGINS

Court of Appeals of Idaho, 1992.
122 Idaho 708, 838 P.2d 311.

WALTERS, CHIEF JUDGE.

This case arises from a dispute between parties to a real estate contract and concerns the ownership of a wood cook stove. On appeal from a decision upholding the trial court's determination that the stove was the personal property of the seller, the purchaser argues (1) that the stove was a fixture passing to him by deed with the real estate, and, alternatively, (2) that the stove passed to him under the terms of the real estate contract. For the reasons explained below, we affirm.

FACTS

The following facts, found by the trial court, are not disputed on appeal. Paul and Shelly Higgins owned a home in Rathdrum, Idaho. Although the home was equipped with a modern, gas heating system, it also contained two antique wood cook stoves, one in the downstairs portion of the home, and one upstairs in the master bedroom. Each stove rested on, but was not attached to, a built-in brick platform, which was slightly higher than the surrounding wood flooring. However, only the downstairs wood stove was connected to the chimney flu[e]. Its heat was incorporated into the forced-air distribution of the home's heating system. The upstairs stove was not operational but exclusively decorative: it had no stove pipe connecting it to the chimney. In fact, prior to the Higgins' occupancy of the home, the chimney flu[e] had been blocked by a concrete plug where the stove pipe would have attached. This plug was never removed but was concealed by a decorative device.

The Higgins decided to put their home on the market and, in 1988, entered into a real estate purchase and sale agreement conveying the property to Jack Everitt. Everitt viewed the home twice prior to the sale but never discussed either wood stove with the Higgins. Nor did the parties explicitly reference the stoves in their written agreement. At the time Everitt took possession of the home, after the sale closed, the upstairs wood stove had been removed. Everitt demanded the stove be returned, claiming it had been conveyed to him in the sale of the home. When the Higgins refused, Everitt filed a complaint seeking to recover the stove, or, in the alternative, for damages. The case was tried before the magistrate judge, sitting without a jury. At the conclusion of the trial the judge denied the complaint, ruling that the stove was not a fixture but was the personal property of the Higgins, and hence did not pass with the realty. The judge further concluded that, because the stove was not otherwise covered by the terms of the contract, it was not included in the sale to Everitt.

The district court affirmed the judgment of the magistrate. On appeal from that decision, Everitt contends that the trial court failed to properly apply the law when it held that the stove was personal property. He further avers that the court misconstrued the real estate contract when it concluded that the stove was not included in the terms of the sale.

* * *

WAS THE STOVE A FIXTURE?

We first examine the trial court's determination that the wood stove was the personal property of the Higgins, and not a fixture which, by operation of law, had passed to Everitt by deed with the real estate. For an object to become a fixture, thus becoming part of the realty, three essential elements must concur: (1) annexation to the realty, either actual or constructive; (2) adaptation or application to the use or purpose to which that part of the realty to which it is connected is appropriated; and (3) intention to make the article a permanent accession to the freehold. Rayl v. Shull Enterprises, Inc., 108 Idaho 524, 527, 700 P.2d 567, 570 (1984); Beebe v. Pioneer Bank & Trust Co., 34 Idaho 385, 391, 201 P. 717, 718 (1921); see also R. Boyer, Survey of the Law of Property, ch. 14, 327–333 (3rd ed. 1981). Once an item becomes a fixture, it is thereafter treated as part of the realty until or unless it is severed by the fee owner.

"Annexation" is usually considered in light of the actual relationship of the object to the realty, although an object may be constructively annexed to the real property. The "adaptation" requirement is generally held to be met when the particular object is clearly adapted to the use to which the realty is devoted. This test frequently focuses on whether the real property is peculiarly valuable in use because of the continued presence of the annexed property. An object placed on the realty may become a fixture if it is a necessary, or at least a useful, adjunct to the realty, considering the purposes to which the realty is devoted.

"Intention" is generally regarded as the most important of the three elements. The relevant inquiry here is whether the objective circumstances manifest an intent that the item was to be permanently annexed to the realty. This objective intention may be inferred from:

(1) the nature of the article; (2) the manner of annexation to the land; (3) the injury to the land, if any, by its removal; (4) the completeness with which the chattel is integrated with the use to which the land is being put; (5) the relation which the annexer has with the land such as licensee, tenant at will or for years or for life or fee owner; (6) the relation which the annexer has with the chattel such as owner, bailee or converter; (7) the local custom respecting treating such chattel as personal property or a fixture; (8) the time, place and degree of social, economic and cultural development, (e.g., a luxury in one generation is a necessity in another * * *); and (9) all other relevant facts surrounding the annexation.

Boyer at 329. Whether an item is a fixture usually presents a mixed question of law and fact to be determined by the trier of fact upon proper application of the three-part test. However, where the facts are undisputed or when the evidence allows but one reasonable conclusion to be drawn therefrom, the question may be decided as a matter of law. In view of the evidence presented at trial and of the magistrate's basic findings—which are not disputed on appeal—we conclude, as a matter of law, that the wood stove at issue in this case was not a fixture.

Plainly, the item in question in this case was not actually annexed to the property. The four-legged stove simply rested upon the brick platform where it had been placed. It was not attached to the chimney, nor did it appear to be attached, as it had no connecting stove pipe. It could have been removed without destruction to the realty simply by lifting it. Although Everitt does not challenge the lower court's finding that the stove was purely decorative, he asks us to presume the wood stove originally had been installed to be operational. He maintains that this historical intent is controlling on the status of the stove as a fixture. The record, however, lacks any evidence showing that the stove was ever functional, and in fact tends to suggest the opposite to be true. Even assuming, *arguendo,* that the stove was once actually annexed to the realty, the fact that its stove pipe had been removed and the chimney flu[e] plugged clearly evidence an intent that it be permanently disconnected. Furthermore, a building inspector testified that reattaching the stove to the chimney would constitute a building violation. Where an owner severs a fixture from realty with the intent that it be permanently severed therefrom, the item reacquires its character as personal property. Thus, even if the stove at one time had been actually annexed, the evidence clearly establishes an intent to permanently sever the stove before the sale of the real estate to Everitt.

Everitt next argues that actual annexation is not essential to the wood stove's status as a fixture because the stove had been *constructively* annexed. Constructive annexation may be found where the object, although not itself attached to the realty, comprises a necessary, integral or working part of some other object which is attached. Everitt contends that the stove was constructively annexed by virtue of its prominence in the room as a decorative focal point. He further submits that the intent to annex the stove should be inferred from the fact that its removal left a brick platform which was both useless and unsightly. The trial court evidently rejected this argument, however, when it found that the platform could accommodate any similarly-sized decorative stove. Certainly, there is nothing in the record suggesting that the brick surface, although permanent, was designed to accommodate the particular stove, or that the stove was especially manufactured, measured, or designed to fit the platform.

Everitt further directs our attention to disputed evidence that Paul Higgins told his wife and the movers that the stove was to remain in the home. However, even if the Higgins had determined to leave the stove behind when they moved, it does not necessarily follow that the stove was intended to be permanently annexed to the realty. The interpretation of the evidence was a matter for the magistrate, who was persuaded ultimately not to accept Everitt's position.

Applying the three-element test to the basic facts found by the magistrate, which are not disputed on appeal, and in light of the evidence presented at trial, we conclude as a matter of law that the stove was not a fixture. Accordingly, we uphold the magistrate's determination that the stove was personal property.

Was The Stove Included Under The Agreement?

Having concluded that the stove did not pass with the realty as a fixture, we turn to Everitt's contention that the stove was conveyed under the terms of the real estate purchase and sale agreement. Where the language of a contract is clear, it is deemed unambiguous and will be interpreted by the court as a matter of law.

The purchase and sale agreement contained a standard clause specifically including all "cooling and heating systems." The contract additionally contained hand-writing expressly including in the sale the "range, refrigerator, washer & dryer," and expressly excluding from the sale the "kitchen light fixture (stain glass), mirrors in both baths & antique lawn ornaments." Everitt first contends that a reasonable interpretation of the term "heating systems" includes the wood stove in question. However, the magistrate found that the stove was exclusively used for decoration at the time of the sale and was not part of an integrated heating system. Given this finding, which is supported by the uncontroverted evidence, the antique wood stove can not reasonably be considered as part of a "heating system" under the contract.

* * *

Conclusion

The wood cook stove was the personal property of the Higgins and did not pass to Everitt by deed with the realty. Although the parties were free to include the stove in the sale by agreement, there is no evidence that any such agreement existed. Consequently, Everitt acquired no rights in the stove, and he has no right to damages for its removal from the home.

The district court's decision upholding the judgment of the magistrate is affirmed.

* * *

METROPOLITAN CABLEVISION, INC. v. COX CABLE CLEVELAND AREA

Court of Appeals of Ohio, Cuyahoga County, 1992.
78 Ohio App.3d 273, 604 N.E.2d 765.

Matia, Chief Justice.

This appeal arises out of the judgment of the Cuyahoga County Court of Common Pleas which found that the cable wiring installed in a subscriber's home by a cable television company was a fixture. Appellant claims error, and assigns this issue for our review. We affirm the decision of the trial court.

Statement of the Facts

Defendant-appellant Cox Cable Television Company ("Cox") is a cable television company with a cable franchise in the city of Parma, Ohio, as well as other communities in Cuyahoga County.

Plaintiff-appellee Metropolitan Cablevision, Inc., d.b.a. MetroTen Cablevision ("MetroTen"), is a cable television company which provides "wireless" cable to the city of Cleveland, and elsewhere in the northeast Ohio area, including Parma, through a technology known as Multichannel Multipoint Distribution System. Unlike other cable companies, MetroTen transmits signals through the air to an antenna located on the subscriber's home. MetroTen and Cox compete for cable customers in Parma.

When Cox installs service in a new subscriber's home, it runs a wire from the cable pole to the house, and through a drilled hole in the house to the television set. If the television is not near the wall, Cox uses clips to attach the wiring to the baseboard. A grounding device is also used and attached with screws to the joists in the basement. Cox runs wiring along the interior walls if necessary. When a subscriber cancels his service, Cox is under no obligation to remove the wiring unless the homeowner requests its removal in writing. Parma Ordinances 717.22.

If a former Cox Cable subscriber switches to MetroTen, MetroTen will use internal wiring previously installed by Cox to provide MetroTen's service to that subscriber. MetroTen installs its antenna and runs wiring from its antenna to the ground-block left by Cox. MetroTen then uses the wiring left by Cox from the ground-block to the subscriber's television set.

Plaintiff-appellee Dawn Mueller is a homeowner in Parma. After cancelling her Cox subscription, she refused to permit Cox's removal of her internal wiring. Both Mueller and MetroTen allege that the internal wiring left in the homes of former subscribers by Cox is a fixture. Cox alleges that the contract between Cox and the homeowner expressly asserts that internal wiring remains the property of Cox and never becomes a fixture.

Statement of the Case

Appellee MetroTen filed for a declaratory judgment and injunctive relief against Cox * * *.

In its complaint for declaratory judgment, MetroTen prayed that the court find * * * that the internal wiring was a fixture * * *. Cox counterclaimed for the reasonable value of the use of its equipment.

* * *

* * * [T]he trial court found that the internal wiring was a fixture and enjoined Cox from prosecuting either civil or criminal actions against MetroTen for its use of the internal wiring and from prosecuting Dawn Mueller based on her refusal to allow Cox to remove the internal wiring from her home. * * * The court also dismissed Cox's counterclaim.

* * * Cox filed a timely notice of appeal from that judgment.

Appellant argues in its sole assignment of error that the trial court erred in finding that internal wiring installed in a home by a cable company is a fixture. Specifically, appellant argues that internal wiring remains the property of the cable company.

This assignment of error is not well taken.

Issue: Whether Cable Wiring Installed in a Subscriber's Home Becomes a Fixture

In determining whether articles annexed to the leasehold by the tenant have become fixtures, the trier of fact must consider the nature of the property, the manner of annexation, the purpose of annexation, the intention of the annexing party, the difficulty of removal, and the damage to the severed property which removal would cause. Brown v. DuBois (1988), 40 Ohio Misc.2d 18, 532 N.E.2d 223.

In the cause *sub judice,* the court is not making a determination regarding fixtures placed in a leasehold by the tenant; however, the holding in *Brown* reaffirms the general rule of law in Ohio since 1853 that a fixture to realty brings into issue not ownership but, rather, whether the fixture becomes a permanent part of the realty and thus capable of passing with the freehold or leasehold estate.

* * *

This general rule has been reviewed, examined, reaffirmed and refined by the Ohio Supreme Court:

"We reaffirm that such a determination must be made in light of the particular facts of each case, taking into account such facts as the nature of the property; the manner in which it is annexed to the realty; the purpose for which annexation is made; the intention of the annexing party to make the property a part of the realty and dedicate it irrevocably to the realty for a particular use; the degree of difficulty and the extent of any economic loss involved in thereafter removing it from the realty; and the damage to the severed property which removal would cause." Masheter v. Boehm (1974), 37 Ohio St.2d 68, 77, 66 O.O.2d 183, 188, 307 N.E.2d 533, 540.

* * *

In reviewing the cause herein, and applying the standards enunciated by precedent, this court finds that the trial court properly found that the cable wiring placed in the subscriber's home by Cox was a fixture and, thus, part of the realty by annexation.

The wiring supplied by Cox is stapled, screwed and clamped to the walls, floorboards, basement joists, and exterior and interior walls of the subscriber's home. The facts indicate that Cox is efficient and as minimally intrusive into the integrity of the structure as possible; however, holes are drilled into the exterior wall of the subscriber's home to permit ingress of the cable service to the subscriber's television. Wires are annexed to the floorboards of the home if necessary. A ground wire is attached, preferably to the cold water line in the basement. Most important, notwithstanding Cox's contract with the subscriber, prior to MetroTen's complaint the cable wiring was customarily left in the home after the subscriber terminated Cox's cable service.

Cox's own testimony revealed that the wire was intentionally left in the subscriber's home due to the high incidence of repeat service either by resubscription or by a new subscription by new tenants or homeowners. Cox further testified that removing the cable cost more than it was worth, and that although the wiring could be removed without causing a great amount of damage, some damage could result from removal of the cable wires.

We find conclusively then that the facts of the cable wiring fit squarely within the rules for determining whether moveable property becomes so attached to the realty as to become a fixture and therefore a part of the real estate. Accordingly, we find that the trial court properly determined that the cable wiring is a fixture.

Issue: Whether Cox Cable Contract Between Cox and Subscriber Circumvents Fixture Law

Cox relies also on the contract between it and the subscriber to counter the fixture argument. The contract states that the subscriber will "allow Cox reasonable access to the customer's premises for the purpose of * * * removal of cable equipment to customer's premises." The front of the contract reads: "Important equipment agreement. I understand and agree that the equipment installed by Cox Cable Cleveland Area remain their property and is to be returned in good working condition when the cable service is terminated."

Cox argues that the trial court's ruling contradicts the intent of the contract between the subscriber and Cox. We find, however, that the equipment that the contract refers to is the moveable components of the cable service, *i.e.*, the cable box and the remote control and any other equipment that is easily removable because it is attached to the realty only by a connection here or there. Therefore, the trial court's judgment does not contradict the intent of the contract between Cox and the subscriber.

Accordingly, finding no error, and for the foregoing reasons, we affirm the judgment of the trial court.

Judgment affirmed.

Notes, Problems and Questions

1. Is a building necessarily a fixture that passes to the purchaser of the land upon which it is located? *See* Abrenilla v. China Insurance Company, Ltd., 870 F.2d 548 (9th Cir.1989); Sigrol Realty Corp. v. Valcich, 12 A.D.2d 430, 212 N.Y.S.2d 224 (1961), *affirmed mem.* 11 N.Y.2d 668, 225 N.Y.S.2d 748, 180 N.E.2d 904 (1962).

2. As indicated in *Metropolitan Cablevision,* fixture issues also arise between landlords and tenants. At the end of a lease, the tenant may remove business or trade items that the tenant installed on the leased premises. This "trade fixture" rule has been expanded generally in this country to include items installed for agricultural and even ornamental use. *See* W. Burby, Handbook of the Law of Real Property 29–30 (3d ed.) (1965); *see also* Willett v. Centerre Bank of Branson, 792 S.W.2d 916 (Mo.App.1990). The tenant, however, may be found to have no right to remove items it installed if removal would cause material injury to the leased premises. Are "trade fixtures" really fixtures? Why was the "trade fixture" rule created? *See* 8 Powell on Real Property ¶ 653 (1998). The "trade fixture" question often arises in connection with distribution of compensation paid upon the condemnation of leased premises. *See, e.g.,* Sweeting v. Hammons, 521 So.2d 226 (Fla.App.1988); State v. Jim Lynch Toyota, Inc., 835 S.W.2d 421 (Mo. App.1992).

3. Suppose the Lloyds wish to remove an expensive chandelier they purchased and installed in the dining room of their apartment. (Installation required three hours of work by a carpenter.) Daze Corporation claims that the chandelier should remain with the apartment when the Lloyds move. Advise the Lloyds.

Chapter 3

INTERESTS IN REAL PROPERTY

Hypothetical Situation—Number 3

Jill and Steve Ryan are a young married couple. Jill is an architect, and Steve is a dentist. The Ryans are renting an apartment, but want to purchase a home. They have noticed a house for-sale-by-owner on the outskirts of Centerville and are also interested in looking at other property. They are, however, unsure as to legal matters involved in purchasing real estate. In particular, the Ryans are confused about the many different property interests, such as fee simple, tenancy by the entirety, and easement, that their friends in the real estate business have mentioned. Thus, they contacted you for general information in anticipation that they will purchase a house in the near future. You agreed to act as their attorney and to be available during the course of their search for a home to help solve any legal problems that arise.

A. HISTORICAL BACKGROUND

In order to advise the Ryans properly, it is necessary that you gain a basic understanding of the historical foundation of our current system of real property ownership. Hence, we offer a brief, but important, excursion through medieval history.

On October 14, 1066, a bloody battle was fought at Hastings in England. It involved tiny armies by today's standards, but it had enduring consequences not only for the British nation generally but for British and American legal systems as well. You, as American law students, must be familiar with the consequences of that distant event because it continues to influence the property law of every jurisdiction in the United States.

Although William of Normandy prevailed in the Battle of Hastings, the English did not immediately surrender. In following years, there were many rebellions against William the Conqueror, as he is now known. William was able to crush these insurrections and to follow them with cruel sanctions of ruthless exploitation and expropriation. He spread terror throughout England and in the process created a feudal system which solidified the English nation and ultimately formed the basis for American property law.

William, as Duke of Normandy, was a rather insignificant feudal figure who could not have mounted a successful campaign against Anglo–Saxon England without the financial and military support of many barons and knights from Flanders and Brittany. These supporters, on a calculated judgment that William had a fair chance of success in enforcing his dubious claim to the crown, committed to the venture. When William did indeed prevail, he was required to compensate his backers.

As an 11th century king, William was far less powerful than the absolute monarchs who reigned later in Europe. But under the feudal theory he imposed, William, as king, "owned" all the land in the kingdom. He proceeded to distribute about three-quarters of the entire territory of England among his backers; the balance he retained for himself. William's task in this distribution was made easier by the fact that he had seized almost the entire holdings of the old Anglo–Saxon–Danish aristocracy, many of whom had been killed in the Battle of Hastings.

A new scheme of property ownership gradually evolved in England. Extraordinarily complex, it governed land and later spread to personal property. We deal primarily with this system as it relates to real property. It is ironic that although the English abandoned many of its more technical and archaic aspects in a series of reforms during the late 19th and early 20th centuries, American jurisdictions retain much of the ancient usage.

There are several steps you should take in dealing with this material. First, master the vocabulary. This is an area of law where precision in expression is essential. A possibility of reverter is not a reversion, and to confuse the two is a certain route to difficulty.

Second, you should see the development of English property law *THE STRUGGLE* largely as the consequence of an ongoing struggle between those who owned land and wanted to assure control of it for themselves and their successors, and those who wished to curtail the privileges of the landed gentry. Often the struggle took the form of taxation and resistance to taxation. Sometimes the tax collector won a skirmish and sometimes a group of resourceful lawyers, known as conveyancers, prevailed. But the battle continued and the advantage shifted from one side to the other.

Third, do not try to grasp the entire mosaic of the feudal system in one sitting. The material tends to build on itself. Thus, each step must be mastered before you proceed to the next. For example, an understanding of the terms "freehold," "non-freehold," "tenure," and "seisin" must be firmly in place before you examine estates in land. These concepts were pragmatic solutions to certain problems existing at the time they were crafted. You should view them in the context of those times and appreciate their impact on the system of estates in land we still use today.

In early feudal society the basis of wealth and power was land, not money. That ancient system was grounded in the theory that the entire nation was the personal fief of the king. Obviously, it was not practical for the king to own and operate such an enormous amount of land; and, as stated earlier, William was obligated to the barons and ecclesiastics who supported his venture into England. For these reasons, he parceled out huge tracts of land to his loyal retainers. William did not, however, sell or give the land in the sense we understand those terms today. Instead, he simply made the recipients his tenants. In theory, William, as king, still "owned" all of the land and his tenants were said to hold "of" him. In fact, his tenants occupied, possessed, and used the land much as absolute owners would today. The concept of holding "of" another is called tenure.[1]

The notion of tenure spawned a complicated property scheme. The immediate tenants of the king, known as tenants in chief, parceled out portions of their tracts to tenants of their own. The tenants in chief then became lords in their own right. The lesser tenants distributed their tracts in a similar manner and this process was repeated until even the lowest orders of society were included. Feudal society, therefore, was organized in the shape of a pyramid, with the king at the top, the tenants in chief immediately under him, their tenants under them, and so on down the line.[2]

The compensation a tenant rendered his lord was known as services and was individually fixed for each tenure. Services took many forms. The tenant might have been required, for example, to furnish troops in times of disorder or, in the case of lesser classes, to work the lord's land. As feudalism deteriorated through the centuries, the tenures came to be supported more and more by the payment of fixed sums of money rather than the performance of personal services. As might be expected, inflation undermined the value of these payments.

Another aspect of tenure involved the duty of incidents. These were certain rights flowing to the lord incidental to the tenurial arrangement. They eventually became more significant than services. Essentially, incidents were a sort of tax the tenant paid the lord for certain privileges.[3] These "taxes" were of great importance to the lords receiving

---

1. Contrast the tenurial system with allodial ownership. The term "allodial" means ownership in absolute terms with no thought of holding "of," or subservient to, anyone.

2. The pyramid continued to expand downward until 1290 when the Statute Quia Emptores was enacted. This statute was interpreted to prohibit the practice of subinfeudation in fee simple estates. Thereafter, no new lord and tenant relationship in fee simple absolute could be created, but free substitution was permitted without the lord's consent. See 3 W. Holdsworth, A History of English Law 80–81 (1926).

3. The most important incidents can be grouped into five general categories: (1) relief—a rough type of inheritance tax, (2) aids—contributions to the lord in certain emergency situations such as the need to pay ransom, (3) escheat—forfeiture of the land to the lord if the tenant was convicted of a felony or died without heirs, (4) wardship—the lord's right to the rents and profits of the land during the minority of a deceased tenant's heirs, and (5) marriage—the lord's right to arrange a marriage for wards and to enjoy advantageous financial arrangements attendant on the marriage. See Walker, Free Consent and Marriage of

them. The struggle to avoid them *(TAXES)* led directly to the enactment of the Statute of Uses (1536). This famous statute, among its consequences, fundamentally altered earlier methods of land transfer. *See* pages 263–265.

Most feudal incidents were abolished on the restoration of the Stuart Monarchy in 1660. In theory, tenure remains the basis for land ownership in England, but it no longer is a meaningful limitation on the rights of owners. Although some land in the original colonies was held in tenure and theoretically lands may still be so held in a few states, as a practical matter virtually all land in this country is owned allodially. Even where a tenurial relationship may exist, it no longer has practical significance. *See* C. Moynihan, Introduction to the Law of Real Property 22–24 (2d ed. 1988); Ely, *Law in a Republican Society: Continuity and Change in the Legal System of Postrevolutionary America*, in Perspectives on Revolution and Evolution 46, 50 (1979).

B. ESTATES IN LAND

We now address estates in land. This is a time when precise use of vocabulary is essential. To be nearly accurate is not enough because lines are technical and narrowly drawn. A slight variation can cause vast differences in result.

Property may be possessed by one person presently with the right in another to possess the same property at a future time. The right of present possession is termed a present estate or a present possessory estate. The right to possession at a future time is called a future estate. The law of future interests will be treated subsequently in this chapter.

[margin note: PRESENT OWNERSHIP VS. FUTURE]

Estates are also classified in terms of their relative dignity in the ancient feudal hierarchy. Freehold estates were the most prestigious. The term "freehold" derives from the fact that these estates were held by free men, not serfs. Non-freehold estates, which originated as a moneylenders' device, were less distinguished. These estates, now called leases, came to be used primarily for agricultural purposes. The principal theoretical difference between the two classes of estates was in their presumed dignity. The principal practical difference lay in access to the courts. *See* T. Plucknett, A Concise History of the Common Law 569–574 (5th ed. 1956).

Certain important and rather rigid rules grew up around freehold estates. These rules flowed from the concept of seisin. The freehold estate holder was seized of property. The non-freehold estate owner was not. Seisin was a murky concept which combined the notion of ownership of property with the right to possession. It was fundamentally important in the feudal system that the lord be able to determine which of the lord's tenants were seized of the lord's holdings because the lord looked to those persons for the production of services and incidents at

Feudal Wards in Medieval England, 8 J. Medieval History 123 (1982) (discussing economic importance of the lord's right to control the marriage of wards).

critical times. Someone had to be seized of every piece of land at all times—there could never be a gap in seisin. It was simply a matter of knowing who was responsible for the performance of feudal obligations.

Freehold estates were transferred by a physical livery of seisin in a feoffment ceremony. The owner and the transferee went to the land where the owner delivered seisin to the transferee by handing the transferee a twig or clod of dirt. A written deed did not suffice to transfer a present possessory freehold. Frequently, however, a written document, called a charter, was prepared to evidence the actual feoffment. *See* T. Bergin & P. Haskell, Preface to Estates in Land and Future Interests 10–11 (2d ed. 1984).

Freehold estates in land consist of four groupings: fee simple absolute, defeasible fees, fee tail, and life estate. The three non-freehold estates are: tenancy for a fixed term (estate for years); periodic tenancy; and tenancy at will. Some observers include a fourth non-freehold estate—tenancy at sufferance. In each case, pay particular attention to the wording required to create the estate and to the peculiar characteristics of that estate, the most important of which is its duration.

1. FEE SIMPLE ABSOLUTE

O, owner of land, conveys the property "to A and his heirs." The words of the conveyance create a fee simple absolute in A. This is the largest possible estate. The property now belongs entirely to A and, in theory, is A's forever. A's heirs take nothing by reason of the conveyance.

D'Arundel's Case (1225) established that A took the entire estate for all time, subject only to A's feudal responsibility for services and incidents. This was a convenient arrangement for both A and A's lord. A could dispose of the property without concern for the rights of A's heirs. However, if A did not dispose of the property during A's lifetime, it descended to A's heirs who were required to pay the lord the incident of relief.

Why did the words "and his heirs" continue in use and hold sway over the nature of the conveyance so that a fee simple could not be created without them? The answer is that they were considered words of limitation, denoting only that the estate conveyed was inheritable. The estate would not necessarily be inherited because A could dispose of it during A's lifetime. But, if A did not, A's heirs would receive it. In time, the words became mandatory. Their absence meant that no fee simple absolute was conveyed. Even a conveyance from O "to A in fee simple absolute" transferred merely a life estate. Only in modern times has this rigid requirement been eliminated.

To summarize, a conveyance "to A and his heirs" means that A takes an estate of indefinite duration. A is a purchaser and the words "to A" are words of purchase. (This is true whether A actually pays something for the land or receives it by gift.) The words "and his heirs" are words of limitation indicating that the estate can be inherited. They are no longer required. Thus, today a conveyance "to A" creates a fee simple absolute in A.[1]

Notes, Problems, and Questions

1. O conveys land "to A and her heirs." A plans to sell the land to take advantage of an unusual opportunity at the racetrack. Given the wording of the conveyance, can A's children prevent A from conveying the property? What kind of estate can A convey?

2. If a mortgage is placed on property owned in fee simple absolute, can the owner convey a fee simple absolute to a third party? Does the amount of the mortgage debt make a difference? *See* pages 498–503.

3. Does the existence of a zoning restriction on or an easement through property prevent the owner from holding a fee simple absolute?

4. It is noted in the text that a fee simple absolute in land is an inheritable estate. Who inherited the estate at common law? Unlike some continental arrangements, the English developed a system of inheritance based on primogeniture. Under this system, land passed at the death of the owner to the owner's eldest son as sole heir. There could, therefore, be only one "heir" in each generation. If there were no sons, the property passed to the family's daughters collectively. For this purpose daughters as a group were regarded as a single heir. The doctrine of primogeniture tended to keep large tracts of land intact from generation to generation. Primogeniture was eliminated in England in 1925. It was never an important concept in this country. In the United States, intestate property generally descends to the decedent's children equally subject to rights of a surviving spouse.

2. DEFEASIBLE FEES

In every generation there are those who wish to transfer property and yet retain a measure of control over its use. To accommodate these yearnings, the common law developed two fee simple estates which involve conditions that might cause them to end.

a. Fee Simple Determinable

O conveys "to A for so long as A uses the property for agricultural purposes."

This defeasible fee estate is the fee simple determinable. It is created by the transfer of a fee simple to endure until the occurrence of a given event. Typically, as illustrated above, a fee simple is created followed by words such as "until," "so long as," or "while." If the event occurs, the estate automatically ends. Note that the estate terminates on its own volition; no action is needed on the part of anyone. This automatic

---

1. After the enactment of the Statute of Wills (1540), it was possible for a landowner to transfer property by will. Such a testamentary transfer is termed a devise; an inter vivos transfer of land is called a conveyance. If a landowner neither conveys nor devises property, it passes to the landowner's heirs by intestate succession.

termination is the key distinction between the fee simple determinable and its cousin, the fee simple subject to a condition subsequent.

Obviously, the specified event may never occur and the transferee may retain the fee indefinitely. But if the event occurs, the property must pass to someone. The common law, therefore, provided that an estate in the transferor was created simultaneously with the creation of a fee simple determinable. This estate is a possibility of reverter. It is necessarily a future interest because it becomes possessory only if the fee simple fails. We will consider the possibility of reverter further in our examination of future interests. *See* page 248.

b. Fee Simple Subject to a Condition Subsequent

O conveys "to A, but if A fails to use the land for agricultural purposes, O may enter and recover the land."

The fee simple subject to a condition subsequent, illustrated above, is closely related to the fee simple determinable. There are, however, important differences in its creation and operation. The fee simple subject to a condition subsequent is an estate in fee simple so conditioned that the happening of a certain event gives the transferor the right to enter and terminate the estate. Generally a fee simple is created, followed by a phrase such as "on condition that" or "provided that" some event does or does not happen. These phrases are not magic ones, and modern courts look to the intent of the grantor. If words such as the ones above are present, and especially if they are followed by words giving the transferor the right to recover the property, it is likely the estate will be considered a fee simple subject to a condition subsequent. When this estate is formed, a future interest is simultaneously created in the transferor. This interest is known as a right of entry or, sometimes, as a power of termination. It becomes possessory only when the condition is met and the owner of the right of entry takes appropriate steps to terminate the present estate. Thus, with respect to termination, the fee simple determinable and the fee simple subject to a condition subsequent are markedly different. *See* page 259 for further discussion of rights of entry.

Because both defeasible fees may be forfeited, courts are loath to construe ambiguous terminology as creating either estate. In modern times, judges strain to construe conditions in deeds or wills as covenants which, if violated, lead only to money damages or injunctive relief. *See generally* Jost, *The Defeasible Fee and the Birth of the Modern Residential Subdivision*, 49 Mo.L.Rev. 695 (1984). If such a construction is not possible, the courts generally prefer to find a fee simple subject to a condition subsequent rather than a fee simple determinable. This is because the former estate must be terminated by affirmative action whereas the latter estate ends automatically on breach of the condition.

MAHRENHOLZ v. COUNTY BOARD OF SCHOOL TRUSTEES OF LAWRENCE COUNTY

Appellate Court of Illinois, Fifth District, 1981.
93 Ill.App.3d 366, 48 Ill.Dec. 736, 417 N.E.2d 138.

JONES, JUSTICE:

This case involves an action to quiet title to real property located in Lawrence County, Illinois. Its resolution depends on the judicial construction of language in a conveyance of that property. The case is before us on the pleadings, plaintiffs' third amended complaint having been dismissed by a final order. The pertinent facts are taken from the pleadings.

On March 18, 1941, W.E. and Jennie Hutton executed a warranty deed in which they conveyed certain land, to be known here as the Hutton School grounds, to the Trustees of School District No. 1, the predecessors of the defendants in this action. The deed provided that "this land to be used for school purpose only; otherwise to revert to Grantors herein." W.E. Hutton died intestate on July 18, 1951, and Jennie Hutton died intestate on February 18, 1969. The Huttons left as their only legal heir their son Harry E. Hutton.

The property conveyed by the Huttons became the site of the Hutton School. Community Unit School District No. 20 succeeded to the grantee of the deed and held classes in the building constructed upon the land until May 30, 1973. After that date, children were transported to classes held at other facilities operated by the District. The District has used the property since then for storage purposes only.

Earl and Madeline Jacqmain executed a warranty deed on October 9, 1959, conveying to the plaintiffs over 390 acres of land in Lawrence County and which included the 40 acre tract from which the Hutton School grounds were taken. When and from whom the Jacqmains acquired the land is not shown and is of no consequence in this appeal. The deed from the Jacqmains to the plaintiffs excepted the Hutton School grounds, but purported to convey the disputed future interest. * * *

On May 7, 1977, Harry E. Hutton, son and sole heir of W.E. and Jennie Hutton, conveyed to the plaintiffs all of his interest in the Hutton School land. This document was filed in the recorder's office of Lawrence County on September 7, 1977. * * *

The plaintiffs filed a complaint in the circuit court of Lawrence County on April 9, 1974, in which they sought to quiet title to the school property in themselves, by virtue of the interests acquired from * * * the Jacqmains and from Harry Hutton. On March 21, 1979, the trial court entered an order dismissing this complaint.

* * *

Plaintiffs have perfected an appeal to this court.

The basic issue presented by this appeal is whether the trial court correctly concluded that the plaintiffs could not have acquired any interest in the school property from the Jacqmains or from Harry Hutton. Resolution of this issue must turn upon the legal interpretation of the language contained in the March 18, 1941, deed from W. E. and Jennie Hutton to the Trustees of School District No. 1:

> "this land to be used for school purpose only; otherwise to revert to Grantors herein."

In addition to the legal effect of this language we must consider the alienability of the interest created and the effect of subsequent deeds.

The parties appear to be in agreement that the 1941 deed from the Huttons conveyed a defeasible fee simple estate to the grantee, and gave rise to a future interest in the grantors, and that it did not convey a fee simple absolute, subject to a covenant. The fact that provision was made for forfeiture of the estate conveyed should the land cease to be used for school purposes suggests that this view is correct.

The future interest remaining in this grantor or his estate can only be a possibility of reverter or a right of re-entry for condition broken. As neither interest may be transferred by will or by *inter vivos* conveyance (Ill.Rev.Stat., ch. 30, par. 37b), and as the land was being used for school purposes in 1959 when the Jacqmains transferred their interest in the school property to the plaintiffs, the trial court correctly ruled that the plaintiffs could not have acquired any interest in that property from the Jacqmains by the deed of October 9, 1959.

Consequently this court must determine whether the plaintiffs could have acquired an interest in the Hutton School grounds from Harry Hutton. The resolution of this issue depends on the construction of the language of the 1941 deed of the Huttons to the school district. As urged by the defendants and as the trial court found, that deed conveyed a fee simple subject to a condition subsequent followed by a right of re-entry for condition broken. As argued by the plaintiffs, on the other hand, the deed conveyed a fee simple determinable followed by a possibility of reverter. In either case, the grantor and his heirs retain an interest in the property which may become possessory if the condition is broken. We emphasize here that although sec. 1 of An Act relating to Rights of Entry or Reeentry for breach of condition subsequent and possibilities of reverter effective July 21, 1947 (Ill.Rev.Stat., ch. 30, par. 37b) provides that rights of re-entry for condition broken and possibilities of reverter are neither alienable or devisable, they are inheritable. The type of interest held governs the mode of reinvestment with title if reinvestment is to occur. If the grantor had a possibility of reverter, he or his heirs become the owner of the property by operation of law as soon as the condition is broken. If he has a right of re-entry for condition broken, he or his heirs become the owner of the property only after they act to retake the property.

It is alleged, and we must accept, that classes were last held in the Hutton School in 1973. Harry Hutton, sole heir of the grantors, did not act to legally retake the premises but instead conveyed his interest in that land to the plaintiffs in 1977. If Harry Hutton had only a naked right of re-entry for condition broken, then he could not be the owner of that property until he had legally re-entered the land. Since he took no steps for a legal re-entry, he had only a right of re-entry in 1977, and that right cannot be conveyed *inter vivos.* On the other hand, if Harry Hutton had a possibility of reverter in the property, then he owned the school property as soon as it ceased to be used for school purposes. Therefore, assuming (1) that cessation of classes constitutes "abandonment of school purposes" on the land [and] (2) that the conveyance from Harry Hutton to the plaintiffs was legally correct * * *, the plaintiffs could have acquired an interest in the Hutton School grounds if Harry Hutton had inherited a possibility of reverter from his parents.

The difference between a fee simple determinable (or, determinable fee) and a fee simple subject to a condition subsequent, is solely a matter of judicial interpretation of the words of a grant. As Blackstone explained, there is a fundamental theoretical difference between a conditional estate, such as a fee simple subject to a condition subsequent, and a limited estate, such as a fee simple determinable.

"A distinction is however made between a *condition in deed* and a *limitation,* which Littleton denominates also a *condition in law.* For when an estate is so expressly confined and limited by the words of it's [sic] creation, that it cannot endure for any longer time than till the contingency happens upon which the estate is to fail, this is denominated in *limitation:* as when land is granted to a man, *so long as* he is parson of Dale, or *while* he continues unmarried, or *until* out of the rents and profits he shall have made 500, and the like. In such case the estate determines as soon as the contingency happens (when he ceases to be parson, marries a wife, or has received the 500,) and the next subsequent estate, which depends upon such determination, becomes immediately vested, without any act to be done by him who is next in expectancy. But when an estate is, strictly speaking, upon *condition in deed* (as if granted expressly *upon condition* to be void upon the payment of 40, by the grantor, or *so that* the grantee continues unmarried, or *provided* he goes to York, etc.), the law permits it to endure beyond the time when such contingency happens, unless the grantor or his heir or assigns take advantage of the breach of the condition, and make either an entry or a claim in order to avoid the estate." (Emphasis in original.) 2 W. Blackstone, Commentaries *155.

A fee simple determinable may be thought of as a limited grant, while a fee simple subject to a condition subsequent is an absolute grant to which a condition is appended. In other words, a grantor should give a fee simple determinable if he intends to give property for so long as it is needed for the purposes for which it is given and no longer, but he should employ a fee simple subject to a condition subsequent if he intends to compel compliance with a condition by penalty of a forfeiture.

Following Blackstone's examples, the Huttons would have created a fee simple determinable if they had allowed the school district to retain the property *so long as* or *while* it was used for school purposes, or *until* it ceased to be so used. Similarly, a fee simple subject to a condition subsequent would have arisen had the Huttons given the land *upon condition that* or *provided that* it be used for school purposes. In the 1941 deed, though the Huttons gave the land "to be used for school purpose only, otherwise to revert to Grantors herein," no words of temporal limitation, or terms of express condition, were used in the grant.

The plaintiffs argue that the word "only" should be construed as a limitation rather than a condition. The defendants respond that where ambiguous language is used in a deed, the courts of Illinois have expressed a constructional preference for a fee simple subject to a condition subsequent. Both sides refer us to cases involving deeds which contain language analogous to the 1941 grant in this case.

We believe that a close analysis of the wording of the original grant shows that the grantors intended to create a fee simple determinable followed by a possibility of reverter. Here, the use of the word "only" immediately following the grant "for school purpose" demonstrates that the Huttons wanted to give the land to the school district only as long as it was needed and no longer. The language "this land to be used for school purpose only" is an example of a grant which contains a limitation within the granting clause. It suggests a limited grant, rather than a full grant subject to a condition, and thus, both theoretically and linguistically, gives rise to a fee simple determinable.

The second relevant clause furnishes plaintiffs' position with additional support. It cannot be argued that the phrase "otherwise to revert to grantors herein" is inconsistent with a fee simple subject to a condition subsequent. Nor does the word "revert" automatically create a possibility of reverter. But, in combination with the preceding phrase, the provisions by which possession is returned to the grantors seem to trigger a mandatory return rather than a permissive return because it is not stated that the grantor "may" re-enter the land.

The terms used in the 1941 deed, although imprecise, were designed to allow the property to be used for a single purpose, namely, for "school purpose." The Huttons intended to have the land back if it were ever used otherwise. Upon a grant of exclusive use followed by an express provision for reverter when that use ceases, courts and commentators have agreed that a fee simple determinable, rather than a fee simple subject to a condition subsequent, is created. Our own research has uncovered cases from other jurisdictions and sources in which language very similar to that in the Hutton deed has been held to create a fee simple determinable.

* * *

We hold, therefore, that the 1941 deed from W. E. and Jennie Hutton to the Trustees of School District No. 1 created a fee simple determinable in the Trustees followed by a possibility of reverter in the Huttons and their heirs. Accordingly, the trial court erred in dismissing plaintiffs' third amended complaint which followed its holding that the plaintiffs could not have acquired any interest in the Hutton School property from Harry Hutton. We must therefore reverse and remand this cause to the trial court for further proceedings.

We refrain from deciding the following issues: (1) whether the 1977 conveyance from Harry Hutton was legally sufficient to pass his interest in the school property to the plaintiffs * * * and [(2)] whether the defendants have ceased to use the Hutton School grounds for "school purposes."

Reversed and remanded.

Notes and Questions

1. What result in this case if the court had found that the provision in question created a fee simple absolute subject to a covenant rather than a fee simple determinable?

2. Why do courts have a constructional preference for a fee simple subject to a condition subsequent over a fee simple determinable? *See* Higbee Corp. v. Kennedy, 286 Pa.Super. 101, 428 A.2d 592 (1981). *Less harsh, respect the condition put on the property.*

3. Why did the *Mahrenholz* court conclude that a fee simple determinable was created when the preference is for a fee simple subject to a condition subsequent? *Compare* DeHart v. Ritenour Consolidated School District, 663 S.W.2d 332 (Mo.App.1983).

4. Does storage constitute use for a "school purpose"? *See* Mahrenholz v. County Board of School Trustees of Lawrence County, 188 Ill.App.3d 260, 135 Ill.Dec. 771, 544 N.E.2d 128 (1989). In a similar vein, consider a situation where property was deeded to a city in fee simple subject to a condition subsequent that the grantee commence "public park development" within seven years. What action is required to satisfy the condition? *See* City of Lincoln v. Townhouser, Inc., 248 Neb. 399, 534 N.W.2d 756 (1995) (noting that conditions subsequent "will be construed most strongly against the holder of a right to entry and a forfeiture will not be enforced unless clearly established").

5. The court indicates that in Illinois neither a possibility of reverter nor a right of entry may be transferred by will or inter vivos conveyance. This is a minority position. *See* pages 258–259 for a discussion of the transferability of these future interests.

6. Some state statutes limit the duration of possibilities of reverter and rights of entry. *See, e.g.*, Fla.Stat. Ann. § 689.18 (West 1994), which with certain exceptions renders such provisions void and unenforceable after twenty-one years from their creation. What estate does the defeasible fee owner hold when such a statute applies? *See* J. C. Vereen & Sons, Inc. v. City of Miami, 397 So.2d 979 (Fla.App.1981). The judiciary also may fashion limits on the duration of possibilities of reverter and rights of entry. Courts

in some jurisdictions have ruled that when a fee simple subject to a condition subsequent is created by an instrument containing no duration, a reasonable length of time for observing the condition will be implied. *See, e.g.,* Mildram v. Town of Wells, 611 A.2d 84 (Me.1992); *see also* Powell, *Defeasible Fees and the Nature of Real Property,* 40 Kan.L.Rev. 411 (1992).

7. General statutes of limitation control the time within which possessory rights may be enforced once the condition of the grant is breached.

3. FEE TAIL

There is another estate with the word "fee" in the title—the fee tail. Of all the estates in land, the fee tail is least important in modern law. But, because the words formerly used to create it are still occasionally employed by conveyancers, you must be familiar with this estate.

The fee tail had its origins in the desire of 13th century property holders to pass their land to future generations without end. Conveyancers put their minds to the problem. The need was to assure the present owner maximum use of the property, but to guarantee that at the owner's death the property passed intact to the next generation. As previously stated, a conveyance "to A and his heirs" would not produce the desired result. These words created a fee simple absolute which A could alienate.

The conveyancers, therefore, created a new estate by using the words "to A and the heirs of his body." Because these words were clearly distinguishable from the fee simple formulation, a judicial response was required. The landed gentry, of course, wanted a decision which would prevent the present holder from alienating the property. The courts ultimately held that a conveyance to "A and the heirs of his body" created a fee simple conditional. (This estate is totally different from the fee simple subject to a condition subsequent despite the similar name.) As holder of a fee simple conditional, A could convey the property after A produced live issue, even if the child died immediately. This judicial interpretation failed to satisfy the needs of the landed gentry. True, if A did not produce issue, A could not convey and at A's death the property returned to A's grantor; or if A produced issue but did not convey, the property passed to A's issue. Nevertheless, the real danger was that issue would be born alive and A would choose or be compelled to alienate. The judicial route had failed. Thus, the landed gentry turned to other means to keep land in the family.

Relief came in the form of the Statute De Donis Conditionalibus (1285) which provided that a conveyance "to A and the heirs of his body" would be enforced according to the manifested intention of the grantor. This meant that A, the tenant in tail, could no longer alienate the land even if A had issue born alive.[2] The estate, known as a fee tail,

---

2. A handful of American states, notably Iowa and South Carolina, do not consider the Statute De Donis part of the common law. Consequently, a fee simple conditional is still recognized in these jurisdictions. *See* 2 Powell on Real Property ¶ 198 (1998). *See*

passed at A's death to A's issue, or if none, the property returned to the grantor or the grantor's successors. The courts subsequently extended this limitation to the tenant in tail in each generation thereby securing the land in the family perpetually. Or so it seemed.

The Statute De Donis was hugely successful as these matters go. For about two centuries it effectively protected the great family estates, and although widely criticized for its negative side-effects, its proponents successfully turned back all legislative attempts to abolish the statute.

The fee tail's most obvious disadvantage was its restriction on alienation. The tenant in tail in possession was for most purposes only a tenant for life and thus could not necessarily use the land in the most productive way. Moreover, creditors were often frustrated in collecting lawful claims.

At length lawyer ingenuity and judicial sympathy with those who wished to undercut the fee tail led to the development of two complex disentailing procedures—common recovery and fine, both of which allowed the tenant in tail to convey a fee simple. Again the balance had shifted, this time against the landed gentry and in favor of free alienation.[3]

In the United States the fee tail has had a spotty and unpopular history. As might be expected, it was employed most often in areas settled by immigrants sympathetic to the feudal system. It is no longer intentionally used anywhere. All states that recognized the fee tail have either abolished the estate or provided easy means to defeat it. Occasionally the language "to A and the heirs of his body" appears in a deed or will and for this reason lawyers must understand its history. States chose different methods to abolish or defeat the fee tail, so it is necessary to determine what judicial or legislative solution has been adopted in a given jurisdiction.

Notes

1. As indicated above, the fee tail is no longer a viable estate. It can be created in only four states (Delaware, Maine, Massachusetts, and Rhode Island), but in each of these jurisdictions the tenant in tail can easily divest the estate by a disentailing conveyance. In most jurisdictions, statutes now provide that fee tail language creates another estate. These statutes fall into three general categories:

    (a) In two or three jurisdictions, statutes preserve the fee tail for one generation. That is, the fee tail exists for the life of the first taker, who may not make any disentailing conveyance. The estate then becomes a fee simple absolute in the first taker's issue.

also Third National Bank in Nashville v. Stevens, 755 S.W.2d 459, 463 (Tenn.Ct.App. 1988) (stating "grant to grantee and his bodily issue creates a fee conditional estate, which is a life estate convertible into a fee by the birth of bodily issue to the grantee").

3. The legal fee tail was abolished in England by the Law of Property Act of 1925.

(b) In a few jurisdictions, statutes convert the fee tail to a life estate with a remainder in fee simple absolute to the life tenant's issue.

(c) In the majority of jurisdictions, statutes provide that fee tail language creates a fee simple absolute in the first taker.

See 2 Powell on Real Property ¶¶ 196–198 (1998); see also Orth, Does the Fee Tail Exist in North Carolina?, 23 Wake Forest L.Rev. 767 (1988).

2. Although widely abolished, the fee tail estate remains the subject of occasional litigation. See Robins Island Preservation Fund, Inc. v. Southold Development Corporation, 959 F.2d 409 (2d Cir.1992) (discussing New York's confiscation of Loyalist property owned in fee tail during American Revolution and subsequent transformation of fee tail estates into fee simple estates); Long v. Long, 45 Ohio St.2d 165, 343 N.E.2d 100 (1976) (concerning nature of interest remaining in grantor after conveying fee tail).

3. The fee tail played an important role in a popular novel. The setting for Daphne Du Maurier's Rebecca (1938) is the entailed de Winter family estate called Manderley. The tenant in tail, Max de Winter, is driven to murder his wife Rebecca by the belief that Manderley will pass as an entailed estate to a child that is not his.

4. LIFE ESTATE

The remaining freehold estate is the life estate. This estate is created by the words "to A for life." As this language indicates, the estate endures for A's life. This estate is not, therefore, typically an inheritable estate. (We shall examine an exception, the estate *pur autre vie*, in a moment.)

Although the life estate is measured by the life of the transferee, the estate may end before the transferee's death. For example, the estate may be defeasible, as when it is created to endure for the period a surviving spouse remains unmarried. It may also terminate early by merging with a greater estate.

An important variation of the life estate is the estate *pur autre vie*, or the estate for the life of another. The formulation for this estate is "to A for the life of B." Here the life tenant is A, but the estate's duration is measured not by A's life, but by that of B.

Questions frequently arise regarding the rights and responsibilities of the life tenant in relation to those who take the estate upon the life tenant's death. Generally, the life tenant has the absolute right to possess the property and enjoy its income. Problems, however, develop when the life tenant depletes the estate by cutting timber or mining minerals. Or suppose the life tenant neglects the property, fails to repair it, or actively damages it. The doctrine of waste was fashioned to solve these problems. See Kimbrough v. Reed, 130 Idaho 512, 943 P.2d 1232 (1997) (finding life tenant committed waste by failing to water lawn, trees, and shrubery). See also pages 37–44 discussing doctrine of waste in landlord-tenant context.

The question of who is responsible for paying of taxes or servicing a mortgage on the property may also arise. Moreover, the property may be taken for a public purpose and compensation paid to its owners. How is this money divided between the life tenant and the future interest holders? *See* United States v. 403.15 Acres of Land, 316 F.Supp. 655 (M.D.Tenn.1970).

Problems

1. A, who owned a life estate in property, conveyed a fee simple absolute to B. What estate does B take?

2. O conveyed an estate "to A for life." B wishes to rent the land for a ten-year term for business purposes. A is agreeable. How can B contract for a secure lease agreement?

3. O conveyed an estate "to A for the life of B." A died before B. What happens to the estate upon A's death? *See* Collins v. Held, 174 Ind.App. 584, 369 N.E.2d 641 (1977).

4. L is the life tenant of a quarter-acre tract containing a residence. R holds the remainder interest. The character of the neighborhood has changed from residential to commercial, and L could not rent the dwelling for enough to pay taxes and insurance on the lot. L then destroyed the building and graded the lot for business use. R sues L for waste. What result? Would it make any difference if the value of the property were enhanced by the alteration? *See* Melms v. Pabst Brewing Co., 104 Wis. 7, 79 N.W. 738 (1899).

5. Is it waste for the life tenant to cut trees on the land? Suppose that the prime use of the tract has been for a commercial timbering. May the life tenant continue this operation? Are any considerations of public policy appropriate? *See* Sauls v. Crosby, 258 So.2d 326 (Fla.App.1972); Pedro v. January, 261 Or. 582, 494 P.2d 868 (1972).

5. LEASE

You have already studied the modern lease. Leases are non-freehold estates. They originated relatively early in post-conquest England as a moneylenders' security device. Their evolution is traced in Chapter 1.

The lease was not a freehold estate because it did not fit any of the recognized categories of freeholds and because it was not created by transfer of seisin. In practical terms, the non-freehold estate differed from the freehold estate in two important particulars: (1) It was not regarded as real property but as a "chattel real" (a form of personal property).[4] (2) It could not be the subject of the so-called "real" actions available for the protection of freehold estates. As the hostility of the courts to the non-freehold estates softened, a new action called ejectment was developed to protect them. Ejectment was so effective and relatively simple as compared to the "real" actions that freeholders began to employ the device through lawsuits alleging fictitious leases.

---

4. Today, for various purposes, modern statutes often define a lease as an interest in land. *See* 2 Powell on Real Property § 16.02[2] (1998).

Non-freehold estates take several forms: tenancy for a fixed term (estate for years), periodic tenancy, and tenancy at will. Some commentators also include tenancy at sufferance. Each of these non-freehold estates is discussed in detail on pages 12–14 of Chapter 1.

C. FUTURE INTERESTS

Future interests are estates which become possessory at a future time. There are five types of future interests: possibility of reverter, right of entry, reversion, remainder, and executory interest.

Future interests have a logic and rhythm of their own. The key to early success in this field is mastery of the classification of the interests and careful attention to vocabulary. Expertise in the future interest area is essential for complex estate planning, and the competent drafting of even a simple deed or will requires at least a general understanding of the subject.[1] Although the system is complex, it is at the same time a marvel of Anglo–American law in its capacity for ingenuity and flexibility. As you read this material, consider the array of options available in the disposition of property. C. Moynihan, Introduction to the Law of Real Property 103–206 (2d ed. 1988); L. Simes, Handbook of the Law of Future Interests (2d ed. 1966); and 1 American Law of Property §§ 4.1– 4.58 (1952) are sources you may wish to consult during your study of this section.

1. CLASSIFICATION

Future interests are divided into two broad categories—those that may be created in the transferor and those that may be created in a third party. The first category includes: possibility of reverter, right of entry, and reversion. These interests permit a property owner to transfer an estate to another, but retain an interest in the property. The estate transferred is a present possessory estate in the transferee. The interest retained is a future interest in the transferor.

a. *Possibility of Reverter*

The possibility of reverter is that interest retained by a transferor who has created a fee simple determinable.[2] It becomes possessory only on the termination of the fee simple estate. For example, O conveys "to A for so long as A uses the land for agricultural purposes." A has a fee simple determinable; O retains a possibility of reverter.

---

1. Although our discussion focuses on future interests in land, most states recognize the full range of future interests in personal property. *See* L. Simes, Handbook of the Law of Future Interests § 7 (2d ed. 1966). Reconsider *Gruen v. Gruen* at page 211 on this point.

2. In addition, in those few states not recognizing the Statute de Donis as part of the common law, a conveyance by O "to A and the heirs of his body" creates a fee simple conditional in A and a possibility of reverter in O.

In most jurisdictions, this future interest is freely alienable, devisable, and descendible. It is also important to note that a possibility of reverter, although contingent in nature, is not subject to the Rule Against Perpetuities.

Recall that the possibility of reverter becomes a present possessory estate automatically. Hence no action on the part of the future interest holder is required for title to revert on the termination of the fee simple determinable.

b. *Right of Entry*

The right of entry, also called a power of termination, is that interest retained by a transferor who has created a fee simple subject to a condition subsequent. It is a future interest which becomes possessory only on the termination of the preceding fee simple estate. In contrast to the possibility of reverter, most courts require that the right of entry be explicitly spelled out in the terms of the transfer. For example, O conveys "to A in fee simple, but if A ever fails to use the land for agricultural purposes, O may enter and recover the land." A has a fee simple subject to a condition subsequent; O retains a right of entry. Under certain circumstances, however, a court may find that a right of entry was created by implication. *See* DeHart v. Ritenour Consolidated School District, 663 S.W.2d 332 (Mo.App.1983); Forsgren v. Sollie, 659 P.2d 1068 (Utah 1983).

This future interest is generally devisable and descendible. It is, however, usually transferable inter vivos only when coupled with a reversion. For example, a landlord may convey the right to enter for breach of a lease covenant along with the transfer of the reversion. The right of entry is contingent in nature, but it is not subject to the Rule Against Perpetuities.

c. *Reversion*

A reversion is that interest remaining in one who transfers a lesser estate than the estate that person owns. There is no need for the transferor to spell out the reversion in the instrument creating the present interest. The law implies a reversion whenever one transfers a lesser estate than that owned.[3] *See* Whittington v. Whittington, 608 So.2d 1274 (Miss.1992).

Reversions are fully alienable, descendible and devisable. They are always vested and thus, are not subject to the Rule Against Perpetuities.

You are already acquainted with the reversion from your study of landlord-tenant law. In the landlord-tenant cases we considered, the landlord (owner in fee simple absolute) conveyed a lesser estate (tenancy

---

3. The possibility of reverter and right of entry follow fee simple estates and thus are not regarded as reversions.

for a fixed term or periodic tenancy) to the tenant. The landlord, therefore, retained a reversion in fee simple absolute.

Problems

What estates are created by the following transfers? (Unless otherwise indicated, assume O owns the land involved in fee simple absolute.)

1. O conveys "to A for life." (O is 80 years old. A is 30 years old. O dies one year after the conveyance.)

2. O conveys "to A so long as the property is not used for commercial purposes."

3. O conveys "to A for 20 years, however, A may be evicted in the event that the property is ever used for commercial purposes."

4. O conveys "to A and her successive generations of lineal descendants."

5. O conveys "to A for life." (One year after the conveyance, O conveys all O's interest in the property to C.)

6. O devises "to A for life, then to B if B survives A."

7. O owns a life estate. O conveys "to A for 99 years."

We turn now to the second category of future interests; those that may be created only in a third party. There are just two interests in this category: remainder and executory interest. Each involves several variations.

d. Remainder

The concept of remainder originally posed theoretical problems because of the rigid requirements of seisin. At early common law, a transferor could not create an estate in a third party to commence in the future. This logically flowed from the requirement that seisin be transferred by a physical act on the land itself. Since a remainder became possessory only on the natural expiration of the preceding freehold estate, how could seisin be transferred at that time without a feoffment ceremony between the original transferor and the remainderman? The common law solved this theoretical difficulty by vaguely recognizing the tenant in tail or the life tenant as holding seisin both for that estate and the remainder.[4]

Remainders can only follow a fee tail, a life estate, or, in modern practice, a leasehold; they can never follow any of the fee simple estates. Further, the remainder must be created at the same time as the preceding supporting estate and must become possessory immediately upon the natural termination of that estate. In other words, the remainder can never cut short the preceding estate, and there can be no gap between the supporting estate and the remainder. This is not to say that remainders must be certain to become possessory at some future time;

---

4. The common law was not as generous in its resolution of other types of attempted shifts and gaps in seisin, as the following discussion of executory interests indicates.

the requirement is only that they become possessory, if at all, on the natural termination of the estate or estates supporting them.

There are two types of remainders: vested remainders and contingent remainders.

(1) Vested Remainder

A remainder is vested when it is transferred to a born and ascertained person, and there is no condition precedent to the taking. Vested remainders take the following forms: totally vested, vested subject to partial divestment (sometimes called vested subject to open), and vested subject to complete divestment. All vested remainders are freely alienable, descendible, and devisable.

Consider these examples of vested remainders:

(a) O conveys "to A for life, remainder to B." B has a totally vested remainder in fee simple absolute. The interest is totally vested because: (1) it is conveyed to an ascertained living person; (2) there is no condition precedent to the taking; and (3) there is no provision for partial or total divestment after the taking.

(b) O conveys "to A for life, remainder to the children of B (a living person)." (At the time of the conveyance, B has one child, C–1.) C–1 has a vested remainder subject to partial divestment in favor of other children who may be born of B before the remainder becomes possessory on A's death.

(c) O conveys "to A for life, then to B, but if B fails to marry before A dies, then to C." The remainder to B is vested. But, following the vesting language is a condition that B must marry before the death of the life tenant or be divested of B's interest. B, therefore, has a vested remainder subject to complete divestment. (C has an executory interest, a topic discussed later.)

(2) Contingent Remainder

Contingent remainders were recognized somewhat later than vested remainders and generally were accorded less protection. Rather restrictive rules grew up around their use. In most jurisdictions, they are now freely alienable, descendible, and devisable.

A remainder is contingent when it is either (1) subject to a condition precedent or (2) created in an unborn or unascertained person. Examples of contingent remainders are:

(a) O conveys "to A for life, remainder to the heirs of A." A's heirs cannot be ascertained until A's death. (There are no heirs of living persons.) Their remainder is, therefore, contingent.

(b) O conveys "to A for life, remainder to the first child of A." (A has no children.) Because the potential taker is unborn, the remainder is contingent.

(c) O conveys "to A for life, then if B marries before A dies, to B." Because B's remainder is subject to a condition precedent, it is contingent.

Notice the similarity between this last contingent remainder and a vested remainder subject to complete divestment. Often it is difficult to distinguish between these two formulations. If a remainder is created, followed by language of divestment (a condition subsequent), the remainder is vested subject to complete divestment. If the conditional language is part and parcel of the formulation of the remainder—if it seems to make the condition a precedent to any taking, the remainder is contingent.

Problems

What estates are created by the following transfers? (Assume O owns the land involved in fee simple absolute.)

1. O conveys "to A for life, then to B for life, then to C."

2. O conveys "to A for life, then to B if B reaches age 25." (B is 20 years old at the time of the conveyance.)

3. O conveys "to A for life, then to A's children that survive A."

4. O conveys "to A for life, then to B if B survives A but to C if B does not survive A."

5. O devises "to A for five years, then to B."

6. O conveys "to A for life, then to the children of B." (B has a daughter, C–1, at the time of the conveyance. B then has another child, C–2. C–1 dies.)

7. O conveys "to A for life, then to B and her heirs."

8. O conveys "to A for life, then to B, but if B does not survive A, then to C."

e. Executory Interest

(1) Historical Background

Until the 16th century, the remainder was the only legal future interest that could be created in a third party. The common law courts, however, had developed two judicial doctrines, the Rule in Shelley's Case and the Doctrine of Worthier Title, which limited the use of contingent remainders to assure payment of services and incidents. A third judicial device, the Doctrine of Destructibility of Contingent Remainders, put contingent remainders at risk and frustrated certain schemes to tie-up property and thereby avoid incidents.

The effectiveness of these rules challenged the ingenuity of those who wished to avoid the increased "taxation" which resulted from their application. Conveyancers representing the landed gentry reasoned that since many incidents were payable only when land descended from an ancestor to an heir, these "taxes" could be avoided by passing property at death other than by descent. This result could not be accomplished at the time by a will. Aside from a few areas where local custom permitted, real estate could not be devised in England prior to 1540.

(2) The "Use"

To meet this problem, conveyancers developed the "use," a handy device that could be employed as a rough substitute for a will. The grantor conveyed fee simple absolute by livery of seisin, but added certain stated uses to which the property had to be put by the grantee. The grantor typically required the grantee to use the property for the grantor's benefit during the grantor's lifetime, and then for the benefit of the grantor's children, their children, and so on. The grantee was often the Church or a friend of the grantor.

The common law courts recognized the transfer of legal title by livery of seisin, but not the attempt to modify the transfer by the imposition of uses. Fortunately for landowners, courts of equity were more sympathetic. Because it was fundamentally unfair to permit the grantee to disregard promises as to the use of the property, equity courts enforced the uses imposed on the legal title.

This result was of critical importance. If the grantee died, the grantee's heir took subject to the use. This rendered the value of legal title minimal. Accordingly, the incidents that attached on its descent became essentially worthless.

The use was employed both to avoid incidents attendant on the descent of property and to evade the rules of seisin. Recall that common law forbade the creation of any legal estate to begin *in futuro*. There could be no gap or shift in seisin. Seisin could be transferred only by a physical act on the land. None of these considerations affected the use because the beneficiary did not hold seisin. Thus, it was possible for O to convey a fee simple absolute to T with provision that T use the property for the benefit of O during O's lifetime, and one day thereafter, use the property for the benefit of O's heirs. There is a gap in the beneficial use but no gap in the seisin because T holds legal title and the accompanying seisin throughout. Under this conveyance, O's heirs have a springing executory use. (The reason for employing this rather curious disposition will be more apparent after you consider the Rule in Shelley's Case.)

Shifting executory uses were also created. For example, O could convey legal title to T for the use of A, but provide that if A did not marry before O died, then the property be used for B's benefit. The equitable title in A might be cut short and the interest shifted to a third party (B) at some future time. This was not possible at law. But, since T held seisin irrespective of whether the condition occurred and the use shifted, the equity courts enforced this formulation.

(3) Statute of Uses

After the enactment of the Statute Quia Emptores (1290), which was construed to forbid further subinfeudation, the tenure system gradually folded in on itself. By the time of the Tudor dynasty, the Crown was the principal recipient of incidents. The value of these incidents, however, had been greatly diminished by the success of the use. King Henry VIII, in need of money as always, sought to enhance his revenues by influencing Parliament to enact the famous Statute of Uses (1536) to put an end to this form of "tax" evasion.

The Statute of Uses did not abolish uses. Indeed, it specifically recognized uses, but immediately transformed them from equitable to legal interests. Hence, the owner of the equitable interest (the beneficiary of the use) owned in law exactly the same interest that person had owned in equity a moment earlier. This was a tidy solution for the Crown, for now the new legal springing and shifting executory interests, formerly "uses," descended to heirs on the death of the owner in the same manner as any other legal interest. The lucrative incidents owed the Crown attached to these estates.

The Statute of Uses had many significant consequences. (1) It made possible a method of conveying legal title to land without the clumsy physical transfer techniques previously required. A bargain and sale deed could be used to create equitable title in the grantee that was transformed by the Statute into legal title as well.[5] (2) The Statute was interpreted to permit beneficial interests to be separated from legal interests where management duties were imposed on the legal title holder (trustee). Thus, it gave rise to the modern law of trusts. (3) The Statute also had significant impact on the law of future interests by making possible legal springing and shifting executory interests. Prior to the Statute, these interests could be created in equity only.

Conveyancers lost little time in taking advantage of court holdings that the old rules restricting contingent remainders did not apply to executory interests. New opportunities were thereby presented to landowners to tie-up land indefinitely.

Notes and Problems

1. It is no longer necessary to employ a use in order to create a legal springing or shifting executory interest.

2. What interests are created by the following transfers? (Assume O owns the land involved in fee simple absolute.)

    a. O conveys "to A upon A's marriage to B."

---

5. A bargain and sale deed worked as follows: O agreed to sell land to A. A paid O the purchase price and O executed a bargain and sale deed to A. Originally legal title did not pass because there was no livery of seisin. Equity courts, however, recognized the agreement and required O to hold legal title for A's benefit. The Statute of Uses then converted A's equitable title into legal title.

   b.   O devises "to A, but if A dies without children living then to B."

   c.   O conveys "to A for life, then to B, but if B does not survive A, then to C."

   d.   O conveys "to A in 2015."

   3.   When an executory interest is created after a defeasible fee, the defeasible fee estate is called a fee simple subject to an executory interest. Consider the following examples: (1) O conveys "to A but if the property is used for commercial purposes then to B." A has a fee simple subject to a shifting executory interest. B has a shifting executory interest. (2) O conveys "to A so long as the property is used solely for residential purposes, then to B." A has a fee simple subject to an executory interest. B has an executory interest.

   4.   In modern law, executory interests are devisable and descendible. They are also alienable inter vivos in most states. *See* L. Simes, Handbook of the Law of Future Interests §§ 33, 35–36 (2d ed. 1966). With uncommon exceptions, executory interests are contingent, and thus subject to the Rule Against Perpetuities.

2.   COMMON LAW RULES LIMITING FUTURE INTERESTS

   We now examine common law rules designed to prevent the landed gentry from utilizing contingent future interests to keep property in a family forever.

a.   *Rule in Shelley's Case*

   It is a quirk of history that Henry Shelley's name should become legendary. This is not by reason of any distinctiveness of doctrine or fact in his Elizabethan lawsuit, but because the famous lawyer, Sir Edward Coke, not only represented Shelley but reported the case. 1 Coke's Reports 93b (1581). Coke embodied in his account legal principles developed centuries earlier. These principles, dealing with certain kinds of contingent remainders, came to be known as the Rule in Shelley's Case.

   Statement of the Rule in Shelley's Case is relatively simple. If in the same instrument (either a deed or will) the transferor creates a fee tail or a life estate in one person, and then creates a contingent remainder in the heirs of that person, the life tenant or tenant in tail takes both the supporting estate and the remainder. For the Rule to apply, the estates must be both legal or both equitable. The Rule does only one thing; it takes the contingent remainder away from the heirs and gives it to the tenant in tail or life tenant. The result is that the tenant in tail or life tenant owns both the supporting estate and the remainder. The estates may merge,[6] but whether they do is immaterial to the Rule in Shelley's

---

   6.   The doctrine of merger provides that whenever successive vested estates come to   be owned by the same person, the smaller one merges into the larger one to become a

Case. In any event, the heirs of the transferee receive nothing under the deed or will. If they take at all, it is by descent subject to incidents. For example, O conveys "to A for life, remainder to A's heirs." A has a life estate; A's heirs have a contingent remainder. The Rule transforms the contingent remainder in A's heirs into a remainder in A. The two interests in A merge to form a present possessory fee simple absolute. If A does not convey or devise the fee, A's heirs will take it by descent on A's death.

The Rule is a rule of law, not a rule of construction. This means that it is invoked irrespective of the transferor's intent. The Rule, however, governs only real estate, not personalty.

Notice that the Rule applies just to contingent remainders in the transferee's heirs, not to any other contingent interest. Hence, it may be avoided by making the future interest in question an executory interest. This is easily accomplished. One might simply create an interval between the life estate and the future interest. For example, O conveys "to A for life, one day thereafter to A's heirs." A's heirs receive a springing executory interest so the Rule does not apply.

The Rule in Shelley's Case was important in England until abolished by the Law of Property Act in 1925. It remained part of American law until well into the 20th century and still exists in a handful of jurisdictions. The Rule's demise is a happy circumstance because it was a technical trap that often produced tortured and unjustified results. In every instance it defeated the stated intention of a transferor whose dispositions fell within its ambit. Yet the Rule had one unmistakable advantage—it promoted free alienability of real estate.

Why spend time studying this anachronism? For three reasons: First, the Rule is the law in a few states that evidently find practical reasons for retaining it.[7] Second, in some states it has been abolished prospectively and still governs conveyances made before the date of abolition.[8] Third, an understanding of the Rule is useful in mastering the Rule Against Perpetuities. *See generally* Reppy, *Judicial Overkill in Applying the Rule in Shelley's Case*, 73 Notre Dame L. Rev. 83 (1997).

Problems and Questions

1. Does the Rule in Shelley's Case apply to the following transfers? (Assume O owns the land involved in fee simple absolute.)

   a.   O conveys "to A for life, then to B for life, then to B's heirs."

   b.   O conveys "to A for life, then to B's heirs."

single estate. For a discussion of merger in another context see pages 635–638.

7. It apparently lingers in Arkansas, Colorado, Delaware, Indiana, and Washington. See L. Simes & A. Smith, The Law of Future Interests § 1563 (2d ed. 1956 & Supp.1996). *See generally* Orth, *Observa-*

tion—Requiem for the Rule in Shelly's Case, 67 N.C.L.Rev. 681 (1989).

8. *See* Society National Bank v. Jacobson, 54 Ohio St.3d 15, 560 N.E.2d 217 (1990); Toler v. Harbour, 589 S.W.2d 529 (Tex.Civ.App.1979).

    c.   O conveys "to A for B's life, then to B's heirs." A devises A's interest to B.

    d.   O devises "to A for life, then to B for life, then to A's heirs."

    2.   Assume you are in a jurisdiction which follows the Rule in Shelley's Case. How could one avoid the Rule?

b. *Doctrine of Worthier Title*

One would think that an equally timely obituary could be written for the Doctrine of Worthier Title. Logic dictates such a fate for this relic of feudalism, but that is not the case. The Doctrine of Worthier Title is a vigorous survivor.

Just as the Rule in Shelley's Case originated in a desire to force the descent of property and insure the collection of incidents, so did the Doctrine of Worthier Title develop to protect incidents in a somewhat different situation. The Rule in Shelley's Case affects contingent remainders created in the heirs of a transferee. In contrast, the Doctrine of Worthier Title applies to contingent remainders created in the heirs of the transferor. It provides that an attempted devise or conveyance to the heirs of the transferor creates no interest in those heirs but instead creates a reversion in the transferor or the transferor's estate. The transferor's heirs receive nothing under the deed or will. If they take at all, it is by descent. For example, O conveys "to A for life, remainder to O's heirs." A has a life estate; O's heirs have a contingent remainder. The Doctrine converts the purported contingent remainder in O's heirs into a reversion in O. If O does not convey or devise the reversion, O's heirs will take it by descent on O's death.

In earlier times the Doctrine applied only to realty and was regarded as a rule of law, not a rule of construction. In these respects it closely resembled the Rule in Shelley's Case; and had the matter ended there, the Doctrine would likely have followed Shelley's Rule to oblivion. However, in the famous case of Doctor v. Hughes, 225 N.Y. 305, 122 N.E. 221 (1919), a New York court resurrected the Doctrine and modified it in a number of ways to make it more acceptable in modern usage. The court held the Doctrine to be a rule of construction, not a rule of law. This meant that henceforth the intent of the transferor would govern the disposition. The court also established a rebuttable presumption that a transferor conveying to the transferor's own heirs intended to create a reversion in the transferor or the transferor's estate, not an interest in the transferor's heirs. It further determined that the Doctrine governed personal as well as real property. This opened the way for the Doctrine to apply to trusts funded with personalty, the most common trust asset today. Moreover, the Doctrine is now deemed applicable to executory interests created in the transferor's heirs.

Originally, there were two branches to the Doctrine, the inter-vivos branch and the testamentary branch. The latter branch is now effectively dead since only in remote circumstances does it make any difference whether an heir receives property by intestacy or by devise. *See* Harris Trust & Savings Bank v. Beach, 118 Ill.2d 1, 112 Ill.Dec. 224, 513 N.E.2d 833 (1987). After *Doctor v. Hughes*, the inter-vivos branch assumed new importance and is still applied in many jurisdictions although not in New York where the case arose. It provides a snare for unwary drafters, but also enhances the alienability of property. For an application of the Doctrine, see All Persons v. Buie, 386 So.2d 1109 (Miss.1980).

c. *Destructibility of Contingent Remainders*

Before the Statute of Uses (1536), the contingent remainder was the only legal contingent future interest that could be created in a third party. The courts, therefore, directed their attention to that potential troublemaker. The medieval notion that there could be no gap in seisin bolstered the efforts of jurists to curtail remote contingent remainders. The courts fashioned the Doctrine of Destructibility of Contingent Remainders, which provides that if a contingent remainder does not vest before or at the termination of the preceding freehold estates, it is destroyed and the next vested estate becomes possessory. For example, O conveys "to A for life, then to B on her twenty-first birthday." A has a life estate; B has a contingent remainder; and O has a reversion because B's interest is contingent. Assume A dies when B is 20. B's contingent remainder is destroyed because it did not vest before or at the time the preceding estate terminated. O's reversion becomes possessory.

The Doctrine applies solely to real property, and does not require that an estate become possessory, only that it vest at or before the critical time. As long as any preceding freehold estate supports the contingent remainder, the Doctrine does not operate to destroy the remainder. For instance, if the remainder is preceded by two life estates, the termination of one does not destroy the remainder since the other life estate continues to support it.

Another means of destruction involves the concept of merger. With certain technical exceptions, contingent remainders lying between two vested estates owned by the same person are destroyed by merger of the vested estates. For example, assume O in our illustration conveys the reversion to A. A's present life estate merges into A's reversion to form a present possessory fee simple absolute. B's contingent remainder is destroyed in the process.

The Destructibility Doctrine was an important mechanism to prevent landowners from tying-up land for long periods. Had it been extended to executory interests after the Statute of Uses, its effectiveness would have continued. The English courts, however, limited the Doctrine to contingent remainders and left executory interests unfettered. As a consequence, the Doctrine's influence declined. Only a handful of states still recognize it.[9] Moreover, the purpose and effect of

---

9. One authority suggests that the Doctrine probably survives in only four states (Florida, Oregon, Pennsylvania and Tennessee). *See* L. Simes & A. Smith, The Law of

the Destructibility Doctrine have been subsumed by the Rule Against Perpetuities so that the Doctrine, even where it survives, is little more than a redundancy.

Problems

Does the Doctrine of Destructibility of Contingent Remainders apply to any of the following situations? (Assume O owns the land involved in fee simple absolute.)

1. O conveys "to A for life, then to B for life." O conveys the reversion ~No~ to A.

2. O conveys "to A for life, then to B ~if~ B survives A." O conveys the ~Yes~ reversion to A. ~CR~

3. O devises "to A for life, then to B." B dies before A. ~No~

4. O devises "to A for life, then to B if B marries C." B has not married ~Yes No~ C at A's death. ~Le~ ~CR~

d. *Rule Against Perpetuities*

The debate over use of long-term contingent future interests to tie-up land reached a critical stage with the famous Duke of Norfolk's Case (1683). The case involved many colorful and controversial figures in Restoration England and laid the basis for what we know today as the Rule Against Perpetuities. The courts then spent almost two centuries working out the details of the Rule. The most widely recognized formulation was set forth by John Chipman Gray in 1886: "No interest is good unless it must vest, if at all, not later than twenty-one years after some life in being at the creation of the interest."[10] The Rule is still the basic tool of perpetuities control, although there are ongoing efforts to improve its operation.

The Rule Against Perpetuities is not about interests which last too long. (In theory, fee simple estates can last forever.) It is about the vesting of contingent interests. More particularly, it requires interests to vest, if at all, within a stipulated time (twenty-one years after the end of some life in being at the time the interest is created). The theory underlying the Rule is that it is reasonable for uncertainty to exist about who will ultimately own property if the uncertainty will be resolved within some life in being plus twenty-one years.

Legal and equitable contingent interests in real and personal property are governed by the Rule.[11] Contingent remainders and executory interests are, of course, included. But as we have seen, rights of entry and possibilities of reverter, though contingent, are not.

Although the Rule Against Perpetuities is widely recognized, it does not further the free alienation of property to the extent it once did.

Future Interests § 209 (1956 & Supp.1996).

10. J. Gray, The Rule Against Perpetuities § 201 (4th ed. 1942).

11. A class gift vested as to some members but not as to all is regarded as contingent for purposes of the Rule.

Several profound developments since the seventeenth century have undercut the Rule's effectiveness: First, the Rule is usually geared to the duration of "lives in being" at the creation of the interest. Average life spans continue to grow, effectively stretching the absolute time available for vesting. Second, the society which the Rule was developed to serve no longer exists. When one considers the pace of change today as compared to the pace of the last century and a half, the antiquity and inappropriateness of a formula fixed two centuries ago becomes apparent. Third, all of the so-called "reforms" of the Rule undertaken recently tend to validate long-lasting contingencies, not to void them. Gray had stipulated that once the Rule was found to apply, it should be applied "remorselessly." This mandate has faded as "wait and see," and "cy pres," and other reform techniques have been adopted to ameliorate the perceived harshness of the Gray directive. Those "reforms" are the very vehicles through which the Rule's effectiveness has been undercut. Doubtless reforms have been popular because there have been popular targets—formulas expressed in archaic terms reflecting assumptions long discredited.

Bostick, *Loosening the Grip of the Dead Hand: Shall We Abolish Legal Future Interests in Land*, 32 Vand.L.Rev. 1061, 1079–1080 (1979). *See also* Haskell, *A Proposal for a Simple and Socially Effective Rule Against Perpetuities*, 66 N.C.L.Rev. 545 (1988); Waggoner, *Perpetuity Reform*, 81 Mich.L.Rev. 1718 (1983).

Problems

Does the common law Rule Against Perpetuities render invalid any interest created by the following transfers? (Assume O owns the land involved in fee simple absolute.)

  1. O devises "to A for life, then to B if B survives A."

  2. O conveys "to A so long as the property is used for commercial purposes, then to B."

  3. O conveys "to A for life, then to B." O is 93 years old and in poor health. A is 10 years old and in excellent health.

  4. O conveys "to A for life, then to A's first child to reach age 25." At the time of the conveyance, A has one child, age 24.

  5. O conveys "to A upon A's marriage to B."

UNITED VIRGINIA BANK/CITIZENS & MARINE v. UNION OIL CO. OF CALIFORNIA

Supreme Court of Virginia, 1973.
214 Va. 48, 197 S.E.2d 174.

CARRICO, JUSTICE.

The question for decision in this appeal is whether the provisions of a land option agreement violate the rule against perpetuities. For reasons to be later discussed, we hold that the rule is violated.

The question arose in a declaratory judgment proceeding brought by United Virginia Bank/Citizens & Marine (hereafter, the Bank), executor and trustee under the last will and testament of William Jonathan Abbitt, deceased, against Union Oil Company of California and Sanford & Charles, Inc. (hereafter, Sanford). The Bank sought a declaration that an option agreement entered into by Abbitt during his lifetime was void and unenforceable on the ground it was in violation of the rule against perpetuities. The trial court held that the agreement was valid and enforceable, and the Bank appeals.

The agreement in question was entered into on April 7, 1966, between Abbitt and Union Oil Company of California. It was later assigned by Union Oil to Sanford, the active appellee here. It granted the optionee the right and option to purchase a parcel of land 200 feet by 200 feet at the northwest corner of an intersection to be formed by two highways, "Boxley Boulevard Extension and new U.S. 60," proposed to be constructed in the city of Newport News.

The option was granted for a period of 120 days. However, the agreement provided as follows:

> "It is expressly understood that the 120 days option period shall begin at the time the City of Newport News, Virginia acquires the right of way of Boxley Boulevard Extension and new U.S. 60."

It is this provision which is the focal point of the controversy between the parties.

* * *

The Bank contends that the provision of the agreement in question, making exercise of the option contingent upon acquisition by the city of the rights-of-way of the proposed highways, violates the rule against perpetuities. The Bank says that on April 7, 1966, the date the agreement was executed, "it was not known when, if ever, the City would acquire the rights-of-way for either of [the] proposed thoroughfares." Therefore, the Bank argues, there was "every possibility" that the option might not expire within the period prescribed by the rule against perpetuities.

Sanford contends, on the other hand, that since the proposed highways were shown on the major thoroughfare plan and were contemplated to be completed at the latest by January, 1987, or within 21 years from April 7, 1966, the date of the option agreement, the limitation created by the agreement did not violate the rule against perpetuities. Alternatively, Sanford contends that if the agreement "poses a technical violation of the rule," we should hold the rule inapplicable to option contracts.

We dispose first of Sanford's alternative contention that the rule against perpetuities should be held inapplicable to option contracts. To so hold, we would have to overrule our decision in Skeen v. Clinchfield Coal Corp., 137 Va. 397, 119 S.E. 89 (1923). While the reasoning of *Skeen* has been the subject of some criticism, the case clearly establishes, and we think properly so, the proposition that option contracts are unenforceable if they do not necessarily expire within the period fixed by the rule against perpetuities. In addition, it is generally recognized that the rule against perpetuities is properly applicable to option contracts. So we decline to depart from our holding in *Skeen*.

A preliminary matter requires attention. We must determine what period is to be employed in testing the validity of the limitation created by the option agreement under consideration. Ordinarily, the rule against perpetuities is expressed in terms of the necessity of an interest vesting within a period measured by a life or lives in being plus 21 years and 10 months. But here, the optionee is a corporate, not a human, entity, and the parties have not contracted with reference to a life or lives in being, but rather with reference to an event contemplated to occur sometime in the future. In such circumstances, a gross term of 21 years is the determinative period.

As applied to an option agreement, the rule against perpetuities requires that the option must be exercised, if at all, within the period fixed by the rule. If there exists at the time the agreement is entered into a possibility that exercise of the option might be postponed beyond the prescribed period, the agreement is invalid because it is in violation of the rule.

The question becomes, therefore, whether there existed at the time the option agreement was entered into in this case a possibility that exercise of the option might be postponed beyond a period of 21 years from the date of the agreement.

Turning to the option agreement itself, it is clear that the parties intended that the optionee would exercise the option, if at all, only upon occurrence of the specific contingency set up in the agreement, that is, the acquisition by the city of the rights-of-way of the proposed highways. It is equally as clear, from the agreement and the surrounding circumstances, that on the date the agreement was executed there existed the distinct possibility that the specified contingency might not occur until after expiration of a period of 21 years from the date of the agreement.

Sanford argues, however, that it was "the dominant intent" of the parties to the option agreement that the city would acquire the rights-of-way in question, if at all, within a reasonable time and that such a time "under the circumstances of this case is less than 21 years." This being true, Sanford asserts, we should exercise the *cy pres* power of the judiciary and imply into the terms of the option agreement a provision that the contingency of the city's acquisition of the rights-of-way would occur within a reasonable time not more than 21 years from the date of the agreement. This, Sanford concludes, would effectuate the intention of the parties and avoid a construction of the agreement which would violate the rule against perpetuities.

The answer to this argument is three-fold. In the first place, "the dominant intent" Sanford refers to does not appear from the option agreement itself or from any other source. Secondly, the asserted intent relates to acts which parties other than those privy to the agreement must perform to bring about occurrence of the agreed contingency. So whatever may have been the intent of the contracting parties, it is of little moment. Lastly, assuming, without deciding, that the power of *cy pres* is otherwise available in a case such as this, it may not be employed in Virginia as a vehicle to alter an agreement so as to evade the rule against perpetuities. * * *

Sanford next urges us to adopt the "wait and see" doctrine which has been legislatively enacted into the law of several states and judicially applied in others. Under this doctrine, the rule against perpetuities is determined to have been violated or not by taking into consideration events which occur after the period fixed by the rule has commenced. If, upon a later look, the event upon which an interest was made contingent is found to have occurred and the interest has vested or has become certain to vest within the period fixed by the rule, the rule is held not to have been violated.

Sanford does not tell us what effect adoption of the "wait and see" doctrine would have upon this case. Presumably, Sanford would say that because "new U.S. 60" is now completed or is nearing completion, we can look at this late development and see that the contingency set up in the option agreement has been or soon will be satisfied at a time within the period fixed by the rule against perpetuities. If that be Sanford's position, it overlooks the fact that the record shows nothing to have yet occurred concerning "Boxley Boulevard Extension" bordering the optioned property, an integral part of the contingency.

But aside from that, the established rule in Virginia, to which we adhere, is that a perpetuities problem may not be solved by resort to what occurs after commencement of the period fixed by the rule. In Claiborne v. Wilson, 168 Va. 469, 474, 192 S.E. 585, 586 (1937), we said, speaking of perpetuities cases:

> " 'Nor is it material in such cases how the fact actually turns out. The possibility that the event may, in point of time, exceed the limits allowed, vitiates the limitation *ab initio.*' "

Finally, Sanford contends that if we should decide, as we do, that the option agreement violates the rule against perpetuities, it is nevertheless entitled to recover damages for breach of contract, and it asks us to remand the case for a hearing on damages. However, an agreement in violation of the rule against perpetuities is void *ab initio*. To allow recovery of damages for the failure of an optionor to comply with such an agreement would have the effect of compelling performance of an invalid contract and would, at the same time, act as a restraint upon alienation. We conclude, therefore, that damages are not allowable in such a case.

For the reasons assigned, we hold the option agreement of April 7, 1966, in violation of the rule against perpetuities and, therefore, invalid and unenforceable. Accordingly, the judgment of the trial court will be reversed and final judgment will be entered here declaring the agreement void.

Reversed and final judgment.

Notes and Questions

1. How would you have drafted the option to avoid application of the Rule Against Perpetuities?

2. What result in the principal case if it had arisen in a "wait and see" or a "cy pres" jurisdiction?

3. The Uniform Statutory Rule Against Perpetuities (1986) adopts the "wait and see" approach and utilizes a 90 year waiting period. This measure has been enacted in a sizeable number of states. *See* 8B Uniform Laws Annotated 53 (Supp.1998). *See also* Fellows, *Testing Perpetuity Reforms: A Study of Perpetuity Cases 1984–89,* 25 Real Prop., Prob. & Tr. J. 597 (1991); Hess, *Freeing Property Owners From the RAP Trap: Tennessee Adopts the Uniform Statutory Rule Against Perpetuities,* 62 Tenn. L. Rev. 267 (1995); Waggoner, *The Uniform Statutory Rule Against Perpetuities: The Rationale of the 90–Year Waiting Period,* 73 Cornell L.Rev. 157 (1988).

4. For other cases applying the Rule Against Perpetuities to options to purchase land, see Symphony Space, Inc. v. Pergola Properties, Inc., 88 N.Y.2d 466, 646 N.Y.S.2d 641, 669 N.E.2d 799 (1996); Garza v. Sun Oil Co., 727 S.W.2d 115 (Tex.App.1986); Crossroads Shopping Center v. Montgomery Ward & Co., 646 P.2d 330 (Colo.1981); Rose v. Chandler, 247 Ga. 382, 279 S.E.2d 423 (1981). The Rule also has been applied to rights of first refusal. *See, e.g.,* Stuart Kingston, Inc. v. Robinson, 596 A.2d 1378 (Del.1991); Village of Pinehurst v. Regional Investments of Moore, Inc., 97 N.C.App. 114, 387 S.E.2d 222 (1990).

5. Courts in some jurisdictions, including Virginia, take the position that the Rule Against Perpetuities does not apply to a tenant's option to purchase leased real property during the term of the lease. *See* Texaco Refining and Marketing, Inc. v. Samowitz, 213 Conn. 676, 570 A.2d 170 (1990); Coomler v. Shell Oil Company, 108 Or.App. 233, 814 P.2d 184 (1991); Citgo Petroleum Corporation v. Hopper, 245 Va. 363, 429 S.E.2d 6 (1993). Is this approach sound?

BERRY v. UNION NATIONAL BANK

Supreme Court of Appeals of West Virginia, 1980.
164 W.Va. 258, 262 S.E.2d 766.

HARSHBARGER, JUSTICE:

This case presents the issue whether a private testamentary trust which violates the rule against perpetuities should be modified to effectuate a testatrix' intent or should fail.

Clara Clayton Post died on June 20, 1975, in Harrison County. Her will and codicil were admitted to probate on June 23, 1975, at which time Josephine H. Berry, appellant, qualified as executrix. After a series of specific bequests to her heirs at law, appellees Ellen Clayton and

Arthur Clayton, and to other parties, Ms. Post created a private educational trust for the descendants of her late husband's brothers and sisters, giving her trustee absolute discretion to provide educational expenses for class members meeting certain criteria. The trust was to endure for twenty-five years after testatrix' death or until the principal was reduced to less than $5,000.00, whichever should first occur. At the termination of the trust the principal and interest were to be distributed per stirpes to the then living descendants of her husband's brothers and sisters. The Union National Bank of Clarksburg, appellee, was named trustee.

Executrix Berry recognized that the trust potentially violated the rule against perpetuities and entered into a trust termination agreement with the trustee. The agreement amended the twenty-five year provision to twenty-one years and required the executrix to initiate a declaratory judgment action in the Circuit Court of Harrison County to determine *inter alia*, whether the trust violated the rule against perpetuities and whether it was proper for the executrix and trustee to enter into a trust termination agreement. A guardian ad litem was appointed for the unborn beneficiaries on April 26, 1977. The trial court granted summary judgment for the heirs at law, finding that the trust provision violated the rule against perpetuities and was therefore void and without force. The court additionally ruled that the executrix and trustee were not authorized to enter into the trust termination agreement. Executrix Berry appealed.

* * *

The rule against perpetuities is a common law rule which reflects the public policy that a testator or trustor cannot control the devolution of his property for an inordinate period of time. To prevent bars to property alienation the rule requires that:

> '[E]very executory limitation, in order to be valid, shall be so limited that it must necessarily vest, if at all, within a life or lives in being, ten months and twenty-one years thereafter, the period of gestation being allowed only in those cases in which it is a factor.' Goetz v. Old National Bank of Martinsburg, 140 W.Va. 422, 84 S.E.2d 759, 772 (1954).[1]

If a testator creates an estate which vests or has the possibility of vesting after a life in being plus twenty-one years and a period of gestation, the estate violates the rule against perpetuities and the testator's intent will be defeated.

It is here that principles of law collide: a testator may not indefinitely control the devolution of his property; but a testator's intent should be

---

1. The most frequently quoted statement of the rule is found in The Rule Against Perpetuities § 201 (4th ed. R. Gray 1942) by John Chipman Gray: "No interest is good unless it must vest, if at all, not later than twenty-one years after some life in being at the creation of the interest." For a better understanding of the rule, *see* Professor Leach's articles, *Perpetuities in a Nutshell*, 51 Harvard L.Rev. 638 (1938) and *Perpetuities: The Nutshell Revisited*, 78 Harvard L.Rev. 973 (1965).

honored and intestacy avoided whenever feasible. To remedy this apparent conflict, we adopt a doctrine of equitable modification which courts should apply to certain devises that on their face appear to violate the rule against perpetuities but meet the conditions enumerated below. Our action accords with a developing trend to ameliorate the harsh consequences of "remorseless application" of the rule.[2] The theory which we endorse today is akin to the doctrine of *cy pres* which was initially developed in the area of charitable trusts and was legislatively enacted in West Virginia in 1931 for that purpose. W.Va.Code, 35–2–2.

The purpose of equitable modification is to revise an instrument in a fashion that effectuates a testator's general intent within the limitations established by the rule.

We support the underlying policies of the rule against perpetuities and will deny validity to an interest which vests beyond the time limitations provided in the rule. However, before a testamentary scheme is totally obliterated by application of the rule, we will determine whether the testamentary disposition can be equitably modified to comport with the rule's underlying policy.

A non-charitable devise or bequest which violates the rule will be modified if the following conditions are met:

(1) The testator's intent is expressed in the instrument or can be readily determined by a court;

(2) The testator's general intent does not violate the rule against perpetuities;

(3) The testator's particular intent, which does violate the rule, is not a critical aspect of the testamentary scheme; and

(4) The proposed modification will effectuate the testator's general intent, will avoid the consequences of intestacy, and will conform to the policy considerations underlying the rule.

The testamentary trust here meets all these criteria for application of the equitable modification doctrine.

Testatrix clearly expressed her general intent in Section IX of her will when she stated:

2. There have been statutory and judicial reforms with respect to the application of the rule against perpetuities. The *cy pres* doctrine, alternatively called equitable reformation or equitable approximation, has been statutorily adopted in fifteen states. It has been judicially accepted in an additional three states.

It is interesting that theories other than *cy pres* have been employed to remedy the harsh results of the rule against perpetuities in its orthodox form. The "wait and see" doctrine has become the law of several jurisdictions and was recently adopted by the American Law Institute for the Restatement (Second) Property, Tentative Draft No. 2 on Donative Transfers. Other jurisdictions have abolished the fertile octagenarian and unborn widow rules. A theory of "separable alternative contingencies" provides for the elimination of a contingency which violates the rule if an alternative is provided in the instrument. By application of that theory, a devise which would be void under the rule can stand in one of its alternative forms.

I believe it was the desire of my husband that such funds as I might have at my death should be used to help such persons [who are later defined in this section] obtain educations. This is the only expression I ever heard him make relative to the disposition of such funds.

Her general intention to provide funds for education of her husband's nieces, nephews and their families does not contravene the rule. Her particular intention—to have the trust continue for twenty-five years after her death or until the principal was less than $5,000.00—violates the rule. There is no indication that the twenty-five year period is a critical aspect of her testamentary scheme. If the trust is modified to reduce that twenty-five year period to twenty-one years before distribution of the remaining principal to the then living descendants of her husband's siblings, the general intent to provide for their education will be effectuated, intestacy for that portion of her estate will be avoided, and property will not be controlled by her beyond the perpetuities' limitation.

* * *

Conclusion

It is not necessary for us to address the other issues raised in the parties' briefs due to our disposition of the main question. We hold, therefore, that the will of Clara Clayton Post should be equitably modified to reduce the duration of the trust from twenty-five years to twenty-one years. The ruling of the circuit court is reversed and the cause remanded for appointment of additional guardians ad litem and further proceedings consistent with this opinion.

Reversed and remanded.

Note

How does the doctrine of equitable modification differ from the cy pres doctrine? *See* Grill, *Perpetuities Reform: A Signal from West Virginia*, 11 Real Est. L.J. 116 (1982).

D. CONCURRENT INTERESTS

Either a present possessory estate or a future interest, may be owned simultaneously by two or more individuals. Such an arrangement is termed concurrent ownership. Both realty and personalty may be owned concurrently, but we focus on the concurrent ownership of realty.

In our hypothetical situation, Steve and Jill Ryan plan to take title to whatever property they purchase as concurrent owners. You must be thoroughly acquainted with this area of property law in order to advise the Ryans as to the form of concurrent ownership most suitable for their purposes.

1. TYPES

Concurrent ownership arrangements are of three types: tenancy in common, joint tenancy, and tenancy by the entirety.

a. *Tenancy in Common*

Tenants in common concurrently own the same or different percentage interests in real or personal property. Regardless of the size of their respective shares, each tenant has a right to possess the property subject to every other tenant's right to possession. Because of this "unity" of possession, tenants in common are said to hold undivided interests in the whole property.

Tenants in common may freely convey their interests. The grantee of such a conveyance steps into the shoes of the grantor and becomes a tenant in common with the other tenants. Similarly, when a tenant in common dies, that tenant's interest in the property passes to that tenant's heirs or devisees.

Problem

A, B, & C each own an undivided 1/3 fee simple interest in a parcel of land as tenants in common. A dies and by will leaves A's interest in the land to X and Y equally. Who owns what interest in the property?

b. *Joint Tenancy*

The traditional rule is that a joint tenancy requires the "unities" of time, title, interest, and possession. That is, a joint tenancy can exist only if the cotenants acquire their interests at the same time, from the same instrument, and the interests are identical and undivided. Although these requirements are frequently overlooked by modern courts when the intent to create or maintain a joint tenancy is clear, they are relics that cannot be ignored. *See* Helmholz, *Realism and Formalism in the Severance of Joint Tenancies*, 77 Neb.L.Rev. 1 (1998). In this regard, consider the following analysis found in Riddle v. Harmon, 102 Cal. App.3d 524, 527–28, 162 Cal.Rptr. 530, 532 (1980):

> At common law, one could not create a joint tenancy in himself and another by a direct conveyance. It was necessary for joint tenants to acquire their interests at the same time (unity of time) and by the same conveyancing instrument (unity of title). So, in order to create a valid joint tenancy where one of the proposed joint tenants already owned an interest in the property, it was first necessary to convey the property to a disinterested third person, a "strawman," who then conveyed the title to the ultimate grantees as joint tenants. This remains the prevailing practice in some jurisdictions. Other states, including California, have disregarded this application of the unities requirement "as one of the obsolete

'subtle and arbitrary distinctions and niceties of the feudal common law,' [and allow the creation of a valid joint tenancy without the use of a strawman]." (4A Powell on Real Property (1979) [¶] 616.)

By amendment to its Civil Code, California became a pioneer in allowing the *creation* of a joint tenancy by direct transfer. Under authority of Civil Code section 683, a joint tenancy conveyance may be made from a "sole owner to himself and others," or from joint owners to themselves and others as specified in the code. The purpose of the amendment was to "avoid the necessity of making a conveyance through a dummy" in the statutorily enumerated situations. Accordingly, in California, it is no longer necessary to use a strawman to *create* a joint tenancy.

Joint tenancy features the right of survivorship. When a joint tenant dies, the interests of the remaining joint tenants are enlarged proportionately. The joint tenant who survives all other joint tenants becomes the sole owner of the entire property. Notwithstanding this survivorship feature, joint tenants may freely convey their individual interests in the property and thereby sever the joint tenancy. A tenancy in common results between the grantee and the remaining tenant or joint tenants. *See* Estate of Gulledge, 673 A.2d 1278 (D.C.1996).

Problems

1. A, B, and C owned land in fee simple as joint tenants. A died and by will devised all A's realty to X and Y equally. Who owns what interest in the land at this point? B then died without a will. B's only heir is Z. Who owns what interest in the land?

2. A owned a parcel of land in fee simple. A conveyed the fee "to A and B as joint tenants with the right of survivorship." A died leaving all A's realty to X by will. Who owns what interest in the land?

3. A, B, and C owned land in fee simple as joint tenants. A conveyed A's interest in the land to X. B then died. Who owns what interest in the land?

4. O conveyed "to A and B equally for the period they are both alive and then to the survivor at the death of the other." A conveyed A's interest to C. A then died. Who owns what interest in the land? *See* Durant v. Hamrick, 409 So.2d 731 (Ala.1981).

c. *Tenancy by the Entirety*

Tenancy by the entirety is limited to married couples. It, like a joint tenancy, includes a right of survivorship. This tenancy, however, cannot be severed unilaterally. Thus, when a married couple takes title to property as tenants by the entirety neither spouse acting individually can destroy the survivorship aspect of the estate. The parties may, of course, join to convey the property to a third person.

The notion that the husband was the dominant marital partner permeated English common law. The husband, therefore, had the power to manage, convey, or encumber tenancy by the entirety property subject only to the wife's right of survivorship.

Tenancy by the entirety has been abolished in the majority of states. Courts in many jurisdictions reasoned that passage of Married Women's Property Acts, beginning in the mid-nineteenth century, abolished spousal unity and necessarily eliminated this form of concurrent ownership. *See* pages 321–322. In those states which retain tenancy by the entirety, the husband and wife are treated as relative equals and the right of survivorship remains indestructible. There is, however, wide diversity among these jurisdictions as to the language necessary to create and the legal effects of a tenancy by the entirety. *See* 7 Powell on Real Property ¶ ¶ 620–622 (1998).

Problem

O owned land in fee simple. O conveyed the land to "A and B, husband and wife, as tenants by the entirety." A and B are not married. Who owns what interest in the land? What if A and B later marry? *See* Kepner, *The Effect of an Attempted Creation of an Estate by the Entirety in Unmarried Grantees*, 6 Rutgers L.Rev. 550 (1952).

2. CREATION

IN RE ESTATE OF MICHAEL

Supreme Court of Pennsylvania, 1966.
421 Pa. 207, 218 A.2d 338.

JONES, JUSTICE.

This is an appeal from a decree of the Orphans' Court of Lycoming County entered in a proceeding brought under the Uniform Declaratory Judgment Act. The purpose of the proceeding was to obtain an interpretation and construction of a deed to determine whether the decedent, Bertha W. Michael, died owning any interest in realty located in Wolf and Moreland Townships, Lycoming County, known as "King Farm."

On February 24, 1947, Joyce E. King deeded certain real estate in Lycoming County, known as "King Farm", to Harry L. Michael and Bertha M. Michael,[1] his wife, and Ford W. Michael (son of Bertha and Harry L. Michael) and Helen M. Michael, his wife. The pertinent provisions of the lawyer-drawn deed are as follows:

"This Indenture Made the 24th day of February in the year of our Lord one thousand nine hundred forty-seven (1947).

Between Joyce E. King, widow, of Milton, Northumberland County, State of Pennsylvania, party of the first part, Harry L. Michael and Bertha M. Michael, his wife, tenants by the entireties and Ford W. Michael and Helen M. Michael, his wife, as tenants by

---

1. It is stipulated that Bertha M. Michael and Bertha W. Michael are one and the same person.

the entireties, *with right of survivorship*, of Hughesville, Lycoming County, Pennsylvania, parties of the second part." (Emphasis supplied.)

" * * * [H]ave granted, bargained, sold, aliened, enfeoffed, released, conveyed and confirmed and by these presents does grant, bargain, sell, alien, enfeoff, release[,] convey and confirm unto the said parties of the second part, their heirs and assigns."

* * *

"To Have and To Hold the said hereditaments and premises hereby granted or mentioned and intended so to be with the appurtenances unto the said parties of the second part, their heirs and assigns to and for the only proper use and behoof of the said parties of the second part, their heirs and assigns forever."

Harry L. Michael died prior to February 20, 1962 leaving to survive him his wife, Bertha W. Michael and two sons, Ford W. Michael, one of the grantees, and Robert C. Michael, the appellant.

Bertha W. Michael died testate, November 26, 1963, leaving to survive her two sons, Ford W. and Robert C. Michael. By her will dated February 20, 1962, she provided inter alia as follows:

"Second. It is my sincere wish and I hereby direct that my Executors settle my estate in such way that my sons Ford W. Michael and Robert C. Michael each receive an equal share of the same. Because of the fact that a good portion of my estate may be in the form of real estate, my Executors shall use their own discretion in the matter of the method to be used to make the division. The following, however, are my desires in this matter and these desires follow closely the wishes of their father, namely: * * *.

(d) That my interest in the 'King Farm' situate partly in Wolf and partly in Moreland Townships go to Robert C. Michael and the sum of $1,000.00, be paid to Ford W. Michael to balance this gift."

The two sons were appointed executors of their mother's estate. Soon thereafter a dispute arose as to what, *if any*, interest Bertha W. Michael had in the real estate known as "King Farm." The answer to this question turns on the construction of the language, above-quoted, contained in the deed of 1947. The court below held that the deed created a joint tenancy with right of survivorship between the two sets of husbands and wives.

The appellant urges that the deed created a tenancy in common as between the two married couples, each couple holding its undivided one-half interest as tenants by the entireties.[2] The appellees, conceding that

---

2. Appellant, in urging the creation of a tenancy in common, points to decedent's will (above-quoted in part) wherein she indicated that she expected her interest in the property to pass under her will. From this appellant argues that the interest was considered by the parties to be one of tenancy in common rather than joint tenancy. Such an argument is insufficient to establish the intention of the parties. The question must

the respective one-half interests were held by husband and wife as tenants by the entireties, contend, however, that *as to each other* the couples held as joint tenants with a right of survivorship. The lower court, predicating its decision on the use in the deed of the phrase "with right of survivorship", held that there was a clear expression of an intended right of survivorship between the two couples. To further support its decision, the court found it significant that the phrase was not used twice in modification of each husband-wife-grantee designation, but rather was utilized after both couples had been named and had been designated severally as tenants by the entireties.

At common law, joint tenancies were favored, and the doctrine of survivorship was a recognized incident to a joint estate. The courts of the United States have generally been opposed to the creation of such estates, the presumption being that all tenants hold jointly as tenants in common, unless a clear intention to the contrary is shown.

In Pennsylvania, by the Act of 1812, the incident of survivorship in joint tenancies was eliminated unless the instrument creating the estate expressly provided that such incident should exist. The Act of 1812 has been repeatedly held to be a statute of construction; it does not *forbid* creation of a joint tenancy if the language creating it *clearly* expresses that intent. Whereas before the Act, a conveyance or devise to two or more persons (not husband and wife or trustees) was presumed to create a joint tenancy with the right of survivorship unless otherwise clearly stated, the presumption is reversed by the Act, with the result that now such a conveyance or devise carries with it no right of survivorship unless clearly expressed, and in effect it creates, not a joint tenancy, but a tenancy in common.

Since passage of the Act of 1812, the question of survivorship has become a matter of intent and, in order to engraft the right of survivorship on a co-tenancy which might otherwise be a tenancy in common, the intent to do so must be expressed with sufficient clarity to overcome the statutory presumption that survivorship is not intended. Whether or not survivorship was intended is to be gathered from the instrument and its language, but no particular form of words is required to manifest such intention. The incident of survivorship may be expressly provided for in a deed or a will or it may arise by necessary implication.

Applying the above-stated principles to the instant facts, we fail to find a sufficiently *clear* expression of intent to create a right of survivorship, as required by the case law, to overcome the presumption against such a right arising from the Act of 1812. Neither the research of the parties involved nor our own has yielded any case involving language or involving facts similar to that in the present litigation.

The lower court found that the use in the deed of the phrase "with right of survivorship" and the location of that phrase in such deed (see

be answered solely by reference to the lan-   ment.
guage employed in the conveying instru-

quoted provision of deed, supra) constituted a clear expression of an intended right of survivorship. The inherent difficulty with such an interpretation is that it is purely conjectural and finds certainty in a totally ambiguous phrase.

The phrase, "with right of survivorship", is capable, as appellant properly urges, of at least three possible interpretations: (1) explanatory of the one of the incidents of the estate, known as tenancy by the entirety; (2) explanatory of the one tenancy by the entirety, the creation of which it follows or (3), as the appellee and the lower court contend, indicative of the creation of a right of survivorship as between the two sets of spouses. Any one of these interpretations is a *possibility* but deciding which was intended by the parties would involve nothing but a mere guess. Such ambiguous terminology falls far short of the *clear* expression of intent required to overcome the statutory presumption.

Nowhere in the deed is the term "joint tenants" employed. To create a right of survivorship the *normal* procedure is to employ the phrase "joint tenants, with a right of survivorship, and not as tenants in common" in describing the manner in which the grantees are to take or hold the property being conveyed or transferred.

The deed herein involved also uses the term "*their* heirs and assigns forever." (Emphasis supplied.) The use of the plural would tend to indicate a tenancy in common. If "*his* or *her*" heirs and assigns had been used a strong argument could be made that the grantor intended a right of survivorship and that the survivor of the four named grantees would have an absolute undivided fee in the property.

Both the Act of 1812 and our case law clearly dictate that joint tenancies with the incident right of survivorship are not to be deemed favorites of the law. We cannot find within the four corners of this deed a *clearly* expressed intention to create a joint tenancy with the right of survivorship. Having failed to find a *clear* intention to overcome the statutory presumption against such estates, the Act of 1812 compels us to find that the deed of 1947 created a tenancy in common as between the two sets of married couples, each couple holding its undivided one-half interest as tenants by the entireties.

Decree reversed. Each party to pay own costs.

Notes and Questions

1. What considerations supported the common law presumption of joint tenancy? Why do modern courts and state legislatures adopt the presumption of tenancy in common?

2. How would you have drafted the deed in *Michael* to create a joint tenancy between the two family groups?

3. Courts continue to be presented with the vexing problem of determining what language is necessary to create a joint tenancy. In a crabbed interpretation of a state statutory provision, the Supreme Court of Virginia ruled that the words "as joint tenants, and not as tenants in common" failed to sufficiently manifest an intent to establish a survivorship estate. Hoover

v. Smith, 248 Va. 6, 444 S.E.2d 546 (1994). In other jurisdictions, such language generally would be considered to create a joint tenancy with right of survivorship. *See* R. Cunningham, W. Stoebuck, & D. Whitman, The Law of Property § 5.3 (2d ed. 1993). Of course, the terminology suggested in *Michael*—"joint tenants, with a right of survivorship, and not as tenants in common"—is preferable and presumably would even satisfy the Virginia court.

4. What type of concurrent ownership is created by the following conveyance in a state that recognizes tenancy by the entirety? O conveys "to A and B, husband and wife." "[A]t common law it was presumed that a conveyance to husband and wife created a tenancy by the entirety even in the absence of language of survivorship or reference to that kind of tenancy." Carver v. Gilbert, 387 P.2d 928, 929 (Alaska 1963). Some states continue this presumption even in light of the general modern preference for tenancy in common. *See, e.g.,* N.C.Gen.Stat. § 39–13.6 (1984). Other states require that tenancy by the entirety be expressly declared. *See Carver v. Gilbert;* 7 Powell on Real Property ¶ 621[2] (1998).

3. RIGHTS OF CREDITORS

SAWADA v. ENDO

Supreme Court of Hawaii, 1977.
57 Hawaii 608, 561 P.2d 1291.

MENOR, JUSTICE.

This is a civil action brought by the plaintiffs-appellants, Masako Sawada and Helen Sawada, in aid of execution of money judgments in their favor, seeking to set aside a conveyance of real property from judgment debtor Kokichi Endo to Samuel H. Endo and Toru Endo, defendants-appellees herein, on the ground that the conveyance as to the Sawadas was fraudulent.

On November 30, 1968, the Sawadas were injured when struck by a motor vehicle operated by Kokichi Endo. On June 17, 1969, Helen Sawada filed her complaint for damages against Kokichi Endo. Masako Sawada filed her suit against him on August 13, 1969. The complaint and summons in each case was served on Kokichi Endo on October 29, 1969.

On the date of the accident, Kokichi Endo was the owner, as a tenant by the entirety with his wife, Ume Endo, of a parcel of real property situate at Wahiawa, Oahu, Hawaii. By deed, dated July 26, 1969, Kokichi Endo and his wife conveyed the property to their sons, Samuel H. Endo and Toru Endo. This document was recorded in the Bureau of Conveyances on December 17, 1969. No consideration was paid by the grantees for the conveyance. Both were aware at the time of the conveyance that their father had been involved in an accident, and that he carried no liability insurance. Kokichi Endo and Ume Endo, while reserving no life interests therein, continued to reside on the premises.

On January 19, 1971, after a consolidated trial on the merits, judgment was entered in favor of Helen Sawada and against Kokichi Endo in the sum of $8,846.46. At the same time, Masako Sawada was awarded judgment on her complaint in the amount of $16,199.28. Ume Endo, wife of Kokichi Endo, died on January 29, 1971. She was survived by her husband, Kokichi. Subsequently, after being frustrated in their attempts to obtain satisfaction of judgment from the personal property of Kokichi Endo, the Sawadas brought suit to set aside the conveyance which is the subject matter of this controversy. The trial court refused to set aside the conveyance, and the Sawadas appeal.

I

The determinative question in this case is, whether the interest of one spouse in real property, held in tenancy by the entireties, is subject to levy and execution by his or her individual creditors. This issue is one of first impression in this jurisdiction.

A brief review of the present state of the tenancy by the entirety might be helpful. Dean Phipps, writing in 1951,[1] pointed out that only nineteen states and the District of Columbia continued to recognize it as a valid and subsisting institution in the field of property law. Phipps divided these jurisdictions into four groups. He made no mention of Alaska and Hawaii, both of which were then territories of the United States.

In the Group I states (Massachusetts, Michigan, and North Carolina) the estate is essentially the common law tenancy by the entireties, unaffected by the Married Women's Property Acts. As at common law, the possession and profits of the estate are subject to the husband's exclusive dominion and control. In all three states, as at common law, the *husband* may convey the entire estate subject only to the possibility that the wife may become entitled to the whole estate upon surviving him. As at common law, the obverse as to the wife does not hold true. Only in Massachusetts, however, is the estate in its entirety subject to levy by the husband's creditors. In both Michigan and North Carolina, the use and income from the estate is not subject to levy during the marriage for the separate debts of either spouse.

In the Group II states (Alaska, Arkansas, New Jersey, New York, and Oregon) the interest of the debtor spouse in the estate may be sold or levied upon for his or her separate debts, subject to the other spouse's contingent right of survivorship. Alaska, which has been added to this group, has provided by statute that the interest of a debtor spouse in any type of estate, except a homestead as defined and held in tenancy by the entirety, shall be subject to his or her separate debts.

In the Group III jurisdictions (Delaware, District of Columbia, Florida, Indiana, Maryland, Missouri, Pennsylvania, Rhode Island, Vermont, Virginia, and Wyoming) an attempted conveyance by either spouse

---

1. Phipps, "Tenancy by Entireties," 25 Temple L.Q. 24 (1951).

is wholly void, and the estate may not be subjected to the separate debts of one spouse only.

In Group IV, the two states of Kentucky and Tennessee hold that the contingent right of survivorship appertaining to either spouse is separately alienable by him and attachable by his creditors during the marriage. The use and profits, however, may neither be alienated nor attached during coverture.

It appears, therefore, that Hawaii is the only jurisdiction still to be heard from on the question. Today we join that group of states and the District of Columbia which hold that under the Married Women's Property Acts the interest of a husband or a wife in an estate by the entireties is not subject to the claims of his or her individual creditors during the joint lives of the spouses. In so doing, we are placing our stamp of approval upon what is apparently the prevailing view of the lower courts of this jurisdiction.

Hawaii has long recognized and continues to recognize the tenancy in common, the joint tenancy, and the tenancy by the entirety, as separate and distinct estates. That the Married Women's Property Act of 1888 was not intended to abolish the tenancy by the entirety was made clear by the language of Act 19 of the Session Laws of Hawaii, 1903 (now HRS § 509-1). The tenancy by the entirety is predicated upon the legal unity of husband and wife, and the estate is held by them in single ownership. They do not take by moieties, but both and each are seized of the whole estate.

A joint tenant has a specific, albeit undivided, interest in the property, and if he survives his cotenant he becomes the owner of a larger interest than he had prior to the death of the other joint tenant. But tenants by the entirety are each deemed to be seized of the entirety from the time of the creation of the estate. At common law, this taking of the "whole estate" did not have the real significance that it does today, insofar as the rights of the wife in the property were concerned. For all practical purposes, the wife had no right during coverture to the use and enjoyment and exercise of ownership in the marital estate. All she possessed was her contingent right of survivorship.

The effect of the Married Women's Property Acts was to abrogate the husband's common law dominance over the marital estate and to place the wife on a level of equality with him as regards the exercise of ownership over the whole estate. The tenancy was and still is predicated upon the legal unity of husband and wife, but the Acts converted it into a unity of equals and not of unequals as at common law. No longer could the husband convey, lease, mortgage or otherwise encumber the property without her consent. The Acts confirmed her right to the use and enjoyment of the whole estate, and all the privileges that ownership of property confers, including the right to convey the property in its entirety, jointly with her husband, during the marriage relation. Jordan v. Reynolds, 105 Md. 288, 66 A. 37 (1907); Hurd v. Hughes, 12 Del.Ch. 188, 109 A. 418 (1920); Frost v. Frost, 200 Mo. 474, 98 S.W. 527 (1906).

They also had the effect of insulating the wife's interest in the estate from the separate debts of her husband.

Neither husband nor wife has a separate divisible interest in the property held by the entirety that can be conveyed or reached by execution. Fairclaw v. Forrest, 76 U.S.App.D.C. 197, 130 F.2d 829 (1942). A joint tenancy may be destroyed by voluntary alienation, or by levy and execution, or by compulsory partition, but a tenancy by the entirety may not. The indivisibility of the estate, except by joint action of the spouses, is an indispensable feature of the tenancy by the entirety.

In *Jordan v. Reynolds, supra,* the Maryland court held that no lien could attach against entirety property for the separate debts of the husband, for that would be in derogation of the entirety of title in the spouses and would be tantamount to a conversion of the tenancy into a joint tenancy or tenancy in common. In holding that the spouses could jointly convey the property, free of any judgment liens against the husband, the court said:

> "To hold the judgment to be a lien at all against this property, and the right of execution suspended during the life of the wife, and to be enforced on the death of the wife, would, we think, likewise encumber her estate, and be in contravention of the constitutional provision heretofore mentioned, protecting the wife's property from the husband's debts.

> It is clear, we think, if the judgment here is declared a lien, but suspended during the life of the wife, and not enforceable until her death, if the husband should survive the wife, it will defeat the sale here made by the husband and wife to the purchaser, and thereby make the wife's property liable for the debts of her husband." 105 Md. at 295, 296, 66 A. at 39.

In *Hurd v. Hughes, supra,* the Delaware court, recognizing the peculiar nature of an estate by the entirety, in that the husband and wife are the owners, not merely of equal interests but of the whole estate, stated:

> "The estate [by the entireties] can be acquired or held only by a man and woman while married. Each spouse owns the whole while both live; neither can sell any interest except with the other's consent, and by their joint act; and at the death of either the other continues to own the whole, and does not acquire any new interest from the other. There can be no partition between them. From this is deduced the indivisibility and unseverability of the estate into two interests, and hence that the creditors of either spouse cannot during their joint lives reach by execution any interest which the debtor had in land so held. * * * One may have doubts as to whether the holding of land by entireties is advisable or in harmony with the spirit of the legislation in favor of married women; but when such an estate is created due effect must be given to its peculiar characteristics." 12 Del.Ch. at 190, 109 A. at 419.

In *Frost v. Frost, supra,* the Missouri court said:

"Under the facts of the case at bar it is not necessary for us to decide whether or not under our married women's statutes the husband has been shorn of the exclusive right to the possession and control of the property held as an estate in entirety; it is sufficient to say, as we do say, that the title in such an estate is as it was at common law; neither husband nor wife has an interest in the property, to the exclusion of the other. Each owns the whole while both live and at the death of either the other continues to own the whole, freed from the claim of any one claiming under or through the deceased." 200 Mo. at 483, 98 S.W. at 528, 529.

We are not persuaded by the argument that it would be unfair to the creditors of either spouse to hold that the estate by the entirety may not, without the consent of both spouses, be levied upon for the separate debts of either spouse. No unfairness to the creditor is involved here. We agree with the court in *Hurd v. Hughes, supra:*

"But creditors are not entitled to special consideration. If the debt arose prior to the creation of the estate, the property was not a basis of credit, and if the debt arose subsequently the creditor presumably had notice of the characteristics of the estate which limited his right to reach the property." 12 Del.Ch. at 193, 109 A. at 420.

We might also add that there is obviously nothing to prevent the creditor from insisting upon the subjection of property held in tenancy by the entirety as a condition precedent to the extension of credit. Further, the creation of a tenancy by the entirety may not be used as a device to defraud existing creditors.

Were we to view the matter strictly from the standpoint of public policy, we would still be constrained to hold as we have done here today. In *Fairclaw v. Forrest, supra,* the court makes this observation:

"The interest in family solidarity retains some influence upon the institution [of tenancy by the entirety]. It is available only to husband and wife. It is a convenient mode of protecting a surviving spouse from inconvenient administration of the decedent's estate and from the other's improvident debts. It is in that protection the estate finds its peculiar and justifiable function." 130 F.2d at 833.

It is a matter of common knowledge that the demand for single-family residential lots has increased rapidly in recent years, and the magnitude of the problem is emphasized by the concentration of the bulk of fee simple land in the hands of a few. The shortage of single-family residential fee simple property is critical and government has seen fit to attempt to alleviate the problem through legislation. When a family can afford to own real property, it becomes their single most important asset. Encumbered as it usually is by a first mortgage, the fact remains that so long as it remains whole during the joint lives of the spouses, it is always available in its entirety for the benefit and use of the entire family.

Loans for education and other emergency expenses, for example, may be obtained on the security of the marital estate. This would not be possible where a third party has become a tenant in common or a joint tenant with one of the spouses, or where the ownership of the contingent right of survivorship of one of the spouses in a third party has cast a cloud upon the title of the marital estate, making it virtually impossible to utilize the estate for these purposes.

If we were to select between a public policy favoring the creditors of one of the spouses and one favoring the interests of the family unit, we would not hesitate to choose the latter. But we need not make this choice for, as we pointed out earlier, by the very nature of the estate by the entirety as we view it, and as other courts of our sister jurisdictions have viewed it, "[a] unilaterally indestructible right of survivorship, an inability of one spouse to alienate his interest, and, importantly for this case, a broad immunity from claims of separate creditors remain among its vital incidents." In re Estate of Wall, 440 F.2d [215] at 218 [1971].

Having determined that an estate by the entirety is not subject to the claims of the creditors of one of the spouses during their joint lives, we now hold that the conveyance of the marital property by Kokichi Endo and Ume Endo, husband and wife, to their sons, Samuel H. Endo and Toru Endo, was not in fraud of Kokichi Endo's judgment creditors.

Affirmed.

KIDWELL, JUSTICE, dissenting.

* * *

The majority reaches its conclusion by holding that the effect of the Married Women's Act was to equalize the positions of the spouses by taking from the husband his common law right to transfer his interest, rather than by elevating the wife's right of alienation of her interest to place it on a position of equality with the husband's. I disagree. I believe that a better interpretation of the Married Women's Acts is that offered by the Supreme Court of New Jersey in King v. Greene, 30 N.J. 395, 412, 153 A.2d 49, 60 (1959):

> It is clear that the Married Women's Act created an equality between the spouses in New Jersey, insofar as tenancies by the entirety are concerned. If, as we have previously concluded, the husband could alienate his right of survivorship at common law, the wife, by virtue of the act, can alienate her right of survivorship. And it follows, that if the wife takes equal rights with the husband in the estate, she must take equal disabilities. Such are the dictates of common equality. Thus, the judgment creditors of either spouse may levy and execute upon their separate rights of survivorship.

One may speculate whether the courts which first chose the path to equality now followed by the majority might have felt an unexpressed aversion to entrusting a wife with as much control over her interest as had previously been granted to the husband with respect to his interest. Whatever may be the historical explanation for these decisions, I feel that the resultant restriction upon the freedom of the spouses to deal independently with their respective interests is both illogical and unnecessarily at odds with present policy trends. Accordingly, I would hold that the separate interest of the husband in entireties property, at least to the extent of his right of survivorship, is alienable by him and subject to attachment by his separate creditors, so that a voluntary conveyance of the husband's interest should be set aside where it is fraudulent as to such creditors, under applicable principles of the law of fraudulent conveyances.

Notes and Problems

1.   Tenancy by the entirety remains a lively topic of debate, and the state groupings set forth in *Sawada* are not fixed. For statutory changes to tenancy by the entirety law since *Sawada* was decided, see, e.g., Mass.Gen. Laws Ann. ch. 209, § 1 (West 1998) (husband and wife "equally entitled" to income, control, and possession of entirety property); N.J.Stat.Ann. 46:3–17.4 (West 1989) (neither husband nor wife can alienate their individual interest without other tenant's written consent); N.C.Gen.Stat. § 39–13.6 (1984) (equalizing position of spouses as to income, possession, and control of entirety property and prohibiting one spouse from alienating property unless other spouse joins in writing). *See also* Coraccio v. Lowell Five Cents Savings Bank, 415 Mass. 145, 612 N.E.2d 650 (1993) (discussing statutory changes in Massachusetts tenancy by the entirety law and holding that either husband or wife may mortgage their individual interest subject to the other tenant's right of survivorship).

2.   An Arkansas appellate court has reaffirmed the state's long-standing rule that a judgment creditor of one spouse can levy upon the debtor spouse's interest in property owned as tenancy by the entirety, subject to the non-debtor spouse's right of possession and survivorship. Morris v. Solesbee, 48 Ark.App. 123, 892 S.W.2d 281 (1995).

3.   Suppose that Steve and Jill Ryan acquire property as tenants in common and that Steve's dental practice is financially unsuccessful. What rights do Steve's creditors have in the property? What rights would Steve's creditors have if Steve and Jill had acquired the property as joint tenants?

4.   RIGHTS AND OBLIGATIONS AMONG COTENANTS

GRAHAM v. INLOW

Supreme Court of Arkansas, 1990.
302 Ark. 414, 790 S.W.2d 428.

GLAZE, JUSTICE.

This second appeal stems from our earlier reversal and remand of this partition suit case wherein we held valid a deed from Robert Inlow to his second wife, Freda, and his three children. Robert had two children, Charles and Carol, by his wife Freda, and he had another child, Patricia Graham, by his first wife. In remanding this case, the trial court was placed in the position of reconsidering Graham's request for partitioning the parties' one-fourth respective interest in the 287 acre farm. The chancellor found the property could not be partitioned in kind and ordered the sale of the farm. The chancellor further held that Graham was entitled to certain rental income and timber sale proceeds after her commencement of the suit as well as attorney fees and costs in connection with prosecuting this partition action. He also awarded Freda the sum of $70,000 for improvements she made on the disputed property. Graham appeals and the Inlows cross appeal from the awards made by the chancellor.

* * *

It is well settled that a tenant in common has the right to make improvements on the land without the consent of his cotenants; and, although he has no lien on the land for the value of his improvements, he will be indemnified for them, in a proceeding in equity to partition the land between himself and cotenants, either by having the part upon which the improvements are located allotted to him or by having compensation for them, if thrown into the common mass. The improvements must be made in good faith and have benefit to the premises.

Here, the record reflects that the appellee Freda made improvements which benefited the land beginning in 1979. The majority of those improvements were in the form of repairs and renovations to already existing buildings such as barns. There is no showing that these benefits were not made in good faith. However, because tenants in common might be improved out of their property, the cotenant can only receive the enhancement value of the improvement to the property. This limitation is analogous to the requirement found in the Betterment Statute. The proper measurement is the difference between the value of the land without the improvements and the value of the land with the improvements in their then condition.

Appellee Freda attempted to prove this value through the testimony of a real estate appraiser, Mr. Hinshaw. Hinshaw testified about improvements made to each separate itemized item and the enhanced value of those improvements on each item. He then explained that this value was not the cost value but the contributory value. Hinshaw explained that the contributory value was determined by comparing a similar piece of property without a building, like the building improved on the land in question, to the value of the land in question with the building. In addition, Hinshaw gave testimony about the difference in value of raw land and the value of the land in question with buildings on it.

Hinshaw's testimony showed the court the following things: (1) the difference in value between raw land and land with buildings; (2) the contributory value of a barn, for instance, to the land, which is figured by knowing the selling price of a similar piece of land without a barn, and (3) the difference in value or enhancement of the building before and after the improvement. However, as shown by the following exchange on cross-examination, Hinshaw did not testify as to the difference in value of property without improvements and the value of property after improvements.

Q. So you're not prepared to tell me and this Court how much these improvements that you made reference to here * * * actually enhanced the value of the entire property? What you're saying is what they enhanced each individual building or item; is that correct?

A. Well, yes, but they in total affected the property also. I'm saying you were trying to get me to compare it with the value of the property before anything was done to 'em and I can't do that without some special work. I can do it * * *. But I don't have the figures here to do it.

Even though Hinshaw later stated that he thought that the values he testified to showed both the enhancement of the individual items that were improved and the value of those improvements to the property as a whole, we do not agree. From our review of Hinshaw's testimony, we cannot find any testimony to support this measure of recovery. Thus, in awarding Freda $70,000 for the improvements as a result of Hinshaw's testimony, we hold that the chancellor erred in determining the proper amount to be allowed for the improvements, and we remand the case with directions to proceed in a manner not inconsistent with this opinion.

In the second issue, the appellant argues that the chancellor erred in holding that she could only recover rents after the commencement of her partition suit. On this same issue, the appellees in their cross appeal argue that the chancellor erred in awarding any rents to the appellant. We find no error in the chancellor's holding on this point.

One of the characteristics of tenancy in common is that each tenant has the right to occupy the premises, and neither tenant can lawfully exclude the other. The occupation of one tenant in common is deemed possession by all. For the possession of one tenant in common to be adverse to that of his cotenants, knowledge of his adverse claim must be brought home to them directly or by such acts that notice may be presumed. We have stated that the dispossession of a cotenant is a question of fact, and we will not reverse the chancellor's determination absent a showing it was clearly erroneous.

Under the property laws of common tenancy, until the appellant asserted her right for common enjoyment of the farm, the other tenants in common were not obligated to stay out. A tenant in possession who does not exclude his cotenants is not liable for rent.

From our review of the record, we cannot say that the chancellor's finding that the appellant did not assert her right for common enjoyment until the filing of her partition suit is clearly erroneous. In so ruling, we note that the appellant lived on part of the farm and there is ample evidence, albeit conflicting, to reflect she had reasonable access to all the property. While we would agree that there seems to be bad blood between the appellant and her stepmother Freda, we cannot conclude that the appellees excluded the appellant prior to her commencement of the partition suit.

* * *

For the reasons above, we affirm in part and reverse and remand in part. * * *

Question

Suppose one tenant in common leased the common property and received rental income. Must the leasing tenant account to the other tenants in common for such income? Consider the following comments from *Lerman v. Levine*, 14 Conn.App. 402, 406–407, 541 A.2d 523, 524–525 (1988):

> Our analysis commences in the ancient common law of property. Under the early rule "a cotenant in possession was not chargeable by his cotenant for the use of the property, since his occupancy was presumed to be his own right as the owner of one half of all and every part of the common property. Unless he was bailiff for his cotenant he was not accountable to him for anything he received from the common estate, and could lawfully appropriate all the rent and profits to his own benefit." *Hill v. Jones*, 118 Conn. 12, 17, 170 A. 154 (1934). In 1709, the English parliament remedied this unfair situation by passage of the Statute of Anne. "This statute made any tenant in common who received more than his just share of the rents and profits liable to his cotenants for the excess; and it was no longer necessary that he should take as bailiff by appointment in order to make him responsible." 20 Am.Jur.2d, Cotenancy and Joint Ownership § 40. Because of its early passage, the Statute of Anne is generally considered to be ingrained in the common law, emigrating to this country with the settlors long before the Revolutionary War, a common historical point of demarcation in legal analysis. This statutory remedy, however, was limited to property that produced rental payments or other tangible receipts from a third party. The English courts did not construe the Statute of Anne as applicable to an action for benefits enjoyed by a cotenant who occupied common property to the exclusion of his cotenants. Phrased differently, mere sole occupancy did not render the occupying cotenant liable to his co-owners.

COGGAN v. COGGAN

Supreme Court of Florida, 1970.
239 So.2d 17.

MOODY, CIRCUIT JUDGE.

This cause is before this court on petition for writ of certiorari to review the decision of the District Court of Appeals, Second District, in the case of Coggan v. Coggan, 230 So.2d 34.

Petitioner, husband, defendant in the trial court, owned an office building jointly with his wife, plaintiff below, which he occupied as his medical office. In 1963 the parties were divorced and they thereby became tenants in common of the property. No provision was made in the decree, or by agreement, as to its use and possession. The defendant continued in possession, paying the taxes, making necessary repairs, and otherwise exercising complete control. In 1967 the former wife filed a partition suit praying for an accounting of one-half the rental value of the office building from the date of the final decree of divorce. The defendant counterclaimed for partition of the plaintiff's home which, by the terms of the final decree, was purchased as a tenancy in common with the exclusive possession granted to the plaintiff. The trial court ordered a partition sale of the office building and an accounting in favor of the plaintiff for one-half the rental value of the premises since the date of the divorce. The counterclaim was denied.

* * *

On the question of the accounting, the District Court * * * affirmed the lower court and in its opinion correctly stated the governing law as follows:

"* * * when one cotenant has exclusive possession of lands owned as tenant in common with another and uses those lands for his own benefit and does not receive rents or profits therefrom, such cotenant is not liable or accountable to his cotenant out of possession *unless* such cotenant in exclusive possession holds adversely or as the result of ouster or the equivalent thereof. This was the rule of common law, as modified by the Statute of Ann[e] and as it was expressly adopted as the law of Florida in 1875 by our Supreme Court in Bird v. Bird (Fla.1875), 15 Fla. 424. The rule has persisted unchanged and has heretofore been recognized by this court. Thus it appears that appellant's point is well taken unless the case falls within one of the exceptions to the rule; i.e., unless it is shown that appellant held exclusive possession of his professional office adversely to appellee, or as the result of ouster *or the equivalent thereof. See,* 51 A.L.R.2d 388, 437, § 13."

It then found, based on the undisputed facts, that the defendant's actions were "the equivalent of ouster." The facts being undisputed, it becomes a question of law as to whether or not the tenant in possession held the property adversely or as a result of ouster or the equivalent thereof.

The possession of a tenant in common is presumed to be the possession of all cotenants until the one in possession brings home to the other the knowledge that he claims the exclusive right or title. What is called "exclusive possession" may amount merely to sole possession without actual exclusion of a cotenant or denial, or invasion of the rights of such cotenant.

There can be no holding adversely or ouster or its equivalent, by one cotenant unless such holding is manifested or communicated to the other. Where a tenant out of possession claims an accounting of a tenant in possession, he must show that the tenant in possession is holding the exclusive possession of the property adversely or holding the exclusive possession as a result of ouster or the equivalent thereof. This possession must be attended with such circumstances as to evince a claim of the exclusive right or title by the tenant in possession imparted to the tenant out of possession.

In the case of Stokely et al. v. Conner (1915) 69 Fla. 412, 68 So. 452, this court stated:

> "But a tenant in common, to show an ouster of his cotenant, must show acts of possession inconsistent with, and exclusive of, the rights of such cotenant and such as would amount to an ouster between landlord and tenant, and knowledge on the part of his cotenant of his claim of exclusive ownership. He has the right to assume that the possession of his cotenant [is] his possession, until informed to the contrary, either by express notice, or by acts and declarations that may be equivalent to notice."

In the case at Bar, although the defendant continued in sole possession of the property after the divorce decree, the record is devoid of any evidence that, prior to the filing of the partition suit, he advised the plaintiff he was claiming adversely to her, or that he had taken any action adverse to her interest or title, or that he had taken any steps to actually or constructively oust her from possession, or that she knew or should have known he was claiming any right of title adverse to her.

The claim of the defendant was manifested for the first time in his unsworn answer to the complaint for partition wherein he denied the existence of any cotenancy. This pleading cannot be considered as evidence. It was not an admission in a pleading eliminating the necessity of proof, but was a general denial of plaintiff's claim or a conclusion of law upon which evidence would be necessary for determination. The District Court based its decisions upon the denial in the pleading and the defendant's testimony at the trial that he had always considered himself to be the sole owner of the property and that his former wife had no rights therein. However, as previously noted, there was no evidence that he had expressed this attitude or belief to her, or that she was otherwise cognizant of this claim.

In consideration of the foregoing, the decision of the District Court is quashed to the extent set forth herein with directions that the case be remanded to the trial court for further proceedings not inconsistent herewith.

Question

Would the court have reached the same result if the husband had changed the locks to the medical office building shortly after the divorce? *See* Patterson v. Patterson, 396 So.2d 821 (Fla.App.1981).

5. TERMINATION

For a helpful analysis of many of the issues addressed in this subsection, see Helmholz, *Realism and Formalism in the Severance of Joint Tenancies*, 77 Neb.L.Rev. 1 (1998).

SHEPHERD v. SHEPHERD

Supreme Court of Mississippi, 1976.
336 So.2d 497.

Before INZER, P.J., and SUGG and LEE, JJ.

INZER, PRESIDING JUSTICE, for the Court.

This is an appeal by the executrix of the estate of Fannie S. Shepherd from a decree of the Chancery Court of Quitman County adjudicating that the tract of land in question became the property of Thomas R. Shepherd by the terms of a deed conveying the land to the parties. We affirm.

At a time when Fannie and Thomas Shepherd were man and wife, they purchased from Flossie K. Chism a house and lot in the town of Lambert. The deed in part stated: "I, Flossie K. Chism, do hereby and by these presents bargain, sell, convey and warrant unto T.R. Shepherd and Fannie S. Shepherd, his wife, as an estate in entirety, with the right of survivorship, and not as tenants in common, the following described real property. * * * " In 1966 Fannie Shepherd filed suit against Thomas Shepherd seeking a divorce, alimony and attorney's fee. The bill of complaint alleged that they owned the house and lot as an estate in entirety but that complainant had paid for the home and her husband should be required to execute to her a quit claim deed to the realty. Thomas Shepherd answered and denied that Fannie was entitled to a divorce, denied that he did not pay a part of the purchase price of the home, and alleged that he sold a house and lot in Memphis and paid on the purchase price of the property in question.

On May 26, 1966, Fannie Shepherd was granted a divorce but was denied alimony or attorney's fee. The decree specifically provided that no property rights were divested out of the defendant Thomas Shepherd. The decree further provided that all property rights in regard to the realty were taken under advisement for rendition of a decree in vacation at a time and place agreeable to the parties and the court. The decree specifically stated that the only issue held in abeyance was whether the grantees in the deed conveying the home as a matter of law, after the divorce became final, became tenants in common or remained joint tenants as an estate in the entirety. The decree then provided that Fannie was to have the exclusive use of the property described in the deed until her death or remarriage.

After rendition of this decree no further action was taken relative to the property and Fannie remained in possession of the property until her death. After her death in 1974, Thomas Shepherd filed a motion in the divorce case for a final hearing for determination of the estate of the parties, alleging that he was the sole owner of the property under the terms of the deed. The executrix of Fannie's estate was made a party to the proceedings. The executrix answered and alleged that the divorce terminated the estate in the entirety and the parties became tenants in common each owning a one-half interest in the property. The answer was made a cross bill praying that the court hold that the title to the property was vested one-half to Thomas Shepherd and one-half to the devisees named in the Last Will and Testament of Fannie Shepherd. The devisees under the will entered their appearance and joined in the prayer of the executrix.

After a hearing the chancellor held that the parties after the divorce continued to hold the property as joint tenants as an estate in the entirety with the right of survivorship and upon the death of Fannie Shepherd, Thomas Shepherd became the sole owner of the land.

After an appeal was perfected to this Court, Thomas Shepherd died and the cause has been revived in the name of Harvey Henderson, executor of his estate.

The only issue presented by this appeal is whether an estate in entirety with the right of survivorship is terminated and becomes an estate in common when the parties are divorced. Appellant's principal contention is that when the Shepherds were divorced they could no longer hold title to the property as tenants by entirety and thereafter held the property as tenants in common. Section 89–1–7, Mississippi Code, 1972 Annotated, provides as follows:

> All conveyances or devises of land made to two or more persons, including conveyances or devises to husband and wife, shall be construed to create estates in common and not in joint tenancy or entirety, unless it manifestly appears from the tenor of the instrument that it was intended to create an estate in joint tenancy or entirety with the right of survivorship. But an estate in joint tenancy or entirety with right of survivorship may be created by such conveyance from the owner or owners to himself, themselves, or others, or to himself, themselves and others.

> This section shall not apply to mortgages or devises or to conveyances made in trust.

Appellants argue that the above section does not abrogate the common law relative to the tenancy by the entirety, and under the common law, tenancy by entirety may exist only between husband and wife. Thus, it is argued that the divorce terminated the tenancy by entirety and the parties owned the land as tenants in common. We find no merit in this contention. In Miller v. Miller, 298 So.2d 704 (Miss. 1974), the deed to the property in question conveyed to husband and wife the property as joint tenants with the right of survivorship. The parties were divorced and some time later decided to sell the property. The dispute arose as to how the proceeds should be divided. In deciding this question we pointed out that in Mississippi it is well settled that the dissolution of the marriage by divorce does not of itself affect title of the respective parties to the real estate owned by them. In deciding the question involved in the case, we stated:

> A legally enforceable agreement to the contrary not having been established, the grantor's conveyance vested in each of the parties, as grantees, an equal estate in joint tenancy. Further, while the conveyance to husband and wife perhaps more accurately might be said to have created in them an estate by the entirety, dissolution of the marriage did not have the effect of altering the character, extent or attributes of the estate conveyed, and upon divorce, it remained one in equal joint tenancy, with the right of survivorship, under the express terms of the instrument which created it. (298 So.2d at 706).

In the case before us the conveyance was to husband and wife as an estate in entirety with the right of survivorship. An estate in entirety is a joint tenancy with the right of survivorship plus the marital relation. If it can be said that after the dissolution of the marriage the parties could no longer be tenants by the entirety, they certainly remained joint tenants with the right of survivorship. The dissolution of the marital relation under the statute as now written did not destroy the joint tenancy with the right of survivorship. The parties continued to own the property as joint tenants with the right of survivorship until the death of Fannie Shepherd.

* * *

For the reasons stated, this case must be and is affirmed.

Affirmed.

Problems and Questions

1.   In Ayers v. Petro, 417 So.2d 912, 914 n. 2 (Miss.1982) the Supreme Court of Mississippi reaffirmed its decision in *Shepherd*, and commented:

> Our holding in *Shepherd* is contrary to the weight of authority. It is generally held that a decree of divorce severs an estate by the entireties and makes the divorced spouses tenants in common. Although not expressed in our opinion in *Shepherd*, the reason for our holding is that only the unity of person is destroyed by the divorce, leaving *intact* the unities of time, title, interest and possession.

Which is the better view? *See* 7 Powell on Real Property ¶ 624[5] (1998).

2.   H and W owned a house as tenants by the entirety. They separated and entered a separation agreement that W would have exclusive possession of the house for a certain period. The agreement further provided that at the end of the specified period the house should be sold and the proceeds divided between H and W. W later filed for divorce. Before the court entered a divorce decree and before the house was sold, W died leaving A as her sole heir. Who owns what interest in the house? *See In re* Estate of Violi, 65 N.Y.2d 392, 492 N.Y.S.2d 550, 482 N.E.2d 29 (1985).

PORTER v. PORTER

Supreme Court of Alabama, 1985.
472 So.2d 630.

ALMON, JUSTICE.

This is an appeal by Mary Jane Porter from a partial summary judgment rendered in favor of Martha Porter. The issue is whether a divorce decree destroyed a joint tenancy with right of survivorship in real estate.

The appellant, Mary Jane Porter, and the late Denis M. Porter were married in 1948. In 1963 they purchased a house and lot in Jefferson County under a deed containing the following habendum clause:

"[Grantors] do grant, bargain, sell and convey unto the said Denis M. Porter and wife, Mary Jane Porter as joint tenants, with right of survivorship, the following described real estate. * * *"

"TO HAVE AND TO HOLD unto the said Denis M. Porter and wife, Mary Jane Porter, as joint tenants, with right of survivorship, their heirs and assigns, forever; it being the intention of the parties to this conveyance, that (unless the joint tenancy hereby created is severed or terminated during the joint lives of the grantees herein), in the event one grantee herein survives the other, the entire interest in fee simple shall pass to the surviving grantee, and if one grantee does not survive the other, then the heirs and assigns of the grantee herein shall take as tenants in common."

The appellant and Denis Porter were divorced in 1976. The final judgment of divorce contained the following references to the real property in question:

"[Fifth] (b) Defendant/Cross–Plaintiff [Mary Jane Porter] shall have the right to exclusive occupancy to the former residence of the parties, property now jointly owned by them until a change in circumstances warrant a modification of this Decree in this respect, and Plaintiff/Cross–Defendant [Denis M. Porter] shall maintain said property in a reasonably good and tenantable condition. Plaintiff/Cross–Defendant [Denis M. Porter] shall maintain adequate insurance on said property; shall pay all charges of utility companies, less charges for long distance telephone calls for persons other than Plaintiff/Cross–Defendant [Denis M. Porter], and shall pay all ad valorem taxes on said property.

(c) During the continuance of the obligations of sub-paragraph (b) above:

Plaintiff/Cross–Defendant [Denis M. Porter] shall pay all indebtedness as or before it matures under the present mortgages on the property involved, which payments as under principal will inure in equal proportion to the parties as joint owners."

Sometime after his divorce from appellant, Denis Porter married Martha Porter, appellee, and remained married to her until his death in 1983. There was no modification of the final judgment of divorce in regard to the real property, and neither Denis Porter nor appellant attempted to convey his or her interest in the real property prior to the death of Denis Porter.

Appellee, as executrix of the estate of Denis Porter (later substituted as Martha Porter, individually) filed a complaint for the sale of the property for division. She alleged that Denis Porter's estate was a tenant in common in the property with appellant, claiming that the final judgment of divorce terminated the survivorship provisions of the 1963 deed and made the parties joint owners of the property subject to a sale for division upon petition of either party. Appellant denied any termination of the joint tenancy and moved for summary judgment upon the pleadings and uncontradicted facts presented. Appellee answered by also moving for summary judgment.

The trial court entered a decree of partial summary judgment, finding that "Plaintiff [appellee] and Defendant [appellant] are co-tenants in the property * * * and each owns a one-half (1/2) undivided interest therein."

* * *

The issue is whether the divorce decree destroyed the unity of possession and converted the joint tenancy with right of survivorship into a tenancy in common by granting exclusive occupancy of the house to appellant. The major distinction between a tenancy in common and a joint tenancy is that the interest held by tenants in common is devisable and descendible, whereas the interest held by joint tenants passes automatically to the last survivor. Thus, if the granting of exclusive possession to appellant destroyed the joint tenancy and converted it into a tenancy in common, appellee would own a half interest in the property through Mr. Porter's will. If the joint tenancy was not destroyed, appellant would own the entire interest by virtue of being the survivor.

Unity of possession requires that the property be held by one and the same undivided possession. Unity of possession means that all joint tenants have a common right to possess and enjoy the property. Possession by one co-tenant is presumed to be possession by all.

Appellee argues that since the divorce decree gave appellant "exclusive occupancy" that means she was given exclusive "possession." This argument concludes that the unity of possession is destroyed, the joint tenancy is destroyed, and a tenancy in common results.

When one or all of the unities of time, title, and interest are destroyed the joint tenancy is severed and a tenancy in common results. This result follows from the rule of law that a tenancy in common requires only one unity, that of possession.

Thus, if we assume that by granting exclusive occupancy to the appellant the unity of possession was destroyed, then the joint tenancy was severed. No other recognized common law joint estate arose and we are left with the conclusion that the divorce court either granted absolute ownership to one of the parties or partitioned the property or some variation of the above. This result is contrary to the divorce decree. The granting of exclusive possession of the house to appellant did not destroy the unity of possession. The divorce decree provides that appellant shall have exclusive occupancy of the house "until a change in the circumstances warrants a modification of this decree in this respect." This retention of jurisdiction, with respect to the jointly owned property, indicates that the court left itself an option to later modify the occupancy or terminate the joint tenancy. This retention of jurisdiction to later modify the decree also indicates that the exclusive occupancy given to the appellant was temporary as opposed to permanent. * * * The mere temporary division of property held by joint tenants, without an intention to partition, will not destroy the unity of possession and amount to a severance of the joint tenancy.

The circuit court has the power to adjust the ownership of property held by joint tenants who are parties to a divorce action. Appellee argues that the divorce decree, when read in its entirety, severs the joint tenancy. No portion of the divorce decree, other than that quoted at the beginning of this opinion, sheds any light on the present controversy. Thus, we must discern from the previously quoted portion of the divorce decree if the joint tenancy was severed.

The decree refers to the property as "jointly owned" and the parties as "joint owners." These are the only attempts by the court to characterize the cotenancy in common law terms. The term "jointly" is consistent with either a joint tenancy or a tenancy in common. Mann v. Bradley, 188 Colo. 392, 535 P.2d 213 (1975), cited with approval in Watford v. Hale, 410 So.2d 885 (Ala.1982).

* * *

The lower court relied on *Watford v. Hale, supra,* and *Mann v. Bradley, supra,* in holding that the divorce decree severed the joint tenancy. Suffice it to say that each of these cases involved a property settlement agreement which expressed the intent of the parties to sell the jointly owned property and divide the proceeds equally. We do not deem these cases controlling under the facts in this case.

A divorce does not necessarily sever a joint tenancy. Although divorcing parties are usually desirous of settling all their property rights, there is no requirement that the divorce modify the previous ownership. A divorce decree which is silent with respect to property held jointly with a right of survivorship does not automatically destroy the existing survivorship provisions. The divorce decree is effectively silent as to the status of the property. To hold that the divorce decree severed the joint tenancy in this case would be to convey the property by implication. Real property cannot be conveyed by implication.

The divorce decree did not destroy the joint tenancy with right of survivorship. Consequently, the property vested in the appellant upon the death of her joint tenant, Mr. Porter. The judgment is therefore reversed and the cause remanded.

Reversed and Remanded.

IN RE ESTATE OF KNICKERBOCKER

Supreme Court of Utah, 1996.
912 P.2d 969.

HOWE, JUSTICE:

This appeal is from a judgment entered in several consolidated actions involving the validity of a will, a revocable trust agreement, [and] the severance of a joint tenancy in real estate * * *.

Plaintiff Bradford E. Knickerbocker and Christine Cannon Knickerbocker married on July 2, 1984. * * * On July 22, 1991, Mrs. Knickerbocker filed a divorce action against her husband. The trial court awarded her exclusive temporary use of the house that she owned in joint tenancy with Mr. Knickerbocker and issued a temporary restraining order prohibiting him from contacting her. On August 7, 1991, the court issued another order prohibiting the parties from "selling, encumbering or mortgaging" their assets. Thereafter, Mr. Knickerbocker left the state and did not return to Utah until after Mrs. Knickerbocker's death on December 7, 1991. The divorce action was pending at that time.

About the time she filed for divorce, Mrs. Knickerbocker learned that she was suffering from a potentially life-threatening disease, diagnosed after her death as malignant intravascular lymphomatosis, a rare blood disease. As Mrs. Knickerbocker's condition worsened, she expressed concern about the welfare of her two children to her attorney, Joseph Henriod, her mother, cross-appellant Elaine Cannon, and her brother, defendant and cross-appellant James Q. Cannon.[1] In an effort to preserve her assets for her children, she decided to establish an inter vivos trust for their benefit, execute a will naming them as her beneficiaries, and appoint Mr. Cannon as her attorney-in-fact. On August 21, 1991, while she was a patient at the University of Utah Medical Center, she executed (1) a declaration of trust and agreement establishing a trust for the benefit of her children and naming herself, Anthony J. Cannon, and Elaine Cannon as trustees; (2) her last will and testament naming Mr. Cannon as the personal representative of her estate; and (3) a durable power of attorney naming Mr. Cannon as her attorney-in-fact.

A few days before executing these documents but after the trial court had prohibited Mr. and Mrs. Knickerbocker from "selling, encumbering or mortgaging" their assets, Mrs. Knickerbocker executed a quitclaim deed "as a Joint Tenant," conveying to herself "as a Tenant in

---

1. James Q. Cannon will be referred to as Mr. Cannon throughout this opinion, and Anthony J. Cannon, another cross-appellant, will be referred to by his full name.

Common" her interest in the house. The deed was promptly recorded. After establishing the trust, she executed a deed conveying her one-half interest in the house to the trustees. * * *

* * *

Mr. Cannon filed a petition for formal probate of Mrs. Knickerbocker's will and formal appointment of himself as personal representative of her estate. The petition was ultimately granted. * * * The court also found that Mrs. Knickerbocker's attempt to sever the joint tenancy in the house was legally ineffective because (1) she did not effectively convey the property to a third party, and (2) it violated the August 7, 1991, order prohibiting the parties from "selling, encumbering or mortgaging" their assets.

* * *

Mr. Cannon, Anthony J. Cannon, and Elaine Cannon cross-appeal, asserting that the trial court erred in ruling that Mrs. Knickbocker failed to sever the joint tenancy in the house. * * *

I. THE JOINT TENANCY

Before examining Mr. Knickerbocker's assignments of error, we address cross-appellants' argument assailing the trial court's ruling that Mrs. Knickerbocker failed to sever the joint tenancy. This issue is most appropriately addressed in three parts. In the first part, we will determine whether Mrs. Knickerbocker's quitclaim deed from herself as joint tenant to herself as tenant in common was valid. Second, we will examine whether the deed violated the trial court's order in the divorce proceeding prohibiting the parties from "selling, encumbering or mortgaging" their assets. Finally, we will determine whether Mrs. Knickerbocker's conveyance of her interest in the house to the trustees violated the order.

A. The Unilateral Severance

Historically, a joint tenant could unilaterally terminate a joint tenancy by destroying one of the four unities essential to joint tenancy— time, title, interest, and possession. A joint tenant could destroy the unities of title and interest by selling or mortgaging his interest to a third party. Alternatively, a joint tenant could arrange a "strawman" transaction, in which he would convey his interest to a third party who would immediately convey it back to the grantor. However, a joint tenant could not terminate a joint tenancy by executing a unilateral self-conveyance because such a conveyance had no legal effect and could not destroy any of the four unities.

This court followed the common law approach in *Nelson v. Davis*, 592 P.2d 594 (Utah 1979). In that case, the plaintiff, Douglas Nelson, filed for a divorce from his wife, Betty Nelson. In the course of the divorce proceeding, the trial court prohibited the parties from disposing of or encumbering their assets prior to the conclusion of the case. A few days later, Mrs. Nelson, who owned a house with Mr. Nelson in joint tenancy, deeded her interest in the house to the defendant, a daughter of a previous marriage. She also executed and recorded a document entitled "Notice of Termination of Joint Tenancy in the house." Before the divorce proceeding was resolved, Mrs. Nelson died. We found the deed to the daughter invalid for lack of delivery and because it was executed in derogation of the trial court's restraining order. In the absence of a valid conveyance by deed, we held that the joint tenancy could not have been severed by Mrs. Nelson's "mere unilateral declaration of termination of such a tenancy."

The instant case is clearly distinguishable on the facts since Mrs. Nelson's notice of termination of joint tenancy was a nonstatutory instrument, containing no words of grant, while Mrs. Knickerbocker severed the joint tenancy by means of a duly recorded quitclaim deed. Therefore, plaintiff erred in relying on our holding in Nelson for the broad proposition that in Utah, a joint tenancy cannot be unilaterally severed by one of the parties. Cross-appellants cite to a number of recent cases which have abolished the need to convey to a strawman in order to sever a joint tenancy and have recognized that a severance may be accomplished by a unilateral self-conveyance. *Riddle v. Harmon*, 102 Cal.App.3d 524, 162 Cal.Rptr. 530, 532 (1980); *Countrywide Funding Corp. v. Palmer*, 589 So.2d 994, 995–96 (Fla.Dist.Ct.App.1991); *Minonk State Bank v. Grassman*, 103 Ill.App.3d 1106, 59 Ill.Dec. 802, 803–04, 432 N.E.2d 386, 387–88 (1982), aff'd, 95 Ill.2d 392, 69 Ill.Dec. 387, 447 N.E.2d 822 (1983); *Hendrickson v. Minneapolis Fed. Sav. & Loan Ass'n*, 281 Minn. 462, 161 N.W.2d 688, 691–92 (1968). * * *

A substantial number of jurisdictions, including those followed in *Nelson v. Davis*, have now recognized that a severance may be accomplished by a unilateral self-conveyance. While it is true that, as Mr. Knickerbocker points out, many states have not abolished the need to convey to a strawman to sever a joint tenancy, we find that the reasoning of those that have abolished it is more convincing.

The reasoning of the Illinois Court of Appeals in *Minonk State Bank*, 59 Ill.Dec. at 805, 432 N.E.2d at 389, is particularly persuasive. In that case, after pointing out that the Illinois legislature had already abolished the strawman requirement for the creation of joint tenancies, Ill.Rev. Stat. ch. 76, § 1(b) (1953), the court observed that "adherence to a rule which would make it more difficult to destroy joint tenancies than to create them, runs contrary to the basic concept of joint tenancy." *Minonk State Bank*, 59 Ill.Dec. at 805, 432 N.E.2d at 389. The court reasoned that if a person can create a joint tenancy by granting to himself and another person, a tenant should also be able to sever the joint tenancy by conveying his interest to himself. In addition, the court stated that the key to determining whether a joint tenancy has been severed is the intent of the parties rather than the four unities. The court held that a joint tenant clearly demonstrates an intent to sever by making a unilateral self-conveyance and courts should not frustrate that intent by refusing to recognize the severance.

We agree with that analysis. Like the Illinois legislature, the Utah legislature has recognized that the use of a strawman to create a joint tenancy is unnecessary. Utah Code Ann. § 57–1–5.[2] Continuing to require the use of a strawman to sever a joint tenancy would create a lopsided body of law wherein property owners are required to perpetrate legal fictions for one purpose but not for another. There is substantial support for the concept that it is the intent of the parties, not the destruction of one of the four unities, that should govern. 4 Thompson on Real Property 48 (David A. Thomas ed., 1994); II American Law of Property § 6.3 (1952); Samuel M. Fetters, An Invitation to Commit Fraud: Secret Destruction of Joint Tenant Survivorship Rights, 55 Fordham L.Rev. 173, 186–89 (1986) [hereinafter Fetters]. A unilateral, recorded self-conveyance sufficiently demonstrates an intent to sever.

We also find the analysis of the California Court of Appeals in *Riddle v. Harmon* persuasive. The court, after referring to the four unities as one of the ancient vestiges of ceremony that remain the law in many states, reasoned:

> "We are given to justifying our tolerance for anachronistic precedents by rationalizing that they have engendered so much reliance as to preclude their liquidation. Sometimes, however, we assume reliance when in fact it has been dissipated by the patent weakness of the precedent. Those who plead reliance do not necessarily practice it." Thus ... resourceful attorneys have worked out an inventory of methods [such as the strawman method] to evade the rule that one cannot be both grantor and grantee simultaneously.

Riddle, 162 Cal.Rptr. at 533 (quoting Roger J. Traynor, No Magic Words Could Do It Justice, 49 Cal.L.Rev. 615, 622–23 (1961)). We also note that other courts have been convinced by similar reasoning and have further asserted that it is contrary to sound public policy to prohibit a party from doing directly what that party could do indirectly through the use of a strawman. We agree and hold that a joint tenant may sever a joint tenancy by executing a unilateral self-conveyance and recording the deed.

In contending that this court should continue to require strawman conveyances to terminate joint tenancies, Mr. Knickerbocker asserts that such conveyances will ensure that one joint tenant cannot defraud the other by conducting a secret severance transaction. He points out that when one joint tenant secretly severs the joint tenancy, he is free to treat the tenancy as a tenancy in common for his own purposes and if the other tenant dies first, he may destroy any evidence of the severance transaction and become the sole owner of the property. Thus, he argues, a secret severance transaction allows the severing joint tenant to " 'have his cake and eat it too.' " Fetters, *supra*, at 179.

2. More than half of the states have statutorily eliminated the need to employ a strawman for the creation of a joint tenan- cy. 4 Thompson on Real Property 16 (David A. Thomas ed., 1994).

Although an unrecorded and unwitnessed unilateral transaction may allow one joint tenant to defraud the other, that is not at issue in this case. Here, Mrs. Knickerbocker severed the joint tenancy by conveying her interest to herself and promptly recording the deed. Not only did recording the deed eliminate the possibility of fraud, but it provided a clear indication of Mrs. Knickerbocker's intent to sever and it afforded Mr. Knickerbocker a reasonable opportunity to discover the severance. In these respects, Mrs. Knickerbocker's recorded self-conveyance is equal to a recorded strawman transaction, and it is superior to an unrecorded one. A joint tenant does not eliminate the possibility of fraud by executing an unrecorded strawman transaction because he may destroy all evidence of the transaction by disposing of the two deeds. Further, a joint tenant who fails to record a strawman transaction has not clearly demonstrated the intent to sever because he has reserved the opportunity to destroy evidence of the transaction. Finally, the nonsevering joint tenant does not have a reasonable opportunity to discover the unrecorded strawman transaction. He is completely dependent upon the severing joint tenant or the "strawman" to inform him of the transaction. Thus, sound reasons support our holding that a joint tenant may effectively sever a joint tenancy by executing and recording a unilateral self-conveyance.

B. The Order in the Divorce Proceeding As Applied to the Unilateral Severance

Next, cross-appellants contend that the trial court erred in finding that Mrs. Knickerbocker's unilateral self-conveyance violated the order in the divorce action providing:

> Each of the parties is restrained from selling, encumbering or mortgaging the assets of the parties, including any assets the parties brought into the marriage, during the pendency of this action.

* * *

* * * Mrs. Knickerbocker's unilateral self-conveyance did not violate the trial court's order unless it resulted in the removal of assets from the jurisdiction of the court. We find that it did not accomplish such a removal; it merely changed the form in which Mr. and Mrs. Knickerbocker held title to their residence. Therefore, the severance was valid, and the residence was held in tenancy in common at Mrs. Knickerbocker's death.

* * *

IV. CONCLUSION

In sum, we hold that the marital home of Mr. and Mrs. Knickerbocker was held in tenancy in common at Mrs. Knickerbocker's death because she severed the joint tenancy by executing and recording a quitclaim deed of her interest from herself as a joint tenant to herself as a tenant in common. This severance did not violate the trial court's order prohibiting Mr. and Mrs. Knickerbocker from "selling, encumbering or mortgaging" their assets because it did not remove the home from the court's jurisdiction. Likewise, Mrs. Knickerbocker's conveyance of her interest to the revocable trust for the benefit of her children did not violate the order.

* * *

Question

As noted in *In re Estate of Knickerbocker*, a joint tenant may secretly sever the joint tenancy. Should such practice be regulated by a statute requiring some form of notice to the other joint tenants? *See* Fetters, *An Invitation to Commit Fraud: Secret Destruction of Joint Tenant Survivorship Rights*, 55 Fordham L.Rev. 173 (1986); Mattis, *Joint Tenancy: Notice of Severance; Mortgages and Survivorship*, 7 N.Ill.U.L.Rev. 41 (1986).

TENHET v. BOSWELL   *leading case*

Supreme Court of California, 1976.
18 Cal.3d 150, 133 Cal.Rptr. 10, 554 P.2d 330.

MOSK, JUSTICE.

A joint tenant leases his interest in the joint tenancy property to a third person for a term of years, and dies during that term. We conclude that the lease does not sever the joint tenancy, but expires upon the death of the lessor joint tenant.

Raymond Johnson and plaintiff Hazel Tenhet owned a parcel of property as joint tenants. Assertedly without plaintiff's knowledge or consent, Johnson leased the property to defendant Boswell for a period of 10 years at a rental of $150 per year with a provision granting the lessee an "option to purchase." Johnson died some three months after execution of the lease, and plaintiff sought to establish her sole right to possession of the property as the surviving joint tenant. After an unsuccessful demand upon defendant to vacate the premises, plaintiff brought this action to have the lease declared invalid. The trial court sustained demurrers to the complaint, and plaintiff appealed from the ensuing judgment of dismissal.

* * *

An understanding of the nature of a joint interest in this state is fundamental to a determination of the question whether the present lease severed the joint tenancy. Civil Code section 683 provides in part: "A joint interest is one owned by two or more persons in equal shares, by a title created by a single will or transfer, when expressly declared in the will or transfer to be a joint tenancy. * * * " This statute, requiring an express declaration for the creation of joint interests, does not abrogate the common law rule that four unities are essential to an estate in joint tenancy: unity of interest, unity of time, unity of title, and unity of possession.

The requirement of four unities reflects the basic concept that there is but one estate which is taken jointly; if an essential unity is destroyed the joint tenancy is severed and a tenancy in common results. Accordingly, one of two joint tenants may unilaterally terminate the joint tenancy by conveying his interest to a third person. Severance of the joint tenancy, of course, extinguishes the principal feature of that estate—the *jus accrescendi* or right of survivorship. Thus, a joint tenant's right of survivorship is an expectancy that is not irrevocably fixed upon the creation of the estate; it arises only upon success in the ultimate gamble—survival—and then only if the unity of the estate has not theretofore been destroyed by voluntary conveyance, by partition proceedings, by involuntary alienation under an execution, or by any other action which operates to sever the joint tenancy.

Our initial inquiry is whether the partial alienation of Johnson's interest in the property effected a severance of the joint tenancy under these principles. It could be argued that a lease destroys the unities of interest and possession because the leasing joint tenant transfers to the lessee his present possessory interest and retains a mere reversion. Moreover, the possibility that the term of the lease may continue beyond the lifetime of the lessor is inconsistent with a complete right of survivorship.

On the other hand, if the lease entered into here by Johnson and defendant is valid only during Johnson's life, then the conveyance is more a variety of life estate *pur autre vie* than a term of years. Such a result is inconsistent with Johnson's freedom to alienate his interest during his lifetime.

We are mindful that the issue here presented is "an ancient controversy, going back to Coke and Littleton." (2 Am.Law of Prop. (1952) § 6.2, p. 10.) Yet the problem is like a comet in our law: though its existence in theory has been frequently recognized, its observed passages are few. Some authorities support the view that a lease by a joint tenant to a third person effects a complete and final severance of the joint tenancy. Such a view is generally based upon what is thought to be the English common law rule.

Others adopt a position that there is a temporary severance during the term of the lease. If the lessor dies while the lease is in force, under this view the existence of the lease at the moment when the right of survivorship would otherwise take effect operates as a severance, extinguishing the joint tenancy. If, however, the term of the lease expires before the lessor, it is reasoned that the joint tenancy is undisturbed because the joint tenants resume their original relation. The single conclusion that can be drawn from centuries of academic speculation on the question is that its resolution is unclear.

As we shall explain, it is our opinion that a lease is not so inherently inconsistent with joint tenancy as to create a severance, either temporary or permanent.

Under Civil Code sections 683 and 686 a joint tenancy must be expressly declared in the creating instrument, or a tenancy in common results. This is a statutory departure from the common law preference in favor of joint tenancy. Inasmuch as the estate arises only upon express intent, and in many cases such intent will be the intent of the joint tenants themselves, we decline to find a severance in circumstances which do not clearly and unambiguously establish that either of the joint tenants desired to terminate the estate.

If plaintiff and Johnson did not choose to continue the joint tenancy, they might have converted it into a tenancy in common by written mutual agreement. They might also have jointly conveyed the property to a third person and divided the proceeds. Even if they could not agree to act in concert, either plaintiff or Johnson might have severed the joint tenancy, with or without the consent of the other, by an act which was clearly indicative of an intent to terminate, such as a conveyance of her or his entire interest. Either might also have brought an action to partition the property, which, upon judgment, would have effected a severance. Because a joint tenancy may be created only by express intent, and because there are alternative and unambiguous means of altering the nature of that estate, we hold that the lease here in issue did not operate to sever the joint tenancy.

Having concluded that the joint tenancy was not severed by the lease and that sole ownership of the property therefore vested in plaintiff upon her joint tenant's death by operation of her right of survivorship, we turn next to the issue whether she takes the property unencumbered by the lease.

In arguing that plaintiff takes subject to the lease, defendant relies on Swartzbaugh v. Sampson (1936) 11 Cal.App.2d 451, 54 P.2d 73. In that case, one of two joint tenants entered into lease agreements over the objection of his joint tenant wife, who sought to cancel the leases. The court held in favor of the lessor joint tenant, concluding that the leases were valid.

But the suit to cancel the lease in *Swartzbaugh* was brought during the lifetime of both joint tenants, not as in the present case after the death of the lessor. Significantly, the court concluded that "a lease to all of the joint property by one joint tenant is not a nullity but is a valid and supportable contract *in so far as the interest of the lessor in the joint property is concerned.*" (Italics added; *id.* at p. 458, 54 P.2d at p. 77.) During the lifetime of the lessor joint tenant, as the *Swartzbaugh* court perceived, her interest in the joint property was an undivided interest in fee simple that encompassed the right to lease the property.

By the very nature of joint tenancy, however, the interest of the nonsurviving joint tenant extinguishes upon his death. And as the lease is valid only "in so far as the interest of the lessor in the joint property is concerned," it follows that the lease of the joint tenancy property also expires when the lessor dies.

This conclusion is borne out by decisions in this state involving liens on and mortgages of joint tenancy property. In Zeigler v. Bonnell (1942) 52 Cal.App.2d 217, 126 P.2d 118, the Court of Appeal ruled that a surviving joint tenant takes an estate free from a judgment lien on the interest of a deceased cotenant judgment debtor. The court reasoned that "The right of survivorship is the chief characteristic that distinguishes a joint tenancy from other interests in property. * * * The judgment lien of [the creditor] could attach only to the interest of his debtor * * *. That interest terminated upon [the debtor's] death." After his death "the deceased joint tenant had no interest in the property, and his judgment creditor has no greater rights."

A similar analysis was followed in People v. Nogarr (1958) 164 Cal.App.2d 591, 330 P.2d 858, which held that upon the death of a joint tenant who had executed a mortgage on the tenancy property, the surviving joint tenant took the property free of the mortgage. The court reasoned (at p. 594, 330 P.2d at p. 861) that "as the mortgage lien attached only to such interest as [the deceased joint tenant] had in the real property[,] when his interest ceased to exist the lien of the mortgage expired with it."

As these decisions demonstrate, a joint tenant may, during his lifetime, grant certain rights in the joint property without severing the tenancy. But when such a joint tenant dies his interest dies with him, and any encumbrances placed by him on the property become unenforceable against the surviving joint tenant. For the reasons stated a lease falls within this rule.

Any other result would defeat the justifiable expectations of the surviving joint tenant. Thus if A agrees to create a joint tenancy with B, A can reasonably anticipate that when B dies A will take an unencumbered interest in fee simple. During his lifetime, of course, B may sever the tenancy or lease his interest to a third party. But to allow B to lease for a term continuing *after* his death would indirectly defeat the very purposes of the joint tenancy. For example, for personal reasons B might execute a 99–year lease on valuable property for a consideration of one dollar a year. A would then take a fee simple on B's death, but would find his right to use the property—and its market value—substantially impaired. This circumstance would effectively nullify the benefits of the right of survivorship, the basic attribute of the joint tenancy.

On the other hand, we are not insensitive to the potential injury that may be sustained by a person in good faith who leases from one joint tenant. In some circumstances a lessee might be unaware that his lessor is not a fee simple owner but merely a joint tenant, and could find himself unexpectedly evicted when the lessor dies prior to expiration of the lease. This result would be avoided by a prudent lessee who conducts a title search prior to leasing, but we appreciate that such a course would often be economically burdensome to the lessee of a residential dwelling or a modest parcel of property. Nevertheless, it must also be recognized that every lessee may one day face the unhappy revelation that his lessor's estate in the leased property is less than a fee simple. For example, a lessee who innocently rents from the holder of a life estate is subject to risks comparable to those imposed upon a lessee of joint tenancy property.

More significantly, we cannot allow extraneous factors to erode the functioning of joint tenancy. The estate of joint tenancy is firmly embedded in centuries of real property law and in the California statute books. Its crucial element is the right of survivorship, a right that would be more illusory than real if a joint tenant were permitted to lease for a term continuing after his death. Accordingly, we hold that under the facts alleged in the complaint the lease herein is no longer valid.

* * *

* * * [T]he judgment is reversed.

Notes, Problems and Questions

1. A and B owned land as joint tenants. A granted a mortgage to C. Does this sever the joint tenancy? *See* Harms v. Sprague, 105 Ill.2d 215, 85 Ill.Dec. 331, 473 N.E.2d 930 (1984); Schaefer v. Peoples Heritage Savings Bank, 669 A.2d 185 (Me.1996); General Credit Co. v. Cleck, 415 Pa.Super. 338, 609 A.2d 553 (1992); R. Cunningham, W. Stoebuck, & D. Whitman, The Law of Property § 5.4 (2d ed. 1993).

2. A and B owned land as joint tenants. A murdered B. Who owns the property?

3. Tenancy in common or joint tenancy may exist in personal property. Further, some states recognize tenancy by the entirety in personal property. *See* 7 Powell on Real Property ¶ 621[6] (1998).

4. A and B owned land as joint tenants. They contracted to sell the property. Before the purchase price was paid, A died. B claims the proceeds by reason of survivorship. C, A's sole heir, claims one-half of the proceeds. What result? *See* In re Estate of King, 572 S.W.2d 200 (Mo.App.1978); Estate of Phillips v. Nyhus, 124 Wash.2d 80, 874 P.2d 154 (1994).

COOLIDGE v. COOLIDGE   *PARTITION*

Supreme Court of Vermont, 1971.
130 Vt. 132, 287 A.2d 566.

BARNEY, JUSTICE.

This is an act for partition of jointly owned property. The matter has proceeded to the point of a judgment ordering partition, but the division proceedings provided for in 12 V.S.A. § 5169 have not yet been ordered. The defendant, who opposes partition, appealed this judgment. * * *

The matter had its beginnings in 1941. The plaintiff and her husband and the defendant, one of their sons, were conveyed the premises involved in this litigation "as joint tenants and not as tenants in common." This, of course, carries with it the implication of eventual full ownership in the survivor of the three tenants. Kennedy v. Rutter, 110 Vt. 332, 340, 6 A.2d 17 (1939). The evidence discloses that this consequence was well understood and intended by all three tenants at the time of the conveyance to them. In 1966 the plaintiff's husband died and she soon moved off the farm. She is now seventy-seven and lives with another son, her only income being a monthly social security check of $64.00.

The statute under which this action is brought is 12 V.S.A. § 5161, which provides:

A person having or holding real estate with others, as joint tenants, tenants in common or coparceners, may have partition thereof.

By its express terms, this statute purports to authorize partition in cases of joint tenancy.

The defendant says it cannot apply where it is understood by the parties that the survivor is intended to be the ultimate owner of the total fee. But, as we have seen in Kennedy v. Rutter, *supra*, 110 Vt. at 340, 6 A.2d 17, survivorship is a particular attribute of joint tenancy. Thus, with the statute already undertaking to deal with common ownership which involves survivorship, the existence of a joint tenancy alone will not forestall its operation. It seems clear that the additional phrase "and not as tenants in common," while clearly delineating the title as a joint tenancy, including the survivorship characteristic, adds no new quality to the tenancy such as to distinguish it from that named in the statute. Indeed, even the addition of words such as "with right of survivorship" would add nothing to the quality or quantum of the joint estate, but merely more particularly describe it. Therefore, to remove the matter from the operation of the statute, it is clear something more must be required, otherwise, every joint estate, in spite of the express statutory language, would be immune from partition.

The defendant asserts the conversations at the time of the conveyance established an agreement barring resort to partition. The general law is that partition is a right incident to common ownership which a co-owner may demand absolutely. But it is also the law that partition may be barred by agreement between the parties, either express or implied, but that the mere contemplation against partition is not sufficient to raise such an implied agreement. Even so, such agreements may run counter to public policy as unreasonable restraints on alienation.

However, in this case the findings do not report any agreement barring [partition]. An examination of the pertinent testimony shows only that the parties understood and accepted the characteristics of joint tenancy, including survivorship, at the time the deed was passed. This falls far short of supporting any ancillary agreement [to] forego the right to partition. The judgment decreeing partition is supported by the findings and the evidence.

* * *

Judgment affirmed and cause remanded for further proceedings in implementation of partition.

* * *

Question

How could the parties have created the type of estate the son seeks? *Through Intervivos mutual Agreement*

VON BEHREN v. OBERG   *Partition*

Missouri Court of Appeals, Eastern District 1995.
902 S.W.2d 338.

CRANDALL JUDGE.

Plaintiffs, Larry L. Von Behren and Nancy C. Von Behren, appeal from the trial court's judgment in a partition action between plaintiffs and defendant, Shirley Oberg. We affirm.

Plaintiffs owned a three-fourths interest in real property consisting of 170 acres in Montgomery County, Missouri (hereinafter property). The property consisted of "some bottom land, some hill ground, some ridge ground and also [a] top field." The Loutre River flowed through the property, cutting off a bottom field. The property was accessible by an easement for a roadway over properties owned by others. The one and one-half mile roadway was mostly dirt and some rock and was in need of extensive repair. There was an old house on the property which plaintiffs valued at $1,000.00 because of its dilapidated condition. Plaintiffs valued the property at $65,000.00.

Defendant owned a one-fourth interest in the property. Her expert, the Gasconade County surveyor and a licensed real estate broker, valued the property at $80,000.00. He testified that the property was capable of being divided to accommodate the respective interests of the parties and that the resultant smaller parcels were more valuable than the property as a whole.

The trial court found that the property was susceptible to division in kind and ordered partition. The commissioners appointed by the court divided the property, allotting defendant 50 acres subject to an easement for ingress and egress and allotting plaintiffs the remaining 120 acres together with an easement for ingress and egress. The court overruled plaintiffs' exceptions to the commissioners' report. Plaintiffs appeal. *Tr. ct. ordered Partition*

In their first point, plaintiffs contend the trial court erred in ordering a partition in kind of the property. They argue that the diverse topography of the land, the difficulties in accessing the land, and some potential boundary disputes rendered the property incapable of division without great prejudice to the parties. *π's Argument against Partition*

In partition, a division in kind is favored unless it would result in great prejudice to the owners. *First Nat. Bank of Carrollton v. Eucalyptus*, 752 S.W.2d 456, 458 (Mo.App.1988). Partition is a question of fact for the trial court; and the findings of the trial court are afforded great weight if there is substantial evidence to support them. The test of whether partition in kind would result in great prejudice to the owners is whether or not the value of the share of each, after partition, would be materially less than the share of the money equivalent that each could probably obtain from the whole.

There was substantial evidence in the record from which the trial court could have found that partition in kind would not result in great injury to the parties. Defendant's expert testified that it was feasible to divide the land between the parties. The expert was experienced in dealing with real estate in Montgomery County and the neighboring counties and in dividing larger pieces of property in those counties into smaller tracts which he then sold as "recreational properties." In his opinion, the property was more valuable divided into smaller tracts than it was in its entirety. *Compare Eucalyptus*, 752 S.W.2d at 459 (partition in kind not as feasible where potential purchasers expressed interest in purchasing entire property, but not a portion thereof). The nature of the property permitted a division which resulted in each party receiving a parcel that incorporated the various terrains found on the property and that could be accessed by the existing road. *Compare Leland Stanford Junior University v. Treat*, 170 S.W.2d 115 (Mo.App.1943) (partition would result in great prejudice to five owners where the property consisted of 120 acres of well improved rolling land south of highway and 80 acres of unimproved flat land north of highway underlaid with hardpan and with a large ditch crossing north portion thereof; and where, after partition, one parcel would be without a road to reach it). The trial court did not err in ordering partition in kind. Plaintiffs' first point is denied.

In their second point, plaintiffs claim the trial court erred in confirming the commissioners' division of the property.

Rule 96.12 authorizes the court to appoint three commissioners to make the partition. Rule 96.16 permits the court either to set aside the commissioners' report "for good cause" or to confirm the report and order judgment thereon. "Good cause" must be that the commissioners did not carry out their duty. *Genetti v. Kesterson*, 775 S.W.2d 536, 537 (Mo.App.1989). That duty as described by statute is to "divide the lands and tenements, and allot the several portions and shares thereof to the respective parties, quantity and quality relatively considered by them...." § 528.260, RSMo (1994).

The approval or rejection of the commissioners' report rests in the sound discretion of the trial court. The commissioners act at the direction of the court and the court delineates the scope of their duty. If the court orders partition in kind, the commissioners' function is to aid the court in fashioning the partition. If the commissioners find they are unable to partition the property in kind without great prejudice to the parties, their sole alternative is to inform the court that they are unable to accomplish its directive. The court, not the commissioners, may then order a sale of the property. *See* Rule 96.18.

In determining whether the commissioners performed their duty when partition in kind is ordered, the court looks to the equality of the division. Equality is not to be decided by the number of acres but by all factors bearing on value. In *Genetti*, the appellate court held that the commissioners' division of property, which allotted 110 acres to a one-half owner and 80 acres to the other one-half owner, was not so disproportionate as to demonstrate that they did not perform their duty.

In the case before us, the court appointed commissioners to partition the property in kind and to make a report of their proceedings "according to law." The commissioners' report stated that they personally viewed the property. They allocated to defendant 50 acres, 7.5 acres more than her one-fourth share; and to plaintiffs 120 acres, 7.5 acres less than their three-fourths share. From the record, we cannot say that the division of the property was so inequitable as to justify our interference with the trial court's discretion. Also, there is nothing in the record to indicate that the commissioners did not act in accordance with the court's directive. Plaintiffs' second point is denied.

The judgment of the trial court is affirmed.

Problems and Questions

1. Although courts consistently express a preference for partition in kind, a split of authority exists over the evidence which justifies partition by sale. A number of courts adopt the position of *Von Behren* and treat the financial interests of the owners as the primary factor. *See, e.g.,* Ashley v. Baker, 867 P.2d 792 (Alaska 1994). Other courts give substantial weight to non-economic considerations and are exceedingly reluctant to force a sale of land. *See, e.g.,* Eli v. Eli, 557 N.W.2d 405 (S.D.1997). Which is the better view? For a decision directing partition by sale because it was impractical to physically divide land into individual parcels, see Chuck v. Gomes, 56 Hawaii 171, 532 P.2d 657 (1975).

2. Suppose one concurrent owner contributes more to the purchase price than the other concurrent owner. Should division of the property upon partition be made according to contribution or on an equal basis? *See* Landay v. Landay, 429 So.2d 1197 (Fla.1983); Jezo v. Jezo, 23 Wis.2d 399, 127 N.W.2d 246 (1964).

3. Now that you are acquainted with the concept of concurrent ownership, how should Jill and Steve Ryan take title to residential property?

4. The Ryans are considering condominiums and cooperatives as options to traditional home ownership, but they are unclear as to their rights as owners in either type of development. Specifically, they wish to know if they could redecorate their unit or use part of the land adjoining the building for a garden.

6. CONDOMINIUMS

Condominiums involve a special form of concurrent interest whereby separate ownership of housing or commercial units in a multi-unit building is possible. Condominiums are of ancient origin, but became a popular form of real estate development in this country only within the last forty years. Several factors have contributed to this condominium boom. First, land in desirable locations has become increasingly scarce thereby creating a greater need for high-density less-expensive housing and commercial units. Second, most individuals desire to purchase rather than rent housing consistent with the American Dream of home-ownership. Third, statutes have been enacted in every state establishing standards for condominium development. Fourth, federal agencies now treat condominiums much the same as traditional housing for purposes of mortgage insurance and financing. As a result, condominiums have become a staple of the housing and commercial marketplace.

a. *Creation and Operation*

A condominium is created when a project sponsor records a declaration that certain property is being developed in accordance with the state condominium statute. Any physical form of housing may be organized as a condominium. Commercial projects such as offices or stores also may be developed as condominiums.

Condominium ownership is defined in spatial terms. Each condominium owner holds title to a particular unit and an undivided interest in the condominium common elements as a co-tenant with all other unit owners. Common elements typically include the land on which the building has been constructed, structural aspects of the building, parking lots, and recreational areas.

Condominium unit owners are responsible for the care of their individual units. They also must arrange separate financing and pay their own real estate taxes. A condominium owners' association insures that the common elements are maintained and that reasonable rules and regulations for condominium living are adopted and enforced. *See* Notes 3–4 on pages 406–407. Each condominium unit owner is a member of the association and must pay an assessment to cover a pro rata share of maintenance costs and other community expenses. *See* Berger, *Condominium: Shelter on a Statutory Foundation,* 63 Colum.L.Rev. 987 (1963); P. Rohan & M. Reskin, Condominium Law and Practice (1998).

Condominium ownership is not without disadvantages. Conflicts often arise over rules governing the use of common areas. *See* Notes 3–4 on pages 406–407. It also is very difficult to remove unit owners whose behavior is undesirable. Moreover, in periods of economic difficulty some owners may default in the payment of common expenses. *See* Cribbet, *Condominium-Home Ownership for Megalopolis?,* 61 Mich.L.Rev. 1207, 1239–1243 (1963).

Notes and Problems

1. Although a condominium may be created by contract under common law principles, several areas of concern caused real estate developers to ignore the condominium concept until statutes were enacted to resolve these problems. Important statutory provisions include:

    (a) A statement that ownership of part of a building, "space" if you will, is real estate for all purposes. Thus, unit owners may convey and mortgage their units in the same manner as owners of single-family dwellings.

    (b) Prohibition against partition of the land and building except in narrowly drawn situations such as substantial destruction of the building by fire.

    (c) Prohibition against separation of the ownership of a unit from the undivided interest in the common areas that goes with the unit.

    (d) Provision for separate taxation of each unit.

    (e) Creation of an owners' association to manage the common areas and facilities.

See Note, *Condominium: A Reconciliation of Competing Interests?*, 18 Vand. L.Rev. 1773, 1775–1776 (1965).

2. The condominium is not the only type of housing development with an association of owners. A subdivision of single-family dwellings or a group of separately owned townhouses with party walls may also have a home-owners' association. The function of the homeowners' association in those cases, however, may differ somewhat from that of the typical condominium owners' association.

An association in a subdivision may be purely voluntary and exercise no more authority than any other private association. Such associations are primarily civic action groups. Other subdivision homeowners' associations are established by the developer, own the recreational facilities in the subdivision, and maintain those facilities by using mandatory assessments on all homeowners.

The townhouse homeowners' association is typically created by the developer, and each townhouse purchaser must join. The association owns the common areas, and maintains the common areas and building exteriors from assessments paid by the townhouse owners.

See The Home Association Handbook, Urban Land Institute Technical Bulletin 50 (1970); 7 Powell on Real Property ¶ ¶ 632.1[1]-[3] (1998). *See generally* R. Natelson, Law of Property Owners Associations (1989 & Supp. 1997).

3. Y, a condominium unit owner, was raped and robbed in her unit. She sued the condominium owners' association, alleging negligence in the failure to provide adequate lighting in the common areas. Does Y's complaint state a cause of action? *See* Frances T. v. Village Green Owners Association, 42 Cal.3d 490, 229 Cal.Rptr. 456, 723 P.2d 573 (1986); Martinez v. Woodmar

IV Condominiums Homeowners Association, Inc., 189 Ariz. 206, 941 P.2d 218 (1997). What result if the condominium unit owners had voted against the installation of expensive security protection? Should a condominium owners' association be treated as the functional equivalent of a landlord? *See* Freyfogle, *A Comprehensive Theory of Condominium Tort Liability*, 39 U.Fla.L.Rev. 877 (1987).

b. *Conversion*

Condominiums may be newly constructed or converted from rental apartments or hotels. The conversion phenomenon, introduced in Chapter 1, is explored further here.

The owner of an apartment building may want to convert it to a condominium for a number of reasons. On this point, consider the following analysis by one authority.

> Disincentives to retain apartment buildings for rental purposes have contributed to the shortage of rental apartments. The underlying factors include: (1) increased costs of ownership and operation of rental buildings, outpacing increases in rental rates; (2) fear of rent control; (3) increased interest rates; and (4) reductions in available federal income tax benefits. For a landlord facing such disincentives, selling the apartment building to a developer for conversion to a condominium often represents the most profitable option. Although the owner can generally sell an apartment building for five to six times its gross annual rent, it is not unusual for converted condominium units to bring fifteen to twenty-five times the gross annual rent.

Mursten, *Florida's Regulatory Response to Condominium Conversion: The Roth Act*, 34 U.Miami L.Rev. 1077, 1082 (1980).

Condominium conversion produces significant legal, social, and economic side-effects. One commentator has ably analyzed these side-effects, noting that advantages of condominium conversion include addition of relatively low-cost units to the housing market and revitalization of urban areas. Disadvantages of the conversion phenomenon involve depletion of rental housing stock and dislocation of existing tenants. Comment, *The Condominium Conversion Problem: Causes and Solutions*, 1980 Duke L.J. 306, 314–320. *See also* Kamer, *Conversion of Rental Housing to Unit Ownership—A Noncrisis*, 10 Real Est.L.J. 187 (1982) for the argument that condominium conversion improves the overall housing picture.

State and local governments have enacted legislation regulating condominium conversion in various ways. These measures include declaring a moratorium on conversions, conditioning conversion upon approval by a percentage of the tenants, and requiring that tenants receive certain advance notice of conversion and a right of first refusal on the unit they occupy. *See* Keenan, *Condominium Conversion Residential Rental Units: a Proposal for State Regulation and a Model Act*, 20

U.Mich.J.L.Reform 639 (1987); Mursten, *Florida's Regulatory Response to Condominium Conversions: The Roth Act*, 34 U.Miami L.Rev. 1077 (1980); Comment, *The Regulation of Rental Apartment Conversions*, 8 Fordham Urb.L.J. 507 (1980); Note, *The Validity of Ordinances Limiting Condominium Conversion*, 78 Mich.L.Rev. 124 (1979); Note, *Condominium Conversion Legislation: Limitation on Use or Deprivation of Rights?—A Re-examination*, 15 New Eng. L.Rev. 815 (1980); Comment, *Protecting the Elderly From Displacement by Condominium Conversions: Troy, Ltd. v. Renna*, 30 Wash.U.J.Urban & Contemp.L. 275 (1986). (The broad issue of governmental regulation of private land use is explored in Chapter 6.)

The condominium conversion phenomenon has slowed. Nonetheless, conversion of rental apartment buildings to condominiums and cooperatives continues in many areas. *See* Keenan, *supra* at 646–649.

c. *Time-sharing*

"Time-sharing" is a relatively recent innovation whereby a condominium unit is divided into time segments, often one or two weeks, and then marketed on that basis. Time-sharing may involve either a fee ownership interest or merely a right to use the property. The latter arrangement may take the form of a "vacation license," "vacation lease," or "club membership." Pollack, *Time-Sharing, or Time is Money But Will It Sell?* 10 Real Est.L.J. 281, 284–286 (1982).

Ownership time-sharing arrangements usually take one of two forms: tenancy in common or interval ownership. Under a tenancy in common ownership program, sometimes called a time-span, each owner receives an undivided fee simple interest in a unit as a tenant in common. By separate agreement among all time-share owners, each also receives the exclusive right to use the unit for a certain time period each year. Under the interval ownership program, every owner receives two property interests: (1) a tenancy for a fixed term for the same time period each year for a specified number of years and (2) an undivided interest in a vested remainder in fee simple which becomes possessory at the end of the specified number of years. *See id.;* Eastman, *Time Sharing Ownership: A Primer,* 57 N.D.L.Rev. 152 (1981); Comment, *Time-Share Condominiums: Property's Fourth Dimension,* 32 Me.L.Rev. 181 (1980). *See generally* M. Henze, The Law and Business of Time–Share Resorts (1990).

7. COOPERATIVES

Housing cooperatives are a well established form of multiple ownership. They were organized in New York City and other urban centers to give apartment renters the opportunity to own the apartment building in which they lived. Although condominium growth has tended to supplant cooperative development in recent times, the cooperative concept is still utilized. Typically a non-profit corporation is formed to hold title to the building. The corporation's stock is allocated among the apartments in the building, usually on the basis of their value. One who wishes to become a member in the cooperative purchases the shares of stock assigned to the apartment to be occupied. Together with this stock, the purchaser receives a long-term "proprietary" lease to the apartment. As a result, the purchaser has an ownership interest (shares of stock) in the entire project and the right to occupy a particular apartment as long as the purchaser retains the ownership interest. The rights and duties of the tenant-owner are set forth in the proprietary lease.

The corporation pays the costs of operation of the apartment building from the rental payments received from cooperative members. Operational costs include debt service (payments on the mortgage on the entire building) and maintenance. This arrangement poses one of the major drawbacks to cooperative housing. Cooperative members are financially interdependent. If several members fail to pay rent, the cooperative corporation may not be able to pay the blanket mortgage. All members then stand to lose their apartments through foreclosure unless they can raise additional funds to make mortgage payments. Usually reserves are available or special assessments may be made to meet the problem. Moreover, cooperative leases commonly prohibit assignment or sublease of the apartment without the consent of the corporation. This permits an assessment of the financial responsibility of prospective tenants.

Another drawback to cooperative housing is that lending institutions in many states are unauthorized or unwilling to accept a cooperative member's shares of stock and proprietary lease as collateral for long-term financing. Thus, the various kinds of mortgage loans available to owners of single-family dwellings and condominiums are not generally available to cooperative members.

See P. Rohan & M. Reskin, Cooperative Housing Law and Practice (1998); Comment, *Legal Characterization of the Individual's Interest in a Cooperative Apartment: Realty or Personalty?*, 73 Colum.L.Rev. 250 (1973).

Questions

1. Can a cooperative utilize summary eviction procedures to evict cooperative members who fail to pay rent or otherwise breach their proprietary leases? *Compare* Kadera v. Superior Court In & For County of Maricopa, 187 Ariz. 557, 563, 931 P.2d 1067, 1073 (App. 1996) (declaring that "the cooperative is a hybrid property arrangement wherein the line between ownership and leasehold blurs," and holding that summary eviction proceedings are inappropriate with respect to cooperative apartments), *rev. denied* (1997) *with* Quality Management Services, Inc. v. Banker, 291 Ill.App.3d 942, 226 Ill.Dec. 264, 685 N.E.2d 367 (1997) (noting that cooperative apartment was dependent on rent received from members, and ruling that there was sufficient indicia of landlord-tenant relationship to bring cooperative within summary eviction process).

2. How would you advise Jill and Steve Ryan regarding their desire to redecorate their unit and maintain a garden in either a condominium or cooperative development?

E. MARITAL INTERESTS

In order to counsel Steve and Jill Ryan about acquiring real estate, you must appreciate the rights of a married person in the property of his or her spouse.

1. AT COMMON LAW (JURE UXORIS, CURTESY, AND DOWER)

We have already considered the common law presumption that a tenancy by the entirety was created when a married couple acquired property as concurrent owners. In this subsection, we examine common law marital interests not based on concurrent ownership.

> By marriage, the husband and wife are one person in law: that is, the very being or legal existence of the woman is suspended during the marriage, or at least is incorporated and consolidated into that of the husband; under whose wing, protection, and cover, she performs everything; and is therefore called in our law-french a feme-covert, * * * under the protection and influence of her husband, * * * and her condition during her marriage is called her coverture.

1 W. Blackstone, Commentaries on the Law of England 430 (1765).[1]

One consequence of this concept of marital unity was a significant limitation on the right of the wife to own or manage the property that she brought to the marriage by gift, inheritance, or her own labor. Personal property, including leaseholds, passed to her husband absolutely and could be reached by his creditors. Choses in action could be reduced to the husband's possession and also became his property. The disposition of real property was more complicated. Title to land remained in the wife, but the husband was entitled to rent or manage her land during the marriage, and could retain any profits. Moreover, the husband could alienate his wife's land to the extent of his interest, and that interest could be reached by his creditors. For her part, a wife was entitled to support and maintenance from her husband. *See* Haskins, *The Estate by the Marital Right*, 97 U.Pa.L.Rev. 345 (1949). The husband's bundle of rights in his wife's property was termed an interest jure uxoris, whereas the wife was said to be under the disability of coverture.

---

1. Even in former times some individuals questioned this legal fiction. In Charles Dickens' *Oliver Twist,* Mr. Bumble is advised: "the law supposes that your wife acts under your direction." Whereupon Mr. Bumble exclaimed:

"If the law supposes that, * * * the law is a ass—a idiot. If that's the eye of the law, the law is a bachelor; and the worst I wish the law is, that his eye may be opened by experience—by experience."

Courts of equity, however, eased the rigidity of the common law by recognizing a wife's separate estate in her property. By trust or antenuptial agreement a married woman's property could be managed for her benefit free of the husband's control. As a practical matter, the benefits of a separate estate in equity were largely restricted to elite women. *See* M. Salmon, *Women and the Law of Property in Early America* (1986).

In the mid–19th century the states began to enact legislation known as Married Women's Property Acts. Mississippi took the lead in 1839. *See* Comment, *Husband and Wife—Memorandum on the Mississippi Woman's Law of 1839,* 42 Mich.L.Rev. 1110 (1944). The Married Women's Property Acts simply provided that the real and personal property of a wife should continue as her separate estate. Such measures effectively removed the disability of coverture and abolished jure uxoris. The wife's property was no longer subject to her husband's disposal nor liable for his debts. *See* N. Basch, In the Eyes of the Law: Women, Marriage, and Property in Nineteenth Century New York (1982); Chused, *Married Women's Property Law: 1800–1850,* 71 Geo.L.J. 1359 (1983).

The husband's interest jure uxoris lasted only during the joint lives of the couple. Hence, the common law gave the husband an additional interest in his wife's real property in the event she should predecease him. If the marriage had produced issue, the husband was entitled to a life estate in all his deceased wife's freeholds under the doctrine of curtesy. The husband's right of curtesy vested on the live birth of a child. It did not depend on the child surviving.

The common law also gave the wife a dower interest in the land of her deceased husband.[2] This interest arose at the time of marriage, but remained inchoate until the husband's death. Unlike curtesy, dower did not require that a child of the marriage be born alive. Under the doctrine of dower, the wife was entitled to a life estate in one-third of all inheritable land of which her husband was seized at any time during the marriage. The wife could release her inchoate dower by joining in a deed or mortgage. Upon the husband's death her dower right became consummate, and an assignment of dower property would be made for her benefit.

Additional characteristics of dower are noteworthy. First, unreleased dower rights remained attached to the husband's land even after he conveyed it away. Second, dower did not attach to equitable interests in land even though curtesy did. Third, creditors of the deceased husband could not reach the wife's dower interest.

The common law doctrines of curtesy and dower have not survived intact. Curtesy has been widely abolished by statute. Even where it still exists, curtesy has usually been modified to resemble dower. The current status of dower is more complex. Although common law dower still exists in some states, it has been materially altered or abolished in many

---

2. The wife eventually received an interest in her deceased husband's personal property. The Statute of Distribution (1670) provided that, after the payment of debts, the chattels of an intestate should be distributed among his spouse and children.

jurisdictions. There are several general schemes governing the wife's marital interest:

(a) Some states have abolished common law dower (and curtesy) in favor of a statutory elective share for the surviving spouse. These statutory shares have sometimes been described as "dower," thereby creating unnecessary confusion. The statutes vary widely, but usually give the surviving spouse a fraction of the decedent's entire estate, often 1/3 or 1/2. Statutory provisions generally expand the spouse's statutory share if the deceased spouse leaves no lineal descendants. The statutory share is in fee simple, not just a life interest, and covers both realty and personalty owned at the time of death. If the deceased spouse leaves a will, the survivor may elect to take under the will or renounce the will in favor of the statutory share.

(b) Some states permit the widow to elect a statutory share, the provisions of her husband's will, or common law dower.

(c) Some states have modified common law dower so that a widow is entitled to dower only in real property owned by her husband at his death.

Dower originally represented a crude form of social security for the widow. The system worked reasonably well so long as land was the principal form of wealth. However, as wealth increasingly took the form of stocks, bonds, bank accounts, and insurance, dower was less appropriate to accomplish this protective function. Today the statutory share is usually more valuable than common law dower. Nonetheless, the statutory share is more tenuous than dower in several respects. Since the statutory share only applies to property owned at the time of death, a husband can defeat his wife's interest by inter vivos or causa mortis gift of his property. Moreover, the claims of the husband's creditors are satisfied before the size of a statutory share is determined.

See 1 American Law of Property §§ 5.1–5.74 (1952).

Problems and Questions

1.　You represent W, a widow, in a state where she can elect either common law dower or a statutory share. At the time of his death her husband owned Blackacre (value $60,000) and a personal estate of $10,000 in excess of debts and taxes. Following his marriage to W, he had conveyed Whiteacre (value $90,000) to X. At the same time he had given his son, S, corporate securities worth $30,000. The husband's will left all his property to S. Advise W.

2.　O conveyed Blackacre to "A and his heirs so long as the property is used for agricultural purposes." A died, survived by his widow, W. The heirs of A used Blackacre for other than agricultural purposes. Can O successfully claim Blackacre free of W's dower?

3.　Can a state constitutionally abolish inchoate dower and curtesy? *Compare* Walker v. Bennett, 107 N.J.Eq. 151, 152 A. 9 (1930) *with* Opinion of the Justices, 337 Mass. 786, 151 N.E.2d 475 (1958).

4. What is the effect of divorce upon inchoate dower? *See* Heaney v. Nagel, 14 Ill.2d 520, 153 N.E.2d 75 (1958).

5. Assume W is entitled to a dower interest in her deceased husband's land. How is her dower interest determined?

6. When Reginald Vanderbilt died in 1925 his will made generous provisions for his wife, Gloria. In fact, Reginald's staggering debts exceeded the value of his estate. Did Gloria have any recourse? In *Little Gloria * * * Happy at Last* (1980) Barbara Goldsmith explains:

> Thomas Gilchrist [family attorney], knowing that it would be futile for Gloria to pursue her bequests, suggested that her only chance to obtain any money would be by exercising her dower rights. In so doing, as Reginald's widow, she would then have claim, before any other creditor, to a one-third share of the revenues yielded on the sale of the New York town house and Sandy Point Farm. But until she could exercise these rights, Gloria was destitute. Alice Vanderbilt gave her the money on which to live. (Dell ed. at 149.)

Would Gloria have received more favorable treatment under a modern statutory share?

2. COMMUNITY PROPERTY

Nine states—Arizona, California, Idaho, Louisiana, Nevada, New Mexico, Texas, Washington and Wisconsin—reject the common law approach to marital property interests in favor of the civil law concept of community property developed in France and Spain.[1] In these community property states, marriage is treated as an equal partnership. All property acquired during the marriage by the efforts of either spouse is community property. Property owned by either spouse before the marriage or received by one spouse during the marriage by gift, descent, or devise is considered separate property. Income from separate property is treated as community property in some states and separate property in other jurisdictions.

The problem of distinguishing between separate and community property is often difficult, and has given rise to much litigation. *See, e.g.,* Haldeman v. Haldeman, 202 Cal.App.2d 498, 21 Cal.Rptr. 75 (1962). There is a rebuttable presumption that all property is part of the community. Detailed records must be maintained to overcome this presumption.

Community property is a statutory creation. Consequently, there are numerous differences in community property law among the states adopting the basic concept. With this in mind, consider the following generalizations about the community property system.

Conveyance. Both spouses must join in a conveyance of community property. Each spouse, however, can individually convey separate property.

---

1. Wisconsin is the latest addition to this group. The Wisconsin legislature enact- ed the Uniform Marital Property Act effective January 1, 1986.

Management. Although the husband formerly controlled community property, today husband and wife are equal managers. Each spouse, of course, manages his or her separate property.

Claims of Creditors. Creditors of either the husband or wife can reach community property for debts incurred for community benefit. Further generalization is virtually impossible because this is the area of greatest variance among community property states.

Divorce. Absent a property settlement, the spouses equally divide community property. Each of the parties retains his or her separate property.

Death. At the death of one spouse, one-half of the community property remains with the surviving spouse. The remaining one-half passes by will or intestate succession along with the decedent's separate property.

Waiver. A spouse may waive community property rights by either antenuptial or postnuptial agreement. These waiver agreements are common.

See 7 Powell on Real Property §§ 53.1–53.09 (1998).

3. HOMESTEAD

Most states have established a marital property interest called homestead that is distinct from those interests previously discussed. Homestead laws are designed to advance family stability and security by protecting the family residence (homestead) from the claims of general creditors. Because homestead rights are of statutory or state constitutional origin, they vary from jurisdiction to jurisdiction. Keep this in mind as you proceed through the following material which by necessity contains many generalizations.

What constitutes homestead property is sometimes a difficult question. Generally, property qualifies for homestead status if the owner's family occupies the premises as its residence. In some states a recorded declaration of homestead is also required. Courts construe such declarations strictly, and failure to comply with statutory requirements renders the homestead exemption invalid. *See* Matcha v. Winn, 131 Ariz. 115, 638 P.2d 1361 (1981).

Homestead property is wholly or partially exempt from the claims of the owner's creditors. The homestead exemption is usually a fixed dollar amount, a stated acreage, or a combination of the two. States that utilize the fixed amount approach often set and maintain such a low exemption figure that the family does not receive the type of protection originally intended. For instance, a Tennessee statute provides that an individual is entitled to a homestead exemption of $5000 on a principal residence. Concurrent owners of a residence are allowed an aggregate exemption of $7500. Tenn.Code Ann. § 26–2–301 (1980). Jurisdictions that formulate the exemption in terms of acreage sometimes distinguish between urban and rural homesteads, providing a larger acreage exemption for rural property.

Obligations incurred by the owner in order to acquire or improve the homestead are not subject to the exemption. Thus, purchase money mortgagees and mechanics' lienors may reach the homestead for payment. Although subject to the homestead exemption, general creditors can reach the property to the extent its value or size exceeds the homestead exemption. *See* Bush & Proctor, *Piercing the Homestead: The Trial of an Excess Value Case,* 34 Baylor L.Rev. 387 (1982).

Homestead property is often subject to other limitations designed to protect the family. In most states it cannot be conveyed by the owner unless the spouse joins in the transaction. This effectively gives each spouse a separate possessory interest in the homestead which can only be lost by death, abandonment, or voluntary transfer. Upon the owner's death the homestead exemption continues for the benefit of the surviving spouse and minor children so long as the property is used as a residence. The precise interest received by the surviving spouse and minor children varies widely.

See 1 American Law of Property §§ 5.75–5.120 (1952); 2 Powell on Real Property § 18.03 (1998); *see also* McKnight, *Protection of the Family Home from Seizure By Creditors: The Sources and Evolution of a Legal Principle,* 86 Southwestern Historical Q. 369 (1983).

F. NON–POSSESSORY RIGHTS AND INTERESTS

Even if the Ryans acquire land in fee simple absolute, other individuals may have nonpossessory rights or interests in the same property. Therefore, in this section we examine easements, licenses, and real covenants.

1. EASEMENTS

An easement is the right to use or limit the use of another person's land. Easements are appurtenant or in gross. An easement appurtenant benefits land owned by the holder of the easement. Such an easement is viewed as attached to that land and is in a sense part of it. An easement in gross personally benefits the holder of the easement.

Land subject to an easement is called a servient tenement. Every easement requires a servient tenement. If the easement is appurtenant, the land that receives the benefit of the easement, and to which the easement is appurtenant, is called the dominant tenement. If the easement is in gross, no dominant tenement exists.

Easements are affirmative or negative in character. Affirmative easements are frequently utilized. They give the holder the right to use the servient tenement in some specified way. Negative easements are employed less often. They enable the holder to prohibit a particular use of the servient tenement.

A special type of easement—the profit a prendre—deserves mention. The profit is a right to enter the servient tenement and remove some part thereof, such as coal, gravel, or timber. The law of easements is applicable to profits, so they are not treated separately.

For a comprehensive treatment of the law governing easements, see J. Bruce & J. Ely, The Law of Easements and Licenses in Land (rev.ed.1995 & Supp.1998).

Problem

The day after you met with the Ryans, they called to say that they had inspected a house for-sale-by-owner on the outskirts of Centerville. They are interested in the property, but are concerned about a path that winds through the trees along one side of the lot. The present owner claims that there is no problem because the path is used only by students from a neighboring private school to travel to and from the nearest bus stop. The owner says that a previous owner had made some sort of agreement with parents of a few of the school children. The Ryans ask whether any legal problems will arise if they should purchase the property and block off the path. At the end of the subsections on easements and licenses you will be asked to advise them. As you proceed, keep this problem in mind.

a. Creation

(1) Express Provision

CORBETT v. RUBEN

Supreme Court of Virginia, 1982.
223 Va. 468, 290 S.E.2d 847.

POFF, JUSTICE.

Bernard R. Corbett and Marie Bullock, d/b/a C & E partnership (collectively, Corbett), filed a bill of complaint against Ralph H. Ruben and Dorothy K. Ruben (collectively, Ruben) seeking to remove a cloud on Corbett's title. The chancellor entered a decree in favor of Ruben on cross motions to strike the pleadings, and we summarize the facts as stated in the pleadings and the stipulations of the parties.

In 1962, Al Baker Maintenance Company, a partnership (the Maintenance Company), owned two parcels of land located at 212–14 South Payne Street (parcel # 1) and 219–21 South Payne Street (parcel # 2). By a document styled "Declaration and Easement" recorded that year (the 1962 document) the Maintenance Company attempted to impress a perpetual automobile parking easement upon the whole of parcel # 1 as an appurtenance to parcel # 2 on which the Maintenance Company planned to construct an apartment building.

In 1964, after the building had been completed, the Maintenance Company conveyed parcel # 2 to Lewis & Thos. Saltz, Inc., and parcel

1 to Albert E. Baker, Thomas Saltz's partner in the Maintenance Company. Later that year, Baker and his wife signed, acknowledged, sealed, and recorded a document styled "Corrected Declaration of Easement" (the 1964 document). Describing parcel # 1 by metes and bounds, the 1964 document recited that the 1962 document had misdefined the scope and term of the easement and that the Bakers "wish to correct * * * and redefine this easement". The 1964 document then stated that the Bakers

> hereby create and establish an easement for the off-street parking of seven (7) passenger automobiles on [parcel # 1] for the use and benefit of the owner and occupants of the apartments located on [parcel # 2], said easement [described by metes and bounds], the duration of this easement to be co-extensive with the life of the building constructed [on parcel # 2] and shall terminate when that structure no longer stands.

This document further provided that the Bakers "covenant and agree that the said easement shall be a covenant running with the title to" parcel # 1.

Corbett, successor in title to parcel # 1, maintained that a landowner cannot make one portion of his estate subservient to another portion and that the 1962 document was void. Ruben, successor in title to parcel # 2, agreed, the case proceeded on that theory, and we treat the agreement as the law of the case. The chancellor ruled that the 1964 document, despite its references to the void document, "is by its terms a grant of an express easement appurtenant to [parcel # 2] and that [parcel # 1] is servient thereto".

Appealing from that ruling, Corbett argues that the 1964 document was void because "one may not modify, change, redefine or otherwise correct that which is null and void." Corbett misconceives the ruling. The question is not whether one document can breathe life into another which was void *ab initio*. The chancellor did not rule that the 1964 document validated the 1962 document; he held that the 1964 document was "by its [own] terms a grant of an express easement", and we address our inquiry to that holding.

Yet, the 1964 document is inoperative, Corbett asserts, because it "does not make an express grant of an easement". Corbett seems to assume an imperative the law does not impose. Neither statutory nor common law requires a grantor to employ words of art so long as "the intention to 'grant' is so manifest on the face of the instrument that no other construction could be put upon it". Albert v. Holt, 137 Va. 5, 10, 119 S.E. 120, 122 (1923). We believe the words "hereby create and establish" employed by the Bakers signify such an intent.

* * *

Assuming the 1964 document created an easement, Corbett maintains that it is not an easement appurtenant, as the chancellor ruled, but an easement in gross, *i.e.*, an easement with a servient estate but no dominant estate, an easement personal to the grantee. And, Corbett says, an easement in gross is not transferable.

In Coal Corporation v. Lester, 203 Va. 93, 97–99, 122 S.E.2d 901, 904–05 (1961), we reaffirmed the principles that an easement is not presumed to be one in gross; that the intent of the parties is the crucial determinant; that one of the tests of appurtenancy is whether the easement is a useful adjunct to the property; and that an easement appurtenant is one capable of being transferred and inherited while an easement in gross is not.[1]

The easement reviewed in *Coal Corporation* was granted "forever", *id.* at 97, 122 S.E.2d at 904, and Corbett argued at bar that an easement is not appurtenant unless its tenure is permanent. We did not consider such an argument in that case, and nothing in our analysis supports the inference Corbett draws. Even when the grant is made without term, courts may presume that an appurtenant easement was intended to terminate when the purpose for which it was created can no longer be served. McCreery v. Chesapeake Corp., 220 Va. 227, 257 S.E.2d 828 (1979); American Oil Company v. Leaman, 199 Va. 637, 101 S.E.2d 540 (1958). When "the easement is intended to endure so long only as the purpose of its creation can be regarded as still existent, the possible duration of the easement corresponds to that of an estate in fee determinable rather than to that of an estate in fee simple." 3 H. Tiffany, The Law of Real Property § 760, at 210 (3d ed. 1939) (footnote omitted).

If courts can presume an easement appurtenant was intended to be determinable, there is no reason why a landowner cannot expressly make it so. Rejecting Corbett's argument, we adopt such a rule.

Pursuing his theory that permanency is essential, Corbett submits that an easement is not appurtenant unless the grantor specifically provide that its life extend to the grantee and his "heirs, successors and assigns". While such words are "language which strongly tends to preclude the idea of [an easement] in gross", French v. Williams, 82 Va. 462, 468, 4 S.E. 591, 594 (1886), they were not considered essential to a grant of an easement appurtenant at common law. Absent a statutory change in the common law rule, we apply it here.

Bringing to bear the principles reviewed in *Coal Corporation*, we hold that the 1964 document created an easement, that the easement is appurtenant to parcel #2, and that parcel #1 is servient thereto.

Even so, Corbett insists that neither the burden nor the benefit passed by conveyance to successors in title in this case. We disagree.

Under the explicit language of the 1964 document, the burden was affixed to parcel #1 as a "covenant running with the title". That document was signed, acknowledged, sealed, and recorded by the grant-

---

1. After our decision in *Coal Corporation*, the General Assembly amended Code § 55–6 (which provides what property interests may be "disposed of by deed or will") to include "easements in gross". Acts 1962, c. 169.

ors. Thus, the title Corbett acquired was burdened by the easement, an encumbrance he accepted with constructive, if not actual, notice.

Clearly, the benefit of the easement passed with the title to parcel # 2. It is wholly immaterial whether the easement was described in the deeds in Ruben's chain of title. " '[T]he easement * * * continues to adhere to the dominant estate to which it is appurtenant and passes with it to the grantee thereof, though not specifically mentioned. * * *' Minor on Real Property (2nd Ed.), page 124." Stokes Inc. v. Matney, 194 Va. at 344, 73 S.E.2d at 272. "Every deed conveying land shall * * * be construed to include all * * * appurtenances of every kind * * *." Code § 55–60.

* * *

Finding no error below, we will affirm the chancellor's decree.

Affirmed.

Questions and Problems

1. Y owns land within the boundaries of a Wildlife Area. The State executed an instrument providing: "Y is hereby granted the right to use the roads existing on other lands of the Wildlife Resources Commission for the purpose of ingress and egress to and from the above described lands by the most direct route." Subsequently the Wildlife Commission placed a locked gate at the entrance to the road and kept out all persons except Y, including Y's brother who came to visit. Y seeks your advice as to Y's right to receive visitors. *See* Shingleton v. State, 260 N.C. 451, 133 S.E.2d 183 (1963).

2. Must the dominant and servient tenements be contiguous in order for an easement to be construed as appurtenant?

3. B granted C a strip of land for use as a "right-of-way." Is C's interest a fee or an easement? See J. Bruce & J. Ely, The Law of Easements and Licenses in Land ¶ 1.06[2] (rev.ed.1995 & Supp.1998).

4. In *Corbett*, the easement was created by express grant. Easements also may be created by express reservation; that is, a transferor of property may reserve an easement to benefit land the transferor retains. *See* J. Bruce & J. Ely, The Law of Easements and Licenses in Land ¶ 3.05 (rev.ed.1995 & Supp.1998). Problems, however, arise when a transferor of land seeks to reserve an easement in the transferred parcel to benefit someone else. Courts are divided as to whether a deed may create an easement in favor of a third party. The traditional view, still held by many courts, is that a grantor cannot reserve an easement to benefit a stranger. *See, e.g.,* Tripp v. Huff, 606 A.2d 792 (Me.1992); Estate of Thomson v. Wade, 69 N.Y.2d 570, 516 N.Y.S.2d 614, 509 N.E.2d 309 (1987). In *Thomson,* the Court of Appeals of New York explained:

> Although application of the stranger-to-the-deed rule may, at times, frustrate a grantor's intent, any such frustration can readily be avoided by the direct conveyance of an easement of record from the grantor to the third party. The overriding considerations of the "public policy

favoring certainty in title to real property, both to protect bona fide purchasers and to avoid conflicts of ownership, which may engender needless litigation" (*Matter of Violi*, 65 N.Y.2d 392, 396, 492 N.Y.S.2d 550, 482 N.E.2d 29), persuade us to decline to depart from our settled rule.

A number of other courts have jettisoned the traditional view, recognizing easements reserved in third persons in order to effectuate the intention of the transferor. *See, e.g.,* Aszmus v. Nelson, 743 P.2d 377 (Alaska 1987); Michael J. Uhes, Ph.D., P.C., Profit Sharing Plan & Trust v. Blake, 892 P.2d 439 (Colo.App.1995); Garza v. Grayson, 255 Or. 413, 467 P.2d 960 (1970). *See generally* J. Bruce & J. Ely, The Law of Easements and Licenses in Land ¶ 3.05 (rev.ed. 1995 & Supp.1998)(discussing division of authority). Which is the better approach?

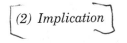

(2) Implication

SCHMIDT v. EGER

Court of Appeals of Michigan, 1980.
94 Mich.App. 728, 289 N.W.2d 851.

PER CURIAM.

Plaintiff appeals as of right the judgment of the trial court in favor of defendants denying the relief requested in plaintiff's complaint.

Plaintiff leased two lots of an industrial complex to a corporation controlled by the defendants on November 12, 1968. Plaintiff subsequently became the owner of a small area of property at the southern end of the two lots, and this property also became a part of the defendants' leasehold. In 1969, this new area was developed, a lawn established, and a ditch put in. This ditch carries water off of other land owned by plaintiff and is the subject of the instant case. Testimony differed as to when it was first developed; plaintiff testified that the work done in 1969 was a modification of a ditch that had existed prior to the acquisition of the property to the south of the original two lots, although he had previously given answers to written interrogatories stating that the ditch was first put in simultaneously with the other improvements. Defendant Frank Eger testified that the ditch did not exist prior to the establishment of the leasehold, but that it was constructed after he commenced occupation.

A history of litigation between the parties commenced in 1972 when defendants' corporation brought suit seeking specific performance of an option to purchase the property that was contained in the lease. A consent judgment was entered and defendants took title to the property. On October 9, 1973, defendants announced to plaintiff their intention to grade and level that portion of the property that contained the ditch, a manhole, access structures, and buried drain tile. Plaintiff filed suit seeking an injunction against the defendants prohibiting them from interfering with the drainage ditch. Accelerated judgment was granted to defendants, but this Court reversed and remanded for trial. Schmidt v.

Eger, 69 Mich.App. 457, 245 N.W.2d 90 (1976), lv. den. 399 Mich. 867 (1977).

* * * Judgment was for defendants and plaintiff has appealed as of right * * *.

I.

Plaintiff claims the drainage ditch represents an easement by implied reservation. To establish an implied easement, three things must be shown: (1) that during the unity of title an apparently permanent and obvious servitude was imposed on one part of an estate in favor of another, (2) continuity, and (3) that the easement is reasonably necessary for the fair enjoyment of the property it benefits. Harrison v. Heald, 360 Mich. 203, 103 N.W.2d 348 (1960); Rannels v. Marx, 357 Mich. 453, 98 N.W.2d 583 (1959). The party asserting the easement has the burden of proving the claim by a preponderance of the evidence. Kahn–Reiss, Inc. v. Detroit & Northern Savings & Loan Ass'n, 59 Mich.App. 1, 12, 228 N.W.2d 816 (1975). The trial court found that the continuity element was established, given the nature of drains, and we agree. Our discussion is limited to the remaining two elements.

A. NECESSITY

On the necessity element, the trial court held that plaintiff needed to establish that the easement was *strictly* necessary before it would be implied. We hold that this was error, and that plaintiff needed only to establish that the easement was *reasonably* necessary. We do note, however, that some confusion in this regard is justified, as Michigan law has been less than clear on the point and as easements by implication may arise under different circumstances.

An implied easement may arise in essentially two ways.[1] First, it can be implied from necessity. In this situation, an estate has been severed, leaving the dominant estate without a means of access. Before an easement will be implied in this situation, the party who would assert the easement must establish that it is strictly necessary for the enjoyment of the property. Mere convenience, or even reasonable necessity, will not be sufficient if there are alternative routes, even if these alternatives prove more difficult or more expensive. All implied easements are based on the presumed intent of the parties, but this sort is additionally supported by the public policy favoring the productive and beneficial enjoyment of property. Easements implied from necessity have been recognized in Michigan as requiring a showing of strict necessity. This sort of implied easement is not dependent on the existence of any established route or quasi-easement prior to the severance of the estate by the common grantor; it is first established after the severance.

The easement with which we are involved in the instant case is of a different type, what Dean Cribbet refers to as easements implied from

---

1. See generally, 2 Thompson on Real Property, §§ 351–355, 362–364, pp. 308– 371, 410–446, Cribbet, Principles of the Law of Property, pp. 335–340.

quasi-easements.[2] It requires that at the severance of an estate an obvious and apparently permanent servitude already exists over one part of the estate and in favor of the other. It also requires a showing of necessity, but whether that necessity needs to be "strict", or only "reasonable", traditionally has depended on whether the easement claimed was an implied *grant,* or an implied reservation.

It appears to be the position of a majority of jurisdictions that an implied grant of an easement requires only a showing of reasonable necessity, while an implied reservation of an easement in the grantor requires a showing of strict necessity. The difference seems based on the idea that a grantor will not be allowed to derogate from the grant by alleging to retain interests which the deed purports to convey.[3] Because the grantor is not allowed to assert the reservation of an implied easement based on the existence of a * * * quasi-easement, the claim of an implied reservation must, under this view, proceed as if no * * * quasi-easement existed, and requires a showing of strict necessity as in the case of an easement implied from necessity.

Several Michigan cases have adopted this position, and held that when an implied reservation is involved, as in the instant case, a showing of strict necessity is required. Brown v. Fuller, 165 Mich. 162, 130 N.W. 621 (1911); von Meding v. Strahl, 319 Mich. 598, 605–606, 30 N.W.2d 363 (1948); Kahn-Reiss, Inc. v. Detroit & Northern Savings & Loan Ass'n, supra; Wilson v. Anglin, 72 Mich.App. 212, 249 N.W.2d 360 (1976). An apparent minority of jurisdictions hold that there is no difference between a grant and a reservation for the purposes of implying an easement from an existing servitude or quasi-easement, and that only reasonable necessity is required for both. Despite the holdings in the cases cited above, this seems to be the most recent position adopted by our Supreme Court. * * * While it is true that the Supreme Court in *Harrison* did not specifically direct itself to the precise issue of what quantum of necessity was to be required in cases of implied reservations, as opposed to implied grants, it is clear that it intended the same rules to apply to each. We thus view *Harrison* as controlling, and as requiring only a showing of reasonable necessity, regardless of whether a grant or reservation is sought to be implied. To the extent that post-*Harrison* decisions of this Court may be read to require a showing of strict necessity when an implied reservation is involved, it is our opinion that they were wrongly decided.

Applying a test of reasonable necessity to the facts of the instant case, we hold plaintiff sufficiently established this element. The trial court found that the several alternative drainage plans open to the plaintiff would require considerable work. One of the expert witnesses

---

2. See note 1, *supra.*

3. An easement implied grant is not, however, without a similar problem, in that it amounts to a conveyance of an interest in land without the writing required by the statute of frauds. Courts have not generally

concerned themselves with this point, perhaps viewing the requirements for establishing an implied easement as stringent enough to satisfy the purposes of the statute.

who testified placed the cost of a new drainage system at between $30,000 and $35,000. Under the facts and circumstances of this case, the effort and expense were great enough for implication of the easement to be reasonably necessary.

B. APPARENTNESS

In order to establish his easement, plaintiff also needs to show that it was apparent at the date of severance. The testimony conflicted as to whether the drain existed prior to November 12, 1968, the date of the lease, but the trial court found that it did not, that it instead came into existence in 1969. The lease contained an option to purchase the property, and on June 22, 1973, the defendants purchased the property they had been leasing. Since the trial court held that the necessity element had not been established, it felt that it was unnecessary to decide the question of when severance took place, but remarked that if called upon to do so, the appropriate date of severance would have been the date of the lease. Since we reach a different result on the necessity element, we must decide the date of severance. If, as the trial court suggested, that date is the date of the lease, then plaintiff has failed to establish the element of apparentness since the drain was found to have first come into existence after the date of the lease. If, on the other hand the plaintiff is right in asserting that severance did not take place until 1973 when defendants took title to the land, then the easement was apparent and plaintiff will have shown all the elements necessary to the establishment of an implied easement.

We have found no Michigan cases directly on point, but our analysis of the purpose of the severance requirement leads us to conclude that the appropriate date of severance is the date of the lease.

Simply put, a severance is required because it is legally impossible to have an "easement" in your own land. If a person owns two adjacent tracts of land and imposes a servitude on one tract for the benefit of the other, there exists only a quasi-easement that may ripen into a full easement when one of the tracts is conveyed. A lease is a conveyance of property for a term, and while the grantor retains a reversionary interest in the land, the right to use and possess the land has passed to the lessee. It is for this reason that while an easement cannot exist over one part of a person's land in favor of another part when both parts remain in that person's possession, an easement may exist when one part is conveyed to a lessee. See 5 Restatement Property, § 475, p. 2976 (Illustration 1). The Restatement's drafters, when addressing the issue of severance, wisely chose to speak in terms of the severance of a single *possessory interest*. 5 Restatement Property, § 474, pp. 2972–2975. The lessor, having conveyed his possessory interest in a tract of land for a period of time, must establish his right to use an easement in the land conveyed in the manner generally provided for establishing easements. In the instant case the defendants took a possessory interest in the land in 1968. In 1973 they joined with this possessory interest all the other property interests in the land that the deed conveyed. Given the nature and purpose of the severance requirement, we hold that the date of severance cannot be placed in the middle of a continuous possessory interest, but must instead be placed at the point where the possessory interest first arose, which in this case is November 12, 1968, the date of the lease. Because the trial court found that the drain did not come into existence until 1969, we hold that it was not "apparent" as of the date of severance. Plaintiff thus failed to satisfy one of the necessary elements, and the trial court did not err in holding that he failed to establish an implied easement.

* * *

Affirmed.

Notes and Questions

1. How do easements implied from quasi-easements differ from easements of necessity?

2. Was the *Schmidt* court correct that the apparentness test would have been met if the drain had been in existence at the time of severance?

3. How may the requisite severance of commonly-owned land occur other than by lease?

4. As indicated in *Schmidt*, necessity is a prerequisite for both easements implied from quasi-easements and easements of necessity. The necessity required to imply an easement from a quasi-easement goes to the question of whether the parties intended an existing use to continue. On the other hand, the necessity required to imply an easement of necessity goes to the question of whether the parties intended a new use to arise. In this latter case, public policy favoring land utilization also provides strong support for the implication of an easement.

As discussed in *Schmidt*, opinion is divided as to the necessity standard for an easement implied from a quasi-easement. Similarly, there is a split of authority as to whether strict or reasonable necessity is required for an easement of necessity, but typically no distinction is drawn between implied grants and implied reservations. *See* J. Bruce & J. Ely, The Law of Easements and Licenses in Land ¶¶ 4.02[2][c], 4.03[2][d] (rev.ed.1995 & Supp. 1998); 4 Powell on Real Property §§ 34.07, 34.08[2][d] (1998); Glenn, *Implied Easements in the North Carolina Courts: An Essay on the Meaning of 'Necessary'*, 58 N.C.L.Rev. 223 (1980).

5. Statutes in many states permit the owner of landlocked property to condemn a right-of-way through a neighbor's land. *See, e.g.*, Ala.Code §§ 18–3–1 to 18–3–3 (1997); Fla.Stat.Ann. §§ 704.01(2), 704.03–704.04 (West 1988 & Supp.1998); Wyo.Stat. §§ 24–9–101 to 24–9–103 (1997 & Supp.1998). The statutes vary but all require that the owner of the landlocked property show necessity and pay the neighbor for the easement. Prior common ownership of the dominant and servient tenements need not be established. Rights-of-way acquired under such statutes are sometimes referred to as statutory ways of necessity. *See* J. Bruce & J. Ely, The Law of Easements and Licenses in Land ¶ 4.02[4] (rev.ed.1995 & Supp.1998); Note, *Real Property: Mortgages: Easements of Necessity*, 47 Cornell L.Q. 293, 298–299 (1962).

WHITT v. FERRIS

Court of Appeals of Indiana, Fourth District, 1992.
596 N.E.2d 230.

CONOVER, JUDGE.

Defendants–Appellants Johnny P. Whitt, Sr. and Bonnie L. Whitt (Whitt) appeal a judgment in favor of Plaintiffs–Appellees Donald E. and Nancy L. Ferris (Ferris), Rick A. and Pamela F. Jones (Jones), and Norman G. and Valna R. Stettler (Stettler).[1]

We affirm in part and reverse in part.

Whitt raises the following restated and consolidated issue: whether the trial court erred in finding an implied easement in favor of the appellees.

In 1967, John and Mary Kumpf purchased approximately eighty-eight acres in Marshall County. In early 1968, they subdivided most of the acreage, calling the subdivision Beechwood County Estates (Beechwood). The plat map was recorded and was approved by the Plymouth City Planning Commission.

During the summer or early fall of 1968, some of the platted roads, including a road running east to west along the southern end of the property called "Tulip Drive", were graded. However, when the Kumpfs discovered each lot as platted was individually taxable, they vacated all the platted lots and streets, except for Lots 1 through 6 abutting a public road called "King Road", by recording a document to that effect in the county recorder's office.[2] No lots had been sold when the plat was vacated.

Lots 5, 6, 7, and 8 are involved in this case. Lots 5 and 6, which are located in Beechwood, as currently platted, both abut the intersection of King Road and former Tulip Drive on the northwest and southwest corners, respectively. Lot 7 abuts Lot 6 on its west boundary and Lot 8 abuts Lot 5 on its west boundary. Both Lots 7 & 8 abut Tulip Drive's former boundaries on the south and north, respectively. Neither Lot 7 nor Lot 8, however, is included in Beechwood, as currently platted.[3]

Ferris owns Lot 5 in Beechwood and former Lot 8 in that part of the subdivision which was vacated by the Kumpfs (vacated Beechwood).

---

1. When Ferris, Jones, and Stettler are referred to collectively, we will use the term "appellees".

2. King Road is a north/south public roadway which bounds Lots 1 through 6 on the east side.

3. Before the vacation of the subdivision, Tulip Drive was planned as a street sixty feet wide and one thousand and fifty feet long. However, only a twenty foot wide strip was ever graded for the road, with twenty foot strips of grass on each side. Even though they contend they have an easement over the entire length of what was planned to be Tulip Drive, the appellees only asked the trial court for use of an area sixty feet wide (the road plus the grassy areas) and three hundred and eighty feet long. Hereinafter, this area, which encompasses part of what was to be Tulip Drive and its boundaries, will be designated the "Disputed Parcel".

Jones owns Lot 6 in Beechwood. Lot 7 in vacated Beechwood is owned by Stettler. Bonnie Whitt purchased the property surrounding these four parcels, including the Disputed Parcel.

The Disputed Parcel is a twenty foot wide dirt and gravel road surrounded by twenty foot wide strips of grass on each side. The road through the Disputed Parcel was used over the years to access vacated Beechwood, most of which was farmland. In 1982, Stettler began using the road through the Disputed Parcel as his only means of ingress and egress to his property, Lot 7 of vacated Beechwood. Ferris used the road to get to his back lot, Lot 8 of vacated Beechwood. Jones also used the road to access the back of his lot, Lot 6 of Beechwood. Ferris, Jones, and Stettler have all used the grassy areas on the sides of the road through the Disputed Parcel for parking.

Whitt protested the appellees' use of the Disputed Parcel, especially the use of the grassy areas for parking. She then constructed a fence alongside the south side of the Disputed Parcel to match the one on the north side erected by Ferris. However, Whitt did leave an opening in the fence for Stettler's driveway. The appellees brought suit seeking to permanently enjoin interference with their use of the Disputed Parcel. Whitt brought a counterclaim for trespass. The trial court granted each of the appellees an implied easement sixty feet in width and three hundred and eighty feet in length. The court opined the easement could be used in the same manner in which a public road is used.

Whitt appeals from the judgment in favor of Jones, Ferris, and Stettler, and the negative judgment on her counterclaim. The standard of review on appeal is whether the trial court's judgment is contrary to law. *McConnell v. Satterfield* (1991), Ind.App., 576 N.E.2d 1300, 1301. Because the trial court entered a general judgment, we will affirm on any theory supported by the evidence.

The appellees claim the trial court's judgment is justified because (1) their lots were sold in reference to a plat showing the Disputed Parcel as a road [and] (2) an implied easement arose upon the severance of the parcels * * *. Stettler also claims he has a way of necessity because his property is landlocked. Except for the way of necessity theory as applied to Stettler's property, the trial court's judgment is unsupported.

I. WAY OF NECESSITY

A way of necessity is implied by law where there has been a severance of the unity of ownership of a tract of land in such a way as to leave one part without access to a public road. Where a grantor conveys a parcel of land which has no outlet to a public road except over his remaining land or over the lands of a stranger, a way of necessity over the remaining lands of the grantor is implied.

In the present case, former Lot 7 was part of larger tract originally owned by the Kumpfs. After a number of conveyances, the large tract ended up in the possession of the Browns. The Browns originally severed Lot 7 from the tract by conveying it to William Brown. Stettler acquired former Lot 7 through mesne conveyances beginning with William. The only access from former Lot 7 to a public road (King Road) is over the Disputed Parcel. The road over the Disputed Parcel has been used to access the public road since the lot was conveyed out of the larger tract by the Browns. Under the facts, the trial court was correct in finding a way of necessity over the road running through the Disputed Parcel.

However, the trial court erred in finding Stettler's way of necessity is sixty feet wide. Easements are limited to the purpose for which they are created. In the present case, where the easement is necessary only as a way to access Stettler's property, access over the twenty foot wide graded roadway through the middle of the Disputed Parcel, coupled with sufficient footage over the grassy area on the south side of the road to allow access to Stettler's driveway, is all that is necessary. There is no need to burden the servient estate further by allowing use of the grassy areas on the sides of the road for parking.

Whitt contends a way of necessity cannot exist because of a provision in both Brown and Stettler's deeds which provides "access to this parcel is not included in the above description." (R. 168, 176). In support of her contention, Whitt cites *Hewitt v. Meaney* (1986), 181 Cal.App.3d 361, 226 Cal.Rptr. 349, and 25 Am.Jur.2d *Easement and Licenses* § 34, which conclude the grant of a way of necessity will not be made where the terms of the conveyance show the parties did not intend the grantee's estate to have access over the grantor's property.

The trial court found the language of the deeds to be ambiguous, a determination which the Whitts do not now challenge. Accordingly, the trial court allowed the drafter of William Brown's deed to testify on the meaning of the limiting language. The drafter opined the language was included in the deed "as a word of caution to a prospective recipient of this deed that there was no public access to this property that was included within this description." (R. 324). The trial court did not err in finding the limiting language to be merely cautionary. Thus, the language of the deed did not prevent the trial court from finding a way of necessity in favor of former Lot 7.

II. EASEMENT BY REFERENCE TO A PLAT MAP

The appellees argue they have an easement over the Disputed Parcel due to the sale of their property with reference to the old plat map. They refer to cases holding that where a conveyance of land describes the property by reference to a plat upon which a street is depicted, an easement is implied over the entire street for the benefit of the lots represented in the plat. The appellees maintain that although the Kumpfs vacated the public easement prior to sale of any lots, a private easement exists to this day.

The cases cited by the appellees do not support the trial court's judgment in this case. The conveyances in the present case, unlike those in the cited cases, were made after the vacation of the plat.

When the Kumpfs laid out the subdivision on March 5, 1968, they conveyed to the public an easement over the Disputed Parcel and retained fee simple ownership in the land. Although the Kumpfs conveyed the easement on that date, they vacated the easement on February 26, 1969, stating "[t]hat they desire to divest all public rights in and to the streets located in said Beechwood Country Estates." (R. 161). * * * Since no lots had been sold at the time of the vacation of the plat, there were no private easements in existence at that time. Fee simple title to the Disputed Parcel, free of any easements, was in the Kumpfs.

* * *

References to the old subdivision in the deeds were for the purpose of showing the buyers where their lots were located; they were obviously not an attempt to reinstate the vacated plat. References to the original plat map did not recreate easements to roads in the now nonexistent old subdivision.

III. IMPLIED EASEMENT UPON THE SEVERANCE OF THE ESTATE

Generally, an easement will be implied where during the unity of title, an owner imposed an apparently permanent and obvious servitude on one part of the land in favor of another part, and the servitude was in use when the parts were severed, if the servitude is reasonably necessary for the fair enjoyment of the land. *McConnell, supra,* at 1302. Stated differently, an easement will be implied where (1) there was common ownership at the time the estate was severed; (2) the common owner's use of part of his land to benefit another part (a quasi-easement) was apparent and continuous; (3) the land was transferred; and (4) at severance it was necessary to continue the preexisting use for the benefit of the dominant estate. *See* J. Bruce & J. Ely, Jr., The Law of Easements and Licenses in Land ¶ 4.01(2) (1988).

Even though the owner of the dominant estate does not need to show absolute necessity, there still must be some necessity shown. *Fischer v. Revett* (1982), Ind.App., 438 N.E.2d 995, 996B997. In Indiana, a landowner seeking an easement to access part of his lot, when only a portion of the land is inaccessible, faces a heavy burden.

In both *Fischer* and *McConnell,* this court emphasized that a means of access will not be granted if another reasonable means exists. Accordingly, in *Fischer* the court found no easement was implied where a loop of a driveway which infringed on a neighbor's property was not necessary for ingress or egress. The court so held even though the loop had been used by the former owner of both tracts. Similarly, in *McConnell* the court found an easement could not be implied over a driveway which was originally a part of a single estate, but became the appellee's property upon severance. This was true even though the appellant presented evidence that if he were not allowed an easement over the appellee's property he would have to tear out part of his pool deck and retaining wall, or place a driveway over a septic system, to gain access to his garage. The court noted "[a] way of reasonable necessity must be more than convenient and beneficial, for if the owner of the land can use another way, he cannot claim by implication the right to pass over that of another to get to his own." 576 N.E.2d at 1302 (*quoting Shandy v. Bell* (1934), 207 Ind. 215, 189 N.E. 627, 631). The court also noted McConnell "could have sought assurances of ready access to the garage by means of Satterfield's driveway when they bought Lot B if that was important to them." *Id.*

Even though the road through the Disputed Parcel was continuously used over the years, its use by the Kumpfs and the Browns (the owners of the unified tracts) was for the purpose of reaching farmland and a dump. Under current case law, use of the road is not reasonably necessary for the fair enjoyment of the appellees' lots.

Fischer and *McConnell* dictate our decision here. Lots 5 and 6 abut a public roadway; there is no reasonable necessity to burden the Whitt's property to benefit the lots. In addition, there is no evidence to indicate that at the time of severance of the larger tract, the road was used to benefit these lots. The road was always used to access farmland and a dump west of Lots 5 and 6.

When Lot 8 was transferred to Ferris as a back lot to Lot 5, there was no garage located there. Ferris constructed the garage at a later date and built a driveway to the road running through the Disputed Parcel. At the time of severance, access to the lot could have been reasonably accomplished through Ferris's front lot. Even now, reasonable access can be accomplished by moving one to three trees to another part of Lot 5. Under *McConnell*, there is no need to use the Disputed Parcel to access the back lot.

* * *

The trial court's judgment is reversed in part and affirmed in part. The case is remanded to the trial court for further proceedings consistent with this opinion.

Note

Easements implied from quasi-easements and easements of necessity are the two traditional forms of common law implied easements. However, as indicated in *Whitt,* courts also commonly imply easements from conveyance of a subdivision lot by reference to a plat upon which roads and parks are designated.

DE RUSCIO v. JACKSON

Supreme Court of New York, Appellate Division, Third Department, 1991.
164 A.D.2d 684, 565 N.Y.S.2d 593.

LEVINE, JUSTICE.

Plaintiff is the owner of certain parcels of real property designated as lots 96 and 97 in the subdivision known as Manning Park on Ballston Lake in Saratoga County. Plaintiff took title to the property in 1983 through deeds from James, Joseph and Elizabeth De Ruscio which described the lots by reference to a " 'Map of Lots at Manning Park on Ballston Lake, Property of the White Farms, J.B. White, Owner, made by S.J. Mott, C.E., 1926', and duly filed in the Saratoga County Clerk's Office". Defendants Herbert L. Jackson, Mrs. Harry W. Deegan, James R. Young and Deborah M. Young (hereinafter collectively referred to as defendants) are also owners of lots within the subdivision, described in their respective deeds by reference to the filed subdivision map.

In 1987, plaintiff sought to build a residence on his lots, but was apparently denied an area variance by defendant Town of Ballston Zoning Board (hereinafter the Board) on the basis of lack of access to his property. According to plaintiff, he was directed by the Board to obtain easements over the paper streets of the subdivision necessary to gain access to his property. When defendants either refused to grant plaintiff an easement or denied him access to his property over the paper streets abutting their property, plaintiff, in December 1987, commenced this action seeking various declaratory and injunctive relief, including a declaration that he has an easement of access over the streets of the subdivision.

Following joinder of issue, plaintiff moved for summary judgment on his complaint. * * * County Court denied plaintiff's motion, concluding that questions of fact remained with regard to his claimed easement, and also denied the Youngs' cross motion. These appeals by plaintiff and the Youngs followed.

Turning to the merits, plaintiff contends on this appeal that he established his entitlement to a declaration that he has an implied easement over certain paper streets shown on the filed subdivision map and, therefore, that County Court improperly denied his motion for summary judgment. It is well settled that " 'when property is described in a conveyance with reference to a subdivision map showing streets abutting on the lot conveyed, easements in the private streets appurtenant to the lot generally pass with the grant' "(*Coccio v. Parisi,* 151 A.D.2d 817, 818, 542 N.Y.S.2d 405, quoting *Fischer v. Liebman,* 137 A.D.2d 485, 487, 524 N.Y.S.2d 720). Nonetheless, whether an implied easement was in fact created depends on the intention of the parties at the time of the conveyance. This requires proof that the deed from the original subdividing grantor referred to the subdivision map or the abutting paper street.

While courts in other jurisdictions have held that such an easement extends to all streets delineated on a subdivision map or plat (*see, e.g., Cohen v. Simpson Real Estate Corp.,* 385 Pa. 352, 123 A.2d 715; *Owens Hardware Co. v. Walters,* 210 Ga. 321, 80 S.E.2d 285; *James v. Delery,* 211 La. 306, 29 So.2d 858; *Danielson v. Sykes,* 157 Cal. 686, 109 P. 87), the prevailing and most current view in this State appears to be that a grantee acquires an easement by implication only over the street on which his property abuts, to the next intersecting streets, i.e., an easement of access.

Here, the filed subdivision map indicates that plaintiff's lots are bounded on the north by a paper street designated Hampton Road, which intersects to the west with Hawkwood Avenue and to the east with Lake Shore Avenue, on the south by the Youngs' property, on the west by Jackson's property and on the east by Lake Shore Avenue. It follows from the foregoing that, at most, plaintiff is entitled to an easement of access only, extending along Hampton Road to Hawkwood Avenue, which is the most direct route to the public highway. Under this view, the only named defendant whose property would be affected is Jackson. Accordingly, summary judgment dismissing the complaint should have been granted in favor of the Youngs and Deegan.

With regard to Jackson, it is our view that summary judgment should have been granted in plaintiff's favor, declaring his right to an easement over Hampton Road and Hawkwood Avenue. We note that plaintiff did not come forward with the requisite proof of the subdivider's intent in the form of the original deed to plaintiff's lots containing a reference to the subdivision map. However, no one appears to have contested that the original grants contained such a reference and Jackson admitted in his answer the existence of an easement of access in plaintiff's favor, provided that plaintiff was the record owner of lots 96 and 97 and that a subdivision map had in fact been filed, both of which were established by plaintiff. * * * Inasmuch as plaintiff seeks injunctive relief directing Jackson to remove trees allegedly planted by him on Hampton Road and/or damages, the matter must be remitted to County Court for further proceedings to determine the appropriate equitable or legal relief.

* * *

Order modified, on the law, without costs, by (1) granting summary judgment dismissing the complaint against defendants James R. Young, Deborah M. Young and Mrs. Harry W. Deegan, and (2) granting partial summary judgment in favor of plaintiff against defendant Herbert L. Jackson declaring plaintiff's right to an easement of access over Hampton Road and Hawkwood Avenue, and, as so modified, affirmed.

Note

Private easements implied from reference to a plat should be distinguished from public rights created by express or implied dedication. *See* Horrighs v. Elfrank, 727 S.W.2d 910 (Mo.App.1987). Subdivision developers frequently offer to dedicate fees or easements for public use. Indeed a municipality may insist upon such an offer as a condition of plat approval. *See* Chapter 6, pages 874–896 (discussing exactions). If the local government accepts the offer, the dedication is accomplished. Lot owners, of course, may use dedicated areas along with the general public. As discussed in *Whitt* and *De Ruscio*, lot owners also may have acquired wholly separate private easements implied from reference to the plat. These private easements may arise even if there has been no dedication. *See* J. Bruce & J. Ely, The Law of Easements and Licenses in Land ¶¶ 3.07, 4.05, 4.06 (rev.ed.1995 & Supp. 1998).

(3) Prescription

WHITE v. RUTH R. MILLINGTON LIVING TRUST

Missouri Court of Appeals, Southern District, 1990.
785 S.W.2d 782.

MAUS, JUDGE.

The plaintiffs * * * seek a declaration they have acquired an easement for ingress and egress by prescription. * * * The judgment of the trial court * * * denied relief upon the petition. The plaintiffs appeal.

The following is a summary of the facts.

* * *

* * * [T]he plaintiffs' 318 acres joins the defendant's 320 acres on the east. Neither tract is fenced. Except for a machine shed and cabin constructed by plaintiffs, neither tract is improved. The tracts are located in a wooded, sparsely settled area of Wayne County.

* * *

At all relevant times, an improved county road has extended generally north and south along the west side of the defendant's tract. An unimproved dirt road (road A) meanders through the woods, west to east, from the county road across the defendant's tract to the plaintiffs' tract. Road A varies in width and is bordered by trees, many of substantial size. The plaintiffs claim an easement by prescription in road A across the defendant's tract.

* * *

Road B, also an unimproved dirt road, runs northeast from a point on the county road, well south of the defendant's tract. Road B extends northeast to the southwest corner of the plaintiffs' tract[.] * * *

The plaintiffs bought their tract by a contract for deed on October 16, 1972. They subsequently received a warranty deed. The plaintiffs, and members of their family, used the tract for recreational purposes. Plaintiff Willis White was 70 years old at the time of trial, December 20, 1988. The plaintiffs have five sons. The plaintiffs and/or members of their family came to the tract to spend most weekends since the plaintiffs bought the tract. Initially, the plaintiffs placed a travel trailer on the tract. The five brothers built a machine shed on plaintiffs' tract using road A to haul materials. They later converted a portion of the machine shed into living quarters, or a cabin. The plaintiffs thought road A was a public road. They primarily used road A in going to and coming from their property. From time to time they graded and filled holes on that road. In the earlier years, when it was wet, they used road B, to avoid causing ruts in road A. At the time of trial, road B had become impass[a]ble by vehicle.

The plaintiffs bought their tract subject to a "timber deed" in favor of John E. Haggett. The timber deed sold all timber ten inches in diameter and above to Haggett and granted him eighteen months in which to remove that timber. He used road A in removing the timber. In an unexplained manner, the defendant learned of his use and directed that he stop using road A unless he paid her $50 per month for the privilege. To avoid delay, Haggett made the payments for several months. When he quit cutting timber, Haggett repaired the road at defendant's request. He said he "hauled gavel [sic] back in there and I had my bulldozer down there, you know, to level and so forth."

The defendant lived in Advance, Missouri. She bought her tract in 1968. She knew of the existence of road A at that time. She considered it a logging road, a type of road commonly found in the area. She did collect $50 per month from Haggett for his use of the road through March 1974. It was difficult for her to estimate how often she saw the tract. She surmised that she had been there once a year since she bought it. Some of her family and friends used the tract for hunting. On more than one occasion in the 1970's she caused barbed wire to be placed across road A at its junction with the county road to bar unauthorized use of the road. The wire was removed. At one time she caused a cable to be placed across road A for that purpose. It, too, was removed. She did not know the plaintiffs were using road A. No one, including her family members, reported to her that the plaintiffs were using road A.

Defendant acknowledged that exhibits D through S (photographs) showed road A in substantially the condition it had been in through the time she owned her tract. Those photographs unmistakably show a well-defined dirt road through the woods.

On July 12, 1983, plaintiff Willis White called the defendant and asked permission to cut some trees along road A. Defendant testified this was the first she knew plaintiffs were using the road. Negotiations between the plaintiffs and the defendant to establish the plaintiffs' right to use the road were futile. On March 19, 1987, the defendant wrote to Willis White. That letter included the following two paragraphs.

"Under no circumstances will your continued use of the logging road which crosses our property be tolerated unless you acknowledge in writing, within ten days of the date of this letter, that your use of the road has been and will be with our express permission only.

As previously indicated, I would be willing to enter into an agreement with you providing for your occasional permissive use of the road for a period of time. However, should you fail to acknowledge in writing that your use has been and will continue to be permissive, an appropriate legal action will be instituted in Wayne County, Missouri, to obtain a court order prohibiting your further use."

The plaintiffs did not terminate their use of road A. They filed this action on August 10, 1987.

The plaintiffs' basic contention is that the overwhelming weight of the evidence established they had acquired an easement for ingress and egress over the route described as road A by prescription and that the trial court misapplied the law in finding they had not acquired such an easement. The fundamental requirements for the acquisition of an easement by prescription are well established.

> "The elements that establish an easement by prescription have been outlined and considered in detail in countless decisions. The requirements have been summarized: 'An easement by prescription may be established by use which is shown to have been continuous, uninterrupted, visible and adverse for a period of ten years.' *Guerin v. Yocum,* [506 S.W.2d 46, 47 (Mo.App.1974)]." *Orvis v. Garms,* 638 S.W.2d 773, 776 (Mo.App.1982).

Of course, those fundamental elements have been refined and amplified where necessary by reason of the issues raised in individual cases. Such amplifications relevant to this case include the following.

> "To be adverse, it is only necessary for the use to proceed without recognition of the owner's authority to permit or prohibit the use; it is not necessary that the user intend to violate the owner's rights." *Johnston v. Bates,* 778 S.W.2d 357, 362 (Mo.App.1989).

A use may be continuous within the meaning of the above requirement, even though it is not daily.

> " 'Continuous enjoyment' simply means that the claimant must exercise the use as frequently as convenience or necessity requires consistent with the character of the property and the nature of the easement asserted." Bruce & Ely, The Law of Easements and Licenses in Land, Para. 5.05[1], p. 5–24 (1988).

* * *

It is not required that the adverse use be exclusive.

> "[T]he fact that the right-of-way traveled by plaintiffs was in fact used by other people did not preclude establishment of an easement by prescription in plaintiffs." *Beldner v. General Electric Company,* 451 S.W.2d 65, 75 (Mo.1970). "The claim of right need not be a claim to possess title as in adverse possession, but it may be a nonexclusive right to use the property." *Fenster v. Hyken,* [759 S.W.2d 869 (Mo.App.1988)] at 870.

The trial court made detailed Findings of Fact and Conclusions of Law. Those Findings substantially included the facts set forth in the above statement of the evidence. The Conclusions of Law included the following.

> "*The crucial element lacking* in plaintiffs' claim in Count I for an easement by prescription is that of notice. The uncontroverted evidence presented before the court is that defendant, or even residents within the area of Road A, have either *never received any actual notice* of plaintiffs' use of logging Road A or, received no such

notice until July of 1983. Plaintiffs therefore did not present proof that they have engaged in the requisite type of use of the roadway, with notice, for a period of ten (10) years and that, at the time of trial, such use, although possibly satisfying all other elements of easement by prescription, only satisfied all of the essential elements, including that of notice, for a little over five (5) years. *For these reasons,* relief requested by plaintiff [sic] in Count I, seeking establishment of an easement by prescription, must be denied." (Emphasis added.)

This is a clear determination by the trial court the plaintiffs established all the elements required for the acquisition of an easement by prescription in the route described as road A, but denied relief because plaintiffs did not prove the defendant had actual notice of their adverse use. The defendant seeks to sustain the judgment upon that basis. The issue presented in her brief is stated in the following terms. "Constructive notice of use is not sufficient." In support of that position, she argues: "Appellants would now have the Court hold that constructive notice of a use or possession will suffice to divest a property owner of its interest. The only constructive notice of ownership interest or claims of ownership interest accorded by the law is that in the recording of enforceable instruments and deeds in a recorder's office which are by statute sanctioned with the authority and ability to provide constructive notice by the mere act of recording." In denying relief, the trial court erroneously declared and applied the law.

It is generally recognized that to establish an easement by prescription, it is not necessary the owner of the servient estate have actual knowledge of an adverse use.

* * *

"The landowner need not have actual knowledge of adverse usage. Rather, the claimant must prove that the use was sufficiently open and notorious to apprise a diligent owner of its existence. In other words, the usage must be of such a nature as to charge the landowner with constructive notice." Bruce & Ely, The Law of Easements and Licenses in Land, Para. 5.04, pp. 5–19–20 (1988).

That principle has been established as the law of this state by the Supreme Court at an early date. In *Boyce v. Missouri Pac. R. Co.,* 168 Mo. 583, 68 S.W. 920 (1902), the Supreme Court was considering whether or not a railroad company had acquired an easement by prescription. In holding that it had, the Supreme Court established the law of this state in the following language.

"Theoretically the use and easement are with the knowledge and acquiescence of the owner as much as is the adverse possession of a defendant in ejectment. For the law presumes that every man knows the condition and status of his land, and if any one ousts him, or trespasses upon his land, or enters into possession and sets up an adverse claim thereto, and the owner does not ask legal aid to dispossess him within the time limited for bringing such actions, the law assumes that the owner has acquiesced in the adverse claim * * *. In point of fact, the owner, like these owners, may have had no actual knowledge, and therefore did not expressly acquiesce; but the law implies knowledge, and therefore consent. This is as true of claims to easements as it is to claims to the land itself." *Id.* 68 S.W. at 922–923.

* * *

The doctrine has been consistently followed.

"While it is correct that appellants and perhaps their predecessors had no actual notice of use, such is not necessary because from the surrounding facts, such notice can be constructive or implied * * *." *Auxier v. Holmes,* [605 S.W.2d 804 (Mo.App.1980)] at 810.

* * *

In the trial court, and in this court, the defendant has emphasized portions of the evidence to establish she had no actual notice of the plaintiffs' use of road A. Such evidence, of course, included her testimony that she had no actual knowledge. It also included testimony that no member of her family or their guests saw or reported use by the plaintiffs. She also in part relied upon the fact that Peck West, who lived in the immediate vicinity for thirty years, never saw the plaintiffs using road A.

This evidence does support the conclusion defendant had no actual notice of the plaintiffs' use. However, as above noted, lack of such actual notice does not defeat the plaintiffs' claim.

Even the defendant's evidence supports the conclusion that the plaintiffs' use was sufficient to provide constructive notice of that use. The members of defendant's family were there only a few days each year. Yet they acknowledged the existence of the road. The defendant was there perhaps only one day each year. The photographs in evidence taken May 21, 1988 establish that road A was well defined. The defendant acknowledged that road A had been in substantially the same condition since 1968. Witness Dee West described road A as better than the average logging road. The defendant acknowledged there had been adverse use of that road by placing wire across road A several times in the 1970's. She knew the wire was later removed. When asked why she placed barbed wire across road A the first time, she replied, "We could see where cars were pulling in, or vehicles were pulling in."

The undisputed evidence established that the plaintiffs and members of their family used road A virtually each weekend since 1972. The plaintiffs' use was readily apparent from the improvements that were placed upon the plaintiffs' property during the period of time in question. The net effect of the evidence in respect to the issue of constructive notice, was established by two witnesses called by the defendant. Witness Mike Clark had lived in the area and had been familiar with road A for twenty-five years. He said, "[i]t's a beaten path" and even though he had not seen anyone using the road, "I knew someone was using it."

When asked if he had seen Willis White use the road, witness Peck West testified as follows:

> "A.   Well, actually see him, I couldn't say that I have.
>
> Q.   Okay.
>
> A.   But I do know that he uses the road."

The weight of the evidence established the plaintiffs' use of road A was sufficient to afford the defendant constructive notice of that use. In denying the plaintiffs' relief, because they did not prove the defendant had actual notice of that use, the trial court misapplied the law and the judgment must be reversed.

The judgment of the trial court is reversed. The cause is remanded for the entry of judgment granting the plaintiffs relief * * * and declaring they have established by prescription an easement appurtenant to the tract owned by them for ingress and egress to that tract over road A as located by the survey in evidence. * * * The costs are assessed against the defendant. The cause is remanded for further proceedings consistent with this opinion.

Notes, Problems, and Questions

1.   How long must adverse use continue in order for the user to acquire a prescriptive easement? Generally, the courts have held that the period of use required is the same as the period of occupancy necessary to obtain title to land by adverse possession. Hence, one must look to the local statute of limitations on actions to recover possession of land, often fifteen or twenty years. In order to satisfy the prescriptive period, the owner of the dominant tenement may "tack" on the time predecessors in title used the claimed easement. *See* 4 Powell on Real Property § 34.10 (1998).

2.   What result in *White* if the landowner had effectively barricaded the roadway during the prescriptive period?

3.   Contrary to the position taken in *White*, courts in many jurisdictions assert that an adverse use must be "exclusive." What is connoted by this requirement? Is usage in common with the owner or another unauthorized user a sufficient basis for a prescriptive easement? *See* Hoffman v. United Iron and Metal Company, 108 Md.App. 117, 671 A.2d 55 (1996); Gilman v. McCrary, 97 N.M. 376, 640 P.2d 482 (1982).

4.   What is the scope of a prescriptive easement once it has been established? *See Clemson University* case on page 366.

5.   What policy justifies the doctrine of prescriptive easement? Should the party obtaining a prescriptive easement be required to compensate the owner of the servient estate? *See* Note, "*Warsaw v. Chicago Metallic Ceilings, Inc.:*" *Compensation for Prescriptive Easements*, 19 Loy.L.A.L.Rev. 111 (1985).

STATE EX REL. HAMAN v. FOX

Supreme Court of Idaho, 1979.
100 Idaho 140, 594 P.2d 1093.

McFADDEN, JUSTICE.

This is an action brought by the Prosecuting Attorney of Kootenai County on behalf of the people of the state of Idaho to establish public rights in and to privately owned water front property on Lake Coeur d'Alene. The district court determined that the public had no right or interest in the property and gave judgment to the property owners. We affirm.

THE FACTS

Defendants-respondents C. R. W. Fox and Eileen Fox, husband and wife, and Burgess K. McDonald, personal representative of the estate of Carmelita K. McDonald, deceased, own adjoining residential properties in the City of Coeur d'Alene. The properties consist of two residential lots in the Lake Shore Addition Plat together with two water front parcels abutting the waters of Lake Coeur d'Alene. The water front property is separated from the platted lots by Lake Shore Drive, a dedicated public street. Respondents' homes and yards are in the platted lots to the north of Lake Shore Drive. The water front lots to the south of Lake Shore Drive are for the most part sandy beach. The beach lots are adjoined on both sides by other privately owned lots, which together comprise what is commonly known as Sander's Beach. The beach has no public access other than from the lake itself. But the public does have access to the lake via a deeded right-of-way to the west of respondents' property and via a ten-foot wide pathway to the east of respondents' property.

Respondents' beach property extends south from Lake Shore Drive to the ordinary mean high water mark of Lake Coeur d'Alene. Their adjoining lots have a combined lake frontage of 250 feet and a depth of from 60 to 75 feet. The property is subject to the seasonal fluctuations of high water in the spring and low water in the late summer and fall. The property is also subject to the washings and erosive forces of the lake.

For many years, at least since the 1920's, respondents and their predecessors have maintained seawalls to protect a portion of their property immediately south of Lake Shore Drive from the erosive forces of the lake. In 1971 respondents obtained the necessary building permits from the City of Coeur d'Alene and constructed a new concrete seawall. The new wall is a three-sided structure extending approximately 20 feet closer to the lake than the earlier walls and running the entire 250 feet across respondents' property. The wall does not interfere with swimming or boating on the lake, nor does it extend to the ordinary high water mark of the lake. The wall has, however, eliminated the public use of the enclosed area for sunbathing, picnicking and other related activities. It is this 20 feet by 250 feet enclosed area which is in dispute here.

This action was brought to force respondents to remove the seawall and to permanently enjoin them from further interfering with the alleged right of the public to use the enclosed areas. The complaint alleged that for over thirty years the general public had enjoyed complete freedom to use the beach for recreational purposes. It was alleged that by virtue of such public use respondents had impliedly dedicated the property to the general public or in the alternative that the public had acquired an easement thereon by prescription or by custom. It was also alleged that the wall interfered with the public trust in which the waters of the lake are held. After a trial to the court sitting without a jury, the people of the state of Idaho were adjudged to have no right or interest whatever to the property. The requested injunctive relief was denied, and judgment was entered in favor of respondents. This appeal followed.

STANDING

* * *

We are of the opinion that the legislative grant of authority to the prosecuting attorney to prosecute actions in which "the people are interested" amounts to a statutory grant of standing in the instant case. The statute empowers the prosecuting attorney to call upon the courts of this state for vindication of public rights which for all practical purposes would otherwise go unprotected. The rights contended for here are of this nature. * * *

THE MERITS

A. *Easement by Prescription*

Appellant claims a right on behalf of the general public of this state to use private property for recreational purposes. In order to establish such a right by prescription, a party must submit "reasonably clear and convincing proof of open, notorious, continuous, uninterrupted use, under a claim of right, with the knowledge of the owner of the servient tenement, for the prescriptive period." West v. Smith, 95 Idaho 550, 557, 511 P.2d 1326, 1333 (1973) (footnotes omitted). The prescriptive right cannot arise, however, if the use of the land is with the permission of the owner.

After hearing the testimony of some seventeen witnesses on the use of respondents' property, the trial court found "that the use herein by the public was open, notorious, continuous, and uninterrupted and with the knowledge of the defendants [respondents] for more than the prescriptive period." The court further found, however, that the public use was in fact "a permissive use" and that "the evidence herein does not establish an adverse or hostile use by the plaintiff [appellant] against the interest of the defendants [respondents] nor any act on the part of any member of the public that would give notice to the defendants [respondents] that the public was claiming an interest adverse to them." The court therefore concluded that no public rights had been established by prescription.

These findings, if supported by substantial and competent evidence in the record, will not be disturbed on appeal. We have carefully reviewed the record and conclude that there is substantial and competent evidence to support these findings. Even so, the court's finding that the use was by permission of respondents can only be sustained from that point in time in which respondents held title to the property. Respondents Fox acquired their property in 1948. Carmelita McDonald, now deceased, acquired hers in 1924. Appellant contends that the prescriptive rights to use the beach were acquired prior to 1948 and 1924, and that respondents took their fee interests subject to the already established public rights. We find it unnecessary to answer this contention. For the reasons stated below, this court is of the opinion that the "general public" or "the people of the state of Idaho" as distinguished from specific individuals cannot, absent specific statutory authorization, acquire prescriptive rights to private property.

As a starting point, it is important that the underlying legal rationale of a prescriptive right be discussed. Many courts have relied upon the fiction of the "lost-grant," i.e. it was presumed, from long possession under claim of right and with acquiescence of the owner, that there must have originally been a grant, from the owner to the claimant, which had become lost during the course of time. Under the lost grant rationale, courts have held that the general public, considered apart from legally organized or political entities, could not acquire prescriptive rights because they could not receive a grant. In Ivons–Nispel, Inc. v. Lowe, 347 Mass. 760, 200 N.E.2d 282 (1964), in a case almost identical to the case at bar, the Supreme Judicial Court of Massachusetts stated that "We are of opinion that 'persons of the local community' and the 'general public' are too broad a group to acquire by prescription an easement to use private beaches for bathing and for recreational purposes. (citations omitted.)" 200 N.E.2d at 283.

Although Idaho long ago abandoned the fiction of the lost grant, we reach the same result as the Massachusetts court in holding that the general public cannot acquire prescriptive rights in private property. In *Last Chance Ditch Co. v. Sawyer,* an action brought by the property owner to enjoin 89 persons from permitting waste water to flow into the canal, 35 Idaho 61, 66B67, 204 P. 654, 655 (1922), the court stated

> We are of the opinion, however, that the recognized fiction of a lost grant should not be given such controlling efficacy. While it is true that the statute of limitations does not in terms apply to the acquisition of title to an easement by prescription, it is generally held that by analogy such statutes are applicable. The use of an easement constitutes a direct invasion of the dominion of the proprietor of the land, and the statute forbids maintenance of an action to prevent such use as has been enjoyed openly, continuously, adversely, and with the acquiescence of the owner for a period of five years or more. The statute announces the policy of the law. It does not appear to be founded upon the fiction of a lost grant, but upon the proposition that it is the policy of the state to discourage litigation of

matters which, through the lapse of time, should be considered as settled. We think the acquiescence of the owner of land in case of continuous and adverse user of an easement is presumed, and can be disproved only by showing acts upon his part which interrupt the continuity of the use, or by appropriate action in court to prevent its continuance. (See Lehigh Valley R. Co. v. McFarlan, 43 N.J.L. 605.)

The statute of limitations discussed in *Last Chance Ditch Co., supra,* upon which prescriptive rights in Idaho are based, is I.C. § 5–203. This statute in effect gives an owner five years to take the necessary and appropriate legal action to have an unauthorized use of his property stopped. If the owner of the property fails to eject the trespasser or enjoin the unauthorized use, after five years his right to do so will be barred. But as against whom would the owner be barred? Only those who had actually made open, notorious, continuous, uninterrupted use, under a claim of right, with the knowledge of the owner, for the five year period. Those persons who had not made such use could be enjoined from further interfering with the owner's superior rights.

In *West v. Smith, supra,* where an individual claimant asserted a prescriptive right to moor his houseboat in front of another person's privately owned lake front lot and to maintain a catwalk onto the owner's property, this court held that any prescriptive right there acquired was purely personal to the individual claimant. The prescriptive right belonged exclusively to the actual user, and not to guests or assignees. The private owner could therefore exclude all others from making any unapproved use of his property.

As in *West v. Smith, supra,* the rights contended for here are in the nature of an easement in gross. Being a personal right, the rule is that one individual's prescriptive use cannot inure to the benefit of anyone else. Personal prescriptive rights are confined to the actual adverse user and are limited to the use exercised during the prescriptive period. The fact that hundreds of individuals have made use of respondents' property for the prescriptive period does not bar respondents from enjoining all future trespass to the property. Nor does the use of respondents' property by certain neighbors or friends or even total strangers accrue or inure to the benefit of others. We therefore hold that the "people of the State of Idaho" as distinguished from specific individuals cannot acquire prescriptive rights in and to private property absent some express statutory authority. The one situation where the legislature has allowed such public prescriptive rights is in public highways. When a right-of-way has been used by the general public for a period of five years and has been maintained at public expense, the right-of-way becomes a public highway. *See* I.C. § 40–103. No similar statute applies to the facts of this case. The district court's denial of the prescriptive easement is affirmed.

B. Dedication

Appellant contends that respondents have made an implied dedication of their property to the public. The district court put the burden on appellant to prove that respondents had by their acts or omissions intended to dedicate the land to public use. The court found that this burden had not been sustained. We concur.

The fundamental principles in this state regarding implied dedications are found in Village of Hailey v. Riley, 14 Idaho 481, 495, 95 P. 686, 691 (1908), quoted with approval in Simmons v. Perkins, 63 Idaho 136, 143, 118 P.2d 740, 744 (1941):

> It is no trivial thing to take another's land without compensation, and for this reason the courts will not lightly declare a dedication to public use. It is elementary law that an intention to dedicate upon the part of the owner must be plainly manifest.

> * * *

> And while long continued user, without objection, and with the knowledge and consent of the owner is some evidence of a right in the public, still there must be joined to that user an intention upon the part of the owner to dedicate, or no dedication will be consummated; for the long-continued user by the public without objection by the owner is entirely consistent with a license to the public to use the land, and therefore evidence of long-continued user alone will not support a finding of fact that a dedication was created. Neither will a finding of fact of mere long-continued user support a conclusion of law that a public highway was created. As previously stated, in order to constitute a dedication of a highway by evidence in pais, there must be convincing evidence that the owner intended to appropriate the land to the public use.

Appellant urges this court to adopt the reasoning of the California per curiam decisions, Gion v. City of Santa Clara and Dietz v. King, 2 Cal.3d 29, 84 Cal.Rptr. 162, 465 P.2d 50 (1970), for the proposition that five years uninterrupted public use of private property creates a conclusive presumption of the owner's intent to dedicate. We decline the opportunity. Instead we adhere to the rule that a party claiming a right by dedication bears the burden of proof on every material issue. The intent of the owner to dedicate his land to public use must be clearly and unequivocally shown and must never be presumed.

* * *

The district court found as a fact that "none of the present defendants [respondents] nor any of their predecessors ever intended to make any dedication of the disputed area to public use * * *. The plaintiff [appellant] did not carry his burden of proof in this regard." Our review of the record discloses substantial and competent evidence to support this finding. Respondents exercised dominion over the property by at various times personally ousting unwelcome users; at other times they enlisted the aid of the city police to do so. Trash cans mistakenly put on the property by the city were ordered removed by respondents. The deed executed in 1923 by John Taylor and Edith Taylor, respondents predecessors in title, conveying to the City of Coeur d'Alene a public right-of-way to the lake over property located to the west of respondents' property expressly limited the public rights to the narrow right of way and expressly prohibited interference with the rights of the private owners. This instrument, together with respondents' own affirmative acts of dominion and unequivocal testimony at trial negative any intent to dedicate the property to the public.

C. Custom

Another theory advanced by appellant is that the public has by customary usage acquired recreation rights to respondents' property. This theory is based upon the English common law of custom, defined as: "a usage or practice of the people, which, by common adoption and acquiescence, and by long and unvarying habit, has become compulsory, and has acquired the force of a law with respect to the place or subject-matter to which it relates." Black's Law Dictionary 461 (rev. 4th ed. 1968). By the law of custom, the general public could, after many years of unrestricted common usage, acquire rights over private property.

The acquisition of a right through custom in England required that the use "must have continued from time immemorial without interruption, and as a right; it must be certain as to the place, and as to the persons; and it must be certain and reasonable as to the subject matter or rights created." 3 H. Tiffany, Law of Real Property, § 935 at 623 (3d ed. 1939). Virtually all commentators are agreed that, until recently, the law of custom was a dead letter in the United States. Aside from two New Hampshire cases decided in the 1850's no state had applied the doctrine. As recently as 1935 New York refused to accept customary usage as a means of claiming an easement in a private beach for bathing and boating. Gillies v. Orienta Beach Club, 159 Misc. 675, 289 N.Y.S. 733 (1935). The doctrine was exhumed, however, by the Supreme Court of Oregon in State ex rel. Thornton v. Hay, 254 Or. 584, 462 P.2d 671 (1969), where it was held that the public had acquired customary rights to a privately owned dry sand stretch of beach on the Oregon sea coast. Because of the tract-by-tract limitations inherent in the prescription theory, the Oregon court chose to apply custom to claimed public use of oceanfront lands.

Whether the doctrine exists in this state is a matter of first impression. I.C. § 73–116 provides that "[t]he common law of England, so far as it is not repugnant to, or inconsistent with, the constitution or laws of the United States, in all cases not provided for in these compiled laws, is the rule of decision in all courts of this state." There being no statute which expressly or impliedly rejects the doctrine of custom, this court is of opinion that the doctrine does obtain in Idaho.

The district court applied the law of custom to the facts of this case and concluded that the requisite elements had not been established. The first element, use from time immemorial, means that the use has existed for so long that "the memory of man runneth not to the contrary." State ex rel. Thornton, v. Hay, *supra*, 462 P.2d at 677. In the instant case, the district court found that usage commenced as early as 1912. We agree with the district court that this does not constitute "from time immemorial." The second requirement, that the use must be uninterrupted, is not met because of the fact that respondents had personally and with police assistance removed members of the public from their land. Without further burdening this opinion, suffice it to say that of the seven essential elements of a customary right, the trial court found adversely to appellant on six of them. We find ample evidence in the record to support the findings, and we therefore affirm the district court's denial of any customary rights in this case.

D.   *Public Trust*

Appellant's final argument is that respondents' lake front property is imbued with a public trust under the principles of the public trust doctrine. That doctrine's leading authority, Professor Sax of the University of Michigan School of Law, articulates the following as the "central substantive thought in public trust litigation":

> [w]hen a state holds a resource which is available for the free use of the general public, a court will look with considerable skepticism upon *any* governmental conduct which is calculated *either* to relocate that resource to more restricted uses *or* to subject public uses to the self-interest of private parties.

J. Sax, *The Public Trust Doctrine in Natural Resource Law: Effective Judicial Intervention*, 68 Mich.L.Rev. 473, 490 (1970) (emphasis in text).

It is undisputed that the land in contention here is private property, traceable to a patent from the United States Government in 1892. It is also undisputed that the seawall constructed by respondents lies above the ordinary mean high water mark of the lake and that it in no way interferes with navigability or the public's use of the lake's waters. Since no natural resource owned by the state is involved here the public trust doctrine is inapposite. The district court judgment is affirmed in all respects. Costs to respondents.

Notes and Questions

1.   As discussed in *Fox,* at one time American courts based the doctrine of prescription on the fiction of a lost grant. If a particular use had continued for twenty years, it was assumed that such usage was made pursuant to a grant, but that the grant itself was now lost. The lost grant theory was grounded on the notion that the claimant was acting rightfully and with the "acquiescence" of the landowner. Today, most courts reject the lost grant theory in favor of a straight adverse use approach to prescriptive easements which is based on use hostile to the rights of the owner. *See* Stoebuck, *The Fiction of Presumed Grant*, 15 U.Kan.L.Rev. 17 (1966). However, the lost grant theory survives in some jurisdictions, and has left terms that often serve to confuse our analysis of prescriptive easements. Is the notion of acquiescence consistent with the adverse use theory?

2. Assume that before the applicable time period has run, the owner of the servient tenement sends a letter to the adverse user demanding that the use stop. Does this interrupt the prescriptive easement?

3. The desire to secure public access to beaches has produced much litigation and legislation. In contrast to *Fox*, some courts have recognized that the general public may acquire a prescriptive easement for recreational use of privately owned beach areas. *See, e.g.*, Opinion of the Justices, 139 N.H. 82, 649 A.2d 604 (1994) (finding that public could acquire prescriptive easements in beachfront property, but holding that proposed statute which would impose public easement on privately-owned dry sands area would constitute taking of property requiring payment of compensation); Villa Nova Resort, Inc. v. State, 711 S.W.2d 120 (Tex.App.1986). Which is the better view?

4. As noted in *Fox*, a few courts have exhumed the ancient doctrine of custom and held that the public acquired a customary right to use privately owned beaches. *See* State ex rel. Thornton v. Hay, 254 Or. 584, 462 P.2d 671 (1969); In re Ashford, 50 Hawaii 314, 440 P.2d 76 (1968); City of Daytona Beach v. Tona–Rama, Inc., 294 So.2d 73 (Fla.1974); Matcha v. Mattox, 711 S.W.2d 95 (Tex.App.1986), *cert. denied*, 481 U.S. 1024 (1987). *See generally* Comment, *Sunbathers Versus Property Owners: Public Access to North Carolina Beaches*, 64 N.C.L.Rev. 159 (1985). The Supreme Judicial Court of Maine, however, has refused to recognize easements based on local custom. Bell v. Town of Wells, 557 A.2d 168 (Me.1989). Two Supreme Court justices have maintained that applying the doctrine of custom to the whole coastline of Oregon raises a significant takings issue that should be heard. Stevens v. City of Cannon Beach, 510 U.S. 1207 (1994) (dissent from denial of writ of certiorari); *see also* Bederman, *The Curious Resurrection of Custom: Beach Access and Judicial Takings*, 96 Colum. L. Rev. 1375 (1996) (noting that concept of custom as applied in Oregon transformed common law doctrine, and arguing that retroactive changes in state property law by judiciary constitute unconstitutional taking of property). For an analysis of customary rights unique to Hawaii, see Public Access Shoreline Hawaii v. Hawai'i County Planning Commission, 79 Hawai'i 425, 903 P.2d 1246 (1995), *cert. denied* 517 U.S. 1163 (1996).

5. Most courts have declined to impose public trust easements for recreational purposes. *See, e.g.*, State ex rel. Meek v. Hays, 246 Kan. 99, 785 P.2d 1356 (1990). However, the Supreme Court of New Jersey has ruled that the public trust doctrine authorized public use of private beach areas "subject to an accommodation of the interests of the owner." Matthews v. Bay Head Improvement Association, 95 N.J. 306, 471 A.2d 355 (1984), *cert. denied*, 469 U.S. 821 (1984).

6. As indicated in *Fox*, the Supreme Court of California has ruled that the public might obtain an easement for recreational purposes by using particular land without obtaining permission. In such case an implied dedication is conclusively presumed. Gion v. City of Santa Cruz, 2 Cal.3d 29, 84 Cal.Rptr. 162, 465 P.2d 50 (1970). In 1971 the California legislature limited the scope of *Gion*, and one judge has argued that the opinion should be overruled. *See* County of Los Angeles v. Berk, 26 Cal.3d 201, 161 Cal.Rptr. 742, 605 P.2d 381 (1980) (Justice Clark's dissenting opinion), *cert.*

denied, 449 U.S. 836 (1980). Moreover, the Supreme Court of Hawaii has joined the Supreme Court of Idaho in specifically rejecting the *Gion* approach. *See* In Matter of Application of Banning, 73 Hawaii 297, 832 P.2d 724 (1992) (long public use may create rebuttable, not conclusive presumption of implied dedication).

FONTAINEBLEAU HOTEL CORP. v. FORTY–FIVE TWENTY–FIVE, INC.

Third District Court of Appeal of Florida, 1959.
114 So.2d 357.

PER CURIAM.

This is an interlocutory appeal from an order temporarily enjoining the appellants from continuing with the construction of a fourteen-story addition to the Fontainebleau Hotel, owned and operated by the appellants. Appellee, plaintiff below, owns the Eden Roc Hotel, which was constructed in 1955, about a year after the Fontainebleau, and adjoins the Fontainebleau on the north. Both are luxury hotels, facing the Atlantic Ocean. The proposed addition to the Fontainebleau is being constructed twenty feet from its north property line, 130 feet from the mean high water mark of the Atlantic Ocean, and 76 feet 8 inches from the ocean bulkhead line. The 14–story tower will extend 160 feet above grade in height and is 416 feet long from east to west. During the winter months, from around two o'clock in the afternoon for the remainder of the day, the shadow of the addition will extend over the cabana, swimming pool, and sunbathing areas of the Eden Roc, which are located in the southern portion of its property.

In this action, plaintiff-appellee sought to enjoin the defendants-appellants from proceeding with the construction of the addition to the Fontainebleau (it appears to have been roughly eight stories high at the time suit was filed), alleging that the construction would interfere with the light and air on the beach in front of the Eden Roc and cast a shadow of such size as to render the beach wholly unfitted for the use and enjoyment of its guests, to the irreparable injury of the plaintiff; further, that the construction of such addition on the north side of defendants' property, rather than the south side, was actuated by malice and ill will on the part of the defendants' president toward the plaintiff's president; and that the construction was in violation of a building ordinance requiring a 100–foot setback from the ocean. It was also alleged that the construction would interfere with the easements of light and air enjoyed by plaintiff and its predecessors in title for more than twenty years and "impliedly granted by virtue of the acts of the plaintiff's predecessors in title, as well as under the common law and the express recognition of such rights by virtue of Chapter 9837, Laws of Florida 1923 * * *." Some attempt was also made to allege an easement by implication in favor of the plaintiff's property, as the dominant, and against the defendants' property, as the servient, tenement.

The defendants' answer denied the material allegations of the complaint, pleaded laches and estoppel by judgment.

The chancellor heard considerable testimony on the issues made by the complaint and the answer and, as noted, entered a temporary injunction restraining the defendants from continuing with the construction of the addition. His reason for so doing was stated by him, in a memorandum opinion, as follows:

"In granting the temporary injunction in this case the Court wishes to make several things very clear. The ruling is not based on any alleged presumptive title nor prescriptive right of the plaintiff to light and air nor is it based on any deed restrictions nor recorded plats in the title of the plaintiff nor of the defendant nor of any plat of record. It is not based on any zoning ordinance nor on any provision of the building code of the City of Miami Beach nor on the decision of any court, nisi prius or appellate. It is based solely on the proposition that no one has a right to use his property to the injury of another. In this case it is clear from the evidence that the proposed use by the Fontainebleau will materially damage the Eden Roc. There is evidence indicating that the construction of the proposed annex by the Fontainebleau is malicious or deliberate for the purpose of injuring the Eden Roc, but it is scarcely sufficient, standing alone, to afford a basis for equitable relief."

This is indeed a novel application of the maxim *sic utere tuo ut alienum non laedas.* This maxim does not mean that one must never use his own property in such a way as to do any injury to his neighbor. It means only that one must use his property so as not to injure the lawful *rights* of another. In Reaver v. Martin Theatres, Fla.1951, 52 So.2d 682, 683, 25 A.L.R.2d 1451, under this maxim, it was stated that "it is well settled that a property owner may put his own property to any reasonable and lawful use, so long as he does not thereby deprive the adjoining landowner of any right of enjoyment of his property *which is recognized and protected by law, and so long as his use is not such a one as the law will pronounce a nuisance.*" [Emphasis supplied.]

No American decision has been cited, and independent research has revealed none, in which it has been held that—in the absence of some contractual or statutory obligation—a landowner has a legal right to the free flow of light and air across the adjoining land of his neighbor. Even at common law, the landowner had no legal right, in the absence of an easement or uninterrupted use and enjoyment for a period of 20 years, to unobstructed light and air from the adjoining land. And the English doctrine of "ancient lights" has been unanimously repudiated in this country.

There being, then, no legal right to the free flow of light and air from the adjoining land, it is universally held that where a structure serves a useful and beneficial purpose, it does not give rise to a cause of action, either for damages or for an injunction under the maxim *sic utere tuo ut alienum non laedas,* even though it causes injury to another by

No LEGAL RIGHT
TO AIR & LIGHT

cutting off the light and air and interfering with the view that would otherwise be available over adjoining land in its natural state, regardless of the fact that the structure may have been erected partly for spite.

We see no reason for departing from this universal rule. If, as contended on behalf of plaintiff, public policy demands that a landowner in the Miami Beach area refrain from constructing buildings on his premises that will cast a shadow on the adjoining premises, an amendment of its comprehensive planning and zoning ordinance, applicable to the public as a whole, is the means by which such purpose should be achieved. (No opinion is expressed here as to the validity of such an ordinance, if one should be enacted pursuant to the requirements of law. Cf. City of Miami Beach v. State ex rel. Fontainebleau Hotel Corp., Fla.App.1959, 108 So.2d 614, 619; certiorari denied, Fla.1959, 111 So.2d 437.) But to change the universal rule—and the custom followed in this state since its inception—that adjoining landowners have an equal right under the law to build to the line of their respective tracts and to such a height as is desired by them (in the absence, of course, of building restrictions or regulations) amounts, in our opinion, to judicial legislation. As stated in Musumeci v. Leonardo, [77 R.I. 255, 75 A.2d 175], "So use your own as not to injure another's property is, indeed, a sound and salutary principle for the promotion of justice, but it may not and should not be applied so as gratuitously to confer upon an adjacent property owner incorporeal rights incidental to his ownership of land which the law does not sanction."

We have also considered whether the order here reviewed may be sustained upon any other reasoning, conformable to and consistent with the pleadings, regardless of the erroneous reasoning upon which the order was actually based. We have concluded that it cannot.

The record affirmatively shows that no statutory basis for the right sought to be enforced by plaintiff exists. The so-called Shadow Ordinance enacted by the City of Miami Beach at plaintiff's behest was held invalid in City of Miami Beach v. State ex rel. Fontainebleau Hotel Corp., supra. It also affirmatively appears that there is no possible basis for holding that plaintiff has an easement for light and air, either express or implied, across defendants' property, nor any prescriptive right thereto—even if it be assumed, arguendo, that the common-law right of prescription as to "ancient lights" is in effect in this state. And from what we have said heretofore in this opinion, it is perhaps superfluous to add that we have no desire to dissent from the unanimous holding in this country repudiating the English doctrine of ancient lights.

* * *

Since it affirmatively appears that the plaintiff has not established a cause of action against the defendants by reason of the structure here in question, the order granting a temporary injunction should be and it is hereby reversed with directions to dismiss the complaint.

Reversed with directions.

Notes and Questions

1. Why do American courts reject the doctrine of "ancient lights?" Should this approach be re-evaluated in light of the development of solar energy systems?

In this regard, consider the following excerpt from Prah v. Maretti, 108 Wis.2d 223, 224, 233–237, 240, 321 N.W.2d 182, 184, 188–190, 191 (1982):

* * * [This case] present[s] an issue of first impression, namely, whether an owner of a solar-heated residence states a claim upon which relief can be granted when he asserts that his neighbor's proposed construction of a residence (which conforms to existing deed restrictions and local ordinances) interferes with his access to an unobstructed path for sunlight across the neighbor's property.

* * *

* * * At English common law a landowner could acquire a right to receive sunlight across adjoining land by both express agreement and under the judge-made doctrine of "ancient lights." Under the doctrine of ancient lights if the landowner had received sunlight across adjoining property for a specified period of time, the landowner was entitled to continue to receive unobstructed access to sunlight across the adjoining property. Under the doctrine the landowner acquired a negative prescriptive easement and could prevent the adjoining landowner from obstructing access to light.

Although American courts have not been as receptive to protecting a landowner's access to sunlight as the English courts, American courts have afforded some protection to a landowner's interest in access to sunlight. American courts honor express easements to sunlight. American courts initially enforced the English common law doctrine of ancient lights, but later every state which considered the doctrine repudiated it as inconsistent with the needs of a developing country. Indeed, for just that reason this court concluded that an easement to light and air over adjacent property could not be created or acquired by prescription and has been unwilling to recognize such an easement by implication.

Many jurisdictions in this country have protected a landowner from malicious obstruction of access to light (the spite fence cases) under the common law private nuisance doctrine. If an activity is motivated by malice it lacks utility and the harm it causes others outweighs any social values. This court was reluctant to protect a landowner's interest in sunlight even against a spite fence, only to be overruled by the legislature. Shortly after this court upheld a landowner's right to erect a useless and unsightly sixteen-foot spite fence four feet from his neighbor's windows, Metzger v. Hochrein, 107 Wis. 267, 83 N.W. 308 (1900), the legislature enacted a law specifically defining a spite fence as an actionable private nuisance. Thus a landowner's interest in sunlight has been protected in this country by common law private nuisance law at least in the narrow context of the modern American rule invalidating spite fences.

This court's reluctance in the nineteenth and early part of the twentieth century to provide broader protection for a landowner's access to sunlight was premised on three policy considerations. First, the right of landowners to use their property as they wished, as long as they did not cause physical damage to a neighbor, was jealously guarded.

Second, sunlight was valued only for aesthetic enjoyment or as illumination. Since artificial light could be used for illumination, loss of sunlight was at most a personal annoyance which was given little, if any, weight by society.

Third, society had a significant interest in not restricting or impeding land development. This court repeatedly emphasized that in the growth period of the nineteenth and early twentieth centuries change is to be expected and is essential to property and that recognition of a right to sunlight would hinder property development. * * *

Considering these three policies, this court concluded that in the absence of an express agreement granting access to sunlight, a landowner's obstruction of another's access to sunlight was not actionable. Miller v. Hoeschler, *supra*, 126 Wis. at 271, 105 N.W. 790. These three policies are no longer fully accepted or applicable. They reflect factual circumstances and social priorities that are now obsolete.

First, society has increasingly regulated the use of land by the landowner for the general welfare.

Second, access to sunlight has taken on a new significance in recent years. In this case the plaintiff seeks to protect access to sunlight, not for aesthetic reasons or as a source of illumination but as a source of energy. Access to sunlight as an energy source is of significance both to the landowner who invests in solar collectors and to a society which has an interest in developing alternative sources of energy.

Third, the policy of favoring unhindered private development in an expanding economy is no longer in harmony with the realities of our society. The need for easy and rapid development is not as great today as it once was, while our perception of the value of sunlight as a source of energy has increased significantly.

Courts should not implement obsolete policies that have lost their vigor over the course of the years. The law of private nuisance is better suited to resolve landowners' disputes about property development in the 1980's than is a rigid rule which does not recognize a landowner's interest in access to sunlight.

* * *

Accordingly we hold that the plaintiff in this case has stated a claim under which relief can be granted. Nonetheless we do not determine whether the plaintiff in this case is entitled to relief. In order to be entitled to relief the plaintiff must prove the elements required to establish actionable nuisance, and the conduct of the defendant herein must be judged by the reasonable use doctrine.

Is this decision consistent with *Fontainebleau* regarding the appropriate use of nuisance law? "[C]ould it be said that the solar energy user is creating the nuisance when others must conform their homes to accommodate his use?" *Id.* at 248 n. 3, 321 N.W.2d at 195 n. 3 (dissent).

2. An instrument may expressly grant an easement of light and air. A solar energy user may obtain access to sunlight in this fashion. Are landowners likely to grant such easements?

b. Scope

HAYES v. AQUIA MARINA, INC.

Supreme Court of Virginia, 1992.
243 Va. 255, 414 S.E.2d 820.

STEPHENSON, JUSTICE.

The principal issue in this appeal is whether an easement across the servient estates will be overburdened by the proposed expanded use of the dominant estate.

Robert C. Hayes and others (collectively, Hayes) brought a chancery suit against Aquia Marina, Inc., Warren E. Gnegy, and Cynthia Gnegy (collectively, Gnegy). Hayes alleged, *inter alia,* that a proposed expansion of a marina located on Gnegy's land (the dominant estate or marina property) would overburden the easement across Hayes's lands (the servient estates). Hayes, therefore, sought to have the trial court enjoin the proposed expanded use of the dominant estate.

The cause was referred to a commissioner in chancery. Following an *ore tenus* hearing, and after taking a view of the subject properties, the commissioner filed a report containing the following findings: (1) a perpetual easement exists across the servient estates for ingress to and egress from the dominant estate; (2) the easement is not limited solely for domestic use, but may be used commercially by the marina and its customers and by boat owners and their guests; (3) the proposed expansion of the marina from 84 to 280 boat slips is a reasonable use of the dominant estate; (4) the resulting increase in traffic over the easement will not change the type, only the degree, of use and will not overburden the easement; and (5) paving the easement is reasonable and a proper means of maintenance.

By a final decree, entered March 5, 1991, the trial court overruled all of Hayes's exceptions to the commissioner's report and confirmed the report in all respects. Hayes appeals.

We must view the evidence in the light most favorable to Gnegy, the prevailing party at trial. The marina property is a 2.58–acre tract situate on Aquia Creek in Stafford County. The easement is the sole means of land access to the marina property.

The litigants' predecessors in title entered into a written agreement, executed February 3, 1951, for "the establishment of a certain roadway or right of way beginning at the Northern terminus of State Highway No. 666, and terminating at the property division line between [the servient estates], and where [the dominant estate] adjoins the same on the North side thereof" and for "the continuation of said right of way." The agreement recited that "the State Department of Highways will be requested * * * to take over into the State Highway System the present roadway beginning at the North terminus of said State Highway No. 666, and leading through [the servient estates]." The roadway that was intended to be taken into the state highway system was "approximately something less than one-half mile in length." The "newly established private roadway" was "approximately 1,120 feet in length" and "fifteen feet wide along its entire distance." The agreement provided that the parties thereto "shall have an easement of right of way over the entire length [thereof]."

The record indicates that the portion of the easement, beginning at the northern terminus of State Highway No. 666, became a part of the state highway system in 1962. The record also indicates that the "private roadway" is constructed of dirt and gravel.

By 1959, three residential buildings and a wooden pier were located on the dominant estate. The pier was approximately 30 feet long and contained about 10 boat slips. This small marina was operated commercially.

Between 1961 and 1962, the current marina was constructed. This marina has been operated commercially for the general public from 1964 until the present. The marina consists of 84 boat slips, a travel lift station,[1] a public boat launch, and a gas dock. Boats and boat parts are sold at the marina. Boats also are repaired on the marina property.

In September 1989, the Board of Supervisors of Stafford County granted Gnegy a special use permit to expand the marina by increasing the number of boat slips to 280. After the proposed expansion, the marina will continue to provide the same services it has provided since 1964.

There has never been a "traffic problem" with the easement. An expert witness on emergency services testified that there never had been a problem with access to the marina property and none was anticipated if the proposed expansion occurred. On weekends, a time of maximum use of the marina property, Gnegy anticipates that only 20 to 30 percent of the boat owners will make use of the marina.

As a general rule, when an easement is created by grant or reservation and the instrument creating the easement does not limit the use to be made of it, the easement may be used for "any purpose to which the dominant estate may then, or in the future, reasonably be devoted." *Cushman Corporation v. Barnes,* 204 Va. 245, 253, 129 S.E.2d 633, 639

---

1. A "travel lift" is a device for moving boats out of the water for repairs.

R

(1963). Stated differently, an easement created by a general grant or reservation, without words limiting it to any particular use of the dominant estate, is not affected by any reasonable change in the use of the dominant estate. However, no use may be made of the easement which is different from that established at the time of its creation and which imposes an additional burden upon the servient estate.

Δ's CONTENTION #1

Hayes contends that, by using the phrase, "private roadway," in the easement agreement, the parties to the agreement intended to limit the use of the easement to domestic purposes, thereby prohibiting commercial uses. Gnegy contends, on the other hand, that the agreement created

π's CONTENTION

an easement for access without limitation. The commissioner and the trial court adopted Gnegy's contention.

When the agreement is read as a whole, it is clear that the phrase, "private roadway," was used to distinguish that portion of the easement that would not become a part of the state highway system from that portion of the easement that could be taken into the system. Thus, the phrase is descriptive, not restrictive.

H

Consequently, we hold that the agreement creating the easement for access contains no terms of limitation upon the easement's use. Additionally, the record supports the conclusion that the operation of a marina is a use to which the dominant estate reasonably can be, and has been, devoted.

Δ's CONTENTION #2

Hayes further contends that the proposed expansion of the marina will impose an additional and unreasonable burden upon the easement. Having alleged that the proposed expansion will impose an additional burden upon the easement, Hayes has the burden of proving this allegation.

CASE LAW

A contention similar to the one advanced by Hayes was presented in *Cushman Corporation, supra.* In *Cushman Corporation,* as in the present case, the instruments creating the easement contain no language limiting the easement's use. 204 Va. at 253, 129 S.E.2d at 640. When the easement was established, the dominant estate, a 126.67–acre tract, was used as a farm and contained two single-family dwellings with appurtenant servant and tenant houses. A controversy arose when the dominant owner proposed to subdivide the tract for residential and commercial uses. The trial court limited the easement to its original uses. We reversed the ruling, stating, *inter alia:*

R

> The fact that the dominant estate is divided and a portion or portions conveyed away does not, in and of itself, mean that an additional burden is imposed upon the servient estate. The result may be that the *degree* of burden is increased, but that is not sufficient to deny use of the right of way to an owner of a portion so conveyed.

Id. at 253, 129 S.E.2d at 640. (Emphasis added.)

Here, after weighing the evidence, both the commissioner and the trial court concluded that the proposed expansion would not unreasonably burden the easement. On appeal, a decree confirming a commissioner's report is presumed to be correct and will be affirmed unless plainly wrong.

In the present case, we cannot say that the trial court's conclusion is plainly wrong. Indeed, we think that it is supported by the evidence and by well-established principles of law. Here, as in *Cushman Corporation*, the proposed expansion will not, "in and of itself," impose an "additional burden" upon the easement, even though the "degree of burden" may be increased. Therefore, assuming, without deciding, that an expanded use of the dominant estate could be of such degree as to impose an additional and unreasonable burden upon an easement, such is not the situation in the present case.

Finally, Hayes contends that Gnegy does not have the right to pave the easement. Hayes acknowledges, and we agree, that the owner of a dominant estate has a *duty* to maintain an easement. However, Hayes reasons that, because the owner of a dominant estate has a duty to maintain an easement, it follows that the owner does not have a *right* to improve the easement. We agree that there is a distinction between maintenance and improvement. However, we do not agree that the owner of a dominant estate does not have the right to make reasonable improvements to an easement.

Although we previously have not addressed the "improvement" issue, courts in other jurisdictions have held that the owner of a dominant estate has the right to make reasonable improvements to an easement, so long as the improvement does not unreasonably increase the burden upon the servient estate. *See, e.g., Stagman v. Kyhos,* 19 Mass.App.Ct. 590, 476 N.E.2d 257 (1985); *Glenn v. Poole,* 12 Mass.App. Ct. 292, 423 N.E.2d 1030 (1981); *Schmutzer v. Smith,* 679 S.W.2d 453 (Tenn.App.1984). Such improvement may include paving a roadway. *See, e.g., Stagman, supra; Schmutzer, supra.* Ordinarily, the reasonableness of the improvement is a question of fact. *Guillet v. Livernois,* 297 Mass. 337, 340, 8 N.E.2d 921, 922 (1937). We adopt these principles of law.

In the present case, the commissioner and the trial court found that the proposed paving of the roadway by Gnegy, under the existing facts and circumstances, is reasonable. We will affirm this finding; it is supported by the evidence and is not plainly wrong.

Accordingly, the trial court's judgment will be

Affirmed.

Notes and Problems

1. An instrument grants B a right of way over O's land. Can B install power lines over the right of way? *Compare* Guild v. Hinman, 695 A.2d 1190 (Me.1997) *with* Kelly v. Schmelz, 439 S.W.2d 211 (Mo.App.1969).

2. A 1799 instrument referred to a "cartway going on to Wills' Island" and granted "all necessary privileges of passing and repassing." Can the

current easement holder use motor vehicles on the right of way? *See* Marden v. Mallard Decoy Club, Inc., 361 Mass. 105, 278 N.E.2d 743 (1972).

3. Easements may be expressly limited to foot travel. *See, e.g.,* Sheftel v. Lebel, 44 Mass.App.Ct. 175, 689 N.E.2d 500 (1998); Buran v. Peryea, 246 A.D.2d 856, 668 N.Y.S.2d 265 (1998). In Tucci v. Salzhauer, 40 A.D.2d 712, 336 N.Y.S.2d 721 (1972), *affirmed mem.* 33 N.Y.2d 854, 352 N.Y.S.2d 198, 307 N.E.2d 256 (1973), the court found that a baby carriage was not a "vehicle" prohibited from utilizing an easement created for pedestrian traffic only.

CLEMSON UNIVERSITY v. FIRST PROVIDENT CORP.

Supreme Court of South Carolina, 1973.
260 S.C. 640, 197 S.E.2d 914.

MOSS, CHIEF JUSTICE:

Clemson University and William B. Douglas, the respondents herein, each instituted an action against First Provident Corporation of South Carolina and others, the appellants herein, seeking a temporary and permanent injunction for an alleged trespass committed by them. The question of the issuance of a temporary injunction was heard before The Honorable W.L. Rhodes, Presiding Judge of the Court of Common Pleas, and an order was issued by him granting the injunction, *pendente lite,* pending a hearing on the merits. Thereafter, a consent order was issued consolidating and transferring the pending actions to the Civil Court of Florence for a determination of all issues involved. The respondents, in their complaints, allege that each is the owner of a tract of land in Florence County situate northwest of the City of Florence and that First Provident Corporation, hereinafter referred to as the appellant, owns a tract of land located in the vicinity of lands of the respondents. It is then alleged that the appellant, through its agents, servants and employees, did enter upon the lands of the respondents, without their consent, and commenced the construction of a drainage canal across and through their lands bringing thereon for said purpose a dragline, bulldozer, trucks and other tools and equipment and did proceed to clear a thirty to forty foot right of way. It is further alleged that the appellant intends to construct such canal as a drainage for its real estate development [Carver Place Annex]. The respondents further allege that unless the appellant is enjoined they will suffer further irreparable damage.

* * *

The trial judge found that First Provident Corporation, the owner of Carver Place Annex, had an easement by prescription with respect to the ditches leading from its property to Beaver Dam Creek and High Hill Creek, both ditches having been in existence for many years. The respondents have not appealed from this finding. The appellants assert that the court was in error, after finding an easement by prescription in favor of First Provident Corporation, to then enjoin its agents, servants or employees from entering the lands of the respondents for the purpose of cleaning or repairing the ditches.

There can be no question that an easement of drainage through a ditch or across the lands of another may be acquired by prescription. In such case, the owner of land over which a prescriptive right has been acquired cannot prevent drainage through his land to the extent of the right acquired by prescription. The rule set forth in 93 C.J.S. Waters § 121, at page 823, is applicable. We quote the following therefrom:

"* * * Thus, while the lower owner has no right to obstruct the flow of surface water where a prescriptive right of drainage has been acquired, such an easement gives no right to enlarge or vary the servitude beyond the conditions under which it has been exercised during the prescriptive period, although the upper owner has a right to clean the ditch. * * *"

In 25 Am.Jur.2d, Easements and Licenses, Section 72, at page 478, we find the following:

"The rights of any person having an easement in the land of another are measured and defined by the purpose and character of the easement. A principle which underlies the use of all easements is that the owner of the easement cannot materially increase the burden of the servient estate or impose thereon a new and additional burden. Though the rights of the easement owner are paramount, to the extent of the easement, to those of the landowner, the rights of the easement owner and of the landowner are not absolute, irrelative, and uncontrolled, but are so limited, each by the other, that there may be a due and reasonable enjoyment of both the easement and the servient tenement. The owner of an easement is said to have all rights incident or necessary to its proper enjoyment, but nothing more. And, if he exceeds his rights either in the manner or in the extent of its use, he becomes a trespasser to the extent of the unauthorized use."

In the case of Capers v. M'Kee, 32 S.C.L.R. 164 (1 Strob. 164), it was held that the owner, by prescription, of a private way over another's land, has no right to cut ditches for the improvement of his way, without the consent of the owner of the soil, unless he has acquired such right also by a prescriptive use.

It is generally held that the owner of a servient estate will be given equitable relief where the owner of the easement makes an unauthorized or excessive use thereof. 28 C.J.S. Easements § 107, at page 797.

There is evidence that the appellants had entered upon the lands of the respondents, without any consent or permission to do so, and had cleared a thirty-five to forty foot strip adjacent to one of the ditches, destroying trees and virtually building a road to be used by heavy equipment in enlarging the ditches. These acts by the appellants placed an additional servitude upon the lands of the respondents. In so doing, the appellants became trespassers to the extent of the unauthorized use.

The trial judge restrained the appellants from clearing any right of way whatsoever or constructing, digging or extending any drainage ditch and from committing any trespass upon the lands of the respondents. The trial judge granted leave to the appellants to apply to the court for permission to clear the ditches upon the lands of the respondents to the depth and width that they had acquired an easement by prescription so to do.

We find no error on the part of the trial judge in granting the injunction. The trial judge has reserved and, upon proper motion, may modify his order to permit the appellants to clean the ditches upon the lands of the respondents. He has the right to fix the means and the methods by which such can be accomplished.

* * *

Notes and Questions

1. On remand, the trial court issued an order allowing First Provident to use a backhoe to excavate one of the ditches to a depth not exceeding 3.3 feet below the existing bottom. The order reflected an attempt to restore the ditch to its former depth and to re-establish the rights that First Provident had obtained by prescription. On appeal, the majority rejected the trial court's finding regarding the original depth of the ditch and held that any order pursuant to this finding would exceed the limit of First Provident's prescriptive right. Douglas v. First Provident Corp., 263 S.C. 199, 209 S.E.2d 49 (1974). (Clemson did not appeal.)

2. May an easement holder ever enter the portion of the servient tenement not covered by the easement in order to resurface the easement or to inspect or repair a water main or an electric line that occupies the easement area?

SCHOLD v. SAWYER

Colorado Court of Appeals, 1997.
944 P.2d 683.

Opinion by CHIEF JUDGE STERNBERG.

Defendants, William and Mary Sawyer, appeal from a summary judgment entered in favor of plaintiffs, Njal and Jane Schold, on plaintiffs' claim for injunctive relief related to an easement across defendants' property. We agree with defendants that the trial court improperly applied the standards for summary judgment, and we reverse and remand for further proceedings.

In 1994, a subdivision was created, dividing a parcel of land into two residential lots, one of which is owned by plaintiffs and the other by defendants. Pursuant to an express grant in the subdivision plat, plaintiffs hold a 40–foot-wide right-of-way easement across defendants' property. On the easement is a driveway which is the sole access route from a public road to plaintiffs' property. Shortly after purchasing the burdened lot, defendants erected fence gates and installed cattle guards at both ends of the driveway.

Plaintiffs sought an injunction to compel defendants to remove the cattle guards and fence gates, characterizing the installations as obstructions which interfered with their rights to use of the easement. The trial court granted summary judgment and ordered defendants to remove the obstructions. This appeal followed.

Defendants contend on appeal that the trial court did not apply the correct standards for granting summary judgment, and that their use of the burdened land was reasonable as a matter of law. Specifically, they argue that the trial court's findings were not supported by undisputed facts in the record, and that the court failed to give reasonable inferences to defendants as the nonmoving party. We agree that the trial court improperly granted the motion for summary judgment.

* * *

Here, it was undisputed that the easement existed, that it had certain boundaries, and that defendants had installed the gates and cattle guards on the easement. However, the parties disagreed as to whether the installation of gates and cattle guards unreasonably interfered with plaintiffs' use of the easement. As a basis for its decision to grant summary judgment, the trial court made findings regarding the intent of the parties and made conclusions based on those findings. The court stated that one factor it considered was the "intention of the parties given the circumstances surrounding the grant," and noted that, at the time of the grant, cattle guards and fences were not contemplated.

The issue of intent is generally a question of fact which can only rarely be resolved by means of a summary judgment. Also, the trial court should not have assessed the weight of the evidence on summary judgment; that process is appropriate only after an evidentiary hearing. The fact that the disputed installations were not contemplated at the time of the grant does not necessarily mean they were prohibited.

If a right-of-way is granted without a reservation of the right to maintain gates, the servient estate owner is not necessarily precluded from installing gates, including cattle guards, unless such gates are expressly prohibited in the grant or unless a prohibition is implied from the circumstances. The servient owner may maintain gates across the way if necessary for the use of the servient estate and if the gates do not unreasonably interfere with the right of passage. Fortner v. Eldorado Springs Resort Co., 76 Colo. 106, 230 P. 386 (1924); see generally Annot., Fence or Gate Across Right of Way, 52 A.L.R.3d 9 at § 3 (1973).

"When an easement exists, so does a dichotomy of interests which must be respected and, as nearly as possible, kept in balance." Lazy Dog Ranch v. Telluray Ranch Corp., 923 P.2d 313, 316 (Colo.App.1996).

In regard to that balance, the owner of land subject to a right-of-way may use the way for any lawful purpose, provided such use does not interfere with the right of passage resting in the owner of the easement.

Also, ordinarily, what may be considered a proper use by the servient owner is a question of fact.

* * *

The necessity for the gates and fences and the reasonableness of interference with the right of passage presented genuine issues of fact. Hence, plaintiffs were not entitled to judgment as a matter of law; instead, the issues should be resolved only after the parties have an opportunity to present evidence regarding the need for and the reasonableness of the installation of the gates and cattle guards.

The judgment is reversed and the cause is remanded to the trial court for further proceedings consistent with this opinion.

Notes and Problems

1. On remand, what considerations should guide the court in ascertaining whether the servient owner can erect gates and cattle guards? Could the servient owner install locked gates, giving a key to the dominant owner? *See* Ballington v. Paxton, 327 S.C. 372, 488 S.E.2d 882 (App.1997).

2. As indicated in *Schold,* adjusting the rights of the owners of the dominant and servient tenements can be difficult. How should the following disputes be resolved?

(a) An instrument conveys a right of way to A and clearly defines its location across O's land. May O build over the right of way, substituting an equally convenient strip for A's use? Suppose the instrument did not specifically describe the location of the right of way, but a particular strip has been used by A since the grant. Same result? *See* Sakansky v. Wein, 86 N.H. 337, 169 A. 1 (1933).

(b) O, the owner of Greenacre, granted a five-foot easement to A for the purpose of installing a water main. A installed water lines, partially occupying the area of the easement. O then granted a similar easement in the same strip to B. A sued B for an injunction to prevent invasion of A's easement. Is A entitled to the injunction? *See* City of Pasadena v. California–Michigan Land and Water Company, 17 Cal.2d 576, 110 P.2d 983 (1941).

c. *Maintenance*

TRIPLETT v. BEUCKMAN

Appellate Court of Illinois, Fifth District, 1976.
40 Ill.App.3d 379, 352 N.E.2d 458.

JONES, JUSTICE.

Plaintiffs appeal from a judgment for defendants rendered in a bench trial in plaintiffs' action for a mandatory injunction requiring defendants to remove a causeway access to an island and replace it with a bridge. Defendants' counterclaim for a judgment for the cost of construction of the causeway resulted in a judgment for plaintiffs, from which no appeal was taken.

On March 10, 1971, Susan Triplett, as executrix of the estate of Francis L. Wortman, and defendants entered into a written contract for the sale of certain real property from the Wortman estate to defendants. The property conveyed consisted of an island, with residential improvements, except for a riparian ten foot circumferential strip, which was retained by the grantor. Defendants were granted the right to use and cross that ten foot strip of land but not to improve it. The lake in which the island was located and all of the land surrounding the lake were also part of the estate of Francis L. Wortman. Defendants were granted "the right to recreational use" of the lake "jointly with the owners of said lake." They were also granted an easement "for roadway purposes" across a described portion of the land surrounding the lake to a bridge, "thence North across said bridge a distance of 60 feet more or less to the island."

The bridge referred to provided the only above-water access to the island. It was wooden; and at the time of the conveyance was in need of repair. According to his uncontradicted testimony, defendant Fred Beuckman attempted to obtain the assistance of plaintiffs in repairing the bridge not long after defendants began to occupy the island residence. However, in response to this request Susan Triplett had stated "that's not my baby, it's all yours." Thereafter defendants repaired the bridge by resurfacing it with concrete and iron reinforcing rods. These repairs proved unsuccessful when a portion of the bridge "gave way." Consequently, defendants removed the bridge, filled the same area with soil, rock, and concrete, paved the surface with asphalt, and covered the sides of the fill with stone.

According to the testimony of Susan Triplett and William Wortman, the removal of the bridge and construction of the causeway deprived the plaintiffs of the fastest or most convenient water access from some points along the lake to other points and cut off plaintiffs' ability to take advantage of the circular nature of the lake for boating and water-skiing activities. Plaintiffs introduced evidence that prior to the construction of the causeway they were able to boat and water-ski completely around the island by passing under the bridge. Accordingly the causeway constituted a severe restriction on the recreational use of their lake. In the opinion of Susan Triplett the property surrounding the lake would decrease in value as a consequence of the construction of the causeway.

Fred Beuckman, on the other hand, testified that at the time the bridge was removed "there was hardly any water underneath the bridge to start with. It was all dried up." In Beuckman's opinion it would not have been possible to water-ski under the bridge "Unless you put wheels on the bottoms of the skis, cause there was no water there at all hardly."

Joan Beuckman testified that the causeway was "[m]uch more attractive" than the bridge. Additionally an engineer and two iron workers testified that they had advised defendants prior to the removal of the bridge that the bridge could not be sufficiently repaired and would have to be replaced.

Based upon the testimony and the trial court's personal viewing (by stipulation of the parties) of the causeway, the court found "[t]he entire result is a practical result to an unusual problem and presents a reasonably attractive access to the 'island' [now 'peninsula']." The court also found that any injury to plaintiffs because of the construction of the causeway "was occasioned by plaintiffs' joint and several acts of disinterest or refusal to cooperate," and refused to issue the requested injunction.

We are of the opinion that the trial court erred in refusing to issue a mandatory injunction requiring the removal of the causeway and reconstruction of the bridge. The easement in this case was determined by express grant. The grant fixed the passage over the water or lakebed as being "across" a bridge then in existence at a described location. This situation is significantly different from one in which the easement is described without reference to a particular structure, such as a bridge, or one in which the easement arises by implication, such as a way of necessity. The parties could have agreed upon some different means of access to the island, as, for example, by ford or ferry or causeway, which could have imposed a lesser or greater burden upon the servient tenement. However, they did not. In light of the fact that the lake was and is used primarily for recreation, the limitation to access by bridge cannot be ignored. As is stated in the Restatement of the Law, Property:

> "The use made of the servient tenement prior to the creation of an easement by conveyance may be a factor in ascertaining the extent of the easement." 5 Restatement of the Law, Property, sec. 483, Comment i, p. 3018.

It is well settled that, in the absence of an agreement to the contrary, the owner of the easement has not only the right but the duty to keep the easement in repair, while the owner of the servient tenement has no duty to either put or keep the easement in repair. The only duty the owner of the servient tenement has is to not interfere with the use of the easement for purposes of access by the owner of the dominant tenement, that is, the owner of the easement.

It has also been stated that once the point or place at which, or line along which, an easement is to be exercised is fixed, whether by express grant or otherwise by agreement or acquiescence, neither of the parties can change such location without the consent of the other. Moreover, although the owner of the dominant estate has the duty to maintain and repair the easement, he cannot make a material alteration in the character of the easement, even though it be more to his convenience to do so, if the alteration places a greater burden upon the servient estate or interferes with the use and enjoyment of the servient estate by its owner.

In the light of the above * * * , it is apparent that the duty to maintain and repair the bridge in the instant case was that of defendants, the Beuckmans. In destroying the bridge and constructing a causeway, defendants materially altered the character of the easement and increased the burden on the servient tenement. Plaintiffs are unable to use and enjoy that portion of the lake or lakebed which was previously accessible under the bridge, but which now is covered by the causeway. Plaintiffs had the right to have the bridge maintained and are entitled to injunctive relief; and the court below erred in refusing to grant that relief.

We expressly decline to conclude, however, that defendants should be required to reconstruct a bridge 60 feet in length. A court of chancery can balance the hardships involved and grant relief upon whatever terms it deems equitable when the owner of either the dominant or the servient estate interferes with the rights of the other, under a mistaken belief that he owns the area or structure in dispute. In the instant case both Susan Triplett and Fred Beuckman testified that they had thought that the Beuckmans owned the bridge as a result of the conveyance discussed above. It was under this mistaken belief that Fred Beuckman had the bridge removed.

Furthermore, although Susan Triplett and William Wortman testified that plaintiffs had at some previous time been able to boat and water-ski under the bridge, Fred Beuckman testified that at the time the bridge was removed there was not a sufficient amount of water beneath the bridge for water-skiing. Neither the testimony of Beuckman nor that of Triplett and Wortman was contradicted.

We, of course, do not have, and cannot have, the benefit of a personal examination of the lake to determine what amount of water may have been in that part of the lake at the time the bridge was destroyed or at the time of the decision of the trial court. Nor do we know what amount of water may have been under the bridge at times prior to its removal or what amount might have been there in the future. The trial court has had the opportunity of personal examination. Based upon that examination, the trial court should be able to determine the length of the bridge span necessary for the reasonable use of the water that can reasonably be expected to be in that portion of the lake. It may very well be that use can be made of some of the causeway and that a bridge of less than 60 feet is sufficient for recreational use of that portion of the lake. If so, the trial court, acting in equity, should frame the relief granted in such terms as will take those factors into account.

We, therefore, reverse the judgment of the trial court with respect to plaintiffs' complaint and remand for further proceedings consistent with this opinion.

Reversed and remanded with directions.

Eberspacher, Justice (dissenting).

I agree, as the majority states, "A court of chancery can balance the hardships involved and grant relief upon whatever terms it deems equitable when the owner of either the dominant or the servient estate interferes with the rights of the other, under a mistaken belief that he owns the area or structure in dispute." That, however, is not the function of an intermediate reviewing court.

It appears that the trial court has applied that principle, after hearing the testimony and examining the premises. It has obviously balanced the hardships involved and granted relief upon terms it deemed equitable. The majority is saying, balance the hardships again and grant relief upon different terms which we consider equitable. If the principle is to be here applied, the uncontradicted testimony that there is and was at the point where the bridge existed, an inadequate amount of water to boat, ski or swim, has to be, and obviously was, taken into consideration.

d. Transferability

Easements appurtenant are transferred with the dominant tenement whether or not they are mentioned in the deed or devise. In this regard, reconsider *Corbett v. Ruben* on page 327. The transfer of easements in gross is a more difficult problem, as the following case demonstrates.

Problem

O owned Blackacre, a dominant tenement with a right of way over Whiteacre, an adjoining parcel. Can O convey Blackacre to Y and the right of way to Z?

MILLER v. LUTHERAN CONFERENCE AND CAMP ASSOCIATION

Supreme Court of Pennsylvania, 1938.
331 Pa. 241, 200 A. 646.

Opinion by MR. JUSTICE STERN, June 30, 1938:

This litigation is concerned with interesting and somewhat novel legal questions regarding rights of boating, bathing and fishing in an artificial lake.

Frank C. Miller, his brother Rufus W. Miller, and others, who owned lands on Tunkhannock Creek in Tobyhanna Township, Monroe County, organized a corporation known as the Pocono Spring Water Ice Company, to which, in September, 1895, they made a lease for a term of ninety-nine years of so much of their lands as would be covered by the backing up of the water as a result of the construction of a 14–foot dam which they proposed to erect across the creek. The company was to have "the exclusive use of the water and its privileges." It was chartered for the purpose of "erecting a dam * * *, for pleasure, boating, skating, fishing and the cutting, storing and selling of ice." The dam was built, forming "Lake Naomi," somewhat more than a mile long and about one-third of a mile wide.

By deed dated March 20, 1899, the Pocono Spring Water Ice Company granted to "Frank C. Miller, his heirs and assigns forever, the exclusive right to fish and boat in all the waters of the said corporation at Naomi Pines, Pa." On February 17, 1900, Frank C. Miller (his wife Katherine D. Miller not joining) granted to Rufus W. Miller, his heirs and assigns forever, "all the one-fourth interest in and to the fishing, boating, and bathing rights and privileges at, in, upon and about Lake Naomi * * * ; which said rights and privileges were granted and conveyed to me by the Pocono Spring Water Ice Company by their indenture of the 20th day of March, A.D. 1899." On the same day Frank C. Miller and Rufus W. Miller executed an agreement of business partnership, the purpose of which was the erection and operation of boat and bath houses on Naomi Lake and the purchase and maintenance of boats for use on the lake, the houses and boats to be rented for hire and the net proceeds to be divided between the parties in proportion to their respective interests in the bathing, boating and fishing privileges, namely, three-fourths to Frank C. Miller and one-fourth to Rufus W. Miller, the capital to be contributed and the losses to be borne in the same proportion. In pursuance of this agreement the brothers erected and maintained boat and bath houses at different points on the lake, purchased and rented out boats, and conducted the business generally, from the spring of 1900 until the death of Rufus W. Miller on October 11, 1925, exercising their control and use of the privileges in an exclusive, uninterrupted and open manner and without challenge on the part of anyone.

Discord began with the death of Rufus W. Miller, which terminated the partnership. Thereafter Frank C. Miller, and the executors and heirs of Rufus W. Miller, went their respective ways, each granting licenses without reference to the other. Under date of July 13, 1929, the executors of the Rufus W. Miller estate granted a license for the year 1929 to defendant, Lutheran Conference and Camp Association, which was the owner of a tract of ground abutting on the lake for a distance of about 100 feet, purporting to grant to defendant, its members, guests and campers, permission to boat, bathe and fish in the lake, a certain percentage of the receipts therefrom to be paid to the estate. Thereupon Frank C. Miller and his wife, Katherine D. Miller, filed the present bill in equity, complaining that defendant was placing diving floats on the lake and "encouraging and instigating visitors and boarders" to bathe in the lake, and was threatening to hire out boats and canoes and in general to license its guests and others to boat, bathe and fish in the lake. The bill prayed for an injunction to prevent defendant from trespassing on the lands covered by the waters of the lake, from erecting or maintaining any structures or other encroachments thereon, and from granting any bathing licenses. The court issued the injunction.

It is the contention of plaintiffs that, while the privileges of boating and fishing were granted in the deed from the Pocono Spring Water Ice Company to Frank C. Miller, no *bathing* rights were conveyed by that instrument. * * * They further contend that even if such bathing rights ever did vest in Frank C. Miller, all of the boating, bathing and fishing privileges were easements in gross which were inalienable and indivisible, and when Frank C. Miller undertook to convey a one-fourth interest in them to Rufus W. Miller he not only failed to transfer a legal title to the rights but, in attempting to do so, extinguished the rights altogether as against Katherine D. Miller, who was the successor in title of the Pocono Spring Water Ice Company. It is defendant's contention, on the other hand, that the deed of 1899 from the Pocono Spring Water Ice Company to Frank C. Miller should be construed as transferring the bathing as well as the boating and fishing privileges, but that if Frank C. Miller did not obtain them by grant he and Rufus W. Miller acquired them by prescription, and that all of these rights were alienable and divisible even if they be considered as easements in gross, although they might more properly, perhaps, be regarded as licenses which became irrevocable because of the money spent upon their development by Frank C. Miller and Rufus W. Miller.

* * *

It is impossible to construe the deed of 1899 from the Pocono Spring Water Ice Company to Frank C. Miller as conveying to the latter any privileges of bathing. It is clear and unambiguous. It gives to Frank C. Miller the exclusive right to *fish and boat.* Expressio unius est exclusio alterius. No *bathing* rights are mentioned. This omission may have been the result of oversight or it may have been deliberate, but in either event the legal consequence is the same. * * *

But, while Frank C. Miller acquired by grant merely boating and fishing privileges, the facts are amply sufficient to establish title to the bathing rights by prescription. True, these rights, not having been granted in connection with, or to be attached to, the ownership of any land, were not easements appurtenant but in gross. There is, however, no inexorable principle of law which forbids an adverse enjoyment of an easement in gross from ripening into a title thereto by prescription. * * * Certainly the casual use of a lake during a few months each year for boating and fishing could not develop into a title to such privileges by prescription. But here the exercise of the bathing right was not carried on sporadically by Frank C. Miller and his assignee Rufus W. Miller for their personal enjoyment but systematically for commercial purposes in the pursuit of which they conducted an extensive and profitable business enterprise. The circumstances thus presented must be viewed from a realistic standpoint. Naomi Lake is situated in the Pocono Mountains district, has become a summer resort for campers and boarders, and, except for the ice it furnishes, its bathing and boating facilities are the factors which give it its prime importance and value. They were exploited from the time the lake was created, and are recited as among the purposes for which the Pocono Spring Water Ice Company was chartered. From the early part of 1900 down to at least the filing of the present bill in 1929, Frank C. Miller and Rufus W. Miller openly carried on their business of constructing and operating bath houses and licensing individuals and camp associations to use the lake for bathing. This was known to the stockholders of the Pocono Spring Water Ice Company and necessarily also to Katherine D. Miller, the wife of Frank C. Miller;

no objection of any kind was made, and Frank C. Miller and Rufus W. Miller were encouraged to expend large sums of money in pursuance of the right of which they considered and asserted themselves to be the owners. Under such circumstances it would be highly unjust to hold that a title by prescription to the bathing rights did not vest in Frank C. Miller and Rufus W. Miller which is just as valid, as far as Katherine D. Miller is concerned, as that to the boating and fishing rights which Frank C. Miller obtained by express grant.

We are thus brought to a consideration of the next question, which is whether the boating, bathing and fishing privileges were assignable by Frank C. Miller to Rufus W. Miller. What is the nature of such rights? In England it has been said that easements in gross do not exist at all, although rights of that kind have been there recognized. In this country such privileges have sometimes been spoken of as licenses, or as contractual in their nature, rather than as easements in gross. These are differences of terminology rather than of substance. We may assume, therefore, that these privileges are easements in gross, and we see no reason to consider them otherwise. It has uniformly been held that a profit in gross—for example, a right of mining or fishing—may be made assignable. In regard to easements in gross generally, there has been much controversy in the courts and by textbook writers and law students as to whether they have the attribute of assignability. There are dicta in Pennsylvania that they are non-assignable. But there is forcible expression and even definite authority to the contrary. Tide-Water Pipe Co. v. Bell, 280 Pa. 104, 112, 113. There does not seem to be any reason why the law should prohibit the assignment of an easement in gross if the parties to its creation evidence their intention to make it assignable. Here, as in *Tide-Water Pipe Company v. Bell,* supra, the rights of fishing and boating were conveyed to the grantee—in this case Frank C. Miller—"his heirs and assigns," thus showing that the grantor, the Pocono Spring Water Ice Company, intended to attach the attribute of assignability to the privileges granted. Moreover, as a practical matter, there is an obvious difference in this respect between easements for personal enjoyment and those designed for commercial exploitation; while there may be little justification for permitting assignments in the former case, there is every reason for upholding them in the latter.

The question of assignability of the easements in gross in the present case is not as important as that of their divisibility. It is argued by plaintiffs that even if held to be assignable such easements are not divisible, because this might involve an excessive user or "surcharge of the easement" subjecting the servient tenement to a greater burden than originally contemplated. The law does not take that extreme position. It does require, however, that, if there be a division, the easements must be used or exercised as an entirety. This rule had its earliest expression in *Mountjoy's Case,* which is reported in Co.Litt. 164b, 165a. It was there said, in regard to the grant of a right to dig for ore, that the grantee, Lord Mountjoy, "might assign his whole interest to one, two, or more; but then, if there be two or more, they could make no division of it, but work together with one stock." In Caldwell v. Fulton, 31 Pa. 475, 477, 478, 72 Am.Dec. 760 and in Funk v. Haldeman, 53 Pa. 229, that case was followed, and it was held that the right of a grantee to mine coal or to prospect for oil might be assigned, but if to more than one they must hold, enjoy and convey the right as an entirety, and not divide it in severalty. There are cases in other jurisdictions which also approve the doctrine of *Mountjoy's Case,* and hold that a mining right in gross is essentially integral and not susceptible of apportionment; an assignment of it is valid, but it cannot be aliened in such a way that it may be utilized by grantor and grantee, or by several grantees, separately; there must be a joint user, nor can one of the tenants alone convey a share in the common right.

These authorities furnish an illuminating guide to the solution of the problem of divisibility of profits or easements in gross. They indicate that much depends upon the nature of the right and the terms of its creation, that "surcharge of the easement" is prevented if assignees exercise the right as "one stock," and that a proper method of enjoyment of the easement by two or more owners of it may usually be worked out in any given instance without insuperable difficulty.

In the present case it seems reasonably clear that in the conveyance of February 17, 1900, it was not the intention of Frank C. Miller to grant, and of Rufus W. Miller to receive, a separate right to subdivide and sublicense the boating, fishing and bathing privileges on and in Lake Naomi, but only that they should together use such rights for commercial purposes, Rufus W. Miller to be entitled to one-fourth and Frank C. Miller to three-fourths of the proceeds resulting from their combined exploitation of the privileges. They were to hold the rights, in the quaint phraseology of *Mountjoy's Case,* as "one stock." Nor do the technical rules that would be applicable to a tenancy in common of a corporeal hereditament apply to the control of these easements in gross. Defendant contends that, as a tenant in common of the privileges, Rufus W. Miller individually was entitled to their use, benefit and possession and to exercise rights of ownership in regard thereto, including the right to license third persons to use them, subject only to the limitation that he must not thereby interfere with the similar rights of his co-tenant. But the very nature of these easements prevents their being so exercised, inasmuch as it is necessary, because of the legal limitations upon their divisibility, that they should be utilized in common, and not by two owners severally, and, as stated, this was evidently the intention of the brothers.

Summarizing our conclusions, we are of opinion (1) that Frank C. Miller acquired title to the boating and fishing privileges by grant and he and Rufus W. Miller to the bathing rights by prescription; (2) that he made a valid assignment of a one-fourth interest in them to Rufus W. Miller; but (3) that they cannot be commercially used and licenses thereunder granted without the common consent and joinder of the present owners, who with regard to them must act as "one stock." It follows that the executors of the estate of Rufus W. Miller did not have the right, in and by themselves, to grant a license to defendant.

The decree is affirmed; costs to be paid by defendant.

Notes and Questions

1. The traditional rule is that easements in gross are not assignable and die with the holder. However, as the *Miller* case indicates, courts have generally found commercial easements in gross assignable. Examples include easements for railroad tracks, telephone lines, and water mains. Further, courts sometimes find noncommercial easements in gross assignable upon a showing that alienability was intended by the original parties. *See* J. Bruce & J. Ely, The Law of Easements and Licenses in Land ¶ 9.03 (rev.ed.1995 & Supp.1998); Note, *The Easement in Gross Revisited: Transferability and Divisibility Since 1945,* 39 Vand.L.Rev. 109 (1986). Why do courts permit the transfer of commercial easements in gross? Why not afford the same treatment for noncommercial easements in gross?

2. Does the court in *Miller* properly balance the principle of free alienability with the need to eliminate potential clogs on title and to protect the servient tenement against an inappropriate surcharge? Is the one-stock rule workable with respect to modern commercial easement arrangements? *See* J. Bruce & J. Ely, The Laws of Easements and Licenses in Land ¶ 9.04 (rev.ed.1995 & Supp.1998).

3. Assume that four adjoining property owners each granted the following easement to XYZ Power Company: "Party of the first part conveys to XYZ Power Company, its successors, assigns, and lessees forever, a right-of-way with the authority to erect, operate, and maintain a line of poles and wires for the purpose of transmitting electric or other power, including telegraph and telephone wires, across the following described lands." Some years later, XYZ Power Company granted Cable TV Company the right to install a television cable on XYZ's poles. May the property owners prevent Cable TV from installing the cable? *See* Jolliff v. Hardin Cable Television Co., 26 Ohio St.2d 103, 269 N.E.2d 588 (1971); *see also* Centel Cable Television Company of Ohio, Inc. v. Cook, 58 Ohio St.3d 8, 567 N.E.2d 1010 (1991).

e. *Termination*

Easements may be terminated in several ways.

1. An express easement may contain provision for its own expiration. For example, a landowner may grant an easement for a set time period or until the occurrence of a particular event. (*See Corbett v. Ruben* on page 327 involving an easement created for the life of a building).

2. An easement implied from necessity alone will end when the necessity ends. This occurs whenever a reasonable alternative to the easement of necessity becomes available to the easement holder. If an implied easement is based upon a quasi-easement, the end of the necessity will not terminate the easement.

3. An easement may be released by its holder.

4. An easement ends by merger when title to both the servient tenement and the dominant tenement come into the same hands.

5. An easement may be terminated by prescription. If the owner of the servient tenement obstructs the easement area or otherwise interferes with the rights of the easement holder for the prescriptive period, the easement is extinguished.

6. An easement terminates when it is abandoned. (See *Lindsey v. Clark* which follows for a discussion of abandonment.)

7. An easement may be extinguished by estoppel. For example, if the owner of the servient tenement improves the servient land in reliance on the easement holder's non-use, the holder may be estopped from using the easement. (See *Lindsey v. Clark* which follows for a discussion of extinguishment by estoppel.)

8. An easement may be terminated by the destruction of a building that serves as the dominant or servient tenement.

9. An easement is extinguished when the holder of the dominant tenement misuses the easement in such a manner that it is impossible for a court to enjoin the misuse. *See* Crimmins v. Gould, 149 Cal.App.2d 383, 308 P.2d 786 (1957).

10. An easement may end when the servient estate is conveyed to a bona fide purchaser without actual, constructive, or inquiry notice of the easement. (See pages 535–553 for a discussion of notice.)

11. An easement may be extinguished when the servient tenement is condemned by the government under the power of eminent domain. The easement holder is, of course, entitled to "just compensation." (See pages 760–818 for a discussion of eminent domain.)

See J. Bruce & J. Ely, The Law of Easements and Licenses in Land ¶¶ 10.01–10.13 (rev.ed.1995 & Supp.1998); 4 Powell on Real Property §§ 34.18–34.23 (1998); 7 Thompson on Real Property §§ 60.08–60.08(d)(2) (1994 & Supp.1998).

LINDSEY v. CLARK

Supreme Court of Appeals of Virginia, 1952.
193 Va. 522, 69 S.E.2d 342.

BUCHANAN, JUSTICE.

This suit was instituted by the Lindseys to enjoin the Clarks from using a driveway along the north side of the Lindsey lots and to have themselves adjudged the fee simple owners of the two lots claimed by them. The trial court held that the Clarks owned a right of way on the south side of the Lindsey lots and, in effect, put the Lindseys on terms to make it available to them or else allow the Clarks to continue using the one on the north side.

There is no controversy about the controlling facts.

In 1937 the Clarks were the owners of four adjoining lots, Nos. 31, 32, 33 and 34, each fronting 25 feet on the east side of Magnolia avenue in West Waynesboro, and running back 150 feet to a 20–foot alley. The Clark residence was on Nos. 31 and 32.

By deed dated July 24, 1937, the Clarks conveyed to C.W. Six and Mabel G. Six, his wife, the latter being a daughter of the Clarks, the front two-thirds of Lots 33 and 34, being a frontage of 50 feet and extending back 100 feet. On the rear one-third of these two lots Clark erected a dwelling and garage for rental purposes. After this conveyance the Sixes built a house on their property, approximately 15 feet from the Clark line on the north and about 8 feet from their own line on the south. The Clark deed to the Sixes contained this reservation: "There is reserved, however, a right-of-way ten (10) feet in width, along the South side of the two lots herein conveyed, for the benefit of the property in the rear."

By deed of January 16, 1939, the Sixes conveyed their property to William H. McGhee and wife, with the same reservation; and by deed of March 16, 1944, the McGhees conveyed the property to the Lindseys, without any reservation.

These three deeds were all made with general warranty and both the deed to the Sixes and the deed to the McGhees were duly recorded prior to the date of the deed to the Lindseys.

Notwithstanding that the 10–foot right of way was reserved by Clark along the south side of the property conveyed to the Sixes, now owned by the Lindseys, Clark proceeded to use it along the north side of the Six property, and has so used it ever since, without objection by the Sixes, or by the McGhees, or by the Lindseys until a few months before this suit was brought. There is no explanation of this change of location. Six, a witness for the Lindseys, testified that Clark stood in the driveway on the north and said, "I am reserving this driveway to get to my back property." The time of that statement is not shown, but the words suggest it was at or before the time of the conveyance to the Sixes. When the McGhees bought the property in 1939, Six pointed out to them the driveway on the north, but the reservation in the deed he made to the McGhees was, as stated, on the south.

In 1946 the Lindseys had their attorney write to Clark, referring to the right of way in the deed to the McGhees, their grantors, and complaining, not of its location, but of its being used for parking purposes. Again, on November 7, 1949, they had their attorney write Clark, calling attention to the fact that the reservation was along the south side of their property and complaining about the use of a water line on their property which had not been reserved. The Lindseys, the letter stated, wanted to erect a line fence and suggested a discussion of the matter before this was done.

The Lindseys contend that the Clarks now have no right of way across their property because none was reserved along the north side and the one reserved on the south side has been abandoned and thereby extinguished. The trial court held it had not been abandoned and that holding was clearly right.

Abandonment is a question of intention. A person entitled to a right of way or other easement in land may abandon and extinguish such right by acts *in pais;* and a cessation of use coupled with acts or circumstances clearly showing an intention to abandon the right will be as effective as an express release of the right.

But mere non-user of an easement created by deed, for a period however long, will not amount to abandonment. In addition to the non-user there must be acts or circumstances clearly manifesting an intention to abandon; or an adverse user by the owner of the servient estate, acquiesced in by the owner of the dominant estate, for a period sufficient to create a prescriptive right. Nor is a right of way extinguished by the habitual use by its owner of another equally convenient way unless there is an intentional abandonment of the former way.

The burden of proof to show the abandonment of an easement is upon the party claiming such abandonment, and it must be established by clear and unequivocal evidence.

Clark specifically reserved a right of way over the lots now owned by the Lindseys. Very clearly he had no intention of abandoning that right of way. He was evidently mistaken as to where it was located; but his grantees, the Sixes, were likewise mistaken, as were also their grantees, the McGhees. Clark's use on the wrong location of the right of way reserved by him did not establish an intention on his part to abandon his right of way on the right location. He could not have intended to abandon his easement on the south of the Lindsey lots when he did not know that that was where his easement was.

The residence built by the Sixes, and now occupied by the Lindseys, encroaches by about two feet on the 10–foot alley when located on the south side, and the Lindsey property on that side within the 10–foot space is terraced and planted with shrubbery and a tree. The Lindseys argue that the Clarks are estopped from claiming a right of way on that side because Clark knew where the Sixes were building the house. The only testimony about that is from Six, who said that Clark was away at work when the house was being built but came and went every day to and from his home on the adjoining property, saw where the house was located and made no objection; but Six also said that Clark had nothing to do with locating the house. There is no evidence that Clark knew, any more than Six knew, that the house was encroaching on the right of way. Clark did not think the right of way was on that side. Even if he had known it was there, he would not likely have known that Six was building on it. The location of the house was not influenced by anything Clark did or said. Clark knew nothing about the matter that Six did not know.

"It is essential to the application of the principles of equitable estoppel, or estoppel *in pais,* that the party claiming to have been influenced by the conduct or declarations of another to his injury, was not only ignorant of the true state of facts, but had no convenient and available means of acquiring such information, and where the facts are known to both parties, and both had the same means of ascertaining the truth, there can be no estoppel." Lindsay v. James, 188 Va. 646, 659, 51 S.E.2d 326, 332.

The Lindseys had both actual and constructive knowledge of the situation. The driveway was there on the north side when they bought the property and Lindsey testified he could see where cars had been using it. They negligently failed to have their title examined but they are, of course, chargeable with the information contained in the recorded deeds.

The suit therefore developed this situation: The Clarks were entitled to a 10–foot right of way along the south side of the Lindsey property. The right of way was partially blocked by the Lindsey house with its terraces and shrubbery. To require their removal would be very expensive to the Lindseys and damaging to their property. The Clarks were willing to let their right of way continue to be located on the north side.

The court was well warranted in resolving the matter by applying the maxim "He who seeks equity must do equity." That means that "he who seeks the aid of an equity court subjects himself to the imposition of such terms as the settled principles of equity require, and that whatever be the nature of the controversy between the parties, and whatever be the nature of the remedy demanded, the court will not confer its equitable relief on the party seeking its interposition and aid, unless he has acknowledged and conceded, or will admit and provide for, all the equitable rights, claims, and demands justly belonging to the adversary party, and growing out of, or necessarily involved in, the subject matter of the controversy." 30 C.J.S. Equity, § 91, p. 461.

A court of equity may in a case in which the principles and rules of equity demand it, condition its granting of the relief sought by the complainant upon the enforcement of a claim or equity held by the defendant which the latter could not enforce in any other way.

The decree of the trial court provided: "The Court will not require the expensive removal of the obstruction, so long as the right-of-way along the north side of the property is made available. However, it is ordered that the defendants desist from the use of the right-of-way for any purpose other than the use of the rear one-third portion of Lots 33 and 34, and only for the right of passage over and across the said right-of-way to and from the property in the rear." And, further, "Should the complainants make an election under this order, a further order will be entered fixing the rights of the respective parties."

The decree appealed from is affirmed and the cause is remanded for further decree as indicated.

Affirmed and remanded.

Note

The rails-to-trails movement, spurred by a 1983 amendment of the National Trails System Act (16 U.S.C.A. § 1247(d) (West 1985 & Supp. 1998)), has raised several easement issues. Creation, overburden, and abandonment concerns exist within the context of the taking controversy which surrounds the statutory scheme designed to facilitate converting unused railroad lines to trails for recreational use. *See* J. Bruce & J. Ely, The Law of Easements and Licenses in Land ¶ 12.08 (rev.ed.1995 & Supp.1998). For a significant decision in the ongoing takings litigation in this area that treats the easement concerns noted, see Preseault v. United States, 100 F.3d 1525 (Fed.Cir.1996)(finding compensation was due servient estate owner for Fifth Amendment taking that occurred when railroad right-of-way was transformed into hiking and bicycling trail).

2. LICENSES

MOSHER v. COOK UNITED, INC.

Supreme Court of Ohio, 1980.
62 Ohio St.2d 316, 405 N.E.2d 720.

Plaintiff-appellant, Arthur J. Mosher, was a member of a food cooperative in which members pooled their grocery money to buy in bulk at lower unit prices. In response to a newspaper advertisement by defendant-appellee, Hudson Food Warehouse Corporation, displaying lower prices than competitive stores and advising shoppers to "check and compare," appellant and his family drove to the food warehouse with the intention to purchase food for the cooperative.

Upon entering the store appellant began to write down prices, as was his custom, in order to make comparisons for the most economical purchases. Appellant was thereupon approached by store employees and informed that it was against store policy to write down prices and that appellant must either cease to do so, or leave the store. Appellant refused either alternative. A police officer, who was called from special duty in an adjacent store, placed appellant under arrest for violating Columbus City Code No. 2305.04(A)(4). This trespass ordinance provided that a person without a privilege to be on premises of another must leave the premises when told to do so by the owner or occupant of the premises. The charge against appellant was reduced and the reduced charge eventually dismissed.

Appellant then brought this action in the Court of Common Pleas of Franklin County asserting several grounds for relief. Following appellant's presentation of his case, the court granted a motion for directed verdict against appellant and dismissed the complaint. The Court of Appeals affirmed.

The cause is now before this court upon allowance of a motion to certify the record.

PER CURIAM.

Because appellant either elected to waive, or failed to make other arguably relevant legal challenges, we are confronted here with but one proposition, that being whether appellant, as a business invitee, possessed an irrevocable license to remain on appellee's premises so long as he behaved in an orderly manner. Our answer is that he did not possess such a privilege.

A license has been defined by this court as "an authority to do a particular act or series of acts upon another's land, without possessing any estate therein." Rodefer v. Pittsburg, O. V. & C. Rd. Co. (1905), 72 Ohio St. 272, 281, 74 N.E. 183, 185–186, citing Wolfe v. Frost, 4 Sanford's Chancery 72. One who possesses a license thus has the authority to enter the land in another's possession without being a trespasser. *Rodefer, supra.* The parties do not dispute that appellant's initial presence on appellee's property was authorized by virtue of a license. The conflict concerns the revocability of the license. If the license was revocable at the will of appellee, appellant became a trespasser at the point of revocation and his basis for relief is unfounded.

5 Restatement of Property 3133–34, Section 519, speaks to revocation of licenses. That section provides:

"(1) Except as stated in Subsections (2), (3) and (4), a license is terminable at the will of the possessor of the land subject to it.

"(2) In the termination of the license of one who has entered upon land under a license, the licensee must be given a reasonable opportunity to remove himself and his effects from the land.

"(3) A license coupled with an interest can be terminated only to such an extent as not to prevent the license from being effective to protect the interest with which it is coupled.

"(4) A licensee under such a license as is described in § 514 [dealing with licenses analogous to easements] who has made expenditures of capital or labor in the exercise of his license in reasonable reliance upon representations by the licensor as to the duration of the license, is privileged to continue the use permitted by the license to the extent reasonably necessary to realize upon his expenditures."

Appellee was, therefore, entitled to revoke appellant's license for any purpose, reasonable or not, unless any of subsections (2) through (4) were applicable. The record is clear that none of these subsections were applicable. Accordingly, upon the theory propounded by appellant before this court, appellee was legally justified in demanding that appellant leave the premises. Since appellant has failed to establish a basis for relief, the judgment of the Court of Appeals is affirmed.

Judgment affirmed.

HOFSTETTER, JUSTICE, dissenting.

The majority, in my opinion, has minimized the issue herein simply to the single proposition of whether appellant, as a business invitee, possessed an irrevocable license to remain on appellee's premises so long as he behaved in an orderly manner.

From the majority opinion concerning this proposition, I must dissent. The appellant, in response to "check and compare" advertising, drove a substantial number of miles in anticipation of buying groceries valued at several hundreds of dollars. The issue, as I see it, is not whether the business invitee had an irrevocable license to remain on appellee's premises on the terms noted in the majority opinion, but whether, having been invited to do exactly what he was doing, which consumed considerable time and expense on his part, he could be forced to leave on the day in question, when the record does not reveal that he behaved in a disorderly manner. On the contrary, it follows he was simply checking and comparing prices pursuant to the solicitation.

Clearly, from the evidence elicited in the instant cause, if the appellant had been able to commit to memory all of the prices, he could have remained on appellee's property so long as he behaved in an orderly manner. By reason of his frailty of being unable to commit to memory the prices he wished to compare, he wrote them down on a pad of paper. The real question then is, would all "comparison" shoppers, no matter how they performed their comparisons, be excluded from the appellee's store?

According to the record, there were no posted regulations concerning comparison shopping as conducted by the appellant. Even if there had been, they were vitiated momentarily to allow a reasonable number of days of comparison shopping as urged by the newspaper advertising. To hold as the majority did, it follows that there must be an absolute right to revoke a customer's privilege to be in the store at *any time*, even if he behaves in an orderly manner.

I would hold that, in this day and age, in order for the common law right to exclude a person from another's premises to become operative, when that person is there by specific invitation to do exactly what the appellant was doing, there must be a reasonable reason to exclude him, and notice must be given him that comports with the effort and expense incurred by the appellant. The rights of the appellant, in my opinion, were violated and the directed verdict should not have been granted.

Problem

B purchased a ticket to a basketball game that provided on its face: "Reserved ($25.00)—Section A, Row 7, Seat 12—Centerville University v. University of Michiana, Centerville Arena, 8:00 p.m., Saturday, November 27, 1999." What is B's interest in the designated seat? What is B's remedy if B is refused admission to the game when B presents the ticket? *See* Soderholm v. Chicago National League Ball Club, Inc., 225 Ill.App.3d 119, 167 Ill.Dec. 248, 587 N.E.2d 517 (1992); Bickett v. Buffalo Bills, 122 Misc.2d 880, 472 N.Y.S.2d 245 (1983).

LINRO EQUIPMENT CORPORATION v. WESTAGE TOWER ASSOCIATES

Supreme Court of New York, Appellate Division, Third Department, 1996.
233 A.D.2d 824, 650 N.Y.S.2d 399.

PETERS, JUSTICE.

* * *

In 1984, plaintiff entered into a seven-year agreement with defendant Westage Towers Associates (hereinafter Westage), the sponsor/developer for defendant Westage Towers West Condominium (hereinafter the Condominium), which obligated plaintiff to install and maintain coin-operated laundry machines on each of the 12 floors of the Condominium. In connection therewith, plaintiff agreed to pay a set sum for "rent", with offsets each month which included, inter alia, the cash equivalent of the price of one washing and one drying cycle per installed machine per day. It also provided that "[i]f during any three (3) month period, after rent, proceeds do not equal * * * one cycle per machine per day, Tenant shall have the right to cancel this lease and to remove the equipment upon thirty (30) days prior written notice". Plaintiff was given the option to renew for an additional seven-year period. In April 1985, after the filing of the declaration and bylaws of the Condominium, Westage was converted to condominium ownership and, thereafter, individual condominiums were sold.

Pursuant to its terms, the agreement commenced on March 1, 1987. By letter dated September 10, 1987, plaintiff notified Parke Rose Management Company, the managing corporation for Westage, that it was exercising its option to renew through March 1, 2001. In January 1989, Parke Rose was replaced by defendant Owen A. Mandeville Inc. (hereinafter Mandeville) as the new managing agent of the Condominium. Upon inquiry by Mandeville in July 1992 as to the expiration date of this agreement, plaintiff notified Mandeville, by letter dated July 16, 1992, that "the expiration date shall be March 1, 2001".

As a result of a myriad of complaints, Mandeville notified plaintiff that it was terminating the agreement, effective March 1, 1994. In November 1994, plaintiff received a letter from defendant Westage Towers West Condominium Board of Managers (hereinafter the Board) insisting that it remove its laundry machines.

Plaintiff commenced this action in December 1994 seeking, inter alia, a declaration that the agreement between itself and Westage was an enforceable lease which was validly extended until March 1, 2001. By order to show cause, plaintiff sought a preliminary injunction pending a hearing and further moved for a temporary restraining order (hereinafter TRO) to prevent defendants from removing the laundry machines or entering into any other commitment for the provision of laundry services during the pendency of the action.

On December 8, 1994 Supreme Court granted the TRO, which prompted a cross motion by defendants to have the TRO vacated and the complaint dismissed. Supreme Court, inter alia, refused to vacate the TRO pending a hearing and, further, denied defendants' motion to dismiss, finding a viable issue as to whether defendants had actual or constructive notice of the agreement. Finally, the court determined, as a matter of law, that the subject agreement was a lease and not a license. Defendants now appeal.

Reviewing first whether the agreement constitutes a lease or a license, it has generally been recognized that an agreement of this nature creates only a license (see, Todd v. Krolick, 96 A.D.2d 695, 466 N.Y.S.2d 788, affd 62 N.Y.2d 836, 477 N.Y.S.2d 609, 466 N.E.2d 149; Dime Laundry Serv. v. 230 Apts. Corp., 120 Misc.2d 399, 466 N.Y.S.2d 117; Kaypar Corp. v. Fosterport Realty Corp., 1 Misc.2d 469, 69 N.Y.S.2d 313, affd 272 App.Div. 878, 72 N.Y.S.2d 405), which "confers a personal privilege to do some act or acts on the land without possessing any interest therein" (Todd v. Krolick, supra, at 696, 466 N.Y.S.2d 788). For the agreement to constitute a lease and thus "create[] a landlord-tenant relationship depends on the intent of the parties and not on their characterization of the agreement" (Dime Laundry Serv. v. 230 Apts. Corp., supra, at 401, 466 N.Y.S.2d 117). To so find, we would have to conclude that, by the terms thereof, plaintiff paid rent "for outright ownership [of a definite space] for the duration of the term" (Kaypar Corp. v. Fosterport Realty Corp., supra, at 471, 69 N.Y.S.2d 313). Such exclusivity, necessary for the creation of a landlord-tenant relationship, could be indicated by "control over the patrons of the laundry services, control of the keys, or exclusion of other vending machines or services" (Dime Laundry Serv. v. 230 Apts. Corp., supra, at 401, 466 N.Y.S.2d 117).

Our review of this agreement reveals that, notwithstanding the terminology used, a mere license was created since the essential element of sole and exclusive dominion and control over the designated space was lacking. Plaintiff was required to keep the equipment in good working order and had only limited access to both the building and the laundry area. This agreement is indistinguishable from most other laundry-servicing agreements which create only a license to use a designated space for the purpose of providing and maintaining a service to the tenants. In so determining the agreement to be a license, which is a "personal, revocable and nonassignable privilege" (Dime Laundry Serv. v. 230 Apts. Corp., supra, at 403, 466 N.Y.S.2d 117), we further conclude that it was extinguished upon the conveyance of the property.

* * *

Accordingly, Supreme Court's order must be modified by granting defendants' cross motion to vacate the TRO and declaring that the agreement between the parties was a license.

ORDERED that the order is modified, on the law, without costs, by reversing so much thereof as denied defendants' cross motion to vacate the temporary restraining order; cross motion granted to that extent and it is declared that the agreement between the parties is a license; and, as so modified, affirmed.

Notes and Problems

1.   The county airport entered into a written agreement with several rental car companies under which the county provided the companies with counter space in the terminal and space in the parking lot. Thereafter the county announced plans to relocate the terminal. The rental companies complained that the projected move violated the terms of the arrangement. Is this contention sound? *See* Hilton Head Air Service, Inc. v. Beaufort County, 308 S.C. 450, 418 S.E.2d 849 (App.1992).

2.   For a well-known decision that distinguishes among leases, licenses, and easements in gross, see Baseball Publishing Co. v. Bruton, 302 Mass. 54, 18 N.E.2d 362 (1938) (discussing nature of written authorization to place sign on building wall).

STONER v. ZUCKER

Supreme Court of California, 1906.
148 Cal. 516, 83 P. 808.

Henshaw, J. Plaintiff pleaded that defendants had entered upon his land in 1899, under license, and had constructed thereon and thereover a ditch for the carrying of water; that he never conveyed or agreed to convey to the defendants any right of way, easement, or interest in the land for the purpose, and their right to construct and maintain the ditch rested wholly upon this license; that in 1900 he served notice upon them that the license to construct and operate the ditch had been revoked and abrogated by him. Notwithstanding this notice of revocation and abrogation, the defendants, disregarding it, have continuously entered upon plaintiff's land, making repairs upon the ditch and restoring the same where it was broken and washed away, and defendants threaten to continue this trespass upon the lands of the plaintiff. Plaintiff therefore prayed that the defendants be adjudged trespassers and be enjoined from the use of the ditch or from in any manner entering upon the lands of the plaintiff to repair or otherwise maintain it. The evidence established, without controversy, that defendants constructed the ditch for the purpose of carrying water for irrigation to their own and other lands, and had expended upon the ditch the sum of seven thousand and more dollars. The court found that "a right of way for the construction and maintenance of the ditch for the purpose of taking water from Santa Ana river for use in connection with and upon defendants' lands was given and granted by the plaintiff to the defendants, and that the defendants are the owners of a right of way for said ditch for the purpose aforesaid." The court further found that there was a consideration for the granting of said right of way, in that defendants contracted and agreed with the plaintiff to deliver to and for the use of the plaintiff on his land lying under said canal sufficient water to irrigate the land, and the defendants have at all times delivered said water so agreed to be delivered. This last finding derives no support from the evidence, and the first finding, to the effect that the plaintiff "granted" a right of way, can be supported only upon the understanding that the court by "grant" meant that "permission" was given to defendants for the construction and maintenance of the ditch. So construing the findings, the question is squarely presented as to the revocability or nonrevocability of an executed parol license, whose execution has involved the expenditure of money, and where, from the very nature of the license given, it was to be continuous in use.

Appellant contends that a parol license to do an act upon the land of the licensor, while it justifies anything done by the licensee before revocation, is revocable at the option of the licensor, so that no further acts may be justified under it, and this, although the intention was to confer a continuing right, and money has been expended by the licensor upon the faith of the license, and that such a license cannot be changed into an equitable right on the ground of equitable estoppel. To the support of this proposition is offered authority of great weight and of the highest respectability. The argument in brief is that a license in its very nature is a revocable permission, that whoever accepts that permission does it with knowledge that the permission may be revoked at any time; that the rule cannot be changed, therefore, because the licensee has foolishly or improvidently expended money in the hope of a continuance of a license, upon the permanent continuance of which he has no right in law or in equity to rely; that to convert such a parol license into a grant or easement under the doctrine of estoppel is destructive of the statute of frauds, which was meant to lay down an inflexible rule; and, finally, that there is no room or play for the operation of the doctrine of estoppel, since the licensor has in no way deceived the licensee by revocation, has put no fraud upon him, and has merely asserted a right which had been absolutely reserved to him by the very terms of his permission. No one has stated this argument more clearly and cogently than Judge Cooley, who, holding to this construction of the law, has expressed it in his work on Torts. Cooley, Torts (2d Ed.) 364. But that the same eminent jurist recognized the injustice and the hardship which followed such a conclusion is plainly to be seen from his opinion in Maxwell v. Bay City Bridge Co., 41 Mich. 453, 2 N.W. 639, where, discussing this subject, he says: "But the injustice of a revocation after the licensee, in reliance upon the license, has made large and expensive improvements, is so serious that it seems a reproach to the law that it should fail to provide some adequate protection against it. Some of the courts have been disposed to enforce the license as a parol contract which has been performed on one side." Indeed, the learned jurist, with equal accuracy, might have stated that the majority of courts have so decided, in accordance with the leading case of Rerick v. Kern, 14 Serg. & R. 267, 16 Am.Dec. 497. That case was carefully considered, and it was held that it would be to countenance a fraud upon the part of the licensor if he were allowed, after expenditure of money by the licensees upon the faith of the license, to cut short by revocation the natural term of its continuance and existence, and that under the doctrine of estoppel, the licensor would not be allowed to do this. The decision was that the licensor would be held to have conveyed an easement commensurate in its extent and duration with the right to be enjoyed. In that case there was a parol license without consideration to use the waters of a stream for a sawmill, and it was held it could not be revoked at the grantor's pleasure, where the grantee, in consequence of the license, had erected a mill. The court in that case says, after discussion: "It is to be considered as if there had been a formal conveyance of the right, and nothing remains but to determine its duration and extent. A right under a license, when not specifically restricted, is commensurate with the thing of which the license is an accessory." * * *

It will not be necessary to multiply citations of authority upon this point. It is sufficient to refer to the very instructive comment of Prof. Freeman to the case of Rerick v. Kern, reported in 16 Am.Dec., at page 497. The learned author of the note concludes his review by saying, as he shows, that "it will be seen that the doctrine of the principal case, though not recognized in some of our state courts, is, nevertheless, expressive of the law as administered by the majority of them." * * * The recognized principle, therefore, is that where a licensee has entered under a parol license and has expended money, or its equivalent in labor, in the execution of the license, the license becomes irrevocable, the licensee will have a right of entry upon the lands of the licensor for the purpose of maintaining his structures or, in general, his rights under his license, and the license will continue for so long a time as the nature of it calls for. Thus, for example, where the license was to erect a lumber mill, the license came to an end when the timber available for use at that mill had been worked up into lumber. The same has been held as to a milldam, the right to maintain the dam continuing so long as there was use for the mill, and the right being lost by abandonment and disuse only when the nonuser had continued for a period sufficient to raise the presumption of release. In the case of irrigating ditches, drains, and the like, the license becomes, in all essentials, an easement, continuing for such length of time, under the indicated conditions, as the use itself may continue.

For these reasons the judgment and order appealed from are affirmed.

Problems and Questions

1. X renovated its meat packing plant at considerable expense in reliance on Y's permission to use a cattle walkway across Y's land. Can Y subsequently demolish the walkway? *See* Pine Valley Meats, Inc. v. Canal Capital Corporation, 566 N.W.2d 357 (Minn.App.1997).

2. Does the concept of an irrevocable license make sense? How can fraud or estoppel exist if a license was originally intended? *See* J. Bruce & J. Ely, The Law of Easements and Licenses in Land ¶ 11.06[2] (rev.ed.1995 & Supp.1998).

3.   Assume that an easement was originally intended in *Stoner*. Would it be rendered unenforceable by the Statute of Frauds? *See* Christensen v. Ruffing, 117 Idaho 1047, 793 P.2d 720 (App.1990).

4.   Recall that the Ryans asked about a path running through property they had inspected. The path was used by children from a neighboring private school to reach a bus stop. This use was based on some sort of agreement between a previous owner and parents of a few children at the school. The Ryans wondered whether they could block off the path if they purchased the property. Consider the following questions: What rights do the school children, their parents, and the private school have to keep the path open? If anyone has the right to continue to use the path, what is the extent of that right? (For example, who has the right or duty to clear a tree that falls across the path?) If someone has a right to use the path, can that right be transferred? (For example, can all children enrolled in the private school use the path? What if the private school is converted to a public school or a drug rehabilitation center?)

After you discussed this problem with the Ryans, they decided to look at additional property. They plan to contact a real estate broker to help them in their search.

3.   REAL COVENANTS

We have already treated covenants in connection with our analysis of the landlord and tenant relationship. We now focus on real covenants, the backbone of private control of land use. (Governmental control of land use is treated in Chapter 6.)

Real covenants, or deed covenants as they are often called, are restrictive (negative) or affirmative. That is, they prohibit certain use of property or require particular action by a property owner. Such covenants are important today as the means by which the development of a subdivision or the operation of a condominium is regulated. *See generally* Winokur, *The Mixed Blessings of Promissory Servitudes: Toward Optimizing Economic Utility, Individual Liberty, and Personal Identity,* 1989 Wis.L.Rev. 1. Covenants are typically recorded with the plat of a subdivision and then incorporated by reference into each conveyance made by the developer. Similarly, numerous covenants binding condominium unit owners are contained in condominium documentation.

The most difficult problem you will encounter in this section is whether purchasers of property are bound by or may enforce existing covenants. Thus, the Ryans must be well advised about the existence and enforceability of any covenants that affect the use of property they are interested in purchasing.

Notes and Questions

1.   An example of a common restrictive covenant is: O, a subdivision developer, conveys lots to A, B, and C, including in each deed a covenant that the property is not to be used for commercial purposes. An example of a common affirmative covenant is: X, Y, and Z purchase condominium units

subject to a covenant in the declaration requiring each owner to pay an annual assessment for maintenance of the condominium common areas.

2. How does the restrictive covenant described in Note 1 differ from a defeasible fee prohibiting use of the land for commercial purposes? *See generally* Korngold, *For Unifying Servitudes and Defeasible Fees: Property Law's Functional Equivalents,* 66 Texas L.Rev. 533 (1988).

3. As we proceed through this section, try to determine how a real covenant differs from an easement. *See* J. Bruce & J. Ely, The Law of Easements and Licenses in Land ¶ 1.07 (rev.ed.1995 & Supp. 1998). In this regard, consider Reichman, *Toward a Unified Concept of Servitudes,* 55 S.Cal.L.Rev. 1177 (1982) and French, *Toward a Modern Law of Servitudes: Reweaving the Ancient Strands,* 55 S.Cal.L.Rev. 1261 (1982), where the term "servitude" is used to include easements and real covenants. Each author suggests ways to unify and modernize the law on these subjects. Both base their analysis on the notion that easements and real covenants should be treated similarly. This approach has been incorporated into the recently completed Restatement (Third) of Property—Servitudes. *See* Restatement (Third) of Property—Servitudes, Tentative Draft No. 1, Introduction (1989); Restatement (Third) of Property—Servitutes, Tenative Draft No. 7, Introduction (1998). *See generally* French, *Servitudes Reform and The New Restatement of Property: Creation Doctrines and Structural Simplification,* 73 Cornell L.Rev. 929 (1988); French, *Design Proposal for the Restatement of the Law of Property—Servitudes,* 21 U.C. Davis L.Rev. 1213 (1988). The Restatement's attempt to unify the law of easements and real covenants, however, is fraught with the risks of eliminating useful distinctions and of generating additional complexity and unsettling disorder in these areas. *See* Berger, *Integration of the Law of Easements, Real Covenants and Equitable Servitudes,* 43 Wash. & Lee L.Rev. 337 (1986); Weaver, *Easements are Nuisances,* 25 Real Prop., Prob. & Tr.J. 103 (1990).

a. Creation (By Express Agreement or By Implication)

Real covenants are usually created in writing. Questions arise, however, as to whether a covenant expressed orally is enforceable or whether a covenant may be implied. The answers to these questions depend upon the court's view of the nature of a real covenant. Is such a covenant an interest in land or a contract about the use of land? If the former, the Statute of Frauds requires a writing. If the latter, a writing is not required. Although there is a split of authority on the question, many jurisdictions view a real covenant as an interest in land and require a writing to satisfy the Statute of Frauds. Courts in these jurisdictions, however, may use equitable principles of estoppel and part performance to grant equitable relief in cases involving oral covenants. Further, in many states a covenant may be implied in equity under certain circumstances. *See* 9 Powell on Real Property §§ 60.02–60.03 (1998).

Equity is also willing to wink at certain law court requirements used to determine whether covenants burden or benefit subsequent purchasers, a topic we shall address shortly. Thus, different treatment is afforded covenants, based in part on the nature of relief sought (damages at law/specific performance or injunction in equity). Covenants enforced in equity are generally called "equitable servitudes."

SANBORN v. MCLEAN

Supreme Court of Michigan, 1925.
233 Mich. 227, 206 N.W. 496.

WIEST, J. Defendant Christina McLean owns the west 35 feet of lot 86 of Green Lawn subdivision, at the northeast corner of Collingwood avenue and Second boulevard, in the city of Detroit, upon which there is a dwelling house, occupied by herself and her husband, defendant John A. McLean. The house fronts Collingwood avenue. At the rear of the lot is an alley. Mrs. McLean derived title from her husband, and, in the course of the opinion, we will speak of both as defendants. Mr. and Mrs. McLean started to erect a gasoline filling station at the rear end of their lot, and they and their contractor, William S. Weir, were enjoined by decree from doing so and bring the issues before us by appeal. Mr. Weir will not be further mentioned in the opinion.

Collingwood avenue is a high grade residence street between Woodward avenue and Hamilton boulevard, with single, double, and apartment houses, and plaintiffs, who are owners of land adjoining and in the vicinity of defendants' land, and who trace title, as do defendants, to the proprietors of the subdivision, claim that the proposed gasoline station will be a nuisance per se, is in violation of the general plan fixed for use of all lots on the street for residence purposes only, as evidenced by restrictions upon 53 of the 91 lots fronting on Collingwood avenue, and that defendants' lot is subject to a reciprocal negative easement barring a use so detrimental to the enjoyment and value of its neighbors. Defendants insist that no restrictions appear in their chain of title and they purchased without notice of any reciprocal negative easement, and deny that a gasoline station is a nuisance per se. We find no occasion to pass upon the question of nuisance, as the case can be decided under the rule of reciprocal negative easement.

This subdivision was planned strictly for residence purposes, except lots fronting Woodward avenue and Hamilton boulevard. The 91 lots on Collingwood avenue were platted in 1891, designed for and each one sold solely for residence purposes, and residences have been erected upon all of the lots. Is defendants' lot subject to a reciprocal negative easement? If the owner of two or more lots, so situated as to bear the relation, sells one with restrictions of benefit to the land retained, the servitude becomes mutual, and, during the period of restraint, the owner of the lot or lots retained can do nothing forbidden to the owner of the lot sold. For want of a better descriptive term this is styled a reciprocal negative easement. It runs with the land sold by virtue of express fastening and abides with the land retained until loosened by expiration of its period of service or by events working its destruction. It is not personal to owners, but operative upon use of the land by any owner having actual or constructive notice thereof. It is an easement passing its benefits and carrying its obligations to all purchasers of land, subject to its affirmative or negative mandates. It originates for mutual benefit and exists with vigor sufficient to work its ends. It must start with a common owner. Reciprocal negative easements are never retroactive; the very nature of their origin forbids. They arise, if at all, out of a benefit accorded land retained, by restrictions upon neighboring land sold by a common owner. Such a scheme of restriction must start with a common owner; it cannot arise and fasten upon one lot by reason of other lot owners conforming to a general plan. If a reciprocal negative easement attached to defendants' lot, it was fastened thereto while in the hands of the common owner of it and neighboring lots by way of sale of other lots with restrictions beneficial at that time to it. This leads to inquiry as to what lots, if any, were sold with restrictions by the common owner before the sale of defendants' lot. While the proofs cover another avenue, we need consider sales only on Collingwood.

December 28, 1892, Robert J. and Joseph R. McLaughlin, who were then evidently owners of the lots on Collingwood avenue, deeded lots 37 to 41 and 58 to 62, inclusive, with the following restrictions:

> "No residence shall be erected upon said premises which shall cost less than $2,500, and nothing but residences shall be erected upon said premises. Said residences shall front on Helene (now Collingwood) avenue and be placed no nearer than 20 feet from the front street line."

July 24, 1893, the McLaughlins conveyed lots 17 to 21 and 78 to 82, both inclusive, and lot 98 with the same restrictions. Such restrictions were imposed for the benefit of the lands held by the grantors to carry out the scheme of a residential district, and a restrictive negative easement attached to the lots retained, and title to lot 86 was then in the McLaughlins. Defendants' title, through mesne conveyances, runs back to a deed by the McLaughlins dated September 7, 1893, without restrictions mentioned therein. Subsequent deeds to other lots were executed by the McLaughlins, some with restrictions and some without. Previous to September 7, 1893, a reciprocal negative easement had attached to lot 86 by acts of the owners, as before mentioned, and such easement is still attached and may now be enforced by plaintiffs, provided defendants, at the time of their purchase, had knowledge, actual or constructive, thereof. The plaintiffs run back with their title, as do defendants, to a common owner. This common owner, as before stated, by restrictions upon lots sold, had burdened all the lots retained with reciprocal restrictions. Defendants' lot and plaintiff Sanborn's lot, next thereto, were held by such common owner, burdened with a reciprocal negative easement, and, when later sold to separate parties, remained burdened therewith, and right to demand observance thereof passed to each purchaser with notice of the easement. The restrictions were upon defendants' lot while it was in the hands of the common owners, and abstract of title to defendants' lot showed the common owners, and the record showed deeds of lots in the plat restricted to perfect and carry out the general plan and resulting in a reciprocal negative easement upon defendants' lot and all lots within its scope, and defendants and their predecessors in title were bound by constructive notice under our recording acts. The original plan was repeatedly declared in subsequent sales of lots by restrictions in the deeds, and, while some lots sold were not so restricted, the purchasers thereof, in every instance, observed the general plan and purpose of the restrictions in building residences. For upward of 30 years the united efforts of all persons interested have carried out the common purpose of making and keeping all the lots strictly for residences, and defendants are the first to depart therefrom.

When Mr. McLean purchased on contract in 1910 or 1911, there was a partly built dwelling house on lot 86, which he completed and now occupies. He had an abstract of title which he examined and claims he was told by the grantor that the lot was unrestricted. Considering the character of use made of all the lots open to a view of Mr. McLean when he purchased, we think, he was put thereby to inquiry, beyond asking his grantor, whether there were restrictions. He had an abstract showing the subdivision and that lot 86 had 97 companions. He could not avoid noticing the strictly uniform residence character given the lots by the expensive dwellings thereon, and the least inquiry would have quickly developed the fact that lot 86 was subjected to a reciprocal negative easement, and he could finish his house, and, like the others, enjoy the benefits of the easement. We do not say Mr. McLean should have asked his neighbors about restrictions, but we do say that with the notice he had from a view of the premises on the street, clearly indicating the residences were built and the lots occupied in strict accordance with a general plan, he was put to inquiry, and, had he inquired, he would have found of record the reason for such general conformation, and the benefits thereof serving the owners of lot 86 and the obligations running with such service and available to adjacent lot owners to prevent a departure from the general plan by an owner of lot 86.

* * *

We notice the decree in the circuit directed that the work done on the building be torn down. If the portion of the building constructed can be utilized for any purpose within the restrictions, it need not be destroyed.

With this modification, the decree in the circuit is affirmed, with costs to plaintiffs.

Notes and Questions

1. The phrase "reciprocal negative easements" used in the *Sanborn* decision refers to restrictive covenants implied in equity or implied "equitable servitudes." For a case utilizing the *Sanborn* terminology and applying the *Sanborn* analysis to a modern development, see Land Developers, Inc. v. Maxwell, 537 S.W.2d 904 (Tenn.1976).

2. The doctrine of implied equitable servitudes retains considerable vitality. *See, e.g.,* Webb v. Smith, 204 Mich.App. 564, 516 N.W.2d 124 (1994);

Webb v. Smith, 224 Mich.App. 203, 568 N.W.2d 378 (1997) (directing that landowner remove house constructed in violation of implied restriction).

3.   Implied equitable servitudes are not recognized in states that strictly apply the Statute of Frauds. *See, e.g.,* Sprague v. Kimball, 213 Mass. 380, 100 N.E. 622 (1913). But if easements are implied, as they are in all states, why are covenants not implied in some jurisdictions?

4.   Equitable servitudes, express or implied, are binding only on subsequent purchasers with notice. Express equitable servitudes are usually recorded so as to give notice to subsequent purchasers of the burdened property. How does a subsequent purchaser receive notice of an implied equitable servitude? *See* Shalimar Ass'n v. D.O.C. Enterprises, Ltd., 142 Ariz. 36, 688 P.2d 682 (App.1984).

b.   *Enforcement at Law Against Subsequent Purchasers*

The relationship between the original parties to a real covenant is governed by contract law. Thus, we will not dwell on the matter of enforcement of a covenant by the covenantee against the covenantor. Instead, we focus in this and the next subsection on the question of whether a successor to the covenantee may enforce the covenant and whether a successor to the covenantor is bound by the covenant. These issues arose initially at a time when contract rights were not assignable and when contract obligations could be enforced only against the covenantor. As a result, special rules were developed to cover covenants concerning land. The law courts established rigid requirements for a covenant to burden or benefit successors of the original parties, that is, for a covenant to run with the land at law. Equity courts established different, more flexible standards for a covenant to run with the land in equity. The approach of the law courts is traced in this subsection. The tack of the equity courts is examined in the next subsection.

Spencer's Case, 77 Eng.Rep. 72 (1583), is generally recognized as the seminal case concerning covenants running with the land at law. In that case, Spencer leased property to a tenant who covenanted that the tenant or the tenant's assigns would build a brick wall on the leased property. The tenant assigned the leasehold estate and when the assignee failed to build the wall, Spencer brought an action against the assignee to recover damages for breach of the covenant. The court ruled in favor of the assignee, specifying requirements for a covenant to run with the land at law, standards that are still applied today. The requirements, as expanded and modified over the years, are: (1) the covenant be enforceable, (2) the original parties intend the covenant to run with the land, (3) the covenant touch and concern the land, (4) privity of estate exist between the original parties, as well as between such parties and their successors, and (5) the purchaser of the burdened property have notice of the covenant.

(1) Enforceable Covenant

In order for a covenant to burden or benefit successors of the original parties, the covenant must be a proper subject of judicial enforcement. Although this issue was not discussed in Spencer's Case, a covenant that is incomprehensibly vague or unreasonable as a matter of public policy will not be enforced even between the original parties.

CAULLETT v. STANLEY STILWELL & SONS, INC.

Superior Court of New Jersey, Appellate Division, 1961.
67 N.J.Super. 111, 170 A.2d 52.

FREUND, J.A.D.

This is an action in the nature of a bill to quiet title to a parcel of land in the Township of Holmdel. Defendant appeals from the entry of summary judgment in favor of plaintiffs.

Defendant, a developer, by warranty deed conveyed the subject property, consisting of a lot approximately one acre in size, to the plaintiffs for a consideration of $4,000. The deed was delivered on January 13, 1959. Following the collapse of negotiations directed towards agreement on the construction by defendant of a dwelling on the transferred premises, the present suit was instituted.

The focal point of the action is a recital in the deed, inserted under the heading of "covenants, agreements and restrictions," to the effect that:

"(i) The grantors reserve the right to build or construct the original dwelling or building on said premises."

The item is one of those designated in the instrument as "covenants running with the land * * * [which] shall bind the purchasers, their heirs, executors, administrators and assigns."

In support of their motion for summary judgment, plaintiffs set forth that no contract exists or ever did exist between the parties for the construction of a dwelling or building on the premises. The principal officer of the defendant corporation, in a countering affidavit, stated that one of the foremost considerations in fixing the price of the lot, and one of the primary conditions of the sale as it was effected, was the understanding that when the purchasers declared themselves ready and able to build, defendant would act as general contractor.

The trial judge held that the provision in question was unenforceable and should properly be stricken from the deed. He granted plaintiffs the relief demanded in their complaint, namely, an adjudication that: (1) defendant has no claim, right or interest in and to the lands by virtue of the clause in question; (2) defendant has no interest, right or cause of action against plaintiffs by virtue of the covenant; and (3) the clause in question is stricken from the deed and declared null, void and of no further force and effect.

The central issue argued on the appeal is whether the recital constitutes an enforceable covenant restricting the use of plaintiffs' land. Defendant urges that it comprises an ordinary property restriction, entered into for the benefit of the grantor and his retained lands. Plaintiff maintains that the clause is too vague to be capable of enforcement and that, in any event, it amounts to no more than a personal covenant which in no way affects or burdens the realty and has no place in an instrument establishing and delimiting the title to same.

While restrictive covenants are to be construed realistically in the light of the circumstances under which they were created, counter considerations, favoring the free transferability of land, have produced the rule that incursions on the use of property will not be enforced unless their meaning is clear and free from doubt. Thus, if the covenants or restrictions are vague or ambiguous, they should not be construed to impair the alienability of the subject property. For a concise and cogent discussion of the unenforceability of restrictive covenants because of vagueness, see Sutcliffe v. Eisele, 62 N.J.Eq. 222, 50 A. 69 (Ch.1901).

Approached from a direction compatible with the constructional principles set forth above, it is clear that the deed item in question is incapable of enforcement and is therefore not restrictive of plaintiffs' title. The clause is descriptive of neither the type of structure to be built, the cost thereof, or the duration of the grantees' obligation. While it might conceivably have been intended to grant to defendant a right of first refusal on construction bids on the property, this is by no means its palpable design. What, for example, would be its effect were plaintiffs to erect a structure by their own hands?

It must be remembered that a restrictive covenant is in its inception a mere contract, subject to the interpretative doctrines of contract law which focus on the parties' mutual purpose. A purported contract so obscure that no one can be sure of its meaning is incapable of remedy at law or equity for its alleged breach, and therefore cannot constitute a valid impediment to title.

* * *

The judgment of the trial court is affirmed.

McHURON v. GRAND TETON LODGE COMPANY

Supreme Court of Wyoming, 1995.
899 P.2d 38.

THOMAS, JUSTICE.

The focus of concern in this case is a restrictive covenant which required approval by a development company of "proposed building plans, specifications, exterior color or finish, building materials, plot plan

* * *, landscaping plan and construction schedule" with respect to lots within the development. More precisely, the question is whether Grand Teton Lodge Company (Company), acting through an Architectural Review Committee (Committee), unreasonably withheld approval of the use of fiberglass shingles by Gregory I. McHuron and Linda L. McHuron (McHurons) on the ground their use was "not in keeping with the surrounding landscape and natural beauty of the area." * * *

* * *

In May of 1975, the McHurons purchased a lot in a subdivision in Teton County called the Jackson Hole Golf and Tennis Club Estates—Second Filing. Their warranty deed stated their lot was subject to the covenants, conditions, and restrictions set forth in an instrument recorded by the Company on May 24, 1973. The document referred to is entitled "Declaration of Protective Covenants Jackson Hole Golf and Tennis Club Estates—Second Filing." The covenants are comprehensive in nature and, with respect to the issues in this case, they provide:

> 2. *APPROVAL OF PLANS.* No building, fence or other structure shall be erected, placed or altered on any lot * * * until the proposed building plans, specifications, exterior color or finish, *building materials*, plot plan * * *, landscaping plan and construction schedule shall have been approved in writing by Grand Teton Lodge Company * * *, its successors or assigns. Approval of plans, location and specifications may not be unreasonably withheld by Company, but refusal may be based by the company upon particularly the ground that the exterior is not in keeping with the surrounding landscape and natural beauty of the area. (Emphasis added.)

* * *

> 24. *VARIANCES.* The Company may allow reasonable variances and adjustments of the within conditions and restrictions in order to overcome practical difficulties, and prevent unnecessary hardships in the application of regulations contained herein, provided this may be done in conformity with the intent and purposes hereof and also provided in every instance that such variance or adjustment will not be materially detrimental or injurious to other property or improvements in the neighborhood.

The Company established the Committee for the purpose of enforcing the covenants.

Almost fifteen years after they acquired their lot, the McHurons sought approval by the Committee of the building plans for a home to be constructed on their lot. After examining the proposed plans, the Committee sent a letter to the McHurons in which the plans as submitted were not approved. The Committee stated in its letter that the plans could not be approved until the McHurons submitted, among other items, a drawing showing the total height of the house to be no more than eighteen feet, and a letter requesting a variance for the roofing materials. That letter advised the McHurons they would have to present a sample of their proposed roofing materials to the Committee.

The McHurons responded to these requests in a letter in which they formally requested a "variance for the section of our proposed house that goes to 19 feet, as you have done for others in the past." The McHurons also asked permission from the Committee to install the fiberglass shingles after explaining their reasons for using them. The Committee granted the request of the McHurons for a variance on the height of the building, but denied the request for use of fiberglass shingles. The McHurons were advised they should "plan to use the standard cedar shakes used by all your neighbors when building your home."

Despite the disapproval by the Committee of the roofing material, the McHurons installed the fiberglass shingles on their home. The Committee demanded the McHurons stop installing those fiberglass shingles, and the demand letter specifically stated the Committee intended to "enforce our right to determine the architectural materials installed on all buildings on the Estates." The Committee did permit the McHurons to complete the roof with fiberglass shingles to prevent water damage to the home and, in a subsequent letter, the Committee agreed it would permit the fiberglass shingles to remain on the home if eighty percent of the homeowners in the subdivision, in a straw poll, agreed to the use of the fiberglass shingles. The results of the poll were not favorable to the McHurons.

The Company then brought this action seeking enforcement of the covenants by a mandatory injunction. The Company filed a Motion for Summary Judgment, and discovery materials, consisting primarily of affidavits, were presented in support of, and in opposition to, that motion.

The trial court held a hearing with respect to the Motion for Summary Judgment. At that hearing, the court sagaciously and prophetically remarked:

> The fact is, of course, that this Court is not going to get itself in the position where it is determining whether a particular home and materials used in the home, the landscaping or any other feature, is in keeping with the natural beauty of the area, nor fitting with the general scheme of the developers in the subdivision.

> If that were to happen, I can see great disaster, if the Court substitutes its judgment for that of the committee that was appointed to represent all of the homeowners and to represent the developer.

> The real issue here is whether or not the decision of the committee was unreasonable, the denial of Mr. McHuron's application for a so-called variance was unreasonable. That's the only issue that this Court needs to determine either today or in a subsequent trial.

* * *

The court then entered its Order Granting Plaintiff's Motion for Summary Judgment requiring the McHurons to remove their fiberglass shingles and replace them with cedar shakes or a gravel roof. This appeal is taken from that order.

We agree with the trial court that the critical issue in this case is whether the decision of the Committee to disapprove the use of fiberglass shingles on the McHurons' home was unreasonable. The covenants in this case are contractual in nature and are to be interpreted in accordance with the principles of contract law. Aesthetic covenants such as these have been found to be enforceable by a majority of the courts if their purpose and intent can be ascertained. *E.g., Rhue v. Cheyenne Homes, Inc.,* 168 Colo. 6, 449 P.2d 361 (1969); *Palmetto Dunes Resort, Div. of Greenwood Dev. Corp. v. Brown,* 287 S.C. 1, 336 S.E.2d 15 (1985).

We said in *Bowers Welding and Hotshot, Inc. v. Bromley,* 699 P.2d 299, 303 (Wyo.1985) (citing *Dawson v. Meike,* 508 P.2d 15 (Wyo.1973)):

A common way in which to uphold restrictive covenants is to find a general plan or scheme for the development of a tract of land. To determine this, we must look to the restrictive covenants and construe them to effectuate the intent of the parties.

The purpose and intent of the covenants at issue are gleaned from the first page of the covenants where this language is found:

WHEREAS, the property is unusually attractive and valuable as a place of residence because of the surrounding landscape, and Declarant [the Company] executing this Declaration intends to offer said property for sale and desires to establish and impose a general plan for the improvement, development, use and occupancy of said property and each and every part thereof; all of which shall be binding on and inure to the benefit of the owners and future owners of said property in order to enhance the value, desirability, attractiveness, and to be in keeping with the surrounding area of Grand Teton National Park, as well as to subserve and promote the sale of said property: * * *.

Summary judgment is appropriate with respect to contract cases in the absence of any ambiguity because the construction of the contract is a question of law. If no ambiguity is discernible from a reading of the covenants, the clear meaning is to be gleaned only from the language of the covenants, although the court may look to the situation of the parties, the subject matter, and the purpose to be served. In this instance, the Declaration of Protective Covenants Jackson Hole Golf and Tennis Club Estates—Second Filing manifests an intent to establish a general scheme for the subdivision and a purpose of preserving aesthetics and property values. That scheme and purpose were to be maintained by the creation of the Committee, which was charged with making reasonable pre-approval decisions concerning all aspects of proposed construction in the subdivision. The Committee could disapprove a planned residence on the ground that it is "not in keeping with the surrounding landscape and natural beauty of the area."

The McHurons contend the quoted phrase manifests ambiguity because it furnishes no notice that roofing materials in the subdivision are limited to "natural materials," namely gravel or wood shingles. They also argue there is no specific requirement in the covenants prescribing any particular type of roofing material. The same argument could be advanced with respect to other aspects of construction materials.

The McHurons had notice of the existence of a general scheme as to approved roofing materials. In the subdivision, it was apparent only wood shake and gravel roofs had been installed. There is no evidence any roofs in the subdivision have ever been constructed with material other than the wooden shakes or gravel. The absence of any other roofing materials suffices to demonstrate the Company had construed the covenants in a way demonstrating a purpose and intent to limit subdivision roofs to natural materials in keeping with the surrounding area of Grand Teton National Park. The McHurons produced no evidence to contradict the existence of such a scheme and plan with respect to this subdivision.

The covenants are unequivocal in their requirement that any conceivable structure must be approved in writing by the Committee. The McHurons not only had actual notice this provision was incorporated in the covenants, but the covenants were imposed in such a way that they would run with the land and be enforceable against any owner. The McHurons' actual knowledge is manifested by their seeking permission from the Committee to use fiberglass shingles when they were told to submit a request for a variance. The McHurons concluded they were not bound by the Committee's decision after they requested a variance, and the variance was denied. The inconsistency of the McHurons' approach is demonstrated by the fact they were granted, and took advantage of, a variance with respect to the height of their building.

Having concluded the covenants are enforceable according to their terms, we must address whether the actions of the Committee were reasonable. The covenants provide the Committee must act "reasonably." In analyzing the claimed issue of material fact with respect to reasonableness, we follow the approach articulated in *McKenney v. Pac. First Fed. Sav. Bank of Tacoma, Washington*, 887 P.2d 927 (Wyo.1994). That analysis leads to the conclusion that the decision of the district court finding the action of the Committee was reasonable is supported by this record. The Company produced affidavits explaining the intent underlying the adoption of the covenants; the historical application of the covenants; and the dialogue with the McHurons. Responding to that showing, the McHurons produced information as to the general desirability of fiberglass shingles; asserted the possible violation of the Uniform Building Code based upon the pitch of the roof provided in their plans in relationship to other materials; and stated their opinion that the fiberglass shingles were aesthetically appropriate.

The record is silent as to the applicability of the Uniform Building Code to the subdivision. If it were applicable, it was not disputed at the hearing on summary judgment that the approved roofing materials would violate code. The covenants, however, make it clear the company assumes no responsibility for compliance with building codes. It was the responsibility of the McHurons to submit plans that would conform to any applicable building codes and still receive the approval of the Committee as to the materials.

The record is clear that, far from allowing a broad spectrum of roofing materials, the Committee had limited roofs in the subdivision to gravel or wooden shakes. Since the Committee in the past had limited other roofs in the subdivision to either gravel or wood shakes, its decision not to permit fiberglass was in keeping with that precedent and, therefore, "reasonable." In effect, the offer of a straw ballot to justify a variance serves only as additional evidence of the attempt of the Company to proceed in a reasonable fashion with respect to the McHurons' building plans.

We find no merit in the McHurons' contention that the Company is not permitted to insist on the utilization of certain materials. The simple fact that fiberglass shingles are generally suitable and desirable for construction does not pose a genuine issue with respect to aesthetic propriety. The McHurons' opinion concerning the aesthetic aspects of the fiberglass shingles is of questionable admissibility at trial but, in any event, a disagreement between the McHurons and the Committee does not manifest a genuine issue of material fact as to the enforceability of the covenants. The discretion with respect to that determination clearly was vested in the Committee.

A contrary holding in this case would place the judicial branch of government in an untenable position. In each instance, a court would be required to determine the application of an aesthetic standard even though the application of that standard was clearly reserved to a developer according to the validly-adopted covenants. It is not the prerogative of this court or that of the district court to determine whether certain materials, such as fiberglass shingles are "in keeping with the surrounding landscape and natural beauty of the area." That determination clearly is vested in the Committee by virtue of the language of the covenants imposed by the Company. We are limited to addressing the reasonableness of the action of the Committee, and we find no issue of fact as to reasonableness in this case.

We are satisfied the district court correctly resolved this case. The Order Granting Plaintiffs' Motion for Summary Judgment is affirmed.

GOLDEN, CHIEF JUSTICE, dissenting, with whom MACY, JUSTICE, joins.

I respectfully dissent. The majority approves the committee's argument that its discretion is unlimited, its decision is final without articulated reason to a lot owner, and a lot owner is precluded from any legal recourse for an arbitrary decision. Aesthetic covenants are generally upheld, however, under a rule which offers dual protection to both parties. By resolving the reasonability issue as a question of law, the majority opinion fails to afford due process protection to a lot owner, a process other jurisdictions do find legally tenable.

Courts uphold aesthetic covenants as enforceable guarantees to a purchaser of a subdivision lot that his house will be protected against adjacent construction which will impair its value and that a general plan of construction will be followed. *Rhue v. Cheyenne Homes, Inc.*, 168 Colo. 6, 449 P.2d 361, 362 (1969). Committee approval is an accepted method of accomplishing and maintaining guarantees of value and general plan. The corollary to enforceability of a covenant requiring committee approval is protection and due process of law to a lot owner, namely, that a committee's refusal to approve plans must be reasonable and made in good faith and must not be arbitrary or capricious. *Rhue*, 449 P.2d at 363.

Whether a particular aesthetic covenant is valid and enforceable is a question of law, but better reasoned cases consider the question whether the committee was reasonable or arbitrary in exercising its power of refusal a factual question to be considered in light of the circumstances. Such approval may not be unreasonably withheld without legal recourse on the part of the party subject to the restriction.

The McHurons are contending, first, that the restriction is invalid and, second, that consent has been unreasonably withheld. Their first contention, that the aesthetic covenant was so vague as to deny due process, is properly resolved against them and found valid. The clear purpose and intent of the aesthetic covenant was to establish a general scheme and then empower a committee to preserve the subdivision against homes inharmonious with the surroundings to such an extent that property value is diminished or the general plan is violated.

The specifics of the McHurons' second contention are the committee is unreasonably rejecting a material (fiberglass shingle) without proof of diminished property value or a disturbed general plan. Generally, a refusal can be proved to be reasonable by a showing the building plans or materials will diminish the value of the subdivision, or so conflict with the architecture of other nearby homes that it causes damages to the property value of those homes, or is specifically prohibited by the covenants or the committee's own lists. *See LeBlanc v. Webster*, 483 S.W.2d 647, 650 (Mo.App.1972); *Syrian Antiochian Orthodox Archdiocese v. Palisades Associates*, 110 N.J.Super. 34, 264 A.2d 257, 262 (1970). McHurons contend none of these harms are present and the committee's refusal unreasonably denies them the use of an attractive, quality, harmonious material safer and more suitable to the surroundings.

A proper ruling by the majority would state the McHurons are entitled to legal recourse when material questions of fact exist on the issue of unreasonably withheld approval. Other jurisdictions require that a committee's power of refusal be exercised objectively, honestly and reasonably and the committee's whims or aesthetic tastes are not subjectively imposed on lot owners. Under this standard, a committee's refusal of a roofing material which does not diminish the value and general plan of the subdivision; which does not violate a specific restriction either of the covenants or the committee's lists; and which is not in conflict with the other homes so that it creates damages would be unreasonable.

McHurons presented summary judgment materials demonstrating material questions of fact exist concerning the issue of reasonableness and, in opposition, the committee only claimed that the roofing material is aesthetically unattractive because it is synthetic. With the barest of assertions, the committee declared that property values would be harmed. Applying the standard articulated above, at trial the committee may very well prevail but only after proving that the variation would be unsightly, causing diminished values, or inharmonious to the extent that the general plan was disturbed. It is difficult to believe that the McHurons would not be able to counter that a fiberglass shingle designed as a cedar shake look-alike does not disturb the general plan, is not unsightly, and actually enhances property values because it is safer, fire resistant and, therefore, more suitable to a wooded area. Regardless, due process requires they be afforded a proper opportunity to present evidence of the roofing material's harmony and suitability with the surroundings. The committee's discretion is not unlimited and the reasonableness of their decision is a material question of fact which should be tried.

I would reverse and remand for a trial on the issue of reasonableness.

Notes and Questions

1. The question of reasonableness arises in other situations involving real covenants. A covenant-not-to-compete may be unenforceable as an unreasonable restraint on competition. Factors considered in determining reasonableness in this context include the covenant's geographic extent, duration, impact on the covenantor, benefit to the covenantee, and effect on the interest of the public in competition. *See* 9 Powell on Real Property § 60.06[3][b] (1998); Comment, *Covenants Not to Compete—Do They Pass?* 4 Cal.W.L.Rev. 131, 141–144 (1968).

2. A restrictive covenant may violate public policy against unreasonable restraints on alienation (*see* the *Casey* case on page 679 or run afoul of constitutional or statutory provisions prohibiting discrimination on various grounds, including race, religion, sex, or national origin. (*See* the cases of *Shelley v. Kraemer* and *Jones v. Mayer* on pages 688 and 695 respectively.) *See generally* Browder, *Running Covenants and Public Policy,* 77 Mich. L.Rev. 12 (1978).

3. The reasonableness issue is also presented when a cooperative apartment or a subdivision or condominium homeowners' association adopts rules and regulations or amends its by-laws contrary to the desires of some of the owners. *See, e.g.,* Liebler v. Point Loma Tennis Club, 40 Cal.App.4th 1600, 47 Cal.Rptr.2d 783 (1995) (rule banning nonresident owners from playing tennis on condominium courts determined to be reasonable); Hidden Harbour Estates, Inc. v. Norman, 309 So.2d 180 (Fla.Dist.Ct.App.1975) (rule prohibiting drinking alcoholic beverages in condominium clubhouse found reasonable); Justice Court Mutual Housing Cooperative, Inc. v. Sandow, 50 Misc.2d 541, 270 N.Y.S.2d 829 (1966) (regulations on playing musical instru-

ments in cooperative apartment held unreasonable). What factors should courts consider in determining the reasonableness of these rules and regulations? *See* Johnson v. Hobson, 505 A.2d 1313 (D.C.App.1986); Schiller, *Limitations on the Enforceability of Condominium Rules,* 22 Stetson L.Rev. 1133 (1993).

4.   The issue of reasonableness is sometimes entwined with the question of notice of the covenant. The relationship between reasonableness and notice is addressed in Nahrstedt v. Lakeside Village Condominium Association, Inc., 8 Cal.4th 361, 33 Cal.Rptr.2d 63, 878 P.2d 1275 (1994). There, the Supreme Court of California took the position that a use restriction included in a recorded condominium declaration is presumed reasonable. Accordingly, the court held that a condominium association restriction against keeping pets in condominium units was enforceable unless an individual unit owner could establish that such restriction was arbitrary, violated public policy, or imposed a burden which substantially outweighed its benefit to residents of the condominium. *See generally* Epstein, *Notice and Freedom of Contract in the Law of Servitudes,* 55 S.Cal.L.Rev. 1353 (1982).

(2) Intent

In order for a real covenant to run with the land, the original parties must intend that their successors be bound by its terms. Intention is ascertained by examining the wording of the covenant and the surrounding circumstances. *See, e.g.,* Lex Pro Corp. v. Snyder Enterprises, Inc., 100 N.M. 389, 671 P.2d 637 (1983) (finding intent that building setback restriction run with land notwithstanding absence of specific language indicating such intent).

Spencer's Case also required that if the covenant concerned something not *in esse, e.g.* an unbuilt wall, it bound successors only if it expressly so stated. *See* Tenstate Distribution Co. v. Averett, 397 F.Supp. 1227 (N.D.Ga.1975). This requirement has been rejected in most states, but still lives in a few jurisdictions. *See* 9 Powell on Real Property § 60.04[2][b] (1998).

(3) Touch and Concern

Regardless of the original parties' intent, a covenant will not run with the land to burden or benefit successors unless it touches and concerns the land. Although it is difficult to define, "touch and concern" requires that the covenant directly relate to the land in some way and not concern merely a collateral matter of a personal nature. *See* C. Clark, Real Covenants and Other Interests Which "Run With Land" 96–100 (2d ed. 1947). Today, this requirement ordinarily does not impede the running of a covenant at law once the court is satisfied as to the intent of the parties. *See* Browder, *Running Covenants and Public Policy,* 77 Mich.L.Rev. 12, 45–46 (1978). Indeed, the drafters of the Restatement (Third) of Property–Servitudes seek to eliminate the touch and concern requirement. *See* Restatement (Third) of Property–Servitudes, Tentative

Draft No. 2, § 3.2 (1991). One authority, however, counsels caution in this regard. After thoroughly analyzing the utility of the touch and concern requirement, he suggests refinements in its application and concludes that its elimination may be unwise. Stake, *Toward an Economic Understanding of Touch and Concern,* 1988 Duke L.J. 925.

Modern covenants are usually found to involve the land in some way as illustrated by the treatment of the touch and concern requirement in *Runyon v. Paley* on page 410. For a case in which a contract to provide landfill to and install utilities on a specific parcel was found not to touch and concern the land, see Bremmeyer Excavating, Inc. v. McKenna, 44 Wn.App. 267, 721 P.2d 567 (1986).

Notes and Questions

1. Courts often experience difficulty in determining whether the burden of an affirmative covenant touches and concerns the land. Does the burden of a covenant to build a bridge, maintain a drainage ditch, satisfy the covenantee's debts, or pay assessments of a homeowners' association satisfy this requirement? *See* 2 American Law of Property § 9.13 (1952); 9 Powell on Real Property § 60.06[2] (1998); *see also* Vulcan Materials Co. v. Miller, 691 So.2d 908 (Miss.1997) (finding agreement to make royalty payments constituted personal covenant that did not run with land). (We will encounter this issue again in the *Neponsit* case on page 419.)

2. Covenants-not-to-compete are subject to close scrutiny under the touch and concern requirement. Are these covenants purely personal in nature or do they touch and concern the land in some way? Today most jurisdictions allow reasonable covenants-not-to-compete to run with the land. The covenant is generally found to touch and concern the burdened land by restricting the way it may be used and to touch and concern the benefited land by enhancing its value. *See* 9 Powell on Real Property § 60.06[3][b] (1998); Comment, *Covenants Not to Compete—Do They Pass?* 4 Cal.W.L.Rev. 131 (1968); Annot., *Covenant Restricting Use of Land Made for Purpose of Guarding Against Competition, As Running With Land,* 25 A.L.R.3d 897 (1969).

In Davidson Bros., Inc. v. D. Katz & Sons, Inc., 121 N.J. 196, 579 A.2d 288 (1990), the Supreme Court of New Jersey struggled to apply the touch and concern requirement to a covenant-not-to-compete and concluded that touching and concerning is a only a factor to be considered in determining whether a covenant satisfies the test of reasonableness. For a critical analysis of this approach, see Franzese, *"Out of Touch:" The Diminished Viability of the Touch and Concern Requirement in the Law of Servitudes,* 21 Seton Hall L.Rev. 235 (1991).

(4) Privity of Estate

The court in Spencer's Case noted that privity of estate is necessary for a covenant to run with the land at law. What sort of privity of estate the court required is unclear. Thus, a variety of interpretations developed in this country. Much of the confusion results from the generally accepted notion that there are two types of privity of estate—horizontal privity and vertical privity—both of which must exist for a covenant to run with the land at law. Horizontal privity refers to a land transaction between the covenantor and covenantee. Vertical privity refers to a land transaction between an original party and that party's successor. *See* Malley v. Hanna, 65 N.Y.2d 289, 491 N.Y.S.2d 286, 480 N.E.2d 1068 (1985) (finding vertical privity because plaintiff and defendant had each derived title through continuous and lawful succession of conveyances from one of original parties).

Horizontal privity is the more troublesome form of privity. The English position is that the horizontal privity requirement demands a landlord-tenant relationship. Such a crabbed view of horizontal privity still may be alive in one or two jurisdictions. Courts in Massachusetts and possibly a few other states have expanded the English approach slightly to include situations in which the covenantor and covenantee each hold a continuing interest in the property covered by the covenant, *e.g.,* fee owner/easement holder and tenants-in-common. A more liberal view of horizontal privity is taken in the remaining states. Courts in most jurisdictions find that horizontal privity is established by a conveyance from one party to the other at the time the covenant is made. No continuing relationship is required. This form of horizontal privity is sometimes called "instantaneous privity." In a few states, the requirement of horizontal privity has been eliminated altogether. *See* 9 Powell on Real Property § 60.04[2][c] (1998); Browder, *Running Covenants and Public Policy,* 77 Mich.L.Rev. 12, 21–26(1978).

Vertical privity of estate has caused the courts relatively little difficulty. It is universally recognized that vertical privity between the original covenantor and the covenantor's successor must exist in order for the burden of the covenant to run with the land at law. Problems arise under this requirement only when the covenantor transfers an estate less than the covenantor owns. In such case, the individual receiving the lesser estate is not bound by the covenant. Distinguish this situation from the case where the covenantor transfers a geographical portion of the burdened estate. There, the purchaser takes subject to a proportionate burden of the covenant. *See* Restatement of Property §§ 535–536 (1944); 2 American Law of Property § 9.15 (1952).

The preceding paragraph about vertical privity focuses on the running of the burden. The running of the benefit also must be considered. The benefit of a covenant is impliedly assigned by the covenantee when the covenantee transfers the covenantee's estate. Thereafter, the covenantee cannot enforce the covenant, but the covenantee's successor can. This is true even if a covenantee who owns in fee simple transfers only a life estate or leasehold. *See* 2 American Law of Property §§ 9.19–9.20 (1952).

Do not be misled into believing that the courts neatly categorize privity of estate problems and then dispatch them with clarity and certainty. Regrettably such is not the case. One writer observed that courts often reach inconsistent results in this area because "the law surrounding privity of estate is so confused, and the rule so confusing, that litigants and judges no longer know what the privity rule requires, and more importantly why it exists." Note, *Covenants Running with the Land: Viable Doctrine or Common–Law Relic?* 7 Hofstra L.Rev. 139, 174 (1978).

Problems and Questions

1.   O, the owner of a parcel of land containing a stream, conveyed a portion thereof to A. Six days later O and A entered into a written agreement to construct a dam and flume. They further agreed to keep the dam and flume in good repair at their joint expense. Several years later X obtained A's title. Thereafter, X refused to pay half of the cost of necessary repairs on the dam, and O brings suit at law to recover that sum. Is X liable to O? *See* Wheeler v. Schad, 7 Nev. 204 (1871); *see also* Bremmeyer Excavating Inc. v. McKenna, 44 Wn.App. 267, 721 P.2d 567 (1986).

2.   What public policy does the horizontal privity requirement serve? *See* C. Clark, Real Covenants and Other Interests Which "Run With Land" 131–137 (2d ed. 1947); Browder, *Running Covenants and Public Policy,* 77 Mich.L.Rev. 12, 25–26 (1978).

(5) Notice

Although Spencer's Case said nothing about notice, the covenantor's successor is bound only if the successor has notice of the covenant. The concept of notice was discussed briefly in connection with *Sanborn v. McLean* (p. 394) and is more fully analyzed in the section of Chapter 4 dealing with recording systems. *See* pages 524–562.

RUNYON v. PALEY

Supreme Court of North Carolina, 1992.
331 N.C. 293, 416 S.E.2d 177.

MEYER, JUSTICE.

This case involves a suit to enjoin defendants from constructing condominium units on their property adjacent to the Pamlico Sound on Ocracoke Island. Plaintiffs maintain that defendants' property is subject to restrictive covenants that prohibit the construction of condominiums. The sole question presented for our review is whether plaintiffs are entitled to enforce the restrictive covenants.

On 17 May 1937, Ruth Bragg Gaskins acquired a four-acre tract of land located in the Village of Ocracoke bounded on the west by the Pamlico Sound and on the east by Silver Lake. By various deeds, Mrs. Gaskins conveyed out several lots, which were later developed for residential use.

One and one-half acres of the sound-front property, part of which is at issue here, were conveyed by Mrs. Gaskins and her husband to plaintiffs Runyon on 1 May 1954. On 6 January 1960, the Runyons reconveyed the one and one-half acre tract, together with a second tract consisting of one-eighth of an acre, to Mrs. Gaskins. By separate deeds dated 8 January 1960, Mrs. Gaskins, then widowed, conveyed to the Runyons a lake-front lot and a fifteen-foot-wide strip of land that runs to the shore of Pamlico Sound from the roadway separating the lake-front and sound-front lots. This fifteen-foot strip was part of the one and one-half acre parcel that the Runyons had reconveyed to Mrs. Gaskins.

The next day, 9 January 1960, Mrs. Gaskins conveyed the remainder of the one and one-half acre parcel to Doward H. Brugh and his wife, Jacquelyn O. Brugh. Included in the deed of conveyance from Mrs. Gaskins to the Brughs was the following:

> BUT this land is being conveyed subject to certain restrictions as to the use thereof, running with said land by whomsoever owned, until removed as herein set out; said restrictions, which are expressly assented to by [the Brughs], in accepting this deed, are as follows:
>
> (1) Said lot shall be used for residential purposes and not for business, manufacturing, commercial or apartment house purposes; provided, however, this restriction shall not apply to churches or to the office of a professional man which is located in his residence, and
>
> (2) Not more than two residences and such outbuildings as are appurtenant thereto, shall be erected or allowed to remain on said lot. This restriction shall be in full force and effect until such time as adjacent or nearby properties are turned to commercial use, in which case the restrictions herein set out will no longer apply. The word "nearby" shall, for all intents and purposes, be construed to mean within 450 feet thereof.
>
> TO HAVE AND TO HOLD the aforesaid tract or parcel of land and all privileges and appurtenances thereunto belonging or in anywise thereunto appertaining, unto them, the [Brughs], as tenants by the entirety, their heirs and assigns, to their only use and behoof in fee simple absolute forever, [b]ut subject always to the restrictions as to use as hereinabove set out.

Prior to the conveyance of this land to the Brughs, Mrs. Gaskins had constructed a residential dwelling in which she lived on lake-front property across the road from the property conveyed to the Brughs. Mrs. Gaskins retained this land and continued to live on this property until her death in August 1961. Plaintiff Williams, Mrs. Gaskins' daughter, has since acquired the property retained by Mrs. Gaskins.

By mesne conveyances, defendant Warren D. Paley acquired the property conveyed by Mrs. Gaskins to the Brughs. Thereafter, defendant Warren Paley and his wife, defendant Claire Paley, entered into a partnership with defendant Midgett Realty and began constructing condominium units on the property.

Plaintiffs brought this suit, seeking to enjoin defendants from using the property in a manner that is inconsistent with the restrictive covenants included in the deed from Mrs. Gaskins to the Brughs. In their complaint, plaintiffs alleged that the restrictive covenants were placed on the property "for the benefit of [Mrs. Gaskins'] property and neighboring property owners, specifically including and intending to benefit the Runyons." Plaintiffs further alleged that the "restrictive covenants have not been removed and are enforceable by plaintiffs."

Defendants moved to dismiss the lawsuit, and plaintiffs thereafter moved for summary judgment. Following a hearing on both motions, the trial court granted defendants' motion to dismiss for failure to state a claim upon which relief could be granted and, pursuant to Rule 54(b), rendered a final judgment after having determined that there was no just reason for delay in any appeal of the matter. The Court of Appeals affirmed the trial court, concluding that the restrictive covenants were personal to Mrs. Gaskins and became unenforceable at her death.

* * *

Having considered the evidence presented to the trial court, we conclude that plaintiff Williams presented sufficient evidence to show that the covenants at issue here are real covenants enforceable by her as an owner of property retained by Mrs. Gaskins, the covenantee. Accordingly, we reverse that part of the Court of Appeals' decision that affirmed the trial court's dismissal of plaintiff Williams' claim. However, we agree with the Court of Appeals that the covenants are not enforceable by the Runyons, and we therefore affirm that part of the Court of Appeals' decision that concerns the dismissal of the Runyons' claim.

It is well established that an owner of land in fee has a right to sell his land subject to any restrictions he may see fit to impose, provided that the restrictions are not contrary to public policy. Such restrictions are often included as covenants in the deed conveying the property and may be classified as either personal covenants or real covenants that are said to run with the land. The significant distinction between these types of covenants is that a personal covenant creates a personal obligation or right enforceable at law only between the original covenanting parties, whereas a real covenant creates a servitude upon the land subject to the covenant ("the servient estate") for the benefit of another parcel of land ("the dominant estate"). As such, a real covenant may be enforced at law or in equity by the owner of the dominant estate against the owner of the servient estate, whether the owners are the original covenanting parties or successors in interest.

I.   REAL COVENANTS AT LAW

A restrictive covenant is a real covenant that runs with the land of the dominant and servient estates only if (1) the subject of the covenant touches and concerns the land, (2) there is privity of estate between the party enforcing the covenant and the party against whom the covenant is being enforced, and (3) the original covenanting parties intended the benefits and the burdens of the covenant to run with the land.

A. Touch and Concern

As noted by several courts and commentators, the touch and concern requirement is not capable of being reduced to an absolute test or precise definition. *See Neponsit Property Owners Ass'n v. Emigrant Indus. Sav. Bank,* 278 N.Y. 248, 256–58, 15 N.E.2d 793, 795–96, *reh'g denied,* 278 N.Y. 704, 16 N.E.2d 852 (1938); Charles E. Clark, *Real Covenants and Other Interests Which "Run With Land"* 96 (2d ed. 1947) [hereinafter Clark, *Real Covenants*]. Focusing on the nature of the burdens and benefits created by a covenant, the court must exercise its best judgment to determine whether the covenant is related to the covenanting parties' ownership interests in their land. Clark, *Real Covenants* 97.

For a covenant to touch and concern the land, it is not necessary that the covenant have a physical effect on the land. It is sufficient that the covenant have some economic impact on the parties' ownership rights by, for example, enhancing the value of the dominant estate and decreasing the value of the servient estate. It is essential, however, that the covenant in some way affect the legal rights of the covenanting parties as landowners. Where the burdens and benefits created by the covenant are of such a nature that they may exist independently from the parties' ownership interests in land, the covenant does not touch and concern the land and will not run with the land. *See Choisser v. Eyman,* 22 Ariz.App. 587, 529 P.2d 741 (1974) (covenant capable of enforcement regardless of status as owner of interest in land is personal in nature); *Flying Diamond Oil Corp.,* 776 P.2d at 623 (Utah) ("[T]o touch and concern the land, a covenant must bear upon the use and enjoyment of the land and be of the kind that the owner of an estate or interest in land may make because of his ownership right.").

Although not alone determinative of the issue, the nature of the restrictive covenants at issue in this case (building or use restrictions) is strong evidence that the covenants touch and concern the dominant and servient estates. As recognized by some courts, a restriction limiting the use of land clearly touches and concerns the estate burdened with the covenant because it restricts the owner's use and enjoyment of the property and thus affects the value of the property. *Net Realty Holding Trust v. Franconia Properties,* 544 F.Supp. 759, 762 (E.D.Va.1982); *see also* 20 Am.Jur.2d *Covenants, Conditions, and Restrictions* '167 (1965). A use restriction does not, however, always touch and concern the dominant estate. *See Stegall v. Housing Authority,* 278 N.C. 95, 178 S.E.2d 824 (1971) (holding that covenant did not meet the touch and concern requirement where the record failed to disclose the location of the grantor's property "in the area" or the distance from the grantor's property to the restricted property). To meet the requirement that the covenant touch and concern the dominant estate, it must be shown that the covenant somehow affects the dominant estate by, for example, increasing the value of the dominant estate.

In the case at bar, plaintiffs have shown that the covenants sought to be enforced touch and concern not only the servient estate owned by defendants, but also the properties owned by plaintiffs. The properties owned by defendants, plaintiff Williams, and plaintiffs Runyon comprise only a portion of what was at one time a four-acre tract bounded on one side by the Pamlico Sound and on the other by Silver Lake. If able to enforce the covenants against defendants, plaintiffs would be able to restrict the use of defendants' property to uses that accord with the restrictive covenants. Considering the close proximity of the lands involved here and the relatively secluded nature of the area where the properties are located, we conclude that the right to restrict the use of defendants' property would affect plaintiffs' ownership interests in the property owned by them, and therefore the covenants touch and concern their lands.

B. Privity of Estate

In order to enforce a restrictive covenant as one running with the land at law, the party seeking to enforce the covenant must also show that he is in privity of estate with the party against whom he seeks to enforce the covenant. Although the origin of privity of estate is not certain, the privity requirement has been described as a substitute for privity of contract, which exists between the original covenanting parties and which is ordinarily required to enforce a contractual promise. 3 *Tiffany Real Property* § 851, at 451 n. 32. Thus, where the covenant is sought to be enforced by someone not a party to the covenant or against someone not a party to the covenant, the party seeking to enforce the covenant must show that he has a sufficient legal relationship with the party against whom enforcement is sought to be entitled to enforce the covenant.

For the enforcement at law of a covenant running with the land, most states require two types of privity: (1) privity of estate between the covenantor and covenantee at the time the covenant was created ("horizontal privity"), and (2) privity of estate between the covenanting parties and their successors in interest ("vertical privity"). William B. Stoebuck, *Running Covenants: An Analytical Primer,* 52 Wash.L.Rev. 861, 867 (1977) [hereinafter Stoebuck, 52 Wash.L.Rev. 861]. The majority of jurisdictions have held that horizontal privity exists when the original covenanting parties make their covenant in connection with the conveyance of an estate in land from one of the parties to the other. A few courts, on the other hand, have dispensed with the showing of horizontal privity altogether, requiring only a showing of vertical privity.

Vertical privity, which is ordinarily required to enforce a real covenant at law, requires a showing of succession in interest between the original covenanting parties and the current owners of the dominant and servient estates. As one scholar has noted:

> The most obvious implication of this principle [of vertical privity] is that the burden of a real covenant may be enforced against

remote parties only when they have succeeded to the covenantor's *estate* in land. Such parties stand in privity of estate with the covenantor. Likewise, the benefit may be enforced by remote parties only when they have succeeded to the covenantee's *estate*. They are in privity of estate with the covenantee.

Stoebuck, 52 Wash.L.Rev. 861, 876 (emphasis added).

We adhere to the rule that a party seeking to enforce a covenant as one running with the land at law must show the presence of both horizontal and vertical privity. In order to show horizontal privity, it is only necessary that a party seeking to enforce the covenant show that there was some "connection of interest" between the original covenanting parties, such as, here, the conveyance of an estate in land.

In the case *sub judice,* plaintiffs have shown the existence of horizontal privity. The record shows that the covenants at issue in this case were created in connection with the transfer of an estate in fee of property then owned by Mrs. Gaskins. By accepting the deed of conveyance, defendants' predecessors in title, the Brughs, covenanted to use the property for the purposes specified in the deed and thereby granted to Mrs. Gaskins a servitude in their property.

To review the sufficiency of vertical privity in this case, it is necessary to examine three distinct relationships: (1) the relationship between defendants and the Brughs as the covenantors; (2) the relationship between plaintiff Williams and the covenantee, Mrs. Gaskins; and (3) the relationship between plaintiffs Runyon and Mrs. Gaskins. The evidence before us shows that the Brughs conveyed all of their interest in the restricted property and that by mesne conveyances defendant Warren Paley succeeded to a fee simple estate in the property. Thus, he is in privity of estate with the covenantors. Any legal interests held by the other defendants were acquired by them from defendant Warren Paley. As successors to the interest held by defendant Warren Paley, they too are in privity of estate with the covenantors. Plaintiff Williams has also established a privity of estate between herself and the covenantee. Following the death of Mrs. Gaskins, the property retained by Mrs. Gaskins was conveyed by her heirs to her daughter, Eleanor Gaskins. Thereafter, Eleanor Gaskins conveyed to plaintiff Williams a fee simple absolute in that property. The mere fact that defendants and plaintiff Williams did not acquire the property directly from the original covenanting parties is of no moment. Regardless of the number of conveyances that transpired, defendants and plaintiff Williams have succeeded to the estates then held by the covenantor and covenantee, and thus they are in vertical privity with their ... [predecessors] in interest. Such would be true even if the parties had succeeded to only a part of the land burdened and benefitted by the covenants. Plaintiffs Runyon have not, however, made a sufficient showing of vertical privity. The Runyons have not succeeded in any interest in land held by Mrs. Gaskins at the time the covenant was created. The only interest in land held by the Runyons was acquired by them prior to the creation of the covenant.

Therefore, they have not shown vertical privity of estate between themselves and the covenantee with respect to the property at issue in this case. Because the Runyons were not parties to the covenant and are not in privity with the original parties, they may not enforce the covenant as a real covenant running with the land at law.

C. Intent of the Parties

Defendants argue that plaintiff Williams is precluded from enforcing the restrictive covenants because the covenanting parties who created the restrictions intended that the restrictions be enforceable only by Mrs. Gaskins, the original covenantee. According to defendants, such a conclusion is necessitated where, as here, the instrument creating the covenants does not expressly state that persons other than the covenantee may enforce the covenants. We disagree.

Defendants correctly note that our law does not favor restrictions on the use of real property. It is generally stated that "[r]estrictions in a deed will be regarded as for the personal benefit of the grantor unless a contrary intention appears, and the burden of showing that they constitute covenants running with the land is upon the party claiming the benefit of the restriction." *Stegall,* 278 N.C. at 101, 178 S.E.2d at 828. This, however, does not mean that we will always regard a restriction as personal to the covenantee unless the restriction expressly states that persons other than the covenantee may enforce the covenant. *See, e.g., Reed v. Elmore,* 246 N.C. 221, 98 S.E.2d 360 (1957) (concluding that covenant was intended to benefit land despite the absence of an express statement to that effect).

"Whether restrictions imposed upon land * * * create a personal obligation or impose a servitude upon the land enforceable by subsequent purchasers [of the covenantee's property] is determined by the intention of the parties at the time the deed containing the restriction was delivered." *Stegall,* 278 N.C. at 100, 178 S.E.2d at 828; *Reed,* 246 N.C. at 224, 98 S.E.2d at 362. The question of the parties' intention is one that the court must decide by applying our well-established principles of contract construction.

* * *

Ordinarily, the parties' intent must be ascertained from the deed or other instrument creating the restriction. *Stegall,* 278 N.C. at 100, 178 S.E.2d at 828. However, when the language used in the instrument is ambiguous, the court, in determining the parties' intention, must look to the language of the instrument, the nature of the restriction, the situation of the parties, and the circumstances surrounding their transaction.

We conclude that the language of the deed creating the restrictions at issue here is ambiguous with regard to the intended enforcement of the restrictions. The deed from Mrs. Gaskins to the Brughs provided that the property conveyed was being made "subject to certain restrictions as to the use thereof, running with said land by whomsoever owned, until removed [due to a change of conditions in the surrounding properties] as herein set out." As noted by the dissent in the Court of Appeals, this provision unequivocally expresses the parties' intention that the burden of the restrictions runs with the land conveyed by the deed. *Runyon v. Paley,* 103 N.C.App. 208, 215, 405 S.E.2d 216, 220 (1991) (Greene, J., concurring in part and dissenting in part). In the habendum clause of the deed, the parties also included language providing that the estate granted shall be *"subject always* to the restrictions as to use as hereinabove set out." (Emphasis added.) We conclude that the language of the deed creating the restrictions is such that it can reasonably be interpreted to establish an intent on the part of the covenanting parties not only to bind successors to the covenantor's interest, but also to benefit the property retained by the covenantee.

Having determined that the instrument creating the restrictions at issue here is ambiguous as to the parties' intention that the benefit of the covenants runs with the land, we must determine whether plaintiff Williams has produced sufficient evidence to show that the covenanting parties intended that the covenants be enforceable by the covenantee's successors in interest. Defendants argue that plaintiff Williams has not met her burden because (1) the covenants do not expressly state that the benefit of the covenant was to run with any land retained by the covenantee; and (2) plaintiff Williams has not shown that the property was conveyed as part of a general plan of subdivision, development, and sales subject to uniform restrictions. While evidence of the foregoing would clearly establish the parties' intent to benefit the covenantee's successors, such evidence is not the only evidence that may be used to prove the parties' intent.

We find strong evidence in the record of this case to suggest that the covenanting parties intended the restrictive covenants to be real covenants, the benefit of which attached to the land retained by Mrs. Gaskins, the covenantee. The covenants at issue here are building and use restrictions that restrict the use of the burdened property to "two residences and such out-buildings as are appurtenant thereto" to be used for "residential purposes." The covenants expressly prohibit the use of the property for "business, manufacturing, commercial or apartment house purposes." The only exception provided by the covenants is that the latter restriction "shall not apply to churches or to the office of a professional man which is located in his residence." As noted by some courts, restrictions limiting the use of property to residential purposes have a significant impact on the value of neighboring land, and thus the very nature of such a restriction suggests that the parties intended that the restriction benefit land rather than the covenantee personally. *See, e.g., Bauby v. Krasow,* 107 Conn. 109, 115, 139 A. 508, 510 (1927) (concluding that only reasonable inference to be drawn from use restriction "is that its sole purpose was to protect the [covenantee's] homestead"). We need not decide whether the nature of a building or use restriction, in and of itself, is sufficient evidence of the parties' intent that the benefit run with the land, however.

In this case, the evidence also shows that the property now owned by defendants was once part of a larger, relatively secluded tract bounded by Silver Lake and the Pamlico Sound. Prior to conveying the property now owned by defendants, Mrs. Gaskins had erected on a portion of the tract a single-family residence in which she lived. At some point, her property was subdivided into several lots. Mrs. Gaskins conveyed several of these lots, on which residences were thereafter erected. Although none of these deeds of conveyance contained restrictions limiting the use of the property to residential purposes, it is reasonable to assume that Mrs. Gaskins, by later restricting the use of defendants' property, intended to preserve the residential character and value of the relatively secluded area. This evidence is further supported by the fact that Mrs. Gaskins retained land across the road from the property now owned by defendants and continued to reside in her dwelling located on the retained land. We believe that this evidence of the parties' situation and of the circumstances surrounding their transaction strongly supports a finding that the covenanting parties intended that the restrictive covenants inure to the benefit of Mrs. Gaskins' land and not merely to Mrs. Gaskins personally.

Moreover, we conclude that the language of the deed creating the restrictive covenants supports a finding that the parties intended the benefit of the covenants to attach to the real property retained by Mrs. Gaskins. The pertinent language of the deed provides that the property was conveyed subject to certain use restrictions "running with said land by whomsoever owned, until removed," and that the property is "subject always to the restrictions." As the Connecticut Appellate Court concluded after analyzing similar language in *Grady v. Schmitz,* 16 Conn.App. 292, 547 A.2d 563, *cert. denied,* 209 Conn. 822, 551 A.2d 755 (1988), we believe that this language suggests a broad, rather than a limited, scope of enforcement. That the deed expressly stated that the covenants were to run with the land and continue indefinitely, unless and until the surrounding property is "turned to commercial use," indicates that the parties intended the restrictive covenants to be enforceable by Mrs. Gaskins as the owner of the land retained by her or by her successors in interest to the retained land.

Having reviewed the language of the deed creating the restrictive covenants, the nature of the covenants, and the evidence concerning the covenanting parties' situation and the circumstances surrounding their transaction, we conclude that plaintiff Williams presented ample evidence establishing that the parties intended that the restrictive covenants be enforceable by the owner of the property retained by Mrs. Gaskins and now owned by plaintiff Williams. Defendants did not offer any contrary evidence of the parties' intent but relied solely upon the theory that plaintiff Williams could not enforce the restrictions because the covenants did not expressly state the parties' intent and because plaintiff Williams had failed to show that the covenants were created as part of a common scheme of development. Based upon the uncontradicted evidence presented by plaintiff Williams, the trial court erred in concluding that plaintiff Williams, the successor in interest to the property retained by Mrs. Gaskins, was not entitled to enforce the restrictive covenants against defendants.

* * *

For the reasons stated herein, we conclude that the restrictive covenants contained in the deed from Mrs. Gaskins to defendants' predecessors are not personal covenants that became unenforceable at Mrs. Gaskins' death but are real covenants appurtenant to the property retained by Mrs. Gaskins at the time of the conveyance to defendants' predecessors in interest. As a successor in interest to the property retained by Mrs. Gaskins, plaintiff Williams is therefore entitled to seek enforcement of the restrictive covenants against defendants. We therefore reverse that part of the Court of Appeals' decision that affirmed the trial court's dismissal of plaintiff Williams' claim and remand this case to that court for further remand to the Superior Court, Hyde County, for further proceedings not inconsistent with this opinion.

We further conclude that the Runyons have not proffered sufficient evidence to show that they have standing to enforce the restrictive covenants * * *. We therefore affirm that part of the Court of Appeals' decision that affirmed the trial court's dismissal of the Runyons' claim.

Affirmed in Part, Reversed in Part, and Remanded.

Note

In Sloan v. Johnson, 254 Va. 271, 491 S.E.2d 725 (1997), the Supreme Court of Virginia found subdivision restrictive covenants that limited development on each subdivision lot to a single residence satisfied all the requirements necessary for the covenants to run with the land at law.

c. *Flexible Approach to Enforcing Covenants at Law*

NEPONSIT PROPERTY OWNERS' ASSOCIATION, INC. v. EMIGRANT INDUSTRIAL SAVINGS BANK

Court of Appeals of New York, 1938.
278 N.Y. 248, 15 N.E.2d 793.

LEHMAN, JUDGE.

The plaintiff, as assignee of Neponsit Realty Company, has brought this action to foreclose a lien upon land which the defendant owns. The lien, it is alleged, arises from a covenant, condition or charge contained in a deed of conveyance of the land from Neponsit Realty Company to a predecessor in title of the defendant. The defendant purchased the land at a judicial sale. The referee's deed to the defendant and every deed in the defendant's chain of title since the conveyance of the land by

Neponsit Realty Company purports to convey the property subject to the covenant, condition or charge contained in the original deed. The answer of the defendant contains, in addition to denials of some of the allegations of the complaint, seven separate affirmative defenses and a counterclaim. The defendant moved for judgment on the pleadings, dismissing the complaint pursuant to rule 112 of the Rules of Civil Practice. The plaintiff moved to dismiss the counterclaim pursuant to rule 109, subdivision 6, and to strike out the affirmative defenses contained in the answer pursuant to rule 103, as well as pursuant to rule 109, subdivision 6, of the Rules of Civil Practice. The motion of the plaintiff was granted and the motion of the defendant denied. The Appellate Division unanimously affirmed the order of the Special Term and granted leave to appeal to this court. * * *

It appears that in January, 1911, Neponsit Realty Company, as owner of a tract of land in Queens county, caused to be filed in the office of the clerk of the county a map of the land. The tract was developed for a strictly residential community, and Neponsit Realty Company conveyed lots in the tract to purchasers, describing such lots by reference to the filed map and to roads and streets shown thereon. In 1917, Neponsit Realty Company conveyed the land now owned by the defendant to Robert Oldner Deyer and his wife by deed which contained the covenant upon which the plaintiff's cause of action is based.

That covenant provides:

"And the party of the second part for the party of the second part and the heirs, successors and assigns of the party of the second part further covenants that the property conveyed by this deed shall be subject to an annual charge in such an amount as will be fixed by the party of the first part, its successors and assigns, not, however exceeding in any year the sum of four ($4.00) Dollars per lot 20x100 feet. The assigns of the party of the first part may include a Property Owners' Association which may hereafter be organized for the purposes referred to in this paragraph, and in case such association is organized the sums in this paragraph provided for shall be payable to such association. The party of the second part for the party of the second part and the heirs, successors and assigns of the party of the second part covenants that they will pay this charge to the party of the first part, its successors and assigns on the first day of May in each and every year, and further covenants that said charge shall on said date in each year become a lien on the land and shall continue to be such lien until fully paid. Such charge shall be payable to the party of the first part or its successors or assigns, and shall be devoted to the maintenance of the roads, paths, parks, beach, sewers and such other public purposes as shall from time to time be determined by the party of the first part, its successors or assigns. And the party of the second part by the acceptance of this deed hereby expressly vests in the party of the first part, its successors and assigns, the right and power to bring all actions against the owner of the premises hereby conveyed or any part thereof for the collection of such charge and to enforce the aforesaid lien therefor.

"These covenants shall run with the land and shall be construed as real covenants running with the land until January 31st, 1940, when they shall cease and determine."

Every subsequent deed of conveyance of the property in the defendant's chain of title, including the deed from the referee to the defendant, contained, as we have said, a provision that they were made subject to covenants and restrictions of former deeds of record.

There can be no doubt that Neponsit Realty Company intended that the covenant should run with the land and should be enforceable by a property owners association against every owner of property in the residential tract which the realty company was then developing. The language of the covenant admits of no other construction. Regardless of the intention of the parties, a covenant will run with the land and will be enforceable against a subsequent purchaser of the land at the suit of one who claims the benefit of the covenant, only if the covenant complies with certain legal requirements. These requirements rest upon ancient rules and precedents. The age-old essentials of a real covenant, aside from the form of the covenant, may be summarily formulated as follows: (1) It must appear that grantor and grantee intended that the covenant should run with the land; (2) it must appear that the covenant is one "touching" or "concerning" the land with which it runs; (3) it must appear that there is "privity of estate" between the promisee or party claiming the benefit of the covenant and the right to enforce it, and the promisor or party who rests under the burden of the covenant. Clark on Covenants and Interests Running with Land, p. 74. Although the deeds of Neponsit Realty Company conveying lots in the tract it developed "contained a provision to the effect that the covenants ran with the land, such provision in the absence of the other legal requirements is insufficient to accomplish such a purpose." Morgan Lake Co. v. New York, N.H. & H.R.R. Co., 262 N.Y. 234, 238, 186 N.E. 685, 686. In his opinion in that case, Judge Crane posed but found it unnecessary to decide many of the questions which the court must consider in this case.

The covenant in this case is intended to create a charge or obligation to pay a fixed sum of money to be "devoted to the maintenance of the roads, paths, parks, beach, sewers and such other public purposes as shall from time to time be determined by the party of the first part [the grantor], its successors or assigns." It is an affirmative covenant to pay money for use in connection with, but not upon, the land which it is said is subject to the burden of the covenant. Does such a covenant "touch" or "concern" the land? These terms are not part of a statutory definition, a limitation placed by the State upon the power of the courts to enforce covenants *intended* to run with the land by the parties who entered into the covenants. Rather they are words used by courts in England in old cases to describe a limitation which the courts themselves created or to formulate a test which the courts have devised and which the courts voluntarily apply. Cf. Spencer's Case, Coke, vol. 3, part 5, 16a. In truth such a description or test so formulated is too vague to be of much assistance and judges and academic scholars alike have struggled, not with entire success, to formulate a test at once more satisfactory and more accurate. "It has been found impossible to state any absolute tests to determine what covenants touch and concern land and what do not. The question is one for the court to determine in the exercise of its best judgment upon the facts of each case." Clark, op.cit. p. 76.

Even though that be true, a determination by a court in one case upon particular facts will often serve to point the way to correct decision in other cases upon analogous facts. Such guideposts may not be disregarded. It has been often said that a covenant to pay a sum of money is a personal affirmative covenant which usually does not concern or touch the land. Such statements are based upon English decisions which hold in effect that only covenants, which compel the covenanter to submit to some *restriction on the use* of his property, touch or concern the land, and that the burden of a covenant which requires the covenanter to do an affirmative act, even on his own land, for the benefit of the owner of a "dominant" estate, does not run with his land. Miller v. Clary, 210 N.Y. 127, 103 N.E. 1114, L.R.A.1918E, 222 Ann.Cas.1915B, 872. In that case the court pointed out that in many jurisdictions of this country the narrow English rule has been criticized and a more liberal and flexible rule has been substituted. In this State the courts have not gone so far. We have not abandoned the historic distinction drawn by the English courts. So this court has recently said: "Subject to a few exceptions not important at this time, there is now in this state a settled rule of law that a covenant to do an affirmative act, as distinguished from a covenant merely negative in effect, does not run with the land so as to charge the burden of performance on a subsequent grantee [citing cases]. This is so though the burden of such a covenant is laid upon the very parcel which is the subject-matter of the conveyance." Guaranty Trust Co. of New York v. New York & Queens County Ry. Co., 253 N.Y. 190, 204, 170 N.E. 887, 892, opinion by Cardozo, Ch.J.

Both in that case and in the case of Miller v. Clary, supra, the court pointed out that there were some exceptions or limitations in the application of the general rule. Some promises to pay money have been enforced, as covenants running with the land, against subsequent holders of the land who took with notice of the covenant. It may be difficult to classify these exceptions or to formulate a test of whether a particular covenant to pay money or to perform some other act falls within the general rule that ordinarily an affirmative covenant is a personal and not a real covenant, or falls outside the limitations placed upon the general rule. At least it must "touch" or "concern" the land in a substantial degree, and though it may be inexpedient and perhaps impossible to formulate a rigid test or definition which will be entirely satisfactory or which can be applied mechanically in all cases, we should at least be able to state the problem and find a reasonable method of approach to it. It has been suggested that a covenant which runs with the land must affect the legal relations—the advantages and the burdens—of the parties to the covenant, as owners of particular parcels of land and not merely as members of the community in general, such as taxpayers or owners of other land. Clark, op.cit. p. 76. That method of approach has the merit of realism. The test is based on the effect of the covenant rather than on technical distinctions. Does the covenant impose, on the one hand, a burden upon an interest in land, which on the other hand increases the value of a different interest in the same or related land?

Even though we accept that approach and test, it still remains true that whether a particular covenant is sufficiently connected with the use of land to run with the land, must be in many cases a question of degree. A promise to pay for something to be done in connection with the promisor's land does not differ essentially from a promise by the promisor to do the thing himself, and both promises constitute, in a substantial sense, a restriction upon the owner's right to use the land, and a burden upon the legal interest of the owner. On the other hand, a covenant to perform or pay for the performance of an affirmative act disconnected with the use of the land cannot ordinarily touch or concern the land in any substantial degree. Thus, unless we exalt technical form over substance, the distinction between covenants which run with land and covenants which are personal, must depend upon the effect of the covenant on the legal rights which otherwise would flow from ownership of land and which are connected with the land. The problem then is: Does the covenant in purpose and effect substantially alter these rights?

* * *

Looking at the problem presented in this case * * * and stressing the intent and substantial effect of the covenant rather than its form, it seems clear that the covenant may properly be said to touch and concern the land of the defendant and its burden should run with the land. True, it calls for payment of a sum of money to be expended for "public purposes" upon land other than the land conveyed by Neponsit Realty Company to plaintiff's predecessor in title. By that conveyance the grantee, however, obtained not only title to particular lots, but an easement or right of common enjoyment with other property owners in roads, beaches, public parks or spaces and improvements in the same tract. For full enjoyment in common by the defendant and other property owners of these easements or rights, the roads and public places must be maintained. In order that the burden of maintaining public improvements should rest upon the land benefited by the improvements, the grantor exacted from the grantee of the land with its appurtenant easement or right of enjoyment a covenant that the burden of paying the cost should be inseparably attached to the land which enjoys the benefit. It is plain that any distinction or definition which would exclude such a covenant from the classification of covenants which "touch" or "concern" the land would be based on form and not on substance.

Another difficulty remains. Though between the grantor and the grantee there was privity of estate, the covenant provides that its benefit shall run to the assigns of the grantor who "may include a Property Owners' Association which may hereafter be organized for the purposes referred to in this paragraph." The plaintiff has been organized to receive the sums payable by the property owners and to expend them for the benefit of such owners. Various definitions have been formulated of "privity of estate" in connection with covenants that run with the land, but none of such definitions seems to cover the relationship between the plaintiff and the defendant in this case. The plaintiff has not succeeded to the ownership of any property of the grantor. It does not appear that it ever had title to the streets or public places upon which charges which are payable to it must be expended. It does not appear that it owns any other property in the residential tract to which any easement or right of enjoyment in such property is appurtenant. It is created solely to act as the assignee of the benefit of the covenant, and it has no interest of its own in the enforcement of the covenant.

The arguments that under such circumstances the plaintiff has no right of action to enforce a covenant running with the land are all based upon a distinction between the corporate property owners association and the property owners for whose benefit the association has been formed. If that distinction may be ignored, then the basis of the arguments is destroyed. How far privity of estate in technical form is necessary to enforce in equity a restrictive covenant upon the use of land, presents an interesting question. Enforcement of such covenants rests upon equitable principles (Tulk v. Moxhay, 2 Phillips, 774; Trustees of Columbia College v. Lynch, 70 N.Y. 440, 26 Am.Rep. 615), and at times, at least, the violation "of the restrictive covenant may be restrained at the suit of one who owns property or for whose benefit the restriction was established, irrespective of whether there were privity either of estate or of contract between the parties, or whether an action at law were maintainable." Chesebro v. Moers, 233 N.Y. 75, 80, 134 N.E. 842, 843, 21 A.L.R. 1270. The covenant in this case does not fall exactly within any classification of "restrictive" covenants, which have been enforced in this State and no right to enforce even a restrictive covenant has been sustained in this State where the plaintiff did not own property which would benefit by such enforcement so that some of the elements of an equitable servitude are present. In some jurisdictions it has been held that no action may be maintained without such elements. But cf. VanSant v. Rose, 260 Ill. 401, 103 N.E. 194, 49 L.R.A.,N.S., 186. We do not attempt to decide now how far the rule of Trustees of Columbia College v. Lynch, supra, will be carried, or to formulate a definite rule as to when, or even whether, covenants in a deed will be enforced, upon equitable principles, against subsequent purchasers with notice, at the suit of a party without privity of contract or estate. There is no need to resort to such a rule if the courts may look behind the corporate form of the plaintiff.

The corporate plaintiff has been formed as a convenient instrument by which the property owners may advance their common interests. We do not ignore the corporate form when we recognize that the Neponsit

Property Owners' Association, Inc., is acting as the agent or representative of the Neponsit property owners. As we have said in another case: when Neponsit Property Owners' Association, Inc., "was formed, the property owners were expected to, and have looked to that organization as the medium through which enjoyment of their common right might be preserved equally for all." Matter of City of New York, Public Beach, Borough of Queens, 269 N.Y. 64, 75, 199 N.E. 5, 9. Under the conditions thus presented we said: "It may be difficult, or even impossible, to classify into recognized categories the nature of the interest of the membership corporation and its members in the land. The corporate entity cannot be disregarded, nor can the separate interests of the members of the corporation" (page 73, 199 N.E. page 8). Only blind adherence to an ancient formula devised to meet entirely different conditions could constrain the court to hold that a corporation formed as a medium for the enjoyment of common rights of property owners owns no property which would benefit by enforcement of common rights and has no cause of action in equity to enforce the covenant upon which such common rights depend. Every reason which in other circumstances may justify the ancient formula may be urged in support of the conclusion that the formula should not be applied in this case. In substance if not in form the covenant is a restrictive covenant which touches and concerns the defendant's land, and in substance, if not in form, there is privity of estate between the plaintiff and the defendant.

* * *

The order should be affirmed, with costs.

* * *

Problems and Questions

1. What sort of privity was at issue in *Neponsit?*

2. Was *Neponsit* a case at law or in equity? If in equity, why did the court discuss privity of estate, an element not necessary for a covenant to run with the land in equity?

3. Suppose the covenant in *Neponsit* had required the property owners to pay dues to the homeowners' association to be used for maintenance of a recreational facility to which outsiders could obtain membership? *See* Regency Homes Association v. Egermayer, 243 Neb. 286, 498 N.W.2d 783 (1993); Riverton Community Association, Inc. v. Myers, 184 A.D.2d 1063, 584 N.Y.S.2d 368 (1992).

4. A sold land to B and included a covenant under which B agreed to furnish heat to A's building on adjacent property. B conveyed the land to C, who purchased with notice of the heating arrangement. C refused to furnish heat, and A sues for specific performance. What result? *See* Nicholson v. 300 Broadway Realty Corp., 7 N.Y.2d 240, 196 N.Y.S.2d 945, 164 N.E.2d 832 (1959).

d. *Enforcement in Equity Against Subsequent Purchasers*

While the English law courts were preoccupied with refining the various technical requirements for a covenant to run with the land, equity courts took a dramatically different tack. The equity approach was so flexible that a new label was applied to covenants enforceable in equity—"equitable servitudes."

TULK v. MOXHAY

Court of Chancery, 1848.
2 Phillips 774, 41 Eng.Rep. 1143.

In the year 1808 the Plaintiff, being then the owner in fee of the vacant piece of ground in Leicester Square, as well as of several of the houses forming the Square, sold the piece of ground by the description of "Leicester Square garden or pleasure ground, with the equestrian statue then standing in the centre thereof, and the iron railing and stone work round the same," to one Elms in fee: and the deed of conveyance contained a covenant by Elms, for himself, his heirs, and assigns, with the Plaintiff, his heirs, executors, and administrators, "that Elms, his heirs, and assigns should, and would from time to time, and at all times thereafter at his and their own costs and charges, keep and maintain the said piece of ground and square garden, and the iron railing round the same in its then form, and in sufficient and proper repair as a square garden and pleasure ground, in an open state, uncovered with any buildings, in neat and ornamental order; and that it should be lawful for the inhabitants of Leicester Square, tenants of the Plaintiff, on payment of a reasonable rent for the same, to have keys at their own expense and the privilege of admission therewith at any time or times into the said square garden and pleasure ground."

The piece of land so conveyed passed by divers mesne conveyances into the hands of the Defendant, whose purchase deed contained no similar covenant with his vendor: but he admitted that he had purchased with notice of the covenant in the deed of 1808.

The Defendant having manifested an intention to alter the character of the square garden, and asserted a right, if he thought fit, to build upon it, the Plaintiff, who still remained owner of several houses in the square, filed this bill for an injunction; and an injunction was granted by the Master of the Rolls to restrain the Defendant from converting or using the piece of ground and square garden, and the iron railing round the same, to or for any other purpose than as a square garden and pleasure ground in an open state, and uncovered with buildings.

On a motion, now made, to discharge that order, * * *

The Lord Chancellor [Cottenham] That this Court has jurisdiction to enforce a contract between the owner of land and his neighbour purchasing a part of it, that the latter shall either use or abstain from using the land purchased in a particular way, is what I never knew disputed. Here there is no question about the contract: the owner of certain houses in the square sells the land adjoining, with a covenant from the purchaser not to use it for any other purpose than as a square garden. And it is now contended, not that the vendee could violate that contract, but that he might sell the piece of land, and that the purchaser from him may violate it without this Court having any power to interfere. If that were so, it would be impossible for an owner of land to sell part of it without incurring the risk of rendering what he retains worthless. It is said that, the covenant being one which does not run with the land [at law], this Court cannot enforce it; but the question is, not whether the covenant runs with the land [at law], but whether a party shall be permitted to use the land in a manner inconsistent with the contract entered into by his vendor, and with notice of which he purchased. Of course, the price would be affected by the covenant, and nothing could be more inequitable than that the original purchaser should be able to sell the property the next day for a greater price, in consideration of the assignee being allowed to escape from the liability which he had himself undertaken.

That the question does not depend upon whether the covenant runs with the land [at law] is evident from this, that if there was a mere agreement and no covenant, this Court would enforce it against a party purchasing with notice of it; for if an equity is attached to the property by the owner, no one purchasing with notice of that equity can stand in a different situation from the party from whom he purchased.

* * *

With respect to the observations of Lord Brougham in *Keppell v. Bailey* [2 M. & K. 547] he never could have meant to lay down that this Court would not enforce an equity attached to land by the owner, unless under such circumstances as would maintain an action at law. If that be the result of his observations, I can only say that I cannot coincide with it.

I think the cases cited before the Vice–Chancellor and this decision of the Master of the Rolls perfectly right, and, therefore, that this motion must be refused, with costs.

Notes and Questions

1.   Why could the covenant in *Tulk* not be enforced at law?

2.   Equity courts eliminate the privity of estate requirement and focus on reasonableness, intent, and notice. What role, if any, does the touch and concern requirement play with respect to equitable servitudes running with the land?

3.   Now that law and equity courts are generally merged, is it appropriate to continue to use different sets of rules for the running of real covenants depending on the relief sought? Indeed, the two sets of elements are often blurred by modern courts. *Neponsit* (page 419) is an illustration of the failure of courts to clearly distinguish between the enforcement of real

covenants at law and in equity. Moreover, a court may analyze a real covenant in terms of the requirements for a covenant to run with the land at common law and then grant equitable relief. *See, e.g.,* Sloan v. Johnson, 254 Va. 271, 491 S.E.2d 725 (1997).

e. Who May Enforce?

Assuming the existence of a covenant that runs in law or equity, the next question is: Who may enforce the covenant? The owner of land benefited by the covenant, of course, may enforce it against successive owners of the burdened land. Conversely, in many jurisdictions, one who does not own benefited land may not enforce the covenant against successive owners of the burdened land on the ground that a covenant with a benefit in gross restrains the use of certain property without resulting in a corresponding advantage to other property. *See* 9 Powell on Real Property § 60.04[2][a] (1998); 2 American Law of Property § 9.32 (1952). Recall, however, that in the *Neponsit* case on page 419, a homeowners' association was allowed to enforce a covenant even though it did not own benefited land. The standing of a homeowners' association to enforce covenants is now relatively well-established. *See, e.g.,* Merrionette Manor Homes Improvement Association v. Heda, 11 Ill.App.2d 186, 136 N.E.2d 556 (1956); Architectural Committee of the Mount Olympus Cove Subdivision No. 3 v. Kabatznick, 949 P.2d 776 (Utah App.1997). *See generally* Roberts, *Promises Respecting Land Use—Can Benefits Be Held In Gross*, 51 Mo.L.Rev. 933 (1986) (re-evaluating and criticizing judicial reluctance to enforce benefits in gross).

CHRISTIANSEN v. CASEY

Missouri Court of Appeals, Western District, 1981.
613 S.W.2d 906.

NUGENT, JUDGE.

This is an appeal on behalf of plaintiffs, Paul A. Christiansen, et al., developers of real estate in Blue Springs, Jackson County, Missouri. The Christiansens' petition for temporary restraining order, temporary and permanent injunctions, and damages for violation of restrictive covenants was dismissed with prejudice by the circuit court for plaintiffs' lack of standing. We reverse.

The Christiansens filed suit August 17, 1979, alleging that in May, 1976, Paul A. Christiansen caused to be prepared and filed a declaration of restrictions against Lots 1–63 in Lake Village, a residential development in eastern Jackson County. Included in the restrictions was a provision giving the Christiansens the power to review and approve all plans for the construction of improvements to any of the sixty-three lots, including any proposed fences. The Christiansens alleged that the Caseys, owners of Lot 5, constructed a fence on Lot 5 with actual knowledge that the fence was violative of the restrictive covenants. The record shows that the parties later stipulated that, at the time of the filing of their petition, the Christiansens no longer owned any of the sixty-three lots in question. The Caseys filed a motion to dismiss based on the theory that, because the declaration of restrictions vests the right to seek judicial enforcement of the restrictions solely in fee simple title holders of Lots 1–63 inclusive, the Christiansens lacked standing to bring the action. Reserving its decision on Caseys' motion, the trial court held a hearing on the temporary injunction. Subsequently, the defendants' motion to dismiss was sustained.

* * *

Lake Village is a 340–acre residential subdivision of which Lots 1–63 constituted the first tract upon which restrictions were placed. The restricting document, wherein the Christiansens variously described themselves as "owners", "developers", and "undersigned", contains two provisions that give rise to this action, to-wit, in relevant parts:

SECTION II—APPROVAL OF PLANS AND SPECIFICATIONS OF IMPROVEMENTS PERMITTED

No building shall be erected, placed or altered on any lot until the building plans, specifications and plot plan showing the location of the improvements or alterations have been approved in writing as to conformity and harmony of external design with existing structures, and as to location with respect to topography and finished ground level, by the undersigned or their representative, and a complete set of plans and specifications permanently filed with the developer.

No outside work on the house, except clean-up work, may be performed by the buyers until the house is finished. Builders must be approved by the developer.

No fencing shall be permitted on any lot unless the same is chain link fencing, and approval for all fencing must be obtained in the manner and method as set out in the foregoing paragraph, except that no fencing shall be permitted nearer to the front street line than the rear lines of the residence improvements * * *

and:

SECTION IV—DURATION AND ENFORCEMENT

These restrictions and covenants are to run with the land and shall be binding on all parties and all persons claiming under them until January 1, 2000 * * *

Each of the restrictions and covenants herein set forth shall run with the land and bind the present owners, its successors and assigns and all parties claiming by, through or under them shall be taken to hold, agree and covenant with the owner of said tract, to conform to and observe said restrictions and covenants. The owner or owners of any portion of the above lands shall have the right to sue for and obtain an injunction, prohibitive or mandatory, to prevent the breach of or to enforce the observance of the restrictions and covenants above set forth, in addition to the ordinary legal action for damages * * *

Although the Christiansens later filed identical restrictions covering Lots 64–84, lands adjacent to the tract at issue, they filed neither a master plat nor one master set of restrictions.

At the hearing evidence was presented to establish the fact that when the Caseys purchased Lot 5 in 1979 from a builder other than the developer they had actual knowledge of the restrictions. Indeed, in June, 1979 the Caseys, in accordance with section II of the restrictions, submitted a plan for a swimming pool to Mr. Christiansen for his approval. Following a procedure used for the purpose of dealing with such requests, Christiansen noted in ink on the plan that a chain link fence was to be placed on the perimeter of the lot and stamped his approval.

The Christiansens were out of town during the time of the construction of the fence. When they returned, they discovered that the Caseys had completed a wooden fence placed not at the property line but two feet inside the line. On August 17, 1979, the Christiansens filed this action.

The trial court in its judgment entry of December 7, 1979, found the evidence to be "conclusive that the defendants are in violation of the Declaration of the Restrictions and that they are obligated to follow those declarations, as land owners, even though not signatory to said Declarations." While noting that the "Declarations prohibit the erection of the type fence herein involved, except one approved by the developer, i.e., the Plaintiffs", the trial court found that "a reading of the entire document" led it to believe that the language in section IV vests the right to seek enforcement only in "fee simple title holders".

In this case there is no dispute as to the facts. The Caseys are clearly in violation of the restrictive covenants; the Christiansens no longer own land in the restricted tract. The only issue is the propriety of the court's dismissal under the facts. In other words, how will the transfer of an original grantor's interest in land affect his continued rights? We hold that under the facts of this case the grantor being the promisee of the covenantor may hold the grantee-covenantor to his promise. That would seem to be especially compelling when an additional ground of the grantor's claim for relief is that he holds nearby land which, although not under the umbrella of the restrictions, may be materially affected by the violation of the restrictions.

Missouri courts have long held to the principles that "the law favors the free and untrammeled use of property" and that "when there is substantial doubt as to the wording of the meaning of any restriction, such doubt should be resolved in the favor of free use of any property". Steve Vogli & Co. v. Lane, 405 S.W.2d 885 (Mo.1966). In the instant case, however, no controversy exists as to the meaning of the restrictions as they relate to the kind of fence that may be constructed or the place where the fence is to be located. Although the Caseys refer to and rely upon the policy of law which favors the untrammeled use of property, in fact, they do not claim that these restrictions are unreasonable or unduly burden the use of their property. Nor do they claim lack of notice. Such matters are not in issue in this case. The Caseys merely claim that their promise to the Christiansens is no longer enforceable by the Christiansens.

Missouri's Supreme Court in Kerrick v. Schoenberg, 328 S.W.2d 595 (Mo.1959), defined a real covenant at 600 as

> one having for its object something annexed to, inherent in, or connected with, land or other real property—one which relates to, touches, or concerns, the land granted or demised and the occupation or enjoyment thereof. A covenant is viewed as real in nature, or one that runs with the land, when either the liability to perform the duties therein enumerated or the right to take advantage thereof passes to the assignee of the land.

However, a promise made to the grantor becomes a personal covenant, or benefit in gross, when the covenantor remains liable to the grantor after the grantor has divested himself of the benefited land.

If the plaintiff still owns land that is benefited by the agreement, courts generally have no difficulty in finding the restriction to be a real covenant and the plaintiff to have standing to enforce. But, if the plaintiff no longer owns the benefited property, courts find that the covenant is personal rather than real. The question of the standing of an original grantor to sue a covenant[or] on a personal covenant is an open one in the United States.[1]

* * *

Apparently, Missouri aligns itself with the states which allow the original grantor to enforce a restrictive covenant when the covenantor has actual or constructive knowledge of the restriction. This approach, although a departure from the leading English case, London County Council v. Allen, 3 K.B. 642 (1914), has practical as well as equitable

---

1. See Oakman v. Marino, 241 Mich. 591, 217 N.W. 794 (1928), holding that the plaintiff, owner of extensive properties in adjoining additions where identical restrictions were being enforced, had an interest in the enforcement of restrictions in the addition where he had earlier sold land; Hills v. Graves, 26 Ohio App. 1, 159 N.E. 482 (1927), in which the court found the promisee still owned adjacent property which would be damaged by the violation of the covenant; Van Sant v. Rose, 260 Ill. 401, 103 N.E. 194 (1913), wherein the court treated the promisee's interest in the restriction as a property interest enforceable even absent damage to the promisee.

Contra, Place v. Cummiskey, 6 A.D.2d 344, 176 N.Y.S.2d 806 (Sup.Ct.1958), in which the court found that no right has ever been sustained in the State of New York to enforce a restrictive covenant where the plaintiff did not own property which would be benefited by such enforcement; Auerbacher v. Smith, 22 N.J.Super. 568, 92 A.2d 492 (N.J.Super.A.D.1952), holding that when the grantor disposed of her remaining lands benefited by the restriction, she no longer had a sufficient interest to maintain an action for breach of covenant; Boyd v. Park Realty Corp., 137 Md. 36, 111 A. 129 (1920), holding that a company which restricted lots and sold them could no longer enforce the restrictions.

appeal. Professor Stone,[2] in an analysis of such covenants would recommend this position:

> And this, it is submitted, is the view which should prevail. There is no reason why equity, which has made a distinct advance over the rules of property recognizing that equitable rights *in personam* are themselves a species of property worthy of protection, should set limits upon the protection which it affords, by analogy to rules of property developed before Sir Edward Coke's time and which it has actually to some extent supplanted. If the plaintiff has an equitable right on his covenant, that is, one which equity will enforce by compelling the covenantor to perform; if the injury to plaintiff is equally great and the act of the defendant is equally unconscientious, as in the case where a specific performance would give the plaintiff a property right; then equity should not deny relief merely because the result of a specific performance does not fall within one of the categories of property recognized as such by the courts of common law.

The defendants' position, supported by the judgment of the trial court, is that the plain language of section IV of the declaration of restrictions does not reserve to the Christiansens the right to enforce the restriction. Examination of section IV reveals that the language is not so plain and, therefore, may need a bit of construing.

This court finds that paragraph 2 of section IV, as quoted earlier in this opinion, is unclear and ambiguous in the use of the words "present owners" and "owners". The first sentence appears to bind the present owners, at that time the Christiansens, as well as their successors and assigns to the restrictions and covenants. The second sentence in referring to "owner or owners" does not identify them as being the present owners or their successors and assigns.

* * *

The Caseys unquestionably had constructive knowledge of the restrictive covenants as well as actual knowledge of the developer's power to approve or disapprove of the proposed fencing. Christiansen gave additional notice and reminder of the restrictions when the Caseys submitted their plans for a swimming pool. This court in Sherwood Estates Homes Ass'n v. Schmidt, 592 S.W.2d 244 (Mo.App.1979), noted that the "power to enforce [a restriction] is a legally sterile power if it does not include the power to grant or withhold approval of plans and specifications falling within its purview". Conversely, under the facts of this case, power to grant or withhold approval of plans might very well be a legally sterile power if it does not include the power to enforce the restriction.

* * *

2. Stone, *The Equitable Rights and Liabilities of Strangers,* 18 Colum.L.Rev. 291, 313 (1918).

Consideration of the surrounding circumstances at the time this covenant was made must include the fact that the sixty-three lots against which these restrictions were filed were part of a larger adjacent neighborhood in which the Christiansens owned property. Their nearby land provides the Christiansens with a continuing interest which would seem to support the concept that even if the grantor has divested himself of fee simple interest in the lots covered by the restrictions, he retains a property interest in their enforcement. Moreover, as indicated above, we see no reason why equity should not allow these plaintiffs to enforce the covenant, be it real or personal.

Since neither party nor the court below addressed the question whether under this declaration of restrictions the developer had a duty to proceed at his expense on behalf of the grantees to enforce the restrictions, we do not undertake to do so. We leave to future plaintiffs and defendants to argue the question of the continuing duty of a subdivision's developer in absence of delegation of his duties to a homes association, or the like.

Under the facts of this case we find the covenants, made for the benefit and protection of the plaintiffs, may be enforced by them. The judgment of the trial court is reversed and the case remanded for further proceedings.

Notes and Questions

1.   Suppose the developers (the Christiansens) had not owned property within the Lake Village residential development. Would the court have reached the same result?

2.   Compare Haldeman v. Teicholz, 197 A.D.2d 223, 611 N.Y.S.2d 669 (1994) (holding restrictive covenants were intended to benefit subdivision lots only, and therefore original grantor had no standing to enforce covenants despite continued ownership of life estate in adjacent property) with *Christiansen*.

3.   The *Christiansen* court cites London County Council v. Allen [1914] 3 K.B. 642, as the leading case for the proposition that the burden of a covenant will not run with the land when the benefit is in gross. In that case the London County Council and Morris Allen, a builder, entered an agreement whereby the Council gave Allen permission to lay out a new street and in return Allen covenanted not to build on certain land he owned. Later Allen conveyed part of the restricted land to his wife who built three houses on the property. In addition, Allen built a wall on the part of the restricted land he retained. The London County Council sought a mandatory injunction to have the houses and wall removed. The Council was successful as to the wall because Mr. Allen was contractually bound on the covenant. It, however, was unsuccessful with respect to the houses built by Mrs. Allen. In this respect, J. Scrutton noted in his opinion that "the plaintiffs must fail on the ground that they never had any land for the benefit of which this * * * [covenant] could be created, and therefore cannot sue a person who bought the [burdened] land with knowledge that there was a restrictive covenant as

to its use, which [s]he proceeds to disregard, because [s]he is not privy to the contract." *Id.* at 672.

4. Another aspect of the "who may enforce?" problem arises when a covenant is designed to benefit land, but it is unclear what land is to be benefited. In this respect the existence of a common building scheme is often of critical importance.

SNOW v. VAN DAM

Supreme Judicial Court of Massachusetts, 1935.
291 Mass. 477, 197 N.E. 224.

LUMMUS, JUSTICE.

This suit, although brought in Middlesex County, relates to land on the seashore at Brier Neck in Gloucester in Essex county, title to which, after the decision in Luce v. Parsons, 192 Mass. 8, 77 N.E. 1032, was registered on September 5, 1906, in the name of one Luce, from whom title soon passed to one Shackelford. The tract so registered was bounded northerly by a line through a pond not far northerly from a county road called Thatcher Road, which ran through the tract from west to east; easterly by land of other owners; southerly by the Atlantic Ocean, where there was a fine bathing beach; and westerly by Witham Road. The entrance to the tract was at the northwesterly corner, where is situated the lot now owned by the defendant Van Dam, which is the larger part of a triangular piece of land lying north of Thatcher Road and enclosed by Thatcher Road, Witham Road and another road.

The northerly part of the tract, including the lot of the defendant Van Dam, is low and marshy. When the tract was registered in 1906, this northerly part was deemed unsuitable for building, and worthless, and consequently was not divided into lots on the earlier plans. Thatcher Road is a public way on which electric cars used to run. There is no summer residence on the north side of that way, and only one bounding on that way on the south side.

From Thatcher Road, going south, there is a fairly sharp ascent to the top of a low hill, from which there is a gentle slope southward to the beach. This hill and slope were in 1906, and still are, well adapted to summer residences. In 1907 the whole tract, except the part north of Thatcher Road, was divided into building lots. By later plans some of the lots were further subdivided and the boundaries of others were changed. In all, about a hundred building lots were laid out. Each of the plaintiffs owns one of these building lots, either on the hill or on the southerly slope, on which he has built a summer residence.

Between July 8, 1907, and January 23, 1923, almost all the lots into which the part of the tract south of Thatcher Road was divided, including the lots of most of the plaintiffs, were sold at various times by the general owner of the tract to various persons. With negligible exceptions, the deeds contained uniform restrictions, of which the material one is that "only one dwelling house shall be erected or maintained thereon at any given time which building shall cost not less than $2500 and no outbuilding containing a privy shall be erected or maintained on said parcel without the consent in writing of the grantor or their [sic] heirs." The entire unsold remainder of the land south of Thatcher Road was conveyed, on June 15, 1923, by Shackelford, the general owner of the unsold parts of the tract, to J. Richard Clark, subject to similar restrictions.

The low and marshy land north of Thatcher Road was first divided, on a revised plan of 1919, into three parcels, called C, D and E. The revised plan covered the whole Brier Neck tract. On January 23, 1923, about five months before the deed to J. Richard Clark, already mentioned, said Shackelford conveyed said lots, C, D and E to one Robert C. Clark, subject to the following restrictions: "Only one dwelling house may be maintained on each of said parcels of land at any given time, which dwelling house shall cost not less than Twenty-five Hundred Dollars ($2500) unless plans and specifications for a dwelling house of less cost shall be approved in writing by the grantor of said parcels of land, and no outbuilding containing a privy shall be maintained on either of said parcels of land without the consent in writing of the grantor. * * * " Lot D is the last of which the larger part is now owned by the defendant Van Dam, having been conveyed to him by Robert C. Clark on February 18, 1933, subject to the restrictions contained in the deed to him "in so far as the same may be now in force and applicable." This phrase did not purport to create any new restriction, and could have no such effect. The defendants have erected on lot D a large building to be used for the sale of ice cream and dairy products and the conducting of the business of a common victualler. The plaintiffs bring this suit for an injunction, claiming a violation of the restrictions. We think that the erection of a building to be used for business purposes was a violation of the language of the restriction. The zoning of the land for business in 1927 by the city of Gloucester could not operate to remove existing restrictions.

Prior to the conveyance from Shackelford to Robert C. Clark on January 23, 1923, there could not have been, under the law of this commonwealth, any enforceable restriction upon lot D. Sprague v. Kimball, 213 Mass. 380, 100 N.E. 622, Ann.Cas.1914A, 431. If any now exists in favor of the lands of the plaintiffs, it must have been created by that deed.

A restriction, to be attached to land by way of benefit, must not only tend to benefit that land itself (Norcross v. James, 140 Mass. 188, 192, 2 N.E. 946), but must also be intended to be appurtenant to that land. If not intended to benefit an ascertainable dominant estate, the restriction will not burden the supposed servient estate, but will be a mere personal contract on both sides. London County Council v. Allen, [1914] 3 K.B. 642.

In the absence of express statement, an intention that a restriction upon one lot shall be appurtenant to a neighboring lot is sometimes inferred from the relation of the lots to each other. But in many cases there has been a scheme or plan for restricting the lots in a tract undergoing development to obtain substantial uniformity in building and use. The existence of such a building scheme has often been relied on to show an intention that the restrictions imposed upon the several lots shall be appurtenant to every other lot in the tract included in the scheme. In some cases the absence of such a scheme has made it impossible to show that the burden of the restriction was intended to be appurtenant to neighboring land. In the present case, unless the lots of the plaintiffs and the defendant Van Dam were included in one scheme of restrictions, there is nothing to show that the restrictions upon the lot of the defendant Van Dam were intended to be appurtenant to the lots of the plaintiffs.

What is meant by a "scheme" of this sort? In England, where the idea has been most fully developed, it is established that the area covered by the scheme and the restrictions imposed within that area must be apparent to the several purchasers when the sales begin. The purchasers must know the extent of their reciprocal rights and obligations, or, in other words, the "local law" imposed by the vendor upon a definite tract. Where such a scheme exists, it appears to be the law of England and some American jurisdictions that a grantee subject to restrictions acquires by implication an enforceable right to have the remaining land of the vendor, within the limits of the scheme, bound by similar restrictions. Sanborn v. McLean, 233 Mich. 227, 206 N.W. 496, 60 A.L.R. 1212. Traces of that idea can be found in our own reports. But it was settled in this commonwealth by Sprague v. Kimball, 213 Mass. 380, 100 N.E. 622, that the statute of frauds prevents the enforcement against the vendor, or any purchaser from him of a lot not expressly restricted, of any implied or oral agreement that the vendor's remaining land shall be bound by restrictions similar to those imposed upon lots conveyed. Only where the vendor binds his remaining land by writing, can reciprocity of restriction between the vendor and the vendee be enforced.

Nevertheless, the existence of a "scheme" continues to be important in Massachusetts for the purpose of determining the land to which the restrictions are appurtenant. Sometimes the scheme has been established by preliminary statements of intention to restrict the tract, particularly in documents of a public nature. More often it is shown by the substantial uniformity of the restrictions upon the lots included in the tract. In some jurisdictions the logic of the English rule, that the extent and character of the scheme must be apparent when the sale of the lots begins, has led to rulings that the restrictions imposed in later deeds are not evidence of the existence or nature of the scheme. Werner v. Graham, 181 Cal. 174, 183B186, 183 P. 945. In the present case there is no evidence of a scheme except a list of conveyances of different lots from 1907 to 1923 with substantially uniform restrictions. Although the point has not been discussed by this court, the original papers show, more clearly than the reports, that subsequent deeds were relied on to show a scheme existing at the time of the earlier conveyances to the parties or their predecessors in title, in [several cases.] Apparently in Massachusetts a "scheme" has legal effect if definitely settled by the common vendor when the sale of lots begins, even though at that time evidence of such settlement is lacking and a series of subsequent conveyances is needed to supply it. In Bacon v. Sandberg, 179 Mass. 396, 398, 60 N.E. 936, 937, it was said, "the criterion in this class of cases is the intent of the grantor in imposing the restrictions."

Neither the restricting of every lot within the area covered, nor absolute identity of restrictions upon different lots, is essential to the existence of a scheme. But extensive omissions or variations tend to show that no scheme exists, and that the restrictions are only personal contracts.

The existence of a "scheme" is important in the law of restrictions for another purpose, namely, to enable the restrictions to be made appurtenant to a lot within the scheme which has been earlier conveyed by the common vendor. In the present case the lots of some of the plaintiffs were sold before, and the lots of others after, the conveyance from Shackelford to Robert C. Clark on January 23, 1923, which first imposed a restriction upon the lot now owned by the defendant Van Dam. The plaintiffs whose lots were sold before January 23, 1923, cannot claim succession to any rights of Shackelford or of land then retained by him. In general, an equitable easement or restriction cannot be created in favor of land owned by a stranger. Nevertheless an earlier purchaser in a land development has long been allowed to enforce against a later purchaser the restrictions imposed upon the latter by the deed to him in pursuance of a scheme of restrictions. * * *

The rationale of the rule allowing an earlier purchaser to enforce restrictions in a deed to a later one pursuant to a building scheme, is not easy to find. The simple explanation that the deed to the earlier purchaser, subject to restrictions, implied an enforceable agreement on the part of the vendor to restrict in like manner all the remaining land included in the scheme, cannot be accepted in Massachusetts without conflict with Sprague v. Kimball, 213 Mass. 380, 100 N.E. 622. In Bristol v. Woodward, 251 N.Y. 275, 288, 167 N.E. 441, 446, Cardozo, C.J., said, "If we regard the restriction from the point of view of contract, there is trouble in understanding how the purchaser of lot A can gain a right to enforce the restriction against the later purchaser of lot B without an extraordinary extension of Lawrence v. Fox, 20 N.Y. 268. * * * Perhaps it is enough to say that the extension of the doctrine, even if illogical, has been made too often and too consistently to permit withdrawal or retreat."

It follows from what has been said, that if there was a scheme of restrictions, existing when the sale of lots began in 1907, which scheme included the lands of the plaintiffs and of the defendant Van Dam, and if the restrictions imposed upon the land of the defendant Van Dam in 1923 were imposed in pursuance of that scheme, then all the plaintiffs are entitled to relief, unless some special defense is shown. The burden is upon the plaintiffs to show the existence of such a scheme. In our opinion they have done so. Unquestionably there was a scheme which included all the land south of Thatcher Road. The real question is, whether in its origin it included the land north of that road, where is situated the lot of the defendant Van Dam. That lot lies at the gateway of the whole development. One must pass it to visit any part of Brier Neck. The use made of that lot tends strongly to fix the character of the entire tract. It is true, that the land north of Thatcher Road was not divided into lots until 1919, but it was shown on all the plans from the beginning. The failure to divide it sooner was apparently due to a belief that it could not be sold, not to an intent to reserve it for other than residential purposes. We think that the scheme from the beginning contemplated that no part of the Brier Neck tract should be used for commercial purposes. When the lot of the defendant Van Dam was restricted in 1923, the restriction was in pursuance of the original scheme and gave rights to earlier as well as to later purchasers.

* * *

The final decree is affirmed, with costs.

Questions

1. Why is it significant that the *Sprague* decision cited in *Snow* strictly interprets the Statute of Frauds so as to prohibit implied reciprocal restrictive covenants in this jurisdiction? *See* Houghton v. Rizzo, 361 Mass. 635, 281 N.E.2d 577 (1972).

2. How did the *Snow* court justify its decision that a prior purchaser from a developer may enforce restrictive covenants the developer puts in deeds to later purchasers?

3. Suppose there is no general plan of development. Can neighboring landowners enforce a covenant burdening a single lot on the theory they are third party beneficiaries of the restrictive covenant? *Compare* Zamiarski v. Kozial, 18 A.D.2d 297, 239 N.Y.S.2d 221 (1963) *and* Rodgers v. Reimann, 227 Or. 62, 361 P.2d 101 (1961) *with* Terry v. James, 72 Cal.App.3d 438, 140 Cal.Rptr. 201 (1977).

NELLE v. LOCH HAVEN HOMEOWNERS' ASSOCIATION, INC.

Supreme Court of Florida, 1982.
413 So.2d 28.

ADKINS, JUSTICE.

The second district acknowledges that two of its sister courts have taken an approach different from the one adopted by the second district in Loch Haven Homeowners' Association v. Nelle, 389 So.2d 697 (Fla. 2d DCA 1980). * * *

Property owners in Loch Haven Subdivision acquired their respective lots subject to duly recorded deed restrictions. These restrictions are comprehensive and detailed. Three of these restrictions are particularly pertinent to the resolution of the legal issue here in question.

g.   These covenants and restrictions are real covenants and restrictions and are to run with the land, and shall be binding on all parties and owners, and on all parties claiming under them * * *.

h.   If any person, firm or corporation, or their heirs, successors or assigns, shall violate or attempt to violate any of the restrictions before their expiration, it shall be lawful for any other person or persons owning any part or parcel of any above described land to prosecute and proceeding [sic] at law or in equity against the person violating or attempting to violate any such covenant or restriction and to either prevent him or them from doing [sic] or to recover damages or other dues for such violation.

* * *

k.   The Developer shall have the right and authority to approve exceptions or variations from these restrictions without notice or liability to the owners of other lots or any persons or authority whatsoever.

These covenants present the question of whether the developer's reservation of the right to approve exceptions to the restrictive covenants prevents enforcement of the remaining covenants by a remote grantee.

Ordinarily, restrictive covenants are unenforceable by one not a party to the conveyance unless the covenants were made by a common grantor for the benefit of all grantees. One method of demonstrating this beneficial intent of the grantor is through a common, uniform, or scheme of restriction imposed on the property transferred out of the common grantor. Thus, a remote grantee may enforce restrictive covenants against another remote grantee when a common grantor intended to create a uniform building plan or scheme of restrictions.

In the past, reservation of the right to modify subdivision restrictions negated the existence of a common, uniform building plan thereby preventing enforcement of the restriction by a remote grantee. We disagree with this rule and affirm the modern view adopted by the second district.

Traditionally, reservation of the right to modify restrictions, without some limit, allowed the grantor to entirely change the character of the subdivision at the grantor's whim with no corresponding benefit to the grantee. Thus, there was no assurance that the subdivision would remain subject to the restrictions which supplied the mutual benefit or consideration necessary to allow enforcement. More recently, however, courts have begun to require that the reserved power be exercised in a reasonable manner so as not to destroy the general plan. Reading this reasonableness requirement into the reservation of power to modify undercuts the grantor's unfettered control and provides the mutual burden and benefit to both grantor and grantees necessary to sustain the covenants. The subdivision will substantially retain the character and restrictions contemplated by the grantor and each grantee at the conveyance.

There may be times, however, when the grantor reserves too much power or other factors support a finding that a common building plan was not intended. Because this intent is critical we cannot subscribe to the "all or nothing" rule previously held. We, therefore, hold that a reservation by the developer of the power to approve exceptions to the restrictive covenants is merely one factor to be considered in determining whether the developer intended to establish a uniform plan of development.

We find that the restrictions in the instant case show an intent on the part of the developer to establish a uniform plan of development. They are comprehensive and detailed. Moreover, the language of covenant g. expresses an intent that the covenants are to run with the land and be binding on and enforceable by all parties and owners. Plaintiffs are entitled to continue their suit for permanent injunction.

In light of the foregoing, the decision of the Second District Court of Appeal is approved.

Problem

As the principal case indicates, a developer may desire to retain some degree of flexibility to deal with future contingencies. How can this best be accomplished? O, a developer, owned sixty acres of vacant land. In 1990, O recorded a declaration of covenants which restricted the area to residential use. The declaration also provided: "But it is understood that special unforeseen conditions may require exceptions in certain cases, which may be permitted by the written consent of the seller providing the spirit and intent of these covenants and restrictions are adhered to." In 1996, O conveyed one lot to A who proceeded to construct a home. Three years later O contracted to sell 15 acres to a hospital. When A objected, O sought a declaratory judgment that the restrictions were no longer enforceable. What result? *See* Rick v. West, 34 Misc.2d 1002, 228 N.Y.S.2d 195 (1962).

f. Termination

There is no common law limitation on the duration of real covenants. Sometimes, however, covenants contain provisions for their own expiration. They also may be restricted by legislative enactment. In a few states, statutes limit their duration to a stated number of years. *See* 9 Powell on Real Property § 60.09 (1998). Further, in several jurisdictions, marketable title acts extinguish covenants that are not periodically rerecorded. *See* Chapter 4, pages 556–561, for treatment of marketable title statutes.

A covenant also may be terminated by virtue of the parties' conduct or because circumstances have changed. *See* 9 Powell on Real Property § 60.10[1] & [2] (1998). The following cases explore these possibilities.

WESTERN LAND CO. v. TRUSKOLASKI

Supreme Court of Nevada, 1972.
88 Nev. 200, 495 P.2d 624.

BATJER, JUSTICE:

The respondents, homeowners in the Southland Heights subdivision in southwest Reno, Nevada, brought an action in the district court to enjoin the appellant from constructing a shopping center on a 3.50–acre parcel of land located within the subdivision at the northeast corner of Plumas and West Plumb Lane. In 1941 the appellant subdivided this 40–acre development, and at that time it subjected the lots to certain restrictive covenants which specifically restricted the entire 40 acres of the subdivision to single family dwellings and further prohibited any stores, butcher shops, grocery or mercantile business of any kind.[1] The district court held these restrictive covenants to be enforceable, and enjoined the appellant from constructing a supermarket or using the 3.5 acres in any manner other than that permitted by the covenants. The appellant contends that the district court erred in enforcing these covenants because the subdivision had so radically changed in recent years as to nullify their purpose. We agree with the holding of the district court that the restrictive covenants remain of substantial value to the homeowners in the subdivision, and that the changes that have occurred since 1941 are not so great as to make it inequitable or oppressive to restrict the property to single-family residential use.

In 1941 the Southland Heights subdivision was outside of the Reno city limits. The property surrounding the subdivision was primarily used

---

1. The agreement as to building restrictions for the Southland Heights Subdivision, signed and filed for record by the Western Land Co., Ltd., provides in pertinent part as follows:

"WHEREAS, the said Western Land Co. Ltd. desires to subject said lots to the conditions and restrictions hereinafter set forth for the benefit of said lots and of the present and subsequent owners thereof.

"NOW, THEREFORE, the Western Land Co. Ltd., for the benefits and considerations herein set forth accrued and accruing to it, does covenant and agree that said lots, pieces, and parcels of land shall be held or conveyed subject to the following conditions and restrictions, to-wit:

"1. No structures shall be erected, altered, placed or permitted to remain on any of said lots or parcels of ground other than one single family dwelling * * *

"* * * *.

"4. No store, butcher shop, grocery or mercantile business of any kind shall

be maintained, carried on, or conducted upon any of said lots or parcels * * *

"* * * *.

"10. These covenants are to run with the land and shall be binding upon all the parties and all persons cla[i]ming under them until January 1st, 1966, at which time said covenants shall be automatically extended for successive periods of ten years unless by a vote of the majority of the then owners of the lots it is agreed to change the said covenants in whole or in part; * * * and whether or not it be so expressed in the deeds or other conveyances of said lots, the same shall be absolutely subject to the covenants, conditions, and restrictions which run with and are appurtenant to said lots or every part thereof as herein expressed as fully as if expressly contained in proper and obligatory covenants and conditions in each and every deed, contract, and conveyance of or concerning any part of the said land or the improvements to be made thereon."

for residential and agricultural purposes, with very little commercial development of any type in the immediate area. At that time Plumb Lane extended only as far east as Arlington Avenue.

By the time the respondents sought equitable relief in an effort to enforce the restrictive covenants, the area had markedly changed. In 1941 the city of Reno had a population of slightly more than 20,000; that figure had jumped to approximately 95,100 by 1969. One of the significant changes, as the appellant aptly illustrates, is the increase in traffic in the surrounding area. Plumb Lane had been extended to Virginia Street, and in 1961 the city of Reno condemned 1.04 acres of land on the edge of the subdivision to allow for the widening of Plumb Lane into a four-lane arterial boulevard. A city planner, testifying for the appellant, stated that Plumb Lane was designed to be and now is the major east-west artery through the southern portion of the city. A person who owns property across Plumas from the subdivision testified that the corner of Plumb Lane and Plumas is "terribly noisy from 5:00 p.m. until midnight." One of the findings of the trial court was that traffic on Plumb Lane had greatly increased in recent years.

Another significant change that had occurred since 1941 was the increase in commercial development in the vicinity of the subdivision. On the east side of Lakeside Drive, across from the subdivision property, is a restaurant and the Lakeside Plaza Shopping Center. A supermarket, hardware store, drug store, flower shop, beauty shop and a dress shop are located in this shopping center. Still further east of the subdivision, on Virginia Street, is the Continental Lodge, and across Virginia Street is the Park Lane Shopping Center.

Even though traffic has increased and commercial development has occurred in the vicinity of the subdivision, the owners of land within Southland Heights testified to the desirability of the subdivision for residential purposes. The traffic density within the subdivision is low, resulting in a safe environment for the children who live and play in the area. Homes in Southland Heights are well cared for and attractively landscaped.

The trial court found that substantial changes in traffic patterns and commercial activity had occurred since 1941 in the vicinity of the subdivision. Although it was shown that commercial activity outside of the subdivision had increased considerably since 1941, the appellant failed to show that the area in question is now unsuitable for residential purposes.

Even though nearby avenues may become heavily traveled thoroughfares, restrictive covenants are still enforceable if the single-family residential character of the neighborhood has not been adversely affected, and the purpose of the restrictions has not been thwarted. Although commercialization has increased in the vicinity of the subdivision, such activity has not rendered the restrictive covenants unenforceable because they are still of real and substantial value to those homeowners living within the subdivision. West Alameda Heights H. Ass'n v. Board of Co. Com'rs, 169 Colo. 491, 458 P.2d 253 (1969).

The appellant asks this court to reverse the judgment of the district court and declare as a matter of law that the objects and purposes for which the restrictive covenants were originally imposed have been thwarted, and that it is now inequitable to enforce such restrictions against the entity that originally created them. This we will not do. The record will not permit us to find as a matter of law that there has been such a change in the subdivision or for that matter in the area to relieve the appellant's property of the burden placed upon it by the covenants. There is sufficient evidence to sustain the findings of the trial court that the objects and purposes of the restrictions have not been thwarted, and that they remain of substantial value to the homeowners in the subdivision.

The case of Hirsch v. Hancock, 173 Cal.App.2d 745, 343 P.2d 959 (1959) as well as the other authorities relied upon by the appellant are inapposite for in those cases the trial court found many changes within as well as outside the subdivision and concluded from the evidence that the properties were entirely unsuitable and undesirable for residential use and that they had no suitable economic use except for business or commercial purposes, and the appellate courts in reviewing those cases held that the evidence supported the findings and sustained the judgments of the trial courts.

On the other hand, in the case of West Alameda Heights H. Ass'n v. Board of Co. Com'rs, supra, upon facts similar to those found in this case, the trial court decided that the changed conditions in the neighborhood were such as to render the restrictive covenants void and unenforceable. The appellate court reversed and held that the trial court misconceived and misapplied the rule as to change of conditions and said, 169 Colo. at 498, 458 P.2d at 256: "As long as the original purpose of the covenants can still be accomplished and substantial benefit will inure to the restricted area by their enforcement, the covenants stand even though the subject property has a greater value if used for other purposes."

There is substantial evidence in the record to support the trial court's findings of fact and conclusions of law that the covenants were of real and substantial value to the residents of the subdivision. Where the evidence is conflicting and the credibility of the witnesses is in issue, the judgment will not be disturbed on appeal if the evidence is substantially in support of the judgment of the lower court. Here the appellant has not carried its burden of showing that the subdivision is not now suitable for residential purposes because of changed conditions.

In another attempt to show that the restrictive covenants have outlived their usefulness, the appellant points to actions of the Reno city council. On August 1, 1968, the council adopted a Resolution of Intent to reclassify this 3.5–acre parcel from R–1 [residential] to C–1(b) [commercial]. The council never did change the zoning, but the appellant contends that since the counsel did indicate its willingness to rezone, it was of the opinion that the property was more suitable for commercial than residential use. This argument of the appellant is not persuasive. A zoning ordinance cannot override privately-placed restrictions, and a trial court cannot be compelled to invalidate restrictive covenants merely because of a zoning change.

Another of the appellant's arguments regarding changed conditions involves the value of the property for residential as compared to commercial purposes. A professional planning consultant, testifying for the appellant, stated that the land in question is no longer suitable for use as a single-family residential area. From this testimony the appellant concludes that the highest and best use for the land is non-residential. Even if this property is more valuable for commercial than residential purposes, this fact does not entitle the appellant to be relieved of the restrictions it created, since substantial benefit inures to the restricted area by their enforcement.

In addition to the alleged changed circumstances, the appellant contends that the restrictive covenants are no longer enforceable because they have been abandoned or waived due to violations by homeowners in the area. Paragraph 3 of the restrictive agreement provides that no residential structure shall be placed on a lot comprising less than 6,000 square feet. Both lot 24 and lot 25 of block E contain less than 6,000 square feet and each has a house located on it. This could hardly be deemed a violation of the restrictions imposed by the appellant inasmuch as it was the appellant that subdivided the land and caused these lots to be smaller than 6,000 feet. Paragraph 7 of the agreement provides that a committee shall approve any structure which is moved onto the subdivision, or if there is no committee, that the structure shall conform to and be in harmony with existing structures. The appellant did show that two houses were moved on to lots within the subdivision, but the appellant failed to show whether a committee existed and if so approved or disapproved, or whether the houses failed to conform or were out of harmony with the existing structures. Finally, in an effort to prove abandonment and waiver, the appellant showed that one house within the subdivision was used as a painting contractor's office for several years in the late 1940's and that more recently the same house had been used as a nursery for a baby sitting business. However, the same witnesses testified that at the time of the hearing this house was being used as a single-family residence.

Even if the alleged occurrences and irregularities could be construed to be violations of the restrictive covenants they were too distant and sporadic to constitute general consent by the property owners in the subdivision and they were not sufficient to constitute an abandonment or waiver. In order for community violations to constitute an abandonment, they must be so general as to frustrate the original purpose of the agreement.

Affirmed.

Notes and Questions

1. If a zoning ordinance permits commercial use, is a restrictive covenant prohibiting such activity still enforceable? *See* Note, *Legal and Policy Conflicts Between Deed Covenants and Subsequently Enacted Zoning Ordinances,* 24 Vand.L.Rev. 1031 (1971).

2. In considering whether to enforce a covenant, how much weight should a court give to changes that have occurred outside the restricted area? In Elliott v. Jefferson County Fiscal Court, 657 S.W.2d 237, 238 (Ky.1983) the Supreme Court of Kentucky observed:

> The Kentucky rule recognizes that *changes outside* the subdivision are beyond the control of the lot owners. The line of demarcation against nonresidential intrusion, once it is drawn, must remain in effect unless the lot owners themselves agree to change the nature of their subdivision. If border lots are released from residential restrictions, the ultimate result could be the destruction of whole subdivisions and there would be a domino effect. (emphasis in original)

Is this view sound? *See* 9 Powell on Real Property § 60.10[2] (1998).

3. For analysis of the theoretical underpinnings of the changed conditions doctrine, see Robinson, *Explaining Contingent Rights: The Puzzle of "Obsolete" Covenants,* 91 Colum.L.Rev. 546 (1991).

4. As suggested in *Western Land Co.,* the right to enforce a restrictive covenant may be waived when landowners acquiesce in its violation. *See* Egan v. Catholic Bishop of Lincoln, 219 Neb. 365, 363 N.W.2d 380 (1985); Fink v. Miller, 896 P.2d 649 (Utah App.1995) (holding that property owners had abandoned right to enforce wood shingle restrictive covenant in view of large number of existing violations). Suppose landowners in a subdivision restricted to residential use acquiesce in the construction of a church in violation of the covenant. Can the landowners later prevent the operation of a dental clinic in the restricted area? *See* Hrisomalos v. Smith, 600 N.E.2d 1363 (Ind.App.1992).

DEMARCO v. PALAZZOLO

Court of Appeals of Michigan, Division Two, 1973.
47 Mich.App. 444, 209 N.W.2d 540.

J.H. GILLIS, PRESIDING JUDGE.

Plaintiffs, individual owners of lots fronting on Ten Mile Road near Mackinac Street in the City of Roseville, Michigan, brought this action seeking to have certain restrictive covenants limiting land use to residential purposes declared void. Defendants are adjacent property owners whose lots front on Mackinac Street. Plaintiffs prevailed below; defendants appeal as of right.

* * *

The evidence at trial showed that 15 or 20 years ago, when plaintiffs purchased their property in the subdivision involved, the neighborhood was pastoral, countrified and generally without commercial use of property. Ten Mile Road was a two-lane street.

Since then, the Edsel Ford Freeway was constructed, substantially eradicating the subdivision of which plaintiff Pantelis' property was a part. Ten Mile Road has become a four-lane thoroughfare, funneling traffic across the freeway at the rate of 24,000 vehicles per day. All other properties in the immediate vicinity that front on Ten Mile Road are now used commercially. Two expert witnesses testified plaintiffs' properties, the only lots in the subdivisions that face Ten Mile Road, were not suitable for residential purposes, as compared to their commercial value.

The trial judge, after viewing the area, held the residential use restrictions void as applied to plaintiffs but required them to create a "greenbelt" to protect defendants' residential property from any detrimental effects of subsequent commercialization.

In spite of the clear evidence adduced by plaintiffs, this is not an easy case. At issue is whether changes *outside* a covenanted subdivision may be considered in determining whether enforcement of reciprocal negative easements such as those here involved would still benefit a dominant estate. There is an apparent split of authority in Michigan jurisprudence on this recurring problem.

A line of cases, apparently headed by Swan v. Mitshkun, 207 Mich. 70, 74, 173 N.W. 529, 530 (1919), hold changes in land use outside covenanted property are *not* relevant, and explain the policy as follows:

> " * * * [T]hose owning property in a restricted residential district or neighborhood, and especially those who have their homes there, and [have] been led to buy or build in such locality by reason of restrictive covenants running with the land imposed upon the street, block or subdivision in which they have purchased, are entitled to protection against prohibited invasion regardless of how close business may crowd around them on unrestricted property, provided the original plan for a residential district has not been departed from in the restricted district, street or block, and the restrictive requirements have been generally enforced, or accepted and complied with by purchasers."

An equally compelling, longstanding and current line of authority holds considerations of land use patterns of surrounding property *are* relevant to the determination of the enforcement of a restrictive covenant. In Windemere–Grand Improvement and Protective Ass'n v. American State Bank, 205 Mich. 539, 548, 172 N.W. 29, 32 (1919), a case factually similar to the one at bar, the Supreme Court stated:

> "Certainly no decree of this court can retain or restore the quiet suburban conditions existing and contemplated when those residential restrictions were imposed. It cannot eliminate the 'vast growth of manufacturing and business institutions out there,' and invasion of traffic which has made 'all Woodward avenue in that vicinity' an exceptionally noisy and busy street. This unforeseen and radical

change in condition and character of the street has defeated the object and purpose of the restrictive covenants upon this lot, which had relations to protecting the home, or dwelling house, and equity does not now, under the concessions and facts shown, demand that defendant be enjoined from improving and using as proposed this lot thus made worthless for residential purposes."

We reiterate, as we attempt to reconcile the divergent authority as applied to the facts of this case, that this lawsuit is, in nature, grounded in principles of equity. Historically, a court of equity seeks to protect to the greatest extent possible the conflicting interests of *both* parties. McClintock, Equity, § 30, p. 78. We, therefore, balance the competing and valid interests of the parties, who, on one side seek to assert their right to maximize the use of their land, and on the other, assert their right to quiet enjoyment of their land intended, as it was, for residential purposes.

The principles of equity announced in the cases on both sides of this issue establish that restrictive covenants are not merely intended to apply and be enforced only so long as it is convenient to do so. However, it is just as certain that restrictive covenants ought not to be enforced when enforcement protects no one. We note this concept is expressed to some degree in cases on either theory of the relevance of marked changes in surrounding areas.

The trial court's opinion clearly makes reference to changes in land use outside the subdivisions *as they have affected the conditions inside the covenanted area.* That is, the traffic, dirt, noise, and inconvenience of the nearby commercialization on Ten Mile Road and along the Edsel Ford Freeway is already an established detriment, for which defendants have no remedy. Thus, the benefit of the restrictive covenant to the remaining residential owners has been substantially impaired. The trial judge, recognizing that, held it would be inequitable to apply the restrictive covenant to plaintiffs' land, the only property in question facing Ten Mile Road. We affirm that decision.

However, that decision only affects plaintiffs' property. For the protection of the remaining residential owners, especially those immediately adjacent to plaintiffs' land, the trial court ordered a "green belt or fence area as provided by the local ordinances" to be established to separate plaintiffs' property from the lots fronting on Mackinac Street. There is authority for such a compromise modification. In Putnam v. Ernst, 232 Mich. 682, 206 N.W. 527 (1925), a 15–foot building line was continued in force even though other restrictions were held inapplicable. A similar balance of the equities was accomplished in Taylor Avenue Improvement Ass'n v. Detroit Trust Co., 283 Mich. 304, 278 N.W. 75 (1938). We are satisfied the modification of restrictions decreed by the trial judge, coupled with the imposition of a "green belt" adequately protects the lot owners whose land faces Mackinac Street.

Affirmed. Costs to plaintiffs.

Notes and Questions

1.   Subdivision covenants usually remain in effect for a certain number of years and often include provision for renewal by the subdivision residents. Many renewal clauses stipulate that the covenants continue for a fixed period unless a stated percentage of the homeowners object. (*See* the building restrictions in *Western Land Co.* in footnote 1 on page 441.) Other renewal clauses require an affirmative vote by the homeowners to extend the covenants for an additional period. Which is the better approach? *See* Zile, *Private Zoning on Milwaukee's Metropolitan Fringe,* 1959 Wis.L.Rev. 451, 459–461.

2.   When property burdened by a restrictive covenant is condemned under the power of eminent domain, the restriction ends and the government takes the property free from limitation on its use. Disagreement exists, however, as to whether parties benefitted by the restrictive covenant are entitled to compensation. Resolution of this question often turns on whether the benefit is viewed as a property right requiring just compensation or a contract right not covered by condemnation awards. *See* 9 Powell on Real Property § 60.10[4] (1998).

Chapter 4

THE MODERN REAL ESTATE TRANSACTION

Hypothetical Situation—Number 4

Shortly after speaking to you about their general interest in purchasing a house or condominium, Jill and Steve Ryan inspected a house for-sale-by-owner. They then contacted Colleen Piper, a real estate broker, for guidance in locating property. Ms. Piper arranged for them to inspect several houses including a three-year old English Tudor in their favorite subdivision—Rolling Hills. After several weeks of searching, the Ryans decided to purchase the house in Rolling Hills. The seller is a corporate executive who was transferred recently to another city. The Ryans have not yet signed a contract. They called you with this information and restated their desire to have you represent them in the transaction. Specifically, they want you to review the real estate contract Ms. Piper has prepared[1] and to advise them about alternative mortgage instruments offered by many lending institutions.

A. INTRODUCTION

1. DIVERSITY OF LAW GOVERNING REAL ESTATE TRANSACTIONS

The law governing real estate transactions differs considerably among the states. Moreover, practice and custom in the field often vary from county to county within a given jurisdiction. This situation is a natural outgrowth of the traditional notion that land transactions have a significant economic and social impact only in the area where the land is located. However, as noted in the preface to this book, the real estate industry has undergone major changes in the last few decades. Today real estate transactions frequently involve persons and businesses in more than one state. Further, many lending institutions make mortgage

---

1. In many areas of the country it is unusual for purchasers of residential property to employ an attorney to examine the sales contract. Most purchasers rely solely on their broker.

loans throughout the country and numerous individuals and financial entities invest in mortgage-backed securities marketed nationally. *See* Uniform Land Transactions Act, prefatory note (1977).

The National Conference of Commissioners on Uniform State Laws concluded from these developments that uniformity in the law of real estate transactions and transfers is desirable. In the 1970's, the Conference created two uniform acts, the Uniform Land Transactions Act (ULTA) and the Uniform Simplification of Land Transfers Act (USLTA), which were designed to achieve uniformity in this area. Although not a single jurisdiction adopted either act, these measures have had an indirect impact on the evolution of legal principles. *See Skendzel v. Marshall* on page 517 (citing ULTA) and *Haner v. Bruce* on page 535 (citing USLTA). *See generally* Bruce, *The Role Uniform Real Property Acts Have Played in the Development of American Land Law: Some General Observations,* 27 Wake Forest L.Rev. 331 (1992). Uniformity has been imposed on certain areas of real estate finance law by federal legislation. *See, e.g.,* page 516 discussing a federal statute governing mortgage due-on-sale clauses.

2. OVERVIEW OF THE MODERN REAL ESTATE TRANSACTION

A special committee of the American Bar Association prepared a report in 1978 reviewing the appropriate role of lawyers in residential real estate transactions. An excerpt from that report is reproduced here in order to provide an overview of the modern real estate transaction. As you read this excerpt, consider whether the report's suggestions regarding increased lawyer participation are realistic or worthwhile. *See generally* Braunstein, *Structural Change and Inter–Professional Competitive Advantage: An Example Drawn From Residential Real Estate Conveyancing,* 62 Mo. L. Rev. 241 (1997) (exploring reasons for declining participation of lawyers in transfer of residential property); Moore, *Lawyers and the Residential Real Estate Transaction,* 26 Real Est.L.J. 351 (1998) (noting that attorney representation in Ohio real property transactions varied widely and that attorneys usually became involved after contract of sale signed).

REPORT, RESIDENTIAL REAL ESTATE TRANSACTIONS: THE LAWYER'S PROPER ROLE—SERVICES—COMPENSATION

14 Real Prop., Prob. & Tr.J. 581, 584–591, 594–595 (1979).

A HYPOTHETICAL HOME PURCHASE TRANSACTION

* * * [I]t is important to inquire what steps are needed to consummate a routine purchase and sale of a home financed by a mortgage given by an institutional lender. In the description which follows, this Paper consciously resorts to what may seem to be overgeneralization. It does so because differences in practice and nomenclature lead many otherwise knowledgeable conveyancers and laymen, at one extreme, to look upon procedures used in their communities as unique, and at the other, as universal. In fact, while there is diversity in the details of practice, there is fundamental unity in the underlying problems facing conveyancers everywhere.

A. The Brokerage Contract

Initially a seller will enter into a brokerage contract with a real estate agent. In many jurisdictions this contract is not required to be in writing with all of the usual dangers of unwritten contracts. A special peril faced by sellers who have not had the advantage of legal counsel is that they may employ more than one broker and, in the absence of a clear understanding concerning the conditions under which the brokerage fee is earned, the seller may become liable to pay more than one fee.

In practice, a high percentage of brokerage contracts are in writing. A common assumption is that the contract is simple and standardized. In fact, a properly drawn contract will anticipate a number of legal problems of some complexity, such as the right of the seller to negotiate on the seller's own behalf, the effect of multiple listings, the disposition of earnest money if the buyer defaults, the rights of the broker if the seller is unable to proffer a marketable title, the duration of any exclusive listing and, as already brought out, the point at which the brokerage fee is earned. Most of the terms are negotiable and, in theory, a new contract should be drawn each time a broker is employed.

Standardized forms, where carefully drawn, have certain advantages. There are no objections to form contracts per se, as used by either brokers or other participants in the land transfer transaction. The objections to form contracts are that they may be inappropriate to the particular transaction, badly drawn initially or incorrectly filled in.

Any seller signing such a contract should have it approved by the seller's lawyer before signing. The seller should have the lawyer explain its meaning and be on hand to see that it is properly executed. (It is presumed that if the seller consults a lawyer, the lawyer will advise against entering into any oral agreement.) In other words, the seller needs the traditional legal services embraced in the expression "advice, representation and drafting." The broker needs similar services at one time or another and receives them from the broker's own lawyer as needed. In routine transactions the broker is sufficiently familiar with the details to be able to handle the matter without resort to professional assistance.

B. The Preliminary Negotiations

When the broker has found a potential buyer, negotiations between the buyer and the seller will begin, with the broker acting in the role of intermediary. In some cases the seller will leave to the broker all the work of negotiation and will merely ratify the agreement reached with the buyer.

It is generally thought that neither the buyer nor the seller needs a lawyer in the course of the negotiations. In theory this assumption is correct because neither party is bound until a written sales contract is signed. In fact, a great deal of trouble can be avoided if both the buyer and the seller consult their own lawyers during the course of the negotiations. If they are to make a proper bargain, they must know what to bargain about.

Aside from the question of price, which seems paramount in the minds of both parties, they should consider such problems as the mode of paying the purchase price and the tax consequences resulting therefrom, the status of various articles as fixtures or personal property, the time set for occupancy and the effect of loss by casualty pending the closing.

They can make whatever agreement they want, but they should anticipate all important questions and be certain a complete understanding has been reached. Failure to do so in the preliminary negotiations may mean, at the time for signing a contract, that they will have to start negotiations all over again. Worse, they may enter into a contract highly disadvantageous to one or the other, so uncertain as to require litigation to determine its meaning, or so ambiguous as to be void for indefiniteness.

C. The Commitment for Financing

Before entering into a sales contract, it would be desirable for the buyer to obtain as much of a commitment as possible for necessary financing.

Many lenders, however, refuse to make the necessary inspections, appraisals and credit investigations to make such a commitment until the buyer can exhibit a signed purchase and sale agreement, and many buyers are reluctant to risk losing the property to a higher offer by deferring the execution of the purchase and sale agreement. All of this leads to the common practice of including in the agreement a "subject to financing" clause which should be examined by the lawyers for the parties before the contract is signed.

Finding a willing lender is not part of a lawyer's professional duties. In practice a lawyer, being a person of affairs, may be able to render this service. Legal expertise is exercised when the lawyer advises the buyer about problems the buyer should anticipate in coming to terms with the lender. By way of illustration, the buyer will seldom have any understanding of the potential effect of an acceleration clause. The buyer should know what the legal and practical consequences of such a clause will be. The buyer should also obtain an estimate of the closing costs that will have to be paid and should obtain legal advice as to all items found in the estimate.

The commitment contract between the lender and buyer will normally be prepared by the lender's lawyer. Before it is accepted, the buyer's lawyer should ascertain that it properly anticipates all important contingencies, comports with the oral agreement previously reached and binds the lender.

Normally the lender has much greater financial expertise than the buyer. This advantage may not have been of as much importance formerly as it is today, because the financing of homes has in many instances become extremely complex. For this reason, when dealing with the lender the buyer is in need of legal assistance.

D. The Contract of Sale

Once an informal agreement has been reached, the buyer and the seller will enter into a formal contract of sale. The importance of this document cannot be overemphasized. Once it is signed, the rights and obligations of the parties are fixed. Each transaction is unique and, in theory, a contract should be specially drafted for each.

The interested parties are the broker, the buyer and the seller. The contract should contain an appropriate provision with regard to the broker's commission. The buyer and the seller want assurance that the writing reflects their understanding. If they have not received legal advice during the preliminary negotiations, they will need to know what questions should have been anticipated and whether firm and advantageous provisions are found in the document. When the instrument is executed, their lawyers should be present to assure that the proper formalities are observed to make it binding. Here again the parties need legal services in the form of drafting, advice, and representation.

This need is not avoided by the use of forms. Even if the form is properly drawn, the printed portion may not adequately express the particular agreement made between the parties, or the words used in filling in blanks may distort its effectiveness. As a matter of practice standardized forms are widely used, and it is recognized that this practice likely will continue. It is recommended that local bar associations draft standard forms of sales agreements, and that joint seminars with real estate brokers and others regarding residential real estate transactions be held regularly. Whenever forms are used, any insertion should be carefully checked by the buyer's and seller's lawyers, and the appropriateness of the form for the particular transaction should be determined by the buyer's and seller's lawyers. The buyer and the seller are often unaware of what the contract means, what they should anticipate, and what steps are needed to make the instrument binding. They should be advised by their own legal counsel.

Prior to the time the contract is signed, the buyer and the seller should have detailed advice about many legal aspects of the transaction. For example, they may not be aware of the need to anticipate the question of who bears the loss or damage to, or destruction of, buildings on the premises between the time the contract is signed and the time of closing. They also may be unaware of the existence of such problems as whether the contract so changes the interest of the seller as to affect insurance policies; whether either the buyer or seller, or both, should execute new wills; whether federal and state gift and death tax matters are involved; whether joint tenancies or tenancies by the entireties will be affected; and the like.

E.   Determining the Status of the Title

After the contract of sale is executed, the state of the seller's title must be determined to the satisfaction of both the buyer and the lender. This is generally the most important legal work connected with the transaction. The initial examination will be made by the lawyer for the buyer, the seller, the lender, or the title insurer, relying upon the official land title records or an abstract thereof, or a title plant maintained by a title insurance company. Where a lawyer's certificate is relied upon, either the lender or the buyer, or both, may desire additional protection in the form of a title insurance policy.

Whoever makes the title examination, the buyer's lawyer should inform the buyer of the limitations, if any, which impair the title. The buyer should also receive formal protection by a written opinion from the lawyer, an owner's title insurance policy, or both. If the buyer applies for title insurance, the buyer's lawyer should negotiate the provisions to be included or excluded from the policy. The lawyer should also make clear to the buyer what the policy means. In particular, the exceptions to coverage contained in the policy should be explained.

The use of standardized exceptions is common to title insurance. They are complex and restrictive and are frequently not understood by the layman.

Each title insurance policy is unique in that it may contain exceptions peculiar to that individual title. The buyer must first be made aware of the existence of these exceptions and must then be made to understand them. If the exception is to a $10,000 mortgage and the buyer sees the provision, the buyer will probably not mistake its meaning. But if the exception is to "all of the conditions and restrictions found in deed of X to Y, recorded in the office of the clerk of the court of Z County, in Deed Book 309 at page 873," the buyer will not, in the first place, realize that the exception is important, or, if the buyer does, will not understand its meaning without assistance from the lawyer.

F.   The Survey

Survey problems arise in many transactions, and the lawyers for all parties should inform their clients of such problems. At some time prior to the approval of title the buyer, the lender, or the title insurance company may demand a survey. The primary purpose of the survey will be to find whether the legal description of the land conforms to the lines laid down on the ground. An additional purpose may be to determine whether structures on the premises violate restrictive covenants or zoning ordinances or constitute an encroachment. When the survey has been completed, the parties should have their lawyers advise them about any legal implications of the surveyor's findings and the scope and extent of the surveyor's certification.

G. Curative Action

In some cases curative action is needed to make titles marketable. Any such curative action should be carried out by a lawyer for the seller, the buyer, or the lender. If the curative action is carried out by the lawyer for the seller, it should be checked for sufficiency by the lawyers for the buyer and lender; if by the lawyer for the buyer, by the lawyer for the lender; and if by the lawyer for the lender, by the lawyer for the buyer.

H. Termite Inspection

In jurisdictions where a termite inspection must be made and a certificate given to the buyer, showing that the premises are free of infestation or damage by termites, the certificate may be ordered by the broker, lender or the lawyer for any of the parties.

In jurisdictions where such certificates are not required, a provision should be added to the contract requiring the seller to provide a current termite certificate by a licensed pest control agency. If there is infestation or damage, the cost of treatment and the cost of necessary repairs of termite-caused damage usually are borne by the seller. The contract should spell out the seller's obligation. A termite clause should be included in all standard form contracts.

I. Drafting Instruments

Before closing, a lawyer should draft the deed, mortgage and the bond or note secured by the mortgage. As a matter of convenience these papers are commonly drafted by the mortgagee's attorney, although the representative of either of the other parties is equally qualified. Whoever does the work, the product should be examined by lawyers for each of the other two parties and the title insurance company, and they should be advised whether the instruments are effective and create the interests intended.

The drafting of these instruments is sometimes considered merely routine work. This is not true. For example, the description of the parties must be so phrased as to prevent confusion, and the description of the land must be complete and accurate. The importance of the form of warranties is often overlooked. By way of illustration, if the title is encumbered by equitable covenants or utility easements, either or both may be acceptable to the buyer and lender, but they should be excepted from the warranty.

How title is to be taken should have been provided in the initial contract between the buyer and the seller, and the buyer should be advised as to the tax and other effects of the manner in which title is taken.

Of equal importance are other special agreements reached earlier in the transaction. The controlling law may provide that the deed supersedes prior understandings so that if they are not embraced in the deed they are nullified. Each deed must therefore be examined to determine whether it carries out what has been agreed upon.

J.   Incidental Paper Work

The Real Estate Settlement Procedures Act requires the preparation of a settlement statement in virtually all residential real estate transactions. In addition, the Truth–In–Lending form must be filled in and executed. If the mortgage loan is to be insured by FHA, VA or by a private mortgage insurance company, more paper work is required. The required documents are standardized and can be completed without resort to legal expertise. They are part of the financing, rather than the legal aspects of the sale and mortgage. Nevertheless, lawyers are frequently called upon to do this work. With a few exceptions, the government has taken the position that whoever performs these services shall receive no compensation therefor.

K.   Obtaining Title Insurance

Where a title insurance policy for the buyer is based on the certificate of a lawyer not employed by a title insurance company, the lawyer may make an application for the initial binder and, after closing, send in a final certificate and procure a policy. This is work for which the lawyer normally, and properly, should be paid by the client to the extent the lawyer is not paid for these services as the agent of the title company. The lawyer should not accept compensation from a title insurance company solely for referring business to that company. This is, of course, clearly improper and contrary to the recorded position of the American Bar Association. The Real Estate Settlement Procedures Act specifically prohibits the acceptance of any "kickbacks" from the title insurance company.

L.   Closing

A closing statement is generally prepared prior to final closing. The statement may take various forms and is designed to indicate the allocation of debits and credits to the various parties. In some cases it is prepared by a layman, in others by a lawyer. The buyer's and seller's lawyers should make certain their clients understand the nature and amount of all closing costs. The American Bar Association supported the adoption of legislation requiring a uniform closing statement in all government-related mortgage transactions. In addition it is recommended that local bar associations draft uniform closing statement forms for use in all other real estate transactions. Even a standard closing form in itself is not sufficient, unless the parties are assured by their own lawyers of the appropriateness of each item.

Unless there is an escrow closing, a further check of title should be made immediately prior to closing. If this check is not made, it is possible that the parties will be unaware that the title has been impaired between the time of the original examination and the closing date. This further check will generally be carried out by the lawyer, abstracter or title insurance company certifying or insuring title.

The closing is the proceeding at which the parties exchange executed instruments, make required payments, and conclude the formal aspects of the transaction. At this point the buyer, the seller, and the lender should be represented by their own lawyers. They require advice and may need representation if a disagreement arises. They should be assured that the legal documents they exchange create the interests intended, that they receive the protection to which they are entitled and that correct payments have been made to those entitled to receive them.

As a part of the closing, arrangements must be made for insurance, taxes, and other incidents of ownership. Instruments must be recorded and a final check of title made. Disbursements must be made and documents distributed to the parties entitled to receive them. Title insurance policies, where called for, must be procured. If a lawyer handles the closing, the lawyer will attend to all or virtually all of these details.

The Conflicts of Interest

At every step set out above it has been said that buyers and sellers should have representation, advice and draftmanship. This is to say, each needs separate legal representation and should not rely on services rendered by a lawyer for some other party. Why, it will be asked, is so much legal service needed to consummate a routine, uncontested transaction? No two transactions are identical, and none is simple. Because of the complexity of property law a "minor" slip may cause great expense and inconvenience. To the buyer, at least, the purchase of a house may be the most important legal and financial transaction of a lifetime.

All of the parties have conflicting interests. Some of them have wide experience with land transfers. To others the transaction may be a once-in-a-lifetime event. Houses are bought and sold by the inexperienced as well as by the sophisticated. The buyer and seller, without representation, will usually not have as much knowledge of conveyancing as the other parties. Only their own attorneys will be motivated to explain fully the transaction.

* * *

How the System Works in Practice

What has gone before is a largely theoretical explanation of the steps taken in completing a residential real estate transaction, the conflicts of interest engendered in the process and the need for the legal services created by these conflicts. To what extent does this explanation comport with what actually takes place?

A great variety of practices are employed throughout the country and generalizations should be expressed with caution. However, it is probably safe to say that in a high percentage of cases the seller is unrepresented and signs the contracts of brokerage and sale on the basis of faith in the broker. The buyer does not employ a lawyer. The contract of sale is signed without reading it and, once financing has been obtained, the details of title search and closing are left to the lender or broker. In many closings no lawyer will appear.

DOES THE SYSTEM WORK WELL OR BADLY?

Because of the large volume of legal services needed by the various parties to the home-buying transaction, any adequate system will necessarily generate substantial legal costs. Costs and services are therefore properly correlative. We have only limited information about patterns of costs and services throughout the country. What little is available leads to the tentative conclusion that in some sections charges may be excessive, in the sense that they are disproportionate to the services received. On the other hand, in other areas they may be so low as to discourage the rendering of needed legal assistance.

What should be apparent is that the system we employ prima facie encourages inequities. The broker, the lender, the escrow company, and the title insurance company are well aware of their legal needs. They require and receive protection. The buyer and seller, who directly or indirectly pay all legal charges, often receive only residual protection and none of the other legal services which they need. They lack both the expertise and the organization to either understand their needs or to make their demands heard. It is therefore the duty of the bar to spell out what services are needed and how these services can be supplied at a reasonable price.

Where the supplying of certain services generates unnecessary expense, the bar should suggest that appropriate measures be adopted to reduce cost. Likewise, where parties to the transaction need services they are not getting, they should be so informed, particularly when they pay for the services.

In the past the bar has not met its responsibility in this respect. The result has been widespread criticism. This criticism has been frequently ill-informed and destructive, but is a warning that unless the bar institutes needed reform it can anticipate political action from those lacking proper skill to do what is needed.

Aside from the question of services and costs, the present system raises ethical problems which lawyers cannot ignore. Although the seller and the buyer are frequently not receiving adequate legal services, they think they are. They have no comprehension of the conflicts of interests between the parties nor of their own need for legal services. They rely upon established institutions and the lawyers of such institutions. They are sometimes advised that they do not need independent representation. The bar is aware of existing practices and has a special responsibility to see that substantial changes are made.

OBJECTIVES

Merely to complain against the present system is not enough. Adequate reform will await a clear understanding of our objectives, the means of obtaining them and the obstacles in the way of success. A primary goal is to simplify present procedures and make them less expensive.

Less well understood is the need to increase the legal services afforded the parties. At first blush these two objectives appear in conflict. However, the thrust of this Position Paper is that, assuming the adoption of adequate reforms, both can be achieved. Many nonlegal costs, such as brokerage fees and real estate transfer taxes, which constitute a large part of closing expenses, are outside the designated scope of this Paper. However, the largest single *legal* expense when homes are bought and sold is created by the need to establish title. If this expense can be reduced, more adequate legal services can be provided without increasing the total cost.[1]

For another overview of this subject, see Johnstone, *Land Transfers: Process and Processors,* 22 Val.U.L.Rev. 493 (1988). Now that you have a general understanding of a residential real property transaction, it is appropriate to examine each facet.

B. REAL ESTATE BROKERS

Recall that Colleen Piper, a real estate broker, helped the Ryans locate the house they plan to purchase. The seller also employed a real estate broker. Questions often arise regarding the legal relationship between brokers and their clients and between brokers and lawyers.

1. EMPLOYMENT AGREEMENT

The relationship between a real estate broker and a prospective purchaser usually is a rather informal arrangement. It is generally understood that the seller will pay the broker, if the broker directs the purchaser to property that the purchaser buys. A broker may work with a prospective purchaser for several hours, several days, or several months. During this period, the broker makes the prospective purchaser aware of properties that may be of interest and "shows" the purchaser those properties the purchaser wishes to inspect. The relationship between the broker and the prospective purchaser ends when a transaction is completed or, just as frequently, when the purchaser is not interested in acquiring any property the broker has shown the purchaser. *See* Sinclair, *The Duty of the Broker to Purchasers and Prospective Purchas-*

---

1. The Committee's plan to reduce the expense of establishing title is reprinted in the section on recording systems. *See* pages 553–556. [Editors' note.]

ers of Real Property in Illinois, 69 Ill.B.J. 260 (1981); Comment, *A Real Estate Broker's Duty to His Purchaser: Washington State's Position and Some Projections for the Future,* 17 Gonz.L.Rev. 79 (1981). *See generally* D. Burke, Law of Real Estate Brokers (2d ed. 1992 & Supp. 1999).

The relationship between the broker and the prospective seller is more *formal.* It is typically governed by a written listing agreement which identifies the property involved and sets the sale price, the amount of the broker's commission, and the duration of the agreement, often three to six months for residential property.

Listing agreements are of three basic kinds: exclusive right to sell, exclusive agency, and open. The exclusive right to sell listing is the one most frequently used by real estate brokers. It requires the seller to pay the listing broker a commission if a purchaser is found by anyone, even the seller.

The exclusive agency listing requires the seller to pay the listing broker a commission if anyone but the seller produces a purchaser. Thus, if a third party locates a purchaser, the listing broker is entitled to a commission.

The open listing obligates the seller to pay a commission only if the broker produces a purchaser. The seller, therefore, may employ several brokers simultaneously under such an arrangement and not be responsible for more than one commission. Under an open listing, if the seller finds a purchaser, the seller is not liable to anyone for a commission. *See* R. Kratovil & R. Werner, Real Estate Law §§ 10.07(b)-(c), 10.08–10.10 (10th ed. 1993).

A sample listing agreement is reproduced below. It is identical to the form that the seller of the house in Rolling Hills executed with a broker.

CHATTANOOGA BOARD OF REALTORS,® INC.

UNIFORM LISTING CONTRACT—IMPROVED RESIDENTIAL—CLASS 1

TO: _____
    LISTING AGENCY WHO IS A MEMBER CHATTANOOGA BOARD OF REALTORS, ® INC.
DATE _____ PROPERTY _____ POSSESSION _____
PRICE $_____ (DOLLARS) TERMS _____
WE HAVE READ AND ACCEPT THE TERMS AND CONDITIONS ON THE RE-VERSE SIDE (_____) AND RECEIVED A COPY OF THIS CONTRACT. WE UN-
    INITIALS

DERSTAND THAT THE SALES COMMISSION IS _____% OF THE CONSIDER-
ATION, THE EXPIRATION DATE OF THIS LISTING CONTRACT IS _____ AND
THE CARRY–OVER PERIOD IS _____ DAYS. INFORMATION BELOW IS FOR
MULTIPLE LISTING SERVICE PURPOSES AND IS ACCURATE TO THE BEST OF
OUR KNOWLEDGE.

ACCEPTED FOR LISTING AGENT:

_____ (L.S.)

OWNER

_____(L.S.)   _____ (L.S.)

OWNER

> [The contract contains space for
> a detailed description of the
> land and improvements.
> Editors' note.]

TERMS AND CONDITIONS*

For one dollar ($1.00) and other good and valuable considerations, including the Listing Agent's agreement to place this listing on the Multiple Listing Service of the CHATTANOOGA BOARD OF REALTORS,® INC. and to try to find a purchaser, the Owner(s) hereby grant to the Listing Agent the exclusive right and privilege to sell the property and on the terms referred to on the reverse side hereof, or at such lesser price or terms to which the Owner(s) may consent. (The expiration time will be at 12 o'clock midnight.)

The Owner(s) agree to pay the Listing Agent the cash commission at the time of closing from the proceeds of the same, provided said property is sold, exchanged or leased with option to purchase by the Listing Agent, or by anyone else, including the Owner(s), during the term of this agreement, or any extension thereof, or should the Listing Agent or anyone else procure a person ready, willing and able to purchase said property at the price and on terms as outlined herein.

CARRY–OVER PERIOD Should the Owner(s) contract to sell, exchange or lease with option to purchase this property within the specified period of carry-over days after expiration of this listing contract to any person who has been introduced to the property during said listing period, or any extensions thereof, the Owner(s) agree to pay the commission as set forth on the reverse side, provided, this paragraph shall not apply if the property is listed with another Broker during this period.

The Owner(s) will furnish Title Insurance Policy and papers and convey by regular form Warranty Deed. Taxes, Insurance and Rent shall be prorated to date of conveyance. The Title is good and merchantable.

The Listing Agent is hereby authorized to advertise the property during this agreement and any extension thereof, to PLACE HIS FOR SALE SIGN AND LOCK BOX ON SAID PROPERTY, to remove any other FOR SALE signs, if any, and to photograph said property and use such photographs in promoting the sale. The Owner(s) further agree to consider the Listing Agent's recommendations to enable the Listing Agent to show this property to his best advantage, to allow the Listing Agent to show it at all reasonable hours and otherwise cooperate with the Listing Agent.

* Found on the reverse side of the contract. [Editors' note.]

Notes and Questions

1. <u>Real estate brokers and salespersons must be licensed</u> in all states. With few exceptions, an unlicensed individual is not entitled to compensation from the seller for finding a purchaser. *See* Comment, *Recovery of Commissions by Unlicensed Real Estate Brokers,* 80 Dick.L.Rev. 500 (1976).

Although the requirements vary from state to state, a broker's license typically may be obtained by an individual who works as a real estate salesperson for a limited period, often one or two years; passes an extensive written examination; and offers proof of good character. A salesperson's license is easier to obtain—good character and a passing grade on a less rigorous examination are generally required. A salesperson must then work with a broker. Frequently brokers employ several salespersons. *See* 15 Powell on Real Property § 84C.03 (1998).

2. In many locales real estate brokers agree to pool their listings. The resulting arrangement is termed a "multiple listing service" (MLS). Member brokers of the MLS obtain exclusive right to sell listings and submit them to the service. The listing broker thereby agrees to split the commission with the MLS member broker who produces the purchaser. *See id.* at § 84C.04[2][e].

Membership in the MLS is frequently the key to success in the real estate brokerage business. Hence, brokers, whose membership applications are rejected, sometimes attack their exclusion from the MLS on antitrust grounds. These attacks are often successful. *See* D. Burke, Law of Real Estate Brokers §§ 11.7–11.8 (2d ed.1992 & Supp.1999); Chang, *Multiple-Listing Services: The Antitrust Issues,* 10 Real Est.L.J. 228 (1982); Comment, *Exclusion from Real Estate Multiple Listing Services as Antitrust Violations,* 14 Cal.W.L.Rev. 298 (1978).

3. Statutes in many states require that the listing agreement be in writing. In other states an oral listing contract is enforceable. Why does the traditional Statute of Frauds not apply? *See* R. Boyer, Survey of the Law of Property 366 (3d ed. 1981); MacGregor v. Labute, 14 Mass.App.Ct. 203, 437 N.E.2d 574 (1982); Murphy v. Nolte & Co., 226 Va. 76, 307 S.E.2d 242 (1983).

2. COMMISSION

Colleen Piper, broker for the Ryans, is a member of the local MLS. The house the Ryans wish to purchase was placed in the MLS system by the seller's broker. The Ryans are anxious to purchase the house and are willing to pay the listing price. What are the rights of the parties if the seller has a change of mind and refuses to sign a contract of sale? What if the seller signs a contract with the Ryans, but they are unable to obtain the financing necessary to complete the purchase?

The broker's right to a commission under each set of circumstances is explored in this subsection. The rights and obligations of the Ryans with respect to the property itself are explored in the following sections on contracts of sale and financing.

TRISTRAM'S LANDING, INC. v. WAIT

Supreme Judicial Court of Massachusetts, 1975.
367 Mass. 622, 327 N.E.2d 727.

TAURO, CHIEF JUSTICE.

This is an action in contract seeking to recover a brokerage commission alleged to be due to the plaintiffs from the defendant. The case was heard by a judge, sitting without a jury, on a stipulation of facts. The judge found for the plaintiffs in the full amount of the commission. The defendant filed exceptions to that finding and appealed.

The facts briefly are these: The plaintiffs are real estate brokers doing business in Nantucket. The defendant owned real estate on the island which she desired to sell. In the past, the plaintiffs acted as brokers for the defendant when she rented the same premises.

The plaintiffs heard that the defendant's property was for sale, and in the spring of 1972 the plaintiff Van der Wolk telephoned the defendant and asked for authority to show it. The defendant agreed that the plaintiffs could act as brokers, although not as exclusive brokers, and told them that the price for the property was $110,000. During this conversation there was no mention of a commission. The defendant knew that the normal brokerage commission in Nantucket was five per cent of the sale price.

In the early months of 1973, Van der Wolk located a prospective buyer, Louise L. Cashman (Cashman), who indicated that she was interested in purchasing the defendant's property. Her written offer of $100,000, dated April 29, was conveyed to the defendant. Shortly thereafter, the defendant's husband and attorney wrote to the plaintiffs that "a counter-offer of $105,000 with an October 1st closing" should be made to Cashman. Within a few weeks, the counter offer was orally accepted, and a purchase and sale agreement was drawn up by Van der Wolk.

The agreement was executed by Cashman and was returned to the plaintiffs with a check for $10,500, representing a ten per cent down payment. The agreement was then presented by the plaintiffs to the defendant, who signed it after reviewing it with her attorney. The down payment check was thereafter turned over to the defendant.

The purchase and sale agreement signed by the parties called for an October 1, 1973, closing date. On September 22, the defendant signed a fifteen day extension of the closing date, which was communicated to Cashman by the plaintiffs. Cashman did not sign the extension. On October 1, 1973, the defendant appeared at the registry of deeds with a deed to the property. Cashman did not appear for the closing and thereafter refused to go through with the purchase. No formal action has been taken by the defendant to enforce the agreement or to recover damages for its breach, although the defendant has retained the down payment.

Van der Wolk presented the defendant with a bill for commission in the amount of $5,250, five percent of the agreed sales price. The defendant, through her attorney, refused to pay, stating that "[t]here has been no sale and consequently the 5% commission has not been earned." The plaintiffs then brought this action to recover the commission.

In the course of dealings between the plaintiffs and the defendant there was no mention of commission. The only reference to commission is found in the purchase and sale agreement signed by Cashman and the defendant, which reads as follows: "It is understood that a broker's commission of five (5) per cent on the said sale is to be paid to * * * [the broker] by the said seller." The plaintiffs contend that, having produced a buyer who was ready, willing and able to purchase the property, and who was in fact accepted by the seller, they are entitled to their full commission. The defendant argues that no commission was earned because the sale was not consummated. We agree with the defendant, and reverse the finding by the judge below.

1. The general rule regarding whether a broker is entitled to a commission from one attempting to sell real estate is that, absent special circumstances, the broker "is entitled to a commission if he produces a customer ready, able, and willing to buy upon the terms and for the price given the broker by the owner." Gaynor v. Laverdure, 291 N.E.2d 617 (1973), quoting Henderson & Beal, Inc. v. Glen, 329 Mass. 748, 751, 110 N.E.2d 373 (1953). In the past, this rule has been construed to mean that once a customer is produced by the broker and accepted by the seller, the commission is earned, whether or not the sale is actually consummated. Furthermore, execution of a purchase and sale agreement is usually seen as conclusive evidence of the seller's acceptance of the buyer.

Despite these well established and often cited rules, we have held that "[t]he owner is not helpless" to protect himself from these consequences. "He may, by appropriate language in his dealings with the broker, limit his liability for payment of a commission to the situation where not only is the broker obligated to find a customer ready, willing and able to purchase on the owner's terms and for his price, but also it is provided that no commission is to become due until the customer actually takes a conveyance and pays therefor." Gaynor v. Laverdure, supra, 291 N.E.2d at 622.

In the application of these rules to the instant case, we believe that the broker here is not entitled to a commission. We cannot construe the purchase and sale agreement as an unconditional acceptance by the seller of the buyer, as the agreement itself contained conditional language. The purchase and sale agreement provided that the commission was to be paid "on the said sale," and we construe this language as requiring that the said sale be consummated before the commission is earned.

While we recognize that there is a considerable line of cases indicating that language providing for payment of a commission when the agreement is "carried into effect" or "when title is passed" does not create a condition precedent, but merely sets a time for payment to be made, we do not think the course of events and the choice of language in this case fall within * * * [the rule of these cases]. * * *

To the extent that there are cases (such as those collected in the *Gaynor* case), unique on their facts, which may appear inconsistent with this holding and seem to indicate a contrary result, we choose not to follow them. In light of what we have said, we construe the language "on the said sale" as providing for a "special agreement," Gaynor v. Laverdure, *supra*, 291 N.E.2d 617, or as creating "special circumstances," Henderson & Beal, Inc. v. Glen, 329 Mass. 748, 751, 110 N.E.2d 373 (1953), wherein consummation of the sale became a condition precedent for the broker to earn his commission. Accordingly, since the sale was not consummated, the plaintiffs were not entitled to recover the amount specified in the purchase and sale agreement.

2.   Although what we have said to this point is determinative of the rights of the parties, we note that the relationship and obligations of real estate owners and brokers inter se has been the "subject of frequent litigation," Henderson & Beal, Inc. v. Glen, *supra,* 329 Mass. at 751, 110 N.E.2d 373. In two of the more recent cases where we were faced with this issue, we declined to follow the developing trends in this area, holding that the cases presented were inappropriate for that purpose. See LeDonne v. Slade, 355 Mass. 490, 492, 245 N.E.2d 434 (1969); Gaynor v. Laverdure, 291 N.E.2d 617. We believe, however, that it is both appropriate and necessary at this time to clarify the law, and we now join the growing minority of States who have adopted the rule of Ellsworth Dobbs, Inc. v. Johnson, 50 N.J. 528, 236 A.2d 843 (1967).[1]

In the *Ellsworth* case, the New Jersey court faced the task of clarifying the law regarding the legal relationships between sellers and brokers in real estate transactions. In order to formulate a just and proper rule, the court examined the realities of such transactions. The court noted that "ordinarily when an owner of property lists it with a broker for sale, his expectation is that the money for the payment of commission will come out of the proceeds of the sale." *Id.* at 547, 236 A.2d at 852. It quoted with approval from the opinion of Lord Justice Denning, in Dennis Reed, Ltd. v. Goody, [1950] 2 K.B. 277, 284–285, where he stated: "When a house owner puts his house into the hands of an estate agent, the ordinary understanding is that the agent is only to receive a commission if he succeeds in effecting a sale * * *. The

1.   Both Kansas and Oregon have adopted the *Ellsworth* rule in its entirety. Additionally, Vermont, Connecticut and Idaho have cited the case with approval. Other States and the District of Columbia also have similar, but more limited, rules which were adopted prior to the *Ellsworth* case.

common understanding of men is * * * that the agent's commission is payable out of the purchase price. * * * The house-owner wants to find a man who will actually buy his house and pay for it. He does not want a man who will only make an offer or sign a contract. He wants a purchaser 'able to purchase and able to complete as well.' "*Id.* at 549, 236 A.2d at 853.

The court went on to say that the principle binding "the seller to pay commission if he signs a contract of sale with the broker's customer, regardless of the customer's financial ability, puts the burden on the wrong shoulders. Since the broker's duty to the owner is to produce a prospective buyer who is financially able to pay the purchase price and take title, a right in the owner to assume such capacity when the broker presents his purchaser ought to be recognized." *Id.* at 548, 236 A.2d at 853. Reason and justice dictate that it should be the broker who bears the burden of producing a purchaser who is not only ready, willing and able at the time of the negotiations, but who also consummates the sale at the time of closing.

Thus, we adopt the following rules: "When a broker is engaged by an owner of property to find a purchaser for it, the broker earns his commission when (a) he produces a purchaser ready, willing and able to buy on the terms fixed by the owner, (b) the purchaser enters into a binding contract with the owner to do so, and (c) the purchaser completes the transaction by closing the title in accordance with the provisions of the contract. If the contract is not consummated because of lack of financial ability of the buyer to perform or because of any other default of his * * * there is no right to commission against the seller. On the other hand, if the failure of completion of the contract results from the wrongful act or interference of the seller, the broker's claim is valid and must be paid." *Id.* at 551, 236 A.2d at 855.

Accordingly, we hold that a real estate broker, under a brokerage agreement hereafter made, is entitled to a commission from the seller only if the requirements stated above are met. This rule provides necessary protection for the seller and places the burden with the broker, where it belongs. In view of the waiver of the counts in quantum meruit, we do not now consider the extent to which the broker may be entitled to share in a forfeited deposit or other benefit received by the seller as a result of the broker's efforts.

We recognize that this rule could be easily circumvented by language to the contrary in purchase and sale agreements or in agreements between sellers and brokers. In many States a signed writing is required for an agreement to pay a commission to a real estate broker. Such a requirement may be worthy of legislative consideration, but we do not think we should establish such a requirement by judicial decision. Informal agreements fairly made between people of equal skill and understanding serve a useful purpose. But many sellers, unlike brokers, are involved in real estate transactions infrequently, perhaps only once in a lifetime, and are thus unfamiliar with their legal rights. In such cases agreements by the seller to pay a commission even though the purchaser defaults are to be scrutinized carefully. If not fairly made, such agreements may be unconscionable or against public policy.

Exceptions sustained.

Judgment for the defendant.

Notes and Questions

1. One commentator has concluded that a majority of jurisdictions continue to adhere to the traditional view that, absent a contractual provision to the contrary, a broker is entitled to a commission upon finding a person ready, willing, and able to purchase on the seller's terms. Zeigler, *Brokers and Their Commissions,* 14 Real Estate L.J. 122 (1985). *See, e.g.,* Sayegusa v. Rogers, 256 Mont. 269, 846 P.2d 1005 (1993). What is the rationale for this rule? *See* D. Burke, Law of Real Estate Brokers § 3.5 (2d ed. 1992).

2. In a jurisdiction following the traditional rule, suppose that the contract of sale contains a clause making the contract contingent upon the purchaser obtaining a mortgage. Is the broker entitled to a commission if the purchaser is unable to secure a mortgage? *See* Stiefvater Real Estate, Inc. v. Hinsdale, 812 F.2d 805 (2d Cir.1987).

3. In a jurisdiction following *Tristram's Landing,* will conduct by the seller that causes a sales transaction to fail render the seller liable for the broker's commission? *See* Margaret H. Wayne Trust v. Lipsky, 123 Idaho 253, 846 P.2d 904 (1993). Suppose that the seller is unable to convey marketable title. What result? *Compare* Bennett v. McCabe, 808 F.2d 178 (1st Cir.1987) *with* Van Winkle & Liggett v. G.B.R. Fabrics, Inc., 103 N.J. 335, 511 A.2d 124 (1986).

3. BROKER'S DUTIES TO SELLER AND BUYER

It has long been recognized that a fiduciary relationship exists between the seller, as principal, and the broker, as agent. Thus, in our hypothetical situation, the listing broker is clearly the seller's agent. Is Colleen Piper, the broker who has been working with the Ryans, an agent for the seller, the Ryans, or both parties? *See* Grohman, *A Reassessment of the Selling Real Estate Broker's Agency Relationship with the Purchaser,* 61 St. John's L.Rev. 560 (1987); Comment, *The Selling Real Estate Broker and the Purchaser: Assessing the Relationship,* 1992 B.Y.U. L.Rev. 1135. Should brokers be required to disclose their agency relationships? *See* Wolf & Jennings, *Seller/Broker Liability in Multiple Listing Service Real Estate Sales: A Case for Uniform Disclosure,* 20 Real Est. L.J. 23 (1991).

If the broker has a fiduciary responsibility to the seller, what duty does the broker owe to the buyer? One authority has observed:

> The broker is understandably bewildered by the legal morass in which he is floundering. On the one hand, the broker is the agent of the seller and owes a fiduciary duty to that seller. On the other

hand, the broker is aware that he has some sort of duty to the buyer and that duty seems to be broadening. The broker needs guidance as to the precise nature and extent of his duty to prospective purchasers of real property.

Murray, *The Real Estate Broker and the Buyer: Negligence and the Duty to Investigate,* 32 Vill.L.Rev. 939, 943 (1987). *See generally* Brown, Grohman, & Valcarcel, *Real Estate Brokerage: Recent Changes in Relations and a Proposed Cure,* 29 Creighton L. Rev. 25 (1995) (suggesting that confusion and controversy regarding broker's duties be addressed by statutory provision that sets forth general principles within which brokers must act).

It is well settled that a broker must exercise good faith and loyalty in representing the broker's principal. Breach of this fiduciary obligation may result in an agent losing the right to any commission. What actions by the broker violate this fiduciary duty? *See* D. Burke, Law of Real Estate Brokers §§ 7.1–7.5 (2d ed. 1992 & Supp.1999).

Some courts have required the seller's real estate agent to disclose known defects in the premises to a potential purchaser. *See, e.g.,* Johnson v. Geer Real Estate Co., 239 Kan. 324, 720 P.2d 660 (1986). Do such decisions place the agent in the untenable position of representing both seller and buyer? *See* Note, *Real Estate Broker Liability in Florida: Is Mandatory Housing Inspection in Florida's Future?,* 11 Nova L.Rev. 825 (1987). Is the seller's agent also under a duty to inspect the property listed for sale in order to determine the existence of possible defects? *Compare* Robinson v. Grossman, 57 Cal.App.4th 634, 67 Cal.Rptr.2d 380 (1997) (discussing statutory duty of brokers to make visual inspection of property and disclose facts materially affecting value to prospective purchasers) *with* Provost v. Miller, 144 Vt. 67, 473 A.2d 1162 (1984) (finding no duty to inspect).

Suppose a real estate agent is aware that a residence for sale has been occupied by a person with AIDS. Is the agent under a duty to disclose this information to a potential purchaser? Several states have enacted statutes which provide that the agent has no obligation to do so. *See, e.g.,* Cal.Civ.Code § 1710.2 (West 1998); Fla.Stat.Ann. § 689.25 (West 1994); Va.Code Ann. § 55–524 (Michie 1995). *See generally* Note, *The Psychological Impact of AIDS on Real Property and a Real Estate Broker's Duty to Disclose,* 36 Ariz.L.Rev. 757 (1994); Note, *A Massachusetts Real Estate Broker's Duty to Disclose: The Quandary Presented by AIDS Stigmatized Property,* 27 New Eng.L.Rev. 1211 (1993).

4. RELATIONSHIP BETWEEN BROKERS AND LAWYERS

As attorney for the Ryans, you are likely to work with Ms. Piper, their broker. What is the relationship between lawyers and brokers?

As has been seen, the initial step in selling a house will probably be the signing of a brokerage contract. Upon the signing of the contract the broker becomes the seller's agent. The broker and seller will have a common interest in obtaining a maximum price from the buyer. So, of course, will the lawyer for the seller. The lawyer has an interest in seeing to it that all other terms of the sale are as favorable to the seller as possible. An apprehension that the signing of the sales contract may be jeopardized by an overmeticulous attention to the other terms sometimes makes the broker reluctant to submit a proposed contract of sale to the seller's lawyer. On the other hand, many brokers realize that the seller's lawyer can help to prepare a contract that is specifically enforceable by the seller. This relieves the broker of the risk that the broker's commission will be nullified by the collapse before the closing of a contract improperly drawn. This may happen when qualifications on the seller's title have not been properly expressed.

It has been indicated that a fear of delay or disruption of the transaction often makes the broker somewhat less than enthusiastic about advising the buyer to submit a proposed contract to a lawyer. The lawyer who lets the contract of sale gather dust does much to foster this feeling. The lawyer should not surrender the client's vital interests, but should remember that the client wants the house, and should not unnecessarily impede the closing. Lawyers are trained in the art of finding fair and reasonable solutions to what might otherwise be deadlocks.

Attention is called to the statement of principles applicable to relations between lawyers and real estate brokers which has been approved by the American Bar Association and the National Association of Realtors, formerly the National Association of Real Estate Boards. (Such principles have been promulgated by the National Conference of Lawyers and Realtors.)

Report, *Residential Real Estate Transactions: The Lawyer's Proper Role—Services—Compensation*, 14 Real Prop., Prob. & Tr.J. 581, 591–592 (1979).

CULTUM v. HERITAGE HOUSE REALTORS, INC.

Supreme Court of Washington, 1985.
103 Wn.2d 623, 694 P.2d 630.

PEARSON, JUSTICE.

At issue in this appeal is whether the completion by a real estate salesperson of a form earnest money agreement containing a contingency clause constitutes the unauthorized practice of law in violation of RCW 2.48.170–.190.

In deciding this issue, the trial court found that this conduct did constitute the unauthorized practice of law and was a per se violation of the Consumer Protection Act, RCW 19.86, warranting damages, attorney fees and injunctive relief. As a consequence, the trial court permanently enjoined defendant, Heritage House Realtors, Inc. (Heritage), from completing, filling in the blanks, or otherwise preparing any clause with respect to any real estate purchase or sale agreement, earnest money agreement, addenda thereto, or any other document intended to create or define contractual rights or obligations in connection with any real estate transaction. In addition, plaintiff, Diane Cultum (Cultum), was awarded damages of $178.65, representing the interest lost during the time Heritage retained the earnest money. Cultum was also awarded attorney fees and costs in excess of $32,000 under the Consumer Protection Act. RCW 19.86.090. We now reverse the decision of the trial court that defendant's actions constituted the unauthorized practice of law, dissolve the injunction, and remand for a determination of contractual attorney fees.

The salient facts are as follows. In 1980 Cultum contacted Heritage in response to an advertisement in the Seattle Times and was put in touch with Yvonne Ramey (Ramey), a real estate agent for Heritage. After viewing several homes, Ramey showed Cultum the home of Arthur and Paula Smith. Cultum decided to make an offer on the Smith home but was concerned that there might be something wrong with the house. Cultum therefore told Ramey that she wanted to have the house inspected and be able to withdraw her offer on the basis of that inspection.

Thereafter Ramey prepared a real estate purchase and sale agreement (earnest money agreement) setting forth Cultum's offer to purchase the Smith home. This agreement and all other subsequent agreements contained an attorney fee clause which provided that

> [i]n the event that either the Buyer, Seller, or Agent, shall institute suit to enforce any rights hereunder, the successful party shall be entitled to court costs and a reasonable attorney's fee.

All agreements were prepared on standardized forms drafted by attorneys. Cultum's offer and a subsequent offer were both rejected. About a month later, Ramey and Cultum resubmitted the earnest money agreement with an addendum which raised the purchase price. Cultum later discovered that the agreement did not contain a structural inspection contingency clause and asked Ramey to prepare a second addendum. This addendum provided: "This offer is contingent on a Satisfactory Structural Inspection, To be completed by Aug. 20, 1980." Both addendums were on forms drafted by an attorney. Ramey merely inserted the desired modifications in a blank space. Ramey did not select the form since her employer used a single standard form.

The Smiths accepted this last offer and Heritage deposited Cultum's $3,000 earnest money into a noninterest bearing trust account. Thereafter, Cultum received a report on the house from Northwest Inspection Engineers. The report noted missing siding and caulking on exterior portions of the home, damage to the siding along one corner of the north entry door, deterioration on the roof which probably caused some leakage, inadequate support on a sheet of plywood on the roof of the new addition causing some softness in the roof, rusted gutters, soft mortar on the chimney, and evidence of minor roof leakage along the living room entry. The inspector found no major problems in the plumbing, heating or electrical systems.

Cultum found the report unsatisfactory and demanded return of her earnest money. Ramey immediately prepared a rescission agreement but the Smiths refused to sign it. The Smiths claimed there was nothing structurally wrong with the house and Cultum was acting in bad faith. The Smiths argued that the language of the inspection contingency meant that the report had to be truly unsatisfactory and reveal real structural defects based upon an objective standard. They therefore threatened to sue Heritage if it returned Cultum's money.

Heritage initially gave Cultum three options: It could continue to hold the money in a noninterest bearing account pending an agreement between Cultum and the Smiths; it could pay the money into a registry of the court; or, it could refund the money to Cultum in exchange for her agreement to indemnify Heritage in an action brought by the Smiths. Subsequently, Heritage also offered to place the money in an interest bearing account pending resolution of the dispute.

Because these options were each substantially less than Cultum had believed the agreement would provide her, she refused to accept them and hired an attorney. Six months later Heritage refunded Cultum's earnest money.

Cultum then filed this action against Heritage seeking damages for loss of the use of her money during the period Heritage held it. She also requested a permanent injunction restraining Heritage from engaging in the unauthorized practice of law. In addition, she sought attorney fees under the Consumer Protection Act, RCW 19.86.090.

I

The holding of the trial court was not surprising. In a series of recent cases this court has broadly defined the practice of law to include

> the selection and completion of form legal documents, or the drafting of such documents, including deeds, mortgages, deeds of trust, promissory notes and agreements modifying these documents * * *

Bowers v. Transamerica Title Ins. Co., 100 Wash.2d 581, 586, 675 P.2d 193 (1983) (quoting Washington State Bar Ass'n v. Great W. Union Fed.Sav. & Loan Ass'n, 91 Wash.2d 48, 55, 586 P.2d 870 (1978)); Hagan & Van Camp, P.S. v. Kassler Escrow, Inc., 96 Wash.2d 443, 635 P.2d 730 (1981).

The trial court's extension of these holdings to completion of form earnest money agreements by real estate salespersons is logical since such agreements fix the legal rights and duties of both buyers and sellers of residential real estate. It therefore fits within the broad definition of the practice of law as we have previously defined it.

Nevertheless, without retreating from our rulings in those three recent cases, we think there are sound and practical reasons why some activities which fall within the broad definition of "the practice of law" should not be unauthorized simply because they are done by laypersons.

As we have so often stated, it is the duty of this court to protect the public from the activity of those who, because of the lack of professional skills, may cause injury whether they are members of the bar or persons never qualified for or admitted to the bar. We have also made it clear that the practice of law is within the sole province of the judiciary and encroachment by the Legislature may violate the separation of powers doctrine. This does not mean, however, that the attorney hegemony over the practice of law must be absolute. Hence, although the completion of form earnest money agreements might be commonly understood as the practice of law, we believe it is in the public interest to permit licensed real estate brokers or licensed salespersons to complete such lawyer prepared standard form agreements; provided, that in doing so they comply with the standard of care demanded of an attorney.

For a long time suppression of the practice of law by nonlawyers has been proclaimed to be in the public interest, a necessary protection against incompetence, divided loyalties, and other evils. It is now clear, however, as several other courts have concluded, that there are other important interests involved. *See* Conway–Bogue Realty Inv. Co. v. Denver Bar Ass'n, 135 Colo. 398, 312 P.2d 998 (1957). These interests include:

(1) The ready availability of legal services.

(2) Using the full range of services that other professions and businesses can provide.

(3) Limiting costs.

(4) Public convenience.

(5) Allowing licensed brokers and salespersons to participate in an activity in which they have special training and expertise.

(6) The interest of brokers and salespersons in drafting form earnest money agreements which are incidental and necessary to the main business of brokers and salespersons.

We no longer believe that the supposed benefits to the public from the lawyers' monopoly on performing legal services justifies limiting the public's freedom of choice. The public has the right to use the full range of services that brokers and salespersons can provide. Christensen, *The Unauthorized Practice of Law: Do Good Fences Really Make Good Neighbors—or Even Good Sense?*, 1980 Am.B.Found.Research J. 159. The fact that brokers and salespersons will complete these forms at no extra charge, whereas attorneys would charge an additional fee, weighs heavily toward allowing this choice.

Another important consideration is the fact that the drafting of form earnest money agreements is incidental to the main business of real estate brokers and salespersons. WAC 308–124D–020. These individuals are specially trained to provide buyers and sellers with competent and efficient assistance in purchasing or selling a home. *See* WAC 308–124H. Because the selection and filling in of standard simple forms by brokers and salespersons is an incidental service, it normally must be rendered before such individuals can receive their commissions. Clearly the advantages, if any, to be derived by enjoining brokers and salespersons from completing earnest money agreements are outweighed by the fact that such conveyances are part of the everyday business of the realtor and necessary to the effective completion of such business. *See* Cowern v. Nelson, 207 Minn. 642, 290 N.W. 795 (1940).

The interest in protecting the public must also be balanced against the inconveniences caused by enjoining licensed brokers and salespersons from completing form earnest money agreements. Although lawyers are also competent to handle these transactions, lawyers may not always be available at the odd hours that these transactions tend to take place. As noted by the Minnesota Supreme Court:

> It is the duty of this court so to regulate the practice of law and to restrain such practice by laymen in a common-sense way in order to protect primarily the interest of the public and not to hamper and burden such interest with impractical technical restraints no matter how well supported such restraint may be from the standpoint of pure logic * * *. We do not think the possible harm which might come to the public from the rare instances of defective conveyances in such transactions is sufficient to outweigh the great public inconvenience which would follow if it were necessary to call in a lawyer to draft these simple instruments.

Cowern, 207 Minn. at 647, 290 N.W. 795.

In a few instances earnest money agreements may be complicated and one or both parties may realize the need for a lawyer to prepare the contract rather than use a standardized form. In fact, if a broker or salesperson believes there may be complicated legal issues involved, he or she should persuade the parties to seek legal advice. More often, however, these transactions are simple enough so that standardized forms will suffice and the parties will wish to avoid further delay or expense by using them. *See* Comment, *The Unauthorized Practice of Law by Laymen and Lay Associations*, 54 Calif.L.Rev. 1331 (1966). *See also* New Jersey State Bar Ass'n v. New Jersey Ass'n of Realtor Bds., 186 N.J.Super. 391, 452 A.2d 1323 (1982).

It should be emphasized that the holding in this case is limited in scope. Our decision provides that a real estate broker or salesperson is *Holding* permitted to complete simple printed standardized real estate forms, which forms must be approved by a lawyer, it being understood that these forms shall not be used for other than simple real estate transactions which arise in the usual course of the broker's business and that such forms will be used only in connection with real estate transactions actually handled by such broker or salesperson as a broker or salesperson and then without charge for the simple service of completing the forms.

* * *

In light of the courts' inherent power to regulate the practice of law, we believe it is totally within our power to allow brokers and salespersons to practice law within the narrow confines that our holding allows * * *.

II

Our decision to allow licensed brokers and salespersons to complete form earnest money agreements is based on the practical needs and interests of the public. The completion of a form earnest money agreement is in most instances less technical and more straightforward than closing a real estate transaction. This is not to say, however, that there is no possibility of injurious consequences from the acts of laypersons. The public still needs protection against incompetence, divided loyalties and other evils. RCW 18.85 controls the licensing of real estate brokers and salespersons. The statute provides some preliminary protection by dictating certain conditions and qualifications with which a person must comply prior to being licensed. However, as the court stated in *Hagan,* the fact that laypersons must comply with licensing requirements does not offer sufficient protection to the public. *Hagan,* 96 Wash.2d at 448–49, 635 P.2d 730. Therefore, we hold that licensed real estate brokers and salespersons, when completing form earnest money agreements, must comply with the standard of care of a practicing attorney.

The trial court awarded Cultum damages based on a finding that the contingency clause as written by Ramey violated the standard of care of a practicing attorney. Whether or not the contingency clause as written by Ramey meets an attorney's standard of care, Ramey is nonetheless liable because the problems in this case were caused by Ramey's failure to follow her client's explicit instructions. This dispute arose because Cultum and the Smiths disagreed on whether the defects noted in the inspection report were sufficient enough to cause the real estate contract to fail. Cultum had wanted her offer conditioned on her subjective approval of the inspection. Ramey, contrary to Cultum's wishes, failed to include a subjective right in the contingency clause. If Ramey had complied with Cultum's request, the dispute with the Smiths could not have arisen and Cultum's earnest money would have been refunded to her immediately.

It is the duty of an agent to obey all reasonable instructions and directions given by the principal and to adhere faithfully to them in all cases where they ought properly to be applied and in which they can be obeyed by the exercise of reasonable and diligent care.

An attorney is liable for all losses caused by his or her failure to follow the explicit instructions of the client. When a broker undertakes to practice law and prepares a contract at variance with the client's instructions, he or she is liable for negligence. Therefore, because Ramey was practicing law and failed to comply with Cultum's wishes she is liable for all damages proximately caused by her negligence. It is irrelevant whether the language in the contingency clause may have somehow been improper.

III

The trial court awarded Cultum damages of $178.65 representing the interest lost during the time that Heritage retained her earnest money. If a real estate broker fails to exercise reasonable care and skill, the real estate broker is liable to the client for damages resulting from such failure. Based on this rule and our conclusion that Ramey failed to exercise the reasonable care and skill of a practicing attorney, we affirm the trial court's award of damages, including the amount, because it is within the range of relevant testimony and therefore will not be disturbed on appeal.

IV

The final issue before us is the award of attorney fees. The trial court determined that Heritage and its agent, Ramey, had violated the Consumer Protection Act, RCW 19.86, and that therefore Cultum was entitled to attorney fees pursuant to the formula articulated by this court in *Bowers v. Transamerica Title Ins. Co., supra.* Unlike the trial court, however, we have concluded that Ramey's conduct did not constitute the unauthorized practice of law. Hence, there is no violation of the Consumer Protection Act and Cultum is not entitled to the attorney fees awarded by the trial judge. However, the earnest money agreement drafted by Ramey specifies that:

> In the event that either the Buyer, Seller, or Agent, shall institute suit to enforce any rights hereunder, the successful party shall be entitled to court costs and a reasonable attorney's fee.

In light of this provision, we remand for further proceedings to determine whether Cultum is entitled to contractual attorney fees. We dissolve the injunction.

BRACHTENBACH, JUSTICE (Concurrence).

* * *

I would reach the same result as the majority by forthrightly recognizing that requiring lawyer preparation of every earnest money agreement is not a practicable alternative to the broker/salesperson preparation which works reasonably well in most instances. I would accept the current practice as a fact of life in the real world. The ultimate protection to the public is the requirement that the broker/salesperson be held to the standard of care of a practicing lawyer. The competent broker/salesperson should recognize when special circumstances require more skilled and knowledgeable drafting. If that decision is made at their peril, hopefully it will be made carefully, keeping in mind the fiduciary relationship and the requirements of the licensing statute.

* * *

Note

In 1983, the Supreme Court of New Jersey approved a consent decree under which real estate brokers and salespersons could prepare contracts of sale and leases for residential property. New Jersey State Bar Association v. New Jersey Association of Realtor Boards, 93 N.J. 470, 461 A.2d 1112 (1983). The decree required that such instruments contain the following language: "THIS IS A LEGALLY BINDING CONTRACT [LEASE] THAT WILL BECOME FINAL WITHIN THREE BUSINESS DAYS. DURING THIS PERIOD YOU MAY CHOOSE TO CONSULT AN ATTORNEY WHO CAN REVIEW AND CANCEL THE CONTRACT [LEASE]." Judge Schreiber dissented, commenting: "The line drawn within which realtors may practice law seems to have been determined by the economic interests of the realtors and attorneys, rather than societal interests. Those who will be subject to the unauthorized practice of law are mostly low and moderate income individuals, who are buying or leasing homes. However, only when the financial stakes are likely to be higher must the realtor step aside to be replaced by the attorney." Id. at 486, 461 A.2d at 1121. Do you agree?

C. REAL ESTATE CONTRACT OF SALE

The Ryans are ready to purchase the English Tudor house in Rolling Hills. They must now negotiate and execute a real estate contract with the owner of the house. The material in this section introduces concepts you must firmly grasp in order to review adequately the contract prepared by Ms. Piper, the Ryan's broker.

Contracts for the sale of land are of two kinds: the standard real estate sales contract and the installment land contract. The standard real estate sales contract is given various names, including offer to purchase, contract of sale, earnest money agreement, and deposit receipt. Regardless of the contract's label, it is designed to be performed within a relatively brief time frame, usually one to three months. During this interval the parties arrange for the necessary performance—payment of the purchase price on one side and delivery of title and possession on the other. Performance is then rendered at a closing or settlement held within the time specified in the contract.

The installment land contract is sometimes called a land contract or contract for deed. This contractual arrangement permits the purchaser to take possession of the land immediately and to pay the purchase price in installments over several years. The seller holds legal title to the property as security until the purchaser pays all of the installments. The installment land contract is actually a financing device. It is used as an alternative to mortgage financing that the purchaser under a standard real estate sales contract usually must obtain from a lending institution in order to pay the purchase price at closing. These different approaches to financing are discussed later in this chapter (*see* pages 498–524, but first it is necessary to examine the unique contractual aspects common to both kinds of agreements for the sale of land.

1. STATUTE OF FRAUDS

a. *Writing Required*

Section 4 of the English Statute of Frauds (1677) provides: "No action shall be brought * * * upon any contract or sale of lands * * * or any interest in * * * them * * * unless the agreement upon which such action shall be brought, or some memorandum or note thereof, shall be in writing and signed by the party to be charged therewith, or by some person thereunto by him lawfully authorized." All states have adopted a similar statute.

The Statute of Frauds does not specify what information the required writing must contain. Although there is some controversy on the subject, courts generally demand that the writing identify the parties, describe the land, state the purchase price, and be signed by the party to be charged.

See R. Kratovil & R. Werner, Real Estate Law § 11.04 (10th ed. 1993); 3 American Law of Property § 11.5 (1952).

CASH v. MADDOX

Supreme Court of South Carolina, 1975.
265 S.C. 480, 220 S.E.2d 121.

NESS, JUSTICE:

John and Sue Maddox allegedly contracted to sell Morris and Betty Cash 15 acres of land. The trial court held there was a binding contract and ordered specific performance. The Maddoxes, appellants, contend the memorandum of the alleged contract of sale is too vague and indefinite to satisfy the Statute of Frauds. We agree and reverse the lower court.

Appellants and respondents are husband and wife respectively. The Cashes lived in Florida. They telephoned the Maddoxes, who lived in Georgia, and discussed the purchase of 15 acres of land owned by the Maddoxes. The only written evidence of the contract is a check mailed by the Cashes for Two Hundred ($200.00) Dollars as part payment. Written on the check was "15 acres in Pickens, S.C., land binder, 30 days from date of check to June 3, 1970." John Maddox endorsed and cashed the check. Subsequently, the Maddoxes advised the Cashes they did not wish to sell as it would cause trouble in the family and returned the Two Hundred ($200.00) Dollars which the Cashes refused. There was testimony the Maddoxes owned a 76 acre tract of land in Pickens County, of which 15.6 acres was south of the Pickens–Greenville highway, outside of the city limits of the town of Pickens.

The Statute of Frauds does not require any particular form of writing. It may be satisfied entirely by a written correspondence. *Speed v. Speed*, 213 S.C. 401, 49 S.E.2d 588 (1948). However, the writings must establish the essential terms of the contract without resort to parol evidence. One of the essential terms of a contract of sale of land is the identification of the land. A decree for specific performance operates as a deed. Hence, the land must be described so as to indicate with reasonable certainty what is to be conveyed. Parol evidence cannot be relied upon to supplement a vague and uncertain description.

The burden of proof was upon the respondents to establish the contract " 'by competent and satisfactory proof, such as is clear, definite, and certain.' * * * (T)he degree of certainty required is reasonable certainty, having regard to the subject-matter of the contract." *Aust v. Beard*, 230 S.C. 515, 521, 96 S.E.2d 558, 561 (1957).

For a contract to meet the requirements of the Statute of Frauds, S.C.Code § 11–101, every essential element of the sale must be expressed therein.

The alleged contract gives no definite location or shape of the 15 acres. The writing does not indicate whether the subject matter of the contract was north or south of the road, or in another area of the county. The fact 15.6 acres of the entire tract may be south of the road is not legally sufficient to satisfy the Statute of Frauds. Parol evidence may be used to explain terms appearing in the description, but the description itself must clearly identify the particular parcel of land.

In the absence of equities removing the case from the operation of the Statute of Frauds, which do not here exist, we hold before a court will decree specific performance of a contract for a sale of land, the writing must contain the essential terms of the contract. They must be expressed with such definiteness, certainty and clarity that it may be understood without recourse to parol evidence to show the intention of the parties. The terms of the contract must be such that neither party can reasonably misunderstand them. It would be inequitable to carry a contract into effect where the court is left to ascertain the intention of the parties by mere guess and conjecture.

The respondents' reliance upon *Speed v. Speed*, supra, is misplaced. That case specifically states, "the writings relied upon must *in and of themselves* furnish the evidence that the minds of the parties met as to the particular property which the one proposed to sell and the other agreed to buy; and, when such evidence is not found in the writings, it cannot be supplied by parol * * *." (Emphasis added). Page 410, 49 S.E.2d p. 592.

There was not a contract between these parties as would satisfy the Statute of Frauds. The land proposed to be sold was not described or designated as would enable a court to render a decree for its conveyance. The words in the check afford no means to adequately identify the property.

The parties should be restored to their original status.

Reversed.

LEWIS, CHIEF JUSTICE (dissenting):

* * *

The pleadings in this case are unverified. Neither of the appellants testified. The testimony of respondents as to the transaction is therefore uncontradicted. There is no testimony by appellants that the consideration was inadequate, nor is there any contention that they were in any manner the victims of a fraud. They simply contend, in effect, that they should be relieved of their part of the bargain because there was no sufficient memorandum of the agreement to sell.

In discussing the memorandum required by the Statute of Frauds, we stated in Blocker v. Hundertmark, 204 S.C. 269, 28 S.E.2d 855:

> "The statute of frauds merely requires some memorandum or note of the agreement relating to real estate to be in writing and signed by the party charged therewith or his agent, and does not require a formally executed contract. There must be written evidence of the contract, if there is no written contract, and our court has gone so far as to hold that a letter which recites the contract, but repudiates it, is sufficient. Colleton Realty Co. v. Folk, 85 S.C. 84, 67 S.E. 156. As stated in 37 C.J.S., Frauds, Statute of, § 174; 'The note or memorandum is not the contract, but only the written evidence of it required by statute.' "

The check and notation thereon leaves no doubt that there was an agreement between the parties for the sale of a 15 acre tract of land, that the check was the *binder* or down payment, and that the transaction was to be closed on or before June 3, 1971.

Appellants contend however that the memorandum fails to meet the requirements of the Statute of Frauds because there is no sufficient description of the land sold by which it can be identified, nor is the consideration stated, relying upon the principles stated in several of our cases that the memorandum, relied upon, must establish the essential terms of the contract, including the identity of the land and the consideration to be paid, without resort to parol evidence. Speed v. Speed, 213 S.C. 401, 49 S.E.2d 588.

The foregoing is not an absolute rule. Certainly it should not be applied when no reason exists to do so.

The purpose of the statute is to protect against fraud. In this case, the fact that there was an agreement for the sale of a trac[t] of "15 acres in Pickens, S. C." is evidenced by the written memorandum.

→ The question of whether parol evidence would be admissible to establish the identity of the particular tract of land referred to in the memorandum and to establish the consideration, where there is a dispute as to these issues, is not before the Court. Testimony was admissible to establish that there was no disagreement as to the identity of the land or the consideration to be paid and that the minds of the parties had met on these issues. If there was a dispute or ground for doubt as to what land was intended and what was to be paid therefor, the rules advanced by appellants should be applied and the parol testimony held inadmissible. That is not the case here.

Since the fact of the agreement for the sale of the land is evidenced by the written memorandum and the testimony shows that the terms of the agreement are not in dispute, there is no reason or basis for the application of the Statute of Frauds. As stated in Beckwith v. Talbot, 95 U.S. 289, 24 L.Ed. 496, 498 (quoted with approval in *Speed v. Speed,* supra), in discussing the admissibility of parol evidence to supply a deficiency in the agreement:

> "There may be cases in which it would be a violation of reason and common sense to ignore a reference which derives its significance from such proof. If there is ground for any doubt in the matter, the general rule should be enforced. But where there is no ground for doubt, its enforcement would aid, instead of discouraging, fraud."

The lower court properly held that a binding agreement for the sale of the land in question had been established entitling respondents to specific performance.

* * *

Notes and Questions

1. Is this a case where strict interpretation of the Statute of Frauds worked an injustice?

2. As the *Cash* case indicates, a memorandum may take any form so long as all necessary information is included. *See, e.g.,* Petition of Schaeffner, 96 Misc.2d 846, 851, 410 N.Y.S.2d 44, 48 (Sur.Ct.1978), where a suicide note was found to be "a sufficient memorandum of the oral agreement between claimant and decedent. It identifies the parties, the business to be sold [an interest in a newsstand], the price and is signed by the party to be charged."

b. Part Performance

An oral contract for the sale of real estate may be specifically enforced under the doctrine of part performance. This equitable doctrine is supported by two theories. The unequivocal reference theory holds that the Statute of Frauds was enacted to prevent one from fabricating a contract. If acts of part performance can only be explained by the existence of an oral contract, then the contract should be specifically enforced.

The fraud or estoppel theory provides that the Statute of Frauds should not be enforced to work a fraud or hardship on one who has acted in reliance on an oral agreement. Stated in another way, the person seeking to avoid the oral contract is estopped from denying the existence of a contract when the other party has acted to that party's detriment in reliance on it.

Almost all states recognize the doctrine on one or both theories, but considerable controversy exists as to what constitutes part performance. Payment of consideration (full or partial), taking possession of the property, and making improvements on it are critical acts. Some courts find that one act is sufficient to constitute part performance, others require a combination of two or three. *See, e.g.,* Green v. Gustafson, 482 N.W.2d 842 (N.D.1992) (finding part performance on basis of possession and improvement). Payment alone generally is not recognized as sufficient. *See* Cain v. Cross, 293 Ill.App.3d 255, 227 Ill.Dec. 659, 687 N.E.2d 1141 (1997)

See J. Cribbet & C. Johnson, Principles of the Law of Property 163–165 (3d ed.1989); *see also* R. Cunningham, W. Stoebuck, & D. Whitman, The Law of Property § 10.2 (2d ed.1993).

Problem

Assume the Ryans make an oral agreement with the seller to purchase the property. In reliance on that oral agreement, they pay part of the purchase price, take possession, and make some improvements on the property. They then decide that they do not like the location of the property. Therefore, they move out and refuse to pay the remainder of the purchase price. Can the seller enforce the contract on the ground that the Ryans' part performance satisfies the Statute of Frauds?

2. SAMPLE CONTRACT

Ms. Piper, the Ryans' real estate broker, proposes to use the following contract form. Notice paragraph 3 entitled "Acceptance." The purchaser typically signs a contract and submits it as an offer to the seller. The purchaser is not bound unless the seller accepts it. In this section we examine various provisions of this sample contract.

CONTRACT OF SALE*

PARTIES: _____, hereinafter called Seller (whether one or more, male, female, or corporate), agrees to sell to _____, hereinafter called Buyer (whether one or more, male, female, or corporate), who agrees to buy from Seller the property hereinafter described upon the terms and conditions hereinafter set forth.

1. LEGAL DESCRIPTION of real estate in _____ County, _____.

Personal property included: _____.

Street Address: _____. Said property fronts _____ feet on said street and runs back _____ feet.

Seller represents that the property can be used for the following purposes: _____
_____

2. PURCHASE PRICE: $_____, payable as follows:

     $_____ earnest money deposited with _____ as escrow agent.

---

*This contract form is found in Duncan & Hill Realty v. Department of State, 62   App.Div.2d 690, 699–700 at n. 4, 405 N.Y.S.2d 339, 344–345 at n. 4 (1978).

$_____ approximate balance of first mortgage, which Buyer assumes. Mortgage holder _____ Interest _____% per annum, payable _____.

$_____ purchase money note and mortgage to Seller. Interest _____%, payable _____

$_____ cash or cashier's check on closing (or such greater or lesser amount as may be required after credits, adjustments and prorations).

3. ACCEPTANCE: If this contract shall not have been signed by both parties on or before _____, the party having signed may declare it void, and if Buyer, he shall receive back his earnest deposit. The date of the last signature shall be the date of this contract.

4. LOAN COMMITMENT: This contract is conditioned upon Buyer's obtaining within 30 days from its date a commitment for a loan of $_____ with interest at _____% or less, and principal and interest payable together in _____ installments.

equitable conversion— "who bears the risk of loss"

5. DAMAGE BY FIRE, ETC.: This contract is further conditioned upon delivery of the improvements in their present condition, and in event of material damage by fire or otherwise before closing, Buyer may declare the contract void and shall be entitled to return of his escrow deposit.

6. CONVEYANCE: The conveyance shall be by general warranty deed, signed by _____ and shall describe the grantee(s) as follows:

_____

7. Seller shall furnish marketable title and shall convey the property free from encumbrances other than those named herein. Seller shall have the option of furnishing either a complete abstract of title or an Owner's Title Insurance Policy, insuring the title in the amount of the purchase price, issued by _____.

If Seller elects to furnish title insurance, he shall place an order therefor within five days from the date of this contract. If he furnishes abstract, Buyer shall have ten days within which to submit in writing any objections to the title. In the event of title objections, either by Buyer's attorney or by the title company, Seller shall have a reasonable time within which to cure them.

On Seller's failure to furnish marketable title within a reasonable time, Buyer may either cancel the contract and receive back his escrow deposit or enforce specific performance.

8. SURVEY: If a survey be required, the cost shall be paid by _____.

9. PRORATIONS: Taxes, insurance, rents, and interest shall be prorated to the date of closing, and Buyer shall assume taxes for the current year and shall take over the unexpired fire and other casualty insurance, except _____.

10. CLOSING: The transaction shall be closed at _____ when title objections have been met; and Seller shall have _____ days after closing within which to deliver possession.

11. COMMISSION: Seller agrees to pay _____, the Broker who negotiated this sale, a commission of $_____; if Buyer shall default, said Broker shall be entitled to half the escrow deposit, or his full commission, whichever shall be smaller.

12. DEFAULT: On default by Buyer, Seller may retain the escrow as liquidated damages or enforce specific performance. On default by Seller, Buyer may reclaim his escrow deposit, <u>sue for damages,</u> or enforce specific performance.

EXECUTED IN QUADRUPLICATE on the dates shown.

_____Date   _____Date
_____Date   _____Date

Note

Suppose that the purchaser is unable to perform on the date set in a contract for the sale of land. Is the seller relieved of obligations on the contract? In Soehnlein v. Pumphrey, 183 Md. 334, 338, 37 A.2d 843, 845 (1944), the court declared:

> The accepted doctrine is that in the ordinary case of contract for the sale of land, even though a certain period of time is stipulated for its consummation, equity treats the provision as formal rather than essential, and permits the purchaser who has suffered the period to elapse to make payments after the prescribed date, and to compel performance by the vendor notwithstanding the delay, unless it appears that time is of the essence of the contract by express stipulation, or by inference from the conduct of the parties, the special purpose for which the sale was made, or other circumstances surrounding the sale.

Hence, each party is allowed a reasonable time after the contract date in which to complete performance.

The parties to a real estate contract can make time of the essence by a specific provision. In this circumstance a delay in closing caused by one party will relieve the other party of obligations on the contract. Where time has been made of the essence, courts can be strict in holding the parties to timely performance. *See* Miceli v. Dierberg, 773 S.W.2d 154 (Mo.App.1989); Gorrie v. Winters, 214 N.J.Super. 103, 518 A.2d 515 (1986). Even where time was not originally made of the essence, either party may, by a distinct notice, fix a reasonable time for performance and make such time of the essence. *See* Dub v. 47 East 74th Street Corporation, 204 A.D.2d 145, 611 N.Y.S.2d 198 (1994). Note, however, that when time is made of the essence, the parties, by their conduct, may waive the requirement. A practice of accepting late payments under an installment land contract may well constitute waiver. *See* 3 American Law of Property § 11.44–11.46 (1952).

3. MARKETABLE TITLE

Paragraph 7 of the sample contract requires that the seller "furnish marketable title and * * * convey the property free from encumbrances other than those named herein." What is marketable title?

G/GM REAL ESTATE CORPORATION v. SUSSE CHALET MOTOR LODGE OF OHIO, INC.

Supreme Court of Ohio, 1991.
61 Ohio St.3d 375, 575 N.E.2d 141.

On March 4, 1985, plaintiff-appellee, G/GM Real Estate Corporation * * * ("G/GM"), and defendant-appellant, Susse Chalet Motor Lodge of

Ohio, Inc. * * * ("Susse"), signed a sales agreement ("Agreement") for a motel and restaurant owned by Susse in Marion. The purchase price was $1,000,000. The Agreement provided for Susse to take back a second mortgage of $250,000. G/GM was obligated to secure funds for the balance of the purchase price. G/GM had intended to convert the motel rooms into condominium units and then sell the individual units as investments. The property would continue to be operated as a motel, but, evidently, the profits would be divided among the unit owners.

The Agreement called for a downpayment of $25,000, which was made. Further, the sale was to close ninety days after the Agreement was signed. There was a provision that allowed the closing date to be moved back thirty days upon payment of an additional $10,000. G/GM exercised that option, extending the closing to July 4, 1985. G/GM subsequently asked that the closing be moved to July 9, which Susse agreed to do at no additional cost. G/GM then made a further request for an extension, this time to July 12. Susse agreed on the condition that another $10,000 be deposited with the seller. The payment was made on or about July 10 with a check from President Harding Inn Corporation, a company formed by one of the former principals in G/GM.

On July 11, 1985, one day prior to the closing, the Wexford Land Title Agency, Inc. ("Wexford"), which had been retained by G/GM, issued a commitment for title insurance through the First American Title Insurance Company of New York. In Schedule B, Section 1 of the commitment, there was a list of seven items that the title company required to be completed, including No. 6: "Proper affidavit cancelling Lease from Susse Chalet Motor Lodge of Ohio, Inc. to Hospitality Systems, Ltd., dated June 28, 1979, and recorded on July 27, 1979, in lease Vol. 37, page 903, Marion County Recorder's Office, Marion County, Ohio." The reference was to a "memorandum of lease" that the parties subsequently agreed did not comply with R.C. 5301.–251, the statute setting forth the requirements for recording a lease, and should not have been accepted for recording. Thomas R. McGrath, an attorney and president of Wexford, testified at trial that he had discovered the memorandum during his title search the last week of June and conveyed that information to all the parties. He also testified that he asked Susse for an affidavit stating that the lease had been canceled for noncompliance with its terms as " * * * just good, prudent underwriting," even though he felt the memorandum presented no risk from a title insurance perspective.

Although the parties met as scheduled for the closing on July 12, 1985, the sale did not close. Appellant alleges that G/GM was unable to tender the purchase price, thus breaching the Agreement. Appellee contends that appellant had breached the Agreement by failing to produce a marketable title, thereby nullifying the requirement that appellee tender the purchase price. There were additional negotiations on the morning of July 13, but the parties were unable to come to terms on a new agreement. Susse subsequently sold the motel on September

13, 1985 for $1,050,000—$50,000 more than the price agreed to between G/GM and Susse.

G/GM subsequently sued Susse and others in the Court of Common Pleas of Marion County, alleging breach of contract. Susse counterclaimed. By the time the case came to trial, Susse was the only defendant remaining, and the only issues remaining were whether either or both of the parties had breached the Agreement and which party was entitled to the $45,000 deposited. The trial court found that Susse had met its obligations under the Agreement by tendering a "good and marketable title." The court ruled that the memorandum of lease, which had formed the basis for G/GM's objections to the title, was recorded improperly and therefore was a nullity.

lower ct. ruling

* * *

On the counterclaim, the trial court found that G/GM had breached the Agreement by failing to produce the funds at closing. The court then ruled that the initial $25,000 deposit should be retained by Susse as liquidated damages per the Agreement. The $10,000 deposit made June 3, 1985, for the first extension of the closing date also belonged to Susse per the Agreement, which provided for one such extension. Finally, the court held that G/GM had not established any right to the second $10,000 deposit, which came from a check drawn on the President Harding Inn account. Consequently, the court held, G/GM had no claim for the return of the funds and, therefore, Susse was entitled to keep the payment.

Upon appeal, the Court of Appeals for Marion County reversed the trial court. The court of appeals, relying on Novogroder v. Di Paola (1919), 11 Ohio App. 374, held that the memorandum of lease, while a nullity for failure to meet the statutory recording requirements, was nonetheless a "cloud on the title." * * * The appellate court also found that G/GM was entitled to restoration of the entire $45,000 deposited.

This cause is now before the court pursuant to the allowance of a motion to certify the record.

* * *

WRIGHT, JUSTICE.

The court would be reluctant to call the precedents in this case elderly, being mindful of adjectives that might be perceived as pejorative, but they were found in volumes yellowed at the margins that left a trail of velvety silt when disturbed.

The question is which trail to follow. The Court of Appeals for Marion County chose the venerable *Novogroder v. Di Paola, supra.* For the reasons set forth, we choose instead the analysis of our nineteenth century colleagues found in Rife v. Lybarger (1892), 49 Ohio St. 422, 31 N.E. 768.

This case sounds in contract, one for the sale of real estate. The terms of that contract set forth in Section 1, Article XV what the seller was obligated to provide: " * * * a Limited Warranty Deed conveying fee simple title, good and marketable, free and clear of all mortgages or deeds of trust * * *."

Issue —

Does the existence of the improperly recorded memorandum of lease represent an impediment of the sort contemplated by the quoted portion of the contract? We think not. There is no dispute that the memorandum did not meet the statutory requirements for filing and, therefore, should not have appeared on the record of title at all. Though appellee cited the memorandum at the closing as a "defect or encumbrance" that rendered the title unmarketable, in fact, the alleged "defect or encumbrance" was a lapsed lease whose recording itself was defective. Further, a lease that is not binding on the purchaser would not render a title unmarketable. There is also little dispute, in the words of the trial court's lucid memorandum of decision, that " * * * the closing would have taken place but for the failure of plaintiff to produce the funds."

The contract did not require the appellant to produce a cloud-free title as asserted by the court of appeals' opinion. Even the *Novogroder* decision, relied upon by that court, noted:

"This contract was peculiarly worded; but it is not the province of the court to make contracts, but to enforce them. It is true that Novogroder may be captious, and his lawyers and his present counsel may be hypercritical, but if he contracted for a cloudless title he has a right to have a cloudless title. * * *

" * * *

" * * * If this suit were based on a contract requiring simply a marketable title, the question which we would have to solve would be different." *Id.* at 377–378.

The court of appeals did not cite to the earlier *Rife* decision for its characterization of *Novogroder,* but there can be little doubt where the *Novogroder* court found its phrasing:

" 'Captious objections to the title ought not to prevail, when made by a purchaser who seeks to avoid the performance of his contract.' "*Rife, supra,* 49 Ohio St. at 429, 31 N.E. at 770, quoting Walsh v. Barton (1873), 24 Ohio St. 28, 40.

Captiousness, absent a contract provision to support it, will not be viewed any more kindly today than it was one hundred eighteen years ago. The real cloud here was the one employed by the appellee in its attempt to divert attention from its failure to secure financing for the purchase. Paraphrasing the language of *Rife, supra,* we hold that an objection to a title must have some substantive merit in order to defeat a claim for specific performance of a contract for the sale of real estate made by a vendor charged with producing "good and marketable" title. A title need not be free of any possible defect in order to be marketable, but must be in a condition as would satisfy a buyer of ordinary prudence. An improperly recorded memorandum of lease intended to provide notice of a lease that has lapsed by its own terms, or has been cancelled for breach of its conditions, does not constitute a defect sufficiently substantive to warrant a purchaser's refusal to perform his obligations under a contract for sale of real estate.

* * *

As the record makes abundantly clear, the real problem was a lack of funds to close the sale, not an unmarketable title. Consequently, we find a breach of the Agreement by the appellee. The trial court cogently analyzed the disposition of the funds at issue.

* * *

The judgment of the court of appeals is reversed, and the judgment of the trial court is reinstated.

Judgment reversed.

Notes and Questions

1. What sort of title must the seller furnish if the contract is silent as to quality of title? It has long been settled that, in the absence of any contrary provision in the contract, a seller must give the purchaser a marketable title. *See* Burwell v. Jackson, 9 N.Y. 535 (1854). Suppose that the seller contracts to convey "such interest as seller has." Must the seller furnish marketable title? What is the consequence of an provision for a "insurable title?" *See* 3 American Law of Property §§ 11.47–11.48 (1952); R. Cunningham, W. Stoebuck, & D. Whitman § 10.12 (2d ed. 1993)

2. As indicated in Note 1, the parties may enlarge or restrict the seller's implied duty to provide marketable title by express provision in the contract. For example, the seller may list certain defects as exceptions to marketable title coverage. Likewise, the contract may require that the seller furnish a title that is both marketable and insurable. In Laba v. Carey, 29 N.Y.2d 302, 327 N.Y.S.2d 613, 277 N.E.2d 641 (1971), the seller agreed to give a marketable and insurable title subject to "covenants, restrictions, utility agreements and easements of records" and "any state of facts an accurate survey may show, provided same does not render title unmarketable." The survey revealed that the sidewalk level was approximately one foot below legal grade. A recorded "Waiver of Legal Grade" restrictive covenant obligated the then owner and the owner's successors to install a sidewalk at legal grade whenever city officials should so direct. The court rejected the purchaser's suit for return of the purchaser's deposit, ruling:

> The contract before us addressed itself to the existence of easements and restrictive covenants and specifically provided that the conveyance was to be subject to these matters of record. The title company, disclosing the existence of a telephone easement and "Waiver of Legal Grades" restrictive covenant, excluded these items from coverage, except insofar as to say that they had not been violated. In so insuring, it was assuming responsibility for no less than that which respondents had expressly agreed to accept. The exceptions were matters specifically contemplated by the contract and, since there is no indication in the record that the parties intended anything other than the interlocking of

the "subject to" and "insurance" clauses, it is our view that they must be read together to determine the scope of the seller's obligation.

Id. at 308, 327 N.Y.S.2d at 618, 277 N.E.2d at 644.

3. What defects will cause a title to be deemed unmarketable? Does the existence of a drainage easement which extends under a patio behind a house impair the marketability of title? *See* Madhavan v. Sucher, 105 Mich.App. 284, 306 N.W.2d 481 (1981). Would private burial easements or perimeter utility easements render title unmarketable? *See* Patten of New York Corporation v. Geoffrion, 193 A.D.2d 1007, 598 N.Y.S.2d 355 (1993).

4. Suppose X contracted to purchase certain low and wet land for homesites. After the contract was signed the area was classified as a wetlands, and thus the purchaser could not develop the land without grading and filling permits. Can X reject the contract on the ground that the wetlands designation rendered the title unmarketable? *See* McMaster v. Strickland, 305 S.C. 527, 409 S.E.2d 440 (App.1991).

5. Does the existence of hazardous waste, possibly requiring expensive remediation, on land subject to a contract of sale render the title unmarketable? For decisions concluding that the seller had marketable title notwithstanding the existence of environmental problems with the property, see HM Holdings, Inc. v. Rankin, 70 F.3d 933 (7th Cir.1995) ("presence of hazardous waste"); Vandervort v. Higginbotham, 222 A.D.2d 831, 634 N.Y.S.2d 800 (1995) ("potential environmental hazards"). *See also* Reitzel, *CERLA and Marketable Title—Is Toxic Contamination a Cloud?*, 26 Real Est.L.J. 253 (1998).

6. Courts have taken the position that the seller does not have to demonstrate marketable title until closing. Why? This principle applies to installment land contracts as well as to standard real estate sales contracts. Do you see any problems in its application to installment land contracts? *See* Luette v. Bank of Italy National Trust & Saving Association, 42 F.2d 9 (9th Cir.1930), *cert. denied* 282 U.S. 884 (1930).

7. If the seller cannot produce marketable title, the purchaser generally may recover the escrow deposit. May the purchaser also recover actual damages? (Consider the wording of paragraph 12 of the sample contract on page 482. Is it clear as to the purchaser's remedies?)

WARNER v. DENIS

Intermediate Court of Appeals of Hawai'i, 1997.
84 Hawai'i 338, 933 P.2d 1372.

BURNS, CHIEF JUDGE.

Plaintiffs Cynthia Warner (Warner), Mark Sheehan (Sheehan), and Ben Bollag (Bollag) (collectively, Plaintiffs) appeal the circuit court's April 22, 1992 Amended Judgment in favor of Defendants Frank Denis (Frank) and Vetra Denis (Vetra) (collectively, Defendants) * * * . * * *

Plaintiffs brought this case against Defendants to enforce a contract for their purchase of land and to recover damages resulting from the breach of the contract. * * *

Frank and Vetra are husband and wife. As joint tenants, they owned adjoining Lots 254, 255, and 256 in the Kalua Koʻi subdivision in West Molokaʻi. * * *

* * *

Plaintiffs do not dispute on appeal that although Vetra owned one-half interest in Lot 256 as a joint tenant with Frank, she never signed any of the documents upon which the Complaint underlying this lawsuit was based. However, Plaintiffs maintain that the trial court was wrong when it concluded, as a matter of law, that Vetra's failure to sign the documents barred any recovery of damages from Frank for breach of contract. * * *

It is a basic principle of contract law "that the promisor ordinarily is bound to perform his [or her] agreement according to its terms or, if he [or she] unjustifiably fails to perform, to respond in damages for his [or her] breach of the contract." Annotation, *Modern status of the rules regarding impossibility of performance as defense in action for breach of contract*, 84 A.L.R.2d 12, 21 (1962). "It is well settled, that when a party promises to do a thing which becomes impossible by contingencies which should have been foreseen and provided against, ... such impossibility is no defense to an action for a breach of the contract." *Bates v. Prendergast*, 1 Haw. 290 (1856). * * *

In transactions involving the sale or purchase of land, "[a] person may contract to sell land which he does not own.... His [or her] only obligation is to be able to convey a clear title at the time agreed upon for a conveyance." *Barkhorn v. Adlib Assoc., Inc.*, 222 F.Supp. 339, 341 (D.Haw.1963), amended 225 F.Supp. 474 (1964); aff'd, 409 F.2d 843 (9th Cir.1969). "Ordinarily, a person is not relieved of liability for breach of a promise to sell property simply because he or she turns out not to have marketable title." In re Ellis, 674 F.2d 1238, 1250 (9th Cir.1982).

In cases involving the sale of marital property, courts in other jurisdictions have uniformly held that where a vendor contracts to sell land jointly owned with a spouse but is thereafter unable to obtain the spouse's consent to the sale, the vendor remains liable to the vendee for damages.

In *Bobst v. Sons*, 252 S.W.2d 303 (Mo.1952), for example, a husband contracted to sell some land that he held with his wife as tenants in the entirety, but his wife refused to sign or consent to the sale. The purchaser subsequently filed an action for specific performance or damages for breach of contract and the circuit court dismissed the action. On appeal by the purchaser, the Missouri Supreme Court held that although the wife's refusal to consent barred the purchaser from obtaining equitable relief from the seller, the purchaser was entitled to damages from the husband. The court reasoned:

> A vendor who alone has contracted to sell land and who is unable to convey a good title because of the refusal of a spouse to join in a conveyance has been held liable in damages for breach of contract. It

is not unlawful for a person to contract to sell and convey something he does not own but expects to acquire, and, if he unqualifiedly undertakes to do that which later he finds he cannot perform, he should suffer the liability the law imposes upon the contract breaker.

Id. at 305 (citations and quotation marks omitted).

In *Raisor v. Jackson*, 311 Ky. 803, 225 S.W.2d 657 (1949), a husband sold property he owned with his wife and was unable to convey to the purchaser because his wife refused to join in the deed. Shortly thereafter, the wife joined in the sale of the property to another party. In concluding that the buyer was entitled to recover substantial damages and was not limited to an award of nominal damages, the Kentucky court of appeals stated:

[T]he buyer may recover substantial damages, if he can prove them, without regard to the seller's good faith, if the breach of contract is occasioned by the failure of the seller to obtain a conveyance of his wife's interest in the property.

This is simply a recognition of the principle that where a seller unconditionally agrees to convey real property, knowing that he has no title or with knowledge of an outstanding interest therein owned by a third party, he is bound by his undertaking to deliver a good deed to the purchaser; the question of good faith is immaterial if he breaches his agreement; and if the buyer is so damaged, he may recover the difference between the contract price and the reasonable market value of the property at the time the contract was executed.

Id. 225 S.W.2d at 660.

Similarly, the (State) Supreme Court of Appeals held in *Greer v. Doriot*, 137 Va. 589, 120 S.E. 291, 293 (1923), that a vendor cannot escape damages for breach of an unconditional land sale contract by showing that his wife refused to consent to the sale, thus preventing conveyance. In accord *Kaufman v. Bell*, 89 Cal.App. 610, 265 P. 317 (1928).

In this case, when Frank signed the Contract to sell to Plaintiffs Lot 256, he knew that he would need Vetra's consent in order to convey marketable title. When he thereafter failed to obtain Vetra's consent to the sale, he breached his Contract with Plaintiffs and, pursuant to the principles outlined above, subjected himself to liability for damages suffered by Plaintiffs as a result of his breach. Although Vetra's failure to consent to the sale rendered it impossible for Plaintiffs to obtain specific performance of Frank's obligations under the Contract, such failure does not shield Frank from liability for damages.

* * *

Accordingly, we vacate the April 22, 1992 Amended Judgment * * *. We remand * * * for the adjudication of Plaintiffs' claim against Frank for damages for breach of the Contract * * *.

Question

Suppose the seller had been unable to provide marketable title because of a title defect of which the seller was unaware. Would the purchaser still have been able to recover actual damages from the seller for breach of contract? There is a split of authority on this question. What is the better view? *See* R. Cunningham, W. Stoebuck, and D. Whitman, The Law of Property § 10.3 (2d ed. 1993).

4. FORFEITURE OF DEPOSIT

Contracts for the sale of real property commonly provide that in the event of default by the purchaser, the seller is entitled to retain the deposit as liquidated damages. *See* paragraph 12 of the sample contract on page 482. Can the seller retain the purchaser's deposit if the land was promptly sold to another individual at a higher price? In Stabenau v. Cairelli, 22 Conn.App. 578, 577 A.2d 1130 (1990), the court declined to enforce an otherwise valid liquidated damages clause where the breach was not willful and the seller suffered no actual loss. Is this result sound? *See also* Nohe v. Roblyn Development Corp., 296 N.J.Super. 172, 686 A.2d 382 (1997) (refusing to enforce liquidated damages clause involving significant amount of money where developer-seller later sold house for considerably more than price specified in breached contract). For discussion of forfeitures under installment land contracts, see pages 517–524.

5. SPECIFIC PERFORMANCE

Paragraph 12 of the sample contract on page 482 provides that upon default of either party, the other party may seek specific performance of the contract. This equitable remedy is generally available to each party even absent such a provision. Why?

PRUITT v. GRAZIANO

Superior Court of New Jersey, Appellate Division, 1987.
215 N.J.Super. 330, 521 A.2d 1313.

The opinion of the court was delivered by FURMAN, P.J.A.D.

Defendants, sellers of a condominium unit, appeal from summary judgment of specific performance in favor of plaintiff purchaser. The condominium unit overlooks woods and a brook and has an addition in back added on by defendants. On appeal defendants contend that plaintiff was not entitled to specific performance in the absence of proof of the uniqueness of the condominium unit. We disagree and affirm.

Under the Condominium Act, *N.J.S.A.* 46:8B–4, each condominium unit "shall constitute a separate parcel of real property." "Condominium" is defined in *N.J.S.A.* 46:8B–3 as "the form of ownership of real property under a master deed providing for ownership by one or more owners of units of improvements together with an undivided interest in common elements appurtenant to each such unit." Under long established equity principles, a contract for the sale of real property is specifically enforceable by the purchaser. Presumptively, real property is unique and damages at law are an inadequate remedy for breach of a contract to sell it. A factual resolution of uniqueness of the real property is immaterial. 11 *Williston on Contracts* (3 ed. Jaeger 1968) § 1418A; *Pomeroy, Equity Jurisprudence* (5 ed. 1941) § 221(b).

Defendants' single argument is that summary judgment should have been denied because of a fact issue as to the uniqueness of the condominium unit under contract of sale, one of approximately 250 in the condominium complex. Defendant relies upon three reported decisions, all clearly distinguishable in our view. Fleischer v. James Drug Stores, 1 N.J. 138, 62 A.2d 383 (1948) involved a suit for specific performance of a business contract. In Blake v. Flaharty, 44 N.J.Eq. 228, 14 A. 128 (E. & A. 1888), specific performance was denied to the purchaser of real property under the unusual circumstance that the purchase price was so low that the seller "will lose the whole purchase-price of his land in costs." Plaintiff there was relegated to his remedy at law "where the costs are much less than in * * * equity."

In the more recent case of Centex Homes Corp. v. Boag, 128 N.J.Super. 385, 320 A.2d 194 (Ch.Div.1974), the seller of a condominium unit was denied specific performance in view of the adequacy of readily measurable damages as a remedy and the absence of any showing of a "unique quality" of "one of hundreds of virtually identical units being offered by [the seller] for sale to the public." The court referred to the trend towards disappearance of the doctrine of mutuality of remedy, which entitled the seller as well as the purchaser of real property to specific performance. * * *

An out-of-state authority awarding specific performance in favor of the purchaser of a condominium unit irrespective of any special showing of uniqueness is Giannini v. First Nat. Bank of Des Plaines, 136 Ill.App.3d 971, 91 Ill.Dec. 438, 483 N.E.2d 924 (1985).

On the appeal before us, we note some indicia of uniqueness of the condominium unit under contract of sale, its view and the addition in its back. Our holding rests, notwithstanding such *prima facie* showing of uniqueness, upon a broader ground: that a contract of sale of a designated condominium unit like any real property is specifically enforceable by the purchaser irrespective of any special proof of its uniqueness.

We affirm.

Questions

Why should the remedy of specific performance be available to sellers? Should a seller be able to obtain specific performance if the purchaser breaches a contract to purchase a condominium unit in a large high-rise complex?

6. EQUITABLE CONVERSION—RISK OF LOSS

The concept of specific performance leads logically to the doctrine of equitable conversion. This doctrine is grounded on the ancient maxim: "Equity regards as done that which ought to be done." It follows that upon execution of the contract, equity courts regard the purchaser as equitable owner of the property and the seller as trustee of bare legal title for the purchaser. Similarly, the seller is considered the equitable owner of the purchase money although it remains in the hands of the purchaser.

The doctrine of equitable conversion is often utilized to determine who bears the risk of loss when the contract is silent on that subject. For example, what are the Ryans' rights and obligations if the house in Rolling Hills is destroyed or damaged by fire after the execution of the contract, but before closing?

BRYANT v. WILLISON REAL ESTATE CO.

Supreme Court of Appeals of West Virginia, 1986.
177 W.Va. 120, 350 S.E.2d 748.

MILLER, CHIEF JUSTICE:

James L. Bryant and James E. Bland, the plaintiffs who were purchasers under a real estate sales contract, appeal from a judgment of the Circuit Court of Harrison County denying their claim for rescission of the contract and permitting the defendants/vendors to retain their down payment. The trial court also awarded damages against the purchasers for property loss suffered by third parties as a result of water flowing from a broken water line into two adjacent businesses.

This case was heard by the trial court judge without a jury by agreement of the parties. The facts are that on January 4, 1980, the plaintiffs entered into a contract to purchase the O.J. Morrison Building in Clarksburg for $175,000. As required by the sales contract, they paid $10,000 to Willison Real Estate Company, the agent for the vendors, at the time the contract was signed. The balance was to be paid upon delivery of the deed, at which time the purchasers would take possession of the property. No date was set for the closing.

On February 18, 1980, before the delivery of the deed, a water line broke in the sprinkler system, permitting water to run throughout the building and into two adjoining businesses. The purchasers had planned to extensively renovate the building for use as a medical office building. The purchasers were informed by an architect and an engineer who inspected the damage that the remodeling of the Morrison Building could be delayed by as much as four to six weeks because the building had to be properly dried out. The purchasers asked the vendors to correct the water damage or to permit the contract to be rescinded. The vendors declined to repair the damage and sold the building to another purchaser in July of 1980 for $140,000. The purchasers then instituted this action for rescission of the contract and return of their down payment. The trial court ruled that the purchasers must bear the risk of loss both to the Morrison Building and for the water damage to the adjoining property owned by third parties.

The purchasers contend that the trial court placed undue reliance on the doctrine of equitable conversion and rejected language in the sales contract placing the risk of loss on the vendors.[1] Our law on the doctrine of equitable conversion with regard to real estate sales contracts is rather minimal. The doctrine of equitable conversion[2] provides that where an executory contract for the sale of real property does not contain a provision allocating the risk of loss and the property is damaged by fire or some other casualty not due to the fault or neglect of the vendor,[3] the risk of loss is on the purchaser. This assumes the vendor has good title.

Our main case is Maudru v. Humphreys, 83 W.Va. 307, 98 S.E. 259 (1919), where the purchaser was in possession of the property under an executory contract of sale. A fire destroyed a building on the property and this Court found the purchaser to have borne the risk of loss, stating in its single Syllabus:

> "Where a vendor, having good title and capacity to perform, makes a valid enforceable contract for the sale of land and, thereafter and before a deed is executed passing the legal title, a fire destroys a building thereon, without his fault or neglect, the loss is sustained by the purchaser. In such case there is no implied warranty that the condition of the property at the time of sale shall continue until after deed is made."

1. The language in the sales contract relied upon by the purchasers is as follows: "It is also understood and agreed that the owner is responsible for said property until the Deed has been delivered to said purchaser."

2. The origins of the doctrine of equitable conversion are traced in 6A R. Powell, Powell on Real Property ¶ 925(6) (1984), where he states that the doctrine was first introduced in "Anglo–American jurisprudence in the landmark English case of Paine v. Meller, 6 Vesey Jr. 349, 31 Eng. Rep. 1088 (Ch.1801)." He points out that it rests on the "concept that 'equity regards as done that which is agreed or ought to be done.'" Id. at 84–75. Thus, at the time the real estate contract is signed, the purchaser becomes the equitable owner, and the seller retains a right to possession and legal title as security for the payment of the balance of the purchase price. Powell also notes that some courts have rejected the doctrine. E.g., Anderson v. Yaworski, 120 Conn. 390,

181 A. 205 (1935); Libman v. Levenson, 236 Mass. 221, 128 N.E. 13, 22 A.L.R. 560 (1920); Skelly Oil Co. v. Ashmore, 365 S.W.2d 582 (Mo.1963); Connell v. Savings Bank of Newport, 47 R.I. 60, 129 A. 803 (1925). Furthermore, Powell points out that several states have adopted the Uniform Vendor and Purchaser Risk Act which generally relieves the purchaser from the contract if he is not in possession and if the property is materially destroyed without fault on the part of the purchaser. The Uniform Act recognizes that risk of loss can be settled by an express provision in the sales contract. Id. at 84–76. He also points out that the Paine case setting the doctrine in England has been rejected by the Law of Property Act of 1925. Id. at 84–80.

3. It would appear that where the risk of loss is on the purchaser and the damage to the property is caused by the negligence of the vendor, the vendor must bear the risk of loss.

The Court in *Maudru* did not make an extensive analysis of the doctrine of equitable conversion, but did state that "[t]here is no warranty or condition in the contract between Mynes and Maudru that the property should be in the same condition when the transaction is completed as it was when the contract was made." 83 W.Va. at 311, 98 S.E. at 261. This appears to be an implied recognition that the parties may allocate the risk of loss in a sales contract and thereby alter the doctrine of equitable conversion.

It is rather universally recognized that the parties to a contract of sale for real property may allocate the risk of loss for fire or other casualty occurring before the actual transfer of the legal title. If the contract allocates the risk to the vendor, then the doctrine of equitable conversion, which places the risk of loss on the purchaser, is no longer applicable.

The trial court was of the view that the contract language stating that "the owner is responsible for said property until the Deed has been delivered to said purchaser" was not sufficient to cast the responsibility on the vendors. This conclusion was based, in part, on testimony of the sales agent for the vendor that this language pertained only to vandalism.

We disagree with this conclusion. The contract was on a printed form and the language is free from ambiguity. Cases in other jurisdictions have held language of similar import to place the burden of risk of loss on the vendor.

To permit this language to be restricted to acts of vandalism cuts across the plain meaning of its wording and would be contrary to the general rule that forecloses oral modification of contract language which is free from ambiguity.

Apparently, the trial court also relied on language in the sales contract which provided: "Purchaser to carry enough fire insurance to protect Self." We do not believe that this provision can be read to place the risk of loss on the purchasers. This provision is nothing more than an acknowledgment of the general rule that both parties to an executory contract for the sale of real property have an insurable interest.

The trial court also referred to the sentence in the contract that "[t]his contract is also subject to 'As Is' condition" as indicating an intention not to deliver the building in a specific condition. We agree with this conclusion insofar as it would dispel any claim by the purchasers to require the vendors to make any improvements to the building from the condition it was in at the time the contract was signed. There was apparently no dispute that the building had been unoccupied for some period of time and was somewhat deteriorated.

However, we do not agree that this language can be read to remove the risk of loss from the vendors. The purpose of this type of provision is not to shift the risk of loss in the event the building is damaged without fault on the part of either party. Rather the use of an "as is" provision in a real estate sales contract is generally intended to negate the existence of any warranty as to the particular fitness or condition of the property. This type of clause simply means that the purchaser must take the premises covered in the real estate sales contract in its present condition as of the date of the contract.

Having determined that the vendors bore the risk of loss under the contract, we believe the purchasers had the right to obtain the return of the initial down payment once the vendors refused to consider an abatement in the sale price as a result of the water damage and then sold the property to a third party.

The particular remedies that may be available where there has been partial destruction or damage to buildings to be sold are not easily categorized as they depend upon particular facts and circumstances. It may be generally stated that where the risk of loss is on the vendor and the casualty damage to the property is not substantial, the purchaser is entitled to sue for specific performance, and the purchase price is abated to the extent the property was damaged. On the other hand where the risk of loss is on the vendor and there is substantial damage to the property, the appropriate remedy ordinarily is to terminate the contract and return the down payment to the purchaser.

We have recognized that a purchaser may have specific performance of his contract to purchase real estate with an abatement in the purchase price where the vendor cannot fully perform his agreement. However, it appears that we have not had occasion to speak to the remedy where the risk of loss is on the vendor and damage has been done to the building.

The purchasers, as we have seen, sued only to recover their down payment. The vendors counterclaimed for the difference in the sales price on the original contract and what they obtained from the subsequent sale of the Morrison Building. The trial court rejected the vendors' counterclaim for reasons that are not entirely clear. However, in view of the risk of loss being placed on the vendors, the trial court's ruling with regard to the vendors' counterclaim would be correct for two reasons.

First, the vendors having the risk of loss for the water damage could not require the purchasers to pay the full purchase price. Consequently, the vendors were wrong in concluding that the purchasers had breached the sales contract when they refused to pay the full purchase price. As a result of this erroneous conclusion, the vendors breached the contract when they sold the property to the third party. If the water damage had not been substantial, the vendors could have sued the purchasers for specific performance while offering an abatement in the purchase price.

As a second alternative, if the vendors had concluded that the damages were substantial, they could have terminated the sales contract and returned the purchasers' down payment. However, with the risk of loss being on the vendors, they would bear the cost of repairing damage to the building.

Holding

Under the particular facts of this case, we conclude that where a contract places the risk of loss on the vendor and insubstantial damage to the property occurs without the fault of either party, the purchaser may recover his down payment where the vendor refuses to repair the damage or to give an abatement in the purchase price.[4]

Finally, we note that with the risk of loss being placed on the vendors, the vendors were not entitled to recover from the purchasers the sums that they had paid to third parties whose adjacent premises were damaged by the water flowing from the vendors' building. The trial court awarded these damages on the basis that the purchasers bore the risk of loss under the doctrine of equitable conversion, which we have found inapplicable because of the terms of the contract.

* * *

We, therefore, reverse the judgment of the Circuit Court of Harrison County and remand the case for further proceedings not inconsistent with this opinion.

Reversed and Remanded.

Notes, Problems and Questions

1. As noted in *Bryant,* courts in some states reject the traditional rule and place the risk of loss on the seller absent a contractual agreement to the contrary. What rationale supports this view?

2. Is the Uniform Vendor and Purchaser Risk Act, discussed in *Bryant* at footnote 2, a sound statutory solution to the risk of loss problem?

3. Assume that the risk of loss is on the purchaser and that the seller has a casualty insurance policy covering a building on the property. The building was destroyed by fire. May the purchaser insist that the insurance proceeds be applied against the purchase price? *See* J. Cribbet & C. Johnson, Principles of the Law of Property 196–200 (3d ed. 1989).

4. What are the Ryans' rights and obligations under paragraph 5 of the sample contract on page 482 if the house in Rolling Hills is partially destroyed by fire before closing?

5. The doctrine of equitable conversion also plays an important role in cases where either the seller or purchaser dies before the transaction is closed. Assume that the seller of the house in Rolling Hills dies while the contract is still executory, leaving by will all the seller's real property to A and all the seller's personal property to B. Who is entitled to the purchase money that the Ryans must pay at closing? *See* 3 American Law of Property § 11.26 (1952). For a discussion of equitable conversion in a similar circumstance, see Bauserman v. Digiulian, 224 Va. 414, 297 S.E.2d 671 (1982).

D. FINANCING

The Ryans, typical home buyers, do not have sufficient ready cash to pay the purchase price. Therefore, they must obtain a loan from the

---

4. We have assumed for purposes of this case that the damages to the building were insubstantial.

seller or an institutional lender. The seller may provide financing by agreeing to sell the property on an installment land contract, or by deeding the property to the Ryans and taking in return a note and mortgage for the unpaid balance of the purchase price. An institutional lender may provide financing by lending the Ryans a substantial part of the purchase price and taking a mortgage on the property to secure repayment, or by allowing the Ryans to assume an existing mortgage.

Usually the purchaser obtains a new mortgage loan from an institutional lender and the seller uses a portion of the purchase money to satisfy the existing mortgage at closing. However, when mortgage money is scarce or expensive, "creative financing" may be required. For example, the purchaser may assume an existing mortgage and give the seller a second mortgage for the balance of the purchase price. The purchaser thereby obtains financing from both an institutional lender and the seller.

1. MORTGAGE

a. *Introduction*

The mortgage, foundation of real estate financing, is a pledge of land to secure the repayment of a loan. In the usual home mortgage arrangement, the purchaser borrows money from an institutional lender, executes a promissory note payable to the lender, uses the loan money to purchase a house, and pledges the property purchased as collateral. In legal parlance, the borrower is known as the mortgagor, the lender as the mortgagee, and the pledge as a mortgage. If the mortgagor fails to repay the loan, the mortgagee may utilize foreclosure procedures to have the mortgaged property sold to satisfy the unpaid balance.

In some areas of the country, the pledge is in the form of an instrument called a deed of trust or trust deed. Whereas the mortgage involves only two parties, a borrower and a lender, the deed of trust is a tripartite agreement involving a borrower, a lender, and a trustee. The deed of trust is designed to be foreclosed outside the court system at a trustee's sale. Thus, deeds of trust are commonly employed in those states where out-of-court foreclosure sales are allowed. The law generally treats deeds of trust and mortgages alike, but in some states a distinction is made between the two in various matters. *See* G. Nelson & D. Whitman, Real Estate Finance Law § 1.6 (3d ed. 1994).

b. *Historical Background and Underlying Theories*

The evolution of mortgage law is discussed in the following excerpt from a leading treatise on real estate finance.

G. NELSON & D. WHITMAN, REAL
ESTATE FINANCE LAW*

§§ 1.2–1.5 (3d ed. 1994).

THE IMPACT OF ENGLISH HISTORY

An understanding of the modern real estate mortgage requires, at least, a limited consideration of its historical antecedents. Although the mortgage has its roots in both Roman law and in early Anglo–Saxon England, the most significant developments for our purposes are the English common law mortgage and the effects on that mortgage of the subsequent intervention of English equity courts. These developments not only substantially influenced the substance of American mortgage law, but they are responsible for much of its terminology as well.

Although the common law mortgage as it developed in the fourteenth and fifteenth centuries varied, in form it was essentially a conveyance of fee simple ownership, but the conveyance was expressly on condition subsequent. For example, assume B loans A $1,000. A would convey Blackacre to B and his heirs, but on the condition that, if A repaid the $1,000 to B on a specified day, A would have the right to reenter and terminate B's estate. There were several important attributes to this transaction. B, the mortgagee, received legal title to the land and the normal incidents of that title. Perhaps the most important feature of this mortgage is that the grantee got the incidents of legal title even though unnecessary or even antagonistic to the sole purpose of the conveyance, namely, security for the performance of an act by the grantor. Thus * * * he had the right to immediate possession. Originally, the mortgagee used possession and the right to collect rents and profits as a method to get a return on his loan, since the charging of any interest was then considered to be usury and unlawful. Later the custom developed to leave the mortgagor in possession, although the mortgagee nevertheless retained the right to obtain possession. If he did obtain possession, however, he was required to account for the rents and profits on the mortgage debt.

The condition with provision for reentry was gradually displaced by a covenant by the mortgagee to reconvey upon full performance by the mortgagor. This covenant had a double operation. It was effective at law as a condition, and also was a promise which equity would enforce specifically. Its development apparently coincided with that of the equity of redemption referred to below, and its popularity was based upon the practical advantages of getting back by a reconveyance, instead of by reentry, the interest conveyed to the mortgagee. Regardless of which form was used, if the mortgagor failed to perform on the day set, the mortgagee's estate became absolute.

This common law mortgage was especially harsh on the mortgagor. The payment date was called the law day. Under the common law, if for any reason the payment was not made on that day, the mortgagor forfeited all interest in Blackacre. This was an absolute rule. It applied even if the mortgagor could not find the mortgagee to pay him. Time was strictly of the essence.

The Intervention of Equity

The excesses and harshness of the common law mortgage inevitably yielded to the moderating influence of English Chancery. Initially, equity intervened to aid the mortgagor who had failed promptly to perform on law day where the mortgagor could establish such traditional equitable grounds for relief as fraud, accident, misrepresentation, or duress. In other words, even though the mortgagee's rights at law were absolute, the mortgagor who had the financial capability to tender the amount due and owing could get his property back after law day so long as he could fit within the grounds described above. However, by the 17th century, the granting of such relief by equity became much more routine so that the mortgagor was able, as a matter of course and right, to redeem his land from the mortgagee if he tendered the principal and interest within a reasonable time after law day. It was no longer necessary to establish the more specific equitable grounds for relief. This right to tardy redemption was referred to as the mortgagor's equity of redemption and became recognized as an equitable estate in land.

The mortgagor's right to tardy redemption obviously created a substantial problem for the mortgagee. Even though the mortgagor had defaulted, the mortgagee could never be reasonably sure that the mortgagor would not sue in equity to redeem. The mortgagee obviously needed to be relieved at some point of the threat of redemption. Thus, this same period saw the concurrent development in equity of the mortgagee's right to foreclosure. When the mortgagor failed to pay on law day or to bring a suit to redeem, at the request of the mortgagee in a bill setting forth the details of the mortgage and default, equity would order the mortgagor to pay the debt, interest and costs within a fixed period. Failure to comply with the decree meant that the mortgagor's right to redeem was forever barred. This type of foreclosure, which is little used today, is known as strict foreclosure because the land is forfeited to the mortgagee no matter what its value in relation to the original mortgage debt. No sale of the land is involved.

Whatever the original reasons for the chancellor's intervention, clearly the later equity view was that the mortgagee's interest was only security and intercession needed no other justification than to limit and protect it for that purpose. * * *

* * *

The American Development

While strict foreclosure is theoretically available in a few states and in some relatively special situations in others, the major method of foreclosure in the United States involves a public sale of the premises. There are two main types of sale foreclosure used in the United States today. The most common type is judicial foreclosure where a public sale results after a full judicial proceeding in which all interested persons must be made parties. In many states this is the sole method of foreclosure. It is time-consuming and costly. The other method of foreclosure is by power of sale. Under this method, after varying types and degrees of notice to the parties, the property is sold at a public sale, either by some public official such as a sheriff, by the mortgagee, or by some other third party. No judicial proceeding is required in a power of sale foreclosure. It is generally available only where the mortgage instrument authorizes it. * * *

It is important to remember that, as a general proposition, an unwilling mortgagor cannot lose his equity of redemption (or equity of tardy redemption, as it is sometimes called) unless there has been a valid foreclosure of the mortgage. In other words, even though the mortgage is in substantial default, normally no agreement of the parties in the mortgage, or contemporaneous with it, can cut off a recalcitrant mortgagor's rights in the mortgaged property without the mortgagee resorting to foreclosure. This concept, which will be considered in greater detail later, is sometimes referred to as the *prohibition against clogging the mortgagor's equity of redemption.*

Suppose, however, that there has been a valid foreclosure and that the mortgagor's equity of redemption has been cut off.[1] Some states, by a variety of legislative methods, have created something called *statutory redemption*. This type of redemption becomes available *only* when the equity of redemption has been effectively cut off by a valid foreclosure. Statutory redemption, as we will see later, varies widely from state to state. In general, however, these statutes permit the mortgagor and sometimes his junior lienors to redeem after the sale for various periods of time as short as a few months in some states to as long as 18 months or more in a few others. The statutory right of redemption was created, in part, to afford the mortgagor or other person entitled to exercise the right additional time to refinance and save his property, but also to put pressure on the mortgagee to bid the value of the property at the foreclosure sale, at least up to the amount of the mortgage debt. To enforce this purpose the redemption amount is usually the *sale price* and *not the mortgage debt*. A secondary purpose of these statutes in some states is to allow an additional period of possession to a hard-pressed

1. "When a mortgage loan goes into default, normally the mortgagee has the right to 'accelerate,' which has the effect of making the entire debt due and payable. The mortgagee may, under some circumstances, simply decide to proceed against the mortgagor personally and forego reliance on the mortgage security. Usually, however, the mortgagee will choose or will be required by law to foreclose the mortgage first. Although methods of foreclosure differ widely, under most circumstances there will be a sale of the mortgaged premises. The proceeds will be used to pay off the mortgage debt and the surplus, if any, will go to any subordinate lien-holders and the mortgagor. If the sale does not yield enough to cover the debt, the mortgagee will often be able to obtain a personal judgment for the deficiency against the mortgagor." G. Nelson & D. Whitman, Real Estate Finance Law § 1.1 (3d ed. 1994). [Editors' note.]

mortgagor. The operation and effectiveness of these statutes will be analyzed in greater detail later in this volume. The important thing to remember at this point is that statutory redemption normally begins *only* after the mortgagor's equity of redemption has been validly terminated by foreclosure.

The Title, Lien, and Intermediate Theories of Mortgage Law

Three "theories" of mortgage law exist today in the United States. One of these, the *title theory*, has its roots in the English common law mortgage discussed earlier. Under this theory, legal "title" is in the mortgagee until the mortgage has been satisfied or foreclosed. While the states that recognize this theory have for the most purposes treated the mortgagee as simply holding a security interest, the mortgagee's "title" does appear to give him the right to possession. Under the more predominant *lien theory*, however, the mortgagee holds no "title" but has security only. The mortgagor, accordingly, has the right to possession until there has been a valid foreclosure. The so-called *intermediate theory* gives the right to possession to the mortgagor at least until default, and generally to the mortgagee after default. The lien theory states, with such exceptions as New York and South Carolina, tend to be west of the Mississippi, and the title and intermediate theory states in the east. Lien theory states have rejected the mortgagee's possessory rights, either by judicial decision or by statute.

While the three theories have tended to interest academics more than practitioners, in certain situations they can prove to have important practical significance. It may come as a surprise that a mortgagee would want possession of the mortgaged premises prior to foreclosure. Most mortgagees, after all, are primarily in the lending business and do not view themselves as managers of real estate. Indeed, in every jurisdiction the mortgagor, at least initially, is in possession of the premises. Then why is the right to possession significant? Primarily because it carries with it not only the right to protect the premises against waste, but more importantly, the right to collect rents and profits. The mortgagee, however, must *account* for any such rents and profits on the mortgage debt.

There may be occasions when a mortgagee may wish to bring ejectment to obtain possession of the premises. Suppose, for example, that the foreclosure proceedings in a particular state are so lengthy that it may take up to three years to bring a foreclosure to successful culmination. Suppose further that a defaulted mortgage on commercial real estate is involved and that the mortgagor is so financially weak as to be judgment-proof. If the mortgagee can gain possession prior to foreclosure, deterioration or destruction of the security can be prevented and the mortgagee will be able to prevent the rents and profits from being diverted to purposes other than payment of the mortgage. * * *

Problem

O owned Blackacre in fee simple absolute. Blackacre had a market value of approximately $100,000. O borrowed $80,000 from Bank and gave Bank an $80,000 promissory note and a mortgage on Blackacre to secure the note. O then borrowed $20,000 from O's Uncle Ed and gave Uncle Ed a $20,000 promissory note and a mortgage on Blackacre to secure the note. O did not pay either debt. Bank commenced foreclosure proceedings and joined O and Uncle Ed. Blackacre brought $90,000 at the foreclosure sale. What are the rights of each party to the proceeds? In other respects?

c. Sample Note and Mortgage

Note and mortgage forms developed by the Federal National Mortgage Association and the Federal Home Loan Mortgage Corporation are reproduced below.

NOTE

...., 19.........   ...., ...
                                                          [City]   [State]

....
                                                   [Property Address]

1. BORROWER'S PROMISE TO PAY

In return for a loan that I have received, I promise to pay U.S. $... (this amount is called "principal"), plus interest, to the order of the Lender. The Lender is .... I understand that the Lender may transfer this Note. The Lender or anyone who takes this Note by transfer and who is entitled to receive payments under this Note is called the "Note Holder."

2. INTEREST

Interest will be charged on unpaid principal until the full amount of principal has been paid. I will pay interest at a yearly rate of ....%.

The interest rate required by this Section 2 is the rate I will pay both before and after any default described in Section 6(B) of this Note.

3. PAYMENTS

(A) Time and Place of Payments

I will pay principal and interest by making payments every month.

I will make my monthly payments on the .... day of each month beginning on ...., 19.......... I will make these payments every month until I have paid all of the principal and interest and any other charges described below that I may owe under this Note. My monthly payments will be applied to interest before principal. If, on ...., ..., I still owe amounts under this Note, I will pay those amounts in full on that date, which is called the "maturity date."

I will make my monthly payments at .... or at a different place if required by the Note Holder.

(B) Amount of Monthly Payments

My monthly payment will be in the amount of U.S. $...

4. BORROWER'S RIGHT TO PREPAY

I have the right to make payments of principal at any time before they are due. A payment of principal only is known as a "prepayment." When I make a prepayment, I will tell the Note Holder in writing that I am doing so.

I may make a full prepayment or partial prepayments without paying any prepayment charge. The Note Holder will use all of my prepayments to reduce the amount of principal that I owe under this Note. If I make a partial prepayment, there will be no changes in the due date or in the amount of my monthly payment unless the Note Holder agrees in writing to those changes.

5. LOAN CHARGES

If a law, which applies to this loan and which sets maximum loan charges, is finally interpreted so that the interest or other loan charges collected or to be collected in connection with this loan exceed the permitted limits, then: (i) any such loan charge shall be reduced by the amount necessary to reduce the charge to the permitted limit; and (ii) any sums already collected from me which exceeded permitted limits will be refunded to me. The Note Holder may choose to make this refund by reducing the principal I owe under this Note or by making a direct payment to me. If a refund reduces principal, the reduction will be treated as a partial prepayment.

6. BORROWER'S FAILURE TO PAY AS REQUIRED

(A) Late Charge for Overdue Payments

If the Note Holder has not received the full amount of any monthly payment by the end of .... calendar days after the date it is due, I will pay a late charge to the Note Holder. The amount of the charge will be ....% of my overdue payment of principal and interest. I will pay this late charge promptly but only once on each late payment.

(B) Default

If I do not pay the full amount of each monthly payment on the date it is due, I will be in default.

MULTISTATE FIXED RATE NOTE—Single Family—FNMA/FHLMC UNIFORM INSTRUMENT   Form 3200 12/83
(E5995)

(C) Notice of Default

If I am in default, the Note Holder may send me a written notice telling me that if I do not pay the overdue amount by a certain date, the Note Holder may require me to pay immediately the full amount of principal which has not been paid and all the interest that I owe on that amount. That date must be at least 30 days after the date on which the notice is delivered or mailed to me.

(D) No Waiver By Note Holder

Even if, at a time when I am in default, the Note Holder does not require me to pay immediately in full as described above, the Note Holder will still have the right to do so if I am in default at a later time.

(E) Payment of Note Holder's Costs and Expenses

If the Note Holder has required me to pay immediately in full as described above, the Note Holder will have the right to be paid back by me for all of its costs and expenses in enforcing this Note to the extent not prohibited by applicable law. Those expenses include, for example, reasonable attorneys' fees.

7. GIVING OF NOTICES

Unless applicable law requires a different method, any notice that must be given to me under this Note will be given by delivering it or by mailing it by first class mail to me at the Property Address above or at a different address if I give the Note Holder a notice of my different address.

Any notice that must be given to the Note Holder under this Note will be given by mailing it by first class mail to the Note Holder at the address stated in Section 3(A) above or at a different address if I am given a notice of that different address.

8. OBLIGATIONS OF PERSONS UNDER THIS NOTE

If more than one person signs this Note, each person is fully and personally obligated to keep all of the promises made in this Note, including the promise to pay the full amount owed. Any person who is a guarantor, surety or endorser of this Note is also obligated to do these things. Any person who takes over these obligations, including the obligations of a guarantor, surety or endorser of this Note, is also obligated to keep all of the promises made in this Note. The Note Holder may enforce its rights under this Note against each person individually or against all of us together. This means that any one of us may be required to pay all of the amounts owed under this Note.

9. WAIVERS

I and any other person who has obligations under this Note waive the rights of presentment and notice of dishonor. "Presentment" means the right to require the Note Holder to demand payment of amounts due. "Notice of dishonor" means the right to require the Note Holder to give notice to other persons that amounts due have not been paid.

10. UNIFORM SECURED NOTE

This Note is a uniform instrument with limited variations in some jurisdictions. In addition to the protections given to the Note Holder under this Note, a Mortgage, Deed of Trust or Security Deed (the "Security Instrument"), dated the same date as this Note, protects the Note Holder from possible losses which might result if I do not keep the promises which I make in this Note. That Security Instrument describes how and under what conditions I may be required to make immediate payment in full of all amounts I owe under this Note. Some of those conditions are described as follows:

Transfer of the Property or a Beneficial Interest in Borrower. If all or any part of the Property or any interest in it is sold or transferred (or if a beneficial interest in Borrower is sold or transferred and Borrower is not a natural person) without Lender's prior written consent, Lender may, at its option, require immediate payment in full of all sums secured by this Security Instrument. However, this option shall not be exercised by Lender if exercise is prohibited by federal law as of the date of this Security Instrument.

If Lender exercises this option, Lender shall give Borrower notice of acceleration. The notice shall provide a period of not less than 30 days from the date the notice is delivered or mailed within which Borrower must pay all sums secured by this Security Instrument. If Borrower fails to pay these sums prior to the expiration of this period, Lender may invoke any remedies permitted by this Security Instrument without further notice or demand on Borrower.

WITNESS THE HAND(S) AND SEAL(S) OF THE UNDERSIGNED.

....(Seal)
-Borrower

....(Seal)
-Borrower

....(Seal)
-Borrower

[Sign Original Only]

(E5996)

MORTGAGE

THIS MORTGAGE ("Security Instrument") is given on .... ,
19 .... The mortgagor is ....
.... ("Borrower"). This Security Instrument is given to ....
.... , which is organized and existing
under the laws of .... , and whose address is ....
.... ("Lender").
Borrower owes Lender the principal sum of ....
.... Dollars (U.S. $ ....). This debt is evidenced by Borrower's note
dated the same date as this Security Instrument ("Note"), which provides for monthly payments, with the full debt, if not
paid earlier, due and payable on .... This Security Instrument
secures to Lender: (a) the repayment of the debt evidenced by the Note, with interest, and all renewals, extensions and
modifications of the Note; (b) the payment of all other sums, with interest, advanced under paragraph 7 to protect the security
of this Security Instrument; and (c) the performance of Borrower's covenants and agreements under this Security Instrument
and the Note. For this purpose, Borrower does hereby mortgage, grant and convey to Lender the following described property
located in .... County, Indiana:

which has the address of .... , ... ,
                                              [Street]   [City]

Indiana .... ("Property Address");
               [Zip Code]

TOGETHER WITH all the improvements now or hereafter erected on the property, and all easements, appurtenances,
and fixtures now or hereafter a part of the property. All replacements and additions shall also be covered by this Security
Instrument. All of the foregoing is referred to in this Security Instrument as the "Property."

BORROWER COVENANTS that Borrower is lawfully seised of the estate hereby conveyed and has the right to mortgage,
grant and convey the Property and that the Property is unencumbered, except for encumbrances of record. Borrower warrants
and will defend generally the title to the Property against all claims and demands, subject to any encumbrances of record.

THIS SECURITY INSTRUMENT combines uniform covenants for national use and non-uniform covenants with limited
variations by jurisdiction to constitute a uniform security instrument covering real property.

INDIANA—Single Family—Fannie Mae/Freddie Mac UNIFORM INSTRUMENT   **Form 3015**   **9/90**   *(page 1 of 6 pages)*
                                                                                                           [G16501]

UNIFORM COVENANTS. Borrower and Lender covenant and agree as follows:

1. Payment of Principal and Interest; Prepayment and Late Charges. Borrower shall promptly pay when due the principal of and interest on the debt evidenced by the Note and any prepayment and late charges due under the Note.

2. Funds for Taxes and Insurance. Subject to applicable law or to a written waiver by Lender, Borrower shall pay to Lender on the day monthly payments are due under the Note, until the Note is paid in full, a sum ("Funds") for: (a) yearly taxes and assessments which may attain priority over this Security Instrument as a lien on the Property; (b) yearly leasehold payments or ground rents on the Property, if any; (c) yearly hazard or property insurance premiums; (d) yearly flood insurance premiums, if any; (e) yearly mortgage insurance premiums, if any; and (f) any sums payable by Borrower to Lender, in accordance with the provisions of paragraph 8, in lieu of the payment of mortgage insurance premiums. These items are called "Escrow Items." Lender may, at any time, collect and hold Funds in an amount not to exceed the maximum amount a lender for a federally related mortgage loan may require for Borrower's escrow account under the federal Real Estate Settlement Procedures Act of 1974 as amended from time to time, 12 U.S.C. § 2601 *et seq.* ("RESPA"), unless another law that applies to the Funds sets a lesser amount. If so, Lender may, at any time, collect and hold Funds in an amount not to exceed the lesser amount. Lender may estimate the amount of Funds due on the basis of current data and reasonable estimates of expenditures of future Escrow Items or otherwise in accordance with applicable law.

The Funds shall be held in an institution whose deposits are insured by a federal agency, instrumentality, or entity (including Lender, if Lender is such an institution) or in any Federal Home Loan Bank. Lender shall apply the Funds to pay the Escrow Items. Lender may not charge Borrower for holding and applying the Funds, annually analyzing the escrow account, or verifying the Escrow Items, unless Lender pays Borrower interest on the Funds and applicable law permits Lender to make such a charge. However, Lender may require Borrower to pay a one-time charge for an independent real estate tax reporting service used by Lender in connection with this loan, unless applicable law provides otherwise. Unless an agreement is made or applicable law requires interest to be paid, Lender shall not be required to pay Borrower any interest or earnings on the Funds. Borrower and Lender may agree in writing, however, that interest shall be paid on the Funds. Lender shall give to Borrower, without charge, an annual accounting of the Funds, showing credits and debits to the Funds and the purpose for which each debit to the Funds was made. The Funds are pledged as additional security for all sums secured by this Security Instrument.

If the Funds held by Lender exceed the amounts permitted to be held by applicable law, Lender shall account to Borrower for the excess Funds in accordance with the requirements of applicable law. If the amount of the Funds held by Lender at any time is not sufficient to pay the Escrow Items when due, Lender may so notify Borrower in writing, and, in such case Borrower shall pay to Lender the amount necessary to make up the deficiency. Borrower shall make up the deficiency in no more than twelve monthly payments, at Lender's sole discretion.

Upon payment in full of all sums secured by this Security Instrument, Lender shall promptly refund to Borrower any Funds held by Lender. If, under paragraph 21, Lender shall acquire or sell the Property, Lender, prior to the acquisition or sale of the Property, shall apply any Funds held by Lender at the time of acquisition or sale as a credit against the sums secured by this Security Instrument.

3. Application of Payments. Unless applicable law provides otherwise, all payments received by Lender under paragraphs 1 and 2 shall be applied: first, to any prepayment charges due under the Note; second, to amounts payable under paragraph 2; third, to interest due; fourth, to principal due; and last, to any late charges due under the Note.

4. Charges; Liens. Borrower shall pay all taxes, assessments, charges, fines and impositions attributable to the Property which may attain priority over this Security Instrument, and leasehold payments or ground rents, if any. Borrower shall pay these obligations in the manner provided in paragraph 2, or if not paid in that manner, Borrower shall pay them on time directly to the person owed payment. Borrower shall promptly furnish to Lender all notices of amounts to be paid under this paragraph. If Borrower makes these payments directly, Borrower shall promptly furnish to Lender receipts evidencing the payments.

Borrower shall promptly discharge any lien which has priority over this Security Instrument unless Borrower: (a) agrees in writing to the payment of the obligation secured by the lien in a manner acceptable to Lender; (b) contests in good faith the lien by, or defends against enforcement of the lien in, legal proceedings which in the Lender's opinion operate to prevent the enforcement of the lien; or (c) secures from the holder of the lien an agreement satisfactory to Lender subordinating the lien to this Security Instrument. If Lender determines that any part of the Property is subject to a lien which may attain priority over this Security Instrument, Lender may give Borrower a notice identifying the lien. Borrower shall satisfy the lien or take one or more of the actions set forth above within 10 days of the giving of notice.

5. Hazard or Property Insurance. Borrower shall keep the improvements now existing or hereafter erected on the Property insured against loss by fire, hazards included within the term "extended coverage" and any other hazards, including floods or flooding, for which Lender requires insurance. This insurance shall be maintained in the amounts and for the periods that Lender requires. The insurance carrier providing the insurance shall be chosen by Borrower subject to Lender's approval which shall not be unreasonably withheld. If Borrower fails to maintain coverage described above, Lender may, at Lender's option, obtain coverage to protect Lender's rights in the Property in accordance with paragraph 7.

All insurance policies and renewals shall be acceptable to Lender and shall include a standard mortgage clause. Lender shall have the right to hold the policies and renewals. If Lender requires, Borrower shall promptly give to Lender all receipts of paid premiums and renewal notices. In the event of loss, Borrower shall give prompt notice to the insurance carrier and Lender. Lender may make proof of loss if not made promptly by Borrower.

Unless Lender and Borrower otherwise agree in writing, insurance proceeds shall be applied to restoration or repair of the Property damaged, if the restoration or repair is economically feasible and Lender's security is not lessened. If the restoration or repair is not economically feasible or Lender's security would be lessened, the insurance proceeds shall be applied to the sums secured by this Security Instrument, whether or not then due, with any excess paid to Borrower. If Borrower abandons the Property, or does not answer within 30 days a notice from Lender that the insurance carrier has offered to settle a claim, then Lender may collect the insurance proceeds. Lender may use the proceeds to repair or restore the Property or to pay sums secured by this Security Instrument, whether or not then due. The 30-day period will begin when the notice is given.

Unless Lender and Borrower otherwise agree in writing, any application of proceeds to principal shall not extend or postpone the due date of the monthly payments referred to in paragraphs 1 and 2 or change the amount of the payments. If under paragraph 21 the Property is acquired by Lender, Borrower's right to any insurance policies and proceeds resulting from damage to the Property prior to the acquisition shall pass to Lender to the extent of the sums secured by this Security Instrument immediately prior to the acquisition.

6. Occupancy, Preservation, Maintenance and Protection of the Property; Borrower's Loan Application: Leaseholds.   Borrower shall occupy, establish, and use the Property as Borrower's principal residence within sixty days after the execution of this Security Instrument and shall continue to occupy the Property as Borrower's principal residence for at least one year after the date of occupancy, unless Lender otherwise agrees in writing, which consent shall not be unreasonably withheld, or unless extenuating circumstances exist which are beyond Borrower's control. Borrower shall not destroy, damage or impair the Property, allow the Property to deteriorate, or commit waste on the Property. Borrower shall be in default if any forfeiture action or proceeding, whether civil or criminal, is begun that in Lender's good faith judgment could result in forfeiture of the Property or otherwise materially impair the lien created by this Security Instrument or Lender's security interest. Borrower may cure such a default and reinstate, as provided in paragraph 18, by causing the action or proceeding to be dismissed with a ruling that, in Lender's good faith determination, precludes forfeiture of the Borrower's interest in the Property or other material impairment of the lien created by this Security Instrument or Lender's security interest. Borrower shall also be in default if Borrower, during the loan application process, gave materially false or inaccurate information or statements to Lender (or failed to provide Lender with any material information) in connection with the loan evidenced by the Note, including, but not limited to, representations concerning Borrower's occupancy of the Property as a principal residence. If this Security Instrument is on a leasehold, Borrower shall comply with all the provisions of the lease. If Borrower acquires fee title to the Property, the leasehold and the fee title shall not merge unless Lender agrees to the merger in writing.

7. Protection of Lender's Rights in the Property.   If Borrower fails to perform the covenants and agreements contained in this Security Instrument, or there is a legal proceeding that may significantly affect Lender's rights in the Property (such as a proceeding in bankruptcy, probate, for condemnation or forfeiture or to enforce laws or regulations), then Lender may do and pay for whatever is necessary to protect the value of the Property and Lender's rights in the Property. Lender's actions may include paying any sums secured by a lien which has priority over this Security Instrument, appearing in court, paying reasonable attorneys' fees and entering on the Property to make repairs. Although Lender may take action under this paragraph 7, Lender does not have to do so.

Any amounts disbursed by Lender under this paragraph 7 shall become additional debt of Borrower secured by this Security Instrument. Unless Borrower and Lender agree to other terms of payment, these amounts shall bear interest from the date of disbursement at the Note rate and shall be payable, with interest, upon notice from Lender to Borrower requesting payment.

8. Mortgage Insurance.   If Lender required mortgage insurance as a condition of making the loan secured by this Security Instrument, Borrower shall pay the premiums required to maintain the mortgage insurance in effect. If, for any reason, the mortgage insurance coverage required by Lender lapses or ceases to be in effect, Borrower shall pay the premiums required to obtain coverage substantially equivalent to the mortgage insurance previously in effect, at a cost substantially equivalent to the cost to Borrower of the mortgage insurance previously in effect, from an alternate mortgage insurer approved by Lender. If substantially equivalent mortgage insurance coverage is not available, Borrower shall pay to Lender each month a sum equal to one-twelfth of the yearly mortgage insurance premium being paid by Borrower when the insurance coverage lapsed or ceased to be in effect. Lender will accept, use and retain these payments as a loss reserve in lieu of mortgage insurance. Loss reserve payments may no longer be required, at the option of Lender, if mortgage insurance coverage (in the amount and for the period that Lender requires) provided by an insurer approved by Lender again becomes available and is obtained. Borrower shall pay the premiums required to maintain mortgage insurance in effect, or to provide a loss reserve, until the requirement for mortgage insurance ends in accordance with any written agreement between Borrower and Lender or applicable law.

Form 3015   9/90   *(page 3 of 6 pages)*

(G16505)

9. Inspection. Lender or its agent may make reasonable entries upon and inspections of the Property. Lender shall give Borrower notice at the time of or prior to an inspection specifying reasonable cause for the inspection.

10. Condemnation. The proceeds of any award or claim for damages, direct or consequential, in connection with any condemnation or other taking of any part of the Property, or for conveyance in lieu of condemnation, are hereby assigned and shall be paid to Lender.

In the event of a total taking of the Property, the proceeds shall be applied to the sums secured by this Security Instrument, whether or not then due, with any excess paid to Borrower. In the event of a partial taking of the Property in which the fair market value of the Property immediately before the taking is equal to or greater than the amount of the sums secured by this Security Instrument immediately before the taking, unless Borrower and Lender otherwise agree in writing, the sums secured by this Security Instrument shall be reduced by the amount of the proceeds multiplied by the following fraction: (a) the total amount of the sums secured immediately before the taking, divided by (b) the fair market value of the Property immediately before the taking. Any balance shall be paid to Borrower. In the event of a partial taking of the Property in which the fair market value of the Property immediately before the taking is less than the amount of the sums secured immediately before the taking, unless Borrower and Lender otherwise agree in writing or unless applicable law otherwise provides, the proceeds shall be applied to the sums secured by this Security Instrument whether or not the sums are then due.

If the Property is abandoned by Borrower, or if, after notice by Lender to Borrower that the condemnor offers to make an award or settle a claim for damages, Borrower fails to respond to Lender within 30 days after the date the notice is given, Lender is authorized to collect and apply the proceeds, at its option, either to restoration or repair of the Property or to the sums secured by this Security Instrument, whether or not then due.

Unless Lender and Borrower otherwise agree in writing, any application of proceeds to principal shall not extend or postpone the due date of the monthly payments referred to in paragraphs 1 and 2 or change the amount of such payments.

11. Borrower Not Released; Forbearance By Lender Not a Waiver. Extension of the time for payment or modification of amortization of the sums secured by this Security Instrument granted by Lender to any successor in interest of Borrower shall not operate to release the liability of the original Borrower or Borrower's successors in interest. Lender shall not be required to commence proceedings against any successor in interest or refuse to extend time for payment or otherwise modify amortization of the sums secured by this Security Instrument by reason of any demand made by the original Borrower or Borrower's successors in interest. Any forbearance by Lender in exercising any right or remedy shall not be a waiver of or preclude the exercise of any right or remedy.

12. Successors and Assigns Bound; Joint and Several Liability; Co-signers. The covenants and agreements of this Security Instrument shall bind and benefit the successors and assigns of Lender and Borrower, subject to the provisions of paragraph 17. Borrower's covenants and agreements shall be joint and several. Any Borrower who co-signs this Security Instrument but does not execute the Note: (a) is co-signing this Security Instrument only to mortgage, grant and convey that Borrower's interest in the Property under the terms of this Security Instrument; (b) is not personally obligated to pay the sums secured by this Security Instrument; and (c) agrees that Lender and any other Borrower may agree to extend, modify, forbear or make any accommodations with regard to the terms of this Security Instrument or the Note without that Borrower's consent.

13. Loan Charges. If the loan secured by this Security Instrument is subject to a law which sets maximum loan charges, and that law is finally interpreted so that the interest or other loan charges collected or to be collected in connection with the loan exceed the permitted limits, then: (a) any such loan charge shall be reduced by the amount necessary to reduce the charge to the permitted limit; and (b) any sums already collected from Borrower which exceeded permitted limits will be refunded to Borrower. Lender may choose to make this refund by reducing the principal owed under the Note or by making a direct payment to Borrower. If a refund reduces principal, the reduction will be treated as a partial prepayment without any prepayment charge under the Note.

14. Notices. Any notice to Borrower provided for in this Security Instrument shall be given by delivering it or by mailing it by first class mail unless applicable law requires use of another method. The notice shall be directed to the Property Address or any other address Borrower designates by notice to Lender. Any notice to Lender shall be given by first class mail to Lender's address stated herein or any other address Lender designates by notice to Borrower. Any notice provided for in this Security Instrument shall be deemed to have been given to Borrower or Lender when given as provided in this paragraph.

15. Governing Law; Severability. This Security Instrument shall be governed by federal law and the law of the jurisdiction in which the Property is located. In the event that any provision or clause of this Security Instrument or the Note conflicts with applicable law, such conflict shall not affect other provisions of this Security Instrument or the Note which can be given effect without the conflicting provision. To this end the provisions of this Security Instrument and the Note are declared to be severable.

16. Borrower's Copy. Borrower shall be given one conformed copy of the Note and of this Security Instrument.

17. Transfer of the Property or a Beneficial Interest in Borrower. If all or any part of the Property or any interest in it is sold or transferred (or if a beneficial interest in Borrower is sold or transferred and Borrower is not a natural person) without Lender's prior written consent, Lender may, at its option, require immediate payment in full of all sums secured by this Security Instrument. However, this option shall not be exercised by Lender if exercise is prohibited by federal law as of the date of this Security Instrument.

If Lender exercises this option, Lender shall give Borrower notice of acceleration. The notice shall provide a period of not less than 30 days from the date the notice is delivered or mailed within which Borrower must pay all sums secured by this Security Instrument. If Borrower fails to pay these sums prior to the expiration of this period, Lender may invoke any remedies permitted by this Security Instrument without further notice or demand on Borrower.

18. Borrower's Right to Reinstate. If Borrower meets certain conditions, Borrower shall have the right to have enforcement of this Security Instrument discontinued at any time prior to the earlier of: (a) 5 days (or such other period as applicable law may specify for reinstatement) before sale of the Property pursuant to any power of sale contained in this Security Instrument; or (b) entry of a judgment enforcing this Security Instrument. Those conditions are that Borrower: (a) pays Lender all sums which then would be due under this Security Instrument and the Note as if no acceleration had occurred; (b) cures any default of any other covenants or agreements; (c) pays all expenses incurred in enforcing this Security Instrument, including, but not limited to, reasonable attorneys' fees; and (d) takes such action as Lender may reasonably require to assure that the lien of this Security Instrument, Lender's rights in the Property and Borrower's obligation to pay the sums secured by this Security Instrument shall continue unchanged. Upon reinstatement by Borrower, this Security Instrument and the obligations secured hereby shall remain fully effective as if no acceleration had occurred. However, this right to reinstate shall not apply in the case of acceleration under paragraph 17.

19. Sale of Note; Change of Loan Servicer. The Note or a partial interest in the Note (together with this Security Instrument) may be sold one or more times without prior notice to Borrower. A sale may result in a change in the entity (known as the "Loan Servicer") that collects monthly payments due under the Note and this Security Instrument. There also may be one or more changes of the Loan Servicer unrelated to a sale of the Note. If there is a change of the Loan Servicer, Borrower will be given written notice of the change in accordance with paragraph 14 above and applicable law. The notice will state the name and address of the new Loan Servicer and the address to which payments should be made. The notice will also contain any other information required by applicable law.

20. Hazardous Substances. Borrower shall not cause or permit the presence, use, disposal, storage, or release of any Hazardous Substances on or in the Property. Borrower shall not do, nor allow anyone else to do, anything affecting the Property that is in violation of any Environmental Law. The preceding two sentences shall not apply to the presence, use, or storage on the Property of small quantities of Hazardous Substances that are generally recognized to be appropriate to normal residential uses and to maintenance of the Property.

Borrower shall promptly give Lender written notice of any investigation, claim, demand, lawsuit or other action by any governmental or regulatory agency or private party involving the Property and any Hazardous Substance or Environmental Law of which Borrower has actual knowledge. If Borrower learns, or is notified by any governmental or regulatory authority, that any removal or other remediation of any Hazardous Substance affecting the Property is necessary, Borrower shall promptly take all necessary remedial actions in accordance with Environmental Law.

As used in this paragraph 20, "Hazardous Substances" are those substances defined as toxic or hazardous substances by Environmental Law and the following substances: gasoline, kerosene, other flammable or toxic petroleum products, toxic pesticides and herbicides, volatile solvents, materials containing asbestos or formaldehyde, and radioactive materials. As used in this paragraph 20, "Environmental Law" means federal laws and laws of the jurisdiction where the Property is located that relate to health, safety or environmental protection.

NON-UNIFORM COVENANTS. Borrower and Lender further covenant and agree as follows:

21. Acceleration; Remedies. Lender shall give notice to Borrower prior to acceleration following Borrower's breach of any covenant or agreement in this Security Instrument (but not prior to acceleration under paragraph 17 unless applicable law provides otherwise). The notice shall specify: (a) the default; (b) the action required to cure the default; (c) a date, not less than 30 days from the date the notice is given to Borrower, by which the default must be cured; and (d) that failure to cure the default on or before the date specified in the notice may result in acceleration of the sums secured by this Security Instrument, foreclosure by judicial proceeding and sale of the Property. The notice shall further inform Borrower of the right to reinstate after acceleration and the right to assert in the foreclosure proceeding the non-existence of a default or any other defense of Borrower to acceleration and foreclosure. If the default is not cured on or before the date specified in the notice, Lender at its option may require immediate payment in full of all sums secured by this Security Instrument without further demand and may foreclose this Security Instrument by judicial proceeding. Lender shall be entitled to collect all expenses incurred in pursuing the remedies provided in this paragraph 21, including, but not limited to, reasonable attorneys' fees and costs of title evidence.

22. Release. Upon payment of all sums secured by this Security Instrument, Lender shall release this Security Instrument without charge to Borrower.

23. Waiver of Valuation and Appraisement. Borrower waives all right of valuation and appraisement.

Form 3015   9/90   *(page 5 of 6 pages)*

[G16504]

24. Riders to this Security Instrument. If one or more riders are executed by Borrower and recorded together with this Security Instrument, the covenants and agreements of each such rider shall be incorporated into and shall amend and supplement the covenants and agreements of this Security Instrument as if the rider(s) were a part of this Security Instrument. [Check applicable box(es)]

☐ Adjustable Rate Rider   ☐ Condominium Rider   ☐ 1—4 Family Rider

☐ Graduated Payment Rider   ☐ Planned Unit Development Rider   ☐ Biweekly Payment Rider

☐ Balloon Rider   ☐ Rate Improvement Rider   ☐ Second Home Rider

☐ Other(s) [specify]

BY SIGNING BELOW, Borrower accepts and agrees to the terms and covenants contained in this Security Instrument and in any rider(s) executed by Borrower and recorded with it.

Witnesses:

....(Seal)
                                                                  —Borrower

Social Security Number...

....(Seal)
                                                                  —Borrower

Social Security Number...

———————————————— [Space Below This Line For Acknowledgment] ————————————————

Form 3815   9/90   *(page 6 of 6 pages)*
(G16602)

d. Underlying Obligation—Interest Rates

An obligation, usually a promissory note, underlies each mortgage. The typical mortgage note bears a fixed-interest rate and is fully amortized with equal-monthly installments over a fifteen to thirty year term. Each installment includes payment of accrued interest and part of the outstanding principal. Early in the loan term, the interest segment of the payment is larger than the principal component. Over time, this situation changes until near the end of the term most of each monthly installment is applied to principal.

Inflation and the fluctuating cost of mortgage money spurred mortgage lenders to devise the adjustable rate mortgage (ARM) as an alternative to the traditional fixed-interest-rate mortgage. An ARM provides for an interest rate that rises and falls over the term of the loan in accordance with a specified economic index. Any modification may be reflected either by adjusting the amount of monthly payments or by varying the loan term. *See* R. Kratovil & R. Werner, Modern Mortgage Law and Practice §§ 29.02(a)–29.02(a)(11) (2d ed. 1981); G. Nelson & D. Whitman, Real Estate Finance Law § 11.4 (3d ed. 1994).

Question

In our hypothetical situation, the Ryans have requested advice about the adjustable rate mortgage (ARM). Assuming that the Ryans are willing to use this mortgage format, what specific provisions in an ARM might prove unduly burdensome to them? What limitations would you require on such provisions?

e. *Subject to Financing Clause*

Because the Ryans need a loan in order to purchase the house in Rolling Hills, they should condition their contractual responsibility upon obtaining the necessary financing. *See* paragraph 4 of the sample contract on page 482, for a subject to financing clause. Such clauses are a frequent source of litigation. *See* Aiken, *'Subject to Financing' Clauses in Interim Contracts for Sale of Realty*, 43 Marq.L.Rev. 265 (1960).

BRUYERE v. JADE REALTY CORP.

Supreme Court of New Hampshire, 1977.
117 N.H. 564, 375 A.2d 600.

Per Curiam.

The issue herein is whether the plaintiffs are entitled to recover their deposit upon a piece of real estate, where the obligations under the purchase and sale agreement were made subject to the buyers' obtaining of bank financing and such financing was first granted but then subsequently revoked due to the plaintiffs' decision to file for divorce. For the reasons which follow below, we hold that the plaintiffs are not entitled to the return of their deposit.

The plaintiffs deposited $1,000 with the defendant in accordance with a purchase and sale agreement between the parties for a piece of residential real estate, dated May 16, 1975, which provided that the contract was "subject to financing at 7 ¾% for thirty (30) years." The closing date was set for August 1, 1975. The plaintiffs applied for financing approval from the Nashua Federal Savings and Loan Association, which was granted on June 17, 1975. Marital problems between the plaintiffs at this time led them to decide to separate and file for divorce. The lender was informed of this development on June 30, 1975, by Mrs. Bruyere, who proposed that she alone purchase the home and assume the financing terms outlined in the bank's previous letter of commitment. The bank declined, stating that one income would not suffice to carry the mortgage in question, and withdrew its financing commitment. Alternative financing could not be arranged, and the deal fell through. The plaintiffs sought the return of their deposit. They argued that they had not breached their agreement, for their obligation was expressly conditioned on the obtaining of financing, and such financing was not available to them as of August 1, 1975, the date of closing. The District Court (*Kfoury,* J.) agreed, and granted a verdict for the plaintiffs. The defendant's exceptions thereto were reserved and transferred.

We cannot adopt the plaintiffs' position. It is true, as they allege, that the grant of bank financing was a condition precedent to the obligations under the contract. The purpose of this frequently utilized provision, however, is merely to protect prospective purchasers from committing a technical breach of contract due to their inability, based on the facts and circumstances present at the time of the signing of the purchase and sale agreement, or due to some fortuitous intervening event, to secure the funds necessary to complete the purchase. The defendant herein contracted with a married couple. The conditional financing provision was inserted under the understanding that the mortgage would be sought by two wage earners. The seller was able to weigh the plaintiffs' likelihood of success under these conditions, and accepted the studied risk of taking its property off the market despite the possibility that the transaction might fail. We do not believe the intent of the financing clause was to place upon the seller the hazard that the plaintiffs would alter their circumstances, and therefore their borrowing potential, through a voluntary act of their own.

We hold that the intent of the financing clause is to protect the buyer from involuntary breach. Where, however, the condition precedent of financing is first satisfied, but then fails because of some action voluntarily undertaken by the buyer, we find that the risk of the failure of the transaction is properly imposed upon the party who so acts and not upon the innocent seller.

Exceptions sustained.

HOMLER v. MALAS

Court of Appeals of Georgia, 1997.
229 Ga.App. 390, 494 S.E.2d 18.

McMURRAY, PRESIDING JUDGE.

Plaintiffs Robert Homler and Barbara Homler filed this breach of contract action against defendant Mohannad Malas. The complaint alleges that defendant Malas agreed to buy and plaintiffs agreed to sell a single family residence, that the agreement was conditioned on defendant obtaining a loan to finance the purchase, and that defendant breached the agreement by failing to diligently pursue in good faith his applications for a loan. The plaintiffs seek damages for the alleged breach of contract, and also expenses of litigation pursuant to OCGA § 13–6–11 and disbursement of $25,000 earnest money paid by defendant and held by the real estate agent who effected the sale, defendant Harry Norman Realtors. Defendant Malas answered denying plaintiffs' claims, and via counterclaim and cross-claim against defendant Harry Norman Realtors sought return of the earnest money. The defendant broker, Harry Norman Realtors, interpleaded the earnest money into the registry of the trial court and sought attorney fees for having to interplead.

Defendant Malas moved for summary judgment on the ground that the contract sought to be enforced is too vague and indefinite to be enforced in that the terms of the loan to be obtained by defendant under the terms of the financing contingency are not sufficiently identified. Summary judgment was granted in favor of defendant Malas both as to plaintiffs' claims and as to defendant's counterclaim seeking return of the earnest money. Attorney fees of $807.50 were awarded to defendant Harry Norman Realtors and the balance of the earnest money was ordered disbursed to defendant. Plaintiffs appeal. Held:

The document executed by the parties was created using a pre-printed contract. The form included a number of blank spaces for insertion of various information. With regard to the loan contingency provisions there were blank spaces for certain terms of the loan to be obtained by the buyer. Blank spaces were completed to indicate that the agreement was conditioned on the buyer "obtaining" a loan in the principal amount of 80 percent of the purchase price to be paid in monthly installments over a term of no less than 30 years. (Although not germane to our decision of the case, we note that the pre-printed contingency clause had been altered by striking a portion of a provision that the agreement was conditional on buyer's "ability to obtain" a loan as described and substituting the word "obtaining.") Two spaces where interest rates could have been provided, as well as a third space where a monthly payment amount could have been provided and from which an interest rate could be calculated, were left blank.

The appellate courts of Georgia have consistently held that such a contract is too vague and indefinite to be enforced since the failure to specify at what rate the buyer is to obtain a mortgage loan causes a failure of a condition precedent to the enforceability of the contract. While plaintiffs assert that there was no need to specify the interest rate of the loan to be obtained by defendant Malas because third-party financing, such as contemplated in the loan contingency executed by the parties, invokes a less stringent requirement to state the specific terms of the anticipated loan, the absence of any authority approving of the omission of such an essential loan term as the interest rate must be noted. Plaintiffs cite Walker v. Anderson, 131 Ga.App. 596, 206 S.E.2d 833, in which the interest rate was not omitted but incorporated by reference to the "prevailing interest rate" and this Court held that a loan contingency anticipating a third-party loan was enforceable under this less stringent standard even though it did not state a payment schedule for the loan such as would be necessary in the case of a deferred-payment-to-seller clause. It must be noted that variations in the payment schedule would be a matter between the lender and the buyer which would not affect a buyer's obligations to a seller. In contrast, the interest rate is an essential term necessary to enable the courts to enforce the contract between buyer and seller.

Contrary to plaintiffs' assertion, Barto v. Hicks, 124 Ga.App. 472, 474, 184 S.E.2d 188, like Walker v. Anderson, 131 Ga.App. 596, 206 S.E.2d 833, supra, is not a case in which there is a failure to specify the interest rate of the anticipated loan. Instead, the interest rate in Barto was specified by reference to the readily ascertainable "current prevailing rate." There is nothing in the document at issue in the present case which amounts to a reference to any source from which an interest rate for the loan which defendant Malas was to seek may be determined.

* * *

The superior court did not err in granting summary judgment in favor of defendant Malas on plaintiffs' claims. It follows that the grant of summary judgment in favor of defendant Malas on his counterclaim seeking the return of the earnest money was proper. * * *

Judgment affirmed.

Notes and Questions

1. Courts have reached different results over whether language in a subject to financing clause was sufficiently precise to be enforced. *Compare* Smith v. Vernon, 6 Ill.App.3d 434, 286 N.E.2d 99 (1972) (provision "subject to purchasers' ability to secure a first mortgage" was not ambiguous because clause interpreted to require that mortgage terms be reasonable) *with* Schreiber v. Delia, 222 A.D.2d 1063, 635 N.Y.S.2d 876 (1995) (language creating financing option at "current commercial loan rates" was enforceable because interest rate could be ascertained by consulting extrinsic standard). Are these decisions consistent with the reasoning in *Homler*?

2. Suppose the contract in *Homler* contained a subject to financing clause that made the contract contingent upon the purchaser securing a mortgage at the "prevailing rate of interest." Would the offer of an adjustable rate mortgage satisfy this condition? *See* Gaynes v. Allen, 116 N.H. 469, 362 A.2d 197 (1976).

3. Courts widely hold that a subject to financing clause imposes an implied duty upon the purchaser to make a good faith effort to obtain a loan. *See* Duncan v. Rossuck, 621 So.2d 1313 (Ala.1993). What constitutes a reasonable effort is often a matter of controversy. Is application to a single lending institution sufficient? See Liuzza v. Panzer, 333 So.2d 689 (La.App. 1976). Must the purchaser submit written loan applications rather than make oral inquiries? *Compare* Case v. Forloine, 266 Ill.App.3d 120, 203 Ill.Dec. 256, 639 N.E.2d 576 (1993) (under circumstances purchaser made good faith effort despite failure to file written application) *with* Scherer v. Nase, 405 Pa.Super. 37, 591 A.2d 1086 (1991) ("good faith effort requires more than an oral inquiry").

f. May the Purchaser Take Over an Existing Mortgage?

When the mortgage money is scarce or available only at high interest rates, the purchaser of mortgaged property may wish to take over an existing mortgage. The purchaser may do this by paying the seller the amount of the seller's "equity"[1] and either taking the property "subject to" the mortgage or "assuming" the mortgage. In both cases the existing mortgage continues on the land, the original mortgagor remains liable as surety unless released by the mortgagee, and the purchaser makes the mortgage payments. *See* Berg v. Liberty Federal Savings and Loan Association, 428 A.2d 347 (Del.1981). The difference between the "subject to" conveyance and the "assumption" conveyance

---

1. The seller's "equity" is the amount by which the purchase price exceeds the unpaid balance of the existing mortgage.

lies in the nature of the rights the mortgagee has against the purchaser. Suppose the purchaser merely takes subject to the mortgage. Upon default the mortgagee may foreclose and have the mortgaged property sold to pay the debt, but cannot hold the purchaser liable for any deficiency. In the assumption conveyance, the purchaser takes the property encumbered by the mortgage and assumes personal liability for the mortgage debt. Thus, upon default the mortgagee may institute foreclosure procedures to have the mortgaged property sold and also may recover any deficiency from the purchaser. *See* G. Nelson & D. Whitman, Real Estate Finance Law §§ 5.1–5.4 (3d ed. 1994).

Most mortgages contain a due-on-sale clause which permits the mortgagee to accelerate the loan if the mortgaged property is conveyed without its consent. *See* paragraph 17 of the sample mortgage on pages 509–510. The due-on-sale clause is utilized by lenders to rid themselves of mortgage loans bearing low interest rates. The Garn–St. Germain Depository Institutions Act of 1982 provides that mortgage due-on-sale clauses are enforceable as specified in the loan contract, with the narrow exception that certain types of transfer of residential mortgaged property "containing less than five dwelling units" will not trigger a due-on-sale clause. 12 U.S.C.A. § 1701j–3 (1989). *See* G. Nelson & D. Whitman, Real Estate Finance Law §§ 5.21–5.24 (3d ed. 1994); Barad & Layden, *Due-on-Sale Law as Preempted by the Garn–St. Germain Act,* 12 Real Est.L.J. 138 (1983); Geier, *Due-on-Sale Clauses under the Garn–St. Germain Depository Institutions Act of 1982,* 17 U.S.F.L.Rev. 355 (1983).

g. *Prepayment*

In a financial climate where mortgage interest rates are falling or have stabilized at a low level, a landowner burdened by a mortgage bearing a relatively high interest rate may wish to prepay that mortgage and refinance at the current lower rate. Mortgagors seeking to prepay an existing mortgage for this or other reasons face certain legal issues.

The mortgagor initially must determine whether the right to prepay exists. Residential mortgage documents commonly grant the mortgagor the right to prepay. *See* paragraph 4 of the sample note on page 504. However, the general rule is that, without such a clause or a statute authorizing prepayment, the mortgagor has no right to pay early and must adhere to the payment schedule specified in the mortgage note. The notion is that the mortgagee is entitled to receive payment in the manner upon which the parties originally agreed.

Even if the mortgage documents grant the mortgagor the right to pay early, prepayment may be conditioned on the remittance of a fee for the opportunity to prepay. Prepayment fees are common in commercial mortgages. A number of states have enacted statutes limiting their use in connection with the prepayment of residential mortgages.

See G. Nelson & D. Whitman, Real Estate Finance Law §§ 6.1–6.5 (3d ed. 1994); Whitman, *Mortgage Prepayment Clauses; An Economic and Legal Analysis,* 40 UCLA L.Rev. 851 (1993).

2. INSTALLMENT LAND CONTRACT

The installment land contract, sometimes called a land contract or contract for deed, is an alternative to mortgage financing. This contractual arrangement for the sale of land permits the purchaser to take possession of the property immediately and to pay the purchase price in installments over several years. The seller holds legal title to the property as security until the purchaser pays all of the installments. The installment land contract typically contains a forfeiture clause which provides that if the purchaser defaults in any payment, the seller may declare the purchaser's rights at an end, retake possession, and keep all payments made. The potential harshness of this traditional remedy has precipitated judicial and legislative action to protect the defaulting purchaser. *See* G. Nelson & D. Whitman, Real Estate Finance Law §§ 3.26–3.29 (3d ed. 1994).

SKENDZEL v. MARSHALL

Supreme Court of Indiana, 1973.
261 Ind. 226, 301 N.E.2d 641, *cert. denied* 415 U.S. 921 (1974).

HUNTER, JUSTICE.

Petitioners seek transfer to this Court as a result of an adverse ruling by the Court of Appeals. Plaintiff-respondents originally brought suit to obtain possession of certain real estate through the enforcement of a forfeiture clause in a land sale contract. Plaintiff-respondents suffered a negative judgment, from which they appealed. The Court of Appeals reversed, holding that the defendant-petitioners had breached the contract and that the plaintiff-respondents had not waived their right to enforce the forfeiture provisions of the contract.

In December of 1958, Mary Burkowski, as vendor, entered into a land sale contract with Charles P. Marshall and Agnes P. Marshall, as vendees. The contract provided for the sale of certain real estate for the sum of $36,000.00, payable as follows:

> "$500.00, at the signing, execution and delivery of this contract, the receipt whereof is hereby acknowledged; $500.00 or more on or before the 25th day of December, 1958, and $2500.00 or more on or before the 15th day of January, 1960, and $2500.00 or more on or before the 15th day of January of each and every year thereafter until the balance of the contract has been fully paid, all without interest and all without relief from valuation and appraisement laws and with attorney fees."

The contract also contained a fairly standard section which provided for the treatment of prepayments—but which the Court of Appeals found to be of particular importance. It provided as follows:

> "Should Vendees have made prepayments or paid in advance of the payments herein required, said prepayments, if any, shall at any

time thereafter be applied in lieu of further principal payments required as herein stated, to the extent of such prepayments only."

The following is the forfeiture/liquidated damages provision of the land sale contract:

for forfeiture clause

"It is further agreed that if any default shall be made in the payment of said purchase price or any of the covenants and/or conditions herein provided, and if any such default shall continue for 30 days, then, after the lapse of said 30 days' period, *all moneys and payments previously paid shall, at the option of the Vendor without notice or demand, be and become forfeited and be taken and retained by the Vendor as liquidated damages* and thereupon this contract shall terminate and be of no further force or effect; provided, however, that nothing herein contained shall be deemed or construed to prevent the Vendor from enforcing specific performance of this agreement in the event of any default on the part of the Vendees in complying, observing and performing any of the conditions, covenants and terms herein contained. * * *." (Id.) (Emphasis added.)

The vendor, Mary Burkowski, died in 1963. The plaintiffs in this action are the assignees (under the vendor's will) of the decedent's interests in the contract. They received their assignment from the executrix of the estate of the vendor on June 27, 1968. One year after this assignment, several of the assignees filed their complaint in this action alleging that the defendants had defaulted through non-payment.

The schedule of payments made under this contract was shown by the evidence to be as follows:

"Date	Amount Paid	Total of Paid Principal
12/1/1958	$ 500.00	$ 500.00
12/25/1958	500.00	1,000.00
3/26/1959	5,000.00	6,000.00
4/5/1960	2,500.00	8,500.00
5/23/1961	2,500.00	11,000.00
4/6/1962	2,500.00	13,500.00
1/15/1963	2,500.00	16,000.00
6/30/1964	2,500.00	18,500.00
2/15/1965	2,500.00	21,000.00"

No payments have been made since the last one indicated above—$15,000.00 remains to be paid on the original contract price.

In response to the plaintiff's attempt to enforce the forfeiture provision, the defendants raised the affirmative defense of waiver. The applicable rule is well established and was stated by the Court of Appeals as follows:

"Where a contract for the sale and purchase of land contains provisions similar to those in the contract in the case at bar, *the vendor may waive strict compliance with the provisions of the contract by accepting overdue or irregular payments,* and having so done, equity requires the vendor give specific notice of his intent that he will no longer be indulgent and that he will insist on his right of forfeiture unless the default is paid within a reasonable and specified time."

* * *

It follows that where the vendor has not waived strict compliance by acceptance of late payments, no notice is required to enforce its provisions.

In essence, the Court of Appeals found that there was no waiver because the vendors were obligated to accept prepayment, and, "the payments made, although irregular in time and amount, were prepayments on the unpaid balance through and including the payment due on January 15, 1965." The Court concluded that up to January 15, 1966, "the vendors waived no rights under the contract, because they were obliged to accept prepayment." and that, "[t]he vendors could not have insisted on forfeiture prior to January 15, 1966, the date of the first missed payment." (We believe the Court of Appeals miscalculated here; the vendors could not have insisted on forfeiture until January 16, 1968.)

If forfeiture is enforced against the defendants, they will forfeit outright the sum of $21,000, or well over one-half the original contract price, as liquidated damages *plus possession.*

Forfeitures are generally disfavored by the law. In fact, "* * * [e]quity abhors forfeitures and beyond any question has jurisdiction, which it will exercise in a proper case to grant relief against their enforcement." 30 C.J.S. Equity § 56 (1965) and cases cited therein. This jurisdiction of equity to intercede is predicated upon the fact that "the loss or injury occasioned by the default must be susceptible of exact compensation." 30 C.J.S., *supra.*

* * *

Paragraph 17 of the contract, *supra,* provides that all prior payments "become forfeited and be taken and retained by the Vendor as liquidated damages." "Reasonable" liquidated damage provisions are permitted by the law. However, the issue before this Court, is whether a $21,000 forfeiture is a "reasonable" measure of damages. If the damages are unreasonable, i.e., if they are disproportionate to the loss actually suffered, they must be characterized as penal rather then compensatory. Under the facts of this case, a $21,000 forfeiture is clearly excessive.

The authors of American Law Reports have provided an excellent analysis of forfeiture provisions in land contracts:

"As is frequently remarked, there is no single rule for the determination of whether a contractual stipulation is one for liquidated damages or a penalty, each case depending largely upon its own facts and equities, and this apothegm is fully applicable to the decisions involving provisions in land contracts for the forfeiture of payments.

"There is a plethora of abstract tests and criteria for the determination of the nature of a contractual provision as one for a penalty or liquidated damages, and in most instances the courts struggle valiantly to make the result reached by them accord reasonably well with one or more of the more prominent of these abstract tests. But it must be observed that in the last analysis, these factors and criteria are so vague and indefinite that it is doubtful if they are of much aid in construing a specific contractual provision, even assuming that the court makes a conscious and conscientious effort to apply them. At any rate, a reading of the cases collected herein conveys the impression that the ultimate catalyst is the court's belief as to the equities of the case before it.

"Granting this, however, certain tendencies of decision are clearly discernible in the cases. If, for example, the contract involved calls for deferred payments of the purchase price which are relatively small in amount and extend over a number of years, and if it appears that at the time of the purchaser's breach and the consequent invocation of the forfeiture clause by the vendor a comparatively small proportion of the total price remains unpaid, the courts are prone to find that the forfeiture clause was one for a penalty, at least if, as is usually the case, such a holding will tend to give the purchaser another chance to complete the purchase.

"On the other hand, if the amount of the payments received by the vendor at the time the purchase was abandoned represents but a small percentage of the total purchase price, and if the purchaser's breach occurred soon after the execution of the agreement (and particularly if the circumstances indicate that the purchase was made for speculative purposes or that the breach represented an effort on the part of the purchaser to escape an unfortunate turn in the market), the courts tend to hold that the forfeiture clause was one for liquidated damages, with the result that the purchaser cannot recover back the payments made." 6 A.L.R.2d 1401 (1949).

If we apply the specific equitable principle announced above—namely, that the amount paid be considered in relation to the total contract price—we are compelled to conclude that the $21,000 forfeiture as liquidated damages is inconsistent with generally accepted principles of fairness and equity. The vendee has acquired a substantial interest in the property, which, if forfeited, would result in substantial injustice.

Under a typical conditional land contract, the vendor retains legal title until the total contract price is paid by the vendee. Payments are generally made in periodic installments. *Legal* title does not vest in the vendee until the contract terms are satisfied, but equitable title vests in the vendee at the time the contract is consummated. When the parties enter into the contract, all incidents of ownership accrue to the vendee. The vendee assumes the risk of loss and is the recipient of all appreciation in value. The vendee, as equitable owner, is responsible for taxes. The vendee has a sufficient interest in land so that upon sale of that interest, he holds a vendor's lien.

This Court * * * in effect, views a conditional land contract as a sale with a security interest in the form of legal title reserved by the vendor. Conceptually, therefore, the retention of the title by the vendor is the same as reserving a lien or mortgage. Realistically, vendor-vendee should be viewed as mortgagee-mortgagor. To conceive of the relationship in different terms is to pay homage to form over substance.

* * *

It is also interesting to note that the drafters of the Uniform Commercial Code abandoned the distinction between a conditional sale and a security interest. Section 1–201 of the UCC defines "security interest" as "an interest in personal property or fixtures which secures payment or performance of an obligation * * * retention or reservation of title by a seller of goods notwithstanding shipment or delivery to the buyer is limited in effect to a reservation of 'security interest.' " We can conceive of no rational reason why conditional sales of real estate should be treated any differently.[1]

A conditional land contract in effect creates a vendor's lien in the property to secure the unpaid balance owed under the contract. This lien is closely analogous to a mortgage—in fact, the vendor is commonly referred to as an "equitable mortgagee." In view of this characterization of the vendor as a lienholder, it is only logical that such a lien be enforced through foreclosure proceedings. Such a lien "[has] all the incidents of a mortgage", one of which is the right to foreclose.

* * *

Forfeiture is closely akin to strict foreclosure—a remedy developed by the English courts which did not contemplate the equity of redemption. American jurisdictions, including Indiana, have, for the most part, rejected strict foreclosure in favor of foreclosure by judicial sale:

"The doctrine of strict foreclosure developed in England at a time when real property had, to a great extent, a fixed value; the vastly different conditions in this country, in this respect, led our courts to introduce modifications to the English rules of foreclosure. Generally, in consonance with equity's treatment of a mortgage as essentially a security for the payment of the debt, foreclosure by judicial sale supplanted strict foreclosure as the more equitable mode of effectuating the mutual rights of the mortgagor and mort-

---

1. In fact, the Commissioners on Uniform State Laws have recognized the transparency of any such distinctions. Section 3–102 of the Uniform Land Transactions Code (working draft of first tentative draft) reads as follows:

"This Article applies to security interests created by contract, including mortgage * * * land sales contract * * * and any other lien or title retention contract intended as security."

We believe this position is entirely consistent with the evolving case law in the area.

gagee; and there is at the present time, in the majority of the American states, no strict foreclosure as developed by the English courts—either at law or in equity—by which a mortgagee can be adjudged absolute owner of the mortgaged property. The remedy of the mortgagee is by an action for the sale of the mortgaged premises and an application of the proceeds of such sale to the mortgage debt, and although usually called an action to foreclose, it is totally different in its character and results from a strict foreclosure. The phrase 'foreclosure of a mortgage' has acquired, in general, a different meaning from that which it originally bore under the English practice and the common law imported here from England. In this country, the modern meaning of the term 'foreclosure' denotes an equitable proceeding for the enforcement of a lien against property in satisfaction of a debt.''

55 Am.Jur.2d, Mortgages, § 549 (1971).

Guided by the above principles we are compelled to conclude that judicial foreclosure of a land sale contract is in consonance with the notions of equity developed in American jurisprudence. A forfeiture—like a strict foreclosure at common law—is often offensive to our concepts of justice and inimical to the principles of equity. This is not to suggest that a forfeiture is an inappropriate remedy for the breach of all land contracts. In the case of an abandoning, absconding vendee, forfeiture is a logical and equitable remedy. Forfeiture would also be appropriate where the vendee has paid a minimal amount on the contract at the time of default and seeks to retain possession while the vendor is paying taxes, insurance, and other upkeep in order to preserve the premises. Of course, in this latter situation, the vendee will have acquired very little, if any, equity in the property. However, a court of equity must always approach forfeitures with great caution, being forever aware of the possibility of inequitable dispossession of property and exorbitant monetary loss. We are persuaded that forfeiture may only be appropriate under circumstances in which it is found to be consonant with notions of fairness and justice under the law.

Holding ✶

In other words, we are holding a conditional land sales contract to be in the nature of a secured transaction, the provisions of which are subject to all proper and just remedies at law and in equity.

Turning our attention to the case at hand, we find that the vendor-assignees were seeking forfeiture, including $21,000 already paid on said contract as liquidated damages and immediate possession. They were, in fact, asking for strict application of the contract terms at law which we believe would have led to unconscionable results requiring the intervention of equity. "Equity delights in justice, but that *not* by halves." (Story, Eq.Pl. § 72.) On the facts of this case, we are of the opinion that the trial court correctly refused the remedy sought by the vendor-assignees, but in so refusing it denied all remedial relief to the plaintiffs. Equity will "look upon that as done which ought to have been done." (Story, Eq.Jur. § 64(g)). Applying the foregoing maxims to the case at bar, where such parties seek unconscionable results in such an action, equity will treat the subject matter as if the final acts and relief contemplated by the parties were accomplished exactly as they should have been in the first instance. Where discretionary power is not exercised by a trial court, under the mistaken belief that it was without this power, a remand and direction by a court of review is necessary and proper. This is not an unwarranted interference with the trial court's function. Upon appeal to this Court, we have the judicial duty to *sua sponte* direct the trial court to apply appropriate equitable principles in such a case. Consistent with such above stated rules, this Court has the undeniable authority to remand with guidelines which will give substantial relief to plaintiffs under their secured interests and will prevent the sacrifice of the vendees' equitable lien in the property.

For all of the foregoing reasons, transfer is granted and the cause is reversed and remanded with instructions to enter a judgment of foreclosure on the vendors' lien, pursuant to Trial Rule 69(C) and the mortgage foreclosure statute (IC 1971, 32–8–16–1 (Ind.Stat.Ann., § 3–1801 [1968 Repl.])) as modified by Trial Rule 69(C). Said judgment shall include an order for the payment of the unpaid principal balance due on said contract, together with interest at 8% per annum from the date of judgment. The order may also embrace any and all other proper and equitable relief that the court deems to be just, including the discretion to issue a stay of the judicial sale of the property, all pursuant to the provisions of Trial Rule 69(C). Such order shall be consistent with the principles and holdings developed within this opinion.

Reversed and remanded with instructions.

PRENTICE, JUSTICE (concurring).

I have some concern that our opinion herein might be viewed by some as indicating an attitude of indifference towards the rights of contract vendors. Such a view would not be a true reflection.

Because the installment sales contract, with forfeiture provisions, is a widely employed and generally accepted method of commerce in real estate in this state, it is appropriate that a vendee seeking to avoid the forfeiture, to which he agreed, be required to make a clear showing of the inequity of enforcement. In any given transaction anything short of enforcing the forfeiture provision may be a denial of equity to the vendor. It has been set forth in the majority opinion that if the vendee has little or no real equity in the premises, the court should have no hesitancy in declaring a forfeiture. It follows that if the vendee has indicated his willingness to forego his equity, if any, whether by mere abandonment of the premises, by release or deed or by a failure to make a timely assertion of his claim, he should be barred from thereafter claiming an equity.

If the court finds that forfeiture, although provided for by the terms of the contract, would be unjust, it should nevertheless grant the vendor the maximum relief consistent with equity against a defaulting vendee. In so doing, it should consider that, had the parties known that the forfeiture provision would not be enforceable, other provisions for the protection of the vendor doubtlessly would have been incorporated into the agreement. Generally, this would require that the transaction be treated as a note and mortgage with such provisions as are generally included in such documents customarily employed in the community by prudent investors. Terms customarily included in such notes and mortgages but frequently omitted from contracts include provisions for increased interest during periods of default, provision for the acceleration of the due date of the entire unpaid principal and interest upon a default continuing beyond a reasonable grace period, provisions for attorneys' fees and other expenses incidental to foreclosure, for the waiver of relief from valuation and appraisement laws and for receivers.

Notes and Questions

1. Would the *Skendzel* court have reached the same result if the purchaser had paid only $5,000 of the $36,000 purchase price and had neglected to obtain casualty insurance as required by the installment land contract? *See* Phillips v. Nay, 456 N.E.2d 745 (Ind.App.1983); Goff v. Graham, 159 Ind.App. 324, 306 N.E.2d 758 (1974); *see also* Looney v. Farmers Home Admin., 794 F.2d 310 (7th Cir.1986); Parker v. Camp, 656 N.E.2d 882 (Ind.App.1995).

2. Courts in an increasing number of jurisdictions are fashioning various forms of protection for the purchaser. *See* G. Nelson & D. Whitman, Real Estate Finance Law § 3.29 (3d ed. 1994). The approach taken by the Indiana court is representative of one type of judicial reform. *See generally* Freyfogle, *Vagueness and the Rule of Law: Reconsidering Installment Land Contract Forfeitures*, 1988 Duke L.J. 609.

3. Legislative reforms also exist. Some state statutes provide for a period of grace before forfeiture can occur. Moreover, an Oklahoma statute requires that installment land contracts be treated as mortgages and foreclosed. *See* G. Nelson & D. Whitman, Real Estate Finance Law § 3.28 (3d ed. 1994). *See also* Uniform Land Security Interest Act §§ 102(b), 111(25), 111 comment 1, & 202 (1985) (foreclosure procedures apply to installment land contracts as well as mortgages). Is either legislative approach desirable?

E. RECORDING SYSTEMS

After the contract of sale is executed, the state of the seller's title must be determined to the satisfaction of both the buyer and the lender. This is generally the most important legal work connected with the transaction. The initial examination will be made by the lawyer for the buyer, the seller, the lender, or the title insurer, relying upon the official land title records or an abstract thereof, or a title plant maintained by a title insurance company.

Report, *Residential Real Estate Transactions: The Lawyer's Proper Role—Services—Compensation*, 14 Real Prop., Prob. & Tr. J. 581, 587–588 (1979).

As attorney for the Ryans you are responsible for advising them regarding the state of the title to the property they are about to purchase. This section is designed to provide you with the necessary background upon which to base your advice.

1. COMMON LAW RULE

At common law, questions of priority between claims to real property were decided on the basis of the familiar maxim "prior in time, prior in right". This system placed a tremendous burden on the purchaser, who ran the risk of not acquiring any interest by reason of a prior conveyance. Even the most thorough investigation would not necessarily reveal the existence of an earlier transaction.

To remedy this situation, the modern system of recording was developed. Today all states have recording statutes designed to provide protection for purchasers by creating a public record of instruments affecting land. In order to fully understand the system of recording, it is necessary to first consider the mechanics involved.

2. MECHANICS OF RECORDING

The recording statute of each state lists instruments that may be recorded. Although statutes vary, the designated instruments typically include deeds, mortgages, long-term leases, and other instruments affecting title to real estate. These instruments generally are valid between the parties even if the instruments are not recorded. Recording preserves the purchaser's interest by imparting notice of the transaction to subsequent purchasers.

The recording process begins when an instrument is taken to the recorder's office in the county where the property is located. The recorder's office copies the document and files the copy in the official records. In many counties literally millions of documents are filed. The recorder's office, therefore, must maintain a system of indexing. The index is the key to title examination. A proper search using the index will disclose any documents affecting title.

Two methods of indexing exist: the grantor-grantee index system and the tract index system. Most states maintain separate indices for each type of instrument but some simplify title searches by maintaining a consolidated index.

The grantor-grantee index system is the method most commonly employed. Separate indices are maintained for grantors and grantees. In the grantor index, the instruments are listed alphabetically under the grantor's surname. Each entry also includes the grantee's name, a description of the land, the type of instrument, the date of recordation, and a reference to the volume and page of the records where the recorder's copy of the instrument is located. The grantee's index contains identical information, except all instruments are listed alphabetically under the grantee's surname. Therefore, under this system it is possible to locate an instrument by conducting a search under the name of either party to the conveyance. Excerpts from both a grantor and a grantee index are reproduced below.

DIRECT [GRANTOR] INDEX TO DEEDS

DAVIDSON COUNTY, TENNESSEE

JULY 1, 1979—JUNE 30, 1982

Number	Surname Given Name	AP1 Code	Reverse Party	AP Code	Date Filed	Book	Page	Brief Description
	HUMPHRIES							
F39946	Mackie J	W	Brown Lectra W Jr	W	7–13–1979	5464	881	Town Park Ests
	HUNEYCUTT							
F44166	Alva C		Northern Murray	W	8–3–1979	5476	901	Creekwood Dr
F44166	Alva N		Northern Murray	W	8–3–1979	5476	901	Creekwood Dr
	HUNKA							
G97334	Robert F	W	Donald R Lovelace	W	6–25–1982	5903	314	Lions Head No 150
	HUNLEY							
F49947	Edith E		Jager Jonathan	W	9–4–1979	5492	860	Compton Ave
F45819	James R	W	Carlisle Ella C		8–13–1979	5481	62	Hibbitts Rd
F45399	Linda H		Tuggle Harry G		8–10–1979	5480	38	Eastland Ave
F80644	Linda H	O	Mabry Nancye L	O	3–14–1980	5578	649	Setliff Pl
G44371	Linda H	O	Betty J Obert	O	6–2–1981	5752	151	Eastland Avenue
F98143	Mary C		Thompson, Thomas S Jr		7–18–1980	5626	137	Goldilocks St
F80644	Nancy J	O	Mabry Nancye L	O	3–14–1980	5578	649	Setliff Pl
G44371	Nancy J	O	Betty J Obert	O	6–2–1981	5752	151	Eastland Avenue
F68331	Patsy R	O	Weatherford Ronald W	W	12–17–1979	5544	439	Raymond Hgts
	HUNNICUTT							
G36770	Robert J	W	Russell B Mabrey, Sr	W	4–9–1981	5731	24	Unit No 4–A Plan of Revised Pointset
	HUNSUCKER							
F73072	Jackie F	O	Toney Charles PBTR		1–21–1980	5557	642	Q C Fortland Dr
G48699	Julia H	H	Carolyn Thompson		6–30–1981	5764	98	Unit No 2 Versailles
F73072	Sue E	O	Toney Charles PBTR		1–21–1980	5557	642	Q C Fortland Dr

REVERSE [GRANTEE] INDEX TO DEEDS

DAVIDSON COUNTY, TENNESSEE

JULY 1, 1979—JUNE 30, 1982

Number	Surname Given Name	AP1 Code	Reverse Party	AP Code	Date Filed	Book	Page	Brief Description
	MABREY							
G36770	Russell B, Sr	W	Robert J Hunnicutt	W	4–9–1981	5731	24	Unit No 4–A Plan of Revised Pointset
G54907	Russell B, Sr	W	Hershel H Brown, Jr		8–12–1981	5781	471	Heritage Village of Priest Lake Park No 34
	MABRY							
G60280	Edith L	O	John R Claibourne, Sr	W	9–17–1981	5795	687	Browndale Ct
G62780	Kenneth R		Ronald W Fuller	W	10–6–1981	5803	852	Q C Old Charlotte Pk
G65224	Kenneth R		Ronald W Fuller	W	10–22–1981	5809	986	Q C Old Charlotte Pike
G50882	Nancy E	O	Ernest M Fleming, Jr		7–15–1981	5770	718	Lease Agreement
F80644	Nancye L	O	Hunley Linda H	O	3–14–1980	5578	649	Setliff Pl
F81864	Nancye L	O	Sharber Irene		3–24–1980	5582	94	Fatherland St
F98615	Nancye L	O	Agee Willis W	W	7–22–1980	5627	399	Fatherland St
G37990	Robert L	W	Karla K Allen, TR		4–20–1981	5734	873	Q C 53rd Ave North
G05538	Teddye A		Mabry James L		9–2–1980	5645	438	CC/Final Decree

1. The AP Code refers to additional persons involved in the transaction. W = wife, H = husband, and O = others. [Editors' note.]

Number	Surname Given Name	AP1 Code	Reverse Party	AP Code	Date Filed	Recorded Book	Page	Brief Description
F53971	MACALUSO Ronald J		Brewer H W	W	9–25–1979	5504	132	Beaumont Pl
F47155	MACBEAN Annette C		King Roy L	O	8–20–1979	5484	701	Woodmont Blvd
G80233	MACDONALD John		Gary A Thomas	W	2–18–1982	5853	271	Horton Property
G03568	Michael J		Phillips Randall Inc		8–21–1980	5640	250	Towne Ridge Dr
G08741	Pamela D M		Maislin Gerald B	W	9–19–1980	5653	664	Franklin Limestone Rd
G89560	Valeria		Florence L Hutchison, Est		5–5–1982	5880	816	Affidavit of Heirship
G10593	MACDONIELS Jay S	W	Philhall Corporation		10–1–1980	5658	960	Wood Bridge Dr

In a tract index system, land transactions are indexed by reference to the particular parcel involved. The burden of searching the records is thereby greatly reduced because the title examiner need only review those instruments listed under the tract in question. Unfortunately, tract indices are maintained in only a few jurisdictions. Many title insurance companies, however, have developed their own unofficial tract index systems.

Under either index system, the title examiner must establish a "chain of title" for the present owner, the seller in our hypothetical situation. A chain of title is the successive conveyances of title to a particular parcel of land beginning with the first or patent deed from the government and ending with the deed to the person presently claiming title. The period of search has been reduced by marketable title statutes in some states to thirty or forty years. In other jurisdictions, the period of search is limited to sixty years or so by custom. Thus, it is generally no longer necessary to establish a chain of title back to the original owner.

See J. Cribbet & C. Johnson, Principles of the Law of Property 306–309 (3d ed. 1989); R. Kratovil & R. Werner, Real Estate Law §§ 9.01–9.14 (10th ed. 1993).

Notes and Questions

1. Two transactions are found in each index excerpt reproduced above. Can you locate them? Note also that two transactions are listed twice in the grantor index. Why?

2. Transfers of property by descent or devise generally are not recorded in the same office with deeds, mortgages, and other inter vivos transactions. Therefore, a title examiner often must search testamentary instruments filed in the appropriate probate court to complete the chain of title.

3. In certain counties recording techniques have not changed greatly for decades. On the other hand, some recording offices have computerized their land records. *See* Report, *Land Information Systems for the Twenty-First Century,* 15 Real Prop., Prob. & Tr. J. 890 (1980).

3. TYPES OF RECORDING STATUTES

Recording an instrument puts the world on constructive notice of its existence and contents. The consequences of failure to record vary from state to state depending on the language of the statute. Generally, a conveyance is valid between the immediate parties whether recorded or not. However, failure to record may pose serious problems if the grantor conveys the same property to a subsequent purchaser.

The nature of the protection afforded a subsequent purchaser depends on the type of recording act in effect. Recording systems are of three major types: race, notice, and race-notice.

Race. Early recording acts were race statutes, under which the first purchaser to record prevailed. Notice was irrelevant. A pure race statute still exists in only a handful of states. *See, e.g.,* Department of Transportation v. Humphries, 496 S.E.2d 563 (N.C.1998) (discussing operation of local race statute).

Notice. The notice statute developed as an alternative to the race statute and was designed to address the inequity of allowing a subsequent purchaser with notice of a prior instrument to prevail over the prior claimant. Under a notice statute, only a subsequent purchaser who takes without notice of prior unrecorded instruments is protected. A subsequent purchaser need not record to prevail over a prior claimant but recordation would be wise to insure protection against further subsequent purchasers.

Race-Notice. The race-notice statute is a combination of the two types of recording acts previously discussed. In order to prevail under a race-notice statute, a subsequent purchaser must be without notice of a prior instrument and record first.

The states are now almost evenly divided into notice and race-notice jurisdictions. Naturally, one should begin analysis of any priority problem by ascertaining the type of recording statute involved.

See 4 American Law of Property § 17.5 (1952) (listing type of recording statute for each state); Johnson, *Purpose and Scope of Recording Statutes,* 47 Iowa L.Rev. 231 (1962).

Problems

Who prevails in the following circumstances under a race, notice, and race-notice statute?

a. O, owner of Blackacre, conveyed to A who failed to record. O conveyed to B who knew of the conveyance to A. B recorded.

b. O, owner of Blackacre, conveyed to A who failed to record. O conveyed to B who knew nothing of the conveyance to A. B failed to record. A recorded.

4. WHO IS PROTECTED?

Generally, the only persons protected by the recording system are bona fide purchasers. In order to qualify as a bona fide purchaser, a person must (a) give valuable consideration and (b) take without notice. (In race jurisdictions, however, one merely must be a purchaser for valuable consideration to be protected by the recording system. The purchaser, of course, must then record first.)

a. *Purchaser for Valuable Consideration*

ANDERSON v. ANDERSON

Supreme Court of North Dakota, 1989.
435 N.W.2d 687.

MESCHKE, JUSTICE.

Plaintiffs appealed from a judgment quieting defendants' title to an undivided one-fourth of 280 acres in McKenzie County. We reverse and remand.

Kari Anderson patented the 280 acres from the United States in 1916. In 1922, Kari conveyed the 280 acres to her four children, A.T. Anderson, James T. Anderson, Julia Anderson, and Theodore T. Anderson, as tenants in common, each acquiring an undivided one-fourth.

This dispute is only about Julia's undivided one-fourth received from Kari. The plaintiffs are children of James T. Anderson's son, George Teleford Anderson. They have record title to three-fourths of the 280 acres and claim the remaining one-fourth * * * through a deed from Julia to James T., dated February 7, 1934, but not recorded until December 14, 1983. The defendants, heirs of Julia's children, Ida Mathews and Willie H. Anderson, claim one-fourth of the 280 acres through a quit-claim deed from Julia to Ida and Willie, dated October 1, 1951, and recorded October 11, 1951.

* * *

The trial court * * * concluded that the recorded 1951 deed from Julia to her children, Ida and Willie, had priority over the unrecorded 1934 deed from Julia to James T. Anderson because, under Section 47–19–41, N.D.C.C., Julia's children were purchasers in good faith and for a valuable consideration. The court quieted defendants' title to one-fourth of the property. Plaintiffs appealed.

We consider the relative priority of the 1934 and 1951 deeds under Section 47–19–41, N.D.C.C., which, in relevant part, says:

"Every conveyance of real estate not recorded shall be void as against any subsequent purchaser in good faith, and for a valuable consideration, of the same real estate, or any part or portion thereof, whose conveyance, * * * first is deposited with the proper officer for record and subsequently recorded, whether entitled to record or not, * * * prior to the recording of such conveyance."

Plaintiffs contended that Ida Mathews and Willie H. Anderson were not good faith purchasers for a valuable consideration in 1951. Defendants responded that Ida and Willie were good faith purchasers for a valuable consideration under Section 47–19–41, N.D.C.C., so that their 1951 deed, recorded in 1951, had priority over the 1934 deed, recorded in 1983. * * *

Although this court has often considered the requirements of notice for a good faith purchase under § 47–19–41, N.D.C.C., the element of valuable consideration has not been directly examined.

Generally, for protection under a recording act as a good faith purchaser for value, the purchase must be for a valuable and not a nominal consideration. *See* cases cited in United States v. Certain Parcels of Land, 85 F.Supp. 986, 1006 (S.D.Cal.1949) fn. 17. The consideration does not have to be an equivalent value in order to be valuable, but it must be substantial and not merely nominal. In Horton v. Kyburz, 53 Cal.2d 59, 346 P.2d 399, 403 (1959), the court quoted an explanation of the rationale:

" 'The recording laws were not enacted to protect those whose ignorance of the title is deliberate and intentional, nor does a mere nominal consideration satisfy the requirement that a valuable consideration must be paid. Their purpose is to protect those who honestly believe they are acquiring a good title, and who invest some substantial sum in reliance on that belief.' "

* * *

The recital of a nominal consideration in a deed is insufficient to establish a valuable consideration or to raise a presumption of value for a good faith purchase. Moreover, the party claiming to be a good faith purchaser has the burden of proof to establish valuable consideration from evidence other than the deed.

In this case, the defendants relied on the abstract of title to establish that Ida and Willie paid Julia "$10.00 & OG & VC" for the 1951 quitclaim deed. The defendants presented no evidence of any actual consideration. We conclude, as a matter of law, that the consideration recited in the 1951 quit-claim deed was a nominal consideration and did not constitute a valuable consideration. Ida and Willie were not good faith purchasers for a valuable consideration under Section 47–19–41, N.D.C.C. Therefore, the defendants cannot claim priority over the plaintiffs by virtue of the 1951 deed.

Accordingly, we reverse the judgment and remand for entry of judgment quieting title in the plaintiffs.

Notes, Problems, and Questions

1. Courts are divided as to whether a purchaser must give substantial consideration in order to qualify for protection under the recording acts. For a case which reached the same result as *Anderson,* see Phillips v. Latham, 523 S.W.2d 19 (Tex.Civ.App.1975) ($691 sale price for property worth over $12,000 "grossly inadequate," thus purchaser did not qualify as good faith purchaser for value). Other courts have taken the position that nominal consideration, absent fraud, is sufficient to make the grantee a purchaser for value under the recording statutes. *See, e.g.,* Walters v. Calderon, 25 Cal. App.3d 863, 102 Cal.Rptr. 89 (1972); Strong v. Whybark, 204 Mo. 341, 102 S.W. 968 (1907) ("natural love and affection and five dollars" found to be valuable consideration). Which is the better approach?

2. As a general rule, donees do not qualify as bona fide purchasers under the recording system because a donee by definition does not give consideration. Consider the following problems in the context of a notice jurisdiction:

(a) O, owner of Blackacre, conveyed Blackacre to A for valuable consideration. A did not record. O then conveyed Blackacre to B as a gift. B did not know about the conveyance to A. B recorded. Who prevails?

(b) O, owner of Blackacre, conveyed Blackacre to A as a gift. A recorded. O then conveyed Blackacre to B for valuable consideration. B recorded. Who prevails?

Same results in a race-notice jurisdiction?

3. X owed Giant Corp. $10,000 for goods and services. X could not pay on time, so Giant Corp. accepted a mortgage on X's warehouse to secure the pre-existing debt. Is Giant Corp. a purchaser under the recording system entitled to protection against prior unrecorded interests in the warehouse? There is a difference of opinion on this issue. *Compare* Gabel v. Drewrys Limited, U.S.A., Inc., 68 So.2d 372 (Fla.1953) (finding mortgagee not purchaser for purposes of recording unless new consideration given) *with* Fox v. Templeton, 229 Va. 380, 385, 329 S.E.2d 6, 9 (1985) ("[I]t is well settled in Virginia that a conveyance of property in satisfaction of a preexisting debt constitutes a purchase for a valuable consideration within the meaning of the recording acts."). Which is the better approach?

4. A mortgagee who gives value qualifies as a purchaser. The protection afforded other creditors by the recording system varies from state to state. *See* Johnson, *Purpose and Scope of Recording Statutes,* 47 Iowa L.Rev. 231, 235–237 (1962); 4 American Law of Property § 17.29 (1952); Note, *Status of Judgment Creditors Under the Recording Acts,* 32 Notre Dame Law. 471 (1957).

ROWE v. SCHULTZ

Court of Appeals of Arizona, Division 1, 1982.
131 Ariz. 536, 642 P.2d 881.

OPINION

McFATE, JUDGE (Retired).

Ben C. Rowe brought this action to quiet title to certain land located in Yuma County. The Yuma County Superior Court granted defendant Arthur C. Schultz, Jr. a summary judgment and Rowe appealed. * * *

The facts material to a resolution of this case are undisputed. On April 12, 1978, Rowe obtained a quitclaim deed to the land in question from the owners, Mr. and Mrs. Michael Peregoy. However, Rowe did not record his deed until May 18, 1978, some five weeks later. During the interim, on May 12, 1978, Schultz obtained a money judgment against Peregoy on an apparently unrelated cause of action and recorded an abstract of judgment the very same day. There is no contention that Rowe was other than a good faith purchaser for value without notice of Schultz's claim. The sole issue on appeal is whether the recording of the abstract of judgment created a lien against the land which Peregoy had previously conveyed to Rowe. We hold that it did and affirm the trial court's summary judgment.

* * * Rowe challenges the trial court's conclusion that, under the given facts, Arizona's judgment lien statute operates in favor of a judgment creditor to reach his debtor's real property sold in an unrecorded transaction prior to perfection of the lien.

The applicable lien statute, A.R.S. § 33–964(A), provides in pertinent part that:

> from and after the time of recording * * * a judgment shall become a lien for a period of five years from the date it is given, upon all real property of the judgment debtor except real property exempt from execution, including the interest in the homestead, * * * whether the property is then owned by the judgment debtor or is later acquired.

In order to determine the respective interests of Peregoy, Rowe and Schultz in the land when Schultz perfected his judgment lien we must consult Arizona's recording statute. The relevant portions of A.R.S. § 33–412 (emphasis added) provide that:

> A. All bargains, sales and other conveyances whatever of lands, tenements and hereditaments * * * *shall be void as to creditors* and subsequent purchasers for valuable consideration without notice, unless they are acknowledged and recorded in the office of the county recorder as required by law * * *.

> B. Such unrecorded instruments, as between the parties and their heirs, and as to all subsequent purchasers with notice thereof, or without valuable consideration, shall be valid and binding.

The two statutes must be considered together and each given effect, if possible. If, under the provisions of A.R.S. § 33–412(B), Peregoy effectively divested himself of ownership before Schultz recorded his abstract of judgment, then the land was not "real property of the judgment debtor" under A.R.S. § 33–964(A) and the lien did not attach. On the other hand, if failure to record the deed prior to perfection of the lien rendered it void as to creditors, including Schultz, then the lien attached to the land as though no conveyance had been made.

Rowe contends that since A.R.S. § 33–412(B) validates an unrecorded conveyance as between the parties to a transaction, Peregoy no longer actually owned the land when Schultz's lien was perfected. As liens authorized under A.R.S. § 33–964 attach only to property of the debtor owned *at the time or acquired after* an abstract of judgment is recorded, Rowe therefore urges that title passed to him by the conveyance and that Schultz's lien cannot apply to land not owned by the judgment debtor when the abstract was first recorded. We do not agree.

At early common law there was no lien on real estate and a creditor had no remedy against his debtor's land. Absent a recording statute such as A.R.S. § 33–412(A), it is true that:

> Where the judgment debtor conveys his realty before judgment is rendered against him, the judgment is not a lien on the realty conveyed * * * [because] as between the parties to it the conveyance is valid, and no interest, legal or equitable, remains in the grantor upon which the lien can rest.

10A G. Thompson on Real Property § 5308, at 662 (1957) (footnote omitted).

Judgment liens are derived from statutes which create them. Unless otherwise provided by statute, a judgment lien is subordinate to prior conveyances even where these are not recorded. However, statutes may expressly or by implication require recording of such conveyances if their priority is to be maintained.

Art. 9 UCC ?

* * *

Appellant contends that since A.R.S. § 33–412(B) declares an unrecorded deed to be valid as between the parties thereto, the conclusion follows with even greater logical certainty that a grantee in a prior unrecorded deed which is by statute declared valid as between the parties prevails over a creditor who subsequently perfects a judgment lien. To strengthen his argument appellant cites the Oregon cases of Wilson v. Willamette Industries, Inc., 280 Or. 45, 569 P.2d 609 (1977) and Thompson v. Hendricks, 118 Or. 39, 245 P. 724 (1926), wherein under statutes quite similar to the Arizona statutes (§§ 33–412 and 33–964(A)) it was held that a judgment creditor could not subject property of an innocent purchaser for value to his judgment lien where the debtor had previously conveyed the property to such purchaser by an unrecorded deed. The court noted that the deed was valid as between the parties and the lien attached only to the debtor's actual interest in the property. The court reasoned that by merely docketing his judgment, a judgment creditor parts with nothing and does not become entitled to have the property of an innocent purchaser for value applied in satisfaction of a debt he does not owe, especially when the judgment lien is limited to property "then owned by the debtor." This argument deserves careful consideration.

On analysis, it is obvious that the rationale of the Oregon cases assumes the validity of the unrecorded conveyance not only as between the parties, but in respect to the creditor, and ignores the impact of the Oregon recording statute (similar to A.R.S. § 33–412(A)) which declares the conveyance void as to creditors. The holdings imply that an unrecorded conveyance "good as between the parties" cannot be void as to a creditor of the transferor. But that is precisely the opposite of what the statute provides. The judgment in the case *sub judice* established the creditor-debtor relationship between Schultz and Peregoy. As to Schultz, section 33–412(A) voids the unrecorded conveyance. This left Peregoy and Rowe in the same situation as though no conveyance had been made. Accordingly, as between Schultz and Peregoy, the latter still owned the property and Rowe acquired no interest therein which could be asserted against Schultz.

Our recording statute was adopted from Texas. In that jurisdiction (although we do not find a judgment lien statute similar to A.R.S. § 33–964) the courts have held that a judgment lien takes precedence over an unrecorded prior conveyance by the judgment debtor under the express terms of the Texas recording statute. * * *

We recognize that the statutory construction herein adopted may, in some instances, cause untoward hardship on innocent purchasers for value who do not record their deeds. However, where the language of a statute is clear in its meaning and no impossibility or absurdity results, courts must give effect to the plain import thereof even if "the result may be harsh, unjust or mistaken policy." Members of Bd. of Educ. v. Leslie, 112 Ariz. 463, 465, 543 P.2d 775, 777 (1975).

In defining the relative rights of creditors, lien claimants and innocent purchasers for value, the legislature occupies an unenviable position. Some unfair or harsh results will surely attend any attempt to classify the diverse factual situations which constantly arise. We surmise that the factors which long ago prompted our legislature to enact the recording statutes here involved were the desirability of encouraging recording and penalizing non-recording of property interests for the protection of all persons involved, including the public interest to be served in deterring debtors from antedating deeds to friendly third parties in order to circumvent the liens of their judgment creditors.

Our interpretation of the statutory provisions is consonant with the view taken by the trial court. Accordingly, the grant of summary judgment is affirmed.

Note

For a thoughtful discussion of the protection afforded judgment lien creditors under the various recording acts, see Schechter, *Judicial Lien Creditors Versus Prior Unrecorded Transferees of Real Property: Rethinking the Goals of the Recording System and Their Consequences*, 62 S.Cal.L.Rev. 105 (1988).

b. *Without Notice*

What does it mean to be "without notice?" The concept of notice encompasses three different forms: actual, constructive, and inquiry.

HANER v. BRUCE

Supreme Court of Vermont, 1985.
146 Vt. 262, 499 A.2d 792.

GIBSON, JUSTICE.

The question raised by this appeal is whether a real estate attachment that is misindexed by the city clerk is valid against a subsequent bona fide purchaser who had no actual notice of the attachment. The trial court dismissed the attaching party's claim. We reverse and remand.

On March 23, 1979, having obtained a writ of attachment in a pending suit against defendant Wendall Bruce, plaintiff filed the attachment with the St. Albans city clerk. At that time, a recorded land contract gave Bruce the right to purchase property at 58–60 Fairfield Street in St. Albans. Although the city clerk recorded and indexed the attachment in an "attachment book," she did not index it in the general index of land records, as required by 24 V.S.A. § 1161. The record does not disclose whether the "attachment book" was the volume in which attachments of personalty only are to be recorded pursuant to 24 V.S.A. § 1163, or a different volume.

On May 29, 1979, Bruce purchased the Fairfield Street property, and one day later, he conveyed the property by warranty deed to defendants David and Gloria Fosgate, whose purchase was financed by defendant-mortgagee Peoples Trust Company of St. Albans. In early 1982, plaintiff obtained a final judgment in his suit against Bruce, which he duly filed and recorded with the city clerk.

It is not disputed that the title search conducted for defendants Fosgate and Peoples Trust in preparation for their purchase did not disclose the misindexed writ of attachment; it is also undisputed that they did not learn of the attachment until May 1982.

Recognizing defendants as bona fide purchasers without notice of the misindexed attachment, and observing that prospective real estate purchasers should not be required to search personal property records, the trial court dismissed plaintiff's claim, with prejudice, on the authority of Burchard, Wilson & Co. v. Town of Fairhaven, 48 Vt. 327 (1875). In that case, a writ of attachment was left at the town clerk's office for recording, but the writ was lost or removed before the town clerk could either record or index it; this Court held that no lien had been established against subsequent bona fide purchasers who had no notice of the attachment.

Subsequent to *Burchard,* this Court was presented with a slightly different case. In Barrett v. Prentiss, 57 Vt. 297, 300 (1884), a mortgage deed was duly recorded but not indexed, despite a statute, R.L. § 2680 (now 24 V.S.A. § 1161), that required the town clerk to keep a general index. Thereafter, a second mortgage was executed and assigned to a person who purchased it without actual knowledge of the first mortgage. Under these facts, the Court held that the first mortgage was superior to the second and could be foreclosed. The Court in *Barrett* followed Curtis v. Lyman, 24 Vt. 338 (1849), a case decided before the enactment of the indexing statute. *Curtis* also had held that the clerk's failure to index a mortgage did not invalidate the effect of its recordation. In a more recent case, Hunn v. Koerber, 129 Vt. 490, 282 A.2d 831 (1971), this Court ruled that an attaching creditor had standing to defend a mortgage foreclosure action although the town clerk had failed to record the attachment. The Court stated:

> The attachment was effected when the officer lodged the copy of the writ, with the endorsement of his return, in the office of the town clerk. The actual recording of the entries respecting the writ was the duty of the town clerk, but such record, or the want of it, does not constitute any part of the attachment itself. The defendant's lien is unaffected by the neglect of the town clerk to enter it in the town records.

Id. at 493, 282 A.2d at 833. Thus, for over a century, it has been the law of Vermont that the proper recording of an instrument has served as constructive notice to the public, notwithstanding clerical errors in indexing.

* * *

Although the result reached by Vermont (and most other states) has been criticized, e.g., 4 A. Casner, American Law of Property § 17.25, at 604–05 (1952), "the rule appears to be well established that in the absence of statutory provision to that effect, an index is not an essential part of the record." *Id.* at 604 (footnote omitted, citing, inter alia, *Barrett, supra*).

* * *

The recently developed Uniform Simplification of Land Transfers Act (not as yet enacted in Vermont) gives priority to the attaching party when his interests conflict with those of subsequent purchasers. Although the Uniform Act imposes responsibility upon a filer to provide detailed indexing information, and makes indexing an essential part of recordation, the filer need not undertake to verify the correctness of indexation after the recording officer has accepted a properly completed submission. See Uniform Simplification of Land Transfers Act §§ 2–302 to 2–304, 3–202(b), 14 U.L.A. 234–37, 244–45 (1980).

As between the parties, the filer can not be held to be more blameworthy than the title searcher. Although the filer could return to the clerk's office to make certain that the instrument was properly recorded, he should not have to do so; he should be entitled to rely on the clerk to do his or her job in a proper manner. Further, a requirement that the filer double-check the clerk would be impractical—the clerk might not complete the recording and indexing promptly, for one reason or another, forcing the filer to make one or more additional visits to the clerk's office, to the inconvenience and annoyance of both individuals. An out-of-state filer would be particularly disadvantaged by such a requirement. The title searcher, on the other hand, is in a position to protect himself by simply asking the clerk about search procedures and whether there are particular volumes or indexing records he or she should check.

The trial court's dismissal of plaintiff's claim was erroneous.

Reversed and remanded.

ALLEN, CHIEF JUSTICE, dissenting.

I disagree with the result reached by the majority. A purchaser of real estate for value without actual or constructive notice of any defect in the title will hold the same against a prior grantee or attaching creditor who has failed to have his conveyance recorded, whether through his fault or that of the town clerk. Burchard, Wilson & Co. v. Town of Fairhaven, 48 Vt. 327 (1875). This is so because purchasers have the implicit right to rely upon the land records required by law to be kept for that purpose. *Id.* at 335.

* * *

Our recording acts were passed for the purpose of providing a method by which an intending purchaser or encumbrancer might safely ascertain the condition of title. An integral part of the recording scheme for real property is the general index.

There may have been a time in our early history when it would have been reasonably possible to examine all of the pages of all of the volumes of land records in a clerk's office to determine the true state of title. Today, there are in some communities hundreds of volumes of recorded materials relating to land transactions. The task of examining the necessary number of volumes to accurately determine the state of title under the majority holding is unduly burdensome. It was the legislative intent to avoid this necessity that led to the requirement of a general index.

It is here agreed that the parties were equally blameless for the error that led to this action, and it may be that an inquiry to the clerk might here have disclosed the location of the attachment. A like inquiry to a clerk or successor clerk would, in all probability, be fruitless in the case of a misplaced or misfiled document. The filer knows of its existence and has the opportunity to make certain that it is properly indexed. The filer should suffer the consequences of improper indexing as he is usually the only one who can make certain that it is done right. Compiano v. Jones, 269 N.W.2d 459, 462 (Iowa 1978). As was stated in Prouty v. Marshall, 225 Pa. 570, 576–77, 74 A. 550, 552 (1909):

If from any cause she fell short of giving legal notice [i.e., by recording and indexing], the consequence must fall upon her. She cannot hide behind the mistake of the recorder. It is an easy matter for a mortgagee, or a grantee in each particular instance, either in person, or by a representative, to look at the record, and see that the instrument has been properly entered.

The dictates of convenience and certainty require that one be able to rely on the general index.

The unreasoned one paragraph holding in *Barrett* has created a general disclaimer for misindexing in certificates of title by the signers of those instruments. The resulting and potentially highly damaging exposure to subsequent innocent purchasers ought to be avoided. This can best be accomplished under our present recording scheme by the simple requirement that one recording an instrument affecting the title to real estate make certain that the instrument is properly indexed.

Notes and Questions

1. For decisions adopting the position expressed by the dissenting judge in *Haner*, see Mortensen v. Lingo, 99 F.Supp. 585 (D.C.Alaska 1951), and Howard Savings Bank v. Brunson, 244 N.J.Super. 571, 582 A.2d 1305 (1990). Which is the better view? *See* 4 American Law of Property § 17.25 (1952).

2. Assume you are in a jurisdiction where an instrument must be indexed in order to impart constructive notice. Suppose an instrument is indexed but under the wrong name or initial. Should the title searcher be required to examine every entry in the index? *See* Prouty v. Marshall, 225 Pa. 570, 74 A. 550 (1909); *see also* 4 American Law of Property §§ 17.18, 17.31 (1952).

FAR WEST SAVINGS AND LOAN ASSOCIATION v. McLAUGHLIN

Court of Appeal of California, Second District, 1988.
201 Cal.App.3d 67, 246 Cal.Rptr. 872.

CROSKEY, ASSOCIATE JUSTICE.

Defendants and appellants, Mary P. McLaughlin and Barbara Nicholls (McLaughlin) appeal from a summary judgment granted in favor of plaintiff and respondent Far West Savings and Loan Association (Far West). Far West claims priority for its deed of trust over an earlier recorded encumbrance given to McLaughlin by an unrecorded grantee whose deed placing him in the chain of title was not recorded until the same date as Far West's deed of trust. As we hold (1) that in order for such earlier recorded encumbrance to impart constructive notice to a subsequent bona fide encumbrancer for value it must be *rerecorded after* its trustor is in the chain of title and (2) that Far West did not have actual knowledge or notice of the earlier encumbrance, we affirm the judgment.

Factual Background

On June 1, 1982, Frederick Geiger (Geiger) acquired record title to real property in Sylmar located at 13553 Polk Street. A purchase money deed of trust from Geiger to Hancock Savings and Loan Association for $92,000 was also recorded that same day.

On July 8, 1982, Geiger executed a grant deed transferring the property to GTB Properties (GTB). However, *that document was not recorded until July 1, 1983,* almost a year later. Meanwhile, on August 3, 1982, GTB executed a deed of trust for $51,888.49 in favor of McLaughlin ("GTB deed of trust") and *on August 10, 1982, this document was recorded.*

On July 1, 1983, * * * the following * * * documents were recorded in the following sequential order: * * * the Geiger grant deed to GTB (dated July 8, 1982) and a grant deed conveying the property from GTB to Thomas and Jean Stapleton (Stapleton). On the same date, * * * a purchase money deed of trust executed by Stapleton in favor of Far West for $105,300, was also recorded. From the $105,300 loan made by Far West, the outstanding first trust deed obligation to Hancock Savings and Loan Association was satisfied.

On February 3, 1984, after Stapleton had failed to make timely payments, Far West recorded a Notice of Default and Election to Sell under Deed of Trust in order to foreclose Stapleton's interest in the Sylmar property. On May 15, 1984, Far West recorded a Notice of Trustee's Sale and, on July 5, 1984, acquired title to the property at a nonjudicial foreclosure sale.

Subsequently, McLaughlin informed Far West of their intention to foreclose under the GTB deed of trust and denied that * * * Far West was a bona fide encumbrancer for value * * *.

Procedural Background

On April 9, 1985, Far West filed a complaint for declaratory relief seeking a declaration that its interest in the property was unencumbered by any claim or right of McLaughlin. * * *

McLaughlin filed an answer, admitting a controversy exists among the parties but *denying* that Far West did not have actual or constructive notice or knowledge of McLaughlin's claim against the property at the time it obtained its purchase money lien. McLaughlin alleged that Far West's right was junior to theirs.

On December 2, 1985 Far West filed a motion for summary judgment and on July 21, 1986, the motion was granted on the ground that "[t]his matter turns on a 'wild deed' of which moving party has no constructive notice. Responding party has presented no evidence moving party had actual notice of 'wild deed.' No constructive notice by virtue of date of execution of deed. Purpose of recordation is to avoid this situation to determine who owns property at any particular time."

* * * This appeal followed.

* * *

DISCUSSION

* * *

Proper recordation of a real property instrument is necessary to impart constructive notice of its contents. (Civ.Code, §§ 1213, 1214.)[1] If an instrument cannot be located by searching the "grantor" and "grantee" indices of the public records, the instrument does not constitute constructive notice and later bona fide purchasers or encumbrances are not charged with knowledge of its existence.

The GTB deed of trust was recorded *before GTB obtained record title*. Therefore, it must be termed a "wild" document, i.e., one recorded outside the chain of title. As such, a search of the grantor/grantee indices could not have disclosed its existence. "One who is not connected by any conveyance whatever with the record title to a piece of property and makes a conveyance thereof, does not thereby create any defect in the record title of another when such title is deducible by intermediate effective conveyances from the original owners to that other * * *. Such a deed would not even be constructive notice." (Bothin v. The California Title Ins. Co. (1908) 153 Cal. 718, 723, 96 P. 500.)

This same rule applies to a conveyance by a person who is in the chain of title, but who makes a conveyance *prior to his acquisition of record title*. His conveyance, at the time it is made, is that of a stranger to the title; and, although he afterwards gains record title and makes another conveyance, the second grantee is not bound, in his search of the record, to determine whether his grantor, or any grantor in the chain, made a conveyance *before such grantor became a part of the chain*. The second grantee who purchases for value and records first will prevail by virtue of the terms of the recording statute (see fn. 1, *ante*). He has no constructive notice of the deed to the first grantee, for the record of such deed, made before the grantor had title, *is not in the chain of title*. For the first grantee to prevail he would have to have recorded his deed *again* (1) *after* record title had come to his grantor and (2) *before* the second grantee had given value.

McLaughlin did not later record again after GTB acquired record title; therefore, the GTB deed of trust remained outside the chain of

---

1. Civil Code section 1213 provides in pertinent part:

"Every conveyance of real property acknowledged or proved and certified and recorded as prescribed by law from the time it is filed with the recorder for record is constructive notice of the contents thereof to subsequent purchasers and mortgagees; * * *"

Civil Code section 1214 provides:

"Every conveyance of real property, other than a lease for a term not exceeding one year, is void as against any subsequent purchaser or mortgagee of the same property, or any part thereof, in good faith and for a valuable consideration, whose conveyance is first duly recorded, and as against any judgment affecting the title, unless such conveyance shall have been duly recorded prior to the record of notice of action."

title. Contrary to McLaughlin's argument, the later recordation, on July 1, 1983, of the July 8, 1982 Geiger grant deed to GTB did not bring the GTB deed of trust into the chain of title. To accomplish that, McLaughlin would have had to record the GTB deed of trust again, *after the grant deed to GTB had been recorded, and before Far West gave value*. This, of course, did not happen. Nor did the earlier date of the Geiger deed to GTB impart a duty to search beyond the chain of title. "Priorities, and the title examination, are determined by the date of recording and not the date of execution." (2 Miller & Starr, Current Law of Cal. Real Estate, Vol. II Supp., § 11:20, p. 24.)

* * *

DISPOSITION

The judgment of dismissal is affirmed. Far West shall recover its costs.

Problems and Questions

1.　O, owner of Blackacre, conveyed to A who failed to record. O conveyed to B who knew nothing of the conveyance to A. Before B recorded, B learned of the prior conveyance to A. B recorded anyway. A then recorded. Who prevails in a notice jurisdiction? In a race-notice jurisdiction?

2.　Can a purchaser under an installment land contract be a bona fide purchaser if such purchaser learned of a prior unrecorded interest in the property before the purchase price was paid in full and before legal title was transferred? *See* Daniels v. Anderson, 162 Ill.2d 47, 204 Ill.Dec. 666, 642 N.E.2d 128 (1994) (concluding that purchaser under installment sale contract who receives notice of superior claim before making full payment is only entitled to protection of bona fide status pro tanto, and upholding decision requiring purchaser to transfer title to superior holder of right of first refusal in exchange for payment of purchase price and reimbursement of property taxes paid); Tomlinson v. Clarke, 118 Wn.2d 498, 825 P.2d 706 (1992)(purchaser under installment land contract may qualify as bona fide purchaser and obtain superior title even though full purchase price remains unpaid).

SABO v. HORVATH ✓

Supreme Court of Alaska, 1976.
559 P.2d 1038.

BOOCHEVER, CHIEF JUSTICE.

This appeal arises because Grover C. Lowery conveyed the same five-acre piece of land twice—first to William A. Horvath and Barbara J. Horvath and later to William Sabo and Barbara Sabo. Both conveyances were by separate documents entitled "Quitclaim Deeds." Lowery's interest in the land originates in a patent from the United States Government under 43 U.S.C. § 687a (1970) ("Alaska Homesite Law"). Lowery's conveyance to the Horvaths was prior to the issuance of patent, and his subsequent conveyance to the Sabos was after the issuance of patent. The Horvaths recorded their deed in the Chitna Recording District on January 5, 1970; the Sabos recorded their deed on December 13, 1973. The transfer to the Horvaths, however, predated patent and title, and thus the Horvaths' interest in the land was recorded "outside the chain of title." Mr. Horvath brought suit to quiet title, and the Sabos counterclaimed to quiet their title.

In a memorandum opinion, the superior court ruled that Lowery had an equitable interest capable of transfer at the time of his conveyance to the Horvaths and further said the transfer contemplated more than a "mere quitclaim"—it warranted patent would be transferred. The superior court also held that Horvath had the superior claim to the land because his prior recording had given the Sabos constructive notice for purposes of AS 34.15.290.[1] The Sabos' appeal raises the following issues:

1. Under 43 U.S.C. § 687a (1970), when did Lowery obtain a present equitable interest in land which he could convey?

2. Are the Sabos, as grantees under a quitclaim deed, "subsequent innocent purchaser[s] in good faith"?

3. Is the Horvaths' first recorded interest, which is outside the chain of title, constructive notice to Sabo?

We affirm the trial court's ruling that Lowery had an interest to convey at the time of his conveyance to the Horvaths. We further hold that Sabo may be a "good faith purchaser" even though he takes by quitclaim deed. We reverse the trial court's ruling that Sabo had constructive notice and hold that a deed recorded outside the chain of title is a "wild deed" and does not give constructive notice under the recording laws of Alaska.[2]

The facts may be stated as follows. Grover C. Lowery occupied land in the Chitna Recording District on October 10, 1964 for purposes of obtaining Federal patent. Lowery filed a location notice on February 24, 1965, and made his application to purchase on June 6, 1967 with the Bureau of Land Management (BLM). On March 7, 1968, the BLM field examiner's report was filed which recommended that patent issue to Lowery. On October 7, 1969, a request for survey was made by the United States Government. On January 3, 1970, Lowery issued a document entitled "Quitclaim Deed" to the Horvaths; Horvath recorded the deed on January 5, 1970 in the Chitna Recording District. Horvath testified that when he bought the land from Lowery, he knew patent and

---

1. AS 34.15.290 states:

A conveyance of real property in the state hereafter made, other than a lease for a term not exceeding one year, is void as against a subsequent innocent purchaser or mortgagee in good faith for a valuable consideration of the property or a portion of it, whose conveyance is first duly recorded. An unrecorded instrument is val- id as between the parties to it and as against one who has actual notice of it.

2. Because we hold Lowery had a conveyable interest under the Federal statute, we need not decide issues raised by the parties regarding after-acquired property and the related issue of estoppel by deed.

title were still in the United States Government, but he did not rerecord his interest after patent had passed to Lowery.

Following the sale to the Horvaths, further action was taken by Lowery and the BLM pertaining to the application for patent and culminating in issuance of the patent on August 10, 1973.

Almost immediately after the patent was issued, Lowery advertised the land for sale in a newspaper. He then executed a second document also entitled "quitclaim" to the Sabos on October 15, 1973. The Sabos duly recorded this document on December 13, 1973.

* * *

The first question this court must consider is whether Lowery had an interest to convey at the time of his transfer to the Horvaths. Lowery's interest was obtained pursuant to patent law 43 U.S.C. § 687a (1970) commonly called the "Alaska Homesite Law". Since Lowery's title to the property was contingent upon the patent ultimately issuing from the United States Government and since Lowery's conveyance to the Horvaths predated issuance of the patent, the question is "at what point in the pre-patent chain of procedures does a person have a sufficient interest in a particular tract of land to convey that land by quitclaim deed." Willis v. City of Valdez, 546 P.2d 570, 575 (Alaska 1976).

* * *

In *Willis* we held that one who later secured a patent under the Solders' Additional Homestead Act had an interest in land which was alienable at the time that he requested a survey. Here, Lowery had complied with numerous requirements under the Homesite Law including those of occupancy, and the BLM had recommended issuance of the patent. Since 43 U.S.C. § 687a (1970) does not prohibit alienation, we hold that at the time Lowery executed the deed to the Horvaths he had complied with the statute to a sufficient extent so as to have an interest in the land which was capable of conveyance.

Since the Horvaths received a valid interest from Lowery, we must now resolve the conflict between the Horvaths' first recorded interest and the Sabos' later recorded interest.

The Sabos, like the Horvaths, received their interest in the property by a quitclaim deed. They are asserting that their interest supersedes the Horvaths under Alaska's statutory recording system. AS 34.15.290 provides that:

> A conveyance of real property * * * is void as against a subsequent innocent purchaser * * * for a valuable consideration of the property * * * whose conveyance is first duly recorded. An unrecorded instrument is valid * * * as against one who has actual notice of it.

Initially, we must decide whether the Sabos, who received their interest by means of a quitclaim deed, can ever be "innocent purchaser[s]" within the meaning of AS 34.15.290. Since a "quitclaim" only transfers the interest of the grantor, the question is whether a "quit-claim" deed itself puts a purchaser on constructive notice. Although the authorities are in conflict over this issue, the clear weight of authority is that a quitclaim grantee can be protected by the recording system, assuming, of course, the grantee purchased for valuable consideration and did not otherwise have actual or constructive knowledge as defined by the recording laws. We choose to follow the majority rule and hold that a quitclaim grantee is not precluded from attaining the status of an "innocent purchaser."

In this case, the Horvaths recorded their interest from Lowery prior to the time the Sabos recorded their interest. Thus, the issue is whether the Sabos are charged with constructive knowledge because of the Horvaths' prior recordation. Horvath is correct in his assertion that in the usual case a prior recorded deed serves as constructive notice pursuant to AS 34.15.290, and thus precludes a subsequent recordation from taking precedence. Here, however, the Sabos argue that because Horvath recorded his deed prior to Lowery having obtained patent, they were not given constructive notice by the recording system. They contend that since Horvaths' recordation was outside the chain of title, the recording should be regarded as a "wild deed".

It is an axiom of hornbook law that a purchaser has notice only of recorded instruments that are within his "chain of title." If a grantor (Lowery) transfers prior to obtaining title, and the grantee (Horvath) records prior to title passing, a second grantee who diligently examines all conveyances under the grantor's name from the date that the grantor had secured title would not discover the prior conveyance. The rule in most jurisdictions which have adopted a grantor-grantee index system of recording is that a "wild deed" does not serve as constructive notice to a subsequent purchaser who duly records.

Alaska's recording system utilizes a "grantor-grantee" index. Had Sabos searched title under both grantor's and grantee's names but limited his search to the chain of title subsequent to patent, he would not be chargeable with discovery of the pre-patent transfer to Horvath.

On one hand, we could require Sabo to check beyond the chain of title to look for pretitle conveyances. While in this particular case the burden may not have been great, as a general rule, requiring title checks beyond the chain of title could add a significant burden as well as uncertainty to real estate purchases. To a certain extent, requiring title searches of records prior to the date of a grantor acquired title would thus defeat the purposes of the recording system. The records as to each grantor in the chain of title would theoretically have to be checked back to the later of the grantor's date of birth or the date when records were first retained.

On the other hand, we could require Horvath to rerecord his interest in the land once title passes, that it, after patent had issued to Lowery. As a general rule, rerecording an interest once title passes is less of a burden than requiring property purchasers to check indefinitely beyond the chain of title.

It is unfortunate that in this case due to Lowery's double conveyances, one or the other party to this suit must suffer an undeserved loss. We are cognizant that in this case, the equities are closely balanced between the parties to this appeal. Our decision, however, in addition to resolving the litigants' dispute, must delineate the requirements of Alaska's recording laws.

Because we want to promote simplicity and certainty in title transactions, we choose to follow the majority rule and hold that the Horvaths' deed, recorded outside the chain of title, does not give constructive notice to the Sabos and is not "duly recorded" under the Alaskan Recording Act, AS 34.15.290. Since the Sabos' interest is the first duly recorded interest and was recorded without actual or constructive knowledge of the prior deed, we hold that the Sabos' interest must prevail. The trial court's decision is accordingly.

REVERSED.

Problem

In early 1998, P and S entered a contract for P to purchase a 40–acre vacant tract of land from S. P looked at the records and found that S had acquired the tract from O by a deed dated and recorded on July 13, 1995. On March 1, 1998, P paid S the purchase price and S deeded the tract to P who recorded immediately. Shortly thereafter, X contacted P and claimed ownership of the tract. X has a deed from S dated and recorded on September 2, 1990. Who prevails?

This problem presents the after-acquired title issue noted, but not addressed, in *Sabo. See* page 542 n.2. The doctrine of after-acquired title, or estoppel-by-deed as it is often called, was developed to prevent a grantor (S in our problem), who did not have title at the time of the conveyance but subsequently acquired it, from denying the grantee's ownership of the land in question. Title automatically passes to the grantee (X in our problem) by operation of law once it is actually acquired by the grantor. The doctrine generally operates, however, only when the grantor warranted title at the time the grantor purportedly conveyed it to the grantee. *See* Wood v. Sympson, 833 P.2d 1239 (Okl.1992); 3 American Law of Property §§ 15.19–15.21 (1952).

Is a person who purchases the land from the grantor after the grantor actually acquired title (P in our problem) bound by the doctrine of after-acquired title? That is, who is entitled to the property in such case, the original grantee (X) or the subsequent purchaser (P)? The answer depends on whether the subsequent purchaser had notice of the interest the original grantee received under the doctrine. Many jurisdictions follow the reasoning in *Sabo* and find for the subsequent purchaser. *E.g.,* Wheeler v. Young, 76 Conn. 44, 55 A. 670 (1903). Some states, however, favor the original grantee on the ground that a subsequent purchaser has constructive notice of documents recorded under the grantor's name *before* as well as after the grantor acquires title. *E.g.,* Ayer v. Philadelphia & Boston Face Brick Co.,

159 Mass. 84, 34 N.E. 177 (1893); *see also* Robben v. Obering, 279 F.2d 381 (7th Cir.1960). Which is the better view? *See* 3 American Law of Property §§ 15.21–15.22 (1952).

WITTER v. TAGGART

Court of Appeals of New York, 1991.
78 N.Y.2d 234, 573 N.Y.S.2d 146, 577 N.E.2d 338.

BELLACOSA, JUDGE.

Plaintiff Witter and defendants Taggarts are East Islip neighboring property owners. Their homes are on opposite sides of a canal on the south shore of Long Island. Witter's home is north of the canal and the Taggarts' home and dock are across the canal on the south side. The Winganhauppauge or Champlin's Creek lies immediately west of both parcels. Their property dispute arose when the Taggarts erected a 70–foot long dock on their canal-side frontage. This was done after a title search revealed that their deed expressly permitted building the dock and reflected no recorded restrictions in their direct property chain against doing so. Witter complained of a violation of his scenic easement to an unobstructed view of the creek and an adjacent nature preserve, which he claims is protected by a restrictive covenant contained in his chain of title. He sued to compel the Taggarts to dismantle and remove the dock and to permanently enjoin any such building in the future.

Supreme Court granted the Taggarts' motion for summary judgment dismissing Witter's complaint and denied Witter's cross motion for summary judgment. Relying principally on Buffalo Academy of Sacred Heart v. Boehm Bros., 267 N.Y. 242, 196 N.E. 42, the trial court held that the Taggarts are not bound by or charged with constructive notice of a restrictive covenant which does not appear in their direct chain of title to the allegedly burdened land. * * *

The Appellate Division affirmed the instant case, reasoning that under Buffalo Academy, 267 N.Y. 242, 196 N.E. 42, *supra* the restrictive covenant contained in the chain of deeds to Witter's allegedly benefited parcel was outside the chain of title to the Taggarts' land and did not constitute binding notice to them (167 A.D.2d 397, 561 N.Y.S.2d 808).

We granted Witter's motion for leave to appeal to decide whether the covenant recited in Witter's chain of title to his purported "dominant" land, which appears nowhere in the direct chain of title to the Taggarts' purported "servient" land, burdens the Taggarts' property. We agree with the lower courts that it does not, and therefore affirm the order of the Appellate Division.

The homes of these neighbors are located on lots which have been separately deeded through a series of conveyances, originally severed and conveyed out by a common grantor, Lawrance. Lawrance conveyed one parcel of his land to Witter's predecessor in title in 1951. The deed contained the restrictive covenant providing that "no docks, buildings, or other structures [or trees or plants] shall be erected [or grown]" on the grantor's (Lawrance's) retained servient lands to the north "which shall obstruct or interfere with the outlook or view from the [dominant] premises" over the Winganhauppauge Creek. That deed provided that the covenant expressly ran with the *dominant* land. William and Susan Witter purchased the dominant parcel in 1963 by deed granting them all the rights of their grantor, which included the restrictive covenant. In 1984, Susan Witter transferred her interest to William Witter alone.

After common grantor Lawrance died, his heirs in 1962 conveyed his retained, allegedly servient, land to the Taggarts' predecessor in title. Lawrance's deed made no reference to the restrictive covenant benefiting the Witter property and neither did the heirs' deed to the Taggarts' predecessors. The restrictive covenant was also not included or referenced in any of the several subsequent mesne conveyances of that allegedly servient parcel or in the deed ultimately to the Taggarts in 1984. Quite to the contrary, the Taggarts' deed specifically permitted them to build a dock on their parcel.

Restrictive covenants are also commonly categorized as negative easements. They restrain servient landowners from making otherwise lawful uses of their property. However, the law has long favored free and unencumbered use of real property, and covenants restricting use are strictly construed against those seeking to enforce them.

The guiding principle for determining the ultimate binding effect of a restrictive covenant is that "[i]n the absence of actual notice before or at the time of * * * purchase or of other exceptional circumstances, an owner of land is only bound by restrictions if they appear in some deed of record in the conveyance to [that owner] or [that owner's] direct predecessors in title." (Buffalo Academy of Sacred Heart v. Boehm Bros., 267 N.Y. at 250, 196 N.E. 42.) Courts have consistently recognized and applied this principle, which provides reliability and certainty in land ownership and use (*see,* Doyle v. Lazarro, 33 A.D.2d 142, 144, 306 N.Y.S.2d 268, aff'd without opn. 33 N.Y.2d 981, 353 N.Y.S.2d 740, 309 N.E.2d 138).

In *Buffalo Academy,* we held that a restrictive covenant did not run with the dominant land, but added that even if it did, the servient landowners were not bound because the deed to the servient land did not reflect the covenant. We noted that this rule is "implicit in the acts providing for the recording of conveyances." (267 N.Y. at 250, 196 N.E. 42.) The recording act (Real Property Law art. 9) was enacted to accomplish a twofold purpose: to protect the rights of innocent purchasers who acquire an interest in property without knowledge of prior encumbrances, and to establish a public record which will furnish potential purchasers with actual or at least constructive notice of previous conveyances and encumbrances that might affect their interests and uses.

The recording statutes in a grantor-grantee indexing system charge a purchaser with notice of matters only in the record of the purchased land's chain of title back to the original grantor. *Buffalo Academy* recognized that a "purchaser is not normally required to search *outside* the chain of title" (*Doyle v. Lazarro, supra* [emphasis added]), and is not chargeable with constructive notice of conveyances recorded outside of that purchaser's direct chain of title where, as in Suffolk County, the grantor-grantee system of indexing is used. This is true even if covenants are included in a deed to another lot conveyed by the same grantor.

To impute legal notice for failing to search each chain of title or "deed out" from a common grantor "would seem to negative the beneficent purposes of the recording acts" and would place too great a burden on prospective purchasers (Buffalo Academy of Sacred Heart v. Boehm Bros., 267 N.Y., *supra,* at 250, 196 N.E. 42). Therefore, purchasers like the Taggarts should not be penalized for failing to search every chain of title branching out from a common grantor's roots in order to unearth potential restrictive covenants. They are legally bound to search only within their own tree trunk line and are bound by constructive or inquiry notice only of restrictions which appear in deeds or other instruments of conveyance in that primary stem. Property law principles and practice have long established that a deed conveyed by a common grantor to a dominant landowner does *not* form part of the chain of title to the servient land retained by the common grantor.

A grantor may effectively extinguish or terminate a covenant when, as here, the grantor conveys retained servient land to a bona fide purchaser who takes title without actual or constructive notice of the covenant because the grantor and dominant owner failed to record the covenant in the servient land's chain of title. One way the dominant landowner or grantor can prevent this result is by recording in the servient chain the conveyance creating the covenant rights so as to impose notice on subsequent purchasers of the servient land.

It goes almost without repeating that definiteness, certainty, alienability and unencumbered use of property are highly desirable objectives of property law. To restrict the Taggarts because of Lawrance's failure to include the covenant in the deed to his retained servient land, or for the failure by Witter's predecessors to insist that it be protected and recorded so as to be enforceable against the burdened property, would seriously undermine these paramount values, as well as the recording acts.

* * *

Order affirmed, with costs.

Notes and Questions

1.   Courts are split on the issue of notice of restrictive covenants in collateral deeds from a common grantor. *See* 4 American Law of Property § 17.24 (1952). The Supreme Court of Kentucky recently switched views on the subject, adopting the approach expressed in *Witter.* Oliver v. Schultz, 885 S.W.2d 699 (Ky.1994) (holding that no longer will restriction set forth in collateral recorded instrument impart notice to subsequent purchaser in that jurisdiction). On the other hand, the Supreme Court of Rhode Island has taken the position that a landowner had constructive notice of an easement

contained in the deeds of adjacent owners from a common grantor. Rowland Family Trust v. Pelletier, 673 A.2d 1081 (R.I.1996).

2. A document in the chain of title may contain information indicating a possible cloud on the title. In such case, a purchaser is obligated to make further inquiry and is charged with knowledge which reasonable inquiry would disclose. *See* Kordecki v. Rizzo, 106 Wis.2d 713, 317 N.W.2d 479 (1982).

BANK OF MISSISSIPPI v. HOLLINGSWORTH

Supreme Court of Mississippi, 1992.
609 So.2d 422.

BANKS, JUSTICE, for the court:

This case concerns an application of the well-established doctrine that physical presence is an indicia of ownership, which may override record title with respect to subsequent purchasers. Here, application of the doctrine serves to defeat a deed of trust filed prior in time to a deed of conveyance to a third party, where the third party had taken possession in a manner sufficient to put the lender on notice that ownership may not be accurately reflected by the deeds of record.

I

On June 16, 1989, in the Chancery Court of Jones County, First Judicial District, Wayne and Debbie Hollingsworth (Hollingsworths) filed a complaint for Injunction and Partial Cancellation of Deed In Trust against the Bank of Mississippi (Bank). The complaint alleged that on April 11, 1983, Mamie Walters Robinson, now deceased, conveyed by warranty deed a certain parcel consisting of approximately 27 acres to the Hollingsworths. On January 24, 1984, William Robinson, Frances E. Robinson and Mamie Walters Robinson executed a deed of trust to James McKenzie, as trustee for the Bank, and recorded the same in the Jones County Chancery Clerk's Office on January 27, 1984, conveying three parcels, consisting of approximately 60 acres, including 18 of the acres previously conveyed to the Hollingsworths.

The Hollingsworths did not record their deed until April 30, 1985. They alleged in their complaint, however, that at all times after April 1, 1983, they "were in open and obvious actual occupancy and possession" of the 18 acres.

The Hollingsworths moved the court for a temporary restraining order without notice to prevent the bank from foreclosing the deed of trust lien. On June 19, 1989, the Chancellor granted the Hollingsworths a Temporary Restraining Order against the Bank and enjoined them from foreclosing on the property in question.

The Bank answered the Hollingsworths' complaint by moving to dismiss for failure to state a cause of action upon which relief could be granted. Additionally, the Bank answered that they filed their deed of trust lien for record on January 27, 1984, prior to the Hollingsworths'

Warranty Deed, thus giving the Hollingsworths constructive notice that the Bank had a deed of trust lien on the subject property. The Bank moved for damages and losses as a result of the Restraining Order granted without notice.

On December 6, 1989, following a trial of the matter on July 18, 1989, the Chancellor entered an order granting a permanent injunction against foreclosure and partial cancellation of the Bank's deed of trust lien as to 18 acres. The Chancellor found that the property had been enclosed by a fence in 1983, prior to the deed of trust being recorded, and that the fence was visible to any one making a physical inspection of the premises. He held that by enclosing the property inside a fence, the Hollingsworths came into possession of the property, prior to the execution of the deed of trust by Mamie Robinson. He further held that had the bank conducted a reasonable inspection of the property, the Bank would have been on notice that someone had the tract of land fenced and enclosed with an adjacent tract. Therefore, a reasonable inquiry into "this act of possession may have revealed the existence of the unrecorded deed, or, at least, put the bank on notice that someone else may be claiming title to the 18–acre tract." The Chancellor held that as a result of the Bank's failure to make a reasonable inspection and inquiry, it is barred from claiming any benefits under the recording statute because possession by someone other than the grantor would constitute actual notice to the lender. The chancellor cancelled the deed of trust lien on the property.

* * *

* * * In a timely manner, the Bank perfected its appeal to this Court.

II

On January 19, 1984, Bill Robinson applied to the Bank for a loan. Following discussions with the Bank's loan officer and after complying with the usual application process, Mr. Robinson provided the Bank a title certificate from his attorney on 60 acres of land. The title opinion indicated that Mamie Robinson was the record owner of the land pledged as security for repayment of the proposed debt to the Bank and that title was free and clear subject to exceptions including: "3. Any facts which a physical survey of the premises would reveal."

Hugh Garraway, Jr., the loan officer who approved the loan, testified that the Bank did not order a survey and never made a visual inspection of the property to determine if anyone else was claiming the property in question, because the title certificate indicated that the land was free and clear of all liens.

Gar[r]away testified that it was customary for the Bank to inspect the property on a map, locate it and place an approximate value in the property for appraisal purposes. Gar[r]away never met Wayne Hollingsworth until June 1989 and did not receive any written notice from the

Hollingsworths as to their claim of ownership of the 18–acre tract in dispute.

Wayne Hollingsworth testified that he bought the property from his wife's grandmother, Mamie, in 1983. He produced two cancelled checks in amounts corresponding to his claim that he paid $750 per acre for the land. He said that he did not record the deed out of ignorance. Prior to 1986, the property in dispute was assessed for tax purposes to Mamie Robinson.

It is undisputed that in 1983 Wayne had a fence placed around the entire 27–acre parcel purchased from Mamie, including the 18 acres in question. The evidence indicated that the fence was distinctive in that all of the posts were painted white at the top. It is also undisputed that there was no fence separating the 18–acre parcel from the 27 acres upon which the Hollingsworths' home is now situated. The home, built in 1985, after the bank's deed of trust had been recorded, is not located on the 18–acre parcel in dispute.

Bill, Francis and Mamie Robinson signed and delivered to the Bank a promissory note and deed of trust covering the 60 acres of land on or about January 23, 1984, securing a loan in the principal sum of $45,000, plus interest. Mr. Robinson received the loan proceeds from the Bank. The loan was renewed several times, but remained secured by the initial deed of trust. The loan ultimately went into default and the Bank attempted to enforce payment by foreclosure of its lien, when the foreclosure sale scheduled for June 20, 1989, was restrained by the chancellor's order in these proceedings.

In this appeal, the bank asks that we find the chancellor erred in fact and law. The Bank's argument is that the chancellor erred in finding that the construction of the fence on the property in question constituted adequate notice to the Bank that someone was in possession of the property and that the court's decision placed upon the bank a duty of inquiry not supported by law.

* * *

IV

The issue is whether the chancellor was correct in determining that as a result of the construction of a fence on the land in question, the Bank had constructive notice that someone was claiming title to the land. The Bank argues that the mere act of possession by the Hollingsworths is not, in and of itself, legally sufficient to constitute actual notice to the Bank, absent a requirement of a physical inspection of the premises or such other inquiry regarding title. Our law is to the contrary.

"Possession of land by one under claim of title is notice to the world of such claim. The rights of such a claimant are protected against a bona fide purchaser for value, although the evidence of his title be not of record." Russell v. Scarborough, 155 Miss. 508, 511, 124 So. 648 (1929); Stevens v. Hill, 236 So.2d 430 (1970); Gulf Refining Co. v. Travis, 201

Miss. 336, 29 So.2d 100 (1947). *Stevens* holds that "possession of real estate is constructive notice of the title in the occupant to the same extent as that imputed by the record of a deed to him thereto." 236 So.2d at 434. *Gulf Refining* holds that "the registration statutes do not affect an owner in possession by himself or by his tenants, and that his actual possession is all the notice necessary to any prospective purchaser." 29 So.2d at 102. This is a principle well established in our law which we have reaffirmed as recently as 1982. Morgan v. Sauls, 413 So.2d 370, 375 n. 5 (Miss.1982).

Although our recordation statutes speak of "actual" notice, this court observed in *Gulf Refining* that the 1924 amendment adding that language was directed at notice of earlier deeds and does not apply to "the established rule with reference to the effect of actual possession of land." 201 Miss. at 366; 29 So.2d at 102.

The sole question in this case is whether the indicia of possession established by the evidence is sufficient. For "possession [to] have the effect of protecting the title under which it is held, it must be of that character which would arrest attention." Loughridge & Bogan v. Bowland, 52 Miss. 546 (1876). We have held that fences satisfy the requirements of "actual, open, notorious, and visible" occupancy in adverse possession cases. Cole v. Burleson, 375 So.2d 1046, 1048 (Miss.1979) citing, Berry v. Houston, 195 So.2d 515, 518 (Miss.1967). Here, the chancellor found that the construction of the fence was sufficient to put the Hollingsworths in possession. We will not disturb that finding.

V

For the foregoing reasons, we affirm.

AFFIRMED.

Notes, Problems, and Questions

1. *Hollingsworth* represents the generally accepted view that a purchaser is charged with inquiry notice from the fact of possession. Some courts, however, apparently require inquiry only if the purchaser actually knows of the possession. *See* J. Cribbet & C. Johnson, Principles of the Law of Property 318–319 (3d ed. 1989). What arguments exist for each position?

2. Recall that the concept of inquiry notice is important with respect to whether an implied equitable servitude is binding on a subsequent purchaser. *See Sanborn v. McLean* (page 394).

3. A and B were record title holders of Blackacre as joint tenants. B was in possession. A conveyed A's undivided one-half interest in Blackacre to B who failed to record. A then conveyed A's undivided one-half interest in Blackacre to X who recorded. Who prevails between B and X? *See* W. Burby, Handbook of the Law of Real Property 330 (3d ed. 1965).

4. Assume you searched the records for the Ryans and found no apparent flaws in the chain of title. The Ryans, however, learned of a rumor that a previous owner of this lot had sold it to an unmarried army officer in the late 1960's. The story goes that the officer was transferred to Vietnam

before recording the deed and was subsequently killed in action. The previous owner then sold the property to the present record title holder. The Ryans have questioned the present owner, but the owner disavows any knowledge of the story. Steve and Jill are concerned that if they decide to close the deal and the rumor proves to be true, their title to the land might be challenged. They ask for your advice.

5. RECENT STATUTORY DEVELOPMENTS

a. *Introduction*

REPORT, RESIDENTIAL REAL ESTATE TRANSACTIONS: THE LAWYER'S PROPER ROLE—SERVICES—COMPENSATION

14 Real Prop., Prob. & Tr.J. 581, 595–598 (1979).

A. TITLE EXAMINATION COSTS

Title examination often is expensive because of the excessive labor input under the present system. This high labor input is the result of the following major causes: (1) Condition of public land title records; (2) Lack of marketable title legislation; and (3) Lack of title curative legislation.

1. *Condition of Public Land Title Records*

Our system of public land title records was designed to fit the needs of a rural community. It was invented by the Massachusetts colonists and has not been essentially changed in the interim. The records often are so scattered in different offices, so voluminous, or so badly indexed, as to make the task of separating the relevant from the irrelevant long and arduous. Where lawyers must resort to direct examination of these records, the cost, in terms of their time, is clearly apparent.

Less apparent is the high cost arising out of the use of private title plants, whether these plants are the property of individuals, abstract companies or title insurance companies. These plants duplicate the public records except that all relevant material is consolidated and efficiently indexed. They should not be needed. They are expensive to create and maintain, and until they are superseded by adequate public records we cannot realistically expect to reduce the cost of title proof.

The creation and maintenance of a title plant in a major city is extremely expensive. Unless something is done to check this expense, title and abstract companies may price themselves out of the market while there is still no practical substitute for the services they perform. The economic repercussions of such an eventuality cannot be assessed but would undoubtedly be serious. These repercussions must be avoided by the creation of adequate public records at government expense.

In some of our largest cities, title companies have ceased to maintain full plants, in others consolidation of facilities has been resorted to, and everywhere efforts are being made to keep costs within manageable limits. Excessive expense entailed in the daily takeoff has led some title insurance executives to become proponents of adequate public records. In 1968 the then treasurer of the American Land Title Association took this position and stigmatized the waste involved in private title plants as "immoral," "unconscionable" and "reprehensible."

At this point it should be made clear there is no criticism of the individuals and corporations who have created title plants in an effort to meet an immediate public demand. However, if the public records were adequate, title plants would not be necessary. It would be unwise to assume we will continue to use them indefinitely; it would be unrealistic to assume we can dispense with them immediately.

It is universally assumed that we can eliminate the need for private title plants and reduce the high cost of title examination only by the creation of an efficient system of public land records. Agreement about the details of any new system is lacking. Currently most investigation is directed toward the creation of computerized land data banks. Computerization offers a fruitful field for investigation and should be the object of further study. At the same time the field of investigation should be expanded to non-computerized systems. Such less sophisticated systems, which can be installed in the near future and at limited expense, are urgently needed. Such systems can undoubtedly be created. Block indexing in New York City, Baltimore and Mississippi, and the official and unofficial tract indexes found in courthouses in Mississippi, Oklahoma and some other states are prototypes upon which highly efficient systems might be developed. Alabama has adopted a self-indexing system along novel lines. None of these approaches is specifically endorsed. Other systems may be practicable. As many systems as possible should be investigated and it should be kept in mind that a system satisfactory for installation in one part of the country may not be suitable elsewhere. National uniformity is not necessary and may not be desirable.

There are reports now nearing completion under the sponsorship of the federal Department of Housing and Urban Development into ways to improve the efficiency of public records and to lower costs for title searching and examination.

2. Lack of Marketable Title Legislation

A second means of reducing title costs can be achieved by shortening the period of search. While the invention of the recording system was a great improvement over the then existing English system, or non-system, it would have been a greater improvement if a limit had been placed on the duration of the notice created by recording.

While the various statutes of limitations can be relied upon to bar many ancient claims, there are other interests as to which the applicable statute does not begin to run until the interest has been violated. A purchaser needs, of course, to know about these. As a consequence, in theory, it is necessary to trace every title back to its origin in the state. To do so is already impractical in much of our country and will ultimately become so elsewhere. As a consequence, conveyancers conventionally limit search to an arbitrary number of years. Aside from the fact that this practice is resorted to at the risk of the lawyer's client, the periods set, ranging up to sixty or more years, result in an enormous and unnecessary input of labor.

What is needed is a theory of title which will permit the examining lawyer to trace the title back for only a relatively short number of years with complete confidence that his client will be protected from all adverse claims antedating a record root of title. This reform should be accompanied by limitations on the period during which title claims, including those of record and those not of record, remain viable. Much legislation is developing piecemeal, in a number of states, some based on shortening the applicable statutes of limitations, others based on a periodic rerecording requirement for certain specific interests, and others based on marketable title acts. All these approaches can be improved and extended. Special attention is directed to the need to amend the existing marketable title acts.

The Uniform Simplification of Land Transfers Act, recently adopted by the National Conference of Commissioners on Uniform State Laws and approved by the American Bar Association, sets forth a uniform marketable title act, and deserves serious consideration by the organized bar and state legislatures.[1]

A prerequisite to completely effective marketable title acts is the adoption of federal legislation permitting the application of these acts to federal lands and federal claims. Unlike statutes of limitation, marketable title acts can be made to apply to federal lands without serious adverse effects even in areas where the government owns large tracts of unimproved and unpoliced property. All that is necessary is to require, as a prerequisite to marketability, the assessment of land for taxes for a given period of time. This provision must be coupled with a requirement that local tax assessors notify the attorney general when public land is assessed to private individuals. This system results in the government being given reasonable warning of any effort to acquire marketable title to its holdings. When so notified the government can, at little or no expense, take necessary steps to prevent loss of title. If adverse possession were to operate against the federal government, the government could lose land without being made aware of the fact. No such result would follow the enactment of properly drafted marketable title legislation.

3. Lack of Title Curative Legislation

Many titles may be unmarketable because of formal defects in the record. These defects are cost-generating because they must be removed by time-consuming investigation and curative action. While adequate marketable title legislation will wipe out the effect of older defects, many

---

1. The National Conference of Commissioners on Uniform State Laws promulgated the Uniform Marketable Title Act in 1990. See pages 556–561. [Editors' note.]

recent defects, not barred by marketable title acts, are the result of highly artificial rules of law or unintentional blunders by the parties. Any such impediments to marketability should be cured in a much shorter time than that set by even the most liberal marketable title act. To achieve this result, a large volume of title curative legislation is required. Some such legislation will be needed because of law peculiar to a particular locality. However, a number of problems are universal. They can be cured by title curative legislation in virtually every state. Adequate models to assist legislatures in their task of systematic reform are required.

B. Other Conveyancing Costs

Other areas of the conveyancing process are ripe for efforts to increase efficiency and to reduce costs. Some inefficiencies are the result of outside forces; others arise from the practice of lawyers themselves. An example of the former is the large and increasing amount of paper work demanded by governmental organizations. The effect of the adoption of the Real Estate Settlement Procedures Act, the effect of the Truth–In–Lending Act and FHA and VA demands for "uncompensated" work has already been alluded to. Increasing federal demands for paper work are incompatible with the efforts to reduce closing costs and it is unrealistic to believe that services demanded by the government will not result in higher closing costs.

Internal inefficiencies may result from improper procedures and allocations of personnel within a given law office. These inefficiencies have been under study by the American Bar Association and many state bar associations for many years and are being eliminated as rapidly as possible. Other internal inefficiencies result in title practice, as in other fields of the law, from an outdated legal structure which compels elaborate and time-consuming procedures to accomplish routine ends.

---

b. *Marketable Title Statutes*

To determine the status of title to a particular parcel of land, a title examiner theoretically must search back to the point when the land passed from government ownership into private hands. In some cases this occurred more than 150 years ago. The potentially overwhelming task facing title examiners has been eased by two developments. First, many bar associations have adopted a customary period of search, often sixty years, as part of a set of informal guidelines for title examiners called title standards. *See* P. Basye, Clearing Land Titles §§ 3, 7 (2d ed. 1970 & Supp.1997). Second and more significantly, approximately twenty states have enacted marketable title statutes that limit the required period of search to a certain period of time, usually thirty or forty years. *See id.* at § 173; 14 Powell on Real Property § 82.04 (1998). Following are salient portions of the Uniform Marketable Title Act promulgated by the National Conference of Commissioners on Uniform State Law in 1990.

UNIFORM MARKETABLE TITLE ACT*

§ 1. Definitions

In this [Act], unless the context otherwise requires:

* * *

(5) "Marketable record title" means a title of record, complying with Section 3, that operates to extinguish interests and claims existing before the effective date of the root of title, as provided in Section 5.

* * *

(14) "Root of title" means a conveyance or other title transaction, whether or not it is a nullity, in the record chain of title of a person, purporting to create or containing language sufficient to transfer the interest claimed by that person, upon which that person relies as a basis for marketability of title, and which was the most recent to be recorded as of a date 30 years before the time marketability is being determined.

* * *

§ 2. Notice; Knowledge; Giving Notice; Receipt of Notice

(a) A person has notice of a fact if:

(1) the person has actual knowledge of it;

(2) the person has received a notice of it; or

(3) from all the facts and circumstances known to the person at the time in question that person has reason to know it exists.

(b) Except as provided in subsection (e), a person has knowledge or learns of a fact or knows or discovers a fact only when the person has actual knowledge of it.

(c) A person notifies or gives or sends notice to another, whether or not the other person actually comes to know of it, by taking steps reasonably required to inform the other in ordinary course, but if this [Act] specifies particular steps to be taken to notify or to give or send notice, those steps must be taken.

(d) A person receives a notice at the time it:

(1) comes to the person's attention; or

(2) is delivered at the place of business through which the person conducted the transaction with respect to which the notice is

---

* Certain comments have been omitted without indication.

given or at any other place held out by the person as the place for receipt of the communication.

(e) Notice, or knowledge of a notice, received by a person is effective for a particular transaction at the earlier of the time it comes to the attention of the individual conducting the transaction or the time it would have come to the individual's attention had the person maintained reasonable routines for communicating significant information to the individual conducting the transaction and had there been reasonable compliance with the routines. Reasonable compliance does not require an individual acting for the person to communicate information unless the communication is part of the individual's regular duties or the individual has reason to know of the transaction and that the transaction would be materially affected by the information.

§ 3. Marketable Record Title

(a) A person who has an unbroken record chain of title to real estate for 30 years or more has a marketable record title to the real estate, subject only to the matters stated in Section 4.

(b) A person has an unbroken chain of title if the official public records disclose a conveyance, or other title transaction, of record not less than 30 years before the time marketability is determined, and the conveyance or other title transaction, whether or not it was a nullity, purports to create the interest in or contains language sufficient to transfer the interest to:

(1) the person claiming the interest; or

(2) some other person from whom, by one or more conveyances or other title transactions of record, the purported interest has become vested in the person claiming the interest.

(c) If anything appears of record, in either case described in subsection (b), purporting to divest the claimant of the purported interest, the chain of title is broken.

Comment

This is the basic section which frees the holder of marketable record title from adverse claims antedating his root of title, even if the root of title is a forgery. *See* Marshall v. Hollywood, Inc., 224 So.2d 743 (Fla.App.1969), affirmed 236 So.2d 114 (Fla.1970).

§ 4. Matters to Which Marketable Record Title Is Subject

The marketable record title is subject to:

(1) all interests and defects that are apparent in the root of title or inherent in the other muniments of which the chain of record title is formed, but a general reference in a muniment to an easement, restriction, encumbrance, or other interest created before the effective date of the root of title is not sufficient to preserve it unless a reference by record location is made in the muniment to a

recorded title transaction that created the easement, restriction, encumbrance, or other interest;

(2) all interests preserved by the recording of proper notice of intent to preserve an interest;

(3) all interests arising out of title transactions recorded after the effective date of the root of title, and which have not been previously extinguished; [and]

(4) all interests preserved under Section 7[; and][.]

[(5) all interests preserved by the [Torrens Title Act].]

Comment

This section states the types of claims to which a marketable record title is subject. * * * [A]ny extension of this list may defeat the whole purpose of marketable title legislation.

* * *

§ 5. **Interests Extinguished by Marketable Record Title**

(a) In this section, "person dealing with the real estate" includes a purchaser of real estate, the taker of a security interest, a levying or attaching creditor, a real estate contract vendee, or another person seeking to acquire an estate or interest therein, or impose a lien thereon.

(b) Subject to Section 4, a marketable record title is held by its owner and is taken by a person dealing with the real estate free and clear of all interests, claims, and charges, the existence of which depends upon an act, transaction, event, or omission that occurred before the effective date of the root of title. All interests, claims, or charges, however denominated, whether legal or equitable, present or future, whether the interests, claims, or charges are asserted by a person who is or is not under a disability, whether the person is within or without the state, whether the person is an individual or an organization, or is private or governmental, are null and void.

(c) Recording an interest after the effective date of the root of title does not revive an interest previously extinguished.

Comment

This section is designed to make absolutely clear what has already been indicated in Section 3, that all interests except those indicated in Section 4 are extinguished by marketable record title.

§ 6. **Effect Upon Marketable Record Title of Recording Notice of Intent to Preserve an Interest**

(a) A person claiming an interest in real estate may preserve and keep the interest, if any, effective by recording during the 30–year period immediately following the effective date of the root of title of the person who would otherwise obtain marketable record title, a notice of intent to preserve the interest. Disability or lack of knowledge of any kind on the part of anyone does not suspend the running of the 30–year period. The notice may be recorded by the claimant or by another person acting on behalf of a claimant who is:

(1) under a disability;

(2) unable to assert a claim on his [or her] own behalf; or

(3) one of a class, but whose identity cannot be established or is uncertain at the time of recording the notice of intent to preserve the interest.

(b) The notice must:

(1) state the name of the person claiming to be the owner of the interest to be preserved;

(2) contain a reference by record location to a recorded document creating, reserving, or evidencing the interest to be preserved or a judgment confirming the interest;

(3) be signed by or on behalf of the person claiming to be the owner of the interest; and

(4) state whether the person signing claims to be the owner or to be acting on behalf of the owner.

(c) A notice recorded to preserve a utility easement claimed in the real estate of another may include a map incorporating the claim.

§ 7. Interests not Barred by [Act]

This [Act] does not bar:

(1) a restriction the existence of which is clearly observable by physical evidence of its use;

(2) a use or occupancy inconsistent with the marketable record title, to the extent that the use or occupancy would have been revealed by reasonable inspection or inquiry;

(3) rights of a person in whose name the real estate or an interest therein was carried on the real property tax rolls within three years before marketability is to be determined, if the relevant tax rolls are accessible to the public when marketability is to be determined; [and]

(4) a claim of the United States not subjected by federal law to the recording requirements of this State and which has not terminated under federal law[; and][.]

[(5) oil, gas, sulphur, coal, and all other mineral interests, whether similar or dissimilar to those minerals specifically named.]

§ 8. Effect of Contractual Liability as to Interests Antedating Root of Title

This [Act] does not relieve a person of contractual liability with respect to an interest antedating the person's root of title to which the person has agreed to be subject by reason of the provision of a deed or contract to which the person is a party, but a person under contractual liability may create a marketable record title in a transferee not otherwise subjected to the interest antedating root of title by this [Act].

Comment

This section is meant to overcome a possible constitutional problem of impairment of the obligations of contracts. Its application is limited so that it should pose no problem for the title examiner.

* * *

Notes and Questions

1. How far back must a title examiner search under this marketable title statute?

2. What is the "root of title?"

3. Can interests on record over thirty years be protected?

4. Do you see any constitutional problems with the application of a marketable title statute to interests existing prior to the enactment of the statute? *Compare* Cline v. Johnson County Board of Education, 548 S.W.2d 507 (Ky.1977) *with* Board of Education v. Miles, 15 N.Y.2d 364, 259 N.Y.S.2d 129, 207 N.E.2d 181 (1965). *See also* Texaco, Inc. v. Short, 454 U.S. 516 (1982); P. Basye, Clearing Land Titles § 175 (2d ed. 1970).

6.   TITLE REGISTRATION—THE TORRENS SYSTEM

Commentators have long attacked current title examination practices as inefficient and expensive. There have been repeated calls to streamline the conveyance process. Chief Justice Warren Burger urged the legal community to reconsider the question of title examination:

> Today, we know that in many states the incidental costs of acquiring a new home, even in the $40,000 category, can run into a very large sum. We know that, in common with others, the operating costs of lawyers have skyrocketed in recent years, but the very cost of the procedure today dictates that we examine the whole business closely.
>
> * * * The basic system of real estate titles and transfers and the related matters concerning financing and purchase of home cries out for reexamination and simplification. In a country that transfers not only expensive automobiles but multi-million dollar airplanes with a few relatively simple pieces of paper covering liens and all, I believe that if American lawyers will put their ingenuity and inventiveness to work on this subject they will be able to devise simpler methods than we now have. (Address before the American Law Institute, May 21, 1974.)

There are two primary areas of complaint. First, under the present system various instruments constituting evidence of title are recorded, but a purchaser must form an independent conclusion as to the state of the title. The purchaser acts at the purchaser's peril. Second, there must be a fresh examination of the title upon every sale of the land regardless of the length of time since the last search. Thus, the costly process of land transfer is repetitious.

The most sweeping proposed reform is title registration. Registration provides a public record of the state of the title so that a purchaser of registered land can verify any interests in the property by examination of the record. Initial registration is based upon a judicial proceeding in rem, and the state thereafter guarantees the accuracy of the registered title by an indemnity fund. Persons wrongfully deprived of an interest in land by virtue of the registration system are paid from this fund. The registrar enters the title in the registry and delivers a certificate of title to the owner. Land may be conveyed only by surrender of the owner's certificate and entry on the public registry. All subsequent transactions affecting the land must be entered on the registry, or they are invalid against a subsequent purchaser. Title registration was developed in the mid–19th century by Sir Robert Torrens in Australia, and thus registration measures are often called Torrens Acts. *See generally* P. Butt, Land Law 686–778 (3d ed.1996); D. Whalen, The Torrens System in Australia (1982); McCormack, *Torrens and Recording: Land Title Assurance in the Computer Age,* 18 Wm. Mitchell L.Rev. 61 (1992); Comment, *Yes Virginia—There is A Torrens Act,* 9 U.Rich.L.Rev. 301 (1975).

A number of states have statutes authorizing title registration of land. Such legislation, however, is not compulsory and the recording system remains in effect. As a result, the registration of titles has moved very slowly. Individuals rarely register residential property. The initial expense of registration, coupled with the opposition of the bar and title insurance companies, helps explain the failure of title registration in the United States. *See generally* Comment, *The Torrens System of Title Registration: A New Proposal for Effective Implementation,* 29 UCLA L.Rev. 661 (1982).

In contrast, title registration has been successful in Great Britain. Under the Land Registration Act of 1925 compulsory registration is gradually being extended, and an estimated 75 percent of conveyances in England and Wales involve registration. For the British experience, see K. Gray & P. Symes, *Real Property and Real People* (1981); Bostick, *Land Title Registration: An English Solution to an American Problem,* 63 Ind.L.J. 55 (1987); Fiflis, *English Registered Conveyancing: A Study in Effective Land Transfer,* 59 Nw.U.L.Rev. 468 (1964).

Title registration has not proved to be a panacea for all conveyancing problems. The claims of parties in possession have been troublesome. Must such persons be joined in the registration proceedings? May title to registered land be acquired by adverse possession? *See* Follette v. Pacific Light and Power Corp., 189 Cal. 193, 208 P. 295 (1922); Konantz v. Stein, 283 Minn. 33, 167 N.W.2d 1 (1969). Another difficulty is the tendency of courts to resurrect the doctrine of notice, thereby undermining the conclusive character of registration. See Rose, *Crystals and Mud in Property Law*, 40 Stan.L.Rev. 577, 588–589 (1988). Finally, title registration is not necessarily a solution for high land transfer expenses. One study has concluded that "Torrens produces no significant reduction in title-related residential closing costs." B. Shick & I. Plotkin, Torrens in the United States 6 (1978).

F. ESTABLISHING TITLE BY ADVERSE POSSESSION

Recordation does not protect a property owner against adverse possessors who may acquire title to the property by occupying it in a certain manner for a particular period of time. The time period is established by the statute of limitations on actions to recover possession of land. Although the period varies considerably from state to state, fifteen to twenty years is common. Some states also have a short-term statute, often seven years, which applies in special situations, such as where the adverse possessor has paid property taxes.

The manner of possession may be spelled out in the statute, but is usually dictated by judicial requirements. Litigation abounds on whether the requirements have been met in a particular case.

See 3 American Law of Property § 15.1 (1952); 16 Powell on Real Property ¶ 1012 (1998).

CHAPLIN v. SANDERS MAJ-VIEW

Supreme Court of Washington, 1984.
100 Wn.2d 853, 676 P.2d 431.

UTTER, JUSTICE.

A judgment was entered by the trial court in favor of Peter and Patricia Sanders, petitioners herein, awarding a part of property claimed by them by virtue of adverse possession from their neighbors Kent and Barbara Chaplin and Kenneth and Hazel Chaplin. The Court of Appeals reversed, finding no "hostility" in Sanders' possession of the property. We reverse the Court of Appeals and hold in favor of petitioners on all aspects of their claim.

This case presents two issues relating to the doctrine of adverse possession. Does a claimant's actual notice of the true owner's interest in the land possessed negate the element of hostility? Does the true owner's actual knowledge of the claimant's use of his land satisfy the element of open and notorious? In light of the historical basis for the development of the adverse possession doctrine, we hold the possessor's subjective belief whether the land possessed is or is not his own and his intent to dispossess or not dispossess another are irrelevant to a finding of hostility. We also hold that, when the true title owner knows of the possessor's adverse use throughout the duration of the statutory period, the element of open and notorious is satisfied.

I

Petitioners Peter and Patricia Sanders, d/b/a Shady Glen Trailer Park, are record title owners of property in Snohomish County. Their property adjoins property owned by respondents Kent and Barbara Chaplin and Kenneth and Hazel Chaplin. The Chaplin property is to the east of the Sanders' property. This action concerns a dispute over a strip of land owned of record by the Chaplins, forming the western portion of their property and bordering the Sanders' eastern boundary line.

In 1957 or 1958, Mr. and Mrs. Hibbard, the Sanders' predecessors in interest, decided to clear their land of woods and overgrowth and set up a trailer park (hereinafter the western parcel). There was no obvious boundary between the western and eastern parcels, so Mr. Hibbard cleared the land up to a deep drainage ditch and opened his park.[1] He, further, installed a road for purposes of ingress and egress to the park.

In 1960, Mr. McMurray, then owner of the eastern parcel, had a survey conducted whereupon he discovered the true boundary. He then informed the Hibbards that their driveway encroached upon his land. Two years later, the Hibbards sold their parcel to the Gilberts. The 1962 Hibbard–Gilbert recorded contract of sale contained the following provision:

> The purchaser here has been advised that the existing blacktop road used by the trailer park encroaches on the adjoining property by approximately 20 feet and purchaser agrees that no claim will be made by him for any ownership of said 20 foot strip of property; and, in the event the owner of the adjoining property should remove blacktop, no claim will be made by the purchaser herein. Purchaser agrees to remove blacktop if requested to do so.

In 1967, the western parcel was sold to a Mr. French, who had no actual notice of the true boundary line. The western parcel changed hands once again before the Sanders purchased it in 1976. None of these subsequent owners were made aware that their road encroached on the eastern parcel; but were informed rather casually that the boundary was the drainage ditch. The Sanders were given actual notice of the contract provision, but purportedly mistook the road to which it referred.

Since its initial development in 1958, there was little change in the use of the western parcel. The road remained in continuous use in connection with the trailer park. The area between the road and the drainage ditch was also used by trailer park residents for parking, storage, garbage removal and picnicking. Grass was mowed up to the

---

1. This drainage ditch forms the eastern leg of the triangular strip of property in dispute, the true boundary line its western leg, and the intersection of the true boundary line and the drainage ditch its apex. The base is formed by a 30-foot wide sec- tion in the southwest corner of the eastern parcel. The strip varies in width from 30 feet at its base to 1 foot at the apex, with the average width being approximately 15 feet.

drainage ditch and flowers were planted in the area by trailer personnel and tenants. In the spring of 1978, the Sanders installed underground wiring and surface power poles in the area between the roadway and the drainage ditch.

In May of 1978, the Chaplins purchased the still undeveloped eastern parcel without the benefit of a survey. Soon thereafter they contacted an architectural consultant for the purpose of designing commercial buildings for their property. They had a survey conducted for this purpose and discovered the Sanders' encroachments. Despite this evidence, which indicated that the Sanders claimed some interest in the land, the Chaplins secured a rezone to a more intensive commercial classification and instructed the architectural engineers to design buildings for the development based on the true survey line. They then brought this action to quiet title to the disputed portion and sought damages for increased construction costs due to the delay necessitated by this action.

The trial court determined that 1967, the date of acquisition by the Sanders' predecessor Mr. French, was the appropriate time from which to compute the 10–year period necessary to establish adverse possession. It then found that the Sanders had satisfied each element of adverse possession with regard to the road and its 3–foot shoulder (Parcel A), and quieted title in them to this portion. It found that the Sanders had not satisfied their burden of proving open and notorious possession with regard to the property between the roadway and the ditch (Parcel B) and quieted title to this portion in the Chaplins. The trial court then issued a mandatory injunction requiring the Sanders to remove their underground wiring and surface power poles at an estimated cost of $20,000.

The Court of Appeals found that, due to the Sanders' actual notice of McMurray's interest, the requirement of hostility had not been satisfied for either parcel. It therefore reversed the trial court's holding with respect to Parcel A, and remanded the cause with directions to quiet title in the Chaplins.

II

A.

In order to establish a claim of adverse possession, the possession must be: 1) exclusive, 2) actual and uninterrupted, 3) open and notorious and 4) hostile and under a claim of right made in good faith. Peeples v. Port of Bellingham, 93 Wash.2d 766, 613 P.2d 1128 (1980). The period throughout which these elements must concurrently exist is 10 years. RCW 4.16.020. Hostility, as defined by this court, "does not import enmity or ill-will, but rather imports that the claimant is in possession as owner, in contradistinction to holding in recognition of or subordination to the true owner." King v. Bassindale, 127 Wash. 189, 192, 220 P. 777 (1923). We have traditionally treated the hostility and claim of right requirements as one and the same.

Although the definition of hostility has remained fairly constant throughout this last century, the import we have attributed to this definition has varied.

* * *

B.

The doctrine of adverse possession was formulated at law for the purpose[s] of, among others, assuring maximum utilization of land, encouraging the rejection of stale claims and, most importantly, quieting titles. Because the doctrine was formulated at law and not at equity, it was originally intended to protect both those who knowingly appropriated the land of others and those who honestly entered and held possession in full belief that the land was their own. Thus, when the original purpose of the adverse possession doctrine is considered, it becomes apparent that the claimant's motive in possessing the land is irrelevant and no inquiry should be made into his guilt or innocence.

Washington is not the only state which [has] look[ed] to the subjective belief and intent of the adverse claimant in determining hostility. However, the requirement has been regarded as unnecessarily confusing by many legal commentators, and has been abandoned by the apparent majority of states. 3 *American Law of Property* § 15.5, at 785.

For these reasons, we are convinced that the dual requirement that the claimant take possession in "good faith" and not recognize another's superior interest does not serve the purpose of the adverse possession doctrine. The "hostility/claim of right" element of adverse possession requires only that the claimant treat the land as his own as against the world throughout the statutory period. The nature of his possession will be determined solely on the basis of the manner in which he treats the property. His subjective belief regarding his true interest in the land and his intent to dispossess or not dispossess another is irrelevant to this determination. Under this analysis, permission to occupy the land, given by the true title owner to the claimant or his predecessors in interest, will still operate to negate the element of hostility. The traditional presumptions still apply to the extent that they are not inconsistent with this ruling.

C.

In the present case, due to the contract language manifesting Hibbard and Gilberts' recognition of McMurray's superior title, the trial court determined that their possession was not hostile to McMurray's interest. Under our holding today the contractual provision is no longer relevant. What is relevant is the objective character of Hibbard's possession and that of his successors in interest. Because the trial court did not make explicit findings regarding the character of the pre–1967 possession, we will look to the 1967–77 period in making our determination.

The trial court found the character of possession to have been hostile for at least a 10–year period. We agree. The Sanders and their predecessors used and maintained the property as though it was their own for over the statutory period. This was sufficient to satisfy the element of hostility.

III

The Sanders also appeal from the trial court's finding that Parcel B was not possessed in an open and notorious manner.

In Hovila v. Bartek, 48 Wash.2d 238, 242, 292 P.2d 877 (1956), we stated that the requirement of open and notorious is satisfied if the title holder has actual notice of the adverse use throughout the statutory period. This is consistent with the purpose of the requirement, which is to ensure that the user makes such use of the land that any reasonable person would assume he is the owner. R. Powell, at ¶ 1013[2][b]. For this reason the owner is held to constructive notice of the possession. When the owner has actual knowledge of the possession, the requirement's purpose has been satisfied.

Here the trial court found that McMurray knew of the Hibbards' encroachments in 1960. He was aware of these encroachments until he sold to the Chaplins in 1978. Although the trial court explicitly found that McMurray knew of the road's encroachment on his land, it did not explicitly so find with regard to the strip running between the roadway and the ditch (Parcel B). Mrs. Hibbard testified at trial that she and her husband consistently maintained and mowed Parcel B. It would have been so maintained in 1960 when Mr. McMurray informed the Hibbards that their road was encroaching on his land. We are compelled to conclude, from this evidence, that McMurray was aware of the Hibbards' use of the strip abutting the roadway. This conclusion is all the more compelling when the disparate condition of McMurray's undeveloped, overgrown property and the cleared, mowed and maintained strip of land separating the roadway and McMurray's land is considered.

Although we could rest our holding that the requirement of open and notorious was satisfied on this alone, we find ample evidence to rest our holding on another ground as well. "[A]dverse possession is a mixed question of law and fact. Whether the essential facts exist is for the trier of fact; but whether the facts, as found, constitute adverse possession is for the court to determine as a matter of law." Peeples v. Port of Bellingham, *supra* at 771, 613 P.2d 1128.

In determining what acts are sufficiently open and notorious to manifest to others a claim to land, the character of the land must be considered. Krona v. Brett, 72 Wash.2d 535, 433 P.2d 858 (1967). "The necessary use and occupancy need only be of the character that a true owner would assert *in view of its nature and location.*" *Krona,* at 539, 433 P.2d 858.

In the present case the trial court found that, during the relevant statutory period, the western parcel was cleared up to the drainage ditch while the eastern parcel remained vacant and overgrown. The residents of the trailer park mowed the grass in Parcel B and put the parcel to various uses: guest parking, garbage disposal, gardening and picnicking. Some residents used portions of Parcel B as their backyard. The trial court concluded that the contrast between the fully developed parcel west of the drainage ditch and the overgrown, undeveloped parcel east of the drainage ditch was insufficient to put the owners of the eastern parcel on notice of the Sanders' claim of ownership. We disagree.

Accordingly, the case is reversed and remanded with directions to quiet title to the disputed property in the Sanders.

Notes and Questions

1.　Although courts struggle to decide whether mistaken belief satisfies the hostility requirement, would it be more appropriate to make good faith a prerequisite to acquiring title by adverse possession? *See* Helmholz, *Adverse Possession and Subjective Intent,* 61 Wash.U.L.Q. 331 (1983). Professor Helmholz's article precipitated a lively discussion of this subject. *See* Cunningham, *Adverse Possession and Subjective Intent: A Reply to Professor Helmholz,* 64 Wash.U.L.Q. 1 (1986); Helmholz, *More on Subjective Intent: A Response to Professor Cunningham,* 64 Wash.U.L.Q. 65 (1986); Cunningham, *More on Adverse Possession: A Rejoinder to Professor Helmholz,* 64 Wash. U.L.Q. 1167 (1986); Merrill, *Property Rules, Liability Rules, and Adverse Possession,* 79 Nw.U.L.Rev. 1122 (1984–85).

2.　As noted in *Chaplin,* the adverse possessor must establish exclusive possession for the statutory period. The claimant is required to exclude others, including the landowner, from the property. When the claimant occupies land in common with third persons or the public generally, the possession is not exclusive. *See* United States v. Tobias, 899 F.2d 1375 (4th Cir.1990); Snowball Corporation v. Pope, 580 N.E.2d 733 (Ind.App.1991).

3.　An adverse possessor may take possession under color of title, i.e., pursuant to a document purporting to transfer ownership that legally fails to do so. Certain states allow adverse possessors claiming under color of title to avail themselves of a short-term statute of limitations. Moreover, the possession of one who holds under color of title extends constructively to the boundaries of the land description in the document, whereas the possession of an individual holding under claim of right only extends to the property actually possessed. Possession under color of title is thus said to involve constructive adverse possession. *See* J. Cribbet & C. Johnson, Principles of the Law of Property 334–338 (3d ed. 1989); 3 American Law of Property §§ 15.4, 15.11 (1952); 16 Powell on Real Property ¶ 1013[2][g] (1998).

4.　The concept of adverse possession has been reexamined from different perspectives. *Compare* Miceli & Sirmans, *An Economic Theory of Adverse Possession,* 15 Int'l Rev.L. & Econ. 161 (1995) (offering economic justification for adverse possession concept) *with* Sprankling, *An Environmental Critique of Adverse Possession,* 79 Cornell L. Rev. 816 (1994) (contending adverse possession doctrine favors development, runs contrary to environmental concerns, and should not apply to "wild lands").

5.　In contrast to adverse possession, a boundary line between adjoining parcels of land may be established by acquiescence. A boundary by acquiescence typically arises when one landowner erects a fence or otherwise marks a line as the boundary, and the other landowner accepts the division line for a long period of time, often measured by the statute of limitations for the recovery of land. *See* Harris v. Robertson, 306 Ark. 258, 813 S.W.2d 252 (1991); Lakeview Farm, Inc. v. Enman, 166 Vt. 158, 689 A.2d 1089 (1997); R. Cunningham, W. Stoebuck, and D. Whitman, The Law of Property 818–823 (2d ed. 1993).

CARPENTER v. HUFFMAN

Supreme Court of Alabama, 1975.
294 Ala. 189, 314 So.2d 65.

JONES, JUSTICE.

This case involves a boundary line dispute between coterminous landowners, Ralph and Dorothy Carpenter (appellants) and Lizzie Huffman (appellee). The land in question is a forty-foot wide strip which runs along the south border of the Carpenters' land and the north boundary of Mrs. Huffman's land. Although the deeds of the two parties are in accord as to their common boundary line, the disputed strip, which Mrs. Huffman claims by adverse possession, begins at the common record boundary and extends 40 feet into the property described in the Carpenters' deed.

After a hearing on the evidence, the trial Court decreed that the true boundary line between the properties of the parties was forty feet north of that shown in the deeds of the parties, thus vesting title in the disputed strip in Mrs. Huffman.

The agreed statement of facts indicates that Phil Alexander, the brother of Mrs. Huffman, bought four acres of land, which included the disputed strip, in 1948; but he did not receive a deed to it until 1953. He fenced in the four acres, running the fence along what he believed to be the correct property line, though in actuality the fence line was incorrectly some 40 feet north of his true boundary.[1]

In 1959, he sold one-half acre to Mrs. Huffman and her northern boundary line was placed along the fence which Alexander had erroneously erected earlier. At that time Mrs. Huffman built a house on the one-half acre, half of which was on the disputed strip. A portion of the fence on her northern border was removed during the construction of her house. Also, a driveway was built which ran across the strip in question and a pump was placed in one of the old fence postholes. In 1968, she conveyed the property back to Alexander who in turn reconveyed it to her in 1971.

---

1. It appears from the transcript of the trial that Phil Alexander purchased the four acres of land in 1948 pursuant to an installment land contract. He immediately took possession of the tract, and received a deed in 1953. The testimony was unclear as to when the fence on the disputed northern boundary was constructed, and apparently the court concluded that the statute of limitations did not begin to run at least until 1953. The authors wish to thank Mr. John Earle Chason of Bay Minette, Alabama, attorney for Mrs. Huffman, for providing us with the transcript of the trial and additional background information. [Editors' note.]

At the time the Carpenters purchased their property, the pump, the driveway, and a portion of the fence were standing. Their grantor informed them that "the fence was in the wrong place," so they had a survey made which showed, as did the original deeds, the true boundary line as 40 feet south of the old fence and running through the middle of Mrs. Huffman's house. This action was commenced on April 10, 1974, when Mrs. Huffman refused to sign an agreement to have her house moved.

This appeal presents the issue whether there is sufficient evidence to sustain the trial Court's holding of privity of possession between Mrs. Huffman and her brother to allow her to tack her periods of possession onto his in order to establish title in Mrs. Huffman to the disputed strip by adverse possession. Because the facts are virtually undisputed, the essence of our function is to determine whether the trial Court correctly applied the law to those facts.

We hold that there was sufficient privity of possession to allow tacking and affirm the decision of the lower court establishing the boundary line between the parties.

* * *

The Carpenters cite Wilson v. Cooper, 256 Ala. 184, 54 So.2d 286 (1951), as authority for their contention that Mrs. Huffman should not be allowed to "tack" her period of possession onto that of her predecessor in order to achieve the minimum ten-year period required to gain title by adverse possession. *Wilson* stated that a party claiming title by deed which describes the land conveyed by government numbers could not acquire title to a disputed area beyond the government line which his predecessors in title had acquired by adverse possession.

We agree that ordinarily title to land gained by adverse possession must be included in the deed of conveyance in order for it to effectively pass to the grantee. But where, as here, the predecessors of Mrs. Huffman had not yet gained title to the disputed strip at the time of their conveyance to her but had possessed it adversely, the failure to include in the deed the description of the disputed strip would not of itself disallow tacking. The rule is aptly summarized in Graham v. Hawkins, 281 Ala. 288, 202 So.2d 74 (1967), quoting from 3 Am.Jur.2d, Adverse Possession, § 65, p. 156:

" * * * Thus, where a person having title by deed to a lot or tract of land described in the deed also has inclosed with it and is in possession of adjoining land to which he has no record title, and conveys the land by the description in the deed and delivers with it possession of the entire inclosure, the continuity of possession will not be broken, and the two possessions may be joined and considered as one continuous possession. So, where a purchaser of land incloses and occupies a tract outside his boundaries, believing it to be included therein, and in that belief conveys to another by the same description, intending that the grantee shall take the whole inclosed area, his possession may be tacked to that of his grantee. * * * "

Thus, *Graham* stands for the applicable proposition that when the grantee is put into actual possession of the disputed land adversely held by his immediate grantor, sufficient privity is established to allow tacking.

The facts of this case fall squarely within the *Graham* rule and the trial Court was correct in holding that the disputed strip should remain with Mrs. Huffman and not belong to the Carpenters.

Affirmed.

Notes and Questions

1. The *Carpenter* case focuses on tacking between adverse possessors. What effect does a change in record ownership of the property have upon the running of the statute of limitations?

2. Many adverse possession statutes do not run against property owners suffering certain disabilities. *See* 3 American Law of Property § 15.12 (1952). For example, the pertinent Georgia statutes provide:

> Possession of real property in conformance with the requirements of Code Section 44–5–161 for a period of 20 years shall confer good title by prescription to the property against everyone except the state and those persons laboring under the disabilities stated in Code Section 44–5–170.

Ga.Code Ann. § 44–5–163 (1991).

> Prescription shall not run against the rights of a minor during his minority, a person incompetent by reason of mental illness or retardation as long as the mental illness or retardation lasts, or a person imprisoned during his imprisonment. After any such disability is removed, prescription shall run against the person holding a claim to realty or personalty.

Ga.Code Ann. § 44–5–170 (1991).

Are such disability provisions wise additions to statutes on adverse possession?

JARVIS v. GILLESPIE

Supreme Court of Vermont, 1991.
155 Vt. 633, 587 A.2d 981.

ALLEN, CHIEF JUSTICE.

Defendant, grantee of a quitclaim deed from the Town of Waterville for a 1.2–acre parcel of land, contests the trial court's ruling that title to the parcel had previously passed from the Town of Waterville to plaintiff by way of adverse possession. We affirm.

The Town of Waterville acquired title to the parcel in 1935 from the administrator of the estate of the then owner. * * *

In 1947, plaintiff purchased over 200 acres of land which surround the disputed parcel on three sides. The fourth side of the parcel is bounded by a road.

On May 7, 1986, the Town of Waterville, by quitclaim deed, conveyed the disputed parcel to defendant. Shortly thereafter, defendant went to the property and removed "No Trespassing" signs which plaintiff had posted on the property. Plaintiff replaced the signs and built a wooden fence on the property.

On February 24, 1988, plaintiff filed a declaratory judgment action to establish his ownership of the disputed parcel by way of adverse possession or, in the alternative, to obtain a prescriptive easement over a roadway which crosses the parcel. Defendant contested the action by denying plaintiff's claims and by asserting as an affirmative defense that plaintiff could not gain title to, nor a prescriptive easement over, the parcel because lands given to a public use are exempted from adverse possession claims by 12 V.S.A. § 462.

The trial court found that at various times between the years 1947 and 1986 plaintiff had used the land for a variety of purposes, such as grazing cattle and horses, parking vehicles, as a staging area for a logging operation on surrounding property, and to store slab wood from a sawmill which was located on adjacent property. The court also found that during that period plaintiff, at various times, maintained a fence on the roadside boundary of the parcel, tapped maple trees on the parcel, planted trees on the parcel, cut Christmas trees and firewood from the parcel, posted "No Trespassing" signs on the parcel, and built a loading ramp on the parcel for the logging operation which remained in use to load and unload his tractor after the logging operation ceased. The court found that these uses were clearly visible from the road which abutted the parcel. Further, the court found that plaintiff was the only person to make use of the property for any reason during the period and that neither the Town of Waterville nor the public made any use of the parcel during that time.

From these facts, the court concluded that plaintiff had established title to the property by adverse possession. The court further concluded that the exemption provided in 12 V.S.A. § 462 did not apply in this instance because the property was not given to a public use. Defendant then brought this appeal contesting both of these conclusions.

* * *

II.

Defendant * * * contends that the trial court erred in finding that plaintiff had established all the elements necessary to gain title to the parcel by adverse possession. One acquires title by adverse possession through " 'open, notorious, hostile and continuous' possession of another's property for a period of fifteen years." Moran v. Byrne, 149 Vt. 353, 355, 543 A.2d 262, 263 (1988) (quoting Laird Properties New England Land Syndicate v. Mad River Corp., 131 Vt. 268, 277, 305 A.2d 562, 567

(1973)). The claimant has the burden of establishing all of these elements.

Defendant argues that except for the logging operation in 1971 and 1972 and storing the slab wood in 1983 and 1984, none of plaintiff's uses of the parcel constituted sufficient possession to establish adverse possession. Defendant relies on case law asserting that certain acts, such as tapping trees or cutting timber, by themselves are insufficient to establish possession. See Caskey v. Lewis, 54 Ky. (15 B.Mon.) 27, 32 (1854) (occasional use for sugaring and cutting timber and firewood did not constitute possession); Adams v. Robinson, 6 Pa. 271, 272 (1847) (annual use of land as a sugar camp constituted a succession of trespasses rather than occupancy). Such a general proposition, however, is not conclusive of the particular controversy before us. "The ultimate fact to be proved in an adverse possession case is that the claimant has acted toward the land in question as would an average owner, taking properly into account the geophysical nature of the land." 7 R. Powell, The Law of Real Property ¶ 1013[2][h], at 91–62 (1990); see Laird, 131 Vt. at 280, 305 A.2d at 569 (acts needed to give rise to constructive possession must be consistent with the nature of the property). Thus, although certain of the acts of possession taken by a claimant may not be sufficient to establish possession in all circumstances, each case must be examined individually, viewing the claimant's acts in light of the nature of the land.

In this case, the land is a 1.2–acre parcel surrounded on three sides by 280 acres of plaintiff's land and bounded on the fourth side by a road. The area in which it is located is rural and agricultural in nature. In 1947 there were no buildings on the property and there had not been any for many years. Grazing cattle and horses, cutting hay, planting and tapping trees, and cutting firewood and Christmas trees are the types of acts which are consistent with the nature of the parcel.

Defendant contends, however, that these acts are not the uses an average owner would have made of the parcel. He argues that because at one point before 1947 there had been a house on the parcel, because the parcel is flat, open, dry and well drained, because more trees could have been planted on it, and because defendant plans to build a house upon it, plaintiff did not use the parcel as an average owner might. We do not agree. Simply because a parcel may be susceptible to uses other than those to which the claimant chose to put it does not necessarily lead to the conclusion that the claimant failed to act toward the parcel as an average owner would have. "'The possession is gauged by the actual state of the land, and not with reference to its capability of being changed into another state which would reasonably admit of a different character of possession.'" Bergen v. Dixon, 527 So.2d 1274, 1278 (Ala. 1988) (quoting Goodson v. Brothers, 111 Ala. 589, 595, 20 So. 443, 445 (1896)). Plaintiff used the parcel for purposes which were consistent with its condition as he found it. He was not required to change nor necessarily improve the land, but was merely required to perform acts of possession which were consistent with the parcel's nature. Plaintiff's acts, while not necessarily sufficient to constitute possession of every piece of land, were sufficient to establish his possession of this parcel of rural, agricultural land.

Defendant argues that plaintiff also failed to establish a continuous fifteen-year period of possession. One basis of the argument is that plaintiff failed to establish the exact date in 1971 on which the loading ramp was constructed on the parcel. This is significant because of defendant's entry on the land in May 1986, which, defendant contends, effectively interrupted plaintiff's possession. This contention ignores the fact that plaintiff's claim predates 1971.

Another basis for the argument raised by defendant is that the acts of possession were merely fragmentary and occasional.

> "To constitute continuous possession of lands, the law does not require the occupant to be present on the site at all times. The kind and frequency of the acts of occupancy, necessary to constitute continuing possession, are dependent on the nature and condition of the premises as well as the uses to which it is adapted." There may be lapses of time between acts of possession.

Montgomery v. Branon, 129 Vt. 379, 386, 278 A.2d 744, 748 (1971) (quoting Amey v. Hall, 123 Vt. 62, 67, 181 A.2d 69, 73 (1962)).

The uses made of the parcel from 1965 until 1986 consisted of cutting firewood and Christmas trees, parking vehicles, staging the logging operation, building the loading ramp, loading and unloading a tractor using the ramp, storing slab wood, cutting brush, and posting "No Trespassing" signs. Further, plaintiff testified that although there were times when he had not been on the parcel for as long as a month, he was never absent for as long as a year.

This Court has held that using property only at certain times of the year for certain activities and not using it for the rest of the year can constitute sufficiently continuous use for adverse possession. Thibault v. Vartuli, 143 Vt. 178, 181, 465 A.2d 248, 250 (1983) (using island only in summer for recreational activities); Montgomery, 129 Vt. at 386, 278 A.2d at 748 (using hunting camp only during season); Amey, 123 Vt. at 67–68, 181 A.2d at 73 (using logging camp only during cutting times). Although plaintiff did not use the parcel constantly, he used it each year during certain seasons in ways which were both consistent with the season and with the nature of the parcel. The uses, therefore, were more than fragmentary and occasional, and were sufficiently continuous. Thus, plaintiff established a continuous period of use from 1965 until 1986, which is more than sufficient to satisfy the statutory requirement of fifteen years.

Defendant also contends that plaintiff's acts were not open and notorious. Acts of possession are deemed sufficiently open and notorious if they are conducted in a manner which would put a person of ordinary prudence on notice of the claim. As the parcel bordered on the road, anyone passing would have been able to see plaintiff's activities. Further, there was testimony from a former town lister and from the town clerk, who had worked in the town clerk's office since 1939, that they both knew that plaintiff claimed to own the parcel. There was no error in finding plaintiff's possession to be open and notorious.

Lastly, defendant argues that the plaintiff's acts were not hostile because they "were beneficial to the Town." Hostility, when used in the context of adverse possession, does not require the presence of ill will toward the actual owner nor destructiveness toward the land. Rather, what is required is that the adverse possessor intends to claim the land and treat it as his own. The trial court properly found that plaintiff's claim was hostile.

III.

Defendant argues that while the parcel was owned by the Town of Waterville it was exempt from adverse possession claims by 12 V.S.A. § 462. The statute reads: "Nothing contained in this chapter [relating to the limitations of actions] shall extend to lands given, granted, sequestered or appropriated to a public, pious or charitable use, or to lands belonging to the state." 12 V.S.A. § 462. While we have applied the statute in the past, we have yet to face the issue presented by this case, namely, how to determine whether property owned by a municipality is "given, granted, sequestered or appropriated to a public * * * use."

Defendant urges that the proper focus of such an inquiry is whether the Town was acting in its "governmental capacity" or its "proprietary capacity" when it acquired the property. The significance of this distinction, defendant contends, is that land which is acquired or held by a municipality in its governmental capacity is within the meaning of the statutory phrase "given * * * to a public * * * use." We do not find this argument persuasive.

Other jurisdictions which have faced the question are split. New Hampshire, for example, in applying N.H.Rev.Stat.Ann. § 477:34 (1983), which reads "[n]o person shall acquire by prescription a right to * * * any public ground by * * * occupying it adversely for any length of time," has held that " 'mere retention of title, without more,' "is a public use for lands owned by a municipality. Kellison v. McIsaac, 131 N.H. 675, 681, 559 A.2d 834, 837 (1989) (quoting McInnis v. Town of Hampton, 112 N.H. 57, 60, 288 A.2d 691, 694 (1972)). This, in essence, exempts all municipal lands from adverse possession claims. This standard, however, is in conflict with our statute which only exempts lands given to a "public, pious, or charitable use." Our statute does not provide a blanket exemption for municipally owned lands, which it easily could have, as evidenced by the provision exempting state-owned land. Therefore, we decline to follow New Hampshire's example.

We find the approach of the Supreme Court of Connecticut to be more in accord with our statute. In American Trading Real Estate Properties, Inc. v. Town of Trumbull, 215 Conn. 68, 574 A.2d 796 (1990), the court held that land which is owned by a municipality is presumed to be given to a public use. However, this presumption can be rebutted by demonstrating that the town has abandoned any plans for the land. Evidence to be considered in determining this issue may include the reason the property was acquired by the town, uses the town has made of the property since acquisition, and whether the town has manifested an intention to use the property in the future.

This standard is a simple, balanced approach for determining which municipal lands are given to a public use and thereby exempt from claims of adverse possession. It allows a municipality to be protected from adverse possession claims on property which it is not using at present but may have future plans for or on property which it has set aside as open space or to be left in its natural state for the benefit of the community and the environment. It does not, however, clash with 12 V.S.A. § 462 by giving a town a blanket exemption to adverse possession claims. It provides only for a presumption that the property is given to a public use which can be rebutted by evidence to the contrary.

* * *

* * * The Town of Waterville acquired the parcel in 1935 * * *. The Town then did nothing with the parcel for fifty-one years. Finally, in 1986, the Town conveyed the property to defendant by quitclaim deed.

Based on these facts, we find that plaintiff has carried his burden of rebutting the presumption that the parcel, while owned by the Town of Waterville, was given to a public use. The Town acquired the parcel as settlement of a debt, the parcel was not used by the public while the Town had title, and by conveying the parcel to defendant, a private individual, the Town manifested that it had no intention of ever using the parcel for a public use. Therefore, the trial court properly concluded that the parcel was not given to a public use and that it was not exempt from claims of adverse possession by 12 V.S.A. § 462.

Affirmed.

Notes and Questions

1. The sufficiency of the acts of possession and dominion by the claimant have been a source of frequent dispute. Is the actual possession requirement satisfied in the following situations?

(a) Claimant cleared a field in a rural area, and cultivated crops, grazed cattle, and erected fences on the tract. *See* Whittemore v. Amator, 148 Ariz. 173, 713 P.2d 1231 (1986); Forester v. Whitelock, 850 S.W.2d 427 (Mo.App. 1993).

(b) Claimant landscaped parcel, and maintained trees, shrubs, and grass. *See* Walker v. Hubbard, 31 Ark.App. 43, 787 S.W.2d 251 (1990).

(c) Claimant cut hay, gathered natural crops, and mowed grass. *See* Thompson v. Hayslip, 74 Ohio App.3d 829, 600 N.E.2d 756 (1991).

(d) Claimant removed sand and gravel from unimproved urban lot and prevented others from engaging in such activity. *See* Ewing v. Burnet, 36 U.S. 41 (1837).

2. A landowner may interrupt the requisite continuity of possession by actions that assert ownership before the statutory period has expired. *See* Mendonca v. Cities Service Oil Co. of Pennsylvania, 354 Mass. 323, 237 N.E.2d 16 (1968) (landowner's occupation and use of disputed strip of land for storage of equipment for three or four weeks destroyed continuity).

MARENGO CAVE CO. v. ROSS

Supreme Court of Indiana, 1937.
212 Ind. 624, 10 N.E.2d 917.

ROLL, JUDGE.

Appellee and appellant were the owners of adjoining land in Crawford county, Ind. On appellant's land was located the opening to a subterranean cavity known as "Marengo Cave." This cave extended under a considerable portion of appellant's land, and the southeastern portion thereof extended under lands owned by appellee. This action arose out of a dispute as to the ownership of that part of the cave that extended under appellee's land. Appellant was claiming title to all the cave and cavities, including that portion underlying appellee's land. Appellee instituted this action to quiet his title as against appellant's claim. Appellant answered by a general denial and filed a cross-complaint wherein he sought to quiet its title to all the cave, including that portion underlying appellee's land. There was a trial by jury which returned a verdict for the appellee. Appellant filed its motion for a new trial which was overruled by the court, and this is the only error assigned on appeal. Appellant assigns as grounds for a new trial that the verdict of the jury is not sustained by sufficient evidence, and is contrary to law. These are the only grounds urged for a reversal of this cause.

The facts as shown by the record are substantially as follows: In 1883 one Stewart owned the real estate now owned by appellant, and in September of that year some young people who were upon that land discovered what afterwards proved to be the entrance to the cavern since known as Marengo Cave, this entrance being approximately 700 feet from the boundary line between the lands now owned by appellant and appellee, and the only entrance to said cave. Within a week after discovery of the cave, it was explored, and the fact of its existence received wide publicity through newspaper articles, and otherwise. Shortly thereafter the then owner of the real estate upon which the entrance was located took complete possession of the entire cave as now occupied by appellant and used for exhibition purposes, and began to charge an admission fee to those who desired to enter and view the cave, and to exclude therefrom those who were unwilling to pay for admission. This practice continued from 1883, except in some few instances when persons were permitted by the persons claiming to own said cave to enter same without payment of the usual required fee, and during the following years the successive owners of the land upon which the entrance to the cave was located, advertised the existence of said cave through newspapers, magazines, posters, and otherwise, in order to attract visitors thereto; also made improvements within the cave, including the building of concrete walks, and concrete steps where there was a difference in elevation of said cavern, widened and heightened portions of passageways; had available and furnished guides, all in order to make the cave more easily accessible to visitors desiring to view the same; and continuously, during all this time, without asking or obtaining consent from any one, but claiming a right so to do, held and possessed said subterranean passages constituting said cave, excluding therefrom the "whole world," except such persons as entered after paying admission for the privilege of so doing, or by permission.

Appellee has lived in the vicinity of said cave since 1903, and purchased the real estate which he now owns in 1908. He first visited the cave in 1895, paying an admission fee for the privilege, and has visited said cave several times since. He has never, at any time, occupied or been in possession of any of the subterranean passages or cavities of which the cave consists, and the possession and use of the cave by those who have done so has never interfered with his use and enjoyment of the lands owned by him. For a period of approximately 25 years prior to the time appellee purchased his land, and for a period of 21 years afterwards, exclusive possession of the cave has been held by appellant, its immediate and remote grantors.

The cave, as such, has never been listed for taxation separately from the real estate wherein it is located, and the owners of the respective tracts of land have paid the taxes assessed against said tracts.

A part of said cave at the time of its discovery and exploration extended beneath real estate now owned by appellee, but this fact was not ascertained until the year 1932, when the boundary line between the respective tracts through the cave was established by means of a survey made by a civil engineer pursuant to an order of court entered in this cause. Previous to this survey neither of the parties to this appeal, nor any of their predecessors in title, knew that any part of the cave was in fact beneath the surface of a portion of the land now owned by appellee. Possession of the cave was taken and held by appellant's remote and immediate grantors, improvements made, and control exercised, with the belief on the part of such grantors that the entire cave as it was explored and held was under the surface of lands owned by them. There is no evidence of and dispute as to ownership of the cave, or any portion thereof, prior to the time when in 1929 appellee requested a survey, which was approximately 46 years after discovery of the cave and the exercise of complete dominion thereover by appellant and its predecessors in title.

It is appellant's contention that it has a fee-simple title to all of the cave; that it owns that part underlying appellee's land by adverse possession. Section 2–602, Burns' Ann.St.1933, section 61, Baldwin's Ind.St.1934, provides as follows: "The following actions shall be commenced within the periods herein prescribed after the cause of action has accrued, and not afterward: * * * Sixth. Upon contracts in writing other than those for the payment of money, on judgments of courts of record, and for the recovery of the possession of real estate, within twenty (20) years.''

It will be noted that appellee nor his predecessors in title had never effected a severance of the cave from the surface estate. Therefore the title of the appellee extends from the surface to the center but actual possession is confined to the surface. Appellee and his immediate and remote grantors have been in possession of the land and estate here in question at all times, unless it can be said that the possession of the cave by appellant as shown by the evidence above set out has met all the requirements of the law relating to the acquisition of land by adverse possession. A record title may be defeated by adverse possession. All the authorities agree that, before the owner of the legal title can be deprived of his land by another's possession, through the operation of the statute of limitation, the possession must have been actual, visible, notorious, exclusive, under claim of ownership and hostile to the owner of the legal title and to the world at large (except only the government), and continuous for the full period prescribed by the statute. The rule is not always stated in exactly the same words in the many cases dealing with the subject of adverse possession, yet the rule is so thoroughly settled that there is no doubt as to what elements are essential to establish a title by adverse possession. Let us examine the various elements that are essential to establish title by adverse possession and apply them to the facts that are established by the undisputed facts in this case.

(1) The possession must be actual. It must be conceded that appellant in the operation of the "Marengo Cave" used not only the cavern under its own land but also that part of the cavern that underlaid appellee's land, and assumed dominion over all of it. Yet it must also be conceded that during all of the time appellee was in constructive possession, as the only constructive possession known to the law is that which inheres in the legal title and with which the owner of that title is always endowed. Whether the possession was actual under the peculiar facts in this case we need not decide.

(2) The possession must be visible. The owner of land who, having notice of the fact that it is occupied by another who is claiming dominion over it, nevertheless stands by during the entire statutory period and makes no effort to eject the claimant or otherwise protect his title, ought not to be permitted, for reasons of public policy, thereafter to maintain an action for the recovery of his land. But, the authorities assert, in order that the possession of the occupying claimant may constitute notice in law, it must be visible and open to the common observer so that the owner or his agent on visiting the premises might readily see that the owner's rights are being invaded. What constitutes open and visible possession has been stated in general terms, thus; it is necessary and sufficient if its nature and character is such as is calculated to apprise the world that the land is occupied and who the occupant is; and such an appropriation of the land by claimant as to apprise, or convey visible notice to the community or neighborhood in which it is situated that it is

in his exclusive use and enjoyment. It has been declared that the disseisor "must unfurl his flag" on the land, and "keep it flying," so that the owner may see, if he will, that an enemy has invaded his domains, and planted the standard of conquest.

(3) The possession must be open and notorious. The mere possession of the land is not enough. It is knowledge, either actual or imputed, of the possession of his lands by another, claiming to own them bona fide and openly, that affects the legal owner thereof. Where there has been no actual notice, it is necessary to show that the possession of the disseisor was so open, notorious, and visible as to warrant the inference that the owner must or should have known of it. In Philbin v. Carr (1920) 75 Ind.App. 560, 129 N.E. 19, 29, it was said: "However, in order that the possession of the occupying claimant may constitute notice in law, it must be visible and open to the common observer so that the owner or his agent on visiting the premises might readily see that the owner's rights are being invaded. In accordance with the general rule applicable to the subject of constructive notice, before possession can operate as such notice, it must be clear and unequivocal."

And again, the possession must be notorious. It must be so conspicuous that it is generally known and talked of by the public. "It must be manifest to the community." Thus, the Appellate Court said in Philbin v. Carr supra, that: "Where the persons who have passed frequently over and along the premises have been unable to see any evidence of occupancy, evidently the possession has not been of the character required by the rule. The purpose of this requirement is to support the principle that a legal title will not be extinguished on flimsy and uncertain evidence. Hence, where there has been no actual notice, the possession must have been so notorious as to warrant the inference that the owner ought to have known that a stranger was asserting dominion over his land. Insidious, desultory, and fugitive acts will not serve that purpose. To have that effect the possession should be clear and satisfactory, not doubtful and equivocal."

(4) The possession must be exclusive. It is evident that two or more persons cannot hold one tract of land adversely to each other at the same time. "It is essential that the possession of one who claims adversely must be of such an exclusive character that it will operate as an ouster of the owner of the legal title; because, in the absence of ouster the legal title draws to itself the constructive possession of the land. A possession which does not amount to an ouster or disseisin is not sufficient." Philbin v. Carr, supra.

The facts as set out above show that appellee and his predecessors in title have been in actual and continuous possession of his real estate since the cave was discovered in 1883. At no time were they aware that any one was trespassing upon their land. No one was claiming to be in possession of appellee's land. It is true that appellant was asserting possession of the "Marengo Cave." There would seem to be quite a difference in making claim to the "Marengo Cave," and making claim to a portion of appellee's land, even though a portion of the cave extended under appellee's land, when this latter fact was unknown to any one. The evidence on both sides of this case is to the effect that the "Marengo Cave" was thought to be altogether under the land owned by appellant, and this erroneous supposition was not revealed until a survey was made at the request of appellee and ordered by the court in this case. It seems to us that the following excerpt from Lewey v. H. C. Frick Coke Co. (1895) 166 Pa. 536, 31 A. 261, 263, 28 L.R.A. 283, 45 Am.St.Rep. 684, is peculiarly applicable to the situation here presented, inasmuch as we are dealing with an underground cavity. It was stated in the above case:

"The title of the plaintiff extends from the surface to the center, but actual possession is confined to the surface. Upon the surface he must be held to know all that the most careful observation by himself and his employés could reveal, unless his ignorance is induced by the fraudulent conduct of the wrongdoer. But in the coal veins, deep down in the earth, he cannot see. Neither in person nor by his servants nor employés can he explore their recesses in search for an intruder. If an adjoining owner goes beyond his own boundaries in the course of his mining operations, the owner on whom he enters has no means of knowledge within his reach. Nothing short of an accurate survey of the interior of his neighbor's mines would enable him to ascertain the fact. This would require the services of a competent mining engineer and his assistants, inside the mines of another, which he would have no right to insist upon. To require an owner, under such circumstances, to take notice of a trespass upon his underlying coal at the time it takes place, is to require an impossibility; and to hold that the statute begins to run at the date of the trespass is in most cases to take away the remedy of the injured party before he can know that an injury has been done him. A result so absurd and so unjust ought not to be possible. * * *

"The reason for the distinction exists in the nature of things. The owner of land may be present by himself or his servants on the surface of his possessions, no matter how extensive they may be. He is for this reason held to be constructively present wherever his title extends. He cannot be present in the interior of the earth. No amount of vigilance will enable him to detect the approach of a trespasser who may be working his way through the coal seams underlying adjoining lands. His senses cannot inform him of the encroachment by such trespasser upon the coal that is hidden in the rocks under his feet. He cannot reasonably be held to be constructively present where his presence is, in the nature of things, impossible. He must learn of such a trespass by other means than such as are within his own control, and, until these come within his reach, he is necessarily ignorant of his loss. He cannot reasonably be required to act until knowledge that action is needed is possible to him."

We are not persuaded that this case falls within the rule of mistaken boundary as announced in Rennert v. Shirk (1904) 163 Ind. 542, 72 N.E. 546, 549, wherein this court said: "Appellant insists, however, that, if one takes and holds possession of real estate under a mistake as to where the true boundary line is, such possession cannot ripen into a title. In this state, when an owner of land, by mistake as to the boundary line of his land, takes actual, visible, and exclusive possession of another's land, and holds it as his own continuously for the statutory period of 20 years, he thereby acquires the title as against the real owner. The possession is regarded as adverse, without reference to the fact that it is based on mistake; it being prima facie sufficient that actual, visible, and exclusive possession is taken under a claim of right."

The reason for the above rule is obvious. Under such circumstances appellant was in possession of the necessary means of ascertaining the true boundary line, and to hold that a mere misapprehension on the part of appellant as to the true boundary line would nullify the well-established law on adverse possession. In that case appellee had actual, visible, notorious, and exclusive possession. The facts in the present case are far different. Here the possession of appellant was not visible. No one could see below the earth's surface and determine that appellant was trespassing upon appellee's lands. This fact could not be determined by going into the cave. Only by a survey could this fact be made known. The same undisputed facts clearly show that appellant's possession was not notorious. Not even appellant itself nor any of its remote grantors knew that any part of the "Marengo Cave" extended beyond its own boundaries, and they at no time even down to the time appellee instituted this action made any claim to appellee's lands. Appellee and his predecessors in title at all times have been in possession of the land which he is now claiming. No severance by deed or written instrument was ever made to the cave, from the surface. In the absence of a separate estate could appellant be in the exclusive possession of the cave that underlies appellee's land.

"If there is no severance, an entry upon the surface will extend downward, and draw to it a title to the underlying minerals; so that he who disseises another, and acquires title by the statute of limitations, will succeed to the estate of him upon whose possession he has entered." Delaware & Hudson Canal Co. v. Hughes (1897) 183 Pa. 66, 38 A. 568, 570, 38 L.R.A. 826, 63 Am.St.Rep. 743.

Even though it could be said that appellant's possession has been actual, exclusive, and continuous all these years, we would still be of the opinion that appellee has not lost his land. It has been the uniform rule in equity that the statute of limitation does not begin to run until the injured party discovers, or with reasonable diligence might have discovered, the facts constituting the injury and cause of action. Until then the owner cannot know that his possession has been invaded. Until he has knowledge, or ought to have such knowledge, he is not called upon to act, for he does not know that action in the premises is necessary and the law does not require absurd or impossible things of any one.

* * *

So in the case at bar, appellant pretended to use the "Marengo Cave" as his property and all the time he was committing a trespass upon appellee's land. After 20 years of secret user, he now urges the statute of limitation, section 2–602, Burns' St.1933, section 61, Baldwin's Ind.St.1934, as a bar to appellee's action. Appellee did not know of the trespass of appellant, and had no reasonable means of discovering the fact. It is true that appellant took no active measures to prevent the discovery, except to deny appellee the right to enter the cave for the purpose of making a survey, and disclaiming any use of appellee's lands, but nature furnished the concealment, or where the wrong conceals itself. It amounts to the taking of another's property without his knowledge of the fact that it is really being taken from him. In most cases the ignorance is produced by artifice. But in this case nature has supplied the situation which gives the trespasser the opportunity to occupy the recesses on appellee's land and caused the ignorance of appellee which he now seeks to avail himself. We cannot assent to the doctrine that would enable one to trespass upon another's property through a subterranean passage and under such circumstances that the owner does not know, or by the exercise of reasonable care could not know, of such secret occupancy, for 20 years or more and by so doing obtained a fee-simple title as against the holder of the legal title. The fact that appellee had knowledge that appellant was claiming to be the owner of the "Marengo Cave," and advertised it to the general public, was no knowledge to him that it was in possession of appellee's land or any part of it. We are of the opinion that appellant's possession for 20 years or more of that part of "Marengo Cave" underlying appellee's land was not open, notorious, or exclusive, as required by the law applicable to obtaining title to land by adverse possession.

We cannot say that the evidence is not sufficient to support the verdict or that the verdict is contrary to law.

Judgment affirmed.

Notes, Problems, and Questions

1. What was accomplished by this lawsuit? How could the problem have been resolved out of court?

2. Mr. Gary T. Roberson, manager of Marengo Cave, advised the authors that as a result of this decision the cave was closed off by a fence at the property line. The fence remained intact for many years. Legend has it that Mr. Ross occasionally bought a ticket and toured the cave to insure that the company was not permitting tourists to go into the cave on his side of the property line. Apparently Mr. Ross' heirs held onto the land for some time after his death and then sold it to a timberman. In 1974, the timberman sold the 2½ acres under which the cave ran to the Marengo Cave Company. It took the cave company several years to improve the site so as to permit easy access for visitors. In 1979, the portion of the cave under the former Ross property was finally opened to the general public.

3. O is record owner of Blackacre, but does not occupy it. A has been in adverse possession of Blackacre for thirteen years. (The statute of limitations for bringing an action to recover possession of land is twenty years in this jurisdiction.) Without permission from either O or A, B began hunting

on Blackacre every weekend. A asked B to stay off Blackacre, but B refused. Does A have any legal recourse against B?

4. The property in Rolling Hills that the Ryans have contracted to purchase is bordered on one side by a large decorative hedge. The next door neighbors have maintained the hedge for many years. The Ryans commissioned a survey which revealed that the hedge lies four feet within the legal boundaries specified in their sales contract. Steve and Jill have asked you to determine whether the seller owns this strip of land and whether they will receive title to it if they decide to close the transaction. What effect will the following information have on your answer:

(a) The seller did not know that the strip of land belonged to the seller.

(b) The seller knew the land belonged to the seller, but did not say anything because the hedge was attractive and the seller did not want to maintain it.

(c) The seller knew the hedge was on the seller's land and informed the neighbors of that fact, but the seller gave the neighbors permission to keep the hedge if they promised to maintain it in good condition.

(d) The neighbors believed the property was theirs because the strip was included in their deed, although the previous owner of their lot did not have legal title to the land.

5. Partly in response to the problem of homelessness, squatters in some urban areas have simply occupied vacant buildings, often those owned by municipalities. Courts have tended to treat squatters as trespassers in illegal occupation and subject to removal. It has proven difficult for squatters to make effective claims of adverse possession. *See* Comment, *Squatters' Rights and Adverse Possession: A Search for Equitable Application of Property Laws*, 8 Ind.Int'l. & Comp.L.Rev. 119, 141–148 (1997); *see also* East 13th Street Homeowners' Coalition v. Lower East Side Coalition Housing Development, 230 A.D.2d 622, 646 N.Y.S.2d 324 (1996) (pointing out that claimants were unlikely to demonstrate elements of adverse possession, and declining to enjoin city from using self-help to remove squatters from buildings).

6. Title to chattels may be acquired by adverse possession. As with real property, the adverse claimant must exercise dominion over the chattels in a manner hostile or adverse to the true owner. The holding must also be open and notorious. Actions for the recovery of personal property are shorter than those relating to land. Actions typically must be commenced between two and six years after the cause of action accrued, but most states enlarge this period in cases of fraudulent concealment. Since chattels are movable and the owner may have difficulty ascertaining who has possession of the property, the rules for adverse possession of chattels are complex. Consequently, there is a large degree of uncertainty in this area of the law. What constitutes open and notorious possession of a chattel? Under what circumstances can a bailee acquire title to the bailor's chattels? Will the statute of limitations run in favor of a thief? Or a bona fide purchaser from a thief? Does it make any difference if the adverse possessor has removed the articles from the state? *See* R. Brown, The Law of Personal Property, §§ 4.1–4.3 (3d ed. 1975); DeWeerth v. Baldinger, 836 F.2d 103 (2d Cir.1987), *cert. denied*

486 U.S. 1056 (1988); O'Keeffe v. Snyder, 83 N.J. 478, 416 A.2d 862 (1980); Solomon R. Guggenheim Foundation v. Lubell, 77 N.Y.2d 311, 567 N.Y.S.2d 623, 569 N.E.2d 426 (1991). *See generally* Gerstenblith, *The Adverse Possession of Personal Property,* 37 Buffalo L.Rev. 119 (1988/89).

G. TITLE INSURANCE

1. INTRODUCTION

REPORT, RESIDENTIAL REAL ESTATE TRANSACTIONS: THE LAWYER'S PROPER ROLE—SERVICES—COMPENSATION

14 Real Prop., Prob. & Tr.J. 581, 604 (1979).

In some sections of the country the use of title insurance has eliminated the lawyer from conveyancing or drastically reduced the lawyer's role. For this reason any statement of the proper role of the lawyer in the residential real estate transaction which ignores the relationship between the title insurers and the bar is unrealistic.

The value of some form of title insurance is recognized. Also, there is no immediate prospect of fundamental change in the traditional system of recording evidence of title. So long as this present system of recording evidence of title is used, national mortgage lenders may insist upon title insurance in addition to the certificate or opinion conventionally furnished by an examining lawyer. Although the national mortgage market is the primary source of demand for title insurance, a lesser but increasing demand comes from local lenders and from home buyers who want owner coverage. The insurance can be provided by commercial companies or by bar-related title insurers.[1]

The objection to private title plants already has been stated. It is to be noted that reliance on private title plants results in absorbing the fee paid for title examination, which frustrates efforts to increase needed legal services to the home buyer.

A legitimate question is whether the public can be better served by commercial title companies or the bar. It has been pointed out that the interests of the insurer and the insured are in conflict and that the insurer cannot, from the nature of the enterprise, furnish needed legal services. The role of the title company should be confined to title insurance. Conveyancing should be left to independent lawyers. The independent lawyer in private practice will protect the client's interests at each stage of the transaction and provide the necessary counseling when any difficulties arise. The objective is to provide needed legal services to the buyer and seller by their own lawyers at reasonable cost.

1. Vigorous competition exists between commercial title companies and bar-related insurance funds. *Compare* Rooney, *Bar-Related Title Insurance: The Positive Perspective,* 1980 S.Ill.U.L.J. 263 *with* Rosenberg, *Why Bar Funds Are Not in the Public Interest,* 59 Title News 11 (1980). [Editors' note.]

Attention is called to the statement of principles with respect to the mutual roles of the lawyer and the title insurer in real estate transactions which have been promulgated by the National Conference of Lawyers, Title Insurance Companies and Abstracters and approved by the American Bar Association and the American Land Title Association.

2. SAMPLE TITLE INSURANCE POLICY

American Land Title Association

Owner's Policy
Revised 10/17/92
Section II-2

POLICY OF TITLE INSURANCE

Issued by

BLANK TITLE INSURANCE COMPANY

SUBJECT TO THE EXCLUSIONS FROM COVERAGE, THE EXCEPTIONS FROM COVERAGE CONTAINED IN SCHEDULE B AND THE CONDITIONS AND STIPULATIONS, BLANK TITLE INSURANCE COMPANY, a Blank corporation, herein called the Company, insures, as of Date of Policy shown in Schedule A, against loss or damage, not exceeding the Amount of Insurance stated in Schedule A, sustained or incurred by the insured by reason of:

1. Title to the estate or interest described in Schedule A being vested other than as stated therein;

2. Any defect in or lien or encumbrance on the title;

3. Unmarketability of the title;

4. Lack of a right of access to and from the land.

The Company will also pay the costs, attorneys' fees and expenses incurred in defense of the title, as insured, but only to the extent provided in the Conditions and Stipulations.
[Witness clause optional]

BLANK TITLE INSURANCE COMPANY

BY:_____
                        PRESIDENT

BY:_____
                        SECRETARY

American Land Title Association

Owner's Policy
Revised 10/17/92
Section II-2

EXCLUSIONS FROM COVERAGE

The following matters are expressly excluded from the coverage of this policy and the Company will not pay loss or damage, costs, attorneys' fees or expenses which arise by reason of:

1.   (a)   Any law, ordinance or governmental regulation (including but not limited to building and zoning laws, ordinances, or regulations) restricting, regulating, prohibiting or relating to (i) the occupancy, use, or enjoyment of the land; (ii) the character, dimensions or location of any improvement now or hereafter erected on the land; (iii) a separation in ownership or a change in the dimensions or area of the land or any parcel of which the land is or was a part; or (iv) environmental protection, or the effect of any violation of these laws, ordinances or governmental regulations, except to the extent that a notice of the enforcement thereof or a notice of a defect, lien or encumbrance resulting from a violation or alleged violation affecting the land has been recorded in the public records at Date of Policy.

         (b)   Any governmental police power not excluded by (a) above, except to the extent that a notice of the exercise thereof or a notice of a defect, lien or encumbrance resulting from a violation or alleged violation affecting the land has been recorded in the public records at Date of Policy.

2.   Rights of eminent domain unless notice of the exercise thereof has been recorded in the public records at Date of Policy, but not excluding from coverage any taking which has occurred prior to Date of Policy which would be binding on the rights of a purchaser for value without knowledge.

3.   Defects, liens, encumbrances, adverse claims or other matters:

         (a)   created, suffered, assumed or agreed to by the insured claimant;

         (b)   not known to the Company, not recorded in the public records at Date of Policy, but known to the insured claimant and not disclosed in writing to the Company by the insured claimant prior to the date the insured claimant became an insured under this policy;

         (c)   resulting in no loss or damage to the insured claimant;

         (d)   attaching or created subsequent to Date of Policy; or

         (e)   resulting in loss or damage which would not have been sustained if the insured claimant had paid value for the estate or interest insured by this policy.

4.   Any claim, which arises out of the transaction vesting in the Insured the estate or interest insured by this policy, by reason of the operation of federal bankruptcy, state insolvency, or similar creditors' rights laws, that is based on:

         (a)   the transaction creating the estate or interest insured by this policy being deemed a fraudulent conveyance or fraudulent transfer; or

         (b)   the transaction creating the estate or interest insured by this policy being deemed a preferential transfer except where the preferential transfer results from the failure:

                 (i)   to timely record the instrument of transfer; or

                 (ii)   of such recordation to impart notice to a purchaser for value or a judgment or lien creditor.

American Land Title Association

Owner's Policy
Revised 10/17/92
Section II-2

<u>SCHEDULE A</u>

[File No.   ]   Policy No.

Amount of Insurance $

[Premium $]

a.m.

Date of Policy   [at   p.m.]

1.   Name of Insured:

2.   The estate or interest in the land which is covered by this policy is:

3.   Title to the estate or interest in the land is vested in:

[4.   The land referred to in this policy is described as follows:]

If Paragraph 4 is omitted, a Schedule C, captioned the same as Paragraph 4, must be used.

American Land Title Association   Owner's Policy
                                                            Revised 10/17/92
                                                            Section II-2

<u>**SCHEDULE B**</u>

[File No.   ]   Policy No.

EXCEPTIONS FROM COVERAGE

This policy does not insure against loss or damage (and the Company will not pay costs, attorneys' fees or expenses) which arise by reason of:

1.

    [POLICY MAY INCLUDE REGIONAL EXCEPTIONS IF SO

2.   DESIRED BY ISSUING COMPANY]

    [VARIABLE EXCEPTIONS SUCH AS TAXES, EASEMENTS, CC & Rs, ETC.]

3.

4.

CONDITIONS AND STIPULATIONS

1.   DEFINITION OF TERMS.

The following terms when used in this policy mean:

(a)   "insured": the insured named in Schedule A, and, subject to any rights or defenses the Company would have had against the named insured, those who succeed to the interest of the named insured by operation of law as distinguished from purchase including, but not limited to, heirs, distributees, devisees, survivors, personal representatives, next of kin, or corporate or fiduciary successors.

(b)   "insured claimant": an insured claiming loss or damage.

(c)   "knowledge" or "known": actual knowledge, not constructive knowledge or notice which may be imputed to an insured by reason of the public records as defined in this policy or any other records which impart constructive notice of matters affecting the land.

(d)   "land": the land described or referred to in Schedule [A][C], and improvements affixed thereto which by law constitute real property. The term "land" does not include any property beyond the lines of the area described or referred to in Schedule [A][C], nor any right, title, interest, estate or easement in abutting streets, roads, avenues, alleys, lanes, ways or waterways, but nothing herein shall modify or limit the extent to which a right of access to and from the land is insured by this policy.

(e)   "mortgage": mortgage, deed of trust, trust deed, or other security instrument.

(f)   "public records": records established under state statutes at Date of Policy for the purpose of imparting constructive notice of matters relating to real property to purchasers for value and without knowledge. With respect to Section 1(a)(iv) of the Exclusions From Coverage, "public records" shall also include environmental protection liens filed in the records of the clerk of the United States district court for the district in which the land is located.

(g)   "unmarketability of the title": an alleged or apparent matter affecting the title to the land, not excluded or excepted from coverage, which would entitle a purchaser of the estate or interest described in Schedule A to be released from the obligation to purchase by virtue of a contractual condition requiring the delivery of marketable title.

2.   CONTINUATION OF INSURANCE AFTER CONVEYANCE OF TITLE.

The coverage of this policy shall continue in force as of Date of Policy in favor of an insured only so long as the insured retains an estate or interest in the land, or holds an indebtedness secured by a purchase money mortgage given by a purchaser from the insured, or only so long as the insured shall have liability by reason of covenants of warranty made by the insured in any transfer or conveyance of the estate or interest. This policy shall not continue in force in favor of any purchaser from the insured of either (i) an estate or interest in the land, or (ii) an indebtedness secured by a purchase money mortgage given to the insured.

3.   NOTICE OF CLAIM TO BE GIVEN BY INSURED CLAIMANT.

The insured shall notify the Company promptly in writing (i) in case of any litigation as set forth in Section 4(a) below, (ii) in case knowledge shall come to an insured hereunder of any claim of title or interest which is adverse to the title to the estate or interest, as insured, and which might cause loss or damage for which the Company may be liable by virtue of this policy, or (iii) if title to the estate or interest, as insured, is rejected as unmarketable. If prompt notice shall not be given to the Company, then as to the insured all liability of the Company shall terminate with regard to the matter or matters for which prompt notice is required; provided, however, that failure to notify the Company shall in no case prejudice the rights of any insured under this policy unless the Company shall be prejudiced by the failure and then only to the extent of the prejudice.

American Land Title Association   Owner's Policy
Revised 10/17/92
Section II-2

4.   <u>DEFENSE AND PROSECUTION OF ACTIONS; DUTY OF INSURED CLAIMANT TO COOPERATE.</u>

(a)   Upon written request by the insured and subject to the options contained in Section 6 of these Conditions and Stipulations, the Company, at its own cost and without unreasonable delay, shall provide for the defense of an insured in litigation in which any third party asserts a claim adverse to the title or interest as insured, but only as to those stated causes of action alleging a defect, lien or encumbrance or other matter insured against by this policy. The Company shall have the right to select counsel of its choice (subject to the right of the insured to object for reasonable cause) to represent the insured as to those stated causes of action and shall not be liable for and will not pay the fees of any other counsel. The Company will not pay any fees, costs or expenses incurred by the insured in the defense of those causes of action which allege matters not insured against by this policy.

(b)   The Company shall have the right, at its own cost, to institute and prosecute any action or proceeding or to do any other act which in its opinion may be necessary or desirable to establish the title to the estate or interest, as insured, or to prevent or reduce loss or damage to the insured. The Company may take any appropriate action under the terms of this policy, whether or not it shall be liable hereunder, and shall not thereby concede liability or waive any provision of this policy. If the Company shall exercise its rights under this paragraph, it shall do so diligently.

(c)   Whenever the Company shall have brought an action or interposed a defense as required or permitted by the provisions of this policy, the Company may pursue any litigation to final determination by a court of competent jurisdiction and expressly reserves the right, in its sole discretion, to appeal from any adverse judgment or order.

(d)   In all cases where this policy permits or requires the Company to prosecute or provide for the defense of any action or proceeding, the insured shall secure to the Company the right to so prosecute or provide defense in the action or proceeding, and all appeals therein, and permit the Company to use, at its option, the name of the insured for this purpose. Whenever requested by the Company, the insured, at the Company's expense, shall give the Company all reasonable aid (i) in any action or proceeding, securing evidence, obtaining witnesses, prosecuting or defending the action or proceeding, or effecting settlement, and (ii) in any other lawful act which in the opinion of the Company may be necessary or desirable to establish the title to the estate or interest as insured. If the Company is prejudiced by the failure of the insured to furnish the required cooperation, the Company's obligations to the insured under the policy shall terminate, including any liability or obligation to defend, prosecute, or continue any litigation, with regard to the matter or matters requiring such cooperation.

5.   <u>PROOF OF LOSS OR DAMAGE.</u>

In addition to and after the notices required under Section 3 of these Conditions and Stipulations have been provided the Company, a proof of loss or damage signed and sworn to by the insured claimant shall be furnished to the Company within 90 days after the insured claimant shall ascertain the facts giving rise to the loss or damage. The proof of loss or damage shall describe the defect in, or lien or encumbrance on the title, or other matter insured against by this policy which constitutes the basis of loss or damage and shall state, to the extent possible, the basis of calculating the amount of the loss or damage. If the Company is prejudiced by the failure of the insured claimant to provide the required proof of loss or damage, the Company's obligations to the insured under the policy shall terminate, including any liability or obligation to defend, prosecute, or continue any litigation, with regard to the matter or matters requiring such proof of loss or damage.

In addition, the insured claimant may reasonably be required to submit to examination under oath by any authorized representative of the Company and shall produce for examination, inspection and copying, at such reasonable times and places as may be designated by any authorized representative of the Company, all records, books, ledgers, checks, correspondence and memoranda, whether bearing a date before or after Date of Policy, which reasonably pertain to the loss or damage. Further, if requested by any authorized representative of the Company, the insured claimant shall grant its permission, in writing, for any authorized representative of the Company to examine, inspect and copy all records, books, ledgers, checks, correspondence and memoranda in the custody or control of a third party, which reasonably pertain to the loss or damage. All information designated as confidential by the insured claimant provided to the Company pursuant to this Section shall not be disclosed to others unless, in the reasonable judgment of the Company, it is necessary in the administration of the claim.

American Land Title Association

Owner's Policy
Revised 10/17/92
Section II-2

Failure of the insured claimant to submit for examination under oath, produce other reasonably requested information or grant permission to secure reasonably necessary information from third parties as required in this paragraph shall terminate any liability of the Company under this policy as to that claim.

6.   OPTIONS TO PAY OR OTHERWISE SETTLE CLAIMS; TERMINATION OF LIABILITY.

In case of a claim under this policy, the Company shall have the following additional options:

(a)   To Pay or Tender Payment of the Amount of Insurance.

(i)   To pay or tender payment of the amount of insurance under this policy together with any costs, attorneys' fees and expenses incurred by the insured claimant, which were authorized by the Company, up to the time of payment or tender of payment and which the Company is obligated to pay.

(ii)   Upon the exercise by the Company of this option, all liability and obligations to the insured under this policy, other than to make the payment required, shall terminate, including any liability or obligation to defend, prosecute, or continue any litigation, and the policy shall be surrendered to the Company for cancellation.

(b)   To Pay or Otherwise Settle With Parties Other than the Insured or With the Insured Claimant.

(i)   to pay or otherwise settle with other parties for or in the name of an insured claimant any claim insured against under this policy, together with any costs, attorneys' fees and expenses incurred by the insured claimant which were authorized by the Company up to the time of payment and which the Company is obligated to pay; or

(ii)   to pay or otherwise settle with the insured claimant the loss or damage provided for under this policy, together with any costs, attorneys' fees and expenses incurred by the insured claimant which were authorized by the Company up to the time of payment and which the Company is obligated to pay.

Upon the exercise by the Company of either of the options provided for in paragraphs (b)(i) or (ii), the Company's obligations to the insured under this policy for the claimed loss or damage, other than the payments required to be made, shall terminate, including any liability or obligation to defend, prosecute or continue any litigation.

7.   DETERMINATION, EXTENT OF LIABILITY AND COINSURANCE.

This policy is a contract of indemnity against actual monetary loss or damage sustained or incurred by the insured claimant who has suffered loss or damage by reason of matters insured against by this policy and only to the extent herein described.

(a)   The liability of the Company under this policy shall not exceed the least of:

(i)   the Amount of Insurance stated in Schedule A; or,

(ii)   the difference between the value of the insured estate or interest as insured and the value of the insured estate or interest subject to the defect, lien or encumbrance insured against by this policy.

(b)   In the event the Amount of Insurance stated in Schedule A at the Date of Policy is less than 80 percent of the value of the insured estate or interest or the full consideration paid for the land, whichever is less, or if subsequent to the Date of Policy an improvement is erected on the land which increases the value of the insured estate or interest by at least 20 percent over the Amount of Insurance stated in Schedule A, then this Policy is subject to the following:

(i)   where no subsequent improvement has been made, as to any partial loss, the Company shall only pay the loss pro rata in the proportion that the amount of insurance at Date of Policy bears to the total value of the insured estate or interest at Date of Policy; or

(ii) where a subsequent improvement has been made, as to any partial loss, the Company shall only pay the loss pro rata in the proportion that 120 percent of the Amount of Insurance stated in Schedule A bears to the sum of the Amount of Insurance stated in Schedule A and the amount expended for the improvement.

The provisions of this paragraph shall not apply to costs, attorneys' fees and expenses for which the Company is liable under this policy, and shall only apply to that portion of any loss which exceeds, in the aggregate, 10 percent of the Amount of Insurance stated in Schedule A.

(c) The Company will pay only those costs, attorneys' fees and expenses incurred in accordance with Section 4 of these Conditions and Stipulations.

8. APPORTIONMENT.

If the land described in Schedule [A][C] consists of two or more parcels which are not used as a single site, and a loss is established affecting one or more of the parcels but not all, the loss shall be computed and settled on a pro rata basis as if the amount of insurance under this policy was divided pro rata as to the value on Date of Policy of each separate parcel to the whole, exclusive of any improvements made subsequent to Date of Policy, unless a liability or value has otherwise been agreed upon as to each parcel by the Company and the insured at the time of the issuance of this policy and shown by an express statement or by an endorsement attached to this policy.

9. LIMITATION OF LIABILITY.

(a) If the Company establishes the title, or removes the alleged defect, lien or encumbrance, or cures the lack of a right of access to or from the land, or cures the claim of unmarketability of title, all as insured, in a reasonably diligent manner by any method, including litigation and the completion of any appeals therefrom, it shall have fully performed its obligations with respect to that matter and shall not be liable for any loss or damage caused thereby.

(b) In the event of any litigation, including litigation by the Company or with the Company's consent, the Company shall have no liability for loss or damage until there has been a final determination by a court of competent jurisdiction, and disposition of all appeals therefrom, adverse to the title as insured.

(c) The Company shall not be liable for loss or damage to any insured for liability voluntarily assumed by the insured in settling any claim or suit without the prior written consent of the Company.

10. REDUCTION OF INSURANCE; REDUCTION OR TERMINATION OF LIABILITY.

All payments under this policy, except payments made for costs, attorneys' fees and expenses, shall reduce the amount of the insurance pro tanto.

11. LIABILITY NONCUMULATIVE.

It is expressly understood that the amount of insurance under this policy shall be reduced by any amount the Company may pay under any policy insuring a mortgage to which exception is taken in Schedule B or to which the insured has agreed, assumed, or taken subject, or which is hereafter executed by an insured and which is a charge or lien on the estate or interest described or referred to in Schedule A, and the amount so paid shall be deemed a payment under this policy to the insured owner.

American Land Title Association

12.   <u>PAYMENT OF LOSS</u>.

     (a)   No payment shall be made without producing this policy for endorsement of the payment unless the policy has been lost or destroyed, in which case proof of loss or destruction shall be furnished to the satisfaction of the Company.

     (b)   When liability and the extent of loss or damage has been definitely fixed in accordance with these Conditions and Stipulations, the loss or damage shall be payable within 30 days thereafter.

13.   <u>SUBROGATION UPON PAYMENT OR SETTLEMENT</u>.

     (a)   <u>The Company's Right of Subrogation</u>.

     Whenever the Company shall have settled and paid a claim under this policy, all right of subrogation shall vest in the Company unaffected by any act of the insured claimant.

     The Company shall be subrogated to and be entitled to all rights and remedies which the insured claimant would have had against any person or property in respect to the claim had this policy not been issued. If requested by the Company, the insured claimant shall transfer to the Company all rights and remedies against any person or property necessary in order to perfect this right of subrogation. The insured claimant shall permit the Company to sue, compromise or settle in the name of the insured claimant and to use the name of the insured claimant in any transaction or litigation involving these rights or remedies.

     If a payment on account of a claim does not fully cover the loss of the insured claimant, the Company shall be subrogated to these rights and remedies in the proportion which the Company's payment bears to the whole amount of the loss.

     If loss should result from any act of the insured claimant, as stated above, that act shall not void this policy, but the Company, in that event, shall be required to pay only that part of any losses insured against by this policy which shall exceed the amount, if any, lost to the Company by reason of the impairment by the insured claimant of the Company's right of subrogation.

     (b)   <u>The Company's Rights Against Non-insured Obligors</u>.

     The Company's right of subrogation against non-insured obligors shall exist and shall include, without limitation, the rights of the insured to indemnities, guaranties, other policies of insurance or bonds, notwithstanding any terms or conditions contained in those instruments which provide for subrogation rights by reason of this policy.

14.   <u>ARBITRATION</u>

     Unless prohibited by applicable law, either the Company or the insured may demand arbitration pursuant to the Title Insurance Arbitration Rules of the American Arbitration Association. Arbitrable matters may include, but are not limited to, any controversy or claim between the Company and the insured arising out of or relating to this policy, any service of the Company in connection with its issuance or the breach of a policy provision or other obligation. All arbitrable matters when the Amount of Insurance is $1,000,000 or less shall be arbitrated at the option of either the Company or the insured. All arbitrable matters when the Amount of Insurance is in excess of $1,000,000 shall be arbitrated only when agreed to by both the Company and the insured. Arbitration pursuant to this policy and under the Rules in effect on the date the demand for arbitration is made or, at the option of the insured, the Rules in effect at Date of Policy shall be binding upon the parties. The award may include attorneys' fees only if the laws of the state in which the land is located permit a court to award attorneys' fees to a prevailing party. Judgment upon the award rendered by the Arbitrator(s) may be entered in any court having jurisdiction thereof.

     The law of the situs of the land shall apply to an arbitration under the Title Insurance Arbitration Rules.

American Land Title Association

A copy of the Rules may be obtained from the Company upon request.

15.   <u>LIABILITY LIMITED TO THIS POLICY; POLICY ENTIRE CONTRACT</u>.

     (a)   This policy together with all endorsements, if any, attached hereto by the Company is the entire policy and contract between the insured and the Company. In interpreting any provision of this policy, this policy shall be construed as a whole.

     (b)   Any claim of loss or damage, whether or not based on negligence, and which arises out of the status of the title to the estate or interest covered hereby or by any action asserting such claim, shall be restricted to this policy.

     (c)   No amendment of or endorsement to this policy can be made except by a writing endorsed hereon or attached hereto signed by either the President, a Vice President, the Secretary, an Assistant Secretary, or validating officer or authorized signatory of the Company.

16.   <u>SEVERABILITY</u>.

     In the event any provision of the policy is held invalid or unenforceable under applicable law, the policy shall be deemed not to include that provision and all other provisions shall remain in full force and effect.

17.   <u>NOTICES, WHERE SENT</u>.

     All notices required to be given the Company and any statement in writing required to be furnished the Company shall include the number of this policy and shall be addressed to the Company at (fill in).

NOTE: Bracketed [ ] material optional

Notes and Questions

     1.   The sample policy insures against loss by reason of unmarketability of title. Not all policies provide such coverage. What is the significance of this difference?

2. Title insurance is also available for lenders. Many mortgagees require that borrowers pay for title insurance policies covering their respective interests.

3. For an excellent practical discussion of title insurance, *see* Rooney, *Title Insurance: A Primer for Attorneys,* 14 Real Prop.Prob. & Tr.J. 608 (1979). *See generally* D. Burke, Law of Title Insurance (2d ed.1993 & Supp.1998).

3. COVERAGE

GREENBERG v. STEWART TITLE GUARANTY COMPANY

Supreme Court of Wisconsin, 1992.
171 Wis.2d 485, 492 N.W.2d 147.

BABLITCH, JUSTICE.

The issue presented is whether the issuance of title commitments and subsequently issued title insurance policies give rise in Wisconsin to a tort cause of action against the title insurer and/or its issuing agent separate and apart from the contractual obligations of the title policy. Martin J. Greenberg (Greenberg), the appellant, obtained from Stewart Title Guaranty Company, through its agent, Southeastern Wisconsin Title Company, four owner's title insurance policies in the amount of $250,000 each, which insured the interest in title in four condominiums. When Greenberg was unable to sell the condominiums because of an alleged defect in title, he contended that Stewart and Southeastern were liable not only under the contract, but in addition, for damage in tort for negligence. The circuit court held that the relationship between the parties involved a contract of indemnity and that no tort liability existed in Wisconsin law. We agree, and affirm the judgment of the circuit court.

The relevant facts follow. Martin Greenberg, the appellant, and John Huber (Huber) purchased four condominium units in Lake Geneva, Wisconsin. Before acquiring the condominiums, Greenberg and Huber contacted Stewart Title Guaranty Company (Stewart) through its agent, Southeastern Wisconsin Title Company (Southeastern). Title commitments were provided to Greenberg and Huber. A title commitment is a document which describes the property as the title insurer is willing to insure it and contains the same exclusions and general and specific exceptions as later appear in the title insurance policy. Greenberg stated in his deposition that he received the title commitments from either Stewart or Southeastern.

Stewart, through its agent, Southeastern, then issued owner's title insurance policies insuring Huber's and Greenberg's title interest in the condominiums. Huber and Greenberg purchased the condominiums and, after acquisition, used the units to secure loans from several banks. Huber quitclaimed his interest in the condominiums to Greenberg, who decided to sell the units. Greenberg alleges that he was unable to sell the units because certain liens and encumbrances against the property made it impossible for him to transfer marketable title. He further alleges that, as a result, his lending institutions obtained a foreclosure judgment, and, after a sheriff's sale of the units, deficiency judgments were entered against him in the amount of $564,771.71.

Greenberg made a claim to Stewart alleging that the titles were unmarketable. Stewart denied the claim and Greenberg brought suit against Stewart and Southeastern. His complaint alleged five claims for relief: (1) negligent misrepresentation; (2) negligence; (3) breach of fiduciary duty; (4) breach of contract; (5) lack of good-faith and fair dealing. Specifically, as to the first cause of action, Greenberg's complaint alleges that Southeastern and Stewart "breached the duties they owed to Greenberg under * * * common law by failing to disclose liens and encumbrances and facts relating to same which were known to * * * [them]." Under the second cause of action the complaint alleges that Stewart and Southeastern "owed Greenberg a duty to base the title insurance commitments and policies for the Units on reasonably diligent searches of the public records," and that they "breached their duties to Greenberg by failing to make reasonably diligent searches * * * which would have disclosed liens and encumbrances of record showing title to the Units to be unmarketable * * *." The circuit court dismissed the first two claims holding that the relationship between the parties involved a contract of indemnity and that no tort liability existed in Wisconsin law. The circuit court dismissed the third claim because Greenberg's complaint did not allege any facts from which the court could find a fiduciary duty. The circuit court ordered further briefing on the breach of contract claim and Greenberg voluntarily dismissed the fifth claim. In addition, the circuit court dismissed Southeastern as a party to the action because the only claim remaining in the lawsuit was the breach of contract claim and, as the agent, Southeastern was not a party to the contract.

Greenberg appealed from the judgment dismissing Southeastern as a party, and the court of appeals certified the following issue to this court: "Is a title insurance company liable in tort for failure to discover a title defect or does such liability sound in contract only?" We accepted certification from the court of appeals.

Greenberg maintains that he can sue a title insurance company for negligence because the issuance of a title commitment and a title insurance policy places a common law duty on a title company to search and disclose any reasonably discoverable defects in title. According to Greenberg, this duty is separate and distinct from the title company's contractual duties under the title insurance policy. We disagree.

Courts in other jurisdictions are split on the question of whether a title insurance company can be exposed to liability in tort for negligence in searching records. Some courts and commentators have concluded that a title company should be liable in tort as well as in contract if it negligently fails to discover and disclose a defect. *See* Title Ins. Co. v. Costain Arizona, 164 Ariz. 203, 207, 791 P.2d 1086, 1090 (Ariz.App.

1990); Shada v. Title & Trust Co. of Fla., 457 So.2d 553 (Fla.App.1984); Ford v. Guarantee Abstract and Title Co., Inc., 220 Kan. 244, 553 P.2d 254 (Kan.1976); Heyd v. Chicago Title Ins. Co., 218 Neb. 296, 354 N.W.2d 154 (1984); Joyce Dickey Palomar, *Title Insurance Companies' Liability For Failure to Search Title and Disclose Record Title*, 20 Creighton L.Rev. 455 (1986–87); Comment, *Title Insurance: The Duty To Search*, 71 Yale L.J. 1161 (1961–62). "The underlying notion [of these opinions] is that the insured has the reasonable expectation that the title company will search the title." Walker Rogge, Inc. v. Chelsea Title & Guar. Co., 116 N.J. 517, 562 A.2d 208, 218 (N.J.1989).

Other jurisdictions have refused to impose tort liability on title insurance companies. *See* Brown's Tie & Lumber v. Chicago Title, 115 Idaho 56, 764 P.2d 423 (Idaho 1988); Anderson v. Title Ins. Co., 103 Idaho 875, 655 P.2d 82 (Idaho 1982); Horn v. Lawyers Title Insurance Corporation, 89 N.M. 709, 557 P.2d 206 (N.M.1976); Stewart Title Guar. Co. v. Cheatham, 764 S.W.2d 315 (Tex.App.1988); Houston Title Co. v. Ojeda De Toca, 733 S.W.2d 325 (Tex.App.1987), rev'd on other grounds Ojeda de Toca v. Wise, 748 S.W.2d 449 (Tex.1988). These courts reason that because a title insurer does not purport to act as anything other than an insurance company, no tort liability exists unless the insurer has voluntarily assumed a duty of searching title for the insured's benefit in addition to the contract to insure title. They further conclude that the issuance of a preliminary report or title commitment is not an independent assumption of a duty to search and disclose reasonably discoverable defects. We find this reasoning, particularly the reasoning of Justice Pollock of the New Jersey Supreme Court in *Walker Rogge,* persuasive.

In *Rogge,* the insured, Walker Rogge, Inc. (Rogge), sued a title insurance company when it discovered that the acreage of the tract of land it purchased was approximately 12 acres, instead of the approximate 19 acres Rogge thought it had purchased. In support of its negligence claim, Rogge pointed to the title company's separate charge for a title examination and to its reliance on the title company to conduct a reasonable search. In response to Rogge's arguments, Justice Pollock, writing for the majority, stated:

> Although we recognize that an insured expects that a title company will conduct a reasonable title examination, the relationship between the company and the insured is essentially contractual. The end result of the relationship between the title company and the insured is the issuance of the policy. To this extent, the relationship differs from other relationships conceivably sounding in both tort and contract, such as the relationship between physician and patient, to which plaintiff alludes. Although the relationship between physician and patient is contractual in its origins, the purpose of the relationship is to obtain the services of the physician in treating the patient. The patient reasonably expects the physician to follow the appropriate standard of care when providing those services. By contrast, the title company is providing not services, but a

policy of insurance. That policy appropriately limits the rights and duties of the parties.

From this perspective, the insured expects that in consideration for payment of the premium, it will receive a policy of insurance. The insurer's expectation is that in exchange for that premium it will insure against certain risks subject to the terms of the policy. If the title company fails to conduct a reasonable title examination or, having conducted such an examination, fails to disclose the results to the insured, then it runs the risk of liability under the policy. In many, if not most, [sic] cases conduct that would constitute the failure to make a reasonable title search would also result in a breach of the terms of the policy. *Id.* 562 A.2d at 220 (citations omitted).

We also find instructive the Texas Court of Appeals' discussion of title insurance in Houston Title Co., 733 S.W.2d at 327 (1987) (citations omitted):

> The title insurance company is not, as is an abstract company, employed to examine title; rather, the title insurance company is employed to guarantee the status of title and to insure against existing defects. Thus, the relationship between the parties is limited to that of indemnitor and indemnitee.

As Southeastern points out in its brief, we have described title insurance in terms similar to those employed by the Texas court. In Blackhawk Prod. v. Chicago Ins., 144 Wis.2d 68, 78, 423 N.W.2d 521 (1988), we explained:

> Title insurance has been described as a contract of indemnity. Its purpose is to indemnify the insured for impairment of its interest due to failure of title as guaranteed in the title insurance report. That is, it protects against losses sustained in the event that a specific contingency, such as the discovery of an unexcepted lien affecting title, occurs.

This language and the language quoted above from other jurisdictions indicate that a title insurance company is not an abstractor of title employed to examine title. Rather, a title insurance company guarantees the status of title and insures up to the policy limits against existing defects. Thus, the only duty undertaken by a title insurance company in issuing a policy of insurance is to indemnify the insured up to the policy limits against loss suffered by the insured if the title is not as stated in the policy. As one court explained:

[handwritten margin note: Duty of Title ins. co.]

> The policy of title insurance, however, does not constitute a representation that the contingency insured against will not occur. Accordingly, when such contingency occurs, no action for negligence or negligent misrepresentation will lie against the insurer based upon the policy of title insurance alone. '[T]he insurer does *not* represent expressly or impliedly that the title is as set forth in the policy; it merely agrees that, * * * the insurer will pay for any losses result-

ing from, or he will cause the removal of, a cloud on the insured's title within the policy provisions.' * * * 'A title policy is *not* a summary of the public records and the insurer is *not* supplying information; to the contrary he is giving a contract of indemnity. A title insurer, as any other insurer, can and does assume the risk of its policy.' Lawrence v. Chicago Title Ins. Co., 192 Cal.App.3d 70, 74–75 [237 Cal.Rptr. 264] (1987) (citations omitted).

Similarly, the issuance of a title commitment does not, as Greenberg suggests, constitute an independent undertaking by the insurer to search the title for the benefit of the insured. Rather, the title commitment "generally constitutes no more than a statement of the terms and conditions upon which the insurer is willing to issue its title policy * * *." Lawrence, 192 Cal.App.3d at 76, 237 Cal.Rptr. 264. Any search done by an insurer in preparation for preparing a title commitment is done to protect itself in deciding whether to insure the property and to protect against losses covered in the policy.

* * *

We therefore hold that a title insurance company and/or its agent is not liable in negligence for an alleged defect in title when it issues a title insurance policy unless it has voluntarily assumed a duty to conduct a reasonable search in addition to the mere contract to insure title.

We further hold that the issuance of a title commitment is not an assumption of an independent duty to search. In this case, the circuit court found that the relationship between Greenberg and the title insurance companies was purely contractual and therefore the companies' liabilities are limited to indemnifying the insured according to the express terms and limits of the insurance policy. This finding is supported by the evidence in the record and is not clearly erroneous. The title companies did not assume an independent duty to Greenberg to examine title and conduct a reasonable search. Greenberg himself acknowledged the lack of such a duty in his deposition testimony:

Q—Can you produce any documents, including either the title commitments or title policies, whereby any of the defendants took on the obligation to warranty title to these four units?

A—I don't understand what warranty title means. Are you talking about insuring title? Are you talking about warranty against certain exceptions? Are you talking about a warranty as to marketability? I don't understand your question.

Q—Okay. As a real estate lawyer and professor, you're generally aware of the content of standard title policies and title commitments; correct?

A—Correct.

Q—And nowhere in those documents is there any warranty of title; is there?

A—There is not a warranty of title, but there is an insurance of marketable title.

Accordingly, we agree with the decision of the circuit court dismissing Greenberg's tort claims and its judgment is affirmed.

* * *

Question

In Heyd v. Chicago Title Insurance Co., 218 Neb. 296, 303, 354 N.W.2d 154, 158–159 (1984), the Supreme Court of Nebraska held:

> * * * [A] title insurance company which renders a title report and also issues a policy of title insurance has assumed two distinct duties. In rendering the title report the title insurance company serves as an abstracter of title and must list all matters of public record adversely affecting title to the real estate which is the subject of the title report. When a title insurance company fails to perform its duty to abstract title accurately, the title insurance company may be liable in tort for all damages proximately caused by such breach of duty. A title insurance company's responsibility for its tortious conduct is distinct from the insurance company's responsibility existing on account of its policy of insurance. Different duties and responsibilities imposed on the title insurance company, therefore, can be the basis for separate causes of action—done cause of action in tort and another in contract.

See also Bank of California, N.A. v. First American Title Insurance Company, 826 P.2d 1126 (Alaska 1992) (title insurance company may be liable in tort for negligence in preparing commitment). Which decision represents the better view—*Greenberg* or *Heyd? See generally* Davis, *More Than They Bargained For: Are Title Insurance Companies Liable in Tort for Undisclosed Title Defects?*, 45 Cath.U.L.Rev. 71 (1995); Palomar, *Title Insurance Companies' Liability for Failure to Search Title and Disclose Record Title*, 20 Creighton L.Rev. 455 (1987).

GATES v. CHICAGO TITLE INSURANCE COMPANY

Missouri Court of Appeals, Western District, 1991.
813 S.W.2d 10.

PER CURIAM:

This is a new opinion.

Plaintiff Ollie Gates on January 9, 1978, acquired title by purchase to a 480–acre tract of land in Torrance County, New Mexico. He got a title insurance policy from Chicago Title Insurance Company, the defendant, in the amount of $75,000. The policy insured against loss or damages sustained or incurred by the insured (the plaintiff), "as of the date of the Policy," by reason of "lack of a right of access to and from the land."

The jury returned a verdict for Gates in the sum of $50,000, but the trial judge granted judgment n.o.v. in favor of Chicago Title Insurance

Company. On Gates's appeal, we must determine whether he made a submissible case against defendant.

At the time Gates purchased the land, he had access by way of a road referred to in the evidence as "the east road," or sometimes "the Halderman road" which extended from a well-maintained gravel road a distance of ¾ mile to the Gates land. Gates was told at the time of the purchase that the east, or Halderman, road was a "county road and a county maintained road." Eighteen months later—in June, 1979—Gates was informed that Halderman had barricaded the road with a chain, and claimed the road as being his private property. Gates's investigation confirmed Halderman's claim. The foregoing facts were shown by Gates's testimony, and no objection was made to his testimony.

Chicago Title claims that, if Gates lacked access to the property by way of the Halderman road, described in the preceding paragraph, he yet had access by another road called the "west road." Gates had entered his property by this route after the Halderman road was closed. He called it a "goat path," and said: "It's indescribable. It comes in as a path through a rocky hill * * *. Makes a beautiful scenery to look at the mountains, but when you try to climb it, it's kind of hard. The boulders are not just rocks. I mean these are old, polished rocks that have over the years been washed by the water and then cleaned, and just rocks on the side of a hill that can be traversed by goats and mountain climbers and that kind of thing * * * I [do not] conceive it to be a road." At one time he negotiated the path with a four-wheel drive vehicle. Passengers walked beside the vehicle "watching that we didn't fall over the side of the mountain * * *. Not in the least am I exaggerating * * *. Extremely dangerous." By this west route, the distance to the Gates land was about twice the distance from the highway as the east (Halderman) route.

Witness Fidel Montoya, who lived in the vicinity of the Gates land, described the west road as one negotiable only by foot or horseback, and if one attempted it in a four-wheel drive, it should not be after rain or snow.

We hold that the trial court correctly sustained defendant's motion for judgment notwithstanding the verdict. Plaintiff's evidence did not show prima facie that he had no right of access to his property at the time he acquired title thereto. It is true that the western road, the route by which plaintiff Gates had a right of access, was a difficult one and, in its present condition, of only limited usefulness, but if plaintiff had a *right of access,* even though over a rough and nearly impassable route, he makes no case under his title insurance policy. A title insurance company may not be expected to investigate the physical condition of a way of legal access to the insured property to determine if it is passable. In fact, the insurance policy expressly excludes from coverage *"loss or damage by reason of * * ** (3) Encroachments, overlaps, conflicts in boundary lines, shortages in area, or *other matters which would be disclosed by* an accurate survey and *inspection of the premises."* (Emphasis added).

In Title & Trust Co. of Florida v. Barrows, 381 So.2d 1088 (Fla.Dist. Ct.App.1979), the title insurance policy insured against "lack of a right of access to and from the land." The access to plaintiff's land, shown on the plat as a street, was only the extension of a sandy beach, and was covered by the tide in the spring and in the fall. The court reversed a judgment in favor of the insured landowner, saying: "In the case here before us, there is no dispute that the public record shows a legal right of access to appellant's property via the platted Viejo Street. The title insurance policy only insured against record title defects and not against physical infirmities of the platted street." *Id.* at 1090.

Another case very close to the present one is Krause v. Title & Trust Co. of Florida, 390 So.2d 805 (Fla.Dist.Ct.App.1980). There the court held that the title insurance policy did not insure against the absence of a "reasonable and practicable" access route, but only the absence of "legal" access. So the insured owner had no claim under his policy although the only way to his land was not passable by ordinary passenger vehicles without a substantial amount of clay or rock fill. See to the same effect Hocking v. Title Insurance & Trust Co., 37 Cal.2d 644, 234 P.2d 625 (1951).

In *Barrows,* the court took note of Marriott Financial Services, Inc. v. Capitol Funds, Inc., 288 N.C. 122, 217 S.E.2d 551 (1975), cited by plaintiff for his position, but elected not to follow it. *Marriott* contains language which tends to support plaintiff's claim. The language is actually *obiter dicta,* though, and the case is different from the present case in its essential facts. *Marriott* seems to stand alone in offering any support for plaintiff's policy claim.

Judgment affirmed.

GAITAN, JUDGE, dissenting.

I must respectfully dissent. I believe the term "right of access" must be given a reasonable, rather than a strict, construction when the right of access does not provide a reasonable access under the circumstances of the intended use of the property. This is tantamount to no access or a denial of "legal access." *See* Marriott Financial Services, Inc. v. Capitol Funds, Inc., 288 N.C. 122, 217 S.E.2d 551, 565 (1975).

Problems

1. Suppose that the purchaser of a parcel of land was compelled to incur costs for the removal and clean-up of hazardous waste. Does the presence of a hazardous substance on the property impair its marketability and constitute a breach of a title policy insuring against "unmarketability of title"? *See* Lick Mill Creek Apartments v. Chicago Title Insurance Company, 231 Cal.App.3d 1654, 283 Cal.Rptr. 231 (1991).

2. A title policy guaranteed a good title, but excepted "Restrictive covenants in instrument recorded in Book 211 of Conveyances at page 13 in the office of the County Register." The excepted instrument provided that, in the event of a breach, the deed should become void and the estate vest in the grantor or the grantor's heirs. The insured owner suffered a loss as a

result of this instrument. Can the owner recover from the title company? *See* Holly Hotel Company v. Title Guarantee & Trust Company, 147 Misc. 861, 264 N.Y.S. 3 (1932), *affirmed* 239 App.Div. 773, 264 N.Y.S. 7 (1933).

STEWART TITLE GUARANTY CO. v. LUNT LAND CORP.

Supreme Court of Texas, 1961.
162 Tex. 435, 347 S.W.2d 584.

NORVELL, JUSTICE.

The trial court granted defendant-petitioner's motion for summary judgment. This judgment was reversed by the Court of Civil Appeals, 342 S.W.2d 376. We reverse this order of the lower appellate court and affirm the trial court's action. The undisputed facts are as follows:

On March 10, 1954, L. D. Tuttle and wife, by warranty deed, conveyed 50.1 acres out of the Henry Gough Survey (Abstract No. 493) Dallas County, Texas, to D. Eldon Lunt for a consideration of $12,500. At that time, the tract was subject to an easement in favor of the Lone Star Gas Company executed by Tuttle in 1949 which gave the gas company the right to lay and maintain an underground high pressure gas transmission line across the premises. The easement contract provided that if the pipe line should interfere with any present or future permanent structure upon the property, the gas company would relocate the line so as to eliminate the interference. This easement was not excepted from the Tuttle warranty.

On May 1, 1957, D. Eldon Lunt and wife conveyed the property by warranty deed to Lunt Land Corporation, the plaintiff-respondent, for a recited consideration of $12,500. The warranty in this deed contained no exception as to the gas company easement.

On June 19, 1959, Lunt Land Corporation secured two policies of title insurance from petitioner, Stewart Title Company; one being a mortgagee's policy covering a $148,400 loan made to the land corporation by Hillcrest State Bank of University Park; the other being an owner's policy. Both policies covered five tracts of land in Dallas County, including the 50.1 acres out of the Henry Gough Survey (Abstract No. 493) which L. D. Tuttle had conveyed to D. Eldon Lunt. The face amount of this policy covering the five tracts was $175,000. The pertinent provisions of the policy were as follows:

> "Stewart Title Guaranty Company * * * does hereby guarantee to Party or Parties named below (Lunt Land Corporation) herein styled assured * * * that the assured has good and indefeasible title to the following described property subject to the following liens: (the Hillcrest Bank lien is then described followed by a description of the five tracts of land covered by the policy) * * *.

> "Said Company shall not be liable in a greater amount than the actual monetary loss of assured, and in no event shall said Company

be liable for more than One Hundred Seventy-five Thousand and No/100 Dollars, * * *.

"Upon the sale of the property covered hereby, this policy automatically thereupon shall become a warrantor's policy and the assured, his heirs, executors and administrators, shall for a period of twenty-five years from date hereof remain fully protected according to the terms hereof, by reason of the payment of any loss he or they may sustain on account of any warranty contained in the deed executed by assured conveying said property. The Company to be liable under said warranty only by reason of defects, liens or encumbrances existing prior to or at the date hereof (and not excepted above) such liability not to exceed the amount above written."

This policy contained no exception relating to the Lone Star Gas Company easement.

In the first part of August, 1959, according to the testimony of D. Eldon Lunt, President of the land corporation (given in deposition form), he and his company for the first time gained knowledge of the gas company's easement.

On September 2, 1959, after he had obtained such knowledge, Lunt, acting for and on behalf of the corporation, entered into a valid contract of sale binding the corporation to convey the 50.1 acre tract out of the Henry Gough Survey (Abstract No. 493) to Bunker Hills, Inc. for a consideration of $1,875 per acre.

On September 11, 1959, nine days after the property was sold, Lunt, in behalf of his corporation, notified petitioner of its claim under the title insurance policy.

On September 17, 1959, Lunt Land Corporation conveyed the 50.1 acre tract by warranty deed to Mayflower Investment Company, the nominee of Bunker Hills, Inc. No exception was made in the warranty as to the Lone Star Gas Company's easement.

Respondent's theory and pleaded measure of damages was that the 50.1 acre tract:

"* * * has a reasonable market value, without the presence of the hereinbefore referred to high pressure gas line, of $130,000.00. That [said] * * * tract of realty, with the high pressure gas line located thereon, has a reasonable market value in Dallas County, Texas of $94,000.00. That as a result of the said pipeline being located on the hereinabove described tract the title in and to the said tract has failed and as a result of such failure of title Plaintiff has been damaged in the sum of $36,000.00, which sum Plaintiff is entitled to recover of and from the Defendant."

In the Annotation relating to "Title Insurance—Amount of Recovery" contained in 60 A.L.R.2d 970, it is pointed out that there is variation as to the methods of measuring the loss sustained by an owner because of undisclosed easements or liens insured against by a title policy. Such methods necessarily differ according to the nature of the defect and the circumstances in the particular case. Where the title defect is the existence of an easement, the measure of liability will generally be the cost of removing the easement.

The circumstances of the present case are unusual and scant authority has been called to our attention which bears upon the situation.

The nature of the easement itself is hardly common and seems to invite negotiation at some future time with reference to change in location or perhaps removal of the pipe line crossing the property.

Then there is the circumstance that in 1957, Lunt conveyed the property to the land corporation with full warranty of title. This was two years prior to the issuance of the Stewart title policy.

While photographs made a part of Lunt's deposition indicate that the gas line easement had been marked by a cindero and signs for some period of time, we accept his statement that he never gained knowledge of the easement until the early part of August, 1959. He did not, however, notify the title company of a prospective sale of the property so they could mitigate an impending loss under their policy by negotiating with the gas company for a removal of the pipe line or the purchase of its easement rights. On the contrary, he sold the property and even then did not notify the title company until nine days after the contract of sale was signed. The deed given by the Lunt Land Corporation in consummation of the contract of sale contained a clause binding it, its successors and assigns "to warrant and forever defend, all and singular the said premises unto the said Mayflower Investment Company, its successors and assigns, against every person whomsoever lawfully claiming or to claim the same or any part thereof." This warranty covered the pipe line easement.

In the trial court the petitioner urged by plea in abatement and by summary judgment (both of which were heard together) that upon the sale of the property, the title policy ceased to be an owner's policy and became a warrantor's policy. This contention went to the merits. The present suit is not based upon the provisions fixing the title company's liability under the contract considered as a warrantor's policy, and the judgment of the trial court would have no effect upon an assertion of liability under such provision.

The language of the policy upon the particular point is clear and certain: "Upon the sale of the property covered hereby, this policy thereupon shall become a warrantor's policy * * *." It is hardly contemplated that the title guarantor would be liable to the same person for the same defect in title under both the "owner's policy" provisions and the "warrantor's title" provisions. The contract provides successive liabilities. This does not mean that liability having once accrued under the "owner's policy" will necessarily be extinguished by a sale of the property, but that the holder of the title policy, when he knows of the title defect, must give notice or take some appropriate action to prevent the automatic conversion of the contract from an owner's to a warrantor's policy. He cannot, having such knowledge, remain silent, sell the property, execute a full warranty deed thereto and then contend that the policy remained in effect as an owner's policy despite the specific wording thereof.

The judgment of the Court of Civil Appeals is reversed and that of the trial court affirmed.

H. DEED

1. STATUTE OF FRAUDS AND DEED FORM

Recall that at early common law possessory freehold estates in land were transferred by livery of seisin in a feoffment ceremony. Although no writing was necessary, a document called a charter of feoffment was often prepared to evidence the transfer of ownership. *See* page 246. The Statutes of Uses (1536) made it possible to transfer legal freehold estates by written document. Thereafter, many grantors forsook the cumbersome feoffment ceremony in favor of the more convenient bargain and sale deed by which a freehold interest could be conveyed without traveling to the land. *See* page 264. It was not, however, until the enactment of the English Statute of Frauds (1677) that a writing signed by the grantor was required for the transfer of all interests in land except short-term leases. Each state has adopted a similar statute. *See* 3 American Law of Property § 12.14 (1952).

Deed forms vary somewhat from state to state, but each must include the following: grantor's name, grantee's name, words of conveyance, description of land, grantor's signature, and in some states, signatures of at least two witnesses. Deeds also usually include other provisions such as the amount of consideration, covenants of title, recitals of existing mortgages, easements, and restrictions on the property, and an acknowledgment clause. *See* R. Kratovil & R. Werner, Real Estate Law §§ 7.03–7.03(k) (10th ed. 1993). The inclusion of covenants of title, redundant words of description and conveyance, and other information caused deeds to become unnecessarily lengthy and complex. Thus, statutes in most states specify a short form deed. *See* 14 Powell on Real Property ¶ 897[2] (1998). Following is a sample short form warranty deed:

WARRANTY DEED*

THIS INDENTURE WITNESSETH, That _____
_____ (Grantor)
of _____ County, in the State of _____, CONVEY _____
AND WARRANT _____ to _____
_____ (Grantee)
of _____ County, in the State of _____, for the sum of _____ Dollars
($_____) and other valuable consideration, the receipt and sufficiency of which is hereby acknowledged, the following described real estate in _____ County, State of Indiana:

* Indianapolis Bar Association Form Rev. 10/91.

Subject to any and all easements, agreements and restrictions of record. The address of such real estate is commonly known as _____

Tax bills should be sent to Grantee at such address unless otherwise indicated below.

IN WITNESS WHEREOF, Grantor has executed this deed this _____ day of _____, 19__.

Grantor: (SEAL)   Grantor: (SEAL)

Signature _____   Signature _____

Printed _____   Printed _____

STATE OF   )
) SS: ACKNOWLEDGMENT
COUNTY OF   )

Before me, a Notary Public in and for said County and State, personally appeared _____

_____

who acknowledged the execution of the foregoing Warranty Deed, and who, having been duly sworn, stated that any representations therein contained are true. Witness my hand and Notarial Seal this _____ day of _____, 19__.

My commission expires: Signature _____

_____   Printed _____, Notary Public

                         Resident of _____ County, Indiana.

This instrument prepared by _____, Attorney at Law.
Return deed to _____
Send tax bills to _____

2. DESCRIPTION OF LAND

Transfer of title occurs only if the deed provides a proper description of the land being conveyed. A street address is inadequate because it does not identify the boundaries of the property. A legal description is required. Realty may be described properly in three general ways: metes and bounds, government survey, and plat.

a. Metes and Bounds

The oldest form of legal description is one utilizing metes and bounds. Such a description starts at a definite point on the boundary of a tract of land and traces its perimeter by reference to appropriate courses (directions) and distances back to the starting point. If the description does not "close," the attempted conveyance generally fails for lack of an identifiable parcel.

Following is a metes and bounds description from a 1903 deed:

* * * [A]ll that tract or parcel of land lying and being in the County of Lumpkin, and State of Georgia, and being a part of lot of land Number (1172) Eleven Hundred and Seventy Two, in the Twelfth District and First Section of said County and State, and Bounded as follows: Commencing on an oak stump on the East side of the McBriar road on said lot of land, and thence running along said road to the corner of the Singleton Ditch: thence in a Southerly direction along said ditch to the pasture fence of J.B. Ricketts: thence a strait line through said pasture to a place called 'Buzzard Roost' [apparently a chestnut stump]; thence West on a straight line to the beginning point; said tract containing ten acres more or less.

Lumpkin Co., Georgia, Deed Book J–1, page 396.[1]

b. *Government Survey*

After the Revolutionary War, the Continental Congress sold some of the country's newly acquired land to settlers. Because most of the land was wilderness, it was impractical to utilize metes and bounds to describe tracts carved from this territory. Thus, the government survey system was developed to identify all land north of the Ohio River and west of the Mississippi River except Texas. Alabama, Florida, and Mississippi were also included in the system.

All this land was divided into rectangular tracts by running parallel lines north and south and then running parallel lines east and west. The initial north and south line drawn in an area is called the principal or prime meridian. Every principal meridian is intersected by a base line running east and west along a latitude. After the principal meridian and base line were located in any area, additional north and south lines and east and west lines were placed six miles apart to create townships.

Townships are identified by reference to the principal meridian and the base line. Each row of townships running east and west is referred to by the number of that row north or south of the base line. For example, the first row north of the base line is Township 1 North. The second row north is Township 2 North and so on. Each row of townships running north and south is a range and is referred to by its location east or west of the principal meridian. For example, the first row west of the principal meridian is Range 1 West. The second row west is Range 2 West and so on. A township, therefore, is identified by combining the range and township numbers. Using this system, identify Township 4 North, Range 3 West on the surveyed tract found in Figure 1 below:

1. Mr. Joe K. Telford an attorney in Gainesville, Georgia, provided the authors with this description.

Figure 1—Townships

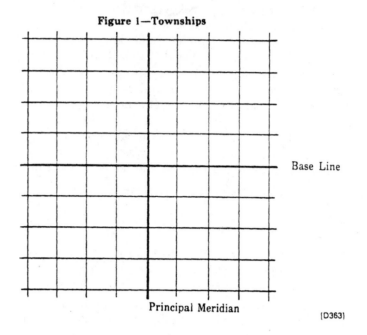

Base Line

Principal Meridian

[D363]

Each township is divided into thirty-six one-square-mile (640 acres) sections. See Figure 2 below:

Figure 2—Township Sections

6	5	4	3	2	1
7	8	9	10	11	12
18	17	16	15	14	13
19	20	21	22	23	24
30	29	28	27	26	25
31	32	33	34	35	36

[O364]

Sections are carved into quarter sections (160 acres). Quarter sections are then frequently subdivided into quarter-quarter sections (40 acres). Using Figure 2 above, locate the N.E. ¼ of the S.W. ¼ of Section 19 of Township 4 North, Range 3 West.

Even quarter-quarter sections are unduly large tracts for many purposes. As a result, it is common practice to describe land both by reference to the government survey and by use of metes and bounds.

Consider the following description:

That portion of the East Half of the Southwest Quarter of Section 12, Township 14 North, Range 2 West of the Gila and Salt River Base and Meridian, Yavapai County, Arizona, being that portion of the tract hereafter described, lying North of the section line dividing Sections 12 and 13, as shown on the survey map of James B. Holmquist recorded in Book 6 of Maps at page 15 in the office of the Yavapai County Recorders, State of Arizona; said tract being described as follows:

Beginning at an iron pipe in a lake, thence North 72 degrees 41 minutes East 135.44 feet, thence North 85 degrees 14 minutes East 121.30 feet to the Westerly right-of-way line of U.S. Highway 89; thence southerly along said right-of-way line 978.92 feet; thence North 51 degrees 39 minutes West 58.12 feet, thence North 0 degrees 22 minutes 20 seconds East 867.53 feet; to said iron pipe at the point of beginning. Said iron pipe in a lake is located as follows: Beginning at a brass cap which marks the East Quarter corner of Section 24, Township 14 North, Range 2 West; thence North 62 degrees 49 minutes 35 seconds West 5953.38 feet to the original stone at the Southwest corner of Section 13, Township 14 North, Range 2 West; thence North 0 degrees 01 seconds East 5268.70 feet to an iron pipe set in bedrock; thence North 89 degrees 33 minutes East 1378.24 feet to said iron pipe in a lake.

Fritts v. Ericson, 103 Ariz. 33, 436 P.2d 582, 583 (1968).

c. *Plat*

Owners of large tracts of land often subdivide their property into lots for purposes of development or sale. A surveyor prepares a map or plat of the subdivision by dividing the area into blocks and the blocks into lots. The blocks and lots are described by metes and bounds on the plat and numbered for ease of reference. The plat is approved by local government officials and recorded in the land records. Each lot in the subdivision then may be described by reference to the recorded plat. Following is a plat description: "Lot 1, Block 4 of Rolling Hills Subdivision, according to the plat thereof recorded in Plat Book 7, page 41 in the Office of the Recorder of Wayne County, Michiana."

See R. Kratovil & R. Werner, Real Estate Law §§ 5.01–5.05 (10th ed. 1993) (discussing each type of legal description); *see also* 3 American Law of Property §§ 12.100, 12.102–12.103, 12.105 (1952).

Notes and Problems

1. Does the following language adequately describe the parcel to be conveyed?

(a) "Part of the Northeast Quarter of the Northeast Quarter of Section 9 Township 16 North Range 13 East all in Douglas County Nebraska as recorded in the Douglas County Register of Deeds office." Haines v. Mensen, 233 Neb. 543, 446 N.W.2d 716 (1989).

(b) "All lands and real estate belonging to the said party of the first part, wherever the same may be situated." Pettigrew v. Dobbelaar, 63 Cal. 396 (1883).

(c) "My farm." Cramer v. Ballard, 315 Mich. 496, 24 N.W.2d 80 (1946).

(d) "The lot on which the residence and Dairy–Joy or ice cream business of Kenneth L. Bennett is located." Bicknell Manufacturing Co. v. Bennett, 431 A.2d 35 (Me.1981).

2. Natural forces may change the boundaries of land lying along a river or lake. This problem is presented in an unusual context in the following case.

HONSINGER v. STATE

Supreme Court of Alaska, 1982.
642 P.2d 1352.

CONNOR, JUSTICE.

This case started as a quiet title action brought against the state in 1973. Plaintiffs are the owners of homestead lands in the Mendenhall Wetlands area northwest of Juneau. Between the time of the original federal homestead patent surveys and 1973, approximately 95 acres of land had emerged contiguous to the seaward side of plaintiffs' property.

Plaintiffs' claimed that the property in dispute was created by accretion and, therefore, should inure to their benefit as littoral, i.e. shoreline, owners. The state responded that all or a portion of the land in question was formed instead by glacio-isostatic uplift[1] and, as a matter of law, should not be subject to the general rule applicable to accretion.

In May, 1979, the parties agreed to submit the legal question to the court in a motion to establish the law of the case. They entered into a stipulation, which provided in part:

"3. [The state does not contest] * * * that if the property in dispute in this action was formed by the process of accretion, it would inure to the littoral owner;

* * *

---

1. "Glacio-isostatic uplift," in simplified terms, refers to the gradual rise of the earth's crust which occurs when the downward pressure exerted by a glacial ice mass diminishes. The result at shorelines is a gradual emergence of land previously submerged.

5. In the event this court should rule that lands formed by isostatic rebound inure to the benefit of the shoreline owner, title to the lands in dispute in this case may be quieted as against [the state];

6. In the event that this court should rule that lands formed entirely, or substantially, by the process of isostatic rebound do not inure to the benefit of the shoreline owner, a trial in this case may be necessary to determine the extent, if any, of the role of isostatic rebound in the formation of said lands."

In its decision, the superior court departed from the traditional law of accretion, holding instead that policy considerations warranted an exception to the common law rule where glacio-isostatic uplift is involved. We granted plaintiffs' petition for review. Because we find that glacio-isostatic uplift falls within the general doctrine of accretion, we now reverse.

* * *

Accretion refers generally to the gradual and imperceptible increase in land area beside a body of water. In this context, it should be distinguished from "avulsion," which refers to a sudden and perceptible change in the shoreline. The benefits of accretion inure to the shoreline owner, while avulsion does not change the legal boundary.

Accretion as used in its specific sense refers to "the process by which an area of land along a waterway is expanded by the gradual deposit of soil there due to the action of contiguous waters." Schafer v. Schnabel, 494 P.2d 802, 806 (Alaska 1972). The counterpart to accretion is "reliction," which comes about by an emergence of existing soil. Accretion and reliction, although physically quite different processes, are subject to the same rule regarding title; i.e. the benefit inures to the shoreline owner.

The state argues that glacio-isostatic uplift is a unique geological phenomenon which does not fall within the doctrine of reliction. The state relies on some dictum from our decision in *Schafer*:

"Reliction involves an increase in the amount of exposed land beside a body of water, *but properly refers only to situations where the water itself has receded.*" (emphasis added).

494 P.2d at 806 n. 16. We cited no authority for the statement, although, as the state points out, reliction has been defined elsewhere as referring only to emergence of land as the result of receding waters. We are now persuaded that reliction properly encompasses the emergence of existing soil either through recession of the water or through rise of the bed. Thus, glacio-isostatic uplift is a form of reliction, and therefore subject to the general common law doctrine of accretion.[2]

2. The superior court adopted and the state urges us to adopt the rationale of State By Kobayashi v. Zimring, 58 Hawaii 106, 566 P.2d 725 (1977). *Zimring* involved new land formed when a volcanic eruption overflowed the shoreline and extended it. Because the court found that these "lava extensions" were the result of neither ac-

We adopt the general rule that where there is a gradual and imperceptible increase in land beside a body of water, by way of accretion or reliction, the shoreline owner is the beneficiary of title to the surfaced land. The judgment of the superior court is Reversed and, pursuant to stipulation by the parties, title to the lands in dispute is quieted as against the state.

Question

Suppose a river which serves as a boundary between two parcels changes course. Does the boundary line change? *See* R. Cunningham, W. Stoebuck, & D. Whitman, The Law of Property 778–780 (2d ed. 1993).

3. COVENANTS OF TITLE

No covenants of title are implied in a deed. The grantor, however, usually makes express covenants about the status of title to the property being conveyed. Such covenants do not affect the validity of the conveyance. They merely give the grantee and the grantee's successors the right to recover damages from the grantor if title to the property is not as covenanted.

Deeds are generally classified by the type of covenants the grantor gives the grantee:

General Warranty Deed. The seller of real estate typically contracts to convey the property by general warranty deed in which the seller promises that the title is free from defects. A general warranty deed includes six covenants of title—three present covenants and three future covenants. Present covenants are those promises regarding title that are broken, if ever, when the deed is delivered. Future covenants are broken only if the grantee is evicted from the property. The statute of limitations begins to run at the time of the breach in each case.

The three present covenants are: (1) The covenant of seisin, by which the grantor promises that the grantor owns the property in question. (2) The covenant of right to convey, by which the grantor promises that the grantor has authority to convey the property. This covenant generally is the functional equivalent of the covenant of seisin, but there are occasions where a legal title holder, such as a trustee, does not have authority to convey. Furthermore, there are situations in which one who has authority to convey does not have legal title, *e.g.,* the holder of a power of attorney. (3) The covenant against encumbrances, by which the grantor promises that the land is not burdened by any mortgages, liens, easements, leases, restrictive covenants, or other encumbrances.

cretion nor avulsion, it relied on equitable principles to determine ownership of the new land. In balancing the state's interest against the individual landowners' interest, the court held that title passed to the state, to be held in trust for the benefit of the people of the state. 566 P.2d at 734–35.

Zimring is not applicable to the case at bar. Here, we are confronted with a phenomenon that falls squarely within established common law; thus, there is no need to resort to a balancing of the interests involved.

The three future covenants are: (1) The covenant of quiet enjoyment, by which the grantor promises that the grantee will not be evicted by a paramount title holder. (2) The covenant of warranty, which is effectively the same as the covenant of quiet enjoyment. Today the covenant of quiet enjoyment and the covenant of warranty are usually considered one covenant. (3) The covenant of further assurance, by which the grantor promises to do any act or execute any document necessary to make title good. *See* 3 American Law of Property §§ 12.126–12.131 (1952) (discussing covenants of title).

In most states the six covenants are no longer spelled out in deeds. Statutes providing for short form warranty deeds allow all covenants to be included by using certain words such as "warrant." *See* 14 Powell on Real Property ¶ 897[2] (1998). The sample short form deed on page 607 is based on an Indiana statute of this type. *See* Ind.Code Ann. § 32–1–2–12 (Burns 1995).

The grantor may limit the scope of the covenants by listing exceptions to title, such as certain mortgages, easements, or restrictive covenants. The grantor, however, may properly list only those items noted as exceptions to marketability of title in the contract of sale.

Special Warranty Deed. A special warranty deed includes the same six covenants as the general warranty deed, except that the grantor promises only that *the grantor* did not create a title defect. For example, if the defect is an easement created by the grantor's predecessor in title, the grantor is not liable for breach of the covenant against encumbrances.

Quitclaim Deed. A quitclaim deed includes no title covenants. The grantor simply conveys whatever interest the grantor has in the property. Hence, if the grantor holds good title to the property, that title passes to the grantee as effectively as it would by a general warranty deed or special warranty deed. *See* Moelle v. Sherwood, 148 U.S. 21 (1893) (discussing reasons why grantor who owns good title might wish to use quitclaim deed).

See R. Kratovil & R. Werner, Real Estate Law §§ 7.02–7.02(b)(1) (10th ed. 1993) (analyzing these basic deed formats).

Problem

Although the Ryans in our hypothetical situation received a general warranty deed (*see* sample deed on pages 607–608), questions may arise regarding breach of covenants and damages available for such breach. For example, assume that the Ryans closed the transaction without resolving the question about the hedge. Later their neighbors establish that the neighbors own the small strip occupied by the hedge, even though the strip was included in the description in the Ryans' deed. What are the Ryans' rights against their grantor? Does it matter that they had some indication at the time of closing that the neighbors might own the strip? Further, what if the Ryans have conveyed the property to someone else before the neighbors establish ownership? The following cases and notes give you the background necessary to answer these questions.

a. Breach of Covenants of Title/Damages

WILCOX v. PIONEER HOMES, INC.

Court of Appeals of North Carolina, 1979.
41 N.C.App. 140, 254 S.E.2d 214.

In October 1976, plaintiffs brought this action to recover damages for breach of warranty against encumbrances contained in a warranty deed from defendant to plaintiffs.

The record tends to show that on 17 November 1974, the parties entered into a contract whereby the defendant agreed to construct a house on Lot I, Clifton Forge Subdivision in Hope Mills, and to convey the house and lot to plaintiffs for $52,000. Defendant agreed to convey a good and marketable title, free of all encumbrances. On 1 May 1975, defendant conveyed the house and lot to plaintiffs by warranty deed. In 1976, plaintiffs entered into a contract to sell the property and prior to closing the sale, the purchasers caused a survey of the property to be made. The survey revealed that the lot was narrower than the defendant had represented. The house was located 3.5 feet from the side line of the lot, in violation of a Hope Mills City ordinance which provided for a minimum side lot requirement of 15 feet. The house was also in violation of a restrictive covenant applicable to lots in the Clifton Forge Subdivision which provided that no structure shall be located less than 7 feet from the side lines of the lot. The plaintiffs thereafter purchased a triangular strip of property adjacent to the lot for $1,500 in order to bring the house and lot into compliance with the ordinance and covenants, and deeded the strip of land to the purchasers of the house and lot.

Plaintiffs then brought this action to recover $1,500, alleging in the complaint that the defendant had breached the covenant against encumbrances contained in the warranty deed to plaintiffs. Both parties moved for summary judgment. On 25 April 1978, the court found that there was no genuine issue of material fact and entered summary judgment in favor of defendant. The court concluded as a matter of law that:

"1. A restriction upon the use which may be made of land, or upon its transfer, which is imposed by a statute or ordinance enacted pursuant to the police power, such as a zoning ordinance or an ordinance regulating the size of lots, fixing building lines or otherwise regulating a subdivision of an area into lots is not an encumbrance upon the land within the meaning of a covenant against encumbrances or a contract or option to convey the land free from encumbrances,

2. The existence of the ordinance and the failure of the defendant to comply with its provisions did not constitute an encum-

brance such as to prevent it (defendants) from giving a deed that is both marketable and free from encumbrances."

CLARK, JUDGE.

The plaintiffs assign as error the court's granting of summary judgment in favor of defendant. Plaintiffs contend that a violation of a municipal ordinance regulating the use of real property at the time of sale constitutes an encumbrance on the land and a breach of the warranty against encumbrances.

An encumbrance, within the meaning of such a covenant, has been defined as "any burden or charge on the land and includes any right existing in another whereby the use of the land by the owner is restricted." *Gerdes v. Shew,* 4 N.C.App. 144, 148, 166 S.E.2d 519, 522 (1969). The general view is that the existence of a public restriction on the use of real property does not constitute an encumbrance within the meaning of the covenant against encumbrances. This view was adopted in North Carolina in *Fritts v. Gerukos,* 273 N.C. 116, 159 S.E.2d 536 (1968). In *Fritts,* the plaintiffs purchased an option on a tract of land containing 49 lots. The defendant agreed to deliver a deed with full covenants and warranty against encumbrances. At the time the parties entered into the option contract, an ordinance of the City of Gastonia prohibited the transfer or sale of land by reference to a subdivision plat without obtaining the city's approval of the plat. After exercising the option, plaintiffs advertised an auction sale of the 49 lots. The City of Gastonia enjoined the sale for failure of plaintiffs to obtain approval of the plat. Plaintiffs then brought suit for breach of warranty against encumbrances contending that the existence of the ordinance constituted an encumbrance. The North Carolina Supreme Court rejected plaintiffs' contention on the grounds that:

> "A restriction upon the use which may be made of land, or upon its transfer, which is imposed by a statute or ordinance enacted pursuant to the police power, such as a zoning ordinance or an ordinance regulating the size of lots, fixing building lines or otherwise regulating the subdivision of an area into lots, is not an encumbrance upon the land within the meaning of a covenant against encumbrances * * * being distinguishable in this respect from restrictions imposed by a covenant in a deed. (Citations omitted.) Thus, the *existence* of the Subdivision Standard Control Ordinance * * * at the time the option agreement was executed did not cause the title of the defendant to be subject to an encumbrance * * *." (Emphasis added.) *Id.* 273 N.C. at 119, 159 S.E.2d at 539.

In the case *sub judice,* however, plaintiffs do not contend that the *existence* of the municipal ordinance constituted an encumbrance on the property, but contend that a *violation* of the ordinance, existing at the time of the conveyance to plaintiffs, constituted an encumbrance. There are no North Carolina cases which consider whether an existing violation of public restrictions on the use of real property constitutes an encumbrance. There is a split of authority among the jurisdictions which have considered this question. Annot., 39 A.L.R.3d 362 § 2 (1971). The majority of the jurisdictions have held that, although the existence of a public restriction on the use of real property is not an encumbrance rendering the title to the real property unmarketable, an existing violation of such an ordinance is an encumbrance within the meaning of a warranty against encumbrances. Lohmeyer v. Bower, 170 Kan. 442, 227 P.2d 102 (1951), (minimum side lot violation); Oatis v. Delcuze, 226 La. 751, 77 So.2d 28 (1954), (non-conforming building); Moyer v. De Vincentis Construction Co., 107 Pa.Super. 588, 164 A. 111 (1933), (violation of set-back requirement).

We hold that the existing violation of the minimum side lot requirement as set forth in the ordinance of the City of Hope Mills, constitutes an encumbrance within the meaning of the covenant against encumbrances contained in the plaintiffs' warranty deed.

The summary judgment for defendant was improvidently entered. The judgment is reversed and the cause remanded for proceedings consistent with this opinion.

Reversed and Remanded.

Problems and Questions

1. Why is an unviolated zoning ordinance restricting the use of real property not a breach of the covenant against encumbrances?

2. As noted in *Wilcox*, courts are divided on the question of whether a violated zoning ordinance constitutes a breach of the covenant against encumbrances. For a view contrary to that taken in *Wilcox*, see Frimberger v. Anzellotti, 25 Conn.App. 401, 594 A.2d 1029 (1991) (violation of wetlands statute not breach of warranty against encumbrances). Which is the better approach?

3. O conveyed Blackacre to A by general warranty deed. A later discovered that there is an outstanding mortgage of record on the property even though the mortgage had been satisfied. A brought an action against O for breach of the covenant against encumbrances. What result? *See* Boulware v. Mayfield, 317 So.2d 470 (Fla.App.1975); *see also* James v. McCombs, 936 P.2d 520 (Alaska 1997).

FOLEY v. SMITH

Court of Appeals of Washington, 1975.
14 Wn.App. 285, 539 P.2d 874.

ANDERSEN, JUDGE.

FACTS OF CASE

This case is another chapter in a decade-long course of litigation relating to a 37–acre parcel of real estate in the Kent Valley area of King County.

The property was repeatedly sold during a boom in the valley land which had been triggered by the announcement of large new industrial facilities to be constructed in the area.

The factual intricacies of the various speculations and transactions involved in this course of litigation are well chronicled in earlier appellate decisions. Hudesman v. Foley, 73 Wash.2d 880, 441 P.2d 532 (1968); Hudesman v. Foley, 4 Wash.App. 230, 480 P.2d 534 (1971).

As decided in the previous litigation, Mr. and Mrs. Foley sold the real estate to Mr. and Mrs. Smith for, $70,000 after having previously contracted to sell it to another. The Foleys received the Smiths' down payment, note and mortgage back on the property. They then conveyed the land to the Smiths by a statutory warranty deed dated November 11, 1965.

The party who had previously contracted to purchase the property from the Foleys brought a specific performance action against the Foleys and the Smiths, seeking to obtain title to the property.

Mr. Foley passed away on May 26, 1967, while the specific performance action was pending. Subsequently, letters of administration were issued to Mrs. Foley on February 9, 1968, and she duly published notice to estate creditors commencing February 10, 1968. No claim was filed against the estate by the Smiths within the 4–month claim period or at any time.

The trial of the specific performance case took place in November of 1968 with Mrs. Foley continuing in that case as an individual defendant and also as the personal representative of her late husband's estate. That trial resulted in a decree for specific performance being entered on December 20, 1968, in favor of the prior purchaser. By the terms of that decree, the Foleys and the Smiths were divested of all title to and interest in the land in question.

* * *

Mrs. Foley and the Smiths were in agreement that the Smiths were entitled to receive back the money the Smiths had previously paid to the Foleys for the property. This was the sum of $41,714.24. Agreement was also reached as to the distribution of certain other portions of the moneys that the prior purchaser had paid to get the property. No agreement could be reached, however, as to distribution of the remaining balance of such proceeds in the amount of $20,471.16.

Thereupon the $20,471.16 was deposited in a savings account with the names of both Mrs. Foley and Mr. Smith on the account. As a part of that transaction, the parties entered into a written agreement dated September 23, 1971. Mrs. Foley signed the agreement individually and as personal representative of the late Mr. Foley's estate, and Mr. Smith signed it also. That agreement essentially provided that the $20,471.16 would be kept in a savings account until such time as the parties agreed in writing as to how the funds should be disbursed.

Mrs. Foley and the Smiths were unable to reach agreement as to the disposition of the $20,471.16 being held in the savings account. Mrs. Foley then filed suit against the Smiths on April 13, 1972, asking that she be declared the rightful owner of this money. The Smiths counterclaimed alleging breach of covenant in the deed by which the property had earlier been conveyed to them, and asking damages.

* * *

ISSUES

* * *

ISSUE TWO. Where grantors convey land to grantees by statutory warranty deed, does a subsequent judgment obtained by a third party which divests both the grantors and grantees of their interest in the land constitute a breach of the grantors' covenants to the grantees?

ISSUE THREE. Does knowledge on the part of the grantees of land of an outstanding potentially superior claim to the land so conveyed of and by itself defeat the grantees' right to recover for the breach of a covenant of warranty?

ISSUE FOUR. When does the statute of limitations commence to run on an action for breach of covenants of warranty and of quiet enjoyment when title litigation is pending?

* * *

ISSUE SIX. Are interest on the moneys paid by grantees for property conveyed to them, and the attorneys' fees incurred by the grantees in unsuccessfully defending their title to such property, allowable items of damage in the grantees' action against the grantors for breach of the covenants of warranty and quiet enjoyment?

DECISION

* * *

ISSUE TWO.

CONCLUSION. The decree of specific performance obtained by the prior purchaser of the land was an eviction and constituted a breach of the covenants of warranty and quiet enjoyment in the deed.

The statutory warranty deed, by which the Foleys conveyed the real estate in question to the Smiths, did by force of statute carry with it certain broad covenants. RCW 64.04.030.[1]

---

1. "Every deed in substance in the above [statutory warranty deed] form, when otherwise duly executed, shall be deemed and held a conveyance in fee simple to the grantee, his heirs and assigns, with covenants on the part of the grantor: (1) That at the time of the making and delivery of such deed he was lawfully seized of an indefeasible estate in fee simple, in and to the premises therein described, and had good right and full power to convey the same; (2) that the same were then free from all encumbrances; and (3) that he warrants to the grantee, his heirs and assigns, the quiet and peaceable possession of such premises, and will defend the title thereto against all persons who may lawfully claim the same, and such covenants shall be obligatory upon any grantor, his heirs and personal representatives, as fully and with like effect as if written at full length in such deed." RCW 64.04.030.

As RCW 64.04.030 shows on its face (*see* footnote 1 *supra*), the covenants thereby engrafted into the deed given by the Foleys to the Smiths included the covenants of warranty and of quiet enjoyment.

The covenant of warranty is usually considered the principal covenant of a deed. It is an assurance or guaranty of title, or an agreement or assurance by the grantor that the grantee and the grantee's heirs and assigns shall enjoy it without interruption by virtue of paramount title, and that they shall not, by force of a paramount title, be evicted from the land or deprived of its possession.

The obligation on the Foleys as the covenantors was that they would defend and protect the Smiths as covenantees against the rightful claims of all persons thereafter asserted.

In the respects stated above, a covenant for warranty and a covenant for quiet enjoyment are substantially the same, and the same basic rules governing breach and damages generally apply to both.

A covenant of warranty is broken only by an actual or constructive eviction under a paramount title existing at the time of the conveyance. The same is true of a covenant of quiet enjoyment.

What constitutes actual or constructive [eviction] can vary according to the circumstances of the eviction, who is in possession and who has actual title.

In the present case, either the grantor or grantee was in possession at all times and the third party was not. It is thus clear the eviction occurred here when the prior purchaser obtained the decree of specific performance divesting the Foleys and the Smiths of their interest in the land, and that such eviction breached the Foleys' covenants of warranty and quiet title to the Smiths.

ISSUE THREE.

CONCLUSION. Knowledge on the part of the grantees of an outstanding potentially superior claim to the land to which they obtained a deed does not bar their claim for breaches of the covenants of warranty and quiet enjoyment in their deed when they are later evicted from the property by judicial action.

Mrs. Foley cites us to the prior litigation commenced by the prior purchaser wherein it was held that as to the prior purchaser "[t]he Smiths were not bona fide purchasers for value." Hudesman v. Foley, 4 Wash.App. 230, 233, 480 P.2d 534, 537 (1971). She argues this as res judicata in the present case and as establishing that the trial court erred in concluding that the Smiths could still be bona fide purchasers as to the Foleys in the present case.

Whether or not the Smiths were bona fide purchasers for value when they obtained the deed from the Foleys is not determinative of the present case. The fact that the Smiths, as grantees under the deed, had knowledge at the time of the execution of the conveyance of an allegedly outstanding superior claim of title, does not bar their right to recover for breaches of the covenant arising from their subsequent eviction.

Such covenants warrant against known as well as unknown defects, and grantees with knowledge of an encumbrance have the right to rely on the covenants in the deed for their protection. The purpose of the covenant is protection against defects, and to hold that grantees can be protected only against unknown defects would rob the covenant of much of its value and destroy the force of its language.

ISSUE FOUR.

CONCLUSION. The 6–year statute of limitations on the covenants of warranty and quiet enjoyment in a deed did not commence to run until the specific performance decree evicting the covenantors and covenantees had become final.

Mrs. Foley argues that the statute of limitations on any breaches of the covenants in the deed had run well prior to the time that the Smiths filed their counterclaim for breach of covenant, and that therefore the Smiths' counterclaim is barred.

Some covenants in deeds are deemed to operate in the present and to be breached, if at all, when made, while others are prospective in operation and are not breached until an eviction or its equivalent.

As expressed above, the covenants of warranty and of quiet enjoyment were not broken in the present case until the eviction by the decree of specific performance. Accordingly, the statute of limitations on the Smiths' claim for breaches of those covenants did not commence running until they, as covenantees, were evicted or ousted, either actually or constructively from the premises conveyed.

The pertinent rule is stated in 95 A.L.R.2d 913, at 931 (1964):

> Where litigation is pending which will be determinative of the title to the premises conveyed as between the covenantee and the third persons claiming paramount title, an eviction such as will commence the running of limitations on the covenantee's action for breach of warranty is not ordinarily held to have occurred until the final decree in such litigation is entered against the covenantee.

The counterclaim by the Smiths was brought well within 6 years of the decree in the specific performance action becoming final. It was, therefore, not barred by RCW 4.16.040.

* * *

ISSUE SIX.

CONCLUSION. Interest and attorneys' fees are allowable items of damage for breach of the covenants of warranty and quiet enjoyment.

After the third party finally established his title to the land, Mrs. Foley voluntarily transferred back to the Smiths the $41,714.24 which the Smiths had previously paid down on the sales price of the property.

Mrs. Foley's position is that since that is all of the purchase price that was paid by the Smiths, that is all they are entitled to recover.

The trial court entered findings of fact to the effect that the costs and attorneys' fees reasonably expended by the Smiths in defense of the prior purchaser's action, and the interest on the money they had paid down on the property during the years that the Foleys had the use of their money, far exceeded the remaining moneys here in controversy. Although that finding is challenged on this appeal, there is substantial evidence in the record to support it. Therefore, it must be taken as a verity on this appeal.

The remaining issue then is whether the items of damage allowed by the trial court are in law proper items of damage for the breach of the covenants here involved.

It is true that as a broad general rule, the measure of damages for a total breach of a covenant of warranty is the consideration paid, or the value of the land as measured by the purchase price.

In addition, however, interest on the consideration paid on the land for which title failed is an allowable element of damages in a suit by covenantees for breach of covenants of warranty and quiet enjoyment.

Reasonable attorneys' fees expended by covenantees in good faith to defend their title are likewise recoverable as damages.

Mrs. Foley, as appellant, did not make out a prima facie case of error.

Judgment affirmed.

Problems and Questions

1. Why did the grantee not seek to recover for breach of the covenant of seisin?

2. Claims of adverse possession and prescriptive easement may raise questions regarding breach of title covenants. For example, a seller who conveys property burdened by a prescriptive easement breaches the covenant against encumbrances. Gill Grain Co. v. Poos, 707 S.W.2d 434 (Mo.Ct.App. 1986). Does a seller breach the covenant of seisin by conveying land which is in the possession of a hostile claimant whose adverse title has not yet ripened? *See* Bosnick v. Hill, 292 Ark. 505, 731 S.W.2d 204 (1987).

3. O owns Blackacre. GR, believing that GR owned Blackacre, conveyed the property to GE by general warranty deed. GE immediately built a warehouse on Blackacre. When O learned of the transaction and the warehouse, O evicted GE. GE can recover the purchase price from GR for breach of covenants of title, but can GE recover anything from GR or O for the value of the improvements? *See* Madrid v. Spears, 250 F.2d 51 (10th Cir.1957). *See also* W. Burby, Handbook of the Law of Real Property 28–29 (3d ed. 1965); 5 American Law of Property § 19.9 (1952).

Betterment statutes granting relief to mistaken improvers of another's property have been enacted in many jurisdictions. These measures vary widely as to the relief available. *See* Dickinson, *Mistaken Improvers of Real*

Estate, 64 N.C.L.Rev. 37 (1985). Moreover, some courts, on equitable grounds, have permitted mistaken improvers to remove structures erected in good faith. *See* Peck v. M.C. Developers, Inc., 261 N.J.Super. 384, 618 A.2d 940 (1992).

Mistaken improvement of another's land is hardly a new problem. Consider the following dialogue from Shakespeare's *Merry Wives of Windsor*, Act 2, Scene 2:

Falstaff: Of what quality was your love, then?

Ford: Like a fair house, built upon another man's ground; so that I have lost my edifice by mistaking the place where I erected it.

See W. Rushton, Shakespeare's Legal Maxims 22–25 (1907) (discussing real property principle to which Ford refers).

b. Running of Covenants of Title

PROFFITT v. ISLEY

Court of Appeals of Arkansas, Division II, 1985.
13 Ark.App. 281, 683 S.W.2d 243.

MAYFIELD, JUDGE.

In 1974 Bobby and Mary Proffitt sold one and one-half acres of real estate to Truman and Earline Atkinson, who sold it to Shirley Carter in 1978, who sold it to Arthur and Bonnie Isley in 1980. About two months after the Isleys bought it they discovered that the land had been mortgaged by the Proffitts and that the mortgage was still outstanding. The Isleys sued Carter, the Atkinsons, and the Proffitts for damages based on the general warranties in the warranty deeds. The jury held for the Atkinsons and Carter, but held the Proffitts liable to the Isleys for $4,390.78 representing the unpaid balance on the mortgage plus interest and costs. The Proffitts appeal. We reverse.

The usual covenants of title in a general warranty deed are the covenants of seisin, good right to convey, against encumbrances, for quiet enjoyment and general warranty. An encumbrance is any right to an interest in land which may subsist in third persons, to the diminution of the value of the land, not inconsistent with the passing of title. Examples of encumbrances are an outstanding lease, a timber deed, dower, an easement, and a mortgage. In Logan v. Moulder, 1 Ark. 313, 320 (1839), the court said:

> The covenants of seizin, and of right to convey, and against incumbrances are personal covenants, not running with the land, nor passing to the assignee, but are declared to be mere *choses in action*, not assignable at common law. The covenants of warranty, and of quiet enjoyment, are in the nature of a real covenant, and run with the land, and descend to the heirs, and are made transferable to the assignee.

In 7 G. Thompson, *Thompson On Real Property* § 3185 at 303 (Repl.1962), the *Logan* case is cited in support of the general rule that a covenant against encumbrances is not assignable and does not pass to a grantee. Since the covenant against encumbrances is personal between the grantor and the grantee, the remedy for a remote grantee, when the encumbrance has not been removed from the property, is against his immediate grantor, whose recourse is against his grantor and so forth back up the chain of title to the original grantor whose conveyance breached the warranty against encumbrances. However, the covenant of general warranty may be breached where steps are taken to enforce an encumbrance.

[handwritten: Laley can only sue Carter/them]

With some exceptions, not applicable here, unless the covenantee is evicted or has satisfied the outstanding encumbrance, he may only recover nominal damages. In Smith v. Thomas, 169 Ark. 1110, 278 S.W. 39 (1925), the court stated:

> The measure of damages for the breach of a covenant against incumbrance is the amount necessary to remove the incumbrance, not exceeding the consideration expressed in the deed containing the covenants of warranty, and ordinarily the covenantee cannot recover on the mere existence of the incumbrance, but must first discharge it by payment, unless he has actually lost the estate in consequence of the incumbrance. In 7 R.C.L. p. 1104, the rule is stated as follows: "In a number of jurisdictions it has been held that, although a covenant against incumbrances, like a covenant of seisin, is broken if at all as soon as made, yet the covenantee can found no right to actual damages on the mere existence of incumbrances, but will be limited to a nominal recovery, unless he has paid off the incumbrance or actually lost the estate in consequence of it."

In the present case the appellees had incurred no expense because of the outstanding mortgage on the property, and the mortgagee had made no effort to either evict appellees or foreclose on the property. Therefore, appellees' only cause of action was a technical breach of the covenant against encumbrances which could be brought against their grantor, Carter, with the recovery of only nominal damages.

Therefore, the judgment against the Proffitts is reversed and dismissed.

Notes, Problems, and Questions

1. A few states take the position that present covenants run with the land to subsequent grantees. *See* Schofield v. The Iowa Homestead Co., 32 Iowa 317 (1871).

2. Should all covenants of title run with the land without regard to privity of estate? If all covenants of title ran with the land, would there be any reason to continue to distinguish between present and future covenants? *See* Levin, *Warranties of Title—A Modest Proposal*, 29 Vill.L.Rev. 649 (1983–84).

3. A conveys Blackacre to B for $60,000 by general warranty deed. B conveys Blackacre to C for $50,000 by a quitclaim deed. C conveys Blackacre to D for $80,000 by general warranty deed. O, the paramount owner, ousts D from the land. At the time of the ouster Blackacre is worth $90,000. From whom and how much can D recover? If D recovers from C, does C have any recourse?

4. Now that you have studied title covenants, what advice would you give the Ryans about the problem posed on pages 615–616?

5. Consider the following assessment of title covenants: "The concept of a general warranty deed is in many ways obsolete today, when title insurance can be purchased at a modest price with an almost absolute guarantee against title defects because title insurance lawyers seldom make mistakes." Booker T. Washington Construction & Design Co. v. Huntington Urban Renewal Authority, 181 W.Va. 409, 415, 383 S.E.2d 41, 47 (1989). Do you agree?

4. DELIVERY

Delivery * * * is essential to the operation, and validity of the conveyance. * * * [D]elivery of a deed is strictly a matter of the intention of the grantor as manifested and evidenced by the words, acts and circumstances surrounding the transaction. Manual transfer of the deed is not indispensable to delivery but is evidence of delivery. The controlling factor in determining the question of delivery in all cases is the intention of grantor. * * *

Berigan v. Berrigan, 413 Ill. 204, 215, 108 N.E.2d 438, 444–445 (1952).

Issues regarding the delivery of deeds of real property are similar to delivery questions presented in the section on gifts. Consequently, you should review pages 208–233.

Deeds are often delivered in escrow. That is, they are given to a third party to be delivered to the grantee upon the satisfaction of a certain condition, such as payment of the purchase price, or upon the occurrence of a particular event, such as the death of the grantor. *See* W. Burby, Handbook of the Law of Real Property § 121 (3d ed. 1965). Escrows may involve either gift or commercial transactions.

Both parties to the sale of real estate may have reasons to close the transaction in escrow. The purchaser may want to avoid complications that might arise if the seller dies before the transaction is completed. The seller may wish to insure that checks for the purchase price have cleared before title is transferred. *See* J. Cribbet & C. Johnson, Principles of the Law of Property 217–219 (3d ed. 1989).

CHANDLER v. CHANDLER

Supreme Court of Alabama, 1981.
409 So.2d 780.

JONES, JUSTICE.

Appellants (Plaintiffs below) are six of the eight children of J. W. and Maggie Chandler. Appellee, J. P. Chandler (Defendant below), is a brother of Appellants. In June, 1964, the Chandler parents executed a deed purportedly conveying to Maggie an undivided one-half interest in 270 acres for life, reserving unto J. W. an undivided one-half interest for life, with right of survivorship for the lifetime of the survivor, and with remainder in fee simple to their son, J. P. The father and mother lived on the subject property for many years, until they died in 1972 and 1975, respectively.

In May, 1980, this action was commenced, seeking to set aside the deed on grounds of undue influence, mental incapacity of the father (grantor), and "no legal delivery" of the deed. This appeal is from the trial court's judgment upholding the validity of the deed.

Appellants, per counsel's brief, state the issue presented for our review:

"Whether there is a valid delivery of a deed where the deed is held by a third party depositary 'for safekeeping,' subject to be returned to the grantors upon request, to be transferred to the grantee upon the death of the grantors."

If we accept the " * * * subject to be returned to the grantors upon request * * * " portion of Appellants' statement of the issue, unquestionably the trial court committed reversible error. The reserved right of a grantor, who has left the deed with a third party, to retrieve the instrument, and thus revoke the grant, voids delivery of the deed which is essential to its validity as a conveyance.

Appellants' brief correctly sets forth the applicable "lack of delivery" rules:

"Delivery of a deed is essential to its validity as a conveyance. Delivery is the final act which consummates the deed, signifying that it is in operation and effect. Generally, where the deed is not delivered during the life of the grantor, no right or title is conferred on the grantee. An exception to the general rule is where the grantor delivers a deed to a third party to be delivered to the grantee after the death of the grantor. However, there is no delivery when the deed is merely given to the third party for safekeeping. If the deed is subject to be recalled by the grantor before delivery to the grantee, there is no effectual delivery by the grantor."

Urging our application of these rules to the evidence of record before us, Appellants conclude:

"The deed in this case was held by the Dozier bank 'for safekeeping,' according to the head cashier of the bank. * * * The grantor had the right to go back to the bank and recover the deed. * * * The trial court failed to recognize the well-established principles of delivery in upholding the sufficiency of delivery, and, thus, ruled incorrectly that the conveyance was valid."

The well-settled, and equally well-understood, "sufficiency of delivery" principle, where delivery is made to a person other than the grantee or his agent, is discussed in Fitzpatrick v. Brigman, 130 Ala. 450, 30 So. 500 (1900):

"[T]he delivery must be so effectual as to deprive the grantor of the right to revoke it. For so long as he reserves to himself the *locus penitentiae,* there is no delivery—no present intention to divest himself of the title to the property. * * * [T]he grantor need not expressly reserve to himself this right to repent, but if his act upon which a delivery is predicated does not place the deed beyond his control, as a matter of law, then his right of revocation is not gone.

" * * * 'The law does not presume, when a deed is handed to a third person, that it has been with the intention to pass title to the grantee. In order to make such an act a delivery to the grantee, the intention of the grantor must be expressed *at the time* in an unmistakable manner.'—5 Am. & Eng. Encyc. Law (1st ed.), note 4, on p. 448."

We look to the record, then, to test the Appellants' assertion that " * * * grantors unquestionably did not place the deed beyond their complete control since the third party depositary would have returned the deed had the grantors requested it; thus, the right of revocation was not gone."

In support of their "lack of delivery" contention, Appellants accurately summarize the evidence:

"The deed in question was not transferred directly to the defendant-grantee, but rather was transferred to the bank vault of the Dozier bank by J. W. Chandler sometime in 1965. Ms. Sport [the head cashier] testified there was only one packet in the Dozier bank vault belonging to J. W. Chandler. She testified that she personally received instructions from J. W. Chandler at the time the deed was put in the vault, * * * [and] that the deed was given to the defendant, pursuant to instructions on a note attached to the deed instructing that the deed be delivered to J. P. Chandler upon the death of J. W. Chandler. * * * Ms. Sport testified that on most of the 'stuff' the bank keeps, since it has no safety deposit boxes, 'you have got to have some kind of instructions as to who to deliver certain items to.' Questioned further, Ms. Sport stated that, '[I]f I delivered the documents to J. P. Chandler, there was some information attached to it * * * .' Pressed further about the presence of a note, she was asked, 'Do you remember whether or not there was any * * * ?' to which Ms. Sport responded, 'There was or I wouldn't have delivered them to J. P.' Asked again, whether she, in fact, remembers a note, she replied, 'Yes.' Finally, referring to the presence of a note with instruction, she stated, 'I told you very distinctly that if I delivered them, that it was on there.' She stated that instructions on the note were typed out by another employee of the bank, Mr. Merrill.

"Ms. Sport testified that when a person, such as J. W. Chandler, leaves a deed with the bank, that person has a right to go back and pick that deed up at any time he desires. She was asked whether 'Mr. Chandler or any other person for that matter [would] have had the right or control to go get the paper from the time that he put them in there at any time prior to [his] death,' and [she] responded that he would have the right to go to the bank and take back the document. Asked the purpose of having this service such as was provided J. W. Chandler when he transferred his deed to the Dozier bank, Ms. Sport replied, 'Just for safekeeping.' "

The question for our resolution is whether the trial court erred, in the face of Ms. Sport's testimony relating to J. W. Chandler's "right to go to the bank and take back the document," in finding a valid delivery of the deed. We hold that the trial court did not err in concluding from Ms. Sport's testimony, when considered along with the totality of the circumstances, that J. W. Chandler, at the time he delivered the deed to the bank for "safekeeping," possessed the requisite intent to relinquish control over the deed and have it take effect as a present conveyance.

Indeed, we are of the opinion that J. W. Chandler's unequivocal instruction to the third party to deliver the deed, upon his death, to his son J. P., absent any expression or conduct on the part of the father relative to his right to retrieve the deed, or otherwise exercise control thereof, precluded a contrary finding on the part of the trial court. The policy of the bank in permitting those who left papers in its vault to take such papers back from the bank is not determinative of the grantor's surrender of control of the instrument in question. The fact of delivery rests in the grantor's intention, which is an issue of fact to be determined from all the attendant circumstances at the time.

Here the grantor, for a valuable consideration expressed in the deed, granted a life estate in a one-half interest to his wife, reserved to himself a life estate in the remaining one-half interest (expressly creating a joint tenancy with right of survivorship), with the remainder to his son J. P. He delivered the deed to the bank with express instructions (both written and oral) to deliver the deed to J. P. upon the grantor's death. The bank's policy of freely returning such papers upon its customers' requests is grounded in the nature of the bank's service to, and relationship with, its customers. Such policy, grounded on institutional good will considerations, is not determinative of the legal requisite of the grantor's intention to so surrender control of the deed as to effectuate the conveyance.

We are clear to the conclusion, and we so hold, that the trial court acted properly in holding, upon consideration of all the attendant circumstances, that J. W. Chandler intended to deliver the deed to the grantee when he deposited it with the bank and instructed its personnel to deliver it to J. P. Chandler upon the event of the grantor's death.

Central to our holding is the undisputed fact that the grantor gave express, unequivocal instructions to the third party for delivery of the deed to the named grantee upon a certain future event—the death of the grantor. Given this fact, along with the other attendant circumstances, including the absence of words or conduct reserving the grantor's right of revocation, the inference of completed delivery, fully executed, is amply sustainable, and in accord with our case law cited above.

Moreover, the trial judge was warranted under the evidence in finding the requisite delivery as between the grantors and the life tenants without reference to any issue of delivery as between the grantors and the remainderman. Nevertheless, we have addressed the issue of "delivery" as between the grantor (the father) and the remainderman (the son) in the context of the issue as framed by the pleadings and tried before the trial court and as presented and argued to this Court.

Affirmed.

TORBERT, CHIEF JUSTICE (dissenting).

I dissent. While the majority correctly set out the law as it has evolved in Alabama, they misapply this law to the facts of this case. The majority states that the testimony of Ms. Sport, an officer of the First National Bank of Dozier, "along with the totality of the circumstances," shows that J. W. Chandler "possessed the requisite intent to relinquish control over the deed" to have it operate as a valid conveyance. This is simply not the case.

For the delivery to be complete, the grantor must completely divest himself of any control over the title. As long as he reserves to himself the *locus penitentiae,* whether by express reservation or by not placing the deed beyond his control, then as a *matter of law* he has not foregone his right of revocation.

The case of Culver v. Carroll, 175 Ala. 469, 57 So. 767 (1911), best described the prerequisites for valid delivery:

> Perhaps the clearest and completest statement of the law on this subject is the following, by Dowling, J., in Osborne v. Eslinger, 155 Ind. 351, 360, 58 N.E. 439, 442, 80 Am.St.Rep. 240, 247: "Where the claim of title rests upon the delivery of the deed to a third person, the deed must have been properly signed by the grantor, and delivered by him, or by his direction, unconditionally, to a third person for the use of the grantee, to be delivered by such person to the grantee, either presently, or at some future date, or upon some inevitable contingency, the grantor parting, and intending to part, with all dominion and control over it, and absolutely surrendering

his possession and authority over the instrument, so that it would be the duty of the custodian or trustee for the grantee, on his behalf, and as his agent and trustee, to refuse to return the deed to the grantor, for any purpose, if demand should be made upon him. And there should be evidence beyond such delivery of the intent of the grantor to part with his title, and the control of the deed, and that such delivery is for the use of the grantee. If the deed is placed in the hands of a third person, as the agent, friend, or bailee of the grantor, for safe-keeping only, and not for delivery to the grantee; if the fact that the instrument is a deed is not made known to such third person, either at the time it is handed over, or at any time before the death of the grantor; if the name of the grantee, or other description of him, is not given; and if there is no evidence beyond the mere fact of such delivery of the intent of the grantor to part with his control over the instrument and his title to the land—then such transfer of the mere possession of the instrument does not constitute a delivery, and the instrument fails for want of execution."

175 Ala. at 476–77, 57 So. 767.

While J. W. Chandler did leave instructions to the bank to deliver the deed upon his death, it is without doubt that the bank held the deed only for safekeeping and that he retained control over the deed. Ms. Sport testified that the deed was in a file at the bank under the name of Mr. J. W. Chandler at the time of his death in 1972. She stated that this was done as part of the normal service rendered by the banks in that area, since these banks do not have safe deposit boxes. When specifically questioned about the issue of control, the following ensued:

> Q. Ms. Sport, I will ask you ma'am, would Mr. Chandler or any other person, for that matter, have the right or control to go get the papers from the time that he put them in there at any time prior to their death?
>
> A. Why, sure.
>
> Q. Would you tell the Court the purpose of your bank having this for your customers, please?
>
> A. Just for safekeeping.
>
> Q. Thank you.

From this testimony, it is quite obvious that Mr. Chandler *did not* place the deed beyond his control. Thus, as a *matter of law* his right of revocation was not gone and no finding of a valid delivery could have been made.

Had J. W. Chandler deposited the deed into a personal safe deposit box, there is no question that the delivery would not have been complete. Here, however, the bank had no safe deposit boxes, but held documents in special files for its customers. Ms. Sport's testimony shows that these files are the functional equivalent of safe deposit boxes. Therefore, there can be no doubt that J. W. Chandler still had the deed within his control and possession.

For these reasons, I cannot agree that there was a valid delivery of the deed. Thus, I would reverse the holding of the trial court.

Notes and Problems

1.   For a decision emphasizing that the requirement of delivery remains crucial to the effectiveness of a deed, see Sargent v. Baxter, 673 So.2d 979 (Fla.App.1996) (delivery to third party not effective when deed was subject to grantor's control).

2.   As a general proposition, the recording of a deed creates a rebuttable presumption of its delivery to the grantee. *See, e.g.,* Johnson v. Ramsey, 307 Ark. 4, 817 S.W.2d 200 (1991); CUNA Mortgage v. Aafedt, 459 N.W.2d 801 (N.D.1990).

3.   The relation back doctrine may govern the time at which a deed delivered in escrow takes effect. In Fuqua v. Fuqua, 528 S.W.2d 896, 898 (Tex.Civ.App.1975), the court stated:

> The rule is that the death of the grantor while grantor's deed is held in escrow does not invalidate the instrument upon its subsequent delivery. Where, after the death of the grantor, the grantee performs the conditions of the escrow agreement, grantee is entitled to delivery of the deed, and grantee's title relates back to the date of the original deposit of the instrument in escrow.

4.   Consider further the application of the relation back doctrine. Assume O, owner of Blackacre, executed a valid deed transferring Blackacre to A in fee simple. O gave the deed to B with instructions to deliver the instrument to A upon O's death. What is the consequence of this transaction in the following situations?

(a)   O conveys Blackacre to P, who pays value and is without notice of the prior transaction.

(b)   O dies leaving a will which devises Blackacre to D.

(c)   O dies without sufficient assets to pay O's debts. O's creditors seek to reach Blackacre.

CHILLEMI v. CHILLEMI

Court of Appeals of Maryland, 1951.
197 Md. 257, 78 A.2d 750.

DELAPLAINE, JUDGE.

This litigation originated in the Circuit Court for Montgomery County when Eugene J. Chillemi, appellee, instituted suit against his estranged wife, Lulu R. Chillemi, appellant, to enjoin her to reconvey his former home in Bethesda to him and her as tenants by the entireties, as it was owned before he conditionally relinquished his interest therein.

* * *

The parties were married in Rockville in 1937. In 1941 appellee received a commission as Lieutenant in the United States Army, and when he was ordered to Florida, Colorado, Louisiana and Oklahoma, his wife accompanied him. They had no children, and in September, 1945, they adopted a daughter slightly over one year old. In January, 1946, while appellee was stationed as a Captain in the Army in Washington, they purchased the home on Irvington Avenue, which is now in controversy. In February appellee was honorably discharged from the military service and was given a civilian position in the War Department.

The marital life became increasingly discordant after a quarrel on July 4, 1946. On that day appellant became enraged at her husband because he refused to accompany her to a party in Southern Maryland. Appellee described the quarrel as follows: "So she told me she was going alone, and I told her to go ahead. And she told me just prior to her departure that she wanted me out of the house when she came back. I told her that I wasn't going to leave. That evening when she came back, * * * I was in the basement ironing some shirts, and * * * she came downstairs alone and she told me that she had ordered me out of the house before she left, and wanted to know why I wasn't out. I told her I was doing my laundry * * * and with that, I don't recall if it was a beer bottle flew at me first or a small China lamp, whichever it was I caught that first, and then I caught either the beer bottle or China lamp that came at me second."

After this episode, appellant consulted an attorney in Washington with the object of inducing her husband to give her complete title to the home in Bethesda. Her husband declined to relinquish his interest in the property. Early in September, 1946, there was a change in the situation. He received an order from the Office of the Chief Engineer to go on a mission to Japan and China. As the Chinese Communists were at war with the Nationalist forces at that time, his mission promised to be a dangerous one. In view of the uncertainty of his return, he consented to execute a deed conveying the home to his wife, but, according to his version, on condition (1) that she would not record the deeds until such time as he "should have been reported missing, killed, or had failed to return," and (2) that if he should return, the deeds would be returned and destroyed. On September 10 he brought the deeds to his wife and that evening they executed before a notary public a deed conveying the title to a third person, who in turn executed a deed conveying it to appellant, and appellee also executed a release of his right of dower. A few days later appellee started on his trip to Japan.

After completing his work in Japan, appellee did not go to China, but returned to the United States much sooner than he had expected. When he arrived home on December 8, his wife demanded that he must not sleep in her bedroom. In order to avoid an argument, he took the back room. He testified that he asked his wife several times to return the deeds, but she refused to give them back. She recorded them on January 7, 1947.

* * *

We now come to the question whether the deeds which the husband delivered to the wife should have been annulled. It has long been held at common law that there cannot be a valid delivery of a deed to the grantee named therein upon a condition not expressed in the deed. The ancient rule that the mere transfer of a deed from the grantor to the grantee overrides the grantor's explicit declaration of intention that the deed shall not become operative immediately is a relic of the primative formalism which attached some peculiar efficacy to the physical transfer of the deed as a symbolical transfer of the land. In England in ancient times there could be no change of possession of land until a livery of seisin had taken place. A knife was produced and a piece of turf was cut, and the turf was handed over to the new owner. Later, under the Roman influence, the written document came into use. These documents, which few people had the art to manufacture, were regarded with mystical awe. Just as the sod had been taken up from the ground to be delivered, so the document was laid upon the ground and then solemnly lifted and delivered as a symbol of ownership. In this way the principle developed that the delivery of the deed was the mark of finality.

Through the centuries the courts have struggled to break away from this strict formalism. The first sign of flexibility in the rule was the concession that the delivery of a deed may be conditioned upon the performance of some act or the occurrence of some event, provided that such conditional delivery, known as delivery in escrow, is accomplished by having the deed placed in the hands of a third person for subsequent handing to the grantee. But the concession of conditional delivery was not allowed where the deed was placed directly in the hands of the grantee in anticipation of some future event. Thus this Court, recognizing the rule that a deed cannot be delivered in escrow to the grantee, said in Buchwald v. Buchwald, 175 Md. 115, 120, 199 A. 800, that if a deed absolute on its face is deposited by the grantor with the grantee, to be held by the grantee in escrow, such a deposit becomes a delivery which operates to vest the title in the grantee immediately.

But there is actually no logical reason why a deed should not be held in escrow by the grantee as well as by any other person. The ancient rule is not adapted to present-day conditions and is entirely unnecessary for the protection of the rights of litigants. After all, conditional delivery is purely a question of intention, and it is immaterial whether the instrument, pending satisfaction of the condition, is in the hands of the grantor, the grantee, or a third person. After the condition is satisfied, there is an operative conveyance which is considered as having been delivered at the time of the conditional delivery, for the reason that it was then that it was actually delivered, although the ownership does not pass until the satisfaction of the conditions. We, therefore, hold that it is the intention of the grantor of a deed that determines whether the delivery of the deed is absolute or conditional, although the delivery is made by the grantor directly to the grantee.

In the case before us the two deeds and the release of dower were delivered conditionally. The husband testified that, before leaving on a dangerous mission in the Orient, he handed the instruments to his wife, but it was understood that the deeds were not to be recorded until such time as he "should have been reported missing, killed, or had failed to return." The wife's version is different. She testified that she promised that when her husband returned home, she would tear up the deeds and let the original title stand upon condition that he would change into a better man. In any event, the wife admitted that her husband did not intend to divest himself of all control over the property. It is undisputed that it was the intention of the parties that the instruments were not to be recorded while the husband was on his mission. The instruments were not recorded by the wife until January 7, 1947, a month after the husband returned home.

As we have indicated, the title to property described in a deed delivered conditionally does not pass as long as the condition attached to the delivery of a deed is not satisfied. Therefore, when it becomes assured that the condition will not be satisfied, the deed loses all possible efficacy. In such a case the grantor will ordinarily desire to have the deed returned to him, in order to preclude the possibility of its being used afterwards to his detriment. In view of the presumption of delivery which naturally arises from the grantee's possession of the deed, the burden rests upon the grantor, when he has delivered the deed to the grantee, to show (1) that the delivery was conditional, and (2) that the condition was not satisfied.

In this case the chancellor believed the grantor's version of the delivery, and held that he sustained the burden of proof. * * * We consider the evidence sufficient to sustain the annulment of the instruments.

Decree affirmed, with costs.

Problems and Questions

1. The common law rule stated in the *Chillemi* opinion is still generally accepted. It is thought to lend stability to titles. Do you agree? *See* W. Burby, Handbook of the Law of Real Property 304 (3d ed. 1965).

2. O, the owner of a farm, prepared and signed a deed transferring the property to S for life, remainder to S's sons. Angry at this disposition, S tore up the deed in O's presence and threw it in the wastebasket. Thereafter O died, leaving the farm by will to S's daughter. S's sons claim the property. Who prevails? *See* Underwood v. Gillespie, 594 S.W.2d 372 (Mo.App.1980).

5. MERGER

AMERICAN NATIONAL SELF STORAGE, INC. v. LOPEZ–AGUIAR

District Court of Appeal of Florida, Third District, 1988.
521 So.2d 303.

DANIEL S. PEARSON, JUDGE.

American National Self Storage, the purchaser of a parcel of real property, sued the seller, Carlos Lopez–Aguiar, alleging that the seller breached the following express warranty contained in the contract of sale:

> "The Seller further represents and warrants that water, sewer and electric service are presently available at the property line or lines of the premises with sufficient capacity to accommodate a 45,000 sq. ft. office/warehouse building."

American alleged that the water and sewer connections were not, as warranted, "presently available at the property line," but rather were so distant from it that American had to pay more than $25,000 to extend the lines for its use. Lopez–Aguiar countered, first, that the contract containing the warranty merged into the deed, which contained no such warranty and, thus, American's right to enforce the provision of the sales contract was extinguished * * *. The trial court entered a summary judgment for the seller. American appeals.

Because we conclude that the execution and delivery of the deed did not, ipso facto, extinguish the warranty of the contract, and because the seller has not otherwise attempted to show that the parties intended that the warranty of the contract be merged into and extinguished by the silent deed, we reverse the summary judgment under review and remand the cause for further proceedings.

Where a provision of a contract to sell land is not performed or satisfied by the execution and delivery of the deed, "[t]he rule that acceptance of a deed tendered in performance of a contract to convey land merges or extinguishes the covenants and stipulations contained in the contract does not apply * * *." Milu, Inc. v. Duke, 204 So.2d 31, 33 (Fla. 3d DCA 1967). It is said that "[i]n such case, the delivery of the conveyance is merely a part performance of the contract, which remains binding as to its further provisions." Gabel v. Simmons, 100 Fla. 526, 529, 129 So. 777, 778 (1930).

The continued efficacy, then, of collateral agreements which are not usually included in the terms of a deed is not affected by the merger rule. Such collateral agreements call for acts by the seller which go beyond merely conveying clear title and placing the purchaser in possession of the property. For example, in Campbell v. Rawls, 381 So.2d 744 (Fla. 1st DCA 1980), the court found that because the seller's warranty in the contract of sale that the air conditioning and heating systems would be in working order at the time of closing was an independent covenant generally excepted from the merger doctrine, the buyer was not required to inspect the property and report discrepancies before closing in order to preserve his rights under the warranty. Likewise, in Mallin v. Good, 93 Ill.App.3d 843, 49 Ill.Dec. 168, 417 N.E.2d 858 (1981), the buyer was entitled to close on the property with knowledge of the seller's breach of covenants in the sales contract without losing the right to enforce them. The court, reversing summary judgment for the seller, found that the covenants—that "all heating, plumbing, electrical and air conditioning would be in working order at the time of closing'' and that "any damage to [the] roof to be repaired by seller''—survived the conveyance of title by deed because they were collateral undertakings, incidental to the transfer of title. Mallin v. Good, 49 Ill.Dec. at 169, 417 N.E.2d at 859. *See also* Stiles v. Bodkin, 43 Cal.App.2d 839, 111 P.2d 675 (1941) (no merger despite acceptance of deed to property on which improvements, called for by the contract of sale, had not yet been made); Mueller v. Banker's Trust Co., 262 Mich. 53, 247 N.W. 103 (1933) (seller's undertaking in contract to build bridge not merged in deed); Caparrelli v. Rolling Greens, Inc., 39 N.J. 585, 190 A.2d 369 (1963) (seller's warranty that panelled section of basement was habitable and usable for normal daily activity deemed to be collateral undertaking which survived delivery and acceptance of deed).

In contrast, where the provision in the contract of sale pertains to the title to the property or warrants that the title is unencumbered—covenants usually included in the deed itself—the merger rule applies. *See, e.g.,* Stephan v. Brown, 233 So.2d 140 (Fla. 2d DCA 1970) (warranty in contract that the realty would be free of encumbrances not enforceable after purchaser accepted a deed which did not contain the warranty); Volunteer Security Co. v. Dowl, 159 Fla. 767, 33 So.2d 150 (1947) (restrictive covenants contained in contract but omitted from deed not enforceable once deed accepted); St. Clair v. City Bank & Trust Co., 175 So.2d 791 (Fla. 2d DCA 1965) (where buyers accepted quitclaim deed at closing, sellers' prior agreement to convey by warranty deed extinguished by merger).

Turning now to the present case, it is clear to us that the seller's agreement—that water, sewer and electrical service are presently available at the property line—calls for acts by the seller that go beyond merely conveying good title and placing the purchaser in possession of the property; it is not an agreement usually contained in a deed, related to the condition of the title to property, or satisfied by the execution and delivery of the deed. We have no difficulty in concluding, then, that the warranty in American's contract was not merged in and extinguished by the deed, and that, therefore, the summary judgment for the seller which concluded otherwise was improper. Our reversal of the summary judgment does not, however, foreclose the seller from attempting to prove, by evidence other than the deed itself, that the parties intended that the warranty of the contract of sale was to be extinguished by the conveyance of the property. Furthermore there remains to be resolved at trial a dispute over whether the warranty—assuming it survived—was fulfilled, that is, whether the water and sewer lines were, as promised, "presently available at the property line" at the time of closing.

Reversed and remanded.

Note

For further discussion of the merger doctrine, see Berger, *Merger by Deed—What Provisions of a Contract for the Sale of Land Survive the*

Closing?, 21 Real Estate L.J. 22 (1992); Dunham, *Merger by Deed—Was It Ever Automatic?*, 10 Ga.L.Rev. 419 (1976).

I. SELLER LIABILITY FOR CONDITION OF PREMISES

1. WARRANTY OF QUALITY

We have seen that covenants of title are not implied in a conveyance. A purchaser, however, usually receives a warranty deed containing express covenants of title. Hence, neither courts nor state legislatures have perceived a need to change the no-implied-covenants-of-title rule. The situation is different with respect to covenants as to the condition of the premises being conveyed. Many purchasers receive no express warranty of quality from their seller. Suppose, for example, that the Ryans received good title to their house in Rolling Hills, but a poorly constructed wall collapsed shortly after they moved in. Do they have any recourse against the person from whom they purchased the property? Do they have any recourse against the builder?

GAITO v. AUMAN

Supreme Court of North Carolina, 1985.
313 N.C. 243, 327 S.E.2d 870.

Appeal from a decision of the Court of Appeals, 70 N.C.App. 21, 318 S.E.2d 555 (1984), affirming the judgment of Burris, J., at the 1 November 1982 Civil Session of District Court, Moore County.

Plaintiffs Sam and Eleanor Gaito brought this action against defendant Howard Frank Auman, Jr. on 19 May 1981, alleging in their complaint that in April 1978 they purchased a home from Auman, its builder, and moved into the home in June 1978. The Gaitos alleged that the purchase price of the home included central air conditioning, but that the air conditioning system in the house never worked properly despite repeated efforts to correct the cooling problems. The plaintiffs alleged that they were damaged in the amount of $3,500 as a result of a breach of warranty on the part of the defendant Auman.

In his answer and amended answer defendant Auman denied liability under a theory of implied warranty of habitability of a recently completed dwelling on grounds that the house was not new at the time plaintiffs purchased it and on grounds that plaintiffs were aware that the house was not new. Defendant Auman also filed a third party complaint against Alvin LeGrand, who Auman alleged supplied and installed the air conditioner in the home. On 30 April 1982 defendant filed a motion for summary judgment which the trial court denied.

The evidence at trial tended to show that the house in dispute was completed by defendant in November 1973 as a speculation house. Defendant was in the business of building houses. The house sat vacant one and one-half years before defendant Auman contracted to sell it to a man named Lee Cole. Although no deed was passed conveying title to him, Cole lived in the house for two months. While living there, Cole bulldozed the area around the house to make a pasture for horses. Cole left the house after he became unable to make a payment and forfeited his down payment.

The house was next rented to a realtor, Jack Vernon, for a period of six months. In 1976 Raymond and Catherine Ashley rented and lived in the house for fifteen months. During the time the Ashleys lived in the house, the air conditioning system did not cool the house properly. During three weeks of 95 degree weather, the Ashleys were unable to get the temperature of the house below 85 degrees. The Ashleys contacted defendant Auman about the problem and defendant LeGrand went to the house to attempt repairs. LeGrand replaced compressors and Freon and did electrical work. Another air conditioning repairman, Metrah Spencer, subsequently replaced the compressor, opened up and rearranged the duct work. He did not change the capacity of the air conditioning unit.

In early 1978 defendant Auman listed the house for sale with a local real estate company, and Thomas Caulk, one of the firm's realtors, showed the house to the Gaitos. Caulk told the Gaitos that the house was four years old and that it had been occupied for two short periods of time. The Gaitos decided to purchase the house and had Caulk inspect it before the closing. The closing on the house was in April 1978 and plaintiffs moved in June. Plaintiffs first turned on the air conditioning at the end of June 1978 when the temperature outside was in the eighties. Although plaintiffs let the system run two days and nights, the system created only a ten degree difference between outside and inside temperatures. The Gaitos contacted Auman several times during the summer of 1978 and had repairs done. The repairs included the installation of power vents, an exhaust fan, and insulation for the duct work, the changing of filters, and the addition of Freon. The ducting system was reworked, and the compressor was replaced two times. In 1979 the Gaitos converted their garage into an apartment. They had duct work added and attached the apartment to the air conditioning system for the house.

Rod Tripp, who was qualified as an expert in the field of heating and air conditioning, testified for the plaintiffs that in 1973 the accepted standard in the air conditioning industry for the differential between outside and inside temperatures was 20 degrees when the outside temperature was 95 degrees. In 1978 the accepted differential was 15 degrees. Tripp stated that in his opinion a four ton air conditioning system rather than the three and one-half ton system originally installed was the proper size for the Gaitos' house. Tripp testified that the cost of installing a four ton system in a house in 1980 would have been approximately $3,655. At the time of trial the cost would have been $3,955.

At the close of the evidence, Judge Burris granted defendant Alvin LeGrand's motion to dismiss the case against him based on the statute of limitations. Defendant Auman's attorney made a motion to dismiss the case on grounds that the implied warranty of habitability theory was inapplicable. The trial court denied his motion and allowed the jury to deliberate on the question of defendant's liability.

The jury returned with a verdict in favor of the plaintiffs in the amount of $3,655. Defendant appealed to the Court of Appeals, which affirmed the trial court. Judge Hedrick dissented.

BRANCH, CHIEF JUSTICE.

The question posed by this appeal is whether the Court of Appeals erred in affirming the judgment in favor of the plaintiffs on a theory of implied warranty of habitability. The majority concluded that a residential structure could be considered new for purposes of the implied warranty within the maximum applicable statute of limitations period. We reject this reasoning.

* * *

The essence of defendant's arguments * * * is that plaintiffs' claim was not cognizable under an implied warranty theory because of the age of the house and its occupation by tenants prior to its purchase by the plaintiffs. Although we held in Griffin v. Wheeler–Leonard & Co., 290 N.C. 185, 225 S.E.2d 557 (1976), that the implied warranty of habitability arises by operation of law, we hold that the applicability of the warranty is to be determined on a case by case basis and that under these facts, plaintiffs presented a legally cognizable claim under a theory of implied warranty of habitability.

The trend of recent judicial decisions has been to invoke the doctrine of implied warranty of habitability or fitness in cases involving the sale of a new house by the builder. *See* Humber v. Morton, 426 S.W.2d 554 (Tex.1968); *Annot.*, 25 A.L.R.3d 372 (1969). The rigid common law rule of *caveat emptor* in the sale of recently completed dwellings was relaxed in this state by this Court's opinion in Hartley v. Ballou, 286 N.C. 51, 209 S.E.2d 776 (1974). In *Hartley* the plaintiffs purchased a "recently" constructed house from defendants. Although they inspected the house prior to moving in, plaintiffs observed nothing amiss. Shortly after moving in[,] the house showed signs of substantial water leakage and insufficient waterproofing in the basement. This Court, in an opinion authored by Chief Justice Bobbitt, concluded that the defendant builder-vendor had an obligation to perform work in a proper, workmanlike and ordinarily skillful manner. Chief Justice Bobbitt then stated the rule as follows:

> [I]n every contract for the sale of a recently completed dwelling, and in every contract for the sale of a dwelling then under construction, the vendor, if he be in the business of building such dwellings, shall be held to impliedly warrant to the initial vendee that, at the time of the passing of the deed or the taking of possession by the initial

vendee (whichever first occurs), the dwelling, together with all its fixtures, is sufficiently free from major structural defects, and is constructed in a workmanlike manner, so as to meet the standard of workmanlike quality then prevailing at the time and place of construction; and that this implied warranty in the contract of sale survives the passing of the deed or the taking of possession by the initial vendee.

Id. at 62, 209 S.E.2d at 783.

The doctrine recited in *Hartley* is known as an implied warranty of habitability and represents a growing trend in the jurisprudence of our states. An implied warranty of habitability is limited to latent defects—those not visible or apparent to a reasonable person upon inspection of a dwelling. Griffin v. Wheeler–Leonard and Co., 290 N.C. 185, 225 S.E.2d 557 (1976) (defect was poor waterproofing which caused standing water in crawl space).

The relaxing of the rigid rule of *caveat emptor* in *Hartley* is based on a policy which holds builder-vendors accountable beyond the passage of title or the taking of possession by the initial vendee for defects which are not apparent to the purchaser at that time. This policy is justified because the innocent purchaser is often making one of the largest investments of a lifetime from one whose experience and expertise places him in a dominating position in that sale.

Defendant appellant argues that the facts of this case are legally insufficient to support a verdict for the plaintiff because the facts do not fall within the exception to the rule of *caveat emptor* established by *Hartley.* Defendant contends that an implied warranty of habitability is inapplicable because both the pretrial pleadings and evidence at trial show that the house was not "recently completed" or under construction at the time of the passing of the deed; the plaintiff claims and the evidence shows instead that the house was built four and one-half years earlier. Defendant also argues that the previous occupancy by tenants invalidated any implied warranty which may have arisen.

We first consider defendant's argument that he must prevail because the house was built four and one-half years before the plaintiffs received a deed or took possession. Our cases do not address the precise limits of our requirement in *Hartley* that a house be "recently completed." We therefore turn to other jurisdictions for instruction on this question.

A number of courts have established a standard of reasonableness in determining how the age of a house affects the application of the warranty. See Sims v. Lewis, 374 So.2d 298 (Ala.1979); Barnes v. Mac Brown and Co., 264 Ind. 227, 342 N.E.2d 619 (1976); Smith v. Old Warson Development, Co., 479 S.W.2d 795 (Mo.1972); Padula v. J.J. Deb–Cin Homes, Inc., 111 R.I. 29, 298 A.2d 529 (1973); Waggoner v. Midwestern Development, Inc., 83 S.D. 57, 154 N.W.2d 803 (1967).

In *Barnes* the plaintiffs in 1971 purchased a home which had been completed in 1967 and had been sold to an intermediate purchaser. After plaintiffs moved in, a large crack appeared in a wall, and the plaintiffs discovered that the basement leaked. In considering the question of the applicability of an implied warranty of habitability, the Indiana Supreme Court applied a reasonableness standard:

> This extension of liability is limited to latent defects not discoverable by a subsequent purchaser's reasonable inspection, manifesting themselves after the purchase. The standard to be applied in determining whether or not there has been a breach of warranty is one of reasonableness in light of the surrounding circumstances. The age of the home, its maintenance, the use to which it has been put are but a few factors entering into this factual determination at trial.

342 N.E.2d at 621.

In a subsequent case, the Indiana Court of Appeals considered whether the warranty extended to a defective septic tank in which the defect appeared five years after the completion of the dwelling. Relying on *Barnes* and the reasonableness standard, the court stated that where a defective septic tank was involved "we cannot say, as a matter of law, that five years is too long a period of time to extend the implied warranty of fitness." Wagner Construction Co. v. Noonan, 403 N.E.2d 1144 (Ind.App.1980).

In a case decided by the Washington Supreme Court, Klos v. Gockel, 87 Wash.2d 567, 554 P.2d 1349 (1976), plaintiffs purchased a home in 1973 which had been completed in July 1972. The builder-vendor had lived in the house approximately one year before plaintiffs purchased it. After plaintiffs moved in, a portion of the slope below the rear wall of the house slid, causing the patio to crack and patio slabs to upend. Although the Court in *Klos* rejected the applicability of the warranty on other grounds, it reasoned that the passage of a year would not necessarily invalidate a warranty of habitability.

> It is true that for purposes of warranty liability, the house purchased must be a "new house", but this is a question of fact. The passage of time can always operate to cancel liability but just how much time need pass varies with each case.

87 Wash.2d at 571, 554 P.2d at 1352. *See also* Tavares v. Horstman, 542 P.2d 1275 (Wyo.1975) (warranty applied where septic tank failed after five years because "we appreciate that different parts of construction may have different expected life").

We are persuaded that the reasoning of these courts is sound and that the standard of reasonableness is the appropriate standard for determining whether a dwelling has been recently completed. Thus, under the facts of this case, it was a question of fact for the fact finder to determine whether the house was "recently completed." Among some of the factors which may be considered in determining this question are the age of the building, the use to which it has been put, its maintenance, the nature of the defects and the expectations of the parties. This standard allows extension of the warranty to vary in lengths of time, depending on the nature of the defect and whether the warranty should reasonably be expected to apply.

Even so, defendant argues that the tenancies which intervened between construction and purchase by plaintiffs rendered the warranty inapplicable. We disagree. We note that the purpose of the warranty is to protect homeowners from defects which can only be within the knowledge of vendors. There are many kinds of major structural defects upon which the presence of tenants can have little or no effect. In other cases intervening tenants may contribute to or directly cause major defects in a dwelling's structure. We hold that the effect of occupation by tenants prior to the passage of the deed to the initial vendee is but one of the factors which a fact finder should consider in determining whether defendant is liable for breach of an implied warranty of habitability. *See* Casavant v. Campopiano, 114 R.I. 24, 327 A.2d 831 (1974) (warranty affected by tenants only if tenants causally connected with defects).

At this point we note that *Hartley* limits the implied warranty of habitability to *initial vendees* at the time of the taking of possession or the passing of the deed. Here plaintiff was an initial vendee and therefore it is unnecessary for us to discuss the applicability of the implied warranty to subsequent purchasers. For the same reason, we disavow any inferences that may arise from the footnote from the decision of the Court of Appeals relating to this question.

Defendant contends that to extend an implied warranty to this factual situation will be disastrous to home builders who would "for all intents and purposes be prevented from renting homes they were unable to sell" for fear that the builders would be liable for damage to the home caused by the tenants.

However, builders are still accorded substantial protection by the requirement that the defect in a dwelling or its fixtures be latent or not reasonably discoverable at the time of sale or possession. Claimants must also show that structural defects had their origin in the builder-seller and in construction which does not meet the standard of workmanlike quality then prevailing at the time and place of construction. *Hartley,* 286 N.C. 51, 209 S.E.2d 776. We have also made it clear that the implied warranty falls short of "an absolute guarantee." *Id.* at 61, 209 S.E.2d at 782. In regard to this argument we wish to make it clear that the test of reasonableness to determine whether a dwelling is "recently completed" does not affect the relevant statutes of limitation and repose.

Although defendant did not raise the argument at the Court of Appeals level, he now argues that an implied warranty is inapplicable to an air conditioning unit because it is not "an absolute essential utility to a dwelling house." In *Hartley* we held that the builder of a recently completed dwelling impliedly warrants that "the dwelling, *together with all its fixtures,* is sufficiently free from major structural defects and is constructed in a workmanlike manner, so as to meet the standard of workmanlike quality then prevailing at the time and place of construction." 286 N.C. at 62, 209 S.E.2d at 783. (Emphasis added).

Courts have found a breach of implied warranty for defects arising in many different areas of construction. *See, e.g.,* Sims v. Lewis, 374 So.2d 298 (Ala.1979) (defective septic tank); Carpenter v. Donohoe, 154 Colo. 78, 388 P.2d 399 (1964) (cracks in basement wall); Weeks v. Slavick Builders, Inc., 24 Mich.App. 621, 180 N.W.2d 503, affirmed, 384 Mich. 257, 181 N.W.2d 271 (1970) (leaky roof); Schipper v. Levitt & Sons, Inc., 44 N.J. 70, 207 A.2d 314 (1965) (failure to install boiler valve which regulated temperature for water used for domestic purposes); Waggoner v. Midwestern Development, Inc., 83 S.D. 57, 154 N.W.2d 803 (1967) (water seepage in basement); Humber v. Morton, 426 S.W.2d 554 (Tex. 1968) (fireplace and chimney defective).

The test of a breach of an implied warranty of habitability in North Carolina is not whether a fixture is an "absolute essential utility to a dwelling house." The test is whether there is a failure to meet the prevailing standard of workmanlike quality. *See* Griffin v. Wheeler–Leonard & Co., 290 N.C. 185, 225 S.E.2d 557 (1976) (breach of standard of workmanlike quality not "liveability" is test of breach of warranty). We hold that under the facts of this case, a jury may properly find a defective air conditioning system in a "recently completed dwelling" to be a major structural defect as between an initial vendee and a builder-vendor.

After a review of the evidence we hold that under a theory of implied warranty of habitability, the plaintiff raised questions of fact and a legally cognizable cause of action sufficient to survive defendant's motions for summary judgment, directed verdict and judgment notwithstanding the verdict.

Since Judge Hedrick in his dissent took exception to the Court of Appeals majority's affirmance of the trial court on the issue of damages, we consider the relevant rules of damages. The rule as stated in *Hartley* is that a vendee can maintain an action against a builder-vender for damages for the breach of implied warranty of habitability "either (1) for the difference between the reasonable market value of the subject property as impliedly warranted and its reasonable market value in its actual condition, or (2) for the amount required to bring the subject property into compliance with the implied warranty." Hartley v. Ballou, 286 N.C. at 63, 209 S.E.2d at 783. The Court in *Hartley* cited Robbins v. C.W. Trading Post, Inc., 251 N.C. 663, 111 S.E.2d 884 (1960) in which Justice Moore explained the principles behind the two measures of damages in the context of a breach of a construction contract:

> "The fundamental principle which underlies the decisions regarding the measure of damages for defect or omissions in the performance of a building or construction contract is that a party is entitled to have what he contracts for or its equivalent. What the equivalent is depends upon the circumstances of the case. *In a majority of jurisdictions, where the defects are such that they may be*

remedied without the destruction of any substantial part of the benefit which the owner's property has received by reason of the contractor's work, the equivalent to which the owner is entitled is the cost of making the work conform to the contract. But where, in order to conform the work to the contract requirements, a substantial part of what has been done must be undone, and the contractor has acted in good faith, or the owner has taken possession, the latter is not permitted to recover the cost of making the change, but may recover the difference in value." 9 Am.Jr., Building and Construction Contracts, sec. 152, p. 89; Twitty v. McGuire, 7 N.C. 501, 504. The difference referred to is the difference between the value of the house contracted for and the value of the house built—the values to be determined as of the date of tender or delivery of possession to the owner.

Id. at 666, 111 S.E.2d at 887. (Emphasis added.)

The evidence in this case shows that the defect complained of may be remedied without destroying a substantial part of the dwelling. Since the appellant did not bring forward the trial court's instructions, we must assume they were correctly given. It appears that the jury's verdict correctly represented the cost of making the builder-vendor's work conform to the implied warranty of habitability—in this case the cost of replacing the original air conditioner. Since plaintiffs do not contest defendant's assertion that he is entitled to receive the original three and one-half ton unit if a four ton unit is installed, we do not consider defendant's argument in this regard. We therefore do not disturb the jury's award of damages.

For the reasons stated, the decision of the Court of Appeals is affirmed.

Affirmed.

Notes and Questions

1. Must the builder-vendor be given notice of the defect and an opportunity to repair before liability arises under an implied warranty of quality? *See* Wagner Construction Co. v. Noonan, 403 N.E.2d 1144 (Ind.App. 1980).

2. Many homebuilders give express written warranties as to the quality of their new homes. Is a purchaser limited to recovery on express warranties when a broader warranty is implied in that jurisdiction? *Compare* Gable v. Silver, 258 So.2d 11 (Fla.App.1972), *affirmed per curiam* 264 So.2d 418 (Fla.1972) *and* Bridges v. Ferrell, 685 P.2d 409 (Okl.App.1984) *with* Dixon v. Mountain City Construction Co., 632 S.W.2d 538 (Tenn.1982).

3. Courts generally recognize the ability of the builder-vendor to disclaim both express and implied warranties by clear and unambiguous language. *See* Tusch Enterprises v. Coffin, 113 Idaho 37, 740 P.2d 1022 (1987); *but see* Melody Home Mfg. Co. v. Barnes, 741 S.W.2d 349 (Tex.1987). Litigation may arise with respect to whether particular language is sufficient for this purpose. *Compare* Schoeneweis v. Herrin, 110 Ill.App.3d 800, 66

Ill.Dec. 513, 443 N.E.2d 36 (1982) *with* Frickel v. Sunnyside Enterprises, Inc., 106 Wn.2d 714, 725 P.2d 422 (1986). *See generally* Abney, *Disclaiming the Implied Real Estate Common–Law Warranties,* 17 Real Estate L.J. 141 (1988) (proposing model disclaimer clause); Powell, *Disclaimers of Implied Warranty in the Sale of New Homes,* 34 Vill.L.Rev. 1123 (1989).

4.   For a proposal for reform of the law of housing warranties based upon a system of disclosure, see Sovern, *Toward a Theory of Warranties in Sales of New Homes: Housing the Implied Warranty Advocates, Law and Economics Mavens, and Consumer Psychologists Under One Roof,* 1993 Wis.L.Rev. 13.

RICHARDS v. POWERCRAFT HOMES, INC.

Supreme Court of Arizona, 1984.
139 Ariz. 242, 678 P.2d 427.

GORDON, VICE CHIEF JUSTICE:

Each of the several individually named plaintiffs purchased houses in the Indian Hills subdivision near Casa Grande, Arizona at varying times during 1975, 1976, and 1977. The houses had been built by defendant Powercraft Homes beginning in 1974. Plaintiffs Woodward, Fillion, Schaar, and Grant purchased their homes directly from Powercraft while plaintiffs Richards, Farina, and White bought repossessed homes from Farmers Home Administration. After occupying the houses, each plaintiff discovered numerous defects. The defects included, *inter alia,* faulty water pipes, improperly leveled yards that resulted in pooling and flooding with any rain, cracking of the interior and exterior walls, separation of the floors from the walls, separation of sidewalks, driveways, and carports from the houses, and doors and windows which were stuck closed or which could not be locked because of misalignment. Powercraft was notified of many of these defects and attempted some repairs. The repairs in most cases provided only temporary or partial relief from the problems.

In the spring of 1978, each of the plaintiffs filed a complaint with the Arizona Registrar of Contractors. The Registrar found that Powercraft had failed to follow certain plans and specifications in the building of each home and that it had failed to properly compact the soil beneath each house before building commenced. Powercraft's contractor's license was revoked on December 6, 1978.

Plaintiffs filed suit against Powercraft on August 17, 1979 alleging violation of the Consumer Fraud Act, A.R.S. § 44–1521 *et seq.,* and breach of the implied warranty that houses be habitable and constructed in a workmanlike manner. A jury awarded the plaintiffs $210,000 in compensatory and punitive damages. Powercraft appealed; the Court of Appeals affirmed in part and reversed in part. Richards v. Powercraft Homes, Inc., 139 Ariz. 264, 678 P.2d 449 (App.1983). The Court of Appeals ordered the consumer fraud count dismissed, the punitive damage award vacated, and the verdicts in favor of plaintiffs Richards,

Farina, and White set aside. The plaintiffs petitioned this Court to review the Court of Appeal's opinion. We have jurisdiction pursuant to Ariz. Const. art. 6, § 5(3) and Ariz.R.Civ.App.P. 23. While we approve the Court of Appeal's decision regarding the consumer fraud claim and the punitive damages, we vacate that portion of the Court of Appeal's decision regarding the verdicts of plaintiffs Richards, Farina, and White. The jury verdict in favor of those three plaintiffs against defendant Powercraft for the breach of the implied warranty of habitability is reinstated for the reasons set forth below.

In setting aside the verdicts in favor of Richards, Farina, and White, the Court of Appeals held that "there must be privity to maintain an action for breach of the implied warranty of workmanship and habitability," *Richards, supra,* 139 Ariz. at 266–267, 678 P.2d at 451–52. * * * In Columbia Western Corp. v. Vela, 122 Ariz. 28, 592 P.2d 1294 (App.1979), builder-vendors of new homes were held to impliedly warrant that construction has been done in a workmanlike manner and that the structure is habitable. The issue before us now is whether this implied warranty extends to subsequent buyers of the homes.

The courts of several states have confronted this issue. Many of those courts have refused to extend the implied warranty of habitability to remote purchasers or to those not in privity with the builder-vendor. *See, e.g.,* H.B. Bolas Enterprises, Inc. v. Zarlengo, 156 Colo. 530, 400 P.2d 447 (1965); Coburn v. Lenox Homes, Inc., 173 Conn. 567, 378 A.2d 599 (1977); Strathmore Riverside Villas Condominium Ass'n, Inc. v. Paver Development Corp., 369 So.2d 971 (Fla.App.1979); Oliver v. City Builders, Inc., 303 So.2d 466 (Miss.1974); John H. Armbruster & Co. v. Hayden Company–Builder Developer, Inc., 622 S.W.2d 704 (Mo.App. 1981); Herz v. Thornwood Acres "D", Inc., 86 Misc.2d 53, 381 N.Y.S.2d 761 (Justice Ct.1976), aff'd, 91 Misc.2d 130, 397 N.Y.S.2d 358 (App. Term.1977); Brown v. Fowler, 279 N.W.2d 907 (S.D.1979). Others, however, have rejected the imposition of a privity requirement and have allowed remote purchasers to maintain a cause of action against a builder-vendor for breach of the implied warranty of habitability. *See, e.g.,* Blagg v. Fred Hunt Co. Inc., 272 Ark. 185, 612 S.W.2d 321 (1981); Redarowicz v. Ohlendorf, 92 Ill.2d 171, 65 Ill.Dec. 411, 441 N.E.2d 324 (1982); Barnes v. Mac Brown & Co., Inc., 264 Ind. 227, 342 N.E.2d 619 (1976); Hermes v. Staiano, 181 N.J.Super. 424, 437 A.2d 925 (Law Div.1981); McMillan v. Brune–Harpenau–Torbeck Builders, Inc., 8 Ohio St.3d 3, 455 N.E.2d 1276 (1983); Elden v. Simmons, 631 P.2d 739 (Okl.1981); Terlinde v. Neely, 275 S.C. 395, 271 S.E.2d 768 (1980); Gupta v. Ritter Homes, Inc., 646 S.W.2d 168 (Tex.1983); Moxley v. Laramie Builders, Inc., 600 P.2d 733 (Wyo.1979). We find the latter group of cases to be more in line with the public policy of this state and hold that privity is not required to maintain an action for breach of the implied warranty of workmanship and habitability.

We agree with the persuasive comments of the Wyoming Supreme Court in *Moxley, supra,* that:

"[t]he purpose of a warranty is to protect innocent purchasers and hold builders accountable for their work. With that object in mind, any reasoning which would arbitrarily interpose a first buyer as an obstruction to someone equally deserving of recovery is incomprehensible."

600 P.2d at 736. In addition, such reasoning might encourage sham first sales to insulate builders from liability.

Since *Columbia Western,* an original homebuyer in this state has been able to rely on the builder-vendor's implied warranty. The same policy considerations that led to that decision—that house-building is frequently undertaken on a large scale, that builders hold themselves out as skilled in the profession, that modern construction is complex and regulated by many governmental codes, and that homebuyers are generally not skilled or knowledgeable in construction, plumbing, or electrical requirements and practices—are equally applicable to subsequent homebuyers. Also, we note that the character of our society is such that people and families are increasingly mobile. Home builders should anticipate that the houses they construct will eventually, and perhaps frequently, change ownership. The effect of latent defects will be just as catastrophic on a subsequent owner as on an original buyer and the builder will be just as unable to justify improper or substandard work. Because the builder-vendor is in a better position than a subsequent owner to prevent occurrence of major problems, the costs of poor workmanship should be his to bear.

The implied warranty of habitability and proper workmanship is not unlimited. It does not force the builder-vendor to "act as an insurer for subsequent vendees" as the Court of Appeals feared, *Richards, supra,* 139 Ariz. at 267, 678 P.2d at 452. It is limited to latent defects which become manifest after the subsequent owner's purchase and which were not discoverable had a reasonable inspection of the structure been made prior to purchase. We adopt the standard set forth by the Indiana Supreme Court in *Barnes, supra.*

"The standard to be applied in determining whether or not there has been a breach of warranty is one of reasonableness in light of surrounding circumstances. The age of a home, its maintenance, the use to which it has been put, are but a few factors entering into this factual determination at trial."

264 Ind. at 229, 342 N.E.2d at 621. The burden is on the subsequent owner to show that the defect had its origin and cause in the builder-vendor and that the suit was brought within the appropriate statute of limitations. Defenses are, of course, available. The builder-vendor can demonstrate that the defects are not attributable to him, that they are the result of age or ordinary wear and tear, or that previous owners have made substantial changes.

In the present case, the plaintiffs met their burden and proved that the defect had its origin and cause in Powercraft. There was no indication that the original owners substantially changed the structure of the homes. The cracking of the exterior and interior walls, the separation of the floors from the walls, and the separation of the sidewalks, driveways, and carports from the homes were due to improper compacting done by Powercraft prior to building the houses coupled with an apparent systematic lack of reinforcement in the floors, walls, ceilings, and roofs of the houses. Such improper compaction and lack of structural reinforcement could not have been determined from a reasonable inspection prior to purchase. Each of the plaintiffs moved into their homes before the end of 1977. The defects became manifest only after extraordinarily heavy rains in early 1978. Therefore, all of the plaintiffs, whether or not in privity with Powercraft, are entitled to the jury verdicts rendered in their favor.

The decision of the Court of Appeals that the consumer fraud count be dismissed and that the punitive damage award be vacated is approved; the decision of the Court of Appeals that the verdicts in favor of plaintiffs Richards, Farina, and White be set aside is vacated; the verdicts in favor of plaintiffs are affirmed in all other respects. The case is remanded for further proceedings not inconsistent with this opinion.

VETOR v. SHOCKEY

Court of Appeals of Indiana, Second District, 1980.
414 N.E.2d 575.

SULLIVAN, JUDGE.

Judy and Richard Shockey filed a small claims action against Thomas Vetor on April 24, 1978, alleging that they had purchased a house from Vetor in October of 1977, that Vetor had warranted that the septic tank was in working order, but that in fact the septic system needed extensive repair. After a bench trial the court found the following:

"[T]he defendant is liable to the plaintiff for latent defects not discoverable by the plaintiff's reasonable inspection which manifested themselves after the purchase of the realty in question. This being specifically, that there was an *implied warranty* that the septic system was in proper working order and that subsequent to the purchase, the plaintiff did find that the septic tank was not in proper working order." (Emphasis supplied.)

Vetor presents one issue for our review, namely: did the trial court err, as a matter of law, when it determined that an implied warranty of habitability existed in the sale of a used home by a non builder-vendor?
* * *

This action was brought in small claims court and under the informal procedures prescribed for such courts, no trial transcript was made. However, pursuant to the procedure outlined in Ind. Rules of Procedure, Appellate Rule 7.2(A)(3)(c), Vetor submitted a statement of the evidence adduced at trial to both the trial judge and the Shockeys. Approximately two weeks later the court, without objection from the Shockeys, certified that statement to be a true and accurate account of the proceedings. The facts as gleaned from that statement are as follows: The Shockeys purchased the house from Vetor in October of 1977; Vetor had owned and occupied the home for four years but had not built it. The purchase agreement specified that Vetor would deliver a general warranty deed conveying the real estate "in the same condition as it now is, ordinary wear and tear excepted. * * * "Prior to taking possession, the Shockeys questioned Vetor about the condition of the septic system, which was installed by an independent contractor in October of 1973, and he informed them that the system was in "satisfactory working condition except for certain times of the year when there would be a lot of water on the ground, the septic system might be a little slow." The Shockeys experienced trouble with the system, manifested by the malfunctioning of the toilet and the washing machine. They obtained an estimate for the cost of repair amounting to $1000.50.

Under the common law tradition, the doctrine of *caveat emptor* governed the purchase of real estate. The theory underlying *caveat emptor* was that buyers and sellers dealt at arm's length and that if the purchaser sought any warranties, those warranties should be negotiated and incorporated into the written contract. Additionally, purchasers were presumed to have the means and the opportunity to examine the property and judge its qualities for themselves.

Recently, *caveat emptor* has been viewed with disfavor and many jurisdictions including Indiana have adopted the doctrine of implied warranty of habitability for the purchase of a new home from a builder-vendor. In part, this is due to a recognition of the sale of goods concept that a sound price merits a sound article. Humber v. Morton (Tex.1968) 426 S.W.2d 554. In addition, the following rationales have been offered:

    1. caveat emptor encourages unscrupulous, shoddy workmanship,

    2. buyers of mass produced development homes are not on equal footing with builder-vendors,

    3. the purchase of a home is not an everyday transaction so, as a result, most purchasers are inexperienced and must rely on the skill and expertise of the builder-vendor.

See Barnes v. Mac Brown & Co. (1976) 264 Ind. 227, 342 N.E.2d 619; Theis v. Heuer (1972) 264 Ind. 1, 280 N.E.2d 300. In the *Barnes* case, *supra,* our Supreme Court extended the protection of the home builders' implied warranty of habitability to a subsequent purchaser. *See also* Wagner Construction Co. v. Noonan, *supra,* 403 N.E.2d at 1146–47.

Our research, however, has uncovered no Indiana cases expanding this implied warranty concept to the purchaser of a *used* house from a *non* builder-vendor. Those jurisdictions which have been confronted with such factual situations have universally rejected such expansion. The refusal to extend the doctrine is seemingly premised on the idea that in the sale of *used* housing, the vendor usually has no greater expertise in determining the quality of a house than the purchaser.

The extension of the doctrine to purchasers of used homes from non builder-sellers is not totally without support however. Paul Haskell in his article *The Case for an Implied Warranty of Quality in Sales of Real Property*, 53 Geo.L.[J.] 633 (1965) argues persuasively:

> "Most sales of personal property involve new goods. Most sales of real property involve used construction. If the implied warranty is recognized only in the sale of new construction, then the law offers only occasional protection to the purchaser. The typical sale of improved real estate involves a good deal of money; in the case of the home purchase, it usually is the largest single investment the purchaser makes in his lifetime. To conclude that there are no implicit assumptions as to quality when the breadwinner earning 13,500 dollars invests 30,000 dollars in a house is absurd. Any distinction between the purchase of the new house and the purchase of the used house with respect to assumptions as to quality is wholly unrealistic; the only difference is in the degree of expectation.

* * *

> [T]here should be an implied warranty of merchantability in every sale of *used* construction, whether the seller be a merchant in the field of real estate or a nonmerchant, subject to the exclusion of known or discoverable defects. The determination of what constitutes merchantability here also must be left to the judgment of individual courts and juries. It is clear that the problem of merchantability is more complex in the case of used construction than it is in the case of new construction. The purchaser's justifiable expectations are quite different in each instance. In view of the fact that this concerns the contingent liability of the nonmerchant, and the rather uncertain nature of merchantability in the case of used construction, a short period of exposure to potential liability is called for." 53 Geo.L.[J.] at 650–52.

Further, the Supreme Court of Wyoming, in discussing the abandonment of *caveat emptor*, remarked in dicta, "We do not include used housing in our holding but visualize that circumstances may require consideration of some sales as included." Tavares v. Horstman (Wyo.1975) 542 P.2d 1275, 1282. While we too recognize that there may be some situations which necessitate the expansion of the implied warranty of habitability to used housing, we decline to extend the doctrine to the case before us. We are not convinced that a non builder-vendor should bear the risk of latent defects. While the public interest may well be served by placing repair or replacement costs of a new home on the responsible vendor-builder who created the defect and is in a better economic position to bear the cost than the purchaser, these policy considerations are inapplicable where the house is an older one and the seller is not its builder. As for defects *known* to the vendor of an older home at the time of sale, the tort theories of misrepresentation or fraudulent concealment are alternatives open to the unknowing buyer. *E.g.*, Wilhite v. Mays (1976) 140 Ga.App. 816, 232 S.E.2d 141, affirmed, (1977) 239 Ga. 31, 235 S.E.2d 532 (seller of a four year old home was liable for damages where he fraudulently misrepresented the condition of a septic system).

Based on the foregoing analysis, we reverse the judgment of the trial court.

* * *

Notes and Problems

1. Should the implied warranty of quality apply to a builder who constructs an addition to an existing house? *See* VonHoldt v. Barba & Barba Construction, Inc., 175 Ill.2d 426, 222 Ill.Dec. 302, 677 N.E.2d 836 (1997).

2. D, a commercial developer, conveyed an unimproved lot to P. Unknown to either party at the time, the lot had severe drainage problems which rendered it unfit for a sewage disposal system. P sues D, alleging breach of an implied warranty of fitness of the land for residential purposes. What result? *Compare* Hinson v. Jefferson, 287 N.C. 422, 215 S.E.2d 102 (1975) *with* Cook v. Salishan Properties, Inc., 279 Or. 333, 569 P.2d 1033 (1977) *and* Jackson v. River Pines, Inc., 276 S.C. 29, 274 S.E.2d 912 (1981).

3. Should the implied warranty of quality extend to environmental defects in land on which new homes are constructed? *See* Powell, *Builder-Vendor Liability for Environmental Contamination In the Sale of New Residential Property*, 58 Tenn.L.Rev. 231 (1991).

4. As indicated by the *Vetor* decision, courts are reluctant to imply a warranty of quality in the sale of used housing. *See, e.g.,* Haygood v. Burl Pounders Realty, Inc., 571 So.2d 1086 (Ala.1990); *but see* Andreychak v. Lent, 257 N.J.Super. 69, 607 A.2d 1346 (1992) (implied warranty applied to used housing). However, the seller of used housing may be liable for fraudulent misrepresentation of the condition of the premises or even for failure to disclose defects. In this regard, consider the material in the following section.

2. MISREPRESENTATION AND NONDISCLOSURE

Would the Ryans have any recourse against the seller if the seller had known about a structural problem with the wall that collapsed, but did not bring the problem to the Ryans' attention? What if the seller had not mentioned to the Ryans the fact that the seller had be brutally assaulted in the house some time ago?

LYONS v. MCDONALD

Court of Appeals of Indiana, Third District, 1986.
501 N.E.2d 1079.

HOFFMAN, JUDGE.

Defendants-appellants Kenneth and Jo Ann Lyons appeal a judgment entered by the trial court against them in favor of Thomas and Joan McDonald. The court awarded $21,992.11 as compensatory damages and $7,330.70 as punitive damages.

The evidence pertinent to this appeal discloses that in late 1983 the McDonalds purchased a house from the Lyons which the Lyons had been using as a residence. The McDonalds toured the house at least once prior to the sale while Kenneth was present. Thomas asked Kenneth if there were any particular problems with the real estate. Kenneth stated that there were none that he knew of.

In their proposition for the purchase of the house on October 17, 1983, the McDonalds noted that the proposition was "[s]ubject to termite inspection and clearance[,]" and "[i]n the event of termites Seller to treat at his expense." The Lyons obtained a document which stated:

"October 19, 1983

TO WHOM IT MAY CONCERN:

The home at 1103 East Thompson has been treated by this Company for termites.

At this time there is no active infestation."

Despite repeated requests for the clearance by Joan McDonald prior to the closing, the Lyons were unable to present this document at closing because Kenneth had left it in the glove compartment of his truck. Nevertheless, the closing was completed on December 12, 1983.

Thomas had told Kenneth that he planned to remodel the home to turn it into an office. After closing, Kenneth stopped by the house and Thomas explained the intended remodeling. Thomas told Kenneth that one of the first things he planned was to remove a bulkhead between two of the rooms. Kenneth responded that he would not do that and that "[y]ou don't know what you'll run into if you tear that bulkhead out."

On the day the remodeling began, the contractor removed the bulkhead and discovered serious termite damage. Upon thorough examination it was discovered that the entire house, except two rooms added by the Lyons, had extensive structural damage caused by termites. After receiving opinions by several contractors the McDonalds determined that the house would have to be gutted in order to repair the damage. After the termite damage was uncovered the termite clearance dated October 19, 1983 was delivered to the McDonalds.

Later, the McDonalds discovered that Milton Garrison, who owned the house prior to the Lyons' ownership, told Kenneth Lyons that the house had termites and had been treated for termites. Further, the contractor who had supervised remodeling work for the Lyons found extensive termite damage to the house which he showed Kenneth Lyons. Because of the termite damage, additional studs were required before a door could be placed between the existing structure and the room addition which the Lyons were having built. The Lyons did nothing to repair the damage, and instead continued the remodeling work which covered the damage.

At trial, the McDonalds' expert witness, Kermit Gasche, testified that he inspected the house and found extensive damage including studs which crumbled at the touch of a probe. Although the Lyons maintained that they knew of no termites or termite damage, they admitted that they had the house treated for termites yearly. Gasche testified that a house is treated for termites only as a preventive measure prior to construction or for an active infestation.

The trial court awarded a judgment to the McDonalds as noted above. This appeal ensued. On appeal, the Lyons raise several issues for review. As restated and consolidated the [issue] dispositive of the appeal [is]:

> whether sufficient evidence supports the trial court's determination that the Lyons fraudulently misrepresented the condition of the house

* * *

The Lyons' first issue questions the trial court's conclusion that they fraudulently misrepresented the condition of the house. The essential elements of fraud are 1) a material representation of a past or existing fact, 2) the representation is false, 3) the representation is made with knowledge or reckless ignorance of its falsity and 4) the representation causes a detrimental reliance by another. Circumstantial evidence may be used to establish fraud if grounds from which fraud may be reasonably inferred exist. Grissom v. Moran (1972), 154 Ind.App. 419, 427, 290 N.E.2d 119, 123, reh. denied, 154 Ind.App. 419, 292 N.E.2d 627.

In the present case Kenneth made a statement to Thomas that there were no particular problems of which he knew regarding the real estate. Although the Lyons contended at trial that they did not know about termites or termite damage, the evidence demonstrated that Kenneth had been told by the former owner that the house had termites; the contractor performing remodeling work for the Lyons showed Kenneth termite damage which was exposed when limestone was removed from the outside of the house; and the Lyons had the house treated for termites yearly.

The termite damage was a particular problem which was known by Kenneth when he stated that there were no particular problems that he knew of. The statement was a material representation of a past or existing fact which Kenneth knew to be false. Additionally, had Kenneth answered truthfully in all likelihood the McDonalds would not have purchased the house or the purchase price would have reflected the lowered value of the house due to the termite damage. Thus, the McDonalds relied upon the misrepresentation to their detriment. The evidence presented to the trial court established the elements of fraud.

The Lyons assert that the statement, made by Kenneth, was merely "puffing" and did not amount to a material representation. In the case of *Grissom v. Moran, supra,* the purchasers of a motel were allowed to rescind the contract for the sale based upon fraudulent misrepresentations made by the sellers. In response to the purchasers' inquiry as to the condition of the motel, the sellers stated that the facilities "were all in fine working condition." *Grissom, supra,* 290 N.E.2d at 120. When specifically questioned regarding the electrical and sewage systems, the sellers responded that "they were all right." The purchasers began experiencing various problems soon after they took possession of the motel. This Court noted that the general representation that the facilities "were all in fine working condition" and other responses to the more specific questions were material representations of existing facts. *Grissom, supra,* 290 N.E.2d at 123.

The Lyons also claim that as non-builder vendors they should not bear the risk of latent defects, those defects not apparent upon reasonable inspection. In support of their argument, the Lyons make citation to Vetor v. Shockey (1980), Ind.App., 414 N.E.2d 575. In *Vetor, supra,* this Court reversed a judgment for the purchasers which was based upon an implied warranty of habitability. *Vetor, supra,* 414 N.E.2d at 578. There was no showing that the defect was known to the sellers or that any misrepresentation regarding the defect was made by the sellers. It was noted in the decision that:

> "As for defects *known* to the vendor of an older home at the time of sale, the tort theories of misrepresentation or fraudulent concealment are alternatives open to the unknowing buyer." (Citations omitted.) (Original emphasis.)

414 N.E.2d at 577.

Consequently, contrary to the contention by the Lyons, *Vetor, supra,* is not an impediment to the judgment in the present case.

While this Court is not bound by the law of other jurisdictions, a recent decision by the South Carolina Court of Appeals is worthy of note. In May v. Hopkinson (1986), S.C.App., 347 S.E.2d 508, the Court affirmed a judgment against the seller of a home which had moisture and termite damage. The seller cosmetically repaired the damage and then listed the home for sale. The seller represented to the purchasers that the house had no problems except a crack in the kitchen vinyl and a fogged window. A termite inspection report stated that subterranean termites had been found and were treated. Soon after closing the purchasers discovered extensive structural damage. The court found that the misrepresentation established fraud and allowed compensatory and punitive damages to stand. *May, supra,* 347 S.E.2d at 513–514.

As in *May, supra,* and *Grissom, supra,* the general statement as to the condition of the real estate in the present case amounted to a material misrepresentation upon which the McDonalds relied. Sufficient evidence supports the trial court's finding of fraud.

* * *

There being no finding of error, the trial court's judgment is affirmed.

Affirmed.

Question

Would the *Lyons* court have reached the same result if the real estate contract had provided that the purchaser was to take the property "as is?" *See* Brewer v. Brothers, 82 Ohio App.3d 148, 611 N.E.2d 492 (1992); George v. Lumbrazo, 184 A.D.2d 1050, 584 N.Y.S.2d 704 (1992); Prudential Insurance Company of America v. Jefferson Associates, Ltd., 896 S.W.2d 156 (Tex.1995); Annot., *Construction and Effect of Provision in Contract for Sale of Realty by Which Purchaser Agrees to Take Property "As Is" or in Its Existing Condition*, 8 ALR 5th 312 (1992).

JOHNSON v. DAVIS

Supreme Court of Florida, 1985.
480 So.2d 625.

ADKINS, JUSTICE.

* * *

In May of 1982, the Davises entered into a contract to buy for $310,000 the Johnsons' home, which at the time was three years old. The contract required a $5,000 deposit payment, an additional $26,000 deposit payment within five days and a closing by June 21, 1982. The crucial provision of the contract, for the purposes of the case at bar, is Paragraph F which provided:

> F.   *Roof Inspection:* Prior to closing at Buyer's expense, Buyer shall have the right to obtain a written report from a licensed roofer stating that the roof is in a watertight condition. In the event repairs are required either to correct leaks or to replace damage to facia or soffit, seller shall pay for said repairs which shall be performed by a licensed roofing contractor.

The contract further provided for payment to the "prevailing party" of all costs and reasonable fees in any contract litigation.

Before the Davises made the additional $26,000 deposit payment, Mrs. Davis noticed some buckling and peeling plaster around the corner of a window frame in the family room and stains on the ceilings in the family room and kitchen of the home. Upon inquiring, Mrs. Davis was told by Mr. Johnson that the window had had a minor problem that had long since been corrected and that the stains were wallpaper glue and the result of ceiling beams being moved. There is disagreement among the parties as to whether Mr. Johnson also told Mrs. Davis at this time that there had never been any problems with the roof or ceilings. The Davises thereafter paid the remainder of their deposit and the Johnsons vacated the home. Several days later, following a heavy rain, Mrs. Davis entered the home and discovered water "gushing" in from around the window frame, the ceiling of the family room, the light fixtures, the glass doors, and the stove in the kitchen.

Two roofers hired by the Johnsons' broker concluded that for under $1,000 they could "fix" certain leaks in the roof and by doing so make the roof "watertight." Three roofers hired by the Davises found that the roof was inherently defective, that any repairs would be temporary because the roof was "slipping," and that only a new $15,000 roof could be "watertight."

The Davises filed a complaint alleging breach of contract, fraud and misrepresentation, and sought re[s]cission of the contract and return of their deposit. The Johnsons counterclaimed seeking the deposit as liquidated damages.

The trial court entered its final judgment on May 27, 1983. The court made no findings of fact, but awarded the Davises $26,000 plus interest and awarded the Johnsons $5,000 plus interest. Each party was to bear their own attorneys' fees.

The Johnsons appealed and the Davises cross-appealed from the final judgment. The Third District found for the Davises affirming the trial court's return of the majority of the deposit to the Davises ($26,-000), and reversing the award of $5,000 to the Johnsons as well as the court's failure to award the Davises costs and fees. Accordingly, the court remanded with directions to return to the Davises the balance of their deposit and to award them costs and fees.

The trial court included no findings of fact in its order. However, the district court inferred from the record that the trial court refused to accept the Davises' characterization of the roof inspection provision of the contract. The district court noted that if there was a breach, the trial court would have ordered the return of the Davises' entire deposit because there is no way to distinguish the two deposit payments under a breach of contract theory. We agree with this interpretation and further find no error by the trial court in this respect.

The contract contemplated the possibility that the roof may not be watertight at the time of inspection and provided a remedy if it was not in such a condition. The roof inspection provision of the contract did not impose any obligation beyond the seller correcting the leaks and replacing damage to the facia or soffit. The record is devoid of any evidence that the seller refused to make needed repairs to the roof. In fact, the record reflects that the Davises' never even demanded that the areas of leakage be repaired either by way of repair or replacement. Yet the Davises insist that the Johnsons breached the contract justifying re[s]cission. We find this contention to be without merit.

We also agree with the district court's conclusions under a theory of fraud and find that the Johnsons' statements to the Davises regarding the condition of the roof constituted a fraudulent misrepresentation entitling respondents to the return of their $26,000 deposit payment. In the state of Florida, relief for a fraudulent misrepresentation may be granted only when the following elements are present: (1) a false statement concerning a material fact; (2) the representor's knowledge that the representation is false; (3) an intention that the representation induce another to act on it; and, (4) consequent injury by the party acting in reliance on the representation.

The evidence adduced at trial shows that after the buyer and the seller signed the purchase and sales agreement and after receiving the $5,000 initial deposit payment the Johnsons affirmatively repeated to the Davises that there were no problems with the roof. The Johnsons subsequently received the additional $26,000 deposit payment from the Davises. The record reflects that the statement made by the Johnsons was a false representation of material fact, made with knowledge of its falsity, upon which the Davises relied to their detriment as evidenced by the $26,000 paid to the Johnsons.

The doctrine of caveat emptor does not exempt a seller from responsibility for the statements and representations which he makes to induce the buyer to act, when under the circumstances these amount to fraud in the legal sense. To be grounds for relief, the false representations need not have been made at the time of the signing of the purchase and sales agreement in order for the element of reliance to be present. The fact that the false statements as to the quality of the roof were made after the signing of the purchase and sales agreement does not excuse the seller from liability when the misrepresentations were made prior to the execution of the contract by conveyance of the property. It would be contrary to all notions of fairness and justice for this Court to place its stamp of approval on an affirmative misrepresentation by a wrongdoer just because it was made after the signing of the executory contract when all of the necessary elements for actionable fraud are present. Furthermore, the Davises' reliance on the truth of the Johnsons' representation was justified and is supported by this Court's decision in Besett v. Basnett, 389 So.2d 995 (1980), where we held "that a recipient may rely on the truth of a representation, even though its falsity could have been ascertained had he made an investigation, unless he knows the representation to be false or its falsity is obvious to him." *Id.* at 998.

In determining whether a seller of a home has a duty to disclose latent material defects to a buyer, the established tort law distinction between misfeasance and nonfeasance, action and inaction must carefully be analyzed. The highly individualistic philosophy of the earlier common law consistently imposed liability upon the commission of affirmative acts of harm, but shrank from converting the courts into an institution for forcing men to help one another. This distinction is deeply rooted in our case law. Liability for nonfeasance has therefore been slow to receive recognition in the evolution of tort law.

In theory, the difference between misfeasance and nonfeasance, action and inaction is quite simple and obvious; however, in practice it is not always easy to draw the line and determine whether conduct is active or passive. That is, where failure to disclose a material fact is calculated to induce a false belief, the distinction between concealment and affirmative representations is tenuous. Both proceed from the same motives and are attended with the same consequences; both are violative of the principles of fair dealing and good faith; both are calculated to produce the same result; and, in fact, both essentially have the same effect.

Still there exists in much of our case law the old tort notion that there can be no liability for nonfeasance. The courts in some jurisdictions, including Florida, hold that where the parties are dealing at arms's length and the facts lie equally open to both parties, with equal opportunity of examination, mere nondisclosure does not constitute a fraudulent concealment. The Fourth District affirmed that rule of law in Banks v. Salina, 413 So.2d 851 (Fla. 4th DCA 1982), and found that although the sellers had sold a home without disclosing the presence of a defective roof and swimming pool of which the sellers had knowledge, "[i]n Florida, there is no duty to disclose when parties are dealing at arms length." *Id.* at 852.

These unappetizing cases are not in tune with the times and do not conform with current notions of justice, equity and fair dealing. One should not be able to stand behind the impervious shield of caveat emptor and take advantage of another's ignorance. Our courts have taken great strides since the days when the judicial emphasis was on rigid rules and ancient precedents. Modern concepts of justice and fair dealing have given our courts the opportunity and latitude to change legal precepts in order to conform to society's needs. Thus, the tendency of the more recent cases has been to restrict rather than extend the doctrine of caveat emptor. The law appears to be working toward the ultimate conclusion that full disclosure of all material facts must be made whenever elementary fair conduct demands it.

The harness placed on the doctrine of caveat emptor in a number of other jurisdictions has resulted in the seller of a home being liable for failing to disclose material defects of which he is aware. This philosophy was succinctly expressed in Lingsch v. Savage, 213 Cal.App.2d 729, 29 Cal.Rptr. 201 (1963):

> It is now settled in California that where the seller knows of facts materially affecting the value or desirability of the property which are known or accessible only to him and also knows that such facts are not known to or within the reach of the diligent attention and observation of the buyer, the seller is under a duty to disclose them to the buyer.

In Posner v. Davis, 76 Ill.App.3d 638, 32 Ill.Dec. 186, 395 N.E.2d 133 (1979), buyers brought an action alleging that the sellers of a home fraudulently concealed certain defects in the home which included a leaking roof and basement flooding. Relying on *Lingsch,* the court concluded that the sellers knew of and failed to disclose latent material defects and thus were liable for fraudulent concealment. *Id.* 32 Ill.Dec. at 190, 395 N.E.2d at 137. Numerous other jurisdictions have followed this view in formulating law involving the sale of homes. *See* Flakus v. Schug, 213 Neb. 491, 329 N.W.2d 859 (1983) (basement flooding); Thacker v. Tyree, 297 S.E.2d 885 (W.Va.1982) (cracked walls and foundation problems); Maguire v. Masino, 325 So.2d 844 (La.Ct.App.1975) (termite infestation); Weintraub v. Krobatsch, 64 N.J. 445, 317 A.2d 68 (1974) (roach infestation); Cohen v. Vivian, 141 Colo. 443, 349 P.2d 366 (1960) (soil defect).

We are of the opinion, in view of the reasoning and results in *Lingsch, Posner* and the aforementioned cases decided in other jurisdictions, that the same philosophy regarding the sale of homes should also be the law in the state of Florida. Accordingly, we hold that where the seller of a home knows of facts materially affecting the value of the property which are not readily observable and are not known to the buyer, the seller is under a duty to disclose them to the buyer. This duty is equally applicable to all forms of real property, new and used.

In the case at bar, the evidence shows that the Johnsons knew of and failed to disclose that there had been problems with the roof of the house. Mr. Johnson admitted during his testimony that the Johnsons were aware of roof problems prior to entering into the contract of sale and receiving the $5,000 deposit payment. Thus, we agree with the district court and find that the Johnsons' fraudulent concealment also entitles the Davises to the return of the $5,000 deposit payment plus interest. We further find that the Davises should be awarded costs and fees.

The decision of the Third District Court of Appeals is hereby approved.

It is so ordered.

BOYD, CHIEF JUSTICE, dissenting.

I respectfully but strongly dissent to the Court's expansion of the duties of sellers of real property. This ruling will give rise to a flood of litigation and will facilitate unjust outcomes in many cases. If, as a matter of public policy, the well settled law of this state on this question should be changed, the change should come from the legislature. Moreover, I do not find sufficient evidence in the record to justify rescission or a finding of fraud even under present law. I would quash the decision of the district court of appeal.

My review of the record reveals that there is not adequate evidence from which the trier of fact could have found any of the following crucial facts: (a) that at the time Johnson told Mrs. Davis about the previous leaks that had been repaired, he knew that there was a defect in the roof; (b) that at that time or the time of the execution of the contract, there were in fact any defects in the roof; (c) that it was not possible to repair the roof to "watertight" condition before closing.

* * *

Homeowners who attempt to sell their houses are typically in no better position to measure the quality, value, or desirability of their houses than are the prospective purchasers with whom such owners come into contact. Based on this and related considerations, the law of Florida has long been that a seller of real property with improvements is under no duty to disclose all material facts, in the absence of a fiduciary relationship, to a buyer who has an equal opportunity to learn all material information and is not prevented by the seller from doing so. *See, e.g.,* Ramel v. Chasebrook Construction Co., 135 So.2d 876 (Fla. 2d DCA 1961). This rule provides sufficient protection against overreaching by sellers, as the wise and progressive ruling in the *Ramel* case shows. The *Ramel* decision is not the least bit "unappetizing."

The majority opinion sets forth the elements of actionable fraud as they are stated in Huffstetler v. Our Home Life Ins. Co., 67 Fla. 324, 65 So. 1 (1914). Those elements were not established by sufficient evidence in this case. There was no competent, substantial evidence to show that Mr. Johnson made a false statement knowing it to be false. There was absolutely no evidence that the statement was made with the intention of causing Mrs. Davis to do anything; she had already contracted to purchase the house. There was no competent evidence that Mrs. Davis in fact relied on Mr. Johnson's statement or was influenced by it to do anything. And the only detriment or injury that can be found is that, when the Davises subsequently decided not to complete the transaction, they stood to forfeit the additional $26,000 deposit paid in addition to the original $5,000. The Davises had already agreed to pay the additional deposit at the time of the conversation. They had to pay the additional deposit if they wanted to preserve their rights under the contract. They chose to do so. Mr. Johnson's statements, even if we believe Mrs. Davis' version of them rather than Mr. Johnson's, did not constitute the kind of representation upon which a buyer's reliance is justified.

I do not agree with the Court's belief that the distinction between nondisclosure and affirmative statement is weak or nonexistent. It is a distinction that we should take special care to emphasize and preserve. Imposition of liability for seller's nondisclosure of the condition of improvements to real property is the first step toward making the seller a guarantor of the good condition of the property. Ultimately this trend will significantly burden the alienability of property because sellers will have to worry about the possibility of catastrophic post-sale judgments for damages sought to pay for repairs. The trend will proceed somewhat as follows. At first, the cause of action will require proof of actual knowledge of the undisclosed defect on the part of the seller. But in many cases the courts will allow it to be shown by circumstantial evidence. Then a rule of constructive knowledge will develop based on the reasoning that if the seller did not know of the defect, he should have known about it before attempting to sell the property. Thus the burden of inspection will shift from the buyer to the seller. Ultimately the courts will be in the position of imposing implied warranties and guaranties on all sellers of real property.

Although as described in the majority opinion this change in the law sounds progressive, high-minded, and idealistic, it is in reality completely unnecessary. Prudent purchasers inspect property, with expert advice if necessary, before they agree to buy. Prudent lenders require inspections before agreeing to provide purchase money. Initial deposits of earnest money can be made with the agreement to purchase being conditional upon the favorable results of expert inspections. It is significant that in the present case the major portion of the purchase price was to be financed by the Johnsons who were to hold a mortgage on the property. If they had been knowingly trying to get rid of what they knew to be a defectively constructed house, it is unlikely that they would have been willing to lend $200,000 with the house in question as their only security.

I would quash the decision of the district court of appeal. This case should be remanded for findings by the trial court based on the evidence already heard. The action for rescission based on fraud should be dismissed. The only issue is whether the Johnsons were in compliance with the contract at the time of the breach by the Davises. Resolving this issue requires a finding of whether the roof could have been put in watertight condition by spot repairs or by re-roofing and in either case whether the sellers were willing to fulfill their obligation by paying for the necessary work. If so, the Johnsons should keep the entire $31,000 deposit.

Notes, Problems and Questions

1.   How does a seller determine which facts materially affect the value of the property? *See* Rose, *Crystals and Mud in Property Law*, 40 Stan.L.Rev. 577, 581–582 (1988).

2.   In states that require a seller to disclose, should this duty apply to the sale of commercial as well as residential property? *See* Haskell Company v. Lane Company, Ltd., 612 So.2d 669 (Fla.App.1993); Futura Realty v. Lone Star Building Centers (Eastern), Inc., 578 So.2d 363 (Fla.App.1991); Brown, *Real Property: 1991 Survey of Florida Law*, 16 Nova L.Rev. 399, 413–415 (1991).

3.   Many states require the seller of residential property to deliver a written disclosure statement describing the premises to the buyer before the transfer of title. *See, e.g.,* Cal.Civ.Code §§ 1102–1102.14 (West Supp.1998); Wis.Stat. Ann. §§ 709.01–709.08 (West Supp. 1997); *see also* Washburn, *Residential Real Estate Condition Disclosure Legislation*, 44 DePaul L.Rev. 381 (1995). *See generally* Weinberger, *Let the Buyer Be Well Informed?— Doubting the Demise of Caveat Emptor*, 55 Md.L.Rev. 387 (1996) (noting that courts increasingly require sellers of residences to disclose material defects, asserting that state disclosure laws serve to limit scope of disclosure, and expressing concern that such statutes increase transaction costs of real estate conveyances).

4.   Should a seller of residential property have a duty to divulge information about conditions existing in the neighborhood that may affect the value of the property? *See* Strawn v. Canuso, 140 N.J. 43, 657 A.2d 420 (1995); Comment, *For Sale: Two–Bedroom Home With Spacious Kitchen, Walk–In Closet, and Pervert Next Door*, 27 Seton Hall L.Rev. 668 (1997); *see also* Nev.Rev.Stat.Ann. § 40.770(2) (Michie Supp.1997) (reprinted on page 666).

REED v. KING

Court of Appeal of California, Third District, 1983.
145 Cal.App.3d 261, 193 Cal.Rptr. 130.

BLEASE, ASSOCIATE JUSTICE.

In the sale of a house, must the seller disclose it was the site of a multiple murder? Dorris Reed purchased a house from Robert King. Neither King nor his real estate agents (the other named defendants) told Reed that a woman and her four children were murdered there ten years earlier. However, it seems "truth will come to light; murder cannot be hid long." (Shakespeare, Merchant of Venice, Act II, Scene II.) Reed learned of the gruesome episode from a neighbor after the sale. She sues seeking rescission and damages. King and the real estate agent defendants successfully demurred to her first amended complaint for failure to state a cause of action. Reed appeals the ensuing judgment of dismissal. We will reverse the judgment.

FACTS

We take all issuable facts pled in Reed's complaint as true. (See 3 Witkin, Cal.Procedure (2d ed. 1971) Pleading, § 800.) King and his real estate agent knew about the murders and knew the event materially affected the market value of the house when they listed it for sale. They represented to Reed the premises were in good condition and fit for an "elderly lady" living alone. They did not disclose the fact of the murders. At some point King asked a neighbor not to inform Reed of that event. Nonetheless, after Reed moved in neighbors informed her no one was interested in purchasing the house because of the stigma. Reed paid $76,000, but the house is only worth $65,000 because of its past.

The trial court sustained the demurrers to the complaint on the ground it did not state a cause of action. The court concluded a cause of action could only be stated "if the subject property, by reason of the prior circumstances, were *presently* the object of community notoriety * * *." (Original italics.) Reed declined the offer of leave to amend.

DISCUSSION

Does Reed's pleading state a cause of action? Concealed within this question is the nettlesome problem of the duty of disclosure of blemishes on real property which are not physical defects or legal impairments to use.

* * *

In general, a seller of real property has a duty to disclose: "where the seller knows of facts *materially* affecting the value or desirability of the property which are known or accessible only to him and also knows that such facts are not known to, or within the reach of the diligent attention and observation of the buyer, the seller is under a duty to disclose them to the buyer. [Emphasis added]" (Lingsch v. Savage, 213

Cal.App.2d at p. 735, 29 Cal.Rptr. 201.) This broad statement of duty has led one commentator to conclude: "The ancient maxim *caveat emptor* ('let the buyer beware.') has little or no application to California real estate transactions." (1 Miller and Starr, Current Law of Cal.Real Estate (rev. ed. 1975) § 1:80.)

Whether information "is of sufficient materiality to affect the value or desirability of the property * * * depends on the facts of the particular case." (*Lingsch,* 213 Cal.App.2d at p. 737, 29 Cal.Rptr. 201.) Materiality "is a question of law, and is part of the concept of right to rely or justifiable reliance." (3 Witkin, Cal.Procedure (2d ed. 1971) Pleading, § 578, p. 2217.) Accordingly, the term is essentially a label affixed to a normative conclusion. Three considerations bear on this legal conclusion: the gravity of the harm inflicted by non-disclosure; the fairness of imposing a duty of discovery on the buyer as an alternative to compelling disclosure, and its impact on the stability of contracts if rescission is permitted.

Numerous cases have found non-disclosure of physical defects and legal impediments to use of real property are material. However, to our knowledge, no prior real estate sale case has faced an issue of non-disclosure of the kind presented here. Should this variety of ill-repute be required to be disclosed? Is this a circumstance where "non-disclosure of the fact amounts to a failure to act in good faith and in accordance with reasonable standards of fair dealing[?]" (Rest.2d Contracts, § 161, subd. (b).)

The paramount argument against an affirmative conclusion is it permits the camel's nose of unrestrained irrationality admission to the tent. If such an "irrational" consideration is permitted as a basis of rescission the stability of all conveyances will be seriously undermined. Any fact that might disquiet the enjoyment of some segment of the buying public may be seized upon by a disgruntled purchaser to void a bargain. In our view, keeping this genie in the bottle is not as difficult a task as these arguments assume. We do not view a decision allowing Reed to survive a demurrer in these unusual circumstances as endorsing the materiality of facts predicating peripheral, insubstantial, or fancied harms.

The murder of innocents is highly unusual in its potential for so disturbing buyers they may be unable to reside in a home where it has occurred. This fact may foreseeably deprive a buyer of the intended use of the purchase. Murder is not such a common occurrence that *buyers* should be charged with anticipating and discovering this disquieting possibility. Accordingly, the fact is not one for which a duty of inquiry and discovery can sensibly be imposed upon the buyer.

Reed alleges the fact of the murders has a quantifiable effect on the market value of the premises. We cannot say this allegation is inherently wrong and, in the pleading posture of the case, we assume it to be true. If information known or accessible only to the seller has a significant and measureable effort on market value and, as is alleged here, the seller is aware of this effect, we see no principled basis for making the duty to disclose turn upon the character of the information. Physical usefulness is not and never has been the sole criterion of valuation. Stamp collections and gold speculation would be insane activities if utilitarian considerations were the sole measure of value.

Reputation and history can have a significant effect on the value of realty. "George Washington slept here" is worth something, however physically inconsequential that consideration may be. Ill-repute or "bad will" conversely may depress the value of property. Failure to disclose such a negative fact where it will have a for[e]seeably depressing effect on income expected to be generated by a business is tortious. Some cases have held that *unreasonable* fears of the potential buying public that a gas or oil pipeline may rupture may depress the market value of land and entitle the owner to incremental compensation in eminent domain. (See Annot., Eminent Domain: Elements and Measure of Compensation for Oil or Gas Pipeline Through Private Property (1954) 38 A.L.R.2d 788, 801–804.)

Whether Reed will be able to prove her allegation the decade-old multiple murder has a significant effect on market value we cannot determine. If she is able to do so by competent evidence she is entitled to a favorable ruling on the issues of materiality and duty to disclose. Her demonstration of objective tangible harm would still the concern that permitting her to go forward will open the floodgates to rescission on subjective and idiosyncratic grounds.

A more troublesome question would arise if a buyer in similar circumstances were unable to plead or establish a significant and quantifiable effect on market value. However, this question is not presented in the posture of this case. Reed has not alleged the fact of the murders has rendered the premises useless to her as a residence. As currently pled, the gravamen of her case is pecuniary harm. We decline to speculate on the abstract alternative.

The judgment is reversed.

Note

Several state legislatures, including California, have enacted statutes that provide that the seller and the seller's real estate agent need not disclose certain facts that might have an adverse psychological impact on prospective purchasers. These measures vary in their particulars. Consider the following Nevada statute.

    1.   In any sale of real property, the fact that the property is or has been:

        (a) The site of a homicide, suicide or death by any other cause, except a death that results from a condition of the property, or the site of any crime punishable as a felony; or

        (b) Occupied by a person exposed to the human immunodeficiency virus or suffering from acquired immune deficiency syndrome or any other disease that is not known to be transmitted through occupancy of the property, is not material to the transaction.

2. In any sale of real property, the fact that a sex offender, as defined in NRS 179D.400, resides or is expected to reside in the community is not material to the transaction, and the seller or any agent of the seller does not have a duty to disclose such a fact to a buyer or any agent of a buyer.

3. A seller or any agent of the seller is not liable to the buyer in any action at law or in equity because of the failure to disclose any fact described in subsection 1 or 2 that is not material to the transaction.

4. Except as otherwise provided in an agreement between the buyer and his agent, an agent of the buyer is not liable to the buyer in any action at law or in equity because of the failure to disclose any fact described in subsection 1 or 2 that is not material to the transaction.

Nev.Rev.Stat.Ann. § 40.770 (Michie Supp.1997). *See also* Cal.Civ.Code § 1710.2 (West 1998) (no disclosure required about death of occupant on premises over three years before offer to purchase/rent or that occupant had or died of AIDS).

Are such statutes appropriate? *See* Brown & Thurlow, *Buyers Beware: Statutes Shield Real Estate Brokers and Sellers Who Do Not Disclose That Properties Are Psychologically Tainted,* 49 Okla. L. Rev. 625 (1996); McEvoy, *Caveat Emptor Redux: "Psychologically Impacted" Property Statutes,* 18 Western St.U.L.Rev. 579 (1991); Murray, *AIDS, Ghosts, Murder: Must Real Estate Brokers and Sellers Disclose?,* 27 Wake Forest L.Rev. 689 (1992).

STAMBOVSKY v. ACKLEY

Supreme Court of New York, Appellate Division, 1991.
169 A.D.2d 254, 572 N.Y.S.2d 672.

RUBIN, JUSTICE.

Plaintiff, to his horror, discovered that the house he had recently contracted to purchase was widely reputed to be possessed by poltergeists, reportedly seen by defendant seller and members of her family on numerous occasions over the last nine years. Plaintiff promptly commenced this action seeking rescission of the contract of sale. Supreme Court reluctantly dismissed the complaint, holding that plaintiff has no remedy at law in this jurisdiction.

The unusual facts of this case, as disclosed by the record, clearly warrant a grant of equitable relief to the buyer who, as a resident of New York City, cannot be expected to have any familiarity with the folklore of the Village of Nyack. Not being a "local," plaintiff could not readily learn that the home he had contracted to purchase is haunted. Whether the source of the spectral apparitions seen by defendant seller are parapsychic or psychogenic, having reported their presence in both a national publication ("Readers' Digest") and the local press (in 1977 and 1982, respectively), defendant is estopped to deny their existence and, as a matter of law, the house is haunted. More to the point, however, no divination is required to conclude that it is defendant's promotional efforts in publicizing her close encounters with these spirits which fostered the home's reputation in the community. In 1989, the house was included in a five-home walking tour of Nyack and described in a November 27th newspaper article as "a riverfront Victorian (with ghost)." The impact of the reputation thus created goes to the very essence of the bargain between the parties, greatly impairing both the value of the property and its potential for resale. The extent of this impairment may be presumed for the purpose of reviewing the disposition of this motion to dismiss the cause of action for rescission (Harris v. City of New York, 147 A.D.2d 186, 188–189, 542 N.Y.S.2d 550) and represents merely an issue of fact for resolution at trial.

While I agree with Supreme Court that the real estate broker, as agent for the seller, is under no duty to disclose to a potential buyer the phantasmal reputation of the premises and that, in his pursuit of a legal remedy for fraudulent misrepresentation against the seller, plaintiff hasn't a ghost of a chance, I am nevertheless moved by the spirit of equity to allow the buyer to seek rescission of the contract of sale and recovery of his downpayment. New York law fails to recognize any remedy for damages incurred as a result of the seller's mere silence, applying instead the strict rule of caveat emptor. Therefore, the theoretical basis for granting relief, even under the extraordinary facts of this case, is elusive if not ephemeral.

"Pity me not but lend thy serious hearing to what I shall unfold" (William Shakespeare, Hamlet, Act I, Scene V [Ghost]).

From the perspective of a person in the position of plaintiff herein, a very practical problem arises with respect to the discovery of a paranormal phenomenon: "Who you gonna' call?" as the title song to the movie "Ghostbusters" asks. Applying the strict rule of caveat emptor to a contract involving a house possessed by poltergeists conjures up visions of a psychic or medium routinely accompanying the structural engineer and Terminix man on an inspection of every home subject to a contract of sale. It portends that the prudent attorney will establish an escrow account lest the subject of the transaction come back to haunt him and his client—or pray that his malpractice insurance coverage extends to supernatural disasters. In the interest of avoiding such untenable consequences, the notion that a haunting is a condition which can and should be ascertained upon reasonable inspection of the premises is a hobgoblin which should be exorcised from the body of legal precedent and laid quietly to rest.

It has been suggested by a leading authority that the ancient rule which holds that mere non-disclosure does not constitute actionable misrepresentation "finds proper application in cases where the fact undisclosed is patent, or the plaintiff has equal opportunities for obtaining information which he may be expected to utilize, or the defendant has no reason to think that he is acting under any misapprehension"

(Prosser, Law of Torts § 106, at 696 [4th ed., 1971]). However, with respect to transactions in real estate, New York adheres to the doctrine of caveat emptor and imposes no duty upon the vendor to disclose any information concerning the premises unless there is a confidential or fiduciary relationship between the parties or some conduct on the part of the seller which constitutes "active concealment". Normally, some affirmative misrepresentation or partial disclosure is required to impose upon the seller a duty to communicate undisclosed conditions affecting the premises.

Caveat emptor is not so all-encompassing a doctrine of common law as to render every act of non-disclosure immune from redress, whether legal or equitable. * * * Common law is not moribund. *Ex facto jus oritur* (law arises out of facts). Where fairness and common sense dictate that an exception should be created, the evolution of the law should not be stifled by rigid application of a legal maxim.

The doctrine of caveat emptor requires that a buyer act prudently to assess the fitness and value of his purchase and operates to bar the purchaser who fails to exercise due care from seeking the equitable remedy of rescission. For the purposes of the instant motion to dismiss the action * * *, plaintiff is entitled to every favorable inference which may reasonably be drawn from the pleadings, specifically, in this instance, that he met his obligation to conduct an inspection of the premises and a search of available public records with respect to title. It should be apparent, however, that the most meticulous inspection and the search would not reveal the presence of poltergeists at the premises or unearth the property's ghoulish reputation in the community. Therefore, there is no sound policy reason to deny plaintiff relief for failing to discover a state of affairs which the most prudent purchaser would not be expected to even contemplate (*see,* Da Silva v. Musso, 53 N.Y.2d 543, 551, 444 N.Y.S.2d 50, 428 N.E.2d 382).

The case law in this jurisdiction dealing with the duty of a vendor of real property to disclose information to the buyer is distinguishable from the matter under review. The most salient distinction is that existing cases invariably deal with the physical condition of the premises, defects in title, liens against the property, expenses or income and other factors affecting its operation. No case has been brought to this court's attention in which the property value was impaired as the result of the reputation created by information disseminated to the public by the seller (or, for that matter, as a result of possession by poltergeists).

Where a condition which has been created by the seller materially impairs the value of the contract and is peculiarly within the knowledge of the seller or unlikely to be discovered by a prudent purchaser exercising due care with respect to the subject transaction, nondisclosure constitutes a basis for rescission as a matter of equity. Any other outcome places upon the buyer not merely the obligation to exercise care in his purchase but rather to be omniscient with respect to any fact which may affect the bargain. No practical purpose is served by imposing such a burden upon a purchaser. To the contrary, it encourages predatory business practice and offends the principle that equity will suffer no wrong to be without a remedy.

Defendant's contention that the contract of sale, particularly the merger or "as is" clause, bars recovery of the buyer's deposit is unavailing. Even an express disclaimer will not be given effect where the facts are peculiarly within the knowledge of the party invoking it. Moreover, a fair reading of the merger clause reveals that it expressly disclaims only representations made with respect to the physical condition of the premises and merely makes general reference to representations concerning "any other matter or things affecting or relating to the aforesaid premises". As broad as this language may be, a reasonable interpretation is that its effect is limited to tangible or physical matters and does not extend to paranormal phenomena. Finally, if the language of the contract is to be construed as broadly as defendant urges to encompass the presence of poltergeists in the house, it cannot be said that she has delivered the premises "vacant" in accordance with her obligation under the provisions of the contract rider.

* * *

In the case at bar, defendant seller deliberately fostered the public belief that her home was possessed. Having undertaken to inform the public at large, to whom she has no legal relationship, about the supernatural occurrences on her property, she may be said to owe no less a duty to her contract vendee. It has been remarked that the occasional modern cases which permit a seller to take unfair advantage of a buyer's ignorance so long as he is not actively misled are "singularly unappetizing" (Prosser, Law of Torts § 106, at 696 [4th ed. 1971]). Where, as here, the seller not only takes unfair advantage of the buyer's ignorance but has created and perpetuated a condition about which he is unlikely to even inquire, enforcement of the contract (in whole or in part) is offensive to the court's sense of equity. Application of the remedy of rescission, within the bounds of the narrow exception to the doctrine of caveat emptor set forth herein, is entirely appropriate to relieve the unwitting purchaser from the consequences of a most unnatural bargain.

* * *

Judgment, Supreme Court, New York County (Edward H. Lehner, J.), entered on April 9, 1990, modified, on the law and the facts and in the exercise of discretion, and the first cause of action seeking rescission of the contract reinstated, without costs.

Smith, Justice (dissenting).

I would affirm the dismissal of the complaint by the motion court.

* * *

The parties herein were represented by counsel and dealt at arm's length. This is evidenced by the contract of sale which, *inter alia*, contained various riders and a specific provision that all prior understandings and agreements between the parties were merged into the contract, that the contract completely expressed their full agreement and that neither had relied upon any statement by anyone else not set forth in the contract. There is no allegation that defendants, by some specific act, other than the failure to speak, deceived the plaintiff. Nevertheless, a cause of action may be sufficiently stated where there is a confidential or fiduciary relationship creating a duty to disclose and there was a failure to disclose a material fact, calculated to induce a false belief. However, plaintiff herein has not alleged and there is no basis for concluding that a confidential or fiduciary relationship existed between these parties to an arm's length transaction such as to give rise to a duty to disclose. In addition, there is no allegation that defendants thwarted plaintiff's efforts to fulfill his responsibilities fixed by the doctrine of caveat emptor.

Finally, if the doctrine of caveat emptor is to be discarded, it should be for a reason more substantive than a poltergeist. The existence of a poltergeist is no more binding upon the defendants than it is upon this court.

* * *

3. ENVIRONMENTAL ISSUES

Environmental law has increasingly affected real estate transactions. Following are summaries of significant areas of impact.

a. CERCLA

The Comprehensive Environmental Response, Compensation and Liability Act of 1980 (CERCLA) is designed to promote the cleanup of hazardous waste sites. CERCLA provides that the current owner or operator of a hazardous waste site is strictly liable for the costs incurred in remedying environmental violations regardless of whether that individual or entity owned the property at the time the contamination occurred. Moreover, courts have generally favored a broad construction of CERCLA liability and narrowly interpreted statutory defenses. *See* Comment, *CERCLA Liability, Where It Is and Where It Should Not Be Going: The Possibility of Liability Release for Environmentally Beneficial Land Transfers,* 23 Envtl.L. 295 (1993).

Since cleanup costs can be prohibitively expensive, prospective purchasers of commercial property must exercise caution to minimize their exposure to hazardous waste liability. It is becoming a routine practice for purchasers to require an environmental assessment to discover previous uses of the property and possible contamination. Such an environmental audit often includes an on-site inspection of the property. Contracts for the sale of commercial property commonly permit the purchaser to terminate the agreement if the purchaser is dissatisfied with the results of the survey. The purchaser also may seek to have the seller share in the expense of preparing the audit and may attempt to secure an indemnification clause to allocate any future cleanup costs to the seller. The desire of purchasers of commercial property to avoid CERCLA liability markedly increases the delay and transaction costs associated with land transfers. Further, the fear of exposure to environmental risk may thwart commercial deals and render parcels of land unmarketable. *See* Carlisle & Johnson, *The Impact of CERCLA on Real Estate Transactions*, 4 S.C. Envtl. L.J. 129 (1995); Note, *The Impact of CERCLA on Real Estate Transactions: What Every Owner, Operator, Buyer, Lender, * * * Should Know*, 6 B.Y.U.Pub.L. 365 (1992); Note, *A Buyer's Catalogue of Prepurchase Precautions to Minimize CERCLA Liability in Commercial Real Estate Transactions*, 15 U.Puget Sound L.Rev. 469 (1992).

CERCLA problems are not restricted to commercial property. The purchaser of a residence, who neither caused nor knew about contamination, may face the risk of liability for hazardous waste. Some commentators have suggested that environmental audits soon may become the norm for residential sales. *See* Boggs, *Real Estate Environmental Damage, The Innocent Residential Purchaser, and Federal Superfund Liability*, 22 Envtl.L. 977 (1992).

b. *Lead–Based Paint*

In 1996, the Environmental Protection Agency and the Department of Housing and Urban Development issued regulations mandated by the Residential Lead–Based Paint Hazard Reduction Act of 1992 (42 U.S.C.A. §§ 4851–4856 (West 1996)). Pursuant to § 4852d of the Act, these regulations require that, with certain exceptions, prescribed lead-based paint disclosure standards be met prior to the sale or rental of pre–1978 housing. *See* Henderson, *Start Spreading the News: EPA and HUD Lead–Based Paint Disclosure Regulations*, 25 Real Est. L.J. 244 (1997); *see also* Fensler & Bernstein, *Lead Poisoning at Home: New Federal Disclosure Duties*, 26 Real Est. L.J. 7 (1997); Rechtschaffen, *The Lead Poisoning Challenge: An Approach for California and Other States*, 21 Harv. Envtl. L. Rev. 387 (1997).

c. *Radon*

A related concern is the presence of radon, a natural radioactive gas, in homes in certain sections of the country. The legal issues posed by radon contamination remain largely unsettled. Contracts for the sale of residences in affected areas sometimes require radon testing and permit the purchaser to cancel the contract if unsafe levels of radon are found. There also have been legislative proposals to mandate radon testing prior to the sale or lease of single-family residences. In addition, sellers, brokers, and builders potentially may be subject to liability for failure to warn purchasers of possible radon problems. *See* King, *The Legal Implications of Residential Radon Contamination: The First Decade*, 18 Wm.

& Mary J.Envtl.L. 107 (1993); Note, *Radon in New Jersey: Is It Time for Mandatory Testing?*, 15 Seton Hall Legis.J. 171 (1991); Note, *Radon Litigation: An Overview of Homeowners' Potential Causes of Action*, 20 Cumb.L.Rev. 825 (1990).

d. State Disclosure Laws

Several states have enacted legislation that requires grantors of sites exposed to hazardous substances to furnish grantees a written disclosure statement with respect to environmental defects. Such statutes generally are not applicable to residential transfers. *See* Andrew & DuSold, *Seller Beware: The Indiana Responsible Property Transfer Law*, 24 Ind.L.Rev. 761 (1991); Inderbitzin, *Taking the Burden Off the Buyer: A Survey of Hazardous Waste Disclosure Statutes*, 1 Envtl. Law. 513 (1995).

Chapter 5

ATTRIBUTES OF OWNERSHIP
OF REAL PROPERTY

Hypothetical Situation—Number 5

A few weeks after the Ryans moved into their home in Rolling Hills, Jill Ryan asked you to meet with the Board of Directors of the Rolling Hills Homeowners' Association about serving as its legal counsel. You agreed to do so.

At the meeting, you discovered that the Association is a non-profit corporation formed by the developer of Rolling Hills. It owns the recreational facilities and green areas in the subdivision, including a swimming pool, tennis courts, and a two-acre unimproved parcel located along the rear boundary of the subdivision. The purchaser of a lot in Rolling Hills automatically becomes a member of the Association and is liable for an annual assessment to maintain the recreational facilities and green areas.

You were retained as legal counsel by the Association. Shortly thereafter, J.A. "Jim" Tyler, president of the Association, contacted you stating he would send you a list of topics that the Association planned to consider over the next few months. He asked that you be prepared to comment on the legal aspects of each topic.

Later in the week you received the following list of discussion topics from Mr. Tyler:

1. Keeping salespersons and solicitors off the premises.

2. Approving prospective homeowners.

3. Regulating noise and other undesirable activity by homeowners.

4. Creating a fishing pond by digging a hole next to a small stream that runs just inside the rear boundary of the property.

5. Insuring that homeowners with solar energy systems receive sunlight undisturbed by buildings and trees.

A. RIGHT TO EXCLUDE

STATE v. SHACK

Supreme Court of New Jersey, 1971.
58 N.J. 297, 277 A.2d 369.

WEINTRAUB, C.J.

Defendants entered upon private property to aid migrant farmworkers employed and housed there. Having refused to depart upon the demand of the owner, defendants were charged with violating N.J.S.A. 2A:170-31 which provides that "[a]ny person who trespasses on any lands * * * after being forbidden so to trespass by the owner * * * is a disorderly person and shall be punished by a fine of not more than $50." Defendants were convicted in the Municipal Court of Deerfield Township and again on appeal in the County Court of Cumberland County on a trial *de novo*. R. 3:23-8(a). We certified their further appeal before argument in the Appellate Division.

* * *

Complainant, Tedesco, a farmer, employs migrant workers for his seasonal needs. As part of their compensation, these workers are housed at a camp on his property.

Defendant Tejeras is a field worker for the Farm Workers Division of the Southwest Citizens Organization for Poverty Elimination, known by the acronym SCOPE, a nonprofit corporation funded by the Office of Economic Opportunity pursuant to an act of Congress, 42 U.S.C.A. §§ 2861–2864. The role of SCOPE includes providing for the "health services of the migrant farm worker."

Defendant Shack is a staff attorney with the Farm Workers Division of Camden Regional Legal Services, Inc., known as "CRLS," also a nonprofit corporation funded by the Office of Economic Opportunity pursuant to an act of Congress, 42 U.S.C.A. § 2809(a)(3). The mission of CRLS includes legal advice and representation for these workers.

Differences had developed between Tedesco and these defendants prior to the events which led to the trespass charges now before us. Hence when defendant Tejeras wanted to go upon Tedesco's farm to find a migrant worker who needed medical aid for the removal of 28 sutures, he called upon defendant Shack for his help with respect to the legalities involved. Shack, too, had a mission to perform on Tedesco's farm; he wanted to discuss a legal problem with another migrant worker there employed and housed. Defendants arranged to go to the farm together. Shack carried literature to inform the migrant farmworkers of the assistance available to them under federal statutes, but no mention seems to have been made of that literature when Shack was later confronted by Tedesco.

Defendants entered upon Tedesco's property and as they neared the camp site where the farmworkers were housed, they were confronted by Tedesco who inquired of their purpose. Tejeras and Shack stated their missions. In response, Tedesco offered to find the injured worker, and as to the worker who needed legal advice, Tedesco also offered to locate the man but insisted that the consultation would have to take place in Tedesco's office and in his presence. Defendants declined, saying they had the right to see the men in the privacy of their living quarters and without Tedesco's supervision. Tedesco thereupon summoned a State Trooper who, however, refused to remove defendants except upon Tedesco's written complaint. Tedesco then executed the formal complaints charging violations of the trespass statute.

I.

The constitutionality of the trespass statute, as applied here, is challenged on several scores.

It is urged that the First Amendment rights of the defendants and of the migrant farmworkers were thereby offended. * * *

Defendants also maintain that the application of the trespass statute to them is barred by the Supremacy Clause of the United States Constitution, Art. VI, cl. 2, and this on the premise that the application of the trespass statute would defeat the purpose of the federal statutes, under which SCOPE and CRLS are funded, to reach and aid the migrant farmworker.

* * *

These constitutional claims are not established by any definitive holding. We think it unnecessary to explore their validity. The reason is that we are satisfied that under our State law the ownership of real property does not include the right to bar access to governmental services available to migrant workers and hence there was no trespass within the meaning of the penal statute.

* * *

II.

Property rights serve human values. They are recognized to that end, and are limited by it. Title to real property cannot include dominion over the destiny of persons the owner permits to come upon the premises. Their well-being must remain the paramount concern of a system of law. Indeed the needs of the occupants may be so imperative and their strength so weak, that the law will deny the occupants the power to contract away what is deemed essential to their health, welfare, or dignity.

Here we are concerned with a highly disadvantaged segment of our society. We are told that every year farmworkers and their families numbering more than one million leave their home areas to fill the seasonal demand for farm labor in the United States.

* * *

The migrant farmworkers are a community within but apart from the local scene. They are rootless and isolated. Although the need for their labors is evident, they are unorganized and without economic or political power. It is their plight alone that summoned government to their aid. * * * It is in this framework that we must decide whether the camp operator's rights in his lands may stand between the migrant workers and those who would aid them. The key to that aid is communication. Since the migrant workers are outside the mainstream of the communities in which they are housed and are unaware of their rights and opportunities and of the services available to them, they can be reached only by positive efforts tailored to that end.

* * *

A man's right in his real property of course is not absolute. It was a maxim of the common law that one should so use his property as not to injure the rights of others. Although hardly a precise solvent of actual controversies, the maxim does express the inevitable proposition that rights are relative and there must be an accommodation when they meet. Hence it has long been true that necessity, private or public, may justify entry upon the lands of another.

The subject is not static. As pointed out in 5 Powell, Real Property (Rohan 1970) ¶ 45, pp. 493–494, while society will protect the owner in his permissible interests in land, yet

" * * * [S]uch an owner must expect to find the absoluteness of his property rights curtailed by the organs of society, for the promotion of the best interests of others for whom these organs also operate as protective agencies. The necessity for such curtailments is greater in a modern industrialized and urbanized society than it was in the relatively simple American society of fifty, 100, or 200 years ago. The current balance between individualism and dominance of the social interest depends not only upon political and social ideologies, but also upon the physical and social facts of the time and place under discussion."

Professor Powell added in ¶ 46, pp. 494–496:

"As one looks back along the historic road traversed by the law of land in England and in America, one sees a change from the viewpoint that he who owns may do as he pleases with what he owns, to a position which hesitatingly embodies an ingredient of stewardship; which grudgingly, but steadily, broadens the recognized scope of social interests in the utilization of things."

* * *

This process involves not only the accommodation between the right of the owner and the interests of the general public in his use of his property, but involves also an accommodation between the right of the owner and the right of individuals who are parties with him in consensual transactions relating to the use of the property. Accordingly substantial alterations have been made as between a landlord and his tenant.

The argument in this case understandably included the question whether the migrant worker should be deemed to be a tenant and thus entitled to the tenant's right to receive visitors, or whether his residence on the employer's property should be deemed to be merely incidental and in aid of his employment, and hence to involve no possessory interest in the realty.

* * *

We see no profit in trying to decide upon a conventional category and then forcing the present subject into it. That approach would be artificial and distorting. The quest is for a fair adjustment of the competing needs of the parties, in the light of the realities of the relationship between the migrant worker and the operator of the housing facility.

Thus approaching the case, we find it unthinkable that the farmer-employer can assert a right to isolate the migrant worker in any respect significant for the workers' well-being. The farmer, of course, is entitled to pursue his farming activities without interference, and this defendants readily concede. But we see no legitimate need for a right in the farmer to deny the worker the opportunity for aid available from federal, State, or local services, or from recognized charitable groups seeking to assist him. Hence representatives of these agencies and organizations may enter upon the premises to seek out the worker at his living quarters. So, too, the migrant worker must be allowed to receive visitors there of his own choice, so long as there is no behavior hurtful to others, and members of the press may not be denied reasonable access to workers who do not object to seeing them.

It is not our purpose to open the employer's premises to the general public if in fact the employer himself has not done so. We do not say, for example, that solicitors or peddlers of all kinds may enter on their own; we may assume for the present that the employer may regulate their entry or bar them, at least if the employer's purpose is not to gain a commercial advantage for himself or if the regulation does not deprive the migrant worker of practical access to things he needs.

And we are mindful of the employer's interest in his own and in his employees' security. Hence he may reasonably require a visitor to identify himself, and also to state his general purpose if the migrant worker has not already informed him that the visitor is expected. But the employer may not deny the worker his privacy or interfere with his opportunity to live with dignity and to enjoy associations customary among our citizens. These rights are too fundamental to be denied on the basis of an interest in real property and too fragile to be left to the unequal bargaining strength of the parties.

It follows that defendants here invaded no possessory right of the farmer-employer. Their conduct was therefore beyond the reach of the trespass statute. The judgments are accordingly reversed and the matters remanded to the County Court with directions to enter judgments of acquittal.

Notes and Problems

1.   Exclusivity has long been deemed an essential element of private property. William Blackstone observed: "There is nothing which so generally strikes the imagination, and engages the affections of mankind, as the right of property; or that sole and despotic dominion which one man claims and exercises over the external things of the world, in total exclusion of the right of any other individual in the universe." 2 Blackstone, Commentaries on the Laws of England 2 (1766). The United States Supreme Court has held that the right to exclude is "universally held to be a fundamental element of the property right." Kaiser Aetna v. United States, 444 U.S. 164, 179–180 (1979).

2.   A much litigated question is whether a privately-owned shopping center has the right to exclude persons who picket or hand out leaflets on shopping center property. In Lloyd Corp. v. Tanner, 407 U.S. 551, 564 (1972), the United States Supreme Court upheld a shopping center ban on persons distributing anti-war leaflets on the ground that the leafleteers' actions "had no relation to any purpose for which the center was built." The Court also noted that the ban did not effectively deprive the leafleteers of any suitable location on which to exercise their First Amendment rights. Nearby public property provided an acceptable alternative site for distributing leaflets. Four years later, the Supreme Court in Hudgens v. NLRB, 424 U.S. 507 (1976), concluded that pickets could be banned from shopping centers when they were employees of a warehouse maintained by a store owner but located away from the center.

3.   Federal courts have found no First Amendment right of access to a migrant farm labor camp and a rest home. See Illinois Migrant Council v. Campbell Soup Co., 574 F.2d 374 (7th Cir.1978); Cape Cod Nursing Home Council v. Rambling Rose Rest Home, 667 F.2d 238 (1st Cir.1981).

4.   State courts have divided sharply over the right of persons to engage in political solicitation or distribution of literature in privately-owned shopping centers. Many courts have held that their state constitutions do not confer the right to engage in expressive activities on private property, and have permitted the owners to exclude such persons from the premises. See, e.g., Cologne v. Westfarms Associates, 192 Conn. 48, 469 A.2d 1201 (1984); Woodland v. Michigan Citizens Lobby, 423 Mich. 188, 378 N.W.2d 337 (1985); SHAD Alliance v. Smith Haven Mall, 66 N.Y.2d 496, 498 N.Y.S.2d 99, 488 N.E.2d 1211 (1985); Charleston Joint Venture v. McPherson, 308 S.C. 145, 417 S.E.2d 544 (1992); Western Pennsylvania Socialist Workers 1982 Campaign v. Connecticut General Life Insurance Company, 512 Pa. 23, 515 A.2d 1331 (1986); Jacobs v. Major, 139 Wis.2d 492, 407 N.W.2d 832 (1987). Some state courts, however, have broadly construed state constitutional

guarantees to permit communicative activities on privately-owned property. The California Supreme Court held that the California constitution guaranteed access to shopping centers by students soliciting signatures for a political petition. Robins v. Pruneyard Shopping Center, 23 Cal.3d 899, 153 Cal.Rptr. 854, 592 P.2d 341 (1979). The United States Supreme Court determined that this decision did not violate the shopping center owner's property rights under the Fifth and Fourteenth Amendments of the U.S. Constitution. PruneYard Shopping Center v. Robins, 447 U.S. 74 (1980). *See also* Batchelder v. Allied Stores International, Inc., 388 Mass. 83, 445 N.E.2d 590 (1983); New Jersey Coalition Against War in the Middle East v. J.M.B. Realty Corporation, 138 N.J. 326, 650 A.2d 757 (1994), *cert. denied* 516 U.S. 812 (1995); Lloyd Corp. v. Whiffen, 89 Or.App. 629, 750 P.2d 1157 (1988); Alderwood Associates v. Washington Environmental Council, 96 Wn.2d 230, 635 P.2d 108 (1981). *See generally* Berger, *"Pruneyard" Revisited: Political Activity on Private Lands,* 66 N.Y.U.L.Rev. 633 (1991).

5. Two state courts have determined that private universities violated the state constitution by prohibiting the distribution of political literature on their campuses without permission. State v. Schmid, 84 N.J. 535, 423 A.2d 615 (1980), *appeal dismissed as moot sub nom.* Princeton University v. Schmid, 455 U.S. 100 (1982); Commonwealth v. Tate, 495 Pa. 158, 432 A.2d 1382 (1981).

6. Can the Rolling Hills Homeowners' Association legally exclude all solicitors and salespersons from the subdivision? *See* Breard v. Alexandria, 341 U.S. 622 (1951).

7. In Uston v. Resorts International Hotel, Inc., 89 N.J. 163, 445 A.2d 370 (1982), a property owner (Resorts) excluded a professional blackjack player (Uston) from the blackjack table in its gambling casino because he used a card counting system. Resorts maintained that it had the right to exclude any person for any reason. Rejecting this position, the court ruled that property owners who open their property to the public may not unreasonably exclude persons. Since Uston had not disrupted the functioning of Resorts' casino, he was entitled to usual access. *But see* Brooks v. Chicago Downs Association, Inc., 791 F.2d 512 (7th Cir.1986) (rejecting *Uston* and recognizing race track operator's common law right to exclude handicappers); *Mosher v. Cook United, Inc.,* page 384 (finding supermarket properly excluded individual shopping for food cooperative). *See generally* Note, *Uston v. Resorts International Hotel: An Unwarranted Intrusion on the Common Law Right of Exclusion,* 20 Cal.W.L.Rev. 511 (1984).

B. FREEDOM OF ALIENATION

1. RESTRAINTS ON ALIENATION

CASEY v. CASEY

Supreme Court of Arkansas, 1985.
287 Ark. 395, 700 S.W.2d 46.

Holt, Chief Justice.

This case involves the interpretation of a restriction placed on a devise to appellee which, if violated, would shift the interest in the inheritance to appellants. The trial court held the restriction was invalid as an unreasonable restraint on alienation and too vague to be enforced and that appellee thus held the property in fee simple absolute. Our jurisdiction is pursuant to Sup.Ct.R. 29(1)(p).

Donald Casey, appellee, is the son of the testator, Fred Casey. The testator left $50.00 to each of six of his seven children and left the rest of his estate to appellee. In 1974, shortly before he died, the testator added a codicil which placed a restriction on appellee's inheritance. The appellee filed a petition to remove the cloud from the title in the Pope County Chancery Court on October 2, 1984 in which he sought to have the restriction declared void. The petition was challenged by appellants, who would take the property upon a violation of the restriction.

The testator's codicil stated in pertinent part:

FIRST: * * * Karen Kim Casey is the daughter of Donald J. Casey. It is my will that Karen Kim Casey shall never own or possess as a tenant, nor be on as a guest for more than one week per each calendar year any of the real estate which I have devised to my son, Donald J. Casey.

SECOND: It is my intent to create a defeasible estate in Donald J. Casey in the nature of, and conditional limitation over, or executory devise, with the fact of termination depending upon the ownership or possession of Karen Kim Casey as set out above. It is my will that in the event Karen Kim Casey should ever own any part of the land which I heretofore bequeathed to Donald J. Casey or in the event she should ever possess said land as a tenant, or in the event she should ever be a guest on said land or any of it for more than one week of each calendar year, that the estate of Donald J. Casey immediately terminate as to that part of my real estate which I have devised and bequeathed to him and that said real estate shall immediately become the property of Sam Casey in fee simple absolute and to his heirs and assigns forever. It is further my will to create a vested estate in Sam Casey and his heirs in fee simple absolute in the nature of the interest created by a springing or shifting use.

We agree with the trial court that the restriction is invalid. The trial court based its ruling in part on a finding that the phrase "never own or possess as a tenant" was vague, in that it could be read two ways, depending on whether a comma is inserted after "own". We see no vagueness or ambiguity, particularly when reading the will as a whole, but we do agree with the chancellor and find that the restriction is an unreasonable restraint on alienation.

A direct restraint is "a provision which, by its terms, prohibits or penalizes the exercise of the power of alienation." Broach v. City of Hampton, 283 Ark. 496, 677 S.W.2d 851 (1984); L. Simes, *Law of Future Interests* 237 (1966). There are three types of direct restraints: disabling restraints, forfeiture restraints and promissory restraints. This case involves a forfeiture restraint, which "exists when, by the terms of an instrument of transfer, the estate will be subject to forfeiture on alienation or will be terminated." *Broach* supra; Simes supra. "In general, the courts adhere to the rule that all forfeiture restraints on the alienation of a legal fee simple interest in land are void. This rule operates to give full effect to the conveyance or devise except that the condition or limitation with respect to alienation is eliminated." *Broach* supra; Simes supra.

Restraints on alienation may be upheld if they are a reasonable means of accomplishing a legal and useful purpose. The Restatement of Property § 406 provides:

> The restraint on the alienation of a legal possessory estate in fee simple which is, or but for the restraint would be, indefeasible is valid if, and only if,
>
> (a) the restraint is a promissory restraint or a forfeiture restraint, and
>
> (b) the restraint is qualified so as to permit alienation to some though not all possible alienees, and
>
> (c) the restraint is reasonable under the circumstances, and
>
> (d) if the restraint is a forfeiture restraint, the requirements of the rule against perpetuities are satisfied.

4 Restatement of Property § 406 (1944).

> Comment a to § 406 further states:

> To uphold restraints on the alienation of such estates it must appear that the objective sought to be accomplished by the imposition of the restraint is of sufficient social importance to outweigh the evils which flow from interfering with the power of alienation or that the curtailment of the power of alienation is so slight that no social danger is involved.

This rule applies even when the restraint on alienation is slight.

All the circumstances of the conveyance should be considered in determining the reasonableness of the restraint. When present, the following factors support the conclusion that a restraint is unreasonable:

1. the restraint is capricious;

2. the restraint is imposed for spite or malice;

3. the one imposing the restraint has no interest in land that is benefited by the enforcement of the restraint;

4. the restraint is unlimited in duration;

5. the number of persons to whom alienation is prohibited is large.

Restatement § 406 comment i.

Applying these and other factors, we conclude that this restraint is unreasonable. The restraint did not protect any interest the testator had in the land while he was living, and only worked to keep his granddaughter off the land after his death. The duration of the restraint is limited to the lifetime of his granddaughter, who is 28, so it will likely remain for the entire period that appellee holds the land.

* * *

Here, there is no worthwhile purpose evident in this restraint; it appears to be capricious, and imposed for spite or malice. At trial, no one could explain why the testator harbored such animosity toward his granddaughter.

Though the restraint is limited directly to only one person, the appellee's daughter would be a natural heir of appellee, which makes the restraint more significant. Further, to find that a restraint is reasonable on this factor alone would lead to difficult and arbitrary line-drawing in determining when a limited number of restricted transferees is too many.

This restraint also had indirect effects which go beyond the direct restriction. "An *indirect* restraint on alienation, arises when an attempt is made to accomplish some purpose other than the restraint of alienability, but with the incidental result that the instrument, if valid, would restrain practical alienability." L. Simes and A. Smith, *The Law of Future Interests,* § 1112 (2d ed. 1956). This litigation was prompted by the suspension of royalties to appellee for a well drilled on the land by Essex Exploration Company because of this cloud on the title. Thus, Essex's present posture is a clear example of a present and continuing restraint on practical alienability resulting from such a restriction.

For public policy reasons, some cases have held that provisions by which the acquisition or retention of property interests was made to depend on the separation of parent and minor child were illegal conditions. "A broader objection has appeared on occasion against any provision which tends to disrupt or interfere with family relations." *American Law of Property,* Vol. VI, § 27.19 (1974). Though this restraint does not require total separation of father and daughter, its obvious effect, if not purpose, is to interfere with family relations.

For these reasons, the restriction is invalid.

Affirmed.

Notes

1. As noted in *Casey,* the Restatement of Property classifies restraints on alienation as disabling, forfeiture, and promissory. A disabling restraint renders void any conveyance by the grantee. A forfeiture restraint terminates the grantee's interest if the grantee tries to convey away the property. A promissory restraint imposes contractual liability on one who conveys in violation of an agreement. *See* Restatement of Property § 404 (1944).

2. You have encountered the policy against unreasonable restraints on alienation in earlier cases. Reconsider the decisions in *Rowe v. Great Atlantic & Pacific Tea Co.* on page 99 and *Julian v. Christopher* on page 105 (each involving lease covenant limiting tenant's right to assign).

SMITH v. MITCHELL

Supreme Court of North Carolina, 1980.
301 N.C. 58, 269 S.E.2d 608.

CARLTON, JUSTICE.

I.

The record reveals that in 1967 W. O. Smith, Jr., and his wife Roberta K. Smith placed certain restrictive covenants expressly running with the land on a plat of real property they owned in Caswell County. In addition to the usual covenants limiting development on the plat to residential dwellings of a certain size and environmental soundness, the Smiths' duly recorded restrictive covenants included Article XIV. which provided:

> If any future owner of lands herein described shall desire to sell the lands owned by him, he shall offer the parties of the first part the option to repurchase said property at a price no higher than the lowest price he is willing to accept from any other purchaser. Parties of the first part agree to exercise said option or to reject same in writing within 14 days of said offer. This covenant shall be binding on the parties of the first part and their heirs, successors, administrators, and executors or assigns for as long as W. Osmond Smith, Jr. shall live and for 20 years from the date of his death unless sooner rescinded.

In 1973, plaintiff, W. Osmond Smith III, succeeded W. O. Smith, Jr. and Roberta K. Smith in interest to the land as their heir, successor and assignee. Plaintiff deeded Lot No. 16 in the plat to defendants Mitchell on 26 September 1974. The Mitchells' deed was made subject to all recorded restrictive covenants, including Article XIV., quoted above. In July 1975, defendants Mitchell deeded Lot No. 16 to defendants Barber without first offering the land to plaintiff as they were required to do under the terms of Article XIV. Defendants Mitchell did this despite plaintiff's notification to them that he stood ready, willing, and able to purchase the lot.

Plaintiff thereafter sued for specific performance, or, in the alternative, for damages of some $2,500.00 for breach of the restrictive covenant. Defendant families each counter-claimed for damages in excess of $5,000.00 alleging breach of certain warranties in their deeds and also alleging that plaintiff's lawsuit had clouded their title. Both sides moved for summary judgment. The trial court granted summary judgment for defendants, stating that Article XIV. was an unlawful restraint on the right to freely alienate property, was against public policy and was therefore void. Plaintiff appealed to the Court of Appeals. That court affirmed the trial court.

We granted plaintiff's petition for discretionary review 4 January 1980.

The Court of Appeals held "squarely" that "*any* restriction on a landowner's right to freely alienate his property, even though limited as to time and certain as to price, is void as an invalid restraint on alienation." 44 N.C.App. at 476, 261 S.E.2d at 233. We disagree. Certain such restrictions on alienability, if defined as preemptive rights and if carefully limited in duration and price, are not void *per se* and will be enforced if reasonable. Moreover, we find the specific restrictive covenant before us here to be a reasonable preemptive right which is not void. We therefore reverse the Court of Appeals.

II.

A preemptive right "requires that, before the property conveyed may be sold to another party, it must first be offered to the conveyor or his heirs, or to some specially designated person." Sometimes termed a "right of first refusal," preemptive provisions, while analogous to options, are technically distinguishable. An option creates in its holder the power to compel sale of land. A preemptive provision, on the other hand, creates in its holder only the right to buy land before other parties if the seller decides to convey it. Preemptive provisions may be contained in leases, in contracts, or, as is the case here, in restrictive covenants contained in deeds or recorded in chains of title.

The defendants and the Court of Appeals relied on Hardy v. Galloway, 111 N.C. 519, 15 S.E. 890 (1892) as authority for the proposition that *any* preemptive right is an impermissible restraint on alienation in North Carolina. We believe defendants and the Court of Appeals have misapplied *Hardy v. Galloway* for the following reasons.

First, the policy considerations behind the common law prohibition of restraints on alienation have never absolutely forbidden all such restraints. Thus the law has long allowed such indirect restraints as conveying a fee subject to a possibility of reverter or to a condition subsequent. Furthermore, while the rationale underlying the common law prohibition of direct restraints on alienation has been traced to the necessity of maintaining a society controlled primarily by its living members and the desirability of facilitating the utilization of wealth, the policy absolutely favoring alienability has always conflicted with another common law tenet that one who has property should be able to convey it subject to whatever condition he or she may desire to impose on the conveyance.

Faced with this tension, the law has evolved in such a way that some direct restraints on alienation are permissible where the goal justifies the limit on the freedom to alienate, or where the interference with alienation in a particular case is so negligible that the major policies furthered by freedom of alienation are not materially hampered. Thus the general rule is that a restraint on alienation which provides that the property cannot be alienated, a disabling restraint, is *per se* invalid, while restraints which provide only that someone's estate may be forfeited or be terminated if he alienates, or that provides damages must be paid if he alienates, may be upheld if reasonable.

As applied in other jurisdictions, these principles have frequently led courts to uphold preemptive rights when those rights were reasonable. *See, e.g.*, Annot., 40 A.L.R.3d 920 (1971 & Supp.1979) and cases cited therein. Their reasoning appears grounded upon the conviction that any interference of a preemptive right with freedom of alienation is so negligible that the major policies of utilization of wealth and economy of land control are not hampered. Indeed, some courts have gone so far as to state that the preemptive right does not limit alienability but enhances it, as the seller is provided two buyers instead of one. Watergate Corporation v. Reagan, 321 So.2d 133, 136 (Fla.App.1975). Other courts have reasoned that the primary purpose of a preemptive right is not to *prevent* an owner from alienating property but to enable a grantor to reacquire it. It seems clear, then, that the minimal interference with alienability presented by a preemptive right does little violence to the primary reason for prohibiting restraints on alienation in the first place, and should not be *per se* void.

Secondly, the reasons courts uphold the nearest analog to preemptive rights, the option, are equally applicable to preemptive provisions. Options have long been upheld as accepted commercial devices to aid in the disposition of property. * * *

By analogy here, the preemptive provision in the deed is an integral part of the bargained-for consideration in the sale of the land to defendants. Just as the commercial device of the option is upheld, if it is reasonable, so too the provisions of a preemptive right should be upheld if reasonable, particularly here where the preemptive right appears to be part of a commercial exchange, bargained for at arm's length.

Thirdly, the preemptive right is a useful tool for creating planned and orderly development, again analogous to similar devices upheld by courts of this State. As plaintiff's intestates attempted here, landowners and developers frequently try to make their land more attractive and desirable to purchasers by establishing a protected residential community free from nonconforming housing and non-residential uses. Settled law in this jurisdiction upholds such restrictive covenants, insuring privately planned development, when those covenants do not materially impair the beneficial enjoyment of the land or violate the public good. A preemptive covenant in a deed is simply one more way of protecting an area by providing that the original planner has some continuing control over his creation. To hold such a provision void *per se* is an unnecessary limiting of the right of a developer and is in contradiction to a general trend to uphold restrictive covenants running with the land if those covenants are reasonable.[1]

Viewed against this framework, defendants' insistence that *Hardy v. Galloway, supra* prohibits *any* restriction on alienability in this jurisdic-

---

1. Generally, however, in this jurisdiction restrictive covenants are strictly construed. We do not believe such a construction necessarily indicates judicial disfavor over the concept of restrictive covenants, but is merely an attempt to prevent future litigation over expanding definitions of specific restrictions.

tion is misguided. *Hardy v. Galloway* involved a preemptive provision which provided that grantors were to have the right of first refusal if their grantees ever decided to reconvey the land. If the grantees failed to allow the grantor this "option," the grantees' deed was "null and void." 111 N.C. at 520, 15 S.E. at 890.

In striking this provision as void, the Court in *Hardy v. Galloway* emphasized that the preemptive right included neither a statement as to the duration of the right nor a method for calculating the price of exercising it. Nowhere did the Court state that *any* restraint on alienation was prohibited. Nowhere did it state that *any* preemptive provision in a deed was void as an impermissible restraint on alienation.

Indeed, decisions of this Court subsequent to *Hardy v. Galloway* indicate that the holding there is authority only when voiding *unreasonable* restraints on alienation.

* * *

The only time, to our knowledge, that this Court reviewed a preemptive right limited as to price and duration, it did not, out of hand, void the provision, but remanded the case to add a necessary third party to the action. *See* Story v. Walcott, 240 N.C. 622, 83 S.E.2d 498 (1954). The inference is clear and we so hold that certain preemptive rights, if reasonable, may be upheld; *Hardy v. Galloway* stands only for the proposition that preemptive provisions which are unreasonable are void as imposing impermissible restraints on alienation.

III.

The question remains whether the preemptive right before us, while not *per se* void, is nevertheless an unreasonable restraint on alienation.

Hardy v. Galloway, supra, makes clear that two primary considerations dictate the reasonableness or unreasonableness of a preemptive right: the duration of the right and the provisions it makes for determining the price of exercising the right.

In *Hardy*, the preemptive provision contained neither a method for determining price of the land nor a time limit on the right to exercise the first refusal. Such vagueness was fatal, the Court held.

The general rule is that as long as the price provision in a preemptive right provides that the price shall be determined either by the market place or by the seller's desire to sell, a preemptive right is reasonable if its duration does not violate the rule against perpetuities. Restatement of the Law of Property § 413. *But see American Law of Property* § 26.66 [1952] suggesting neither the rule against perpetuities, nor apparently any time limit, should apply despite considerable authority *contra.*

While some courts have not imposed the Restatement's rule against perpetuities limit, and have only stated that the duration of a preemptive right must be for a reasonable time, or have said nothing about time, most generally agree there must be some limit on time, and all agree that reasonableness in pricing includes some way of linking the price to the fair market value of the land or to the price the seller is willing to take from third parties.

We believe the better rule is to limit the duration of the right to a period within the rule against perpetuities and thus avoid lengthy litigation over what is or is not a reasonable time within the facts of any given case. We further agree with the authorities that a reasonable price provision in a preemptive right is one which somehow links the price to the fair market value of the land, or to the price the seller is willing to accept from third parties.

Viewed against these requirements, the terms of the preemptive right *sub judice* are reasonable. The provisions of Article XIV. expressly provide that the preemptive right here shall last the lifetime of the grantor, W. O. Smith, Jr., plus *twenty* years. This is well within the rule against perpetuities requirement that a property interest shall vest, if at all, within a life-in-being plus *twenty-one* years.

* * *

In like manner, the provisions of Article XIV. clearly reflect a price tied to the fair market price of the land, or the price that the seller is willing to accept from third parties. Here the grantor provided that the price the grantor or his successor was to pay upon exercise of the right was "a price no higher than the lowest price [grantee] is willing to accept from any other purchaser." This provision is clearly reasonable and imposes no undue restraint upon defendants' ability to alienate their land.

Defendants vigorously argue however that upholding both preemptive rights in general and the reasonableness of this particular preemptive right denies them the right to give their land as a gift or devise. We believe defendants are misstating the case. By its very terms, the preemptive right is exercisable only when and if the seller decides to *sell*, not give or devise his land. Defendants continue to have the unhampered right to give or devise.

The preemptive clause before us, therefore, is not void *per se* nor is it an unreasonable restraint on alienation. Summary judgment for the defendants was improperly granted.

Accordingly, we reverse the decision of the Court of Appeals and remand this case to that court to remand to the trial court for further proceedings in accordance with this opinion.

Because of the analogy between preemptive rights and options to purchase land, on remand we note this case will be controlled by the usual rules in this jurisdiction pertaining to specific performance. These include the ability of the preemptive right holder to enforce that preemptive right against subsequent purchasers for value who are charged with notice of the right in the recorded chain of title, Chandler v. Cameron, 229 N.C. 62, 47 S.E.2d 528 (1948), provided there is no equitable matter precluding this ability.

Reversed and remanded.

Problems and Questions

1. Suppose a covenant, recorded at the time the Rolling Hills subdivision was created, provides that a homeowner who wants to sell must give the Rolling Hills Homeowners' Association a right of first refusal to purchase the property at a price established by impartial appraisal. The covenant further states that if the Association does not exercise its right within 60 days, the property may be sold on the open market. Advise the Association of the validity of this covenant. Could a condominium owners' association or a cooperative corporation enforce a similar provision? *See* Browder, *Restraints on the Alienation of Condominium Units (The Right of First Refusal),* 1970 U.Ill.L.F. 231; Di Lorenzo, *Restraints on Alienation in a Condominium Context: An Evaluation and Theory for Decision Making,* 24 Real Prop., Prob. & Tr.J. 403 (1989); Gale v. York Center Community Cooperative, Inc., 21 Ill.2d 86, 171 N.E.2d 30 (1960).

2. What result if the preemptive price were fixed in the provision creating the right? *See* Lawson v. Redmoor Corp., 37 Wn.App. 351, 679 P.2d 972 (1984); Miller, *Fixed Price Preemptive Rights in California: The Quality of Mercer is Strained,* 31 Hastings L.J. 617 (1980).

2. OPEN HOUSING

SHELLEY v. KRAEMER

Supreme Court of the United States, 1948.
334 U.S. 1.

Mr. Chief Justice Vinson delivered the opinion of the Court.

These cases present for our consideration questions relating to the validity of court enforcement of private agreements, generally described as restrictive covenants, which have as their purpose the exclusion of persons of designated race or color from the ownership or occupancy of real property. Basic constitutional issues of obvious importance have been raised.

The first of these cases comes to this Court on certiorari to the Supreme Court of Missouri. On February 16, 1911, thirty out of a total of thirty-nine owners of property fronting both sides of Labadie Avenue between Taylor Avenue and Cora Avenue in the city of St. Louis, signed an agreement, which was subsequently recorded, providing in part:

" * * * the said property is hereby restricted to the use and occupancy for the term of Fifty (50) years from this date, so that it shall be a condition all the time and whether recited and referred to as [sic] not in subsequent conveyances and shall attach to the land, as a condition precedent to the sale of the same, that hereafter no part of said property or any portion thereof shall be, for said term of Fifty years, occupied by any person not of the Caucasian race, it being intended hereby to restrict the use of said property for said period of time against the occupancy as owners or tenants of any portion of said property for resident or other purpose by people of the Negro or Mongolian Race."

The entire district described in the agreement included fifty-seven parcels of land. The thirty owners who signed the agreement held title to forty-seven parcels, including the particular parcel involved in this case. At the time the agreement was signed, five of the parcels in the district were owned by Negroes.

* * *

On August 11, 1945, pursuant to a contract of sale, petitioners Shelley, who are Negroes, for valuable consideration received from one Fitzgerald a warranty deed to the parcel in question. The trial court found that petitioners had no actual knowledge of the restrictive agreement at the time of the purchase.

On October 9, 1945, respondents, as owners of other property subject to the terms of the restrictive covenant, brought suit in the Circuit Court of the city of St. Louis praying that petitioners Shelley be restrained from taking possession of the property and that judgment be entered divesting title out of petitioners Shelley and revesting title in the immediate grantor or in such other person as the court should direct. The trial court denied the requested relief. * * *

The Supreme Court of Missouri sitting *en banc* reversed and directed the trial court to grant the relief for which respondents had prayed. That court held the agreement effective and concluded that enforcement of its provisions violated no rights guaranteed to petitioners by the Federal Constitution. At the time the court rendered its decision, petitioners were occupying the property in question.

The second of the cases under consideration comes to this Court from the Supreme Court of Michigan. The circumstances presented do not differ materially from the Missouri case. In June, 1934, one Ferguson and his wife, who then owned the property located in the city of Detroit which is involved in this case, executed a contract providing in part:

> "This property shall not be used or occupied by any person or persons except those of the Caucasian race.

> "It is further agreed that this restriction shall not be effective unless at least eighty percent of the property fronting on both sides of the street in the block where our land is located is subjected to this or a similar restriction."

The agreement provided that the restrictions were to remain in effect until January 1, 1960. The contract was subsequently recorded; and similar agreements were executed with respect to eighty percent of the lots in the block in which the property in question is situated.

By deed dated November 30, 1944, petitioners, who were found by the trial court to be Negroes, acquired title to the property and thereupon entered into its occupancy. On January 30, 1945, respondents, as owners of property subject to the terms of the restrictive agreement, brought suit against petitioners in the Circuit Court of Wayne County. After a hearing, the court entered a decree directing petitioners to move from the property within ninety days. Petitioners were further enjoined and restrained from using or occupying the premises in the future. On appeal, the Supreme Court of Michigan affirmed, deciding adversely to petitioners' contentions that they had been denied rights protected by the Fourteenth Amendment.

* * *

[P]etitioners urge that they have been denied the equal protection of the laws, deprived of property without due process of law, and have been denied privileges and immunities of citizens of the United States. We pass to a consideration of those issues.

I.

Whether the equal protection clause of the Fourteenth Amendment inhibits judicial enforcement by state courts of restrictive covenants based on race or color is a question which this Court has not heretofore been called upon to consider.

* * *

It is well, at the outset, to scrutinize the terms of the restrictive agreements involved in these cases. In the Missouri case, the covenant declares that no part of the affected property shall be [355 Mo. 814, 198 S.W.2d 681] "occupied by any person not of the Caucasian race, it being intended hereby to restrict the use of said property * * * against the occupancy as owners or tenants of any portion of said property for resident or other purpose by people of the Negro or Mongolian Race." Not only does the restriction seek to proscribe use and occupancy of the affected properties by members of the excluded class, but as construed by the Missouri courts, the agreement requires that title of any person who uses his property in violation of the restriction shall be divested. The restriction of the covenant in the Michigan case seeks to bar occupancy by persons of the excluded class. It provides that [316 Mich. 614, 25 N.W.2d 642] "This property shall not be used or occupied by any person or persons except those of the Caucasian race."

It should be observed that these covenants do not seek to proscribe any particular use of the affected properties. Use of the properties for residential occupancy, as such, is not forbidden. The restrictions of these agreements, rather, are directed toward a designated class of persons and seek to determine who may and who may not own or make use of the properties for residential purposes. The excluded class is defined wholly in terms of race or color; "simply that and nothing more."[1]

It cannot be doubted that among the civil rights intended to be protected from discriminatory state action by the Fourteenth Amendment are the rights to acquire, enjoy, own and dispose of property.

---

1. Buchanan v. Warley, 1917, 245 U.S. 60, 73.

Equality in the enjoyment of property rights was regarded by the framers of that Amendment as an essential pre-condition to the realization of other basic civil rights and liberties which the Amendment was intended to guarantee. Thus, § 1978 of the Revised Statutes, derived from § 1 of the Civil Rights Act of 1866 which was enacted by Congress while the Fourteenth Amendment was also under consideration, provides:

> "All citizens of the United States shall have the same right, in every State and Territory, as is enjoyed by white citizens thereof to inherit, purchase, lease, sell, hold, and convey real and personal property."

This Court has given specific recognition to the same principle. Buchanan v. Warley, 1917, 245 U.S. 60.

It is likewise clear that restrictions on the right of occupancy of the sort sought to be created by the private agreements in these cases could not be squared with the requirements of the Fourteenth Amendment if imposed by state statute or local ordinance. We do not understand respondents to urge the contrary. In the case of Buchanan v. Warley, supra, a unanimous Court declared unconstitutional the provisions of a city ordinance which denied to colored persons the right to occupy houses in blocks in which the greater number of houses were occupied by white persons, and imposed similar restrictions on white persons with respect to blocks in which the greater number of houses were occupied by colored persons. During the course of the opinion in that case, this Court stated: "The Fourteenth Amendment and these statutes enacted in furtherance of its purpose operate to qualify and entitle a colored man to acquire property without state legislation discriminating against him solely because of color."

In Harmon v. Tyler, 1927, 273 U.S. 668, a unanimous court, on the authority of Buchanan v. Warley, supra, declared invalid an ordinance which forbade any Negro to establish a home on any property in a white community or any white person to establish a home in a Negro community, "except on the written consent of a majority of the persons of the opposite race inhabiting such community or portion of the City to be affected."

The precise question before this Court in both the Buchanan and Harmon cases, involved the rights of white sellers to dispose of their properties free from restrictions as to potential purchasers based on considerations of race or color. But that such legislation is also offensive to the rights of those desiring to acquire and occupy property and barred on grounds of race or color, is clear, not only from the language of the opinion in Buchanan v. Warley, supra, but from this Court's disposition of the case of City of Richmond v. Deans, 1930, 281 U.S. 704. There, a Negro, barred from the occupancy of certain property by the terms of an ordinance similar to that in the Buchanan case, sought injunctive relief in the federal courts to enjoin the enforcement of the ordinance on the grounds that its provisions violated the terms of the Fourteenth Amendment. Such relief was granted, and this Court affirmed, finding the citation of Buchanan v. Warley, supra, and Harmon v. Tyler, supra, sufficient to support its judgment.

But the present cases, unlike those just discussed, do not involve action by state legislatures or city councils. Here the particular patterns of discrimination and the areas in which the restrictions are to operate, are determined, in the first instance, by the terms of agreements among private individuals. Participation of the State consists in the enforcement of the restrictions so defined. The crucial issue with which we are here confronted is whether this distinction removes these cases from the operation of the prohibitory provisions of the Fourteenth Amendment.

Since the decision of this Court in the Civil Rights Cases, 1883, 109 U.S. 3, the principle has become firmly embedded in our constitutional law that the action inhibited by the first section of the Fourteenth Amendment is only such action as may fairly be said to be that of the States. That Amendment erects no shield against merely private conduct, however discriminatory or wrongful.

We conclude, therefore, that the restrictive agreements standing alone cannot be regarded as a violation of any rights guaranteed to petitioners by the Fourteenth Amendment. So long as the purposes of those agreements are effectuated by voluntary adherence to their terms, it would appear clear that there has been no action by the State and the provisions of the Amendment have not been violated.

But here there was more. These are cases in which the purposes of the agreements were secured only by judicial enforcement by state courts of the restrictive terms of the agreements. The respondents urge that judicial enforcement of private agreements does not amount to state action; or, in any event, the participation of the State is so attenuated in character as not to amount to state action within the meaning of the Fourteenth Amendment. Finally, it is suggested, even if the States in these cases may be deemed to have acted in the constitutional sense, their action did not deprive petitioners of rights guaranteed by the Fourteenth Amendment. We move to a consideration of these matters.

II.

That the action of state courts and of judicial officers in their official capacities is to be regarded as action of the State within the meaning of the Fourteenth Amendment, is a proposition which has long been established by decisions of this Court. That principle was given expression in the earliest cases involving the construction of the terms of the Fourteenth Amendment.

* * *

The short of the matter is that from the time of the adoption of the Fourteenth Amendment until the present, it has been the consistent ruling of this Court that the action of the States to which the Amendment has reference, includes action of state courts and state judicial officials. Although, in construing the terms of the Fourteenth Amendment, differences have from time to time been expressed as to whether particular types of state action may be said to offend the Amendment's prohibitory provisions, it has never been suggested that state court action is immunized from the operation of those provisions simply because the act is that of the judicial branch of the state government.

III.

Against this background of judicial construction, extending over a period of some three-quarters of a century, we are called upon to consider whether enforcement by state courts of the restrictive agreements in these cases may be deemed to be the acts of those States; and if so, whether that action has denied these petitioners the equal protection of the laws which the Amendment was intended to insure.

We have no doubt that there has been state action in these cases in the full and complete sense of the phrase. The undisputed facts disclose that petitioners were willing purchasers of properties upon which they desired to establish homes. The owners of the properties were willing sellers; and contracts of sale were accordingly consummated. It is clear that but for the active intervention of the state courts, supported by the full panoply of state power, petitioners would have been free to occupy the properties in question without restraint.

These are not cases, as has been suggested, in which the States have merely abstained from action, leaving private individuals free to impose such discriminations as they see fit. Rather, these are cases in which the States have made available to such individuals the full coercive power of government to deny to petitioners, on the grounds of race or color, the enjoyment of property rights in premises which petitioners are willing and financially able to acquire and which the grantors are willing to sell. The difference between judicial enforcement and nonenforcement of the restrictive covenants is the difference to petitioners between being denied rights of property available to other members of the community and being accorded full enjoyment of those rights on an equal footing.

The enforcement of the restrictive agreements by the state courts in these cases was directed pursuant to the common-law policy of the States as formulated by those courts in earlier decisions.

* * *

We hold that in granting judicial enforcement of the restrictive agreements in these cases, the States have denied petitioners the equal protection of the laws and that, therefore, the action of the state courts cannot stand. We have noted that freedom from discrimination by the States in the enjoyment of property rights was among the basic objectives sought to be effectuated by the framers of the Fourteenth Amendment. That such discrimination has occurred in these cases is clear. Because of the race or color of these petitioners they have been denied rights of ownership or occupancy enjoyed as a matter of course by other citizens of different race or color.

* * *

Respondents urge, however, that since the state courts stand ready to enforce restrictive covenants excluding white persons from the ownership or occupancy of property covered by such agreements, enforcement of covenants excluding colored persons may not be deemed a denial of equal protection of the laws to the colored persons who are thereby affected. This contention does not bear scrutiny. The parties have directed our attention to no case in which a court, state or federal, has been called upon to enforce a covenant excluding members of the white majority from ownership or occupancy of real property on grounds of race or color. But there are more fundamental considerations. The rights created by the first section of the Fourteenth Amendment are, by its terms, guaranteed to the individual. The rights established are personal rights. It is, therefore, no answer to these petitioners to say that the courts may also be induced to deny white persons rights of ownership and occupancy on grounds of race or color. Equal protection of the laws is not achieved through indiscriminate imposition of inequalities.

* * *

For the reasons stated, the judgment of the Supreme Court of Missouri and the judgment of the Supreme Court of Michigan must be reversed.

Reversed.

Notes, Problems, and Questions

1. May a party to a racially restrictive covenant recover damages for its breach? In Barrows v. Jackson, 346 U.S. 249, 258 (1953), the Supreme Court held that it would "not permit or require California to coerce respondent to respond in damages for failure to observe a [racially] restrictive covenant that this Court would deny California the right to enforce in equity."

2. The full implications of *Shelley v. Kraemer* are best explored in another course. Nonetheless, you should be aware that legislative encouragement or judicial enforcement of private conduct concerning land has often been challenged under the 14th Amendment.

(a) Does a nonjudicial foreclosure under a deed of trust constitute state action where the state has enacted comprehensive regulations governing the process?

(b) Does it constitute state action for a court to enforce private covenants restricting occupancy by age?

3. O conveyed a 40 acre pasture "to A but if A attempts to convey the property to a non-white then it shall revert in fee simple to the grantor." A conveyed to B, a black citizen. O brings suit to quiet title in O's name. In light of *Shelley v. Kraemer*, does O have any legal basis for this action? *Compare* Capitol Federal Savings & Loan Association v. Smith, 136 Colo. 265, 316 P.2d 252 (1957) *with* Charlotte Park & Recreation Commission v.

Barringer, 242 N.C. 311, 88 S.E.2d 114 (1955), *cert. denied* 350 U.S. 983 (1956). *See also* Evans v. Abney, 396 U.S. 435 (1970), in which the Supreme Court found no state action in a reverter by operation of law to the heirs of a grantor who had devised land in trust for a public park for whites only. *See generally* Entin, *Defeasible Fees, State Action, and the Legacy of Massive Resistance,* 34 Wm. & Mary L.Rev. 769 (1993).

Assume that there is no state action in this situation. Is this forfeiture restraint on alienation valid under the test discussed in *Casey?*

JONES v. ALFRED H. MAYER CO.

Supreme Court of the United States, 1968.
392 U.S. 409.

Mr. Justice Stewart delivered the opinion of the Court.

In this case we are called upon to determine the scope and constitutionality of an Act of Congress, 42 U.S.C. § 1982, which provides that:

> "All citizens of the United States shall have the same right, in every State and Territory, as is enjoyed by white citizens thereof to inherit, purchase, lease, sell, hold, and convey real and personal property."

On September 2, 1965, the petitioners filed a complaint in the District Court for the Eastern District of Missouri, alleging that the respondents had refused to sell them a home in the Paddock Woods community of St. Louis County for the sole reason that petitioner Joseph Lee Jones is a Negro. Relying in part upon § 1982, the petitioners sought injunctive and other relief. The District Court sustained the respondents' motion to dismiss the complaint, and the Court of Appeals for the Eighth Circuit affirmed, concluding that § 1982 applies only to state action and does not reach private refusals to sell. We granted certiorari to consider the questions thus presented. For the reasons that follow, we reverse the judgment of the Court of Appeals. We hold that § 1982 bars *all* racial discrimination, private as well as public, in the sale or rental of property, and that the statute, thus construed, is a valid exercise of the power of Congress to enforce the Thirteenth Amendment.

I.

At the outset, it is important to make clear precisely what this case does *not* involve. Whatever else it may be, 42 U.S.C. § 1982 is not a comprehensive open housing law. In sharp contrast to the Fair Housing Title (Title VIII) of the Civil Rights Act of 1968, Pub.L. 90–284, 82 Stat. 81, the statute in this case deals only with racial discrimination and does not address itself to discrimination on grounds of religion or national origin. It does not deal specifically with discrimination in the provision of services or facilities in connection with the sale or rental of a dwelling. It does not prohibit advertising or other representations that indicate discriminatory preferences. It does not refer explicitly to discrimination in financing arrangements or in the provision of brokerage services. It does not empower a federal administrative agency to assist aggrieved parties. It makes no provision for intervention by the Attorney General. And, although it can be enforced by injunction, it contains no provision expressly authorizing a federal court to order the payment of damages.

Thus, although § 1982 contains none of the exemptions that Congress included in the Civil Rights Act of 1968, it would be a serious mistake to suppose that § 1982 in any way diminishes the significance of the law recently enacted by Congress. Indeed, the Senate Subcommittee on Housing and Urban Affairs was informed in hearings held after the Court of Appeals had rendered its decision in this case that § 1982 might well be "a presently valid federal statutory ban against discrimination by private persons in the sale or lease of real property." The Subcommittee was told, however, that even if this Court should so construe § 1982, the existence of that statute would not "eliminate the need for congressional action" to spell out "responsibility on the part of the federal government to enforce the rights it protects." The point was made that, in light of the many difficulties confronted by private litigants seeking to enforce such rights on their own, "legislation is needed to establish federal machinery for enforcement of the rights guaranteed under Section 1982 of Title 42 even if the plaintiffs in Jones v. Alfred H. Mayer Company should prevail in the United States Supreme Court."

On April 10, 1968, Representative Kelly of New York focused the attention of the House upon the present case and its possible significance. She described the background of this litigation, recited the text of § 1982, and then added:

> "When the Attorney General was asked in court about the effect of the old law [' 1982] as compared with the pending legislation which is being considered on the House floor today, he said that the scope was somewhat different, the remedies and procedures were different, and that the new law was still quite necessary."

Later the same day, the House passed the Civil Rights Act of 1968. Its enactment had no effect upon § 1982 and no effect upon this litigation, but it underscored the vast differences between, on the one hand, a general statute applicable only to racial discrimination in the rental and sale of property and enforceable only by private parties acting on their own initiative, and, on the other hand, a detailed housing law, applicable to a broad range of discriminatory practices and enforceable by a complete arsenal of federal authority. Having noted these differences, we turn to a consideration of § 1982 itself.

* * *

III.

We begin with the language of the statute itself. In plain and unambiguous terms, § 1982 grants to all citizens, without regard to race or color, "the same right" to purchase and lease property "as is enjoyed by white citizens." As the Court of Appeals in this case evidently recognized, that right can be impaired as effectively by "those who place property on the market" as by the State itself. For, even if the State and its agents lend no support to those who wish to exclude persons from their communities on racial grounds, the fact remains that, whenever property "is placed on the market for whites only, whites have a right denied to Negroes." So long as a Negro citizen who wants to buy or rent a home can be turned away simply because he is not white, he cannot be said to enjoy "the *same* right * * * as is enjoyed by white citizens * * * to * * * purchase [and] lease * * * real and personal property." 42 U.S.C. § 1982. (Emphasis added.)

On its face, therefore, § 1982 appears to prohibit *all* discrimination against Negroes in the sale or rental of property—discrimination by private owners as well as discrimination by public authorities. Indeed even the respondents seem to concede that, if § 1982 "means what it says"—to use the words of the respondents' brief—then it must encompass every racially motivated refusal to sell or rent and cannot be confined to officially sanctioned segregation in housing. Stressing what they consider to be the revolutionary implications of so literal a reading of § 1982, the respondents argue that Congress cannot possibly have intended any such result. Our examination of the relevant history, however, persuades us that Congress meant exactly what it said.

* * *

V.

The remaining question is whether Congress has power under the Constitution to do what § 1982 purports to do: to prohibit all racial discrimination, private and public, in the sale and rental of property. Our starting point is the Thirteenth Amendment, for it was pursuant to that constitutional provision that Congress originally enacted what is now § 1982. The Amendment consists of two parts. Section 1 states:

> "Neither slavery nor involuntary servitude, except as a punishment for crime whereby the party shall have been duly convicted, shall exist within the United States, or any place subject to their jurisdiction."

Section 2 provides:

> "Congress shall have power to enforce this article by appropriate legislation."

As its text reveals, the Thirteenth Amendment "is not a mere prohibition of state laws establishing or upholding slavery, but an absolute declaration that slavery or involuntary servitude shall not exist in any part of the United States." Civil Rights Cases, 109 U.S. 3, 20. It has never been doubted, therefore, "that the power vested in Congress to enforce the article by appropriate legislation," ibid., includes the power to enact laws "direct and primary, operating upon the acts of individuals, whether sanctioned by state legislation or not." Id., at 23.

Thus, the fact that § 1982 operates upon the unofficial acts of private individuals, whether or not sanctioned by state law, presents no constitutional problem. If Congress has power under the Thirteenth Amendment to eradicate conditions that prevent Negroes from buying and renting property because of their race or color, then no federal statute calculated to achieve that objective can be thought to exceed the constitutional power of Congress simply because it reaches beyond state action to regulate the conduct of private individuals. The constitutional question in this case, therefore, comes to this: Does the authority of Congress to enforce the Thirteenth Amendment "by appropriate legislation" include the power to eliminate all racial barriers to the acquisition of real and personal property? We think the answer to that question is plainly yes.

"By its own unaided force and effect," the Thirteenth Amendment "abolished slavery, and established universal freedom." Civil Rights Cases, 109 U.S. 3. Whether or not the Amendment *itself* did any more than that—a question not involved in this case—it is at least clear that the Enabling Clause of that Amendment empowered Congress to do much more. For that clause clothed "Congress with power to pass *all laws necessary and proper for abolishing all badges and incidents of slavery in the United States.*" Ibid. (Emphasis added.) * * *

Negro citizens, North and South, who saw in the Thirteenth Amendment a promise of freedom—freedom to "go and come at pleasure" and to "buy and sell when they please"—would be left with "a mere paper guarantee" if Congress were powerless to assure that a dollar in the hands of a Negro will purchase the same thing as a dollar in the hands of a white man. At the very least, the freedom that Congress is empowered to secure under the Thirteenth Amendment includes the freedom to buy whatever a white man can buy, the right to live wherever a white man can live. If Congress cannot say that being a free man means at least this much, then the Thirteenth Amendment made a promise the Nation cannot keep.

* * *

The judgment is reversed.

Mr. Justice Harlan, dissenting.

* * * I have concluded that this is one of those rare instances in which an event which occurs after the hearing of argument so diminishes a case's public significance, when viewed in light of the difficulty of the questions presented, as to justify this Court in dismissing the writ as improvidently granted.

The occurrence to which I refer is the recent enactment of the Civil Rights Act of 1968, Pub.L. 90–284, 82 Stat. 73. Title VIII of that Act contains comprehensive "fair housing" provisions, which by the terms of '803 will become applicable on January 1, 1969, to persons who, like the petitioners, attempt to buy houses from developers. Under those provisions, such persons will be entitled to injunctive relief and damages from developers who refuse to sell to them on account of race or color, unless the parties are able to resolve their dispute by other means. Thus, the type of relief which the petitioners seek will be available within seven months' time under the terms of a presumptively constitutional Act of Congress. In these circumstances, it seems obvious that the case has lost most of its public importance, and I believe that it would be much the wiser course for this Court to refrain from deciding it. I think it particularly unfortunate for the Court to persist in deciding this case on the basis of a highly questionable interpretation of a sweeping, century-old statute which, as the Court acknowledges contains none of the exemptions which the Congress of our own time found it necessary to include in a statute regulating relationships so personal in nature. In effect, this Court, by its construction of § 1982, has extended the coverage of federal "fair housing" laws far beyond that which Congress in its wisdom chose to provide in the Civil Rights Act of 1968. The political process now having taken hold again in this very field, I am at a loss to understand why the Court should have deemed it appropriate or, in the circumstances of this case, necessary to proceed with such precipitate and insecure strides.

* * *

Notes and Problems

1. The *Jones v. Mayer* decision recognized the inherently limited application of § 1982 to discrimination in housing and made extensive reference to the more comprehensive Fair Housing Chapter of the Civil Rights Act of 1968. 42 U.S.C.A. §§ 3601 *et seq.* (West 1994 & Supp.1998). The Fair Housing Act, as amended, provides sanctions against many forms of discrimination in housing and is applicable to a large segment of the private sector. The Act extends not only to racial discrimination, but also to any discrimination based on color, religion, sex, handicap, familial status, or national origin. Among other things, the Act prohibits persons from discriminating on the basis of any of these characteristics by (1) refusing to sell or rent; (2) altering the terms or conditions of a sale or rental; (3) misrepresenting the availability of certain properties; (4) withholding services or facilities; (5) denying or limiting home loans; or (6) refusing membership in or access to brokerage organizations or services.

These prohibitions, however, are inapplicable to certain situations. The Fair Housing Act does not apply to single family homes sold or rented by the owner without the assistance of a realtor. Nor does it apply to units in a dwelling occupied by the owner provided no more than four families are living independently of one another in the building. *See* Note, *Is the U.S. Committed to Fair Housing? Enforcement of the Fair Housing Act Remains a Critical Problem*, 29 Cath.U.L.Rev. 641 (1980).

2. The Fair Housing Act also forbids any advertisement or notice that states a preference or limitation on the basis of race, color, religion, sex, handicap, familial status, or national origin. (a) Does a developer violate the Act by mounting an advertising campaign featuring exclusively models of a particular race? *See* Spann v. Colonial Village, Inc., 899 F.2d 24 (D.C.Cir.

1990), *cert. denied* 498 U.S. 980 (1990); Ragin v. Harry Macklowe Real Estate Co., Inc., 801 F.Supp. 1213 (S.D.N.Y.1992), *aff'd in part, rev'd in part* 6 F.3d 898 (2d Cir.1993); Saunders v. General Services Corp., 659 F.Supp. 1042 (E.D.Va.1987). (b) Suppose a female law student rented a small house. She wants a roommate to share expenses, but wishes to live only with another female. She placed a written notice on the university's housing office bulletin board asking for interested female students. She published a similar advertisement in the school newspaper. Has she violated the Fair Housing Act? *See* Holmgren v. Little Village Community Reporter, 342 F.Supp. 512 (N.D.Ill.1971); *see also* Annot., *Validity, Construction, and Application of § 804(c) of Civil Rights Act of 1968 (Fair Housing Act) (42 U.S.C.A. § 3604(c)); Prohibiting Discriminatory Notice, Statement, or Advertisement With Respect to Sale or Rental of Dwelling,* 22 A.L.R.Fed. 359 (1975).

3. Congress amended the Fair Housing Act to prohibit discrimination on the basis of "familial status," which is defined as referring to a child under 18 years of age living with a parent, guardian, or other authorized individual. However, "housing for older persons" is exempt from the "familial status" provisions of the Act. A complicated formula is established for determining what constitutes "housing for older persons." 42 U.S.C. §§ 3602(k), 3604, 3607(b) (1994). *See* Seniors Civil Liberties Association, Inc. v. Kemp, 965 F.2d 1030 (11th Cir.1992) (upholding constitutionality of "familial status" provision).

4. State or local housing statutes may prohibit discrimination on a larger number of characteristics than federal law. For example, the District of Columbia code prohibits discrimination on the basis of "race, color, religion, national origin, sex, age, marital status, personal appearance, sexual orientation, family responsibilities, disability, matriculation, political affiliation, source of income, or place of residence or business * * *." D.C.Code Ann. § 1–2515 (1992 & Supp. 1998).

COUNTY OF DANE v. NORMAN

Supreme Court of Wisconsin, 1993.
174 Wis.2d 683, 497 N.W.2d 714.

STEINMETZ, JUSTICE.

The issue in this case is whether Dwight Norman discriminated against potential tenants on the basis of "marital status," contrary to Chapter 31 of the Dane county ordinances, when he refused to rent a three-bedroom duplex to two groups of potential tenants, on separate occasions, on the ground that his policy as a landlord is not to rent to groups of unrelated individuals seeking to live together. One group seeking to rent Norman's property consisted of three single women, and the other group consisted of two single women and one of the women's two children.

We hold that Norman's policy does not violate Chapter 31 of the Dane county ordinances which proscribes discrimination based on "marital status." Norman refused to rent to the prospective tenants in this case because they intended to live together. Living together is "conduct" not "status."

This action was commenced pursuant to a summons and complaint filed on February 26, 1990. The complaint alleged that Norman violated Dane county's fair housing ordinance by refusing to rent a three-bedroom duplex to (a) three single women and (b) two single women and the two children of one of the women. The complaint alleged that the refusal was impermissibly based on the "marital status" of the prospective tenants.

The Dane county circuit court, Judge Richard J. Callaway, issued a decision and order denying Dane County's motion for summary judgment and granting Norman's cross motion for summary judgment. The court found no violation of Dane county's fair housing ordinance. The court of appeals reversed the circuit court judgment, concluding that Norman's motion for summary judgment dismissing the complaint should have been denied and that Dane county's motion for summary judgment should have been granted. County of Dane v. Norman, 168 Wis.2d 675, 484 N.W.2d 367 (Ct.App.1992).

* * *

In May, 1989, Joyce Anderton contacted Dwight Norman and asked if he had any three-bedroom duplexes available. He said some would be available in July and asked how large Anderton's family was. She said she was not married and would be living with two single women. Norman replied that he would rent to her individually but not to groups of unrelated individuals. He rejected an offer that one of the three be solely responsible for the rent.

In August, 1989, Norman showed one of his apartments to Deb Dana and her two children. Dana told Norman that she and the children would be living with another woman. He refused to rent to Dana on that basis.

It is undisputed that under Norman's policy individuals who are married, divorced, widowed, separated, or single are eligible to rent from him. Norman's policy is not to rent to groups of unrelated individuals. Neither Anderton nor Dana inquired about renting as single persons.

Chapter 31 of the Dane county ordinances, entitled "Fair Housing" prohibits "unlawful discrimination in housing" based on "marital status." Section 31.02, Dane county ordinances. More specifically, Chapter 31 provides as follows:

> Section 31.02 INTENT. It is the intent of this chapter to render unlawful discrimination in housing. It is the declared policy of the County of Dane that all persons shall have an equal opportunity for housing regardless of * * * [the] marital status of the person maintaining a household * * *.

Section 31.03 DEFINITIONS. The following words and phrases have the meanings indicated unless the context requires otherwise:

* * *

(2) Discriminate and Discrimination mean to segregate, separate, exclude or treat any person or class of persons unequally because of * * * [the] marital status of the person maintaining the household * * *.

* * *

(5) Marital status means being married, divorced, widowed, separated, single or a cohabitant.

Section 31.10 DISCRIMINATION PROHIBITED. It shall be unlawful for any person to discriminate:

(1) By refusing to sell, lease, finance or contract to construct housing or by refusing to discuss the terms thereof * * *.

As stated above, "marital status" under Dane county ordinance sec. 31.03(5) is defined as "being married, divorced, widowed, separated, single or a cohabitant." The term "status," is not specifically defined in Chapter 31 but means in its common and approved usage "state or condition." Black's Law Dictionary (6th ed. 1990). Thus, the Dane county ordinance prohibits discrimination based on the state or condition of being married, the state or condition of being single, and the like.

Dane county argues that the inclusion of the term "cohabitant"[1] in the definition of "marital status" indicates that the term "marital status" was intended to cover groups of unrelated individuals seeking to live together. As a result, Norman's rental policy violates Chapter 31. We reject this argument. Chapter 31 is invalid to the extent that it seeks to protect "cohabitants." Because Dane county's argument turns on an invalid provision, it is unpersuasive.

Sections 31.02, 31.03 and 31.10, Dane county ordinances, were passed pursuant to the enabling authority contained in sec. 66.432(2), Stats. The authority granted to municipalities through enabling legislation like sec. 66.432 is not unlimited. "[A] municipality may not pass ordinances 'which infringe the spirit of a state law or are repugnant to the general policy of the state.'" Anchor Savings & Loan Ass'n v. Madison EOC, 120 Wis.2d 391, 397, 355 N.W.2d 234 (1984) (quoting Fox v. Racine, 225 Wis. 542, 545, 275 N.W. 513 (1937)); see also 5 Eugene McQuillin, The Law of Municipal Corporations sec. 15.21 (3rd ed. 1989). McQuillin elaborates on this rule as follows:

The rule requires at least substantial conformity, and under it an ordinance cannot prohibit what the public policy permits, or permit

---

1. Chapter 31 does not specifically define "cohabitant." Webster's Dictionary defines the term as follows: "to live together as husband and wife * * * without a legal marriage having been performed." Webster's Third New International Dictionary (1966).

that which public policy forbids. Nor, under a general grant of power, can a municipal corporation adopt ordinances which infringe the spirit, or are repugnant to the policy, of the state as declared in its legislation. It follows that if the state has expressed through legislation a public policy with reference to a subject, a municipality cannot ordain an effect contrary to or in qualification of the public policy so established, unless there is a specific, positive, lawful grant of power by the state to the municipality to so ordain.

5 McQuillin, *supra,* sec. 15.21.

Chapter 31's requirement that landlords make available their rental units to "cohabitants" is inconsistent with the public policy of this state which seeks to promote the stability of marriage and family. As a result, it is outside the enabling authority of sec. 66.432(2), Stats., and invalid.

Chapters 765–768, Stats., clearly set forth Wisconsin's policy of encouraging and protecting marriage. The preamble of intent to those sections states as follows:

(2) INTENT. It is the intent of chs. 765 to 768 to promote the stability and best interests of marriage and the family. It is the intent of the legislature to recognize the valuable contributions of both spouses during the marriage and at termination of the marriage by dissolution or death. Marriage is the institution that is the foundation of the family and of society. Its stability is basic to morality and civilization, and of vital interest to society and the state. The consequences of the marriage contract are more significant to society than those of other contracts, and the public interest must be taken into account always. The seriousness of marriage makes adequate premarital counseling and education for family living highly desirable and courses thereon are urged upon all persons contemplating marriage. The impairment or dissolution of the marriage relation generally results in injury to the public wholly apart from the effect upon the parties immediately concerned. Under the laws of this state, marriage is a legal relationship between 2 equal persons, a husband and wife, who owe to each other mutual responsibility and support. Each spouse has an equal obligation in accordance with his or her ability to contribute money or services or both which are necessary for the adequate support and maintenance of his or her minor children and of the other spouse. No spouse may be presumed primarily liable for support expenses under this subsection.

(3) CONSTRUCTION. Chapters 765 to 768 shall be liberally construed to effect the objectives of sub. (2).

Section 765.001(2), (3), Stats.; *see also* Phillips v. Wisconsin Personnel Commission, 167 Wis.2d 205, 220, 482 N.W.2d 121 (Ct.App.1992) (the court of appeals noted that unmarried cohabitants do not receive the same statutory protections, *i.e.,* a mutual duty of general support, as do spouses); Federated Elec. v. Kessler, 131 Wis.2d 189, 214, 388 N.W.2d 553 (1986) (recognizing that an employer's prohibition against extramarital affairs among its employees conforms with the policy set forth in sec. 765.001(2)).

Norman's motivation for denying rental to the individuals in this case was triggered by their "conduct," not their "marital status." As explained above, "marital status" refers to the state or condition of being married, the state or condition of being single, and the like. "Conduct," on the other hand, is defined by Black's Law Dictionary (6th ed. 1990) to mean "[p]ersonal behavior; deportment; mode of action; [and] any positive or negative act." It is undisputed that Norman would have rented to any of the prospective tenants, regardless of their individual "marital status," if they had not intended to live together. Their living together is "conduct," not "status."

* * *

We hold that Norman's policy does not violate Chapter 31 of the Dane county ordinances. Chapter 31 proscribes discrimination based on the state or condition of being married, the state or condition of being single, and the like. Norman refused to rent to the prospective tenants in this case because they intended to live together. Living together is "conduct" not "status".

The decision of the court of appeals is reversed.

HEFFERNAN, CHIEF JUSTICE (*dissenting*).

In upholding Dwight and Patricia Norman's right to refuse to lease apartments to groups of unrelated persons, today's holding defies legal examination and legislative resolve alike. I thus reject the majority's reasoning and instead conclude that the Normans' actions are in violation of Chapter 31 of Dane county's fair housing ordinance which specifically forbids landlords to discriminate against persons on the basis of "marital status." Accordingly, I dissent from the majority's opinion.

The majority begins its assault on Chapter 31 by holding that insofar as the Dane county ordinance permits cohabitation among unrelated persons it violates existing public policy and therefore exceeds the scope of municipal powers authorized in sec. 66.432, Stats. Specifically, the majority maintains that chapters 765–768, Stats., which set forth this state's policy in respect to the promotion of marriage and family, render this portion of the county ordinance invalid. In so holding, the majority misconstrues the scope of municipal authority in the state of Wisconsin and mistakes legislative support for marriage for advocacy of marriage as the only acceptable relationship between Wisconsin citizens.

In 1965, the state legislature enacted Wisconsin's first fair housing statute, now numbered sec. 101.22. Although initially concerned with race discrimination, the statute gradually has expanded to guarantee equal access to housing for all persons regardless of "sex, race, color, sexual orientation, disability, religion, national origin, marital status, family status, lawful source of income, age or ancestry * * *." Wis. Stats., sec. 101.22(1). Subsequent to enacting the state statute, the legislature passed sec. 66.432, Stats., authorizing municipalities to enact analogous local ordinances prohibiting housing discrimination among suspect classes. In the statement of intent to sec. 66.432 the legislature spelled out its vision for future such statutes:

[t]he right of all persons to have equal opportunities for housing * * * is a matter both of statewide concern under s. 101.22 and also of local interest under this section and s. 66.433. The enactment of s. 101.22 by the legislature shall not preempt the subject matter of equal opportunities in housing from consideration by political subdivisions, and *shall not exempt political subdivisions from their duty, nor deprive them of their right, to enact ordinances which prohibit discrimination in any type of housing solely on the basis of an individual being a member of a protected class.* (emphasis added)

Wis.Stats., sec. 66.432(1). As the quoted portion indicates, the legislature not only anticipated but in fact urged localities to enact laws such as the one at issue today.

In keeping with the legislature's evident concern over the scope of the problem confronting local municipalities, section 66.432(2) granted municipalities wide latitude in enacting these local ordinances: they could either adopt a model similar to sec. 101.22, or draft an ordinance "even more inclusive in its terms * * *."

Dane county's fair housing ordinance closely mirrors its progenitor, sec. 101.22(1), Stats. Exercising the right under sec. 66.432 to make its local ordinance "even more inclusive in its terms," however, the county opted to broaden the definition of "marital status" contained in sec. 101.22 to include "cohabitation." Contrary to the majority's holding, I conclude that this addition to the classification "marital status" was within the scope of authority granted the county under section 66.432, Stats.

* * *

In the case of Dane county, there are obvious reasons, of which we appropriately take judicial notice, for the local fair housing ordinance to contain a provision prohibiting discrimination against groups of unrelated persons. Dane county hosts both the state government and the state's largest university campus. Both of these institutions tend to attract large numbers of young, single individuals—people for whom rent-sharing is often the only means of obtaining affordable housing. One can imagine the ensuing chaos if property owners on the Madison isthmus decided to rent only to single individuals or related cohabitants; thousands of residents thus displaced would be unable to find adequate, affordable housing in Madison.

Regardless of the meritorious necessity for adding "cohabitation" to the list of suspect classifications protected from housing discrimination, the majority maintains that by doing so Dane county has enacted an ordinance in violation of the Wisconsin Family Code. Implicit in the reasoning of the majority is the assumption that "cohabitants" include only unrelated persons residing together in a sexual relationship. Unfortunately, this premise is based entirely on a partial definition of "cohabitation." Had the majority considered more complete definitions it might have arrived at a conclusion more in keeping with contemporary mores. For example Webster's New Collegiate Dictionary (1980) defines the verb "cohabit" as: "1: to live together as husband and wife 2a: to live together or in company * * * b: to exist together * * *." Similarly, Webster's New World Dictionary of the American Language (1972) defines the noun "cohabitant" as "a person living together with another or others." It is this broad definition of "cohabitation" that is implicated in the Normans' rental policy which affects all groups of unrelated persons who reside together, not only those who "cohabitate" as husband and wife. The Normans' prospective tenants included a single mother of two seeking to share an apartment with a second woman, and three single women. Absent any evidence that these individuals were involved in anything other than a cost-sharing relationship, I can not conceive how allowing these individuals to live together co-operatively would in any way affect the health and well-being of Wisconsin families and marriages.

* * *

For the foregoing reasons, I conclude that today's holding misconstrues existing law and, without legislative sanction, unwisely engages in *ultra vires* moralizing from the bench. Dane county's ordinance protecting "cohabitants" from housing discrimination is fully consistent with the state legislature's anti-discrimination laws. Accordingly, the Normans' policy of refusing to rent apartments to groups of unrelated individuals violates the county's completely appropriate and legislatively authorized ordinance. I would affirm the decision of the court of appeals.

Notes and Questions

1. Would the court in *Norman* have reached the same result if the landlord had refused for religious reasons to rent to an unmarried couple who planned to live together? *Compare* Swanner v. Anchorage Equal Rights Commission, 874 P.2d 274 (Alaska 1994) (concluding that landlord's refusal on religious grounds to rent residences to unmarried cohabiting couples violated state and municipal fair housing statutes prohibiting discrimination on basis of marital status, and finding that enforcement of statutes against landlord did not deprive landlord of right to free exercise of religion), *cert. denied* 513 U.S. 979 (1994), *and* Smith v. Fair Employment and Housing Commission, 12 Cal.4th 1143, 51 Cal.Rptr.2d 700, 913 P.2d 909 (1996) (holding that state statutory ban on discrimination because of "marital status" protected unmarried cohabiting couples, and that statute did not violate landlord's free exercise of religion), *cert. denied* 117 S.Ct. 2531 (1997), *and* McCready v. Hoffius, 586 N.W.2d 723 (Mich.1998) (determining that landlord violated state civil rights law by refusing on basis of religious beliefs to rent to unmarried couples) *with* Thomas v. Anchorage Equal Rights Commission, 165 F.3d 692 (9th Cir.1999) (recognizing free exercise exemption from state and municipal fair housing statutes prohibiting "marital status" discrimination for landlords who declined on religious grounds to rent to unmarried cohabiting couples), *and* State by Cooper v. French, 460 N.W.2d 2 (Minn.1990) (ruling that landlord's refusal to rent house because prospective tenant planned to live with fiancé did not violate state law

prohibiting discrimination on basis of martial status, and opining that whatever interest prospective tenant had in cohabiting with fiancé was subordinate to landlord's religious liberty as protected by state constitution).

2. The Americans with Disabilities Act (ADA) has potentially far-reaching implications for owners of public accommodations and commercial facilities. Such owners and operators are required to make their facilities "readily accessible" to the disabled. Many unresolved issues exist with respect to the scope of the ADA, but owners and operators of existing buildings are obligated to remove barriers to access by disabled persons, where such removal is "readily achievable." More exacting requirements are imposed for alteration of existing buildings and construction of new facilities. 42 U.S.C.A. §§ 12101–12213 (West 1995 & Supp.1998). *See* Jones, *Real Estate Impact of the Americans With Disabilities Act,* 21 Real Est.L.J. 3 (1992); Moore, *The Americans With Disabilities Act Title III—The "New" Building Code,* 71 Neb.L.Rev. 1145 (1992).

C. FREEDOM OF USE (NUISANCE)

As a general rule, an owner is at liberty to use his property as he sees fit, without objection or interference from his neighbor, provided such use does not violate an ordinance or statute. There is, however, a limitation to this rule; one made necessary by the intricate complex, and changing life of today. The old and familiar maxim that one must so use his property as not to injure that of another (sic utere tuo ut alienum non laedas) is deeply imbedded in our law. An owner will not be permitted to make an unreasonable use of his premises to the material annoyance of his neighbor, if the latter's enjoyment of life or property is materially lessened thereby. * * *

Such a rule is imperative, or life to-day in our congested centers would be intolerable and unbearable. If a citizen was given no protection against unjust harassment arising from the use to which the property of his neighbor was put, the comfort and value of his home could easily be destroyed by any one who chose to erect an annoyance nearby, and no one would be safe, unless he was rich enough to buy sufficient land about his home to render such disturbance impossible. When conflicting rights arise, a general rule must be worked out which, so far as possible, will preserve to each party that to which he has a just claim.

While the law will not permit a person to be driven from his home, or to be compelled to live in it in positive distress or discomfort because of the use to which other property nearby has been put, it is not every annoyance connected with business which will be enjoined. Many a loss arises from acts or conditions which do not create a ground for legal redress. Damnum absque injuria is a familiar maxim. Factories, stores, and mercantile establishments are essential to the prosperity of the nation. They necessarily invade our cities, and interfere more or less with the peace and tranquility of the neighborhood in which they are located.

One who chooses to live in the large centers of population cannot expect the quiet of the country. Congested centers are seldom free from smoke, odors, and other pollution from houses, shops, and factories, and one who moves into such a region cannot hope to find the pure air of the village or outlying district. A person who prefers the advantages of community life must expect to experience some of the resulting inconveniences. Residents of industrial centers must endure without redress a certain amount of annoyance and discomfiture which is incident to life in such a locality. Such inconvenience is of minor importance compared with the general good of the community.

Whether the particular use to which one puts his property constitutes a nuisance or not is generally a question of fact, and depends upon whether such use is reasonable under all the surrounding circumstances. * * * Each case is unique. No hard and fast rule can be laid down which will apply in all instances.

Bove v. Donner–Hanna Coke Corp., 236 App.Div. 37, 39, 258 N.Y.S. 229, 231–32 (1932).

Notes and Questions

1. Consider the following analysis of nuisance law:

*Common law nuisances are classified as public or private nuisances. * * * A public nuisance impairs the health, safety, morals and comfort of the general community without necessarily harming particular property rights in any special way. A private nuisance unreasonably interferes with the use and enjoyment of another's land. Although theoretically quite distinct, the distinction between the two may be of little practical significance. A public nuisance often is also a private nuisance, individuals are frequently granted rights to sue under regulatory ordinances, and many plaintiffs may be joined in one action.

D. Hagman, Urban Planning and Land Development Control Law § 158 (1971).

2. Private nuisances have been found in a variety of situations. *See, e.g.,* Collier v. Ernst, 31 Del.Co. 49, 46 Pa.D. & C. 1 (1943) (playing marimba in residential neighborhood continuously for long periods, and playing certain tunes to annoy neighbors); Tichenor v. Vore, 953 S.W.2d 171 (Mo.App. 1997) (periodic but consistent barking, both day and night, of dogs housed in kennel).

---

* Reprinted from D. Hagman, Urban Planning and Land Development Control Law (1971) with permission of the West Group.

3.   Is nuisance law adequate to regulate noise and other undesirable activity by homeowners in Rolling Hills? What steps could the Homeowners' Association take to deter nuisance-like activity within the subdivision?

BOOMER v. ATLANTIC CEMENT CO.

Court of Appeals of New York, 1970.
26 N.Y.2d 219, 309 N.Y.S.2d 312, 257 N.E.2d 870.

BERGAN, JUDGE.

Defendant operates a large cement plant near Albany. These are actions for injunction and damages by neighboring land owners alleging injury to property from dirt, smoke and vibration emanating from the plant. A nuisance has been found after trial, temporary damages have been allowed; but an injunction has been denied.

The public concern with air pollution arising from many sources in industry and in transportation is currently accorded ever wider recognition accompanied by a growing sense of responsibility in State and Federal Governments to control it. Cement plants are obvious sources of air pollution in the neighborhoods where they operate.

* * *

It seems apparent that the amelioration of air pollution will depend on technical research in great depth; on a carefully balanced consideration of the economic impact of close regulation; and of the actual effect on public health. It is likely to require massive public expenditure and to demand more than any local community can accomplish and to depend on regional and interstate controls.

A court should not try to do this on its own as a by-product of private litigation and it seems manifest that the judicial establishment is neither equipped in the limited nature of any judgment it can pronounce nor prepared to lay down and implement an effective policy for the elimination of air pollution. This is an area beyond the circumference of one private lawsuit. It is a direct responsibility for government and should not thus be undertaken as an incident to solving a dispute between property owners and a single cement plant—one of many—in the Hudson River valley.

The cement making operations of defendant have been found by the court at Special Term to have damaged the nearby properties of plaintiffs in these two actions. That court, as it has been noted, accordingly found defendant maintained a nuisance and this has been affirmed at the Appellate Division. The total damage to plaintiffs' properties is, however, relatively small in comparison with the value of defendant's operation and with the consequences of the injunction which plaintiffs seek.

The ground for the denial of injunction, notwithstanding the finding both that there is a nuisance and that plaintiffs have been damaged substantially, is the large disparity in economic consequences of the nuisance and of the injunction. This theory cannot, however, be sustained without overruling a doctrine which has been consistently reaffirmed in several leading cases in this court and which has never been disavowed here, namely that where a nuisance has been found and where there has been any substantial damage shown by the party complaining an injunction will be granted.

The rule in New York has been that such a nuisance will be enjoined although marked disparity be shown in economic consequence between the effect of the injunction and the effect of the nuisance.

* * *

Although the court at Special Term and the Appellate Division held that injunction should be denied, it was found that plaintiffs had been damaged in various specific amounts up to the time of the trial and damages to the respective plaintiffs were awarded for those amounts. The effect of this was, injunction having been denied, plaintiffs could maintain successive actions at law for damages thereafter as further damage was incurred.

The court at Special Term also found the amount of permanent damage attributable to each plaintiff, for the guidance of the parties in the event both sides stipulated to the payment and acceptance of such permanent damage as a settlement of all the controversies among the parties. The total of permanent damages to all plaintiffs thus found was $185,000. This basis of adjustment has not resulted in any stipulation by the parties.

This result at Special Term and at the Appellate Division is a departure from a rule that has become settled; but to follow the rule literally in these cases would be to close down the plant at once. This court is fully agreed to avoid that immediately drastic remedy; the difference in view is how best to avoid it.

One alternative is to grant the injunction but postpone its effect to a specified future date to give opportunity for technical advances to permit defendant to eliminate the nuisance; another is to grant the injunction conditioned on the payment of permanent damages to plaintiffs which would compensate them for the total economic loss to their property present and future caused by defendant's operations. For reasons which will be developed the court chooses the latter alternative.

If the injunction were to be granted unless within a short period—e.g., 18 months—the nuisance be abated by improved methods, there would be no assurance that any significant technical improvement would occur.

The parties could settle this private litigation at any time if defendant paid enough money and the imminent threat of closing the plant would build up the pressure on defendant. If there were no improved techniques found, there would inevitably be applications to the court at Special Term for extensions of time to perform on showing of good faith efforts to find such techniques.

Moreover, techniques to eliminate dust and other annoying by-products of cement making are unlikely to be developed by any research the defendant can undertake within any short period, but will depend on the total resources of the cement industry nationwide and throughout the world. The problem is universal wherever cement is made.

For obvious reasons the rate of the research is beyond control of defendant. If at the end of 18 months the whole industry has not found a technical solution a court would be hard put to close down this one cement plant if due regard be given to equitable principles.

On the other hand, to grant the injunction unless defendant pays plaintiffs such permanent damages as may be fixed by the court seems to do justice between the contending parties. All of the attributions of economic loss to the properties on which plaintiffs' complaints are based will have been redressed.

The nuisance complained of by these plaintiffs may have other public or private consequences, but these particular parties are the only ones who have sought remedies and the judgment proposed will fully redress them. The limitation of relief granted is a limitation only within the four corners of these actions and does not foreclose public health or other public agencies from seeking proper relief in a proper court.

It seems reasonable to think that the risk of being required to pay permanent damages to injured property owners by cement plant owners would itself be a reasonable effective spur to research for improved techniques to minimize nuisance.

The power of the court to condition on equitable grounds the continuance of an injunction on the payment of permanent damages seems undoubted.

The damage base here suggested is consistent with the general rule in those nuisance cases where damages are allowed. "Where a nuisance is of such a permanent and unabatable character that a single recovery can be had, including the whole damage past and future resulting therefrom, there can be but one recovery" (66 C.J.S. Nuisances § 140, p. 947). It has been said that permanent damages are allowed where the loss recoverable would obviously be small as compared with the cost of removal of the nuisance.

* * *

Thus it seems fair to both sides to grant permanent damages to plaintiffs which will terminate this private litigation. The theory of damage is the "servitude on land" of plaintiffs imposed by defendant's nuisance.

The judgment, by allowance of permanent damages imposing a servitude on land, which is the basis of the actions, would preclude future recovery by plaintiffs or their grantees.

* * *

The orders should be reversed, without costs, and the cases remitted to Supreme Court, Albany County to grant an injunction which shall be vacated upon payment by defendant of such amounts of permanent damage to the respective plaintiffs as shall for this purpose be determined by the court.

JASEN, JUDGE (dissenting).

I agree with the majority that a reversal is required here, but I do not subscribe to the newly enunciated doctrine of assessment of permanent damages, in lieu of an injunction, where substantial property rights have been impaired by the creation of a nuisance.

It has long been the rule in this State, as the majority acknowledges, that a nuisance which results in substantial continuing damage to neighbors must be enjoined. To now change the rule to permit the cement company to continue polluting the air indefinitely upon the payment of permanent damages is, in my opinion, compounding the magnitude of a very serious problem in our State and Nation today.

* * *

I see grave dangers in overruling our long-established rule of granting an injunction where a nuisance results in substantial continuing damage. In permitting the injunction to become inoperative upon the payment of permanent damages, the majority is, in effect, licensing a continuing wrong. It is the same as saying to the cement company, you may continue to do harm to your neighbors so long as you pay a fee for it. Furthermore, once such permanent damages are assessed and paid, the incentive to alleviate the wrong would be eliminated, thereby continuing air pollution of an area without abatement.

* * *

I would enjoin the defendant cement company from continuing the discharge of dust particles upon its neighbors' properties unless, within 18 months, the cement company abated this nuisance.

Note

For a thoughtful analysis of *Boomer*, see Dobris, *"Boomer" Twenty Years Later: An Introduction, With Some Footnotes About "Theory"*, 54 Albany L.Rev. 171 (1990).

BUCHANAN v. SIMPLOT FEEDERS LIMITED PARTNERSHIP

Supreme Court of Washington, 1998.
134 Wash.2d 673, 952 P.2d 610.

DOLLIVER, JUSTICE.

The certified question in this case stems from the Buchanans' federal lawsuit against Defendants Simplot Feeders Limited Partnership (Simplot) and IBP, Inc. (IBP). The lawsuit complains of manure dust, flies, and odors allegedly emanating from Defendants' feedlot and meat processing plant adjacent to the Buchanans' farm.

* * * The Buchanans own and operate a 320–acre farm near Pasco, Washington. They have farmed and lived on the land since 1961. When they purchased the property, the adjacent properties were primarily used as rangeland. In approximately 1969, a small cattle feeding operation opened on land to the southeast of the Buchanan farm. The Buchanans allege Simplot purchased the feedlot in fall 1992. The Simplot operation now allegedly covers over 580 acres of pens and holds over 40,000 cows. The Buchanans allege Simplot's operation of the lot since 1992 has resulted in a significant increase of flies and foul and obnoxious odors.

The Buchanans allege a small meat processing plant began operation on property to the southeast of the Buchanan farm on or about 1970. They allege IBP purchased and has operated the facility since 1976. The Buchanans claim IBP has significantly expanded its meat processing and rendering plant since 1993, adding a new, large wastewater storage lagoon, a new, large storage pond for brine, and several new "cookers." The Buchanans allege this expansion has resulted in a significant increase in foul and obnoxious odors crossing onto the Buchanans' farm and residence.

The Buchanans sued Simplot and IBP in federal court, alleging nuisance, trespass and negligence. Under the trespass action, the Buchanans complained of flies and manure dust which were damaging the Buchanans' crops. Under the nuisance claim, they complained of the foul and obnoxious odors.

As to the nuisance claim, Simplot and IBP argued to the federal court that their operations were exempt from nuisance suits under RCW 7.48.305, a "right-to-farm" statute. RCW 7.48.305 declares certain agricultural activities do not constitute a nuisance under certain conditions.

The Buchanans disputed Defendants' reliance on RCW 7.48.305. They argued to the federal court that the statute cannot apply since the Buchanan farm allegedly was in operation *before* Defendants' activities. The Buchanans then argued that, even if Defendants could rely upon RCW 7.48.305, the Buchanans could still seek damages in their nuisance action pursuant to a 1992 amendment to the statute. The Buchanans claim the 1992 amendment to RCW 7.48.305 changed the whole statute so as to prohibit just those nuisance actions where injunctive relief is sought.

The federal court issued an order partially granting Defendants' motions for summary judgment. The court dismissed some of the Buchanans' negligence and trespass claims, but it withheld ruling on the nuisance claim, finding there was "a question of interpretation of RCW ch. 7.48 on which there are no relevant Washington authorities." The federal court certified the following question:

Does the 1992 amendment to RCW § 7.48.305 which added the passage "Nothing in this section shall affect or impair any

right to sue for damages" limit application of the balance of the section to actions seeking extraordinary relief?

During the 1970's and early 1980's, every state except South Dakota enacted what are generally referred to as right-to-farm statutes. Neil D. Hamilton & David Bolte, *Nuisance Law and Livestock Production in the United States: A Fifty–State Analysis*, 10 J. Agric. Tax'n & L. 99, 101 (1988). Right-to-farm statutes were created to address a growing concern that too much farmland was being overtaken by urban sprawl. Margaret Rosso Grossman & Thomas G. Fischer, *Protecting the Right to Farm: Statutory Limits on Nuisance Actions Against the Farmer*, Wis. L.Rev. 95, 97 (1983) (hereinafter Grossman & Fischer). As more urban dwellers moved into agricultural areas, nuisance lawsuits by those urbanites threatened the existence of many farms. Nuisance suits frustrated farming operations and encouraged farmers to sell to developers, continuing the cycle.

Most of the right-to-farm statutes adopted across the country codified the common law defense of "coming to the nuisance." Plaintiffs who purchase or improve property, after the establishment of a local nuisance activity, have "come to the nuisance." While this fact did not absolutely bar the plaintiff's nuisance action, it was one factor to be considered in whether to grant the plaintiff relief.

The Washington State Legislature embraced the right-to-farm issue in 1979, when it passed an act entitled "Agricultural Activities—Protection from Nuisance Lawsuits." Laws of 1979, ch. 122 (codified at RCW 7.48.300–.310 & .905). We will refer to this legislation as the Right-to-Farm Act, or the Act. * * * In 1992 the Legislature * * * [amended] RCW 7.48.305. * * * Part of the new law added the following sentence to RCW 7.48.305: "Nothing in this section shall affect or impair any right to sue for damages." Laws of 1992, ch. 151, § 1. The certified question from the federal court questions the effect of this damages sentence on the remainder of the statute.

Before we address the certified question, we must comment on the distinct, yet related, question of whether Defendants may properly rely on the Right-to-Farm Act in defense of this nuisance action. The Buchanans argued to the federal court that the nuisance exemption cannot be raised as a defense by Defendants:

> The Right to Farm Act was intended to protect existing farms from the pressures associated with urbanization. Urbanization is not at issue in this case. Instead, it is the Buchanan family farm that is being forced out by the expanding cattle feedlot and industrial-like beef processing facility. The Right to Farm Act neither expressly nor impliedly applies to this situation.

The Buchanans further argued RCW 7.48.305 applies only to the following situation:

> [I]f a farm or agricultural activity pre-exists at a particular location and then a non-farm activity, such as a residential community,

moves into the area, the non-farm activity is precluded from bringing an action for nuisance against the pre-existing farm.

Since the Buchanan farm allegedly does not constitute "encroaching urbanization," and since the Buchanans' farm was allegedly in operation before Defendants' activities giving rise to the nuisance, the Buchanans argued the Defendants should not be able to raise RCW 7.48.305 as a defense.

In their memoranda submitted to the federal court, Simplot and IBP argued they can rely on RCW 7.48.305. They claimed the only time a farm is *not* exempt from a nuisance suit under the statute is if the farm locates in preexisting urban areas. Simplot and IBP assert their activities were established before any surrounding nonagricultural activities, allowing them to rely on RCW 7.48.305 as a defense. The record shows no indication of any nonagricultural activities existing in the area.

The certified question does not raise the issue of whether Defendants may rely on the Right-to-Farm Act, and we observe that the federal court has yet to rule on the question. We also note there is no case law clarifying the issue of who exactly may raise the Right-to-Farm Act as a defense. Given the lack of authority on the issue, we feel compelled to discuss the scope of RCW 7.48.305. While the issue is not directly before this court, we feel the following analysis will be helpful to the federal court's pending resolution of the matter.

As written, RCW 7.48.305 is not very structured. The statute provides:

> Notwithstanding any other provision of this chapter, agricultural activities conducted on farmland and forest practices, if consistent with good agricultural and forest practices and established prior to surrounding nonagricultural and nonforestry activities, are presumed to be reasonable and shall not be found to constitute a nuisance unless the activity has a substantial adverse effect on the public health and safety.

> If those agricultural activities and forest practices are undertaken in conformity with all applicable laws and rules, the activities are presumed to be good agricultural and forest practices not adversely affecting the public health and safety for purposes of this section and RCW 7.48.300. An agricultural activity that is in conformity with such laws and rules shall not be restricted as to the hours of the day or day or days of the week during which it may be conducted.

> Nothing in this section shall affect or impair any right to sue for damages.

Three conditions can be derived from this statute. An agricultural activity is presumed to be reasonable and shall not constitute a nuisance when: (1) the activity does not have a substantial adverse effect on public health and safety; (2) the activity is consistent with good agricultural practices, laws, and rules; and (3) the activity was established prior to surrounding nonagricultural activities. * * *

The third condition requires the challenged agricultural activity to have been established prior to surrounding nonagricultural activities before the nuisance exemption applies. This condition also suggests an established farm may not be able to institute a new or radically expanded "activity" and maintain nuisance immunity, because the language of the statute focuses on agricultural activity that has been established prior to the urban encroachment. *Cf. Payne v. Skaar*, 127 Idaho 341, 900 P.2d 1352, 1355 (1995) (Idaho Right-to-Farm Act does not protect an established feedlot from nuisance suits if the nuisance arises because of expansion of the agricultural activity). This third condition presents an ambiguity within the structure of RCW 7.48.305: One would assume the statute's nuisance exemption is limited to situations where the nuisance suit arises because of the subsequent surrounding nonagricultural activities, since the Legislature expressly states the statute is designed to protect farms "in *urbanizing areas*" from nuisance suits. RCW 7.48.300 (emphasis added). The language of the statute, however, does not explicitly make this connection between the nuisance suit and the urbanization.

Since the statute contains an ambiguity, this court must look to legislative intent when applying the statute. When analyzing the ambiguous language in RCW 7.48.305 along with the Legislature's finding and purpose in RCW 7.48.300, it becomes clear the nuisance immunity should be allowed just in those cases where the nuisance suit arises because of urban encroachment into an established agricultural area.

Our ability to interpret and apply the Right-to-Farm Act is enhanced by the Legislature's express statement of findings and purpose. See RCW 7.48.300. The first sentence of the statute clearly connects the design of the Act to protecting farms in urbanizing areas:

> The legislature finds that agricultural activities conducted on farmland and forest practices in urbanizing areas are often subjected to nuisance lawsuits, and that such suits encourage and even force the premature removal of the lands from agricultural uses and timber production.

RCW 7.48.300. The second sentence of the statute, however, offers a more sweeping statement:

> It is therefore the purpose of RCW 7.48.300 through 7.48.310 and 7.48.905 to provide that agricultural activities conducted on farmland and forest practices be protected from nuisance lawsuits.

RCW 7.48.300. This second sentence broadly offers nuisance protection for all agricultural activities. In their arguments to the federal court, Defendants focused on this second sentence.

When determining the legislative intent of the nuisance exemption, we cannot blindly focus on the second sentence—we must read it in context with the first sentence. * * * The Legislature is concerned farmlands *in urbanizing areas* are prematurely being closed to agricultural use because of nuisance lawsuits *in those urbanizing areas*. This first sentence expresses the specific problem the Legislature intended to address. We read the second sentence in a narrow sense as responding to the specific problem of farming operations being threatened by urbanization.

The Legislature's stated purpose of the Right-to-Farm Act supports a narrow interpretation of RCW 7.48.305. A narrow reading is also supported by the legislative history of the statute, which is an important tool to ascertain intent. The Senate floor debate concerning passage of the Right-to-Farm Act clearly shows RCW 7.48.305 was intended to protect farms *in urbanizing areas* from nuisance suits.

* * *

The express legislative purpose and the legislative history behind the Right-to-Farm Act support this court's reading the phrase "established prior to surrounding nonagricultural ... activities" as including the premise that the only nuisance suits barred by RCW 7.48.305 are those which arise because of subsequent nonagricultural development and which are filed by one of those nonagricultural activities referenced in the language of the statute. This narrow reading of the ambiguous condition serves the narrowly tailored legislative intent of protecting farms "in urbanizing areas" from nuisance lawsuits which arise because of the encroaching urbanization.

Additionally, we find public policy considerations urge a narrow application of the Act. The protection afforded by the nuisance exemption is similar to a prescriptive easement. When a farm establishes a particular activity which potentially interferes with the use and enjoyment of adjoining land, and urban developments subsequently locate next to the farm, those developers presumably have notice of those "farm" activities. The Right-to-Farm Act gives the farm a quasi easement against the urban developments to continue those nuisance activities.

* * *

We have commented on the issue of who may raise RCW 7.48.305 as a defense only because we find no case law clarifying the ambiguous statute. We are unprepared to rule on the merits of Defendants' reliance on the statute in this case, nor does the certified question ask for such a ruling. Our analysis is solely intended to aid the federal court in deciding the question when the federal proceedings resume.

We now turn to the question of whether the 1992 amendment to RCW 7.48.305 allows the Buchanans to seek damages in this nuisance action. As originally enacted in 1979, the Right-to-Farm Act plainly stated agricultural activities which met the three listed conditions "do not constitute a nuisance." This left little room for a plaintiff to pursue a nuisance claim. If the approved agricultural activity, by statutory proclamation, did not constitute a nuisance, there would be no legal basis for seeking either injunctions or damages under a nuisance theory. In 1992 the Legislature amended RCW 7.48.305 by adding the following damages sentence: "Nothing in this section shall affect or impair any right to sue for damages." RCW 7.48.305 (as amended by Laws of 1992, ch. 151, § 1).

Defendants interpret the damages sentence as referring to a plaintiff's ability to seek damages under related causes of action, such as trespass. Defendants claim the Right-to-Farm Act, as a whole, was designed to protect farms in urbanizing areas from nuisance lawsuits. * * *

* * *

In conclusion, we agree with Defendants' reading of the damages sentence in RCW 7.48.305. We hold the language merely refers to a plaintiff's ability to seek damages in other causes of action, such as trespass. Assuming Defendants can rely on the Right-to-Farm Act as a defense, the 1992 amendment does not allow the Buchananas to seek nuisance damages for the foul odors allegedly emanating from Defendants' properties.

Notes

1. The Supreme Court of Iowa has held a right to farm statute unconstitutional because it conferred immunity from nuisance claims and thus amounted to a taking of neighbors' property rights without providing just compensation. Bormann v. Board of Supervisors in and for Kossuth County, 584 N.W.2d 309 (Iowa 1998) (finding easement to operate nuisance imposed on neighboring land), *cert. denied,* 1999 WL 80820 (U.S.)

2. Spur Industries, Inc. v. Del E. Webb Development Co., 108 Ariz. 178, 494 P.2d 700 (1972) involved an unusual application of the "coming to the nuisance" doctrine in the absence of the type of statute discussed in *Buchanan.* In *Spur Industries,* a developer constructed a residential community (Sun City) near a cattle feedlot. Webb, the developer, sought to have Spur Industries enjoined from operating the feedlot. The court awarded the injunction because odor and flies from the feedlot threatened the health of the purchasers of homes in Sun City. However, having brought people to the nuisance, Webb was required to indemnify Spur Industries for the cost of moving or shutting down.

D. RIGHT TO LATERAL AND SUBJACENT SUPPORT

The right to lateral and subjacent support is a common law incident of land ownership. Lateral support is provided by adjoining parcels of land. Subjacent support is provided by soil beneath the surface and may become an issue when a property owner conveys away mineral rights. *See* 6A American Law of Property §§ 28.36–28.54 (1954); 9 Powell on Real Property ¶¶ 698–703 (1998). Our discussion focuses on lateral support. The law of subjacent support is similar and hence is not treated separately.

NOONE v. PRICE

Supreme Court of West Virginia, 1982.
171 W.Va. 185, 298 S.E.2d 218.

NEELY, JUSTICE:

In 1960 the plaintiffs below, and appellants in this Court, Mr. and Mrs. William H. Noone, bought a house located on the side of a mountain in Glen Ferris, West Virginia. This house had been constructed in 1928 or 1929 by Union Carbide, and in 1964, four years after plaintiffs purchased the house, plaintiffs became aware that the wall under their front porch was giving way and that the living room plaster had cracked.

The defendant below, appellee in this Court, Mrs. Marion T. Price, lived directly below the plaintiffs at the foot of the hill in a house that was built in 1912. Sometime between 1912 and 1919 a wall of stone and concrete was constructed along the side of the hill, ten to twelve feet behind the defendant's house. This wall was a hundred to a hundred and twenty-five feet long, approximately four feet high, and of varying degrees of thickness. The wall lay entirely on the defendant's property, and was approximately ten to twelve feet from the property line that divided the defendant's property from the plaintiffs' property. The defendant purchased her house in 1955 and lived there until 1972, when she sold the property. Before the defendant's purchase, the wall had fallen into disrepair.

When the plaintiffs discovered that their house was slipping down the hill, they complained to the defendant that their problem was the result of deterioration in the defendant's retaining wall. The defendant did nothing to repair the wall and the plaintiffs repaired the damage to their house at a cost of approximately $6,000.

The action before us now was filed in 1968 for damages of $50,000 for failure of the defendant to provide lateral support for the plaintiffs' land, and her negligent failure to provide lateral support for their house. Plaintiffs alleged that the wall was constructed to provide support to the slope upon which their house was built, and that the disrepair and collapse of the wall caused the slipping and eventual damage to their property.

The defendant denied that the wall on her property provided support to the slope, or that the condition of her wall caused the slipping and damage to the plaintiffs' property. In addition, the defendant asserted that the plaintiffs were negligent in failing to take reasonable precautions to protect their own property and were estopped from suing her because the wall on her property was erected by her predecessor in title and the plaintiffs had purchased their property with knowledge of the wall's deteriorating condition.

Defendant made a motion for summary judgment that the circuit court granted in part. The circuit court concluded that the plaintiffs had no right to recover for damage to their dwelling house and buildings, but the court left open the question of whether plaintiffs could recover for damage to their land. The circuit court stated on the record that "there is a duty of lateral support to the land but not to a structure on the land." Unfortunately, while the circuit court stated an entirely correct principle of law, his disposition of this case on summary judgment was inappropriate. While an adjacent landowner has an obligation only to support his neighbor's property in its raw or natural condition, if the support for land in its raw, natural condition is insufficient and the land slips, the adjacent landowner is liable for both the damage to the land and the damage to any buildings that might be on the land. Consequently, we reverse and remand.

I

This case provides an opportunity that we have not had for many years to address the obligations of adjoining landowners to provide lateral support to each other's land. Support is lateral when the supported and supporting lands are divided by a vertical plane. The withdrawal of lateral support may subject the landowner withdrawing the support to strict liability or to liability for negligence. We have recognized both forms of liability in Walker v. Strosnider, 67 W.Va. 39, 67 S.E. 1087 (1910) and this case, remarkably enough, is still in harmony with the modern weight of authority as articulated in the *Restatement (Second) of Torts*.

As a general rule, "[a] landowner is entitled, *ex jure naturae*, to lateral support in the adjacent land for his soil." Point 2, syllabus, McCabe v. City of Parkersburg, 138 W.Va. 830, 79 S.E.2d 87 (1953). Therefore, as we said in syllabus point 2 of *Walker, supra*:

> "An excavation, made by an adjacent owner, so as to take away the lateral support, afforded to his neighbor's ground, by the earth so removed, and cause it, of its own weight, to fall, slide or break away, makes the former liable for the injury, no matter how carefully he may have excavated. Such right of support is a property right and absolute."

An adjacent landowner is strictly liable for acts of commission and omission on his part that result in the withdrawal of lateral support to his neighbor's property. This strict liability, however, is limited to land in its natural state; there is no obligation to support the added weight of buildings or other structures that land cannot naturally support. However, the majority of American jurisdictions hold that if land in its natural state would be capable of supporting the weight of a building or other structure, and such building or other structure is damaged because of the subsidence of the land itself, then the owner of the land on which the building or structure is constructed can recover damages for both the injury to his land and the injury to his building or structure. The West Virginia cases are largely consistent with this position, although none has expressly so held.

The converse of the preceding rule is also the law: where an adjacent landowner provides sufficient support to sustain the weight of land in its natural state, but the land slips as a direct result of the additional weight of a building or other structure, then in the absence of negligence on the part of the adjoining landowner, there is no cause of action against such adjoining landowner for damage either to the land, the building, or other structure.

The issue in the case before us concerns the proper application of the strict liability rule. The circuit court improperly awarded summary judgment because the plaintiffs should have been allowed to prove that their land was sufficiently strong in its natural state to support the weight of their house, and that their house was damaged as a result of a chain reaction that began when the land in its natural state, toward the bottom of the hill, slipped as a result of the withdrawal of lateral support occasioned by the deterioration of the retaining wall, causing, in turn, successive parts of the hillside to subside until the ripple effect reached the foundation of the plaintiffs' house.

The cases recognize that lateral support sufficient to hold land in its natural state may be insufficient to support the additional weight of a building or other structure. If, therefore, as a result of the additional weight of a building or other structure, so much strain is placed upon existing natural or artificial lateral support that the support will no longer hold, then in the absence of negligence, there is no liability whatsoever on the part of an adjoining landowner. In the case before us, this means that if the weight of the plaintiff's house placed so much pressure on the soil that the house itself caused the subsidence, and the land would not have subsided without the weight of the house, then the plaintiffs cannot recover.

II

A theoretical problem that presents itself in all of these cases is the extent to which the obligation of support runs with the land. The weight of authority appears to be that where an actor, whether he be an owner, possessor, lessee, or third-party stranger, removes necessary support he is liable, and an owner cannot avoid this liability by transferring the land to another. Nevertheless, when an actor who removes natural lateral support substitutes artificial support to replace it, such as a retaining wall, the wall then becomes an incident to and a burden on the land upon which it is constructed, and subsequent owners and possessors have an obligation to maintain it.

In the case *sub judice,* the plaintiffs' land had no buildings erected on it at the time the defendant's predecessor in title built the retaining wall on his property; therefore, he needed only to erect a retaining wall sufficient to provide support for their soil. He was not required to furnish a wall sufficient to support any structure which they might erect upon their property. The defendant, as his successor, merely had the obligation to maintain the wall to support the plaintiffs' land in its natural condition. Defendant was not required to strengthen the wall to the extent that it would provide support for the weight of plaintiffs' buildings.

III

Since the pleadings in the case before us make reference to negligence, it is appropriate here to address the scope of a negligence theory. In general, it has been held that while an adjoining landowner has no obligation to support the buildings and other structures on his neighbor's land, nonetheless, if those structures are *actually being supported,* a neighbor who withdraws such support must do it in a non-negligent way. In an action predicated on strict liability for removing support for the land in its natural state, the kind of lateral support withdrawn is material, but the quality of the actor's conduct is immaterial; however, in a proceeding based upon negligence, the kind of lateral support withdrawn is immaterial, and the quality of the actor's conduct is material. Comment e, *Restatement (Second) of Torts* § 819 succinctly explains the nature of liability for negligence.

"The owner of land may be unreasonable in withdrawing lateral support needed by his neighbor for artificial conditions on the neighbor's land in either of two respects. First, he may make an unnecessary excavation, believing correctly that it will cause his neighbor's land to subside because of the pressure of artificial structures on the neighbor's land. If his conduct is unreasonable either in the digging or in the intentional failure to warn his neighbor of it, he is subject to liability to the neighbor for the harm caused by it. The high regard that the law has by long tradition shown for the interest of the owner in the improvement and utilization of his land weighs heavily in his favor in determining what constitutes unreasonable conduct on his part in such a case. Normally the owner of the supporting land may withdraw lateral support that is not naturally necessary, for any purpose that he regards as useful provided that the manner in which it is done is reasonable. But all the factors that enter into the determination of the reasonableness or unreasonableness of the actor's conduct must be considered, and in a particular case the withdrawal itself may be unreasonable. Thus, if the actor's sole purpose in excavating his land is to harm his neighbor's structures, the excavation itself is unreasonable. Furthermore, although for the purpose of permanently leveling the land it may be reasonable to withdraw support that is not naturally necessary, it may be unreasonable to make an excavation for a building that will itself require a foundation, without providing for the safeguarding of the neighbor's structures during the progress of the work. Likewise it is normally unreasonable not to notify an adjacent landowner of excavations that certainly will harm his structures, unless the neighbor otherwise has notice.

"Secondly, the owner of land may be negligent in failing to provide against the risk of harm to his neighbor's structures. This negligence may occur either when the actor does not realize that any harm will occur to his neighbor's structures or when the actor realizes that there is a substantial risk to his neighbor's land and fails to take adequate provisions to prevent subsidence, either by himself taking precautions or by giving his neighbor an opportunity to take precautions. Although the law accords the owner of the supporting land great freedom in withdrawing from another's land support that is not naturally necessary in respect to the withdrawal itself, it does not excuse withdrawal in a manner that involves an unreasonable risk of harm to the land of another. The owner in making the excavation is therefore required to take reasonable precautions to minimize the risk of causing subsidence of his neighbor's land. In determining whether a particular precaution is reasonably required, the extent of the burden that the taking of it will impose upon the actor is a factor of great importance."

* * *

The plaintiffs contend that the defendant should be held liable for negligence in removing the support required by their dwelling, in addition to the strict liability for removing support for their soil, relying on *Walker v. Strosnider, supra* [and] Beaver v. Hitchcock, 151 W.Va. 620, 153 S.E.2d 886 (1967). * * * *Walker* and *Beaver* imposed liability for damages to structures caused by negligent excavation and failure to shore up an excavation; however, they involved situations where the structures were already in existence at the time of the acts that deprived them of lateral support, and the owner of the property was the actor who caused the excavation to be made. If there are no structures on the land at the time of the excavation, the excavator owes no further duty than to refrain from removing the lateral support for the soil, or to substitute artificial support for that which is removed. His duty of support cannot be enlarged by the addition of artificial structures to the land; therefore, the duty of his successor in title cannot be greater, where she has done no act to deprive the structures of their support.

IV

It would appear that the case before us either stands or falls on a question of strict liability. It is admitted that the retaining wall on the defendant's property was constructed at least sixty years ago, before the construction of the plaintiffs' house, and that all parties to this action were aware of the condition of the wall. Furthermore, there is no allegation that the defendant did anything to cause the collapse of the wall, but rather only failed to keep it in repair. Therefore, if the plaintiffs can recover, they must do so by proving that the disrepair of the retaining wall would have led ineluctably to the subsidence of their land in its natural condition. If, on the other hand, the land would not have subsided but for the weight of the plaintiffs' house, then they can recover nothing.

Since the proper resolution of this issue will require the development of an appropriate factual record, the judgment of the Circuit Court of Fayette County is reversed and the case is remanded for further proceedings consistent with this opinion.

Reversed and remanded.

Notes and Problems

1. Is a subsequent purchaser of land liable for the removal of lateral support of adjoining land caused by the previous owner? *See* Vecchio v. Pinkus, 833 S.W.2d 300 (Tex.App.1992). Would the court in *Noone* have reached the same result if the original excavator had not constructed a retaining wall?

2. Assume that the Rolling Hills Homeowners' Association decided to create a fishing pond in the green area it owns near the boundary of the subdivision. The site for the pond was excavated in a careful and workmanlike manner. Nonetheless, the excavation caused the adjoining land to subside in several places, including under a barn and a section of fence. O, the adjoining landowner, established that the land would have subsided even if it had been in its natural, unimproved state. O can recover damages to the land, but can O recover damages to the barn and fence? Would a rule permitting such recovery cause landowners to refrain from improving their land for fear of damaging valuable improvements on adjoining property?

3. A person who removes minerals from the ground is liable if such action causes neighboring property to subside. However, one may withdraw groundwater from a well and, absent negligence, is not liable if adjoining land is thereby damaged through settling. For a case which examines the validity of such a distinction, see Friendswood Development Co. v. Smith–Southwest Industries, Inc., 576 S.W.2d 21 (Tex.1978). *See also* 6A American Law of Property § 28.46 (1954).

E.   WATER RIGHTS

1.   LAKES, PONDS, RIVERS, AND STREAMS

GAME & FRESH WATER FISH COMMISSION v. LAKE ISLANDS, LTD.

Supreme Court of Florida, 1981.
407 So.2d 189.

OVERTON, JUSTICE.

This is an appeal from a trial court judgment holding chapter 65–1841, Laws of Florida, and the implementing administrative rule, unconstitutional as applied to appellees. Chapter 65–1841 authorizes the Game and Fresh Water Fish Commission to regulate the use of motorboats on the public waters of Lake Iamonia in Leon County. By rule 16E–14.02, Florida Administrative Code, the commission invoked this authority to absolutely prohibit the use of motorboats, including airboats, on the lake during duck hunting season. The trial court found the law and the rule to be constitutional as applied to the general public, but to be unreasonable and arbitrary as applied to island owners seeking access to their property. We have jurisdiction under article V, section 3(b)(1) of the Florida Constitution, and we affirm.

Lake Iamonia is a navigable lake in northern Leon County. In it are a number of islands some of which are owned by appellees. The navigability of the lake is described by the trial court as follows:

3. The shallowness as well as the vegetation upon the lake has made navigation upon the lake difficult. While boat paths have been cut by persons using the lake, they do not provide ready access to some of the islands. For access to some of the islands boats must be poled or an airboat used. As to a few of the islands, the water level is too low for even a poled boat and an airboat is the only method of reaching them.

4. Navigation upon the lake has been made more difficult by a drawdown begun by the [commission] in 1977. This drawdown was deemed necessary because the natural outlet, a sinkhole at the eastern end of the lake, had been dammed off several years earlier. The dam had been constructed to prevent the lake from going periodically dry. Natural fluctuations from completely dry to flood had previously occurred with some regularity for decades, perhaps centuries before. After the dam had had its desired effect of keeping the water in the lake basin, it was discovered that the natural fluctuations were required to maintain the ecology of the lake. The lack of periodic drying out resulted in an "undesirable" plant growth, the white water lily, becoming predominant. The purpose of the drawdown was to allow the lake to again go dry. The hope is that this will result in killing off the white water lily so that more desirable vegetation will return along with open water.

During the 1978 duck hunting season, Lake Islands, Ltd., a limited partnership that owns some of the lake islands, requested from the commission a permit to use airboats on the lake in order to take prospective purchasers out to see the property. When the commission refused, Lake Islands sought and obtained from the circuit court of Leon County a temporary injunction restraining the commission from enforcing its rule against Lake Islands during the hunting season. The court later entered a final judgment requiring the commission to issue permits to the island owners for reasonable use of motorboats and airboats on the lake during the hunting season.

* * *

We agree with this holding. Riparian rights under both common law and Florida statute include the right of ingress and egress. In Ferry Pass Inspectors' & Shippers' Association v. White's River Inspectors' & Shippers' Association, 57 Fla. 399, 48 So. 643 (1909), this Court, speaking through Chief Justice Whitfield, set forth in detail the rights of riparian owners as follows:

Riparian rights are incident to the ownership of lands contiguous to and bordering on navigable waters. The common-law rights of riparian owners with reference to the navigable waters are incident to the ownership of the uplands that extend to high-water mark. The shore or space between high and low water mark is a part of the bed of navigable waters, the title to which is in the state in trust for the public. If the owner of land has title to high-water mark, his land borders on the water, since the shore to high-water mark is a part of the bed of the waters; and, if it is a navigable waterway, he has as incident to such title the riparian rights accorded by the common law to such an owner.

Among the common-law rights of those who own land bordering on navigable waters apart from rights of alluvion and dereliction are the right of access to the water from the land for navigation and other purposes expressed or implied by law, the right to a reasonable use of the water for domestic purposes, the right to the flow of the water without serious interruption by upper or lower riparian owners or others, the right to have the water kept free from pollution, the right to protect the abutting property from trespass and from injury by the improper use of the water for navigation or other purposes, *the right to prevent obstruction to navigation or an unlawful use of the water or of the shore or bed that specially injures the riparian owner in the use of his property, the right to use the water in common with the public for navigation, fishing, and other purposes in which the public has an interest. Subject to the superior rights of the public as to navigation and commerce, and to the concurrent rights of the public as to fishing and bathing and the like,* a riparian owner may erect upon the bed and shores adjacent to his riparian holdings bath houses, wharves, or other structures to facilitate his business or pleasure; but these privileges are subject to the rights of the public to be enforced by proper public authority or by individuals who are specially and unlawfully injured. Riparian owners have no exclusive right to navigation in or commerce upon a navigable stream opposite the riparian holdings, and have no right to so use the water or land under it as to obstruct or unreasonably impede lawful navigation and commerce by others, or so as to unlawfully burden or monopolize navigation or commerce. The exclusive rights of a riparian owner are such as are necessary for the use and enjoyment of his abutting property and the business lawfully conducted thereon; and these rights may not be so exercised as to injure others in their lawful rights. * * *

The rights of the public in navigable streams for purposes of navigation are to use the waters and the shores to high-water mark in a proper manner for transporting persons and property thereon subject to controlling provisions and principles of law. The right of navigation should be so used and enjoyed as not to infringe upon the lawful rights of others. All inhabitants of the state have concurrent rights to navigate and to transport property in the public waters of the state. As to mere navigation in and commerce upon the public waters, riparian owners as such have no rights superior to other inhabitants of the state. * * *

Id., 57 Fla. at 402–03, 48 So. at 644–45 (citations omitted; emphasis supplied).

It is a recognized general rule of law that a riparian owner's interest in waterway navigation is the same as a member of the public *except where there is some special injury to the riparian owner*. We fully recognized this special injury exception in Webb v. Giddens, 82 So.2d 743 (Fla.1955). In that case Giddens was the owner of a parcel of land located on a small arm of Lake Jackson in Leon County. He was in the business of renting boats to people who came to fish. To reach the main part of Lake Jackson, his customers had to pass under a wooden state highway bridge that stretched across this arm of the lake. The state road department improved this road by removing the wooden bridge and replacing it with a fill completely spanning the arm and blocking Giddens and his customers from the main part of the lake. The trial court rejected the state road department's contention that one's riparian rights ended when he reached the water and held that the owner had a legal right of access to the main body of the lake for purposes of fishing, hunting, and boating. We approved that lower court decision, holding that one common law riparian right was ingress and egress to and from the water over the owner's land and that the issue was whether the denial of ingress and egress deprived the owner of "a practical incident of his riparian proprietorship." We concluded that Giddens' right of ingress and egress would be virtually meaningless unless he were allowed access to the main body of the lake.

* * *

For the riparian right of ingress and egress to mean anything, it must at the very least establish a protectable interest when there is a special injury. To hold otherwise means the state could absolutely deny reasonable access to an island property owner or block off both ends of a channel without being responsible to the riparian owner for any compensation. A waterway is often the street or public way; when one denies its use to a property owner, one denies him access to his property. This is particularly so in the case of island property. As stated rhetorically in F. Maloney, *supra*, "What good is access to a thirty-foot-deep channel a hundred yards or so long and blocked at both ends?" *Id.* at 104. Reasonable access must, of course, be balanced with the public good, but a substantial diminution or total denial of reasonable access to the property owner is a compensable deprivation of a property interest.

* * *

The rule is, however, constitutional in general application. When the question of ingress and egress of an island property owner is removed, we do not find that the mere restriction on the means of navigation on the lake violates any constitutional rights.

* * *

For the reasons expressed, the judgment is affirmed.

SUNDBERG, CHIEF JUSTICE, dissenting.

I must respectfully dissent to that portion of the majority opinion which holds that the act and implementing rule is unreasonable, arbitrary and unconstitutional as applied to island owner appellees. The majority finds the law and rule to be a reasonable exercise of the police power vis-a-vis the general public, but unreasonable as it affects the appellees because it unreasonably limits their common law riparian rights of ingress and egress.

Regrettably, the majority misconceives both the issue and the extent of the right of ingress and egress inuring to riparian ownership. As is clear from both the trial court's judgment and this Court's opinion, the issue is one of *navigation* across the waters of Lake Iamonia. This case has nothing to do with ingress and egress to and from the uplands from the waters edge, i.e., "access to and from the navigable waters." Merrill–Stevens Co. v. Durkee, 62 Fla. 549, 558, 57 So. 428, 431 (1912). The distinction is crucial, because while the right to ingress and egress is an exclusive right adhering in riparian ownership, the right to navigation is not.

As framed by the pleadings, adjudged by the trial court and held by the majority, the riparian owners enjoy a greater *right of navigation across the waters of Lake Iamonia*, than does the public in general. This simply is not the law. If the act and regulation is efficacious as to the public in general, then it is valid as applied to the island owners. This is so because the right of a riparian owner to navigation rises no higher than the right of the public in general. "The common-law riparian proprietor enjoys [the right of ingress and egress] and that of unobstructed view over the waters and *in common with the public the right of navigating,* bathing, and fishing, * * *." (Emphasis supplied.) Thiesen v. Gulf, F. & A. Ry. Co., 75 Fla. 28, 58, 78 So. 491, 501 (1917). * * * No statutory rights are involved here. Section 197.228, Florida Statutes (1979), merely recognizes such riparian rights as exist at common law.[1] * * * The *Webb* case [relied upon by the majority] to me represents an erroneous interpretation of *Thiesen* principles under the guise of applying equitable principles. By defining the landowner's navigational access to the main body of the lake as "a practical incident of his riparian proprietorship," the Court was less than faithful to the principles carefully articulated in *Thiesen*. There is much mischief in this. Although the *Webb* decision may have wrought an equitable result just as

---

1. Section 197.228(1), Florida Statutes (1979), provides:

Riparian rights are those incident to land bordering upon navigable waters. They are rights of ingress, egress, boating, bathing and fishing and such others as may be or have been defined by law. Such rights are not of a proprietary nature. They are rights inuring to the owner of the riparian land but are not owned by him. They are appurtenant to and are inseparable from the riparian land. The land to which the owner holds title must extend to the ordinary high watermark of the navigable water in order that riparian rights may attach. Conveyance of title to or lease of the riparian land entitles the grantee to the riparian rights running therewith whether or not mentioned in the deed or lease of the upland.

the result of the majority here may be equitable, nevertheless, such a result-oriented decision does a disservice to a body of law which has a pervasive effect on a state with such an abundance of riparian or littoral lands. I would recede from *Webb v. Giddens.*

Consequently, once the majority finds the act and regulation in the instant case a reasonable exercise of the police power over navigation insofar as the general public is concerned, it must be found reasonable as to the island owners because they enjoy no greater rights to navigation on the lake than does the public in general. I would reverse the judgment of the trial court.

Notes and Questions

1.   A riparian owner is one whose land is contiguous to a stream or river. One who owns land bordering a pond or lake is technically a littoral owner. The law, however, generally treats riparian and littoral owners the same. *See* 6A American Law of Property § 28.55 (1954). Thus, it is common for courts and commentators to use the term "riparian" to refer to both types of ownership.

2.   Contrary to indications in the *Lake Islands* case, the common law doctrine of riparian rights also applies to non-navigable waters. *See* J. Cribbet, Principles of the Law of Property 382 (2d ed. 1975).

3.   Does a riparian owner's right to use water constitute a constitutionally protected property interest? Does a statute limiting the future use of a stream by riparian owners represent an unconstitutional taking of property without just compensation? *See* Franco–American Charolaise Ltd. v. Oklahoma Water Resources Board, 855 P.2d 568 (Okl.1990).

PYLE v. GILBERT

Supreme Court of Georgia, 1980.
245 Ga. 403, 265 S.E.2d 584.

HILL, JUSTICE.

This is a water rights case involving a non-navigable watercourse. It presents a confrontation between the past and the present. Plaintiffs are the owners of a 140–year-old water-powered gristmill. They emphasize the natural flow theory. Defendants are upper riparians using water to irrigate their farms. They emphasize the reasonable use theory of water rights.

The plaintiffs, Willie and Arlene Gilbert, own property commonly known as Howard's Mill located on Kirkland's Creek, a non-navigable stream in Early County which goes into the Chattahoochee River. * * * Until August 31, 1978, the Gilberts owned and operated a water-powered gristmill on their property. They also rented boats for profit and permitted fishing and swimming in the 40–acre pond. (On August 31, 1978, the mill was destroyed by fire.)

On July 7, 1978, the Gilberts filed a complaint against Sanford Hill, who is an owner of property that is upper riparian in relation to the

Gilbert's property, alleging that since 1975 he has been diverting and using water from Kirkland's Creek for irrigation. * * * The Gilberts characterized Hill's diversion of waters from Kirkland's Creek for irrigation as both a nuisance and a trespass and sought injunctive relief as well as actual and punitive damages and attorney fees.

The testimony at a hearing on July 18, 1978, revealed to plaintiffs that other upper riparian owners also had irrigated with water from the creek. The plaintiffs subsequently added four defendants * * *. * * * [T]he trial court made an extensive examination of our water law and granted the plaintiffs' motions for summary judgment as to liability against all defendants, holding that the defendants' use of the water for irrigation constituted a diversion, a trespass, a nuisance and an unreasonable use as a matter of law, and enjoining any future use. The issue of damages was reserved for trial. The defendants appeal.

1. Over 100 years ago, when this court first considered riparian rights in Hendrick v. Cook, 4 Ga. 241 (1848), several bedrock principles were established. First, the court firmly rejected the doctrine of appropriation and instead applied riparian principles to the dispute.[1] And in stating the principles of riparian rights, the court also adopted the doctrine of reasonable use. As stated by the court (4 Ga. at 256): "Each proprietor of the land on the banks of the creek, has a natural and equal right to the use of the water which flows therein as it was *wont to run,* without diminution or alteration. Neither party has the right to use the water in the creek, to the *prejudice* of the other. The plaintiff cannot divert or diminish the quantity of water which would naturally flow in the stream, so as to prejudice the rights of the defendants, without their consent * * * Each riparian proprietor is entitled to a *reasonable use* of the water, for *domestic, agricultural* and *manufacturing* purposes; provided, that in making such use, he does not work a *material injury* to the other proprietors." (Emphasis supplied.) The court also held that an injury to one's riparian rights gave rise to an action for damages for trespass even in the absence of proof of actual damage.

Subsequently, two statutes were enacted and codified in the Code of 1863. Section 2206 of the Code of 1863 appears today almost verbatim at Code § 85–1301: "Running water, while on land, belongs to the owner of the land, but he has *no right to divert it* from the usual channel, nor may he so use or adulterate it as to interfere with the enjoyment of it by the next owner." (Emphasis supplied.) Section 2960 of the Code of 1863 now appears at Code § 105–1407: "The owner of land through which nonnavigable watercourses may flow is entitled to have the water in such streams come to his land in its natural and usual flow, subject only to such detention or diminution as may be caused by a *reasonable use* of it by other riparian proprietors; and the *diverting of the stream, wholly or in part,* from the same, or the obstructing thereof so as to impede its

---

1. In the continental United States, the eastern or "humid" states apply the doctrine of riparian rights with some legislative modifications, while the western or "semi-arid" states apply the doctrine of prior appropriation or hybrid riparian-appropriation doctrines. See 1 Clark, Waters and Water Rights 29–32, § 4.1 (1967).

course or cause it to overflow or injure his land, or any right appurtenant thereto, or the pollution thereof so as to lessen its value to him, shall be a trespass upon his property." (Emphasis supplied.) The words "subject only to such detention or diminution as may be caused by a reasonable use of it by other riparian proprietors" first appear in the Code of 1933, § 105–1407, and appear to have been taken from White v. East Lake Land Co., 96 Ga. 415, 416, 23 S.E. 393 (1895).

Thus it is clear that under both court decisions and statutes, Georgia's law of riparian rights is a natural flow theory modified by a reasonable use provision. The reasons for the rule and its contradictory reasonable use provision were well stated by the court in Price v. High Shoals Mfg. Co., 132 Ga. 246, 248–249, 64 S.E. 87, 88 (1909): "Under a proper construction [of the pertinent Code sections], every riparian owner is entitled to a reasonable use of the water in the stream. *If the general rule that each riparian owner could not in any way interrupt or diminish the flow of the stream were strictly followed, the water would be of but little practical use to any proprietor, and the enforcement of such rule would deny, rather than grant, the use thereof.* Every riparian owner is entitled to a reasonable use of the water. Every such proprietor is also entitled to have the stream pass over his land according to its natural flow, subject to such disturbances, interruptions, and diminutions as may be necessary and unavoidable on account of the reasonable and proper use of it by other riparian proprietors. Riparian proprietors have a common right in the waters of the stream, and the necessities of the business of one can not be the standard of the rights of another, but each is entitled to a reasonable use of the water with respect to the rights of others." (Emphasis supplied.)

In this case, the trial court found that irrigation with modern equipment was a "diversion" which is entirely prohibited by Georgia law, Code §§ 85–1301, 105–1407, supra; i.e., the trial court found that irrigation with modern equipment constituted a trespass as a matter of law. We disagree. The use of water for agricultural purposes was recognized as a reasonable use along with domestic use in the first reported Georgia case on riparian rights. *Hendrick v. Cook,* supra.

* * *

The first question, then, is whether the use of water for irrigation is a diversion under our laws and thus is prohibited. We find that it is not. When our riparian rights statutes were enacted, irrigation apparently was practiced only moderately here and in other "humid" states. Thus the General Assembly would not have contemplated prohibiting the use of water for irrigation in enacting these laws. This conclusion is buttressed by the absence of any litigation in Georgia on this topic. Additionally, the legislation largely tracks the case of *Hendrick v. Cook,* supra, and its progeny, and the court therein specified that a reasonable use of riparian water could be made for agricultural purposes. This use for agricultural purposes would have been primarily by some form of irrigation.

In prohibiting "diversion", Code §§ 85–1301, 105–1407, we do not find that the General Assembly intended to prevent the use of riparian water for irrigation, even though irrigation is accomplished by removing water from its natural watercourse. Rather we think the General Assembly intended to prohibit the diversion of water from a watercourse for other purposes, such as to drain one's own property or to create a new watercourse on the diverter's property. * * *

* * *

In sum, we find that the right of the lower riparian to receive the natural flow of the water without diversion or diminution is subject to the right of the upper riparian to its reasonable use, for agricultural purposes, including irrigation.

2. In addition to holding that the use of water for irrigation was a prohibited diversion, the trial court also ruled that the uses at issue here were unreasonable as a matter of law. The trial court granted summary judgment as to liability based on several findings of fact as to which we find a conflict in the evidence.

* * *

* * * [W]e do not find that the record supports the conclusion that the uses complained of were unreasonable as a matter of law. Whether the use of water for irrigation is reasonable or unreasonable presents a triable question. It was error to grant summary judgment to the plaintiffs.

3. In its detailed analysis of Georgia water law, the trial court had to apply Hendrix v. Roberts Marble Co., 175 Ga. 389, 394, 165 S.E. 223, 226 (1932), to the effect that " * * * riparian rights are appurtenant only to lands which actually touch on the watercourse, or through which it flows, and that a riparian owner or proprietor can not himself lawfully use or convey to another the right to use water flowing along or through his property * * * " Thus *Hendrix* held water could only be used on riparian lands. * * *

A major study of Georgia water law concluded that "Another disadvantage of this doctrine is that it permits the use of stream water only in connection with riparian land." Institute of Law and Government, University of Georgia Law School, *A Study of the Riparian and Prior Appropriation Doctrines of Water Law* (1955), p. 104. Likewise, the American Law Institute now recommends allowing use of water by riparian owners on non-riparian land, Rest. Torts 2d § 855, as well as allowing non-riparian owners to acquire a right to use water from riparian owners. Id., § 856(2). The Restatement relies on two principles: that riparian rights are property rights and as such could normally be transferred, and that water law should be utilitarian and allow the best use of the water. Id., comment b. Also, the Institute considers the acquisition of water rights by condemnation a "grant of riparian right." Id., comment c.

Georgia recognizes the power to condemn riparian rights. * * * We agree with the American Law Institute that the right to use water on non-riparian land should be permitted and if that right can be acquired by condemnation, it can also be acquired by grant. Thus we find that the right to the reasonable use of water in a non-navigable watercourse on non-riparian land can be acquired by grant from a riparian owner. The contrary conclusion in *Hendrix v. Roberts Marble Co.,* supra, will not be followed.

4. In summary, the grant of summary judgment, and the permanent injunction based thereon, against each of the defendants must be reversed. On remand, the issues must be tried in accordance with the foregoing decision, looking always to see if, insofar as injunctive relief is concerned, all the uses of the creek and pond can be accommodated.

Judgment reversed.

Notes and Problems

1. Is a lower riparian owner liable to an upper riparian owner if beavers build a dam on the lower riparian owner's land that causes flooding of the upper riparian owner's property? *See* Bracey v. King, 199 Ga.App. 831, 406 S.E.2d 265 (1991).

2. Assume that the Rolling Hills Homeowners' Association has settled the problems caused by the excavation for a fishing pond. The excavation runs parallel to and a few feet from a stream that flows through the subdivision. The Association plans to open both ends of the excavation to the stream so that the stream flows in, creates a pond, and then continues down its natural course. It will take approximately three days for the stream to fill the excavation and continue on course. A farmer downstream waters dairy cattle each day at the stream. The cattle need water readily available. Thus, the farmer threatens to use legal means to prevent the Association from creating the pond. Advise the Association of its rights and obligations, then propose ways to settle this matter.

3. With some exceptions, each state holds title to the bed of navigable water within its boundaries. Navigable water is, however, subject to the public right of navigation and to regulation by the federal government under the commerce clause. *See* 9 Powell on Real Property § 65.11[2] (1998); 3 American Law of Property § 12.27b (1952).

Title to the bed of non-navigable water is vested in the owners of adjoining lands. Thus, ownership of land bordering a non-navigable stream or lake extends to the middle of the stream or lake bed. *See* R. Boyer, Survey of the Law of Property 276 (3d ed. 1981); A. Tarlock, Law of Water and Resources § 3.09 [3][b] (1998).

4. How does one know whether water is navigable? The Court of Appeals of North Carolina noted: "If a body of water is navigable in fact, then it is navigable in law. The test is 'the capability of being used for purposes of trade and travel in the usual and ordinary mode * * * and not the extent and manner of such use.'" Steel Creek Development Corporation v. James, 58 N.C.App. 506, 511, 294 S.E.2d 23, 27 (1982). *See also* A. Tarlock, Law of Water Rights and Resources §§ 8.02–8.03 (1998).

5. In People v. Emmert, 198 Colo. 137, 597 P.2d 1025 (1979), the owner of the bed of a non-navigable stream sought to exclude rafters from floating on the stream across the owner's land. The court upheld a criminal trespass conviction against the rafters stating:

It is the general rule of property law recognized in Colorado that the land underlying non-navigable streams is the subject of private ownership and is vested in the proprietors of the adjoining lands. Hartman v. Tresise, 36 Colo. 146, 84 P. 685 (1906). It is clear, therefore, that since the section of the Colorado River here involved is non-navigable the title to the stream bed is owned by the riparian landowner, the Ritschard Cattle Company. Defendants do not dispute the ownership by the Ritschard Cattle Company of the riverbed in question.

The common law rule holds that he who owns the surface of the ground has the exclusive right to everything which is above it (*"cujus est solum, ejus est usque ad coelum"*). This fundamental rule of property law has been recognized not only judicially but also by our General Assembly when in 1937 it enacted what is now codified as section 41–1–107, C.R.S.1973:

"The ownership of space above the lands and waters of this state is declared to be vested in the several owners of the surface beneath, subject to the right of flight of aircraft."

Applying this rule, which was implicitly adopted by the court in *Hartman, supra,* the ownership of the bed of a non-navigable stream vests in the owner the exclusive right of control of everything above the stream bed, subject only to constitutional and statutory limitations, restrictions and regulations. Thus, in *Hartman, supra,* ownership of the stream bed was held to include the exclusive right of fishery in the waters flowing over it. It follows that whoever "breaks the close"— intrudes upon the space above the surface of the land—without the permission of the owner, whether it be for fishing or for other recreational purposes, such as floating, as in this case, commits a trespass.

We have not been cited to any Colorado decisions interpreting constitutional or statutory provisions which may have modified the common law rule of property law upon which we predicate this decision. And we do not feel constrained to follow the trend away from the coupling of bed title with the right of public recreational use of surface waters as urged by defendants. We recognize the various rationales employed by courts to allow public recreational use of water overlying privately owned beds, *i.e.,* (1) practical considerations employed in water rich states such as Florida, Minnesota and Washington; (2) a public easement in recreation as an incident of navigation; (3) the creation of a public trust based on usability, thereby establishing only a limited private usufructuary right; and (4) state constitutional basis for state ownership. We consider the common law rule of more force and effect, especially given its longstanding recognition in this state. As noted in Smith v. People, 120 Colo. 39, 206 P.2d 826 (1949): "If a change in long established judicial precedent is desirable, it is a legislative and not a judicial function to make any needed change." We specifically note that it is within the competence of the General Assembly to modify rules of common law within constitutional parameters.

* * *

Id. at 140–141, 597 P.2d at 1027. For a case reaching a similar result, *see* State ex rel. Meek v. Hays, 246 Kan. 99, 785 P.2d 1356 (1990).

6. In both *Lake Islands* and *Pyle* reference is made to the riparian owner's common law right to the flow of water free from pollution. Again the question of reasonableness arises, but resolution of this issue between riparian owners has little effect on overall water quality. Congress, therefore, enacted the Clean Water Act which, among other things, established nation-wide controls on the discharge of water pollutants. 33 U.S.C.A. §§ 1251 *et seq.* (West 1994 & Supp.1998). The Act is much too complex to cover at this point and is best left for a course on environmental law.

COFFIN v. LEFT HAND DITCH CO.

Supreme Court of Colorado, 1882.
6 Colo. 443.

HELM, J. Appellee, who was plaintiff below, claimed to be the owner of certain water by virtue of an appropriation thereof from the south fork of the St. Vrain creek. It appears that such water, after its diversion, is carried by means of a ditch to the James creek, and thence along the bed of the same to Left Hand creek, where it is again diverted by lateral ditches and used to irrigate lands adjacent to the last named stream. Appellants are the owners of lands lying on the margin and in the neighborhood of the St. Vrain below the mouth of said south fork thereof, and naturally irrigated therefrom.

In 1879 there was not a sufficient quantity of water in the St. Vrain to supply the ditch of appellee and also irrigate the said lands of appellant. A portion of appellee's dam was torn out, and its diversion of water thereby seriously interfered with by appellants. The action is brought for damages arising from the trespass, and for injunctive relief to prevent repetitions thereof in the future.

* * *

* * * [T]rial was had before a jury * * * and verdict and judgment given for appellee [plaintiff below]. Such recovery was confined, however, to damages for injury to the dam alone, and did not extend to those, if any there were, resulting from the loss of water.

* * *

* * * [T]wo important questions upon the subject of water rights are fairly presented by the record, and we cannot well avoid resting our decision upon them.

It is contended by counsel for appellants that the common law principles of riparian proprietorship prevailed in Colorado until 1876, and that the doctrine of priority of right to water by priority of appropriation thereof was first recognized and adopted in the constitution. But we think the latter doctrine has existed from the date of the earliest appropriations of water within the boundaries of the state. The climate is dry, and the soil, when moistened only by the usual rainfall, is arid and unproductive; except in a few favored sections, artificial irrigation for agriculture is an absolute necessity. Water in the various streams thus acquires a value unknown in moister climates. Instead of being a mere incident to the soil, it rises, when appropriated, to the dignity of a distinct usufructuary estate, or right of property. It has always been the policy of the national, as well as the territorial and state governments, to encourage the diversion and use of water in this country for agriculture; and vast expenditures of time and money have been made in reclaiming and fertilizing by irrigation portions of our unproductive territory.

* * *

We conclude, then, that the common law doctrine giving the riparian owner a right to the flow of water in its natural channel upon and over his lands, even though he makes no beneficial use thereof, is inapplicable to Colorado. Imperative necessity, unknown to the countries which gave it birth, compels the recognition of another doctrine in conflict therewith. And we hold that, in the absence of express statutes to the contrary, the first appropriator of water from a natural stream for a beneficial purpose has, with the qualifications contained in the constitution, a prior right thereto, to the extent of such appropriation.

* * *

It is urged, however, that even if the doctrine of priority or superiority of right by priority of appropriation be conceded, appellee in this case is not benefited thereby. Appellants claim that they have a better right to the water because their lands lie along the margin and in the neighborhood of the St. Vrain. They assert that, as against them, appellee's diversion of said water to irrigate lands adjacent to Left Hand creek, though prior in time, is unlawful.

In the absence of legislation to the contrary, we think that the right to water acquired by priority of appropriation thereof is not in any way dependent upon the *locus* of its application to the beneficial use designed. And the disastrous consequences of our adoption of the rule contended for, forbid our giving such a construction to the statutes as will concede the same, if they will properly bear a more reasonable and equitable one.

The doctrine of priority of right by priority of appropriation for agriculture is evoked, as we have seen, by the imperative necessity for artificial irrigation of the soil. And it would be an ungenerous and inequitable rule that would deprive one of its benefit simply because he has, by large expenditure of time and money, carried the water from one stream over an intervening watershed and cultivated land in the valley of another. It might be utterly impossible, owing to the topography of the country, to get water upon his farm from the adjacent stream; or if possible, it might be impracticable on account of the distance from the point where the diversion must take place and the attendant expense; or the quantity of water in such stream might be entirely insufficient to supply his wants.

* * *

* * * [T]his is an action of trespass; the defendants below were, according to the verdict of the jury, and according to the views herein expressed, wrong-doers * * *.

The judgment of the court below will be affirmed.

Affirmed.

Notes

1. At common law, no right to divert water could be obtained by prior appropriation. Yet *Left Hand Ditch* indicates the importance of the prior appropriation doctrine in the arid regions of the United States. Many western states have enacted appropriation statutes in recognition of the need to protect the prior appropriator's water needs, especially during periods of short supply. *See* 6 Thompson on Real Property §§ 50.07(c), 50.09 (1994 & Supp.1998).

2. Most prior appropriation states have adopted a permit system, under which all appropriations are a matter of public record. Rather than rely exclusively upon the user's previous acts to determine the amount which can be appropriated, the permit system empowers a state administrative agency to determine the amount of water needed by each appropriator and to allocate the finite supply of water among the users. Each permit determines the amount of the diversion, and the period of time for which that allocation is guaranteed. The permit system offers greater certainty concerning water rights, as well as a degree of regulation for public benefit.

This approach is not limited to states which have recognized the right of prior appropriation, but has been used by several riparian eastern states as well. Some of these eastern states have adopted the permit system as a replacement for the riparian system in order to guarantee greater control over how the state's water system is managed, and to help deal with any water problems in the future. Other eastern states have maintained the riparian system but now require permits for certain watersheds or for certain uses, such as irrigation and industry. *See* A. Tarlock, J. Corbridge, & D. Getches, Water Resource Management 104–110, 235–244 (4th ed. 1993); *see also* Corbridge, *Historical Water Use and the Protection of Vested Rights: A Challenge for Colorado Water Law,* 69 U.Colo.L.Rev. 503 (1998); *see generally* Note, *Reallocating Western Water: Beneficial Use, Property, and Politics,* 1986 U.Ill.L.Rev. 277.

3. Does the right of prior appropriation include the storage of water from a stream for later application to some beneficial use? *See* Matter of Applications for Water Rights of the Upper Gunnison River Water Conservancy District, 838 P.2d 840 (Colo.1992).

4.　Natural forces can alter the boundaries of a riparian or littoral owner's land. *See* the *Honsinger* case on page 612.

2.　DIFFUSED SURFACE WATER

HEINS IMPLEMENT COMPANY v. MISSOURI HIGHWAY & TRANSPORTATION COMMISSION

Supreme Court of Missouri, 1993.
859 S.W.2d 681.

PRICE, JUDGE.

The principal issue raised by this appeal is whether the modified common enemy doctrine should be applied to bar recovery by landowners and tenants whose property was flooded because a culvert under a highway bypass was not designed to handle the normal overflows from a nearby creek. We conclude that the common enemy doctrine no longer reflects the appropriate rule in situations involving surface water runoff and adopt a doctrine of reasonable use in its stead. We reverse the trial court's grant of judgment notwithstanding the verdict and remand.

I.　BACKGROUND

* * *

Appellants own or rent commercial and agricultural property along the bottomlands of Wakenda Creek, near the intersection of State Route 10 and U.S. Route 65 south of Carrollton. At this location, Route 10 runs east-west and Route 65 runs north-south. Before the obstructing bypass was built, Wakenda Creek regularly escaped its banks after heavy rainfalls. The floodwaters ran south over Route 10 and collected in a small artificial lake. When the lake's capacity was exceeded, the waters headed east over portions of appellants' lands before crossing Route 65 and returning to the creek farther downstream. These floods were always brief and had never reached any of appellants' buildings.

The Missouri Highway & Transportation Commission (MHTC) condemned some of the property owned by each of the appellants, or their predecessors in title, to build a bypass for Route 65. Mel Downs was the chief design engineer for this project. Downs testified that, although he knew Wakenda Creek was prone to flooding toward the north, he did not know that it also commonly overflowed to the south across Routes 10 and 65. Consequently, he designed a five-foot culvert under the bypass to handle normal rainfall drainage from the area west of the bypass. Downs admitted that this culvert was inadequate to drain the creek's other normal overflows.

Work on the bypass project began in 1975 and ended in 1977. The late 1970s happened to be a period of severe drought in the area. But in July 1981, heavy rains swelled Wakenda Creek once more. The errant waters coursed south and east over appellants' lands as they had done before. However, when they reached Route 65 they met the new bypass arching above Route 10. The raised bypass with its inadequate drainage culvert acted as a dam, pooling the water on appellants' lands, where it remained for seven days. Commercial buildings were invaded by up to thirty inches of water. Numerous items of business and farm equipment and hundreds of acres of crops were destroyed. Similar floods recurred in June 1982, April 1983, February 1985, October 1985, and June 1990.

Appellants filed suit in 1985 against MHTC; Mel Downs; Frank Trager & Sons, the general contractor for the bypass project; and Carroll County Recreation Club, owner of the lake through which the floodwaters passed on their way to appellants' lands. The trial court granted summary judgment on all claims against the contractor, the engineer, and the club, and on the claims of negligence and nuisance against MHTC. The two remaining counts alleging inverse condemnation against MHTC were tried to a jury.

The jury returned verdicts in favor of appellants and assessed their damages at $298,175. * * * MHTC filed a motion for judgment n.o.v., arguing that appellants' action was barred by the original condemnation proceedings and by the common enemy doctrine. The trial court sustained MHTC's motion and entered judgment in its favor.

II. Res Judicata

Appellants first challenge the grant of MHTC's motion for judgment n.o.v., asserting that their action was not barred by res judicata by reason of the original condemnation proceedings for the construction of the bypass. * * *

Appellants could not be expected to discern in the bypass plans a consequence that the designer himself did not foresee. It is true that appellants possessed a crucial bit of knowledge that Downs did not—the fact that the Wakenda regularly flooded Routes 10 and 65. However, appellants could not be aware of, and are not responsible for, this omission. The public has a right to expect that the designers of major public works projects will consider all relevant factors, especially when the necessary information is readily available.

Moreover, the risk of subsequent flooding could not have been asserted in the original condemnation proceedings because it would have been considered too remote or speculative at that time. A judgment is not conclusive of any question that could not have been adjudicated in the case in which it was rendered. Therefore, the fact that each of the appellants (or their predecessors) received some compensation in the initial condemnation does not bar this action for damages subsequently caused by unanticipated flooding.

III. The Common Enemy Doctrine/Natural Flow
(Civil Law) Rule/Reasonable Use Rule

A.

At the heart of this appeal lies the parties' dispute over the applicability of the modified common enemy doctrine, which has directed the law of surface waters in our state since 1884. See Abbott v. Kansas City, St. Joseph & Council Bluffs R.R. Co., 83 Mo. 271, 286 (1884). It was initially formulated as follows:

> But in the case of surface water, which is regarded as a common enemy, [each owner] is at liberty to guard against it, or divert it from his premises, provided he exercises reasonable care and prudence in accomplishing that object * * *. [T]he owner of the dominant or superior heritage 'must improve and use his own lands in a reasonable way, and in so doing he may turn the course of, and protect his own land from, the surface water flowing thereon; and he will not be liable for any incidental injury occasioned to others by the changed course in which the water may naturally flow, and for its increase upon the land of others. Each proprietor, in such case, is left to protect his own lands against the common enemy of all.'

Hosher v. K.C., St.J. & C.B. R.R. Co., 60 Mo. 329, 333 (1875) (quoting McCormick v. K.C., St.J. & C.B. R.R. Co., 57 Mo. 433, 438 (1874)).[1]

Later decisions assuaged the Court's discomfort with the harshness of this doctrine by developing a series of mitigating exceptions. Unfortunately, the decisions have not always agreed on the scope of these exceptions or the reasoning behind them. In fact, a recent opinion by our court of appeals flatly states that the precedents cannot be reconciled. Brown v. H & D Duenne Farms, Inc., 799 S.W.2d 621, 628 (Mo.App. 1990).

* * *

* * * It is apparent that the confusion resulting from the various applications of the modified common enemy doctrine in Missouri now justifies a reexamination of our surface water law.

B.

American courts have developed three distinct approaches to controversies involving the diversion or impoundment of diffuse surface waters: the civil law or natural flow rule, the common enemy doctrine, and the reasonable use rule.[2] * * *

Extensive analyses of these doctrines have been undertaken by several courts; they need not be repeated here.[3] Briefly, the civil law rule appears to be derived from the French and Spanish civil codes, which in turn have their roots in Roman law. It imposes liability for any interference with the natural surface drainage pattern that causes injury to

1. This rule is applied directly to private persons and indirectly to public entities. Any action of a public entity found to be privileged under the common enemy doctrine does not infringe upon a viable property right of adjacent landowners, and therefore it does not constitute a taking.

2. See generally Kinyon & McClure, Interferences with Surface Waters, 24 Minn. L.Rev. 891 (1940); Beck, Waters and Water Rights, vol. 2, § 10.03 (1991). The ensuing discussion is freely adapted from these two sources without further attribution.

3. See, e.g., Keys v. Romley, 412 P.2d 529 (Cal.1966); Armstrong v. Francis Corp., 120 A.2d 4 (N.J.1956); Pendergrast v. Aiken, 236 S.E.2d 787 (N.C.1977); Butler v. Bruno, 341 A.2d 735 (R.I.1975).

another's land. Each parcel of land is said to be subject to a natural servitude or easement for the flow of surface water, so that the lower or servient estate is obliged to accept the water that would naturally drain into it, and the higher or dominant estate is precluded from retaining the water that would naturally drain out of it.

The civil law doctrine, with its comforting allusions to the "natural" law, was sometimes adopted or retained as a gentler alternative to the perceived crudity of the common enemy doctrine. Many courts rejected it, however, out of concern that it would impede the development of land and thus would retard the march of progress that was so dear to the nineteenth century. Courts also encountered difficulties in determining "what was the exact course of the 'natural flow' of the surface water before the bulldozers arrived on the scene." Butler v. Bruno, 341 A.2d at 738.

The common enemy doctrine, in contrast, was once believed to derive from the English common law, but it is now accepted that the English law of surface waters was unsettled when the doctrine first appeared in Massachusetts. It is based on an exaggerated view of the notion of absolute ownership of land, as reflected by the rather primitive analysis that justified its original formulation:

> [T]he right of a party to the free and unfettered control of his own land above, upon and beneath the surface cannot be interfered with or restrained by any considerations of injury to others which may be occasioned by the flow of mere surface water in consequence of the lawful appropriation of land by its owner to a particular use or mode of enjoyment.

Gannon v. Hargadon, 10 Allen 106, 110 (Mass.1865). As a consequence of this short-sighted focus on "the due exercise of dominion over [one's] own soil", id., the doctrine completely ignores the fact that invasion by an unwanted and destructive volume of water might otherwise have been viewed as a classic trespass.

At one time, the common enemy doctrine held sway over most of the United States. Many courts were persuaded that it would best promote land development and economic growth, particularly as compared to the civil law rule. On the other hand, the practical consequence of adherence to this rule has been described as "a neighborhood contest between pipes and dikes from which 'breach of the peace is often inevitable.' "R. Timothy Weston, *Gone with the Water: Drainage Rights and Storm Water Management in Pennsylvania,* 22 Vill.L.Rev. 901, 908 (1977). The enduring objection to the common enemy doctrine was aptly put by a member of this Court: "This is a mere reiteration of the doctrine of 'sauve qui peut,' or as popularly translated into our vernacular 'the devil take the hindmost.' "Shane v. K.C., St.J. & C.B. R.R. Co., 71 Mo. 237, 252 (1879).

Predictably, neither of these rigid doctrines has proved workable in the real world. In short order each was encrusted with a myriad of mitigating exceptions, in some cases harsh and capricious and in most cases confusing and unpredictable. Perhaps the most telling fact is that courts applying these ostensibly opposite rules often reach similar results. In their frequently cited analysis of surface water law, Kinyon and McClure concluded that "in many types of situation, though by no means in all, the actual decisions under both rules are harmonious." 24 Minn.L.Rev. at 934. Over the years, through the accretion of complementary exceptions and qualifications, the two doctrines have been laboriously drifting towards confluence—and, not coincidentally, toward the third doctrine of surface water use.

The rule of reasonable use differs from the other two rules in that it does not purport to lay down any specific rights or privileges with respect to surface waters, but leaves each case to be determined on its own facts, in accordance with general principles of fairness and common sense. Under the common enemy and civil law regimes, the law of surface waters is treated as a branch of property law. The reasonable use doctrine has a dual nature. While it has been recognized as a distinct property law concept, it has also been recognized as a tort. The Restatement (Second) of Torts, § 833 (1977), declares that "[a]n invasion of one's interest in the use and enjoyment of land resulting from another's interference with the flow of surface water" is to be analyzed as a form of nuisance.

Under either theory, the thrust and elements of the rule of reasonableness are the same: "each possessor is legally privileged to make a reasonable use of his land, even though the flow of surface waters is altered thereby and causes some harm to others, but incurs liability when his harmful interference with the flow of surface waters is unreasonable." Armstrong v. Francis Corp., 120 A.2d at 8. Reasonableness is a question of fact, to be determined in each case by weighing the gravity of the harm to the plaintiff against the utility of the defendant's conduct. Pendergrast v. Aiken, 236 S.E.2d at 797. Liability arises when the defendant's conduct is either (1) intentional and unreasonable; or (2) negligent, reckless, or in the course of an abnormally dangerous activity. Restatement (Second) of Torts § 822 (1977). Perhaps the rule can be stated most simply to impose a duty upon any landowner in the use of his or her land not to needlessly or negligently injure by surface water adjoining lands owned by others, or in the breach thereof to pay for the resulting damages. The greatest virtue of the reasonable use standard is its ability to adapt to any set of circumstances while remaining firmly focused on the equities of the situation.

Some have suggested that the reasonable use rule might be too unpredictable for users of land to follow, or for courts to administer. See, e.g., Argyelan v. Haviland, 435 N.E.2d 973, 976 (Ind.1982). However, those fears have not materialized. Today, the overwhelming majority of American jurisdictions have either adopted the reasonable use rule outright, or have overlaid a reasonableness requirement upon the existing civil law or common enemy jurisprudence—which, in practical effect, may be a distinction without a difference. Only a handful of courts cling to the common enemy or civil law rule and a few employ different rules in different situations.[4]

C.

Upon consideration, we are persuaded that the common enemy doctrine, even as modified, has outlived its usefulness in our state. The rule's harsh origins and labyrinth of exceptions are unduly complicated and confusing and threaten arbitrary and unjust results. In its stead, we adopt the rule of reasonable use as the one most likely to promote the optimum development and enjoyment of land, while ensuring that their true costs are equitably distributed among the competing interests at hand. Moreover, its simplicity of concept will allow for a more flexible and sure application to the many factual situations that inevitably will arise.

4. The reasonable use rule has been adopted by the following courts: Weinberg v. Northern Alaska Dev. Corp., 384 P.2d 450, 452 (Alaska 1963); Page Motor Co., Inc., v. Baker, 438 A.2d 739, 741 (Conn. 1980); Weldin Farms, Inc., v. Glassman, 414 A.2d 500, 505 (Del.Supr.Ct.1980); Westland Skating Center, Inc., v. Gus Machado Buick, 542 So.2d 959, 962 (Fla.1989); Rodrigues v. State, 472 P.2d 509, 516 (Haw. 1970); Klutey v. Commonwealth, Dept. of Highways, 428 S.W.2d 766, 769 (Ky.1967); Tucker v. Badoian, 384 N.E.2d 1195, 1201 (Mass.1978); Enderson v. Kelehan, 32 N.W.2d 286, 289 (Minn.1948); Hall v. Wood, 443 So.2d 834, 840 (Miss.1983); County of Clark v. Powers, 611 P.2d 1072, 1076 (Nev. 1980); City of Franklin v. Durgee, 51 A. 911, 913 (N.H.1901); Armstrong v. Francis Corp., 120 A.2d 4, 10 (N.J.1956); Pendergrast v. Aiken, 236 S.E.2d 787, 796 (N.C. 1977); Jones v. Boeing Co., 153 N.W.2d 897, 904 (N.D.1967); McGlashan v. Spade Rockledge Terrace Condo Dev. Corp., 402 N.E.2d 1196, 1200 (Ohio 1980); Butler v. Bruno, 341 A.2d 735, 740 (R.I.1975); Sanford v. University of Utah, 488 P.2d 741, 744 (Utah 1971); Morris Associates, Inc., v. Priddy, 383 S.E.2d 770, 774 (W.Va.1989); State v. Deetz, 224 N.W.2d 407, 416 (Wis. 1974).

Courts that have imposed a reasonableness requirement upon the civil law rule include: Keys v. Romley, 412 P.2d 529, 536–37 (Cal.1966); Templeton v. Huss, 311 N.E.2d 141, 146 (Ill.1974); Burgess v. Salmon River Canal Co., 805 P.2d 1223, 1230 (Idaho 1991); O'Tool v. Hathaway, 461 N.W.2d 161, 163 (Iowa 1990); Whitman v. Forney, 31 A.2d 630, 633 (Md.1943). Those that have done so for the common enemy doctrine include: Pirtle v. Opco, Inc., 601 S.W.2d 265, 267 (Ark.App.1980); Mattoon v. City of Norman, 617 P.2d 1347, 1349 (Okla. 1980); Irwin v. Michelin Tire Corp., 341 S.E.2d 783, 785 (S.C.1986); Mullins v. Greer, 311 S.E.2d 110, 112 (Va.1984).

The following courts adhere to the civil rule: Fisher v. Space of Pensacola, Inc., 483 So.2d 392, 393 (Ala.1986); Dougan v. Rossville Drainage Dist., 757 P.2d 272, 275 (Kan.1988); Lee v. Schultz, 374 N.W.2d 87, 90 (S.D.1985); Powers v. Judd, 553 A.2d 139, 140 (Vt.1988). The common enemy doctrine is observed by the following courts: Gillespie Land & Irrigation Co. v. Gonzalez, 379 P.2d 135, 146 (Ariz.1963); Ballard v. Ace Wrecking Co., 289 A.2d 888, 890 (D.C. 1972); Argyelan v. Haviland, 435 N.E.2d 973, 976 (Ind.1982); State By & Through Dept. of Highways v. Feenan, 752 P.2d 182, 184 (Mont.1988); Buffalo Sewer Auth. v. Town of Cheektowaga, 228 N.E.2d 386, 389 (N.Y.1967).

Among the courts that observe more than one rule are the following: Nebraska applies the common enemy rule to diffuse surface water, but switches to the civil law rule once the water has reached a drainway. Nu–Dwarf Farms v. Stratbucker Farms, 470 N.W.2d 772, 777 (Neb.1991). Pennsylvania applies the civil law rule in rural areas and the reasonable use rule where artificial uses of land exist. Westbury Realty Corp. v. Lancaster Shopping Center, Inc., 152 A.2d 669, 671–72 (Pa.1959). This rule has been modified by statute. See Pastore v. State System of Higher Educ., 618 A.2d 1118, 1121 (Pa.Commw.Ct.1992). In Texas, the civil law rule governs the conduct of landowners whose title derives from Spain and Mexico, whereas the common enemy doctrine applies to landowners whose title derives from the Republic or the State of Texas. The conduct of non-owners, however, is subject to the civil law rule by statutory mandate. Kraft v. Langford, 565 S.W.2d 223, 229 (Tex.1978).

The standard we sanction today is in harmony with the most basic tenets of our law. "Reasonableness is the vital principle of the common law." City of Franklin v. Durgee, 51 A. at 913. Reasonable use concepts already govern the rights of users of our watercourses, subterranean streams, and subterranean percolating waters. See Bollinger v. Henry, 375 S.W.2d 161, 166 (Mo.1964); Higday v. Nickolaus, 469 S.W.2d 859, 869 (Mo.App.1971). To some extent, they have also applied to upper land owners through the modified common enemy doctrine. Their extension to the management of all diffuse surface waters finally "bring[s] into one classification all waters over the use of which controversy may arise." Higday, 469 S.W.2d at 869–70.

D.

All that remains then is the application of this standard to the facts before us. The instructions given to the jury have not been preserved, but the record reflects that the cause was tried and submitted as an inverse condemnation claim. As it happens, that submission was entirely correct, because MHTC is empowered to exercise the right of eminent domain. § 227.120, RSMo 1986.

Article I, § 26 of the Missouri Constitution provides: "That private property shall not be taken or damaged for public use without just compensation." We have considered whether a "taking" has occurred in surface water situations in terms of the common enemy doctrine. Haferkamp v. City of Rock Hill, 316 S.W.2d 620, 630 (Mo.1958). There, it was noted:

> If defendants' acts in disposing of the surface water were within the permitted limits, there could be no taking or damaging of plaintiffs' property within the meaning of Art. I, § 26, Constitution of Missouri 1945.

This approach would also hold true when the reasonable use rule is substituted for the common enemy doctrine. Accordingly, we hold that when, as a result of a public works project, private property is damaged by an unreasonable diversion of surface waters, whether by design or by mistake, the owner may bring an action for inverse condemnation.

In the case before us, the extent and regularity of the flooding caused by the bypass, coupled with the MHTC's negligence in installing an inadequate culvert would be sufficient to allow a jury to find an unreasonable use and, thereby, an inverse condemnation. Thus, the judgment n.o.v. appears to be in error. However, because the actual instructions which were used to submit the case to the jury are not available, we remand the case to the trial court. If the instructions submitted this matter to the jury consistent with the principles announced here, judgment for plaintiff should be entered in accordance with the verdict * * *. If not, a new trial should be ordered.

* * *

Notes and Questions

1. Although jurisdictions remain widely split over the disposal of surface water, a plurality of states have adopted the reasonable use rule. *See, e.g.,* Kral v. Boesch, 557 N.W.2d 597 (Minn.App.1996). Debate continues as to which rule promotes the most economically efficient and equitable results. *See* Cole, *Liability Rules for Surface Water Drainage: A Simple Economic Analysis,* 12 Geo. Mason U.L.Rev. 35 (1990); Comment, *The Reasonable Use Rule in Surface Water Law,* 57 Mo.L.Rev. 223 (1992).

2. In a jurisdiction following the common enemy doctrine, can a riparian owner alter a natural watercourse for the purpose of alleviating a surface water problem where such action adversely affects other riparian owners? *See* McIntyre v. Guthrie, 596 N.E.2d 979 (Ind.App.1992).

3. UNDERGROUND WATER

MacARTOR v. GRAYLYN CREST III SWIM CLUB, INC.

Court of Chancey of Delaware, 1963.
41 Del.Ch. 26, 187 A.2d 417.

Seitz, Chancellor.

This is the decision after final hearing on plaintiffs' application to enjoin defendant Swim Club from further use of its well * * * and for damages in the sum of $73.49.

This case raises in capsule form very important problems of allocation of rights in percolating water. It is not susceptible of an easy solution, because the controlling test is "objective" reasonableness.

Plaintiffs live on the east side of Marsh Road in Brandywine Hundred and have for their water supply what I will call a bricked well 4 feet 7 inches long, 2 feet 11 inches wide, and just over 4 feet deep. The "normal" water depth is of course much less than the height of the well. The defendant leased land[1] directly across Marsh Road but back about 150 feet from the road and constructed thereon a swimming pool with accompanying facilities. The parties' wells are about 200 feet apart. Defendant proceeded to sink a well of approximately 200 feet. * * *

Defendant began pumping operations from its well on the afternoon of July 7, 1960 for the purpose of filling its pool. The plaintiffs' water fell below the intake pipe at least by the next morning. There followed a series of disagreements resulting in the filing of this action. At the motion stage this court rejected the so-called English rule of absolute ownership of percolating water. The court stated that it preferred to adopt an appropriate legal principle in the light of the fully developed facts. MacArtor v. Graylyn Crest III Swim Club, Inc. (Del.Ch.), 173 A.2d 344.

---

1. For purposes of this dispute defen- dant will be treated as a land owner.

[At the motion stage, the court made the following statements about legal principles governing the use of underground water:

> The issues presented are almost without precedent in the decisions of the Delaware courts. Moreover, there were no decisions in the British courts on the subject of subterranean waters at the time of the separation from the Crown. This court is not bound by the later English common-law rule of so-called absolute ownership. Under the English rule an owner has the absolute right to use percolating water without regard to the effect on his neighbors.

> In the United States, in the absence of binding precedent, courts have adopted rules which seem best suited to the hydrological conditions prevailing in their respective jurisdictions. The result has been a proliferation of doctrines parading under a variety of titles. A common thread binding these decisions is the outright rejection of the English rule of absolute ownership. The American authorities reflect a number of gradations in determining the extent to which one landowner may use water filtering beneath his land to the detriment of his neighbors. Some courts have merely tempered the English rule by requiring that the use be without waste and without malice. California has taken a more extreme view which apparently would require a proration of waters among competing landowners without regard for reasonable use. Between these positions lies the rather amorphous 'reasonable use' doctrine which has itself been subdivided into several categories.

> The court must find that balance which not only will protect the rights of competing property owners but will guarantee as well the fullest beneficial use of the water resources of the state. The English doctrine of absolute ownership lacks the flexibility and reasonableness required by present day conditions. It will therefore not be adopted as the governing law here.

Id. at 345–346.]

The trial resulted in one important change in the record from that presented at the motion stage. At the motion stage, it was contended on affidavit by plaintiffs' expert, and denied by defendant's expert, that there was a hydrological connection between the two wells. At the trial defendant's expert stated that he then agreed with plaintiffs' expert that such a connection did exist. Thus, as strange as it may seem, in view of their relative depths and the other factors mentioned, both wells are drawing from a common pool or reservoir of water.

The defendant's swimming pool requires about 240,000 gallons to fill. It appears that defendant's pump must run constantly for about three weeks to fill the pool. I find that this results in plaintiffs' well being unusable for at least the same period. It also would appear that the amount drawn out by defendant intermittently for miscellaneous pool use during the swimming "season" continues to render plaintiffs' well unusable. Are plaintiffs entitled to relief under the circumstances?

The answer to the question posed first requires the court to determine the applicable legal principle. The doctrine of "reasonable user" commends itself here. This rule permits the court to consider and evaluate the various factors on both sides and arrive at an "accommodation" of the conflicting rights, if that is feasible. It also permits the court to consider the intentions of the offending party and his actions subsequent to the discovery of the consequences of his use of the water.

Before examining the factors relevant to the application of this announced legal principle, certain important preliminary observations are in order. First of all, plaintiffs are not entitled to have the defendant restrained from using its well merely because it can purchase the water commercially at a reasonable rate. I say this because a land owner is entitled to make "reasonable" use of the percolating water under his land. This is one of his "bundle of sticks". Indeed, defendant attempts to bring the same argument to bear against plaintiffs and the court merely reiterates its position. Nor do I think that a prior use by one party automatically preempts the water for such party merely because of such priority.

Nor does the fact that plaintiffs' well may be objectively marginal necessarily deprive them of relief. They are entitled to protection if their use is impaired by an unreasonable use of the water by plaintiff. The marginal nature of the well is however pertinent evidence in evaluating the reasonableness of the comparative uses both for the purpose of determining liability and for the purpose of affording relief.

* * *

What are the facts pertinent to the reasonable user issue? It seems clear that defendant believed and was reasonably entitled to believe that the well it sank would not interfere with wells such as plaintiffs'. Moreover, plaintiffs' well is objectively marginal with a weak recovery rate. In contrast, it appears that defendant's use is recreational. While such use is not to be condemned, it is not entitled to quite the same consideration as a household use. I recognize however that the comparative number of users may also be a relevant factor. So far as appears only a few property owners are apparently affected, and only the plaintiffs complain legally. Next, the defendant is withdrawing water from the land area it occupies in amounts which far exceed what would be the "normal" residential water need for such area, assuming its building density would be about the same as that which surrounds the area. Finally the defendant takes a very large volume of water in concentrated periods.

The foregoing factors, when considered with the balance of the record, lead me to conclude that defendant's initial use of its well was made without an awareness of its consequences on plaintiffs' well. However, after it became aware of such effect defendant's use at least during the period when it pumped to fill the pool was not unqualifiedly reasonable. Whether it will be deemed reasonable after exploration of possible remedies, as hereinafter provided, I need not now decide.

What relief is here warranted? Certainly there are "equities" on both sides. As noted, I do not believe this case justifies a permanent injunction against the use of defendant's well. One immediately asks whether defendant could not pump in amounts and over a time period that would not result in plaintiffs' well going dry. On the record before me there seems to be substantial doubt that the schedule could be sufficiently drawn out to accomplish its purpose without being impractical at least time wise. At least this is so with respect to the filling operation.

The next suggestion that comes to mind is to consider whether plaintiffs' well could be deepened with the hope of obviating the problem. There is of course no assurance that the deepening of plaintiffs' type of well to a reasonable extent would solve the problem created by defendant's pumping. But there is testimony that a nearby similar type of well of some 14 feet is adequate despite the pumping. I think the first approach to a balancing of the conflicting interests for purpose of affording relief is to deepen plaintiffs' well a reasonable distance and see what happens. This can be accomplished by an order made subject to appropriate later change.

I therefore conclude that plaintiffs' request to enjoin defendant from pumping from its well will be granted until further order of the court on the condition that plaintiffs deepen or agree to permit defendant to cause their well to be deepened to a reasonable depth with the cost to be equally divided. Plaintiffs must run the risk of permanent loss of water inherent in deepening the well. Defendant must also arrange for a substitute water supply for plaintiffs in the interim.

As an alternative remedy, if not objectionable to third parties involved, plaintiffs may elect to run at their own expense a permanent connection to the defendant's supply of water from the Suburban Water Company which they may thereafter use so long as they bear their proportion of the costs attributable to such use. If the parties accept one of the alternative remedies and the conditions applicable to it, the order will fix a time schedule and provide for a report on the results of the work. If plaintiffs reject both alternatives or the applicable conditions, no injunction will be granted against the use of the defendant's well. If defendant rejects the conditions applicable to the remedy selected by plaintiffs, a permanent injunction against the use of its well will be granted.

* * *

Finally, I consider plaintiffs' claim for damages. Defendant does not challenge the amount or reasonableness of the expenses. Its defense is that it offered plaintiffs a substitute water supply which was rejected. I accept defendant's defense and decline to assess damages. Unless defendant desires to be heard court costs will be assessed against it.

F. MINERAL RIGHTS

UNITED STATES v. 3,218.9 ACRES OF LAND, MORE OR LESS, SITUATED IN THE COUNTY OF WARREN, STATE OF PENNSYLVANIA

United States Court of Appeals, Third Circuit, 1980.
619 F.2d 288.

ROSENN, CIRCUIT JUDGE.

This appeal asks us to determine whether a government condemnation of a surface tract of land constituted a taking of the subsurface mineral estates so as to entitle the subsurface owners to monetary compensation. The trial court submitted the issue to a jury which awarded damages to the subsurface owners. We conclude it was error to allow the jury to determine the damages to the subsurface estates under the terms of the declaration of taking and reverse that portion of the district court's judgment.

I.

The United States acquired certain lands for the Allegheny National Forest in Warren County, Pennsylvania by condemnation. The federal interest in acquiring the land as stated in the declaration of taking is to promote and protect the navigation of streams, production of timber, and development and management of adequate outdoor recreation resources in connection with the Allegheny Reservoir Project. The land which is the subject of this dispute was not held in fee by any one owner. In addition to the surface landowners, there were several owners of subsurface mineral interests, most importantly oil and gas. Some of the subsurface mineral owners also had interests in the surface. Included among the subsurface owners are the defendants in this case. There is no issue as to the Government's statutory authority to take the land; the question is whether the taking of the surface, reserving a right of access for mining the subsurface limited by government regulations, constitutes a taking of the subsurface mineral interests and therefore entitles owners of such interests to compensation.

The Government's declaration of taking and its complaint exempt from the condemnation any interest in coal, oil, gas or other minerals which are held by parties who have no other connected interest in the land other than a record title to coal, oil, gas, or other minerals. Individuals with any interest in coal, gas, or other minerals who also owned any additional interest in the fee were left with their mineral interests, subject, however, to the constraint that their right to enter upon the land to mine conform to the rules and regulations of the Secretary of Agriculture governing mining in the National Forest.

* * *

II.

Pennsylvania law recognizes that there may be three separate estates in land: the surface, the right of support, and the subsurface mineral rights. Pennsylvania Bank and Trust Co., Youngsville Branch v. Dickey, 232 Pa.Super. 224, 335 A.2d 483, 485 (1975); Smith v. Glen Alden Coal Co., 347 Pa. 290, 32 A.2d 227 (1943). There may be situations where interests in a piece of land may be severed and owned by different persons. In Duquesne Natural Gas Co. v. Fefolt, 203 Pa.Super. 102, 198 A.2d 608, 610 (1964), the Superior Court, quoting from the lower court, stated:

> The right of property in natural gas and oil ordinarily belongs to the owner of the land. The oil and gas are a part of the land so long as they are on it or in it or are subject to control therein. In other words, they are part of the land while they are in place. *They can be severed from ownership of the surface by grant or exception as separate corporeal rights.* Accordingly, they may be the subject of a sale, separate and apart from the surface and from any minerals beneath it; they belong to the owner in fee, or his grantee, as long as they remain part of his property, although use of them is not possible until they are severed from the freehold exactly as done in the case of all other minerals beneath the surface. Hence, a freehold of inheritance may be created in oil and gas.

(Emphasis added; citation omitted).

In this case the interests of the mineral holders had been severed from the surface fee *prior* to the plaintiff's declaration of taking. As to these properties, the declaration sought only to condemn the surface estate, with the reservation to the owners of the right to mine, subject however to the imposition of the Secretary of Agriculture's rules on future drilling on the surface estate. The parties holding only subsurface estates retained the same conditions and rights after the taking as they possessed previously.

* * *

III.

We conclude that it was error for the district court to permit the jury to consider damages to the subsurface estates. The case will be remanded to the district court with instructions to vacate the $485,912 award in favor of the owners of the subsurface estates.

Costs taxed against the defendant-appellees.

Note

A landowner's interest in solid minerals is an attribute of the ownership of the land. Characterization of ownership rights in oil and gas is more difficult. Pennsylvania follows the predominate "ownership in place" theory which recognizes a landowner's property interest in oil and gas lying below the surface of the land. Other states adhere to a "nonownership" theory. Under either theory, landowners who drill on their own land may acquire, by virtue of the rule of capture, oil and gas drained from beneath neighboring property. Oil and gas production is heavily regulated by the states, and statutes modify the rule of capture. *See* E. Kuntz, J. Lowe, O. Anderson, &

E. Smith, Cases and Materials on Oil and Gas Law 19–136 (2d ed.1993); H. Williams & C. Meyer, 1 Oil and Gas Law §§ 203–204.9 (1997).

G. RIGHT TO AIRSPACE

It is ancient doctrine that at common law ownership of the land extended to the periphery of the universe—*Cujus est solum ejus est usque ad coelum.* But that doctrine has no place in the modern world. The air is a public highway, as Congress has declared. Were that not true, every transcontinental flight would subject the operator to countless trespass suits. Common sense revolts at the idea. To recognize such private claims to the airspace would clog these highways, seriously interfere with their control and development in the public interest, and transfer into private ownership that to which only the public has a just claim.

* * *

We have said that the airspace is a public highway. Yet it is obvious that if the landowner is to have full enjoyment of the land, he must have exclusive control of the immediate reaches of the enveloping atmosphere. Otherwise buildings could not be erected, trees could not be planted, and even fences could not be run. The principle is recognized when the law gives a remedy in case overhanging structures are erected on adjoining land. The landowner owns at least as much of the space above the ground as he can occupy or use in connection with the land. The fact that he does not occupy it in a physical sense—by the erection of buildings and the like—is not material.

United States v. Causby, 328 U.S. 256, 260–261, 264 (1946).

Note

Airspace rights are encountered elsewhere in this book. As discussed in Chapter 3, a condominium involves the subdivision of airspace; each condominium unit owner holds title to the space encompassed by the walls of the unit. *See* pages 316–318. Further, the *Penn Central* case in Chapter 6 deals with New York City's plan to preserve historic landmarks by permitting transfer of the right to develop airspace above such buildings to other sites. *See* page 777.

MACHT v. DEPARTMENT OF ASSESSMENTS OF BALTIMORE CITY

Court of Appeals of Maryland, 1972.
266 Md. 602, 296 A.2d 162.

SINGLEY, JUDGE.

This case poses a novel question, apparently one of first impression in this State: Are there circumstances where airspace superjacent to real property may be made the subject of a separate assessment on which state and local real estate taxes can be levied?

The hoary common law concept, *cujus est solum, ejus est usque ad coelum et ad inferos,*[1] has been substantially eroded by technology.[2] For example, Maryland Code (1957, 1968 Repl. Vol.) Art. 1A, § 7, while recognizing that ownership of space above lands and waters is vested in the owners of the surface, subjects the ownership, however, to the right of others to fly aircraft over lands and waters in any fashion which does not interfere with the use to which the surface and the airspace over it is then being put. Judge Delaplaine, speaking for the Court in Friendship Cemetery v. Baltimore, 197 Md. 610, 621–622, 81 A.2d 57, 62 (1951), articulated the modern view:

> "It is true that if a landowner is to have full enjoyment of his land, he must have exclusive control of the immediate reaches of the enveloping atmosphere. Otherwise buildings could not be erected. The landowner owns at least as much of the space above the ground as he can occupy or use in connection with the land."

This quotation is substantially taken from United States v. Causby, 328 U.S. 256, 264 (1946).

As a consequence, the owner of land in fee holds all the complex elements of a single right, a bundle of sticks, if you will, which include not only the right to use the surface, but so much of the superjacent airspace as he can use, as well as the subjacent reaches below. And it is obvious that when a landowner utilizes his airspace for the erection of a building, or quarries or mines below the surface, such use will ordinarily enhance the market value of his property as well as its value for purposes of taxation. Here, however, the question is, what are the tax consequences if he leases his airspace to another?

Philip Macht and Sophia Romm Macht (the Machts), as trustees, hold fee simple title to the property at 11–13 East Fayette Street in Baltimore City, fronting 24 feet on Fayette Street with a depth of approximately 113 feet, improved by a small building some 100 feet in height. In 1961, Charles Street Development Corporation (the Blaustein Building) determined to erect a multi-storied office building on property immediately to the west of that now owned by the Machts. Apparently aware that the doctrine of ancient lights had been rejected by our predecessors, Cherry v. Stein, 11 Md. 1, 21–22 (1857), some positive assurance that the building's eastern face would have unimpeded access to light and air was a problem of immediate concern. To that end, the Blaustein Building opened negotiations with the Machts' predecessor in title. These culminated in an agreement under which the Machts' predecessor leased to the Blaustein Building the airspace over 11–13 East Fayette Street above an altitude of 124 feet. The lease term was 98

---

1. To whomsoever the soil belongs, he owns also to the sky and to the depths, *see* I Coke upon Littleton L.1.C.1. Sect. 1.4a (1st Am. ed. 1853).

2. Mr. Justice Douglas, in United States v. Causby, 328 U.S. at 261 concluded "that doctrine has no place in the modern world."

years and nine months from 1 April 1961, without provision for extension or renewal. The rent from and after 1 January 1962 was fixed at twice the annual real estate taxes imposed on the "entire property" at 11–13 East Fayette Street, "(land, improvements and airspace)" less any increase in taxes attributable to improvements made by the Machts' predecessor, but not more than $8,000.00 or less than $2,000.00 in each of the calendar years 1962 through 1970.

While the lease gave the Blaustein Building two purchase options and reserved a sale option to the lessors, only two of the options are significant here: the right of the Blaustein Building to purchase the airspace at the end of the lease term for a base price of $100,000.00, adjusted, however, for fluctuations in the purchasing power of the dollar, and the obligation of the Blaustein Building to purchase the fee, the improvements and the airspace for $200,000.00 if demanded by the Machts.

The Department of Assessments of the City of Baltimore (the City) first endeavored to value the airspace and place the valuation on the assessment rolls for the fiscal year ended 30 June 1966. For procedural reasons not here important, the City's efforts came to naught, and two years passed until the "air rights" were valued at $50,700.00 and placed on the assessment rolls at that figure for the tax year ended 30 June 1969.

The Machts appealed to the City's Board of Municipal and Zoning Appeals (the Board), which vacated the assessment. The City, in turn, appealed to the Maryland Tax Court (the Tax Court), which reversed the Board, and reinstated the assessment. The Machts then entered this appeal from the order of the Tax Court.

* * *

* * * [T]he Machts seem to concede that the revenue derived from the lease of the airspace could properly be considered, like any other rent, in reaching a valuation of the property as a whole. * * * [W]e see no reason why land, improvements and airspace could not be separately valued for assessment purposes, so long as the sum of the elements did not exceed the value of the whole.

* * *

In 52 Op.Att'y Gen. 425, 426 (1967), the Attorney General, in response to an inquiry from the State Roads Commission as to the propriety of disposing of unused airspace over highways, stated what we understand to be the law:

"* * * The landowner's right to use and *develop* the airspace above his land is well established in Maryland, however, there is little authority concerning the right to *convey* or *lease* airspace. In other jurisdictions, the trend of authority definitely favors a liberal interpretation of the landowner's rights in airspace. The modern trend is to recognize airspace as an 'independent unit of real property', the owner of which is entitled to all the rights associated with land ownership. [Note], 64 Columbia Law Rev. 338 (1964). It appears that the prevailing authority would allow airspace to be conveyed, leased, subdivided, and have interests created in it, and estates carved out of it in the same manner as land." (emphasis in original)

Cf. Horizontal Property Act, Ch. 387 of the Laws of 1963, Code (1957, 1966 Repl.Vol.) Art. 21, §§ 117A–142, which provides that owners of units in condominiums take title in fee simple and sets up a mechanism for the assessment and taxation of the units.

So long as the Machts made no use of the airspace over their property, it was not, nor could it be made the subject of an assessment. Once they denied themselves the use of it for a price, it took on value for the purposes of assessment, a value which could be derived by an appraisal based on income, the option price, or both.

* * *

It should be remembered that this case reaches us in an unusual posture. The taxpayers' attack is levelled at the method by which valuation for tax purposes was reached, and not at the amount of the assessment. If the Machts can demonstrate that the sum of the values separately attributable to land, improvements and airspace exceeds the figure at which the property should have been assessed as a whole, relief may be available. However, this point is not made here.

* * *

It certainly should have been no surprise to the parties that the practical effect of the lease of the airspace was the enhancement of the value of the servient estate because of the rent reserved. In fact, the terms of the agreement are ample proof that this very result was contemplated. In fixing the term of the lease at 98 years and nine months, the parties carefully skirted the provisions of Code (1957, 1969 Repl.Vol., 1971 Supp.) Art. 81, § 8(7)(a) which provides that where a lease is for a term of 99 years or for a shorter term and perpetually renewable, the leaseholder pays the taxes just as if he owned the fee. Had the lease been for 99 years, taxes on the airspace would have been paid by the Blaustein Building directly, and would not have been included in the determination of the annual rent.

In setting up the formula upon which the rent was to be based, the parties carefully stipulated that the base rent was to be twice the annual real estate taxes on the "entire property" at 11–13 East Fayette Street "(land, improvements and airspace)." There was not only no element of surprise, but it may well be that the Machts are estopped from denying that the value of the airspace was an element to be considered in the assessment process. It seems to us that whether the value of the airspace was separated out or included in the valuation of the fee for assessment purposes is indeed a distinction without a difference, so long as the aggregate value of the components does not exceed the value of the whole.

Order affirmed, costs to be paid by appellants.

MACMILLAN, INC. v. CF LEX ASSOCIATES

Court of Appeals of New York, 1982.
56 N.Y.2d 386, 452 N.Y.S.2d 377, 437 N.E.2d 1134.

JONES, JUDGE.

"Tract of land" as used in the New York City Zoning Resolution refers to surface land only and does not include buildings erected thereon. Accordingly, even a very substantial space tenant is not a party in interest whose consent is required for an effective declaration of zoning lot restrictions and the attendant zoning lot merger under the resolution.

Plaintiff is a space tenant in the Macmillan Building, a 31–story building located at 866 Third Avenue in the Borough of Manhattan, New York City. Under its lease as amended which, subject to the tenant's exercise of options, runs until 2008, plaintiff occupies 100% of the usable area of the building above the first floor and 95% of the usable area of the building as a whole.

The Macmillan Building occupies the eastern third of the block bounded by Third Avenue on the east, 52nd Street on the south, Lexington Avenue on the west, and 53rd Street on the north. Adjoining the Macmillan Building to the west are two smaller buildings, an eight-story garage to the north (156 East 53rd Street) and a nine-story apartment building on the south (155–161 East 52nd Street). In the western half of the block, facing on Lexington Avenue, is the proposed development lot which is the genesis of the present litigation.

In July, 1981 Campeau Corporation (U.S.), Inc., purchased the Macmillan Building from The John Hancock Mutual Life Insurance Company, thereby succeeding Hancock as plaintiff's landlord. On September 30, 1981, Campeau, CF Lex Corp. (a general partner of CF Lex Associates, the entity which held title to the development lot), and others, being the holders of separate fee titles to all the underlying land in the block, executed a declaration of zoning lot restrictions to effect a zoning lot merger with respect to the block pursuant to the provisions of the New York City Zoning Resolution as amended. On the same day CF Lex Corp. purchased from Campeau the "air rights" associated with the land on which the Macmillan Building stands for $5,060,000. The objective of the zoning lot merger and the acquisition of these air rights was to enable CF Lex Corp. to erect a larger building on the development lot than could otherwise have been constructed.

In anticipation of these transactions, plaintiff instituted the present action in August, 1981 seeking a declaration that the transfer of air rights by a zoning lot merger of the properties in the block could not be effected without first obtaining the written consent thereto of plaintiff. The contention was that its consent was required because it was a "party in interest" under the zoning resolution.

Defendants moved * * * to dismiss the complaint for failure to state a cause of action, on the ground that plaintiff was not a "party in interest" within the contemplation of the zoning resolution. Supreme Court granted the motions and denied as academic applications by defendants for other relief and cross motions of plaintiff. The Appellate Division reversed the determinations of Supreme Court, reinstated the complaint, temporarily enjoined defendants from proceeding with construction pursuant to the zoning lot merger and the purchase of air rights, and remitted the case to Supreme Court for further proceedings. Defendants appealed to our court pursuant to leave granted by the Appellate Division, 86 A.D.2d 15, 448 N.Y.S.2d 668. We now reverse.

Under the New York City Zoning Resolution as amended in 1977, before a tract of land may be treated as a single zoning lot, a written declaration consenting to the zoning lot merger must be executed by each party in interest, unless such a party has waived its right with respect thereto. Once the separate parcels have been so "merged", the maximum bulk of a building permissible under the zoning resolution is calculated on the basis of the merged zoning lot. Thus, by this means excess square footage associated with an existing building can be made available for use on an adjoining parcel. An "air rights" transfer can thus be effected, making permissible construction on the adjoining parcel of a larger building than would otherwise have been allowable under the resolution. By recourse to these procedures in the present case, defendants sought to acquire air rights associated with the land on which the Macmillan Building stood to enable the construction on the development lot of a larger building than would otherwise have been permissible.

The controversy between the parties is whether plaintiff is a "party in interest" within the prescription of the zoning resolution—if so, the declaration without its participation is unavailing to effect the desired zoning lot merger; if not, the merger is effective and the transfer of the air rights will make possible the desired construction on the development lot. Section 12–10 (subd. [d], par. [iv] ["zoning lot"]) of the zoning resolution provides: "A 'party in interest' in the portion of the tract of land covered by a Declaration shall include only (W) the fee owner or owners thereof, (X) the holder of any enforceable recorded interest in all or part thereof which would be superior to the Declaration and which could result in such holder obtaining possession of any portion of such tract of land, (Y) the holder of any enforceable recorded interest in all or part thereof which would be adversely affected by the Declaration, and (Z) the holder of any unrecorded interest in all or part thereof which would be superior to and adversely affected by the Declaration and which would be disclosed by a physical inspection of the portion of the tract of land covered by the Declaration." Plaintiff asserts that it is a party in interest under one or both of clauses (X) and (Y). This, in turn, depends for present purposes on what is intended by the phrase, "tract of land". If it refers only to the underlying surface land, plaintiff, having no cognizable interest in the land itself, is not a party in interest; on the other hand if it comprehends the buildings and improvements on the land, plaintiff is the holder of a substantial recorded interest therein and thus is a party in interest.

We conclude that the phrase "tract of land" refers only to the underlying surface land and does not embrace buildings on that land. After remarking that the phrase "tract of land" is not defined in the zoning resolution, we base our conclusion on several convergent considerations. In the first place, the denotation of the word "tract" is "a region or stretch (as of land) that is [usually] indefinitely described or without precise boundaries", or "a precisely defined or definable area of land" (Webster's Third New International Dictionary) and the word "land" means "the solid part of the surface of the earth in contrast to the water of oceans and seas" (id.). Neither alone nor in combination do these words in their lexigraphic sense connote buildings or improvements. Moreover it is significant that the draftsmen of the resolution chose not to use the familiar and readily available "land and improvements". Second, as used elsewhere in the zoning resolution we find nothing to suggest that a broader connotation was intended to be attached to the phrase. The words "tract" and "lot" are used to refer to equivalent concepts (see, e.g., § 12–10, "zoning lot", subds. [b], [c]) and it would be a strained interpretation to include buildings and structures.

Finally, it would ill serve the achievement of the objective of the zoning resolution to hold that each party having an interest in a building on the land must join in execution of the declaration. Although it may be acknowledged that in the case before us plaintiff has a very substantial interest in the building, nothing in the phrase "tract of land" would permit a quantum differentiation. To require the consent of every space tenant with a recorded interest in the building, and thus to bestow on each such tenant a power of veto, would be so to encumber the procedure for zoning lot merger as to make it of questionable practical utility. Any such consequence would be inconsistent with the purposes of the zoning resolution, one of which is stated to be, "[t]o promote the most desirable use of land and direction of building development in accord with a well-considered plan, to promote stability of commercial development, to strengthen the economic base of the City" (§ 31–00, subd. [k]).

Moreover, air rights, at the heart of the concept of zoning lot merger, have historically been conceived as one of the bundle of rights associated with ownership of the land rather than with ownership of the structures erected on the land. Air rights are incident to the ownership of the surface property—the right of one who owns land to utilize the space above it. This right has been recognized as an inherent attribute of the ownership of land since the earliest times as reflected in the maxim, *"[c]ujus est solum, ejus est usque ad coelum et ad inferos"* ["to whomsoever the soil belongs, he owns also to the sky and to the depths"] (see Ball, Vertical Extent of Ownership in Land, 76 U. of Pa.L.Rev. 631 in which the maxim is attributed to the early 14th century scholar Cino da Pistoia).[1]

1. The assertion of plaintiff that air rights owe their origin to the New York

For the reasons stated, the order of the Appellate Division should be reversed, with costs, and the case remitted to Supreme Court for entry of a declaratory judgment in accordance with this opinion.

Notes and Problems

1. "An Irish lawyer named Sullivan once argued an air rights case before the highest court of Great Britain. A member of the court asked during oral argument: 'Mr. Sullivan, have your clients not heard of the maxim, *cujus est solum, ejus est usque ad coelum et ad inferos?*' Mr. Sullivan responded: 'My lords, the peasants of Northern Ireland speak of little else.' " Steel Creek Development Corporation v. James, 58 N.C.App. 506, 512, 294 S.E.2d 23, 27 (1982).

2. The question of limits on the right to build in the airspace above one's land may arise in a variety of contexts. Suppose several homeowners in Rolling Hills installed solar panels to reduce their monthly energy bills. They are worried that a neighbor might build a structure or plant a tree which would prevent the sunlight from reaching the panels. What are the rights of these homeowners? Before answering, review the *Fontainebleau Hotel* case on page 357 and the excerpt from the *Prah* case in Note 1 on page 360. *See also* J. Bruce & J. Ely, *The Law of Easements and Licenses in Land* & 12.04 (rev.ed.1995 & Supp.1998); Gergacz, *Solar Energy Law: Easements of Access to Sunlight,* 10 N.M.L.Rev. 121 (1979–80).

3. X and Y own adjacent parcels of land. There are large oak trees located on X's property near its border with Y's land. Can Y cut down tree limbs that grow across the boundary line above Y's property? Can Y remove tree roots that cross the boundary line beneath Y's parcel? See Harding v. Bethesda Regional Cancer Treatment Center, 551 So.2d 299 (Ala.1989).

City Zoning Resolution must be rejected. The zoning resolution provides sophisticated procedures to facilitate the functional transfer of air rights. In so doing it treats * * * property rights long antedating the enactment of the resolution.

Chapter 6

GOVERNMENTAL CONTROL OF PRIVATE LAND USE

Hypothetical Situation—Number 6

Centerville is facing a land use crisis because many people from a nearby metropolis have begun moving into the community. As a result, city utility services are becoming overtaxed and many longtime residents are concerned about Centerville's changing character. The city council asked you to serve as the city's legal counsel to advise it on problems that will arise as the city deals with rapid growth. You agreed and resigned from your firm to devote your full attention and efforts to your new position.

During your first week on the job, the city council asked you to work with the city planner to develop a plan for future growth of the community that will: (1) preserve Centerville's historical sites, open spaces, environmentally-fragile areas, and general character without requiring much money to condemn land; (2) prevent a rapid influx of new residents; and (3) provide for the construction of new sewers and parks at little cost to current residents.

A. INTRODUCTION

Housing, growth management, urban deterioration, and environmental problems plague our society. Federal, state, and local governments have become involved in the real estate marketplace in an attempt to solve these problems. *See* D. Mandelker & R. Cunningham, Planning and Control of Land Development: Cases and Materials 20–31 (1979).

Extensive governmental land use planning and control is a relatively recent phenomenon in this country. Before the turn of the 20th century, most land use control was exercised by private individuals through easement, real covenant, and nuisance law discussed in previous chapters. *See* 1 Rathkopf's The Law of Zoning and Planning § 1.01 (4th ed.1998). Although these doctrines are still significant, their influence on land use has been lessened by governmental involvement of two types: (1) taking private property under the power of eminent domain, and (2) regulating the use of private property under the police power through zoning and subdivision ordinances. The practical distinction between these two forms of governmental action is that under eminent domain the landowner receives just compensation, whereas under the police power the landowner receives no compensation. Naturally, controversy frequently arises as to whether a particular governmental action is a taking or a regulation. *See generally* S. Eagle, Regulatory Takings (1996 & Supp. 1998). In this regard, governmental imposition of exactions as a condition of development has been increasingly a subject of dispute.

As you proceed through these materials be sensitive to takings issues and attempt to formulate a means by which you can distinguish between the two forms of governmental action discussed above. *See generally* F. Bosselman, D. Callies, & J. Banta, The Taking Issue (1973); R. Epstein, Takings: Private Property and the Power of Eminent Domain (1985); W. Fischel, Regulatory Takings: Law, Economics, and Politics (1995). If you hit upon a ready answer, you will be ahead of scholars in the field.

B. EMINENT DOMAIN

This section deals with legal issues that arise when the government acquires private property through the power of eminent domain. How the government manages the property it owns is beyond the purview of this book.

The Fifth Amendment to the United States Constitution provides in part:

> " * * * nor shall private property be taken for public use, without just compensation."

The right to compensation for private property appropriated for public purposes was well established in practice before the American Revolution. The Takings Clause gave constitutional status to the compensation principle and circumscribed the exercise of eminent domain power. *See* Ely, *"That due satisfaction be made:" The Fifth Amendment and the Origins of the Compensation Principle,* 36 Amer. J. Legal History 1 (1992). This provision is made applicable to the states by the due process clause of the Fourteenth Amendment. *See* Ely, *The Fuller Court and Takings Jurisprudence,* 1996:Vol.2 J.Sup.Ct.Hist. 120. Further, virtually every state constitution contains an eminent domain clause and many require compensation for "damaging" as well as "taking" private property. *See* 2A Nichols on Eminent Domain § 6.02 (3d rev.ed. 1998).

Four critical words or phrases are contained in the Taking Clause: "private property," "taken," "public use," and "just compensation." The following cases explore their legal significance, beginning with the concept of public use.

Note

Whether a particular interest constitutes property entitled to constitutional protection is sometimes a matter of dispute. Since the Constitution does not define property, the Supreme Court usually determines the existence of a property interest by reference to state law. Applying this precept, the Supreme Court in Phillips v. Washington Legal Foundation, 118 S.Ct. 1925 (1998) concluded that, under state law, interest earned on a deposit of money accrues to the owner of the principal. Accordingly, the Court determined that interest earned on lawyers' trust accounts is private property for purposes of the Takings Clause. The Court added that "a State may not sidestep the Takings Clause by disavowing traditional property interests long recognized under state law." *Id.* at 1931. *See generally* Note, *IOLTAs Unmasked: Legal Aid Programs' Funding Results in Taking of Clients' Property,* 50 Vand.L.Rev. 1297 (1997).

HAWAII HOUSING AUTHORITY v. MIDKIFF

Supreme Court of the United States, 1984.
467 U.S. 229.

JUSTICE O'CONNOR delivered the opinion of the Court.

The Fifth Amendment of the United States Constitution provides, in pertinent part, that "private property [shall not] be taken for public use, without just compensation." These cases present the question whether the Public Use Clause of that Amendment, made applicable to the States through the Fourteenth Amendment, prohibits the State of Hawaii from taking, with just compensation, title in real property from lessors and transferring it to lessees in order to reduce the concentration of ownership of fees simple in the State. We conclude that it does not.

I

A

The Hawaiian Islands were originally settled by Polynesian immigrants from the western Pacific. These settlers developed an economy around a feudal land tenure system in which one island high chief, the ali'i nui, controlled the land and assigned it for development to certain subchiefs. The subchiefs would then reassign the land to other lower ranking chiefs, who would administer the land and govern the farmers and other tenants working it. All land was held at the will of the ali'i nui and eventually had to be returned to his trust. There was no private ownership of land.

Beginning in the early 1800's, Hawaiian leaders and American settlers repeatedly attempted to divide the lands of the kingdom among the crown, the chiefs, and the common people. These efforts proved largely unsuccessful, however, and the land remained in the hands of a few. In the mid–1960's, after extensive hearings, the Hawaii Legislature discovered that, while the State and Federal Governments owned almost 49% of the State's land, another 47% was in the hands of only 72 private landowners. The legislature further found that 18 landholders, with tracts of 21,000 acres or more, owned more than 40% of this land and that on Oahu, the most urbanized of the islands, 22 landowners owned 72.5% of the fee simple titles. The legislature concluded that concentrated land ownership was responsible for skewing the State's residential fee simple market, inflating land prices, and injuring the public tranquility and welfare.

To redress these problems, the legislature decided to compel the large landowners to break up their estates. The legislature considered requiring large landowners to sell lands which they were leasing to homeowners. However, the landowners strongly resisted this scheme, pointing out the significant federal tax liabilities they would incur. Indeed, the landowners claimed that the federal tax laws were the primary reason they previously had chosen to lease, and not sell, their lands. Therefore, to accommodate the needs of both lessors and lessees, the Hawaii Legislature enacted the Land Reform Act of 1967 (Act), Haw.Rev.Stat., ch. 516, which created a mechanism for condemning residential tracts and for transferring ownership of the condemned fees simple to existing lessees. By condemning the land in question, the Hawaii Legislature intended to make the land sales involuntary, thereby making the federal tax consequences less severe while still facilitating the redistribution of fees simple.

Under the Act's condemnation scheme, tenants living on single-family residential lots within developmental tracts at least five acres in size are entitled to ask the Hawaii Housing Authority (HHA) to condemn the property on which they live. Haw.Rev.Stat. §§ 516–1(2), (11), 516–22 (1977). When 25 eligible tenants,[1] or tenants on half the lots in the tract, whichever is less, file appropriate applications, the Act authorizes HHA to hold a public hearing to determine whether acquisition by the State of all or part of the tract will "effectuate the public purposes" of the Act. § 516–22. If HHA finds that these public purposes will be served, it is authorized to designate some or all of the lots in the tract for acquisition. It then acquires, at prices set either by condemnation trial or by negotiation between lessors and lessees,[2] the former fee owners' full "right, title, and interest" in the land. § 516–25.

After compensation has been set, HHA may sell the land titles to tenants who have applied for fee simple ownership. HHA is authorized to lend these tenants up to 90% of the purchase price, and it may condition final transfer on a right of first refusal for the first 10 years following sale. §§ 516–30, 516–34, 516–35. If HHA does not sell the lot to the tenant residing there, it may lease the lot or sell it to someone else, provided that public notice has been given. § 516–28. However, HHA

1. An eligible tenant is one who, among other things, owns a house on the lot, has a bona fide intent to live on the lot or be a resident of the State, shows proof of ability to pay for a fee interest in it, and does not own residential land elsewhere nearby. Haw.Rev.Stat. §§ 516–33(3), (4), (7) (1977).

2. See § 516–56 (Supp.1983). In either case, compensation must equal the fair market value of the owner's leased fee interest. § 516–1(14). The adequacy of compensation is not before us.

may not sell to any one purchaser, or lease to any one tenant, more than one lot, and it may not operate for profit. §§ 516–28, 516–32. In practice, funds to satisfy the condemnation awards have been supplied entirely by lessees. While the Act authorizes HHA to issue bonds and appropriate funds for acquisition, no bonds have issued and HHA has not supplied any funds for condemned lots.

B

In April 1977, HHA held a public hearing concerning the proposed acquisition of some of appellees' lands. HHA made the statutorily required finding that acquisition of appellees' lands would effectuate the public purposes of the Act. Then, in October 1978, it directed appellees to negotiate with certain lessees concerning the sale of the designated properties. Those negotiations failed, and HHA subsequently ordered appellees to submit to compulsory arbitration.

Rather than comply with the compulsory arbitration order, appellees filed suit, in February 1979, in United States District Court, asking that the Act be declared unconstitutional and that its enforcement be enjoined. The District Court temporarily restrained the State from proceeding against appellees' estates. Three months later, while declaring the compulsory arbitration and compensation formulae provisions of the Act unconstitutional,[3] the District Court refused preliminarily to enjoin appellants from conducting the statutory designation and condemnation proceedings. Finally, in December 1979, it granted partial summary judgment to appellants, holding the remaining portion of the Act constitutional under the Public Use Clause. See 483 F.Supp. 62 (Haw.1979). The District Court found that the Act's goals were within the bounds of the State's police powers and that the means the legislature had chosen to serve those goals were not arbitrary, capricious, or selected in bad faith.

The Court of Appeals for the Ninth Circuit reversed. 702 F.2d 788 (1983). First, the Court of Appeals decided that the District Court had permissibly chosen not to abstain from the exercise of its jurisdiction. Then, the Court of Appeals determined that the Act could not pass the requisite judicial scrutiny of the Public Use Clause. It found that the transfers contemplated by the Act were unlike those of takings previously held to constitute "public uses" by this Court. The court further determined that the public purposes offered by the Hawaii Legislature were not deserving of judicial deference. The court concluded that the Act was simply "a naked attempt on the part of the state of Hawaii to take the private property of A and transfer it to B solely for B's private use and benefit." *Id.*, at 798. One judge dissented.

---

3. As originally enacted, lessor and lessee had to commence compulsory arbitration if they could not agree on a price for the fee simple title. Statutory formulae were provided for the determination of compensation. The District Court declared both the compulsory arbitration provision and the compensation formulae unconstitutional. No appeal was taken from these rulings, and the Hawaii Legislature subsequently amended the statute to provide only for mandatory negotiation and for advisory compensation formulae. These issues are not before us.

On applications of HHA and certain private appellants who had intervened below, this Court noted probable jurisdiction. 464 U.S. 932 (1983). We now reverse.

* * *

III

The majority of the Court of Appeals * * * determined that the Act violates the "public use" requirement of the Fifth and Fourteenth Amendments. On this argument, however, we find ourselves in agreement with the dissenting judge in the Court of Appeals.

A

The starting point for our analysis of the Act's constitutionality is the Court's decision in Berman v. Parker, 348 U.S. 26 (1954). In *Berman,* the Court held constitutional the District of Columbia Redevelopment Act of 1945. That Act provided both for the comprehensive use of the eminent domain power to redevelop slum areas and for the possible sale or lease of the condemned lands to private interests. In discussing whether the takings authorized by that Act were for a "public use," the Court stated:

> "We deal, in other words, with what traditionally has been known as the police power. An attempt to define its reach or trace its outer limits is fruitless, for each case must turn on its own facts. The definition is essentially the product of legislative determinations addressed to the purposes of government, purposes neither abstractly nor historically capable of complete definition. Subject to specific constitutional limitations, when the legislature has spoken, the public interest has been declared in terms well-nigh conclusive. In such cases the legislature, not the judiciary, is the main guardian of the public needs to be served by social legislation, whether it be Congress legislating concerning the District of Columbia * * * or the States legislating concerning local affairs. * * * This principle admits of no exception merely because the power of eminent domain is involved. * * * " *Id.,* at 32 (citations omitted).

The Court explicitly recognized the breadth of the principle it was announcing, noting:

> "Once the object is within the authority of Congress, the right to realize it through the exercise of eminent domain is clear. For the power of eminent domain is merely the means to the end. * * * Once the object is within the authority of Congress, the means by which it will be attained is also for Congress to determine. Here one of the means chosen is the use of private enterprise for redevelopment of the area. Appellants argue that this makes the project a taking from one businessman for the benefit of another businessman. But the means of executing the project are for Congress and Congress alone to determine, once the public purpose has been established." *Id.,* at 33.

The "public use" requirement is thus coterminous with the scope of a sovereign's police powers.

There is, of course, a role for courts to play in reviewing a legislature's judgment of what constitutes a public use, even when the eminent domain power is equated with the police power. But the Court in *Berman* made clear that it is "an extremely narrow" one. *Id.,* at 32. The Court in *Berman* cited with approval the Court's decision in Old Dominion Co. v. United States, 269 U.S. 55, 66 (1925), which held that deference to the legislature's "public use" determination is required "until it is shown to involve an impossibility." The *Berman* Court also cited to United States ex rel. TVA v. Welch, 327 U.S. 546, 552 (1946), which emphasized that "[a]ny departure from this judicial restraint would result in courts deciding on what is and is not a governmental function and in their invalidating legislation on the basis of their view on that question at the moment of decision, a practice which has proved impracticable in other fields." In short, the Court has made clear that it will not substitute its judgment for a legislature's judgment as to what constitutes a public use "unless the use be palpably without reasonable foundation." United States v. Gettysburg Electric R. Co., 160 U.S. 668, 680 (1896).

To be sure, the Court's cases have repeatedly stated that "one person's property may not be taken for the benefit of another private person without a justifying public purpose, even though compensation be paid." Thompson v. Consolidated Gas Corp., 300 U.S. 55, 80 (1937). Thus, in Missouri Pacific R. Co. v. Nebraska, 164 U.S. 403 (1896), where the "order in question was not, *and was not claimed to be,* * * * a taking of private property for a public use under the right of eminent domain," *id.,* at 416 (emphasis added), the Court invalidated a compensated taking of property for lack of a justifying public purpose. But where the exercise of the eminent domain power is rationally related to a conceivable public purpose, the Court has never held a compensated taking to be proscribed by the Public Use Clause.

On this basis, we have no trouble concluding that the Hawaii Act is constitutional. The people of Hawaii have attempted, much as the settlers of the original 13 Colonies did,[4] to reduce the perceived social and economic evils of a land oligopoly traceable to their monarchs. The land oligopoly has, according to the Hawaii Legislature, created artificial deterrents to the normal functioning of the State's residential land market and forced thousands of individual homeowners to lease, rather than buy, the land underneath their homes. Regulating oligopoly and the evils associated with it is a classic exercise of a State's police powers. We cannot disapprove of Hawaii's exercise of this power.

4. After the American Revolution, the colonists in several States took steps to eradicate the feudal incidents with which large proprietors had encumbered land in the Colonies. See, *e.g.,* Act of May 1779, 10 Henning's Statutes At Large 64, ch. 13, § 6 (1822) (Virginia statute); Divesting Act of 1779, 1775–1781 Pa.Acts 258, ch. 139 (1782) (Pennsylvania statute). Courts have never doubted that such statutes served a public purpose. See, e.g., Wilson v. Iseminger, 185 U.S. 55, 60–61 (1902); Stewart v. Gorter, 70 Md. 242, 244–245, 16 A. 644, 645 (1889).

Nor can we condemn as irrational the Act's approach to correcting the land oligopoly problem. The Act presumes that when a sufficiently large number of persons declare that they are willing but unable to buy lots at fair prices the land market is malfunctioning. When such a malfunction is signalled, the Act authorizes HHA to condemn lots in the relevant tract. The Act limits the number of lots any one tenant can purchase and authorizes HHA to use public funds to ensure that the market dilution goals will be achieved. This is a comprehensive and rational approach to identifying and correcting market failure.

Of course, this Act, like any other, may not be successful in achieving its intended goals. But "whether *in fact* the provision will accomplish its objectives is not the question: the [constitutional requirement] is satisfied if * * * the * * * [state] Legislature *rationally could have believed* that the [Act] would promote its objective." Western & Southern Life Ins. Co. v. State Bd. of Equalization, 451 U.S. 648, 671–672 (1981). When the legislature's purpose is legitimate and its means are not irrational, our cases make clear that empirical debates over the wisdom of takings—no less than debates over the wisdom of other kinds of socioeconomic legislation—are not to be carried out in the federal courts. Redistribution of fees simple to correct deficiencies in the market determined by the state legislature to be attributable to land oligopoly is a rational exercise of the eminent domain power. Therefore, the Hawaii statute must pass the scrutiny of the Public Use Clause.

B

The Court of Appeals read our cases to stand for a much narrower proposition. First, it read our "public use" cases, especially *Berman,* as requiring that government possess and use property at some point during a taking. Since Hawaiian lessees retain possession of the property for private use throughout the condemnation process, the court found that the Act exacted takings for private use. 702 F.2d, at 796–797. Second, it determined that these cases involved only "the review of * * * *congressional* determination[s] that there was a public use, *not* the review of * * * state legislative determination[s]." *Id.,* at 798 (emphasis in original). Because state legislative determinations are involved in the instant cases, the Court of Appeals decided that more rigorous judicial scrutiny of the public use determinations was appropriate. The court concluded that the Hawaii Legislature's professed purposes were mere "statutory rationalizations." We disagree with the Court of Appeals' analysis.

The mere fact that property taken outright by eminent domain is transferred in the first instance to private beneficiaries does not condemn that taking as having only a private purpose. The Court long ago rejected any literal requirement that condemned property be put into use for the general public. "It is not essential that the entire community, nor even any considerable portion, * * * directly enjoy or participate in any improvement in order [for it] to constitute a public use." Rindge Co. v. Los Angeles, 262 U.S., at 707. "[W]hat in its immediate aspect [is] only a private transaction may * * * be raised by its class or character to a public affair.'' Block v. Hirsh, 256 U.S., at 155. As the unique way titles were held in Hawaii skewed the land market, exercise of the power of eminent domain was justified. The Act advances its purposes without the State's taking actual possession of the land. In such cases, government does not itself have to use property to legitimate the taking; it is only the taking's purpose, and not its mechanics, that must pass scrutiny under the Public Use Clause.

Similarly, the fact that a state legislature, and not the Congress, made the public use determination does not mean that judicial deference is less appropriate.[5] Judicial deference is required because, in our system of government, legislatures are better able to assess what public purposes should be advanced by an exercise of the taking power. State legislatures are as capable as Congress of making such determinations within their respective spheres of authority. See Berman v. Parker, 348 U.S., at 32. Thus, if a legislature, state or federal, determines there are substantial reasons for an exercise of the taking power, courts must defer to its determination that the taking will serve a public use.

IV

The State of Hawaii has never denied that the Constitution forbids even a compensated taking of property when executed for no reason other than to confer a private benefit on a particular private party. A purely private taking could not withstand the scrutiny of the public use requirement; it would serve no legitimate purpose of government and would thus be void. But no purely private taking is involved in these cases. The Hawaii Legislature enacted its Land Reform Act not to benefit a particular class of identifiable individuals but to attack certain perceived evils of concentrated property ownership in Hawaii—a legitimate public purpose. Use of the condemnation power to achieve this purpose is not irrational. Since we assume for purposes of these appeals that the weighty demand of just compensation has been met, the requirements of the Fifth and Fourteenth Amendments have been satisfied. Accordingly, we reverse the judgment of the Court of Appeals, and remand these cases for further proceedings in conformity with this opinion.

It is so ordered.

Notes

1. Although numerous tenants of long-term leases have purchased land under the scheme sustained in *Midkiff,* the program has done little to alleviate Hawaii's housing problem. Strict land use control laws and a

---

5. It is worth noting that the Fourteenth Amendment does not itself contain an independent ''public use'' requirement. Rather, that requirement is made binding on the States only by incorporation of the Fifth Amendment's Eminent Domain Clause through the Fourteenth Amendment's Due Process Clause. See Chicago, B. & Q. R. Co. v. Chicago, 166 U.S. 226 (1897). It would be ironic to find that state legislation is subject to greater scrutiny under the incorporated ''public use'' requirement than is congressional legislation under the express mandate of the Fifth Amendment.

growing population have contributed to the lack of affordable housing. Individual tenants who purchased land, on the other hand, have often gained a substantial profit through resale or lease to others. *See* Lourne, *"Hawaii Housing Authority v. Midkiff:" A New Slant on Social Legislation: Taking From the Rich and Giving to the Well–To–Do*, 25 Nat.Resources J. 772 (1985); Comment, *Extending Land Reform to Leasehold Condominiums in Hawai'i*, 14 U.Haw.L.Rev. 681, 703–706 (1992).

2.   Does "public use" still impose any limit on the government's power of eminent domain? During the late 1800's and the early 1900's, many courts interpreted "public use" to mean "use by the public." As *Midkiff* indicates, a much broader interpretation gained favor in the 20th century, leading commentators to conclude that the "public use" limitation is virtually dead. *See* Comment, *The Public Use Limitation of Eminent Domain: An Advance Requiem*, 58 Yale L.J. 599 (1949); R. Epstein, Takings: Private Property and the Power of Eminent Domain 161–181 (1985). However, withhold judgment on this issue until you have considered the *Edward Rose Realty* case which follows. *See generally* Berger, *The Public Use Requirement in Eminent Domain*, 57 Or.L.Rev. 203 (1978); Rubenfeld, *Usings*, 102 Yale L.J. 1077 (1993).

3.   Soon after the Revolutionary War, American lawmakers granted the right of eminent domain to privately-owned corporations. For example, South Carolina extended eminent domain power to canal companies during the 1780's. *See* Ely, *American Independence and the Law: A Study of Post–Revolutionary South Carolina Legislation*, 26 Vand.L.Rev. 939, 956–957 (1973). The delegation of eminent domain power was especially important for transportation companies in the 19th century. Courts generally sustained these grants of eminent domain to private corporations, reasoning that the whole of society would benefit by encouraging enterprise. *See* J. Ely, The Guardian of Every Other Right: A Constitutional History of Property Rights 76–78 (2d ed.1998); J. Hurst, Law and the Conditions of Freedom in the Nineteenth–Century United States 63–64 (1956); Freyer, *Reassessing the Impact of Eminent Domain in Early American Economic Development*, 1981 Wis.L.Rev. 1263.

CITY OF LANSING v. EDWARD ROSE REALTY, INC.

Supreme Court of Michigan, 1993.
442 Mich. 626, 502 N.W.2d 638.

RILEY, JUSTICE.

In this case we are asked to review a city ordinance providing for mandatory access to private property by the grantee of a city franchise for provision of cable television services. We hold the ordinance to be unreasonable and beyond the authority of the city to exercise the power of eminent domain.

I

In April 1974, the City of Lansing entered into a franchise agreement with Continental Cablevision, Inc., providing Continental with the nonexclusive right to operate its cable system in the City of Lansing.

This agreement was amended several times and is currently in effect until the year 2004. Among other requirements, Continental agreed to provide nine designated access channels, an emergency override system, universal service, and to pay three percent of its gross revenues as a franchise fee to the city, retaining 0.35 percent of its gross revenues for funding of community cable services.

Defendants Rose own two apartment complexes, Trappers Cove and Waverly Park. In August 1980, Rose's predecessors in interest entered into a private agreement with Continental providing Continental with the exclusive right to install and operate its cable system for the properties. The agreement provided for amendment, modification, or cancellation if agreed to in writing by both parties, and established the rights and obligations of the parties upon termination. On December 23, 1986, Rose gave Continental notice of an intention not to renew the contract upon its expiration on June 30, 1987.[1] Rose also informed Continental of an intention to install a private cable system, a "satellite master antenna television system" (SMATV), which would provide comparable cable service to the tenants of the apartment complexes.

In March 1987, Continental submitted a proposed ordinance to the city that would prohibit an owner of a multiple-unit residential dwelling from interfering with a tenant's choice to receive cable service from the city's franchisee. On June 1, 1987, the city adopted ordinance 753, providing:

> "No owner, agent or representative of the owner of any dwelling shall directly or indirectly prohibit any resident of such dwelling from receiving cable communication installation, maintenance and services from a Grantee operating under a valid franchise issued by the City."

If an owner refused access by the franchised cable service, upon request of the franchisee the city could commence condemnation proceedings. The franchisee was responsible for indemnification of all expenses and costs incurred by the city.

Rose indicated that it would refuse access to Continental upon expiration of their agreement, and on June 11, 1987, Continental requested that the city commence condemnation proceedings. On August 31, 1987, the city council passed resolution no. 0446, providing that the city council deemed "multi-channel CATV service to Trappers Cover [sic] and Waverly Park to be in the public interest, and to constitute both a public use and a public purpose." Pursuant to the authority of ordinance 753, the city resolved to retain an appraiser to determine the fair-market value of Rose's property occupied by Continental, to make an offer to purchase the property, and to take steps necessary to acquire the property.[2] On November 9, 1987, the city council passed resolution no.

1. The cable service agreement was extended until September 30, 1987.

2. Resolution no. 0446 indicated that multichannel CATV services to Waverly Park and Trappers Cove would:

0557, confirming "its finding in Resolution 0446 that the service provided by Continental Cablevision, as a licensed franchisee, to residents of Trappers Cove and Waverly Park, is in the public interest, and constitutes a public use, a public purpose, and a public necessity." Resolution 557 also authorized the city attorney to take steps to acquire Rose's property pursuant to the Uniform Condemnation Procedures Act, M.C.L. § 213.51 *et seq.;* M.S.A. § 8.265(1) *et seq.,* including offering to purchase the property from Rose or, failing an agreement regarding the purchase, filing a complaint asking the court to "ascertain and determine just compensation to be paid for the acquisition of the Property."

Following the inability of the parties to agree to the purchase, on March 3, 1988, the city filed two complaints for condemnation. * * *

The trial court denied Rose's motions to review necessity and upheld the validity of the condemnation proceedings. After the jury was impaneled to determine just compensation, Rose's application for leave to appeal to the Court of Appeals was granted and all proceedings in the trial court were stayed. The Court of Appeals reversed the judgment of the trial court, finding the proposed condemnation exceeded the city's authority to take private property through eminent domain. The Court concluded that "the primary beneficiary of the taking is not the public, but rather Continental Cablevision." 192 Mich.App. 551, 557, 481 N.W.2d 795 (1992). Further, "the proposed condemnation is an attempt by a private entity to use the city's taking powers to acquire what it could not get through arm's length negotiations with defendants." *Id.* at 558, 481 N.W.2d 795.

The city's application for leave to appeal to this Court was granted on November 4, 1992.

II

Resolution of the question posed in this case requires that we turn first to our state and federal constitutions, mandating that private property shall not be taken for public use without just compensation. Const.1963, art. 10, § 2; U.S. Const., Am.V. Because a municipality has no inherent power to condemn property even for public benefit or use, the power of eminent domain must be specifically conferred upon the municipality by statute or the constitution, or by necessary implication from delegated authority.

* * * In the instant case, the city asserts authority to condemn Rose's property pursuant to a general statute applicable to acquisitions

"2. * * * encourage the growth and development of cable systems and assure that cable systems are responsive to the needs and interests of the City and its residents;

"3. * * * assure that Continental Cable provides and is encouraged to provide the widest possible diversity of information sources and services to the public including informing the public of the operation of local, state and federal government;

"4. * * * promote competition in cable communications and minimize unnecessary regulation that will or might impose an undue economic burden on cable systems * * *."

by state agencies and public corporations and the home rule cities act. M.C.L. § 213.23; M.S.A. § 8.13 provides:

> "Any public corporation or state agency is authorized to take private property necessary for a public improvement or for the purposes of its incorporation or for public purposes within the scope of its power for the use or benefit of the public and to institute and prosecute proceedings for that purpose."

A public corporation or state agency may commence condemnation proceedings when it has:

> "declared * * * public purposes within the scope of its powers make it necessary, and * * * that it deems it necessary to take private property for such * * * public purposes within the scope of its powers, designating the same, and that the improvement is for the use or benefit of the public." M.C.L. § 213.24; M.S.A. § 8.14.

In addition, the home rule cities act, M.C.L. § 117.4e; M.S.A. § 5.2078 provides:

> "Each city may in its charter provide:
>
>   * * *
>
> "(2) For the acquisition by * * * condemnation * * * of private property * * * for any public use or purpose within the scope of its powers, whether herein specifically mentioned or not."
>
>   * * *

The city is authorized to condemn private property for any public use within the scope of its powers. The cited enabling statutes, however, do not specifically authorize the takings in the present case. There is no state statute identifying as a public use or purpose the mandatory access onto private property by a city-franchised cable television provider. Ordinances passed under such general authority are open to inquiry by the courts and, in order to be held valid, must be reasonable and not oppressive. Powers implied by general delegations of authority must be "essential or indispensable to the accomplishment of the objects and purposes of the municipality."[3]

We are therefore required to determine whether ordinance 753 is reasonable and serves a public purpose. Ordinances are presumed to have a reasonable relation to a permissible governmental purpose. We will not substitute our judgment for that of the city's officials, but rather will determine whether the city's proposed conduct is "within the range of conferred discretionary powers and then determine if it is reasonable." Square Lake Hills Condominium Ass'n v. Bloomfield Twp., 437 Mich. 310, 317, 471 N.W.2d 321 (1991). Although we assume the validity of the public interest advanced by the city, we find that the private interest to be benefited predominates over the asserted public interest.

---

3. McQuillin, [Municipal Corporations   (3d rev.ed.)] § 15.20, p. 102.

The asserted public interest therefore does not justify the proposed taking of private property by the city.

While this is an issue of first impression in Michigan, several states have enacted legislation requiring some type of mandatory access to rental properties by franchised cable services. Some statutes have been held to be invalid because they failed to provide just compensation for the property taken to install and operate the cable systems.[4] Other statutes would preclude the city's action in the present case if Rose's SMATV service is considered comparable to the CATV provided by Continental.[5] Still others are distinguishable from the city's ordinance in the present case because they require a tenant request for cable services before a cable operator must be provided access to residential property.[6] Other out-of-state statutes if in effect in Michigan would appear to prohibit Rose from refusing Continental access to the property.[7] We are not persuaded, however, that the judicial interpretation of those statutes is applicable to the present case.

The New Jersey Court of Chancery determined that the purpose of the state law mandating access to multiple-dwelling units was to prevent landowners from excessively charging tenants who desire franchised cable services. Princeton Cablevision, Inc. v. Union Valley Corp., 195 N.J.Super. 257, 478 A.2d 1234 (1983). In the present case, the city does not assert that a purpose of its proposed conduct was to protect Rose's tenants from discriminatory rates by Rose or that Rose was gouging the tenants with regard to previous franchised cable services or its current SMATV services.

In New York, the supreme court, again confronted with a state legislative enactment, reviewed the state statute articulating the public purposes to be furthered by cable television. Loretto v. Teleprompter Manhattan CATV Corp., 53 N.Y.2d 124, 139–140, 440 N.Y.S.2d 843, 423 N.E.2d 320 (1981).[8] The court determined that the tenant's right to

---

4. The mandatory access statutes in Florida and Massachusetts were held invalid for failure to provide for just compensation. Fla.Stat.Ann. 83.66, repealed, Storer Cable T.V. v. Summerwinds Apts., 493 So.2d 417 (Fla.1986); Mass.Law Ann., ch. 166A, § 22, Greater Worcester Cablevision, Inc. v. Carabetta Enterprises, Inc., 682 F.Supp. 1244 (D.Mass.1985); Waltham Tele–Communications v. O'Brien, 403 Mass. 747, 532 N.E.2d 656 (1989).

5. See Fla.Stat.Ann. 83.66, repealed. See also proposed § 633 of the federal Cable Act, which was not enacted.

6. See Mass.Law Ann., ch. 166A, § 22. In addition, see Conn.Gen.Stat.Ann. 16–333; 65 Ill.Comp.Stat.Ann. 5/11–42–11.1; 68 Pa.Stat. 250.503–B.

Lack of judicial interpretation of the following statutes leaves unclear whether the state statutes require a tenant request be-

fore a franchised cable operator may demand access to private property. Me.Rev. Stat.Ann., tit. 14, § 6041; Nev.Rev.Stat. 711.255; R.I.Gen.Laws 39–19–10; Wis.Stat. Ann. 66.085.

7. D.C. Code 43–1844.1; Minn.Stat.Ann. 238.23; N.J.Stat.Ann. 48:5A–49; N.Y., Executive Law, § 828. Although listed by the city as providing for mandatory access, Delaware's statute simply allows piggybacking by cable companies on easements used by public utilities. Del.Code, tit. 26, § 613. Virginia prohibits discriminatory rent requirements for tenants who choose to have cable, but does not provide for mandatory access by cable operators. Va.Code 55–248.13:2.

8. This decision was reversed for failure to provide just compensation for the taking of private property in Loretto v. Teleprompter Manhattan CATV Corp., 458 U.S. 419 (1982).

receive communications, the educational and community aspects of CATV, the assurance of maximum penetration by cable systems, and the promotion of its rapid development, supported the mandatory access statute in light of previous "onerous fees and conditions" imposed by landlords on franchised cable systems that inhibited the franchised systems. *Id.* at 141, 440 N.Y.S.2d 843, 423 N.E.2d 320.

The Michigan Legislature has not enunciated as a general public purpose that city-franchised cable operators have mandatory access to all rental properties. There is no extensive regulation of the industry or any legislative pronouncement of the public benefits of franchised cable services as in New York and New Jersey.[9] Because the city passed ordinance 753 without an express delegation of authority by the state, we may review the city's asserted public purpose. Judicial deference granted state legislative determinations of public use[10] is not similarly employed when reviewing determinations of public purpose made by a municipality pursuant to broad, general enabling statutes. Thus, we scrutinize the city's actions bearing in mind that a state statute would affect all municipalities in Michigan and several cable companies, while ordinance 753 is directed toward and would benefit a single private entity, Continental.

In Poletown Neighborhood Council v. Detroit, 410 Mich. 616, 629, 304 N.W.2d 455 (1981), this Court addressed a proposed taking that benefited a private entity. The precise issue considered was:

> "Can a municipality use the power of eminent domain granted to it by the Economic Development Corporations Act, MCL 125.1601 *et seq.;* MSA 5.3520(1) *et seq.*, to condemn property for transfer to a private corporation * * *?"

The "heart" of the dispute was "whether the proposed condemnation [was] for the primary benefit of the public or the private user." *Id.* at 632, 304 N.W.2d 455. The role of this Court to review whether the project was for the primary benefit of the public was limited, mainly because of three circumstances: 1) the Legislature had determined that the government conduct proposed by the city served "an essential public purpose," 2) the Legislature expressly delegated to municipalities the authority to determine if a proposed project constituted a public purpose, and 3) the city followed all procedures established in the legislative enabling statute. The Court then held that the proposed project was a valid exercise of the city's power of eminent domain, finding: 1) the benefit to the municipality was clear and significant, 2) the project was an intended and legitimate object of the Legislature, 3) the power to

---

9. See N.J.Stat.Ann. 48:5A–2; N.Y., Executive Law, § 811.

10. See Berman v. Parker, 348 U.S. 26 (1954); Hawaii Housing Authority v. Midkiff, 467 U.S. 229 (1984).

While state legislative determinations of public purpose may be "well-nigh conclusive" in judicial actions, *Berman, supra,* 348 U.S. at 32, a municipality acting without specific legislative authority must "specify definitely the purpose of the appropriation" to show that its conduct is within its authority. Cincinnati v. Vester, 281 U.S. 439, 447 (1930). Mere statements that the proposed action furthers a public use is not conclusive.

undertake the proposed action was expressly delegated [to] the munici-pality, and 4) the public benefit predominated over the benefit received by the private party. Because a private party would benefit from the city's proposed project, eminent domain would not be proper without substantial proof that the public would be the primary beneficiary of the project. Where the project "benefits specific and identifiable private interests," the assertion of a predominant public interest will be examined by the Court with "heightened scrutiny." Id. at 634, 635, 304 N.W.2d 455.

> "Such public benefit cannot be speculative or marginal but must be clear and significant if it is to be within the legitimate purpose as stated by the Legislature." *Id.* at 635, 304 N.W.2d 455.

Hence, where a proposed government action confers a benefit on a private interest, unless that benefit is merely incidental, a reviewing court will inspect with heightened scrutiny the assertion by the governmental entity of a public purpose.

In the present case, as discussed above, there is no determination by the Legislature that the city's proposed action serves an essential public purpose. The Legislature did not delegate to the city the power to condemn private property for the purpose of providing mandatory access by a city-franchised cable system. Although the city will retain owner-ship of the easement it proposed to obtain through condemnation, Continental will receive more than an incidental benefit. The easement will not merely provide access for public, education, and government (PEG) channels or an emergency override, but will allow Continental to offer its full panoply of services to the tenants of Rose's apartments. Continental could receive substantial revenue through subscription pay-ments and increased market value of its overall system. We therefore apply heightened scrutiny to the city's assertion that a public interest is predominant because a "specific and identifiable" interest will be bene-fited by the city's proposed action. Finally, as explained below, the asserted benefit to the public is not clear and significant, and does not predominate over the specific and identifiable private interest of Conti-nental.

The city asserts that the requirements of PEG channels, universal service, and emergency override support its determination of public use.[11] We agree with the conclusion by the Court of Appeals that the requirement of universal service is not, in and of itself, a public purpose. If the service does not further a public purpose, then universal provision

---

11. The city also advances in support of its position several cases requiring judi-cial deference to legislative determinations of public use. The cases are plainly distin-guishable from the present case either be-cause the only issue involved just compen-sation, *Loretto, supra,* 458 U.S. 419, or because the state legislature had deter-mined the public use and benefit of CATV, and had extensively regulated the taking of private property to require ac-cess. *Loretto, supra,* 53 N.Y.2d 124, 440 N.Y.S.2d 843, 423 N.E.2d 320; Lake Louise Improvement Ass'n v. Multimedia Cablevision of Oak Lawn, Inc., 157 Ill. App.3d 713, 109 Ill.Dec. 914, 510 N.E.2d 982 (1987); Times Mirror Cable Television of Springfield, Inc. v. First Nat'l Bank of Springfield, 221 Ill.App.3d 340, 164 Ill. Dec. 8, 582 N.E.2d 216 (1991).

of that service does not advance a public purpose. Furthermore, the universal service requirement is primarily a restraint on the franchised cable operator, precluding the company from refusing service to poorer communities. It is not an enabling provision authorizing the cable operator to demand access to every dwelling despite the owner's desire for such service. We also agree with the conclusion by the Court of Appeals that the emergency override capacity of CATV is largely duplicative of commercial stations and does not support invasion of an owner's private property.

We do not dispute that PEG channels can provide the public with political and educational benefits. In fact, Congress has declared that government has a substantial interest in ensuring the continuation and availability of both local origination programming and local noncommercial educational stations. Despite these clear statements of policy recognizing the benefits to the public provided by the availability of PEG channels, in light of the countervailing private benefits conferred by the mandatory access ordinance, we find that the primary beneficiary of this ordinance is Continental, a private user, not the public.

Ordinance 753 presents no definition of the public purpose allegedly served by requiring access by its franchised cable operator. Resolution 446 includes three asserted purposes: to encourage growth, development, and responsiveness of Continental; to encourage provision by Continental of the widest possible diversity of information; and to promote competition and minimize unnecessary regulation that might impose undue economic burdens on the cable system.[12] In light of Continental's extensive private interest, we find these asserted rationales for mandatory access to Rose's properties to be insufficient to overcome Rose's right to exclude others from its private property.

There is no explanation regarding how mandatory access to Rose's two apartment complexes encourages growth, development, and responsiveness of Continental, or how such access encourages Continental to provide the widest possible diversity of information. Mere statements that a proposed action furthers a public benefit are not conclusive. Cincinnati v. Vester, 281 U.S. 439, 447 (1930).

The argument is persuasive that ordinance 753 will not increase competition in the cable industry. While allowing Continental to initiate condemnation proceedings to secure cable access to any dwelling in Lansing, no corollary rights are granted other cable systems. Continental will be guaranteed the ability to compete with private cable systems where it decides to compete, without an equivalent right of competition guaranteed to private systems. Access to private dwellings pursuant to ordinance 753 is enforceable only by the franchised cable operator. Neither Rose, the city, nor tenants could initiate condemnation proceedings to ensure competition of cable systems. Moreover, Continental has

---

12. Identical reasons are cited as purposes of the federal Cable Act, 47 U.S.C. § 521. It is instructive to note here that, although considered, a mandatory access provision was not included in the Cable Act.

entered into exclusive cable service contracts in ninety percent of its contracts in Lansing. Even if private systems were allowed to compete, ninety percent of the market is already secured by Continental.

* * *

III

The city's proposed conduct to require mandatory access by its franchised cable operator, Continental, onto Rose's private property does not result from a state legislative pronouncement of public purpose, nor has the Legislature specifically delegated to municipalities the authority to undertake the actions proposed by the city. Rather, the city enacted resolutions 446 and 557 on the basis of its own general assertion that mandatory access by its only franchisee furthers a public purpose. The conduct by the city, however, benefits Continental, a specific and identifiable private interest. We are persuaded that this benefit to Continental predominates over the asserted public benefits. The ordinance and resolutions are therefore invalid as unreasonable because the public would not be the primary beneficiary. Hence, the proposed conduct is beyond the city's authority to exercise the power of eminent domain.

The decision of the Court of Appeals is affirmed.

Notes

1. As demonstrated by *Edward Rose Realty*, some state courts more closely examine the issue of public use than do federal courts and will invalidate the exercise of eminent domain when undertaken primarily for private benefit. *See* Merrill, *The Economics of Public Use*, 72 Cornell L. Rev. 61 (1986) (surveying decisions considering public use rendered from 1954 through 1985). *See also* Cohen v. Larson, 125 Idaho 82, 867 P.2d 956 (1993); Morley v. Jackson Redevelopment Authority, 632 So.2d 1284 (Miss.1994); *In re* City of Seattle, 96 Wn.2d 616, 638 P.2d 549 (1981).

2. In City of Oakland v. Oakland Raiders, 32 Cal.3d 60, 183 Cal.Rptr. 673, 646 P.2d 835 (1982), the Supreme Court of California faced an unusual "public use" question. Shortly after the Oakland Raiders professional football team announced plans to move to Los Angeles, the city of Oakland began eminent domain proceedings to acquire the Raiders' franchise. The trial court issued a summary judgment for the Raiders on the ground that condemnation of a professional football team was not a public use. On appeal, the California Supreme Court remanded the case saying: "[W]e do not decide whether City has a meritorious condemnation claim in this case. City's ability to prove a valid public use for its proposed action remains untested. We hold only that City should be given the opportunity to prove its case * * *." *Id.* at 683, 646 P.2d at 845. On remand the trial court ultimately found for the Raiders, holding, *inter alia,* that the City's avowed objective did not constitute a public use. The appellate court affirmed on the ground that the City's action violated the Commerce Clause and noted that such a decision "obviates the need for further consideration of the public use" issue. City of Oakland v. Oakland Raiders, 174 Cal.App.3d 414, 220 Cal.Rptr. 153 (1985), *cert. denied,* 478 U.S. 1007 (1986). *See generally*

Casenote, *Eminent Domain and the Commerce Clause Defense: "City of Oakland v. Oakland Raiders,"* 41 U.Miami L.Rev. 1185 (1987).

PENN CENTRAL TRANSPORTATION CO. v. NEW YORK CITY

Supreme Court of the United States, 1978.
438 U.S. 104.

MR. JUSTICE BRENNAN delivered the opinion of the Court.

The question presented is whether a city may, as part of a comprehensive program to preserve historic landmarks and historic districts, place restrictions on the development of individual historic landmarks—in addition to those imposed by applicable zoning ordinances—without effecting a "taking" requiring the payment of "just compensation." Specifically, we must decide whether the application of New York City's Landmarks Preservation Law to the parcel of land occupied by Grand Central Terminal has "taken" its owners' property in violation of the Fifth and Fourteenth Amendments.

I

A

Over the past 50 years, all 50 States and over 500 municipalities have enacted laws to encourage or require the preservation of buildings and areas with historic or aesthetic importance. These nationwide legislative efforts have been precipitated by two concerns. The first is recognition that, in recent years, large numbers of historic structures, landmarks, and areas have been destroyed without adequate consideration of either the values represented therein or the possibility of preserving the destroyed properties for use in economically productive ways. The second is a widely shared belief that structures with special historic, cultural, or architectural significance enhance the quality of life for all.

* * *

New York City, responding to similar concerns and acting pursuant to a New York State enabling act, adopted its Landmarks Preservation Law in 1965. See N.Y.C.Admin. Code, ch. 8–A, § 205–1.0 *et seq.* (1976). The city acted from the conviction that "the standing of [New York City] as a world-wide tourist center and world capital of business, culture and government" would be threatened if legislation were not enacted to protect historic landmarks and neighborhoods from precipitate decisions to destroy or fundamentally alter their character.

* * *

The New York City law is typical of many urban landmark laws in that its primary method of achieving its goals is not by acquisitions of historic properties, but rather by involving public entities in land-use decisions affecting these properties and providing services, standards, controls, and incentives that will encourage preservation by private owners and users. While the law does place special restrictions on landmark properties as a necessary feature to the attainment of its larger objectives, the major theme of the law is to ensure the owners of any such properties both a "reasonable return" on their investments and maximum latitude to use their parcels for purposes not inconsistent with the preservation goals.

The operation of the law can be briefly summarized. The primary responsibility for administering the law is vested in the Landmarks Preservation Commission (Commission), a broad based, 11–member agency assisted by a technical staff. The Commission first performs the function, critical to any landmark preservation effort, of identifying properties and areas that have "a special character or special historical or aesthetic interest or value as part of the development, heritage or cultural characteristics of the city, state or nation." If the Commission determines, after giving all interested parties an opportunity to be heard, that a building or area satisfies the ordinance's criteria, it will designate a building to be a "landmark," situated on a particular "landmark site," or will designate an area to be a "historic district". After the Commission makes a designation, New York City's Board of Estimate, after considering the relationship of the designated property "to the master plan, the zoning resolution, projected public improvements and any plans for the renewal of the area involved," may modify or disapprove the designation, and the owner may seek judicial review of the final designation decision. Thus far, 31 historic districts and over 400 individual landmarks have been finally designated, and the process is a continuing one.

Final designation as a landmark results in restrictions upon the property owner's options concerning use of the landmark site. First, the law imposes a duty upon the owner to keep the exterior features of the building "in good repair" to assure that the law's objectives not be defeated by the landmark's falling into a state of irremediable disrepair. Second, the Commission must approve in advance any proposal to alter the exterior architectural features of the landmark or to construct any exterior improvement on the landmark site, thus ensuring that decisions concerning construction on the landmark site are made with due consideration of both the public interest in the maintenance of the structure and the landowner's interest in use of the property.

In the event an owner wishes to alter a landmark site, three separate procedures are available through which administrative approval may be obtained. First, the owner may apply to the Commission for a "certificate of no effect on protected architectural features": that is, for an order approving the improvement or alteration on the ground that it will not change or affect any architectural feature of the landmark and will be in harmony therewith. Denial of the certificate is subject to judicial review.

Second, the owner may apply to the Commission for a certificate of "appropriateness." Such certificates will be granted if the Commission concludes—focusing upon aesthetic, historical, and architectural values—that the proposed construction on the landmark site would not unduly hinder the protection, enhancement, perpetuation, and use of the landmark. Again, denial of the certificate is subject to judicial review. Moreover, the owner who is denied either a certificate of no exterior effect or a certificate of appropriateness may submit an alternative or modified plan for approval. The final procedure—seeking a certificate of appropriateness on the ground of "insufficient return,"—provides special mechanisms, which vary depending on whether or not the landmark enjoys a tax exemption, to ensure that designation does not cause economic hardship.

Although the designation of a landmark and landmark site restricts the owner's control over the parcel, designation also enhances the economic position of the landmark owner in one significant respect. Under New York City's zoning laws, owners of real property who have not developed their property to the full extent permitted by the applicable zoning laws are allowed to transfer development rights to contiguous parcels on the same city block. A 1968 ordinance gave the owners of landmark sites additional opportunities to transfer development rights to other parcels.

* * *

B

This case involves the application of New York City's Landmarks Preservation Law to Grand Central Terminal (Terminal). The Terminal, which is owned by the Penn Central Transportation Co. and its affiliates (Penn Central), is one of New York City's most famous buildings. Opened in 1913, it is regarded not only as providing an ingenious engineering solution to the problems presented by urban railroad stations, but also as a magnificent example of the French beaux-arts style.

The Terminal is located in midtown Manhattan. Its south facade faces 42d Street and that street's intersection with Park Avenue. At street level, the Terminal is bounded on the west by Vanderbilt Avenue, on the east by the Commodore Hotel, and on the north by the Pan–American Building. Although a 20–story office tower, to have been located above the Terminal, was part of the original design, the planned tower was never constructed. The Terminal itself is an eight-story structure which Penn Central uses as a railroad station and in which it rents space not needed for railroad purposes to a variety of commercial interests. The Terminal is one of a number of properties owned by appellant Penn Central in this area of midtown Manhattan. The others include the Barclay, Biltmore, Commodore, Roosevelt, and Waldorf–Astoria Hotels, the Pan–American Building and other office buildings along Park Avenue, and the Yale Club. At least eight of these are eligible to be recipients of development rights afforded the Terminal by virtue of landmark designation.

On August 2, 1967, following a public hearing, the Commission designated the Terminal a "landmark" and designated the "city tax block" it occupies a "landmark site." The Board of Estimate confirmed this action on September 21, 1967. Although appellant Penn Central had opposed the designation before the Commission, it did not seek judicial review of the final designation decision.

On January 22, 1968, appellant Penn Central, to increase its income, entered into a renewable 50–year lease and sublease agreement with appellant UGP Properties, Inc. (UGP), a wholly owned subsidiary of Union General Properties, Ltd., a United Kingdom corporation. Under the terms of the agreement, UGP was to construct a multistory office building above the Terminal. UGP promised to pay Penn Central $1 million annually during construction and at least $3 million annually thereafter. The rentals would be offset in part by a loss of some $700,000 to $1 million net rentals presently received from concessionaires displaced by the new building.

Appellants UGP and Penn Central then applied to the Commission for permission to construct an office building atop the Terminal. Two separate plans, both designed by architect Marcel Breuer and both apparently satisfying the terms of the applicable zoning ordinance, were submitted to the Commission for approval. The first, Breuer I, provided for the construction of a 55–story office building, to be cantilevered above the existing facade and to rest on the roof of the Terminal. The second, Breuer II Revised, called for tearing down a portion of the Terminal that included the 42d Street facade, stripping off some of the remaining features of the Terminal's facade, and constructing a 53–story office building. The Commission denied a certificate of no exterior effect on September 20, 1968. Appellants then applied for a certificate of "appropriateness" as to both proposals. After four days of hearings at which over 80 witnesses testified, the Commission denied this application as to both proposals.

* * *

Appellants did not seek judicial review of the denial of either certificate. Because the Terminal site enjoyed a tax exemption, remained suitable for its present and future uses, and was not the subject of a contract of sale, there were no further administrative remedies available to appellants as to the Breuer I and Breuer II Revised plans. Further, appellants did not avail themselves of the opportunity to develop and submit other plans for the Commission's consideration and approval. Instead, appellants filed suit in New York Supreme Court, Trial Term, claiming, *inter alia*, that the application of the Landmarks Preservation Law had "taken" their property without just compensation in violation of the Fifth and Fourteenth Amendments and arbitrarily deprived them of their property without due process of law in violation of the Fourteenth Amendment. Appellants sought a declaratory judgment, injunctive relief barring the city from using the Landmarks Law to impede the construction of any structure that might otherwise lawfully be constructed on the Terminal site, and damages for the "temporary taking" that occurred between August 2, 1967, the designation date, and the date when the restrictions arising from the Landmarks Law would be lifted. The trial court granted the injunctive and declaratory relief, but severed the question of damages for a "temporary taking."

Appellees appealed, and the New York Supreme Court, Appellate Division, reversed. 50 App.Div.2d 265, 377 N.Y.S.2d 20 (1975).

* * *

The New York Court of Appeals affirmed. 42 N.Y.2d 324, 366 N.E.2d 1271 (1977).

* * *

II

The issues presented by appellants are (1) whether the restrictions imposed by New York City's law upon appellants' exploitation of the Terminal site effect a "taking" of appellants' property for a public use within the meaning of the Fifth Amendment, which of course is made applicable to the States through the Fourteenth Amendment, and, (2), if so, whether the transferable development rights afforded appellants constitute "just compensation" within the meaning of the Fifth Amendment. We need only address the question whether a "taking" has occurred.

A

Before considering appellants' specific contentions, it will be useful to review the factors that have shaped the jurisprudence of the Fifth Amendment injunction "nor shall private property be taken for public use, without just compensation." The question of what constitutes a "taking" for purposes of the Fifth Amendment has proved to be a problem of considerable difficulty. While this Court has recognized that the "Fifth Amendment's guarantee * * * [is] designed to bar Government from forcing some people alone to bear public burdens which, in all fairness and justice, should be borne by the public as a whole," Armstrong v. United States, 364 U.S. 40, 49 (1960), this Court, quite simply, has been unable to develop any "set formula" for determining when "justice and fairness" require that economic injuries caused by public action be compensated by the government, rather than remain disproportionately concentrated on a few persons. See Goldblatt v. Hempstead, 369 U.S. 590, 594 (1962). Indeed, we have frequently observed that whether a particular restriction will be rendered invalid by the government's failure to pay for any losses proximately caused by it depends largely "upon the particular circumstances [in that] case."

In engaging in these essentially ad hoc, factual inquiries, the Court's decisions have identified several factors that have particular significance. The economic impact of the regulation on the claimant and, particularly, the extent to which the regulation has interfered with distinct investment-backed expectations are, of course, relevant considerations. See

Goldblatt v. Hempstead, supra, at 594. So, too, is the character of the governmental action. A "taking" may more readily be found when the interference with property can be characterized as a physical invasion by government, see, *e.g.,* United States v. Causby, 328 U.S. 256 (1946), than when interference arises from some public program adjusting the benefits and burdens of economic life to promote the common good.

"Government hardly could go on if to some extent values incident to property could not be diminished without paying for every such change in the general law," Pennsylvania Coal Co. v. Mahon, 260 U.S. 393, 413 (1922), and this Court has accordingly recognized, in a wide variety of contexts, that government may execute laws or programs that adversely affect recognized economic values. Exercises of the taxing power are one obvious example. A second are the decisions in which this Court has dismissed "taking" challenges on the ground that, while the challenged government action caused economic harm, it did not interfere with interests that were sufficiently bound up with the reasonable expectations of the claimant to constitute "property" for Fifth Amendment purposes. See, *e.g.,* United States v. Willow River Power Co., 324 U.S. 499 (1945) (interest in high-water level of river for runoff for tailwaters to maintain power head is not property); United States v. Chandler–Dunbar Water Power Co., 229 U.S. 53 (1913) (no property interest can exist in navigable waters).

More importantly for the present case, in instances in which a state tribunal reasonably concluded that "the health, safety, morals, or general welfare" would be promoted by prohibiting particular contemplated uses of land, this Court has upheld land-use regulations that destroyed or adversely affected recognized real property interests. See Nectow v. Cambridge, 277 U.S. 183, 188 (1928). Zoning laws are, of course, the classic example, see Euclid v. Ambler Realty Co., 272 U.S. 365 (1926) (prohibition of industrial use); Gorieb v. Fox, 274 U.S. 603, 608 (1927) (requirement that portions of parcels be left unbuilt); Welch v. Swasey, 214 U.S. 91 (1909) (height restriction), which have been viewed as permissible governmental action even when prohibiting the most beneficial use of the property.

Zoning laws generally do not affect existing uses of real property, but "taking" challenges have also been held to be without merit in a wide variety of situations when the challenged governmental actions prohibited a beneficial use to which individual parcels had previously been devoted and thus caused substantial individualized harm. Miller v. Schoene, 276 U.S. 272 (1928), is illustrative. In that case, a state entomologist, acting pursuant to a state statute, ordered the claimants to cut down a large number of ornamental red cedar trees because they produced cedar rust fatal to apple trees cultivated nearby. Although the statute provided for recovery of any expense incurred in removing the cedars, and permitted claimants to use the felled trees, it did not provide compensation for the value of the standing trees or for the resulting decrease in market value of the properties as a whole. A unanimous Court held that this latter omission did not render the statute invalid.

The Court held that the State might properly make "a choice between the preservation of one class of property and that of the other" and since the apple industry was important in the State involved, concluded that the State had not exceeded "its constitutional powers by deciding upon the destruction of one class of property [without compensation in order to save another which, in the judgment of the legislature, is of greater value to the public." *Id.,* at 279.

Again, Hadacheck v. Sebastian, 239 U.S. 394 (1915), upheld a law prohibiting the claimant from continuing his otherwise lawful business of operating a brickyard in a particular physical community on the ground that the legislature had reasonably concluded that the presence of the brickyard was inconsistent with neighboring uses. * * *

Goldblatt v. Hempstead, supra, is a recent example. There, a 1958 city safety ordinance banned any excavations below the water table and effectively prohibited the claimant from continuing a sand and gravel mining business that had been operated on the particular parcel since 1927. The Court upheld the ordinance against a "taking" challenge, although the ordinance prohibited the present and presumably most beneficial use of the property and had, like the regulations in *Miller* and *Hadacheck,* severely affected a particular owner. The Court assumed that the ordinance did not prevent the owner's reasonable use of the property since the owner made no showing of an adverse effect on the value of the land. Because the restriction served a substantial public purpose, the Court thus held no taking had occurred. It is, of course, implicit in *Goldblatt* that a use restriction on real property may constitute a "taking" if not reasonably necessary to the effectuation of a substantial public purpose, or perhaps if it has an unduly harsh impact upon the owner's use of the property.

Pennsylvania Coal Co. v. Mahon, 260 U.S. 393 (1922), is the leading case for the proposition that a state statute that substantially furthers important public policies may so frustrate distinct investment-backed expectations as to amount to a "taking." There the claimant had sold the surface rights to particular parcels of property, but expressly reserved the right to remove the coal thereunder. A Pennsylvania statute, enacted after the transactions, forbade any mining of coal that caused the subsidence of any house, unless the house was the property of the owner of the underlying coal and was more than 150 feet from the improved property of another. Because the statute made it commercially impracticable to mine the coal, *id.,* at 414, and thus had nearly the same effect as the complete destruction of rights claimant had reserved from the owners of the surface land, see *id.,* at 414–415, the Court held that the statute was invalid as effecting a "taking" without just compensation.

Finally, government actions that may be characterized as acquisitions of resources to permit or facilitate uniquely public functions have often been held to constitute "takings." United States v. Causby, 328 U.S. 256 (1946), is illustrative. In holding that direct overflights above the claimant's land, that destroyed the present use of the land as a chicken farm, constituted a "taking," *Causby* emphasized that Government had not "merely destroyed property [but was] using a part of it for the flight of its planes." *Id.*, at 262–263, n. 7.

* * *

B

In contending that the New York City law has "taken" their property in violation of the Fifth and Fourteenth Amendments, appellants make a series of arguments, which, while tailored to the facts of this case, essentially urge that any substantial restriction imposed pursuant to a landmark law must be accompanied by just compensation if it is to be constitutional. Before considering these, we emphasize what is not in dispute. Because this Court has recognized, in a number of settings, that States and cities may enact land-use restrictions or controls to enhance the quality of life by preserving the character and desirable aesthetic features of a city, appellants do not contest that New York City's objective of preserving structures and areas with special historic, architectural, or cultural significance is an entirely permissible governmental goal. They also do not dispute that the restrictions imposed on its parcel are appropriate means of securing the purposes of the New York City law. Finally, appellants do not challenge any of the specific factual premises of the decision below. They accept for present purposes both that the parcel of land occupied by Grand Central Terminal must, in its present state, be regarded as capable of earning a reasonable return, and that the transferable development rights afforded appellants by virtue of the Terminal's designation as a landmark are valuable, even if not as valuable as the rights to construct above the Terminal. In appellants' view none of these factors derogate from their claim that New York City's law has effected a "taking."

They first observe that the airspace above the Terminal is a valuable property interest, citing *United States v. Causby, supra.* They urge that the Landmarks Law has deprived them of any gainful use of their "air rights" above the Terminal and that, irrespective of the value of the remainder of their parcel, the city has "taken" their right to this superjacent airspace, thus entitling them to "just compensation" measured by the fair market value of these air rights.

Apart from our own disagreement with appellants' characterization of the effect of the New York City law, the submission that appellants may establish a "taking" simply by showing that they have been denied the ability to exploit a property interest that they heretofore had believed was available for development is quite simply untenable. Were this the rule, this Court would have erred not only in upholding laws restricting the development of air rights, but also in approving those prohibiting both the subjacent, and the lateral development of particular parcels. "Taking" jurisprudence does not divide a single parcel into discrete segments and attempt to determine whether rights in a particular segment have been entirely abrogated. In deciding whether a particular governmental action has effected a taking, this Court focuses rather both on the character of the action and on the nature and extent of the interference with rights in the parcel as a whole—here, the city tax block designated as the "landmark site."

Secondly, appellants, focusing on the character and impact of the New York City law, argue that it effects a "taking" because its operation has significantly diminished the value of the Terminal site. Appellants concede that the decisions sustaining other land-use regulations, which, like the New York City law, are reasonably related to the promotion of the general welfare, uniformly reject the proposition that diminution in property value, standing alone, can establish a "taking," see Euclid v. Ambler Realty Co., 272 U.S. 365 (1926) (75% diminution in value caused by zoning law); Hadacheck v. Sebastian, 239 U.S. 394 (1915) (87½% diminution in value) and that the "taking" issue in these contexts is resolved by focusing on the uses the regulations permit. Appellants, moreover, also do not dispute that a showing of diminution in property value would not establish a "taking" if the restriction had been imposed as a result of historic-district legislation, see generally Maher v. New Orleans, 516 F.2d 1051 (C.A.5 1975), but appellants argue that New York City's regulation of individual landmarks is fundamentally different from zoning or from historic-district legislation because the controls imposed by New York City's law apply only to individuals who own selected properties.

Stated baldly, appellants' position appears to be that the only means of ensuring that selected owners are not singled out to endure financial hardship for no reason is to hold that any restriction imposed on individual landmarks pursuant to the New York City scheme is a "taking" requiring the payment of "just compensation." Agreement with this argument would, of course, invalidate not just New York City's law, but all comparable landmark legislation in the Nation. We find no merit in it.

It is true, as appellants emphasize, that both historic-district legislation and zoning laws regulate all properties within given physical communities whereas landmark laws apply only to selected parcels. But, contrary to appellants' suggestions, landmark laws are not like discriminatory, or "reverse spot," zoning: that is, a land-use decision which arbitrarily singles out a particular parcel for different, less favorable treatment than the neighboring ones. In contrast to discriminatory zoning, which is the antithesis of land-use control as part of some comprehensive plan, the New York City law embodies a comprehensive plan to preserve structures of historic or aesthetic interest wherever they might be found in the city, and as noted, over 400 landmarks and 31 historic districts have been designated pursuant to this plan.

Equally without merit is the related argument that the decision to designate a structure as a landmark "is inevitably arbitrary or at least subjective, because it is basically a matter of taste," Reply Brief for Appellants 22, thus unavoidably singling out individual landowners for disparate and unfair treatment. The argument has a particularly hollow ring in this case. For appellants not only did not seek judicial review of either the designation or of the denials of the certificates of appropriateness and of no exterior effect, but do not even now suggest that the Commission's decisions concerning the Terminal were in any sense arbitrary or unprincipled. But, in any event, a landmark owner has a right to judicial review of any Commission decision, and, quite simply, there is no basis whatsoever for a conclusion that courts will have any greater difficulty identifying arbitrary or discriminatory action in the context of landmark regulation than in the context of classic zoning or indeed in any other context.

Next, appellants observe that New York City's law differs from zoning laws and historic-district ordinances in that the Landmarks Law does not impose identical or similar restrictions on all structures located in particular physical communities. It follows, they argue, that New York City's law is inherently incapable of producing the fair and equitable distribution of benefits and burdens of governmental action which is characteristic of zoning laws and historic-district legislation and which they maintain is a constitutional requirement if "just compensation" is not to be afforded. It is, of course, true that the Landmarks Law has a more severe impact on some landowners than on others, but that in itself does not mean that the law effects a "taking." Legislation designed to promote the general welfare commonly burdens some more than others. The owners of the brickyard in *Hadacheck*, of the cedar trees in *Miller v. Schoene*, and of the gravel and sand mine in *Goldblatt v. Hempstead*, were uniquely burdened by the legislation sustained in those cases. Similarly, zoning laws often affect some property owners more severely than others but have not been held to be invalid on that account. For example, the property owner in *Euclid* who wished to use its property for industrial purposes was affected far more severely by the ordinance than its neighbors who wished to use their land for residences.

In any event, appellants' repeated suggestions that they are solely burdened and unbenefited is factually inaccurate. This contention overlooks the fact that the New York City law applies to vast numbers of structures in the city in addition to the Terminal—all the structures contained in the 31 historic districts and over 400 individual landmarks, many of which are close to the Terminal. Unless we are to reject the judgment of the New York City Council that the preservation of landmarks benefits all New York citizens and all structures, both economically and by improving the quality of life in the city as a whole—which we are unwilling to do—we cannot conclude that the owners of the Terminal have in no sense been benefited by the Landmarks Law. Doubtless appellants believe they are more burdened than benefited by the law, but that must have been true, too, of the property owners in *Miller, Hadacheck, Euclid,* and *Goldblatt.*

Appellants' final broad-based attack would have us treat the law as an instance, like that in *United States v. Causby,* in which government, acting in an enterprise capacity, has appropriated part of their property for some strictly governmental purpose. Apart from the fact the *Causby* was a case of invasion of airspace that destroyed the use of the farm beneath and this New York City law has in nowise impaired the present use of the Terminal, the Landmarks Law neither exploits appellants' parcel for city purposes nor facilitates nor arises from any entrepreneurial operations of the city. The situation is not remotely like that in *Causby* where the airspace above the property was in the flight pattern for military aircraft. The Landmarks Law's effect is simply to prohibit appellants or anyone else from occupying portions of the airspace above the Terminal, while permitting appellants to use the remainder of the parcel in a gainful fashion. This is no more an appropriation of property by government for its own uses than is a zoning law prohibiting, for "aesthetic" reasons, two or more adult theaters within a specified area, see Young v. American Mini Theatres, Inc., 427 U.S. 50 (1976), or a safety regulation prohibiting excavations below a certain level. See *Goldblatt v. Hempstead.*

C

Rejection of appellants' broad arguments is not, however, the end of our inquiry, for all we thus far have established is that the New York City law is not rendered invalid by its failure to provide "just compensation" whenever a landmark owner is restricted in the exploitation of property interests, such as air rights, to a greater extent than provided for under applicable zoning laws. We now must consider whether the interference with appellants' property is of such a magnitude that "there must be an exercise of eminent domain and compensation to sustain [it]." Pennsylvania Coal Co. v. Mahon, 260 U.S., at 413. That inquiry may be narrowed to the question of the severity of the impact of the law on appellants' parcel, and its resolution in turn requires a careful assessment of the impact of the regulation on the Terminal site.

Unlike the governmental acts in *Goldblatt, Miller, Causby, Griggs,* and *Hadacheck,* the New York City law does not interfere in any way with the present uses of the Terminal. Its designation as a landmark not only permits but contemplates that appellants may continue to use the property precisely as it has been used for the past 65 years: as a railroad terminal containing office space and concessions. So the law does not interfere with what must be regarded as Penn Central's primary expectation concerning the use of the parcel. More importantly, on this record, we must regard the New York City law as permitting Penn Central not only to profit from the Terminal but also to obtain a "reasonable return" on its investment.

Appellants, moreover, exaggerate the effect of the law on their ability to make use of the air rights above the Terminal in two respects. First, it simply cannot be maintained, on this record, that appellants have been prohibited from occupying *any* portion of the airspace above the Terminal. While the Commission's actions in denying applications to construct an office building in excess of 50 stories above the Terminal may indicate that it will refuse to issue a certificate of appropriateness for any comparably sized structure, nothing the Commission has said or done suggests an intention to prohibit *any* construction above the Terminal. The Commission's report emphasized that whether any construction would be allowed depended upon whether the proposed addition "would harmonize in scale, material, and character with [the Terminal]." Record 2251. Since appellants have not sought approval for the construction of a smaller structure, we do not know that appellants will be denied any use of any portion of the airspace above the Terminal.

Second, to the extent appellants have been denied the right to build above the Terminal, it is not literally accurate to say that they have been denied *all* use of even those pre-existing air rights. Their ability to use these rights has not been abrogated; they are made transferable to at least eight parcels in the vicinity of the Terminal, one or two of which have been found suitable for the construction of new office buildings. Although appellants and others have argued that New York City's transferable development-rights program is far from ideal, the New York courts here supportably found that, at least in the case of the Terminal, the rights afforded are valuable. While these rights may well not have constituted "just compensation" if a "taking" had occurred, the rights nevertheless undoubtedly mitigate whatever financial burdens the law has imposed on appellants and, for that reason, are to be taken into account in considering the impact of regulation.

On this record, we conclude that the application of New York City's Landmarks Law has not effected a "taking" of appellants' property. The restrictions imposed are substantially related to the promotion of the general welfare and not only permit reasonable beneficial use of the landmark site but also afford appellants opportunities further to enhance not only the Terminal site proper but also other properties.

Affirmed.

MR. JUSTICE REHNQUIST, with whom THE CHIEF JUSTICE and MR. JUSTICE STEVENS join, dissenting.

Of the over one million buildings and structures in the city of New York, appellees have singled out 400 for designation as official landmarks. The owner of a building might initially be pleased that his property has been chosen by a distinguished committee of architects, historians, and city planners for such a singular distinction. But he may well discover, as appellant Penn Central Transportation Co. did here, that the landmark designation imposes upon him a substantial cost, with little or no offsetting benefit except for the honor of the designation. The question in this case is whether the cost associated with the city of New York's desire to preserve a limited number of "landmarks" within its borders must be borne by all of its taxpayers or whether it can instead be imposed entirely on the owners of the individual properties.

Only in the most superficial sense of the word can this case be said to involve "zoning." Typical zoning restrictions may, it is true, so limit the prospective uses of a piece of property as to diminish the value of that property in the abstract because it may not be used for the forbidden purposes. But any such abstract decrease in value will more than likely be at least partially offset by an increase in value which flows from similar restrictions as to use on neighboring properties. All property owners in a designated area are placed under the same restrictions, not only for the benefit of the municipality as a whole but also for the common benefit of one another. In the words of Mr. Justice Holmes, speaking for the Court in Pennsylvania Coal Co. v. Mahon, 260 U.S. 393, 415 (1922), there is "an average reciprocity of advantage."

Where a relatively few individual buildings, all separated from one another, are singled out and treated differently from surrounding buildings, no such reciprocity exists. The cost to the property owner which results from the imposition of restrictions applicable only to his property and not that of his neighbors may be substantial—in this case, several million dollars—with no comparable reciprocal benefits. And the cost associated with landmark legislation is likely to be of a completely different order of magnitude than that which results from the imposition of normal zoning restrictions. Unlike the regime affected by the latter, the landowner is not simply prohibited from using his property for certain purposes, while allowed to use it for all other purposes. Under the historic-landmark preservation scheme adopted by New York, the property owner is under an affirmative duty to *preserve* his property *as a landmark* at his own expense. To suggest that because traditional zoning results in some limitation of use of the property zoned, the New York City landmark preservation scheme should likewise be upheld, represents the ultimate in treating as alike things which are different. The rubric of "zoning" has not yet sufficed to avoid the well-established proposition that the Fifth Amendment bars the "Government from forcing some people alone to bear public burdens which, in all fairness and justice, should be borne by the public as a whole." Armstrong v. United States, 364 U.S. 40, 49 (1960).

* * *

I

The Fifth Amendment provides in part: "nor shall private property be taken for public use, without just compensation." In a very literal sense, the actions of appellees violated this constitutional prohibition. Before the city of New York declared Grand Central Terminal to be a landmark, Penn Central could have used its "air rights" over the Terminal to build a multistory office building, at an apparent value of several million dollars per year. Today, the Terminal cannot be modified in *any* form, including the erection of additional stories, without the permission of the Landmark Preservation Commission, a permission which appellants, despite good-faith attempts, have so far been unable to obtain. Because the Taking Clause of the Fifth Amendment has not always been read literally, however, the constitutionality of appellees' actions requires a closer scrutiny of this Court's interpretation of the three key words in the Taking Clause—"property," "taken," and "just compensation."

A

Appellees do not dispute that valuable property rights have been destroyed. And the Court has frequently emphasized that the term "property" as used in the Taking Clause includes the entire "group of rights inhering in the citizen's [ownership]." United States v. General Motors Corp., 323 U.S. 373 (1945). The term is not used in the

> "vulgar and untechnical sense of the physical thing with respect to which the citizen exercises rights recognized by law. [Instead, it] * * * denote[s] the *group of rights* inhering in the citizen's relation to the physical thing, *as the right to possess, use and dispose of it.* * * * The constitutional provision is addressed to *every sort of interest* the citizen may possess." *Id.,* at 377–378 (emphasis added).

While neighboring landowners are free to use their land and "air rights" in any way consistent with the broad boundaries of New York zoning, Penn Central, absent the permission of appellees, must forever maintain its property in its present state. The property has been thus subjected to a nonconsensual servitude not borne by any neighboring or similar properties.

B

Appellees have thus destroyed—in a literal sense, "taken"—substantial property rights of Penn Central. While the term "taken" might have been narrowly interpreted to include only physical seizures of property rights, "the construction of the phrase has not been so narrow. The courts have held that the deprivation of the former owner rather than the accretion of a right or interest to the sovereign constitutes the taking." *Id.,* at 378. Because "not every destruction or injury to property by governmental action has been held to be a 'taking' in the constitutional sense," Armstrong v. United States, 364 U.S., at 48, however, this does not end our inquiry. But an examination of the two exceptions where the destruction of property does *not* constitute a taking demonstrates that a compensable taking has occurred here.

1

* * * [T]here is no "taking" where a city prohibits the operation of a brickyard within a residential area, see Hadacheck v. Sebastian, 239 U.S. 394 (1915), or forbids excavation for sand and gravel below the water line, see Goldblatt v. Hempstead, 369 U.S. 590 (1962). Nor is it relevant, where the government is merely prohibiting a noxious use of property, that the government would seem to be singling out a particular property owner. *Hadacheck, supra,* at 413.

* * *

Appellees are not prohibiting a nuisance. The record is clear that the proposed addition to the Grand Central Terminal would be in full compliance with zoning, height limitations, and other health and safety requirements. Instead, appellees are seeking to preserve what they believe to be an outstanding example of beaux arts architecture. Penn

Central is prevented from further developing its property basically because *too good* a job was done in designing and building it. The city of New York, because of its unadorned admiration for the design, has decided that the owners of the building must preserve it unchanged for the benefit of sightseeing New Yorkers and tourists.

Unlike land-use regulations, appellees' actions do not merely *prohibit* Penn Central from using its property in a narrow set of noxious ways. Instead, appellees have placed an *affirmative* duty on Penn Central to maintain the Terminal in its present state and in "good repair." Appellants are not free to use their property as they see fit within broad outer boundaries but must strictly adhere to their past use except where appellees conclude that alternative uses would not detract from the landmark. While Penn Central may continue to use the Terminal as it is presently designed, appellees otherwise "exercise complete dominion and control over the surface of the land," United States v. Causby, 328 U.S. 256, 262 (1946), and must compensate the owner for his loss.

* * *

2

Even where the government prohibits a noninjurious use, the Court has ruled that a taking does not take place if the prohibition applies over a broad cross section of land and thereby "secure[s] an average reciprocity of advantage." Pennsylvania Coal Co. v. Mahon, 260 U.S., at 415. It is for this reason that zoning does not constitute a "taking." While zoning at times reduces *individual* property values, the burden is shared relatively evenly and it is reasonable to conclude that on the whole an individual who is harmed by one aspect of the zoning will be benefited by another.

Here, however, a multimillion dollar loss has been imposed on appellants; it is uniquely felt and is not offset by any benefits flowing from the preservation of some 400 other "landmarks" in New York City. Appellees have imposed a substantial cost on less than one one-tenth of one percent of the buildings in New York City for the general benefit of all its people. It is exactly this imposition of general costs on a few individuals at which the "taking" protection is directed.

* * *

As Mr. Justice Holmes pointed out in *Pennsylvania Coal Co. v. Mahon,* "the question at bottom" in an eminent domain case "is upon whom the loss of the changes desired should fall." 260 U.S., at 416. The benefits that appellees believe will flow from preservation of the Grand Central Terminal will accrue to all the citizens of New York City. There is no reason to believe that appellants will enjoy a substantially greater share of these benefits. If the cost of preserving Grand Central Terminal were spread evenly across the entire population of the city of New York, the burden per person would be in cents per year—a minor cost appellees would surely concede for the benefit accrued. Instead, however, appellees would impose the entire cost of several million dollars per year on Penn Central. But it is precisely this sort of discrimination that the Fifth Amendment prohibits.

* * *

C

Appellees, apparently recognizing that the constraints imposed on a landmark site constitute a taking for Fifth Amendment purposes, do not leave the property owner empty-handed. As the Court notes, the property owner may theoretically "transfer" his previous right to develop the landmark property to adjacent properties if they are under his control. Appellees have coined this system "Transfer Development Rights," or TDR's.

Of all the terms used in the Taking Clause, "just compensation" has the strictest meaning. The Fifth Amendment does not allow simply an approximate compensation but requires "a full and perfect equivalent for the property taken." Monongahela Navigation Co. v. United States, 148 U.S., at 326.

> "[I]f the adjective 'just' had been omitted, and the provision was simply that property should not be taken without compensation, the natural import of the language would be that the compensation should be the equivalent of the property. And this is made emphatic by the adjective 'just.' There can, in view of the combination of those two words, be no doubt that the compensation must be a full and perfect equivalent for the property taken."

* * *

Appellees contend that, even if they have "taken" appellants' property, TDR's constitute "just compensation." Appellants, of course, argue that TDR's are highly imperfect compensation. Because the lower courts held that there was no "taking," they did not have to reach the question of whether or not just compensation has already been awarded. The New York Court of Appeals' discussion of TDR's gives some support to appellants:

> "The many defects in New York City's program for development rights transfers have been detailed elsewhere * * *. The area to which transfer is permitted is severely limited [and] complex procedures are required to obtain a transfer permit." 42 N.Y.2d 324, 334–335, 366 N.E.2d 1271, 1277 (1977).

And in other cases the Court of Appeals has noted that TDR's have an "uncertain and contingent market value" and do "not adequately preserve" the value lost when a building is declared to be a landmark. French Investing Co. v. City of New York, 39 N.Y.2d 587, 591, 350 N.E.2d 381, 383, appeal dismissed, 429 U.S. 990 (1976). On the other hand, there is evidence in the record that Penn Central has been offered substantial amounts for its TDR's. Because the record on appeal is relatively slim, I would remand to the Court of Appeals for a determination of whether TDR's constitute a "full and perfect equivalent for the property taken."

* * *

Notes and Problems

1. The famous *Pennsylvania Coal Co.* case, cited in *Penn Central,* was re-examined and distinguished by the Supreme Court in Keystone Bituminous Coal Ass'n v. DeBenedictis, 480 U.S. 470 (1987).

2. The transferable development rights (TDRs) concept is a relatively new tool for land use control that still is being refined. *See* Costonis, *Development Rights Transfer: An Exploratory Essay,* 83 Yale L.J. 75 (1973); Malone, *The Future of Transferable Development Rights in the Supreme Court,* 73 Ky.L.J. 759 (1985); Merriam, *Making TDR Work,* 56 N.C.L.Rev. 77 (1978); Richards, *Transferable Development Rights: Corrective, Catastrophe, or Curiosity?,* 12 Real Est.L.J. 26 (1983). Indeed, the appropriate role of TDRs in takings litigation remains unsettled. In a 1997 regulatory takings case decided on ripeness grounds, three concurring members of the Supreme Court distinguished *Penn Central* and maintained that the transferable development rights involved in the instant controversy should not be factored into an evaluation of the takings aspect of the dispute, but should be given weight just with respect to calculating any compensation owed the landowner. The majority withheld judgment on this matter. Suitum v. Tahoe Regional Planning Agency, 520 U.S. 725 (1997).

Recall that the Centerville City Council wishes to preserve environmentally fragile areas without condemning land. Could TDRs be used to accomplish this purpose? If so, how?

3. The designation of theaters as historic landmarks has generated litigation regarding the constitutionality of such action. *See* Shubert Organization, Inc. v. Landmarks Preservation Commission of the City of New York, 166 A.D.2d 115, 570 N.Y.S.2d 504 (1991) (upholding designation), *appeal dismissed* 78 N.Y.2d 1006, 575 N.Y.S.2d 456, 580 N.E.2d 1059 (1991), *motion for leave to appeal denied* 79 N.Y.2d 751, 579 N.Y.S.2d 651, 587 N.E.2d 289 (1991), *cert. denied* 504 U.S. 946 (1992); United Artists' Theater Circuit, Inc. v. City of Philadelphia, Philadelphia Historical Commission, 535 Pa. 370, 635 A.2d 612 (1993) (finding designation did not constitute taking under state constitution, but vacating designation on other grounds). *See generally* Note, *The "United Artists Theater" Case: First Step in a New Test?,* 12 J.Law & Commerce 317 (1993).

4. The application of local landmark preservation ordinances to churches also has presented constitutional issues. Religious institutions have attacked the landmarking of churches as an uncompensated taking and as a burden on the free exercise of religion in violation of the First Amendment. *Compare* St. Bartholomew's Church v. City of New York, 914 F.2d 348 (2d Cir.1990) (sustaining preservation ordinance against free exercise claim), *cert. denied* 499 U.S. 905 (1991) *with* First Covenant Church v. City of Seattle, 120 Wn.2d 203, 840 P.2d 174 (1992) (invalidating landmark designation of church as infringement of free exercise of religion).

LORETTO v. TELEPROMPTER MANHATTAN CATV CORP.

Supreme Court of the United States, 1982.
458 U.S. 419.

JUSTICE MARSHALL delivered the opinion of the Court.

This case presents the question whether a minor but permanent physical occupation of an owner's property authorized by government constitutes a "taking" of property for which just compensation is due under the Fifth and Fourteenth Amendments of the Constitution. New York law provides that a landlord must permit a cable television company to install its cable facilities upon his property. N.Y.Exec.Law § 828(1) (McKinney Supp.1982). In this case, the cable installation occupied portions of appellant's roof and the side of her building. The New York Court of Appeals ruled that this appropriation does not amount to a taking. Loretto v. Teleprompter Manhattan CATV Corp., 53 N.Y.2d 124, 440 N.Y.S.2d 843, 423 N.E.2d 320 (1981). Because we conclude that such a physical occupation of property is a taking, we reverse.

* * *

In Penn Central Transportation Co. v. New York City, 438 U.S. 104 (1978), the Court surveyed some of the general principles governing the Takings Clause. The Court noted that no "set formula" existed to determine, in all cases, whether compensation is constitutionally due for a government restriction of property. Ordinarily, the Court must engage in "essentially ad hoc, factual inquiries." *Id.,* at 124. But the inquiry is not standardless. The economic impact of the regulation, especially the degree of interference with investment-backed expectations, is of particular significance. "So, too, is the character of the governmental action. A 'taking' may more readily be found when the interference with property can be characterized as a physical invasion by government, * * * than when interference arises from some public program adjusting the benefits and burdens of economic life to promote the common good." *Id.*

As *Penn Central* affirms, the Court has often upheld substantial regulation of an owner's use of his own property where deemed necessary to promote the public interest. At the same time, we have long considered a physical intrusion by government to be a property restriction of an unusually serious character for purposes of the Takings Clause. Our cases further establish that when the physical intrusion reaches the extreme form of a permanent physical occupation, a taking has occurred. In such a case, "the character of the government action" not only is an important factor in resolving whether the action works a taking but is determinative.

* * *

The historical rule that a permanent physical occupation of another's property is a taking has more than tradition to commend it. Such an appropriation is perhaps the most serious form of invasion of an owner's property interests. To borrow a metaphor, the government does not simply take a single "strand" from the "bundle" of property rights: it chops through the bundle, taking a slice of every strand.

Property rights in a physical thing have been described as the rights "to possess, use and dispose of it." United States v. General Motors Corp., 323 U.S. 373, 378 (1945). To the extent that the government permanently occupies physical property, it effectively destroys *each* of these rights. First, the owner has no right to possess the occupied space himself, and also has no power to exclude the occupier from possession and use of the space. The power to exclude has traditionally been considered one of the most treasured strands in an owner's bundle of property rights.[1] Second, the permanent physical occupation of property forever denies the owner any power to control the use of the property; he not only cannot exclude others, but can make no non-possessory use of the property. Although deprivation of the right to use and obtain a profit from property is not, in every case independently sufficient to establish a taking, it is clearly relevant. Finally, even though the owner may retain the bare legal right to dispose of the occupied space by transfer or sale, the permanent occupation of that space by a stranger will ordinarily empty the right of any value, since the purchaser will also be unable to make any use of the property.

* * *

The traditional rule also avoids otherwise difficult line-drawing problems. Few would disagree that if the State required landlords to permit third parties to install swimming pools on the landlords' rooftops for the convenience of the tenants, the requirement would be a taking. If the cable installation here occupied as much space, again, few would disagree that the occupation would be a taking. But constitutional protection for the rights of private property cannot be made to depend on the size of the area permanently occupied. Indeed, it is possible that in the future, additional cable installations that more significantly restrict a landlord's use of the roof of his building will be made. Section 828 requires a landlord to permit such multiple installations.

Finally, whether a permanent physical occupation has occurred presents relatively few problems of proof. The placement of a fixed structure on land or real property is an obvious fact that will rarely be

---

1. The permanence and absolute exclusivity of a physical occupation distinguish it from temporary limitations on the right to exclude. Not every physical *invasion* is a taking. * * * [T]emporary limitations are subject to a more complex balancing process to determine whether they are a taking. The rationale is evident: they do not absolutely dispossess the owner of his rights to use, and exclude others from, his property.

The dissent objects that the distinction between a permanent physical occupation and a temporary invasion will not always be clear. This objection is overstated, and in any event is irrelevant to the critical point that a permanent physical occupation *is* unquestionably a taking. In the antitrust area, similarly, this Court has not declined to apply a *per se* rule simply because a court must, at the boundary of the rule, apply the rule of reason and engage in a more complex balancing analysis.

subject to dispute. Once the fact of occupation is shown, of course, a court should consider the *extent* of the occupation as one relevant factor in determining the compensation due. For that reason, moreover, there is less need to consider the extent of the occupation in determining whether there is a taking in the first instance.

Teleprompter's cable installation on appellant's building constitutes a taking under the traditional test. The installation involved a direct physical attachment of plates, boxes, wires, bolts and screws to the building, completely occupying space immediately above and upon the roof and along the building's exterior wall.

* * *

Our holding today is very narrow. We affirm the traditional rule that a permanent physical occupation of property is a taking. In such a case, the property owner entertains an historically-rooted expectation of compensation, and the character of the invasion is qualitatively more intrusive than perhaps any other category of property regulation. We do not, however, question the equally substantial authority upholding a State's broad power to impose appropriate restrictions upon an owner's *use* of his property.

Furthermore, our conclusion that § 828 works a taking of a portion of appellant's property does not presuppose that the fee which many landlords had obtained from Teleprompter prior to the law's enactment is a proper measure of the value of the property taken. The issue of the amount of compensation that is due, on which we express no opinion, is a matter for the state courts to consider on remand.[2]

The judgment of the New York Court of Appeals is reversed and the case is remanded for further proceedings not inconsistent with this opinion.

Notes and Questions

1. The Court did not address the question of compensation. Does the statutory scheme satisfy the just compensation requirement? *See* Payne,

2. Prior to 1973, Teleprompter routinely obtained authorization for its installations from property owners along the cable's route, compensating the owners at the standard rate of 5% of the gross revenues that Teleprompter realized from the particular property. To facilitate tenant access to CATV, the State of New York enacted § 828 of the Executive Law, effective January 1, 1973. Section 828 provides that a landlord may not "interfere with the installation of cable television facilities upon his property or premises," and may not demand payment from any tenant for permitting CATV, or demand payment from any CATV company "in excess of any amount which the [State Commission on Cable Television] shall, by regulation, determine to be reasonable." The landlord may, how-ever, require the CATV company or the tenant to bear the cost of installation and to indemnify for any damage caused by the installation. Pursuant to § 828(1)(b), the State Commission has ruled that a one-time $1 payment is the normal fee to which a landlord is entitled. The Commission ruled that this nominal fee, which the Commission concluded was equivalent to what the landlord would receive if the property were condemned pursuant to New York's Transportation Corporations Law, satisfied constitutional requirements "in the absence of a special showing of greater damages attributable to the taking." Statement of General Policy, App. 52. [This paragraph is from a portion of the opinion that was deleted. Editors' note.]

Just Compensation in a Breadbox, 11 Real Est.L.J. 264 (1983). On remand, the New York Court of Appeals determined that "the due process requirements of just compensation" would be satisfied by a decision as to the amount of compensation by the State Commission on Cable Television. Loretto v. Teleprompter Manhattan CATV, 58 N.Y.2d 143, 459 N.Y.S.2d 743, 446 N.E.2d 428 (1983).

2. For a case demonstrating the continuing importance of *Loretto,* see GTE Northwest, Inc. v. Public Utility Commission, 321 Or. 458, 900 P.2d 495 (1995) (regulations which required telephone carriers to allow installation of collocation equipment by other service providers effected a physical taking of property under *Loretto*), *cert. denied* 517 U.S. 1155 (1996).

3. Courts have wrestled with the question of whether local rental occupancy laws that in effect create leases of indefinite duration constitute a physical taking of the landlord's property. *Compare* Yee v. City of Escondido, 503 U.S. 519 (1992) *with* Seawall Associates v. City of New York, 74 N.Y.2d 92, 544 N.Y.S.2d 542, 542 N.E.2d 1059 (1989), *cert. denied* 493 U.S. 976 (1989). For a general discussion of rent control see pages 155–162.

4. The "per se" rule fashioned in *Loretto* extends to personal property. For an application of this doctrine to congressional legislation asserting control over the presidential papers of former President Richard M. Nixon, see Nixon v. United States, 978 F.2d 1269 (D.C.Cir.1992).

FIRST ENGLISH EVANGELICAL LUTHERAN CHURCH OF GLENDALE v. COUNTY OF LOS ANGELES

Supreme Court of the United States, 1987.
482 U.S. 304.

CHIEF JUSTICE REHNQUIST delivered the opinion of the Court.

In this case the California Court of Appeal held that a landowner who claims that his property has been "taken" by a land-use regulation may not recover damages for the time before it is finally determined that the regulation constitutes a "taking" of his property. We disagree, and conclude that in these circumstances the Fifth and Fourteenth Amendments to the United States Constitution would require compensation for that period.

In 1957, appellant First English Evangelical Lutheran Church purchased a 21–acre parcel of land in a canyon along the banks of the Middle Fork of Mill Creek in the Angeles National Forest. The Middle Fork is the natural drainage channel for a watershed area owned by the National Forest Service. Twelve of the acres owned by the church are flat land, and contained a dining hall, two bunkhouses, a caretaker's lodge, an outdoor chapel, and a footbridge across the creek. The church operated on the site a campground, known as "Lutherglen," as a retreat center and a recreational area for handicapped children.

In July 1977, a forest fire denuded the hills upstream from Lutherglen, destroying approximately 3,860 acres of the watershed area and creating a serious flood hazard. Such flooding occurred on February 9 and 10, 1978, when a storm dropped 11 inches of rain in the watershed. The runoff from the storm overflowed the banks of the Mill Creek, flooding Lutherglen and destroying its buildings.

In response to the flooding of the canyon, appellee County of Los Angeles adopted Interim Ordinance No. 11,855 in January 1979. The ordinance provided that "[a] person shall not construct, reconstruct, place or enlarge any building or structure, any portion of which is, or will be, located within the outer boundary lines of the interim flood protection area located in Mill Creek Canyon. * * * "The ordinance was effective immediately because the county determined that it was "required for the immediate preservation of the public health and safety. * * * " The interim flood protection area described by the ordinance included the flat areas on either side of Mill Creek on which Lutherglen had stood.

The church filed a complaint in the Superior Court of California a little more than a month after the ordinance was adopted. As subsequently amended, the complaint alleged two claims against the county and the Los Angeles County Flood Control District. The first alleged that the defendants were liable under Cal.Gov't Code Ann. § 835 (West 1980) for dangerous conditions on their upstream properties that contributed to the flooding of Lutherglen. As a part of this claim, appellant also alleged that "Ordinance No. 11,855 denies [appellant] all use of Lutherglen." App. 12, 49. The second claim sought to recover from the Flood District in inverse condemnation and in tort for engaging in cloud seeding during the storm that flooded Lutherglen. Appellant sought damages under each count for loss of use of Lutherglen. The defendants moved to strike the portions of the complaint alleging that the county's ordinance denied all use of Lutherglen, on the view that the California Supreme Court's decision in Agins v. Tiburon, 24 Cal.3d 266, 157 Cal.Rptr. 372, 598 P.2d 25 (1979), aff'd on other grounds, 447 U.S. 255 (1980), rendered the allegation "entirely immaterial and irrelevant[, with] no bearing upon any conceivable cause of action herein." * * *

In *Agins v. Tiburon, supra,* the Supreme Court of California decided that a landowner may not maintain an inverse condemnation suit in the courts of that State based upon a "regulatory" taking. In the court's view, maintenance of such a suit would allow a landowner to force the legislature to exercise its power of eminent domain. Under this decision, then, compensation is not required until the challenged regulation or ordinance has been held excessive in an action for declaratory relief or a writ of mandamus and the government has nevertheless decided to continue the regulation in effect. Based on this decision, the trial court in the present case granted the motion to strike the allegation that the church had been denied all use of Lutherglen. It explained that "a careful re-reading of the *Agins* case persuades the Court that when an ordinance, even a non-zoning ordinance, deprives a person of the total use of his lands, his challenge to the ordinance is by way of declaratory relief or possibly mandamus." Because the appellant alleged a regulatory taking and sought only damages, the allegation that the ordinance denied all use of Lutherglen was deemed irrelevant.

On appeal, the California Court of Appeal read the complaint as one seeking "damages for the uncompensated taking of all use of Lutherglen by County Ordinance No. 11,855. * * * '' It too relied on the California Supreme Court's decision in *Agins* in rejecting the cause of action, declining appellant's invitation to reevaluate *Agins* in light of this Court's opinions in San Diego Gas & Electric Co. v. San Diego, 450 U.S. 621 (1981). The court found itself obligated to follow *Agins* "because the United States Supreme Court has not yet ruled on the question of whether a state may constitutionally limit the remedy for a taking to nonmonetary relief * * *.'' It accordingly affirmed the trial court's decision to strike the allegations concerning appellee's ordinance. The Supreme Court of California denied review.

This appeal followed, and we noted probable jurisdiction. 106 S.Ct. 3292. Appellant asks us to hold that the Supreme Court of California erred in *Agins v. Tiburon* in determining that the Fifth Amendment, as made applicable to the States through the Fourteenth Amendment, does not require compensation as a remedy for "temporary" regulatory takings—those regulatory takings which are ultimately invalidated by the courts. Four times this decade, we have considered similar claims and have found ourselves for one reason or another unable to consider the merits of the *Agins* rule. See MacDonald, Sommer & Frates v. Yolo County, 106 S.Ct. 2561 (1986); Williamson County Regional Planning Comm'n v. Hamilton Bank, 473 U.S. 172 (1985); *San Diego Gas & Electric Co., supra; Agins v. Tiburon, supra.* For the reasons explained below, however, we find the constitutional claim properly presented in this case, and hold that on these facts the California courts have decided the compensation question inconsistently with the requirements of the Fifth Amendment.

I

* * *

II

Consideration of the compensation question must begin with direct reference to the language of the Fifth Amendment, which provides in relevant part that "private property [shall not] be taken for public use, without just compensation." As its language indicates, and as the Court has frequently noted, this provision does not prohibit the taking of private property, but instead places a condition on the exercise of that power. This basic understanding of the Amendment makes clear that it is designed not to limit the governmental interference with property rights *per se,* but rather to secure *compensation* in the event of otherwise proper interference amounting to a taking. Thus, government action that works a taking of property rights necessarily implicates the "constitutional obligation to pay just compensation." Armstrong v. United States, 364 U.S. 40 (1960).

We have recognized that a landowner is entitled to bring an action in inverse condemnation as a result of " 'the self-executing character of the constitutional provision with respect to compensation. * * * ' " United States v. Clarke, 445 U.S. 253, 257 (1980), quoting 6 P. Nichols, Eminent Domain § 25.41 (3d rev. ed. 1972). As noted in Justice Brennan's dissent in San Diego Gas & Electric Co., 450 U.S., at 654–655, it has been established at least since Jacobs v. United States, 290 U.S. 13 (1933), that claims for just compensation are grounded in the Constitution itself * * *.

* * *

It has also been established doctrine at least since Justice Holmes' opinion for the Court in Pennsylvania Coal Co. v. Mahon, 260 U.S. 393 (1922) that "[t]he general rule at least is, that while property may be regulated to a certain extent, if regulation goes too far it will be recognized as a taking." Id., at 415. While the typical taking occurs when the government acts to condemn property in the exercise of its power of eminent domain, the entire doctrine of inverse condemnation is predicated on the proposition that a taking may occur without such formal proceedings. * * *

While the Supreme Court of California may not have actually disavowed this general rule in Agins, we believe that it has truncated the rule by disallowing damages that occurred prior to the ultimate invalidation of the challenged regulation. The Supreme Court of California justified its conclusion at length in the Agins opinion, concluding that:

> "In combination, the need for preserving a degree of freedom in the land-use planning function, and the inhibiting financial force which inheres in the inverse condemnation remedy, persuade us that on balance mandamus or declaratory relief rather than inverse condemnation is the appropriate relief under the circumstances." Agins v. Tiburon, 24 Cal.3d, at 276–277, 157 Cal.Rptr., at 378, 598 P.2d, at 31.

We, of course, are not unmindful of these considerations, but they must be evaluated in the light of the command of the Just Compensation Clause of the Fifth Amendment. The Court has recognized in more than one case that the government may elect to abandon its intrusion or discontinue regulations. Similarly, a governmental body may acquiesce in a judicial declaration that one of its ordinances has affected an unconstitutional taking of property; the landowner has no right under the Just Compensation Clause to insist that a "temporary" taking be deemed a permanent taking. But we have not resolved whether abandonment by the government requires payment of compensation for the period of time during which regulations deny a landowner all use of his land.

In considering this question, we find substantial guidance in cases where the government has only temporarily exercised its right to use private property. * * *

These cases reflect the fact that "temporary" takings which, as here, deny a landowner all use of his property, are not different in kind from permanent takings, for which the Constitution clearly requires compensation. Cf. San Diego Gas & Electric Co., 450 U.S., at 657 (Brennan, J., dissenting) ("Nothing in the Just Compensation Clause suggests that 'takings' must be permanent and irrevocable"). It is axiomatic that the Fifth Amendment's just compensation provision is "designed to bar Government from forcing some people alone to bear public burdens which, in all fairness and justice, should be borne by the public as a whole." Armstrong v. United States, 364 U.S., at 49. See also Penn Central Transportation Co. v. New York City, 438 U.S., at 123–125; Monongahela Navigation Co. v. United States, 148 U.S., at 325. In the present case the interim ordinance was adopted by the county of Los Angeles in January 1979, and became effective immediately. Appellant filed suit within a month after the effective date of the ordinance and yet when the Supreme Court of California denied a hearing in the case on October 17, 1985, the merits of appellant's claim had yet to be determined. The United States has been required to pay compensation for leasehold interests of shorter duration than this. The value of a leasehold interest in property for a period of years may be substantial, and the burden on the property owner in extinguishing such an interest for a period of years may be great indeed. Where this burden results from governmental action that amounted to a taking, the Just Compensation Clause of the Fifth Amendment requires that the government pay the landowner for the value of the use of the land during this period. Cf. United States v. Causby, 328 U.S., at 261 ("It is the owner's loss, not the taker's gain, which is the measure of the value of the property taken"). Invalidation of the ordinance or its successor ordinance after this period of time, though converting the taking into a "temporary" one, is not a sufficient remedy to meet the demands of the Just Compensation Clause.

* * *

Nothing we say today is intended to abrogate the principle that the decision to exercise the power of eminent domain is a legislative function, " 'for Congress and Congress alone to determine.' " Hawaii Housing Authority v. Midkiff, 467 U.S. 229, 240 (1984), quoting Berman v. Parker, 348 U.S. 26, 33 (1954). Once a court determines that a taking has occurred, the government retains the whole range of options already available—amendment of the regulation, withdrawal of the invalidated regulation, or exercise of eminent domain. Thus we do not, as the Solicitor General suggests, "permit a court, at the behest of a private person, to require the * * * Government to exercise the power of eminent domain * * *." We merely hold that where the government's activities have already worked a taking of all use of property, no subsequent action by the government can relieve it of the duty to provide compensation for the period during which the taking was effective.

We also point out that the allegation of the complaint which we treat as true for purposes of our decision was that the ordinance in question denied appellant all use of its property. We limit our holding to the facts presented, and of course do not deal with the quite different questions that would arise in the case of normal delays in obtaining building permits, changes in zoning ordinances, variances, and the like which are not before us. We realize that even our present holding will undoubtedly lessen to some extent the freedom and flexibility of land-use planners and governing bodies of municipal corporations when enacting land-use regulations. But such consequences necessarily flow from any decision upholding a claim of constitutional right; many of the provisions of the Constitution are designed to limit the flexibility and freedom of governmental authorities and the Just Compensation Clause of the Fifth Amendment is one of them. As Justice Holmes aptly noted more than 50 years ago, "a strong public desire to improve the public condition is not enough to warrant achieving the desire by a shorter cut than the constitutional way of paying for the change." Pennsylvania Coal Co. v. Mahon, 260 U.S., at 416.

Here we must assume that the Los Angeles County ordinances have denied appellant all use of its property for a considerable period of years, and we hold that invalidation of the ordinance without payment of fair value for the use of the property during this period of time would be a constitutionally insufficient remedy. The judgment of the California Court of Appeals is therefore reversed, and the case is remanded for further proceedings not inconsistent with this opinion.

It is so ordered.

JUSTICE STEVENS, with whom JUSTICE BLACKMUN and JUSTICE O'CONNOR join as to Parts I and III, dissenting.

One thing is certain. The Court's decision today will generate a great deal of litigation. Most of it, I believe, will be unproductive. But the mere duty to defend the actions that today's decision will spawn will undoubtedly have a significant adverse impact on the land-use regulatory process. The Court has reached out to address an issue not actually presented in this case, and has then answered that self-imposed question in a superficial and, I believe, dangerous way.

* * *

Notes

1. The California Court of Appeal on remand held that the ordinance at issue in *First English Evangelical* did not constitute a temporary taking of property in violation of the Fifth Amendment. First English Evangelical, Lutheran Church of Glendale v. County of Los Angeles, 210 Cal.App.3d 1353, 258 Cal.Rptr. 893 (1989). The court concluded that the ordinance "substantially advanced the preeminent state interest in public safety and did not deny appellant all use of its property." *Id.* at 1355, 258 Cal.Rptr. at 894. Moreover, the "ordinance only imposed a reasonable moratorium for a

reasonable period of time while the respondent conducted a study and determined what uses, if any, were compatible with public safety." *Id.*

2. Inverse condemnation is discussed in *First English Evangelical.* Justice Brennan described the concept as follows:

> The phrase "inverse condemnation" generally describes a cause of action against a government defendant in which a landowner may recover just compensation for a "taking" of his property under the Fifth Amendment, even though formal condemnation proceedings in exercise of the sovereign's power of eminent domain have not been instituted by the government entity. In the typical condemnation proceeding, the government brings a judicial or administrative action against the property owner to "take" the fee simple or an interest in his property; the judicial or administrative body enters a decree of condemnation and just compensation is awarded. In an "inverse condemnation" action, the condemnation is "inverse" because it is the landowner, not the government entity, who institutes the proceeding.

San Diego Gas & Electric Co. v. City of San Diego, 450 U.S. 621, 638 n. 2 (1981) (dissenting opinion).

LUCAS v. SOUTH CAROLINA COASTAL COUNCIL

Supreme Court of the United States, 1992.
505 U.S. 1003.

JUSTICE SCALIA delivered the opinion of the Court.

In 1986, petitioner David H. Lucas paid $975,000 for two residential lots on the Isle of Palms in Charleston County, South Carolina, on which he intended to build single-family homes. In 1988, however, the South Carolina Legislature enacted the Beachfront Management Act, S.C.Code § 48–39–250 *et seq.* (Supp.1990) (Act), which had the direct effect of barring petitioner from erecting any permanent habitable structures on his two parcels. A state trial court found that this prohibition rendered Lucas's parcels "valueless." This case requires us to decide whether the Act's dramatic effect on the economic value of Lucas's lots accomplished a taking of private property under the Fifth and Fourteenth Amendments requiring the payment of "just compensation."

I

A

South Carolina's expressed interest in intensively managing development activities in the so-called "coastal zone" dates from 1977 when, in the aftermath of Congress's passage of the federal Coastal Zone Management Act of 1972, the legislature enacted a Coastal Zone Management Act of its own. In its original form, the South Carolina Act required owners of coastal zone land that qualified as a "critical area" (defined in the legislation to include beaches and immediately adjacent sand dunes) to obtain a permit from the newly created South Carolina Coastal Council (respondent here) prior to committing the land to a "use other than the use the critical area was devoted to on [September 28, 1977]."

In the late 1970's, Lucas and others began extensive residential development of the Isle of Palms, a barrier island situated eastward of the City of Charleston. Toward the close of the development cycle for one residential subdivision known as "Beachwood East," Lucas in 1986 purchased the two lots at issue in this litigation for his own account. No portion of the lots, which were located approximately 300 feet from the beach, qualified as a "critical area" under the 1977 Act; accordingly, at the time Lucas acquired these parcels, he was not legally obliged to obtain a permit from the Council in advance of any development activity. His intention with respect to the lots was to do what the owners of the immediately adjacent parcels had already done: erect single-family residences. He commissioned architectural drawings for this purpose.

The Beachfront Management Act brought Lucas's plans to an abrupt end. Under that 1988 legislation, the Council was directed to establish a "baseline" connecting the landward-most "point[s] of erosion * * * during the past forty years" in the region of the Isle of Palms that includes Lucas's lots. In action not challenged here, the Council fixed this baseline landward of Lucas's parcels. That was significant, for under the Act construction of occupiable improvements[1] was flatly prohibited seaward of a line drawn 20 feet landward of, and parallel to, the baseline. The Act provided no exceptions.

B

Lucas promptly filed suit in the South Carolina Court of Common Pleas, contending that the Beachfront Management Act's construction bar effected a taking of his property without just compensation. Lucas did not take issue with the validity of the Act as a lawful exercise of South Carolina's police power, but contended that the Act's complete extinguishment of his property's value entitled him to compensation regardless of whether the legislature had acted in furtherance of legitimate police power objectives. Following a bench trial, the court agreed. Among its factual determinations was the finding that "at the time Lucas purchased the two lots, both were zoned for single-family residential construction and * * * there were no restrictions imposed upon such use of the property by either the State of South Carolina, the County of Charleston, or the Town of the Isle of Palms." The trial court further found that the Beachfront Management Act decreed a permanent ban on construction insofar as Lucas's lots were concerned, and that this prohibition "deprive[d] Lucas of any reasonable economic use of the lots, * * * eliminated the unrestricted right of use, and render[ed] them valueless." The court thus concluded that Lucas's properties had been "taken" by operation of the Act, and it ordered respondent to pay "just compensation" in the amount of $1,232,387.50.

---

1. The Act did allow the construction of certain nonhabitable improvements, *e.g.*, "wooden walkways no larger in width than six feet," and "small wooden decks no larg-er than one hundred forty-four square feet." §§ 48–39–290(A)(1) and (2) (Supp. 1988).

The Supreme Court of South Carolina reversed. * * *

* * *

We granted certiorari.

II

As a threshold matter, we must briefly address the Council's suggestion that this case is inappropriate for plenary review. After briefing and argument before the South Carolina Supreme Court, but prior to issuance of that court's opinion, the Beachfront Management Act was amended to authorize the Council, in certain circumstances, to issue "special permits" for the construction or reconstruction of habitable structures seaward of the baseline. According to the Council, this amendment renders Lucas's claim of a permanent deprivation unripe, as Lucas may yet be able to secure permission to build on his property. "[The Court's] cases," we are reminded, "uniformly reflect an insistence on knowing the nature and extent of permitted development before adjudicating the constitutionality of the regulations that purport to limit it." MacDonald, Sommer & Frates v. County of Yolo, 477 U.S. 340, 351 (1986). See also Agins v. Tiburon, 447 U.S. 255, 260 (1980). Because petitioner "has not yet obtained a final decision regarding how [he] will be allowed to develop [his] property," Williamson County Regional Planning Comm'n of Johnson City v. Hamilton Bank, 473 U.S. 172, 190 (1985), the Council argues that he is not yet entitled to definitive adjudication of his takings claim in this Court.

We think these considerations would preclude review had the South Carolina Supreme Court rested its judgment on ripeness grounds, as it was (essentially) invited to do by the Council. The South Carolina Supreme Court shrugged off the possibility of further administrative and trial proceedings, however, preferring to dispose of Lucas's takings claim on the merits. This unusual disposition does not preclude Lucas from applying for a permit under the 1990 amendment for *future* construction, and challenging, on takings grounds, any denial. But it does preclude, both practically and legally, any takings claim with respect to Lucas's *past* deprivation, *i.e.*, for his having been denied construction rights during the period before the 1990 amendment. See generally First English Evangelical Lutheran Church of Glendale v. County of Los Angeles, 482 U.S. 304 (1987) (holding that temporary deprivations of use are compensable under the Takings Clause). Without even so much as commenting upon the consequences of the South Carolina Supreme Court's judgment in this respect, the Council insists that permitting Lucas to press his claim of a past deprivation on this appeal would be improper, since "the issues of whether and to what extent [Lucas] has incurred a temporary taking * * * have simply never been addressed." Yet Lucas had no reason to proceed on a "temporary taking" theory at trial, or even to seek remand for that purpose prior to submission of the case to the South Carolina Supreme Court, since as the Act then read, the taking was unconditional and permanent. Moreover, given the breadth of the South Carolina Supreme Court's holding and judgment,

Lucas would plainly be unable (absent our intervention now) to obtain further state-court adjudication with respect to the 1988–1990 period.

In these circumstances, we think it would not accord with sound process to insist that Lucas pursue the late-created "special permit" procedure before his takings claim can be considered ripe. Lucas has properly alleged Article III injury-in-fact in this case, with respect to both the pre–1990 and post–1990 constraints placed on the use of his parcels by the Beachfront Management Act. That there is a discretionary "special permit" procedure by which he may regain—for the future, at least—beneficial use of his land goes only to the prudential "ripeness" of Lucas's challenge, and for the reasons discussed we do not think it prudent to apply that prudential requirement here. We leave for decision on remand, of course, the questions left unaddressed by the South Carolina Supreme Court as a consequence of its categorical disposition.

III

A

Prior to Justice Holmes' exposition in Pennsylvania Coal Co. v. Mahon, 260 U.S. 393 (1922), it was generally thought that the Takings Clause reached only a "direct appropriation" of property, Legal Tender Cases, 12 Wall. 457, 551 (1871), or the functional equivalent of a "practical ouster of [the owner's] possession." Transportation Co. v. Chicago, 99 U.S. 635, 642 (1879). Justice Holmes recognized in *Mahon*, however, that if the protection against physical appropriations of private property was to be meaningfully enforced, the government's power to redefine the range of interests included in the ownership of property was necessarily constrained by constitutional limits. 260 U.S., at 414–415. If, instead, the uses of private property were subject to unbridled, uncompensated qualification under the police power, "the natural tendency of human nature [would be] to extend the qualification more and more until at last private property disappear[ed]." *Id.*, at 415. These considerations gave birth in that case to the oft-cited maxim that, "while property may be regulated to a certain extent, if regulation goes too far it will be recognized as a taking." *Ibid.*

Nevertheless, our decision in *Mahon* offered little insight into when, and under what circumstances, a given regulation would be seen as going "too far" for purposes of the Fifth Amendment. In 70–odd years of succeeding "regulatory takings" jurisprudence, we have generally eschewed any " 'set formula' " for determining how far is too far, preferring to "engag[e] in * * * essentially ad hoc, factual inquiries," Penn Central Transportation Co. v. New York City, 438 U.S. 104, 124 (1978) (quoting Goldblatt v. Hempstead, 369 U.S. 590, 594 (1962)). We have, however, described at least two discrete categories of regulatory action as compensable without case-specific inquiry into the public interest advanced in support of the restraint. The first encompasses regulations that compel the property owner to suffer a physical "invasion" of his property. In general (at least with regard to permanent invasions), no matter how minute the intrusion, and no matter how weighty the public purpose behind it, we have required compensation. For example, in Loretto v. Teleprompter Manhattan CATV Corp., 458 U.S. 419 (1982), we determined that New York's law requiring landlords to allow television cable companies to emplace cable facilities in their apartment buildings constituted a taking, even though the facilities occupied at most only 1½ cubic feet of the landlords' property. See also United States v. Causby, 328 U.S. 256, 265, and n. 10 (1946) (physical invasions of airspace); cf. Kaiser Aetna v. United States, 444 U.S. 164 (1979) (imposition of navigational servitude upon private marina).

The second situation in which we have found categorical treatment appropriate is where regulation denies all economically beneficial or productive use of land. See *Agins,* 447 U.S., at 260; see also Nollan v. California Coastal Comm'n, 483 U.S. 825, 834 (1987); Keystone Bituminous Coal Assn. v. DeBenedictis, 480 U.S. 470, 495 (1987). As we have said on numerous occasions, the Fifth Amendment is violated when land-use regulation "does not substantially advance legitimate state interests *or denies an owner economically viable use of his land." Agins, supra,* 447 U.S., at 260 (emphasis added).[2]

We have never set forth the justification for this rule. Perhaps it is simply * * * that total deprivation of beneficial use is, from the landowner's point of view, the equivalent of a physical appropriation. "[F]or what is the land but the profits thereof[?]" 1 E. Coke, Institutes, ch. 1, § 1 (1st Am. ed. 1812). Surely, at least, in the extraordinary circumstance when *no* productive or economically beneficial use of land is permitted, it is less realistic to indulge our usual assumption that the legislature is simply "adjusting the benefits and burdens of economic life," Penn Central Transportation Co., 438 U.S., at 124 in a manner that secures an "average reciprocity of advantage" to everyone concerned. Pennsylvania Coal Co. v. Mahon, 260 U.S., at 415. And the *functional* basis for permitting the government, by regulation, to affect property values without compensation—that "Government hardly could go on if to some extent values incident to property could not be diminished without paying for every such change in the general law," *id.,* at 413—does not apply to the relatively rare situations where the government has deprived a landowner of all economically beneficial uses.

---

2. Regrettably, the rhetorical force of our "deprivation of all economically feasible use" rule is greater than its precision, since the rule does not make clear the "property interest" against which the loss of value is to be measured. When, for example, a regulation requires a developer to leave 90% of a rural tract in its natural state, it is unclear whether we would analyze the situation as one in which the owner has been deprived of all economically beneficial use of the burdened portion of the tract, or as one in which the owner has suffered a mere diminution in value of the tract as a whole. * * * The answer to this difficult question may lie in how the owner's reasonable expectations have been shaped by the State's law of property—*i.e.,* whether and to what degree the State's law has accorded legal recognition and protection to the particular interest in land with respect to which the takings claimant alleges a diminution in (or elimination of) value. In any event, we avoid this difficulty in the present case, since the "interest in land" that Lucas has pleaded (a fee simple interest) is an estate with a rich tradition of protection at common law, and since the South Carolina Court of Common Pleas found that the Beachfront Management Act left each of Lucas's beachfront lots without economic value.

On the other side of the balance, affirmatively supporting a compensation requirement, is the fact that regulations that leave the owner of land without economically beneficial or productive options for its use—typically, as here, by requiring land to be left substantially in its natural state—carry with them a heightened risk that private property is being pressed into some form of public service under the guise of mitigating serious public harm. As Justice Brennan explained: "From the government's point of view, the benefits flowing to the public from preservation of open space through regulation may be equally great as from creating a wildlife refuge through formal condemnation or increasing electricity production through a dam project that floods private property." San Diego Gas & Elec. Co., *supra,* 450 U.S., at 652, 101 S.Ct., at 1304 (Brennan, J., dissenting). The many statutes on the books, both state and federal, that provide for the use of eminent domain to impose servitudes on private scenic lands preventing developmental uses, or to acquire such lands altogether, suggest the practical equivalence in this setting of negative regulation and appropriation.

We think, in short, that there are good reasons for our frequently expressed belief that when the owner of real property has been called upon to sacrifice *all* economically beneficial uses in the name of the common good, that is, to leave his property economically idle, he has suffered a taking.[3]

B

The trial court found Lucas's two beachfront lots to have been rendered valueless by respondent's enforcement of the coastal-zone construction ban. Under Lucas's theory of the case, which rested upon our "no economically viable use" statements, that finding entitled him to compensation. Lucas believed it unnecessary to take issue with either the purposes behind the Beachfront Management Act, or the means chosen by the South Carolina Legislature to effectuate those purposes. The South Carolina Supreme Court, however, thought otherwise. In its view, the Beachfront Management Act was no ordinary enactment, but involved an exercise of South Carolina's "police powers" to mitigate the harm to the public interest that petitioner's use of his land might

---

3. Justice STEVENS criticizes the "deprivation of all economically beneficial use" rule as "wholly arbitrary", in that "[the] landowner whose property is diminished in value 95% recovers nothing," while the landowner who suffers a complete elimination of value "recovers the land's full value." This analysis errs in its assumption that the landowner whose deprivation is one step short of complete is not entitled to compensation. Such an owner might not be able to claim the benefit of our categorical formulation, but, as we have acknowledged time and again, "[t]he economic impact of the regulation on the claimant and * * * the extent to which the regulation has interfered with distinct investment-backed expectations" are keenly relevant to takings analysis generally. Penn Central Transportation Co. v. New York City, 438 U.S. 104, 124 (1978). It is true that in at least *some* cases the landowner with 95% loss will get nothing, while the landowner with total loss will recover in full. But that occasional result is no more strange than the gross disparity between the landowner whose premises are taken for a highway (who recovers in full) and the landowner whose property is reduced to 5% of its former value by the highway (who recovers nothing). Takings law is full of these "all-or-nothing" situations.

* * *

occasion. 304 S.C., at 384, 404 S.E.2d, at 899. By neglecting to dispute the findings enumerated in the Act[4] or otherwise to challenge the legislature's purposes, petitioner "concede[d] that the beach/dune area of South Carolina's shores is an extremely valuable public resource; that the erection of new construction, *inter alia,* contributes to the erosion and destruction of this public resource; and that discouraging new construction in close proximity to the beach/dune area is necessary to prevent a great public harm." *Id.,* at 382–383, 404 S.E.2d, at 898. In the court's view, these concessions brought petitioner's challenge within a long line of this Court's cases sustaining against Due Process and Takings Clause challenges the State's use of its "police powers" to enjoin a property owner from activities akin to public nuisances. See Mugler v. Kansas, 123 U.S. 623 (1887) (law prohibiting manufacture of alcoholic beverages); Hadacheck v. Sebastian, 239 U.S. 394 (1915) (law barring operation of brick mill in residential area); Miller v. Schoene, 276 U.S.

---

4. The legislature's express findings include the following:

"The General Assembly finds that:

"(1) The beach/dune system along the coast of South Carolina is extremely important to the people of this State and serves the following functions:

"(a) protects life and property by serving as a storm barrier which dissipates wave energy and contributes to shoreline stability in an economical and effective manner;

"(b) provides the basis for a tourism industry that generates approximately two-thirds of South Carolina's annual tourism industry revenue which constitutes a significant portion of the state's economy. The tourists who come to the South Carolina coast to enjoy the ocean and dry sand beach contribute significantly to state and local tax revenues;

"(c) provides habitat for numerous species of plants and animals, several of which are threatened or endangered. Waters adjacent to the beach/dune system also provide habitat for many other marine species;

"(d) provides a natural health environment for the citizens of South Carolina to spend leisure time which serves their physical and mental well-being.

"(2) Beach/dune system vegetation is unique and extremely important to the vitality and preservation of the system.

"(3) Many miles of South Carolina's beaches have been identified as critically eroding.

"(4) * * * [D]evelopment unwisely has been sited too close to the [beach/dune] system. This type of development has jeopardized the stability of the beach/dune system, accelerated erosion, and endangered adjacent property. It is in both the public and private interests to protect the system from this unwise development.

"(5) The use of armoring in the form of hard erosion control devices such as seawalls, bulkheads, and rip-rap to protect erosion-threatened structures adjacent to the beach has not proven effective. These armoring devices have given a false sense of security to beachfront property owners. In reality, these hard structures, in many instances, have increased the vulnerability of beachfront property to damage from wind and waves while contributing to the deterioration and loss of the dry sand beach which is so important to the tourism industry.

"(6) Erosion is a natural process which becomes a significant problem for man only when structures are erected in close proximity to the beach/dune system. It is in both the public and private interests to afford the beach/dune system space to accrete and erode in its natural cycle. This space can be provided only by discouraging new construction in close proximity to the beach/dune system and encouraging those who have erected structures too close to the system to retreat from it.

* * *

"(8) It is in the state's best interest to protect and to promote increased public access to South Carolina's beaches for out-of-state tourists and South Carolina residents alike." S.C. Code § 48–39–250 (Supp.1991).

272 (1928) (order to destroy diseased cedar trees to prevent infection of nearby orchards); Goldblatt v. Hempstead, 369 U.S. 590 (1962) (law effectively preventing continued operation of quarry in residential area).

It is correct that many of our prior opinions have suggested that "harmful or noxious uses" of property may be proscribed by government regulation without the requirement of compensation. For a number of reasons, however, we think the South Carolina Supreme Court was too quick to conclude that that principle decides the present case. The "harmful or noxious uses" principle was the Court's early attempt to describe in theoretical terms why government may, consistent with the Takings Clause, affect property values by regulation without incurring an obligation to compensate—a reality we nowadays acknowledge explicitly with respect to the full scope of the State's police power. * * *

The transition from our early focus on control of "noxious" uses to our contemporary understanding of the broad realm within which government may regulate without compensation was an easy one, since the distinction between "harm-preventing" and "benefit-conferring" regulation is often in the eye of the beholder. It is quite possible, for example, to describe in *either* fashion the ecological, economic, and aesthetic concerns that inspired the South Carolina legislature in the present case. One could say that imposing a servitude on Lucas's land is necessary in order to prevent his use of it from "harming" South Carolina's ecological resources; or, instead, in order to achieve the "benefits" of an ecological preserve. Compare, *e.g.,* Claridge v. New Hampshire Wetlands Board, 125 N.H. 745, 752, 485 A.2d 287, 292 (1984) (owner may, without compensation, be barred from filling wetlands because land-filling would deprive adjacent coastal habitats and marine fisheries of ecological support), with, *e.g.,* Bartlett v. Zoning Comm'n of Old Lyme, 161 Conn. 24, 30, 282 A.2d 907, 910 (1971) (owner barred from filling tidal marshland must be compensated, despite municipality's "laudable" goal of "preserv[ing] marshlands from encroachment or destruction"). Whether one or the other of the competing characterizations will come to one's lips in a particular case depends primarily upon one's evaluation of the worth of competing uses of real estate. A given restraint will be seen as mitigating "harm" to the adjacent parcels or securing a "benefit" for them, depending upon the observer's evaluation of the relative importance of the use that the restraint favors. Whether Lucas's construction of single-family residences on his parcels should be described as bringing "harm" to South Carolina's adjacent ecological resources thus depends principally upon whether the describer believes that the State's use interest in nurturing those resources is so important that *any* competing adjacent use must yield.

When it is understood that "prevention of harmful use" was merely our early formulation of the police power justification necessary to sustain (without compensation) *any* regulatory diminution in value; and that the distinction between regulation that "prevents harmful use" and that which "confers benefits" is difficult, if not impossible, to discern on an objective, value-free basis; it becomes self-evident that noxious-use logic cannot serve as a touchstone to distinguish regulatory "takings"—which require compensation—from regulatory deprivations that do not require compensation. *A fortiori* the legislature's recitation of a noxious-use justification cannot be the basis for departing from our categorical rule that total regulatory takings must be compensated. If it were, departure would virtually always be allowed. The South Carolina Supreme Court's approach would essentially nullify *Mahon's* affirmation of limits to the noncompensable exercise of the police power. Our cases provide no support for this: None of them that employed the logic of "harmful use" prevention to sustain a regulation involved an allegation that the regulation wholly eliminated the value of the claimant's land.[5]

Where the State seeks to sustain regulation that deprives land of all economically beneficial use, we think it may resist compensation only if the logically antecedent inquiry into the nature of the owner's estate shows that the proscribed use interests were not part of his title to begin with. This accords, we think, with our "takings" jurisprudence, which has traditionally been guided by the understandings of our citizens regarding the content of, and the State's power over, the "bundle of rights" that they acquire when they obtain title to property. It seems to us that the property owner necessarily expects the uses of his property to be restricted, from time to time, by various measures newly enacted by the State in legitimate exercise of its police powers; "[a]s long recognized, some values are enjoyed under an implied limitation and must yield to the police power." Pennsylvania Coal Co. v. Mahon, 260 U.S., at 413. * * * In the case of land, however, we think the notion pressed by the Council that title is somehow held subject to the "implied limitation" that the State may subsequently eliminate all economically valuable use is inconsistent with the historical compact recorded in the Takings Clause that has become part of our constitutional culture.

Where "permanent physical occupation" of land is concerned, we have refused to allow the government to decree it anew (without compensation), no matter how weighty the asserted "public interests" involved, Loretto v. Teleprompter Manhattan CATV Corp., 458 U.S., at 426—though we assuredly *would* permit the government to assert a permanent easement that was a pre-existing limitation upon the landowner's title. Compare Scranton v. Wheeler, 179 U.S. 141, 163 (1900) (interests of "riparian owner in the submerged lands * * * bordering on a public navigable water" held subject to Government's navigational servitude), with Kaiser Aetna v. United States, 444 U.S., at 178–180 (imposition of navigational servitude on marina created and rendered navigable at private expense held to constitute a taking). We believe

---

5. *E.g.,* Mugler v. Kansas, 123 U.S. 623 (1887) (prohibition upon use of a building as a brewery; other uses permitted); Plymouth Coal Co. v. Pennsylvania, 232 U.S. 531 (1914) (requirement that "pillar" of coal be left in ground to safeguard mine workers; mineral rights could otherwise be exploited); Reinman v. Little Rock, 237 U.S. 171 (1915) (declaration that livery stable constituted a public nuisance; other uses of the property permitted); Hadacheck v. Sebastian, 239 U.S. 394 (1915) (prohibition of brick manufacturing in residential area; other uses permitted); Goldblatt v. Hempstead, 369 U.S. 590 (1962) (prohibition on excavation; other uses permitted).

similar treatment must be accorded confiscatory regulations, *i.e.,* regulations that prohibit all economically beneficial use of land: Any limitation so severe cannot be newly legislated or decreed (without compensation), but must inhere in the title itself, in the restrictions that background principles of the State's law of property and nuisance already place upon land ownership. A law or decree with such an effect must, in other words, do no more than duplicate the result that could have been achieved in the courts—by adjacent landowners (or other uniquely affected persons) under the State's law of private nuisance, or by the State under its complementary power to abate nuisances that affect the public generally, or otherwise.

On this analysis, the owner of a lake bed, for example, would not be entitled to compensation when he is denied the requisite permit to engage in a landfilling operation that would have the effect of flooding others' land. Nor the corporate owner of a nuclear generating plant, when it is directed to remove all improvements from its land upon discovery that the plant sits astride an earthquake fault. Such regulatory action may well have the effect of eliminating the land's only economically productive use, but it does not proscribe a productive use that was previously permissible under relevant property and nuisance principles. The use of these properties for what are now expressly prohibited purposes was *always* unlawful, and (subject to other constitutional limitations) it was open to the State at any point to make the implication of those background principles of nuisance and property law explicit. In light of our traditional resort to "existing rules or understandings that stem from an independent source such as state law" to define the range of interests that qualify for protection as "property" under the Fifth (and Fourteenth) amendments, Board of Regents of State Colleges v. Roth, 408 U.S. 564, 577 (1972), this recognition that the Takings Clause does not require compensation when an owner is barred from putting land to a use that is proscribed by those "existing rules or understandings" is surely unexceptional. When, however, a regulation that declares "off-limits" all economically productive or beneficial uses of land goes beyond what the relevant background principles would dictate, compensation must be paid to sustain it.[6]

The "total taking" inquiry we require today will ordinarily entail (as the application of state nuisance law ordinarily entails) analysis of, among other things, the degree of harm to public lands and resources, or adjacent private property, posed by the claimant's proposed activities, the social value of the claimant's activities and their suitability to the locality in question, and the relative ease with which the alleged harm can be avoided through measures taken by the claimant and the government (or adjacent private landowners) alike. The fact that a particular

---

6. Of course, the State may elect to rescind its regulation and thereby avoid having to pay compensation for a permanent deprivation. See First English Evangelical Lutheran Church, 482 U.S., at 321. But "where the [regulation has] already worked a taking of all use of property, no subsequent action by the government can relieve it of the duty to provide compensation for the period during which the taking was effective." *Ibid.*

use has long been engaged in by similarly situated owners ordinarily imports a lack of any common-law prohibition (though changed circumstances or new knowledge may make what was previously permissible no longer so[)]. So also does the fact that other landowners, similarly situated, are permitted to continue the use denied to the claimant.

It seems unlikely that common-law principles would have prevented the erection of any habitable or productive improvements on petitioner's land; they rarely support prohibition of the "essential use" of land, Curtin v. Benson, 222 U.S. 78 (1911). The question, however, is one of state law to be dealt with on remand. We emphasize that to win its case South Carolina must do more than proffer the legislature's declaration that the uses Lucas desires are inconsistent with the public interest, or the conclusory assertion that they violate a common-law maxim such as *sic utere tuo ut alienum non laedas*. As we have said, a "State, by *ipse dixit*, may not transform private property into public property without compensation * * *." Webb's Fabulous Pharmacies, Inc. v. Beckwith, 449 U.S. 155, 164 (1980). Instead, as it would be required to do if it sought to restrain Lucas in a common-law action for public nuisance, South Carolina must identify background principles of nuisance and property law that prohibit the uses he now intends in the circumstances in which the property is presently found. Only on this showing can the State fairly claim that, in proscribing all such beneficial uses, the Beachfront Management Act is taking nothing.

The judgment is reversed and the cause remanded for proceedings not inconsistent with this opinion.

So ordered.

JUSTICE KENNEDY, concurring in the judgment.

The case comes to the Court in an unusual posture, as all my colleagues observe. After the suit was initiated but before it reached us, South Carolina amended its Beachfront Management Act to authorize the issuance of special permits at variance with the Act's general limitations. Petitioner has not applied for a special permit but may still do so. The availability of this alternative, if it can be invoked, may dispose of petitioner's claim of a permanent taking. As I read the Court's opinion, it does not decide the permanent taking claim, but neither does it foreclose the Supreme Court of South Carolina from considering the claim or requiring petitioner to pursue an administrative alternative not previously available.

The potential for future relief does not control our disposition, because whatever may occur in the future cannot undo what has occurred in the past. The Beachfront Management Act was enacted in 1988. It may have deprived petitioner of the use of his land in an interim period. If this deprivation amounts to a taking, its limited duration will not bar constitutional relief. It is well established that temporary takings are as protected by the Constitution as are permanent ones. First English Evangelical Lutheran Church of Glendale v. County of Los Angeles, 482 U.S. 304, 318 (1987).

The issues presented in the case are ready for our decision. The Supreme Court of South Carolina decided the case on constitutional grounds, and its rulings are now before us. There exists no jurisdictional bar to our disposition, and prudential considerations ought not to militate against it. The State cannot complain of the manner in which the issues arose. Any uncertainty in this regard is attributable to the State, as a consequence of its amendment to the Beachfront Management Act. If the Takings Clause is to protect against temporary deprivations as well as permanent ones, its enforcement must not be frustrated by a shifting background of state law.

Although we establish a framework for remand, moreover, we do not decide the ultimate question of whether a temporary taking has occurred in this case. The facts necessary to the determination have not been developed in the record. Among the matters to be considered on remand must be whether petitioner had the intent and capacity to develop the property and failed to do so in the interim period because the State prevented him. Any failure by petitioner to comply with relevant administrative requirements will be part of that analysis.

The South Carolina Court of Common Pleas found that petitioner's real property has been rendered valueless by the State's regulation. The finding appears to presume that the property has no significant market value or resale potential. This is a curious finding, and I share the reservations of some of my colleagues about a finding that a beach front lot loses all value because of a development restriction. While the Supreme Court of South Carolina on remand need not consider the case subject to this constraint, we must accept the finding as entered below. Accepting the finding as entered, it follows that petitioner is entitled to invoke the line of cases discussing regulations that deprive real property of all economic value.

The finding of no value must be considered under the Takings Clause by reference to the owner's reasonable, investment-backed expectations. The Takings Clause, while conferring substantial protection on property owners, does not eliminate the police power of the State to enact limitations on the use of their property. The rights conferred by the Takings Clause and the police power of the State may coexist without conflict. Property is bought and sold, investments are made, subject to the State's power to regulate. Where a taking is alleged from regulations which deprive the property of all value, the test must be whether the deprivation is contrary to reasonable, investment-backed expectations.

There is an inherent tendency towards circularity in this synthesis, of course; for if the owner's reasonable expectations are shaped by what courts allow as a proper exercise of governmental authority, property tends to become what courts say it is. Some circularity must be tolerated in these matters, however, as it is in other spheres. The definition, moreover, is not circular in its entirety. The expectations protected by the Constitution are based on objective rules and customs that can be understood as reasonable by all parties involved.

In my view, reasonable expectations must be understood in light of the whole of our legal tradition. The common law of nuisance is too narrow a confine for the exercise of regulatory power in a complex and interdependent society. The State should not be prevented from enacting new regulatory initiatives in response to changing conditions, and courts must consider all reasonable expectations whatever their source. The Takings Clause does not require a static body of state property law; it protects private expectations to ensure private investment. I agree with the Court that nuisance prevention accords with the most common expectations of property owners who face regulation, but I do not believe this can be the sole source of state authority to impose severe restrictions. Coastal property may present such unique concerns for a fragile land system that the State can go further in regulating its development and use than the common law of nuisance might otherwise permit.

The Supreme Court of South Carolina erred, in my view, by reciting the general purposes for which the state regulations were enacted without a determination that they were in accord with the owner's reasonable expectations and therefore sufficient to support a severe restriction on specific parcels of property. The promotion of tourism, for instance, ought not to suffice to deprive specific property of all value without a corresponding duty to compensate. Furthermore, the means as well as the ends of regulation must accord with the owner's reasonable expectations. Here, the State did not act until after the property had been zoned for individual lot development and most other parcels had been improved, throwing the whole burden of the regulation on the remaining lots. This too must be measured in the balance.

With these observations, I concur in the judgment of the Court.

JUSTICE BLACKMUN, dissenting.

Today the Court launches a missile to kill a mouse.

The State of South Carolina prohibited petitioner Lucas from building a permanent structure on his property from 1988 to 1990. Relying on an unreviewed (and implausible) state trial court finding that this restriction left Lucas' property valueless, this Court granted review to determine whether compensation must be paid in cases where the State prohibits all economic use of real estate. According to the Court, such an occasion never has arisen in any of our prior cases, and the Court imagines that it will arise "relatively rarely" or only in "extraordinary circumstances." Almost certainly it did not happen in this case.

Nonetheless, the Court presses on to decide the issue, and as it does, it ignores its jurisdictional limits, remakes its traditional rules of review, and creates simultaneously a new categorical rule and an exception (neither of which is rooted in our prior case law, common law, or common sense). I protest not only the Court's decision, but each step taken to reach it. More fundamentally, I question the Court's wisdom in issuing sweeping new rules to decide such a narrow case. Surely, as Justice KENNEDY demonstrates, the Court could have reached the result it wanted without inflicting this damage upon our Takings Clause jurisprudence.

My fear is that the Court's new policies will spread beyond the narrow confines of the present case. For that reason, I, like the Court, will give far greater attention to this case than its narrow scope suggests—not because I can intercept the Court's missile, or save the targeted mouse, but because I hope perhaps to limit the collateral damage.

* * *

Notes and Questions

1. The Supreme Court of South Carolina subsequently determined that a temporary taking had occurred in *Lucas* and remanded the case to the trial court to ascertain the measure of damages. Lucas v. South Carolina Coastal Council, 309 S.C. 424, 424 S.E.2d 484 (1992). Before trial, the parties reached a settlement by which the state of South Carolina agreed to purchase the two lots in question from Lucas for $1.5 million. Purportedly, the state planned to sell the lots for residential development. *Keeping Current—Property* (N. White ed.), Prob. & Prop., Sept.–Oct. 1993, at 48, 49.

2. What impact will *Lucas* have on land use regulation? The decision precipitated an outpouring of analysis. *See, e.g.,* After *Lucas:* Land Use Regulation and the Taking of Property Without Compensation (D. Callies ed., 1993); Symposium, *"Lucas v. South Carolina Coastal Council,"* 45 Stan.L.Rev. 1369 (1993).

3. Courts continue to wrestle with whether land use regulations have deprived property owners of their property. *Compare* Loveladies Harbor, Inc. v. United States, 28 F.3d 1171 (Fed.Cir.1994) (wetlands regulation stripped landowner of all beneficial use and constituted regulatory taking) *and* Moroney v. Mayor and Council of Borough of Old Tappan, 268 N.J.Super. 458, 633 A.2d 1045 (1993) (zoning ordinance which deprived residential lot owner of all effective use amounted to inverse condemnation), *cert. denied* 136 N.J. 295, 642 A.2d 1004 (1994) *with* Florida Game and Fresh Water Fish Commission v. Flotilla, Inc., 636 So.2d 761 (Fla.App.1994) (imposition of preservation zones prohibiting development of approximately 48 acres of 173 acre tract in order to preserve bald eagle nesting sites did not amount to unconstitutional taking), *review denied* 645 So.2d 452 (Fla.1994) *and* Zealy v. Waukesha, 201 Wis.2d 365, 548 N.W.2d 528 (1996) (placing substantial portion of landowner's property in "conservancy district" did not constitute uncompensated taking). *See generally* Mandelker, *New Property Rights Under the Taking Clause,* 81 Marq.L.Rev. 9 (1997) (discussing importance of ascertaining what segment of land in question should be considered in takings analysis).

4. Suppose a landowner is deprived of less than all economically viable use of the property. *See* footnote 3 in *Lucas.* How should a court go about determining whether a regulatory taking has occurred? *See* Reahard v. Lee

County, 968 F.2d 1131 (11th Cir.1992); Iowa Coal Mining Company, Inc. v. Monroe County, 494 N.W.2d 664 (Iowa 1993).

5. O owned a large stand of trees. A few of the trees had been found to be infested with a disease that can be communicated to fruit-bearing trees. Most of O's trees were healthy. A state agency, acting under authority of state law, ordered O's entire stand of trees destroyed to prevent spread of the disease. Is O entitled to just compensation for O's trees? *Compare* Miller v. Schoene, 276 U.S. 272 (1928) *with* Department of Agriculture & Consumer Services v. Mid–Florida Growers, Inc., 521 So.2d 101 (Fla.1988).

6. The prospect of damage awards against excessive regulation caused President Ronald Reagan to issue an executive order in 1988 directing federal agencies to evaluate the effect of their actions "on constitutionally protected property rights" in order to reduce the risk of unlawful regulation. Exec. Order No. 12,630, 53 Fed.Reg. 8,859 (1988), *reprinted in* 5 U.S.C. § 601 (1994). *See* Wise, *The Changing Doctrine of Regulatory Taking and the Executive Branch: Will Takings Impact Analysis Enhance or Damage the Federal Government's Ability to Regulate?*, 44 Admin.L.Rev. 403 (1992).

7. The private property rights movement continues to gain ground. An increasing number of states have enacted legislation that requires public agencies to ascertain whether governmental actions may constitute a taking of private property. E.g., Tenn. Code Ann. §§ 12–1–201 to 12–1–206 (1998 Supp.); Utah Code Ann. §§ 63–90–1 to 63–90a–4 (1997 & Supp.1998). Texas has gone a step further by enacting a statute that requires payment of compensation when any regulatory program reduces the market value of property more than twenty-five percent. Tex.Gov't Code Ann. §§ 2007.001–2007.026 (West 1998). Likewise, Florida has passed a private property rights act that authorizes compensation when a property owner demonstrates that government action "has inordinately burdened" the use of land. Fla.Stat. Ann. § 70.001 (West 1998 Supp.). *See* Juergensmeyer, *Florida's Private Property Rights Protection Act: Does It Inordinately Burden the Public Interest?*, 48 Fla.L.Rev. 695 (1996). Congress and other state legislatures have considered similar proposals. Such measures represent an attempt to legislatively define the concept of regulatory taking and to afford more certain protection to the owners of private property. *See* Cordes, *Leapfrogging the Constitution: The Rise of State Takings Legislation*, 24 Ecology L.Q. 187 (1997); Rose, *A Dozen Propositions on Private Property, Public Rights, and the New Takings Legislation*, 53 Wash. & Lee L.Rev. 265 (1996); Thomas, *The Illusory Restraints and Empty Promises of New Property Protection Laws*, 28 Urb.Law. 223 (1996).

8. Landowners have increasingly relied on civil rights suits under 42 U.S.C. § 1983 to contest land use regulations. The case of Bateson v. Geisse, 857 F.2d 1300 (9th Cir.1988) involved such a claim. There the court upheld a developer's claim that a city's capricious refusal to issue a building permit amounted to a violation of substantive due process rights. Similarly, in Sintra, Inc. v. City of Seattle, 119 Wn.2d 1, 829 P.2d 765 (1992), the Supreme Court of Washington held that an oppressive land use regulation constituted a denial of due process and supported a claim under § 1983. Moreover, the Supreme Court of Rhode Island ruled in Pitocco v. Harring-

ton, 707 A.2d 692 (R.I.1998), that landowners "established a prima facie case under § 1983 that they were deprived of their constitutionally protected due-process rights" when a local official, among other things, arbitrarily declined to grant a building permit. *See generally* D. Mandelker, Land Use Law §§ 8.26–8.36 (4th ed. 1997); Pearlman, *Section 1983 and the Liability of Local Officials for Land Use Decisions,* 23 Urb.L.Ann. 57 (1982).

9. As indicated by the material in this section, actions for inverse condemnation continue to raise procedural and substantive problems. Among these is the question—does a claimant have an entitlement to a jury trial on the issue of whether governmental land use regulatory activity constitutes a taking? *See* Del Monte Dunes at Monterey, Ltd. v. City of Monterey, 95 F.3d 1422 (9th Cir.1996) (concluding regulatory taking issue in § 1983 suit properly submitted to jury), *cert. granted,* 118 S.Ct. 1359 (1998).

C. ZONING

"Zoning merely means the division of land into districts having different regulations." E. Bassett, Zoning 9 (1940). As noted previously, zoning was not widely utilized by local governments until the 20th century. Between 1916 and 1926, zoning came of age through three significant occurrences: (1) in 1916 New York City enacted a much emulated comprehensive zoning ordinance, (2) in 1922 the Department of Commerce published an initial draft of the Standard State Zoning Enabling Act, and (3) in 1926 the Supreme Court decided the famous *Euclid* case. *See* R. Ellickson & A. Tarlock, Land–Use Controls 39 (1981). *See generally* J. Ely, The Guardian of Every Other Right: A Constitutional History of Property Rights 113–114 (2d ed. 1998).

1. FOUNDATION

VILLAGE OF EUCLID v. AMBLER REALTY CO.

Supreme Court of the United States, 1926.
272 U.S. 365.

Mr. Justice Sutherland delivered the opinion of the Court.

The Village of Euclid is an Ohio municipal corporation. It adjoins and practically is a suburb of the City of Cleveland. Its estimated population is between 5,000 and 10,000, and its area from twelve to fourteen square miles, the greater part of which is farm lands or unimproved acreage. It lies, roughly, in the form of a parallelogram measuring approximately three and one-half miles each way. East and west it is traversed by three principal highways: Euclid Avenue, through the southerly border, St. Clair Avenue, through the central portion, and Lake Shore Boulevard, through the northerly border in close proximity to the shore of Lake Erie. The Nickel Plate railroad lies from 1,500 to 1,800 feet north of Euclid Avenue, and the Lake Shore railroad 1,600 feet farther to the north. The three highways and the two railroads are substantially parallel.

Appellee is the owner of a tract of land containing 68 acres, situated in the westerly end of the village, abutting on Euclid Avenue to the south and the Nickel Plate railroad to the north. Adjoining this tract, both on the east and on the west, there have been laid out restricted residential plats upon which residences have been erected.

On November 13, 1922, an ordinance was adopted by the Village Council, establishing a comprehensive zoning plan for regulating and restricting the location of trades, industries, apartment houses, two-family houses, single family houses, etc., the lot area to be built upon, the size and height of buildings, etc.

The entire area of the village is divided by the ordinance into six classes of use districts, denominated U–1 to U–6, inclusive; three classes of height districts, denominated H–1 to H–3, inclusive; and four classes of area districts, denominated A–1 to A–4, inclusive. The use districts are classified in respect of the buildings which may be erected within their respective limits, as follows: U–1 is restricted to single family dwellings, public parks, water towers and reservoirs, suburban and interurban electric railway passenger stations and rights of way, and farming, noncommercial greenhouse nurseries and truck gardening; U–2 is extended to include two-family dwellings; U–3 is further extended to include apartment houses, hotels, churches, schools, public libraries, museums, private clubs, community center buildings, hospitals, sanitariums, public playgrounds and recreation buildings, and a city hall and courthouse; U–4 is further extended to include banks, offices, studios, telephone exchanges, fire and police stations, restaurants, theatres and moving picture shows, retail stores and shops, sales offices, sample rooms, wholesale stores for hardware, drugs and groceries, stations for gasoline and oil (not exceeding 1,000 gallons storage) and for ice delivery, skating rinks and dance halls, electric substations, job and newspaper printing, public garages for motor vehicles, stables and wagon sheds (not exceeding five horses, wagons or motor trucks) and distributing stations for central store and commercial enterprises; U–5 is further extended to include billboards and advertising signs (if permitted), warehouses, ice and ice cream manufacturing and cold storage plants, bottling works, milk bottling and central distribution stations, laundries, carpet cleaning, dry cleaning and dyeing establishments, blacksmith, horseshoeing, wagon and motor vehicle repair shops, freight stations, street car barns, stables and wagon sheds (for more than five horses, wagons or motor trucks), and wholesale produce markets and salesrooms; U–6 is further extended to include plants for sewage disposal and for producing gas, garbage and refuse incineration, scrap iron, junk, scrap paper and rag storage, aviation fields, cemeteries, crematories, penal and correctional institutions, insane and feeble minded institutions, storage of oil and gasoline (not to exceed 25,000 gallons), and manufacturing and industrial operations of any kind other than, and any public utility not included in, a class U–1, U–2, U–3, U–4 or U–5 use. There is a seventh class of uses which is prohibited altogether.

Class U–1 is the only district in which buildings are restricted to those enumerated. In the other classes the uses are cumulative; that is to say, uses in class U–2 include those enumerated in the preceding class, U–1; class U–3 includes uses enumerated in the preceding classes, U–2 and U–1; and so on. In addition to the enumerated uses, the ordinance provides for accessory uses, that is, for uses customarily incident to the principal use, such as private garages. Many regulations are provided in respect of such accessory uses.

The height districts are classified as follows: In class H–1, buildings are limited to a height of two and one-half stories or thirty-five feet; in class H–2, to four stories or fifty feet; in class H–3, to eighty feet. To all of these, certain exceptions are made, as in the case of church spires, water tanks, etc.

The classification of area districts is: In A–1 districts, dwellings or apartment houses to accommodate more than one family must have at least 5,000 square feet for interior lots and at least 4,000 square feet for corner lots; in A–2 districts, the area must be at least 2,500 square feet for interior lots, and 2,000 square feet for corner lots; in A–3 districts, the limits are 1,250 and 1,000 square feet, respectively; in A–4 districts, the limits are 900 and 700 square feet, respectively. The ordinance contains, in great variety and detail, provisions in respect of width of lots, front, side and rear yards, and other matters, including restrictions and regulations as to the use of bill boards, sign boards and advertising signs.

A single family dwelling consists of a basement and not less than three rooms and a bathroom. A two-family dwelling consists of a basement and not less than four living rooms and a bathroom for each family; and is further described as a detached dwelling for the occupation of two families, one having its principal living rooms on the first floor and the other on the second floor.

Appellee's tract of land comes under U–2, U–3 and U–6. The first strip of 620 feet immediately north of Euclid Avenue falls in class U–2, the next 130 feet to the north, in U–3, and the remainder in U–6. The uses of the first 620 feet, therefore, do not include apartment houses, hotels, churches, schools, or other public and semi-public buildings, or other uses enumerated in respect of U–3 to U–6, inclusive. The uses of the next 130 feet include all of these, but exclude industries, theatres, banks, shops, and the various other uses set forth in respect of U–4 to U–6, inclusive.

Annexed to the ordinance, and made a part of it, is a zone map, showing the location and limits of the various use, height and area districts, from which it appears that the three classes overlap one another; that is to say, for example, both U–5 and U–6 use districts are in A–4 area districts, but the former is in H–2 and the latter in H–3 height districts. The plan is a complicated one and can be better understood by an inspection of the map, though it does not seem necessary to reproduce it for present purposes.

The lands lying between the two railroads for the entire length of the village area and extending some distance on either side to the north and south, having an average width of about 1,600 feet, are left open, with slight exceptions, for industrial and all other uses. This includes the larger part of appellee's tract. Approximately one-sixth of the area of the entire village is included in U–5 and U–6 use districts. That part of the village lying south of Euclid Avenue is principally in U–1 districts. The lands lying north of Euclid Avenue and bordering on the long strip just described are included in U–1, U–2, U–3 and U–4 districts, principally in U–2.

The enforcement of the ordinance is entrusted to the inspector of buildings, under rules and regulations of the board of zoning appeals. Meetings of the board are public, and minutes of its proceedings are kept. It is authorized to adopt rules and regulations to carry into effect provisions of the ordinance. Decisions of the inspector of buildings may be appealed to the board by any person claiming to be adversely affected by any such decision. The board is given power in specific cases of practical difficulty or unnecessary hardship to interpret the ordinance in harmony with its general purpose and intent, so that the public health, safety and general welfare may be secure and substantial justice done. Penalties are prescribed for violations, and it is provided that the various provisions are to be regarded as independent and the holding of any provision to be unconstitutional, void or ineffective shall not affect any of the others.

The ordinance is assailed on the grounds that it is in derogation of § 1 of the Fourteenth Amendment to the Federal Constitution in that it deprives appellee of liberty and property without due process of law and denies it the equal protection of the law, and that it offends against certain provisions of the Constitution of the State of Ohio. The prayer of the bill is for an injunction restraining the enforcement of the ordinance and all attempts to impose or maintain as to appellee's property any of the restrictions, limitations or conditions. The court below held the ordinance to be unconstitutional and void, and enjoined its enforcement.

Before proceeding to a consideration of the case, it is necessary to determine the scope of the inquiry. The bill alleges that the tract of land in question is vacant and has been held for years for the purpose of selling and developing it for industrial uses, for which it is especially adapted, being immediately in the path of progressive industrial development; that for such uses it has a market value of about $10,000 per acre, but if the use be limited to residential purposes the market value is not in excess of $2,500 per acre; that the first 200 feet of the parcel back from Euclid Avenue, if unrestricted in respect of use, has a value of $150 per front foot, but if limited to residential uses, and ordinary mercantile business be excluded therefrom, its value is not in excess of $50 per front foot.

It is specifically averred that the ordinance attempts to restrict and control the lawful uses of appellee's land so as to confiscate and destroy a great part of its value; that it is being enforced in accordance with its terms; that prospective buyers of land for industrial, commercial and residential uses in the metropolitan district of Cleveland are deterred from buying any part of this land because of the existence of the ordinance and the necessity thereby entailed of conducting burdensome and expensive litigation in order to vindicate the right to use the land for lawful and legitimate purposes; that the ordinance constitutes a cloud upon the land, reduces and destroys its value, and has the effect of diverting the normal industrial, commercial and residential development thereof to other and less favorable locations.

The record goes no further than to show, as the lower court found, that the normal, and reasonably to be expected, use and development of that part of appellee's land adjoining Euclid Avenue is for general trade and commercial purposes, particularly retail stores and like establishments, and that the normal, and reasonably to be expected, use and development of the residue of the land is for industrial and trade purposes. Whatever injury is inflicted by the mere existence and threatened enforcement of the ordinance is due to restrictions in respect of these and similar uses; to which perhaps should be added—if not included in the foregoing—restrictions in respect of apartment houses. Specifically, there is nothing in the record to suggest that any damage results from the presence in the ordinance of those restrictions relating to churches, schools, libraries and other public and semipublic buildings. It is neither alleged nor proved that there is, or may be, a demand for any part of appellee's land for any of the last named uses; and we cannot assume the existence of facts which would justify an injunction upon this record in respect of this class of restrictions. For present purposes the provisions of the ordinance in respect of these uses may, therefore, be put aside as unnecessary to be considered. It is also unnecessary to consider the effect of the restrictions in respect of U–1 districts, since none of appellee's land falls within that class.

We proceed, then, to a consideration of those provisions of the ordinance to which the case as it is made relates, first disposing of a preliminary matter.

A motion was made in the court below to dismiss the bill on the ground that, because complainant [appellee] had made no effort to obtain a building permit or apply to the zoning board of appeals for relief as it might have done under the terms of the ordinance, the suit was premature. The motion was properly overruled. The effect of the allegations of the bill is that the ordinance of its own force operates greatly to reduce the value of appellee's lands and destroy their marketability for industrial, commercial and residential uses; and the attack is directed, not against any specific provision or provisions, but against the ordinance as an entirety. Assuming the premises, the existence and maintenance of the ordinance, in effect, constitutes a present invasion of appellee's property rights and a threat to continue it. Under these circumstances, the equitable jurisdiction is clear.

It is not necessary to set forth the provisions of the Ohio Constitution which are thought to be infringed. The question is the same under both Constitutions, namely, as stated by appellee: Is the ordinance invalid in that it violates the constitutional protection "to the right of property in the appellee by attempted regulations under the guise of the police power, which are unreasonable and confiscatory?"

Building zone laws are of modern origin. They began in this country about twenty-five years ago. Until recent years, urban life was comparatively simple; but with the great increase and concentration of population, problems have developed, and constantly are developing, which require, and will continue to require, additional restrictions in respect of the use and occupation of private lands in urban communities. Regulations, the wisdom, necessity and validity of which, as applied to existing conditions, are so apparent that they are now uniformly sustained, a century ago, or even half a century ago, probably would have been rejected as arbitrary and oppressive. Such regulations are sustained, under the complex conditions of our day, for reasons analogous to those which justify traffic regulations, which, before the advent of automobiles and rapid transit street railways, would have been condemned as fatally arbitrary and unreasonable. And in this there is no inconsistency, for while the meaning of constitutional guaranties never varies, the scope of their application must expand or contract to meet the new and different conditions which are constantly coming within the field of their operation. In a changing world, it is impossible that it should be otherwise. But although a degree of elasticity is thus imparted, not to the *meaning*, but to the *application* of constitutional principles, statutes and ordinances, which, after giving due weight to the new conditions, are found clearly not to conform to the Constitution, of course, must fall.

The ordinance now under review, and all similar laws and regulations, must find their justification in some aspect of the police power, asserted for the public welfare. The line which in this field separates the legitimate from the illegitimate assumption of power is not capable of precise delimitation. It varies with circumstances and conditions. A regulatory zoning ordinance, which would be clearly valid as applied to the great cities, might be clearly invalid as applied to rural communities. In solving doubts, the maxim *sic utere tuo ut alienum non laedas,* which lies at the foundation of so much of the common law of nuisances, ordinarily will furnish a fairly helpful clew. And the law of nuisances, likewise, may be consulted, not for the purpose of controlling, but for the helpful aid of its analogies in the process of ascertaining the scope of, the power. Thus the question whether the power exists to forbid the erection of a building of a particular kind or for a particular use, like the question whether a particular thing is a nuisance, is to be determined, not by an abstract consideration of the building or of the thing considered apart, but by considering it in connection with the circumstances and the locality. A nuisance may be merely a right thing in the wrong place,—like a pig in the parlor instead of the barnyard. If the validity of the legislative classification for zoning purposes be fairly debatable, the legislative judgment must be allowed to control.

There is no serious difference of opinion in respect of the validity of laws and regulations fixing the height of buildings within reasonable limits, the character of materials and methods of construction, and the adjoining area which must be left open, in order to minimize the danger of fire or collapse, the evils of over-crowding, and the like, and excluding from residential sections offensive trades, industries and structures likely to create nuisances.

Here, however, the exclusion is in general terms of all industrial establishments, and it may thereby happen that not only offensive or dangerous industries will be excluded, but those which are neither offensive nor dangerous will share the same fate. But this is no more than happens in respect of many practice-forbidding laws which this Court has upheld although drawn in general terms so as to include individual cases that may turn out to be innocuous in themselves. The inclusion of a reasonable margin to insure effective enforcement, will not put upon a law, otherwise valid, the stamp of invalidity. Such laws may also find their justification in the fact that, in some fields, the bad fades into the good by such insensible degrees that the two are not capable of being readily distinguished and separated in terms of legislation. In the light of these considerations, we are not prepared to say that the end in view was not sufficient to justify the general rule of the ordinance, although some industries of an innocent character might fall within the proscribed class. It can not be said that the ordinance in this respect "passes the bounds of reason and assumes the character of a merely arbitrary fiat." Purity Extract Co. v. Lynch, 226 U.S. 192, 204. Moreover, the restrictive provisions of the ordinance in this particular may be sustained upon the principles applicable to the broader exclusion from residential districts of all business and trade structures, presently to be discussed.

It is said that the Village of Euclid is a mere suburb of the City of Cleveland; that the industrial development of that city has now reached and in some degree extended into the village and, in the obvious course of things, will soon absorb the entire area for industrial enterprises; that the effect of the ordinance is to divert this natural development elsewhere with the consequent loss of increased values to the owners of the lands within the village borders. But the village, though physically a suburb of Cleveland, is politically a separate municipality, with powers of its own and authority to govern itself as it sees fit within the limits of the organic law of its creation and the State and Federal Constitutions. Its governing authorities, presumably representing a majority of its inhabitants and voicing their will, have determined, not that industrial development shall cease at its boundaries, but that the course of such development shall proceed within definitely fixed lines. If it be a proper exercise of the police power to relegate industrial establishments to localities separated from residential sections, it is not easy to find a sufficient reason for denying the power because the effect of its exercise is to divert an industrial flow from the course which it would follow, to the injury of the residential public if left alone, to another course where such injury will be obviated. It is not meant by this, however, to exclude the possibility of cases where the general public interest would so far outweigh the interest of the municipality that the municipality would not be allowed to stand in the way.

We find no difficulty in sustaining restrictions of the kind thus far reviewed. The serious question in the case arises over the provisions of the ordinance excluding from residential districts, apartment houses, business houses, retail stores and shops, and other like establishments. This question involves the validity of what is really the crux of the more recent zoning legislation, namely, the creation and maintenance of residential districts, from which business and trade of every sort, including hotels and apartment houses, are excluded. Upon that question this Court has not thus far spoken. The decisions of the state courts are numerous and conflicting; but those which broadly sustain the power greatly outnumber those which deny altogether or narrowly limit it; and it is very apparent that there is a constantly increasing tendency in the direction of the broader view.

* * *

The matter of zoning has received much attention at the hands of commissions and experts, and the results of their investigations have been set forth in comprehensive reports. These reports, which bear every evidence of painstaking consideration, concur in the view that the segregation of residential, business, and industrial buildings will make it easier to provide fire apparatus suitable for the character and intensity of the development in each section; that it will increase the safety and security of home life; greatly tend to prevent street accidents, especially to children, by reducing the traffic and resulting confusion in residential sections; decrease noise and other conditions which produce or intensify nervous disorders; preserve a more favorable environment in which to rear children, etc. With particular reference to apartment houses, it is pointed out that the development of detached house sections is greatly retarded by the coming of apartment houses, which has sometimes resulted in destroying the entire section for private house purposes; that in such sections very often the apartment house is a mere parasite, constructed in order to take advantage of the open spaces and attractive surroundings created by the residential character of the district. Moreover, the coming of one apartment house is followed by others, interfering by their height and bulk with the free circulation of air and monopolizing the rays of the sun which otherwise would fall upon the smaller homes, and bringing, as their necessary accompaniments, the disturbing noises incident to increased traffic and business, and the occupation, by means of moving and parked automobiles, of larger portions of the streets, thus detracting from their safety and depriving children of the privilege of quiet and open spaces for play, enjoyed by those in more favored localities,—until, finally, the residential character of the neighborhood and its desirability as a place of detached residences are utterly destroyed. Under these circumstances, apartment houses, which in a different environment would be not only entirely unobjectionable but highly desirable, come very near to being nuisances.

If these reasons, thus summarized, do not demonstrate the wisdom or sound policy in all respects of those restrictions which we have indicated as pertinent to the inquiry, at least, the reasons are sufficiently cogent to preclude us from saying, as it must be said before the ordinance can be declared unconstitutional, that such provisions are clearly arbitrary and unreasonable, having no substantial relation to the public health, safety, morals, or general welfare.

It is true that when, if ever, the provisions set forth in the ordinance in tedious and minute detail, come to be concretely applied to particular premises, including those of the appellee, or to particular conditions, or to be considered in connection with specific complaints, some of them, or even many of them, may be found to be clearly arbitrary and unreasonable. But where the equitable remedy of injunction is sought, as it is here, not upon the ground of a present infringement or denial of a specific right, or of a particular injury in process of actual execution, but upon the broad ground that the mere existence and threatened enforcement of the ordinance, by materially and adversely affecting values and curtailing the opportunities of the market, constitute a present and irreparable injury, the court will not scrutinize its provisions, sentence by sentence, to ascertain by a process of piecemeal dissection whether there may be, here and there, provisions of a minor character, or relating to matters of administration, or not shown to contribute to the injury complained of, which, if attacked separately, might not withstand the test of constitutionality. In respect of such provisions, of which specific complaint is not made, it cannot be said that the land owner has suffered or is threatened with an injury which entitles him to challenge their constitutionality.

* * *

The relief sought here is of the same character, namely, an injunction against the enforcement of any of the restrictions, limitations or conditions of the ordinance. And the gravamen of the complaint is that a portion of the land of the appellee cannot be sold for certain enumerated uses because of the general and broad restraints of the ordinance. What would be the effect of a restraint imposed by one or more of the innumerable provisions of the ordinance, considered apart, upon the value or marketability of the lands is neither disclosed by the bill nor by the evidence, and we are afforded no basis, apart from mere speculation, upon which to rest a conclusion that it or they would have any appreciable effect upon those matters. Under these circumstances, therefore, it is enough for us to determine, as we do, that the ordinance in its general scope and dominant features, so far as its provisions are here involved, is a valid exercise of authority, leaving other provisions to be dealt with as cases arise directly involving them.

And this is in accordance with the traditional policy of this Court. In the realm of constitutional law, especially, this Court has perceived the embarrassment which is likely to result from an attempt to formulate rules or decide questions beyond the necessities of the immediate issue. It has preferred to follow the method of a gradual approach to the general by a systematically guarded application and extension of constitutional principles to particular cases as they arise, rather than by out of hand attempts to establish general rules to which future cases must be fitted. This process applies with peculiar force to the solution of questions arising under the due process clause of the Constitution as applied to the exercise of the flexible powers of police, with which we are here concerned.

Decree reversed.

MR. JUSTICE VAN DEVANTER, MR. JUSTICE MCREYNOLDS and MR. JUSTICE BUTLER, dissent.

Notes and Questions

1. The property involved in the *Euclid* case eventually became the site of a General Motors factory. *See* C. Haar & M. Wolf, Land–Use Planning 190 (4th ed. 1989).

2. After the *Euclid* decision, comprehensive zoning ordinances were enacted by communities nationwide and became the primary means by which local governments exercise land use control. What would our cities look like if the Supreme Court had agreed with the trial court judge who found Euclid's zoning ordinance unconstitutional?

> The plain truth is that the true object of the ordinance in question is to place all the property in an undeveloped area of 16 square miles in a strait-jacket. The purpose to be accomplished is really to regulate the mode of living of persons who may hereafter inhabit it. In the last analysis, the result to be accomplished is to classify the population and segregate them according to their income or situation in life. The true reason why some persons live in a mansion and others in a shack, why some live in a single-family dwelling and others in a double-family dwelling, why some live in a two-family dwelling and others in an apartment, or why some live in a well-kept apartment and others in a tenement, is primarily economic. It is a matter of income and wealth, plus the labor and difficulty of procuring adequate domestic service. Aside from contributing to these results and furthering such class tendencies, the ordinance has also an esthetic purpose; that is to say, to make this village develop into a city along lines now conceived by the village council to be attractive and beautiful. The assertion that this ordinance may tend to prevent congestion, and thereby contribute to the health and safety, would be more substantial if provision had been or could be made for adequate east and west and north and south street highways. Whether these purposes and objects would justify the taking of plaintiff's property as and for a public use need not be considered. It is sufficient to say that, in our opinion, and as applied to plaintiff's

property, it may not be done without compensation under the guise of exercising the police power.

Ambler Realty Co. v. Village of Euclid, 297 Fed. 307, 316 (N.D.Ohio 1924), rev'd 272 U.S. 365 (1926). *See also* Siegan, *Non-Zoning in Houston,* 13 J.Law and Econ. 71 (1970). *See generally* Epstein, *A Conceptual Approach to Zoning: What's Wrong with* Euclid, 5 N.Y.U.Entvl.L.J. 277 (1996).

3. Each state has adopted the Standard State Zoning Enabling Act or a similar statute thereby delegating its police power to zone to municipalities. Consequently, most land use regulation has been implemented by local governments. *See* 1 Anderson's American Law of Zoning §§ 2.14–2.29 (4th ed. 1996); J. Juergensmeyer & T. Roberts, Land Use Planning and Control Law §§ 3.5–3.6 (1998).

4. The relationship between zoning and planning is complex. Section 3 of the Standard State Zoning Enabling Act provides that zoning "regulations shall be made in accordance with a comprehensive plan." This provision apparently requires that local governments prepare a blueprint for development and then zone consistently with the blueprint. Many courts, however, interpreted the Act to mean only that the zoning ordinance be comprehensive in nature, not that a separate plan be prepared and followed. *See, e.g.,* Iowa Coal Mining Company, Inc. v. Monroe County, 494 N.W.2d 664 (Iowa 1993). This interpretation may be attributed in large part to the failure of the Department of Commerce to promulgate the Standard City Planning Enabling Act until six years after it published the Standard Zoning Act. In many states, therefore, cities were given the power to zone before they were specifically authorized to engage in land use planning. Moreover, under the Standard Planning Act, local government planning was permitted, not required. *See* D. Mandelker, Land Use Law §§ 3.05, 3.13–3.14 (4th ed. 1997); Haar, *'In Accordance with a Comprehensive Plan,'* 68 Harv.L.Rev. 1154 (1955); Mandelker, *The Role of the Local Comprehensive Plan in Land Use Regulation,* 74 Mich.L.Rev. 899 (1976).

Even where a community has prepared a separate comprehensive plan, courts disagree about the weight to accord the plan in evaluating zoning actions. Traditionally, the plan was viewed merely as a guide, but some courts now require that zoning be "consistent" with it. *See id.* at 901–909, 920–951. *See also* Dimento, *The Consistency Doctrine: Continuing Controversy* in 1982 Zoning and Planning Law Handbook §§ 6.01–6.07. In addition, a number of states have adopted statutes requiring local governments to prepare an independent comprehensive plan and to zone consistently with that plan. *See, e.g.,* Cal.Gov't.Code §§ 65300, 65860(a) (West 1997); Fla.Stat. Ann. §§ 163.3161, 163.3194 (West 1990 & Supp.1998); Or.Rev.Stat.Ann. §§ 197.175(2)(a) & (b) (Lexis 1998 Supp.).

5. Zoning rarely predates all private use of land in the zoned area. Existing use inconsistent with the ordinance is termed "nonconforming."

> A brief survey of the cases and authorities * * * disclose nonconforming uses have been a problem since the inception of zoning. It was originally thought such uses would be few, and would naturally eliminate themselves through the passage of time, with restrictions on their expansion. But during the past two decades it has become increasingly evident pre-existing nonconformities have no natural tendency to fade

away. On the contrary it appears they tend to continue and prosper because of the artificial monopoly accorded them by the law. However, it still remains, the basic aim and ultimate purpose of zoning is to confine certain classes of buildings and uses to specified localities. Nonconforming uses are inconsistent with that objective. In an effort to change nonconformance to conformance as speedily as possible, with due regard for the legitimate interests of the private property owner and the general public, legislative bodies have attempted different means to eradicate undesired uses.

The methods so employed include, (1) condemnation by use of eminent domain; (2) invoking the law of nuisance; (3) forbidding resumption of nonconforming uses after a period of nonuse or abandonment; (4) prohibiting or limiting extensions or repairs; and (5) amortizing the nonconformity over a reasonable period of time.

* * *

* * * [I]t has been reasonably determined the only effective method of eliminating nonconforming uses yet devised is to amortize the offending building, structure or business operation, and prohibit the owner or operator from maintaining it after expiration of a designated period or date.

* * *

However, there has been a conflict in the views adopted by various courts on the power of a municipality, in the adoption of zoning ordinances, to terminate nonconforming uses upon expiration of a prescribed period.

But * * * recent judicial decisions reveal the pronounced trend is toward elimination of nonconformities by the amortization process. And the test most commonly employed by courts in determining reasonableness of the liquidation period is based upon a balancing of public good against private loss. This unavoidably necessitates an examination of the factual situation presented in each case.

Board of Supervisors of Cerro Gordo County v. Miller, 170 N.W.2d 358, 361–362 (Iowa 1969).

Courts in a few jurisdictions, however, have disapproved of the use of amortization as a method of eliminating nonconforming uses. For example, in PA Northwestern Distributors, Inc. v. Zoning Hearing Board of Township of Moon, 526 Pa. 186, 584 A.2d 1372 (1991), the Supreme Court of Pennsylvania ruled that amortization of a lawful preexisting use was a confiscation of property without just compensation in violation of the state constitution.

NECTOW v. CITY OF CAMBRIDGE

Supreme Court of the United States, 1928.
277 U.S. 183.

MR. JUSTICE SUTHERLAND delivered the opinion of the Court.

A zoning ordinance of the City of Cambridge divides the city into three kinds of districts: residential, business and unrestricted. Each of these districts is sub-classified in respect of the kind of buildings which may be erected. The ordinance is an elaborate one, and of the same general character as that considered by this Court in Euclid v. Ambler Co., 272 U.S. 365. In its general scope it is conceded to be constitutional within that decision. The land of plaintiff in error was put in district R–3, in which are permitted only dwellings, hotels, clubs, churches, schools, philanthropic institutions, greenhouses and gardening, with customary incidental accessories. The attack upon the ordinance is that, as specifically applied to plaintiff in error, it deprived him of his property without due process of law in contravention of the Fourteenth Amendment.

The suit was for a mandatory injunction directing the city and its inspector of buildings to pass upon an application of the plaintiff in error for a permit to erect any lawful buildings upon a tract of land without regard to the provisions of the ordinance including such tract within a residential district. The case was referred to a master to make and report findings of fact. After a view of the premises and the surrounding territory, and a hearing, the master made and reported his findings. The case came on to be heard by a justice of the court, who, after confirming the master's report, reported the case for the determination of the full court. Upon consideration, that court sustained the ordinance as applied to plaintiff in error, and dismissed the bill.

A condensed statement of facts, taken from the master's report, is all that is necessary. When the zoning ordinance was enacted, plaintiff in error was and still is the owner of a tract of land containing 140,000 square feet, of which the locus here in question is a part. The locus contains about 29,000 square feet, with a frontage on Brookline street, lying west, of 304.75 feet, on Henry street, lying north, of 100 feet, on the other land of the plaintiff in error, lying east, of 264 feet, and on land of the Ford Motor Company, lying southerly, of 75 feet. The territory lying east and south is unrestricted. The lands beyond Henry street to the north and beyond Brookline street to the west are within a restricted residential district. The effect of the zoning is to separate from the west end of plaintiff in error's tract a strip 100 feet in width. The Ford Motor Company has a large auto assembling factory south of the locus; and a soap factory and the tracks of the Boston & Albany Railroad lie near. Opposite the locus, on Brookline street, and included in the same district, there are some residences; and opposite the locus, on Henry street, and in the same district, are other residences. The locus is now vacant, although it was once occupied by a mansion house. Before the passage of the ordinance in question, plaintiff in error had outstanding a contract for the sale of the greater part of his entire tract of land for the sum of $63,000. Because of the zoning restrictions, the purchaser refused to comply with the contract. Under the ordinance, business and industry of all sorts are excluded from the locus, while the remainder of the tract is unrestricted. It further appears that provision has been made for widening Brookline street, the effect of which, if carried out, will be to reduce the depth of the locus to 65 feet. After a statement at length of further facts, the master finds "that no practical use can be made of the land in question for residential purposes, because among other reasons herein related, there would not be adequate return on the amount of any investment for the development of the property." The last finding of the master is:

> "I am satisfied that the districting of the plaintiff's land in a residence district would not promote the health, safety, convenience and general welfare of the inhabitants of that part of the defendant City, taking into account the natural development thereof and the character of the district and the resulting benefit to accrue to the whole City and I so find."

It is made pretty clear that because of the industrial and railroad purposes to which the immediately adjoining lands to the south and east have been devoted and for which they are zoned, the locus is of comparatively little value for the limited uses permitted by the ordinance.

We quite agree with the opinion expressed below that a court should not set aside the determination of public officers in such a matter unless it is clear that their action "has no foundation in reason and is a mere arbitrary or irrational exercise of power having no substantial relation to the public health, the public morals, the public safety or the public welfare in its proper sense." *Euclid v. Ambler Co., supra.*

An inspection of a plat of the city upon which the zoning districts are outlined, taken in connection with the master's findings, shows with reasonable certainty that the inclusion of the locus in question is not indispensable to the general plan. The boundary line of the residential district before reaching the locus runs for some distance along the streets, and to exclude the locus from the residential district requires only that such line shall be continued 100 feet further along Henry street and thence south along Brookline street. There does not appear to be any reason why this should not be done. Nevertheless, if that were all, we should not be warranted in substituting our judgment for that of the zoning authorities primarily charged with the duty and responsibility of determining the question. But that is not all. The governmental power to interfere by zoning regulations with the general rights of the land owner by restricting the character of his use, is not unlimited, and other questions aside, such restriction cannot be imposed if it does not bear a substantial relation to the public health, safety, morals, or general welfare. *Euclid v. Ambler Co., supra.* Here, the express finding of the master, already quoted, confirmed by the court below, is that the health, safety, convenience and general welfare of the inhabitants of the part of the city affected will not be promoted by the disposition made by the ordinance of the locus in question. This finding of the master, after a hearing and an inspection of the entire area affected, supported, as we think it is, by other findings of fact, is determinative of the case. That the invasion of the property of plaintiff in error was serious and highly injurious is clearly established; and, since a necessary basis for the support of that invasion is wanting, the action of the zoning authorities comes within the ban of the Fourteenth Amendment and cannot be sustained.

Judgment reversed.

2. FLEXIBILITY

Zoning is an imprecise tool for land use control. Consequently, methods for providing flexibility were built into the system by the drafters of the Standard State Zoning Enabling Act and similar state statutes. The local legislative body—city council or county commission— may amend the zoning ordinance when appropriate. Moreover, an administrative body, usually called the board of adjustment or the board of zoning appeals, may grant variances to existing zoning and authorize conditional uses[1] provisionally permitted in the ordinance. *See* J. Juergensmeyer & T. Roberts, Land Use Planning and Control Law §§ 5.1, 5.3, 5.6–5.26 (1998).

a. *Zoning Amendment*

PHARR v. TIPPITT

Supreme Court of Texas, 1981.
616 S.W.2d 173.

POPE, JUSTICE.

E.A. Tippitt and fourteen other landowners filed suit against the City of Pharr, Mayfair Minerals, Inc., and Urban Housing Associates seeking a judgment declaring a zoning ordinance invalid. The district court upheld the ordinance, but the court of civil appeals nullified it. 600 S.W.2d 951. We reverse the court of civil appeals judgment and affirm that of the trial court.

Mayfair Minerals, Inc. is the owner of 10.1 acres of land which the City of Pharr rezoned from R–1, single-family residence use to R–3, multi-family residence use. Urban Housing Associates, the developer, made the application for change of the single-family classification so that it could build fifty family units consisting of duplexes and quadruplexes. The Planning and Zoning Commission rejected its staff's recommendation that the zoning request be approved; but the City Council, by a four to one vote, enacted an ordinance which rezoned the property. After the district court upheld the validity of the zoning ordinance, Tippitt was the only person who appealed from that judgment. Tippitt's single point of error, which point was sustained by the court of civil appeals, was that the City acted arbitrarily because the amendatory ordinance was spot zoning that was not warranted by any change in conditions in the area.

* * *

1. Conditional uses are also known as special exceptions, special uses, and special permits.

Zoning is an exercise of a municipality's legislative powers. The validity of an amendment to City of Pharr's comprehensive zoning ordinance presents a question of law, not fact. In making its determination, courts are governed by the rule stated in Hunt v. City of San Antonio, 462 S.W.2d 536, 539 (Tex.1971): "If reasonable minds may differ as to whether or not a particular zoning ordinance has a substantial relationship to the public health, safety, morals or general welfare, no clear abuse of discretion is shown and the ordinance must stand as a valid exercise of the city's police power." We wrote in City of Fort Worth v. Johnson, 388 S.W.2d 400, 402 (Tex.1964), that "a zoning ordinance, duly adopted pursuant to Arts. 1011a–1011k, is presumed to be valid and the burden is on the one seeking to prevent its enforcement, whether generally or as to particular property, to prove that the ordinance is arbitrary or unreasonable in that it bears no substantial relationship to the health, safety, morals or general welfare of the community."

The burden on the party attacking the municipal legislative action is a heavy one. As expressed in Weaver v. Ham, 149 Tex. 309, 232 S.W.2d 704 (1950):

> The City had the power to enact the basic zoning ordinance, and to amend it, if a public necessity demanded it. While the presumption would be that the enactment of the amendatory ordinance was valid, that presumption disappears when the facts show and it was determined by the court that the City acted arbitrarily, unreasonably, and abused its discretion; that the ordinance is discriminatory and violates the rights of petitioners under the basic ordinance, and does not bear any substantial relation to the public health, safety, morals or general welfare; that it "constitutes unjustifiable spot zoning"; and that the ordinance is void.

These general rules for review of zoning ordinances have often been stated, but there has been little discussion of the actual legal criteria or standards against which legislative action should be tested. It has been suggested that such a statement would help to restrain arbitrary, capricious and unreasonable actions by city legislative bodies; improve the quality of the legislation; assist in eliminating *ad hoc* decisions, and focus the evidence from interested parties upon the real issues. We call attention to some of the important criteria:

First: A comprehensive zoning ordinance is law that binds the municipal legislative body itself. The legislative body does not, on each rezoning hearing, redetermine as an original matter, the city's policy of comprehensive zoning. The law demands that the approved zoning plan should be respected and not altered for the special benefit of the landowner when the change will cause substantial detriment to the surrounding lands or serve no substantial public purpose. The duty to obey the existing law forbids municipal actions that disregard not only the pre-established zoning ordinance, but also long-range master plans and maps that have been adopted by ordinance.

The adoption of a comprehensive zoning ordinance does not, however, exhaust the city's powers to amend the ordinance as long as the action is not arbitrary, capricious and unreasonable.

Second: The nature and degree of an adverse impact upon neighboring lands is important. Lots that are rezoned in a way that is substantially inconsistent with the zoning of the surrounding area, whether more or less restrictive, are likely to be invalid. For example, a rezoning from a residential use to an industrial use may have a highly deleterious effect upon the surrounding residential lands.

Third: The suitability or unsuitability of the tract for use as presently zoned is a factor. The size, shape and location of a lot may render a tract unusable or even confiscatory as zoned. An example of this is found in City of Waxahachie v. Watkins, 154 Tex. 206, 275 S.W.2d 477 (1955), in which we approved the rezoning of a residential lot for local retail use, because the lot was surrounded by a de facto business area. This factor, like the others, must often be weighed in relation to the other standards, and instances can exist in which the use for which land is zoned may be rezoned upon proof of a real public need or substantially changed conditions in the neighborhood.

Fourth: The amendatory ordinance must bear a substantial relationship to the public health, safety, morals or general welfare or protect and preserve historical and cultural places and areas. The rezoning ordinance may be justified, however, if a substantial public need exists, and this is so even if the private owner of the tract will also benefit.

Mr. Tippitt's attack upon the amendatory ordinance in this case is that it is spot zoning. The term, "spot zoning," is used in Texas and most states to connote an unacceptable amendatory ordinance that singles out a small tract for treatment that differs from that accorded similar surrounding land without proof of changes in conditions. Mr. Tippitt's present complaint of spot zoning invokes mainly inquiries about the second and third criteria stated above. Spot zoning is regarded as a preferential treatment which defeats a pre-established comprehensive plan. It is piecemeal zoning, the antithesis of planned zoning.

Spot zoning has uniformly been denied when there is a substantial adverse impact upon the surrounding land. The size of a rezoned tract in relation to the affected neighboring lands has been said by some authorities to be the most significant consideration in rezoning.

Amendatory ordinances which have rezoned a single city lot when there have been no intervening changes or other saving characteristic, have almost always been voided in Texas.

Proof that a small tract is unsuitable for use as zoned or that there have been substantial changes in the neighborhood have justified some amendatory ordinances. Here, too, the size, shape and characteristics of the tract have been determinative factors in upholding the amendments.

Amendatory zoning ordinances should be judicially tested against the same criteria that govern the action of the municipal legislative body.

In this case, the 10.1–acre tract was not, as urged by the developer who made the application, an interim or automatic R–1 zoning following annexation. The tract had been previously comprehensively zoned, along with vast areas reaching south and southeast to the city limits after study, notice, and hearing. The zoning ordinance had classified lands of the city into districts known as residential, single-family (R–1); residential, two-family (R–2); residential, multi-family (R–3); residential, mobile home parks (R–MH); residential, mobile home subdivision (R–MHS); residential, townhouse subdivision (R–TH); general commercial (C), and industrial (M).

* * *

We do not regard the ordinance as spot zoning. The ten-acre tract is located in an undeveloped farming area. Large expanses of rural lands are located to the east, south and southeast, the direction which the town must grow. To hold that the undeveloped land cannot be used for anything other than single-family residences (R–1) would mean, for all practical purposes, that there can be no more multiple housing in Pharr within its present city limits, since there is almost no presently undeveloped area which is available for R–3 housing. The size of this tract is large enough for planning as a self-contained orderly development which can in advance provide for the direction and the flow of traffic and assure a careful development of necessary public utilities. The development will not cause that measure of disharmony that occurs when there is a rezoning ordinance that permits a use that affects lands or tracts that are already developed. This is not an instance of an unplanned or piecemeal zoning of an isolated lot or small tract.

There is also evidence that rezoning would benefit and promote the general welfare of the community. The City of Pharr has a great need for multiple housing, the population has markedly increased since 1974, and there are only three small areas in Pharr that are presently zoned for multiple housing (R–3) which are not fully developed. The mayor testified that the need for multi-family housing will continue to grow. The City of Pharr, from the data included in the minutes of the zoning hearing, has 703 acres zoned for residential purposes of all kinds. Only 49 acres are actually used for multiple housing (R–3), and nine acres are actually used for duplexes (R–2). To relieve the City of Pharr's housing and utility needs, the City had agreed with the Housing and Urban Development Department to provide more space for multiple housing (R–3) construction. A block grant to the City of $3,000,000 had been made which included sums to provide needed extensions of sewer and water lines and the construction of a water reservoir. From the record it does not appear that the one complaining of the rezoning ordinance discharged his burden to prove that the City of Pharr acted arbitrarily, capriciously or unreasonably.

The judgment of the court of civil appeals is reversed and the judgment of the district court upholding the ordinance rezoning the tract in question is affirmed.

Note

In Fasano v. Board of County Commissioners of Washington County, 264 Or. 574, 586, 507 P.2d 23, 29 (1973), *overruled in part on other grounds* 288 Or. 585, 607 P.2d 722 (1980), the Supreme Court of Oregon concluded that rezoning a particular parcel is quasi-judicial, not legislative in nature and thus, "the burden of proof should be placed, as is usual in judicial proceedings, upon the one seeking change." A number of states have adopted the *Fasano* approach. What is its value? *See* J. Juergensmeyer & T. Roberts, Land Use Planning and Control Law § 5.9 (1998); Comment, *Zoning Amendments—The Product of Judicial or Quasi–Judicial Action*, 33 Ohio St.L.J. 130 (1972).

COLLARD v. INCORPORATED VILLAGE OF FLOWER HILL

Court of Appeals of New York, 1981.
52 N.Y.2d 594, 439 N.Y.S.2d 326, 421 N.E.2d 818.

JONES, JUDGE.

Where a local municipality conditions an amendment of its zoning ordinance on the execution of a declaration of covenants providing, in part, that no construction may occur on the property so rezoned without the consent of the municipality, absent a provision that such consent may not be unreasonably withheld the municipality may not be compelled to issue such consent or give an acceptable reason for failing to do so.

Appellants now own improved property in the Village of Flower Hill. In 1976, the then owners of the subject premises and appellants' predecessors in title, applied to the village board of trustees to rezone the property from a General Municipal and Public Purposes District to a Business District. On October 4 of that year the village board granted the rezoning application by the following resolution:

"RESOLVED that the application of Ray R. Beck Company for a change of Zone of premises known and designated as Section 6, Block 73, Lots 9, 12 and 13 on the land and tax map of Nassau County from General Municipal and Public Purposes District be and the same hereby is granted upon the following conditions:

"(a) The Subject Premises and any buildings, structures and improvements situated or to be situated thereon, will be erected, altered, renovated, remodelled, used, occupied and maintained for the following purposes and no other;

"(i) Offices for the practice of the professions of medicine, dentistry, law, engineering, architecture or accountancy;

"(ii) Executive offices to be used solely for the management of business concerns and associations and excluding therefrom, but without limitation, retail or wholesale sales offices or agencies, brokerage offices of all types and kinds, collection or employment agencies or offices, computer programming centres or offices, counseling centres or offices and training offices or business or trade schools.

"(b) No more than four separate tenancies or occupancies are to be permitted on the subject premises or in any building, structure or improvement situated therein at any one time.

"(c) No building or structure or any portion thereof situated or to be situated on the Subject Premises is to be occupied by more than one person (excluding visitors, clients or guests of any tenant or occupant of such building or structure) for each 190 square feet of the gross floor area of such building or structure;

"(d) No building or structure situated on the Subject Premises on the date of this Declaration of Covenants will be altered, extended, rebuilt, renovated or enlarged without the prior consent of the Board of Trustees of the Village.

"(e) There will be maintained on the Subject Premises at all times, no less than twenty-six paved off-street, onsite parking spaces for automobiles and other vehicles, each such parking space to be at least 9N H 20N in dimensions and will be served by aisles and means of ingress and egress of sufficient width to permit the free movement and parking of automobiles and other vehicles.

"(f) Trees and shrubs installed on the Subject Premises pursuant to a landscape plan heretofore filed with the Village in or about 1964, will be maintained in compliance with said landscape plan."

Subsequently, appellants' predecessors in title entered into the contemplated declaration of covenants which was recorded in the office of the Clerk of Nassau County on November 29, 1976. Consistent with paragraph (d) of the board's resolution, that declaration provided that "[n]o building or structure situated on the Subject Premises on the date of this Declaration of Covenants will be altered, extended, rebuilt, renovated or enlarged without the prior consent of the Board of Trustees of the Village."

Appellants, after acquiring title, made application in late 1978 to the village board for approval to enlarge and extend the existing structure on the premises. Without any reason being given that application was denied. Appellants then commenced this action to have the board's determination declared arbitrary, capricious, unreasonable, and unconstitutional and sought by way of ultimate relief an order directing the board to issue the necessary building permits.

Asserting that the board's denial of the application was beyond review as to reasonableness, respondent moved to dismiss the complaint for failure to state a cause of action. Special Term denied the motion * * * . The Appellate Division 75 A.D.2d 631, 427 N.Y.S.2d 301, reversed and dismissed the complaint * * * . We now affirm.

At the outset this case involves the question of the permissibility of municipal rezoning conditioned on the execution of a private declaration of covenants restricting the use to which the parcel sought to be rezoned may be put. Prior to our decision in Church v. Town of Islip, 8 N.Y.2d 254, 203 N.Y.S.2d 866, 168 N.E.2d 680 in which we upheld rezoning of property subject to reasonable conditions, conditional rezoning had been almost uniformly condemned by courts of all jurisdictions—a position to which a majority of States appear to continue to adhere. Since *Church,* however, the practice of conditional zoning has become increasingly widespread in this State, as well as having gained popularity in other jurisdictions.

Because much criticism has been mounted against the practice, both by commentators and the courts of some of our sister States, further exposition is in order.

Probably the principal objection to conditional rezoning is that it constitutes illegal spot zoning, thus violating the legislative mandate requiring that there be a comprehensive plan for, and that all conditions be uniform within, a given zoning district. When courts have considered the issue, the assumptions have been made that conditional zoning benefits particular landowners rather than the community as a whole and that it undermines the foundation upon which comprehensive zoning depends by destroying uniformity within use districts. Such unexamined assumptions are questionable. First, it is a downward change to a less restrictive zoning classification that benefits the property rezoned and not the opposite imposition of greater restrictions on land use. Indeed, imposing limiting conditions, while benefiting surrounding properties, normally adversely affects the premises on which the conditions are imposed. Second, zoning is not invalid per se merely because only a single parcel is involved or benefited; the real test for spot zoning is whether the change is other than part of a well-considered and comprehensive plan calculated to serve the general welfare of the community. Such a determination, in turn, depends on the reasonableness of the rezoning in relation to neighboring uses—an inquiry required regardless of whether the change in zone is conditional in form. Third, if it is initially proper to change a zoning classification without the imposition of restrictive conditions notwithstanding that such change may depart from uniformity, then no reason exists why accomplishing that change subject to condition should automatically be classified as impermissible spot zoning.

Both conditional and unconditional rezoning involve essentially the same legislative act—an amendment of the zoning ordinance. The standards for judging the validity of conditional rezoning are no different from the standards used to judge whether unconditional rezoning is illegal. If modification to a less restrictive zoning classification is warranted, then a fortiori conditions imposed by a local legislature to minimize conflicts among districts should not in and of themselves violate any prohibition against spot zoning.

Another fault commonly voiced in disapproval of conditional zoning is that it constitutes an illegal bargaining away of a local government's police power. Because no municipal government has the power to make contracts that control or limit it in the exercise of its legislative powers and duties, restrictive agreements made by a municipality in conjunction with a rezoning are sometimes said to violate public policy. While permitting citizens to be governed by the best bargain they can strike with a local legislature would not be consonant with notions of good government, absent proof of a contract purporting to bind the local legislature in advance to exercise its zoning authority in a bargained-for manner, a rule which would have the effect of forbidding a municipality from trying to protect landowners in the vicinity of a zoning change by imposing protective conditions based on the assertion that that body is bargaining away its discretion, would not be in the best interests of the public. The imposition of conditions on property sought to be rezoned may not be classified as a prospective commitment on the part of the municipality to zone as requested if the conditions are met; nor would the municipality necessarily be precluded on this account from later reversing or altering its decision.

Yet another criticism leveled at conditional zoning is that the State enabling legislation does not confer on local authorities authorization to enact conditional zoning amendments. On this view any such ordinance would be *ultra vires*. While it is accurate to say there exists no explicit authorization that a legislative body may attach conditions to zoning amendments, neither is there any language which expressly forbids a local legislature to do so. Statutory silence is not necessarily a denial of the authority to engage in such a practice. Where in the face of nonaddress in the enabling legislation there exists independent justification for the practice as an appropriate exercise of municipal power, that power will be implied. Conditional rezoning is a means of achieving some degree of flexibility in land-use control by minimizing the potentially deleterious effect of a zoning change on neighboring properties; reasonably conceived conditions harmonize the landowner's need for rezoning with the public interest and certainly fall within the spirit of the enabling legislation.

One final concern of those reluctant to uphold the practice is that resort to conditional rezoning carries with it no inherent restrictions apart from the restrictive agreement itself. This fear, however, is justifiable only if conditional rezoning is considered a contractual relationship between municipality and private party, outside the scope of the zoning power—a view to which we do not subscribe. When conditions are incorporated in an amending ordinance, the result is as much a "zoning regulation" as an ordinance, adopted without conditions. Just as the scope of all zoning regulation is limited by the police power, and thus local legislative bodies must act reasonably and in the best interests of public safety, welfare and convenience, the scope of permissible conditions must of necessity be similarly limited. If, upon proper proof, the conditions imposed are found unreasonable, the rezoning amendment as well as the required conditions would have to be nullified, with the affected property reverting to the preamendment zoning classification.

Against this backdrop we proceed to consideration of the contentions advanced by appellants in the appeal now before us. It is first useful to delineate arguments which they do not advance. Thus, they do not challenge the conditional zoning change made in 1976 at the behest of their predecessors in title; no contention is made that the village board was not authorized to adopt the resolution of October 4, 1976, conditioned as it was on the execution and recording of the declaration of covenants, or that the provisions of that declaration were in 1976 arbitrary, capricious, unreasonable or unconstitutional. The reason may be what is apparent, namely, that any successful challenge to the adoption of the 1976 resolution would cause appellants' premises to revert to their pre–1976 zoning classification—a consequence clearly unwanted by them.

The focus of appellants' assault is the provision of the declaration of covenants that no structure may be extended or enlarged "without the prior consent of the Board of Trustees of the Village". Appellants would have us import the added substantive prescription—"which consent may not be unreasonably withheld". Their argument proceeds along two paths: first, that as a matter of construction the added prescription should be read into the provision; second, that because of limitations associated with the exercise of municipal zoning power the village board would have been required to include such a prescription.

Appellants' construction argument must fail. The terminology employed in the declaration is explicit. The concept that appellants would invoke is not obscure and language to give it effect was readily available had it been the intention of the parties to include this added stipulation. Appellants point to no canon of construction in the law of real property or of contracts which would call for judicial insertion of the missing clause. Where language has been chosen containing no inherent ambiguity or uncertainty, courts are properly hesitant, under the guise of judicial construction, to imply additional requirements to relieve a party from asserted disadvantage flowing from the terms actually used.

The second path either leads nowhere or else goes too far. If it is appellants' assertion that the village board was legally required to insist on inclusion of the desired prescription, there is no authority in the court to reform the zoning enactment of 1976 retroactively to impose the omitted clause. Whether the village board at that time would have enacted a different resolution in the form now desired by appellants is open only to speculation; the certainty is that they did not then take such legislative action. On the other hand, acceptance of appellants' proposition would produce as the other possible consequence the conclusion that the 1976 enactment was illegal, throwing appellants unhappily back to the pre–1976 zoning of their premises, a destination which they assuredly wish to sidestep.

* * *

For the reasons stated the Board of Trustees of the Incorporated Village of Flower Hill may not now be compelled to issue its consent to the proposed enlargement and extension of the existing structure on the premises or in the alternative give an acceptable reason for failing to do so. Accordingly, the order of the Appellate Division should be affirmed, with costs.

Notes, Problems, and Questions

1. X owns a large city lot. The city wishes to acquire X's lot. The city and X enter an agreement by which X will deed the lot to the city in exchange for city land which the city will rezone from single-family use to multi-family use so that X can construct an apartment complex on the site. X and the city exchange deeds. X seeks the rezoning agreed upon. Is X entitled to have the property X obtained in the exchange rezoned to multi-family use? *See* Dacy v. Village of Ruidoso, 114 N.M. 699, 845 P.2d 793 (1992).

2. The floating zone is a flexibility device of relatively recent origin.

  * A floating zone is an unmapped district with detailed and conditional use requirements. Metaphorically, the zone "floats" over the city until affixed to a particular parcel. Floating zones generally involve predictable uses that have significant community impacts such as shopping centers and planned unit developments, or uses that the city wishes to encourage such as industrial parks, affordable housing, and housing for the elderly.

  Use of the floating zone involves a two-step process. The city first creates a zone with listed characteristics, for example, a planned unit development with minimums set for acreage, open space, and a mix of uses. This ordinance provides that land meeting these characteristics may be so zoned by a second ordinance when a property owner applies for it, if the action will otherwise promote the public interest. Upon receipt of an application meeting the criteria of the initial ordinance, the zone floats down to the surface by enactment of the second ordinance. Once affixed, it is similar to any other zone, except that the invitation remains open to apply it wherever an applicant meets the conditions.

J. Juergensmeyer & T. Roberts, Land Use Planning and Control Law § 4.16 (1998).

Does a floating zone differ from spot zoning?

3. As indicated in Note 2, a planned unit development (PUD) is often designated as a floating zone. But the PUD is a flexibility device itself and may be used independently of the floating zone technique. In any case, the PUD typically includes a mixture of uses blended with atypical density and open space components. Because of these features, the PUD has been attacked, usually unsuccessfully, as not permitted by zoning enabling legislation. *See id.* at §§ 7.15–7.19; D. Mandelker, Land Use Law §§ 9.24–9.30 (4th ed. 1997).

---

* Reprinted from J. Juergensmeyer & T. Roberts, Land Use Planning and Control Law (1998) with permission of the West Group.

b. Variance

PURITAN–GREENFIELD IMPROVEMENT
ASSOCIATION v. LEO

Court of Appeals of Michigan, Div. 1, 1967.
7 Mich.App. 659, 153 N.W.2d 162.

LEVIN, JUDGE.

Defendant-appellant John L. Leo claims the circuit judge erred in setting aside a use variance granted by the Detroit Board of Zoning Appeals.

Leo owns a one-story, one-family dwelling at the northwest corner of Puritan avenue and Prest avenue, located in the northwest section of Detroit in an R–1 (single family residence) zoning district. On application and after hearing, the board granted Leo a variance to permit the use of the property as a dental and medical clinic (an RM–4 use) and to use the side yard for off-street parking on certain conditions.

* * *

Plaintiff-appellee, Puritan–Greenfield Improvement Association, filed a complaint with the circuit court. * * * The matter was heard by the circuit judge on the record made before the board. The circuit judge reversed the decision of the board, stating *inter alia* that it had not been shown the land could not yield a reasonable return or be put to a proper economic use if used only for a purpose allowed by existing zoning and that such showing of hardship as had been made was of "self-created" hardship attributable to the character of the structure thereon.

The applicable enabling act provides for a board of zoning appeals authorized to grant a variance upon a showing of practical difficulties or unnecessary hardship. The Detroit ordinance requires evidence of special conditions[1] and unnecessary hardship or practical difficulties.

* * *

Although there has been a great deal of judicial effort expended in Michigan in considering challenges to the reasonableness or constitutionality of zoning as applied to individual properties, we find no Michigan appellate decisions construing the words "unnecessary hardship or practical difficulties."

The first modern zoning regulations were adopted by the city of New York and the phrase "practical difficulties or unnecessary hardship" was fashioned as the applicable standard to guide New York's board of appeals in considering applications for variances. A comparison

---

1. * * * In Ackerman v. Board of Commissioners of Town of Belleville (1948), 1 N.J.Super. 69, 62 A.2d 476, 479, the court stated that the term "special conditions" refers to "circumstances uniquely touching his (the applicant's) land as distinguished from conditions that affect the whole neighborhood." As will appear, without regard to whether the term "special conditions" is used, courts generally have ruled that a variance in the use of land may only be granted under the circumstances so described in *Ackerman.* * * *

of the relevant language of the applicable Michigan enabling act with that of the original New York city legislation shows that the Michigan provision authorizing the vesting in a board of zoning appeals the authority to grant variances parallels the corresponding New York city provision.

It appears that most State enabling acts, and ordinances based thereon, use "unnecessary hardship" as the governing standard. In those States (like Michigan and New York) where the applicable standard is "unnecessary hardship *or* practical difficulties," the phrase "practical difficulties" has been regarded as applicable only when an area or a dimension variance is sought, and in determining whether a use variance will be granted the decisive words are "unnecessary hardship." In the light of this history, we have turned for guidance to decisions of other States applying the "unnecessary hardship" standard.

A text writer, Rathkopf, states that courts have held, variously, that a property owner seeking a variance on the ground of "unnecessary hardship" must show credible proof that the property will not yield a reasonable return if used only for a purpose allowed by the ordinance or must establish that the zoning gives rise to hardship amounting to virtual confiscation or the disadvantage must be so great as to deprive the owner of all reasonable use of the property. He concedes that the showing required "is substantially equivalent to that which would warrant a court in declaring the ordinance confiscatory, unreasonable, and unconstitutional in its application to the property involved." 2 Rathkopf, The Law of Zoning and Planning, p. 45–14.

These principles also find expression in the frequently stated generalizations that variances should be sparingly granted, that it is not sufficient to show that the property would be worth more or could be more profitably employed if the restrictions were varied to permit another use, and that the board of appeals, being without legislative power, may not in the guise of a variance amend the zoning ordinance or disregard its provisions.

The judicial attitudes so expressed could well have been influenced by the early history of the boards of zoning appeal and the need to declare more precise standards than the somewhat nebulous "unnecessary hardship." When zoning was in its infancy it was thought by some that without a board of zoning appeals the individual declarations of zoning ordinance invalidity would be so numerous it would become necessary to declare the legislation void as a whole and, thus, "the chief value of the board of appeals in zoning is in protecting the ordinance from attacks upon its constitutionality." [Baker, Legal Aspects of Zoning (1927), pp. 79, 81.]

* * *

It has been said that the function of a board of zoning appeals is to protect the community against usable land remaining idle and it is that purpose which gives definition to "unnecessary hardship."

* * *

Whatever the rationale may be, it has been held that a variance should not be granted until it appears the property cannot be put reasonably to a conforming use. * * *

* * *

The New York Court of Appeals has stated:

"Before the Board may exercise its discretion and grant a [use] variance upon the ground of unnecessary hardship, the record must show that (1) the land in question cannot yield a reasonable return if used only for a purpose allowed in that zone; (2) that the plight of the owner is due to unique circumstances and not to the general conditions in the neighborhood which may reflect the unreasonableness of the zoning ordinance itself; and (3) that the use to be authorized by the variance will not alter the essential character of the locality." Otto v. Steinhilber (1939), 282 N.Y. 71, 24 N.E.2d 851.

* * *

We find overwhelming support for the proposition—expressed in *Otto*—that the hardship must be unique or peculiar to the property for which the variance is sought.

"Difficulties or hardships shared with others go to the reasonableness of the ordinance generally and will not support a variance as to one parcel upon the ground of hardship." 2 Rathkopf, op. cit., p. 45–3.

Under these definitions even if the land cannot yield a reasonable return if used only for a purpose permitted by existing zoning, a use variance may not be granted unless the landowner's plight is due to unique circumstances and not to general conditions in the neighborhood that may reflect the unreasonableness of the zoning.

This limitation on the board's powers is related to the third limitation expressed in *Otto*—that a use authorized by a variance shall not alter the essential character of the locality. In this connection we note that the Detroit ordinance prohibits a variance that would be contrary to the public interest or inconsistent with the spirit of the ordinance.

* * *

While we have discussed the foregoing statements that the hardship must be unique and that there are limitations on a zoning appeal board's power to frame a remedy when the hardship is shared with others—such statements being so inextricably a part of judicial, text and scholarly definitions of "unnecessary hardship" that the construction of that term could not accurately be discussed without reference to those statements—we do not here express our views thereon, as it is not necessary to do so in order to decide this case. We limit our holding to that expressed in the next paragraph.

Our review of the authorities leads us to hold that a use variance should not be granted unless the board of zoning appeals can find on the basis of substantial evidence that the property cannot reasonably be used in a manner consistent with existing zoning.

* * *

In the case of Leo's property, we perceive the question to be whether the property can continue reasonably to be used as a single family residence. The appeal board made no determination in that regard, resting its finding of unnecessary hardship solely on the "heavy traffic and the closeness to the business section immediately to the west."

Leo's property has been used for some time as a single family residence. While the board found there was "testimony" that Leo had not received any offers from residence-use buyers during the period of over a year the property had been listed and offered for sale, the asking price for the house and adjoining lot was $38,500 in a neighborhood where, according to the only record evidence, houses generally sell for $20,000 to $25,000. There was no evidence of efforts to sell the property at any price lower than $38,500; indeed, there was no testimony at all as to the extent of the sales effort or the income that could be derived from the property as zoned.

Testimony that the house and lot could not be sold for $38,500 in a neighborhood where houses generally sell for substantially less than that amount does not, in our opinion, constitute any evidence that the property could not continue reasonably to be used as a single family residence.

Thus there was not only a failure to find that the property could not reasonably be used in a manner consistent with existing zoning, but, as we read the record, there was no evidence upon which such a finding could have been based. In this connection, it should be remembered that the fact that the property would be worth more if it could be used as a doctor's clinic and that the corner of Puritan and Prest has disadvantages as a place of residence does not authorize the granting of a variance. Heavy traffic is all too typical of innumerable admittedly residential streets. Adjacency to gasoline stations or other commercial development is characteristic of the end of a business or commercial district and the commencement of a residential district. "A district has to end somewhere." Real Properties, Inc. v. Board of Appeal of Boston (1946), 319 Mass. 180, 65 N.E.2d 199, 201.

It can readily be seen that unless the power of the board of zoning appeals to grant a use variance is defined by objective standards, the appeal board could [and we do not in any sense mean to suggest this would be deliberate] rezone an entire neighborhood—a lot or two lots at a time. The variance granted in response to one "hardship" may well beget or validate another claim of hardship and justify still another variance. If it is a hardship to be next to a gasoline station, it could be a hardship to be across from one, to be behind one, or diagonally across from one. If heavy traffic is a valid basis, variances might become the rule rather than the sparingly granted exception.

We do not wish to be understood as challenging the judgment of the board of zoning appeals. A doctor's office with the appearance of a single family residence on a busy street which already has other commercial uses may very well be a logical, sensible and unobjectionable use. However the question before us is not whether the board of zoning appeals has acted reasonably, but whether on the proofs and findings the board could grant a variance on the ground of unnecessary hardship. We have concluded that neither the proofs nor the findings justified the variance granted.

We have given careful consideration to the considerable number of cases we found where the result was based on the reviewing court's conclusion that the appeal board had not abused the discretion confided to it. If there is substantial evidence to support the necessary findings, such a decision is, indeed, the correct one. However, there must be such evidence and such findings.

* * * We have also considered appellee's contention that the board's action should be reversed because the hardship alleged by Leo was "self-created." However, the hardship found by the board in this case could not be said to have been self-created—Leo neither created the traffic conditions on Puritan nor the gasoline station immediately to the west of his property.

Affirmed. Costs to appellee.

c. Conditional Use

In Archdiocese of Portland v. County of Washington, 254 Or. 77, 458 P.2d 682 (1969), the Archdiocese was denied "a conditional use permit to build a church, school and gymnasium facility in an area zoned for residential purposes." In upholding a decree dismissing the Archdiocese's suit for declaratory judgment, the Supreme Court of Oregon commented on the nature of a conditional use:

> The original ordinance itself expressly provides for the specified "conditional uses" which might be made in the zone. In this sense the granting of an application for a conditional use does not constitute a deviation from the ordinance but is in compliance with it. The Washington County ordinance expressly declares that "A conditional use shall not be construed to be a zone change * * *." One author has explained that the "granting of a conditional use permit or exception permits a use contemplated by the zoning ordinance; a variance permits a use not contemplated by the ordinance except where necessary to avoid hardship."[1] Further, it may be observed that generally the conditional uses specified as permissible in an R–10 zone are uses which are compatible with the purpose of the zone. As the New Jersey Supreme Court observed, "Exceptions fulfill the

1. Gaylord, Zoning: Variances, Exceptions and Conditional Use Permits in California, 5 UCLA L.Rev. 179 at 194 (1958).

practical recognition that certain uses of property are compatible with the essential design of a particular zone although the use is contrary to the restrictions imposed thereon."[2]

Thus the Washington County ordinance provides for such compatible uses as auditoriums, boat moorages, cemeteries, churches, colleges, community buildings, golf courses, greenhouses, hospitals, libraries, etc. Because these uses are generally compatible with the design of the zone the possibility that a permitted use will not comport with the comprehensive plan is not as great as it is when a variance or amendment is sought. Nor is there the same likelihood that such uses will be sought for and obtained as a matter of special privilege by those seeking private gain as there is where a variance or amendment is requested.

But more important than these considerations is the fact that the ordinance itself reveals the legislative plan forecasting the likelihood that certain specified uses will be needed to maximize the use of land in the zone for residential purposes. The Board's discretion is thus narrowed to those cases in which an application falls within one of the specified uses. The fact that these permissible uses are pre-defined and have the legislative endorsement of the governing body of the county as a tentative part of the comprehensive plan for the area limits the possibility that the Board's action in granting a permit will be inimical to the interests of the community. The suspicion which is cast upon the approval of a change involving an incompatible use * * * is not warranted where the change has been anticipated by the governing body. Therefore, unlike the spot zoning cases the granting of permits for conditional uses is not likely to cause the "erosive effect upon the comprehensive zoning plan" * * *.

Id. at 83–85, 458 P.2d at 685–686.

3. ZONING FOR AESTHETICS

STATE v. JONES

Supreme Court of North Carolina, 1982.
305 N.C. 520, 290 S.E.2d 675.

Defendant was charged in a warrant with a violation of Buncombe County Ordinance 16401 in that he failed to erect a fence as required by the ordinance to enclose his junkyard from the adjacent residential area. Defendant moved to quash the warrant on the grounds that the ordinance upon which the warrant was based was unconstitutional. District Court Judge W.M. Styles quashed the warrant as being unconstitutional on 25 September 1980 and pursuant to the State's appeal Judge Kirby

2. Ranney v. Instituto Pontificio Delle A.2d 142, 146 (1955).
Maestre Filippini, 20 N.J. 189, 199, 119

entered an order on 22 October 1980 finding the ordinance unconstitutional and granting the motion to quash. The State appealed to the Court of Appeals which reversed and remanded.

* * *

Buncombe County Ordinance No. 16401 * * * states in pertinent part:

SECTION FOUR. PROHIBITIONS

Except as hereinafter provided, it shall be unlawful after the effective date of this Ordinance for any person, firm or corporation, or other legal entity to operate or maintain in any unincorporated area of Buncombe County a junkyard or automobile graveyard within one hundred yards of the center line of any "public road" within one quarter mile of any "school" or within any residential area. For the purposes of this Ordinance, a junkyard or automobile graveyard shall be within a residential area if there are twenty-five (25) or more housing units within a geographical area comprised of a one-fourth (¼) mile wide strip contiguous and parallel to the external boundary lines of the tract of real property on which said automobile graveyard or junkyard is located.

SECTION FIVE. EXCEPTIONS

A. This Ordinance shall not apply to service stations, repair shops or garages.

B. Junkyards or automobile graveyards may be operated and/or maintained without restrictions if and providing that said junkyard or automobile graveyard shall be entirely surrounded by a fence, or by a wire fence and substantial vegetation of sufficient height and density as to prevent as nearly as is practical any contents of said junkyard from being visible from any public road or residence, taking into consideration the surrounding terrain. The fence or wire fence shall have at least one and not more than two gates for purposes of ingress and egress. The gates shall be closed and securely locked at all times, except during business hours.

In the event that an operator or maintainer of an automobile graveyard or junkyard prohibited herein chooses to surround said automobile graveyard or junkyard with a fence or a wire fence and substantial vegetation as hereinabove provided for, the Environmental Health Services Division of the Buncombe County Health Department shall have the discretion to determine whether or not the said fencing and/or vegetation is substantial and of sufficient height and density as to prevent as nearly as is practical any contents of said automobile junkyards or graveyards from being visible from any public road or residence, taking into consideration the surrounding terrain. The said Environmental Health Services Division shall be available to assist an operator or maintainor of an automobile graveyard or junkyard, upon request by the said operator or maintainor, in the formulation of plans for said fencing and/or vegetation. The fence or wire fence and vegetation shall be maintained in good order and shall not be allowed to deteriorate.

BRANCH, CHIEF JUSTICE.

* * *

Defendant contends that the ordinance in question violates Article I, § 19 of the Constitution of North Carolina and the Fourteenth Amendment to the United States Constitution. Article I, § 19 of our State Constitution states that:

> No person shall be taken, imprisoned, or disseized of his freehold, liberties, or privileges, or outlawed, or exiled, or in any manner deprived of his life, liberty, or property, but by the law of the land.

The Fourteenth Amendment to the United States Constitution, § 1, provides:

> All persons born or naturalized in the United States, and subject to the jurisdiction thereof, are citizens of the United States and of the state wherein they reside. No state shall make or enforce any law which shall abridge the privileges or immunities of citizens of the United States; nor shall any state deprive any person of life, liberty, or property, without due process of law; nor deny to any person within its jurisdiction the equal protection of the laws.

This Court initially considered the question of whether regulation based on aesthetic reasons alone was an unconstitutional exercise of the police powers by the State in requiring the screening from view of certain junkyards in State v. Brown, 250 N.C. 54, 108 S.E.2d 74 (1959). We concluded there that the provisions of G.S. 14–399 conflicted with the rights guaranteed the citizens of this State by Article I, sections 1 and 17 (presently section 19), of the Constitution of North Carolina, commonly referred to as the "law of the land" clause, and held G.S. 14–399 to be unconstitutional. *Brown* recognized that while

> [w]e are in sympathy with every legitimate effort to make our highways attractive and to keep them clean; even so, we know of no authority that vests our courts with the power to uphold a statute or regulation based purely on aesthetic grounds without any real or substantial relation to the public health, safety or morals, or the general welfare.

Id. at 59, 108 S.E.2d at 78.

One year later the holding in *Brown* was reaffirmed in Restaurant, Inc. v. Charlotte, 252 N.C. 324, 113 S.E.2d 422 (1960), wherein an injunction was affirmed prohibiting the enforcement of a Charlotte ordinance which prohibited the maintenance of business signs over sidewalks in a designated area of that city. This Court although acknowledging the presumptive validity of legislative acts stated that:

> Courts are properly hesitant to interfere with a legislative body when it purports to act under the police power, but the exercise of

that power must rest on something more substantial than mere aesthetic considerations. If it appears that the ordinance is arbitrary, discriminatory, and based solely on aesthetic considerations, the court will not hesitate to declare the ordinance invalid.

Id. at 326, 113 S.E.2d at 424.

* * *

Finally, this Court espoused a balancing test applicable in situations involving exercise of the police power in the preservation of historically significant structures in A–S–P Associates v. City of Raleigh, 298 N.C. 207, 258 S.E.2d 444 (1979). *A–S–P Associates* concerned a challenge of two Raleigh city ordinances creating a historic district in the Oakwood neighborhood and adopting architectural guidelines and design standards to be applied by a Historic District Commission with provision for civil and criminal penalties for property owners failing to comply with the ordinance. Although noting the *Vestal* acknowledgement of the growing body of authority in other jurisdictions recognizing that the police power may be broad enough to include reasonable regulation of property for aesthetic reasons alone, we stated that we were not prepared to endorse such a broad concept of the scope of the police power, but we found no difficulty in holding that the police power encompasses the right to control the exterior appearance of private property when the object of such control was the preservation of the State's legacy of historically significant structures. We cited with approval A. Rathkopf, The Law of Zoning and Planning § 15.01, p. 15–4 (4th ed. 1975), that historic district zoning is not primarily concerned with aesthetics, but rather with preservation for educational, cultural, and economic values. Thus, the general welfare under the police power is served by such historical preservation ordinances through contributing to economic and social stability, preserving past noteworthy architectural techniques, and promoting tourism revenues.

* * *

The former majority rule that aesthetic considerations alone could not support an exercise of police power is now the minority rule. According to one commentator, the balance shifted in 1975 with the result that by 1980 the alignment stood at sixteen jurisdictions (including the District of Columbia) authorizing regulation based on aesthetics alone,[1] nine state jurisdictions, including North Carolina, prohibiting regulation based solely on aesthetics,[2] sixteen state jurisdictions where purely aesthetic regulation was an open question,[3] and ten state jurisdic-

1. California, Colorado, Delaware, District of Columbia, Florida, Hawaii, Massachusetts, Michigan, Mississippi, Montana, New Jersey, New York, Ohio, Oregon, Utah, and Wisconsin.

2. Illinois, Maryland, Nebraska, North Carolina, Rhode Island, Tennessee, Texas, Vermont, and Virginia.

3. Arkansas, Connecticut, Indiana, Iowa, Kansas, Kentucky, Louisiana, Maine, Minnesota, Missouri, New Hampshire, New Mexico, North Dakota, Pennsylvania, Washington, and West Virginia. According to the commentator this group of jurisdictions includes some with cases "authorizing regulation based partially upon aesthetic consider-tions having no reported cases on aesthetic regulation.[4] Bufford, *Beyond the Eye of the Beholder: A New Majority of Jurisdictions Authorize Aesthetic Regulation,* 48 U.M.K.C.L.Rev. 125 (1980). Indeed by 1980, nine jurisdictions had joined the new majority position since 1972.[5] Our research indicates that since the publication of that law review article one of the "minority" jurisdictions prohibiting regulation based solely on aesthetics has now joined the "majority" jurisdictions authorizing regulation based on aesthetics alone. State v. Smith, 618 S.W.2d 474 (Tenn. 1981). A previously "silent" jurisdiction has now joined the state jurisdictions where regulation based solely on aesthetics is an open question. Rockdale County v. Mitchell's Used Auto Parts, Inc., 243 Ga. 465, 254 S.E.2d 846 (1979).

With the 1981 Tennessee decision, the new majority includes seventeen jurisdictions where regulation based exclusively upon aesthetics is permissible, while the minority rule is adhered to by eight jurisdictions, including our own.

Since 1972 four state jurisdictions have considered regulation of junkyards based solely on aesthetics and concluded that such regulation was valid. National Used Cars, Inc. v. City of Kalamazoo, 61 Mich.App. 520, 233 N.W.2d 64 (1975); State v. Bernhard, 173 Mont. 464, 568 P.2d 136 (1977); *State v. Smith, supra;* and Buhler v. Stone, 533 P.2d 292 (Utah 1975).

Buhler v. Stone, supra, involved a county ordinance which prohibited the collection of, among other items, "junk, scrap metal * * * or * * * abandoned * * * vehicles" if such items were "unsightly and in public view." 533 P.2d at 293. In response to plaintiff's attack upon the ordinance as not within the police powers and in holding the ordinance constitutional, the Utah Supreme Court answered that:

> It is true that the police power is generally stated to encompass regulation of matters pertaining to the health, morals, safety or welfare. But those are generic terms. The promotion of the general welfare does not rigidly limit governmental authority to a policy that would "scorn the rose and leave the cabbage triumphant." Surely among the factors which may be considered in the general welfare, is the taking of reasonable measures to minimize discordant, unsightly and offensive surroundings; and to preserve the beauty as well as the usefulness of the environment.

Id. at 294.

ations, but have left open the issues of the validity of regulation supported by no other factors and thus based exclusively upon aesthetic considerations." Bufford, 48 U.M.K.C.L.Rev., *supra* at 127.

4. Alabama, Alaska, Arizona, Georgia, Idaho, Nevada, Oklahoma, South Carolina, South Dakota, and Wyoming. *Id.* at 130–31.

5. California (1979), Colorado (1978), Massachusetts (1975), Michigan (1975), Mississippi (1974), Montana (1977), New Jersey (1974), New York (1977), and Utah (1975). *See id.* at 131–44.

The Court of Appeals of Michigan held that a city ordinance requiring that junkyards be shielded from view may be upheld on aesthetic grounds alone in *National Used Cars, Inc. v. City of Kalamazoo, supra.* In noting that the plurality view in 1975 seemed to be that an ordinance based upon aesthetic consideration alone was invalid, the court remarked that:

> [i]t is our opinion that the plaintiff advocates an obsolete and refuted point of view which is based on an overly-restrictive perception of a City's police power.
>
> We are well aware of the traditional judicial reluctance to uphold legislation on aesthetic grounds alone. [Citing *Brown, supra,* in a footnote.] But we find persuasive the reasoning of the more recent decisions, which espouse the contrary and we believe more modern view.

61 Mich.App. at 523, 233 N.W.2d at 66. That court concluded that "a community's desire to enhance the scenic beauty of its neighborhoods by keeping junkyards concealed from view is clearly a legitimate feature of the public welfare." *Id.* at 524, 233 N.W.2d at 67. The Michigan court upheld a "very specific enactment" which required junkyards to be concealed from view by a solid fence eight feet high.

* * *

Most recently the Tennessee Supreme Court in *State v. Smith, supra,* repudiated its prior adherence to the traditional view that aesthetics alone could not support the exercise of the police power. *Smith* involved a conviction for violating a statute which prohibited the establishment of an automobile junkyard within a specified distance from a state highway and operating such a junkyard without a proper permit or license.

* * *

The Tennessee court concluded that modern societal aesthetic considerations such as concern for environmental protection, control of pollution, and prevention of unsightliness may well constitute a legitimate basis for the exercise of the police power. We agree with the rationale expressed in *Smith* and the other decisions representing the new majority.

In light of our * * * general agreement with the views expressed in the recent cases above cited, we expressly overrule our previous cases to the extent that they prohibited regulation based upon aesthetic considerations alone. We do not grant blanket approval of all regulatory schemes based upon aesthetic considerations. Rather, we adopt the test expressed in *A–S–P Associates* that the diminution in value of an individual's property should be balanced against the corresponding gain to the public from such regulation. Some of the factors which should be considered and weighed in applying such a balancing test include such private concerns such as whether the regulation results in confiscation of the most substantial part of the value of the property or deprives the property owner of the property's reasonable use, and such public concerns as the purpose of the regulation and the manner in achieving a permitted purpose. Aesthetic regulation may provide corollary benefits to the general community such as protection of property values, promotion of tourism, indirect protection of health and safety, preservation of the character and integrity of the community, and promotion of the comfort, happiness, and emotional stability of area residents. *See,* Rowlett, *Aesthetic Regulation Under the Police Power: The New General Welfare and the Presumption of Constitutionality,* 34 Vand.L.Rev. 603 (1981). Such corollary community benefits would be factors to be considered in balancing the public interests in regulation against the individual property owner's interest in the use of his property free from regulation. The test focuses on the reasonableness of the regulation by determining whether the aesthetic purpose to which the regulation is reasonably related outweighs the burdens imposed on the private property owner by the regulation.

* * *

We therefore hold that reasonable regulation based on aesthetic considerations may constitute a valid basis for the exercise of the police power depending on the facts and circumstances of each case. We feel compelled to caution the local legislative bodies charged with the responsibility for and the exercise of the police power in the promulgation of regulations based *solely* upon aesthetic considerations that this is a matter which should not be delegated by them to subordinate groups or organizations which are not authorized to exercise the police power by the General Assembly.

* * *

Affirmed.

Notes and Questions

1. Should local governments judge individual taste? Is not beauty, and for that matter ugliness, in the eye of the beholder? In this regard consider the following discussion between two authorities:

"I never heard of 'uglification'," Alice ventured to say. "What is it?"

The Gryphon lifted up both its paws in surprise. "Never heard of uglifying?!" it exclaimed. "You know what to beautify is, I suppose?"

"Yes," said Alice, doubtfully: "it means—to make anything prettier."

"Well then," the Gryphon went on, "if you don't know what to uglify is, you are a simpleton."

L. Carroll, Alice in Wonderland 66 (Classic Pub. Corp. ed. 1970). *See generally* Dukeminier, *Zoning for Aesthetic Objectives: A Reappraisal,* 20 Law & Contemp.Probs. 218 (1955).

2. Aesthetics have served as a basis for municipal imposition of architectural standards on local landowners via administrative review boards. *See, e.g.,* State of Missouri ex rel. Stoyanoff v. Berkeley, 458 S.W.2d 305 (Mo. 1970); Reid v. Architectural Board of Review of the City of Cleveland Heights, 119 Ohio App. 67, 192 N.E.2d 74 (1963).

3. Aesthetic considerations also support land use regulations limiting the display of signs, but such measures commonly precipitate free speech challenges. *See* Metromedia, Inc. v. City of San Diego, 453 U.S. 490 (1981) (involving ordinance restricting use of signs and billboards); City of Ladue v. Gilleo, 512 U.S. 43 (1994) (finding city sign ordinance that prohibited all signs on residential property except identification, for-sale, or warning signs violated First Amendment).

4. EXCLUSIONARY ZONING

VILLAGE OF BELLE TERRE v. BORAAS

Supreme Court of the United States, 1974.
416 U.S. 1.

Mr. Justice Douglas delivered the opinion of the Court.

Belle Terre is a village on Long Island's north shore of about 220 homes inhabited by 700 people. Its total land area is less than one square mile. It has restricted land use to one-family dwellings excluding lodging houses, boarding houses, fraternity houses, or multiple-dwelling houses. The word "family" as used in the ordinance means, "[o]ne or more persons related by blood, adoption, or marriage, living and cooking together as a single housekeeping unit, exclusive of household servants. A number of persons but not exceeding two (2) living and cooking together as a single housekeeping unit though not related by blood, adoption, or marriage shall be deemed to constitute a family."

Appellees the Dickmans are owners of a house in the village and leased it in December 1971 for a term of 18 months to Michael Truman. Later Bruce Boraas became a colessee. Then Anne Parish moved into the house along with three others. These six are students at nearby State University at Stony Brook and none is related to the other by blood, adoption, or marriage. When the village served the Dickmans with an "Order to Remedy Violations" of the ordinance, the owners plus three tenants thereupon brought this action under 42 U.S.C. § 1983 for an injunction and a judgment declaring the ordinance unconstitutional. The District Court held the ordinance constitutional, 367 F.Supp. 136, and the Court of Appeals reversed, one judge dissenting, 476 F.2d 806. The case is here by appeal, and we noted probable jurisdiction.

* * *

The present ordinance is challenged on several grounds: that it interferes with a person's right to travel; that it interferes with the right to migrate to and settle within a State; that it bars people who are uncongenial to the present residents; that it expresses the social preferences of the residents for groups that will be congenial to them; that social homogeneity is not a legitimate interest of government; that the restriction of those whom the neighbors do not like trenches on the newcomers' rights of privacy; that it is of no rightful concern to villagers whether the residents are married or unmarried; that the ordinance is antithetical to the Nation's experience, ideology, and self-perception as an open, egalitarian, and integrated society.

We find none of these reasons in the record before us. It is not aimed at transients. It involves no procedural disparity inflicted on some but not on others. * * * It involves no "fundamental" right guaranteed by the Constitution, such as voting; the right of association; the right of access to the courts; or any rights of privacy. We deal with economic and social legislation where legislatures have historically drawn lines which we respect against the charge of violation of the Equal Protection Clause if the law be " 'reasonable, not arbitrary' " and bears "a rational relationship to a [permissible] state objective." Reed v. Reed, 404 U.S. 71, 76.

It is said, however, that if two unmarried people can constitute a "family," there is no reason why three or four may not. But every line drawn by a legislature leaves some out that might well have been included. That exercise of discretion, however, is a legislative, not a judicial, function.

It is said that the Belle Terre ordinance reeks with an animosity to unmarried couples who live together. There is no evidence to support it; and the provision of the ordinance bringing within the definition of a "family" two unmarried people belies the charge.

The ordinance places no ban on other forms of association, for a "family" may, so far as the ordinance is concerned, entertain whomever it likes.

The regimes of boarding houses, fraternity houses, and the like present urban problems. More people occupy a given space; more cars rather continuously pass by; more cars are parked; noise travels with crowds.

A quiet place where yards are wide, people few, and motor vehicles restricted are legitimate guidelines in a land-use project addressed to family needs. This goal is a permissible one within Berman v. Parker, 348 U.S. 26. The police power is not confined to elimination of filth, stench, and unhealthy places. It is ample to lay out zones where family values, youth values, and the blessings of quiet seclusion and clean air make the area a sanctuary for people.

* * *

Reversed.

Mr. Justice Marshall, dissenting.

* * * In my view, the disputed classification burdens the students' fundamental rights of association and privacy guaranteed by the First and Fourteenth Amendments. Because the application of strict equal protection scrutiny is therefore required, I am at odds with my Brethren's conclusion that the ordinance may be sustained in a showing that it bears a rational relationship to the accomplishment of legitimate governmental objectives.

* * *

My disagreement with the Court today is based upon my view that the ordinance in this case unnecessarily burdens appellees' First Amendment freedom of association and their constitutionally guaranteed right to privacy. Our decisions establish that the First and Fourteenth Amendments protect the freedom to choose one's associates. Constitutional protection is extended, not only to modes of association that are political in the usual sense, but also to those that pertain to the social and economic benefit of the members. The selection of one's living companions involves similar choices as to the emotional, social, or economic benefits to be derived from alternative living arrangements.

The freedom of association is often inextricably entwined with the constitutionally guaranteed right of privacy. The right to "establish a home" is an essential part of the liberty guaranteed by the Fourteenth Amendment. And the Constitution secures to an individual a freedom "to satisfy his intellectual and emotional needs in the privacy of his own home." Stanley v. Georgia, 394 U.S. 557, 565 (1969). Constitutionally protected privacy is, in Mr. Justice Brandeis' words, "as against the Government, the right to be let alone * * * the right most valued by civilized man." Olmstead v. United States, 277 U.S. 438, 478 (1928) (dissenting opinion). The choice of household companions—of whether a person's "intellectual and emotional needs" are best met by living with family, friends, professional associates, or others—involves deeply personal considerations as to the kind and quality of intimate relationships within the home. That decision surely falls within the ambit of the right to privacy protected by the Constitution.

The instant ordinance discriminates on the basis of just such a personal lifestyle choice as to household companions. It permits any number of persons related by blood or marriage, be it two or twenty, to live in a single household, but it limits to two the number of unrelated persons bound by profession, love, friendship, religious or political affiliation, or mere economics who can occupy a single home. Belle Terre imposes upon those who deviate from the community norm in their choice of living companions significantly greater restrictions than are applied to residential groups who are related by blood or marriage, and compose the established order within the community. The village has, in effect, acted to fence out those individuals whose choice of lifestyle differs from that of its current residents.

This is not a case where the Court is being asked to nullify a township's sincere efforts to maintain its residential character by preventing the operation of rooming houses, fraternity houses, or other commercial or high-density residential uses. Unquestionably, a town is free to restrict such uses. Moreover, as a general proposition, I see no constitutional infirmity in a town's limiting the density of use in residential areas by zoning regulations which do not discriminate on the basis of constitutionally suspect criteria. This ordinance, however, limits the density of occupancy of only those homes occupied by unrelated persons. It thus reaches beyond control of the use of land or the density of population, and undertakes to regulate the way people choose to associate with each other within the privacy of their own homes.

* * *

Because I believe that this zoning ordinance creates a classification which impinges upon fundamental personal rights, it can withstand constitutional scrutiny only upon a clear showing that the burden imposed is necessary to protect a compelling and substantial governmental interest. And, once it be determined that a burden has been placed upon a constitutional right, the onus of demonstrating that no less intrusive means will adequately protect the compelling state interest and that the challenged statute is sufficiently narrowly drawn, is upon the party seeking to justify the burden.

A variety of justifications have been proffered in support of the village's ordinance. It is claimed that the ordinance controls population density, prevents noise, traffic and parking problems, and preserves the rent structure of the community and its attractiveness to families. As I noted earlier, these are all legitimate and substantial interests of government. But I think it clear that the means chosen to accomplish these purposes are both overinclusive and underinclusive, and that the asserted goals could be as effectively achieved by means of an ordinance that did not discriminate on the basis of constitutionally protected choices of lifestyle. The ordinance imposes no restriction whatsoever on the number of persons who may live in a house, as long as they are related by marital or sanguinary bonds—presumably no matter how distant their relationship. Nor does the ordinance restrict the number of income earners who may contribute to rent in such a household, or the number of automobiles that may be maintained by its occupants. In that sense the ordinance is underinclusive. On the other hand, the statute restricts the number of unrelated persons who may live in a home to no more than two. It would therefore prevent three unrelated people from occupying a dwelling even if among them they had but one income and no vehicles. While an extended family of a dozen or more might live in a small bungalow, three elderly and retired persons could not occupy the large manor house next door. Thus the statute is also grossly overinclusive to accomplish its intended purposes.

There are some 220 residences in Belle Terre occupied by about 700 persons. The density is therefore just above three per household. The village is justifiably concerned with density of population and the related problems of noise, traffic, and the like. It could deal with those problems by limiting each household to a specified number of adults, two or three perhaps, without limitation on the number of dependent children. The burden of such an ordinance would fall equally upon all segments of the community. It would surely be better tailored to the goals asserted by the village than the ordinance before us today, for it would more realistically restrict population density and growth and their attendant environmental costs. Various other statutory mechanisms also suggest themselves as solutions to Belle Terre's problems—rent control, limits on the number of vehicles per household, and so forth, but, of course, such schemes are matters of legislative judgment and not for this Court. Appellants also refer to the necessity of maintaining the family character of the village. There is not a shred of evidence in the record indicating that if Belle Terre permitted a limited number of unrelated persons to live together, the residential familial character of the community would be fundamentally affected.

By limiting unrelated households to two persons while placing no limitation on households of related individuals, the village has embarked upon its commendable course in a constitutionally faulty vessel. I would find the challenged ordinance unconstitutional. But I would not ask the village to abandon its goal of providing quiet streets, little traffic, and a pleasant and reasonably priced environment in which families might raise their children. Rather, I would commend the village to continue to pursue those purposes but by means of more carefully drawn and even-handed legislation.

I respectfully dissent.

Note

In Moore v. City of East Cleveland, 431 U.S. 494, 495–496 (1977), the Supreme Court struck down a city ordinance that "limit[ed] occupancy of a dwelling unit to members of single family," and "recognize[d] as a 'family' only a few categories of related individuals." The Court distinguished *Belle Terre* on the ground that "[t]he ordinance there affected only *unrelated* individuals." *Id.* at 498. Noting that constitutional protection of the family extends beyond the nuclear family, the Court concluded that the City of East Cleveland could not prevent members of the extended family from sharing a house.

BRITTON v. TOWN OF CHESTER

Supreme Court of New Hampshire, 1991.
134 N.H. 434, 595 A.2d 492.

BATCHELDER, JUSTICE.

In this appeal, the defendant, the Town of Chester (the town), challenges a ruling by the Master * * * approved by the Superior Court * * *, that the Chester Zoning Ordinance is invalid and unconstitutional. In addition, the town argues that the relief granted to plaintiff Remillard, permitting him to construct multi-family housing on a parcel not currently zoned for such development, violates the separation of powers provision of the New Hampshire Constitution, *N.H. Const.* pt. I, art. 37, and creates an unreasonable use for this parcel. We modify the trial court's ruling that the ordinance as a whole is invalid, but we affirm the granting of specific relief to plaintiff Remillard as well as the court's ruling that the ordinance, on the facts of this case, is unlawful as applied.

The plaintiffs brought a petition in 1985, for declaratory and injunctive relief, challenging the validity of the multi-family housing provisions of the Chester Zoning Ordinance. The master's report, filed after a hearing, contains extensive factual findings which we summarize here. The town of Chester lies in the west-central portion of Rockingham County, thirteen miles east of the city of Manchester. Primary highway access is provided by New Hampshire Routes 102 and 121. The available housing stock is principally single-family homes. There is no municipal sewer or water service, and other municipal services remain modest. The town has not encouraged industrial or commercial development; it is a "bedroom community," with the majority of its labor force commuting to Manchester. Because of its close proximity to job centers and the ready availability of vacant land, the town is projected to have among the highest growth rates in New Hampshire over the next two decades.

* * *

The plaintiffs in this case are a group of low-and moderate-income people who have been unsuccessful in finding affordable, adequate housing in the town, and a builder who, the master found, is committed to the construction of such housing. At trial, two plaintiffs testified as representative members of the group of low-and moderate-income people. Plaintiff George Edwards is a woodcutter who grew up in the town. He lives in Chester with his wife and three minor children in a one-bedroom, thirty-foot by eight-foot camper trailer with no running water. Their annual income is $14,040, which places them in the low-income category. Roger McFarland grew up and works in the town. He lives in Derry with his wife and three teenage children in a two-bedroom apartment which is too small to meet their needs. He and his wife both work, and their combined annual income is $24,000. Under the area standards, the McFarlands are a moderate-income family. Raymond Remillard is the plaintiff home builder. A long-time resident of the town, he owns an undeveloped twenty-three-acre parcel of land on Route 102 in the town's eastern section. Since 1979, he has attempted to obtain permission from the town to build a moderate-sized multi-family housing development on his land.

The zoning ordinance in effect at the beginning of this action in 1985 provided for a single-family home on a two-acre lot or a duplex on a three-acre lot, and it excluded multi-family housing from all five zoning districts in the town. In July, 1986, the town amended its zoning ordinance to allow multi-family housing. Article six of the amended ordinance now permits multi-family housing as part of a "planned residential development" (PRD), a form of multi-family housing required to include a variety of housing types, such as single-family homes, duplexes, and multi-family structures.

After a hearing, the master recommended that judgment be ordered for the plaintiffs; that the town's land use ordinances, including the zoning ordinance, be ruled invalid; and that plaintiff Remillard be awarded a "builder's remedy." We will uphold the findings and rulings of a court-approved master's recommendation unless they are unsupported by the evidence or are erroneous as a matter of law. * * *

We first turn to the ordinance itself, because it does, on its face, permit the type of development that the plaintiffs argue is being prohibited. The master found, however, that the ordinance placed an unreasonable barrier to the development of affordable housing for low-and moderate-income families. Under the ordinance, PRDs are allowed on tracts of not less than twenty acres in two designated "R–2" (medium-density residential) zoning districts. Due to existing home construction and environmental considerations, such as wetlands and steep slopes, only slightly more than half of all the land in the two R–2 districts could reasonably be used for multi-family development. This constitutes only 1.73% of the land in the town. This fact standing alone does not, in the confines of this case, give rise to an entitlement to a legal remedy for those who seek to provide multi-family housing. However, it does serve to point out that the two R–2 districts are, in reality, less likely to be developed than would appear from a reading of the ordinance. A reviewing court must read the entire ordinance in the light of these facts.

Article six of the ordinance also imposes several subjective requirements and restrictions on the developer of a PRD. Any project must first receive the approval of the town planning board as to "whether in its judgment the proposal meets the objectives and purposes set forth [in the ordinance] in which event the Administrator [i.e., the planning board] may grant approval to [the] proposal subject to reasonable conditions and limitations." Consequently, the ordinance allows the planning board to control various aspects of a PRD without reference to any objective criteria. One potentially onerous section permits the planning board to "retain, at the applicant's expense, a registered professional engineer, hydrologist, and any other applicable professional to represent the [planning board] and assist the [planning board] in determining compliance with [the] ordinance and other applicable regulations." The master found such subjective review for developing multi-family housing to be a substantial disincentive to the creation of such units, because it would escalate the economic risks of developing affordable housing to the point where these projects would not be realistically feasible. In addition, we question the availability of bank financing for such projects, where the developer is required to submit a "blank check" to the planning board along with his proposal, and where to do so could halt, change the character of, or even bankrupt the project.

The defendant first argues that the trial court erred in ruling that the zoning ordinance exceeds the powers delegated to the town by the zoning enabling legislation, RSA 674:16–30. In support of this argument, the town asserts that the zoning enabling act does not require it to zone for the low-income housing needs of the region beyond its boundaries. Further, the town maintains that even if it were required to consider regional housing needs when enacting its zoning ordinance, the Chester Zoning Ordinance is valid because it provides for an adequate range of housing types. These arguments fail to persuade us of any error in the master's proposed order.

RSA 674:16 authorizes the local legislative body of any city or town to adopt or amend a zoning ordinance "[f]or the purpose of promoting the health, safety, or *the general welfare of the community.*" (Emphasis added.) The defendant asserts that the term "community" as used in the statute refers only to the municipality itself and not to some broader region in which the municipality is situated. We disagree.

The possibility that a municipality might be obligated to consider the needs of the region outside its boundaries was addressed early on in our land use jurisprudence by the United States Supreme Court, paving the way for the term "community" to be used in the broader sense. In Village of Euclid v. Ambler Realty Co., 272 U.S. 365 (1926), the Court recognized "the possibility of cases where the general public interest would so far outweigh the interest of the municipality that the municipality would not be allowed to stand in the way." *Id.* at 390. When an ordinance will have an impact beyond the boundaries of the municipality, the welfare of the entire affected region must be considered in determining the ordinance's validity. Associated Home Builders v. City of Livermore, 18 Cal.3d 582, 557 P.2d 473, 487, 135 Cal.Rptr. 41, 55 (1976).

We have previously addressed the issue of whether municipalities are required to consider regional needs when enacting zoning ordinances which control growth. In Beck v. Town of Raymond, 118 N.H. 793, 394 A.2d 847 (1978), we held that "[growth] controls must not be imposed simply to exclude outsiders, especially outsiders of any disadvantaged social or economic group." *Beck,* 118 N.H. at 801, 394 A.2d at 852. We reasoned that "each municipality [should] bear its fair share of the burden of increased growth." *Id.* Today, we pursue the logical extension of the reasoning in *Beck* and apply its rationale and high purpose to zoning regulations which wrongfully exclude persons of low-or moderate-income from the zoning municipality.

In *Beck,* this court sent a message to zoning bodies that "[t]owns may not refuse to confront the future by building a moat around themselves and pulling up the drawbridge." *Id.* The town of Chester appears willing to lower that bridge only for people who can afford a single-family home on a two-acre lot or a duplex on a three-acre lot. Others are realistically prohibited from crossing.

Municipalities are not isolated enclaves, far removed from the concerns of the area in which they are situated. As subdivisions of the State, they do not exist solely to serve their own residents, and their regulations should promote the general welfare, both within and without their boundaries. Therefore, we interpret the general welfare provision of the zoning enabling statute, RSA 674:16, to include the welfare of the "community", as defined in this case, in which a municipality is located and of which it forms a part.

A municipality's power to zone property to promote the health, safety, and general welfare of the community is delegated to it by the State, and the municipality must, therefore, exercise this power in conformance with the enabling legislation. Because the Chester Zoning Ordinance does not provide for the lawful needs of the community, in that it flies in the face of the general welfare provision of RSA 674:16 and is, therefore, at odds with the statute upon which it is grounded, we hold that, as applied to the facts of this case, the ordinance is an invalid exercise of the power delegated to the town pursuant to RSA 674:16–30. We so hold because of the master's finding that "there are no substantial and compelling reasons that would warrant the Town of Chester, through its land use ordinances, from fulfilling its obligation to provide low[-] and moderate[-]income families within the community and a proportionate share of same within its region from a realistic opportunity to obtain affordable housing."

The town further asserts that the trial court erred in ruling that the zoning ordinance is repugnant to the New Hampshire Constitution, part I, articles 2 and 12, and part II, article 5. In keeping with our longstanding policy against reaching a constitutional issue in a case that can be decided on other grounds, however, we do not reach the defendant's constitutional arguments.

The trial court's order declared the Chester Zoning Ordinance invalid and unconstitutional; as a result, but for this appeal, the town has been left "unzoned." To leave the town with *no* land use controls would be incompatible with the orderly development of the general community, and the court erred when it ruled the ordinance invalid. It is not, however, within the power of this court to act as a super zoning board. "Zoning is properly a legislative function, and courts are prevented by the doctrine of separation of powers from invasion of this field." Godfrey v. Zoning Bd. of Adjustment, 317 N.C. 51, 58, 344 S.E.2d 272, 276 (1986). Moreover, our decision today is limited to those sections of the zoning ordinance which hinder the construction of multi-family housing units. Accordingly, we defer to the legislative body of the town, within a reasonable time period, to bring these sections of its zoning ordinance into line with the zoning enabling legislation and with this opinion. Consequently, we will temporarily allow the zoning ordinance to remain in effect.

As to the specific relief granted to plaintiff Remillard, the town contends that the court's order effectively rezones the parcel in violation of the separation of powers provision found in part I, article 37 of the New Hampshire Constitution. It further asserts that, even if it were lawful for a court to rezone or grant specific relief, plaintiff Remillard's proposed development does not qualify for such a remedy.

The master found that the requirement that multi-family housing may be built only as part of a PRD containing a variety of housing types violated plaintiff Remillard's rights under the equal protection clause of the New Hampshire Constitution, part I, article 2. The master also found that plaintiff Remillard was "unalterably committed to develop [his] tract to accommodate low[-] and moderate[-]income families." Accordingly, he granted specific relief to plaintiff Remillard, ordering that the town allow him to build his development as proposed.

The trial court has the power, subject to our review for abuse of discretion, to order definitive relief for plaintiff Remillard. In Soares v. Town of Atkinson, 129 N.H. 313, 529 A.2d 867 (1987), we upheld the master's finding that granting a "builder's remedy," *i.e.,* allowing the plaintiff builder to complete his project as proposed, is discretionary. Although we there upheld the decision that such relief was inappropriate, noting that the master determined that the ordered revision of the town ordinances would permit the building of the plaintiff's project, we did not reject such relief as a proper remedy in appropriate zoning cases. In this appeal, the master found such relief to be appropriate, and the town has not carried its burden on appeal to persuade us to the contrary. A successful plaintiff is entitled to relief which rewards his or her efforts in testing the legality of the ordinance and prevents retributive action by the municipality, such as correcting the illegality but taking pains to leave the plaintiff unbenefitted. The Pennsylvania Supreme Court reasoned in Casey v. Zoning Board of Warwick Township, 459 Pa. 219, 328 A.2d 464 (1974), that "[t]o forsake a challenger's reasonable development plans after all the time, effort and capital invested in such a challenge is grossly inequitable." *Id.* 328 A.2d at 469.

The master relied on Southern Burlington County N.A.A.C.P. v. Township of Mount Laurel, 92 N.J. 158, 456 A.2d 390 (1983), (*Mt. Laurel II*), in determining that plaintiff Remillard was entitled to build his development as proposed. In *Mount Laurel I,* the New Jersey Supreme Court held that the municipality's zoning ordinance violated the general welfare provision of its State Constitution by not affording a realistic opportunity for the construction of its "fair share" of the present and prospective regional need for low-and moderate-income housing. So. Burlington Cty. N.A.A.C.P. v. Mt. Laurel Tp., 67 N.J. 151, 174, 336 A.2d 713, 724, appeal dismissed, 423 U.S. 808 (1975). *Mt. Laurel II* was a return to the New Jersey Supreme Court, eight years later, prompted by the realization that *Mt. Laurel I* had not resulted in realistic housing opportunities for low-and moderate-income people, but in "paper, process, witnesses, trials and appeals." *Mt. Laurel II, supra* 92

N.J. at 199, 456 A.2d at 410. The court noted that the "builder's remedy," which effectively grants a building permit to a plaintiff/developer, based on the development proposal, as long as other local regulations are followed, should be made more readily available to insure that low-and moderate-income housing is actually built.

Since 1979, plaintiff Remillard has attempted to obtain permission to build a moderate-sized multi-family housing development on his land in Chester. He is committed to setting aside a minimum of ten of the forty-eight units for low-and moderate-income tenants for twenty years. "Equity will not suffer a wrong without a remedy." 2 *Pomeroy's Equity Jurisprudence* § 423 (5th ed. 1941). Hence, we hold that the "builder's remedy" is appropriate in this case, both to compensate the developer who has invested substantial time and resources in pursuing this litigation, and as the most likely means of insuring that low-and moderate-income housing is actually built.

Although we determine that the "builder's remedy" is appropriate in this case, we do not adopt the *Mt. Laurel* analysis for determining whether such a remedy will be granted. Instead, we find the rule developed in Sinclair Pipe Line Co. v. Richton Park, 19 Ill.2d 370, 167 N.E.2d 406 (1960), is the better rule as it eliminates the calculation of arbitrary mathematical quotas which *Mt. Laurel* requires. That rule is followed with some variation by the supreme courts of several other States, and awards relief to the plaintiff builder if his development is found to be reasonable, *i.e.,* providing a realistic opportunity for the construction of low-and moderate-income housing and consistent with sound zoning concepts and environmental concerns. Once an existing zoning ordinance is found invalid in whole or in part, whether on constitutional grounds or, as here, on grounds of statutory construction and application, the court may provide relief in the form of a declaration that the plaintiff builder's proposed use is reasonable, and the municipality may not interfere with it. The plaintiff must bear the burden of proving reasonable use by a preponderance of the evidence. *Id.* Once the plaintiff's burden has been met, he will be permitted to proceed with the proposed development, provided he complies with all other applicable regulations.

The town's argument that the specific relief granted to plaintiff Remillard violates the separation of powers provision found in part I, article 37 of the New Hampshire Constitution, to the extent that the trial court exercised legislative power specifically delegated to the local zoning authority, is without merit. The rule we adopt today does not produce this result. *See Opinion of the Justices,* 121 N.H. 552, 556, 431 A.2d 783, 785–86 (1981) ("complete separation of powers would interfere with the efficient operation of government * * * consequently there must be some overlapping of the power of each branch"). This rule will permit the municipality to continue to control its own development, so long as it does so for the general welfare of the community. It will also accommodate the construction of low-and moderate-income housing that had been unlawfully excluded.

* * *

The zoning ordinance evolved as an innovative means to counter the problems of uncontrolled growth. It was never conceived to be a device to facilitate the use of governmental power to prevent access to a municipality by "outsiders of any disadvantaged social or economic group." *Beck*, 118 N.H. at 801, 394 A.2d at 852. The town of Chester has adopted a zoning ordinance which is blatantly exclusionary. This court will not condone the town's conduct.

Affirmed in part and reversed in part.

Notes

1. The Supreme Court of New Jersey pioneered a judicial assault on the use of zoning to exclude low income persons from residential areas. In Southern Burlington County NAACP v. Township of Mount Laurel, 67 N.J. 151, 336 A.2d 713 (1975), *appeal dismissed and cert. denied* 423 U.S. 808 (1975), the court struck down local land use regulations that had the effect of preventing the construction of low and moderate income housing in developing communities. The court directed that localities must permit the building of low-cost housing to the extent of the municipality's "fair share" of the regional need for such units.

Despite the potentially broad impact of *Mount Laurel*, there was little change in New Jersey housing patterns. Confronted with this situation, in 1983 the Supreme Court of New Jersey issued a sweeping decision designed to secure implementation of the "fair share" requirement. It adopted several novel enforcement remedies and fashioned an affirmative obligation on the part of affected localities to provide an opportunity for low and moderate income housing. Southern Burlington County NAACP v. Township of Mount Laurel, 92 N.J. 158, 456 A.2d 390 (1983) (Mount Laurel II). *See generally* Payne, *Starting Over—Mount Laurel II,* 12 Real Est.L.J. 85 (1983); Rose, *The Mount Laurel II Decision: Is It Based on Wishful Thinking?,* 12 Real Est.L.J. 115 (1983).

In 1985 the New Jersey legislature enacted the Fair Housing Act, which created the Council on Affordable Housing. The Council, an administrative agency, was designed to replace the courts in the implementation of the "fair share" concept. The Council has issued complex guidelines to determine a community's "fair share" and has secured a degree of compliance by reducing the number of required low-cost housing units based upon local circumstances. The Supreme Court of New Jersey upheld the constitutionality of the Fair Housing Act and transferred pending judicial cases to the Council. Hills Development Company v. Township of Bernards, 103 N.J. 1, 510 A.2d 621 (1986) (Mount Laurel III). *See generally* Payne, *Rethinking Fair Share: The Judicial Enforcement of Affordable Housing Policies,* 16 Real Est.L.J. 20 (1987); Franzese, *Mount Laurel III: The New Jersey Supreme Court's Judicious Retreat,* 18 Seton Hall L.Rev. 380 (1988).

The *Mount Laurel* decisions remain highly controversial. Commentators have debated whether the Fair Housing Act satisfies the "fair share" mandate. *See* Fox, *The Selling Out of Mount Laurel: Regional Contribution Agreements in New Jersey's Fair Housing Act,* 16 Fordham Urb.L.J. 535 (1988); McGuire, *The Judiciary's Role in Implementing The Mount Laurel Doctrine: Deference or Activism?,* 23 Seton Hall L.Rev. 1276 (1993). One scholar has questioned whether poor persons are in fact getting the benefit of housing built under *Mount Laurel* programs and has argued that the mandatory set asides for affordable housing constitute an unconstitutional taking of property under the Fifth Amendment. Berger, *Inclusionary Zoning Devices as Takings: The Legacy of the Mount Laurel Cases,* 70 Neb.L.Rev. 186 (1991). *See also* D. Coyle, Property Rights and the Constitution: Shaping Society Through Land Use Regulation 61–72, 75–84 (1993). For studies of the implementation of the *Mount Laurel* decisions, see C. Haar, Suburbs Under Siege: Race, Space, and Audacious Judges (1996); D. Kirp, J. Dwyer, & L. Rosenthal, Our Town: Race, Housing and the Soul of Suburbia (1995).

2. With the exception of *Britton,* the *Mount Laurel* approach has attracted scant judicial support in other jurisdictions. New York courts, for instance, have rejected the "fair share" formula. *See* Asian Americans for Equality v. Koch, 72 N.Y.2d 121, 531 N.Y.S.2d 782, 527 N.E.2d 265 (1988).

3. In several jurisdictions, statutes require municipalities to plan for low and moderate income housing. *See* D. Mandelker, Land Use Law § 3.11 (4th ed. 1997).

4. The exclusionary effect of large lot zoning is implicitly addressed in *Britton.* This issue is directly discussed in the leading case of National Land and Investment Co. v. Kohn, 419 Pa. 504, 215 A.2d 597 (1965). There the Supreme Court of Pennsylvania struck down a zoning ordinance requiring a four-acre minimum lot size. It commented:

> There is no doubt that in Pennsylvania, zoning for density is a legitimate exercise of the police power. Every zoning case involves a different set of facts and circumstances in light of which the constitutionality of a zoning ordinance must be tested. Therefore, it is impossible for us to say that any minimum acreage requirement is unconstitutional per se.
>
> The relative advantages of a one acre lot over a one-half acre lot are easy to comprehend. Similarly, a two acre lot has advantages over a one acre lot and three acres may be preferred over two acres or ten acres over three. The greater the amount of land, the more room for children, the less congestion, the easier to handle water supply and sewage, and the fewer municipal services which must be provided. At some point along the spectrum, however, the size of lots ceases to be a concern requiring public regulation and becomes simply a matter of private preference. The point at which legitimate public interest ceases is not a constant one, but one which varies with the land involved and the circumstances of each case.

Id. at 523–524, 215 A.2d at 607–608.

VILLAGE OF ARLINGTON HEIGHTS v. METROPOLITAN HOUSING DEVELOPMENT CORPORATION

United States Supreme Court, 1977.
429 U.S. 252.

MR. JUSTICE POWELL delivered the opinion of the Court.

In 1971 respondent Metropolitan Housing Development Corporation (MHDC) applied to petitioner, the Village of Arlington Heights, Ill., for the rezoning of a 15–acre parcel from single-family to multiple-family classification. Using federal financial assistance, MHDC planned to build 190 clustered townhouse units for low-and moderate-income tenants. The Village denied the rezoning request. MHDC, joined by other plaintiffs who are also respondents here, brought suit in the United States District Court for the Northern District of Illinois. They alleged that the denial was racially discriminatory and that it violated, *inter alia,* the Fourteenth Amendment and the Fair Housing Act of 1968, 82 Stat. 81, 42 U.S.C. § 3601 *et seq.* Following a bench trial, the District Court entered judgment for the Village, 373 F.Supp. 208 (1974), and respondents appealed. The Court of Appeals for the Seventh Circuit reversed, finding that the "ultimate effect" of the denial was racially discriminatory, and that the refusal to rezone therefore violated the Fourteenth Amendment. 517 F.2d 409 (1975). We granted the Village's petition for certiorari, 423 U.S. 1030 (1975), and now reverse.

I

Arlington Heights is a suburb of Chicago, located about 26 miles northwest of the downtown Loop area. Most of the land in Arlington Heights is zoned for detached single-family homes, and this is in fact the prevailing land use. The Village experienced substantial growth during the 1960's, but, like other communities in northwest Cook County, its population of racial minority groups remained quite low. According to the 1970 census, only 27 of the Village's 64,000 residents were black.

The Clerics of St. Viator, a religious order (Order), own an 80–acre parcel just east of the center of Arlington Heights. Part of the site is occupied by the Viatorian high school, and part by the Order's three-story novitiate building, which houses dormitories and a Montessori school. Much of the site, however, remains vacant. Since 1959, when the Village first adopted a zoning ordinance, all the land surrounding the Viatorian property has been zoned R–3, a single-family specification with relatively small minimum lot-size requirements. On three sides of the Viatorian land there are single-family homes just across a street; to the east the Viatorian property directly adjoins the backyards of other single-family homes.

The Order decided in 1970 to devote some of its land to low-and moderate-income housing. Investigation revealed that the most expeditious way to build such housing was to work through a nonprofit developer experienced in the use of federal housing subsidies under § 236 of the National Housing Act, 48 Stat. 1246, as added and amended, 12 U.S.C. § 1715z–1.[1]

MHDC is such a developer. It was organized in 1968 by several prominent Chicago citizens for the purpose of building low-and moderate-income housing throughout the Chicago area. In 1970 MHDC was in the process of building one § 236 development near Arlington Heights and already had provided some federally assisted housing on a smaller scale in other parts of the Chicago area.

After some negotiation, MHDC and the Order entered into a 99–year lease and an accompanying agreement of sale covering a 15–acre site in the southeast corner of the Viatorian property. MHDC became the lessee immediately, but the sale agreement was contingent upon MHDC's securing zoning clearances from the Village and § 236 housing assistance from the Federal Government. If MHDC proved unsuccessful in securing either, both the lease and the contract of sale would lapse. The agreement established a bargain purchase price of $300,000, low enough to comply with federal limitations governing land-acquisition costs for § 236 housing.

MHDC engaged an architect and proceeded with the project, to be known as Lincoln Green. The plans called for 20 two-story buildings with a total of 190 units, each unit having its own private entrance from the outside. One hundred of the units would have a single bedroom, thought likely to attract elderly citizens. The remainder would have two, three, or four bedrooms. A large portion of the site would remain open, with shrubs and trees to screen the homes abutting the property to the east.

The planned development did not conform to the Village's zoning ordinance and could not be built unless Arlington Heights rezoned the parcel to R–5, its multiple-family housing classification. Accordingly, MHDC filed with the Village Plan Commission a petition for rezoning, accompanied by supporting materials describing the development and specifying that it would be subsidized under § 236. The materials made clear that one requirement under § 236 is an affirmative marketing plan designed to assure that a subsidized development is racially integrated. MHDC also submitted studies demonstrating the need for housing of this type and analyzing the probable impact of the development. To prepare for the hearings before the Plan Commission and to assure compliance with the Village building code, fire regulations, and related requirements, MHDC consulted with the Village staff for preliminary review of the development. The parties have stipulated that every change recommended during such consultations was incorporated into the plans.

---

1. Section 236 provides for "interest reduction payments" to owners of rental housing projects which meet the Act's requirements, if the savings are passed on to the tenants in accordance with a rather complex formula.

During the spring of 1971, the Plan Commission considered the proposal at a series of three public meetings, which drew large crowds. Although many of those attending were quite vocal and demonstrative in opposition to Lincoln Green, a number of individuals and representatives of community groups spoke in support of rezoning. Some of the comments, both from opponents and supporters, addressed what was referred to as the "social issue"—the desirability or undesirability of introducing at this location in Arlington Heights low-and moderate-income housing, housing that would probably be racially integrated.

Many of the opponents, however, focused on the zoning aspects of the petition, stressing two arguments. First, the area always had been zoned single-family, and the neighboring citizens had built or purchased there in reliance on that classification. Rezoning threatened to cause a measurable drop in property value for neighboring sites. Second, the Village's apartment policy, adopted by the Village Board in 1962 and amended in 1970, called for R–5 zoning primarily to serve as a buffer between single-family development and land uses thought incompatible, such as commercial or manufacturing districts. Lincoln Green did not meet this requirement, as it adjoined no commercial or manufacturing district.

At the close of the third meeting, the Plan Commission adopted a motion to recommend to the Village's Board of Trustees that it deny the request. * * * After a public hearing, the Board denied the rezoning by a 6–1 vote.

The following June MHDC and three Negro individuals filed this lawsuit against the Village, seeking declaratory and injunctive relief. A second nonprofit corporation and an individual of Mexican–American descent intervened as plaintiffs. The trial resulted in a judgment for petitioners. Assuming that MHDC had standing to bring the suit, the District Court held that the petitioners were not motivated by racial discrimination or intent to discriminate against low-income groups when they denied rezoning, but rather by a desire "to protect property values and the integrity of the Village's zoning plan." 373 F.Supp., at 211. The District Court concluded also that the denial would not have a racially discriminatory effect.

A divided Court of Appeals reversed. It first approved the District Court's finding that the defendants were motivated by a concern for the integrity of the zoning plan, rather than by racial discrimination. Deciding whether their refusal to rezone would have discriminatory effects was more complex. The court observed that the refusal would have a disproportionate impact on blacks. Based upon family income, blacks constituted 40% of those Chicago area residents who were eligible to become tenants of Lincoln Green, although they composed a far lower percentage of total area population. The court reasoned, however, that under our decision in James v. Valtierra, 402 U.S. 137 (1971), such a disparity in racial impact alone does not call for strict scrutiny of a municipality's decision that prevents the construction of the low-cost housing.

There was another level to the court's analysis of allegedly discriminatory results. Invoking language from Kennedy Park Homes Assn. v. City of Lackawanna, 436 F.2d 108, 112 (C.A.2 1970), cert. denied, 401 U.S. 1010 (1971), the Court of Appeals ruled that the denial of rezoning must be examined in light of its "historical context and ultimate effect." Northwest Cook County was enjoying rapid growth in employment opportunities and population, but it continued to exhibit a high degree of residential segregation. The court held that Arlington Heights could not simply ignore this problem. Indeed, it found that the Village had been "exploiting" the situation by allowing itself to become a nearly all-white community. The Village had no other current plans for building low-and moderate-income housing, and no other R–5 parcels in the Village were available to MHDC at an economically feasible price.

Against this background, the Court of Appeals ruled that the denial of the Lincoln Green proposal had racially discriminatory effects and could be tolerated only if it served compelling interests. Neither the buffer policy nor the desire to protect property values met this exacting standard. The court therefore concluded that the denial violated the Equal Protection Clause of the Fourteenth Amendment.

* * *

III

Our decision last Term in Washington v. Davis, 426 U.S. 229 (1976), made it clear that official action will not be held unconstitutional solely because it results in a racially disproportionate impact. "Disproportionate impact is not irrelevant, but it is not the sole touchstone of an invidious racial discrimination." *Id.*, at 242. Proof of racially discriminatory intent or purpose is required to show a violation of the Equal Protection Clause. Although some contrary indications may be drawn from some of our cases, the holding in *Davis* reaffirmed a principle well established in a variety of contexts. *E.g.*, Keyes v. School Dist. No. 1, Denver, Colo., 413 U.S. 189, 208 (1973) (schools); Wright v. Rockefeller, 376 U.S. 52, 56–57 (1964) (election districting); Akins v. Texas, 325 U.S. 398, 403–404 (1945) (jury selection).

Davis does not require a plaintiff to prove that the challenged action rested solely on racially discriminatory purposes. Rarely can it be said that a legislature or administrative body operating under a broad mandate made a decision motivated solely by a single concern, or even that a particular purpose was the "dominant" or "primary" one. In fact, it is because legislators and administrators are properly concerned with balancing numerous competing considerations that courts refrain from reviewing the merits of their decisions, absent a showing of arbitrariness or irrationality. But racial discrimination is not just another competing consideration. When there is a proof that a discriminatory purpose has been a motivating factor in the decision, this judicial deference is no longer justified.

Determining whether invidious discriminatory purpose was a motivating factor demands a sensitive inquiry into such circumstantial and direct evidence of intent as may be available. The impact of the official action—whether it "bears more heavily on one race than another," *Washington v. Davis, supra,* at 242—may provide an important starting point. Sometimes a clear pattern, unexplainable on grounds other than race, emerges from the effect of the state action even when the governing legislation appears neutral on its face. Yick Wo v. Hopkins, 118 U.S. 356 (1886); Guinn v. United States, 238 U.S. 347 (1915); Lane v. Wilson, 307 U.S. 268 (1939); Gomillion v. Lightfoot, 364 U.S. 339 (1960). The evidentiary inquiry is then relatively easy. But such cases are rare. Absent a pattern as stark as that in *Gomillion* or *Yick Wo,* impact alone is not determinative, and the Court must look to other evidence.

The historical background of the decision is one evidentiary source, particularly if it reveals a series of official actions taken for invidious purposes. The specific sequence of events leading up to the challenged decision also may shed some light on the decisionmaker's purposes. For example, if the property involved here always had been zoned R–5 but suddenly was changed to R–3 when the town learned of MHDC's plans to erect integrated housing, we would have a far different case. Departures from the normal procedural sequence also might afford evidence that improper purposes are playing a role. Substantive departures too may be relevant, particularly if the factors usually considered important by the decisionmaker strongly favor a decision contrary to the one reached.

The legislative or administrative history may be highly relevant, especially where there are contemporary statements by members of the decisionmaking body, minutes of its meetings, or reports. In some extraordinary instances the members might be called to the stand at trial to testify concerning the purpose of the official action, although even then such testimony frequently will be barred by privilege.

The foregoing summary identifies, without purporting to be exhaustive, subjects of proper inquiry in determining whether racially discriminatory intent existed. With these in mind, we now address the case before us.

IV

This case was tried in the District Court and reviewed in the Court of Appeals before our decision in *Washington v. Davis, supra.* The respondents proceeded on the erroneous theory that the Village's refusal to rezone carried a racially discriminatory effect and was, without more, unconstitutional. But both courts below understood that at least part of their function was to examine the purpose underlying the decision. In making its findings on this issue, the District Court noted that some of the opponents of Lincoln Green who spoke at the various hearings might have been motivated by opposition to minority groups. The court held, however, that the evidence "does not warrant the conclusion that this motivated the defendants." 373 F.Supp., at 211.

On appeal the Court of Appeals focused primarily on respondents' claim that the Village's buffer policy had not been consistently applied and was being invoked with a strictness here that could only demonstrate some other underlying motive. The court concluded that the buffer policy, though not always applied with perfect consistency, had on several occasions formed the basis for the Board's decision to deny other rezoning proposals. "The evidence does not necessitate a finding that Arlington Heights administered this policy in a discriminatory manner." 517 F.2d, at 412. The Court of Appeals therefore approved the District Court's findings concerning the Village's purposes in denying rezoning to MHDC.

We also have reviewed the evidence. The impact of the Village's decision does arguably bear more heavily on racial minorities. Minorities constitute 18% of the Chicago area population, and 40% of the income groups said to be eligible for Lincoln Green. But there is little about the sequence of events leading up to the decision that would spark suspicion. The area around the Viatorian property has been zoned R–3 since 1959, the year when Arlington Heights first adopted a zoning map. Single-family homes surround the 80–acre site, and the Village is undeniably committed to single-family homes as its dominant residential land use. The rezoning request progressed according to the usual procedures. The Plan Commission even scheduled two additional hearings, at least in part to accommodate MHDC and permit it to supplement its presentation with answers to questions generated at the first hearing.

The statements by the Plan Commission and Village Board members, as reflected in the official minutes, focused almost exclusively on the zoning aspects of the MHDC petition, and the zoning factors on which they relied are not novel criteria in the Village's rezoning decisions. There is no reason to doubt that there has been reliance by some neighboring property owners on the maintenance of single-family zoning in the vicinity. The Village originally adopted its buffer policy long before MHDC entered the picture and has applied the policy too consistently for us to infer discriminatory purpose from its application in this case. Finally, MHDC called one member of the Village Board to the stand at trial. Nothing in her testimony supports an inference of invidious purpose.

In sum, the evidence does not warrant overturning the concurrent findings of both courts below. Respondents simply failed to carry their burden of proving that discriminatory purpose was a motivating factor in the Village's decisions. This conclusion ends the constitutional inquiry. The Court of Appeals' further finding that the Village's decision carried a discriminatory "ultimate effect" is without independent constitutional significance.

V

Respondents' complaint also alleged that the refusal to rezone violated the Fair Housing Act of 1968, 42 U.S.C. § 3601 *et seq.* They continue to urge here that a zoning decision made by a public body may, and that petitioners' action did, violate § 3604 or § 3617. The Court of Appeals, however, proceeding in a somewhat unorthodox fashion, did not decide the statutory question. We remand the case for further consideration of respondents' statutory claims.

Reversed and remanded.

Notes and Questions

1. On remand, the Seventh Circuit concluded that a "violation of section 3604(a) [of the Fair Housing Act] can be established by a showing of racially discriminatory effect without a showing of discriminatory intent." Metropolitan Housing Development Corp. v. Village of Arlington Heights, 558 F.2d 1283, 1290 (7th Cir.1977), *cert. denied* 434 U.S. 1025 (1978). It then held that "if there is no land other than plaintiff's property within Arlington Heights which is both properly zoned and suitable for federally subsidized low-cost housing, the Village's refusal to rezone constituted a violation of section 3604(a)." 558 F.2d at 1294. The Seventh Circuit directed the district court to make this determination. The district court, however, did not address the issue. Rather, it entered a consent decree approving a settlement whereby Arlington Heights was required to annex and rezone land to permit the construction of low and moderate income housing units. Metropolitan Housing Development Corp. v. Village of Arlington Heights, 469 F.Supp. 836 (N.D.Ill.1979), *affirmed* 616 F.2d 1006 (7th Cir.1980). For a case in which a city's exclusionary zoning ordinance was found to violate the Fair Housing Act, *see* Huntington Branch, NAACP v. Town of Huntington, 844 F.2d 926 (2d Cir.1988), *affirmed* 488 U.S. 15 (1988).

2. Based on your reading of the material in this subsection is it legally possible to exclude all mobile homes from Centerville as some members of the city council advocate? *See* Bibco Corporation v. City of Sumter, 332 S.C. 45, 504 S.E.2d 112 (1998); J. Juergensmeyer & T. Roberts, Land Use Planning and Control Law § 6.5 (1998); Strom, *Current Trends in Mobile Home Zoning* in 1981 Zoning and Planning Law Handbook §§ 11.01–11.11; 1982 Zoning and Planning Law Handbook § 4.05; 2 Williams American Land Planning Law § 57.27 (1987); Note, *Behind the Smokescreen: Exclusionary Zoning of Mobile Homes*, 25 Wash.U.J.Urb. & Contemp.L. 235 (1983).

3. In City of Cleburne v. Cleburne Living Center, Inc., 473 U.S. 432 (1985), the Supreme Court reviewed a zoning ordinance that required a property owner to obtain a special use permit in order to locate a group home for the mentally retarded in an area zoned for apartments, boarding houses, hospitals, nursing homes, and similar uses. The Court held that the denial of a special use permit violated the Equal Protection Clause.

D. EXACTIONS

NEW JERSEY BUILDERS ASS'N
v. BERNARDS TOWNSHIP

Supreme Court of New Jersey, 1987.
108 N.J. 223, 528 A.2d 555.

STEIN, J.

The narrow issue that we address in this appeal is whether Bernards Township's Ordinance 672 is a valid exercise of the authority conferred upon municipalities by the Municipal Land Use Law (MLUL), specifically N.J.S.A. 40:55D–42. We hold that that portion of the ordinance that requires new developers to pay their pro-rata share of the Township's long term, twenty-million dollar road improvement plan exceeds the Township's authority under the MLUL and is therefore invalid. Accordingly, we affirm the judgment of the Appellate Division.

I

The material provisions of Ordinance 672 are set forth at length in Judge D'Annunzio's well-reasoned opinion below, New Jersey Builders Ass'n v. Bernards Township, 211 N.J.Super. 290, 511 A.2d 740 (Law Div.1985). We reiterate them only to the extent necessary to permit a full understanding of the ordinance's purpose and intended implementation.

Bernards Township, bisected by Interstate Highways 78 and 287, is a rapidly-developing municipality in northern Somerset County. During the late 1970's, and in response to the impact of new and increased development, the Township authorized a consulting firm to undertake a comprehensive transportation and traffic study of the entire Township. The study summarized the existing traffic conditions in the community, made traffic projections based on current and projected development in accordance with the zoning ordinance, and set forth road improvements deemed necessary to accommodate current and anticipated development throughout the Township. The result of the study was a Transportation Management Plan that was substantially incorporated into the circulation element of the Township's Master Plan. Reflecting the consultant's recommendations, the Master Plan proposed an extensive roadway improvement program involving improvements to twenty-two township roads, seventeen intersections, seven county roads, two county bridges, and off-street commuter parking facilities. It was anticipated that the improvements would be constructed over a twenty-year period at an estimated cost of twenty million dollars.

As recommended by the Master Plan, Ordinance 672 was adopted to provide a mechanism for allocating the cost of the road improvement program between the Township and its residential and commercial developers. The premise underlying Ordinance 672 is that all new development within the Township contributes to the need for Township-wide road improvements. Thus, allocating the cost of such roadway improvements, on the basis of "trip generation" forecasts, between the Township—to reflect the impact of existing development—and new developers was a reasonable and appropriate exercise of the Township's regulatory authority under the MLUL.

* * *

The ordinance requires developers to pay 50% of their share of the road improvement cost upon issuance of a building permit, to post security for the unpaid balance, and to pay the balance upon issuance of a certificate of occupancy. The ordinance permits payment on the basis of construction in stages, or payment on a per-unit basis at an accelerated rate. Money paid to the Township pursuant to Ordinance 672 is to be segregated, until spent, in a separate dedicated account. The ordinance permits a developer, or its successor in title, to apply for a refund if the funds paid are not spent by the Township within twenty years, or ten years after execution of the particular Developer's Agreement, whichever is later. If no refund claim is made within one year after the date on which it may first be asserted, the money reverts to the Township for general capital purposes.

Plaintiffs New Jersey Builders Association and its local affiliate, Builders Association of Somerset and Morris, are trade organizations consisting of builders and developers, some of whom allegedly own property in Bernards Township that they intend to develop. Plaintiff Mill Race Limited is a purchaser of land in the Township that has since been developed. * * *

The Law Division held that the road improvement provisions of Ordinance 672 violated the limited grant of authority, set forth in N.J.S.A. 40:55D–42, permitting municipalities to require developers to pay their share of "reasonable and necessary" off-site improvements. 211 N.J.Super. at 297, 511 A.2d 740. The Law Division did not determine the validity of the ordinance's provisions relating to off-tract drainage improvements. The court also declined to rule on the Township's motion that the decision invalidating the ordinance should apply prospectively only. The Appellate Division, affirming on the basis of the opinion below, specifically ruled that the judgment would not be limited to prospective application. 219 N.J.Super. at 539, 530 A.2d 1254. We granted the Township's petition for certification. 104 N.J. 421, 517 A.2d 417 (1986).

II

Although our disposition of this appeal is controlled by what we discern to be the intended scope of N.J.S.A. 40:55D–42, a broader context is indispensable to a full understanding of the implications of the issue before us. We acknowledge that our experience with municipal attempts to charge developers for off-site improvements has heretofore been limited to the cost of facilities closely related to needs generated by the specific development. *See, e.g.,* Divan Builders v. Township of Wayne,

66 N.J. 582, 334 A.2d 30 (1975) (municipality sought contribution toward improvement of drainage basin serving subdivision and adjacent area); * * * Longridge Builders v. Planning Bd. of Princeton Township, 52 N.J. 348, 245 A.2d 336 (1968) (municipality required developer to pave dedicated right-of-way from subdivision boundary to public street); *cf.* Daniels v. Point Pleasant, 23 N.J. 357, 129 A.2d 265 (1957) (municipality enacted invalid ordinance amendment increasing building permit fees for the purpose of raising revenue to meet increased school costs). In other states, local governments have attempted to impose a variety of indirect capital costs on new developers, a trend that appears to have gained momentum during the past decade. Bauman & Ethier, "Development Exactions and Impact Fees: A Survey of American Practices," *Law & Contemp. Probs.*, Winter 1987, at 51. *See generally* Exactions: A Controversial New Source for Municipal Funds, Symposium, *Law & Contemp. Probs.*, Winter 1987 (discussing economic and legal factors affecting the use and validity of governmentally-imposed exactions); Heyman & Gilhool, "The Constitutionality of Imposing Increased Community Costs on New Suburban Residents Through Subdivision Exactions," 73 *Yale L.J.* 1119 (1964) (urging a "reasonableness" standard to evaluate the validity of subdivision exaction ordinances).

There is wide variation in the types of exactions that governmental entities impose on developers. The most common are those that require dedication of land within the subdivision for public purposes and the construction of improvements such as streets, sidewalks, and water and sewer lines. Connors & High, "The Expanding Circle of Exactions: From Dedication to Linkage," *Law & Contemp. Probs.*, Winter 1987, at 70. Another common type of exaction requires developers to construct off-site improvements, usually on property adjacent to the subdivision for road or drainage purposes. Smith, "From Subdivision Improvement Requirements to Community Benefit Assessments and Linkage Payments: A Brief History of Land Development Exactions," *Law & Contemp. Probs.*, Winter 1987, at 5, 7–8.

Less common but frequently sustained are requirements for dedication of land for recreational purposes, or payments in lieu of dedication, where the purpose of the dedication or payment is primarily, but not exclusively, to benefit the residents of the new development. Connors & High, *supra* at 71; *see also* City of College Station v. Turtle Rock Corp., 680 S.W.2d 802 (Tex.1984) (upholding ordinance requiring dedication of one acre of land for each 133 housing units, or payment of fee in lieu of dedication, to be used for neighborhood park purposes); Aunt Hack Ridge Estates v. Planning Comm'n, 160 Conn. 109, 273 A.2d 880 (1970) (sustaining ordinance requiring dedication of area equal to 4% of subdivision, but not less than 10,000 square feet, for recreational use); Jenad, Inc. v. Village of Scarsdale, 18 N.Y.2d 78, 218 N.E.2d 673, 271 N.Y.S.2d 955 (1966) (upholding ordinance requiring dedication of land, or payment of fee of $250 per lot, for park purposes); Jordan v. Village of Menomonee Falls, 28 Wis.2d 608, 137 N.W.2d 442 (1965) (upholding ordinance requiring payment of $200 per lot, or dedication of land of equal value, for school, park, and recreational purposes). *But cf.* Pioneer Trust v. Village of Mt. Prospect, 22 Ill.2d 375, 176 N.E.2d 799 (1961) (invalidating municipal ordinance requiring dedication of one acre per sixty housing units for public use).

Another type of municipal exaction, typified by the Bernards ordinance and by ordinances challenged in a series of Florida cases, is the impact fee, described generally as a "charge[ ] against new development for the purpose of raising money to defray the costs of basic services local government provides to its citizens." Currier, "Legal and Practical Problems Associated with Drafting Impact Fee Ordinances," 1984 *Institute on Planning, Zoning and Eminent Domain* at 273–74. Impact fees are described as a cost-shifting device that contribute to "the efforts of local governments to cope with the economic burdens of population growth such as the need for new roads, schools, parks, and sewer and water treatment facilities." Juergensmeyer & Blake, "Impact Fees: An Answer to Local Governments' Capital Funding Dilemma," 9 *Fla.St. U.L.Rev.* 415, 417 (1981). They are justified on the theory that "it is possible to allocate to each development its proportionate share of the future cost of providing public services * * *." Smith, *supra* at 16.

In Contractors & Builders Ass'n v. City of Dunedin, 329 So.2d 314, 318 (1976), the Florida Supreme Court concluded that a city had the authority under Florida's constitution and statutory law to impose an impact fee to defray the capital cost of improving the city's water and sewerage system to meet the increased demand created by new development. The Court concluded that such an ordinance is valid "where expansion is reasonably required, *if use of the money collected is limited to meeting the cost of expansion.*" *Id.* at 320.[1]

In Hollywood Inc. v. Broward County, 431 So.2d 606 (Fla.Dist.Ct. App.), petition for review denied, 440 So.2d 352 (1983), the court upheld a county ordinance that required a dedication of land or a fee payment to assist the county in developing its park system. The ordinance required three acres of park land to be dedicated for each 1,000 residents, or payment of either the value of the required dedication or an impact fee prescribed by the ordinance. The funds had to be expended within a reasonable period of time to acquire new park land within fifteen miles of the subdivision. The court held that the ordinance was valid insofar as its requirements "offset needs sufficiently attributable to the subdivision and so long as the funds collected are sufficiently earmarked for the substantial benefit of the subdivision residents." *Id.* at 611.

Two Florida impact-fee cases involved attempts to collect funds for road improvement purposes. In Broward County v. Janis Dev. Corp., 311 So.2d 371 (Fla.Dist.Ct.App.1975), a county ordinance imposed a fee of $200 for each housing unit constructed, to be deposited in a trust fund

---

1. Although the Florida Supreme Court invalidated the ordinance because of inadequate restriction on the use of the fees collected, *id.* at 321–22, the ordinance was amended and later upheld, City of Dunedin v. Contractors & Builders Ass'n, 358 So.2d 846 (Fla.Dist.Ct.App.1978), *cert. denied,* 370 So.2d 458, cert. denied, 444 U.S. 867 (1979).

"for the purpose of constructing or improving roads, streets, highways, and bridges * * *." *Id.* at 374. In that case, however, the court found "no specifics provided in the ordinance as to where and when these monies are to be expended." *Id.* at 375. Accordingly, the court refused to uphold the ordinance, concluding that the impact fee imposed by the ordinance was a tax prohibited by the Florida constitution.

The second road-improvement case, Home Builders & Contractors Ass'n v. Board of County Comm'rs, 446 So.2d 140 (Fla.Dist.Ct.App. 1983), petition for review denied, 451 So.2d 848, appeal dismissed, 469 U.S. 976 (1984), involved an ordinance that imposed an impact fee on developers to pay for road construction required by increased traffic generated from new developments. The ordinance relied on a formula that took into account the cost of road construction and the number of motor vehicle trips generated by different types of development. The ordinance divided the county into forty zones, establishing a trust fund for each zone and requiring that funds collected from development could be expended only in the zone in which the development was located. The court concluded that the ordinance imposed a regulatory fee and not a tax, observing that the estimated cost of new road construction would far exceed the fees imposed by the ordinance, that the ordinance permitted developers to demonstrate that their required contribution should be lower than that provided in the ordinance, and that expenditures of funds collected were to be allocated by zones. The court sustained the ordinance, concluding that such an imposition was valid "as long as the fee does not exceed the cost of the improvements required by the new development and the improvements adequately benefit the development which is the source of the fee." *Id.* at 143–44.

Another novel type of municipal exaction is the fixed benefit assessment, a fund-raising mechanism employed in California to impose the cost of broad categories of public improvements on the owners of undeveloped property. In J.W. Jones Companies v. City of San Diego, 157 Cal.App.3d 745, 203 Cal.Rptr. 580 (Ct.App.1984), the court upheld a fixed benefit assessment of approximately twenty-seven million dollars imposed by San Diego on undeveloped parcels to cover about half the cost of street and park improvements intended to serve the area of the city assessed. In sustaining the ordinance the court concluded that it was "a valid exercise of San Diego's power to require undeveloped land to bear the costs of the public facilities necessary for the health and welfare of the future residents * * *." *Id.* at 758, 203 Cal.Rptr. at 589; *see also* Smith, *supra* at 19–24 (for a general discussion of fixed benefit assessments).

Recently, some municipalities, such as San Francisco and Boston, have enacted "linkage" ordinances that condition the right to develop commercial properties on construction of or contribution to the cost of low-and moderate-income housing. *See* Smith, *supra,* 25–28; Connors & High, *supra,* 77–83. *See generally* Kayden & Pollard, "Linkage Ordinances and Traditional Exactions Analysis: The Connection Between Office Development and Housing," *Law & Contemp. Probs.,* Winter

1987, at 127 (asserting that ordinances linking housing needs with office development are sustainable under "reasonable relationship" test used by courts to analyze development exactions).

The variety of governmental devices used to impose public facility costs on new development reflect a policy choice that higher taxes for existing residents are less desirable than higher development costs for builders, and higher acquisition costs for new residents. An obvious concern is that the disproportionate or excessive use of development exactions could discourage new development or inflate housing prices to an extent that excludes large segments of the population from the available market. *See generally* Nicholas, "Impact Exactions: Economic Theory, Practice, and Incidence," *Law & Contemp. Probs.,* Winter 1987 at 85 (arguing for more restricted use of developer exactions). The complex legal and policy issues affecting both the decision to authorize impact-fee-type ordinances, and if authorized, their sustainable limits, are not before us in this case. We are convinced that when the Legislature enacted the MLUL, it did not authorize the exaction imposed on developers by Bernards Township's Ordinance 672.

III

Most, but not all, of the cases considering the validity of impact fees or other municipal exactions do so in the context of the underlying statutes that set forth the powers of local governments in reviewing subdivision and development applications. *See* Johnston, "Constitutionality of Subdivision Control Exactions: The Quest for a Rationale," 52 *Cornell L.Q.* 871, 887 (1967); *see also* 4 Anderson, *American Law of Zoning,* § 23.40 at 145 (2d ed.1977) ("The most common rationale of the decisions which disapprove the exaction of money in lieu of land for parks is that the enabling acts do not authorize the requirement.")

Our evaluation of the validity of Bernards Township's Ordinance 672 depends on whether the power to enact it is expressly conferred by, or may fairly be inferred from, the relevant provisions of the MLUL. It is fundamental that laws concerning municipal corporations are to be "liberally construed in their favor," N.J. Const. of 1947 art. IV, sec. 7, para. 11, and the MLUL expressly requires that its provisions be broadly construed. N.J.S.A. 40:55D–92. Nevertheless, in determining the legislative intent, we are constrained by the plain language of N.J.S.A. 40:55D–42 and are informed by decisional law concerning municipal subdivision regulation that preceded the statute's enactment.

The predecessor to N.J.S.A. 40:55D–42 was N.J.S.A. 40:55–1.21 (repealed), a section of the Municipal Planning Act of 1953 that authorized municipalities to require construction of on-site improvements in connection with subdivision approval, but contained no reference to off-site improvements. *See* Divan Builders v. Township of Wayne, *supra,* 66 N.J. at 595, 334 A.2d 30. Prior to the *Divan* decision, municipal authority to compel installation of or payment for off-site improvements had not been established.

* * *

It was not until *Divan Builders v. Township of Wayne, supra,* that the issue of a municipality's power to require off-site improvements was definitively resolved. There the developer's building site was substantially covered by a pond, and the preliminary subdivision plan contemplated draining the pond and "construct[ing] a conduit to pipe the water from its upstream source through the development and into an existing drainage facility on the downstream border of the site." 66 N.J. at 587, 334 A.2d 30. Subsequent to the grant of preliminary subdivision approval, the governing body amended the subdivision ordinance to establish procedures authorizing the construction of off-site improvements as a condition of subdivision approval. The planning board's recommendation for final approval of the subdivision included the condition that the applicant contribute to the township the sum of $20,000 as its "share of improving the downstream conditions of the stream which carries the drainage from the subdivision." *Id.* at 589, 334 A.2d 30. One other developer was also required to contribute to the cost of the drainage improvement.

The primary issue in *Divan* was the authority of the planning board, pursuant to the Municipal Planning Act of 1953, to require the developer to contribute to the cost of an off-site improvement. Acknowledging that the statute was silent with regard to off-site improvements, the Court concluded that recognition of a municipality's authority to require construction of or contribution to the cost of off-site improvements "comports with the overall legislative purpose to require developers in the first instance to assume the legitimate expenses of subdivision." *Id.* at 597, 334 A.2d 30. The Court observed that

> the constitutional and legislative direction to resolve questions of municipal authority broadly in favor of the local unit, compels the conclusion that, by necessary implication, N.J.S.A. 40:55–1.21 empowers a planning agency to require both on-site and off-site improvements of the physical character and type referred to in N.J.S.A. 40:55–1.20 and N.J.S.A. 40:55–1.21, *including off-site improvements made necessary by reason of the subdivision's effect on lands other than the subdivision property,* provided that the agency acts pursuant to a valid local ordinance containing suitable standards governing construction and installation of improvements. [*Id.* at 596, 334 A.2d 30 (emphasis added).]

It is against this rather sparse backdrop of New Jersey case law considering municipal power to require off-site improvements that we assess the Legislature's intent in adopting N.J.S.A. 40:55D–42. We note counsels' concurrence that although the MLUL became effective in August 1976, more than a year after the decision in *Divan,* the drafting of the MLUL was substantially completed before the opinion in *Divan* was published. Nevertheless, when the Legislature enacted the MLUL in 1976, it is presumed to have had knowledge of the relevant judicial decisions. Had its intent been to expand significantly municipal power to require contribution for off-site improvements, we are confident that this intention would have been manifested in the legislative history of the

MLUL. In its absence, we construe N.J.S.A. 40:55D–42 in a manner consistent with the rationale expressed in our [decision] in *Divan* * * *.

Thus, the critical language of the statute permits a municipality to require a developer "to pay his pro rata share of the cost of providing only *reasonable and necessary street improvements* and water, sewerage and drainage facilities, and easements therefor, located outside the property limits of the subdivision or development *but necessitated or required by construction or improvements within such subdivision or development.*" N.J.S.A. 40:55D–42 (emphasis added). We conclude that the plain meaning and obvious legislative intent was to limit municipal authority only to improvements the need for which arose as a direct consequence of the particular subdivision or development under review. The phrase "necessitated or required by construction * * * within such subdivision or development" precludes the more expansive statutory interpretation urged upon us by counsel for Bernards Township.

It is indisputable that subdivisions and development applications, in addition to their direct impact on municipal facilities in the surrounding area, have a cumulative and wide-ranging impact on the entire community. We cannot fault the logic or the foresight that induces a municipality such as Bernards Township to consider the long-term impact of permitted development on municipal resources and public facilities. But as yet the Legislature has not delegated to municipalities the far-reaching power to depart from traditionally authorized methods of financing public facilities so as to allocate the cost of substantial public projects among new developments on the basis of their anticipated impact.

For the reasons stated, we hold that Ordinance 642 is an invalid exercise of municipal authority. We are in accord with the Appellate Division's conclusion that the invalidation of the ordinance should not be limited to prospective application only.

The judgment of the Appellate Division is affirmed.

NOLLAN v. CALIFORNIA COASTAL COMMISSION

Supreme Court of the United States, 1987.
483 U.S. 825.

JUSTICE SCALIA delivered the opinion of the Court.

James and Marilyn Nollan appeal from a decision of the California Court of Appeal ruling that the California Coastal Commission could condition its grant of permission to rebuild their house on their transfer to the public of an easement across their beachfront property. 177 Cal.App.3d 719, 223 Cal.Rptr. 28 (1986). The California Court rejected their claim that imposition of that condition violates the Takings Clause of the Fifth Amendment, as incorporated against the States by the Fourteenth Amendment. We noted probable jurisdiction.

I

The Nollans own a beachfront lot in Ventura County, California. A quarter-mile north of their property is Faria County Park, an oceanside public park with a public beach and recreation area. Another public beach area, known locally as "the Cove," lies 1,800 feet south of their lot. A concrete seawall approximately eight feet high separates the beach portion of the Nollans' property from the rest of the lot. The historic mean high tide line determines the lot's oceanside boundary.

The Nollans originally leased their property with an option to buy. The building on the lot was a small bungalow, totaling 504 square feet, which for a time they rented to summer vacationers. After years of rental use, however, the building had fallen into disrepair, and could no longer be rented out.

The Nollans' option to purchase was conditioned on their promise to demolish the bungalow and replace it. In order to do so, under California Public Resources Code §§ 30106, 30212, and 30600 (West 1986), they were required to obtain a coastal development permit from the California Coastal Commission. On February 25, 1982, they submitted a permit application to the Commission in which they proposed to demolish the existing structure and replace it with a three-bedroom house in keeping with the rest of the neighborhood.

The Nollans were informed that their application had been placed on the administrative calendar, and that the Commission staff had recommended that the permit be granted subject to the condition that they allow the public an easement to pass across a portion of their property bounded by the mean high tide line on one side, and their seawall on the other side. This would make it easier for the public to get to Faria County Park and the Cove. The Nollans protested imposition of the condition, but the Commission overruled their objections and granted the permit subject to their recordation of a deed restriction granting the easement.

On June 3, 1982, the Nollans filed a petition for writ of administrative mandamus asking the Ventura County Superior Court to invalidate the access condition. They argued that the condition could not be imposed absent evidence that their proposed development would have a direct adverse impact on public access to the beach. The court agreed, and remanded the case to the Commission for a full evidentiary hearing on that issue.

On remand, the Commission held a public hearing, after which it made further factual findings and reaffirmed its imposition of the condition. It found that the new house would increase blockage of the view of the ocean, thus contributing to the development of "a 'wall' of residential structures" that would prevent the public "psychologically * * * from realizing a stretch of coastline exists nearby that they have every right to visit." The new house would also increase private use of the shorefront. These effects of construction of the house, along with other area development, would cumulatively "burden the public's ability to traverse to and along the shorefront." Therefore the Commission could properly require the Nollans to offset that burden by providing additional lateral access to the public beaches in the form of an easement across their property. The Commission also noted that it had similarly conditioned 43 out of 60 coastal development permits along the same tract of land, and that of the 17 not so conditioned, 14 had been approved when the Commission did not have administrative regulations in place allowing imposition of the condition, and the remaining 3 had not involved shorefront property.

The Nollans filed a supplemental petition for a writ of administrative mandamus with the Superior Court, in which they argued that imposition of the access condition violated the Takings Clause of the Fifth Amendment, as incorporated against the States by the Fourteenth Amendment. The Superior Court ruled in their favor on statutory grounds, finding, in part to avoid "issues of constitutionality," that the California Coastal Act of 1976, Cal.Pub.Res.Code Ann. § 3000 *et seq.,* authorized the Commission to impose public access conditions on coastal development permits for the replacement of an existing single-family home with a new one only where the proposed development would have an adverse impact on public access to the sea. In the Court's view, the administrative record did not provide an adequate factual basis for concluding that replacement of the bungalow with the house would create a direct or cumulative burden on public access to the sea. Accordingly, the Superior Court granted the writ of mandamus and directed that the permit condition be struck.

The Commission appealed to the California Court of Appeal. While that appeal was pending, the Nollans satisfied the condition on their option to purchase by tearing down the bungalow and building the new house, and bought the property. They did not notify the Commission that they were taking that action.

The Court of Appeal reversed the Superior Court. 177 Cal.App.3d 719, 223 Cal.Rptr. 28 (1986). It disagreed with the Superior Court's interpretation of the Coastal Act, finding that it required that a coastal permit for the construction of a new house whose floor area, height or bulk was more than 10% larger than that of the house it was replacing be conditioned on a grant of access. It also ruled that the requirement did not violate the Constitution under the reasoning of an earlier case of the Court of Appeal, Grupe v. California Coastal Comm'n, 166 Cal. App.3d 148, 212 Cal.Rptr. 578 (1985). In that case, the court had found that so long as a project contributed to the need for public access, even if the project standing alone had not created the need for access, and even if there was only an indirect relationship between the access exacted and the need to which the project contributed, imposition of an access condition on a development permit was sufficiently related to burdens created by the project to be constitutional. The Court of Appeal ruled that the record established that that was the situation with respect to the Nollans' house. It ruled that the Nollans' taking claim also failed because, although the condition diminished the value of the Nollans' lot, it did not deprive them of all reasonable use of their property. Since, in the Court of Appeal's view, there was no statutory or constitutional obstacle to imposition of the access condition, the Superior Court erred in granting the writ of mandamus. The Nollans appealed to this Court, raising only the constitutional question.

II

Had California simply required the Nollans to make an easement across their beachfront available to the public on a permanent basis in order to increase public access to the beach, rather than conditioning their permit to rebuild their house on their agreeing to do so, we have no doubt there would have been a taking. To say that the appropriation of a public easement across a landowner's premises does not constitute the taking of a property interest but rather, (as Justice Brennan contends [in his dissenting opinion]) "a mere restriction on its use," is to use words in a manner that deprives them of all their ordinary meaning. Indeed, one of the principal uses of the eminent domain power is to assure that the government be able to require conveyance of just such interests, so long as it pays for them. Perhaps because the point is so obvious, we have never been confronted with a controversy that required us to rule upon it, but our cases' analysis of the effect of other governmental action leads to the same conclusion. We have repeatedly held that, as to property reserved by its owner for private use, "the right to exclude [others is] 'one of the most essential sticks in the bundle of rights that are commonly characterized as property.' " Loretto v. Teleprompter Manhattan CATV Corp., 458 U.S. 419, 433 (1982), quoting Kaiser Aetna v. United States, 444 U.S. 164, 176 (1979). In *Loretto* we observed that where governmental action results in "[a] permanent physical occupation" of the property, by the government itself or by others, see 458 U.S., at 432–433, n. 9, "our cases uniformly have found a taking to the extent of the occupation, without regard to whether the action achieves an important public benefit or has only minimal economic impact on the owner," *id.*, at 434–435. We think a "permanent physical occupation" has occurred, for purposes of that rule, where individuals are given a permanent and continuous right to pass to and fro, so that the real property may continuously be traversed, even though no particular individual is permitted to station himself permanently upon the premises.

* * *

Given, then, that requiring uncompensated conveyance of the easement outright would violate the Fourteenth Amendment, the question becomes whether requiring it to be conveyed as a condition for issuing a land use permit alters the outcome. We have long recognized that land use regulation does not effect a taking if it "substantially advance[s] legitimate state interests" and does not "den[y] an owner economically viable use of his land," Agins v. Tiburon, 447 U.S. 255, 260 (1980). See also Penn Central Transportation Co. v. New York City, 438 U.S. 104, 127 (1978) ("a use restriction may constitute a 'taking' if not reasonably necessary to the effectuation of a substantial government purpose"). Our cases have not elaborated on the standards for determining what constitutes a "legitimate state interest" or what type of connection between the regulation and the state interest satisfies the requirement that the former "substantially advance" the latter. They have made clear, however, that a broad range of governmental purposes and regulations satisfies these requirements. See Agins v. Tiburon, *supra,* 447 U.S., at 260–262 (scenic zoning); *Penn Central Transportation Co. v. New York City, supra* (landmark preservation); Euclid v. Ambler Realty Co., 272 U.S. 365 (1926) (residential zoning). The Commission argues that among these permissible purposes are protecting the public's ability to see the beach, assisting the public in overcoming the "psychological barrier" to using the beach created by a developed shorefront, and preventing congestion on the public beaches. We assume, without deciding, that this is so—in which case the Commission unquestionably would be able to deny the Nollans their permit outright if their new house (alone, or by reason of the cumulative impact produced in conjunction with other construction)[1] would substantially impede these purposes, unless the denial would interfere so drastically with the Nollans' use of their property as to constitute a taking.

The Commission argues that a permit condition that serves the same legitimate police-power purpose as a refusal to issue the permit should not be found to be a taking if the refusal to issue the permit would not constitute a taking. We agree. Thus, if the Commission attached to the permit some condition that would have protected the public's ability to see the beach notwithstanding construction of the new house—for example, a height limitation, a width restriction, or a ban on fences—so long as the Commission could have exercised its police power (as we have assumed it could) to forbid construction of the house altogether, imposition of the condition would also be constitutional. Moreover (and here we come closer to the facts of the present case), the condition would be constitutional even if it consisted of the requirement that the Nollans provide a viewing spot on their property for passersby with whose sighting of the ocean their new house would interfere. Although such a requirement, constituting a permanent grant of continuous access to the property, would have to be considered a taking if it were not attached to a development permit, the Commission's assumed power to forbid construction of the house in order to protect the public's view of the beach must surely include the power to condition construction upon some concession by the owner, even a concession of property

---

1. If the Nollans were being singled out to bear the burden of California's attempt to remedy these problems, although they had not contributed to it more than other coastal landowners, the State's action, even if otherwise valid, might violate either the incorporated Takings Clause or the Equal Protection Clause. One of the principal purposes of the Takings Clause is "to bar Government from forcing some people alone to bear public burdens which, in all fairness and justice, should be borne by the public as a whole." Armstrong v. United States, 364 U.S. 40, 49 (1960); see also San Diego Gas & Electric Co. v. San Diego, 450 U.S. 621, 656 (1981) (Brennan, J., dissenting); Penn Central Transportation Co. v. New York City, 438 U.S. 104 (1978). But that is not the basis of the Nollans' challenge here.

rights, that serves the same end. If a prohibition designed to accomplish that purpose would be a legitimate exercise of the police power rather than a taking, it would be strange to conclude that providing the owner an alternative to that prohibition which accomplishes the same purpose is not.

The evident constitutional propriety disappears, however, if the condition substituted for the prohibition utterly fails to further the end advanced as the justification for the prohibition. When that essential nexus is eliminated, the situation becomes the same as if California law forbade shouting fire in a crowded theater, but granted dispensations to those willing to contribute $100 to the state treasury. While a ban on shouting fire can be a core exercise of the State's police power to protect the public safety, and can thus meet even our stringent standards for regulation of speech, adding the unrelated condition alters the purpose to one which, while it may be legitimate, is inadequate to sustain the ban. Therefore, even though, in a sense, requiring a $100 tax contribution in order to shout fire is a lesser restriction on speech than an outright ban, it would not pass constitutional muster. Similarly here, the lack of nexus between the condition and the original purpose of the building restriction converts that purpose to something other than what it was. The purpose then becomes, quite simply, the obtaining of an easement to serve some valid governmental purpose, but without payment of compensation. Whatever may be the outer limits of "legitimate state interests" in the takings and land use context, this is not one of them. In short, unless the permit condition serves the same governmental purpose as the development ban, the building restriction is not a valid regulation of land use but "an out-and-out plan of extortion."

III

The Commission claims that it concedes as much, and that we may sustain the condition at issue here by finding that it is reasonably related to the public need or burden that the Nollans' new house creates or to which it contributes. We can accept, for purposes of discussion, the Commission's proposed test as to how close a "fit" between the condition and the burden is required, because we find that this case does not meet even the most untailored standards. The Commission's principal contention to the contrary essentially turns on a play on the word "access." The Nollans' new house, the Commission found, will interfere with "visual access" to the beach. That in turn (along with other shorefront development) will interfere with the desire of people who drive past the Nollans' house to use the beach, thus creating a "psychological barrier" to "access." The Nollans' new house will also, by a process not altogether clear from the Commission's opinion but presumably potent enough to more than offset the effects of the psychological barrier, increase the use of the public beaches, thus creating the need for more "access." These burdens on "access" would be alleviated by a requirement that the Nollans provide "lateral access" to the beach.

Rewriting the argument to eliminate the play on words makes clear that there is nothing to it. It is quite impossible to understand how a requirement that people already on the public beaches be able to walk across the Nollans' property reduces any obstacles to viewing the beach created by the new house. It is also impossible to understand how it lowers any "psychological barrier" to using the public beaches, or how it helps to remedy any additional congestion on them caused by construction of the Nollans' new house. We therefore find that the Commission's imposition of the permit condition cannot be treated as an exercise of its land use power for any of these purposes. Our conclusion on this point is consistent with the approach taken by every other court that has considered the question, with the exception of the California state courts.

Justice Brennan argues that imposition of the access requirement is not irrational. In his version of the Commission's argument, the reason for the requirement is that in its absence, a person looking toward the beach from the road will see a street of residential structures including the Nollans' new home and conclude that there is no public beach nearby. If, however, that person sees people passing and repassing along the dry sand behind the Nollans' home, he will realize that there is a public beach somewhere in the vicinity. The Commission's action, however, was based on the opposite factual finding that the wall of houses completely blocked the view of the beach and that a person looking from the road would not be able to see it at all.

Even if the Commission had made the finding that Justice Brennan proposes, however, it is not certain that it would suffice. We do not share Justice Brennan's confidence that the Commission "should have little difficulty in the future in utilizing its expertise to demonstrate a specific connection between provisions for access and burdens on access," that will avoid the effect of today's decision. We view the Fifth Amendment's property clause to be more than a pleading requirement, and compliance with it to be more than an exercise in cleverness and imagination. As indicated earlier, our cases describe the condition for abridgement of property rights through the police power as a *"substantial advanc[ing]"* of a legitimate State interest. We are inclined to be particularly careful about the adjective where the actual conveyance of property is made a condition to the lifting of a land use restriction, since in that context there is heightened risk that the purpose is avoidance of the compensation requirement, rather than the stated police power objective.

We are left, then, with the Commission's justification for the access requirement unrelated to land use regulation:

> "Finally, the Commission notes that there are several existing provisions of pass and repass lateral access benefits already given by past Faria Beach Tract applicants as a result of prior coastal permit decisions. The access required as a condition of this permit is part of a comprehensive program to provide continuous public access along Faria Beach as the lots undergo development or redevelopment."

That is simply an expression of the Commission's belief that the public interest will be served by a continuous strip of publicly accessible beach along the coast. The Commission may well be right that it is a good idea, but that does not establish that the Nollans (and other coastal residents) alone can be compelled to contribute to its realization. Rather, California is free to advance its "comprehensive program," if it wishes, by using its power of eminent domain for this "public purpose," see U.S. Const., Amdt. V; but if it wants an easement across the Nollans' property, it must pay for it.

Reversed.

Notes and Questions

1. Justice Brennan's characterization of the access easement on the Nollans' property as "a mere restriction on its use" is open to question. An access easement is affirmative in nature, permitting use of the servient property. *See* J. Bruce & J. Ely, *The Law of Easements and Licenses in Land* ¶ 2.03 (rev.ed.1995 & Supp.1998).

2. Suppose that the California Coastal Commission conditioned a building permit upon the grant of an easement of view. Would the Supreme Court have reached the same result?

DOLAN v. CITY OF TIGARD

Supreme Court of the United States, 1994.
512 U.S. 374.

CHIEF JUSTICE REHNQUIST delivered the opinion of the Court.

Petitioner challenges the decision of the Oregon Supreme Court which held that the city of Tigard could condition the approval of her building permit on the dedication of a portion of her property for flood control and traffic improvements. 317 Ore. 110, 854 P.2d 437 (1993). We granted certiorari to resolve a question left open by our decision in *Nollan v. California Coastal Comm'n*, 483 U.S. 825 (1987), of what is the required degree of connection between the exactions imposed by the city and the projected impacts of the proposed development.

I

The State of Oregon enacted a comprehensive land use management program in 1973. Ore.Rev.Stat. §§ 197.005–197.860 (1991). The program required all Oregon cities and counties to adopt new comprehensive land use plans that were consistent with the statewide planning goals. The plans are implemented by land use regulations which are part of an integrated hierarchy of legally binding goals, plans, and regulations. Pursuant to the State's requirements, the city of Tigard, a community of some 30,000 residents on the southwest edge of Portland, developed a comprehensive plan and codified it in its Community Development Code (CDC). The CDC requires property owners in the area zoned Central Business District to comply with a 15% open space and landscaping requirement, which limits total site coverage, including all structures and paved parking, to 85% of the parcel. After the completion of a transportation study that identified congestion in the Central Business District as a particular problem, the city adopted a plan for a pedestrian/bicycle pathway intended to encourage alternatives to automobile transportation for short trips. The CDC requires that new development facilitate this plan by dedicating land for pedestrian pathways where provided for in the pedestrian/bicycle pathway plan.

The city also adopted a Master Drainage Plan (Drainage Plan). The Drainage Plan noted that flooding occurred in several areas along Fanno Creek, including areas near petitioner's property. The Drainage Plan also established that the increase in impervious surfaces associated with continued urbanization would exacerbate these flooding problems. To combat these risks, the Drainage Plan suggested a series of improvements to the Fanno Creek Basin, including channel excavation in the area next to petitioner's property. Other recommendations included ensuring that the floodplain remains free of structures and that it be preserved as greenways to minimize flood damage to structures. The Drainage Plan concluded that the cost of these improvements should be shared based on both direct and indirect benefits, with property owners along the waterways paying more due to the direct benefit that they would receive. [The] CDC * * * and the Tigard Park Plan carry out these recommendations.

Petitioner Florence Dolan owns a plumbing and electric supply store located on Main Street in the Central Business District of the city. The store covers approximately 9,700 square feet on the eastern side of a 1.67–acre parcel, which includes a gravel parking lot. Fanno Creek flows through the southwestern corner of the lot and along its western boundary. The year-round flow of the creek renders the area within the creek's 100–year floodplain virtually unusable for commercial development. The city's comprehensive plan includes the Fanno Creek floodplain as part of the city's greenway system.

Petitioner applied to the city for a permit to redevelop the site. Her proposed plans called for nearly doubling the size of the store to 17,600 square feet and paving a 39–space parking lot. The existing store, located on the opposite side of the parcel, would be razed in sections as construction progressed on the new building. In the second phase of the project, petitioner proposed to build an additional structure on the northeast side of the site for complementary businesses and to provide more parking. The proposed expansion and intensified use are consistent with the city's zoning scheme in the Central Business District.

The City Planning Commission (Commission) granted petitioner's permit application subject to conditions imposed by the city's CDC. The CDC establishes the following standard for site development review approval:

"Where landfill and/or development is allowed within and adjacent to the 100–year floodplain, the City shall require the dedication of sufficient open land area for greenway adjoining and within the floodplain. This area shall include portions at a suitable elevation for the construction of a pedestrian/bicycle pathway within the floodplain in accordance with the adopted pedestrian/bicycle plan."

Thus, the Commission required that petitioner dedicate the portion of her property lying within the 100–year floodplain for improvement of a storm drainage system along Fanno Creek and that she dedicate an additional 15–foot strip of land adjacent to the floodplain as a pedestrian/bicycle pathway. The dedication required by that condition encompasses approximately 7,000 square feet, or roughly 10% of the property. In accordance with city practice, petitioner could rely on the dedicated property to meet the 15% open space and landscaping requirement mandated by the city's zoning scheme. The city would bear the cost of maintaining a landscaped buffer between the dedicated area and the new store.

Petitioner requested variances from the CDC standards. Variances are granted only where it can be shown that, owing to special circumstances related to a specific piece of the land, the literal interpretation of the applicable zoning provisions would cause "an undue or unnecessary hardship" unless the variance is granted. Rather than posing alternative mitigating measures to offset the expected impacts of her proposed development, as allowed under the CDC, petitioner simply argued that her proposed development would not conflict with the policies of the comprehensive plan. The Commission denied the request.

The Commission made a series of findings concerning the relationship between the dedicated conditions and the projected impacts of petitioner's project. First, the Commission noted that "[i]t is reasonable to assume that customers and employees of the future uses of this site could utilize a pedestrian/bicycle pathway adjacent to this development for their transportation and recreational needs." The Commission noted that the site plan has provided for bicycle parking in a rack in front of the proposed building and "[i]t is reasonable to expect that some of the users of the bicycle parking provided for by the site plan will use the pathway adjacent to Fanno Creek if it is constructed." In addition, the Commission found that creation of a convenient, safe pedestrian/bicycle pathway system as an alternative means of transportation "could offset some of the traffic demand on [nearby] streets and lessen the increase in traffic congestion."

The Commission went on to note that the required floodplain dedication would be reasonably related to petitioner's request to intensify the use of the site given the increase in the impervious surface. The Commission stated that the "anticipated increased storm water flow from the subject property to an already strained creek and drainage basin can only add to the public need to manage the stream channel and floodplain for drainage purposes." Based on this anticipated increased storm water flow, the Commission concluded that "the requirement of dedication of the floodplain area on the site is related to the applicant's plan to intensify development on the site." Ibid. The Tigard City Council approved the Commission's final order, subject to one minor modification; the city council reassigned the responsibility for surveying and marking the floodplain area from petitioner to the city's engineering department.

* * *

II

The Takings Clause of the Fifth Amendment of the United States Constitution, made applicable to the States through the Fourteenth Amendment, *Chicago, B. & Q.R. Co. v. Chicago*, 166 U.S. 226, 239 (1897), provides: "[N]or shall private property be taken for public use, without just compensation." One of the principal purposes of the Takings Clause is "to bar Government from forcing some people alone to bear public burdens which, in all fairness and justice, should be borne by the public as a whole." *Armstrong v. United States*, 364 U.S. 40, 49, (1960). Without question, had the city simply required petitioner to dedicate a strip of land along Fanno Creek for public use, rather than conditioning the grant of her permit to redevelop her property on such a dedication, a taking would have occurred. Such public access would deprive petitioner of the right to exclude others, "one of the most essential sticks in the bundle of rights that are commonly characterized as property." *Kaiser Aetna v. United States*, 444 U.S. 164, 176 (1979).

On the other side of the ledger, the authority of state and local governments to engage in land use planning has been sustained against constitutional challenge as long ago as our decision in *Village of Euclid v. Ambler Realty Co.*, 272 U.S. 365 (1926). "Government hardly could go on if to some extent values incident to property could not be diminished without paying for every such change in the general law." *Pennsylvania Coal Co. v. Mahon*, 260 U.S. 393 (1922). A land use regulation does not effect a taking if it "substantially advance[s] legitimate state interests" and does not "den[y] an owner economically viable use of his land." *Agins v. City of Tiburon*, 447 U.S. 255, 260 (1980).

The sort of land use regulations discussed in the cases just cited, however, differ in two relevant particulars from the present case. First, they involved essentially legislative determinations classifying entire areas of the city, whereas here the city made an adjudicative decision to condition petitioner's application for a building permit on an individual parcel. Second, the conditions imposed were not simply a limitation on the use petitioner might make of her own parcel, but a requirement that she deed portions of the property to the city. In *Nollan*, we held that governmental authority to exact such a condition was circumscribed by the Fifth and Fourteenth Amendments. Under the well-settled doctrine of "unconstitutional conditions," the government may not require a person to give up a constitutional right—here the right to receive just compensation when property is taken for a public use—in exchange for a discretionary benefit conferred by the government where the benefit sought has little or no relationship to the property.

Petitioner contends that the city has forced her to choose between the building permit and her right under the Fifth Amendment to just compensation for the public easements. Petitioner does not quarrel with the city's authority to exact some forms of dedication as a condition for the grant of a building permit, but challenges the showing made by the city to justify these exactions. She argues that the city has identified "no special benefits" conferred on her, and has not identified any "special quantifiable burdens" created by her new store that would justify the particular dedications required from her which are not required from the public at large.

III

In evaluating petitioner's claim, we must first determine whether the "essential nexus" exists between the "legitimate state interest" and the permit condition exacted by the city. *Nollan*, 483 U.S., at 837. If we find that a nexus exists, we must then decide the required degree of connection between the exactions and the projected impact of the proposed development. We were not required to reach this question in *Nollan*, because we concluded that the connection did not meet even the loosest standard. Here, however, we must decide this question.

A

We addressed the essential nexus question in *Nollan*. The California Coastal Commission demanded a lateral public easement across the Nollans' beachfront lot in exchange for a permit to demolish an existing bungalow and replace it with a three-bedroom house. The public easement was designed to connect two public beaches that were separated by the Nollan's property. The Coastal Commission had asserted that the public easement condition was imposed to promote the legitimate state interest of diminishing the "blockage of the view of the ocean" caused by construction of the larger house.

We agreed that the Coastal Commission's concern with protecting visual access to the ocean constituted a legitimate public interest. We also agreed that the permit condition would have been constitutional "even if it consisted of the requirement that the Nollans provide a viewing spot on their property for passersby with whose sighting of the ocean their new house would interfere." We resolved, however, that the Coastal Commission's regulatory authority was set completely adrift from its constitutional moorings when it claimed that a nexus existed between visual access to the ocean and a permit condition requiring lateral public access along the Nollans' beachfront lot. How enhancing the public's ability to "traverse to and along the shorefront" served the same governmental purpose of "visual access to the ocean" from the roadway was beyond our ability to countenance. The absence of a nexus left the Coastal Commission in the position of simply trying to obtain an easement through gimmickry, which converted a valid regulation of land use into " 'an out-and-out plan of extortion.' " *Ibid.*, quoting *J.E.D. Associates, Inc. v. Atkinson*, 121 N.H. 581, 584, 432 A.2d 12, 14–15 (1981).

No such gimmicks are associated with the permit conditions imposed by the city in this case. Undoubtedly, the prevention of flooding along Fanno Creek and the reduction of traffic congestion in the Central Business District qualify as the type of legitimate public purposes we have upheld. It seems equally obvious that a nexus exists between preventing flooding along Fanno Creek and limiting development within the creek's 100–year floodplain. Petitioner proposes to double the size of her retail store and to pave her now-gravel parking lot, thereby expanding the impervious surface on the property and increasing the amount of storm water runoff into Fanno Creek.

The same may be said for the city's attempt to reduce traffic congestion by providing for alternative means of transportation. In theory, a pedestrian/bicycle pathway provides a useful alternative means of transportation for workers and shoppers. * * *

B

The second part of our analysis requires us to determine whether the degree of the exactions demanded by the city's permit conditions bears the required relationship to the projected impact of petitioner's proposed development. * * *

The city required that petitioner dedicate "to the City as Greenway all portions of the site that fall within the existing 100–year floodplain [of Fanno Creek] ... and all property 15 feet above [the floodplain] boundary." Id., at 113, n. 3, 854 P.2d, at 439, n. 3. In addition, the city demanded that the retail store be designed so as not to intrude into the greenway area. The city relies on the Commission's rather tentative findings that increased storm water flow from petitioner's property "can only add to the public need to manage the [floodplain] for drainage purposes" to support its conclusion that the "requirement of dedication of the floodplain area on the site is related to the applicant's plan to intensify development on the site."

The city made the following specific findings relevant to the pedestrian/bicycle pathway:

"In addition, the proposed expanded use of this site is anticipated to generate additional vehicular traffic thereby increasing congestion on nearby collector and arterial streets. Creation of a convenient, safe pedestrian/bicycle pathway system as an alternative means of transportation could offset some of the traffic demand on these nearby streets and lessen the increase in traffic congestion."

The question for us is whether these findings are constitutionally sufficient to justify the conditions imposed by the city on petitioner's building permit. Since state courts have been dealing with this question a good deal longer than we have, we turn to representative decisions made by them.

In some States, very generalized statements as to the necessary connection between the required dedication and the proposed development seem to suffice. We think this standard is too lax to adequately protect petitioner's right to just compensation if her property is taken for a public purpose.

Other state courts require a very exacting correspondence, described as the "specifi[c] and uniquely attributable" test. * * * We do not think the Federal Constitution requires such exacting scrutiny, given the nature of the interests involved.

A number of state courts have taken an intermediate position, requiring the municipality to show a "reasonable relationship" between the required dedication and the impact of the proposed development. * * *

* * *

We think the "reasonable relationship" test adopted by a majority of the state courts is closer to the federal constitutional norm than either of those previously discussed. But we do not adopt it as such, partly because the term "reasonable relationship" seems confusingly similar to the term "rational basis" which describes the minimal level of scrutiny under the Equal Protection Clause of the Fourteenth Amendment. We think a term such as "rough proportionality" best encapsulates what we hold to be the requirement of the Fifth Amendment. No precise mathematical calculation is required, but the city must make some sort of individualized determination that the required dedication is related both in nature and extent to the impact of the proposed development.[1]

* * * We turn now to analysis of whether the findings relied upon by the city here, first with respect to the floodplain easement, and second with respect to the pedestrian/bicycle path, satisfied these requirements.

It is axiomatic that increasing the amount of impervious surface will increase the quantity and rate of storm water flow from petitioner's property. Therefore, keeping the floodplain open and free from development would likely confine the pressures on Fanno Creek created by petitioner's development. In fact, because petitioner's property lies within the Central Business District, the CDC already required that petitioner leave 15% of it as open space and the undeveloped floodplain would have nearly satisfied that requirement. But the city demanded more—it not only wanted petitioner not to build in the floodplain, but it also wanted petitioner's property along Fanno Creek for its greenway system. The city has never said why a public greenway, as opposed to a private one, was required in the interest of flood control.

The difference to petitioner, of course, is the loss of her ability to exclude others. As we have noted, this right to exclude others is "one of

---

1. JUSTICE STEVENS' dissent takes us to task for placing the burden on the city to justify the required dedication. He is correct in arguing that in evaluating most generally applicable zoning regulations, the burden properly rests on the party challenging the regulation to prove that it constitutes an arbitrary regulation of property rights. See, e.g., *Village of Euclid* v. *Ambler Realty Co.,* 272 U.S. 365 (1926). Here, by contrast, the city made an adjudicative decision to condition petitioner's application for a building permit on an individual parcel. In this situation, the burden properly rests on the city. See *Nollan,* 483 U.S., at 836. * * *

the most essential sticks in the bundle of rights that are commonly characterized as property." *Kaiser Aetna*, 444 U.S., at 176. It is difficult to see why recreational visitors trampling along petitioner's floodplain easement are sufficiently related to the city's legitimate interest in reducing flooding problems along Fanno Creek, and the city has not attempted to make any individualized determination to support this part of its request.

* * *

If petitioner's proposed development had somehow encroached on existing greenway space in the city, it would have been reasonable to require petitioner to provide some alternative greenway space for the public either on her property or elsewhere. But that is not the case here. We conclude that the findings upon which the city relies do not show the required reasonable relationship between the floodplain easement and the petitioner's proposed new building.

With respect to the pedestrian/bicycle pathway, we have no doubt that the city was correct in finding that the larger retail sales facility proposed by petitioner will increase traffic on the streets of the Central Business District. The city estimates that the proposed development would generate roughly 435 additional trips per day. Dedications for streets, sidewalks, and other public ways are generally reasonable exactions to avoid excessive congestion from a proposed property use. But on the record before us, the city has not met its burden of demonstrating that the additional number of vehicle and bicycle trips generated by petitioner's development reasonably relate to the city's requirement for a dedication of the pedestrian/bicycle pathway easement. The city simply found that the creation of the pathway "could offset some of the traffic demand ... and lessen the increase in traffic congestion."

As Justice Peterson of the Supreme Court of Oregon explained in his dissenting opinion, however, "[t]he findings of fact that the bicycle pathway system '*could* offset some of the traffic demand' is a far cry from a finding that the bicycle pathway system *will*, or is *likely to*, offset some of the traffic demand." 317 Ore., at 127, 854 P.2d, at 447 (emphasis in original). No precise mathematical calculation is required, but the city must make some effort to quantify its findings in support of the dedication for the pedestrian/bicycle pathway beyond the conclusory statement that it could offset some of the traffic demand generated.

IV

Cities have long engaged in the commendable task of land use planning, made necessary by increasing urbanization, particularly in metropolitan areas such as Portland. The city's goals of reducing flooding hazards and traffic congestion, and providing for public greenways, are laudable, but there are outer limits to how this may be done. "A strong public desire to improve the public condition [will not] warrant achieving the desire by a shorter cut than the constitutional way of paying for the change." *Pennsylvania Coal*, 260 U.S., at 416.

The judgment of the Supreme Court of Oregon is reversed, and the case is remanded for further proceedings not inconsistent with this opinion.

It is so ordered.

Notes, Problems, and Questions

1. In late 1997, the *Dolan* case was settled. The parties' agreement included provision that the landowners be paid $1,500,000 by the City of Tigard. *See* Ottey, *Tigard will pay Dolans $1.5 million,* Portland Oregonian, Nov. 19, 1997, at E6.

2. Application of the *Dolan* test to land use exactions has generated a good deal of litigation. *See, e.g.,* Sparks v. Douglas County, 127 Wash.2d 901, 904 P.2d 738 (1995) (finding rights-of-way dedication as condition of development approval did not constitute unconstitutional taking). Controversy also exists as to the long-range impact of *Dolan. Compare* Johnson, *Avoid, Minimize, Mitigate: The Continuing Constitutionality of Wetlands Mitigation After* Dolan v. City of Tigard, 6 Fordham Envtl.L.J. 689 (1995) (arguing for limited reading of *Dolan) with* Kmiec, *At Last, The Supreme Court Solves the Takings Puzzle,* 19 Harv. J.L. & Pub.Pol'y 147 (1995) (contending *Dolan* broadly applicable).

3. In Ehrlich v. City of Culver City, 12 Cal.4th 854, 50 Cal.Rptr.2d 242, 911 P.2d 429 (1996), *cert. denied* 117 S.Ct. 299 (1996), a fragmented Supreme Court of California ruled that the *Dolan* test applied to the payment of monetary exactions as well as to mandated dedications of land. But the court limited its holding to exactions imposed on individual projects through the exercise of discretion rather than by general legislation governing a class of property owners. The court upheld the imposition of a fee on the developer to install public art as prescribed by ordinance, but struck down a fee imposed on the project to fund recreational facilities. *See* Kanner, *Tennis Anyone? How California Judges Made Land Ransom and Art Censorship Legal,* 25 Real Est.L.J. 214 (1997) (criticizing *Ehrlich* decision, and asserting that exactions are being used in lieu of local taxes to acquire social goods at expense of targeted landowners).

4. Under the *Dolan* approach, could a city charge a subdeveloper a fee in lieu of dedication and then use the fee to acquire park land in another part of the community?

5. Can the Centerville City Council achieve its goal of constructing new sewers and parks at little or no cost to current residents by employing subdivision exactions and sewer connection charges?

6. In a portion of the *Dolan* opinion not including in this edited version of the decision, the Supreme Court signaled an intention to continue to give careful attention to the protection of the interests of property owners. The majority noted: "We see no reason why the Takings Clause of the Fifth Amendment, as much a part of the Bill of Rights as the First Amendment or Fourth Amendment, should be relegated to the status of a poor relation...." 512 U.S. at 392.

E. GROWTH MANAGEMENT

GOLDEN v. PLANNING BOARD OF THE TOWN OF RAMAPO

Court of Appeals of New York, 1972.
30 N.Y.2d 359, 334 N.Y.S.2d 138, 285 N.E.2d
291, appeal dismissed 409 U.S. 1003.

SCILEPPI, JUDGE.

* * *

Experiencing the pressures of an increase in population and the ancillary problem of providing municipal facilities and services, the Town of Ramapo, as early as 1964, made application for grant under section 801 of the Housing Act of 1964 (78 U.S.Stat. 769) to develop a master plan. The plan's preparation included a four-volume study of the existing land uses, public facilities, transportation, industry and commerce, housing needs and projected population trends. The proposals appearing in the studies were subsequently adopted pursuant to section 272–a of the Town Law, Consol.Laws, c. 62, in July, 1966 and implemented by way of a master plan. The master plan was followed by the adoption of a comprehensive zoning ordinance. Additional sewage district and drainage studies were undertaken which culminated in the adoption of a capital budget, providing for the development of the improvements specified in the master plan within the next six years. Pursuant to section 271 of the Town Law, authorizing comprehensive planning, and as a supplement to the capital budget, the Town Board adopted a capital program which provides for the location and sequence of additional capital improvements for the 12 years following the life of the capital budget. The two plans, covering a period of 18 years, detail the capital improvements projected for maximum development and conform to the specifications set forth in the master plan, the official map and drainage plan.

Based upon these criteria, the Town subsequently adopted the subject amendments for the alleged purpose of eliminating premature subdivision and urban sprawl. Residential development is to proceed according to the provision of adequate municipal facilities and services, with the assurance that any concomitant restraint upon property use is to be of a "temporary" nature and that other private uses, including the construction of individual housing, are authorized.

The amendments did not rezone or reclassify any land into different residential or use districts, but, for the purposes of implementing the proposals appearing in the comprehensive plan, consist, in the main, of additions to the definitional sections of the ordinance, section 46–3, and the adoption of a new class of "Special Permit Uses", designated "Residential Development Use." "Residential Development Use" is defined as "The erection or construction of dwellings or any vacant plots,

lots or parcels of land" (§ 46–3, as amd.); and, any person who acts so as to come within that definition, "shall be deemed to be engaged in residential development which shall be a separate use classification under this ordinance and subject to the requirement of obtaining a special permit from the Town Board" (§ 46–3, as amd.).

The standards for the issuance of special permits are framed in terms of the availability to the proposed subdivision plat of five essential facilities or services: specifically (1) public sanitary sewers or approved substitutes; (2) drainage facilities; (3) improved public parks or recreation facilities, including public schools; (4) State, county or town roads—major, secondary or collector; and, (5) firehouses. No special permit shall issue unless the proposed residential development has accumulated 15 development points, to be computed on a sliding scale of values assigned to the specified improvements under the statute. Subdivision is thus a function of immediate availability to the proposed plat of certain municipal improvements; the avowed purpose of the amendments being to phase residential development to the Town's ability to provide the above facilities or services.

Certain savings and remedial provisions are designed to relieve of potentially unreasonable restrictions. Thus, the board may issue special permits vesting a present right to proceed with residential development in such year as the development meets the required point minimum, but in no event later than the final year of the 18–year capital plan. The approved special use permit is fully assignable, and improvements scheduled for completion within one year from the date of an application are to be credited as though existing on the date of the application. A prospective developer may advance the date of subdivision approval by agreeing to provide those improvements which will bring the proposed plat within the number of development points required by the amendments. * * * Finally, upon application to the Town Board, the development point requirements may be varied should the board determine that such a variance or modification is consistent with the on-going development plan.

The undisputed effect of these integrated efforts in land use planning and development is to provide an over-all program of orderly growth and adequate facilities through a sequential development policy commensurate with progressing availability and capacity of public facilities. While its goals are clear and its purposes [i]ndisputably laudatory, serious questions are raised as to the manner in which these ends are to be effected, not the least of which relates to their legal viability under present zoning enabling legislation, particularly sections 261 and 263 of the Town Law. The owners of the subject premises argue, and the Appellate Division has sustained the proposition, that the primary purpose of the amending ordinance is to control or regulate population growth within the Town and as such is not within the authorized objectives of the zoning enabling legislation. We disagree.

In enacting the challenged amendments, the Town Board has sought to control subdivision in all residential districts, pending the provision (public or private) at some future date of various services and facilities. A reading of the relevant statutory provisions reveals that there is no specific authorization for the "sequential" and "timing" controls adopted here. That, of course, cannot be said to end the matter for the additional inquiry remains as to whether the challenged amendments find their basis within the perimeters of the devices authorized and purposes sanctioned under current enabling legislation. Our concern is, as it should be, with the effects of the statutory scheme taken as a whole and its role in the propagation of a viable policy of land use and planning.

* * *

It is argued * * * that the timing controls currently in issue are not legislatively authorized since their effect is to prohibit subdivision absent precedent or concurrent action of the Town, and hence constitutes an unauthorized blanket interdiction against subdivision.

* * *

Undoubtedly, current zoning enabling legislation is burdened by the largely antiquated notion which deigns that the regulation of land use and development is uniquely a function of local government—that the public interest of the State is exhausted once its political subdivisions have been delegated the authority to zone. While such jurisdictional allocations may well have been consistent with formerly prevailing conditions and assumptions, questions of broader public interest have commonly been ignored.

Experience, over the last quarter century, however, with greater technological integration and drastic shifts in population distribution has pointed up serious defects and community autonomy in land use controls has come under increasing attack by legal commentators, and students of urban problems alike, because of its pronounced insularism and its correlative role in producing distortions in metropolitan growth patterns, and perhaps more importantly, in crippling efforts toward regional and State-wide problem solving, be it pollution, decent housing, or public transportation.

Recognition of communal and regional interdependence, in turn, has resulted in proposals for schemes of regional and State-wide planning, in the hope that decisions would then correspond roughly to their level of impact. Yet, as salutary as such proposals may be, the power to zone under current law is vested in local municipalities, and we are constrained to resolve the issues accordingly. * * *

* * *

Unless we are to ignore the plain meaning of the statutory delegation, this much is clear: phased growth is well within the ambit of existing enabling legislation. And, of course, it is no answer to point to emergent problems to buttress the conclusion that such innovative schemes are beyond the perimeters of statutory authorization. These considerations, admittedly real, to the extent which they are relevant, bear solely upon the continued viability of "localism" in land use regulation; obviously, they can neither add nor detract from the initial grant of authority, obsolescent though it may be. The answer which Ramapo has posed can by no means be termed definitive; it is, however, a first practical step toward controlled growth achieved without forsaking broader social purposes.

The evolution of more sophisticated efforts to contend with the increasing complexities of urban and suburban growth has been met by a corresponding reluctance upon the part of the judiciary to substitute its judgment as to the plan's over-all effectiveness for the considered deliberations of its progenitors. Implicit in such a philosophy of judicial self-restraint is the growing awareness that matters of land use and development are peculiarly within the expertise of students of city and suburban planning, and thus well within the legislative prerogative, not lightly to be impeded. * * *

* * *

It is the nature of all land use and development regulations to circumscribe the course of growth within a particular town or district and to that extent such restrictions invariably impede the forces of natural growth. Where those restrictions upon the beneficial use and enjoyment of land are necessary to promote the ultimate good of the community and are within the bounds of reason, they have been sustained. "Zoning [, however,] is a means by which a governmental body can plan for the future—it may not be used as a means to deny the future", National Land & Inv. Co. v. Easttown Twp. Bd. of Adj., 419 Pa. 504, 528, 215 A.2d 597, 610 (1965). Its exercise assumes that development shall not stop at the community's threshold, but only that whatever growth there may be shall proceed along a predetermined course. * * *

What we will not countenance, then, under any guise, is community efforts at immunization or exclusion. But, far from being exclusionary, the present amendments merely seek, by the implementation of sequential development and timed growth, to provide a balanced cohesive community dedicated to the efficient utilization of land. The restrictions conform to the community's considered land use policies as expressed in its comprehensive plan and represent a bona fide effort to maximize population density consistent with orderly growth. True other alternatives, such as requiring off-site improvements as a prerequisite to subdivision, may be available, but the choice as how best to proceed, in view of the difficulties attending such exactions cannot be faulted.

Perhaps even more importantly, timed growth, unlike the minimum lot requirements recently struck down by the Pennsylvania Supreme Court as exclusionary, does not impose permanent restrictions upon land use (see National Land & Inv. Co. v. Easttown Twp. Bd. of Adj., 419 Pa.

504, 215 A.2d 597, *supra*). Its obvious purpose is to prevent premature subdivision absent essential municipal facilities and to insure continuous development commensurate with the Town's obligation to provide such facilities. They seek, not to freeze population at present levels but to maximize growth by the efficient use of land, and in so doing testify to this community's continuing role in population assimilation. In sum, Ramapo asks not that it be left alone, but only that it be allowed to prevent the kind of deterioration that has transformed well-ordered and thriving residential communities into blighted ghettos with attendant hazards to health, security and social stability—a danger not without substantial basis in fact.

We only require that communities confront the challenge of population growth with open doors. Where in grappling with that problem, the community undertakes, by imposing temporary restrictions upon development, to provide required municipal services in a rational manner, courts are rightfully reluctant to strike down such schemes. * * *

* * *

The proposed amendments have the effect of restricting development for onwards to 18 years in certain areas. Whether the subject parcels will be so restricted for the full term is not clear, for it is equally probable that the proposed facilities will be brought into these areas well before that time. Assuming, however, that the restrictions will remain outstanding for the life of the program, they still fall short of a confiscation within the meaning of the Constitution.

An ordinance which seeks to permanently restrict the use of property so that it may not be used for any reasonable purpose must be recognized as a taking * * *. An appreciably different situation obtains where the restriction constitutes a *temporary* restriction, promising that the property may be put to a profitable use within a reasonable time. The hardship of holding unproductive property for some time might be compensated for by the ultimate benefit inuring to the individual owner in the form of a substantial increase in valuation; or, for that matter, the landowner, might be compelled to chafe under the temporary restriction, without the benefit of such compensation, when that burden serves to promote the public good.

* * *

In sum, where it is clear that the existing physical and financial resources of the community are inadequate to furnish the essential services and facilities which a substantial increase in population requires, there is a rational basis for "phased growth" and hence, the challenged ordinance is not violative of the Federal and State Constitutions. Accordingly, the order appealed from should be reversed and the actions remitted to Special Term for entry of a judgment declaring section 46–13.1 of the Town Ordinance constitutional.

BREITEL, JUDGE (dissenting).

The limited powers of district zoning and subdivision regulation delegated to a municipality do not include the power to impose a moratorium on land development. Such conclusion is dictated by settled doctrine that a municipality has only those powers, and especially land use powers, delegated or necessarily implied.

* * *

By the unsupportable extrapolation from existing enabling acts, one may not usurp the unique responsibility of the Legislature, even where it has failed to act. What is worse, to do this, as a State legislature would not, without considering the social and economic ramifications for the locality, region, and State, and without limitations essential to an intelligent delegation, is unsound as well as invalid. Moreover, to allow Ramapo's idiosyncratic solution, which would then be available to any other community like Ramapo, may end indefinitely the possibility of commanding better legislation for land planning, just because such legislation requires some diminution in the local control now exercised under the zoning acts.

* * *

American society is at a critical crossroads in the accommodation of urbanization and suburban living, with effects that are no longer confined, bad as they are, to ethnic exclusion or "snob" zoning. Ramapo would preserve its nature, delightful as that may be, but the supervening question is whether it alone may decide this or whether it must be decided by the larger community represented by the Legislature. Legally, politically, economically, and sociologically, the base for determination must be larger than that provided by the town fathers.

* * *

Notes and Questions

1. A somewhat different growth management plan withstood constitutional challenge in Construction Industry Association of Sonoma County v. City of Petaluma, 522 F.2d 897 (9th Cir.1975), cert. denied 424 U.S. 934 (1976). The Petaluma Plan was a five-year program limiting to 500 the number of housing units that could be built each year. The Plan was designed to promote orderly development and preserve the community's "small town character and surrounding open space." It exempted housing units built in connection with projects containing less than five units, created a greenbelt that served as an urban expansion line, established a point system to determine which developers would receive building permits, and provided for construction of both single-family and multifamily dwellings. The Ninth Circuit concluded that "the Petaluma Plan represents a reasonable and legitimate exercise of the police power" and "is rationally related to the social and environmental welfare of the community." 522 F.2d at 909.

2. In City of Boca Raton v. Boca Villas Corp., 371 So.2d 154 (Fla.App. 1979), cert. denied 381 So.2d 765 (Fla.1980), cert. denied 449 U.S. 824 (1980),

an unusual growth management approach was considered. The citizens of Boca Raton adopted by referendum a city charter amendment putting a cap on housing density at 40,000 dwelling units. The City then amended its zoning ordinances to conform to the charter amendment. Certain landowner/developers brought suit challenging the validity of the Cap. "The trial judge held that the City had the power to establish a 'cap' or maximum number of dwelling units allowable with the city boundaries." 371 So.2d at 155. However, the judge "found that the charter amendment (the Cap) and the implementing zoning ordinance did not bear a reasonable relationship to a valid municipal purpose * * *." *Id.* at 157. The appellate court affirmed, noting that the trial judge had made specific findings of fact that the City's utility system and water resources were adequate and that much of the evidence supporting the Cap was based on "after-the-fact studies."

3. Growth management plans continue to be the subject of controversy. *See, e.g.,* Long Beach Equities v. County of Ventura, 231 Cal.App.3d 1016, 282 Cal.Rptr. 877 (1991). *See generally* Kushner, *Growth Management and the City,* 12 Yale L. & Pol'y Rev. 68 (1994); Myren, *Growth Control as a Taking,* 25 Urb.Law. 385 (1993); Siemon, *Successful Growth Management Techniques: Observations from the Monkey Cage,* 29 Urb.Law. 233 (1997).

4. What advice would you give the Centerville City Council about its desire to prevent a rapid influx of new residents?

*

Index

References are to Pages

---

†